AA

GUIDE TO GOLF COURSES
IN BRITAIN
WHERE TO PLAY, WHERE TO STAY

CW00607381

Produced by the Publishing Division of the Automobile Association
Editor: Betty Sheldrick
Editorial assistant: Karen Kemp
Designer: Bob Johnson
Picture researcher: Wyn Voysey
Maps: Prepared by the Cartographic Department of the Automobile Association

Head of Advertisement Sales: Christopher Heard
Tel 0256 20123 (ext 2020)
Advertisement Production: Karen Weeks
Tel 0256 20123 (ext 3525)
Advertisement Sales Representatives:
London, East Anglia, East Midlands, Central Southern and South-east England: Edward May
Tel 0256 20123 (ext 3524) or 0256 467568
South-west, West, West Midlands: Bryan Thompson
Tel 0272 393296
Wales, North of England & Scotland: Arthur Williams
Tel 0222 620267

Filmset by Avonset, Midsomer Norton, Bath, Avon
Colour section printed by J. B. Shears & Sons Ltd, Homesteads Road, Kempshott, Basingstoke, Hants.
Printed and bound in Great Britain by Purnell Book Production Ltd.

Every effort is made to ensure accuracy, but the publishers do not hold themselves
responsible for any consequences that may arise from errors or omissions. While the
contents are believed correct at the time of going to press, changes may have occurred since
that time or will occur during the currency of this book.

Published by The Automobile Association, Fanum House, Basingstoke, Hampshire RG21 2EA

ISBN 0 86145 385 9
AA Reference 59585

CONTENTS

3

FOREWORD

Last year I was honoured to be invited to write the Foreword for the last edition of the *AA Guide to Golf Courses in Britain* and you must all agree that, in retrospect, the previous 12 months had been a fantastic year for golf in Europe and for Europeans overseas. With Sandy Lyle's Open victory, Bernhard Langer's US Masters and the Ryder Cup alone, it will surely be remembered as a milestone in European golf — on both sides of the Atlantic.

I am pleased again this year to add a few words to this magnificent little book, filled from end to end with interesting data, and I cannot help but wonder how the coming year will be remembered in the annals of golf. We Spaniards at least feel that, as newly-hatched members of the EEC and now considered officially as 'Europeans' (whether or not we always were is beside the point), great things are likely to happen, this year and for many more to come, that will go down in golfing history. Many of you may be asking yourselves what is so significant about Europe. The Continent has naturally always existed in geography books but, as European golfers, it has only been over the last few years that we have been able to pride ourselves as being a force to be taken into account.

Personally, that is no surprise to me, having played on every important golf course in Europe and in all weathers — The Belfry, St Nom-la-Bretêche, Cannes, Turnberry, El Saler. All are perfectly designed, fit for top-class tournaments on an international scale, and nowadays language is no problem for anyone, with English of course being predominant wherever one goes. Even the kids at my home course of Pedreña are capable of holding their own with visitors from Japan, Holland, Australia, etc.

We Continentals have indeed finally gained self-confidence and are prepared to challenge the world when it comes to golf and, in all fairness, this achievement has been largely due to British initiative, under the auspices of the ETPD, the instigator of the European Tour circuit. Great Britain has always been a forerunner in golf course design, technical improvements, developments and organisation, and we have all cut our teeth on the British golf courses. The incredible thing about Britain is that there are golf courses for everybody. There always seems to be one nearby — an oasis of tranquillity or excitement, depending upon one's frame of mind.

My own feelings are inevitably geared to my personal experiences in tournaments I have played — St Andrews, Lytham St Annes, Wentworth — above all, those fantastic links that in all climates are sheer joy to any individual who appreciates a good personal battle, whether with himself, the elements or his opponent. The links are a kind of doctorate, to be studied and treated with affection and respect for the results obtained can be greatly humbling.

However, if the links are extraordinarily important to some golfers, that by no means excludes the inland courses, of a quality and quantity that are the envy of all overseas visitors. All that rain, you see, is a blessing in disguise when you think that in places like Spain, for instance, they have to work miracles in order to achieve a similar effect, spending enormous effort and large sums of money to permeate the grounds with that precious liquid element.

What more can I say except that you in Great Britain have the good fortune to be surrounded by the best golf courses in the world so, go out and enjoy your game, that is the prime objective. I wish you all happy golfing for many years to come.

SF179

MIDDLE TAR As defined by H.M. Government
Warning: SMOKING CAN CAUSE
LUNG CANCER, BRONCHITIS
AND OTHER CHEST DISEASES
Health Departments' Chief Medical Officers

In the annual golfing calendar, the professional and amateur tournaments are crucial dates for players and spectators alike. The professional matches, catching the headlines and the TV screens, attract attention because of the top-ranking 'names' taking part, but they are really just the shop window for a sport that depends for its existence on thousands of amateur enthusiasts. The amateur tournaments are no less competitive than their professional equivalents; they are sometimes more fascinating to watch and often provide the grounding for future stars. Tom Scott, an ardent golfer and writer on the sport for most of his life, here recalls some of the more memorable highlights of tournaments in both categories of the sport.

The 1987 Open Championship returns to Muirfield, home of the Honourable Company of Edinburgh Golfers and the most famous of all golf clubs dating back to 1744. Muirfield is situated in the little Lothians village of Gullane some miles to the east of Edinburgh, Scotland's capital. This is the third home of the Company, which had its

Undulating links at Muirfield

1987 TOURNAMENT ROUND UP

Slazenger.
A matter   of course

To create the world's finest clubs. This was Seve's goal when he set about designing Supremo.

So the woods were made from the finest USA persimmon. The stainless steel irons were forged in the traditional way. The result was a set of clubs that combined style, craftsmanship and performance. Only then did the world's finest golfer put his name to them.

Superb performance wa also the key factor in th Slazenger B51 range. For extr distance, play the B51XD. Th durable two piece ball with totally new dimple pattern. Fo extra touch and control, play th B51XTC. The ball that deliver all the benefits of tour wound

construction without compr mising on length.

"I'd recommend Slazenge to all serious golfers–nobod knows more about golf."

Seve Ballesteros

Whatever your golfing need there's only one name to choos Slazenger–as a matter of cours

Slazenger

The great Alfred Perry driving off

roots on Leith Links where its forerunner, the
Company of Gentlemen Golfers, first
introduced the game of golf to Scotland. The
first course was one of five holes.

In 1800 the title 'the Honourable Company
of Edinburgh Golfers' was adopted but, alas,
did not survive for long because in 1830 the
Company was wound up. After six years,
though, it found a new home at Musselburgh
near Leith where it remained for over 50
years before moving to Muirfield. The
Company of Edinburgh Golfers deserves an
honoured place in the history of the game
because it was the Leith golfers who
established a set of rules, and they were the
first golfers to be bound together as a club.

There have been 12 Open Championships
at Muirfield. One of the strangest, perhaps,
was that of 1935 because it was one of the
very few which was won by a comparatively
unknown golfer. The winner was a modest
English professional, Alfred Perry, who had
some small reputation but had never been
looked on as a potential champion. Alf Perry
was a brave golfer, never slow to take risks —
perhaps it was this tendency which
hampered his career — and he was a very
fine putter in his day. He qualified for the
Championship of 1935 with one stroke to
spare but in the event proper he started off
with a round of 69. Perry's putting touch
deserted him on the second day and he
returned a 75 which put him down the list.

On the third day, however, Perry, who was
professional at the Leatherhead club in
Surrey, played the greatest round of his life.
He went for everything and returned a round
of 67, which gave him a lead of one stroke
from the great Charles Whitcombe. In the
final round Whitcombe went to pieces while
other challengers fell by the wayside, except
Perry. He was a late starter — the lowest
scorers did not go out last in those days —
and news soon came over the course that he
was playing well. In his usual carefree
manner he was hitting long drives, slashing
shots to the green and hitting the back of the
hole with his putts. There were many
spectators who feared he could not keep up
the momentum, but he did and, despite the
presence of so many great golfers, he became
what some would describe as a most unlikely
champion. I knew Alf Perry well and found
him a delightful but shy man. The sad thing
about his momentous victory was that he

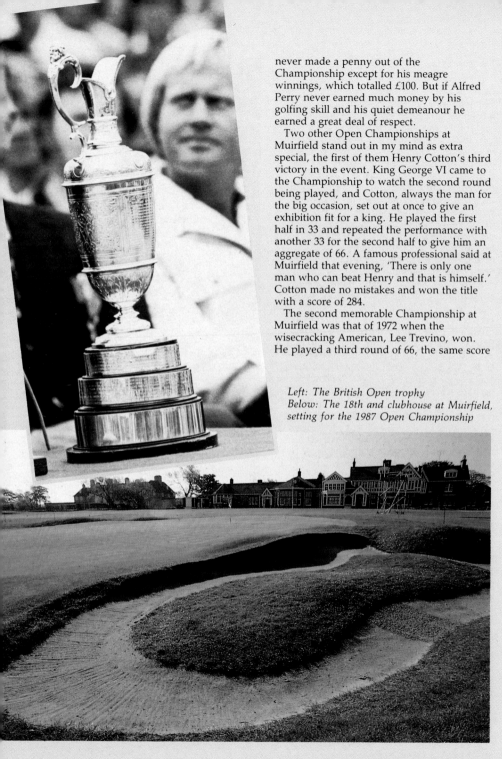

never made a penny out of the Championship except for his meagre winnings, which totalled £100. But if Alfred Perry never earned much money by his golfing skill and his quiet demeanour he earned a great deal of respect.

Two other Open Championships at Muirfield stand out in my mind as extra special, the first of them Henry Cotton's third victory in the event. King George VI came to the Championship to watch the second round being played, and Cotton, always the man for the big occasion, set out at once to give an exhibition fit for a king. He played the first half in 33 and repeated the performance with another 33 for the second half to give him an aggregate of 66. A famous professional said at Muirfield that evening, 'There is only one man who can beat Henry and that is himself.' Cotton made no mistakes and won the title with a score of 284.

The second memorable Championship at Muirfield was that of 1972 when the wisecracking American, Lee Trevino, won. He played a third round of 66, the same score

Left: The British Open trophy
Below: The 18th and clubhouse at Muirfield, setting for the 1987 Open Championship

CHANGE UP

*I*f you have to push a system beyond its limits to get so-called high power, there's only one thing you end up with.

Distortion. And a system that's not long for this world.

That's the difference between high volume and High Power.

With Pioneer High Power, you don't need to push the stick to max to get maximum results – thanks to high tech, single-board advanced electronics that can take all the available power – and then some.

Pioneer High Power is power in reserve, and amplifiers that can deliver up to a crushing 150W per channel.

Change up for the better.
Change up to Pioneer.

KEH-6030 HIGH POWER (2 - 20W) AUTO-REVERSE CAR STEREO WITH QUARTZ PLL SYNTHESIZER STEREO TUNER. TS-1616 16CM FLUSH-MOUNT 3-WAY, 3-SPEAKER SYSTEM. 60 WATTS MAX. MUSIC POWER.

Find your nearest Pioneer dealer by calling 01-200 0200 anytime.

ⓟ PIONEER

I N - C A R   S T E R E O

How to lower your handicap before you leave the clubhouse.

as Cotton had produced on the way to his victory. It was a score which was too much for Tony Jacklin, who looked a good bet to win. In the end Jacklin missed being runner-up, Jack Nicklaus slipping in to take that place.

In 1987 the cream of the world's golfers will be competing at Muirfield and the competition will be intense partly due to the fact that the European professionals in no way play second fiddle to the Americans as they did for so many years.

Apart from the World's Match Play Championship, which has a permanent venue at Wentworth, the London area does not do particularly well as far as important golf events are concerned, certainly not important amateur events, but in 1987 Sunningdale is to stage the Walker Cup match, which is played between the amateurs of Britain & Ireland and the United States. This is a match which is keenly contested, but for the most part the Americans have had

Right: The Walker Cup. Below: Final hole for the Old course at Sunningdale where the Walker Cup will be held this year

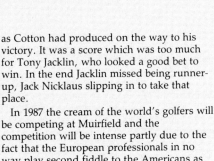

much the better of the exchanges because they have a steady stream of fine young amateurs who come up through the universities where golf scholarships are in abundance. We have no such source from which to draw talent and, to make matters worse, most good young amateurs in Britain have one ambition and that is to become professional. The result is that there is a constant drain to the paid ranks.

We have had our successes, nevertheless, and the Walker Cup matches best remembered are the ones in which our men

Michael Bonallack, one of the victorious 1971 British Walker Cup team

were the victors. The 1971 match at St Andrews was such an encounter. Our players made a brilliant start, winning all the four first-day foursomes. In the afternoon singles, though, it was a different story, with the home team losing by 6½ points to 1½ points, so the day which had started so brightly ended on a sombre note with the Americans leading by 6½ points to 5½ points.

On the second day the Americans were one point further ahead at lunchtime, having won the second-day foursomes by 2½ points to 1½ points. This meant our men were 2 points down going into the second series of singles. A formidable task lay ahead, especially when the leading British player, Michael Bonallack,

H'eau'le in one?

You are now eligible to join the Perrier *H'eau'le in one* club and to wear the *H'eau'le in one* scarf or tie pictured here. Your golf pro has the details.

For your free *H'eau'le in one* certificate write to:
H'eau'le in one Club
Infoplan Limited
30 Eastbourne Terrace
London W2 6LF.

was beaten by the brilliant American, Lanny Wadkins.

Then came one of the biggest turnarounds in the history of international golf matches — the home players won the next six matches to get home by two points! That to my mind was the most exciting Walker Cup match ever played, certainly the most exciting I have ever seen. At St Andrews thousands of spectators can circle the last home, and that afternoon they had a field day for three of the matches came to the 18th. The excitement was tremendous, and the locals who take their golf seriously were joined by visitors in substantial celebrations after the event.

No doubt the home team will have a hard task at Sunningdale, but we do have some good young amateurs always coming along, and the great thing is they have plenty of courage and are not afraid of any opposition. So hopefully Sunningdale will stage another exciting event. Previously Sunningdale was best known for hosting professional tournaments, including the old Dunlop Masters and the Colgate European Women's Professional Championship.

Like Sunningdale, Prestwick is better known for the professional events that take

This year Prestwick, on the west coast of Scotland, stages the Amateur Championship.

place there, but in 1987 it is the stage for the Amateur Championship. Prestwick's claim to tournament fame is that it was there in 1860 that eight professionals, caddies and greenkeepers, with their few clubs actually under their arm, played the first Open Championship. In fact it was the Prestwick Club which instituted the Championship

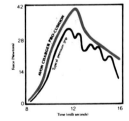

17

because the members fancied their professional, the great Tom Morris, could beat anybody. In fact he failed to win the very first one, that honour going to Willie Park. The first twelve Open Championships were played at Prestwick. Then other venues came into use but Prestwick continued to be used until 1925. The first Amateur Championship was played at Prestwick in 1888 and has been back several times since.

Perhaps the most sensational of the championships played at Prestwick was that of 1934. The finalists were the very good American, Lawson Little, and a local artisan, Jimmy Wallace. Of course the great crowds which turned out to watch were cheering for the local all the way. But it was not his day. Never having been in the final of any major event before he was badly stricken by nerves and could hardly hit a shot. In the end he was beaten 14 and 13 to play the biggest margin ever recorded in a 36-hole final (at least in an important event). The massacre of the genial Wallace had, it seemed, put an end to his aspirations as a golfer and relegated him to obscurity. Not a bit of it. He at once turned professional and was appointed to the Purley Downs Club in Surrey. He served the club for many years.

The Ladies' Golf Union have also chosen an old and famous course for their championship which in 1987 goes to Royal St David's, Harlech, where it has been played several times. Overlooked by the massive old castle, Royal St David's is as picturesque a golf course as can be found anywhere and is much favoured by golfing visitors.

It is often said by experts that it takes a good golf course to produce a good champion. If that is true then Royal St David's must be a good course for it has produced several fine champions. Cecil Leitch, one of the best lady golfers of her era, won there in 1926. Miss Frances Stephens was the winner of the Ladies' Championship there in 1949, and in 1960 Miss Barbara McIntyre, one of America's best ever players, won the Ladies' Championship at Royal St David's.

The Amateur Championships of England, Scotland, Ireland and Wales are controlled by the respective home unions, and to encourage golf throughout each country its main event is taken round, sometimes to major championship courses but also to good golf courses not quite so prominent, like St Andrews and others on the Open

Championship rota. So, for example, in 1987 we find that the English Amateur Championship is at Frilford Heath in Oxfordshire. It is a fine parkland course, in fact there are two courses. No major event has been played there before.

Nairn on the Moray coast is one of Scotland's best seaside courses but because of its rather remote situation does not host as many important events as it would otherwise have done. However, it has been the venue of previous Scottish Amateur Championships. In 1964, Ronnie Shade, one of Scotland's best amateurs was on a winning streak — from 1963 to 1967 he won five Scottish Championships in a row, the second being at Nairn, where he defeated a luckless player by the name of McBeath in the final. The margin was 8 and 7!

The Irish Amateur Championship goes to Tramore near Waterford. I regret to say it is not a golf course I know and not one which has played any prominent part in staging Irish events in the past. Ireland has another important amateur fixture in 1987 — playing host to the Home Internationals. The venue is the splendid Lahinch course in County Clare, not a particularly long course, but very testing. It has staged some important Irish events. Christy O'Connor won one of his numerous Irish Professional Championships there, and Miss Philomena Garvey won two of her Irish Championships at Lahinch, one of them by the wide margin of 12 and 10, which I think would be a record for the final of any Ladies' Championship.

The Welsh Golf Union have fewer courses from which to choose but what they have are good courses, and it is to Royal Porthcawl, one of the best of them, that they take the 1987 Welsh Amateur Championship. Royal Porthcawl is a fine old seaside course of great character and tradition which has housed several important events, including the 1964 Curtis Cup match between the lady golfers of Great Britain & Ireland and the United States. I remember that as an exciting encounter finally won by an exceptionally strong American team.

I think perhaps Prestwick, the chosen venue for the Amateur Championship, is the most inspired piece of planning as far as the 1987 calendar is concerned. I wonder what some of the younger amateurs will think of it. Certainly not many of them will have seen a course quite like it before, which if they wish to gain experience is not a bad thing.

Pro Quip rainsuits.
Strong enough to wear in a car wash.

However strong the wind and rain when you're playing golf, it will never be as violent as standing between the flailing brushes and high pressure water jets of a car wash. Yet we were so confident of our rainsuits that that's exactly what we did. Through it all the golfer remained completely dry and unaffected. The secret is in the GORE-TEX fabric, a unique material composed of billions of microscopic pores that stop the wind and rain getting in but let body moisture out, leaving you comfortable and totally damp free. So when you buy a rainsuit choose the tough one – Pro Quip. Others may make claims, we deliver.

RCR Associates, Wisloe Road, Cambridge, Gloucester, GL2 7AF. Tel. (0453) 89707. Telex 437127 RCR PQG
Pro Quip is the registered trademark of RCR Associates. Gore-tex is a trademark of W. L. Gore and Associates Inc.

Calendar of Tournaments

United Kingdom and Ireland — amateur
Lytham Trophy 2–3 May at Royal Lytham & St Annes
The Brabazon Trophy 15–17 May at Ganton
Senior Interprovincial Championship 15–17 May at Lahinch
Welsh Ladies' Championship 17–20 May at Aberdovey
English Ladies' Championship 19–23 May at Alwoodley
Scottish Ladies' Championship 19–23 May at Nairn
Irish Ladies' Championship 20–23 May at Lahinch
The Walker Cup, Britain & Ireland v. USA 27–28 May at Sunningdale
The Amateur Championship 1–6 June at Prestwick and Prestwick St
  Nicholas
Ladies' Championship 9–13 June at Harlech
The Berkshire Trophy 13–14 June at The Berkshire
European Amateur Team Championship 24–28 June at Muirhof (Austria)
European Amateur Ladies' Team Championship 8–12 July at Turnberry
The Open Championship 16–19 July at Muirfield
Welsh Amateur Championship 25 July–1 August at Royal Porthcawl
English Amateur Championship 27 July–1 August at Frilford Heath
The Seniors' Championship 5–7 August at the Royal Cinque Ports
Irish Amateur Close Championship 8–12 August at Tramore
Youths' Amateur Open Championship 20–22 August at Hollingwell
Home Internationals 9–11 September at Lahinch
Vagliano Trophy, Great Britain & Ireland v. Europe 25–26 September at
  The Berkshire
Ladies' British Open Championship: date and venue to be fixed

North American PGA — principal tournaments
Tournament Players' Championship 26–29 March at the Tournament
  Players' Club at Sawgrass, Ponte Vedra, Florida
The Masters 9–12 April at Augusta National Golf Club, Augusta, Georgia
United States Open 18–21 June at the Olympic Club (Lakeside course),
  San Francisco, California
Canadian Open 2–5 July at Glen Abbey Golf Club, Oakville, Ontario

Only the best is good enough

**Changes In Clothes and Equipment
by Tom Scott**

Time was when golfers — in Britain at least — were content to play with any old clubs and to wear any old pullover or jacket which was too old and too shabby to do service elsewhere. In those days to enter some locker rooms constituted a health hazard, for pullovers and cardigans hung on the pegs for years, some of them long after their owners had stopped playing golf.

As regards clothes the revolution was slow in coming, but gradually manufacturers realised there was an opening for leisure sales. The revolution started, I think, when so many British golfers started to go overseas for winter golf. To play golf in Spain or Portugal they wore lighter clothes, and lighter clothes meant brighter clothes, although to start with those were hard to find in Britain. But gradually colourful, lightweight slacks appeared in sports shops and in pro's shops while sports shirts with striking designs also made their appearance. And of course there were many pullovers, a field in which Britain has always been strong.

So gradually the old torn jerseys were discarded and disappeared from the hooks in the changing rooms which had been their permanent home for years. The result was that locker rooms became tidier and fresher places, for the new sports shirts and sweaters were too valuable to leave hanging about.

Now in general golfers are a fairly well-dressed set of people. Naturally some of the diehards stick to their old waterproof jerkins which are worn whatever the weather. These selfsame veterans are strong supporters of the good old grey flannel trousers which also used to serve on family days to the seaside. But they are in the minority, and more and more are going in for checked slacks, patterned sports shirts and tartan caps. Indeed to golfers in Scotland, both natives' and visitors' tartan caps are the in thing, favoured especially by our American cousins who can claim that their great- great-grandfather was an immigrant from St Andrews or Carnoustie.

Then there are golf shoes. In the early days of golf any kind of shoes were good enough and what was on the market were really adaptations of everyday shoes rather than ones specially designed. Many golfers were loath to buy golf shoes which were specially designed because some are rather expensive, but they do last a long time. Incidentally the greatest advance made in the design of golf shoes is the introduction of rubber studs, something which is comparatively new. Apart from being comfortable to wear they please the golf course managements because they cause less damage to greens.

So much, then, for men golfers. What about the ladies? It is true to say, I think, that they were even slower to break away from the waterproof jerkin and ear muff era than were the men to break away from their smelly cardigans. But the revolution has been achieved, partly because of the women professionals who now play in tournaments in this country and partly because some firms have done wonders in making available attractive and elegant golf clothes. No doubt at all that the image of battle-axe lady golfers is now dead. However, many golf professionals could cater more for lady golfers than they do at present.

Sadly only a few pro shops at golf clubs have a room where ladies can try clothes. They have to take the pullover or pair of slacks over their arm to the changing room in the golf clubhouse, which is not a very satisfactory procedure. I feel that lady golfers are good spenders if they get what they want and many professionals at golf clubs are missing the boat.

Golf pros at clubs are not without their problems. In the old days club members remained loyal to their pros and bought all their golfing gear from them. But those days have gone. The many golf shops and golf discount stores which have been set up have taken much trade from the club pros for the simple reason that they have a bigger turnover, buy in larger quantities and so can sell cheaper. This means that golfers buy from them even if on a Sunday morning they have to revert to going into the pro's shop to buy a golf ball or a packet of tees.

A few firms sell to professionals only; one specialises in supplying golf clubs to suit individual golfers' needs — i.e. tailor-made clubs.

The number of makes of golf club now on the market is staggering and the only problem for golfers who set out to buy a new set of clubs is to know which set to buy. The pro is usually able to advise on that question. A beginner would do well to choose a modest set of clubs or even a half set to start off with. It is even possible to buy second-hand clubs both at golf club pro's shops or at the big discount centres. I make this suggestion because golf clubs are now rather expensive, at least those at the top of the range are. Prices vary of course but the best American clubs can cost around £600 for 3 woods and 9 irons.

Once a golfer has become proficient he or she can seek out better — and more expensive — clubs.

It is said that when the first Open Championship was played at Prestwick in 1860 the eight competitors arrived carrying half a dozen or so clubs under their arm. Later someone invented a container in which clubs could be carried. At first these containers were simple affairs in which clubs could be slipped, but now golf bags are very different, and those carried by the tournament players' caddies are enormous.

When he was an active golfer the great Henry Cotton used to use a donkey to carry his clubs round the Penina course in Portugal. Watching the caddies at work in the big tournaments, one could easily come to the conclusion that donkeys would be gainfully employed in the same calling. Unfortunately they would be unable to give their masters advice on how to play the shots, and this advice some of the tournament stars seem to find invaluable.

But nowadays most club golfers do not carry their own clubs, they use a simple push trolley which is easy to handle and is in every way a distinct improvement on having to stoop and lift a golf bag and then place it on the shoulder, although there are still many golfers who prefer to do that.

But there is something of a revolution going on at British golf clubs. That is the introduction of golf buggies so extensively used in the United States and indeed in other parts of the world. Buggies have been slow to catch on in Britain but are now appearing more and more. They range from the simple push type up to the fine twin-seater battery-operated or petrol-engined ones. There are several different makes on the market now, mostly the twin-seater types, but there are also single-seaters which are ideal for elderly

golfers who find walking round the holes of a golf course difficult or even out of the question.

One of the reasons why golf buggies have been slow to make a general appearance in Britain is that many golf clubs objected to them because they thought they would ruin the courses. In addition, many golfers traditionally think that golf is a game where you should hit the ball and walk after it, thus getting the maximum exercise.

Golf has become so popular that there is now a wide range of equipment for sale to suit all needs, the beginner and the expert,

the young and the old, the casual player or the enthusiast. You can spend £1000 on kitting yourself out or you can do it relatively cheaply.

One thing to remember is that the more golf you play the cheaper it is, because the golf club subscription becomes better value each round you play.

When one considers that a seat at a London theatre may now cost as much as £20, golf can be rated as a very inexpensive game even if you are a member of a golf club around a big city, which is likely to have a high subscription.

25

About this book . . .

This gazetteer provides a guide, for the visiting golfer, to golf courses and clubs throughout England, Scotland and Wales. Information is given about how to reach each course, whether the course or club in question requires an introduction or advance notice of your arrival, what facilities, including catering, will be available to you and what type of course to expect.

For the travelling golfer, a nearby AA-appointed hotel is recommended for most clubs. Many of these have been nominated by the individual golf club secretaries. Where such a nomination was not made, the AA's Hotel Services department have given the hotel closest to the main entrance of the golf course. The AA classification of each establishment is given, along with the full name, address, telephone number and details of the total number of rooms and the number of rooms with bath or bath and shower.

All the towns listed are also shown on the maps at the end of the book.

Within the gazetteer, additional

HOW TO USE THE GAZETTEER

Symbols and abbreviations have been used to convey the information given in each entry.

(IA1)

After the name of each town there is a map reference, given in parentheses. The first figure is the map page number (turn to the map sections, pages I-VII, at the end of the book). The second two figures give the grid reference for the town: read the letter across the map and the number vertically.

Ambridge Golf Club

When a course's name is shown in **bold italics** the details have not been confirmed by management.

T:

STD code and telephone number.

☎

Visitors are required to telephone or write to the club secretary in advance.

✉

Visitors should have an introduction from the secretary of their own golf club or evidence, such as a handicap certificate or a membership card, that they belong to a club.

••

Low green fees
(up to £6 per day at the time of printing).

•∴•

Moderate green fees
(between £6.25-£10 per day at the time of printing).

::

Moderate to high green fees
(over £10 per day at the time of printing).

✱

Green fees have not been confirmed for 1987.

M

Member (of the golf club in question); when followed by a number, as M450, this indicates the total membership of the club.

B

Light lunch or snacks available every day, unless otherwise stated.

L

Full lunch available every day, unless otherwise stated.

☕

Tea or coffee available every day, unless otherwise stated.

D

Dinner available every day, unless otherwise stated.

⌂

Changing rooms available.

♟

Bar open at midday and in the evening, unless otherwise stated.

＼

Golf clubs available for hire.

⋈

Partners may be found.

④

Restricted times for 4 balls; this symbol is followed by the times when 4 balls are not allowed.

TR

Times reserved for members; this symbol is followed by the times when members only may play on the course.

descriptive detail is given for a selection of courses. These courses, for which the entries are in green, have been chosen as being of particular interest to the visiting golfer for varying reasons. Many historic clubs have been included; other clubs have been chosen because their courses are particularly testing or enjoyable to play; yet more clubs have been included because they are in holiday areas and have proved popular with visiting golfers.

Such a selection cannot be either exhaustive or totally objective and the courses included are not intended to represent any formal category on quality or any other grounds. In the case of many of these, an artist's impression of the course, or of individual holes, has been given and in other cases a score card of the course is given.

At the end of the gazetteer there is a list of some golf ranges throughout the country. Details are given of the name, address and telephone number of each range and the times when it is open.

A small number of clubs have chosen not to have an entry in the gazetteer, usually because they do not have facilities for visitors or because they are private.

All information is believed correct at the time of printing.

ʒ
Professional at the club.

S
Well stocked golf shop at the club.

Abbreviations
Mon, Monday; Tu, Tuesday; W, Wednesday; Th, Thursday; F, Friday; S, Saturday; Sun, Sunday; WE, Weekend; BH, Bank Holiday

KEY TO HOTEL CLASSIFICATIONS:
The AA star classification of hotels introduced and used since 1912, in addition to providing an indication of the type of hotel, may be regarded as a universally-accepted standard in all classifications, from the simplest inn to the most luxurious hotel. Some hotels may satisfy several of the requirements of a classification higher than that awarded. In provincial 5 Star hotels, some of the services are provided on a more informal and restricted basis than similarly classified London hotels.

★
Hotels and inns generally of small scale with good facilities and furnishings. All bedrooms with hot and cold water; adequate bath and lavatory arrangements. Meals are provided for residents but their availability to non-residents may be limited.

★★
Hotels offering a higher standard of accommodation and some private bathrooms/showers with lavatory.

★★★
Well-appointed hotels with more spacious accommodation with the majority of bedrooms having private bathrooms/showers.

Fuller meal facilities are provided, which should normally be available to chance callers.

★★★★
Exceptionally well-appointed hotels offering a high standard of comfort and service with all bedrooms providing private bathrooms/showers and lavatory.

★★★★★
Luxury hotels offering the highest international standards.

Country House. Used to denote an AA country house hotel, often secluded but not always rurally situated, where a relaxed informal atmosphere and personal welcome prevail. However some of the facilities may differ from those found in urban hotels of the same classification.

Rosettes highlight those hotels or classified restaurants where it is judged that food can be specially recommended.

○
Denotes hotels which are considered to be of outstanding merit within their classification.

Hotel symbols
Private bathroom/shower with own toilet.

ABERDARE
Mid Glamorgan
Map **III** E8

Aberdare Abernant (¾m E of Aberdare)
T:(0685) 871188
Pleasant parkland course with outstanding valley views 18 | 5875 yds | Par 69 | SSS 69
Visitors welcome without M | ∴ per day | B L ☕ D | △ 🍸 ⟍ | ⋈ 🏌 | M 426 | [S]
★★★Maes Manor, Blackwood. T:(0495) 224551.10rm (7 ⇌ 🚿). Annexe: 16rm (10 ⇌ 3 🚿)

ABERDEEN
Grampian, *Aberdeenshire*
Map **VII** K6

Balnagask St Fitticks Rd, Aberdeen (2m E of city centre)
T:(0224) 876407
Links course. Societies welcome by arrangement. 18 | 5486 metres | SSS 69
Visitors welcome | B L ☕ | △ 🍸
★★Gordon, Wellington Rd. T:(0224) 873012. 26rm (3 ⇌ 13 🚿)

Bon Accord 19 Golf Rd, (¾m NE of city centre)
T:(0224) 633464
Links coastal course. Municipal course used by three private clubs. 18 | 6384 yds | Par 71 | SSS 70
B L D ☕ | △ 🍸 | ⋈
★★Gloucester, 102 Union St. T:(0224) 641095. 72rm ⇌)

Deeside Bieldside, Aberdeen (4½m W of city centre off A93)
T:(0224) 867697
Parkland course. 18 | 5972 yds | Par 71 | SSS 69
Visitors welcome ☎ ✉ | without M :: per day WE | with M •• per day WE | B L ☕ prior arrangement | △ 🍸 | ⋈ | [TR] first and third W of each month | 🏌 | M 500 | [S]
★★★Stakis Treetops, 161 Springfield Rd. T:(0224) 313377. 94rm (86 ⇌)

Hazelhead Public Hazelhead, Aberdeen (4m W of city centre off A944)
T: No tel. personal bookings only.
A tree-lined course. 2 courses of 18, one of 9. No 1 course 18 | 6595 yds | Par 70 | SSS 70
Visitors welcome with M | △ [S] ⟍
★★★Stakis Treetops, 161 Springfield Rd. T:(0224) 313377. 94rm (86 ⇌)

Murcar Murcar, Bridge of Don (2m N of city centre off A92)
T:(0224) 704354
Seaside course, prevailing NE wind, hard walking. Testing 4th, 14th holes. 18 | 6226 yds | Par 71 | SSS 70
Visitors welcome, restricted WE | without M :: per day WE | B L ☕ | D | △ 🍸 ⟍ ⋈ | [4] | [TR] WE, W afternoon, other weekdays after 1500 | M 750 | [S]
★★★Skean Dhu Dyce, Farburn Ter, Dyce. T:(0224) 723101. Annexe: 222rm ⇌ 🚿

Nigg Bay St Fitticks Rd, Aberdeen (plays over Balnagask course)
T:(0224) 871286
Seaside course, hard walking. 18 | 5984 yds | Par 69 | SSS 69
Visitors welcome only with M | B | △ 🍸 | M 800
★★★Skean Dhu Dyce, Farburn Ter, Dyce. T:(0224) 723101. Annexe: 222rm ⇌ 🚿

Northern 22 Gold Rd, Aberdeen (Adjacent to beach)
T:(0224) 636440
Exposed and windy seaside course, testing hole: 10th. 18 | Par 72 | SSS 72
One of 3 clubs playing over King's Links municipal course •• per day | B L ☕ D △ 🍸 | M 1000
★★★★Bucksburn Moat House, Old Meldrum Rd, Bucksburn. T:(0224) 713911. 98rm ⇌ 🚿

Royal Aberdeen Balgownie, Bridge of Don, Aberdeen (2½m N of city centre off A92)
T:(0224) 702571
Championship Links course. Windy, easy walking. (Also short course.) Societies welcome. 18 | 6372 yds (4033) | Par 70 (64) | SSS 71
Visitors welcome ✉ | ☎ to Pro T:(0224) 702221) | B L D ☕ prior arrangement | △ | 🍸 | ⋈ sometimes | [4] [TR] WE until 1430 | 🏌 | M 500 | [S]
★★★★Bucksburn Moat House, Old Meldrum Rd, Bucksburn. T:(0224) 713911. 98rm ⇌ 🚿

Westhill Westhill Heights, Westhill, Skene, Aberdeen. (6m W of city centre off A944)
T:(0224) 740159
A highland course. 18 | 5866 yds | Par 69 | SSS 68
Visitors welcome without M ∴ weekdays, :: WE, BH | B L ☕ | D prior arrangement | △ 🍸 | [4] competition days | 🏌 | [TR] 1630-1800, S 0700- 1530, Sun until 1000 | M 570 | [S]
★★★Westhill Inn, Westhill. T:(0224) 740388. 38rm ⇌ Annexe: 14rm (6 ⇌ 8 🚿)

ABERDOUR
Fife
Map **VI** G2

Aberdour Seaside Pl, (S side of village)
T:(0383) 860256
Parkland course with lovely views over the Firth of Forth. Society meetings by arrangement. 18 | 5469 yds | Par 67 | SSS 67
Visitors welcome, restricted Sun | ∴ per day :: WE | B L ☕ D prior arrangement (not Tu) | △ 🍸 ⟍ | [TR] Sun G | M 600 | [S]
★★Woodside, High St. T:(0383) 860328. 15rm (2 ⇌ 4 🚿)

ABERDOVEY
Gwynedd
Map **III** D4

Aberdovey (½m W of Aberdovey, on A493)
T:(065472) 2493
18 | 6449 yds | Par 71 | SSS 71
Visitors welcome ✉ | ☎ advisable | * | B L D prior arrangement (not some Mon) | ☕ | △ 🍸 | 🏌 ⟍ prior arrangement ⋈ | [4] S pm Sun am off white tees (during competitions) | [TR] 0830-0930, 1300-1400 (summer) | M 800 | [S]
★★★Trefeddian. T:(065472) 213. 46rm (41 ⇌ 5 🚿)

A beautiful championship course at the mouth of the Dovey estuary, Aberdovey has all the true characteristics of a seaside links. It has some fine holes among them the 3rd, the 12th, an especially good short hole, and the 15th. There are some striking views to be had from the course.

KEY

(IA1) atlas grid reference
T: telephone number
☎   advance letter/telephone
       call required
⊠   introduction from own club
       sec/handicap
       certificate/club
       membership card required
..   low fees
∴   medium fees
::   high fees
*   green fees not confirmed for
       1987
B   light lunch
L   full lunch
☻   tea
D   dinner
⚗   changing rooms/showers
Ⴤ   bar open mid-day and
       evenings
⚲   clubs for hire
⋈   partners may be found
④   restricted time for 4 balls
TR   times reserved for members
𝔍   professional
S   well-stocked shop
M   member
Mon Tu W Th F S Sun
WE   weekend
BH   bank holiday

ABERFELDY
Tayside, *Perthshire*
Map **VII**   G7

Aberfeldy Taybridge Rd, (N side of
town centre)
T:(0887) 20535
*Parkland course, situated by River Tay
near the famous Wade Bridge and Black
Watch Museum. Easy walking. 9 |
5400 yds | Par 68 | SSS 67*
Visitors welcome | .. per day WE |
B L ☻ ⚗ Ⴤ | ⋈ | TR Tu W
evenings | M 250 | S
★★*Weem Weem. T:(0887) 20381.
12rm (5 ⇌ 2 ⌗)*

ABERFOYLE
Central, *Perthshire*
Map **VI**   D1

Aberfoyle Braeval (¾m SE of
Aberfoyle, on A81)
T:(08772) 493
*Heathland course with mountain
views. Societies welcome by
arrangement. 18 | 5205 yds | Par 66 |
SSS 66*
Visitors welcome | .. per day | B L

☻ D (WE only) | ⚗ Ⴤ ⚲ | M 250 |
TR to 0930 WE
★★*Forest Hills, Kinlochard,
Aberfoyle. T:(08777) 277. 19rm ⇌ ⌗*

ABERGELE
Clwyd
Map **III**   E2

Abergele & Pensarn Tan-y-Goppa
Rd, (½m W of Abergele, off A547)
T:(0745) 824034
*A beautiful parkland course with views
of the Irish Sea and Gwyrch Castle.
There are splendid finishing holes, a
testing par 5 16th, a 185 yd 17th to an
elevated green, and a superb par 5 18th
with out of bounds just behind the
green. Societies welcome by
arrangement. 18 | 6086 yds | Par 70 |
SSS 69*
Visitors welcome | with or without
M ∴ per day WE | B (not Mon) | L
☻ D prior arrangement | ⚗ Ⴤ | ⋈ |
TR competitions 𝔍 | M 1180 | S
★★*Kinmel Manor, St Georges Rd,
Abergele. T:(0745) 822014.
22rm (20 ⇌ 2 ⌗)*

ABERLADY
Lothian, *East Lothian*
Map **VI**   H2

Kilspindie Aberlady, (W side of
village off A198)
T:(08757) 216
*Seaside course, short but tight and well
bunkered. Testing holes: 2nd, 3rd, 4th,
7th. Societies welcome by arrangement.
18 | 5410 yds | Par 69 | SSS 66*
Visitors welcome | * | B L ☻ | ⚗ Ⴤ |
④ subject to demand on course |
TR M have priority at all times |
M 640
★★*Kilspindie House, Main St,
Aberlady. T:(08757) 319. 12rm
(8 ⇌ 4 ⌗)*

Luffness New (1m E of Aberlady
on A198)
T:(0620) 843336
*Seaside course 18 | 6085 yds | Par 69 |
SSS 69*
Visitors welcome only with M ⊠ ☎
| L ☻ D | ⚗ Ⴤ | TR WE | M 650
⊕ ○ ○ ○ ⚬⚬*Greywalls, Duncar Rd,
Gullane. T:(0620) 842144. 18rm (3 ⌗)*

ABERSOCH
Gwynedd
Map **III**   C3

Abersoch (S side of village).
T:(075881) 2622
*Seaside links, with easy walking and
several holes notable for scenic beauty.
9 | 5892 yds | Par 70 | SSS 68 (18 holes)*
Visitors welcome with M | B L D |
☻ (July Aug) | ⚗ ⋈ | M 650 | 𝔍 | S
TR competitions
⊕ ★★★⚬⚬*Porth Tocyn, Bwlch Tocyn.
T:(075881) 2966. 17rm ⇌ ⌗*

ABERYSTWYTH
Dyfed
Map **III**   D5

Aberystwyth Bryn-y-Mor Rd, (N
side of town)
T:(0970) 615104
*Undulating meadowland course.
Testing holes: 16th The Loop par 3;
17th par 4; 18th par 3. Good views
over Cardigan Bay. 18 | 5750 yds | Par
68 | SSS 68*
Visitors welcome | ⊠ during Open
Week (last wk in July) | without M
∴ per day | with M ∴ per day WE |
B L ☻ | D prior arrangement | ⚗ | Ⴤ
| ⚲ | ⋈ usually | ④ competition
days BH & WE | TR club
competitions | 𝔍 | M 400 | S
★★*Belle Vue Royal, Marine Ter.
T:(0970) 617558. 42rm (12 ⇌ 3 ⌗)*

ABOYNE
Grampian, *Aberdeenshire*
Map **VII** J6

Aboyne Formaston Park, (E side of
village, N of A93)
T:(0339) 2328
*Parkland/heathland course with
outstanding views.* 18 | 5330 yds | Par
66 | SSS 66
Visitors welcome | B L ♥ prior
arrangement | ⚲ ¥ | ④ 5am | M 700
★★*Bainacoil House.* T:(0339) 2252.
11rm (3 ➪ 2 🛏)

ACCRINGTON
Lancashire
Map **V**   D6

Baxenden & District Top o' th'
Meadow, Baxenden, (1½m SE of
Accrington, off A680)
T:(0254) 34555
Moorland course. Societies welcome. 9 |
5740 yds | SSS 68
Visitors welcome | .. per day | B L
♥ (not Thu) | ⚲ ¥ | M 350
★★★*Keirby, Keirby Walk, Burnley.*
T:(0282) 27611. 49rm ➪

Green Haworth Green Haworth,
(2m S of Accrington)
T:(0254) 37580
*Moorland course dominated by
quarries. Easy walking. Societies
welcome by arrangement WE.* 9 | 5470
yds(18) | Par 68 | SSS 67
Visitors welcome, Sun only with M
| B (WE only) ♥ (not Mon to F)
prior arrangement | D prior
arrangement | ⚲ ¥ | ⋈ | ④ Tu Th S
| M 170 | TR after 5 pm W (Ladies
Day), WE competitions
★★★*Blackburn Moat House, Preston
New Rd, Blackburn.* T:(0254) 64441.
98rm ➪

ADDINGTON
Greater London
Map **II** F4

Addington Court Featherbed Ln,
(1m S of Addington, off A2022)
T:01-657 0281
*Challenging well-drained courses
designed by F. Hawtree. Two 18-hole
courses, 9-hole course and a pitch and
putt course. Societies welcome by
arrangement. Reduced rates for
children.* Old(18) 5604 yds, New(18)
5515 yds, Lower(9) 4610 yds | Par 68,
67, 64 | SSS 67, 67, 63.
All courses open to public ☎ | B L

ABRIDGE
Essex
Map **II** F3

Abridge Stapleford Tawney (1¾m NE of Abridge)
T:(04028) 396
18 | 6703 yds | Par 72 | SSS 72
Visitors welcome restricted WE BH | ☎ | with M only Sat | B L ♥ (not F) D
(society bookings only) | ⚲ ¥ | TR Sun (ladies Tu am) | M 400 | S
★★★*Post House, High Rd, Bell Common, Epping.* T:(0378) 73137. 82rm ➪
A parkland course with easy walking. The quick drying course is by
no means easy to play. This has been the venue of several
professional tournaments. Abridge is a Country Club and has all
the attendant facilities.

♥ | ⚲ ¥ ↖ S
★★★★*Selsdon Park, Sanderstead.*
T:01-657 8811. 150rm ➪

Addington Palace Gravel Hill (½m
SW of Addington, on A212)
T:01-654 3061
*Hard walking parkland course, with 2
par 4 testing holes (2nd and 10th).
Societies welcome by arrangement Tu
W F.* 18 | 6262 yds | Par 71 | SSS 71
Visitors welcome weekdays | WE
BH with M | B ♥ (not Mon) | L prior
arrangement (not Mon) | ⚲ ¥ | ④
TR WE BH | ♪ | M 600 | S
★★★★*Selsdon Park, Sanderstead.*
T:01-657 8811. 150rm ➪

ADDINGTON
Kent
Map **II** G4

West Malling London Rd,
Addington (1m S of Addington off
A20)
T:(0732) 844785
*Parkland course. 6 squash courts. No
facilities for children.* 18 | 7029 (Kings)
6222 (Princes) yds | Par 73 (71) | SSS
73 (70)
Visitors welcome, with M only WE
(pm) ☎ preferred | without M ∷ |
with M .. per day ∴ WE | B ♥ | L
D prior arrangement | ⚲ ¥ |
prior arrangement | TR WE until
1130 | ♪ | M 350 | S
★★★*Great Danes, Ashford Rd,
Hollingbourne.* T:(0622) 30022.
127rm ➪ 🛏

AIRDRIE
Strathclyde, *Lanarkshire*
Map **VI** E2

Airdrie Rochsoles, (1m N of
Airdrie, on B802)
T:(02364) 62195
Picturesque parkland course. 18 | 6004

yds | Par 69 | SSS 69
Visitors welcome ☎ ⊠ | B L ♥ D
prior arrangement | ⚲ prior
arrangement ¥ | TR WE M 450 | S
★★*Tudor, Alexander St.* T:(02364)
63295. 21rm (10 ➪)

ALDENHAM
Hertfordshire
Map **II** E2

Aldenham Radlett Rd, (W side of
village)
T:(09276) 7775
*Undulating parkland course. Societies
welcome by arrangement.*
Visitors welcome | fees ∴ per day
∷ WE | B L ♥ | D prior
arrangement | ¥ (x3) ⚲ ⋈ | M 450 |
S
★★★*Ladbroke, Elton Way, Watford
Bypass.* T:(0923) 35881. 155rm ➪

ALDERLEY EDGE
Cheshire
Map **III** H2

Alderley Edge Brook Ln, (1m NW
of Alderley Edge, on B5085)
T:(0625) 585583
*Well wooded undulating pastureland
course. A stream crosses 7 of the 9
holes.* 9 | 5829 yds | Par 68 | SSS 68
Visitors welcome ⊠ | ∴ per day | B
♥ not Mon | ⚲ ¥ ⋈ | ♪ | M 300 | S
TR Tu, Sat
★★★*De Trafford Arms, London Rd.*
T:(0625) 583881. 37rm ➪

ALDERSHOT
Hampshire
Map **II** C5

Army Laffans Rd, Aldershot. (1½m
N of town centre, off A323/A325)
T:(0252) 540638
*Picturesque heathland course with 3
par 3's over 200 yds.* 18 | 6553 yds | ➟

Par 71 | *SSS 71*
Visitors welcome | with M only WE
BH | ⊠ (Mon to F) | without M ∷
per day | with M .. per day WE | B
L ☎ D | ⚘ ♈ ↘ ♃ | M 650 | Ⓢ
★★★*Queens, Lynchford Rd,*
Farnborough. T:(0252) 545051.
79rm ⇌ 爵

ALDRIDGE
West Midlands
Map III J4

Druids Heath Stonnal Rd, Aldridge
(NE side of town centre off A454)
T:(0922) 55595
Testing undulating heathland course.
Societies welcome by arrangement. 18 |
6914 yds | *Par 72* | *SSS 73*
Visitors welcome, but WE only with
M | ∴ per day | B ☎ | ⚘ ♈ ⋈ | ♃ |
M 400 | Ⓢ
★★★*Fairlawns, 178 Little Ashton Rd,*
Aldridge, Walsall. T:(0922) 55122.
30rm ⇌

ALFRETON
Derbyshire
Map III K2

Alfreton Wingfield Rd, (1m W of
Alfreton, on A615)
T:(0773) 832070
A small parkland course with tight
fairways, many natural hazards. 9 |
5012 yds | *Par 66* | *SSS 65*
Visitors welcome with M only Mon
WE BH | without M ∴ per day |
with M ∴ per day | B ☎ (not Mon) |
L D prior arrangement (not Mon) |
⚘ ♈ ⋈ | ⓉⓇ after 1630 | M 230
★*Hurt Arms, Ambergate. T:(077385)*
2006. 6rm

ALLENDALE
Northumberland
Map VI J6

Allendale Thornley Gate, (¾m W

of Allendale town)
T:091-2675875
Slightly hilly rural course with fine
views. Club room available to
picnickers. 9 | *4610 yds (played twice)* |
Par 66 | *SSS 63*
Visitors welcome | .. per day WE |
☎ | ⚘ ↘ | ⋈ | M 107 | Ⓢ
★★*County, Priestpopple, Hexham.*
T:(0434) 602030. 10rm (9 爵)

ALLOA
Central, *Clackmannanshire*
Map VI E1

Alloa Schawpark, Sauchie (1½m
NE of Alloa on A908)
T:(0259) 722745
Parkland course. 18 | *6240 yds* | *Par 70*
| *SSS 70*
Visitors welcome | ∴ per day | B L
☎ D prior arrangement (not Mon) |
⚘ ♈ ↘ | ⋈ | M 600 | Ⓢ
★★★*Royal, Henderson St, Bridge of*
Allan. T:(0786) 832284. 33rm (25 ⇌)

Braehead Cambus, Alloa (2m W of
Alloa on A907)
T:(0259) 722078
Attractive long-holed parkland course
at the foot of the Ochil Hills with
stream running through. Particularly
difficult finish. Societies welcome by
arrangement. 18 | *6013 yds* | *Par 70* |
SSS 69
Visitors welcome | ☎ advisable WE
| .. per day ∴ WE | B ☎ | ⋈ | ⓉⓇ
☎ for details | ④ WE | M 500
★★*King Robert, Glasgow Rd,*
Bannockburn. T:(0786) 811666.
21rm ⇌

ALNESS
Highland, *Ross and Cromarty*
Map VII F4

Alness (½m N of Alness, off A9)
T:(0349) 883877

A short, but testing, 9-hole parkland
course with beautiful views over Moray
Firth. First 7 holes guarded by walls
and fences which are out of bounds. 9 |
2359 yds | *Par 66* | *SSS 63*
Visitors welcome .. per day WE |
ⓉⓇ 1800-1900 competition days |
M 250
★★*Novar Arms, Evanton. T:(0349)*
830210. 10rm

ALNMOUTH
Northumberland
Map VI K4

Alnmouth Foxton Hall, (1m NE of
Alnmouth)
T:(0665) 830368
Coastal course. 18 | *6414 yds* | *Par 71* |
SSS 71
Visitors welcome ∴ per day | ∷
WE | BH B L D ☎ ♈ ⚘ ⋈ ④F |
M 600
★★*Saddle, 24-25 Northumberland St.*
T:(0665) 830476. 9rm (3 ⇌ 6 爵)

Alnmouth Village Marine Rd,
(E side of village)
T:(0665) 830370
Seaside course with partial coast view.
Societies welcome by arrangement. 9 |
6078 yds | *Par 70* | *SSS 70*
Visitors welcome | B L ☎ D | ⚘ ♈
⋈ | ⓉⓇ competition days | M 480
★★*Saddle, 24-25 Northumberland St.*
T:(0665) 830476. 9rm (3 ⇌ 6 爵)

ALNWICK
Northumberland
Map VI K4

Alnwick Swansfield Park, (S side
of town)
T:(0665) 602632
This parkland course offers a fair test of
golfing skills using the contours of land
and trees to create a well laid-out
natural course. 9 | *5379 yds* | *Par 66* |
SSS 66
Visitors welcome, restricted
competition days | without M ..
per day | with M .. per day WE | ⚘
| ♈ evenings only | ⋈ | ⓉⓇ
competition days | M 380
★★★*White Swan, Bondgate Within.*
T:(0665) 602109. 41rm (40 ⇌)

ALRESFORD
Hampshire
Map II B6

Alresford, Cheriton Rd, (1m S of
Alresford, on B3046)

ALDEBURGH
Suffolk
Map IV K7

Aldeburgh Saxmundham Rd (1m W of Aldeburgh, on A1094)
T:(072885) 2890
Societies welcome by arrangement. 18 (9) | *6330 yds (4228)* | *Par 68 (64)* | *SSS 71 (64)*
Visitors welcome ⊠ | ☎ preferred | * | B ☎ | L prior arrangement | ⚘ ♈ ↘
prior arrangement | M 715 | Ⓢ
★★★*Wentworth, Sea Front, T:(072885) 2312. 33rm (19 ⇌ 4 爵)*
A most enjoyable and not unduly difficult seaside course; ideal for
golfing holidaymakers. A bracing and fairly open terrain with some
trees and heathland.

ALVECHURCH
Hereford and Worcester
Map **III** J5

Kings Norton Brockhill Ln,
Weatheroak, (3m NE of
Alvechurch), Birmingham
T:(0564) 826706
*3 9-hole courses. 27 | 3567 yds (3518
yds) 3290 yds | Par 72 | SSS 72*
Visitors welcome but with M only
WE BH ☎ | ✳ | B L ☙ (not Mon) | D
(not Sun Mon) | ⚴ ⅄ ↘ (by
arrangement) | [TR] WE BH | ♩ |
M 600 | [S]
*★★★St Johns Swallow, 651 Warwick
Rd, Solihull. T:021-705 6777.
213rm (192 ⇆)*

Kings Norton course plan

An old club with 3 9-hole courses, the Blue, Red and Yellow. A
parkland course, with some exacting water hazards, it has housed
important events. There is also a 12-hole par 3 course available for
play.

T:(096273) 3746
*Undulating parkland course with
testing 6th and 10th holes (par 4). 18
tees. 9 | 5931 yds | Par 70 | SSS 69*
Visitors welcome | without M ••
per round ∴ WE | with M •• per
round | B L ☙ (not Mon) | D prior
arrangement (not Mon) | ⚴ ⅄ ↘ |
⋈ | [TR] until 1100 WE, BH,
matches and special events | ♩ |
M 450 | [S]
*★★Grange, 17 London Rd,
Holybourne, Alton. T:(0420) 86565.
9rm (6 ⇆ 3 🌢). Annexe: 4rm (2 ⇆
2 🌢)*

ALTRINCHAM
Greater Manchester
Map **V** D8

Altrincham Stockport Rd, (¾m E of
Altrincham, on A560)
T:061-928 0671
*Parkland course with easy walking, and
some natural hazards. 18 | 6204 yds |
Par 71 | SSS 69*
Visitors welcome ☎ | •• per day
WE | ☙ | ⚴ L ↘ | ⋈ | ♩ | M 324 | [S]
[TR] WE
*★★★Cresta Court, Church St.
T:061-928 8017. 139rm ⇆ 🌢*

Dunham Forest Oldfield Ln, (1½m
W of Altrincham off A56)
T:061-928 2605
*Attractive parkland course cut through
magnificent beech woods. Societies
welcome M Th F. 18 | 6800 yds | Par 72
| SSS 72*
Visitors welcome, except WE BH |
∷ per day | with M ∴ per day WE |
B L ☙ D (not F) | ⚴ ⅄ ↘ | [TR]
1245-1345 | ♩ | M 600 | [S]
*★★★Bowdon, Langham Rd, Bowdon.
T:061-928 7121. 41rm (38 ⇆)*

Ringway Hale Mount, Hale Barns,
Altrincham (2½m SE of Altrincham
on A538)
T:061-980 2630
*Parkland course, with interesting
natural hazards. Easy walking, good
views. Societies welcome Th by
arrangement. 18 | 6494 yds | Par 71 |
SSS 71*
Visitors welcome ☎ | without M ∷
per day ∷ WE | with M •• per day
WE | B ☙ (not Mon) | L D prior
arrangement (not Mon) | ⚴ ⅄ | ⋈
sometimes | [TR] not before 0930
w/days. Not between 1300-1400
w/days. Fri-members only | ♩ |
M 650 | [S]
*★★★Cresta Court, Church St.
T:061-928 8017. 139rm ⇆ 🌢*

ALYTH
Tayside, *Perthshire*
Map **VII** H7

Alyth Pitcrocknie, (1m E of Alyth,
on B954)
T:(08283) 2268
*Windy heathland course with easy
walking. Society meetings by*   ➡

arrangement. 18 | 6226 yds | Par 70 | SSS 70
Visitors welcome ☎ ✉ | without M ∴ per day ∷ WE | with M ∴ per day WE | B L ☕ D prior arrangement (not F) | ⛺ | 🍸 variable | ④ WE | M 750 | [S]
★★*Kings of Kinloch, Meigle. T:(08284) 273. 7rm (1 ⇨ 1 ⋒)*

AMLWCH
Gwynedd
Map **III** C1

Bullbay Anglesey (1m NW of Amlwchy on A5025)
T:(0407) 831188/830960
Pleasant seaside course with natural meadow, rock, gorse and wind hazards. Views from all tees across Irish Sea to Isle of Man. Parties at special rates by arrangement. 18 | 6160/5952 yds | Par 70/69 | SSS 70/69
Visitors welcome ✉ | without M ‥ per day ∴ WE | with M ‥ per day WE | B ☕ (not Tu) | L D prior arrangement (not Tu) | ⛺ 🍸 ↘ | ⋈ by arrangement | M 450 | [S]
★★*Trecastell, Bull Bay, Amlwch. T:(0407) 830651. 12rm (8 ⇨ 2 ⋒)*

ALWOODLEY
West Yorkshire
Map **V** F6

Alwoodley Wigton Ln, Alwoodley (5m N of Leeds, off A61)
T:(0532) 681680
18 | 6301 yds | Par 70 | SSS 72
Visitors welcome, restricted F WE BH | * | B L ☕ D | ⛺ 🍸 ↘ | [TR] 1230-1330 | M 450 | [S] | ℷ
★*Hartrigg, Shire Oak Rd, Headingley. T:(0532) 751568. 28rm*

SCORE CARD: White Tees

1	405	10	472
2	305	11	168
3	510	12	366
4	480	13	396
5	371	14	207
6	420	15	405
7	142	16	417
8	546	17	437
9	193	18	439

A fine heathland course with length, trees and abundant heather. Many attractive situations — altogether a severe test of golf.

ANGMERING
West Sussex
Map **II** D7

Ham Manor (¾m SW of Angmering)
T:(0903) 783288
18 | 6216 yds | Par 70 | SSS 70
Visitors welcome, restricted competition days | ✉ ☎ | fees on application | B ☕ | L (not Mon) | ⛺ 🍸 | ④ 1st tee 1000-1130, other times for 10th tee | [TR] competitions | ℷ | M 800 | [S]
★★★*Chatsworth, The Steyne, Worthing. T:(0903) 36103. 97rm (76 ⇨ 3 ⋒)*
Two miles from the sea and easily reached from London, this parkland course has fine springy turf and provides an interesting test in two loops of nine holes each.

AMPFIELD
Hampshire
Map **II** A6

Ampfield Par Three Winchester Rd, (3m NE of Romsey on A31)
T:(0794) 68480
Pretty parkland course designed by Henry Cotton, easy walking. Societies welcome by arrangement. No facilities for children. 18 | 2478 yds | Par 54 | SSS 53
Visitors welcome | ‥ per day ∴ WE | ☕ | B D prior arrangement (not Tu) | ⛺ 🍸 ↘ ⋈ (probable) ℷ | M 500 | [S] ④ Sun
★★★*Potters Heron, Chandlers Ford. T:(04215) 66611. 60rm ⇨*

ANDOVER
Hampshire
Map **II** A5

Andover 51 Winchester Rd, (1m S of Andover, on A3057)
T:(0264) 23980
Hilly downland course, fine views. Societies welcome by arrangement. Junior section. 9 | 5933 yds | Par 69 | SSS 68
Visitors welcome, restricted WE BH (am) | ‥ per round | B ☕ L | D | ⛺ 🍸 ↘ | ⋈ (possible) | [TR] Sun am BH ℷ | M 400 | [S]
★★*Danebury, High St. T:(0264) 23332. 24rm ⇨*

ANSTRUTHER
Fife, *Fife*
Map **VI** H1

Anstruther Shore Road, Marsfield, (SW of town, off A917)
T:(0333) 310224
Seaside course with some excellent par 3 holes always in good condition. 9 | 4504 yds | Par 62 | SSS 63
Visitors welcome | ‥ per day WE | B L D ☕ | ⛺ 🍸 | [TR] competition days | M 470
★★★*Craw's Nest, Bankwell Rd. T:(0333) 310691. 50rm ⇨*

ARBROATH
Tayside, *Angus*
Map **VII** J8

Arbroath 33 Commerce St (2m SW of Arbroath, on A92)
T:(0241) 72272/72069
Two clubs (Arbroath 72272 and Artisan 72069) with facilities playing on same course. Municipal seaside links course. Society meetings by arrangement. 18 | 6078 yds | Par 70 | SSS 69
Visitors welcome | ∴ per day WE | B L ☕ D prior arrangement (not Th) | ⛺ | 🍸 (not Th) ↘ | ℷ | M 500 | [S]
★★*Hotel Seaforth, Dundee Rd. T:(0241) 72232. 20rm (11 ⇨)*

Letham Grange Colliston, By Arbroath (off the Forfar Arbroath Rd)
T:(024189) 373
A course of great variety including woodland and fine parkland holes. Picturesque lakes. 18 | 6742 yds | Par 72 | SSS 72
Visitors welcome | without M ∴ per day WE | with M ‥ per day WE | B L ☕ D | ⛺ 🍸 ↘ | ℷ | [S]
★★★*Letham Grange, Colliston, Arbroath. T:(024189) 373*

ARRAN, ISLE OF
Strathclyde, *Bute*
Map **VI**

See Blackwaterfoot, Brodick, Corrie, Lochranza and Whiting Bay

APPLEBY in WESTMORELAND
Cumbria
Map V   D3

Appleby Brackenber Moor, (2m SE of Appleby, off A66)
T:(0930) 51432
Societies welcome (Mon to F). 18 | 5895 yds | Par 68 | SSS 68
Visitors welcome | B ☎ (not Tu) | ⚐
| ♈ | M 600
***⚘Appleby Manor, Roman Rd.*
T:(07683) 51571. 12rm (8 ⇄)

SCORE CARD:

1	341	10	186
2	401	11	457
3	344	12	265
4	174	13	315
5	304	14	436
6	419	15	178
7	359	16	425
8	305	17	165
9	420	18	420

This remotely situated heather and moorland course offers interesting holiday golf with the rewarding bonus of several long par 4 holes that will be remembered. There are superb views.

ASCOT
Berkshire
Map II   D4

Swinley Forest Ascot (1½m S of Ascot off A330)
T:(0990) 20197
18 | 6001 yds | Visitors welcome with M only | ☎ L prior arrangement (not Mon F) | ⚐ | M 250 | ⓢ
**Cricketers, London Rd, Bagshot. T:(0276) 73196. 21rm (3 ⇄ 1 ஐ)*
Annexe: 8rm ⇄
An immaculate heathland course. The 17th is as good a short hole as will be found with a bunkered plateau green.

ASCOT
Berkshire
Map II   D4

Berkshire Swinley Rd, Ascot (2½m NW of M3 Jct 3, on A332)
T:(0990) 21495/6
Heathland course, difficult walking. Societies welcome (Tu to F) by arrangement. 36 | 6356 yds (6258) | Par 72(71) | SSS 70(70)
Visitors welcome ✉ ☏ | with M only WE BH | without M :: per day

| B | L ☎ (not Mon) | ⚐ 🜊 | M 800 |
ⓢ | TR | WE
★★★★*Berystede, Bagshot Rd, Sunninghill. T:(0990) 23311.*
88rm ⇄ ஐ

Lavender Park Swinley Rd, (3½m SW of Ascot on A332)
T:(0344) 884074
Public parkland course. Driving range with 3 path one-course, floodlit till 2200. 9 | 1104 yds | Par 28

Visitors welcome .. per round | ♈
B L D ☎ | ⟍ | ⓢ 🜊
★★★★*Berystede, Bagshot Rd, Sunninghill. T:(0990) 23311.*
88rm ⇄ ஐ

Royal Ascot Winkfield Rd, Ascot (On Royal Ascot Racecourse, ½m N of Ascot on A330)
T:(0990) 25175
Heathland course exposed to weather. Small societies welcome (Mon to F) by arrangement. 18 | 5653 yds | Par 68 | SSS 67
Visitors welcome, restricted WE BH | * | B L ☎ D prior arrangement | ⚐ ♈ | TR WE BH | M 575 | ⓢ
★★★★*Berystede, Bagshot Rd, Sunninghill. T:(0990) 23311.*
88rm ⇄ ஐ

ASHBOURNE
Derbyshire
Map III   J3

Ashbourne Clifton, (1½m SW of Ashbourne on A515)
T:(0335) 42078
Undulating parkland course. Societies by arrangement. 9 | 5359 yds | Par 66 | SSS 66
Visitors welcome | without M .. per day WE | with M .. per day WE | B ☎ | L D by prior arrangement | ⚐ ♈ ⋈ | M 300
★★*Bentley Brook Inn, Fenny Bentley. T:(033529) 278. 8rm (3 ⇄)*

ASHBY-DE-LA-ZOUCH
Leicestershire
Map III   K4

Willesley Park Tamworth Rd, Ashby de la Zouch (SW side of ↳

town centre on A453)
T:(0530) 414596
*Undulating heathland and parkland
course with quick draining sandy sub-
soil. Societies welcome (W Th F) by
arrangement. 18 | 6310 yds | Par 70 |
SSS 70*
Visitors welcome ✉ without M ∴
per day ∷ WE | with M .. per day
WE | B L ☛ prior arrangement (not
Mon) | D prior arrangement (not
Sun and Mon) | ⚥ ⅄ ⟍ | TR WE
until 0930 | ④ ☎ for details | 🏌 | M
620 | Ⓢ
★★★*Royal Crest, Station Rd. T:(0530)
412833. 31rm (25 ⇄ 6 🛏)*

ASHFORD
Kent
Map II J5

Ashford Sandyhurst Ln, (1½m NW
of Ashford, off A20)
T:(0233) 20180
*Parkland course with good views and
easy walking. Narrow fairways and
tightly bunkered greens ensure a
challenging game. Societies welcome by
arrangement. 18 | 6246 yds | Par 71 |
SSS 70*
Visitors welcome, restricted WE BH
(am) | without M ∴ per day | B ☛ |
L D | ⚥ ⅄ ⟍ ⋉ | ④ sometimes
start at 10th | TR WE BH (until
1130) 🏌 | M 560 | Ⓢ
★★★*Spearpoint, Canterbury Rd,
Kennington. T:(0233) 36863.
37rm (30 ⇄ 4 🛏)*

ASHTON-IN-MAKERFIELD
Greater Manchester
Map V C7

Ashton in Makerfield Garswood
Park, Liverpool Rd, (½m W of M6
(Jct 24) on A58)
T:(0942) 727267
*Well wooded parkland course. 18 | 6190
yds | Par 70 | SSS 69*
Visitors welcome ✉, restricted WE,
BH | ∴ per day | B L ☛ D prior
arrangement (not Mon) | ⚥ ⅄ | M
370 | Ⓢ
★★★*Post House, Lodge Ln, Newton-le-
Willows, Haydock. T:(0942) 717878.
98rm ⇄*

ASHTON-UNDER-LYNE
Greater Manchester
Map V E7

Ashton-under-Lyne Kings Rd,
Higher Hurst, (1½m NE of

Ashton-under-Lyne).
T:061-330 1537
*A testing, varied moorland course, with
large greens. Easy walking. Three new
holes have improved the course.
Societies welcome (Mon-F) by
arrangement. 18 | 6157 yds | Par 70 |
SSS 69*
Visitors welcome, only with M WE
| without M ∴ per day | with M ..
per day WE | B ☛ ☎ (not F) | L D
prior arrangement (not F) | ⚥ ⅄ |
TR WE ⟍ | 🏌 | M 600 | Ⓢ
★★*York House, York Place, off
Richmond St. T:061-330 5899.
26rm (8 ⇄ 3 🛏)*

Dukinfield Lyne Edge, Dukinfield,
Ashton-under-Lyne, (S side of
Dukinfield off B6175)
T:061-338 2340
*Small but tricky moorland course with
several difficult par 3 holes. Societies
welcome weekdays by arrangement. 16 |
5544 yds | Par 68 | SSS 67*
Visitors welcome | without M ..
per day WE | with M .. per day WE
| B ☛ | L D prior arrangement ☎ |
⚥ ⅄ ⋉ | TR WE W (ladies' day) |
M 200
★★*York House, York Pl, off Richmond
St, Ashton-under-Lyne. T:061-330
5899. 26rm (8 ⇄ 3 🛏)*

ASKAM-in-FURNESS
Cumbria
Map V B4

Dunnerholme (1m N of
Askam-in-Furness)
T:(0229) 62675
*Unique 10-hole links course with view
of Lakeland hills and stream running
through. Societies welcome weekdays by
arrangement. 10 | 6101 yds | Par 71 |*

ASPLEY GUISE
Bedfordshire
Map IV C8

Aspley Guise & Woburn Sands West Hill, (2m W of M1 (Jct 13), on W side of
Aspley Guise)
T:(0908) 583596
Societies welcome (W F) by arrangement ✉. *18 | 6115 yds | Par 71 | SSS 69*
Visitors welcome, with M only WE BH | ☎ advisable | ∴ per day | ☛ (not
Mon) | B L D prior arrangement (not Mon) | ⚥ ⅄ | ⋉ prior arrangement | 🏌 |
M 600 | TR WE, BH | ⟍ | Ⓢ
★★★🏌*Flitwick Manor, Church Rd, T:(0525) 712242. 6rm (4 ⇄ 2 🛏).*
A fine undulating course in expansive heathland interspersed with
many attractive clumps of gorse, broom and bracken. Some well-
established silver birch are a feature. The 7th, 8th and 9th are really
tough holes to complete the first half.

SSS 69
Visitors welcome except Sun | ..
per day WE | ⚥ ⅄ ⋉ | TR Sun |
M 330
★★*Eccle Riggs, Foxfield Rd,
Broughton-in-Furness. T:(06576) 398.
13rm (4 ⇄)*

ASKERNISH
Isle of South Uist, Western Isles,
Outer Hebrides
Map VII A5

Askernish Western Isles (5m NW of
Lochboisdale, off A865 via ferry
from Oban)
(No telephone)
*Golfers play on machair, close to the
Atlantic shore. 9 (18 tees) | 5312 yds |
Par 68 | SSS 67*
Visitors welcome without M .. per
day | ⟍ | M 20
★★*Lochboisdale. T:(08784) 322.
20rm (10 ⇄)*

ATHERSTONE
Warwickshire
Map III K4

Atherstone The Outwoods, (½m S
of Atherstone on B4116)
T:(08277) 3110
*Ninety-year-old parkland course laid
out on some hilly ground. 11 | 6239 yds
| Par 72 | SSS 70*
Visitors welcome | with M only WE
| ＊ | B L D prior arrangement (not
WE and Tu) | ☛ | ⚥ ⅄ | TR S Sun
🏌 | M 300 | Ⓢ
★*Old Red Lion. T:(08277) 3156.
10rm (5 🛏)*

**Purley Chase Golf and Country
Club** Pipers Lane, Ridge Lane,
Atherstone, (2m S of Atherstone off
B4114)

T:(0203) 395348/393118
Meadowland course with tricky water hazards and undulating greens. 18 | 6604 yds | Par 71 | SSS 71
Visitors welcome | without M ∷ per day WE | with M ∴ per day WE | B L ☕ D | △ 🍸 ↘ | ⋈ | [TR] Sun am | M 450 | [S]
★*Old Red Lion, Atherstone. T:(08277) 3156. 10rm (5 🚿)*

AUCHINBLAE
Grampian, *Kincardineshire*
Map **VII** J7

Auchinblae Laurencekirk, (½m NE of Auchinblae)
Picturesque small parkland/heathland course, good views. 9 | 2174 yds | Par 32 | SSS 30
Visitors welcome | ‥ per day | B ⋈ | M 50 | [S]
★★★*Commodore, Cowie Park, Stonehaven. T:(0569) 62936. 40rm ⇔ 🚿*

AUCHTERARDER
Tayside, *Perthshire*
Map **VI** F1

Auchterarder Orchil Rd, (¾m SW of Auchterarder on A824)
T:(07646) 2804
Parkland course with easy walking. 18 | 5737 yds | Par 69 | SSS 68
Visitors welcome except W pm | ☎ for parties | ‥ per day | B L ☕ D | △ 🍸 | M 450
○○○○○*Gleneagles. T:(07646) 2231. 254rm ⇔*

Gleneagles Hotel Auchterarder (2m SW of Auchterarder off A823)
T:(07646) 3543
Famous moorland courses. King's course: 18 | 6452 yds | Par 70 | SSS 71 | Queen's course: 18 | 5964 yds | Par 68 | SSS 69 | Prince's course: 18 | 4678 yds | Par 63 | SSS 64 | Glendevon course: 18 | 5762 yds | Par 67 | SSS 68
Visitors welcome ☎ | ∷ per day WE | B L ☕ D | △ 🍸 ↘ | [TR] until 1030, 1330-1430 | ℑ | M 450 | [S]
○○○○○*Gleneagles, Auchterarder. T:(07646) 2231. 254rm ⇔*

AXMOUTH
Devon
Map **I** G6

Axe Cliff Axmouth, Seaton, (¾m S of Axmouth on B3172)
T:(0297) 20499
Undulating links course with coastal views. Societies welcome. 18 | 4998 yds | Par 67 (ladies 69) | SSS 64
Visitors welcome | Sun only after 1330 | ☎ preferable | B ☕ not Tu | L D prior arrangement (not Tu) | △ 🍸 ↘ ⋈ | [TR] Sun until 1330 | M 400
★★*Bay, East Walk, Seaton. T:(0297) 20073. 33rm (11 ⇔)*

AYR
Strathclyde, *Ayrshire*
Map **VI** D4

Belleisle Doonfoot Road, Ayr, (2m S of Ayr on A719)
T:(0292) 41258
Parkland course with beautiful sea views. First-class conditions. 18 | 6540 yds | Par 70 | SSS 71
Visitors welcome ‥ per day ∴ WE | B L D ☕ | △ 🍸 | [S] ↘ | ⋈ | [4] [TR] ☎
★★★*Belleisle House, Belleisle Park, Ayr. T:(0292) 42331. 17rm (9 ⇔ 5 🚿)*

Dalmilling Westwood Av, Ayr, (1½m E of town centre, off A719)
T:(0292) 63893
Meadowland course, with easy walking. 18 | 5401 yds | Par 68 | SSS 66
Visitors welcome ☎ | 🍸 B ☕ | L D prior arrangement | △ | ↘ ℑ | M 151 | [S]
★★★*Carlton, Prestwick. T:(0292) 76811. 39rm ⇔ 🚿*

Seafield Doonfoot Road, Ayr, (2m S of Ayr on A719)
T:(0292) 41258
Public self-starting course of parkland type. 18 | 5205 yds | Par 66 | SSS 66
‥ per day | △ | ↘ | ⋈ | [S]

BACKWORTH
Tyne and Wear
Map **VI** K6

Backworth The Hall, Backworth, Shiremoor (W side of Backworth on B1322)
T:(0632) 2681048
Parkland course, easy walking, natural hazards, good scenery. 9 | 5930 yds | Par 71 | SSS 69
Visitors welcome except Tu, W, Th after 1700, Sun am | B | △ 🍸 ☕ | [TR] S (April-Sept) | M 400
★★★★*Holiday Inn, Great North Rd, Seaton Burn. T:091-236 5432. 150rm ⇔ 🚿*

BACUP
Lancashire
Map **V** D6

Bacup Maiden Road, Bankside Ln (W side of town off A671)
T:(0706) 873170
Moorland course, predominantly flat except climbs to 1st and 10th holes. 9 | 5652 yds | Par 68 | SSS 67
Visitors welcome comp days | ‥ per day | ∴ WE | B L ☕ D prior arrangement (not F) | △ | 🍸 M 400
★★★*Keirby, Keirby Walk, Burnley. T:(0282) 27611. 49rm ⇔*

BAILDON
West Yorkshire
Map **V** E6

Baildon Moorgate, Baildon, Shipley (N side of Baildon)
T:(0274) 584266
Moorland course with much bracken rough. The 5th is a hard climb. Societies welcome by arrangement. Children welcome. 18 | 6178 yds | Par 70 | SSS 69
Visitors welcome restricted WE (not before 1030) | B L ☕ D prior arrangement (not Mon) | △ 🍸 ↘ | ⋈ by arrangement | [TR] Tu (Ladies Day 0900-1030) WE (until 1030) | ℑ |

AYLESBURY
Buckinghamshire
Map **II** C2

Ellesborough Butlers Cross, (1m E of Ellesborough on B4010)
T:(0296) 622114
18 | 6215 yds | Par 71 | SSS 70
Visitors welcome, restricted Tu F WE BH ☎ with or without M ∷ per day | B L ☕ D prior arrangement (not Mon) | △ 🍸 | ℑ | M 800 | [S]
❀○○○*Bell Inn, Aston Clinton. T:(0296) 630252. 21rm ⇔*
Used to be part of the property of Chequers, and under the shadow of the famous monument at the Wendover end of the Chilterns. A downland course, it is rather hilly with most holes enhanced by far-ranging views over the Aylesbury countryside.

M 700 | S
★★★*Bankfield, Bradford Rd, Bingley.*
T:(0274) 567123. 69rm (67 ⇄ 2 🏠)

BAKEWELL
Derbyshire
Map III   J2

Bakewell Station Rd (E side of town on B6408)
T:(062981) 2307
Parkland course, hilly, plenty of natural hazards to test the golfer and magnificent views across the Wye Valley. 9 | 5240 yds | Par 66 | SSS 66
Visitors welcome | * | B L ☛ D | ⩜ Ⴓ open mid-day and evenings except M | ⋈ prior arrangement | ℑ | M 400 | S
★★*Milford House, Mill St. T:(062981) 2130. 11rm (7 ⇄)*

BALA
Gwynedd
Map III   E3

Bala Penlan (¾m SW of Bala off A494)
T:(0678) 520539
Mountainous course with natural hazards. 10 | 4935 yds | Par 66 | SSS 64
Visitors welcome .. per day | B L ☛ D | ⩜ Ⴓ ゝ ⋈ | TR WE ④ WE M 200
★★*Plas Coch, High St. T:(0678) 520309. 10rm (2 ⇄ 6 🏠)*

BALLATER
Grampian, *Aberdeenshire*
Map VII   H6

Ballater Victoria Road, Ballater, Grampian (W side of town)
T:(0338) 55567
Moorland course with testing long holes and beautiful scenery. 18 | 6106 yds | Par 69 | SSS 69
Visitors welcome | .. weekdays ∴ WE | B L ☛ D | ⩜ Ⴓ ゝ | ⋈ | TR variable | ℑ M 700
★★*Darroch Learg, Ballater. T:(0338) 55443. 15rm (13 ⇄ 2 🏠). Annexe: 8rm (3 ⇄ 2 🏠)*

BALMORE
Strathclyde, *Lanarkshire*
Map VI   E2

Balmore By Torrance (N of Balmore, off A807)
T:(0360) 20240
Parkland course with fine views. 18 | 5516 yds | Par 67 | SSS 67
Visitors welcome | without M ∴ per day | with M .. per day | B L ☛ D | ⩜ Ⴓ | ℑ | M 400 | S
★★★*Black Bull Thistle, Main St, Milngavie. T:041-956 2291. 28rm (27 ⇄)*

BAMFORD
Derbyshire
Map V   F8

Sickleholme Bamford, Sheffield (¾m S of Bamford on A6013)
T:(0443) 51306
Downland type course in the lovely Peak District. Fine views. 18 | 6064 yds | Par 69 | SSS 69
Visitors welcome restricted WE BH W am | ⊠ ☎ | ∴ per day | B L ☛ | D prior arrangement (not F) | ⩜ Ⴓ ゝ | TR W am (Ladies) | ④ before 1030 WE | M 550 | S
★★*George, Main Rd, Hathersage. T:(0433) 50436. 18rm (16 ⇄ 2 🏠)*

BANCHORY
Grampian, *Kincardineshire*
Map VII   J6

Banchory Kinneskie, Banchory (S side of town)
T:(03302) 2365
Sheltered parkland course, with easy walking and woodland scenery. 11th and 12th holes testing. Society meetings by arrangement. 18 | 5284 yds | Par 67 | SSS 66
Visitors welcome | ∴ per day | B L ☛ High Tea | ⩜ Ⴓ 1100-2300 | ゝ ⋈ ℑ | M 700 | S
❍❍❍♨*Banchory Lodge. T:(03302) 2625. 25rm (24 ⇄ 1 🏠)*

BANFF
Grampian, *Banffshire*
Map VII   J4

Duff House Royal The Barnyards, Banff (½m S of Banff on A98)
T:(02612) 2062
Well manicured flat parkland, bounded by woodlands and River Deveron. Society meetings by arrangement. 18 | 6161 yds | Par 68 | SSS 69
Visitors welcome | ∴ per round | B

SCORE CARD:			
1	182	10	196
2	213	11	334
3	510	12	413
4	476	13	406
5	314	14	149
6	224	15	404
7	279	16	268
8	162	17	260
9	361	18	314

This is not a long course, but there are those who have played golf all over the world who say that for sheer breathtaking beauty this northern seaside gem cannot be bettered. And the course itself is the greatest fun to play.

L ☎ D prior arrangement | ⚐ ♈ ⚊ |
⋈ | [TR] July Aug | 1600-1730 July
and Aug WE 0800-1000, 1230-1430,
1700-1830 | M 900 | [S]
★★★*Seafield Arms, Seafield St,
Cullen. T:(0542) 40791. 24rm (22 ⇌ 1
🏠)*

BANGOR
Gwynedd
Map III   D2

St Deiniol Bangor (E side of town
centre off A5122)
T:(0248) 353098
*Elevated parkland course with
panoramic views of Snowdonia, Menai
Straits, and Anglesey. Societies
welcome by arrangement. 18 | 5545 yds
| Par 68 | SSS 67*
Visitors welcome ∴ per day WE | B
L ☎ D prior arrangement | ⚐ ♈ ⋈
| M 325 | [S]
★★*Ty Uchaf, Tal-y-Bont. T:(0248)
352219. 9rm (6 ⇌ 3 🏠)*

BANSTEAD
Surrey
Map II   E4

Banstead Downs Burdon Ln,
Belmont, Sutton (1½m N of
Banstead on A217)
T:01-642 2284
*Downland course with narrow fairways
and hawthorns. 18 | 6169 yds | Par 69 |
SSS 69*
Visitors welcome ⊠ weekdays | WE
BH with M | without M ∴ per day |
with M .. per day | B L | D prior
arrangement (not Mon) | ☎ (not
Mon) | ⚐ ♈ | ④ S | [TR] S Sun until
1200 | ♩ | M 542 | [S]
★★*Heathside, Brighton Rd. T:(07373)
53355. 44rm 🏠*

BARASSIE
Strathclyde, *Ayrshire*
Map VI   D4

Kilmarnock (Barassie) 29 Hillhouse
Rd, Barassie, Troon
(E side of village on B746)
T:(0292) 311077(Club) 313920(Office)
18 | 6460 yds | Par 71 | SSS 71
Visitors welcome | without M ∷
per day | with M ∴ per day | B L ☎
D | ⚐ ♈ ⚊ | ⋈ | [TR] 1230-1330 | ♩ |
M 550 | [S]
★★★★*Marine, Crosbie Rd, Troon.
T:(0292) 314444. 69rm ⇌*

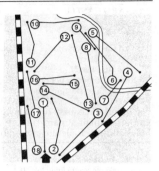

A magnificent seaside course, relatively flat with much heather.
The turf and greens are quite unequalled. The 15th is a testing par 3
at 220 yards.

Cuddington Banstead Rd (N of
Banstead station, off A2022)
T:01-393 0952
*Parkland course with easy walking and
providing good views. Societies
welcome by arrangement (Th). 18 |
6282 yds | Par 70 | SSS 70*
Visitors welcome restricted Tu WE
BH (until 1400) | ☎ | B prior
arrangement (not Tu F) | L (not
Mon Tu W F) D prior arrangement |
☎ ⚐ ♈ ⚊ | ♩ | M 800 | ④ various |
[TR] Tu, WE BH (before 1100) | [S]
★★*Heathside, Brighton Rd. T:(07373)
53355. 44rm 🏠*

BARGOED
Mid Glamorgan
Map I   G2

Bargoed Heolddu (NW side of
Bargoed)
T:(0443) 830143
*Mountain parkland course, testing par
4 13th hole. Societies welcome
weekdays by arrangement. 18 |
5850 yds | Par 70 | SSS 69*
Visitors welcome weekdays | WE
only with M | B L D ☎ prior
arrangement | ⚐ ♈ | ♩ | M 375
★★★*Maes Manor, Blackwood.
T:(0495) 224551. 10rm (7 ⇌ 🏠)
Annexe: 16rm (10 ⇌ 3 🏠)*

BARHAM
Kent
Map II   K5

Broome Park Barham, nr.
Canterbury (2m SE of Barham, on
A260)
T:(0227) 831701

BARNARD CASTLE
Durham
Map **V**   E3

Barnard Castle Marwood, (¾m N of Barnard Castle on B6278)
T:(0833) 38355
18 | 5838 yds | Par 71 | SSS 68
Visitors welcome | .. per day ∴ WE | B L ☞ D prior arrangement (not Mon F)
| ⚐ ♀ | ⋈ | TR starting times WE ④ competitions | ♉ | M 400 | S
**Rose & Crown*, Romaldkirk. T:(0833) 50213. 12rm (2 ⇌ 3 ▥). Annexe: 6rm ⇌
Flat moorland course high above the River Tees and presenting fine views. A small stream runs in front of or alongside many of the holes adding challenge and enjoyment to the game.

Parkland course in a valley, with a 300-year-old mansion/clubhouse. 18 | 6606 yds | Par 72 | SSS 72
Visitors welcome, advisable to ☎ | ∴ per round weekdays ∷ per round WE ∷ per day | B L D ☞ | ⚐
♀ | S ↘ | M 300 | ♉
****County, High St, Canterbury. T:(0227) 66266. 74rm ⇌

BARNEHURST
Greater London
Map **II**   F4

Barnehurst Mayplace Rd East (¾m NW of Crayford, off A2000)
T:(0322) 523746
Parkland course, easy walking. 9 | 5320 yds | Par 66 | SSS 66
Visitors welcome, restricted Tu Th S (pm) and Sun | B ☞ not Mon | ⚐
♀ ↘ ⋈ | ♉ | M 300 | S
***Crest, Black Prince Interchange, Southwold Rd, Bexley. T:(0322) 526900. 78rm ⇌

BARNET
Greater London
Map **II**   E3

Arkley Rowley Green Rd, (2m W of Barnet, off A411)
T:01-449 0394
Wooded parkland course situated on highest spot in Hertfordshire with fine views. 9(18 tees) | 6045 yds | Par 69 | SSS 69
Visitors welcome ☎ advisable | without M ∴ per day | with M .. per day | B L D prior arrangement (not Mon Tu WE) | ☞ ⚐ ♀ | TR
Tu, WE ♉ | M 350 | S
***Elstree Moat House, Barnet-by-Pass, Boreham Wood. T:01-953 1622. 60rm ⇌ ▥

Dyrham Park Galley Ln (3m NW of Barnet off A1081)

T:01-440 3361
Parkland course. 18 | 6369 yds | Par 71 | SSS 70
Visitors welcome only with M. Societies W only. | ∴ per day | B L ☞ | D prior arrangement | ⚐ ♀ ↘ | ♉ | M 1200 | S
***Crest, Bignells Corner, (junct A1/A6) South Mimms. T:(0707) 43311. 120rm ⇌

Old Fold Manor Old Fold Ln, Hadley Green, Barnet (N side of town centre on A1000)
T:01-449 2266
Parkland course, good test of golf. Societies welcome by arrangement. 18 | 6449 yds | Par 71 | SSS 71
Visitors welcome weekdays | WE BH with M or ⊠ | ☎ preferred | ∷ per day | B ☞ (not Mon W) | L D (prior arrangement not Mon W) | ⚐ ♀ ↘ | ④ TR ☎ for details | M 400 | S ♉
***Royal Chace, The Ridgeway, Enfield. T:01-366 6500. 92rm (51 ⇌ 41 ▥)

BARNHAM BROOM
Norfolk
Map **IV**   H4

Barnham Broom (1m N of Barnham Broom, S of A47)
T:(060545) 393
Attractive river valley course. 18 | 6603 yds | Par 72 | SSS 72
Visitors welcome with M WE only ⊠ ☎ | ♀ B L D ☞ | ↘ | ⋈ | M 550 | ♉
***Barnham Broom Golf & Country Club. T:(060545) 393. 39rm ⇌

BARNOLDSWICK
Lancashire
Map **V**   E5

Ghyll Ghyll Brow (1m NE of

Barnoldswick on B6252)
T:(0282) 842466
Parkland course with outstanding views, especially from the 8th tee where you can see the three peaks. Testing 3rd hole is an uphill par 4. 9 | 5722 yds | Par 68 | SSS 68
Visitors welcome | ♀ evenings and WE | B WE only | ⚐ ⋈ | TR ladies day (Tu) competition days | M 250
***Stirk House, Gisburn. T:(02005) 581. 40rm (37 ⇌ 3 ▥). Annexe: 12rm ⇌

BARNSLEY
South Yorkshire
Map **V**   F7

Barnsley Wakefield Rd, Staincross (3m N of Barnsley on A61)
T:(0226) 382856
Undulating meadowland course with easy walking apart from last 4 holes. Testing 8th and 18th holes. Junior section of 200 M, with weekly competitions. 18 | 6048 yds | Par 69 | SSS 69
Visitors welcome | .. per day | B L ☞ D (not T) | ⚐ ♀ ↘ | ⋈ | ④ WE ♉ | M 730 | S
*Royal, Church St. T:(0226) 203658. 17rm (1 ⇌)

BARRHEAD
Strathclyde, Renfrewshire
Map **VI**   D3

Fereneze Fereneze Av (NW side of town off B774)
T:041-881 1519
Moorland course, good view at the end of a hard climb. 18 | 5821 yds | Par 70 | SSS 68
Visitors welcome with M only WE ⊠ ☎ | ∴ per day (Sun per round) | B L ☞ D prior arrangement (not Mon) | ⚐ ♀ | TR ☎ for details | M 450 | S
**Dalmeny Park, Lochlibo Rd, Barrhead. T:041-881 9211. 20rm 10 ▥

BARROW-IN-FURNESS
Cumbria
Map **V**   B5

Barrow Rakesmoor Ln, Hawcoat (2m N of Barrow, off A590)
T:(0229) 25444
Pleasant course laid out on meadowland with extensive views of the nearby lakeland fells. 18 | 6209 yds | Par 71 | SSS 70

BARROW-IN-FURNESS
Cumbria
Map **V**   B5

Furness Central Dr, Walney Island, Barrow-in-Furness
(1¾m E of town centre off A590)
T:(0229) 41232
18 | 6400 *(white)* 6000 *(yellow)* yds | *Par* 71 | *SSS* 70
Visitors welcome | without M **.. per day WE | with M .. per day WE | B ☂ D**
*(prior arrangement) | ⚲ ♈ ⋈ usually pm | TR competition days, Ladies Day
Wed | ♩ | M 600 | S*
**White House, Abbey Rd. T:(0229) 27303. 29rm (3 ⇔)*
Links golf with a fairly flat first half but a much sterner second nine played across subtle sloping ground. Some of the par 4 holes are particularly testing. There are good views of the Lakes, North Wales and the Isle of Man.

BARRY
Tayside, *Angus*
Map **VII**   J8

Panmure Burnside Rd, Barry
(S side of village off A930)
T:(0241) 53120
Societies welcome by arrangement, and
children if playing with adults. 18 |
6302 yds | Par 70 | SSS 70
Visitors welcome (with M only S) |
∴ per round ∷ per day | B ☂ | L D
(not Mon) | ⚲ ♈ | ④ not am if party
more than 12 | M 500 | S
***Glencoe Hotel, Links Pde,*
Carnoustie. T:(0241) 53273.
11rm (3 ⇔ 5 ♨)

SCORE CARD:			
1	289	10	416
2	480	11	164
3	398	12	363
4	348	13	398
5	148	14	535
6	387	15	234
7	418	16	382
8	360	17	401
9	174	18	408

A nerve-testing, adventurous course set amongst sandhills — its hazards belie the quiet nature of the opening holes. Panmure has been used as a qualifying course for the Open Championship.

Visitors welcome with/without M
.. per day | B L ☂ D prior
arrangement (not Mon Tu) | ⚲ ♈ |
TR F (Ladies Day) | ♩ | M 600 | S
**White House, Abbey Rd. T:(0229)*
27303. 29rm (3 ⇔)

BARRY
South Glamorgan
Map **I**   G3

Brynhill (Barry) Port Rd (1½m N of
Barry on B4050)
T:(0446) 735061
Meadowland course with some hard
walking. Prevailing west wind.
Societies welcome (Mon to F) by
arrangement. 18 | 5511 *metres* | *Par* 71
| *SSS* 69
Visitors welcome ⋈ | B (not Mon) |
L (not Mon) ☂ D (prior
arrangement) | ⚲ ♈ ⋋ | ♩ | M 600 |
S
****Mount Sorrell, Porthkerry Rd.*

T:(0446) 740069. 33rm (20 ⇔ 13 ♨).
Annexe: 4rm ⇔

BASILDON
Essex
Map **II**   G3

BARTON ON SEA
Hampshire
Map **II**   A7

Barton on Sea Marine Drive East, (E side of town)
T:(0425) 615308
18 | 5565 yds | *Par* 67 | *SSS* 67
Visitors welcome, restricted WE BH ⋈ ☎ | ∴ per day ∷ WE BH | B L (Sun by
prior arrangement) ☂ | ⚲ ♈ ⋋ | ⋈ prior arrangement | TR WE BH (before
1145) | ♩ | ④ before 10.00 am, 12.30-2.00 pm | M 700 | S
❀❀○○○⚯*Chewton Glen, Christchurch Rd, New Milton. T:(04252) 5341.*
44rm ⇔ ♨
Though not strictly a links course, it is right on a cliff edge with views over the Isle of Wight and Christchuch Bay. On a still day (unusual) there is nothing much to it - but when it blows the course undergoes a complete change in character. Testing 576-yard par 5 12th.

Basildon Bells Hill Ln, Kingswood,
(1m S of Basildon, off A176)
T:(0268) 3297
Undulating municipal parkland course.
Testing 13th hole - double dog leg
(par 4). 18 | 6225 yds | *Par* 70 | *SSS* 69
Open to public .. per day ∴ WE | B
L ☂ D | ⚲ ♈ ⋋ | ⋈ | Club facilities
available by prior arrangement | ♩ |
TR Alternate Suns am | M 300 | S
****Crest, Cranes Farm Rd. T:(0268)*
3955. 116rm ⇔

Pipps Hill Country Club Cranes
Farm Rd, Basildon (N side of town
centre off A127)
T:(0268) 27278
Flat course with ditches and pond. 9 |
2829 yds | Par 34 | SSS 34
Visitors welcome | without M ..
per day | ⚲ ♈ | L D B ☂ | ⋈
(possibly) | M 400
****Crest, Cranes Farm Rd. T:(0268)*
3955. 116rm ⇔

BATH
Avon
Map **I**   J3

Lansdown Lansdown (3m NW of
Bath exit 18 off M4)
T:(0225) 22138
A flat parkland course in open
situation. 18 | 6267 yds | *Par* 71 |
SSS 70
Visitors welcome ☎ advisable WE |
∴ per day ∴ per round WE | B ☂ L
D | ⚲ ♈ ⋋ ⋈ | TR ☎ for details |
M 600 | S
****Lansdown Grove, Lansdown Rd.*
T:(0225) 315891. 41rm (38 ⇔ 3 ♨)

BASINGSTOKE
Hampshire
Map **II**   B5

Basingstoke Kempshott Park,
(3½m on SW of Basingstoke, on
A30)

	SCORE CARD:		
T:(0256) 465990	1 499	10	415
Societies welcome (W Th F) by	2 368	11	412
*arrangement. 18	6263 yds	Par 70	*	3 157	12	209
SSS 70	4 466	13	402
Visitors welcome ⊠	with M only	5 177	14	431
Mon-F	with M ⁚ per day	B L ☛	6 362	15	343
D (high tea) (not Mon)	⚘ ℣ ↘		7 422	16	364
TR WE BH	♩	M 600	Ⓢ	8 251	17	166
★★★*Crest, Grove Rd. T:(0256) 468181.*	9 334	18	485
86rm ⇨			

A well-maintained parkland course with wide and inviting
fairways. You are inclined to expect longer drives than are actually
achieved - partly on account of the trees. There are many two-
hundred-year-old beech trees, since the course was built on an old
deer park.

BATH
Avon
Map **I**   J3

Bath Sham Castle, North Rd (1½m E of Bath city centre)
T:(0225) 63834
Societies welcome (W F) by arrangement. 18 | 6369 yds | Par 71 | SSS 70
Visitors welcome ⊠ | ☎ preferred | without M ∴ per day | with M ‥ per day
| B L D ☛ | ⚘ ℣ ↘ | TR competitions | M 600 | Ⓢ
★★★★*Francis, Queen Sq. T:(0225) 24257. 94rm* ⇨
Considered to be one of the finest courses in the west, this is the site
of Bath's oldest golf club. An interesting course situated on high
ground overlooking the city and with splendid views over the
surrounding countryside. The rocky ground supports good quality
turf and there are many good holes. The 17th is a dog-leg right past
or over the corner of out-of-bounds wall and thence on to an
undulating green.

BATHGATE
Lothian, *West Lothian*
Map **VI**   F2

Bathgate Edinburgh Rd, Bathgate
(E side of town off A89)
T:(0506) 52232
*Moorland course. Easy walking.
Testing 11th hole par 3. 18 | 6345 yds |
Par 71 | SSS 70*
Visitors welcome | B L ☛ | D prior
arrangement | ⚘ ℣ ↘ | ♩ | TR
competition days | M 515 | Ⓢ
★★★*Golden Circle, Blackburn Rd.
T:(0506) 53771. 75rm* ⇨ 🍴

BAWTRY
South Yorkshire
Map **V**   G7

Austerfield Park Cross Ln

(2m NE of Bawtry on A614)
T:(0302) 710841
*Long moorland course with postage
stamp 8th and testing 618 yd 7th.
Driving range attached. Societies
welcome by arrangement. 18 | 6828 yds
| Par 73 | SSS 73*
Visitors welcome | B L | ☛ D | ⚘ | ℣
| ↘ by arrangement | ⋈ TR
competition days (until 1000) |
M 460 | Ⓢ
★★★*Crown, High St, Bawtry.
T:(0302) 710341. 57rm* ⇨ 🍴

BEARSDEN
Strathclyde, *Dumbartonshire*
Map **VI**   D2

Bearsden Thorn Rd (1m W of
Bearsden off A809)
T:041-942 2351

*Parkland course, with easy walking and
views over city. 9 | 5862 yds | Par 68 |
SSS 70*
Visitors welcome ☎ only with M
except overseas visitors |
restrictions ladies juniors | ‥ per
day WE | B L ☛ (not Mon) | D prior
arrangement (not Mon) | ⚘ ℣ |
M 650 | Ⓢ
★★★*Black Bull Thistle, Main St,
Milngavie. T:041-956 2291.
28rm (27* ⇨*)*

Douglas Park Hillfoot (E side of
town on A81)
T:041-942 2220
*Parkland course. Societies by
arrangement. 18 | 5957 yds | Par 69 |
SSS 69*
Visitors welcome only with M ☎
not WE | with M ∴ per day | B L ☛
| D | ⚘ ℣ ↘ | ④ not allowed |
M 800 | Ⓢ
★★★*Black Bull Thistle, Main St,
Milngavie. T:041-956 2291.
28rm (27* ⇨*)*

Glasgow Killermont (SE side of
Bearsden off A81)
T:041-942 2011
*One of the finest parkland courses in
Scotland. Private members club, no
ladies. 18 | 5968 yds | Par 70 | SSS 69*
Visitors welcome only with M ⁚
per day | B L ☛ | ⚘ ℣ | ♩ | M 760 |
Ⓢ
★★★*Stakis Burnbrae, Milngavie Rd,
Bearsden. T:041-942 5951.
18rm (17* ⇨ *1* 🍴*)*

Windyhill (2m NW of Bearsden off
B8050)
T:041-942 2349
*Hard walking on moorland course;
testing hole: 12th (par 4). 18 | 6257 yds
| Par 71 | SSS 70*
Visitors welcome, except WE |
without M ∴ per day | with M ‥
per day | B ☛ | L D prior
arrangement (not Tu) | ⚘ ℣ ↘ | ♩
| M 684 | TR WE and competition
days | Ⓢ
★★★*Black Bull Thistle, Main St,
Milngavie. T:041-956 2291.
28rm (27* ⇨*)*

BEARSTED
Kent
Map **II**   H5

Bearsted Ware St, Bearsted (2½m E
of Maidstone, off A20)

T:(0622) 38198
Parkland course with fine views of the
North Downs. Societies welcome by
arrangement. 18 | 6253 yds | Par 72 |
SSS 70
Visitors welcome, with club
handicap only WE | B ☕ (not Tu) | L
D (societies only - prior
arrangement) (not Tu) | ⚐ ⛳ ♪ |
M 620 | Ⓢ
★★★*Great Danes, Ashford Rd,*
Hollingbourne. T:(0622) 30022.
127rm ⇌ 🍴

BEAUMARIS
Gwynedd
Map **III** D2
Baron Hill (1m SW of Beaumaris
off A545)
T:(0248) 810231
Undulating course, with natural
hazards of rock and gorse. Testing 3rd
and 4th holes (par 4s). 9 | 5062 mtrs |
Par 68 | SSS 67
Visitors welcome | without M ..
per day WE | with M .. per day WE
| B ☕ (not Mon) | ⚐ ⛳ ⋈ ♪ ④ TR
competition days | M 400 | Ⓢ
★★*Bulkeley Arms, Castle St. T:(0248)*
810415. 41rm (34 ⇌ 7 🍴)

BEBINGTON
Merseyside
Map **V** C8
Brackenwood Brackenwood Park,
Bebington, Wirral (On B5151, ¾m
N of M53 Jct 4)
T:051-608 3093
Municipal parkland course with easy
walking. 18 | 6285 yds | Par 70 |
SSS 70
Open to public .. per round | B L
☕ D | ⚐ ⛳ ⋎ | ⋈ | TR Sun
(0700-0900) | ♪ | Ⓢ
★★★*Bowler Hat, 2 Talbot Rd, Oxton.*
T:051-652 4931. 29rm ⇌

BECCLES
Suffolk
Map **IV** K5
Beccles The Common (NE side of
town)
T:(0502) 712244
Heathland course with natural hazards
and particularly exposed to wind. 9 |
2781 yds | Par 68 | SSS 67
Visitors welcome with M only WE |
⚐ ⛳ B ☕ ⋈ ♪ | TR Sun before
1030 | M 200 | Ⓢ
★★*Waveney House, Puddingmoor.*
T:(0502) 712270. 13 rm (4 ⇌ 4 🍴)

BECKENHAM
Greater London
Map **II** F4

Beckenham Place Park The
Mansion (½m N of Beckenham on
B2015)
T:01-658 5374
Picturesque course in the grounds of a
public park. 18 | 5722 yds | Par 68 |
SSS 68
The course is played over by the
Braeside Golf Club | .. per round
WE | B ☕ | ⚐ ⛳ L D ⋎ ⋈ ♪ | TR
WE am | M 200 | Ⓢ
★★★*Bromley Court, Bromley Hill,*
Bromley. T:01-464 5011. 130rm ⇌

BEDALE
North Yorkshire
Map **V** F4

Bedale Leyburn Rd (N side of
town, on A684)

BEACONSFIELD
Buckinghamshire
Map II D3

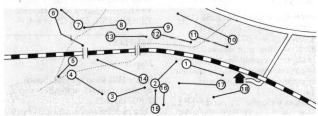

Beaconsfield Seer Green, (2m E of Beaconsfield, S of Seer Green)
T:(04946) 6545
Societies welcome (Tu W) Mar-Nov by arrangement. 18 | 6469 yds | Par 72 | SSS 71
Visitors welcome by arrangement ✉ | with M only WE BH | ⋮ per day | B ☕
L | D prior arrangement | ⚐ ⛳ ⋎ | ♪ | M 832 | Ⓢ
★★★*Bell House (2m E A40). T:(0753) 887211.* 120rm ⇌
An interesting and, at times, a testing course which frequently
plays longer than appears on the card! Each hole differs to
considerable degree and here lies the charm. Walking is easy,
except perhaps to the 8th.

BECKENHAM
Greater London
Map II F4

Langley Park Barnfield Wood Rd, Beckenham (S side of town centre)
T:01-658 6849
Societies welcome (W) by arrangement 18 | 6488 yds | Par 69 | SSS 71
Visitors welcome ✉ ☎ no visitors WE | without M ⋮ per day | with M .. per
day | B L ☕ | D (prior arrangement) | ⚐ ⛳ ⋎ | ⋈ sometimes | M 650 | Ⓢ
★★★*Bromley Court, Bromley Hill. T:01-464 5011.* 130rm ⇌
This is a pleasant, well-wooded, parkland course with natural
hazards including a lake at the 18th hole.

T:(0677) 22580
Secluded parkland course with many
trees. Societies welcome by
arrangement. 18 | 5687 yds | Par 69 |
SSS 68
Visitors welcome | ✳ | B L D ☕
parties only by prior arrangement |
⚐ ⋎ | ⛳ | ♪ | M 500 | Ⓢ
★★*Motel Leeming, Leeming Bar.*
T:(0677) 23611. 40rm ⇌

BEDFORD
Bedfordshire
Map **IV** C7

Bedford & County Green Ln,
Clapham (2m N of Bedford off A6)
T:(0234) 52617
Pleasant parkland course with views
over Bedford and surrounding
countryside. The 15th is a testing par
4. Societies welcome by arrangement.
18 | 6347 yds | Par 70 | SSS 70   ➥

Visitors welcome | without M ∴ per day WE | with M ∴ per day WE | B | ♥ | L D prior arrangement (not Mon) | ⚑ 𝗬 | [TR] WE | 𝗝 | ∞ | M 600 | [S]
★★★*Woodlands Manor, Green Ln, Clapham. T:(0234) 63281.*
18rm (8 ⇌ 10 🏠)

Bedfordshire Bromham Rd, Biddenham (1m W of Bedford on A428)
T:(0234) 61669
Parkland course, tree hazards, easy walking. Societies welcome by arrangement. 18 | 6196 yds | Par 70 | SSS 69
Visitors welcome | .. per round ∴ per day weekdays, ∴ per round ∷ per day WE BH | B ♥ | L prior arrangement | ⚑ 𝗝 | M 600 | [S]
★★*De Parys, De Parys Ave. T:(0234) 52121. 33rm (5 ⇌ 17 🏠)*

BEDLINGTON
Northumberland
Map **VI** K5

BedlingtonshireAcorn Bank (1m SW of Bedlington on A1068)
T:(0670) 822087/822457
Parkland course with easy walking. Under certain conditions the wind can be a distinct hazard. Societies welcome by arrangement. 18 | 6546 mtrs | Par 73 | SSS 73
Visitors welcome | .. per day | B L D ♥ | ⚑ 𝗬 | ⤫ [TR] WE (0700-0930, 1200-1400) | 𝗝 | M 750 | [S]
★★★★*Holiday Inn, Great North Rd, Seaton Burn. T:091-236 5432. 150rm ⇌ 🏠*

BEITH
Strathclyde, *Ayrshire*
Map **VI** D3

Beith Threepwood, Beith (1½m NE of Beith off A737)
T:(05055) 3166
Moorland course, with panoramic views over 7 counties. 9 | 5532 yds | Par 68 | SSS 67
Visitors welcome, restricted WE | .. per day WE | B | L (prior arrangement) | ♥ | ⚑ 𝗬 | ∞ | ④ S [TR] WE pm | M 400
★★*Dalmeny Park, Lochlibo Rd, Barrhead. T:041-881 9211. 20rm (10 🏠)*

BELLINGHAM
Northumberland
Map **VI** J5

Bellingham Boggle Hole, nr. Hexham (N side of village on B6320)
T:(0660) 20530
Downland course with natural hazards. 9 | 5226 yds | Par 67 | SSS 66
Visitors welcome | * | B L ♥ D | ⚑ | 𝗬 evenings only | [TR] competition days | M 230
★★★*Riverdale Hall. T:(0660) 20254. 11rm (9 ⇌ 2 🏠)*

BELLSHILL
Strathclyde, *Lanarkshire*
Map **VI** E3

Bellshill Orbiston, Bellshill (1m SE of Bellshill off A721)
T:(0698) 745124
Parkland course. 18 | 6205 yds | Par 70 | SSS 70
Visitors welcome | .. per day ∴ WE | B | ♥ | L D prior arrangement | ⚑ ∞ | [TR] S | M 410 | [S]
★★★*Garrion, Merry St, Motherwell. T:(0698) 64561. 52rm (28 ⇌ 8 🏠)*

BENFLEET
Essex
Map **II** H3

Boyce Hill Vicarage Hill, South Benfleet (¾m NE of Benfleet sta)
T:(03745) 3625
Hilly parkland course with good views. 18 | 5287 yds | Par 68 | SSS 68
Visitors welcome, with M only WE. Societies only on Th. | * | B L D ♥ | ⚑ 𝗬 | ∞ S ⤫ | M 600 | [TR] WE | 𝗝
★★★*Crest, Cranes Farm Rd, Basildon. T:(0268) 3955. 116rm ⇌*

BENTHAM
North Yorkshire
Map **V** D5

Bentham Robin Ln (N side of High Bentham)
T:(0468) 61018
Moorland course with glorious views. 9 | 5752 yds | Par 70 | SSS 69
Visitors welcome | .. per day WE | B L ♥ D | ⚑ Y | ∞ | [TR] major competitions | M 220
★★★*Royal, Main St, Kirkby Lonsdale. T:(0468) 71217. 22rm (15 ⇌ 1 🏠)*

BERWICK-upon-TWEED
Northumberland
Map **VI** J3

Berwick upon Tweed (Goswick) Goswick (7m SE of Berwick, off A1)
T:(0289) 87348(Sec), 87380(Pro)
Seaside links course playable all year round. 18 | 6399 yds | Par 72 | SSS 71
Visitors welcome ∴ per day WE | B L ♥ D (not Mon winter) | ⚑ 𝗬 (not Mon winter) ⤫ | ∞ | 𝗝 | M 360 | [S]
★★★*Turret House, Etal Rd. T:(0289) 307344. 10rm (7 ⇌)*

Magdalene Fields Magdalene Fields, Berwick upon Tweed (E side of town centre)
Seaside course with natural hazards formed by sea bays. Last 9 holes exposed to winds, hard walking. Testing 14th hole over bay (par 3). Junior section with competitions. 18 | 6551 yds | Par 72 | SSS 71
Visitors welcome | B ♥ L | ⚑ 𝗬 ⤫ ∞ | [TR] Sun to 1000 and Competition days | M 100 | [S]
★★★*Kings Arms, Hide Hill, Berwick upon Tweed. T:(0289) 307454. 36rm (30 ⇌ 6 🏠)*

BERKHAMSTED
Hertfordshire
Map **II** D2

Berkhamsted The Common (1m NE of Berkhamsted)
T:(04427) 5832
Societies welcome (W F) by arrangement. 18 | 6546 yds | Par 71 | SSS 72
Visitors welcome, restricted W F | ☎ | ∷ per 2 rounds WE BH (1 or 2 rounds) | B ♥ | L D prior arrangement (not Mon) | ⚑ 𝗬 ⤫ prior arrangement | [TR] Sun am Tu am | ④ Sun am | 𝗝 | M 800 | [S]
Swan, High St. T:(04427) 71451. 13rm (5 ⇌ 2 🏠)
There are no sand bunkers on this heathland course but this does not make it any easier to play. The natural hazards will test the skill of the most able players, with a particularly testing hole at the 11th, 566 yards par 5. The clubhouse is very comfortable.

BEXHILL
East Sussex
Map II   G7

Cooden Beach Cooden (2m W of Bexhill on B2182)
T:(0424) 2040
Societies welcome (Mon to F) by arrangement. 18 | 6411 yds | Par 72 | SSS 71
Visitors welcome ☎ preferred | ☞ (not Mon) B L D prior arrangement (not Mon) | ⚐ ☂ | ⤸ | ⋈ | ④ by arrangement | ♩ | TR competition days | M 650 | Ⓢ
★★★Cooden Beach, Cooden Sea Rd. T:(04243) 2281. 33rm (27 ⇄ 4 ⓕ)
The course is close by the sea, but is not real links in character. Despite that it is dry and plays well throughout the year. There are some excellent holes such as the 4th played to a built up green, the short 12th, and three good holes to finish.

BETWS-Y-COED
Gwynedd
Map III   D2

Betws-y-Coed (NE side of village)
T:(06902) 556
Attractive parkland course set between two rivers in Snowdonia National Park. Societies welcome. 9 | 4996 yds | Par 64 | SSS 64
Visitors welcome | .. per day ∴ WE| B L ☞ D | ⚐ ☂ | ⤸ | M 250 | Ⓢ
⋈
★★★Royal Oak, Holyhead Rd. T:(06902) 219. 21rm ⇄

BEVERLEY
Humberside
Map V   H6

Beverley & East Riding The Westwood (1m SW of Beverley, on B1230)
T:(0482) 867190
Picturesque parkland course with some hard walking and natural hazards - trees and gorse bushes. Cattle and sheep spring to autumn, horse-riders occasionally early morning. 18 |

5937 yds | Par 69 | SSS 66
Visitors welcome, restricted WE BH | ✳ | B ☂ (not W) | L ☞ D | ⚐ | ♩ | M 460 | Ⓢ
★★★Beverley Arms, North Bar Within. T:(0482) 869241. 61rm ⇄

BEWDLEY
Hereford and Worcester
Map III   H5

Little Lakes Golf and Country Club Lye Head (2¼m W of Bewdley off A456)
T:(0299) 266385
This testing 9-hole course offers alternative tees for the second 9 with some pleasing views. A swimming pool and tennis courts are available. 9 | 6247 yds | Par 73 | SSS 72
Visitors welcome | without M .. | B L D ☞ | ⚐ ☂ | ⋈ | ♩ | M 300 | Ⓢ
★★Black Boy, Kidderminster Rd, Bewdley. T:(0299) 402119. 19rm (7 ⇄ 14 ⓕ) Annexe: 8rm (2 ⇄ 2 ⓕ)

BEXHILL
East Sussex
Map II   G7

Highwoods Ellerslie Lane, E Sussex (1½m NW of Bexhill)
T:(0424) 212625
Undulating course. 18 | 6218 yds | Par 70 | SSS 70
Visitors welcome ⋈, with M only Sun BH | ☎ advisable | without M ∴ per day ∷ WE | with M .. per day | ☞ | B L| D prior arrangement | ⚐ ☂ ⤸ | ④ from 10th tee (0830-0945, 1245-1415, after 1600) | ♩ | M 800 | Ⓢ
★★★Cooden Beach, Cooden Sea Rd, Cooden Beach. T:(04243) 2281. 32rm (24 ⇄ 5 ⓕ)

BEXLEYHEATH
Greater London
Map II   F4

Bexleyheath Mount Drive, Mount Rd (1m SW of Bexleyheath)
T:01-303 6951
Undulating course. 9 | 5239 yds | Par 66 | SSS 66
Visitors welcome | B L D prior arrangement | ☞ ⚐ ☂ | Ⓢ | M 350 | TR|WE, and pm after 1330 | ♩
★★★Crest, Black Prince Interchange, Southwold Rd. T:(0322) 526900. 78rm ⇄

BIGBURY-ON-SEA
Devon
Map I   E7

Bigbury Kingsbridge (1m S of Bigbury, on B3392)
T:(054881) 207
Downland course with easy walking. Exposed to winds. 18 | 6038 yds | ⇛

Par 69 | SSS 69
Visitors welcome weekdays | ☎ WE | B L D prior arrangement (not F) | ☂ ♨ Ⴤ ↘ | ⋈ usually | TR WE | ') | M 700 | S
*Henley, Bigbury on Sea. T:(0548) 810240. 9rm (4 ⇌ 1 ⚱)

BIGGAR
Strathclyde, *Lanarkshire*
Map **VI**   F3

Biggar Municipal Public Park, Broughton Rd (S side of town)
T:(0899) 20618
Flat parkland course, easy walking and fine views. 18 | 5256 yds | Par 67 | SSS 66
Open to public | * | B L ☂ D | ♨ Ⴤ | TR WE (am, most summer eves) | M 250 | S

★★★Tontine, High St, Peebles. T:(0721) 20892. 37rm (36 ⇌ 1 ⚱)

BIGGIN HILL
Kent
Map **II**   F4

Cherry Lodge Jail Ln (1m E of Biggin Hill)

T:(09594) 73762
Undulating parkland course with good views. 18 | 6908 yds | Par 75 | SSS 74
Visitors welcome without M weekdays | Ⴤ L D B ☂ ♨ | TR WE | M 840 | S
★★Hand & Sceptre, 21 London Rd, Southborough, nr Tunbridge Wells. T:(0892) 37055. 25rm (21 ⇌ 2 ⚱)

BILLINGHAM
Cleveland
Map **V**   G3

Billingham Sandy Ln, Billingham (1m W of town centre, E of A19)
T:(0642) 554494
Parkland course on edge of urban-rural district with hard walking and water hazards, testing 15th hole. Societies and parties welcome (Mon to F) by arrangement. 18 | 6430 yds | Par 73 | SSS 71
Visitors welcome, restricted WE BH until 1000 | ∴ per day | B (not Mon) | L D prior arrangement on arrival (not Mon) | ♨ Ⴤ (not Mon) | ') | TR WE, Mon-F until 1000 | M 720 (including juniors) | S
★★★Billingham Arms, The Causeway, Stockton-on-Tees. T:(0642) 553661. 62rm (41 ⇌ 12 ⚱)

BINGLEY
West Yorkshire
Map **V**   E6

Bingley (St Ives) St Ives Mansion, Harden, (¾m W of Bingley, off B6429)
T:(0274) 562506
Parkland/heathland course. 18 | 6466 yds | Par 71 | SSS 71
Visitors welcome, restricted WE BH | without M .. per day | ∴ WE | B L ☂ | ♨ Ⴤ ') ⋈ | TR Tu, Th 1630-1800 in summer | M 620 | S
★★★Bankfield, Bradford Rd. T:(0274) 567123. 69rm (67 ⇌ 2 ⚱)

BIRKENHEAD
Merseyside
Map **V**   C8

Arrowe Park Woodchurch, (1m W of M53, (Jct 3), on A551)
T:051-677 1527
Pleasant municipal parkland course. 18 | 6435 yds | Par 72 | SSS 71
Open to public | .. per day WE | B ☂ | ♨ ↘ ⋈ | TR WE am; W ladies day | ') | M 250 | S

★★★Bowler Hat, 2 Talbot Rd, Oxton. T:051-652 4931. 29rm ⇌

Prenton Golf Links Rd, Prenton, Birkenhead, (S side of town centre off B5151)
T:051-608 1053
Parkland course with easy walking and views of the Welsh Hills. Societies welcome (W) by arrangement. 18 | 6411 yds | Par 71 | SSS 71
Visitors welcome | without M ∴ per day : WE | with M .. per day WE | B L ☂ D | ♨ Ⴤ ↘ ⋈ | TR S (competition days) | M 762 | S
★★Riverhill, Talbot Rd, Oxton. T:051-652 4847. 10rm (5 ⇌ 2 ⚱)

Wirral Ladies 93 Bidston Rd, Oxton, Birkenhead, (W side of town centre on B5151)
T:051-652 1255
Heathland course with heather and birch. 18(18) | 4744 yds (5157 yds men) | Par 68 | SSS 68
Visitors welcome ✉ ☎ | :: per day | B (not Sun, Tu) ☂ | L D prior arrangement | ♨ Ⴤ | ') | TR competition days | M 450 | S
★★★Bowler Hat, 2 Talbot Rd, Oxton. T:051-652 4931. 29rm ⇌

BIRMINGHAM
West Midlands
Map **III**   J5

Brandhall Heron Rd, Warley, Birmingham, (5½m W of city centre off A4123)
T:021-552 2195
Private golf club on municipal parkland course, easy walking, good hazards. Testing holes: 1st 516 yds (par 5) 10th 497 yds dog leg (par 5). 18 | 5813 yds | Par 70 | SSS 69
* | B L D ☂ | Ⴤ (not Mon, S, Sun lunch time only) | ♨ ↘ ⋈ | TR WE 0800-1000 | ') | M 250 | S
★★★Post House, Chapel Ln, Great Barr. T:021-357 7444. 204rm ⇌

Cocks Moors Woods Municipal Alcester Rd S, Kings Heath, (5m S of city centre on A435)
T:021-444 3584, Birmingham
Tree-lined parkland course. 18 | 5888 yds | Par 69 | SSS 68
Visitors welcome without M | B L ☂ ♨ | S ↘ ⋈ | M 250
★★★★Albany, Smallbrook, Queensway, Birmingham. T:021-643 8171. 254rm ⇌

Edgbaston Church Rd, Edgbaston, Birmingham, (2m S of city centre on B4217 off A38)
T:021-454 1736
Parkland course in lovely country. 18 | 6118 yds | Par 69 | SSS 69
Visitors welcome ☎ | ∴ per round ∷ per day | B not Sun | L ☕ | D prior arrangement | ⛛ | 🍸 not Sun eve | ↘ | ℨ | M 800 | [S]
★★★★*Plough and Harrow, Hagley Rd, Edgbaston. T:021-454 4111. 44rm* ⇄

Great Barr Chapel Ln, Great Barr, Birmingham (6m N of city centre off A34)
T:021-357 1232
Parkland course with easy walking. Pleasant views of Barr Beacon National Park. Societies welcome by arrangement. 18 | 6545 yds | Par 73 | SSS 72
Visitors welcome but with M only WE BH | ∴ per day | ∷ WE | B ☕ | L D prior arrangement | ⛛ 🍸 ↘ | ℨ | M 500 | [S]
★★★*Post House, Chapel Ln, Great Barr. T:021-357 7444. 204rm* ⇄

Handsworth Sunningdale Close, Handsworth Wood, Birmingham, (3½m NW of city centre off A4040)
T:021-554 0599
Undulating parkland course with some tight fairways but subject to wind. Societies welcome by arrangement. 18 | 6312 yds | Par 70 | SSS 70
Visitors welcome but with M only WE BH | B ☕ | L D (not Sun Mon) | ⛛ 🍸 | ↘ prior arrangement [TR] Sun | M 350 | [S] | ⋈ ④ WE before 1145 am
★★★*West Bromwich Moat House, Birmingham Rd, West Bromwich. T:021-553 6111. 181rm* ⇄ 🚿

Harborne 40 Tennal Rd, Harborne, Birmingham (3½m SW of city centre off A4040)
T:021-427 1728
Parkland course in hilly situation. Societies welcome (Mon to F) by arrangement. 18 | 6280 yds | Par 70 | SSS 70
Visitors welcome but with M only WE | without M ∴ per day | with M ‥ per round | B L (not Mon) | ☕ D prior arrangement (not Mon) | ⛛ 🍸 ⋈ ④ WE | [TR] WE, BH | ↘ | ℨ | M 450 | [S]
★★★★*Plough & Harrow, Hagley Rd, Edgbaston. T:021-454 4111. 44rm* ⇄

Harborne Church Farm Vicarage Rd, Harborne, Birmingham, (3½m SW of city centre off A4040)
T:021-427 1204
Parkland course with easy walking. Some holes might prove difficult. 9 | 2257 yds | Par 66 | SSS 64
Visitors welcome | ‥ per round | B L ☕ D | ⛛ ↘ | M 320 | [S]
★★★*Apollo, 243-247 Hagley Rd, Edgbaston. T:021-455 0271. 130rm* ⇄ 🚿

Hatchford Brook Coventry Rd, Sheldon, Birmingham, (6m E of city centre on A45)
T:021-743 9821
Fairly flat municipal parkland course. 18 | 6164 yds | Par 69 | SSS 68
Open to public | ‥ per round | B L ☕ D | ⛛ ↘ ⋈ | ℨ | M 200 | [S]
★★★★*Excelsior, Coventry Rd, Elmdon, Birmingham Airport. T:021-743 8141. 141rm* ⇄

Hilltop & Manwood Farm Park Ln, Handsworth, Birmingham, (3½m N of city centre off A4040)
T:021-554 4463
Testing and hilly municipal parkland course. 18 | 6204 yds | Par 71 | SSS 70
Open to public ‥ per round | B ☕ | ⛛ ↘ | ⋈ | ℨ | M 300 | [S]
★★★*West Bromwich Moat House, Birmingham Rd, West Bromwich. T:021-553 6111. 181rm* ⇄ 🚿

Lickey Hills Rednal, (10m SW of city centre on B4096)
T:021-453 3159, Birmingham
Hilly municipal course overlooking the city. 18 | 6610 yds | Par 69 | SSS 69
Visitors welcome | B ☕ | ⛛ ↘ | ⋈ | ℨ | M 300 | [S]
★★★*Perry Hall, Kidderminster Rd, Bromsgrove. T:(0527) 31976. 53rm (36* ⇄ *17* 🚿*)*

Moseley Springfield Rd, Kings Heath, Birmingham (4m S of city centre on B4146 off A435)
T:021-444 2115
Parkland course with a lake, pond and stream to provide natural hazards. The par 3 5th goes through a cutting in woodland to a tree and garden-lined amphitheatre, and the par 4 6th entails a drive over lake to a dog-leg fairway. Societies by arrangement. 18 | 6227 yds | Par 70 | SSS 70
Visitors welcome but ✉ | without M ∴ per day WE | B ☕ L D | ⛛ 🍸 | [TR] Tu (ladies day) | ℨ | M 560 | [S]
★★*Cobden, 166 Hagley Rd, Edgbaston. T:021-454 6621. 210rm (25* ⇄ *112* 🚿*)*

Rose Hill Rednall (10m SW of city centre on B4096)
T:021-453 3159
Club plays over Lickey Hills Municipal Course, in elevated situation with long ➡

reaching views. 18 | 5781 yds | Par 68 | SSS 68
Course open to public | B L ♥ | ⚲ ↘ ⋈ | M 320 | Ⓢ
★★★*Perry Hall, Kidderminster Rd, Bromsgrove. T:(0527) 31976. 53rm (36 ⇄ 17 🍴)*

Warley Lightswood Hill, Bearwood, Birmingham, (4m W of city centre off A456)
T:021-429 2440
Municipal parkland course in Warley Woods. One of the nearest courses to Birmingham centre. 9 | 2606 yds | Par 33 | SSS 64
Open to public | B ♥ | D | L | ⚲ ⋈ ↘ 🎯 | M 150 | Ⓢ
★★*Norfolk, 257-267 Hagley Rd, Edgbaston. T:021-454 8071. 175rm (32 ⇄ 56 🍴)*

BIRSTALL
Leicestershire
Map **IV**   A4

Birstall Station Rd, Birstall (SW side of town centre off A6)
T:(0533) 674322
Parkland course. 18 | 6203 yds | Par 70 | SSS 70
Visitors welcome, restricted certain times | without M ∴ per day | with M .. per day WE | B ♥ | L D (not Mon) | ⚲ Υ | ⓣⓡWE | 🎯 | M 600 | Ⓢ
★★★*Eaton Bray, Abbey St, Leicester. T:(0533) 50666. 73rm (31 ⇄ 42 🍴)*

BISHOPBRIGGS
Strathclyde, *Lanarkshire*
Map **VI**   E2

Bishopbriggs Brackenbrae Rd (½m NW of Bishopbriggs off A803)
T:041-772 1810
Parkland course. Organised parties by arrangement. 18 | 6041 yds | Par 69 | SSS 69
Visitors welcome only with M | B | L ♥ D | ⚲ Υ | M 400
★★★*Black Bull Thistle, Main St, Milngavie. T:041-956 2291. 28rm (27 ⇄)*

Cawder Cadder Estate, Bishopbriggs, (1m NE of Bishopbriggs, off A803)
T:041-772 7101
Two parkland courses. Cawder course hilly, with 5th, 9th, 10th, 11th testing holes. Keir course flat. Visiting parties by arrangement Mon to F Cawder 36 |

6244/5900 yds | Par 71/68 | SSS 71 | Keir: 18 | 5900 yds | Par 68 | SSS 68
Visitors welcome midweek | ✱ | B L D ♥ prior arrangement | ⚲ Υ ↘ | ⓣⓡcompetition days | 🎯 | M 1200 | Ⓢ
★★★*Black Bull Thistle, Main St, Milngavie. T:041-956 2291. 28rm (27 ⇄)*

BISHOPS CANNINGS
Wiltshire
Map **I**   K3

North Wilts Devizes (2m NW of Bishops Cannings)
T:(038 086) 627
High downland course with fine views. Societies welcome by arrangement. 18 | 6450 yds | Par 72 | SSS 71
Visitors welcome | without M ∴ per day WE BH | with M .. per day WE | B L ♥ D | ⚲ Υ | ⋈ | 🎯 | M 500 | Ⓢ
★★*Bear, Market Pl, Devizes. T:(0380) 2444. 27rm (15 ⇄)*

BISHOP'S STORTFORD
Hertfordshire
Map **II**   F1

Bishop's Stortford Dunmow Rd, (1m W of M11 Jct 8, on A1250)
T:(0279) 54715
Parkland course, fairly flat. 18 | 6440 yds | Par 71 | SSS 71
Visitors welcome, not WE BH | ⋈ ☎ | ∴ per round ∶∶ per day | B (not WE) L D | ⚲ Υ | ⓣⓡWE | 🎯 | M 800 | Ⓢ
★★*Saracen's Head, High St, Great Dunmow. T:(0371) 3901. 24rm ⇄*

BISHOPTON
Strathclyde, *Renfrewshire*
Map **VI**   D2

Erskine The Clubhouse, Bishopton, (¾m NE of Bishopton off B815)
T:(0505) 862302
Parkland course. 18 | 6287 yds | Par 71 | SSS 70
Visitors welcome with M only if ⊠ | ∶∶ per day | B L D ♥ | ⚲ Υ ↘ | ⓣⓡ WE | 🎯 | M 700 | Ⓢ
★★★*Crest Hotel Erskine Bridge, North Barr, Inchinnan. T:041- 812 0123. 200 rm ⇄*

BLACKBURN
Lancashire
Map **V**   D6

Blackburn Beardwood Brow, Blackburn, (1¼m NW of town centre, off A677)
T:(0254) 51122
Parkland course on a high plateau with stream and hills. Societies welcome by arrangement. 18 | 6099 yds | Par 71 | SSS 70
Visitors welcome | ∴ per day WE, BH | B L ♥ | D prior arrangement | ⚲ Υ | M 655 | Ⓢ ↘ ⋈ ⓣⓡ 12.30-1.30, Tue ladies day
★★★*Blackburn Moat House, Preston New Rd. T:(0254) 64441. 98rm ⇄*

BLACKWATERFOOT
Strathclyde, *Bute*
Map **VI**   B4

Shiskine Blackwaterfoot, (W side of village off A841)
T:(077 086) 226
Seaside course. Other attractions include tennis courts and bowling green. 12 | 3000 yds | Par 42 | SSS 41
Visitors welcome | .. per day WE | B ♥ L (summer only) | ⚲ | ↘ by arrangement | M 315 | Ⓢ
★★*Kinloch, Blackwaterfoot. T:(077086) 286. 49rm ⇄*

48   35   [3-37 Th.]   Lansdowne 8-30   Rosemount 2-00

BLACKWOOD
Gwent
Map I G2

Blackwood Cwmgelli, (¾m N of `
Blackwood, off A4048)
T:(0495) 223152
*Heathland course with sand bunkers.
Undulating, with hard walking.
Testing 2nd hole par 4. Good views. 9 |
5304 yds | Par 66 | SSS 66*
Visitors welcome weekdays ☎ ⊠ |
.. per day | ⌂ prior arrangement |
♈ evngs and WE 1200-1400 | M 250
★★★*Maes Manor. T:(0495) 224551.
10rm (7 ⇄ ⏶). Annexe: 16rm (10 ⇄ 3
⏶).*

BLAIR ATHOLL
Tayside, *Perthshire*
Map VII G7

Blair Atholl Blair Atholl (½m S of
Blair Atholl off B8079)
T:(079681) 407
*Parkland course, river runs alongside 3
holes, easy walking. 9| 5710 yds |
Par 70 | SSS 69*
Visitors welcome | .. per day WE |
B L ☛ | ⌂ ♈ ⟋ | M 200
❀★★*Killiecrankie, Killiecrankie.
T:(0796) 3220. 12rm (4 ⇄ 6 ⏶)*

BLAIRGOWRIE
Tayside, *Perthshire*   *01250*
Map VII H7   *873116 pro*

Blairgowrie Rosemount, *872594*
Blairgowrie, (1m S of Blairgowrie
off A93)
T:(0250) 2622
*2 18-hole heathland courses, also a
9-hole course. 18(18) | 6592(6621) yds |
Par 72(71) | SSS 72(72)*
Visitors welcome ⊠ ☎ Mon, Tu,
Th, limited on F, between 0830 and

1600. Very restricted WE | without
M ∷ per day | B L ☛ D prior
arrangement | ♈ ⌂ ⟍ | ④ until
1000 and 1300-1400 daily | TR ☎ W
WE competitions; alternate starting
times | ⅃ | S
❀★★★⛳*Kinloch House.
T:(025084) 237. 12rm (7 ⇄ 5 ⏶)*

BLAIRMORE
Strathclyde, *Argyllshire*
Map VI C2

Blairmore & Strone Blairmore by
Dunoon, (W side of Strone, off
A880) Argyll
T:(036 984) 677(Club), 217(Sec)
*Heathland/seaside course with fine
views over the Firth of Clyde. Testing
holes: 2nd (par 3), 7th (par 3), 8th (par
4). 9 | 2112 yds | Par 62 | SSS 62*
Visitors welcome, restricted W
(evng) S (pm) | .. per day WE | ☛ |
⟍ ⌂ ♈ | M 170
★★*Ardentinny, Ardentinny.
T:(036981) 209. 11rm (6 ⇄ 5 ⏶)*

BLAKEDOWN
Hereford and Worcester
Map III H5

Churchill and Blakedown
5 Churchill Ln, Blakedown, (W side
of village, off A456)
T:(0562) 700200, Kidderminster
*Pleasant course on hilltop with
extensive views. Societies by special
arrangement only. 9 | 5399 yds |
Par 68 | SSS 67*
Visitors welcome but with M only
WE BH | B ☛ (not Mon) | L D prior
arrangement (not Mon) | ⌂ ♈ ⟍ ⋈
| M 300 | S
★★*Gainsborough House, Bewdley Hill,
Kidderminster. T:(0562) 754041.
42rm ⇄*

BLANDFORD FORUM
Dorset
Map I J5

Ashley Wood, The Wimborne Rd,
(2m E of Blandford Forum on
B3082)
T:(0258) 52253
*Undulating downland course with rare
flora. Societies welcome by
arrangement. 18 | 6227 yds | Par 70 |
SSS 70*
Visitors welcome | B L ☛ | ⌂ ♈ |
TR WE, Tu ⅃ | ⋈ | M 400
★★★*Crown, 1 West St. T:(0258)
56626. 28rm (27 ⇄ 1 ⏶)*

BLANKNEY
Lincolnshire
Map IV C2

Blankney (1m SW of
Metheringham, on B1188)
T:(0526) 20263
*Peaceful parkland course, fairly flat.
Societies welcome by arrangement. 18 |
6232 yds | Par 70 | SSS 70*
Visitors welcome, with M only at
WE Nov to March ☎ | ∴ per day
WE | B L ☛ D order before play (not
Tu) | ⌂ ♈ ⟍ | ⋈ | TR WE | M 450 |
S
★★★*Eastgate Post House, Eastgate,
Lincoln. T:(0522) 20341. 71rm ⇄*

BLETCHLEY
Buckinghamshire
Map IV B8

Windmill Hill Tattenhoe Ln,
Bletchley (W side of town centre on
A421)
T:(0908) 648149, Bucks
*Municipal parkland course. 18 |
6773 yds | Par 73 | SSS 72*
Open to public | B L ☛ D | ⌂ ♈ ⟍ ⇨

BLUNDELLSANDS
Merseyside
Map **V** B7

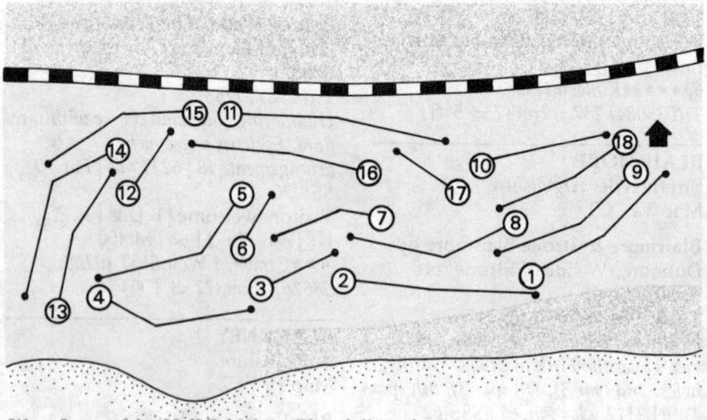

West Lancashire Hall Rd West, Blundellsands, Liverpool (N side of village)
T:051-924 1036
Society meetings by arrangement Th. 18 | 6756 yds | Par 72 | SSS 73
Visitors welcome, restricted Tu (ladies day) weekdays before 0930, 1300-1400, WE BH before 1030, 1500 | B ☕ (not Mon) | L prior arrangement (not Mon) | ⛺ | 🍸 lunchtime | ⟍ | [TR] weekdays before 0930, 1300-1400 Tu until 1600 (ladies) | 🏌 | M 650 | [S]
★★★*Blundellsands, Serpentine, Crosby. T:051-924 6515. 43rm (24 ⇄ 6 ⌂)*

This challenging links with its sandy subsoil provides excellent golf throughout the year. There are many fine holes, particularly the four short ones.

⋈ | [TR] some WE | 🏌 | M 420 | [S]
★★★*Swan, High St, Leighton Buzzard. T:(0525) 372148. 35rm ⇄*

BOLDON
Tyne and Wear
Map **V** F1

Boldon Dipe Ln, East Boldon, (S side of village off A184)
T:(0783) 364182/365835
Meadowland links course, easy walking, distant sea view, windy. 18 | 6318 yds | Par 71 | SSS 70
Visitors welcome, restricted WE | without M ∴ per day ∷ WE | with M ‥ per day ∴ WE | B ☕ D prior arrangement preferable (not Th) | ⛺ 🍸 | ⋈ | [TR] WE (am) | 🏌 | M 560 | [S]
★★★*Seaburn, Queen's Pde, Seaburn, Sunderland. T:(0783) 292041. 82rm (79 ⇄ 3 ⌂)*

BOLTON
Greater Manchester
Map **V** D7

Bolton Municipal Links Rd, (3m W of Bolton, on A673)
T:(0204) 42336
A parkland course. 18 | 6160 yds | Par 70 | SSS 69
Visitors welcome without M | B L D ☕ | ⛺ 🍸 [S] ⋈ ⟍ | [TR] alternative S
★★★*Crest, Beaumont Rd, Bolton. T:(0204) 651511. 100rm ⇄*

Breightmet Red Bridge, Ainsworth, Bolton, (E side of town centre off A58)
T:(0204) 27381
Long parkland course. 9 | 6500 yds | Par 72 | SSS 71
Visitors welcome, ☎ advisable | restricted competition days | without M ‥ per day WE | with M ‥ per day WE | B ☕ (not Mon) | L D prior arrangement (not Mon) | ⛺ | 🍸 (not Mon) | ⋈ | M 170
★★★*The Pack Horse, Bradshawgate, Nelson Sq. T:(0204) 27261. 74rm (72 ⇄ 2 ⌂)*

Dunscar Longworth Ln, Bromley Cross, Bolton, (3m N of Bolton off A666)
T:(0204) 53321
A scenic moorland course with panoramic views, a warm friendly club, visitors welcome. 18 | 5957 yds | Par 71 | SSS 69
Visitors welcome, restrictions WE | without M ∴ per round WE | with M ‥ per day WE | B ☕ (not Mon) | L D prior arrangement (not Th) | ⛺ 🍸 ⟍ | ⋈ | [TR] Tu-ladies, Wed-men | ④ [TR] S/Sun/W 🏌 | M 400 | [S]
★★★♣*Egerton House, Egerton. T:(0204) 57171. 25rm ⇄*

Great Lever & Farnworth Lever Edge Ln, Bolton, (SW side of town centre off A575)
T:(0204) 656650, Gtr Manchester
Downland course with easy walking. 18 | 5859 yds | Par 70 | SSS 69
Visitors welcome restricted certain times | ✉ ☎ | ‥ per round WE | B L ☕ | D prior arrangement, not Mon | ⛺ 🍸 | [TR] WE, Wed | ④ ☎ | M 300 | [S]
★★★*Pack Horse, Bradshawgate, Nelson Sq. T:(0204) 27261. 74rm (72 ⇄ 2 ⌂)*

Harwood Springfield, Roading Brook Rd, Harwood, (2½m NE of Bolton off B6196)
T:(0204) 22878
Parkland course. 9 | 6013 yds | Par 71 | SSS 69
Visitors welcome ☎ | B L ☕ D prior arrangement | ⛺ 🍸 | [TR] WE & BH | 🏌 | M 210 | [S]
★★★♣*Egerton House, Egerton, Bolton. T:(0204) 57171. 25rm ⇄*

Old Links Chorley Old Rd, Bolton, (NW of town centre on B6226)
T:(0204) 42307
Moorland course. 18 | 6406 yds | Par 72 | SSS 72
Visitors welcome ☎ | without M ∴ per day ∷ WE | with M ‥ per day WE | B L ☕ D | 🍸 ⛺ ⟍ | [TR] S and competition days | 🏌 | M 550 | [S]
★★★*Pack Horse, Bradshawgate, Nelson Sq, Bolton. T:(0204) 27261. 74rm (72 ⇄ 2 ⌂)*

Regent Park Municipal Golf Course, Chorley New Rd, Bolton, (3½m W of Bolton off A673)
T:(0204) 42336
Parkland course. 18 | 6160 yds | Par 70 | SSS 69
Open to public | B L ☕ D | ⛺ 🍸 ⟍ ⋈ [TR] S (alternative starting times) | M 200 | [S]
★★★*Crest, Beaumont Rd. T:(0204) 651511. 100rm ⇄*

BOAT OF GARTEN
Highland, *Inverness-shire*
Map VII   G5

£ 14/day

Boat of Garten (E side of village)
T:(047983) 282/351
18 | 5690 yds | Par 69 | SSS 68
Visitors welcome | .. per day WE | B ♛ L | ☖ ☂ ④ competition days | TR
0800-1000, 1300-1400, 1630-1830 | ④ competition days | M 350 | S
★★*Craigard, Kinchurdy Rd. T:(047983) 206. 20rm (7 ⇌ 1 ⌗)*
This parkland course was cut out from a silver birch forest though the fairways are adequately wide. There are natural hazards of broom and heather, good views and walking is easy. A round provides great variety. Testing holes include the 13th and 18th.

BONAR BRIDGE
Highland, *Sutherland*
Map VII   F3

Bonar Bridge - Ardgay (½m E of Bonar Bridge)
T:(086 32) 577(Sec)
Wooded moorland course with picturesque views of hills and loch. 9 | 4626 yds | Par 64 | SSS 64
Visitors welcome .. per day | M 80
★★*Bridge, Bonar Bridge. T:(08632) 204. 16rm (5 ⇌ 5 ⌗)*

BONHILL
Strathclyde, *Dumbartonshire*
Map VI   D2

Vale of Leven North Field Rd, Bonhill (E side of town off A813)
T:(0389) 52351
Moorland course, very scenic, tricky with many natural hazards - gorse, burns, trees. Junior mem. 18 | 5162 yds | Par 68 | SSS 66
Visitors very welcome | .. per day ∴ WE | B L ♛ | D prior arrangement | ☖ ☂ (closed Tu lunchtime) ⋈ | TR S April-September | M 650 | S

★★*Balloch, Balloch. T:(0389) 52579. 13rm (6 ⇌)*

BONNYBRIDGE
Central, *Stirlingshire*
Map VI   E2

Bonnybridge Larbert Rd, Bonnybridge (1m NE of Bonnybridge off A883)
T:(0324) 812822
Testing heathland course, with tightly guarded greens. Easy walking. Facilities for societies. 9 | 6060 yds | Par 72 | SSS 69
Visitors welcome ☎ ✉ with M only | .. per day WE | B L D (WE only) | ♛ | ☖ ☂ ⋈ | M 325 | S
★★★*Inchyra Grange, Grange Rd. T:(0324) 711911. 30rm ⇌ ⌗*

BONNYRIGG
Lothian, *Midlothian*
Map VI   G2

Broomieknowe 36 Golf Course Rd, Bonnyrigg, (½m NE of Bonnyrigg off B704)
T:031-663 9317
Easy walking parkland course laid out

by Ben Sayers and extended by James Braid. Elevated site with excellent views. 18 | 6046 yds | Par 70 | SSS 69
Visitors welcome, restricted W WE BH | without M ∴ per day | with M .. per day WE | B (not Mon) | L ♛ D prior arrangement | ☖ ☂ ↘ ⋈ |
TR competition days | ♩ | M 450 | S
★★★*Donmaree, 21 Mayfield Gdns, Edinburgh. T:031-667 3641. 9rm (4 ⇌ 15 ⌗). Annexe: 8rm (3 ⇌ 2 ⌗)*

BOOTLE
Merseyside
Map V   C7

Bootle Dunnings Bridge Rd, Bootle, (2m NE of Bootle on A5036)
T:051-928 1371
Municipal seaside course, with NW wind. Testing holes: 5th 200 yds Par 3; 7th 415 yds Par 4. 18 | 6362 yds | Par 70 | SSS 70
Open to public | Children reduced rate per round | B L ♛ | ☖ ☂ ↘ ⋈ |
TR Sun am | ♩ | S
★★★*Park, Park Lane West, Netherton. T:051-525 7555. 60rm (23 ⇌ 37 ⌗)*

BOROUGH GREEN
Kent
Map II   G4

Wrotham Heath Seven Mile Ln, Borough Green (2¼m E of Borough Green on B2016)
T:(0732) 884800
Parkland course, hilly, good views. 9 | 5851 yds | Par 69 | SSS 68
Visitors welcome ✉ certificate of handicap required | with M only on WE BH | ∴ per day | B prior arrangement (not Mon) | ☖ ☂ | ♛ | L D prior arrangement (not Mon) | ⇢

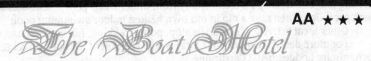

BOGNOR REGIS
West Sussex
Map II D7

Bognor Regis Downview Rd,
Felpham (1½m NE of Bognor, off
A259)
T:(0243) 865867
Societies welcome by arrangement. 18 |
6219 *yds* | *Par* 70 | *SSS* 70
Visitors welcome, restricted Tu
(ladies day), with M only WE
(April-Oct) handicap certificate
required | ☎ advisable | ∴ per day
:: WE | ☜ B | ⚖ ♈ | TR WE
competitions | ʒ | M 725 | S
★★★*Royal Norfolk, The Esplanade.*
T:(0243) 826222. 53rm (38 ⇌ 1 ⋒)

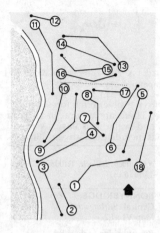

*Bognor Regis
course plan*

This flattish, parkland course has more variety than is to be found
on some of the South Coast courses. The club is also known far and
wide for its enterprise in creating a social atmosphere, much
appreciated by residents of the town and also by visitors. The
course is open to the prevailing wind.

④ WE | TR competitions | ʒ | M 350
| S
★★★★*Post House, London Rd,
Wrotham Heath (At junc M26/A20).
T:(0732) 883311. 119rm ⇌*

BORTH
Dyfed
Map III D5

Borth & Ynslas (½m N of Borth, on
B4353)
T:(097 081) 202
*Seaside links with strong winds
sometimes. Some narrow fairways.* 18 |
6094 *yds* | *Par* 70 | *SSS* 70
Visitors welcome ⊠ or with M | B
☜ L prior arrangement | ⚖ ♈ | ⋈
prior arrangement | TR competition
days | ʒ | M 300 | S
★★*Court Royale, Eastgate,
Aberystwyth. T:(0970) 611722.
10rm (6 ⇌ 4 ⋒)*

BOSTON
Lincolnshire
Map IV E2

Boston Cowbridge, Horncastle Rd,
(2m N of Boston off B1183)
T:(0205) 62306

BOLTON
Greater Manchester
Map **V** D7

Bolton Lostock Park, Chorley New Rd (3m W of Bolton, on A673)
T:(0204) 43067
Societies welcome by arrangement Mon Th F. 18 | 6215 yds | Par 70 | SSS 70
Visitors welcome, Mon to F | restricted WE | ✳ | B ☎ | L D prior arrangement (not Sun Mon) | ⚐ ⵁ ⟍ | ⎘TR⎙ 1330-1400 | ♩ | M 600 | ⎣S⎦
✳✳✳*Pack Horse, Bradshawgate, Nelson Sq.* T:(0204) 27261. *74rm (72 ⇌ 2 ⫪)*
This well-maintained parkland course is always a pleasure to visit. The 9th hole should be treated with respect and so too should the final four holes which have ruined many a card.

BORDON
Hampshire
Map **II** C5

Blackmoor Whitehill (1m SW of Bordon, off A325 at Whitehill)
T:(04203) 2775
Societies welcome by long arrangement. 18 | 6213 yds | Par 69 | SSS 70
Visitors welcome ✉, restricted WE BH | ☎ preferred | ∴ per round | ∷ per day | with M ∴ per day | ☎ | B (not Tu) | L D prior arrangement | ⚐ ⵁ ⟍ | ⋈ | ④ 1330-1415 (from 10th, after 1500 (from 1st) | ♩ | M 500 | ⎣S⎦
✳✳*Bishops Table, 27 West St, Farnham.* T:(0252) 715545. *7rm* ⇌. *Annexe: 9rm (2⇌4 ⫪)*
A first-class moorland course with a great variety of holes. Fine greens and wide pine tree-lined fairways are a distinguishing feature. The ground is mainly flat and walking easy.

Parkland course with many water hazards. Small societies welcome by arrangement. 18 | 5764 yds | Par 69 | SSS 68
Visitors welcome, restricted WE BH | B ☎ (not Tu) | L D prior arrangement (not Tu) | ⚐ ⵁ ⋈ (possibly) | ⟍ (not Mon) | ⎘TR⎙ Sun (am) | ♩ | M 630 | ⎣S⎦
✳✳✳*New England, Wide Bargate.* T:(0205) 65255. *25rm* ⇌

BOTHWELL
Strathclyde, *Lanarkshire*
Map **VI** E3

Bothwell Castle Blantyre Rd, Bothwell (NW of village of B7071)
Flat parkland course. 18 | 6433 yds | Par 71 | SSS 71
Visitors welcome weekdays | ✳ | B L D ☎ | ⚐ ⵁ ⟍ | ⎣S⎦ ⋈ sometimes | ⎘TR⎙ WE | M 800 | ♩
✳✳*Silvertrees, Silverwells Cres, Bothwell.* T:(0698) 852311. *7rm* ⇌ ⫪. *Annexe: 19rm* ⇌ ⫪

BOURNEMOUTH
Dorset
Map **I** K6

KEY

(IA1)	*atlas grid reference*
T:	*telephone number*
☎	*advance letter/telephone call required*
✉	*introduction from own club sec/handicap certificate/club membership card required*
..	*low fees*
∴	*medium fees*
::	*high fees*
*	*green fees not confirmed for 1987*
B	*light lunch*
L	*full lunch*
♥	*tea*
D	*dinner*
⚎	*changing rooms/showers*
♉	*bar open mid-day and evenings*
↘	*clubs for hire*
⋈	*partners may be found*
④	*restricted time for 4 balls*
TR	*times reserved for members*
𝕁	*professional*
S	*well-stocked shop*
M	*member*
Mon Tu W Th F S Sun	
WE	*weekend*
BH	*bank holiday*

Knighton Heath Francis Av, West Howe, Bournemouth (N side of town centre off A348)
T:(0202) 572633
Heathland course on high ground inland from Bournemouth. Easy walking on undulating heather-lined fairways. 18 | 6207 yds | Par 70 | SSS 70
Visitors welcome ✉ restricted Tu (ladies day) ☎ WE | without M : :

BOW BRICKHILL
Buckinghamshire
Map **IV** C8

Woburn Bow Brickhill, Milton Keynes (½m E of Bow Brickhill)
T:(0908) 70756
18 | 6839 yds | Par 72 | SSS 73
Visitors welcome ✉ midweek (prior booking) | : : per day including lunch | L
♥ ⚎ ↘ ♉ ↘ | TR | ④ ☎ for details | 𝕁 | S
∗∗*Swan Revived, High St, Newport Pagnell. T:(0908) 618555. 31rm (12 ⇌ 19 ⌂)*
These two 18-hole golf courses are set amid the beautiful surroundings of the Duke of Bedford's estate near Woburn, and are suitably named the Duke's and the Duchess's.

BOWNESS-ON-WINDERMERE
Cumbria
Map **V** C4

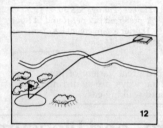
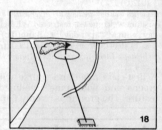

Windermere Cleabarrow, Bowness-on-Windermere (1m E of Bowness-on-Windermere on B5284)
T:(09662) 3123
Societies welcome by arrangement. 18 | 5002 yds | Par 67 | SSS 65
Visitors welcome | without M ∴ per day WE | with M .. per day WE | B ♥ prior arrangement winter | D prior arrangement | ⚎ | ♉ winter hours differ ↘ | ⋈ quite often | TR midweek (1230-1330) WE competition times | 𝕁 | M 700 | S
∗∗∗*Wild Boar, Crook. T:(09662) 5225. 38rm (33 ⇌ 5 ⌂)*
Enjoyable holiday golf on a short slightly hilly but sporting course in this delightful area of the Lake District National Park, with superb views of the mountains as the backcloth to the lake and the course.

per day WE | with M .. per day WE | ☕ B L (not Mon) | D prior arrangement (not Mon) | ☖ ☖ ☖ | TR before 0930 | 🎵 | M 750 | Ⓢ ★★★*Heathlands, Grove Rd, East Cliff* T:(0202) 23336. 116rm (113 ⇌ 3 🍴)

Meyrick Park Municipal Course Meyrick Park, Bournemouth (¾m NW of town centre) T:(0202) 290871 *Wooded parkland course played over by 4 clubs (Meyrick Park, Meyrick Park Ladies, Bournemouth, Bournemouth Ladies). Testing holes are 1st and 4th (par 3), 14th (par 5). 18 | 5878 yds | Par 69 | SSS 69* Open to public but no play after 1100 Sun | .. per round | B ☕ | L D prior arrangement | ☖ ☖ ☖ ☖ | M 300 | Ⓢ ★★★*Heathlands, Grove Rd, East Cliff, Bournemouth. T:(0202) 23336. 116rm (113 ⇌ 3 🍴)*

Queen's Park West Drive (2m NE of town centre off A338) *Undulating parkland course of pine and heather, with narrow, tree-lined fairways. Public course played over by Boscombe Golf Club and Bournemouth Artisans Golf Club. 18 | 6505 yds | Par 72 | SSS 72* Visitors welcome ☎ advisable | B L ☕ (parties prior arrangement) | ☖ (lunchtime only Sun) | ☖ | 🎵 | no M-season ticket | last tee off 1100 on Sun | Ⓢ ★★*Hotel Riviera, West Cliff Gardens. T:(0202) 22845. 34rm (20 ⇌ 3 🍴)*

BRADFORD
West Yorkshire
Map **V** F6

Bradford Moor Scarr Hall, Pollard Ln, Bradford, (2m NE of city centre off A658) T:(0274) 638313 *Parkland course, hard walking. 9 | 5854 yds | Par 70 | SSS 68* Visitors welcome | B L ☕ D prior arrangement | ☖ ☖ ☖ (limited) | TR competition days (up to 1600) | 🎵 | M 376 | Ⓢ | ☖ ★★★★*Stakis Norfolk Gardens, Hall Ings. T:(0274) 734734. 126rm ⇌*

Clayton Thornton View Rd, Clayton (2½m W of city centre on A647) T:(0274) 880047, Bradford

Moorland course, windy. Annual junior competition for M of Bradford Union of Golf Clubs. 9 | 5515 yds | Par 68 | SSS 67 Visitors welcome, restricted WE | .. per day WE | B L D prior arrangement (not Mon) | ☖ ☖ | TR WE | 🎵 | M 210 ★★★*Novotel Bradford, Merrydale Rd. T:(0274) 683683. 136rm ⇌*

East Bierly South View Rd, East Bierly, Bradford (4m SE of city centre off A650) T:(0274) 681023 *Downland course with narrow fairways, easy walking, two par 3 holes over 200 yds. 9 | 4308 yds | Par 64 | SSS 63* Visitors welcome ☎ | restricted S am, Sun | B (not Th) | ☕ L D ☖ ☖ 🎵 | M 200 ★★★*Victoria, Bridge St. T:(0274) 728706. 60rm (45 ⇌ 6 🍴)*

Headley Lower Kipping Ln, Thornton, Bradford (4m W of city centre, off B6145 at Thornton) T:(0274) 833348 *Hilly moorland course, short but very testing, windy, fine views. Societies welcome by arrangement. 9 | 4914 yds | Par 64 | SSS 64* Visitors welcome, restricted Sun (until 1600) | .. per day WE | ☖ ☖ | L D by prior arrangement | M 250 ★★★★*Stakis Norfolk Gardens, Hall Ings, Bradford. T:(0274) 734734. 126rm ⇌*

Phoenix Park Phoenix Park, Thornbury, Bradford, (E side of city on A647) T:(0274) 667573 *Very short, tight moorland course, rather testing. 9 | 4776 yds | Par 66 | SSS 64* Visitors welcome | B L ☕ | ☖ ☖ | 🎵 ★★★★*Stakis Norfolk Gardens, Hall Ings, Bradford. T:(0274) 734734. 126rm ⇌*

South Bradford Pearson Rd, Odsal, Bradford (2m S of city centre off A638) T:(0274) 679195 *Testing meadowland course with trees and ditches. Interesting short 2nd hole par 3 200 yds, well bunkered and play from an elevated tee. 9 | 6004 yds | Par 70 | SSS 69* Visitors welcome weekdays | WE

after 1530 | without M .. weekdays ∴ WE, BH | with M .. per day | B ☕ | L D prior arrangement | ☖ ☖ ☖ | ☖ | ④ | TR WE competitions | M 250 | Ⓢ ★★★*Novotel Bradford, Merrydale Rd. T:(0274) 683683. 136rm ⇌*

West Bowling Newall Hall, Rooley Ln, Bradford (S side of city centre on A6177) T:(0274) 724449 *Parkland average course, easy going. Testing hole: 'the coffin' short par 3, very narrow. Societies welcome by arrangement. 18 | 5769 yds | Par 69 | SSS 68* Visitors welcome, restricted S (winter only 1st, 3rd in each month) | without M .. per day | :: WE | with M .. per day and WE | B (not Mon) | L ☕ D prior arrangement (not Mon) | ☖ ☖ ☖ | 🎵 | M 400 | Ⓢ ★★★*Victoria, Bridge St. T:(0274) 728706. 60rm (45 ⇌ 6 🍴)*

West Bradford Chellow Grange Rd, Bradford (NE side of city centre off B6144) T:(0274) 427671 *Parkland course, windy, especially holes 3, 4, 5 and 6. Hilly but not hard. 7m from Haworth (home of Brontes). 18 | 5705 yds | Par 69 | SSS 68* Visitors welcome ☎ preferred, restricted Tu WE | B ☕ (no catering Mon) | L D by arrangement (not Mon) | ☖ ☖ (evenings only Mon) ☖ ☖ | 🎵 | M 400 | Ⓢ ★★★*Bankfield, Bradford Rd, Bingley. T:(0274) 567123. 69rm (67 ⇌ 2 🍴)*

BRAEMAR
Grampian, *Aberdeenshire*
Map **VII** H6

Braemar Cluniebank Rd (½m S of village) T:(033 83) 618 *Set amid beautiful countryside on Royal Deeside, the course is within easy walking distance of the village and new caravan club site. 18 | 5011 yds | Par 67 | SSS 64* Visitors welcome without M .. Mon-F, ∴ WE | B L D ☕ | ☖ ☖ ☖ | M 220 | Ⓢ ★★*Darroch Learg, Ballater. T:(0338) 55443. 15rm (13 ⇌ 2 🍴). Annexe: 8rm (3 ⇌ 2 🍴)*

BRAINTREE
Essex
Map **IV** G8

Braintree Kings Ln, Stisted (2m E of Braintree, off A120)
T:(0376) 24117
Parkland course with many rare trees. Societies welcome by arrangement. 18 | 6105 yds | Par 70 | SSS 69
Visitors welcome, restricted Sun (am) | ∴ per round ∷ per day weekdays ∷ WE | B L ☕ | D prior arrangement | ⛳ 🍸 | TR Sun am, competition days | ④ various (starting board) | ♪ | M 600 | S
★★*Saracen's Head, High St, Great Dunmow. T:(0371) 3901. 24rm ⇄*

BRAMHALL
Greater Manchester
Map **V** E8

Bramhall The Club House, Ladythorn Rd, Bramhall (E side of town centre off A5102)
T:061-439 4057
Well-wooded parkland course with splendid views of the Pennines. 18 | 6300 yds | Par 70 | SSS 70
Visitors welcome ☎ advisable | without M ∴ per day ∷ WE | with M ‥ per day WE | B prior arrangement Sun (not F) | L D prior arrangement (not F) | ⛳ 🍸 ⟍ | ④ TR Thu, S, competition days | ♪ | M 700 | S ⋈
★★★*Bramhall Moat House, Bramhall Lane South. T:061-439 8116. 40rm ⇄*

Bramhall Park 20 Manor Rd, Bramhall (NW side of town centre off A5149)
T:061-485 3119
Undulating parkland course, easy walking. Societies welcome Tu only, by arrangement. 18 | 6214 yds | Par 71 | SSS 70
Visitors welcome only with M or ✉ | ✻ | B L ☕ | D prior arrangement (not F) | ⛳ 🍸 ⋈ | TR WE | M 700 | S
★★★*Bramhall Moat House, Bramhall Lane South. T:061-439 8116. 40rm ⇄*

BRAMLEY
Surrey
Map **II** D5

Bramley (½m N on A281)
T:(0483) 892696
Downland course, fine views from top. Societies welcome (W to F) by arrangement. 18 | 5910 yds | Par 69 | SSS 68
Visitors welcome, but with M only WE BH | without M ∷ per day | with M ∴ per day ‥ WE | B ☕ | L D prior arrangement | ⛳ 🍸 | ⟍ ⋈ prior arrangement | TR WE | ♪ | M 720 | S
★★*Angel, High St, Guildford. T:(0483) 64555. 27rm ⇄ 🚿*

BRANDESBURTON
Humberside
Map **V** J5

Hainsworth Park Burton Holme, Brandesburton (SW side of village on A165)
T:(0401) 42362
A parkland course with easy walking 9 | 5320 yds | Par 68 | SSS 66
Visitors welcome without M ‥ per day | B L D ☕ 🍸 ⟍ ⋈ | TR some WE | M 200
★★★*Tickton Grange Hotel, Tickton, Beverley. T:(0401) 43666. 16rm (8 ⇄ 8 🚿)*

BRAMPTON
Cumbria
Map **VI** H6

Brampton Talkin Tarn (2m SE of Brampton, on B6413)
T:(09677) 2255
Societies welcome, preferably midweek, 18 | 6420 yds | Par 72 | SSS 71
Visitors welcome, without M ‥ per day ∴ WE | with M ‥ per day WE | B L ☕ D prior arrangement (snacks only Mon F except for booked parties) | ⛳ ⟍ 🍸 | ⋈ (possibly) | ♪ | M 700 | S
❀★★*Tarn End, Talkin Tarn. T:(06977) 2340. 6rm (3 ⇄)*
Challenging golf across glorious rolling fell country demanding solid driving and many long second shots. A number of particularly fine holes, the pick of which may arguably be the 3rd and 11th. The course offers unrivalled panoramic views from its hilly position.

BRANDON
Warwickshire
Map **III** K5

City of Coventry - Brandon Wood
Brandon Ln, Coventry (1m W of Brandon)
Municipal parkland course surrounded by fields and bounded by R Avon on east side. 18 | 6530 yds | Par 72 | SSS 71
Open to public | B L ☕ D | ⛳ 🍸 S ⟍ ⋈
★★★*Chace Crest, London Rd, Willenhall. T:(0203) 303398. 68rm ⇄*

BRECHIN
Tayside, *Angus*
Map **VII** J7

Brechin Trinity, Brechin (1m N of Brechin on B966)
T:(03562) 2383
Parkland course, with easy walking and good views of Strathmore Valley and Grampian Mountains. Society meetings by arrangement. 18 | 5267 yds | Par 65 | SSS 66
Visitors welcome ‥ per day ∴ WE | B L D ☕ | ⛳ 🍸 TR WE (0800-1000) W 1300-1345, 1700-1745 | ④ WE | M 681 | S
★★*Northern, Clerk St. T:(03562) 2156. 17rm (4 ⇄ 11 🚿)*

BRECON
Powys
Map **III** E7

Brecon Newton Park (¾m W of town centre on A40)
T:(0874) 2004
Parkland course, with easy walking. Natural hazards include 2 rivers on boundary of course. Good river and mountain scenery. 9 | 5218 yds | Par 66 | SSS 66
Visitors welcome | ⛳ | 🍸 | ☕ ⋈ | TR competition days, Mon (ladies day) | M 425 | S
★★*Castle of Brecon, The Avenue. T:(0874) 2551. 28rm (6 ⇄ 3 🚿) Annexe: 12rm 🚿*

Cradoc Penoyre Park, Cradoc (2m NW Brecon)
T:(0874) 3658
Parkland with wooded areas, lakes, spectacular views over the Brecon Beacons, challenging course. 18 | 6300 yds | Par 71 | SSS 71
Visitors welcome without M | ‥ per day ∴ WE, BH | L D B ☕ | ⛳ 🍸

BRANCASTER
Norfolk
Map **IV**   G2

Royal West Norfolk Brancaster, Kings Lynn
(1m N of Brancaster off A149)
T:(0485) 210223
Small societies welcome by arrangement. 18 | 6428 yds | Par 71 | SSS 71
Visitors welcome with M or ⊠ preferred, with M only WE, 1st July-30th Sept
| ☎ advisable | ∴ per day ∷ WE | B ☙ | L D prior arrangement | ⚖ ⵂ ⌇ | ④
not permitted | ⊤ᴿ Tu, Th am | M 500 | ⓢ
∗∗*Manor, Titchwell. T:(0485) 210221. 7rm (4 ⇆ 1 🏵) Annexe: 3rm* ⇆

If you want to see what golf courses were like years ago, then go to
the Royal West Norfolk where tradition exudes from both clubhouse and course. The course is close by the sea, which one can say
almost laps against the walls of the clubhouse. Cross bunkering is a
feature of this links. Testing holes at the 3rd (par 4), 4th (par 3),
8th (par 5), 9th (par 4) and 14th (par 4).

BRIDGEND
Mid Glamorgan
Map **I**   F3

Southerndown Ewenny, Bridgend (3m SW of Bridgend on B4524)
T:(0656) 880326
Societies Tu Th by arrangement. 18 | 6615 yds | Par 70 | SSS 73
Visitors welcome ⊠ ☎ preferred | Sun only with M ∴ per day ∷ WE | B ☙
(not Mon) | L D prior arrangement (not Mon) ⚖ ⵂ | ⌇ prior arrangement | 𝔍
| M 598 | ⓢ
∗∗∗*Heronston, Ewenny, Bridgend. T:(0656) 68811. 40rm ⇆ 🏵*

A unique course standing on high downs close to the sea. The views
are entrancing, and the golf completely natural. Close to Royal
Porthcawl and overshadowed perhaps by this famous neighbour.
Well worth a visit.

ⓢ ⌇ ⋈ | M 400
∗∗*Castle of Brecon, The Avenue,
Brecon. T:(0874) 2551.
28rm (6 ⇆ 3 🏵) Annexe: 12rm* 🏵

BRENTWOOD
Essex
Map **II**   G3

Bentley Ongar Rd (3m NW of
Brentwood, on A128)
T:(0277) 73179
*Parkland course, water hazards. 18 |
6709 yds | Par 72 | SSS 72*
Visitors welcome weekdays | ∴ per
day | L D by arrangement only | B
☙ ⚖ ⵂ | ⋈ prior arrangement | ⊤ᴿ
WE BH | 𝔍 | M 450 | ⓢ
∗∗∗*Post House, Brook St. T:(0277)
210888. 120rm* ⇆

Hartswood King George's Playing
Fields, Ingrave Rd (¾m SE of
Brentwood on A128)
T:(0277) 218850
*Municipal parkland course, easy
walking. 18 | 6238 yds | Par 70 |
SSS 70*

Visitors welcome | B L ☙ | ⚖ ⵂ ⌇ |
⋈ | M 500 | ⓢ
∗∗∗*Post House, Brook St, Brentwood.
T:(0277) 210888. 120rm* ⇆

Warley Park Magpie Ln, Little
Warley (2½m S of Brentwood off
B186)
T:(0277) 224891
*Parkland course with reasonable
walking. Numerous water hazards.
There is also a golf practice ground.
Snooker room. 27(3x9 hole) |
2993/3142/3240 yds | Par 35/35/36 |
SSS 69/69/71*
Visitors welcome ⊠ | ☎ advisable |
B L ☙ D | ⚖ ⵂ | ⌇ ⋈ | 𝔍 | M 650 |
ⓢ
∗∗∗*Post House, Brook St. T:(0277)
210888. 120rm* ⇆

BRICKENDON
Hertfordshire
Map **II**   F2

Brickendon Grange (W side of
village)
T:(099 286) 259

*Parkland course. 18 | 6315 yds | Par 71
| SSS 70*
Visitors welcome, but with M only
WE BH | without M ∷ per day WE
| with M ·· per day ∴ WE | B | L ☙
D | ⚖ ⵂ ⌇ | 𝔍 | M 650 | ⓢ | ⋈ ⊤ᴿ
Wed am (ladies day)
∗∗∗*White Horse Inn, Hertingfordbury,
Hertford. T:(0992) 56791. 30rm* ⇆

BRIDGE OF ALLAN
Central, *Stirlingshire*
Map **VI**   E1

Bridge of Allan Sunnylaw, Bridge
of Allan (½m N of Bridge of Allan
off A9)
T:(0786) 83233
*Parkland course, very hilly with good
views. Testing 1st hole 221 yds par 3
uphill, 6 ft wall 25 yds before green. 9 |
4932 yds | Par 66 | SSS 65*
Visitors welcome | ·· per day | B ☙
| ⚖ | ⵂ (evenings and WE only) |
⊤ᴿ after 1730 Mon to F, all day S |
M 270
∗∗∗*Royal, Henderson St. T:(0786)
832284. 33rm (25 ⇆)*

BRIDGNORTH
Shropshire
Map **III**   H5

Bridgnorth Stanley Ln (1m N of
Bridgnorth off B4373)
T:(074 62) 3315
*A pleasant course laid out on
meadowland on the bank of the River
Severn. 18 | 6627 yds | Par 73 | SSS 72*
Visitors welcome without M. | B ☙
(not Mon) | L D prior arrangement
(not Mon) | ⚖ ⵂ | ⋈ possible | 𝔍 |
M 700 | ⓢ
∗∗*Falcon, St John St, Lowtown.
T:(07462) 3134. 16rm (3 ⇆)*

BRIDLINGTON
Humberside
Map **V**   J5

Bridlington Belvedere Rd (1m S of
Bridlington off A165)
T:(0262) 672092
*Clifftop, seaside course, windy at times.
18 | 6320 yds | Par 71 | SSS 70*
Visitors welcome ∴ per day WE BH
| ⵂ B L D | ☙ | ⚖ | ⓢ ⌇ | ⋈ | M 700
| ⊤ᴿ Sun am | 𝔍
∗∗*Monarch, South Marine Dr.
T:(0262) 674447. 43rm (23 ⇆ 1 🏵)*

BRIDPORT
Dorset
Map I   H5

Bridport & West Dorset East Cliff,
West Bay (At West Bay, 2m S of
Bridport)
T:(0308) 22597
*Seaside course on the top of the east
cliff, with fine views over Lyme Bay
and surrounding countryside. At the
13th hole par 3, the green is 70 feet
below the tee.* 18 | 5246 yds | Par 67 |
SSS 66
Visitors welcome ∴ per day | B ☛ |
L D (not Mon) | ⚎ ⌇ ↘ | ⋈ | ℑ |
M 500 | ⓢ
★★★*Haddon House, West Bay.
T:(0308) 23626. 13rm (11 ⇄ 2 ⅷ)*

BRIGHTON
East Sussex
Map II   E7

Brighton & Hove Dyke Rd (4m NW
of Brighton)
T:(0273) 556482
*Downland course with sea views.
Societies welcome by arrangement.
Children welcome.* 9 | 5722 yds |
Par 68 | SSS 68
Visitors welcome, restricted Sun
(am) | ∴ per day | L ☛ D | B (not
Tu) | ⚎ ⌇ ↘ | ⋈ | M 270 | ⒯⒭ Sun
(am) W (2nd & 3rd am) Ladies days
(0900-1000) competition days | ④
Sun (am)
★★★★*Dudley, Lansdowne Pl, Hove.
T:(0273) 736266. 79rm ⇄*

East Brighton Roedean Rd,
Brighton (E side of town centre on
B2118)
T:(0273) 604838
*Downland course overlooking sea,
windy. Societies welcome by
arrangement.* 18 | 6291 yds | Par 71 |
SSS 70
Visitors welcome | B L ☛ (not Mon)
| ⚎ ⌇ | ⒯⒭ 0800-1000 daily, Thu
(ladies day) | ℑ | ↘ | M 400 | ⓢ
★★★*Sackville, 189 Kingsway, Sea
Front, Hove. T:(0273) 736292.
45rm (43 ⇄ 2 ⅷ)*

Hollingbury Park Ditchling Rd,
Brighton (2m N of town centre)
T:(0273) 552010
*Municipal course in hilly situation on
the Downs overlooking the sea.* 18 |
6502 yds | Par 72 | SSS 71
Visitors welcome restricted WE ☎ |
.. per day | B ☛ | L D prior

BRIGHTON
East Sussex
Map II   E7

Dyke Dyke Rd (6½m NW of Brighton)
T:(079156) 296
Societies welcome by arrangement. 18 | 6519 yds | Par 72 | SSS 71
Visitors welcome (not Sun am) ☎ | without M ∴ per day ∷ WE | with M half
rate | B L ☛ D not Tu | ⚎ ⌇ | ④ time board | ⒯⒭ Sun (am) major competitions
| ℑ | M 750 | ⓢ
★★★*Old Ship, King's Rd, Brighton. T:(0273) 29001. 153rm (147 ⇄ 6 ⅷ)*
This, one of the several courses in the Brighton area, is generally
conceded to be the best, because it has more variety. It also has
some glorious views both towards the sea and inland. The best hole
on the course is probably the 17th; it is one of those teasing short
holes of just over 200 yards, and is played across a gully to a high
green. The course is subject to very high winds, especially in the
winter months.

BRISTOL
Avon
Map I   H3

Bristol and Clifton Failand (4m W of Bristol on B3129, off A369)
T:(0272) 393474
18 | 6294 yds | Par 70 | SSS 70
Visitors welcome restricted WE 1100-1230, after 1700 | ∴ per day ∷ WE | B ☛
L D prior arrangement | ⚎ ⌇ ↘ | ⋈ | ⒯⒭ WE (until 1100) | ℑ | M 600 | ⓢ
★★★*Redwood Lodge, Beggar Bush Ln, Failand. T:(0272) 393901. 72rm ⇄ ⅷ*
A downland course with splendid turf and fine tree-lined fairways.
The 200-yard par 3 13th with the green well below, and the par 4
16th with its second shot across an old quarry are outstanding.
There are splendid views over the Bristol Channel towards Wales.
The Coca Cola Professional Tournament has been held here.

BRISTOL
Avon
Map I   H3

Henbury Henbury Hill, Westbury-on-Trym, Bristol
(3m NW of city centre on B4055, off A4018)
T:(0272) 500044(Sec) 500660(Club)
Societies (Tu and F only) by prior arrangement. 18 | 6039 yds | Par 70 | SSS 70
Visitors welcome weekdays | with M BH WE | ☎ for parties for 10 or more
| without M ∴ per day | with M .. per day | B ☛ L (not Mon) | D prior
arrangement | ⚎ ⌇ ↘ ⋈ | ⒯⒭ competition days | ℑ | M 650 | ⓢ
★★★*St Vincent's Rocks, Sion Hill, Clifton, Bristol. T:(0272) 739251. 46rm ⇄*
A parkland course tree-lined and on two levels. The 3rd is a difficult
par 3 and the River Trym comes into play on the 7th drop-hole (par
3) with its green set just over the stream. The last nine holes have
the beautiful Blaise Castle woods for company.

arrangement | ⚎ ⌇ ↘ | ⋈ | ℑ | ⒯⒭
WE am | M 300 | ⓢ
★★★*Old Ship, Kings Rd. T:(0273)
.29001. 153rm (147 ⇄ 6 ⅷ)*

Waterhall Brighton & Hove
(4m NW of Brighton off A27)
T:(0273) 508658
*Hilly downland course with hard
walking and open to the wind. Private*

*club playing over municipal course.
Societies welcome (W Th F) by
arrangement. No children allowed on
course.* 18 | 5900 yds | Par 69 | SSS 68
Open to public. Visitors welcome
but restricted Sun (am) | B L ☛ (no
catering Tu) | D prior arrangement
WE | ⚎ ⌇ ↘ ⋈ | ⒯⒭ Sun
0800-1030 | ℑ | M 375 | ⓢ
★★★*Courtlands, 22 The Drive, Hove.*

T:(0273) 731055. 55rm (44 ⇔ 6 ⋒)
Annexe: 5rm ⇔

BRISTOL
Avon
Map I H3

Filton Golf Course Ln, Filton,
Bristol (5m N of Bristol off A38)
T:(0272) 694169
*Parkland course with a par 4 testing
hole dog-leg 383 yds. 18 | 6277 yds |
Par 70 | SSS 70*
*Visitors welcome with M ✉ | ∴ per
day | B L (not Mon & Tu) | ⬤ (not
Mon) | D prior arrangement (not
Mon) | ⚹ Ỵ ⤳ ✕ | M 600 | ⸤TR⸥ WE |
Ⓢ*
★★★*Crest, Filton Rd, Hambrook.
T:(0272) 564242. 151rm ⇔*

Mangotsfield Carsons Rd,
Mangotsfield, Bristol (6m NE of city
centre off B4465)
T:(0272) 565501
*An easy hilly parkland course. Caravan
site. Societies welcome by arrangement.
18 | 5337 yds | Par 68 | SSS 66*
*Visitors welcome ☎ | B L ⬤ D | ⚹
Ỵ ⤳ | Ɉ | M 400 | Ⓢ*
★★★*Crest, Filton Rd, Hambrook.
T:(0272) 564242. 151rm ⇔*

BROADSTONE
Dorset
Map I K5

Broadstone (Dorset) Wentworth
Drive, Off Station Approach,
Broadstone (N side of village off
B3074)
T:(0202) 692595
*Heathland course. Societies welcome by
arrangement. 18 | 6129 yds (summer)
5914 (winter) | Par 69 | SSS 70
(summer) 69 (winter)*
*Visitors welcome ✉ with M WE
(winter) | without M ∶∶ per day |
with M ∙∙ per day ∴ WE | B | L ⬤ |
D prior arrangement | ⚹ Ỵ ⤳ | ④
Th (am) | ⸤TR⸥ Mon-F (until 0930)
WE (until 1000) | Ɉ | M 800 | Ⓢ*
★★★*King's Head, The Square,
Wimborne Minster. T:(0202) 880101.
22rm (10 ⇔)*

BROADWAY
Hereford and Worcester
Map III J7

Broadway Willersey Hill (2m NE of
Broadway)
T:(0386) 853683

BRISTOL
Avon
Map I H3

Knowle Fairway, Brislington, Bristol (3m SE of city centre off A37)
T:(0272) 770660)
Societies on Th only. 18 | 6016 yds | Par 69 | SSS 68
Visitors welcome weekdays | WE only with M | without M ∴ per day | with M
∙∙ per day | B ⬤ | L D (not Th) | ⚹ Ỵ ⤳ | ✕ prior arrangement | ④ ⸤TR⸥ ☎ for
details | Ɉ | M 700 | Ⓢ
○○○⛪*Hunstrete House, Chelwood, Hunstrete. T:(07618) 578. 13rm ⇔.*
Annexe: 8rm ⇔
A parkland course with nice turf but now somewhat naked after the
loss of its fine elm trees. The first five holes climb up and down hill
but the remainder are on a more even plain.

BRISTOL
Avon
Map I H3

Shirehampton Park Park Hill, Shirehampton, Bristol
(4m W of city centre on A4)
T:(0272) 822083
Societies welcome by arrangement. 18 | 5493 yds | Par 68 | SSS 67
Visitors welcome weekdays | with M BH WE | ☎ advisable | ✳ | B ⬤ | L prior
arrangement (not Th) | D prior arrangement | ⚹ Ỵ | ⸤TR⸥ ☎ for details | M 600
| Ⓢ
★★★*Redwood Lodge, Beggar Bush Ln, Failand. T:(0272) 393901. 72rm ⇔ ⋒*
A lovely course in undulating parkland comprising two loops, an
inner and outer half, each starting and finishing at the Clubhouse.
There are views over the Portway beside the River Avon where
sliced balls at the opening hole are irretrievable.

BROADSTAIRS
Kent
Map II K4

North Foreland Convent Rd, Kingsgate (1½m N of Broadstairs off B2052)
T:(0843) 62140
Societies welcome by arrangement. 18 | 6382 yds | Par 71 | SSS 70
Visitors welcome, restricted WE BH ✉ ☎ | without M ∶∶ per day | with M ∙∙
per day WE | B ⬤ L D | ⚹ Ỵ ⤳ | ⸤TR⸥ WE BH | Ɉ | M 896 | Ⓢ
★★★*Castle Keep, Kingsgate. T:(0843) 65222. 29rm (25 ⇔ 3 ⋒)*
A picturesque course situated where the Thames Estuary widens
towards the sea. North Foreland always seems to have a breath of
tradition of golf's earlier days about it. Perhaps the ghost of one of
its earlier professionals, the famous Abe Mitchell, still haunts the
lovely soft turf of the fairways. Walking is easy and the wind is
deceptive. The 8th and 17th, both par 4, are testing holes. There is
also an approach and putt course.

*At the edge of the Cotswolds lies this
downland course at an altitude of 900
feet above sea level with extensive
views. 18 | 5970 yds | Par 72 | SSS 69*
Visitors welcome ✉ | without M ∴
per day ∶∶ WE | with M ∙∙ per day |
B L (not Mon) ⬤ D (not Mon) | ⚹
Ỵ | ⸤TR⸥ competitions | Ɉ | M 630 | Ⓢ
★★★*Dormy House, Willersey Hill.
T:(0386) 852711. 26rm ⇔ ⋒*
Annexe: 23rm ⇔

BROCTON
Staffordshire
Map III H4

Brocton Hall Stafford (NW side of
village, off A34)
T:(0785) 661901
*Parkland course undulating in places,
easy walking. 18 | 6095 yds | Par 69 |
SSS 69*
Visitors welcome | ✳ | B L D ⬤ | ⚹ ➥

Ⴘ | ∞ Ⓢ↘ | M 550 | Ɉ | TR
competitions
★★*Garth, Wolverhampton Rd, Moss Pit, Stafford. T:(0785) 56124.*
32rm (24 ⇔)

BRODICK
Strathclyde, *Bute*
Map **VI** C3

Brodick (N side of village)
T:(0770) 2349, Isle of Arran
Short seaside course, very flat. 18 |
4500 yds | Par 62 | SSS 62
Visitors welcome ☎ preferred |
without M .. per day ∴ WE | with
M free | B | ♟ Ⴘ ↘ | TR Sun
(0930-1000) Tu W (1700-1800) |
M 525 | Ⓢ
★*Cameronia, Whiting Bay, Isle of Arran. T:(07707) 254. 6rm*

BROMBOROUGH
Merseyside
Map **V** C8

Bromborough Raby Hall Rd,
Bromborough (½m W of
Bromborough station)

BROCKENHURST
Hampshire
Map **II** A7

Brockenhurst Manor Sway Rd (¾m S of Brockenhurst on B3055)
T:(0590) 23332
Societies welcome by arrangement. 18 | 6216 yds | Par 70 | SSS 70 (winter 69)
Visitors welcome, restricted Sun (am) ⊠ ☎ | :: per day ∴ after 1600 | B ☛ | L
D prior arrangement | ♟ Ⴘ | ④ | TR ☎ for details | Ɉ | M 800 | Ⓢ
★★★*Ladbroke Balmer Lawn, Lyndhurst Rd. T:(0590) 23116. 59rm (55 ⇔ 2 ⬚)*
An attractive woodland course set at the edge of the New Forest
with the unusual feature of three loops of six holes each to complete
the round. Fascinating holes include the short 5th and 12th, the
long 16th, and the 4th and 17th both dog-legged.

T:051-334 2155
Parkland course. Societies welcome W by arrangement. 18 | 6650 yds | Par 72 | SSS 73
Visitors welcome, not Sun | without M ∴ per day :: WE | with M .. per day WE | B D (prior arrangement) | L prior arrangement (not Sun) | ☛ | ♟ Ⴘ ∞ | ④ 1630-1730 (Mon to F) | Ɉ | M 700 | Ⓢ
★★★*Bowler Hat, 2 Talbot Rd, Oxton, Birkenhead. T:051-652 4931. 29rm ⇔*

BROMLEY
Greater London
Map **II** F4

Bromley Magpie Hall Ln, (2m SE of Bromley on A21)
T:01-462 7014/8001
Suburban municipal parkland course with easy walking. 9 | 2745 yds | Par 70 | SSS 67
Open to public | .. per round | B ☛ Ⴘ ↘ ∞ | Ɉ | M 100 | Ⓢ
★★★*Bromley Court, Bromley Hill. T:01-464 5011. 130rm ⇔*

Magpie Hall Lane Magpie Hall Ln. (2m SE of Bromley off A21)
T:01-462 7014, London
Flat course ideal for beginners. 9 | 2745 yds | Par 35
Visitors welcome | Ⴘ B ☛ | Ⓢ↘ | ∞ | M 100 | Ɉ
★★★*Bromley Court, Bromley Hill, Bromley. T:01-464 5011. 130rm ⇔*

Shortlands Meadow Rd,
Shortlands, Bromley (¾m W of Bromley off A222)
T:01-460 2471
Easy walking parkland course with brook as natural hazard. 9 | 5261 yds | Par 65 | SSS 66
Visitors welcome weekdays ⊠ | with M .. weekdays ∴ WE | L ☛ D prior arrangement (not Mon) | ♟ Ⴘ | TR competition days | M 310 | Ⓢ
★★★*Bromley Court, Bromley Hill, Bromley. T:01-464 5011. 130rm ⇔*

BROOK
Hampshire
Map **II** A6

Bramshaw Brook, Lyndhurst (In Brook village, on B3079 1m W of M27 Jct 1)
T:(0703) 813433
Two 18-hole courses. Manor course - parkland; Forest course in New Forest. Easy walking, well wooded with streams. Societies by arrangement. 18(18) | 6273(5774) yds | Par 72(69) | SSS 70(68)
Visitors welcome ☎ advisable | not WE BH on Forest course | B L ☛ D prior arrangement | ♟ Ⴘ ④ WE | TR WE (before 1000) | Ⓢ | M 1000
★★*Bell Inn, Brook. T:(0703) 812214. 14rm (8 ⇔)*

BROMLEY
Greater London
Map II F4

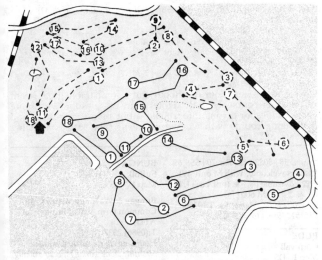

Sundridge Park Garden Rd, Bromley (N side of town centre off A2212)
T:01-460 0278
Societies welcome by arrangement. East: 18 | 6148 yds | Par 70 | SSS 69 | West. 18 | 5708 yds | Par 68 | SSS 68
Visitors welcome weekdays ⊠ | WE with M | ☎ preferred | ∷ per day | B L ☛ | ☖ ♈ ☌ | ⋈ | TR WE | M 1200 | S
★★★*Bromley Court, Bromley Hill, Bromley. T:01-464 5011. 130rm ⇔*
A club with a huge membership and two courses of the best inland type. The East course is some 400 yds longer than the West course but many think the shorter of the two courses is the more difficult. The East is surrounded by trees while the West is more hilly, with good views. The brook comes into play on both and there are several testing par 3 and par 4 holes. Both are certainly good test of golf.

BROOKMANS PARK
Hertfordshire
Map II E2

Brookman's Park Golf Club Road, Hatfield (N side of village, off A1000)
T:(0707) 52487
18 | 6438 yds | Par 70 | SSS 71
Visitors welcome, with M only WE BH | ☎ advisable | B L ☛ (not Mon) | ☖ ♈ ☌ | ④ 1st Tee (0845-1300 and after 1415) 10th Tee (before 0845, 1045-1400 and after 1545) | ♩ | M 550 | S
★★★*Crest, Bignells Corner, South Mimms. T:(0707) 43311. 120rm ⇔*
A popular course with golfers who live to the north of London, although the course itself is in Hertfordshire, a county which has golf courses in great profusion and of wide variety. Brookman's Park is an undulating parkland course, with several cleverly constructed holes. But it is a fair course, although it can play long. The 11th, par 3, is a testing hole which plays across a lake.

BRORA
Highland, *Sutherland*
Map VII G3

Brora Golf Rd (E side of village)
T:(0408) 21417
Fairly easy seaside links with little rough and fine views. Some testing holes. Society meetings catered for with 3 weeks' notice. 18 | 6110 yds | Par 69 | SSS 69
Visitors welcome | ✳ | B L ♈ ☛ (mid-May - mid-Sept, parties by prior arrangement) | ☖ | ⋈ prior arrangement | TR competition days | M 200 | S
★★★*Links, Golf Rd. T:(0408) 21225. 26rm (23 ♨)*

BROUGH
Humberside
Map V H6

Brough Cave Rd (½m N of Brough)
T:(0482) 667374
Parkland course. 18 | 6012 yds | Par 68 | SSS 69
Visitors welcome but not WE or W before 1400. ☎ preferred | ∴ per day | B ☛ ☖ ♈ ☌ | TR 1230-1330 | ♩ | M 650 | S
★★★*Crest Hotel, Humber Bridge, Ferriby High Rd, North Ferriby. T:(0482) 645212. 102rm ⇔*

BUCKIE
Grampian, *Banffshire*
Map VII H4

Buckpool Barhill Road, Buckpool, Buckie (W side of town off A990)
T:(0542) 32236
Windy. Seaside course, with easy walking. Overlooking Moray Firth. 18 | 6257 yds | Par 70 | SSS 70
Visitors welcome | ∙∙ per day WE | B ☛ | L D prior arrangement | ☖ ♈ (not Mon-Th lunchtime) ⋈ | M 260
★★*Cluny, High St. T:(0542) 32922. 10rm (8 ⇔ 2 ♨)*

Strathlene Strathlene Rd, Buckie (Eastern Boundary) (3m E of Buckie on A942)
T:(0542) 31072
Windy seaside course, magnificent view, offering testing golf, including difficult 4th (par 3). Societies welcome by arrangement. 18 | 5925 yds | Par 68 | SSS 68
Visitors welcome | B ☛ L D prior arrangement | ☖ ♈ | ⋈ | TR Tu, Th, F, S (eve) - medals | M 300 ➡

KEY

(IA1) *atlas grid reference*
T: *telephone number*
☎   *advance letter/telephone call required*
✉   *introduction from own club sec/handicap certificate/club membership card required*
· ·   *low fees*
∴   *medium fees*
: :   *high fees*
*   *green fees not confirmed for 1987*
B   *light lunch*
L   *full lunch*
♨   *tea*
D   *dinner*
⚖   *changing rooms/showers*
Ⴤ   *bar open mid-day and evenings*
↘   *clubs for hire*
⋈   *partners may be found*
④   *restricted time for 4 balls*
TR   *times reserved for members*
ℑ   *professional*
S   *well-stocked shop*
M   *member*
Mon Tu W Th F S Sun
WE   *weekend*
BH   *bank holiday*

**Cluny, High St, Buckie. T:(0542) 32922. 10rm (8 ⇄ 2 ♨)

BUCKINGHAM
Buckinghamshire
Map **IV** B8

Buckingham Tingewick Rd (1½m W of Buckingham on A421)
T:(0280) 815566
Undulating parkland course cut by

BROOKWOOD
Surrey
Map **II** D4

West Hill Bagshot Rd, Brookwood, Surrey (E side of village on A332)
T:(04867) 2110
Societies welcome. 18 | 6307 yds | Par 69 | SSS 70
Visitors welcome, restricted WE BH | ✉ | without M : : per day | with M ∴ per day WE | B ♨ | L D prior arrangement | ⚖ Ⴤ ↘ | ④ by arrangement | TR ④
☎ for details | ℑ | M 550 | S
****⚖Pennyhill Park, College Rd, Bagshot. T:(0276) 71774. 17rm (12 ⇄).
Annexe: 33rm (12 ⇄)
Worplesdon's next-door neighbour and a comparably great heath and heather course. Slightly tighter than Worplesdon with more opportunities for getting into trouble — but a most interesting and challenging course with wonderful greens. The 15th is a testing 220-yard par 3.

stream. 18 | 6082 yds | Par 70 | SSS 69
Visitors welcome, with M only WE | ☎ advisable | * | ♨ (not Tu) | L D B | ⚖ Ⴤ | ℑ | M 600 | S
**White Hart, Market Sq. T:(0280) 815151. 19rm (16 ⇄ 3 ♨)

BUDE
Cornwall
Map **I** D5

Bude & North Cornwall Burn View (N side of town)
T:(0822) 2006
Seaside links course has natural sand bunkers and watered greens in excellent condition. Societies by arrangement on weekdays. 18 | 6202 yds | Par 71 | SSS 70
Visitors welcome | B L (not W) | D prior arrangement (not W & Sun) | ⚖ Ⴤ ↘ | ⋈ by arrangement | ℑ | M 550 | S
*Camelot, Downs View Rd. T:(0288) 2361. 13rm (4 ⇄ 9 ♨)

BUNGAY
Suffolk
Map **IV** J5

Bungay & Waveney Valley Outney Common (½m NW of Bungay on A143)
T:(0986) 2337
Heathland course partly comprising Neolithic stone workings, easy walking. 18 | 6000 yds | Par 69 | SSS 68
Visitors welcome, with M only BH WE | ☎ | without M ∴ per week day | B | ⚖ Ⴤ ↘ L D ♨ | ⋈ prior arrangement | TR WE | ℑ | M 600 | S
**Swan, The Thoroughfare, Harleston. T:(0379) 852221. 10rm (7 ⇄)

BUNTINGFORD
Hertfordshire
Map **IV** E8

East Herts Hamels Park, Buntingford (1m N of Puckeridge

off A10)
T:(0920) 821978
An attractive undulating parkland
course with magnificent specimen trees.
Societies welcome weekdays (not Tu).
18 | 6416 yds | Par 71 | SSS 71
Visitors welcome, with M only WE
| ✉ | B ☕ (not Tu) | L D prior
arrangement | ♿ ⅄ ⚲ | ⋈ | M 750 |
S
★★★*Ware Moat House, Baldock St,*
Ware. T:(0920) 5011. 50rm (44 ⇄ 6
🍶*)*

BURFORD
Oxfordshire
Map I   K1

Burford Swindon Rd (½m S of
Burford on A361)
T:(099382) 2583, Oxon
Created out of open farmland, this
parkland course has high quality
fairways and greens. Societies welcome
by arrangement. 18 | 6405 yds | Par 71
| SSS 71
Visitors welcome | B L ☕ D | ♿ ⅄
⚲ | TR competition WE | 𝕁 | M 680 |
S | ⋈
★★*Cotswold Gateway (on A40).*
T:(099382) 2148. 12rm (2 ⇄)

BURLEY
Hampshire
Map I   K5

Burley Burley, Ringwood (E side of
village)
T:(04253) 2431
Undulating heather and gorseland. The
7th requires an accurately placed tee
shot to obtain par 4. 9 | 6140 yds |
Par 71 | SSS 69
Visitors welcome | without M ‥
weekdays ∴ WE | with M ‥ per

BUDLEIGH SALTERTON
Devon
Map I   F6

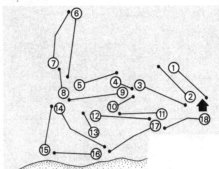

East Devon North View Rd, Budleigh Salterton
(W side of town centre off A376)
T:(0394) 3370
18 | 6214 yds | Par 70 | SSS 70
Visitors welcome with M or ✉ only | ☎ | ∴ per day | B ☕ (not Mon) | L D
prior arrangement (not Mon) | ♿ ⅄ ⚲ | ④ before 0930 from 10th, after 1030 &
after 1415 from 1st | 𝕁 | ⋈ | M 800 | S
★★*Manor, The Beacon, Exmouth. T:(0395) 2725429. 40rm (36 ⇄ 2* 🍶*)*
An interesting course with downland turf, much heather and gorse
and superb views over the bay. The early holes climb to the cliff
edge. The 443-yard downhill 17th has a heather section in the
fairway leaving a good second to the green.

day | TR WS | M 430
★★♨*Moorhill House. T:(04253) 3285.*
24rm (17 ⇄ 7 🍶*)*

BURNHAM-ON-CROUCH
Essex
Map II   H3

Burnham-on-Crouch Ferry Ln,
Creeksea (1¼m W of Burnham-on-
Crouch off B1010)
T:(0621) 782282

Undulating meadowland course, easy
walking, windy. Societies welcome (Tu
F) by arrangement. 9 | 4866 yds |
Par 68 | SSS 68
Visitors welcome, with M only WE
(am) BH (am) | without M ∴ per
day WE | with M ‥ per day WE | ☕
(not Mon) | B L prior arrangement
(not Mon) | ♿ | ⅄ (not Mon) | ⚲ |
TR Thu (ladies day), Sun am |
M 400   ➡

BURNHAM
Buckinghamshire
Map **II**   D3

Burnham Beeches Green Ln (½m NE of Burnham)
T:(0628) 61448
18 | 6415 yds | Par 71 | SSS 71
Visitors welcome, weekdays only :: per day | B ♟ | D prior arrangement | L prior arrangement (not Mon) | ♉ ♈ ↘ | ∞ (possible) | TR competition days | ♌ | M 600 | S
★★★*Holiday Inn, Ditton Rd, Langley. T:(0753) 44244. 308rm ⇄ ∰*
In the centre of the lovely Burnham Beeches countryside. Wide fairways, carefully maintained greens, some hills, and some devious routes to a few holes. A good finish.

★*Ye Olde White Harte, The Quay. T:(0621) 782106. 11rm (3 ⇄ 3 ∰)
Annexe: 4rm*

BURNHAM-ON-SEA
Somerset
Map **I**   G3

Burnham & Berrow St Christopher's Way (N side of town off B3140)
T:(0278) 783137
Links championship course with large sandhills. Societies welcome by arrangement. 18(9) | 6327(3275) yds | Par 71(36) | SSS 71
Visitors welcome ✉ | ∴ per day :: WE | B ♟ | L D prior arrangement | ♉ ♈ ↘ | ∞ prior arrangement | ④ TR ☎ for details | ♌ | M 845 | S
★★*Battleborough Grange Country Hotel, Bristol Rd, Brent Knoll. T:(0278) 760208. 11rm (3 ⇄ 4 ∰)*

BURNHILL GREEN
West Midlands
Map **III**   H4

Patshull Park Burnhill Green, Wolverhampton (1m E of Burnhill

Green)
T:(0902) 700100
Picturesque woodland course. 18 | 6275 yds | Par 72 | SSS 71
Visitors welcome | without M ∴ per day | B ♟ L D | ♉ ♈ | M 270 | S
★★★*Patshull Park, Pattingham. T:(0902) 700100. 28rm ⇄*

BURNLEY
Lancashire
Map **V**   D6

Burnley Glen View (1½m S of Burnley off A646)
T:(0282) 21045
Moorland course with hilly surrounds. Societies welcome by arrangement. 18 | 5900 yds | Par 69 | SSS 69
Visitors welcome | without M ·· per day ∴ WE | B L ♟ D prior arrangement (not Mon W) | ♉ ♈ | TR Thu pm (ladies day) S | ♌ | M 300 | S
★★★*Keirby, Keirby Walk. T:(0282) 27611. 49rm ⇄*

Towneley Towneley Park, Todmorden Rd, Burnley (1m SE of

town centre on A671)
T:(0282) 38473
Parkland course, with other sporting facilities available. 18 | 5812 yds | Par 70 | SSS **68**
Visitors welcome, ☎ WE | ♈ B ♟ | ♉ ↘ | ♌ | M 200 | S
★★★*Keirby, Keirby Walk. T:(0282) 27611. 49rm ⇄*

BURNOPFIELD
Durham
Map **VI**   K6

Hobson Municipal Hobson (¾m S of Burnopfield on A692)
T:(0207) 70941
Five-year-old meadowland course. 18 | 6582 yds | Par 71 | SSS 71
Visitors are welcome without M . . per day | L D B ♟ | ♉ ♈ | S ↘ ∞ | TR S 0800-0930 | M 450
★★★*Five Bridges, High West St. Gateshead. T:091-477 1105. 106rm ⇄*

BURNSIDE
Strathclyde, *Lanarkshire*
Map **VI**   E3

Blairbeth Burnside, Rutherglen (S of Burnside off A749)
T:041-634 3355
Parkland course. Society meetings by arrangement. 18 | 5448 yds | Par 68 | SSS 67
Visitors welcome only with M | B L ♟ D prior arrangement (not Tu) | ♉ ♈ | ∞ possible | ♌ | M 400
★★★*MacDonald Thistle, Eastwood Toll Rbt, Giffnock. T:041-638 2225. 56rm ⇄ ∰*

Cathkin Braes Cathkin Rd, Rutherglen, Glasgow (1m S of Burnside on B759)

T:041-634 4007
Moorland course, prevailing W wind, small loch hazard at 5th hole. 18 | 6266 yds | Par 70 | SSS 71
Visitors welcome only with M | parties only by prior arrangement | ∷ per day | B L ☕ D (not Mon) prior arrangement | △ 🍸 ↘ | M 900 | [S]
★★★*Stuart, 2 Cornwall Way, East Kilbride. T:(03552) 21161. 30rm (26 ⇌ 4 🚿)*

BURNTISLAND
Fife, *Fife*
Map **VI** G2

Burntisland Dodhead, Burntisland (1m E of Burntisland on B923)
T:(0592) 874093
This parkland course has fine sea views. 18 | 5871 yds | Par 69 | SSS 68
Visitors welcome with M ∴ per day ∷ WE | B L D ☕ | △ 🍸 | [S] | ⋈ | [TR] competition days | M 735
★★★*Dean Park, Chapel Level, Kirkcaldy. T:(0592) 261635. 19rm (13 ⇌ 6 🚿) Annexe: 4rm*

BURTON-UPON-TRENT
Staffordshire
Map **III** J3

Branston Burton Rd, Branston (1½m SW of Burton-upon-Trent on A5121)
T:(0285) 43207
Adjacent to River Trent on undulating ground with natural water hazards. 18 | 6458 yds | Par 73 | SSS 71
Visitors welcome | 🍸 B L D ☕ | △ | [S] | M 400 | J
★★★*Riverside Inn, Riverside Dr, Branston. T:(0283) 63117. 22rm (21 ⇌ 🚿)*

Burton-upon-Trent 43 Ashby Rd East (2m E of Burton-upon-Trent on A50)
T:(0283) 44551
Parkland course. 18 | 6555 yds | Par 71 | SSS 71
Visitors welcome restricted competition days (usually S up to 1700) | without M ∷ per day WE | with M ‥ per day WE | B L ☕ D (not Mon) | △ | 🍸 (not Mon) ↘ | ⋈ | J | M 420 | [S]
★★★*Newton Park, Newton Solney. T:(0283) 703568. 27rm (26 ⇌ 1 🚿)*

BURY
Greater Manchester
Map **V** D7

Bury Unsworth Hall, Blackford Bridge (2m S of Bury on A56)
T:061-766 4897
Hard walking on hilly course. Societies of up to 50 welcome by arrangement. 18 | 5962 yds | Par 69 | SSS 69
Visitors welcome ☎ advisable | * | B L (not Mon) | ☕ D | △ 🍸 ↘ | ⋈ sometimes | [TR] 1200-1400 | J | M 340 | [S]
★*Woolfield House, Wash Ln. T:061-764 7048. 13rm (1 🚿)*

Lowes Park Hill Top, Bury (N side of town centre off A56)
T:061-764 1231
Moorland course, with easy walking. Usually windy. 9 | 6035 yds | Par 69 | SSS 69
Visitors welcome | without M ‥ per day | B | L ☕ D | 🍸 △ ⋈ | [TR] WE | ④ WE | M 200
★*Woolfield House, Wash Ln, Bury. T:061-764 7048. 13rm (1 🚿)*

Walmersley Garretts Close, Walmersley (3m N of Bury off A56)
T:061-764 1429
Moorland hillside course, with wide fairways and large greens. Testing holes: 2nd 442 yds par 5; 4th 444 yds par 4. Society meetings considered on application. 9 | 6114 yds | Par 72 | SSS 70
Visitors welcome ☎ ✉ restricted S on competition days | B L ☕ (no catering Mon) | D prior arrangement | △ | 🍸 (including Mon evening in summer) | ⋈ prior arrangement | J | M 350
★*Woolfield House, Wash Ln, Bury. T:061-764 7048. 13rm (1 🚿)*

BURY ST EDMUNDS
Suffolk
Map **IV** G6

Bury St Edmunds Tuthill, Fornham All Saints (2m NW of Bury St Edmunds, on B1106, off A45)
T:(0284) 5979
Undulating parkland course with easy walking and attractive short holes. Societies welcome (Mon to F) by arrangement. 18 | 6615(6295) yds | Par 72(71) | SSS 72(70)
Visitors welcome but with M only Sun until 1000 | ☎ | B | L D (by arrangement) | ☕ △ 🍸 ↘ | ⋈ | J | M 848 | [S]
★★★*Angel, Angel Hill. T:(0284) 3926. 43rm (38 ⇌ 1 🚿)*

Fornham Park Fornham St Martin (2m N of Bury St Edmunds off A134)
T:(0284) 63426
Downland course with many water hazards. Also a country club where facilities include sauna, snooker, bars and restaurant. 18 | 6218 yds | Par 72 | SSS 70
Visitors welcome | B L ☕ D | △ 🍸 ↘ | ⋈ by arrangement | ④ ☎ J | M 500 | [S]
★★★*Angel, Angel Hill, Bury St Edmunds. T:(0284) 3926. 43rm (38 ⇌ 1 🚿)*

BURRY PORT
Dyfed
Map **I** D2

Ashburnham The Club House, Cliffe Terrace, Burry Port (W side of town on B4311)
T:(05546) 2269
Parties by arrangement. 18 | 7016 yds | Par 72 | SSS 73/74
Visitors welcome ✉ | * | B L ☕ D prior arrangement (not Mon) | △ | 🍸 (not Mon lunchtime) | ↘ limited | ⋈ sometimes | ④ competitions and matches have priority | [TR] competition days | M 800 | [S] | J
★★★*Stradey Park, Furnace, Llanelli. T:(0554) 758171. 80rm ⇌*
This course has a lot of variety. In the main it is of the seaside type although the holes in front of the clubhouse are of an inland character. They are, however good holes which make a very interesting finish.

BUSHEY
Hertfordshire
Map **II** E2

Bushey Hall Bushey Hall Dr, (1½m NW of Bushey on A4008)
T:(0923) 25802
Parkland course. Societies welcome (Mon Tu Th F). 18 | 6070 yds | Par 70 | SSS 69

BUXTON
Derbyshire
Map III J2

Cavendish Gadley Ln, Buxton (¾m W of town centre of A53)
T:(0298) 3494
Societies welcome by arrangement, book well in advance. 18 | 5815 yds | Par 68 |
SSS 68
Visitors welcome | without M ∴ per day ∴ per round WE | with M .. per day
WE | B ✆ | L D prior arrangement | ⚐ ⌁ ╲ | ⋈ | TR WE (until 1000) | ⌡ |
M 650 | S
★★★ *Palace, Palace Rd, Buxton. T:(0298) 2001. 120rm* ⇄
This parkland/downland course with its comfortable clubhouse
nestles below the rising hills. Generally open to the prevailing west
wind, it is a course to suit all levels of competence. Noted for greens
of excellent surfaces yet containing many deceptive subtleties.
Good holes include the 8th (par 4, 9th (par 3) and 18th (par 4).

Visitors welcome, with M only WE
BH | B ✆ | D (not Tu) L prior
arrangement (not Tu) | ⚐ ⌁ | ⌡ |
M 450 | S
★★★ *Ladbroke (& Conferencentre),
Elton Way, Watford Bypass. T:(0923)
35881. 155rm* ⇄

**Hartsbourne Golf and Country
Club** Hartsbourne Av, Bushey
Heath (S side of Bushey, off A4140)
T:01-950 1133
Parkland course with good views. 18(9)
| 6305(4968) yds | Par 71(68) |
SSS 70(66)
L B ✆ | ⚐ ⌁ ④ after 1000 TR WE
and Tu am ladies | M 460 | S ⋈
★★★ *Ladbroke, Elton Way, Watford
Bypass. T:(0923) 35881. 155rm* ⇄

BUTE, ISLE OF
Strathclyde, *Bute*
Map VI
See Bute and Port Bannatyne

BUTE
Strathclyde, *Bute*
Map VI C3

Kingarth Isle of Bute (1m W of
Kingarth, off A844)
T:(070083) 242
*Flat seaside course with good fenced
greens.* 9 | 2497 yds | Par 68 | SSS 64
Visitors welcome | ⚐ | M 80
★ *St Ebba, 37 Mountstuart Rd,
Craigmore, Rothesay. T:(0700) 2683.
15rm (1* ⇄ *8* 🍴*)*

BUXTON
Derbyshire   ,
Map III J2

Buxton and High Peak Town End,
Fairfield (1m NE of Buxton, off A6)

T:(0298) 3453
*Meadowland course in the lovely Peak
District. Societies welcome by
arrangement.* 18 | 5920 yds | Par 70 |
SSS 68
Visitors welcome ☎ for parties | B L
✆ D (not Th) | ⚐ ⌁ | ⋈ | TR ④ ☎
for details | ⌡ | M 450 | S
★★ *Grove, Grove Pde. T:(0298) 3804.
21rm (4* ⇄ *1* 🍴*)*

CAERNARFON
Gwynedd
Map III C2

Caernarfon Llanfaglan (1¾m SW of
Caernarfon)
T:(0286) 3783
Parkland course with gentle gradients.
18 | 5859 yds | Par 69 | SSS 69
Visitors welcome | .. per day | B ⚐
| ⌁ | M 250
★★★ *Stables, Llanwnda. T:(0286)
830711. Annexe: 12rm* ⇄

CALDY
Wirral
Map V B8

Caldy Links Hey Rd, Caldy (SE side of village)
T:051-625 5660
Societies welcome by arrangement. 18 | 6665(6251) yds | Par 73(71) | SSS 73(71)
Visitors welcome ⌗ ☎ | restricted WE BH | ⁑ per day | ∴ after 1400 | B L ✆ D
prior arrangement | ⚐ ⌁ | ④ ☎ for details | TR 0900-0930, 1300-1400 | ⌡ |
M 782 | S
★★ *Parkgate, Boathouse Ln, Parkgate. T:051-336 5101. 30rm* ⇄ 🍴
A parkland course situated on the estuary of the River Dee with
many of the fairways running parallel to the river. Of
Championship length, the course is subject to variable winds that
materially alter the day to day playing of each hole. There are
excellent views of North Wales and Snowdonia. The clubhouse has
good facilities.

CAERPHILLY
Mid Glamorgan
Map I G2

Caerphilly Pencapel, Mountain Rd
(½m S of Caerphilly on A469)
T:(0222) 883481
*Undulating mountain course. Good
views especially from 10th hole 700 ft
above sea level.* 14 | 6063 yds | Par 73 |
SSS 71
Visitors welcome weekdays | WE
only with M | ∴ per round | B L ✆
D | ⚐ ⌁ ╲ | ⋈ (sometimes) | ⌡ |
M 700 | S
★★ *Griffin Inn Motel, Rudry. T:(0222)
869735. Annexe: 23rm (20* ⇄*)*

Castell Heights Blaengwynlais
(2m SW of Caerphilly)
'Pay as you play' course. 9 | 2688 yds |
Par 34 | SSS 33
Visitors welcome | B L D ✆ | ⚐ ⌁
╲ | S | ⋈ | M 500
★★ *Griffin Inn Motel, Rudry. T:(0222)
869735. Annexe: 23rm (20* ⇄*)*

CAIRNBULG
Grampian, *Aberdeenshire*
Map VII K4

Inverallochy 24 Shore St, Cairnbulg
(E side of village off B9107)
*Windy seaside course, natural hazards,
easy walking. Panoramic views of
North Sea at every hole.* 18 | 5137 yds |
Par 64 | SSS 65
Visitors welcome | .. per day WE |
B ✆ | ⋈ | M 200
★★ *Tufted Duck, St Combs. T:(03465)
2481. 17rm (11* ⇄ *6* 🍴*)*

CALLANDER
Central, *Perthshire*
Map VI E1

CAMBERLEY
Surrey
Map **II** D4

Camberley Heath Golf Drive,
Camberley (1¼m SE of town
centre, off A325)
T:(0276) 23258
*Societies welcome by arrangement. 18 |
6402 yds | Par 72 | SSS 71*
Visitors welcome, with M only WE |
⊠ ☎ | without M ∶∶ per day | with
M ∴ per day WE | B ☞ | L prior
arrangement | ⚥ ⅋ | ④ until 1000,
1200-1400 | ♩ | M 700 | ⓢ
∗∗∗∗♨*Pennyhill Park, College Ride,
Bagshot. T:(0276) 71774. 19rm ⇄.
Annexe: 33rm (12 ⇄)*

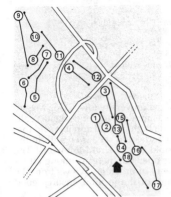

*Camberley Heath
course plan*

One of the great 'heath and heather' courses so frequently
associated with Surrey. Several very good short holes - especially
the 8th. The 10th is a difficult and interesting par four as also is the
17th where the drive must be held well to the left - perdition lurks
on the right.

CAMBORNE
Cornwall
Map **I** B7

Tehidy Park Camborne (2m NE of Camborne, off A30)
T:(0209) 842208
18 | 6222 yds | Par 72 | SSS 70
Visitors welcome ⊠ | ∗ | B ☞ | L D prior arrangement | ⚥ ⅋ ∖ | ⋈ probably
| ⓉⓇ competitions | ♩ | M 550 | ⓢ
∗∗∗*Penventon, Redruth. T:(0209) 214141. 55rm (35 ⇄ 10 ⅋)*
A very good parkland course with splendid trees and four notable
holes (6th, 7th 8th and 9th) in the pretty wooded and rhododendron
area. A well-maintained course providing good holiday golf. A
shorter round may be played by using alternative tees.

Callander Aveland Rd, Callander
(E side of town off A84)
T:(0877) 30090.
*Parkland course, with fairly tightly
guarded greens. Testing 6th hole (par
4) and 15th (par 3). Society meetings
by arrangement. 18 | 5090 yds | Par 66
| SSS 66*
Visitors welcome | ∴ per day WE |
B L ☞ full catering every day | ⚥ ⅋
bar open all day | ∖ ⋈ ♩ | ④ Sun |
ⓉⓇ competition days | M 500 | ⓢ
∗∗∗♨*Roman Camp. T:(0877) 30003.
11rm (9 ⇄ 2 ⅋)*

CAMBRIDGE
Cambridgeshire
Map **IV** E6

Cambridgeshire Moat House Hotel
Bar Hill (5m NW of Cambridge on
A604)
T:(0954) 80555
*Undulating parkland course with lake
and water hazards, easy walking.
Societies welcome by arrangement. 18 |
6734 yds | Par 72 | SSS 72*
Visitors welcome ☎ | ∴ per day ∶∶
WE BH | B L D | ☞ prior
arrangement | ⚥ ⅋ ∖ | ⓉⓇ Sun
(0800-1000) | ♩ | M 400 | ⓢ
∗∗∗*Cambridgeshire Moat House, Bar
Hill. T:(0954) 80555. 100rm ⇄*

CAMBUSLANG
Strathclyde, *Lanarkshire*
Map **VI** E2

Cambuslang Westburn Dr,
Cambuslang (¼m N of Cambuslang
off A724)
T:041-641 3130
*Parkland course. 9 | 6146 yds | Par 70 |
SSS 69*
Visitors welcome ⊠ ☎ | B L ☞ D |
⚥ ⅋ | M 200
∗∗*Silvertrees, Silverwells Cres,
Bothwell. T:(0698) 852311.
11rm 7⇄ ⅋. Annexe: 19rm ⇄ ⅋*

CANTERBURY
Kent
Map **II** J4

Canterbury Scotland Hills,
Littlebourne Rd (1½m E of
Canterbury on A257)
T:(0227) 63586/453532
*Undulating parkland course, natural
hazards. Societies welcome by
arrangement. 18 | 6245 yds | Par 70 |
SSS 70*
Visitors welcome, restricted WE
(until 1130) | without M ∴ per day
∶∶ WE | B ☞ | L D prior
arrangement | B prior arrangement
(not Mon-Fri) | ⚥ ⅋ | ⓉⓇ Sun until
1130 | ♩ | M 600 | ⓢ
∗∗∗*Chaucer, Ivy Ln. T:(0227)
464427. 47rm (41 ⇄)*

CARDIFF
South Glamorgan
Map **I** G2

Cardiff Sherborne Av, Cyncoed
(3m N of city centre)
T:(0222) 753320
*Parkland course, trees form natural
hazards. Interesting variety of holes,
mostly bunkered. Societies welcome by
arrangement. 18 | 6016 yds | Par 70 |
SSS 70*
Visitors welcome ⊠ ☎ preferred |
WE BH only with M | ∴ per day |
with M ∴ weekdays | B (not Sun) |
☞ | L D (not Sun) prior
arrangement | ⚥ ⅋ ∖ ④ ⓉⓇ
competition days always ☎ | ♩ |
M 930 | ⓢ
∗∗∗*Post House, Pentwyn Rd,
Pentwyn. T:(0222) 731212. 150rm ⇄*

Llanishen Cwm Lisvane, Cardiff
(7m N of city centre off A469)
T:(0222) 755078
*Undulating parkland course, with hard
walking. Societies welcome by
arrangement. 18 | 5296 yds | Par 68 |
SSS 66*

CAMBRIDGE
Cambridgeshire
Map IV   E6

Gog Magog, The Shelford Bottom (3m SE of Cambridge, on A1307)
T:(0223) 247626
Societies welcome by arrangement. Old Course: 18 | 6386 yds | Par 70 | SSS 70.
New Course: 9 | 5833 yds | Par 70 | SSS 68
Visitors welcome weekdays ⊠ ☎ | WE only with M | ∷ (Old) and ∴ (New)
per day | B L ☽ D (prior arrangement WE BH) | ⚠ ⅄ | ④ ☎ for details | TR
WE, W (am) | ♩ | M 1000 | Ⓢ
★★★*Gonville, Gonville Pl, Cambridge.* T:(0223) 66611. *62rm* ⇄
Situated just outside the centre of the university town, Gog Magog
is known as the nursery of Cambridge undergraduate golf,
established in 1901. The course is on high ground and it is said that
if you stand on the highest point and could see far enough to the
east the next highest ground would be the Ural Mountains! The
courses (there are two of them) are open but there are enough trees
and other hazards to provide plenty of problems. Views from the
high parts are superb. The nature of the ground ensures good
winter golf.

CARDIFF
South Glamorgan
Map I   G2

St Mellons St Mellons, Cardiff (5m
NE of Cardiff, off A48)
T:(0633) 680408
18 | 6275 yds | Par 70 | SSS 70
Visitors welcome ☎ ⊠ or with M |
∴ per day | B ☽ (not Mon) | L D⁻
prior arrangement (not Mon) | ⚠ ⅄
\ | ⊠ | TR WE & BH | M 1000 | Ⓢ
★★★*Post House, Pentwyn Rd,*
Pentwyn. T:(0222) 731212. *150rm* ⇄

SCORE CARD:			
1	333	10	454
2	411	11	135
3	199	12	487
4	320	13	480
5	172	14	160
6	470	15	334
7	477	16	357
8	186	17	437
9	361	18	452

This parkland course comprises quite a few par 3 holes and provides
some testing golf. It is indeed a challenge to the single handicap
golfer. The 12th hole runs over a stream, making an accurate drive
virtually essential.

CARLISLE
Cumbria
Map V   C2

Carlisle Aglionby, Carlisle (On A69 1m E of M6 jct 43)
T:(022872) 303
18 | 6099 yds | Par 71 | SSS 70
Visitors welcome, ☎ | restricted competition days and Tu pm (ladies day) |
without M ∴ per day WE | with M ∴ per day WE | B L ☽ D prior arrangement
(not Mon) | ⚠ ⅄ \ | ♩ | M 900 | Ⓢ
★★★*Cumbrian, Court Sq.* T:(0228) 31951. *70rm (66 ⇄ 4* 🍴*)*
Majestic looking parkland course with great appeal. A complete but
not too severe test of golf, with fine turf, natural hazards, a stream
and many beautiful trees.

Visitors welcome | ∴ per day | B L
☽ D | ⚠ ⅄ \ | ♩ | M 800 | Ⓢ
★★★*Post House, Pentwyn Rd,*
Pentwyn, Cardiff. T:(0222) 731212.
150rm ⇄

Radyr Drysgol Rd, Radyr, Cardiff
(4½m NW of city centre off A4119)
T:(0222) 842408
Hillside, parkland course which can be
windy. Good views. Societies welcome
W by arrangement. 18 | 6031 yds |

Par 69 | SSS 70
Visitors welcome ☎ | B ☽ (not Th) |
⚠ ⅄ \ | ④ ☎ for details | TR WE
and competitions ☎ | M 820 | Ⓢ
★★★*Stakis Inn on the Avenue, Circle*
Way East, Llanedeyrn. T:(0222)
732520. *150rm* ⇄ 🍴

Whitchurch (Cardiff) Whitchurch,
Cardiff (4m N of city centre on
A470)
T:(0222) 620985
Parkland course, with easy walking. 18
| 6245 yds | Par 71 | SSS 70
Visitors welcome ⊠ | restricted S
April to October | B ☽ (not Mon) | L
D prior arrangement (not Mon) | ⚠
⅄ \ | TR S Apr to Oct | ♩ | M 860 |
Ⓢ
★★★★*Park, Park Pl.* T:(0222) 383471.
108rm ⇄

CARDIGAN
Dyfed
Map III   B6

Cardigan Gwbert-on-Sea (At
Gwbert-on-Sea, 3m N of Cardigan
off B4548)
T:(0239) 612035
A links course, very dry in winter with
wide fairways, light rough and gorse.
Every hole overlooks the sea. Societies
welcome by arrangement. 18 | 6207 yds
| Par 71 (white) 70 (yellow) | SSS 70
(white) 69 (yellow)
Visitors welcome ☎ | ∗ | B L D ☽
(not Mon) | ⚠ ⅄ \ | ⊠ prior
arrangement | ♩ | M 500 | TR
(1300-1415) | Ⓢ
★★★*Cliff.* T:(0239) 613241.
70rm (56 ⇄ 14 🍴*)*

CARDROSS
Strathclyde, *Dumbartonshire*
Map VI   D2

Cardross Cardross, Dumbarton (In
centre of village on A814)
T:(0389) 841213
Undulating parkland course, testing
with good views. 18 | 6082 yds | Par 71
| SSS 71
Visitors welcome ☎ advisable |
only with M F after 1630 and WE |
∴ per day | B (not Mon) | L ☽ D
prior arrangement (not Mon) | ⚠ ⅄
\ | ⊠ | TR Tu am | ♩ | M 700 | Ⓢ
★★★*Commodore, 112 West Clyde St,*
Helensburgh. T:(0436) 6924. *45rm* ⇄

CARLISLE
Cumbria
Map **VI** G6

Stony Holme Municipal St Aidans Rd, Carlisle (3m E of Carlisle off A69)
T:(0228) 34856
Municipal parkland course, bounded on 3 sides by River Eden. Easy walking. Testing 1st hole 387 yards par 4, left hand dog leg. Children encouraged. 18 | 5773 yds | Par 68 | SSS 68
Open to public ☎ advisable | .. per round | B L ☎ | ⚐ ⌇ ↘ | ⋈ possible | ♩ | M 300 | ⓢ
★★*Cumbria Park, 32 Scotland Rd. T:(0228) 22887. 44rm (40 ⇄)*

CARLUKE
Strathclyde, *Lanarkshire*
Map **VI** E3

Carluke Mauldslie Rd, Hallcraig, Carluke (1m W of Carluke off A73)
T:(0555) 71070
Parkland course. Testing 11th hole par 3. 18 | 5805 yds | Par 70 | SSS 68
Visitors welcome, restricted Mon to F before 1630 (no bus parties) |

CARLYON BAY
Cornwall
Map **I** C7

Carlyon Bay Carlyon Bay (2½m E of St Austell, off A3082)
T:(072681) 4228
18 | 6501 yds | Par 72 | SSS 71
Visitors welcome ☎ preferable | B L ☎ D prior arrangement (not Mon) | ⚐ ⌇ | ⒯ 0915-0945 and 1700-1800 | ♩ | ↘ | M 550 | ⓢ
★★★★*Carlyon Bay, Sea Rd, Carlyon Bay. T:(072681) 2304. 73rm (68 ⇄)*
High on the cliff edge overlooking Par Harbour and St Austell Bay, with interesting lay-out, good turf and magnificent views. The 230-yard par 3 18th with railway and road out-of-bounds holds the player's interest to the end.

without M ∴ per day | with M .. per round | B L ☎ D prior arrangement (not Th) | ⚐ ⌇ ⋈ | M 460 | ⒯ ☎ | ④ W (from 1430) until end June | M 600 | ⓢ
★★★*Popinjay, Rosebank. T:(055 586) 441. 36rm (29 ⇄ 7 ⒡)*

CARMARTHEN
Dyfed
Map **III** C7

Carmarthen Blaenycoed Rd (4m NW of Carmarthen)
T:(026787) 493

Mixed downland and heathland type course with fairly hard walking and open to the wind. 18 | 6212 yds | Par 71 | SSS 71
Visitors welcome | without M ∴ WE | B ☎ | L D prior arrangement | ⚐ ⌇ ↘ | M 600 | ⒯ competition days | ⓢ
★★★*Ivy Bush Royal, Spilman St. T:(0267) 235111. 80rm ⇄ ⒡*

CARNOUSTIE
Tayside, *Angus*
Map **VII** J8

KEY

(IA1) *atlas grid reference*
T: *telephone number*
☎ *advance letter/telephone call required*
✉ *introduction from own club sec/handicap certificate/club membership card required*
.. *low fees*
∴ *medium fees*
:: *high fees*
* *green fees not confirmed for 1987*
B *light lunch*
L *full lunch*
♥ *tea*
D *dinner*
⚐ *changing rooms/showers*
🍸 *bar open mid-day and evenings*
✎ *clubs for hire*
⋈ *partners may be found*
④ *restricted time for 4 balls*
[TR] *times reserved for members*
'J *professional*
[S] *well-stocked shop*
M *member*
Mon Tu W Th F S Sun
WE *weekend*
BH *bank holiday*

Dalhousie Links Parade, Carnoustie
T:(0241) 3208
Plays over the Carnoustie golf courses (Medal and Burnside) seaside. 18(18) | M 6809 yds B 5935 | Par M 72 B 68 | SSS M 74 | B 69
Visitors welcome ✉ ☎ Societies apply course committee before applying club | B ♥ | L D prior arrangement | ⚐ 🍸 ⋈
★★*Glencoe, Links Pde. T:(0241) 53273. 11rm (3 ⇌ 5 🛏)*

CARNWATH
Strathclyde, *Lanarkshire*
Map **VI**   F3

Carnwath 1 Main St, Carnwath (W side of village on A70)
T:(0555) 840251
Picturesque parkland course. 18 | 5860 yds | Par 69 | SSS 68
Visitors welcome, restricted after 1700 | without M ∴ per day ∴ Sun | B L ♥ D (not Tu Th) | ⚐ 🍸 | M 380
★★★*Popinjay, Rosebank. T:(055 586) 441. 36rm (29 ⇌ 7 🛏)*

CARNOUSTIE
Tayside, *Angus*
Map **VII**   J8

Carnoustie Golf Links, Starters Box Building, Links Parade, Carnoustie (SW side of town, off A930)
T:(0241) 53789
Medal course seaside links 18(18)(18) | 6809(5935)(6445) yds | Par 72(68)(71) | SSS 74(68)(71)
Visitors welcome ☎ | :: per day | B L ♥ D (prior arrangement all catering) | ⚐ 🍸 ✎ | ⋈ | [TR] usually WE | M 1200
★★*Glencoe, Links Pde. T:(0241) 53273. 11rm (3 ⇌ 5 🛏)*

CARRADALE
Strathclyde, *Argyll*
Map **VI**   B3

Carradale Carradale (S side of village)
T:(05833) 624
Pleasant and not too testing seaside holiday course with extensive views. Natural terrain and small greens are the most difficult natural hazards. Described as the most sporting 9-hole golf course in Great Britain. Testing 7th hole, 240 yds par 3. 9 | 2718 yds | Par 63 (18 holes) | SSS 62
Visitors welcome | B L ♥ D (at Carradale Hotel on course) | ⚐ | M 212 | [S]
★★*Carradale. T:(05833) 223. 15rm (2 ⇌ 3 🛏). Annexe: 6rm (1 ⇌ 3 🛏)*

CARRBRIDGE
Highland, *Inverness-shire*
Map **VII**   G5

Carrbridge (N side of village)
T:(047 984) 674
Part parkland, part moorland 'family' course with good views of the Cairngorms. 9 | 2626 yds | Par 70 | SSS 66
Visitors welcome without M | M 134 | ⚐ ✎ | [TR] competitions
⊛★★🍴*Muckrach Lodge, Dulnain Bridge. T:(047 985) 257. 9rm (8 ⇌)*

CARSHALTON
Greater London
Map **II**   E4

Oaks Park Sports Centre
Woodmansterne Rd (½m S of Carshalton on B278)
T:01-643 8363
Public parkland course with floodlit covered driving range. Societies welcome but no tee booking en bloc. 18(9) | 5873(1590) yds | Par 70(29) |

SSS 68(29)
Open to public, advisable to ☎ WE | B L ♥ D | ⚐ 🍸 ✎ | ⋈ | ④ WE until 1100 | [TR] WE 0700-1000 | 'J | M 500 | [S]
★★★*Croydon Court, Purley Way, Croydon. T:01-688 5185. 86rm ⇌*

CASTLE DOUGLAS
Dumfries and Galloway, *Kirkcudbrightshire*
Map **VI**   E6

Castle Douglas Abercromby Rd, Castle Douglas (W side of town)
T:(0556) 2801
Parkland course, one severe hill. 9 | 5408 yds | Par 68 | SSS 66
Visitors welcome | ⚐ 🍸 | [TR] ☎ | M 450
★★*Kings Arms, St Andrew's St. T:(0556) 2626. 15rm (5 ⇌ 3 🛏)*

CATTERICK CAMP
North Yorkshire
Map **V**   F4

Catterick Garrison Leyburn Rd (1m W of Catterick Garrison)
T:(0748) 833268
Parkland/moorland course with good views of the Pennines and Cleveland hills. Testing 1st and 3rd holes. 18 | 6332 yds | Par 71 | SSS 70
Visitors welcome | ∴ per day WE | B ♥ (not Mon) | L D prior arrangement (not Mon) | ⚐ 🍸 ✎ | ⋈ | M 450 | [S]
★★ *Bridge House, Catterick Bridge. T:(0748) 818331. 18rm (4 ⇌ 2 🛏)*

CHACOMBE
Northamptonshire
Map **III**   K6

Cherwell Edge nr Banbury (½m S of Chacombe, off B4525)
T:(0295) 711591
18 | 5819 yds | Par 70 | SSS 68

Visitors welcome | .. per day | ▼ B
L D ▼ | ⚇ | ⓢ ⌇ | ⋈ | ♌
★★★*Whately Hall, Banbury Cross,
Banbury. T:(0295) 3451.
72rm (63 ⇄ 9 ⌸)

CHADDLEWORTH
Berkshire
Map II A3

West Berkshire Chaddleworth (1m
S of village, off A338)
T:(04882) 574
*Challenging and interesting downland
course with testing 635 yds (par 5) 5th
hole.* 18 | 7053 yds | Par 73 | SSS 74
Visitors welcome ☎ | .. per day ∴
WE (round) | B | L ▼ D prior
arrangement | ⚇ ▼ ⋈ | ♌ | M 314
★★★*Bear, Hungerford. T:(0488)
82512.* 28rm (24 ⇄)

CHALFONT ST GILES
Buckinghamshire
Map II D3

Harewood Downs Cokes Ln (2m N
of Chalfont St Giles, off A413)
T:(02404) 2026
A testing parkland course. 18 |
5958 yds | Par 69 | SSS 69
Visitors welcome but with M only
WE BH | ☎ advisable | ▼ B ▼ (not
Mon) | L D prior arrangement (not
Mon) | ⚇ | ⋈ by arrangement | ♌ |
TR ☎ for details ④ ☎ for details |
M 500 | ⓢ
★★★*Bellhouse, Beaconsfield. T:(0753)
887211.* 120rm ⇄

CHANNEL ISLANDS
Map I
Information is shown under
individual islands. Refer to
Guernsey and **Jersey** for details.

CHAPEL-en-le-FRITH
Stockport
Map V E8

Chapel-en-le-Frith The Cockyard,
Manchester Rd. (1m W of Chapel-
en-le-Frith, on A6)
T:(0298) 812118
*Fairly easy parkland course, with
testing holes at the 15th (par 4) and
17th (511 yds, par 5). Good views.* 18 |
6065 yds | Par 70 | SSS 69
Visitors welcome, not W | ☎ for
more than 8 players | without M ..
per day ∴ WE | with M .. per day
WE | B ▼ (not Mon) | L D prior
arrangement (not Mon) | ⚇ ▼ ⌇ ♌
| ⋈ | TR competitions | M 400 | ⓢ
★★*Buckingham, 1 Burlington Rd,
Buxton.* T:(0298) 70481.
36rm (10 ⇄ 16 ⌸)

CHARD
Somerset
Map I G5

Windwhistle Cricket St Thomas, nr
Chard (3m E of Chard, on A30)
T:(046 030) 231
Parkland course at 735 ft above sea level

*with outstanding views of the Channel
and South Wales.* 12 | 6055 yds |
Par 71 | SSS 69
Visitors welcome | ☎ advisable | B
(no food Sun) ▼ ⚇ ▼ | ⋈ probable
| ④ TR ☎ for details | ♌ | M
limited | ⓢ
★★*Shrubbery, Ilminster. T:(04605)
2108.* 13rm (8 ⇄ 1 ⌸)

CHEADLE
Greater Manchester
Map V E8

Cheadle Cheadle Rd, Cheadle (S
side of village, off A5149)
T:061-428 2160
*Parkland course. Society meetings by
arrangement.* 9 | 5006 yds | Par 64 |
SSS 65
Visitors welcome ⊠ with M |
restricted Tu | B L D prior
arrangement (not Th) | ▼ (not Th) |
⚇ ▼ | ④ TR occasionally ♌ | M 300
| ⓢ
★★*Wycliffe Villa, 74 Edgeley Rd,
Stockport. T:061-477 5395.* 12rm ⇄ ⌸

CHELMSFORD
Essex
Map II G2

Channels Belstead, Farm Lane,
Little Waltham (3½m NE of
Chelmsford, off A130)
T:(0245) 440005
*Built on land from reclaimed gravel
pits, 18 very exciting holes and an
excellent test of golf. 18 | 6033 yds |
Par 69 | SSS 69*
Visitors welcome without M (not
WE) | ♟ L D (no Sun) B ♛ ♣ ☒ |
TR WE | M 600
★★★*South Lodge, 196 New London
Rd, Chelmsford. T:(0245) 264564.
26rm (25 ⇄ 1 ♨)*

CHELTENHAM
Gloucestershire
Map III H7

Cotswold Hills Ullenwood (3m S of
Cheltenham, off A436)
T:(0242) 515264
*A gently undulating course with open
aspects and views of the Cotswolds.
Societies welcome by arrangement. 18 |
6345 yds | Par 70 | SSS 72*
Visitors welcome ☒ | without M ∴
per day ∷ WE | with M .. per day
WE | B L (not Mon) | ♛ | ♣ ♟ ↘ | 🏌
| M 750 | S ☒ TR (☎ for details)
★★★*Crest Hotel, Crest Way,
Barnwood. T:(0452) 63311. 100rm ⇄*

Lilley Brook Cirencester Rd,
Charlton Kings (3m S of
Cheltenham, on A435)
T:(0242) 526785
*Undulating parkland course.
Magnificent views over Cheltenham
and countryside. Societies welcome by*

---

*arrangement. 18 | 6226 yds | Par 69 |
SSS 70*
Visitors welcome | .. per round ∴
per day | B ♛ | L D | ♣ ♟ ↘ | ☒
occasionally | M 750 | S | TR S and
Sun am
★★★★ *Queens, Promenade,
Cheltenham. T:(0242) 514724. 77rm ⇄*

CHERTSEY
Surrey
Map II D4

Barrow Hills Longcross (3m W of
Chertsey, on B386)
T:(0276) 72037
*Parkland course with natural hazards.
18 | 2950 yds | Par 56 | SSS 56*
Visitors welcome with M only,
restricted WE BH (pm) | | TR WE
BH | M 235
★★*Thames Lodge, Thames St, Staines.
T:(0784) 64433. 47rm ⇄*

Laleham Laleham Reach (1½m N of
Chertsey)
T:(09328) 64211
*Well bunkered parkland/meadowland
course. Societies welcome by
arrangement. 18 | 6203 yds | Par 70 |
SSS 70*
Visitors welcome, restricted WE BH
| ∴ members only | B L ♛ | D
(prior arrangement) | ♣ ♟ ☒ | 🏌 |
④ ☎ | M 600 | S
★★*Thames Lodge, Thames St, Staines.
T:(0784) 64433. 47rm ⇄*

CHESHAM
Buckinghamshire
Map II D2

Chesham & Ley Hill Ley Hill
Common (2m E of Chesham)

T:(0494) 784541
*Heathland course on hilltop with easy
walking among trees, gorse and
heather. Subject to wind. 9 | (14 tees)
5158 yds | Par 67 | SSS 65*
Visitors welcome, restricted Tu F
(pm) WE | ♛ not Th | B L D prior
arrangment (not Th) | ♣ | ♟ | TR
Tu, F pm, WE & competitions | S
↘ ☒ | M 350
★★*Crown, High St, Amersham.
T:(02403) 21541. 19rm (6 ⇄)*

CHESHUNT
Hertfordshire
Map II F2

Cheshunt Park Park Ln, (1½m NW
of Cheshunt, off B156)
T:(0992) 29777
*Municipal parkland course, well
bunkered with ponds, easy walking. 18
| 6602 yds | Par 71 | SSS 71*
Visitors welcome with M | L D B ♛ |
♣ (members only) ♟ ↘ 🏌 | M 380 |
S
★★★*Post House, High Rd, Bell
Common, Epping. T:(0378) 73137.
Annexe: 82rm ⇄*

CHESTER
Cheshire
Map III G2

Upton by Chester Upton Ln, Upton
by Chester (N side of city centre, off
A5116)
T:(0244) 381183
*Pleasant tree-lined parkland course.
Not easy for low handicap players to
score well. Testing holes are 2nd (par 4)
14th (par 4) 15th (par 3). Societies
welcome weekdays by arrangment. 18 |
5875 yds | Par 69 | SSS 68*
Visitors welcome restricted BH | ☎
advisable | without M ∴ per day
WE | with M .. per day ∴ WE | B L
♛ (not Th) | D prior arrangement |
♣ ♟ | 🏌 | TR Sun and first W in
month | M 700 | S
★★★*Mollington Banastre, Parkgate
Rd. T:(0244) 851471. 72rm ⇄*

Vicars Cross Littleton, Chester (3m
E of Chester on A51)
*Parkland course, with undulating
terrain. 18 | 5804 yds (5612) |
Par 69(68) | SSS 68(67)*
Visitors welcome | B L ♛ D (not Tu)
| ♣ ♟ ☒ possible | M 650 | S
★★★*Mollington Banastre, Parkgate
Rd. T:(0244) 851471. 72rm ⇄*

CHEPSTOW
Gwent
Map I H2

St Pierre St Pierre Park, Chepstow (3m SW of Chepstow, off A48)
T:(02912) 5261
18(18) | 6700 yds (New 5762) | Par 71(68) | SSS 73(68)
Visitors welcome ☒ | ☎ advisable | ∷ per round ∷ per day WE | with M ..
per round ∴ per day WE | B L ♛ D ♣ ♟ ↘ | ☒ | 🏌 | M 450 | S
★*Lambsquay, Coleford. T:(0594) 33127. 10rm (5 ⇄).*
This parkland/meadowland championship course (the Old), venue
of a Silk Cut Master Tournament, has numerous large trees making
play quite difficult for the average player. The 18th hole is a testing
par 3, played directly across a very picturesque lake. There are
several par 5s, making it difficult to play to handicap. There are
additional facilities at the St Pierre Country Club.

CHESTERFIELD
Derbyshire
Map III K2

Chesterfield Walton (2m SW of Chesterfield, off A632)
T:(0246) 79256
18 | 6356(6110) yds | Par 71 | SSS 70
Visitors welcome restricted WE BH ☎ advisable | ∴ per day | B ☕ | L D prior arrangement | △ 🍸 | ④ Sun | [TR] ☎ | ℷ | M 800 | [S]
★★★Chesterfield, Corporation St. T:(0246) 71141. 61rm ⇌ 🚿

A varied and interesting parkland course with trees picturesquely adding to the holes and the outlook alike. A moderately difficult first half leads to a tough second nine which is overlooked by a fine commodious clubhouse. A stream is a hazard on several of the later holes.

CHIGWELL
Essex
Map II F3

Chigwell High Rd (½m S of Chigwell, on A113)
T:01-500 2059
Societies welcome by arrangement. 18 | 6279 yds | Par 71 | SSS 70
Visitors welcome ✉ ☎ | without M :: per day | with M .. per day | B L ☕ (not Mon) D prior arrangement, also not Mon | △ 🍸 | [TR] Tu WE, and Tu after 1430 ④ ☎ | ℷ | M 600 | [S]
★★Roebuck, North End, Buckhurst Hill. T:01-505 4636. 23rm ⇌

A course of high quality, mixing meadowland with parkland. For those who believe 'all Essex is flat' the undulating nature of Chigwell will be a refreshing surprise. The greens are excellent and the fairways wide.

CHESTERFIELD
Derbyshire
Map III K2

Stanedge Walton Hay Farm, Walton, Chesterfield (5m SW of Chesterfield, off B5057)
T:(0246) 566156
Moorland course in hilly situation open to strong winds. Some fairways are narrow. 9 | 4867 yds | Par 64 | SSS 64
Visitors welcome (except Sun), S, BH with M only | .. per day WE | △ 🍸 | ⋈ sometimes | [TR] after 1400 | M 250
★★★Chesterfield, Corporation St. T:(0246) 71141. 61rm ⇌ 🚿

Tapton Park Murray House, Tapton, Chesterfield (½m E of Chesterfield Station)
T:(0246) 73887
Parkland course with some fairly hard walking. The 626 yd par 5 5th is a testing hole. Pitch and putt course. 18 | 6069 yds | Par 72 | SSS 69
Visitors welcome .. per day | 🍸 L B D ☕ ☎ to confirm catering | ⟍ △ ⋈ | ℷ | M 400 | [S]
★★★Chesterfield, Corporation St. T:(0246) 71141. 61rm ⇌ 🚿

CHESTER-le-STREET
Durham
Map VI K6

Chester-le-Street Lumley Park (1m E of Chester-le-Street, off B1284)
T:(0385) 883218
Parkland course in castle grounds, good views, easy walking. Children admitted to clubhouse until 2000 hrs. 18 | 6245 yds | Par 71 | SSS 70
Visitors welcome | without M ∴ per day WE | with M .. per day WE | B L ☕ | △ 🍸 [TR] WE (before 10.30) | M 600 | ℷ | [S]
★★★Lumley Castle, Lumley Castle. T:(0385) 891111. 8rm ⇌ Annexe: 42rm (33 ⇌ 9 🚿)

CHESTERTON
Oxfordshire
Map II B1

Chesterton Country nr Bicester (½m W of Chesterton, on A4095)
T:(0869) 241204
Laid out over one-time farmland. Well bunkered, and water hazards increase the difficulty of the course. 18 | 6520 yds | Par 71 | SSS 71
Visitors welcome | without M ∴ per day WE | with M .. per day ∴ WE | B ☕ (not Mon) | L prior arrangement | △ 🍸 | ⟍ | M 470 | [S]
★★★Weston Manor, Weston-on-the-Green. T:(0869) 50621. 17rm ⇌ 🚿. Annexe: 6rm ⇌

CHICHESTER
West Sussex
Map II C7

Goodwood (4½m NE of Chichester, off A27)
T:(0243) 774968
Originally designed by James Braid, this mixed downland/parkland course has superb views of the downs and the coast. 18 | 6370 yds | Par 72 | SSS 70
Visitors welcome ☎ advisable | without M ∴ per day :: WE | B (not Mon) | L ☕ | △ 🍸 ⟍ (possible) [TR] | societies competitions and matches only | ℷ | M 900 | [S] | ④ WE
★★★Goodwood Park, Waterbeach. T:(0243) 775537. 50rm ⇌ 🚿

CHIGWELL ROW
Essex
Map II F3

Hainault Forest Romford Rd, Chigwell Row (1¼m SE of Chigwell Row, on A1112)
T:01-500 2097
Club playing over GLC public courses, hilly parkland subject to wind. 18(18) | 5874 yds (6479) | Par 70(71) | SSS 67(71)
Private club but courses open to public | 🍸 B L D ☕ | △ ⟍ | [S] ⋈ | ℷ | M 600
★★★Ladbroke, Southend Arterial Rd, Hornchurch. T:(04023) 471236. 136rm ⇌ 🚿

CHIPPENHAM
Wiltshire
Map I J3

Chippenham Malmesbury Rd (1½m N of Chippenham, on A429)
T:(0249) 652040
Easy walking on downland course. Testing holes at 1st and 15th. Societies welcome on weekdays. 18 | 5540 yds | Par 69 | SSS 67
Visitors welcome, preferably weekdays | ∴ per day WE | B L ☕ D prior arrangement (not Mon) | △ ⟍ | 🍸 | ⋈ prior arrangement | ④ displayed at 1st and 10th tees | ℷ | M 475 | [S]
★★★♣♣Manor House. T:(0249) ➡

782206. 13rm (10 ⇌ 3 🛏).
Annexe: 20rm ⇌

CHIPPING NORTON
Oxfordshire
Map **III** K7

Chipping Norton Southcombe
(1½m E of Chipping Norton, on
A44)
T:(0608) 2383
Pleasant course open to winds. 9 |
6158 yds | Par 71 | SSS 69
Visitors welcome restricted after
1530 (May-Sept) and with M only
WE BH | ∴ per day WE | B L ☛ D |
⚲ | ♈ evenings only | ↘ | ⋈ | TR |
WE BH (after 1530) May-Sept | 🔪 |
M 400 | S |
**Crown & Cushion, High Street.*
T:(0608) 2533. 14rm ⇌ 🛏

CHIPSTEAD
Surrey
Map **II** E4

Chipstead How Ln₊ Chipstead (½m
N of village)
T:(07375) 55781
Hilly downland course, hard walking,
good views. Testing 18th hole. 18 |
5454 yds | Par 67 | SSS 67
Visitors welcome, Mon-F only | ∴
per day | ♈ B L (not Mon) ☛ | ⚲ ↘
TR Tu (am) | 🔪 | M 500 | S |
****Selsdon Park, Sanderstead.*
T:01-657 8811. 150rm ⇌

CHISLEHURST
Greater London
Map **II** F4

Chislehurst Camden Pk Rd,
Chislehurst
T:01-467 2782
Pleasantly wooded undulating
parkland-heathland course.
Magnificent clubhouse with historical
associations. Societies welcome by
arrangement. 18 | 5128 yds | Par 66 |
SSS 65
Visitors welcome weekdays ⋈ | WE
BH with M | ☎ advisable | without
M ∷ per day | with M ‥ per day |
B L D (societies only) ☛ order by
1100 | ⚲ ↘ ♈ | ④ (various) | TR WE
| 🔪 | M 730 | S |
***Bromley Court, Bromley Hill,*
Bromley. T:01-464 5011. 130rm ⇌

CHOPWELL
Tyne and Wear
Map **VI** K6

Garesfield (½m N of Chopwell)
T:(0207) 561278
Undulating parkland course with good
views and picturesque woodland
surround. 18 | 6216 yds (yellow) 6610
(white) | Par 72 | SSS 70(72)
Visitors welcome restricted WE
(until 1000, 1300-1430) | ‥ per
round ∴ WE | B L ☛ D | ⚲ ♈ ↘ |
M 350 | S |
***Swallow, Newgate Arcade,*
Newcastle upon Tyne. T:(0632)
325025. 94rm ⇌ 🛏

CHORLEY
Lancashire
Map **V** C7

Duxbury Jubilee Park Duxbury
Park (2½m S of Chorley, off A6)
T:(02572) 77049
Municipal parkland course. 18 |
6390 yds | Par 71 | SSS 70
Open to public ☎ advisable.
***TraveLodge, Mill Ln, Charnock*
Richard. T:(0257) 791746. 108rm ⇌

CHORLEYWOOD
Buckinghamshire
Map **II** D2

Chorleywood Common Rd,
Chorleywood (E side of village, off
A404)
T:(09278) 2009
Heathland course with natural hazards
and good views. 9 | 5676 yds | Par 68 |
SSS 67
Visitors welcome restricted Tu (am)
| without M ‥ per day WE | with
M ‥ per day WE | B | ☛ L prior
arrangement | ⚲ ♈ | ④ S (until
1130) Sun | TR Tu, Thu, S, Sun | 🔪 |
M 250
***Bedford Arms Thistle, Chenies.*
T:(09278) 3301. 10rm ⇌ 🛏

CHRISTCHURCH
Dorset
Map **I** K5

Iford Bridge Barrack Rd,
Christchurch (W side of town
centre, on A5)
T:(0202) 473817
Parkland course with the River Stour
running through. 5th hole is par 4 over

the river. A driving range and tennis courts are also available. 9 | 4662 yds | *Par 66* | *SSS 63*
Visitors welcome | B ♥ ♈ ⚲ ⋈ ⚲ | ♩ | M 200 | S
★★*Commodore, Overcliffe Dr, Southbourne. T:(0202) 423150. 18rm*

CHULMLEIGH
Devon
Map **I** E5

Chulmleigh Leigh Rd, Chulmleigh (SW side of village)
T:(0769) 80519
Challenging short course, interesting to any experienced golfer. 18 | 1400 yds | *Par 54* | *SSS 54*
Visitors welcome without M | .. per day | ⚲ S ⚲ | M 100
★★*Fox and Hounds, Eggesford. T:(0769) 80345. 10rm (6 ⇋).*
Annexe: 2rm ⇋

CHURCH STRETTON
Shropshire
Map **III** G5

Church Stretton Trevor Hill, Church Stretton (NW side of village, off B4370)
T:(0694) 722281
Moorland course with very fine turf. 18 | 5008 yds | *Par 66* | *SSS 65*
Visitors welcome restricted WE BH | .. per day ∴ WE | B L prior arrangement | ⚲ ♈ | TR WE BH (1000-1200, 1300-1500) | ♩ | M 350 | S (WE only)
★★★*Stretton Hall, All Stretton. T:(0694) 723224. 12rm (10 ⇋ 2 ♨)*

CIRENCESTER
Gloucestershire
Map **III** J8

Cirencester Cheltenham Rd, Bagendon (2m N of Cirencester on A435)
T:(0285) 2465
Undulating Cotswold course. Societies welcome by arrangement on weekdays. 18 | 6007 yds | *Par 70* | *SSS 69*
Visitors welcome ☎ advisable | without M ∴ per day | with M .. weekdays WE | B ♥ | L D prior arrangement (not Mon) | ⚲ ♈ ✉ | ♩ | M 600 | S
★★★*Stratton House, Gloucester Rd. T:(0285) 61761. 26rm (22 ⇋)*

CLACTON-ON-SEA
Essex
Map **II** J2

Clacton West Rd, Clacton-on-Sea (1¼m SW of town centre)
T:(0255) 421919
Seaside, windy course. 18 | 6217 yds | *Par 70* | *SSS 70*
Visitors welcome ✉ | ☎ advisable WE only after 1100 (men), 1200 (ladies) | without M ∴ per day ∷

WE | with M half rate | B ♥ (not Mon) | L D prior arrangement (not Mon) | ⚲ ♈ | ⚲ (limited) | ④ WE (☎ for details) | TR competitions (☎ for details) | ♩ | M 500 | S
★★*Maplin, The Esplanade, Frinton-on-Sea. T:(02556) 3832.*
12rm (9 ⇋ 1 ♨)

CLARKSTON
Strathclyde, *Renfrewshire*
Map **VI** E3

Cathcart Castle Mearns Rd, Clarkston, Glasgow (¾m SW of Clarkston, off A726)
T:041-638 0082
Parkland course, with undulating terrain. Society meetings by arrangement Tu Th. 18 | 5832 yds | *Par 68* | *SSS 68*
Visitors only with M | B | L ♥ D | ⚲ ♈ ⚲ | ♩ | S
★★★*MacDonald Thistle, Eastwood Toll, Giffnock. T:041-638 2225.*
56rm ⇋ ♨

CLECKHEATON
West Yorkshire
Map V F6

Cleckheaton & District Bradford
Rd (1½m NW of Cleckheaton, on
A638)
T:(0274) 874118
*Parkland course with gentle hills. 18 |
5994 yds | Par 71 | SSS 69*
Visitors welcome ⊠ | ∴ per day WE
| B ☎ (not Mon) | L D prior
arrangement (not Mon) | ⚲ ♉ ↘ ⋈
(possible) prior arrangement | ♩ |
M 500 | Ⓢ | Ⓣᴿ Tu 1200-1400, Th
1300-1330, S all day.
★★★*Novotel Bradford, Merrydale Rd,
Bradford. T:(0274) 683683. 136rm* ⇌

CLEETHORPES
Humberside
Map V J7

Cleethorpes Kings Rd (1½m S of
Cleethorpes, off A1031)
T:(0472) 814060
*Seaside course, with a beck running
across it. 18 | 6015 yds | Par 70 |
SSS 69*
Visitors welcome ⊠ restricted W
(pm) | B | L ☎ (not Mon) | D prior
arrangement (not Mon) | ⚲ ♉ | ⋈ |
♩ | M 800 | Ⓢ
★★★*Kingsway, Cleethorpes. T:(0472)
601122. 55rm (50* ⇌)

CLEEVE HILL
Gloucestershire
Map III J7

Cleeve Hill nr Prestbury,
Cheltenham (1m NE of Cleeve Hill,
on A46)
T:(024267) 2592
Hilly commonland course. Societies

*welcome by arrangement. 18 | 6400 yds
| Par 71 | SSS 70*
Visitors welcome (☎ at WE) | .. per
round | B L ☎ | D prior
arrangement | ⚲ ♉ ↘ | ⋈ | Ⓣᴿ
Sun (0700-1000) | M 350 | Ⓢ
★★★*Hotel de la Bere, Southam.
T:(0242) 37771. 24rm (23* ⇌ 1 ⋒*)
Annexe: 11rm (10 ⇌ 1 ⋒*)*

CLEVEDON
Avon
Map I H3

Clevedon Castle Rd, Walton St Mary (1m NE of town centre)
T:(0272) 874057
Societies (Mon) by arrangement. 18 | 5835 yds | Par 69 | SSS 68
Visitors welcome on weekdays ☎ | WE BH ⊠ | ∴ per day :: WE | B | ☎ (not
Tu) | L D prior arrangement (not Tu) | ⚲ ♉ | ↘ prior arrangement | Ⓣᴿ
competitions | ♩ | ⋈ | M 700 | Ⓢ
★★★*Walton Park, Wellington Ter. T:(0272) 874253. 35rm (24* ⇌ 3 ⋒*)
Situated on the cliff-top overlooking the Severn estuary and with
distant views of the Welsh coast. Excellent parkland course in first-
class condition overlooking the Severn Estuary. Magnificent
scenery and some tremendous 'drop' holes.

CLITHEROE
Lancashire
Map V D6

Clitheroe (2m S of Clitheroe, on A671)
T:(0200) 22618
18 | 6280 yds | Par 70 | SSS 71
Visitors welcome, ☎ | without M ∴ per day ∴ WE | with M .. per day WE |
B L ☎ D (not F) | ⚲ ♉ ↘ | ④ Tu Th pm | Ⓣᴿ Ladies day (Th 1240-1415), S,
Sun (☎ for details) competitions | ④ Mon, W, F (1700-1900) | ♩ | M 750 | Ⓢ
★★*Shireburn Arms, Hurst Green, Blackburn. T:(025486) 518. 11rm (6* ⇌ 1 ⋒*)
One of the best inland courses in the country. Clitheroe is a
parkland type course with water hazards and good scenic views,
particularly on towards Longridge and of Pendle Hill. The Club has
been the venue for the Lancashire Amateur Championships.

CLYDACH
West Glamorgan
Map I E2

Inco Clydach (¾m SE of Clydach,
on B4291)
T:(0792) 844216
*Flat meadowland course. 18 | 5976 yds
| Par 71 | SSS 69*
Visitors welcome | B | ♉ ⚲ | M 300
★★*Glyn Clydach House, Longford Rd,*

Neath Abbey. T:(0792) 813701.
8rm (1 ⇄ 4 ⋒)

CLYDEBANK
Strathclyde, *Dumbartonshire*
Map **VI** D2

Dalmuir Park (2m NW of town
centre)
T:041-952 6372
*Hilly parkland course with tough
finishing holes. 18 | 5349 yds | Par 67 |
SSS 66*
Visitors welcome | without M ..
per round | B L D ⚑ | ⚓ ↖ | S | TR
S 1130-1430 | ℐ
★★*Cameron House, Main St,
Hardgate. T:(0389) 73535. 16rm (4 ⇄
12 ⋒)*

COATBRIDGE
Strathclyde, *Lanarkshire*
Map **VI** F2

Drumpellier Drumpellier,
Coatbridge (¾m W of Coatbridge,
off A89)
T:(0236) 24139
*Parkland course. 18 | 6205 yds | Par 71
| SSS 70*
Visitors welcome, ☎ ⊠ | B (not Th)

| L ⚑ D prior arrangement (not Th)
| ⚓ ℣ | TR WE | ℐ | M 450 | S
★★*Tudor, Alexander St, Airdrie.
T:(02364) 63295. 21rm (10 ⇄)*

COBHAM
Surrey
Map **II** D4

Silvermere Redhill Rd, Cobham
(2¼m NW of Cobham, off A245)
T:(0932) 66007
*Parkland course with many very tight
holes through woodland, 17th with
170 yds carry over lake. Societies
welcome. 18 | 6704 yds | Par 73 |
SSS 72*
Visitors welcome with M only | B L
⚑ D ⚓ ℣ ↖ | ⋈ WE | ④ WE |
M 300 | S
★★★*Ladbroke Seven Hills &
Conferencentre, Seven Hills Rd,
Cobham. T:(0932) 64471.
90rm ⇄. Annexe: 25rm ⇄*

COCKERMOUTH
Cumbria
Map **V** B2

Cockermouth Embleton (3m E of
Cockermouth, off A66)

T:(059 681) 223
*Fell land course, fenced, with
exceptional views and a hard climb on
3rd and 11th holes. Testing holes: 10th
and 16th (rearranged by James Braid).
18 | 5496 yds | Par 69 | SSS 67*
Visitors welcome ⊠ restricted WE
(before 1030) | without M .. per day
WE | with M .. per day WE | B L D
⚑ prior arrangement (not Mon) | ⚓
℣ | TR W (1715-1800) WE
(1430-1500)
★★★*Trout, Crown St. T:(0900)
823591. 16rm (11 ⇄ 4 ⋒)*

CODNOR
Derbyshire
Map **III** K3

Ormonde Fields Nottingham Rd
(1m SE of Codnor on A610)
T:(0773) 42987
*Parkland course with undulating
fairways and natural hazards. The par
4 4th and the par 3 11th are notable.
There is a practice area. 18 | 6007 yds |
Par 70 | SSS 69*
Visitors welcome ☎ at WE | ✳ | B ⚑
(not Mon) | L D prior arrangement
(not Sun or Mon) | ⚓ | ⋈ ➡

KEY
(IA1) *atlas grid reference*
T: *telephone number*
☎ *advance letter/telephone call required*
✉ *introduction from own club sec/handicap certificate/club membership card required*
∴ *low fees*
∴ *medium fees*
∷ *high fees*
* *green fees not confirmed for 1987*
B *light lunch*
L *full lunch*
♨ *tea*
D *dinner*
⚐ *changing rooms/showers*
Ⴤ *bar open mid-day and evenings*
↘ *clubs for hire*
∞ *partners may be found*
④ *restricted time for 4 balls*
TR *times reserved for members*
ᴶ *professional*
S *well-stocked shop*
M *member*
Mon Tu W Th F S Sun
WE *weekend*
BH *bank holiday*

sometimes | Ⴤ (not Mon) | TR WE
☎ for details | M 350 | S
★★★*Post House, Bostocks Ln, Sandiacre. T:(0602) 397800. 107rm* ⇄

COLCHESTER
Essex
Map **IV** H8

Birch Grove Layer Rd, Kingsford (2½m S of Colchester, on B1026)
T:(020634) 276
A pretty, undulating course surrounded by woodland - small but challenging. 9 | *2828 yds* | *Par 54* | *SSS 54*
Visitors welcome | .. per day WE |
B L D S♨ | ⚐ ↘ | Ⴤ ∞ | TR Sun (am) | M 172
★★*Kings Ford Park, Layer Rd. T:(0206) 34301. 14rm (11* ⇄ *2* 🏠*)*

Colchester Braiswick (1½m NW of town centre, on B1508)
T:(0206) 853396
A fairly flat parkland course. 18 | *6319 yds* | *Par 70* | *SSS 70*
Visitors welcome without M Mon-

F, with M only WE | without M ∷ per day | with M .. per day | Ⴤ B L
♨ | ⚐ ↘ ∞ (occasionally) | M 700 |
S TR WE
○○*Dedham Vale, Stratford Rd, Dedham. T:(0206) 322273. 6rm* ⇄

Stoke by Nayland Keepers Ln, Leavenheath, Colchester (1½m NW of Stoke-by-Nayland on B1068)
T:(0206) 262836
Two undulating courses (Gainsborough and Constable) situated in Dedham Vale; some water hazards and hedges. On Gainsborough the 10th (par 4) takes 2 shots over lake; very testing par 3 at 11th. Squash courts available. Societies and large evening functions catered for. 18 | *6471 (6498) yds* | *Par 72* | *SSS 71*
Visitors welcome weekdays ☎ advisable, restricted Th, WE BH only with ✉ | without M ∷ per day WE | with M .. per day | B L ♨ | D prior arrangement | ⚐ Ⴤ ↘ | ∞ |
TR competition days | M 900 | S
❀○○○⚌*Maison Talbooth, Stratford Rd, Dedham. T:(0206) 322367. 10rm (9* ⇄ *1* 🏠*)*

COLD ASHBY
Northamptonshire
Map **IV** B6

Cold Ashby Stanford Rd (1m W of Cold Ashby)
T:(0604) 740099/740548
Undulating parkland course, nicely matured, with superb views. 18 | *5809 yds* | *Par 70* | *SSS 69*
Visitors welcome without M | ∴ per day Ⴤ L D B ♨ ♨ S ↘ | TR S 1200-1400 Sun before 1000 | M 550
★★★*Post House, Crick. T:(0788) 822101. 96rm* ⇄

COLDSTREAM
Borders, *Berwickshire*
Map **VI** J3

Hirsel Kelso Rd (SW side of town, off A698)
T:(0890) 2678
Parkland course, with hard walking and sheltered by trees. Testing 3rd and 6th holes. Parties accepted by arrangement. 9 | *5680 yds* | *Par 70* | *SSS 67*
Visitors welcome | .. per day WE |
B L ♨ prior arrangement | ⚐ Ⴤ | ∞ prior arrangment | ④ evngs, WE |
TR matches | M 300

★*Majicado. 71 High St. T:(0890) 2112. 7rm*

COLESHILL
Warwickshire
Map **III** J5

Maxstoke Park Castle Ln, Birmingham (2m E of Coleshill)
T:(0675) 62158
Parkland course with easy walking. Numerous trees and a lake form natural hazards. 18 | *6444 yds* | *Par 71* | *SSS 71*
Visitors welcome restricted WE BH | ∴ per round | ∷ per day | with M .. per day WE | B ♨ not Mon Nov-Mar | L D prior arrangement (not Mon Nov-Mar) | ⚐ Ⴤ ↘ | ∞ | TR
☎ for details | ᴶ | M 500 | S
★★*Swan, High St. Coleshill. T:(0675) 62212. 34rm (23* 🏠*)*

COLNE
Lancashire
Map **V** E6

Colne Law Farm, Skipton Old Rd (¾m NE of Colne, off A6068)
T:(0282) 863391
Moorland course. 9 | *5961 yds* | *Par 70* | *SSS 69*
Visitors welcome | without M .. per day WE | with M .. | Ⴤ ⚐ B L
♨ D prior arrangement (not Mon) |
④ Th | TR competitions | ∞ |
M 320
★★*Great Marsden, Barkerhouse Rd, Nelson. T:(0282) 64749. 14rm (3* ⇄ *3* 🏠*)*

COLONSAY
Strathclyde, *Argyllshire*
Map **VI** A1

Colonsay c/o Colonsay Hotel (2m W of Scalasaig, on A870)
T:(09512) 316
Traditional links course on natural Machair (hard wearing short grass) challenging, primitive. 18 | *4775 yds* | *Par 72* | *SSS 78*
Visitors welcome without M | .. per member or family per year | L D B ♨ | Ⴤ ↘ | ∞ | M 60
★*Colonsay, Scalasaig. T:(09512) 316. 11rm (8* 🏠*)*

COLVEND
Dumfries and Galloway, *Kirkcudbrightshire*
Map **VI** F6

Colvend (1¼m east of village, on

A710)
T:(055 663) 398, Dalbeattie
Hilly seaside course, short but tricky.
Good view. 9 | 2103 yds | Par 62 |
SSS 61
Visitors welcome | * | ♿ ↘ | ✕ |
TR summer Tu (from 1400) Th
(from 1700) | M 300 | S
★★★♨*Barons Craig, Rockcliffe.*
T:(055 663) 225. 26rm (20 ⇥)

COLWYN BAY
Clwyd
Map III E1

Old Colwyn The Club House,
Woodland Av, Old Colwyn (E side
of town centre, on B5383)
T:(0492) 515581
Hilly meadowland course with sheep
and cattle grazing on it in parts. 9 |
5000 yds | Par 68 | SSS 66
Visitors welcome, restricted WE | ••
per day WE | B ☛ D | L (WE only) |
♿ ⅄ ✕ | TR S 1215-1600, Sun
1300-1600 | M 250
★★★*Hopeside, Princes Dr, Colwyn*
Bay. T:(0492) 33244. 19rm (13 ⇥ 6 🍽)

COMRIE
Tayside, *Perthshire*
Map VII G8

Comrie Comrie (E side of village,
off A85)
T:(0764) 70544
Scenic highland course. 9 | 2980 yds |
Par 70 | SSS 69
Visitors welcome | •• per day WE |
B ☛ | ♿ | ✕ ↘ | TR Mon (from
1630) | 🎯 | M 250
★★*Royal. T:(0764) 70200. 9rm ⇥.*
Annexe: 5rm (5 ⇥ 1 🍽)

CONGLETON
Cheshire
Map III H2

Astbury Peel Ln, Astbury (1½m S
of Congleton, between A34 and
A527)
T:(0260) 272772
Parkland course in open countryside,
bisected by a canal. Society applications
considered (Th only). 18 | 6269 yds |
Par 71 | SSS 70
Visitors welcome | without M ∴ per
day WE | with M •• per day WE | B
L ☛ D prior arrangement (not Tu) |
♿ ⅄ 🎯 | M 510 | S
★★★*Saxon Cross, Holmes Chapel Rd,*
Sandbach (M6 junc 17). T:(0270)
763281. 52rm ⇥

Congleton Biddulph Rd (1½m SE
of Congleton on A527)
T:(02602) 273540
Parkland course. 9 | 5055 yds | Par 68 |
SSS 65
Visitors welcome ✉ | * | B L ☛ D
prior arrangement (not Mon) | ♿ ⅄
↘ | TR competition days (usually
WE) Tu (ladies day) | M 350 | S
★★★*Chimney House, Congleton Rd,*
Sandbach. T:(09367) 4141. 20rm ⇥

CONISBROUGH
South Yorkshire
Map V G7

Crookhill Park Municipal
Doncaster (1½m SE of Conisbrough
on B6094)
T:(0709) 862979
A rolling parkland course. 18 |
5846 yds | Par 70 | SSS 68
Visitors are welcome without M,
restricted S Sun before 0900 | B ☛ |

♿ ⅄ S ↘ ✕ TR s Sun till 0900
★★★*Danum, High St, Doncaster.*
T:(0302) 62261. 66rm (59 ⇥ 7 🍽)

CONSETT
Durham
Map VI K6

Consett & District Elmfield Rd (N
side of town on A691)
T:(0207) 502186
Undulating parkland/moorland course,
variable walking, prevailing SW wind,
good views. 18 | 6001 yds | Par 71 |
SSS 69
Visitors welcome ✉ parties
midweek by arrangement,
restrictions WE 🕿 | without M ••
per day ∴ WE | with M •• per day
WE | B | L ☛ D prior arrangement |
♿ ⅄ ✕ | TR competitions | 🎯 |
M 650
★★*Lord Crewe Arms, Blanchland.*
T:(043475) 251. 8rm (6 ⇥ 2 🍽)
Annexe: 7rm ⇥

COOKHAM
Berkshire
Map II D3

Winter Hill Grange Ln, Cookham
(1m NW of Cookham off B4447)
T:(06285) 27613
Parkland course set in a curve of the
Thames, with magnificent river
scenery. Societies welcome by
arrangement. 18 | 6432 yds (Men)
5777 (Ladies) | Par 72(73) | SSS 71(73)
Visitors welcome, restricted WE.
Certificate of handicap required for
WE before 1200. | without M ∴ per
day ∶∶ WE | with M ∴ per day WE |
B ☛ | L D prior arrangement | ♿ ⅄ |
④ ☛ 🕿 for details | 🎯 | M 650 | S ↦

CONSTANTINE
Cornwall
Map I   B6

Trevose Constantine Bay, Padstow (N side of village)
T:(0841) 520208
18(9) | 6461(1357) yds | Par 69(29) | SSS 71
Visitors welcome ⊠ | ∷ per day | B L ☕ | D (not Mon in winter) | ⚐ ♈ | ⋈
④ ☎ for details | M 683 | S
***Treglos, Constantine Bay. T:(0841) 520727. 44rm ➾ ⌂*
A pleasant holiday seaside course with early holes close to the sea on excellent springy turf. It is a good and enjoyable test of the golfer's skill. Additional facilities include a good 9-hole course, tennis courts, a games room and a swimming pool. Self catering accommodation in Bungalows, Chalets, Flats and Dormy Suites available at Club — apply Secretary for details.

CONWY
Gwynedd
Map III   D2

Conwy, (Caernarfonshire) The Morfa, Conwy
(¾m NW of town centre, off A55)
T:(049263) 3400/2423
Flat seaside links championship course with much gorse and open to strong winds. 18 | 9001 yds | Par 72 | SSS 73
Visitors welcome ⊠ | restricted WE BH | without M ∴ per day WE | with M ‥ per day WE | B ☕ (not Tu) | L D prior arrangement (not Tu) | ⚐ ♈ ⋈ | TR
WE (until 1030, 1230-1430) | J | M 480 | S
***Bryn Cregin Garden, TyMawr Rd, Deganwy. T:(0492) 83402. 16rm (12 ➾ 4 ⌂)*
This course close by the old town of Conwy is a real seaside links with gorse, rushes, sandhills and fine old turf. There are plenty of natural hazards, the gorse providing more than its share. The course has a spectacular setting between sea and mountains.

****Compleat Angler, Marlow Bridge, Marlow. T:(06284) 4444. 46rm ➾*

COPMANTHORPE
North Yorkshire
Map V   G6

Pike Hills Tadcaster Rd, Copmanthorpe, York (N side of village on A64)
T:(0904) 706566
Parkland course surrounding nature reserve. 18 | 5718 yds | Par 69 | SSS 68
Visitors welcome | without M ∴ per day | with M ‥ per day WE | B ☕ | D prior arrangement | ⚐ ♈ | TR
WE | M 850 | S
***Chase, Tadcaster Rd. T:(0904) 707171. 80rm (63 ➾ 17 ⌂)*

COPTHORNE
West Sussex
Map II   F5

Effingham Park (2m E of Copthorne, on B2028)
T:(0342) 716528
Parkland course. 9 | 1749 yds | Par 30
Visitors welcome with M | ✳ | ☕ | ⚐
S ⤬ | TR ⋈ occasionally | M 200
****Copthorne, Copthorne Rd. T:(0342) 714971. 223rm (177 ➾ 46 ⌂)

CORBY
Northamptonshire
Map IV   C5

Corby Stamford Rd, Weldon (4m NE of Corby, on A43)
T:(05363) 60756
Municipal course laid out on made up quarry ground and open to prevailing wind. 18 | 6657 yds | Par 72 | SSS 72
Open to public | ‥ per day | B L ☕ D (not Tu) | ⚐ ♈ ⤬ ⋈ | J | M 200 | S
***Talbot, New St, nr Oundle. T:(0832) 73621. 39rm ➾*

CORHAMPTON
Hampshire
Map II   B6

Corhampton (1m W of Corhampton, off B3035)
T:(0489) 877279
Downland course on high elevation, windy. Societies welcome by arrangement. 18 | 6088 yds | Par 69 | SSS 69
Visitors welcome with M only WE BH | B L ☕ D (not Tu) | ⚐ ♈ ⤬ | TR WE 0800-1000, competitions ④ 1st tee WE 0800-1000 | J | M 600 | S
✿**Old House, Wickham. T:(0329) 833049. 10rm ➾ ⌂

COPTHORNE
West Sussex
Map II F5

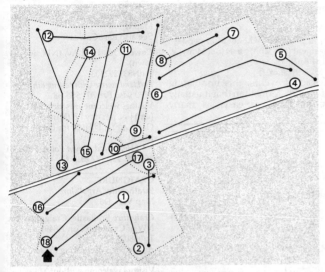

Copthorne Borers Arms Rd (E side of village, off A264)
T:(0342) 712033
18 | 6505 yds | Par 71 | SSS 71
Visitors welcome but with M only WE | B L ♣ | ⚎ ♈ | TR | WE BH until 13.30
| ℑ | M 550 | S |
★★★★*Copthorne, Copthorne Rd (on A264 2m E off A264/B2036 rbt). T:(0342)*
714971. 223rm (177 ⇌ 46 ☖)
Despite it having been in existence since 1892 this club remains one of the lesser known Sussex courses. It is hard to know why because it is most attractive with plenty of trees and much variety.

CORRIE
Strathclyde, *Bute*
Map VI C3

Corrie Sannox (2m N of Corrie on A841)
T:(077082) 223, Isle of Arran

A heathland course on the coast with mountain scenery. 9 | 3896 (18) yds | Par 62 (18 holes) | SSS 61
Visitors are welcome without M | ..
per day | B ♣ | S | ↘ | TR | S 1300 | M 200
★*Cameronia, Whiting Bay. T:(07707) 254. 6rm*

COSBY
Leicestershire
Map IV A5

Cosby Chapel Ln, (S side of village)
T:(0533) 864759
Parkland course. Societies welcome by arrangement. 18 | 6280 yds | Par 71 | SSS 70
Visitors welcome Mon-F until 1600 with M only WE | ✉ ☎ preferred | without M ∴ per day | with M .. per day WE | B ♣ (not Mon) | L D prior arrangement (not Mon) | ⚎ ♈ ↘ | ⋈ (probable) ℑ | M 590 | S |
★★★*Post House, Braunstone Ln East, Leicester. T:(0533) 896688. 182rm ⇌*

COULSDON
Greater London
Map II E4

Coulsdon Court Coulsdon Court
Rd (¾m E of Coulsdon, off B2030)
T:01-660 0468/01-668 0414
Parkland course with good views. Clubhouse formerly owned by Lord Byron. 18 | 6030 yds | Par 70 | SSS 68
Public course | .. per round | L D B ♣ | ⚎ ♈ S | ⋈ | ℑ
★★★★*Selsdon Park, Sanderstead. T:01-657 8811. 150rm ⇌*

Woodcote Park Meadow Hill, Bridle Way, Coulsdon (1m N of ➥

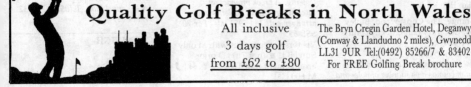

COVENTRY
West Midlands
Map III   K5

Coventry Finham Park (3m S of city centre, on A444)
T:(0203) 414152
Societies by arrangement. 18 | 6613 yds | Par 73 | SSS 72
Visitors welcome WE BH with M only | ☎ preferred | without M ∶∶ per day |
with M ·· per day WE | B L prior arrangement (not Mon) | ☛ D (not Mon) | ⚘
♈ \ | ∞ sometimes | 𝄞 | TR Tu, WE | M 810 | S
★★★★*Hotel Leofric, Broadgate. T:(0203) 21371. 91rm* ⇄ 🍴
The scene of several major professional events, this undulating
parkland course has a great deal of quality. More than that it usually
plays its length, and thus scoring is never easy, as many
professionals have found to their cost.

CRAIL
Fife
Map VI   H1

Crail Golfing Society Balcomie
Clubhouse, Fifeness, Crail
(2m NE of Crail, off A917)
T:(0333) 50278
Society meetings by arrangement.
No children. 18 | 5720 yds | Par 69 |
SSS 68
Visitors welcome, restricted WE |
without M ∴ per day ∶∶ WE | B L
☛ | ♈ ⚘ | TR (until 1000,
1300-1400, 1700-1830) | ④ at all
times | M 700
*Marine, 54 Nethergate. T:(0333)
50207. 13rm

SCORE CARD:

1	312	10	209
2	480	11	500
3	179	12	489
4	348	13	215
5	346	14	149
6	334	15	265
7	421	16	163
8	306	17	461
9	334	18	209

Perched on the very edge of the North Sea on the very point of the
golfing county of Fife, the Crail Golfing Society's course at Balcomie
is picturesque and sporting. And here again golf history has been
made for Crail Golfing Society began its life in 1786. The course is
highly thought of by students of the game both for its testing holes
and the standard of its greens.

town centre, off A237)
T:01-668 2788
Slightly undulating parkland course.
18 | 6624 yds | Par 71 | SSS 71
Visitors welcome weekdays with M
| ∶∶ per day | B | L ☛ prior
arrangement | ⚘ ♈ \ | ∞ | ④
1200-1500 | ④ WE pm | TR WE | 𝄞 |
M 700 | S
★★★*Croydon Court, Purley Way,*
Croydon. T:01-688 5185. 86rm ⇄

COVENTRY
West Midlands
Map III   K5

Grange, The Copsewood, Binley
Rd, Coventry (2m E of city centre
on A428)
T:(0203) 451645
Flat parkland course with very tight
out of bounds on a number of holes and

a river which affects play on five of
them. Well bunkered, with plenty of
new trees. 9 | 6002 yds | Par 72 |
SSS 69
Visitors welcome | ✳ | ⚘ ♈ | TR
Mon-F (after 1400), S (all day), Sun
(until 1200) | M 350
★★★*Chace Crest, London Rd,*
Willenhall. T:(0203) 303398. 68rm ⇄

Hearsall Beechwood Ave, Coventry
(1½m SW of city centre, off A429)
T:(0203) 713470
Parkland course with fairly easy
walking. A brook provides an
interesting hazard. Societies by
arrangement. 18 | 5951 yds | Par 70 |
SSS 69
Visitors welcome but with M only
Sun | B L ☛ (not Tu) | D prior
arrangement (not Tu) | ⚘ ♈ ∞ | 𝄞 |
M 600 | S

★★★★*Hotel Leofric, Broadgate,*
Coventry. T:(0203) 21371. 91rm ⇄ 🍴

COWES
Isle of Wight
Map II   B7
See also East Cowes

Cowes Crossfield Av, (NW side of
town)
T:(0983) 292303
Parkland course with testing 8th. 9 |
5880 yds | Par 70 | SSS 68
Visitors welcome, restricted WE
(am) | ·· per day | B (Mon-S, April-
Oct) | ⚘ ♈ | TR (☎ for details) |
M 250
★★★*Holmwood, Egypt Point. T:(0983)*
292508. 19rm (7 ⇄ *7* 🍴)

CRAIGNURE
Strathclyde, *Argyllshire*
Map VII   D8

Craignure Scallastle, Craignure (1m
NW of Craignure, on A849)
T:(06802) 370
A flat course, overlooking the sea. 9 |
2454 yds | Par 66 | SSS 66
Visitors welcome without M | \ |
M 50
★★★*Isle of Mull, Craignure.*
T:(06802) 351. 60rm ⇄

CRANBROOK
Kent
Map II   H5

Cranbrook Benenden Rd (2m E of
Cranbrook)
T:(0580) 712934/712833
Scenic parkland course with easy
terrain, backed by Hemstead Forest and
near Sissinghurst Castle (1m) and
Bodiam Castle (6m). Testing hole at
7th (530 yds, par 5). Societies up to 50
welcome any time; juniors and schools
accommodated. Venue for the County
Championship. 18 | 6136 yds | Par 70 |
SSS 70
Visitors welcome | without M ∴ per
day | with M ∴ per day | B ☛ | L D
(not Mon Tu) | ⚘ ♈ \ | ∞ prior
arrangement | ④ 0815-0915,
1230-1330 | TR major competition
days | 𝄞 | M 600 | S
★★🏨*Kennel Holt. T:(0580) 712032.*
7rm (4 ⇄)

CRANLEIGH
Surrey
Map II   D5

Fernfell Golf and Country Club

Bar Hatch Ln (1m N of Cranleigh
on Ewhurst Rd)
T:(0483) 276626
*Scenic wooded parkland course at the
base of the Surrey hills, easy walking.
Clubhouse in 400-year-old barn.
Societies welcome by arrangement.* 18 |
5780 yds | Par 70 | SSS 68
Visitors welcome weekdays, with
M only WE | .. per round ∴ per
day | B L ♥ D | ⚲ Y \ | ④ Sun
before 0930 | TR WE | 𝔍 | M 550 | S
★★*Angel, High St, Guildford.*
T:(0483) 64555. 27rm ⇄ 🏠

CRAWLEY
West Sussex
Map II   E5

Cottesmore Buchan Hill, Pease
Pottage (3m SW of Crawley 1m W
of M23 Jct 11)
T:(0293) 28256
*The Old Course is undulating with
birch and rhododendrons. Four holes
are over water. The New Course is
short parkland.* 36 | 6100 (5400) yds |
Par 72 | SSS 71
Visitors welcome | B | L D prior
arrangement | ♥ ⚲ Y | ④ WE only
TR competitions | M 1500 | S
★★★*George, High St, Crawley.*
T:(0293) 24215. 76rm ⇄

Gatwick Manor Lowfield Heath
(2m N of Crawley on A23)
T:(0293) 24470
*Interesting short course. Societies
welcome by arrangement. Expert
tuition. Course owned by hotel with
full catering facilities.* 9 | 1109 yds |
Par 27 | SSS 27
Visitors welcome | ∞ usually | S
★★★*George, High St, Crawley.*
T:(0293) 24215. 76rm ⇄

Ifield Golf and Country Club
Rusper Rd, Ifield, Crawley (W side
of town centre off A23)
T:(0293) 20222
Parkland course. 18 | 6265 yds | Par 70
| SSS 70
Visitors welcome with Club
handicap | ∴ per round | :: per day
| B ♥ | L D prior arrangement | ⚲
Y | ④ W 0930-1200 | TR Tu W am |
𝔍 | M 850 | S
★★★*George, High St, T:(0293) 24215.
76rm ⇄*

CREDITON
Devon
Map I   F5

Downes Crediton Hookway (1½m
SE of Crediton off A377)
T:(03632) 3991
*Converted farmland course with lovely
views.* 18 | 5967 yds | Par 69 | SSS 69
Visitors welcome | without M ∴ per
day WE | With M .. per day | B L ♥
| D prior arrangement | ⚲ Y \ |
TR competitions | 𝔍 | M 500 | S
★★*King's Arms Inn, Tedburn St
Mary.* T:(06476) 224. 5rm (1 ⇄)

CREIGIAU (CREIYIAU)
Mid Glamorgan
Map I   F2

Creigiau Creigiau, nr Cardiff (W
side of village, off A4119)
T:(0222) 890263
*Downland course, with small greens.
Juniors welcome if members of clubs.* 18
| 5715 yds | Par 69 | SSS 68
Visitors welcome | WE BH only
with M | ∴ per day | B L ♥ D prior
arrangement (not M) | ⚲ Y \ | 𝔍 |
M 335 | S | TR ladies day Tu
★★★*Crest, Westgate St, Cardiff.*
T:(0222) 388681. 160rm ⇄

CREWE
Cheshire
Map III   H2

Crewe Fields Rd (2¼m E of Crewe,
E side of Haslington, off A534)
T:(0270) 585032/584099, Cheshire
Undulating parkland course. 18 |
6277 yds | Par 71 | SSS 70
Visitors welcome | ∴ per day not
WE | B L D ♥ | ⚲ Y S \ | TR |
major competitions | M 550

★★★*Crewe Arms, Nantwich Rd.*
T:(0270) 213204. 37rm (35 ⇄)

CRICCIETH
Gwynedd
Map III   C3

Criccieth Ednyfed Hill (1m NE of
Criccieth)
T:(076671) 2154
*Hilly course on Lleyn Peninsula. Good
views.* 18 | 5587 yds | Par 69 | SSS 68
Visitors welcome | without M ..
per day | with M .. per day WE | B
L ♥ D May-Sept only | ⚲ Y | TR
WE 1400-1430 | 𝔍 part-time | M 234 |
S ∞
★★*George IV.* T:(076671) 2168.
34rm (15 ⇄ 9 🏠)

CROMER
Norfolk
Map IV   J2

Royal Cromer 145 Overstrand Rd,
Cromer (1m E of Cromer, on B1159)
T:(0263) 512884
*Seaside course set out on cliff edge, hilly
and subject to wind. Societies welcome
(Mon to F) by arrangement.* 18 |
6508 yds | Par 72 | SSS 71
Visitors welcome restricted WE BH |
without M ∴ per day | :: WE | with
M ∴ per day WE | B L ♥ D prior
arrangement (not Tu) | ⚲ Y | M 600
| S
★★*Cliftonville, Runton Rd.* T:(0263)
512543. 46rm (9 ⇄ 3 🏠)

CRONDALL
Hampshire
Map II   C5

Crondall Oak Park, Heath Lane
(½m E of village on Heath Lane) ⤙

CRIEFF
Tayside, *Perthshire*
Map VII   G8

Crieff Perth Rd, Crieff (½m NE of Crieff, on A85)
T:(0764) 2909
Limited number of society meetings by arrangement. Ferntower Course: 18 |
5818 metres | Par 71 | SSS 70 — *Dornock Course:* 9 | 4364 metres | Par 64 | SSS 63
Visitors welcome ☎ advisable | without M | B | L ♥ D | ⚲ Y \ | ④ | TR ☎ |
𝔍 | M 580 | S
★★*Murray Park, Connaught Ter.* T:(0764) 3731. 15rm (10 ⇄)
Near the famous Gleneagles, this course is what you might call 'up
and down' but the turf is beautiful and the highland air fresh and
invigorating. There are views from the course over Strathearn.
Crieff itself is a popular tourist resort. Of the two courses, the
Ferntower is the most challenging while the smaller Dornock course
is a delight to play.

CROWBOROUGH
East Sussex
Map II F6

Crowborough Beacon Beacon Rd
(1m SW of Crowborough, on A26)
T:(08926) 61511
Societies welcome by arrangement. 18 |
6304 yds | Par 71 | SSS 70
Visitors welcome, restricted WE BH
(am) ☎ preferred | without M ∷
per day WE | with M .. per day WE
| B ☛ | L D prior arrangement (not
Th) | ⚕ Υ ↘ | ④ | TR 0800-0915 | ℐ
| M 500 | S
★★★*Spa, Mount Ephraim, Tunbridge*
Wells. T:(0892) 20331. 70rm (67 ⇄ 3
🁢)

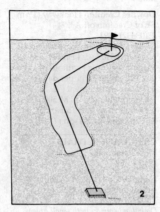

Crowborough Beacon
2nd hole

A picturesque course in pleasant heathland. Though most fairways
are wide and open, one or two are distinctly tight where a wayward
shot results in a lost ball. By no means an easy course, with testing
holes at the 2nd, 6th and 16th

CROWTHORNE
Berkshire
Map II C4

East Berkshire Ravenswood Ave, Crowthorne
(W side of town centre, off B3348)
T:(0344) 2041
Societies welcome (Th F) by arrangement. 18 | 6315 yds | Par 69 | SSS 70
Visitors welcome ✉, with M only WE BH | ☎ advisable | B L ☛ (not Mon) | L
prior arrangement (not Mon) | ⚕ Υ ↘ ⋈ TR WE BH | ℐ | M 500 | S
★★★★🏨*Pennyhill Park, College Ride, Bagshot. T:(0276) 71774. 19rm ⇄*
Annexe: 31rm ⇄
An attractive heathland course with an abundance of heather and
pine trees. Walking is easy and the greens are exceptionally good.
Some fairways become tight where the heather encroaches on the
line of play. The course is testing and demands great accuracy.

T:(0252) 850880
Gently undulating course overlooking
pretty village. 9 (18 tee) | 6000 yds |
Par 70 | SSS 69
Visitors welcome | ✳ | B L D ☛ Υ |
⚕ ↘ ⋈ | ℐ | TR WE and
competition days | S
★★★*Bush, The Borough, Farnham.*
T:(0252) 715237. 65rm (62 ⇄ 3 🁢)

CROOK
Durham
Map V E2

Crook Low Jobs Hill (½m E of
Crook, off A690)
T:(0388) 762429

Meadowland course with natural
hazards, varied holes and terrain, hilly
view. Testing 4th hole - The Copse.
Societies welcome by arrangement, also
accompanied juniors. 18 | 6075 yds |
Par 68 | SSS 69
Visitors welcome | B L ☛ D prior
arrangement | ⚕ Υ | ⋈ (probable)
④ | TR S, Sun (1130-1330) | M 420
★★*Queens Head, Market Pl, Bishop*
Auckland. T:(0388) 603477.
10rm (4 ⇄ 1 🁢)

CROYDON
Greater London
Map II F4

Croham Hurst Croham Rd (1½m
SE of Croydon)
T:01-657 2075
Parkland course with tree-lined
fairways and bounded by wooded hills.
Easy walking. 18 | 6274 yds | Par 70 |
SSS 70
Visitors welcome restricted Tu (am)
WE BH | B L not Mon S | ☛ | ⚕ Υ |
↘ ⋈ possible | TR ④ ☎ | ℐ |
M 950 | S
★★★★*Selsdon Park, Sanderstead.*
T:01-657 8811. 150rm ⇄

Selsdon Park Hotel Addington Rd,
Sanderstead, Croydon (3m S of
Croydon, on A2022)
T:01-657 8811
Surrey parkland course. Societies
welcome by arrangement. 18 | 6402 yds
| Par 73 | SSS 71
Visitors welcome ☎ | ∴ weekdays
∷ WE | B ☛ | L D | Υ ⚕ ↘ ℐ | S
★★★★*Selsdon Park, Sanderstead.*
T:01-657 8811. 150rm ⇄

CULLEN
Grampian, *Banffshire*
Map VII J4

Cullen The Links, Cullen (½m W of
Cullen, off A98)
T:(0542) 40685
Seaside links on two levels with rocks
and ravines. Societies welcome Sun (not
July-3rd Sun August) by arrangement.
18 | 4610 yds | Par 63 | SSS 62
Visitors welcome | B L ☛ | ⚕ ⋈ | Υ
Sun Oct to March lunchtime only |
TR medal days | M 470 | S
★★★*Seafield Arms, Seafield St.*
T:(0542) 40791. 24rm (22 ⇄ 1 🁢)

CUMBERNAULD
Strathclyde, *Dumbartonshire*
Map VI E2

Dullatur Golf Club Dullatur,
Glasgow (1½m N of Cumbernauld)
T:(02367) 23230
Parkland course, with natural hazards
and wind. Testing 17th hole par 5.
Society meetings by arrangement. 18 |
6195 yds | Par 70 | SSS 70
Visitors welcome weekdays ☎ | WE
only with M ✉ | restricted WE BH
& comp days | without M ∴ per
day | with M .. per day WE | B (not
Tu) | L ☛ D prior arrangement (not
Tu) | ⚕ | ℐ | M 420 | S
★★*George, High St, Market Place,*
Castle Cary. T:(0963) 50761.
17rm (15 ⇄ 2 🁢)

CROYDON
Greater London
Map **II** F4

Shirley Park Addiscombe Rd, Croydon (E side of town centre, on A232)
T:01-654 1143
18 | 6210 yds | Par 71 | SSS 70
No societies of W | Visitors welcome weekdays ☎ | with M only WE BH | ∷ per day | B L ☛ | D prior arrangement parties only | ⚷ ⛳ | ♂ | ④ check beforehand | M 800 | Ⓢ
★★★★*Holiday Inn, 7 Altyre Rd. T:01-680 9200. 214rm ⇄ 🍴*
This parkland course lies amid fine woodland with good views of Shirley Hills. The more testing holes come in the middle section of the course. The remarkable 7th hole calls for a 187 yard iron or wood shot diagonally across a narrow valley to a shelved green set right-handed into a ridge. The par 4 11th calls for two long and accurate shots. The Clubhouse is equipped with two snooker tables and card rooms.

CUPAR
Fife, *Fife*
Map **VII** H8

Cupar Hilltarvit, Cupar (¾m S of Cupar, off A92)
T:(0334) 53549
Hillside course with fine view. Societies welcome by arrangement. 9 | 5074 yds | Par 68 | SSS 65
Visitors welcome, with M only WE

| B L ☛ D | ⚷ ⛳ | TR WE | M 420
★★★☘️*Fernie Castle, Letham.
T:(033781) 381. 15rm (6 ⇄ 9 🍴)*

CWMBRAN
Gwent
Map **I** G2

Pontnewydd Maesgwyn Farm, West Pontnewydd, Cwmbran (N side of town centre)

T:(06333) 2170
Mountainside course, with hard walking. Good views across the Severn Estuary. 10 | 5321 yds | Par 68 | SSS 67
Visitors welcome, only with M WE BH | .. per day | B L ☛ | ⚷ ⛳ | ♂ | M 250
★★★*Hotel Commodore, Mill Ln, Llanyravon, Cwmbran. T:(06333) 4091. 60rm (47 ⇄ 11 🍴)*

DAGNALL
Buckinghamshire
Map **II** D2

Whipsnade Studham Ln (1m E of Dagnall off B4506)
T:(044284) 2330
Parkland course situated on downs adjoining Whipsnade Zoo. Easy walking, good views. Societies welcome. 18 | 6800 yds | Par 72 | SSS 72
Visitors welcome | ∴ per day | B | L ☛ D prior arrangement | ⚷ ⛳ ♂ | ♂ prior arrangement | ♂ | M 400 | Ⓢ
★★★*Old Palace Lodge, Church St, Dunstable. T:(0582) 62201. 50rm ⇄*

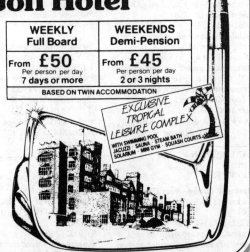

KEY
(IA1) *atlas grid reference*
T: *telephone number*
☎ *advance letter/telephone call required*
✉ *introduction from own club sec/handicap certificate/club membership card required*
•• *low fees*
∴ *medium fees*
:: *high fees*
* *green fees not confirmed for 1987*
B *light lunch*
L *full lunch*
☕ *tea*
D *dinner*
⚠ *changing rooms/showers*
Y *bar open mid-day and evenings*
↘ *clubs for hire*
⋈ *partners may be found*
④ *restricted time for 4 balls*
[TR] *times reserved for members*
ℑ *professional*
[S] *well-stocked shop*
M *member*
Mon Tu W Th F S Sun
WE *weekend*
BH *bank holiday*

CRUDEN BAY
Grampian, *Aberdeenshire*
Map **VII** K5

Cruden Bay Peterhead (SW side of village, on A975)
T:(077 981) 2285
18 & 9 | 6373 yds | Par 70 | SSS 71
Visitors welcome | without M ∴ per day WE | with M •• per day | B L ☕ D prior arrangement | ⚠ Y ↘ | ④ certain competition days | [TR] WE no visitors before 1530 on competition days. Restricted starting times otherwise. Wed 1630-1830 | ④ Summer WE | ℑ | M 1035 | [S]
****Waterside Inn, Fraserburgh Rd. T:(0779) 71121. 80rm ⇌ ⌸ Annexe: 40rm ⇌ ⌸*
A seaside links which provides golf of a high order. It was designed by a master architect, Tom Simpson and although changed somewhat from his original design it is still a great golf course.

CUMMERTREES
Dumfries and Galloway, *Dumfriesshire*
Map **VI** F6

Powfoot (½m S of Cummertrees, off B724)
T:(046 17) 227
18 | 6283 yds | Par 71 | SSS 70
Visitors welcome | B L ☕ ⋈ | ⚠ Y ↘ S 0800-0930, 1200-1400 and 1630-1800, W 0830-0930 then as S | [TR] Sun until 1030, 1245-1445 | ℑ | M 820 | [S]
***Golf, Links Av, Powfoot. T:(04617) 254. 21rm (7 ⇌ 7 ⌸)*
The Cumberland Hills, away beyond the Solway Firth, and from time to time a sight of the Isle of Man, make playing at this delightfully compact and sporting seaside course a scenic treat to remember. Lovely holes include the 2nd, the 8th and the 11th.

DALKEITH
Lothian, *Midlothian*
Map **VI** G2

Newbattle Abbey Rd, Dalkeith (SW side of town off A68)
T:031-663 2123
Undulating parkland course on three levels, surrounded by woods. 18 | 6012 yds | Par 69 | SSS 69
Visitors welcome ☎ restricted until 1600, with M only or ✉ | B L ☕ D prior arrangement (not Mon) | ⚠ | Y (not Mon winter) | [TR] Mon-F after 1600, WE BH | M 650 | [S]
****⚘*Dalhousie Castle, Bonnyrigg. T:(0875) 20153. 24rm ⇌ ⌸*

DARLINGTON
Durham
Map **V** F3

Blackwell Grange Briar Close, Blackwell (1m SW of Darlington off A66)
T:(0325) 464464
Pleasant parkland course with good views, easy walking. Societies welcome by arrangement. 18 | 5587 yds | Par 68 | SSS 67
Visitors welcome, restricted W (pm) | B L ☕ D prior arrangement (not Tu Sun) | ⚠ Y ↘ | ⋈ sometimes | [TR] WE | ℑ | M 600 | [S]
*****Blackwell Grange Moat House, Blackwell Grange. T:(0325) 460111. 98rm ⇌*

Stressholme Snipe Ln, Darlington (SW side of town centre on A67)
T:(0325) 461002
Picturesque municipal course. 18 | 6511 yds | Par 71 | SSS 71
Open to public | B ☕ L (not Tu) | ⚠ Y ↘ ⋈ | M 650 | [S]
*****Blackwell Grange Moat House, Blackwell Grange. T:(0325) 460111. 98rm ⇌*

DARTFORD
Kent
Map **II** G4

Dartford The Club House, Dartford Heath (2m SW of Dartford off B2174)
T:(0322) 23616
Parkland/heathland course. Societies welcome (F) by arrangement. 18 | 5914 yds | Par 69 | SSS 68
Visitors welcome ✉, with M only WE BH | without M :: per day | with M •• per day | B ☕ | L D prior arrangement | ⚠ Y | ℑ | M 600 | [S]
****Crest, Black Prince Interchange, Southwold Rd, Bexley. T:(0322) 526900. 78rm ⇌*

DARWEN
Lancashire
Map **V** D6

Darwen Winter Hill (1m NW of Darwen)
T:(0254) 71287
Moorland course. 18 | 5752 yds | Par 68 | SSS 68
Visitors welcome without M | L D B (not Mon) ☕ | ⚠ Y [S] ↘ | ℑ | [TR] competition days | M 500
****Whitehall, Springbank, Whitehall. T:(0254) 71595. 18rm (14 ⇌)*

DATCHET
Berkshire
Map **II** D3

Datchet Buccleuch Rd, Slough (NW side of Datchet off B470)

DARLINGTON
Durham
Map **V** F3

Darlington Haughton Grange, Darlington (N side of town centre off A1150)
T:(0325) 463936
18 | 6271 yds | Par 70 | SSS 70
Visitors welcome ⊠ ☎ advisable | ∴ per day | B ☛ | L D prior arrangement |
♿ ♟ ↘ | ⋈ | ♩ | M 670 | Ⓢ
★★★★*Blackwell Grange Moat House, Blackwell Grange, Darlington. T:(0325) 460111. 98rm* ⇌
Fairly flat course with tree lined fairways. Course championship standard.

DELAMERE
Cheshire
Map **III** G2

Delamere Forest Station Rd, Northwich (1½m N of Delamere off B5152)
T:(0606) 882807
18 | 6287 yds | Par 72 | SSS 70
Visitors welcome if course is not occupied by a visiting society | ☎ advisable
| without M ∴ per day :: WE | with M ∴ per day WE | B L D prior
arrangement (not F) | ☛ | ♿ ♟ ↘ | ④ WE (visitors permitted 2 ball matches
only) ☎ (Mon-F) | ♩ | M 460 | Ⓢ
★★★*Hartford Hall, School Ln., Hartford. T:(0606) 75711. 21rm* ♫
Played mostly on open heath there is great charm in the way this course drops down into the occasional pine sheltered valley.

T:(0753) 43887
Meadowland course, easy walking. 9 | 5978 yds | Par 70 | SSS 69
Visitors welcome | B ☛ | ♿ ♟ ↘ |
Ⓣ WE | ♩ | M 385 | Ⓢ
★★*Manor, Village Green. T:(0753) 43442. 29rm (21 ⇌ 8* ♫)

DAVENTRY
Northamptonshire
Map **IV** A6

Daventry & District Norton Rd (1m NE of Daventry)
T:(0327) 702829

A hilly course with hard walking. 9 | 5555 yds | Par 69 | SSS 67
Visitors welcome restricted Sun am and WE Oct to March | ☎ | ♿ ♟ ♟ B
☛ ↘ ⋈ | Ⓣ Sun am (summer) WE (winter) | ♩ | M 300 | Ⓢ
★★★*Northampton Moat House, Silver St, Town Centre, Northampton.
T:(0604) 22441. 134rm* ⇌ ♫

DAWLISH WARREN
Devon
Map **I** F6

Warren Dawlish (W side of village)

T:(0626) 862255
*Typical flat links course lying on spit between sea and Exe estuary.
Picturesque scenery - a few trees, much gorse. Societies welcome by arrangement. 18 | 5968 yds | Par 69 | SSS 69*
Visitors welcome | ⊠ ☎ preferred |
B L ☛ (not F) | D ♿ ♟ ↘ | ⋈
possible | Ⓣ Ladies Th ☎ to check
| ♩ | M 450 | Ⓢ
★★★*Langstone Cliff, Dawlish Warren.
T:(0626) 865155. 68rm ⇌* ♫)

DEAL
Kent
Map **II** K5

Royal Cinque Ports Golf Rd, Deal
(Along seafront at N end of Deal)
T:(0304) 374007
Seaside links course, windy, easy walking. Societies welcome by arrangement. 18 | 6744 yds (championship) 6409 yds (medal) | Par 70 (72 champ) | SSS 71 (72 champ)
Visitors welcome ⊠, restricted WE
BH | ☎ preferred | ☛ | B (not Tu) | L
D prior arrangement (not Mon-S) |
♿ ♟ ↘ | ④ no four balls | M 650 | Ⓢ
★★★*Dover Motel, Whitfield, Dover.
T:(0304) 821222. 67rm ⇌* ♫

DENBIGH
Clwyd
Map **III** E2

Denbigh Henllan Rd (1½m NW of Denbigh on B5382)
T:(074571) 4159
Parkland course, giving a testing and ➠

DENHAM
Buckinghamshire
Map II   D3

Denham Tilehouse Ln (2m NW of Denham)
T:(0895) 832022
Societies welcome (Tu Wed Th) by arrangement. 18 | 6439 yds | Par 70 | SSS 71
Visitors welcome, not Sun, with M only S | ☎ | without M ∶∶ per day | with M •• per day WE | B L ♥ prior arrangement (not F) | �†ᴛ Ⴤ ∖ | ⊺ᴿ M F WE | ♪ | M 770 | ⓢ
★★★*Bull, Gerrards Cross.* T:(0753) 885995. *40rm* ⇌
A beautifully maintained parkland/heathland course, home of many county champions. Slightly hilly and calling for good judgement of distance in the wooded areas.

---

varied game. Good views. 18 | 5650 yds | Par 69 | SSS 67
Visitors welcome | without M •• per day WE | ⚹ | Ⴤ B L ♥ D by arrangement with caterer | ⊺ᴿ Tu (Ladies priority) Th S (Gents competitions) | M 340
★★*Bull, Hall Sq.* T:(074571) 2582. *13rm (3* ⇌*)*

DENTON
Greater Manchester
Map V   E7

Denton Manchester Rd, Denton (1½m W of Denton on A57)
T:061-336 3218
Easy, flat parkland course with brook running through. Notable hole is one called Death and Glory. 18 | 6290 yds | Par 72 | SSS 70
Visitors welcome ☎ | restricted WE | B L | ♥ D prior arrangement | ⚹ Ⴤ ⋈ | ♪ | M 600 | ⓢ
★★★*Old Rectory, Meadow Ln, Haughton Green, Denton.* T:061-336 7516. *26rm* ⇌ 🍴

DENVER
Norfolk
Map IV   F4

Ryston Park Denver, Downham Market (½m S of Denver on A10)
T:(0366) 382133
Parkland course. 9 | 6292 yds | Par 70 | SSS 70
Visitors welcome, restricted WE BH | without M ∴ per day | with M •• per day | B L ♥ | D prior arrangement | ⚹ Ⴤ | ⊺ᴿ some competitions and match days | M 300 | ⓢ
★*Crown, Bridge St.* T:(0366) 382322. *10rm (5* ⇌ *2* 🍴*)*

DERBY
Derbyshire
Map III   K3

Allestree Park Allestree Hall (3m N of Derby on A6)
T:(0332) 550616
Municipal parkland course in rather hilly country. Societies welcome (Mon to F) by arrangement. 18 | 5749 yds | Par 68 | SSS 68
Visitors welcome, restricted WE BH | B D (not Mon) prior arrangement | ⚹ Ⴤ ∖ | ⋈ | ⊺ᴿ Sun (am) | ♪ | M 250 | ⓢ
★★★*Breadsall Priory (3½m N of Derby).* T:(0332) 832235. *17rm (14* ⇌ *3* 🍴*)*

Derby Sinfin Lane (3½m S of city centre)
Parkland course. Societies welcome by arrangement. 18 | 6200 yds | Par 70 | SSS 70
Visitors welcome ⊠ ☎ or with M | B ♥ | ⚹ Ⴤ ∖ ♪ | M 350 | ⓢ
★★★*International, 288 Burton Rd.* T:(0332) 369321. *44rm (42* ⇌ *2* 🍴*)*

Mickleover Uttoxeter Rd, Mickleover (2½m SW of Derby off B5020)
T:(0332) 512092
Undulating parkland course in pleasant setting. Societies welcome by arrangement. 18 | 5621 yds | Par 69 | SSS 68
Visitors welcome but restricted WE | B L D ♥ | ⚹ Ⴤ ∖ ⋈ | ⊺ᴿ S |
M 550 | ⓢ
★★*Clarendon, Midland Rd, Derby.* T:(0332) 365235. *50rm (21* ⇌ *7* 🍴*)*

DEREHAM
Norfolk
Map IV   H4

Dereham Quebec Rd, Dereham (N

---

side of town centre off B1110)
T:(0362) 5900
Parkland course. 9 | 6225 yds | Par 71 | SSS 70
Visitors welcome ⊠ during week but only allowed with a M at WE | ☎ advisable | without M •• per day ∴ WE | with M •• per day WE | B ♥ (not Th) | L D prior arrangement (not Th) | ⚹ Ⴤ ∖ ⊺ᴿ competition days | ♪ | M 575 | ⓢ
★★*Phoenix, Church St.* T:(0362) 2276. *28rm (17* ⇌*)*

DEWSBURY
West Yorkshire
Map V   F6

Hanging Heaton White Cross Rd (¾m NE of Dewsbury off A653)
T:(0924) 461606
Arable land course, easy walking, fine views. Testing 4th hole (par 3). Societies welcome by arrangement. 9 | 2917 yds | Par 70 | SSS 68
Visitors welcome, restricted Sun (am) and competition days | B L ♥ D (not Mon) | ⚹ Ⴤ | ♪ | ⊺ᴿ WE | M 450 | ⓢ
★★★*Post House, Queens Dr. Ossett.* T:(0924) 276388. *96rm* ⇌

DIBDEN PURLIEU
Hampshire
Map II   A7

Dibden Southampton Rd (2m NW of Dibden Purlieu)
T:(0703) 845596
Municipal parkland course with views over Southampton Water. A pond guards the green at the par 5, 3rd hole. Societies welcome by arrangement. 18 | 6206 yds | Par 71 | SSS 70
Open to public | •• weekdays WE | B L ♥ | D prior arrangement | ⚹ Ⴤ ∖ | ♪ | ⋈ usually | ⓢ
★★*Pikes Hill Forest Lodge, Pikes Hill, Romsey Rd, Lyndhurst.* T:(042128) 3677. *20rm (11* ⇌ *4* 🍴*)*

DINAS POWIS
South Glamorgan
Map I   G3

Dinas Powis Old High Walls, Dinas Powis (NW side of village)
T:(0222) 512727
Parkland/downland course with views over the Bristol Channel and the seaside resort of Barry. 18 | 5377 yds | Par 66 | SSS 65
Visitors welcome weekdays ⊠ ☎ |

∴ per day | B ♨ (not Th) | L D prior arrangement (not Th) | ⚘ ☂ ⚲ | ④ competitions | ⟦TR⟧ WE (competition days) | ⟧ | M 350 | ⟦S⟧
★★★*Mount Sorrell, Porthkerry Rd, Barry. T:(0446) 740069. 33rm (20 ⇋ 13 ⚐). Annexe: 4rm ⇋*

DISLEY
Cheshire
Map **V** E8

Disley Jacksons Edge, Stanley Hall Ln, Disley (NW side of village off A6)
T:(06632) 2107
Parkland/moorland course with trees and often breezy. Good views. Testing hole: 5th par 5. Societies welcome Mon to F. 18 | 5448 mtrs | Par 69 | SSS 69
Visitors welcome, restricted WE (competitions) | B L ♨ D prior arrangement advisable (not Tu) | ⚘ ☂ ⚲ | ⟧ | ⟦TR⟧ Ladies Day Thu, WE BH | M 380 | ⟦S⟧
★★★*Alma Lodge, 149 Buxton Rd, Stockport. T:061-483 4431. 70rm (53 ⇋)*

DISS
Norfolk
Map **IV** H5

Diss Stuston (1½m SE of Diss on B1118)
T:(0379) 2847
Commonland course with natural hazards. Societies welcome by arrangement. 9 | 5900 yds | Par 69 | SSS 68
Visitors welcome, restricted WE BH | B L ♨ D (not Sun Mon) | ⚘ | ☂ (not Mon) ⚲ | ⟧ | ⋈ ⟦TR⟧ 1630 onwards, WE | M 350 | ⟦S⟧
★★*Scole Inn, Scole. T:(0379) 740481. 8rm (2 ⇋ 2 ⚐) Annexe: 12rm ⇋ ⚐*

DOLGELLAU
Gwynedd
Map **III** D4

Dolgellau Pencefn Rd (¾m N of Dolgellau)
T:(0341) 422603
Undulating parkland course. Ideal course for middle/high handicap players. Good views of mountains and Mawddach estuary. Small societies welcome by arrangement. Children can play golf. 9 | 2310 yds | Par 56 | SSS 62
Visitors welcome | B ♨ | L D prior arrangement | ⚘ ☂ ⚲ | ⋈ prior arrangement | ⟦TR⟧ competition days (usually S) | M 150
★★*Royal Ship. T:(0341) 422209. 23rm (8 ⇋ 1 ⚐)*

DOLLAR
Central, *Clackmannanshire*
Map **VI** F1

Dollar Brewlands House, Dollar (½m N of Dollar off A91)
T:(02594) 2400
Compact hillside course. Societies welcome (Mon to F) by arrangement. 18 | 4692 yds | Par 68 | SSS 63
Visitors welcome, with M only WE | B ♨ (not Th) | L D prior arrangement (not Th) | ⚘ ☂ | ⋈ (usually) | ⟦TR⟧ competition days, usually WE | M 400
★★*King Robert, Glasgow Rd, Bannockburn, Stirling. T:(0786) 811666. 21rm ⇋*

DONCASTER
South Yorkshire
Map **V** G7

Doncaster 278 Bawtry Rd, Bessacarr (5m SE of Doncaster on A638)
T:(0302) 868316

Pleasant undulating heathland course with wooded surroundings, quick drying, ideal autumn, winter and spring. Societies welcome by arrangement. 18 | 6016 yds | Par 69 | SSS 69
Visitors welcome ⋈, with M only at WE | ♨ | B (not Tu) | L D prior arrangement (not Tu) | ⚘ ☂ ⋈ | ⟦TR⟧ WE BH | ⟧ | M 400 | ⟦S⟧
★★*Punch's, Bawtry Rd, Bessacarr. T:(0302) 535235. 25rm (15 ⇋)*

Doncaster Town Moor Neatherd's House, Belle Vue (1½m E of Doncaster at racecourse on A638)
T:(0302) 535286
Easy walking but testing heathland course with good true greens. Friendly club. Notable hole is 11th par 4 474 yds. 18 | 6100 yds | Par 69 | SSS 69
Visitors welcome except Sun am | without M .. weekdays WE | with M .. per day | B ♨ (not Mon) | L D prior arrangement (not Mon) | ⚘ ☂ ⚲ | ⋈ probably ⟦TR⟧ Sat (pm competitions) Sun (am) | ⟧ | M 500 | ⟦S⟧
★★★*Danum Swallow, High St. T:(0302) 62261. 66rm (59 ⇋ 7 ⚐)*

Wheatley Armthorpe Rd, Doncaster (W side of town centre off A18)
T:(0302) 831203
Fairly flat well-bunkered parkland course. Societies welcome (Mon to F) by arrangement. 18 | 6345 yds | Par 72 | SSS 70
Visitors welcome ⋈ or with M | ☎ advisable | without M ∴ per day ∷ WE | with M .. per day WE | B L ♨ D (not Tu) | ⚘ ☂ | ⋈ prior arrangement | ⟧ | ⟦TR⟧ ladies have ➥

DORCHESTER
Dorset
Map I J6

Came Down Came Down (3m S of Dorchester off A354)
T:(030581) 2531
Societies welcome weekdays by arrangement. 18 | 6109 yds | Par 69 | SSS 70
Visitors welcome, restricted Sun BH (am) | ☎ if more than 8 visitors in party
| without M ∴ per day WE | with M ‥ per day | B ☛ | L D prior arrangement
(not F) | ⚘ Υ ↘ | ④ not before 1000 on 1st tee, 1215 and 1300 on 1st tee | TR
Sun some Tu and S | J | M 621 | S
***King's Arms, Dorchester.* T:(0305) 65353. 27rm (23 ⇆)
Scene of the West of England Championships on several occasions,
this fine course lies on a high plateau commanding glorious views
over Portland. Three par 5 holes add interest to a round. The turf is
of the springy downland type and the chalky subsoil quickly drains
after rain.

priority W | M 550 | S
***Earl of Doncaster, Bennetthorpe.*
T:(0302) 61371. 53rm (49 ⇆ 4 🏠)

DORKING
Surrey
Map II E5

Betchworth Park Reigate Rd (1m E
of Dorking on A25)
T:(0306) 882052
Parkland course, with hard walking. 18

| 6244 yds | Par 69 | SSS 70
Visitors welcome, restricted Tu am,
with M only WE BH | ☎ | B | ☛ | L
D prior arrangement (not Mon) | ⚘
Υ ↘ | TR ④ ☎ for details | J |
M 800 | S
***White Horse, High St.* T:(0306)
881138. 36rm ⇆ 🏠. Annexe: 32rm ⇆

Dorking Chart Park (1m S of
Dorking on A24)
T:(0306) 889786

*Dry undulating parkland course, easy
slopes, wind-sheltered. Testing holes:
5th Tom's Puddle (par 4) 7th Rest and
Be Thankful (par 4) 9th Double Decker
(par 4). Small societies welcome by
arrangement.* 9 | 5106 yds | Par 66 |
SSS 65
Visitors welcome, not WE BH | ☎
preferred | B ☛ prior arrangement
(not Mon) | L D prior arrangement
(WE only) | ⚘ Υ ↘ | TR WE;
0900-1000 W (ladies day) | J | M 300
| S
****Burford Bridge, Burford Bridge,*
Box Hill. T:(0306) 884561. 48rm ⇆

DORNOCH
Highland, *Sutherland*
Map VII G3

Royal Dornoch Golf Rd, Dornoch
(E side of town)
T:(0862) 810219
*Very challenging seaside links. Societies
welcome (not July August).* 18 |
6577 yds | Par 70 | SSS 72
Visitors welcome ☎ beforehand | B
L ☛ High Tea (not Mon) | ⚘ Υ
(1100-1430, 1700-2300) ↘ ✕ | ④
until 0945 (also three balls) | M 730 |

$\boxed{S}$
****Dornoch Castle, Castle St. T:(0862)
810216. 20rm (15 ⇌ 3 🛏)**

DOUGLAS
Isle of Man
Map **V** A6

Pulrose (1m W of Douglas off A1)
T:(0624) 75952
*Hilly mainly moorland course under
the control of Douglas Corporation. 18 |
6080 yds | Par 70 | SSS 69*
Visitors welcome | B L 🍸 (May to
Sept) | D prior arrangement (May to
Sept) | ⚖ 🍸 ⟍ | ⋈ limited ⎡TR⎤
before 0900 | 🍴 | M 430 | $\boxed{S}$
**Woodbourne, Alexander Dr. T:(0624)
21766. 12rm*

DOWNE
Kent
Map **II** F4

High Elms High Elms Rd (1½m NE
of Downe)
T:(0689) 58175
*Municipal parkland course. Very tight
13th-230 yds (par 3). 18 | 6340 yds |
Par 71 | SSS 70*
Open to public .. per day WE | B
prior arrangement | ⚖ 🍸 ⟍ ⋈
***Sevenoaks Park, Seal Hollow Rd,
Seal, Sevenoaks. T:(0732) 454245.
16rm (3 ⇌ 3 🛏)*

West Kent West Hill Downe (¾m
SW of Downe)
T:(0689) 51323
*Partly hilly downland course. 18 |
6392 yds | Par 70 | SSS 70*
Visitors welcome ⋈, not WE BH |
🕾 advisable | without M :: per day
| with M .. per day | B L 🍸 | ⚖ 🍸 |
🍴 | ⎡TR⎤ WE BH | M 800 | $\boxed{S}$
****Bromley Court, Bromley Hill,
Bromley. T:01-464 5011. 130rm ⇌*

DRIFFIELD, GREAT
Humberside
Map **V** H5

Driffield Sunderlandwick (2m S of
Great Driffield off A164)
T:(0377) 43116
*An easy walking parkland course. 9 |
6202 yds | Par 70 | SSS 70*
Visitors are welcome without M | L
D B (not Mon) 🍸 | ⚖ 🍸 | $\boxed{S}$ M 320 |
⎡TR⎤ WE
***🍴Wold House, Nafferton. T:(0377)
44242. 11rm (3 ⇌ 3 🛏)*

DROITWICH
Hereford and Worcester
Map **III** H6

Droitwich Ford Ln (1½m N of
Droitwich off A38)
T:(0905) 774344/770207
*Parkland course. 18 | 6036 yds | Par 70
| SSS 69*
Visitors welcome | 🕾 advisable |
without M ∴ per day | with M ..
per day WE | B L 🍸 (not Mon) | D
prior arrangement (not Mon) | ⚖ 🍸
| ⎡TR⎤ WE | 🍴 | M 730 | $\boxed{S}$
*****Château Impney. T:(0905)
774411. 67rm (63 ⇌ 4 🛏)*

DRONFIELD
Derbyside
Map **III** K2

Hallowes Hallowes Lane, Dronfield
(S side of town)
T:(0246) 413734
*Attractive moorland course set in the
Derbyshire hills. Several testing Par 4s
and splendid views. 18 | 6342 yds |
Par 71 | SSS 71*
Visitors welcome 🕾 ⋈ | without M
∴ per day | with M .. per day WE |
B L 🍸 D prior arrangement (not
Mon) | ⚖ 🍸 ⟍ | ⋈ | ⎡TR⎤ 🕾 for
details | 🍴 | M 500 | $\boxed{S}$
***Manor, 10 High St, Dronfield.
T:(0246) 413971. 10rm (1 ⇌ 9 🛏)*

DRYMEN
Central, *Stirlingshire*
Map **VI** D2

Buchanan Castle Drymen (1m W of
Drymen)
T:(0360) 60307
*Parkland course, with easy walking and
good views. 18 | 6032 yds | Par 68 |
SSS 69*
Visitors welcome 🕾 ⋈ or with M |
restricted WE | B L 🍸 D prior
arrangement | ⚖ 🍸 ⟍ | ④ ⎡TR⎤ as
required | 🍴 | M 850 | $\boxed{S}$
****Buchanan Arms. T:(0360) 60588.
35rm ⇌ 🛏*

Strathendrick Drymen, Glasgow (S
side of village off A811)
*Attractive parkland course. 9 | 5063 yds
| Par 66 | SSS 65*
Visitors welcome with M only,
restricted competition days | M 300
****Buchanan Arms. T:(0360) 60588.
35rm ⇌*

DUDLEY
Northumberland
Map **VI** K6

Arcot Hall Dudley, Cramlington
(2m SW of Cramlington, off A1)
T:(091) 2362794
*A wooded parkland course, reasonably
flat. 18 | 6389 yds | Par 70 | SSS 70*
Visitors welcome, restricted
competition days | without M ∴
per day WE | with M .. per day | B
L 🍸 D prior arrangement (not Mon)
| ⚖ 🍸 ⟍ | ⋈ | ⎡TR⎤ 1300-1400 and
1700-1800 (F 1300-1500) | 🍴 | M 620 |
$\boxed{S}$
*****Holiday Inn, Gt North Rd,
Seaton Burn. T: Tyneside (091) 236
5432. 150rm ⇌ 🛏*

DUDLEY
West Midlands
Map **III** H5

Blackhill Wood Bridgnorth Rd,
Swindon (5m W of Dudley on
B4176)
T:(0902) 892279
*Parkland course with coniferous forest.
18 | 5987 yds | Par 70 | SSS 69*
Visitors welcome B L 🍸 D | ⚖ 🍸
⟍ | ⋈ | ⎡TR⎤ WE | M 575 | $\boxed{S}$
****Goldthorn, Penn Rd,
Wolverhampton. T:(0902) 29216. 70rm
(62 ⇌ 4 🛏) Annexe: 16rm (8 ⇌ 3 🛏)*

Dudley Turner's Hill, Dudley
(1½m SE of town centre off B4171)
T:(0384) 54020
*Exposed and very hilly parkland course.
18 | 6000 yds | Par 68 | SSS 67*
Visitors welcome with M only,
restricted W pm | B L 🍸 D prior
arrangement | ⚖ 🍸 ⟍ | ④ WE | ⎡TR⎤
WE | 🍴 | M 300 | $\boxed{S}$
***Station, Birmingham Rd. T:(0384)
53418. 29rm (9 ⇌ 2 🛏)*

DUFFIELD
Derbyshire
Map **III** K3

Chevin Golf Ln, Duffield (N side of
town, off A6)
T:(0332) 841864
*A mixture of parkland and moorland,
this course is rather hilly which makes
for some hard walking. The 8th calls for
a very hard drive, possibly the hardest
in the area. 18 | 6046 yds | Par 69 |
SSS 69*
Visitors welcome 🕾 advisable |
with M only WE BH | B 🍸 (not ➡

Mon) | L D prior arrangement (not Mon) | ⌂ ♈ | TR WE BH (☎ for details) | ♓ | M 500 | S
★★★*Pennine, Macklin St, Derby.*
T:(0332) 41741. 100rm (56 ⇌ 44 🍴)

DUFFTOWN
Grampian, *Banffshire*
Map **VII** H5

Dufftown (¾m SW of Dufftown off B9009)
T:(0340) 20325
Hilly heathland course with good views. Highest hole over 1000 ft above sea level. It is hard to play to handicap here. 9 | 4556 yds | Par 64 | SSS 63
Visitors welcome | .. per day WE | ⌂ | ♈ evngs only | TR Tu W 1730-2000 | ✕ | M 150
★★★**♨**Rothes Glen, Rothes. T:(03403) 254. 16rm (13 ⇌)

DUMBARTON
Strathclyde, *Dumbartonshire*
Map **VI** D2

Dumbarton Broadmeadow, Dumbarton (¼m N of Dumbarton off A814)
T:(0389) 32830
Flat parkland course. Testing holes: 4th (par 4), 15th (par 5). Societies welcome by arrangement. 18 | 5981 yds | Par 71 | SSS 69
Visitors welcome weekdays, restricted WE BH | without M ∴ per day | with M .. per day | ♛ lunchtime only | B L not Tu | D prior arrangement | ⌂ ♈ | ✕ prior arrangement | ④ TR WE BH | M 700
★★★*Lomond Castle, Arden.*
T:(038985) 681. 21rm (16 ⇌ 5 🍴)

DUMFRIES
Dumfries and Galloway, *Dumfries*
Map **VI** F6

Dumfries & County Edinburgh Rd (1m NE of Dumfries off A701)
T:(0387) 53585
Parkland course. Society meetings by arrangement. 18 | 5928 yds | Par 69 | SSS 68
Visitors welcome, restricted competition days | without M ∴ per day WE | with M .. per day WE | B L ♛ (high tea also available) | ⌂ ♈ ✓ | TR 1200-1400 weekdays, before 1000, 1200-1400 WE | ♓ | M 800 | S
★★★*Station, 49 Lovers Walk,*

Dumfries. T:(0387) 54316. 30rm (18 ⇌ 12 🍴)

Dumfries & Galloway
2 Lauriston Av, Castle Douglas Rd, Dumfries (W side of town centre on A75)
T:(0387) 63848/3582
Parkland course. 18 | 5782 yds | Par 68 | SSS 68
Visitors welcome, restricted during competitions | without M .. per day ∴ WE | with M .. per day WE | B (not F) | L ♛ prior arrangemnent (not F) | ⌂ ♈ | M 600
★★★*Station, 49 Lovers Walk. T:(0387) 54316. 30rm (18 ⇌ 12 🍴)*

DUNBAR
Lothian, *East Lothian*
Map **VI** H2

Winterfield North Rd, Dunbar (W side of town off A1087)
T:(0368) 63562
Seaside course with superb views. 18 | 5220 yds | SSS 64
Visitors welcome ☎ advisable | B L ♛ D (not Th) prior arrangement | ⌂ ♈ ✓ | TR until 0930, 1200-1330 | M 200 | S
★★*Bayswell, Bayswell Park. T:(0368) 62225. 12rm (11 ⇌ 1 🍴)*

DUNBLANE
Central, *Perthshire*
Map **VI** E1

Dunblane New Golf Club Ltd.
Perth Rd, Dunblane (E side of town on A9)
T:(0786) 823711
Parkland course, with reasonably hard

DUNBAR
Lothian, *East Lothian*
Map **VI** H2

Dunbar East Links, Dunbar (SE side of town off A1087)
T:(0368) 62317
18 | 6426 yds | Par 71 | SSS 71
Visitors welcome, restricted WE | TR WE until 1030 | B L ♛ D prior arrangement (not Tu) | ⌂ ♈ ✓ | ✕ | ♓ | M 620 | S
★★*Bayswell, Bayswell Park. T:(0368) 62225 12rm (11 ⇌ 1 🍴)*

walking. Testing 6th and 9th holes. Party bookings by arrangement. 18 | 5876 yds | Par 69 | SSS 68
Visitors welcome | without M ∴ per day WE | with M .. per day WE | B | L ♛ D prior arrangement | ⌂ ♈ ✓ | ✕ prior arrangement | ④ after 1430, not on competition days | TR until 0930, and from 1300-1400 | ♓ | M 600 | S
❀★★★**♨***Cromlix House, Kinbuck. T:(0786) 822125. 14rm (13 ⇌ 1 🍴)*

DUNDEE
Tayside, *Angus*
Map **VII** H8

Caird Park Mains Loan, Dundee (1½m N of city centre off A972)
T:(0382) 453606
Municipal parkland course. 18 | 6281 yds | Par 72 | SSS 70
Open to public | B ♈ | ✕ | TR WE 0800-0900 | ♓ | M 400 | S
★★*Queen's, 160 Nethergate. T:(0382) 22515. 56rm (11 ⇌ 1 🍴)*

Camperdown Camperdown House, Camperdown Park, Dundee (3m NW of city centre off A923)
T:(0382) 645450
Parkland course. Testing 2nd hole. Societies welcome by arrangement. Other sporting facilities available. 18 | 6561 yds | Par 72 | SSS 72
Visitors welcome, ☎ | B L prior arrangement (not Tu) | ♛ prior arrangement | ⌂ ♈ (not Tu am) | ✓ | TR S Sun am alternately 0800-1000 | ♓ | M 500 | S
★★★*Angus Thistle, 10 Marketgait, Dundee. T:(0382) 26874. 58rm ⇌ 🍴*

SCORE CARD:			
1	476	10	203
2	495	11	422
3	174	12	464
4	349	13	365
5	150	14	515
6	350	15	333
7	387	16	171
8	371	17	340
9	514	18	441

Another of Scotland's old links. It is said that it was some Dunbar members who first took the game of golf to the North of England. The club dates back to 1856, but doubtless golf was played here before that. As with many Scottish courses, a 'burn' or brook comes into play. The wind, if blowing from the sea, is another problem.

9.20 – 11-50 2-18 – 3-42

£30r £45d Tr ?

DUNDEE
Tayside, *Angus*
Map **VII** H8 Ro 889246

Downfield Turnberry Av, Dundee (2½m NW of city centre off A972)
T:(0382) 825595
18 | 6899 yds | Par 73 | SSS 73
Visitors welcome, with M only WE ☎ | ∷ per day | B L ☕ (not Th winter) | D prior arrangement (not Th winter) | ⚠ 🍸 ↘ | ⋈ possible | TR WE also before 0930, 1200-1418, after 1600 weekdays | 🏌 | M 711 | S
★★★*Swallow, Kingsway West, Invergowrie. T:(0382) 641122. 69rm* ⇄
A fine inland course of recent Championship rating set in undulating woodland to the north of Dundee. The Gelly burn provides a hazard for several holes.

DUNSTABLE
Bedfordshire
Map **II** D1

Dunstable Downs Whipsnade Rd (2m S of Dunstable off B4541)
T:(0582) 604472
18 | 6184 yds | Par 70 | SSS 70
Visitors welcome but with M only WE BH | ☎ | without M ∷ per day | with M ∴ per day WE | B L ☕ D prior arrangement (not Mon) | ⚠ 🍸 | ⋈ | TR WE | 🏌 | M 565 | S
★★★*Old Palace Lodge, Church St, Dunstable. T:(0582) 62201. 50rm* ⇄
A fine downland course set on two levels with far-reaching views and frequent sightings of graceful gliders. The 9th hole is one of the best short holes in the country. There is a modernized clubhouse.

DURNFORD, GREAT
Wiltshire
Map **I** K4

High Post Great Durnford, Salisbury (1¾m SE of Great Durnford on A345)
T:(0722) 73231
Societies welcome preferably Mon & F. 18 | 6267 yds | Par 70 | SSS 70
Visitors welcome ☎ preferred | without M ∴ weekdays ∷ WE | with M ‥ weekdays ∴ WE | B ☕ L D | ⚠ 🍸 | 🏌 | ⋈ | M 600 | S
★★★*Rose & Crown, Harnham Rd, Harnham, Salisbury. T:(0722) 27908. 27rm* ⇄ 🏛
An interesting course on Wiltshire chalk with good turf and splendid views over the southern area of Salisbury Plain. The par 3 17th and the two-shot 18th require good judgment.

DUNFERMLINE
Fife, *Fife*
Map **VI** F2

Dunfermline Pitfirrane, Crossford, Dunfermline (2½m W of Dunfermline on A994)
T:(0383) 723534
Parkland course. The clubhouse is an old historic mansion. Parties by arrangement Mon Tu W F. 18 | 6214 yds | Par 71 | SSS 70
Visitors welcome, ☎ or with M | without M ∷ per day | with M ‥ per round | B L D prior arrangement (not Tu) | ☕ (not Tu) | ⚠ 🍸 summer | 🏌 | M 500 | S
★★★*King Malcolm Thistle, Queensferry Rd, Wester Pitcorthie. T:(0383) 722611. 48rm* ⇄ 🏛

Pitreavie Queensferry Rd, Dunfermline (SE side of town on A823)
T:(0383) 722591
Picturesque course with panoramic view of the River Forth Valley. Testing golf. 18 | 6086 yds | Par 70 | SSS 69
Visitors welcome | without M ‥ per round weekdays ∴ per day WE | with M ‥ per day WE | B ☕ L D | ⚠ 🍸 ↘ | TR ④ ☎ for details | 🏌 | M 500 | S
★★★*King Malcolm Thistle, Queensferry Rd, Wester Pitcorthie. T:(0383) 722611. 48rm* ⇄ 🏛

DUNKELD
Tayside, *Perthshire*
Map **VII** G8

Dunkeld & Birnam Fungarth, Dunkeld (E side of village on A923)
T:(03502) 524
Interesting 9 hole heathland course ➡

DURSLEY
Gloucestershire
Map I J2

Stinchcombe Hill Stinchcombe
Hill, Dursley (1m W of Dursley off
A4135)
T:(0453) 2015
18 | 5710 yds | Par 68 | SSS 68
Visitors welcome weekdays | with
M BH WE | without M ∴ weekdays
:: WE | with M .. per day | B ♛ | L
prior arrangement (not Mon) | D
prior arrangement | ⚎ ♈ ↘ | ⋈ | ④
TR ☎ for details | 𝄐 | M 500 | S
∗∗*Old School House, Berkeley Hotel,*
Cannonbury St, Berkeley. T:(0453)
811711. 7rm (2 ⇌ 5 ∰)
High on the hill with spendid views of the Cotswolds, the River
Severn and to the Welsh hills. A downland course with good turf,
some trees and an interesting variety of greens.

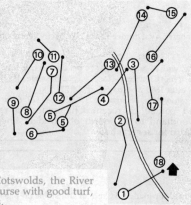

with spectacular views of surrounding
countryside. 9 | 5264 yds | Par 68 |
SSS 66
Visitors welcome | without M ..
per day WE | with M .. per round |
♈ B L ♛ D (April-Oct) | ⚎ (April-
Oct) | TR certain competitions |
M 230 | S
★★★♨*Dunkeld House. T:(03502) 771.*
31rm (25 ⇌ 1 ∰)

DUNOON
Strathclyde, *Argyll*
Map VI C2

Cowal Ardenslate Rd (1m N of
Dunoon)
T:(0369) 5673/2216
Moorland course. Panoramic views of
Clyde Estuary and surrounding hills.
Societies welcome by arrangement. 18 |
5802 yds | Par 70 | SSS 70
Visitors welcome | B ♛ | L D prior
arrangement | ⚎ | ♈ ↘ | ⋈ prior
arrangement | TR weekdays
0900-0930, 1245-1330, 1700-1830;
WE (0800-1000, 1200-1400) | 𝄐 |
M 600 | S
∗∗*Enmore, Marine Pde, Kirn,*
Dunoon. T:(0369) 2230. 13rm (5 ⇌ 3
∰)   See advertisement on page 93.

See advertisement on page 93.

DUNS
Borders, *Berwickshire*
Map VI J3

Duns Longformacus Rd, Duns
(1½m W of Duns off A6105)
Interesting course - natural hazards eg.
water hazards and hilly slopes. 9 |
5826 yds | Par 68 | SSS 68

Visitors welcome | .. per day WE |
♈ | ⚎ ⋈ | TR Tu evng | M 150+
★♨*Chirnside Country House,*
Chirnside. T:(089081) 219. 14rm (3 ∰)

DURHAM
Durham
Map VI K7

Durham City Littleburn, Langley
Moor (1½m S of Durham off A1050)
T:(0385) 780806
Parkland course. 18 | 6070 yds | Par 71
| SSS 69
Visitors welcome | restricted WE BH
| B L ♛ (not Mon) | D prior
arrangement (not Mon Thu or Sun)
| ⚎ ♈ ⋈ | TR competition days,
WE ☎ for details | 𝄐 | M 600 | S
★★★*Three Tuns, New Elvet. T:(0385)*
64326. 54rm ⇌ ∰

Mount Oswald South Rd, Durham
City (1m S of Durham off A1050)
T:(0385) 67527
Parkland course with Georgian
clubhouse. 18 | 6009 yds | Par 71 |
SSS 69
B ♛ L D | ♈ ⚎ ↘ ⋈ | TR |
0800-1000 | M 100
★★★*Bridge, Croxdale, Durham.*
T:(0385) 780524. Annexe: 46rm ⇌ ∰

EAGLESHAM
Strathclyde, *Lanarkshire*
Map VI D3

Bonnyton Eaglesham, Glasgow
(1¼m W of Eaglesham off B764)
T:(03553) 2781
Windy moorland turf course. 18 |

6252 yds | Par 72 | SSS 71
Visitors welcome ☎ ⊠ restricted
WE | ∴ per day | B L ♛ D | ⚎ ♈ |
⋈ by arrangement | TR WE | 𝄐 |
M 500 | S
★★★*Bruce, Cornwall St, East Kilbride.*
T:(03552) 29771. 84rm (32 ⇌ 52 ∰)

EASINGWOLD
North Yorkshire
Map V G5

Easingwold Stillington Rd (1½m SE
of Easingwold)
T:(0347) 21486
Parkland course with easy walking. On
6 holes there are water hazards which
come into play. 18 | 6262 yds | Par 71 |
SSS 70
Visitors welcome with M ⊠ |
without M ∴ per day | WE | with
M .. per day WE | B ♛ | L D prior
arrangement (not M) | ⚎ | ♈ ↘
(limited) | ⋈ (sometimes) | TR
before 0930 and 1245-1430 | M 565 |
S
★★*George, Market Pl. T:(0347)*
21698. 18rm (16 ⇌ 2 ∰)

EASTBOURNE
East Sussex
Map II G7

Eastbourne Downs East Dean
Road, Eastbourne (W side of town
centre on A259)
T:(0323) 20827
Downland/seaside course. 18 | 6684 yds
| Par 71 | SSS 72
Visitors welcome, restricted WE |
without M ∴ per day WE | with M

KEY

- (IA1) *atlas grid reference*
- T: *telephone number*
- ☎ *advance letter/telephone call required*
- ✉ *introduction from own club sec/handicap certificate/club membership card required*
- ·· *low fees*
- ∴ *medium fees*
- ∷ *high fees*
- * *green fees not confirmed for 1987*
- B *light lunch*
- L *full lunch*
- ☕ *tea*
- D *dinner*
- 🚿 *changing rooms/showers*
- 🍸 *bar open mid-day and evenings*
- 🏌 *clubs for hire*
- ⋈ *partners may be found*
- [4] *restricted time for 4 balls*
- [TR] *times reserved for members*
- 👤 *professional*
- [S] *well-stocked shop*
- M *member*
- *Mon Tu W Th F S Sun*
- WE *weekend*
- BH *bank holiday*

EAGLESCLIFFE
Cleveland
Map **V** F3

Eaglescliffe course plan

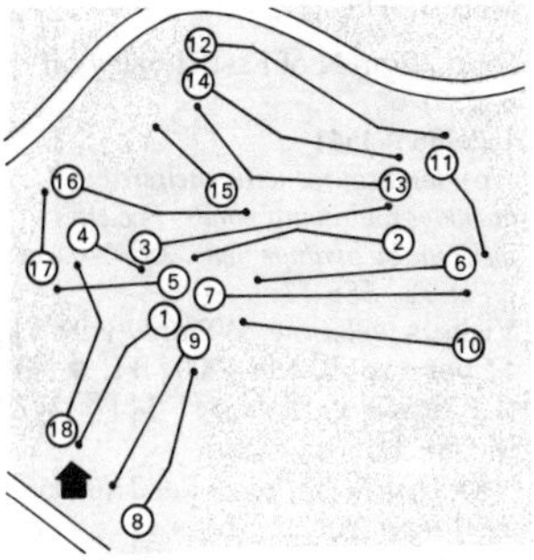

Eaglescliffe and District Yarm Rd, Eaglescliffe (E side of village on A19)
T:(0642) 780098
Societies welcome (Mon to F) by arrangement. 18 | 6275 yds | Par 72 | SSS 69
Visitors welcome restricted Tu and F (1200-1600 Ladies Days) and WE (am) | without M ∴ per day WE | with M ·· per day WE | B | L ☕ D prior arrangement | 🚿 🍸 🏌 | ⋈ | 👤 | [TR] WE am | M 750 | [S]
★★★★*Swallow, 10 John Walker Sq, Stockton-on-Tees. T:(0642) 679721. 127rm* ⇌ 🛁
This hilly course offers both pleasant and interesting golf to all classes of player. It lies in a delightful setting on a rolling plateau shelving to the River Tees. There are fine views to the Cleveland Hills.

EASTBOURNE
East Sussex
Map **II** G7

Royal Eastbourne Paradise Drive, Eastbourne (½m W of town centre)
T:(0323) 29738
Societies welcome by arrangement. Billiard room. 18(9) | 6084 yds (2147) | Par 70(32) | SSS 69 (61)
Visitors welcome ☎ advisable | without M ∴ per day WE | B L (not Mon) ☕ D by arrangement | 👤 [S] 🚿 🍸 🏌 (limited) | [TR] ☎ | [4] after 0930 (Tu after 1400) | M850
★★★*Lansdowne, King Edward's Pde. T:(0323) 25174. 136rm (83* ⇌ *19* 🛁*)*
A famous club within striking distance of its centenary for it dates back to 1887. Sussex has many downland type courses but none with the great tradition of Royal Eastbourne. The course plays longer than it measures, which is always a sign of quality for it means that the holes present many problems. Testing holes are the 8th, a 171-yard par 3 played to a high green and the 16th, a 486-yard par 5 right-hand dog-leg.

·· per day | B ☕ (not Mon) L D | 🚿 🍸 🏌 | ⋈ | [TR] S (until 1000) Sun (until 1100) | M 600 | [S]
★★★★*Cavendish, Grand Pde. T:(0323) 27401. 114rm* ⇌

Willingdon Southdown Rd, Eastbourne (N side of town centre off A22)
T:(0323) 32383
Hilly downland course. Societies welcome (Mon to F) by arrangement. 18 | 6049 yds | Par 69 | SSS 69
Visitors welcome, with M only WE BH | ✉ | without M ∴ per day ∷ WE | with M ·· per day WE | ☕ | B (not Mon WE) | L D prior arrangement | 🚿 🍸 🏌 | ⋈ | 👤 | [4] ☎ for details | M 494 | [S]
★★★*Sandhurst, Grand Pde. T:(0323) 27868. 62rm (35* ⇌ *12* 🛁*)*

EAST COWES
Isle of Wight
Map **II** B7
See also Cowes

Osborne East Cowes (E side of town centre off A3021)
T:(0983) 297758
Undulating parkland course in the grounds of Osborne House. Quiet and peaceful situation. Societies welcome by arrangement. 9 | 6286 yds | Par 70 | SSS 70
Visitors welcome | without M ∴ per day WE | with M ·· per day | 🚿 🍸 🏌 | [TR] Tu 1100-1430 L, Sun before 1200 | 👤 | M 350 | [S]
★★*Padmore House, Beatrice Ave, Whippingham. T:(0983) 293210. 11rm (6* ⇌ *1* 🛁*)*

EASTHAM
Merseyside
Map **V** C8

Eastham Lodge 117 Ferry Rd, Eastham, Wirral (1½m N of Eastham)
T:051-327 1483
A new parkland course. Societies welcome by arrangement, Tu only. 15 | 5826 yds | Par 70 | SSS 68
Visitors welcome with M only WE | without M ∴ per day | with M ·· per day | B ☕ | L D prior arrangement | 🚿 🍸 | 👤 | M 425 | [S]
★★★*Bowler Hat, 2 Talbot Rd, Oxton. T:051-652 4931. 29rm* ⇌

EAST HORSLEY
Surrey
Map II D5

Drift (1½m N of East Horsley off B2039)
T:(04865) 4641
Woodland course with sheltered fairways and many ponds. Societies welcome by arrangement. 18 | 6404 yds | Par 72 | SSS 71
Visitors welcome, WE only with M | :: per day ∴ after 1200 | B L ✿ | D (F S only) | ⚠ ♈ ↘ | ⋈ | 𝄐 | TR WE | M 600 | S
★★★*Thatchers, Epsom Rd. T:(04865) 4291. 6rm. Annexe: 24rm* ⇄

EAST KILBRIDE
Glasgow
Map VI E3

East Kilbride Nerston, East Kilbride (N side of town off A749)
T:(03552) 20913
Parkland course, with hard walking. Very windy. Testing 7th 9th 14th holes. 18 | 6419 yds | Par 71 | SSS 71
Visitors welcome only with M | ∴ per day WE | B (not We) | L D prior arrangement (not WE) | ⚠ ♈ | 𝄐 TR competition days | M 450 | S
★★★*Bruce, Cornwall St. T:(03552) 29771. 84rm (32 ⇄ 52 ▥)*

Torrance House Strathaven Rd, East Kilbride (1½m SE of Kilbride on A726)
T:(03552) 33451
A parkland course. 18 | 6614 yds | Par 72 | SSS 71
Visitors welcome. Booking system - seven days notice required. | Controlled by East Kilbride District Council | ♈ L B ✿ ⚠ 𝄐 S⋈
★★★*Bruce, Cornwall St, East Kilbride. T:(03552) 29771. 84rm (32 ⇄ 52 ▥)*

EAST LEAKE
Nottinghamshire
Map IV A3

Rushcliffe Stocking Lane, East Leake, Nr Nottingham (1m N of East Leake)
T:050-982 2209
Parkland course. Billiards. Societies by arrangement. 18 | 6100 yds | Par 71 | SSS 69
Visitors welcome restricted Tu | without M ∴ per day WE | with M .. per WE | B L ✿ D prior

arrangement | ⚠ ♈ ↘ | M 750 | S
★★★*Novotel Nottingham Derby, Bostock Ln (S of M1 jct 25), Long Eaton. T:(0602) 720106. 112rm* ⇄ ▥

EASTLEIGH
Hampshire
Map II A6

Fleming Park Magpie Ln, Eastleigh (E side of town centre)
T:(0703) 612797
Parkland course with stream 'Monks Brook' running through. Pro interested in teaching the young. 18 | 4436 yds | Par 65 | SSS 62
Visitors welcome | ✳ | B L ✿ D | ⚠ ♈ ↘ | ⋈ | 𝄐 | M 300 | S | TR S am
★★★*Southampton Park, Cumberland Pl, Southampton. T:(0703) 223467. 77rm* ⇄

ECCLESTON
Cheshire
Map III G2

Eaton Chester (1m S of Eccleston)
T:(0244) 671420
A very testing well wooded parkland course. Societies welcome by arrangement. 18 | 6446 yds | Par 72 | SSS 72
Visitors welcome with M or ☎ ✉ | B ✿ | L D prior arrangement (not Mon) | ⚠ | ④ | TR Sun BH (start at 10th tee before 1030 and 1300-1430) | M 433 | S
○○○○*Chester Grosvenor, Eastgate St. T:(0244) 24024. 98rm* ⇄ ▥

EDINBURGH
Map VI G2

Royal Burgess GS181 Whitehouse Rd, Edinburgh (5m W of city centre, off A90)
T:031-339 2075
18 | 6604 yds | Par 71 | SSS 72
Visitors welcome ✉ ☎ WE or Mon to F (pm) | without M :: per day WE | with M .. per day WE | B L ✿ | ⚠ (no ladies' changing room) ♈ ↘ | TR 1200-1400 | ④ not permitted | M 620 | S
★★★*Barnton Thistle, Queensferry Rd, Barnton. T:031-339 1144. 50rm* ⇄ ▥

EDENBRIDGE
Kent
Map II F5

Edenbridge Golf and Country Club Crouch House Rd, Edenbridge (W side of town centre)
T:(0732) 865097
Gently undulating course with a driving range. 18 | 6635 yds | Par 72 | SSS 72
Visitors welcome without M not WE 0800-1000 1st tee | .. per day | 9 hole par 3 course for beginners. Function room for hire | ♈ L D B ✿ | ⚠ S↘ | TR WE 0800-1000 1st tee | M 550
✿○○○▥*Gravetye Manor, Sharpthorne, East Grinstead. T:(0342) 810567. 14rm (12 ⇄ 2 ▥)*

EDINBURGH
Lothian, Midlothian
Map VI G2

Baberton Juniper Green (5m SW of city centre, off A70)
T:031-453 4911
Parkland course. Societies welcome by arrangement. 18 | 6140 yds | Par 69 | SSS 69
Visitors welcome but only with M | ∴ per day | ✉ | B L D ✿ | ⚠ ♈ |
M 800 | S
★★★*Bruntsfield, 69-74 Bruntsfield Pl. T:031-229 1393. 54rm (48 ⇄ 3 ▥)*

Braid Hills Braid Hills Approach, Edinburgh (2½m S of city centre off A702)
T:031-447 6666

SCORE CARD:

1	396	10	385
2	322	11	366
3	440	12	320
4	465	13	205
5	174	14	395
6	484	15	435
7	440	16	482
8	169	17	454
9	420	18	252

No mention of golf clubs would be complete without mention of the Royal Burgess which was instituted in 1735, thus being the oldest golfing society in the world. Its course is a pleasant parkland, and one with much variety. A club which all those interested in the history of the game should visit.

Municipal heathland course with good views of Edinburgh and the Firth of Forth. 18 | 5731 yds | Par 70 | SSS 68 Open to public except S morning and evenings | B ☎ | ♨ ↘ | 🏌 | Ⓢ ★★★Braid Hills, 134 Braid Rd, Braid Hills. T:031-447 8888. 68rm (47 ⇄ 21 ⏴)

Bruntsfield Links 32 Barnton Av, Davidsons Mains, Edinburgh (4m NW of city centre off A90) T:031-336 2006 Parkland course with good views of Forth Estuary. 4th and 14th holes testing. 18 | 6407 yds | Par 71 | SSS 71 Visitors welcome ☎ ✉ or with M | restricted Mon F WE BH | ✳ | L☎ | D Tu-Th summer only | ♨ 🏌 ↘ | TR ☎ for details | 🏌 | M 600 | Ⓢ ★★★Barnton Thistle, Queensferry Rd, Barnton. T:031-339 1144. 50rm ⇄ ⏴

Carrick Vale Carricknowe Municipal, Glendevon Park, Edinburgh (3m W of city centre, S of A8) T:031-337 1932 Flat parkland course suitable for beginners. 18 | 6299 yds | Par 71 | SSS 70 Visitors welcome | 🏌 B ☎ | L D prior arrangement | ↘ ✉ | M 400 | TR WE am | ✉ for bookings ★★★Post House, Corstorphine Rd. T:031-334 8221. 207rm ⇄

Craigmillar Park Observatory Rd, Edinburgh (2m S of city centre, off A7) T:031-667 2837 Parkland course, with good view. 18 | 5846 yds | Par 70 | SSS 68

Visitors welcome without M ∴ per day WE | with M ‥ per day WE | B L ☎ (not Tu) D | ♨ 🏌 ↘ | ✉ | TR club medals | M 650 | Ⓢ ★★★Donmaree, 21 Mayfield Gdns. T:031-667 3641. 9rm (4 ⇄ 5 ⏴) Annexe: 8rm (3 ⇄ 2 ⏴)

Dalmahoy Country Club Kirknewton, Edinburgh, Lothian (7m W of city centre on A71) T:031-333 2055/1436 Two upland courses-one championship (East). 18 | 6664 (East) 5212 (West) yds | Par 72 (East) 67 (West) | SSS 72 (East) 66 (West) Visitors welcome | B L ☎ D | ♨ 🏌 ↘ | ✉ | ④ WE (or for parties) | 🏌 | M 700 | Ⓢ ★★★Post House, Corstorphine Rd, Edinburgh. T:031-334 8221. 207rm ⇄

Duddingston Duddingston Rd West, Edinburgh (2½m SE of city centre off A1) T:031-661 7688/1005 Parkland semi-seaside course, with burn as a natural hazard. Testing 11th hole. Easy walking and windy. View. 18 | 6647 yds | Par 72 | SSS 72 Visitors welcome, ☎ no visiting parties after 1530 | without M ‥ per day WE ∴ per round | party by prior arrangement ∴ per day/round | B (not Mon) | L ☎ D prior arrangement (not Mon) | ♨ 🏌 ↘ | ✉ ④ not permitted | TR before 0900 | 🏌 | M 700 | Ⓢ ★★★Donmaree, 21 Mayfield Gdns. T:031-667 3641. 9rm (4 ⇄ 5 ⏴) Annexe: 8rm (3 ⇄ 2 ⏴)

Kingsknowe Lanark Rd, Edinburgh (4m SW of city centre on A70) T:031-441 1145 Hilly parkland course with prevailing SW winds. Society meetings by arrangement. 18 | 5966 yds | Par 69 | SSS 68/69 Visitors welcome ☎ advisable restricted WE | without M ∴ per day WE | with M ‥ per day WE | B ☎ | L | ♨ 🏌 ↘ ✉ | ④ if course is busy | TR WE | 🏌 | M 700 | Ⓢ ★★★Bruntsfield, 69-74 Bruntsfield Pl, Edinburgh. T:031-229 1393. 54rm (48 ⇄ 3 ⏴)

Liberton 297 Gilmerton Rd, Edinburgh (3m SE of city centre on A7) T:031-664 3009 Undulating wooded parkland course. 18 | 5299 yds | Par 67 | SSS 66 Visitors welcome ∴ per day ∷ WE | B L ☎ | ♨ 🏌 | ✉ | ④ TR ☎ for details | 🏌 | M 700 | Ⓢ ★★★Donmaree, 21 Mayfield Gdns, Edinburgh. T:031-667 3641. 9rm (4 ⇄ 5 ⏴). Annexe: 8rm (3 ⇄ 2 ⏴)

Lothianburn Biggar Rd, Edinburgh (4½m S of city centre on A702) T:031-445 2206 Hilly with a 'T' shaped wooded-area on the course in the Pentland foothills. Sheep on course. 18 | 5671 yds | Par 71 | SSS 69 Visitors welcome | ‥ per day ∴ WE | B L ☎ | ♨ 🏌 | 🏌 | TR WE 1700-1900 | Ⓢ ★★★Braid Hills, 134 Braid Rd, Braid Hills. T:031-447 8888. 68rm (47 ⇄ 21 ⏴)

EDZELL
Tayside, *Angus*
Map VII   J7

Edzell (S side of village on B966)
T:(03564) 235
18 | 6300 yds | Par 71 | SSS 70
Visitors welcome ☎ | ✳ | B L ♥ D prior arrangement (not Tu) | ♨ ♈ ⚲ ⋈ | ④
WE | TR Mon-F 1700-1815, WE 0800-0930, 1200-1400 | ♩ | M 450 | S
★★★*Glen Esk, High St. T:(03564) 319. 25rm (14 ⇄ 6 🛏)*
This delightful course is situated in the foothills of the Scottish
highlands and provides good golf as well as conveying to everyone
who plays there a feeling of peace and quiet. The village of Edzell is
one of the most picturesque in Scotland.

EFFINGHAM
Surrey
Map II   E5

Effingham Guildford Rd, Effingham (W side of village on A246)
T:(0372) 52203
18 | 6488 yds | Par 71 | SSS 71
Visitors welcome weekdays ☎ with M only WE BH with or without M ∴ per
day | B L ♥ | ♨ ♈ ⚲ | ④ on certain tees ☎ | TR 0800-0830, WE, BH | ♩ |
M 1190 | S
★★★*Thatchers, Epsom Rd, East Horsley. T:(04865) 4291. 6rm ⇄. Annexe: 24rm ⇄*
Easy walking downland course laid out on 270 acres with tree-lined
fairways. It is one of the longest of the Surrey courses with subtle
greens that provide a provocative but by no means
exhausting challenge. Facilities include 4 tennis courts and 2 squash
courts.

Merchants of Edinburgh 10
Craighill Gdns, Edinburgh (2m S of
city centre off A702)
T:031-447 1219
*Testing hill course. Limited number of
societies by arrangement. 18 | 4938 yds
| Par 64 | SSS 65*
Visitors welcome with M only | ∴
per day WE | B L D ♥ | ♨ ♈ | TR
WE | M 650
★★★*Braid Hills, 134 Braid Rd,
Braid Hills. T:031-447 8888. 68rm (47
⇄ 21 🛏)*

Mortonhall Braid Rd, Edinburgh
(3m S of city centre off A702)
T:031-447 2411
*Moorland course with views over
Edinburgh. Societies welcome by
arrangement. 18 | 6557 yds | Par 72 |
SSS 71*
Visitors welcome ☎ advisable WE |
✳ | ♥ B L | ♨ ♈ ⚲ | M 500 | S
★★★*Braid Hills, 134 Braid Rd,
Braid Hills. T:031-447 8888. 68rm (47
⇄ 21 🛏)*

Murrayfield Murrayfield Rd,
Edinburgh (2m W of city centre off
A8)

T:031-337 1009
*Parkland course with fine views. 18 |
5724 yds | Par 70 | SSS 68*
Visitors welcome with member or,
restricted WE | ⊠ ☎ first | B L ♥
(not Sun) | ♨ ♈ | ♩ | M 750 | S
★★★*Post House, Corstophine Rd.
T:031-334 8221. 207rm ⇄*

Portobello Stanley St, Edinburgh
(3m E of city centre, off A1)
T:031-669 4361
*Public parkland course, easy walking. 9
| 2405 yds | Par 32 | SSS 32*
Visitors welcome, no Sun play | ∴
per round | ⋈ (possible) | TR S
★★★*Donmaree, 21 Mayfield Gdns.
T:031-667 3641. 9rm (4⇄ 5 🛏)*

Prestonfield Priestfield Rd North,
Edinburgh (1½m S of city centre off
A68)
T:031-667 1273
*Parkland course with beautiful views.
18 | 6216 yds | Par 70 | SSS 70*
Visitors welcome | ∴ per day WE |
B L ♥ | ♨ ♈ ⚲ | TR S not
between 1200-1530, Sun not before
1130 | M 500 | S
★★★*Donmaree, 21 Mayfield Gdns,*

*Edinburgh. T:031-667 3641. 9rm (4 ⇄
5 🛏). Annexe: 8rm (3 ⇄ 2 🛏)*

Ravelston 24 Ravelston Dykes Rd.
Edinburgh (3m W of city centre, off
A90)
T:031-332 4630
*Parkland course. 9 | 5322 yds | Par 66 |
SSS 66*
Visitors welcome | ♥ B | ♨ | S | ⋈ |
M 540 | TR WE
★★★*Crest, Queensferry Rd. T:031-332
2442. 120rm ⇄*

Silverknowes Silverknowes,
Parkway, Edinburgh (4m NW of
city centre, N of A902)
T:031-336 3483
*Links course on coast overlooking the
Firth of Forth. 18 | 6210 yds | Par 72 |
SSS 71*
Visitors welcome | B ♥ | ♨ ♈ ⚲ |
M 500
★★*Murrayfield, 18 Corstorphine Rd.
T:031-337 1844. 22rm (7 ⇄ 2 🛏)*

Swanston Swanston Rd,
Fairmilehead, Edinburgh (4m S of
city centre, off B701)
T:031-445 2239
*Hillside course with steep climb at
12th, 13th holes. Children's TV room.
18 | 5024 yds | Par 66 | SSS 65*
Visitors welcome, (no parties at
WE, ☎) | ∴ per day ‥ per round
‥ per day WE | B ♥ L | D prior
arrangement | ♨ ♈ | TR club
competitions | M 400
★★★*Braid Hills, 134 Braid Rd,
Braid Hills. T:031-447 8888. 68rm (47
⇄ 21 🛏)*

Torphin Hill Torphin Rd, Colinton,
Edinburgh (5m SW of city centre, S
of A720)
T:031-441 1100
*Beautiful hillside course. Societies
welcome (Mon to F) by arrangement.
18 | 5030 yds | Par 67 | SSS 66*
Visitors welcome, restricted Mon to
F (1700-1830) Sun (am) | ‥ per day
∴ WE | B L ♥ D (not Th) | ♨ ♈ ⋈ |
M 450
★★★*Braid Hills, 134 Braid Rd,
Braid Hills. T:031-447 8888. 68rm (47
⇄ 21 🛏)*

Turnhouse Turnhouse Rd,
Edinburgh (6m W of city centre, N
of A8)
T:031-339 1014
*Parkland/heathland course, good views.
18 | 6171 yds | Par 69 | SSS 69*

Visitors welcome, not WE ☎ | without M ∴ per day | with M .. per day | B ☞ | L D prior arrangement (not Mon) | ⏃ ⏆ ⤳ ⋈ | ✴ | TR competition W S | M 500 | S

★★★*Barnton Thistle, Queensferry Rd, Barnton. T:031-339 1144. 50rm ⇄ ⋔*

ELLAND
West Yorkshire
Map **V** E6

Elland Hammerstones, Leach Ln (1m SW of Elland)
T:(0422) 72505
Parkland course. 9 | 2763 yds | Par 66 | SSS 67

£13 £19

Elgin Hardhillock, Birnie Rd, New Elgin, Elgin (1m S of Elgin off A941)
T:(0343) 2338   0343 542338
Society meetings, preferably Mon to F, by arrangement. 18 | 6401 yds | Par 69 | SSS 71
Visitors welcome ☎ restricted competition days | without M ∴ per day WE | with M .. per day WE | B L ☞ prior arrangement (not Tu) D (not Tu Th) | ⏃ ⏆ ⤳ | ⋈ possible | ✴ | M 790 | S
★★★⚑*Rothes Glen, Rothes. T:(03403) 254. 16rm (13 ⇄)*
Possibly the finest inland course in the north of Scotland, with undulating greens and compact holes that demand the highest accuracy. There are 13 par 4 and 1 par 5 holes.

ELIE
Fife, *Fife*
Map **VI** H1

Golf House Club Elie (W side of village off A917)
T:(0333) 330 301
18 | 6241 yds | Par 70 | SSS 70
Visitors welcome | ✱ | B L ☞ | ⏃ ⏆ ⤳ | TR ☎ for details | ✴ | M 450 | S
★★*Golf, Bank St, Elie. T:(0333) 330209. 22rm (9 ⇄ 6 ⋔)*
One of Scotland's most delightful holiday courses and a great favourite with visitors. The course has panoramic views over the Firth of Forth. Some of the holes out towards the rocky coastline are splendid. This is the course which has produced many good professionals, including the immortal James Braid.

Visitors welcome | without M .. per day WE | with M .. per day WE | B L ☞ D prior arrangement (not W) | ⏃ ⏆ | ⋈ | ④ TR S afternoons | M 240 | S
★★★*Ladbroke (& Conferencentre), Ainley Top, Huddersfield. T:(0422) 75431. 118rm ⇄ ⋔*

ELLESMERE PORT
Cheshire
Map **III** G2

Ellesmere Port Chester Rd, Hooton (NW side of town centre on A41)
T:051-339 7689
Municipal parkland course with natural hazards of woods, brook and ponds. Greens set inside on many holes. 17th hole is good par 3. Children welcome accompanied by adult. 18 | 6432 yds | Par 71 | SSS 71
Visitors welcome ☎ | restricted WE BH | .. per round WE | B L D ☞ | ⏃ ⏆ ⤳ | TR WE 0700-0830 | ✴ | M 300+ | S
★★★*Ladbroke, Backford Cross Rdbt. T:(0244) 851551. 121rm ⇄ ⋔*

ELLON
Grampian, Aberdeenshire
Map **VII** K5

McDonald Hospital Rd (¼m N of Ellon on A948)
T:(0358) 20576
Tight parkland course with streams and a pond. 18 | 5986 yds | Par 70 | SSS 69
Visitors welcome .. per day ∴
WE | B L ☞ D | ⏃ ⏆ | ⤳ ⋈ prior arrangement | TR Sun medals, Tu 1530-1830 | ④ medal competitions | M 710
★*Buchan, Ellon. T:(0358) 20208. 17rm (1 ⋔)*

ELSHAM
Humberside
Map **V** H7

Elsham Barton Rd, South Humberside (2m SW of Elsham on B1206)
T:(0652) 680291
Parkland course, easy walking. No facilities for children. 18 | 6500 yds | Par 71 | SSS 71
Visitors welcome with M only WE BH ⋈ | without M ∴ per day | with M .. per day | B L ☞ D prior arrangement | ⏃ ⏆ ⤳ | ⋈ | TR WE | ✴ | M 600 | S
★★★*Wortley House, Rowland Rd, Scunthorpe. T:(0724) 842223. 28rm ⇄*

ELY
Cambridgeshire
Map **IV** F5

Ely City Cambridge Rd, Ely (SW side of city centre on A10)
T:(0353) 2751
Parkland course with water hazards formed of lakes and natural dykes. Testing 13th hole (par 3). Societies welcome by arrangement. 18 | 6686 yds | Par 72 | SSS 72
Visitors welcome ☎ advisable | with or without M ∴ per day ∷ WE | Full bar and restaurant facilities | ⚐ | ⅃ | M 750 | Ⓢ
★★★*Fenlands Lodge, Soham Rd, Stuntney. T:(0353) 67047.*
Annexe: 9rm ⇌ 🍽

EMBLETON
Alnwick, *Northumberland*
Map **VI** K4

Dunstanburgh Castle Golf Course
(1m NE of Embleton)
T:(066576) 562
Rolling links with Castle and Bird Sanctuary either side, superb views. 15 | 5817 mtrs | Par 70 | SSS 70
Visitors welcome without M | ∴ per day | L D B ☂ | ⚐ Ⓨ | Ⓣ Sun until 0830 | M 150
★★*Dunstanburgh Castle, Embleton. T:(066576) 203. 17rm (9 ⇌)*

ENFIELD
Greater London
Map **II** F2

Crews Hill Cattlegate Rd, Crews Hill (3m NW of Enfield, off A1005)
T:01-363 6674
Parkland course in country surroundings. Societies welcome by arrangement. 18 | 6230 yds | Par 70 | SSS 70
Visitors welcome, with M only WE

⊠ ☎ | without M ∷ per day ∴ per round | B ☂ (not Mon) | L D prior arrangement (not Mon) | ⚐ Ⓨ | ④ Mon-F (before 0900) F (1400-1600) | Ⓣ WE | ④ ☎ | ⅃ | M 500 | Ⓢ
★★★*Royal Chace, The Ridgeway, Enfield. T:01-366 6500. 92rm (51 ⇌ 41 🍽)*

Enfield Old Park Rd South, Windmill Hill (W side of town centre off A110)
Parkland course, Salmons Brook crosses 7 holes. Saxon Moat ancient monument. Societies welcome by arrangement. 18 | 6123 yds | Par 72 | SSS 70
Visitors welcome weekdays ⊠ ☎ | ∷ per day | ∴ per round | B L prior arrangement | ☂ ⚐ Ⓨ | ⟍ | ⅃ | M 650 | Ⓢ
★★★*Royal Chace, The Ridgeway, Enfield. T:01-366 6500. 92rm (51 ⇌ 41 🍽)*

Enfield Municipal Beggars Hollow, Clay Hill, Enfield (N side of town centre)
T:01-363 4454
Municipal flat wooded parkland course. 9th hole is a left-hand dog leg with second shot over a brook. 18 | 5881 yds | Par 68 | SSS 68
Open to public | Club facilities only with M
★★★*Royal Chace, The Ridgeway, Enfield. T:01-366 6500. 92rm (51 ⇌ 41 🍽)*

ENMORE
Somerset
Map **I** G4

Enmore Park (1m E of Enmore)
T:(0278) 67481
Parkland course on foothills of Quantocks. Wooded countryside and

views of Quantocks and Mendips. 1st & 10th are testing holes. Societies welcome on weekdays. 18 | 6423 yds | Par 71 | SSS 71
Visitors restricted at WE | B ☂ (not Mon) L D | ⚐ Ⓨ ⟍ | ⋈ probably | ⅃ | Ⓣ ☎ advised | M 600 | Ⓢ
★★⚑⚑*Alfoxton Park, Holford. T:(027874) 211. 16rm (15 ⇌).*
Annexe: 2 ⇌

ENVILLE
Staffordshire
Map **III** H5

Enville Highgate Common, Enville, nr Stourbridge (2m NE of Enville)
T:(0384) 872551
Easy walking on two fairly flat parkland/moorland courses - the Highgate and the Lodge. Societies welcome by arrangement. 36 | 6541(6207) yds | Par 72(70) | SSS 72(70)
Visitors welcome weekdays | ☎ advisable | B L ☂ D | ⚐ Ⓨ | Ⓣ WE Thu am Ladies day (Highgate course) | ⅃ | M 750 | Ⓢ
★★*Talbot, High St, Stourbridge. T:(0384) 394350. 21rm (6 ⇌ 1 🍽)*

EPSOM
Surrey
Map **II** E4

Epsom Longdown Ln South, Epsom Downs, Epsom (SE side of town centre on B288)
T:(03727) 21666
Downland course. Small societies welcome (not WE) by arrangement. 18 | 5290 yds | Par 67 | SSS 66
Visitors welcome, WE not before 1100 | ∴ per round weekdays ∴ per round WE | visitors - Yellow tees only - for men. Red tees only - for ladies | ⚐ | Ⓨ (not Mon) B | ④ after 0830 Ⓣ Tu (0830-1200) ladies and WE | ⅃ | M 600 | Ⓢ
★★★*Ladbroke Seven Hills, Seven Hills Rd, Cobham. T:(0932) 64471. 90rm ⇌*
Annexe: 25rm ⇌

ESHER
Surrey
Map **II** E4

Moore Place Portsmouth Rd, Esher (SW side of town centre on A244)
T:(0372) 63533
Public course on attractive undulating parkland laid out 60 years ago by Harry Vardon. Examples of most of the trees

that will survive in the UK are to be found on the course. Testing short holes at 4th, 5th and 7th. 9 | 3512 yds | Par 58 | SSS 58
Open to public | .. per day | B L D (☎ to check) | ᴧ ꠸ ꜀ | ⋈ sometimes | M 100 | ꒯ | Ⓢ
★★★*Ship Thistle, Monument Gdn, Weybridge. T:(0932) 48364. 39rm* ⇋ 🛏

Sandown Golf Centre Sandown Park, More Ln, Esher (1m NE of Esher off A307)
T:(0372) 63340
Parkland course. Additional facilities include a driving range, and a pitch and putt course. 9 | 2950 yds | Par 70 | SSS 67
Visitors welcome, restricted WE BH | .. per round | B L ♛ | ᴧ ꠸ ꜀ ⋈ | M 300 | Ⓢ
★★★*Ladbroke Seven Hills, Seven Hills Rd, Cobham. T:(0932) 64471. 90rm* ⇋ *Annexe: 25rm* ⇋

Thames Ditton & Esher Marquis of Granby, Portsmouth Rd, Esher (1m NE of Esher on A307)
T:01-398 1551
Easy walking commonland course without bunkers. 9(18) | 5400 yds | Par 64 | SSS 65
Visitors welcome except Su (am) | B L ♛ | ᴧ ꠸ ⋈ | ④ S mornings | TR Sun am | M 300 | Ⓢ
★★*Haven, Portsmouth Rd. T:01-398 0023. 16rm (2* ⇋ *4* 🛏). *Annexe: 4rm (2* ⇋ *2* 🛏)

ESSENDON
Hertfordshire
Map **II** E2

P L London Bedwell Park, Essendon, Hatfield (1m S of Essendon off B158)
T:(0707) 42624
Parkland course with many varied hazards, including ponds, a stream and a ditch. Nineteenth century manor clubhouse. 18 | 6878 yds | Par 72 | SSS 73
Visitors welcome | ☎ advisable WE | L ♛ | ᴧ ꠸ ꜀ | Ⓢ
★★★*Comet, 301 St Albans Rd West, Hatfield. T:(07072) 65411. 57rm (53* ⇋ *2* 🛏)

EXETER
Devon
Map **I** F5

Exeter Topsham Rd, Countess Wear, Exeter (SE side of city centre off A379)
T:(039287) 4139
A sheltered parkland course known as the flattest course in Devon. 15th & 17th are testing par 4 holes. Facilities for tennis, swimming, squash, snooker. Societies welcome by arrangement. 18 | 5205 yds | Par 68 | SSS 68
Visitors welcome ☎ ⊠ | ∴ per day | B ♛ | L D prior arrangement | ᴧ ꠸ ꜀ | TR competition days | ꒯ | M 700 | Ⓢ
★★★*Exeter Moat House, Topsham Rd, Exeter By-Pass. T:(039287) 5441. 44rm* ⇋ 🛏

EYEMOUTH
Borders, *Berwickshire*
Map **VI** J2

Eyemouth Gunsgreen House, Eyemouth (E side of town)
T:(0390) 50551
With the exception of a steep climb to the 1st tee, this is a compact, flat and popular seaside course. 9 | 5446 yds | Par 66 | SSS 66
Visitors welcome | .. per day | catering by prior arrangement (at least one week's notice) | ᴧ ꠸ open every evening and midday at weekends | M 200 | TR competition days
★★*Shieling, Coldingham. T:(03903) 216. 10rm (4* ⇋ *1* 🛏)

FAILSWORTH
Manchester
Map **V** E7

Brookdale Ashbridge, Woodhouses, Failsworth (N side of Manchester)
T:061-681 4534
Undulating parkland course, with river crossed 5 times in play. Hard walking. 18 | 6040 yds | Par 68 | SSS 68
Visitors welcome ⊠, ☎ if more than 4 in party | restricted Tu WE BH | without M .. per day ∴ WE with M .. per day WE | B (not Mon) | L ♛ D prior arrangement (not Mon) | ᴧ ꠸ | ⋈ prior arrangement | ④ Sun | TR Sun | ꒯ ꜀ | M 600 | Ⓢ
★★*Midway, Manchester Rd, Castleton, Rochdale. T:(0706) 32881. 30rm (2* ⇋ *20* 🛏)

KEY

(IA1) *atlas grid reference*
T: *telephone number*
☎ *advance letter/telephone call required*
⊠ *introduction from own club sec/handicap certificate/club membership card required*
· · *low fees*
∴ *medium fees*
: : *high fees*
* *green fees not confirmed for 1987*
B *light lunch*
L *full lunch*
♥ *tea*
D *dinner*
⚐ *changing rooms/showers*
Ⴤ *bar open mid-day and evenings*
↘ *clubs for hire*
⋈ *partners may be found*
④ *restricted time for 4 balls*
TR *times reserved for members*
𝖩 *professional*
S *well-stocked shop*
M *member*
Mon Tu W Th F S Sun
WE *weekend*
BH *bank holiday*

FALKIRK
Central, *Stirlingshire*
Map **VI** F2

Falkirk Stirling Rd, Camelon, Falkirk (1½m W of Falkirk on A9)
T:(0324) 23457
Parkland course with trees, gorse, streams. 18 | 6090 yds | Par 70 | SSS 69
Visitors welcome up to 1600 Mon-F, with M only WE ☎ for visiting parties | ∴ per day | B L ♥ (not Th) | ⚐ Ⴤ ⋈ | ④ none for visitors | TR
WE, Mon-F after 1600 | M 800
★★★*Stakis Park, Arnot Hill, Camelon Rd.* T:(0324) 28331. *55rm* ⇄

FALKLAND
Fife, *Fife*
Map **VI** G1

Falkland The Myre (N side of town on A912)
T:(0337) 57404/57356
A well kept 'L' shaped course with excellent greens. 9 | 5216 yds | Par 68 | SSS 65
Visitors welcome without M · · per day | B L D all by arrangement | ♥ ⚐ Ⴤ | TR competitions | M 230
★★★*Stakis Albany, 1 North St, Glenrothes, Kirkcaldy.* T:(0592) 752292. *30rm (9* ⇄ *18* 🛏*)*

FALMOUTH
Cornwall
Map **I** B8

Falmouth Swanpool Rd, Falmouth (SW side of town centre)
T:(0326) 311262
Seaside/parkland course with outstanding coastal views. The course is sufficiently bunkered to punish any inaccurate shots. 5 acres of practice grounds, putting green and indoor games. 18 | 5581 yds | Par 69 | SSS 67
Visitors welcome | ∴ per day · · per round | B L ♥ | D prior arrangement | ⚐ Ⴤ ↘ | ⋈ possible | TR competition days | 𝖩 | M 600 | S
★★★🛏*Penmere Manor, Mongleath Rd.* T:(0326) 314545. *28rm (24* ⇄ *4* 🛏*)*

FARNBOROUGH
Hampshire
Map **II** C5

Southwood Ively Rd, Farnborough (1m W of Farnborough)
T:(0252) 548700
Municipal parkland course with stream running through. 9 | 2263 yds | Par 32 | SSS 31
Open to public | · · per round | B ♥ | L D prior arrangement | ⚐ Ⴤ | ⋈ | TR competition days | M 350 | S
★★★*Queen's, Lynchford Rd.* T:(0252) 545051. *79rm* ⇄ 🛏

FARNHAM
Surrey
Map **II** C5

Farnham Park (Par 3) Folly Hill (N side of Farnham town centre on A287)
T:(0252) 715216
Municipal parkland course in Farnham Park. 9 | 1200 yds | Par 27 | SSS 54
Open to public · · per day | B ♥ | ↘ | ⋈ | S
★★★*Bush, The Borough.* T:(0252) 715237. *65rm (62* ⇄ *3* 🛏*)*

FARTHINGSTONE
Northamptonshire
Map **IV** A7

Woodlands Farthingstone, Towcester (1m W of Farthingstone)
T:(032736) 291
Pleasant rambling course with open aspect and widespread views. Additional facilities include four championship squash courts, a health centre (sauna etc) and a fully-equipped gym. 18 | 6229 yds | Par 71 | SSS 71

Visitors welcome without M •• per day ∴ WE | with M •• per day WE | B L ☕ D | △ 🍸 ⟍ ⋈ | 🛒 | M 550 | [S]
★★★*Crossroads, Weedon. T:(0327) 40354. 28rm* ⇄

FELIXSTOWE
Suffolk
Map **IV** J8

Felixstowe Ferry Felixstowe (NE side of town centre)
T:(0394) 286834
Seaside links course, pleasant views, easy walking. Testing 491-yd 7th hole. Societies welcome (weekdays) by arrangement. 18 | 6308 yds | Par 72 | SSS 70
Visitors welcome ✉ | with M only WE BH (until 1030) | ∴ per day ∷ WE BH | B ☕ | L D prior arrangement (not Tu) | △ | 🍸 (not evng) | ⟍ | [TR] competitions | M 740 | [S]
★★★★*Orwell Moat House, Hamilton Rd, Felixstowe. T:(0394) 285511. 60rm* ⇄ 🚿

FELLING
Tyne and Wear
Map **VI** K6

Heworth Gingling Gate, Heworth, Gateshead (On A195, ½m NW of jct with A1(M)
T:(0632) 692137
Fairly flat downland course. 18 | 6462 yds | Par 72 | SSS 71
Visitors welcome, restricted WE (am) BH (am) | without M •• per day WE | with M •• per day WE | B L ☕ D prior arrangement | △ 🍸 | ⋈ | M 500 | [S] (summer season) | [TR] before 1200 competition days (usually S)

★★★*Post House, Emerson District 5, Washington. T:091-416 2264. 138rm* ⇄

FENAY BRIDGE
West Yorkshire
Map **V** E7

Woodsome Hall Fenay Bridge, nr Huddersfield (1½m SW of Fenay Bridge off A629)
T:(0484) 602971
Historic clubhouse; parkland course with views. 18 | 6068 yds | Par 70 | SSS 69
Visitors welcome, restricted Tu to 1600 | ☎ | without M ∷ per day | with M •• per day | B ☕ (not Mon) | L D prior arrangement (not Mon) | △ 🍸 ⟍ | [TR] 0845-0930, 1230-1400 | 🛒 | M 700 | [S]
★★★*George, St Georges Sq, Huddersfield. T:(0484) 25444. 62rm (38* ⇄*)*

FARNHAM
Surrey
Map **II** C5

Farnham The Sands (3m E of Farnham off A31)
T:(02518) 2109
Societies welcome by arrangement. 18 | 6221 yds | Par 72 | SSS 70
Visitors welcome (with H/C certificate) ✉ restricted Tu WE BH | ☎ | without M ∷ per day | with M •• per day | B L ☕ | D | △ 🍸 | 🛒 | ④ 1st tee 0930-1100, 1400-1500 | M 660 | [S]
★★★*Bush, The Borough. T:(0252) 715237. 65rm (62* ⇄ *3* 🚿*)*
A mixture of meadowland and heath with quick drying sandy subsoil. Several of the earlier holes have interesting features, the finishing holes rather less.

FAVERSHAM
Kent
Map **II** J4

Faversham Belmont Park (3½m S of Faversham)
T:(079 589) 275
Societies welcome by arrangement. 18 | 5979 yds | Par 70 | SSS 69
Visitors welcome ✉, with M only WE BH ☎ advisable | without M ∷ per day WE | L ☕ D prior arrangement | B prior arrangement (not Fri) | 🍸 | △ ⟍ | [TR] WE | 🛒 | M 700 | [S]
★★★★*County, High St, Canterbury. T:(0227) 66266. 74rm* ⇄ 🚿*)*
A beautiful inland course laid out over part of a large estate and with pheasants walking the fairways quite tamely. Play follows two heavily wooded valleys but the trees affect only the loose shots going out of bounds. There are first-rate views of the surrounding terrain.

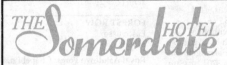

FERNDOWN
Dorset
Map I   K5

Ferndown 119 Golf Links Rd,
Ferndown (S side of town centre off
A347)
T:(0202) 872022
*Two links courses in a pretty situation
amongst pine trees, heather and gorse.
Societies welcome by arrangement. Old
course. 18 | 6422 yds | Par 71 | SSS 71
| New course. 9(18 tee positions) |
5604 yds | Par 70 | SSS 68*
Visitors welcome⊠ | ☎ preferred |
∴ per day (Old course) | .. per day
(New course) | ♈ B L ♛ D prior
arrangement | ⚴ ⚬ | ④ contact
secretary | TR before 0930 (Old)
before 0830 (New) | ♙ | M 650 | S
★★★★*Dormy, New Rd. T:(0202)
872121. 60rm (54 ⇄ 6 ₰).
Annexe: 30rm (27 ⇄ 3 ₰)*

FFESTINIOG
Gwynedd
Map III   D3

Ffestiniog Y Cefn (1m E of
Ffestiniog on B4391)
T:(076676) 2612
*Moorland course set in Snowdonia
National Park. 9 | 4536 yds | Par 68 |
SSS 66*
Visitors welcome .. per day | ♛ | ⚴
♈ | ∝ | M 120
★★⚶*Maes y Neuadd, Talsarnau.
T:(0766) 780200. 14rm (11 ⇄ 1 ₰)*

FILEY
North Yorkshire
Map V   J4

Filey South Cliff (½m S of Filey)
T:(0723) 513293
*Parkland course with good views,
windy. Stream runs through course.
Testing 9th and 13th holes. Societies
welcome by arrangement. 18 | 6030 yds
| Par 70 | SSS 69*
Visitors welcome ⊠ | restricted Tu
(am) Th (am) | with or without M ∴
per day WE | B L D ♛ (not Tu am
Th am) (April-Oct, prior
arrangement) | ⚴ ♈ ⚬ | ∝ | TR
Mon to F (0900-0945, 1230-1345) WE
(until 1015) | M 900 | S
★★*Wrangham House, Stonegate,
Hunmanby. T:(0723) 891333.
9rm (2 ⇄ 5 ₰)*

FLACKWELL HEATH
Buckinghamshire

Map II   D3

Flackwell Heath Treadaway Rd,
High Wycombe (NE side of town
centre)
T:(06285) 20027
*Parkland course on hills overlooking
Loudwater and the M40. Quick drying.
18 | 6150 yds | Par 71 | SSS 69*
Visitors welcome, with M only WE
| ⊠ ☎ preferred | without M ∴ per
day ∴ WE | with M .. per day WE |
♈ B L ♛ D prior arrangement | ∝ |
TR WE 0830-1010, 1315-1345 |
M 600 | S
★★★*Bellhouse, Beaconsfield. T:(0753)
887211. 120rm ⇄*

FLADBURY
Hereford and Worcester
Map III   J6

Evesham Craycombe Links,
Fladbury, Pershore (¾m N of
Fladbury on B4084)
T:(0386) 860395
*Parkland course with good views. Small
societies welcome by arrangement. 18 |
6418 yds | Par 72 | SSS 71*
Visitors welcome but with M only
S. Sun BH ☎ advisable | without M
∴ per day | with M .. per day WE |
B ♛ (not Mon) | L D prior
arrangement (not Mon) | ⚴ ♈ | ⚬
by arrangement | ④ TR
competition days | ♙ | M 320 | S
★★★*Evesham Hotel, Coopers Ln, off
Waterside, Evesham. T:(0386) 49111.
34rm (28 ⇄ 5 ₰)*

FLAMBOROUGH
North Humberside
Map V   J5

Flamborough Head Lighthouse Rd
(2m E of Flamborough off B1259)
T:(0262) 850333
*Undulating seaside course. 18 |
5438 yds | Par 66 | SSS 66*
Visitors welcome | without M ..
per day ∴ WE | with M .. per day
WE | B ♛ | L D prior arrangement
(not Mon) | ⚴ ♈ | M 370 | TR Sun
before 1100
★*Flaneburg, North Marine Rd.
T:(0262) 850284. 13rm (6 ₰)*

FLEMPTON
Suffolk
Map IV   G6

Flempton Bury St Edmunds (½m
W of Flempton on A1101)

T:(028484) 219
*Breckland course. 9 | 6080 yds | Par 70
| SSS 69*
Visitors welcome, with M only WE
BH | ☎ | without M ∴ per day |
with M .. per day WE | B L ♛ D ♈
prior arrangement (not W) | ⚴ | ④
Sun (1300-1700) | ♙ | M 300 | S
★★*Suffolk, 38 The Buttermarket,
Bury St Edmunds. T:(0284) 3995.
41rm (13 ⇄)*

FLINT
Clwyd
Map III   F2

Flint Cornish Park (1m W of Flint)
T:(03526) 2327
*Parkland course incorporating woods
and streams. The 1st and 10th are
testing holes. 9 | 5829 yds | Par 68 |
SSS 68*
Visitors welcome weekdays | WE
only with M .. per day | B D
prior arrangement | ⚴ | ♈ (evngs
only Mon to F) | TR competition
days WE only | M 350 | S
★★★*Chequers, Northophall. T:(0244)
816181. 29rm (27 ⇄ 2 ₰)*

FLIXTON
Greater Manchester
Map V   D7

William Wroe Municipal
Pennybridge Ln, Flixton (E side of
village off B5158)
T:061-748 8680
*Parkland course, with easy walking. 18
| 4395 yds | Par 64 | SSS 61*
Municipal course open to public
although it is played over by Acre
Gate GC | B | ♛ L D WE | ⚴ ⚬ | ∝ |
④ TR ☎ for details | ♙ | M 180 | S
★*Beaucliffe, 254 Eccles Old Rd,
Pendleton, Salford. T:061-789 5092.
22rm (2 ⇄ 20 ₰)*

FOREST ROW
East Sussex
Map II   F5

Royal Ashdown Forest Chapel Ln,
Forest Row (SE side of village)
T:(034282) 2018
*Undulating heathland course. Long
carries off the tees, magnificent views
over the forest. Not a course for
beginners. (Also shorter course through
wood and moorlands). 18 (x2) |
6525 yds (5572) | Par 72 (69) | SSS 71*
Visitors welcome, restrictions apply
☎ | without M ∴ per day WE |

FLEET
Hampshire
Map II C5

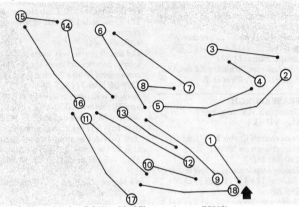

North Hants Minley Rd (¼m N of Fleet station on B3013)
T:(02514) 6443
Societies welcome (Tu W) by arrangement. 18 | 6257 yds | Par 69 | SSS 70
Visitors welcome, restricted WE Th Ladies Day | ④ BH | ⌗ ☎ | ∴ per round
| B ☎ | L D prior arrangement (not Mon) | ⚖ ⅄ | M 730 | Ⓢ
***Lismoyne, Church Rd, Fleet. T:(02514) 28555. 40rm (29 ⇔ 3 ⋔)*
Picturesque tree-lined course with much heather and gorse close to
the fairways. A comparatively easy par four first hole may lull the
golfer into a false sense of security, only to be rudely awakened at
the testing holes which follow. The ground is rather undulating
and, though not tiring, does offer some excellent 'blind' shots, and
more than a few surprises in judging distance.

FLEETWOOD
Lancashire
Map V C5

Fleetwood Princes Way, Fleetwood (W side of town centre)
T:(03917) 3661
Societies welcome by arrangement (not Tu Th S). 18 | 6723 yds | Par 72 | SSS 71
Visitors welcome, restricted Tu S | green fees on application | B ☎ | L D | ⚖ ⅄
\ | ⟦TR⟧ WE variable | '⅃' | ⋈ | M 750 | Ⓢ
***North Euston, The Esplanade. T:(03917) 6525. 57rm (35 ⇔ 10 ⋔)*
Long flat seaside links where the player must always be alert to
changes of direction or strength of the wind.

FORRES
Grampian, *Morayshire*
Map VII G4

Forres Muiryshade (SE side of town centre off B9010)
T:(0309) 72949
Societies welcome Mon to F by arrangement. 18 | 6141 yds | Par 70 | SSS 69
Visitors welcome | .. per day WE | B L D prior arrangement | ☎ | ⚖ ⅄ \ | ⋈
prior arrangement | ⟦TR⟧ competitions and open tournaments | '⅃' | M 830 | Ⓢ
***Ramnee Victoria Rd. T:(0309) 72410. 19rm (9 ⇔ 4 ⋔) Annexe: 2rm ⋔*
An all-year parkland course laid on light, well-drained soil in
wooded countryside. Walking is easy despite some undulations.
The holes are tests for the best golfers.

with M ∴ per day | B L ☎ prior
arrangement | ⚖ ⅄ | \ prior
arrangement | ④ WE | ⟦TR⟧
0930-1000 Mon, 0900-1000 and
1230-1400 Tu, before 1030 approx
WE BH '⅃' | M 450 | Ⓢ
***Roebuck, Wych Cross, Forest
Row. T:(034-282) 3811. 31rm ⇔*

FORFAR
Tayside, *Angus*
Map VII H7

Forfar Cunninghill, Arbroath Rd,
Forfar (1m E of Forfar on A932)
T:(0307) 62120
*Moorland course with wooded
undulating fairways and fine views.
Organised parties by arrangement. 18 |
5522 mtrs | Par 69 | SSS 69*
Visitors welcome | without M ∴ per
day ∷ WE | with M .. per round |
B ☎ | L D prior arrangement | ⚖ ⅄
⋈ | ⟦TR⟧ competition days | '⅃' |
M 850 | Ⓢ
***Royal, Castle St. T:(0307) 62691.
22rm (8 ⇔)*

FORMBY
Merseyside
Map V C7

Formby Golf Rd, Formby (N side of
town)
T:(07048) 72164
*Championship seaside links course.
Societies welcome Tu Th. 18 | 6871 yds
| Par 72 | SSS 73*
Visitors welcome ⌗ ☎ | restricted
W WE | without M ∷ per day WE |
with M .. per day ∴ WE | B
sandwiches only L (not Mon) ☎ | ⚖
⅄ | ④ ⟦TR⟧ on application | '⅃' |
M 600 | Ⓢ
****Prince of Wales, Lord St,
Southport. T:(0704) 36688.
101rm (82 ⇔ 18 ⋔)*

Formby Ladies Golf Rd, Formby (N
side of town)
T:(07048) 73493
*Seaside links - one of the few
independent ladies clubs in the country.
Course has contrasting hard hitting
holes in flat country and tricky holes in
sandhills and woods. Fine short 5th
hole (par 3). Societies welcome. 18 |
5374 yds | Par 71 | SSS 71*
Visitors welcome (⌗ ☎
appreciated) restricted Th | ∴ per
day ∷ WE | with M .. per day WE |
B ☎ (not Th) | L prior arrangement ➦

| ⚠ ⛳ ↘ | ④ Sun 1100-1300 | TR |
Th competition day | ♩ | S |
★★★★*Prince of Wales, Lord St,
Southport. T:(0704) 36688.
101rm (82 ⇌ 18 🏠)*

FORT AUGUSTUS
Highland, *Inverness-shire*
Map **VII**   F6

Fort Augustus Markethill (1m SW
of Fort Augustus on A82)
T:(0320) 6460
*Moorland course, with narrow fairways
and good views adjacent to the
Caledonian Canal. 9 | 5454 yds |
Par 70 | SSS 66*
Visitors welcome | ⚠ ↘ few | ⋈
prior arrangement | TR
competitions | M 100
★★*Lovat Arms. T:(0320) 6206.
20rm (14 ⇌ 1 🏠)*

FORTROSE
Highland, *Ross and Cromarty*
Map **VII**   F4

Fortrose & Rosemarkie Ness Rd
East, Fortrose (W side of town
centre)
T:(0381) 20529
*Seaside course, with sea on 3 sides.
Easy walking. Suitable as a holiday
course. Testing 4th hole par 5. Good
views. 18 | 5973 yds | Par 71 | SSS 69*
Visitors welcome | B L ⚑ D | ⚠ ⛳ |
④ | TR before 1030 and 1300-1430 | ♩
| M 550 | S |
★*Royal, Union St, Fortrose. T:(0381)
20236. 12rm*

FORT WILLIAM
Highland, *Inverness-shire*
Map **VII**   E7

Fort William (3m NE of Fort

William on A82)
T:(0397) 4464
*Moorland course with fine views. Tees
and greens very good, in between can be
very soft in wet weather. 18 | 5640 yds
| Par 70 | SSS 68*
Visitors welcome | ‥ per day WE |
⚑ B (bar times) | ⚠ ⛳ ⋈ | TR
competitions | M 220
★★★*Ladbroke, Achintore Rd (on A82).
T:(0397) 3117. 85rm ⇌ 🏠*

FRASERBURGH
Grampian, *Aberdeenshire*
Map **VII**   K4

Fraserburgh Corbie Hill (1m SE of
Fraserburgh on B9033)
T:(0346) 28287
*Testing seaside course. 4 hole course for
children. 18+4 | 6217 yds | Par 70 |
SSS 70*
Visitors welcome | ‥ per day WE |
B ⚑ L D prior arrangement | ⚠ ⛳ |
⋈ | TR some competitions | ④ WE
0800-0930, 1130-1330 | ♩ | M 500
★★*Tufted Duck, St Combs. T:(03465)
2481. 17rm (11 ⇌ 6 🏠)*

FRESHWATER BAY
Isle of Wight
Map **II**   A8

Freshwater Bay Afton Down,
Freshwater Bay (E side of village off
A3055)
T:(0983) 752955
*A downland/seaside links with wide
fairways and spectacular coastal views
of the Solent and Channel. 18 |
5628 yds | Par 68 | SSS 68*
Visitors welcome | ‥ per day ∴
WE | ⚑ | ⚠ ↘ ⋈ ④ competition
Sun am | M 300 | S |
★★★*Albion, Freshwater. T:(0983)
753631. 43rm (37 ⇌)*

FRINTON-ON-SEA
Essex
Map **II**   K1

Frinton-on-Sea The Club House, 1
The Esplanade (SW side of town
centre)
T:(02556) 4618
*Flat seaside course, easy walking,
windy. Societies welcome (Mon to F) by
arrangement. Also a 9-hole course. 18 |
6259 yds | Par 71 | SSS 70*
Visitors welcome, restricted WE BH
and Th (before 1100) (until 1100) ✉ |
without M ∷ per day WE | ⛳ ⚑ | B
(not Tu) | ⚠ | ⋈ prior arrangement
(not Tu) | ⚠ | ⋈ prior arrangement
L ④ ☎ for details L TR Th until
1100, WE BH until 1130 | ♩ | M 800 |
S |
★★*Maplin. The Esplanade T:(02556)
3832. 12rm (9 ⇌ 1 🏠)*

GAINSBOROUGH
Lincolnshire
Map **V**   H8

Thonock The Belt, Gainsborough
(1m N of Gainsborough off A159)
T:(0427) 3088
*Scenic parkland course. 18 | 5704 yds |
Par 68 | SSS 68*
Visitors welcome, restricted WE BH
| B ⚑ (not Tu) | L D prior
arrangement (not Tu) | ⚠ ⛳ ↘ | ⋈
| TR Sun (am) | M 550 | S |
★★*Hickman-Hill, Cox's Hill. T:(0427)
3639. 8rm (3 ⇌ 1 🏠)*

GAIRLOCH
Highland, *Ross and Cromarty*
Map **VII**   D4

Gairloch (1m S of Gairloch on
A832)
T:(0445) 2407
*Fine seaside course running along
Gairloch Sands with good views across
the loch to Skye. 9 | 2093 yds | Par 62
(over 18) | SSS 63*
Visitors welcome without M ‥ per
day | ⚑ | ⚠ ↘ few | ⋈ | TR
competition days | M 150 | S |
★★★*Gairloch. T:(0445) 2001.
51rm (36 ⇌ 12 🏠)*

GALASHIELS
Borders, *Selkirkshire*
Map **VI**   H3

Galashiels Ladhope Recreation
Ground, Galashiels (N side of town
centre off A7)

T:(0896) 3724
Hillside course, superb views from the top, 10th hole very steep. 18 | 5309 yds | Par 69 | SSS 67
Visitors welcome | △ Y ⟍ | [TR]WE | M 250 | [S]
★★★*Kingsknowes, Selkirk Rd. T:(0896) 3478. 11rm (8 ⇄ 1 🚿)*

Torwoodlee Galashiels (1¾m NW of Galashiels off A7)
T:(0896) 2260
Parkland course with natural hazards. Testing 3rd hole (par 3). 9 | 5912 yds | Par 68 | SSS 68
Visitors welcome, restricted competition S | ∴ per day ‥ per round | B L D ☕ (not Tu) | △ Y ⟍ | [TR]Th (evng) S | M 330 | no shop but some items on sale
★★*Burt's, The Square, Melrose. T:(089682) 2285. 22rm (6 ⇄ 3 🚿)*

GALSTON
Strathclyde, *Ayrshire*
Map **VI** D3

Loudoun Golf Edinburgh Rd, Galston (NE side of town on A71)
T:(0563) 821993
Pleasant testing parkland course. 18 | 5824 yds | Par 68 | SSS 68
Visitors welcome, restricted WE | ∴ per day | B L ☕ D | △ Y ⋈ | [TR] WE, W 1300-1400 | ℨ | M 475
★★★*Howard Park, Glasgow Rd, Kilmarnock. T:(0563) 31211. 46rm ⇄ 🚿*

GANTON
North Yorkshire
Map **V** H4

Ganton Scarborough (¼m NW of Ganton off A64)
T:(0944) 70329
Championship course, variable winds. 18 | Club 6371/Medal 6693 yds | Par C71/M72 | SSS C71/M73
Visitors welcome, restricted Mon to F ☎ (prior arrangement only) | B ☕ | L D prior arrangement | △ Y ⟍ | [TR]0830-0900, 1215-1415, Sun until 1015 | ℨ | M 600 | [S]
★★*Downe Arms, Wykeham. T:(0723) 862471. 9rm (7 ⇄ 🚿)*

GARFORTH
Leeds
Map **V** F6

Garforth (1m N of Garforth)
T:(0532) 862021
Moorland course with fine views, easy walking. Societies welcome by arrangement. 18 | 6005 yds | Par 70 | SSS 70
Visitors welcome, with M only WE BH | ∴ per day WE | B L ☕ D (not Tu) | △ Y ⟍ | [TR]before 0930, 1200-1400, after 1630 | M 400 | [S]
★★★*Ladbroke, Wakefield Rd, Garforth Rbt. T:(0532) 866556. 143rm ⇄ 🚿*

GARMOUTH
Grampian, *Morayshire*
Map **VII** H4

Garmouth & Kingston Garmouth (In village on B9015)
T:(034-387) 388
Seaside/parkland with tidal waters. 5 miles from Fochabers. 9 | 5649 yds | Par 67 | SSS 67
Visitors welcome, restricted WE | ‥ per day WE | B ☕ catering by arrangement | △ Y | [TR]Tu 1715-1900 | M 400
★★*Gordon Arms, Fochabers. T:(0343) 820508. 10rm ⇄. Annexe: 2rm (1 ⇄ 1 🚿)*

GARTCOSH
Strathclyde, *Lanarkshire*
Map **VI** E2

Mount Ellen Gartcosh (¾m N of Gartcosh off A752)
T:(0236) 872277
Downland course with 73 bunkers. Testing hole: 10th (Bedlay) 156 yds par 3. Societies welcome by arrangement. 18 | 5525 yds | Par 68 | SSS 68
Visitors welcome only with M ✉ | ‥ per day WE | B L ☕ D | △ Y | [TR]WE BH | M 500 | [S]
★★*Garfield House, Cumbernauld Rd, Stepps. T:041-779 2111. 27rm ⇄ 🚿*

GATESHEAD
Tyne and Wear
Map **VI** K6

Ravensworth Moss Heaps, Wrekenton, Gateshead (2½m SE of Gateshead off A6127)
T:(091) 4876014
Moorland/parkland course 600 ft above sea level with fine views. Testing 13th hole (par 3). Societies welcome by arrangement. 18 | 5872 yds | Par 68 | SSS 68
Visitors welcome | ‥ per day ∴ WE | ☕ | B (not Mon) | L D prior arrangement (not Mon) | △ Y | ⋈ | ⟍ [TR]WE | M 500 | [S]
★★★*Five Bridges, High West St. T:(091) 4771105. 106rm ⇄*

GATEHOUSE-of-FLEET
Dumfries and Galloway, *Kirkcudbrightshire*
Map **VI** E6

Gatehouse Laurieston Rd, Gatehouse-of Fleet (N side of village)
T:(05574) 654
Set against a background of rolling hills with scenic views of Fleet Bay and the Solway Firth. 9 | 2398 yds | Par 33 | SSS 63
Visitors welcome | △ ⋈ [TR]Sun 0830-1130 am | M 183
★★★*Murray Arms, Gatehouse-of-Fleet. T:(05574) 207. 14rm (11 ⇄ 1 🚿)*

GATLEY
Greater Manchester
Map **V** E7

Gatley Waterfall Farm, Styal Rd, Heald Green, Cheadle (S side of village off B5166)
T:061-437 2091

GERRARDS CROSS
Buckinghamshire
Map **II** D3

Gerrards Cross Chalfont Park, Gerrards Cross (NE side of town centre off A413)
T:(0753) 883263
18 | 6305 yds | Par 70 | SSS 69
Visitors welcome | ✉ ☎ advisable | without M ∷ per round | with M ‥ per round | B ☕ (not Mon) | L D prior arrangement (not Mon) | △ Y | [TR] 1300-1400 daily (1230- 1300 winter), Tu is Ladies Day, WE BH up to 1500 | ℨ | M 780 | [S]
★★★*Bellhouse, Beaconsfield. T:(0753) 887211. 120rm ⇄*

A wooded parkland course which has been modernised in recent years and is now a very pleasant circuit with infinite variety. The best part lies on the plateau above the clubhouse where there are some testing holes.

*Parkland course. Moderately testing. 9
| 5934 yds | Par 68 | SSS 68*
Visitors welcome ⊠ restricted Tu S
| .. per day | B ♥ (not Mon) | L D
prior arrangement (not Mon) | ⚲ ⛾
| TR competition days Tu S | ♩ | ∝
| M 340 | S
✪★★★★*Belfry, Stanley Rd,
Handforth. T:061-437 0511. 92rm* ⇄

GIFFORD
Lothian, *East Lothian*
Map VI H2

Gifford c/o Secretary, Cawdor
Cottage, Gifford (1m SW of Gifford
off B6355)
T:062-081 267
*Parkland course, with easy walking. 9 |
6138 yds | Par 71 | SSS 69*
Visitors welcome .. per day WE
per two rounds | changing rooms
only - no showers | ∝ | TR Sun
after 1200, Tu W after 1600 | M 350
★★*Tweeddale Arms. T:(062081) 240.
10rm (2 ⇄ 4 🍴)*

GILLINGHAM
Kent
Map II H4

Gillingham Woodlands Rd (1½m
SE of Gillingham on A2)
T:(0634) 55862
*Seaside links course. 18 | 5997 yds |
Par 70 | SSS 68*
Visitors welcome, ☎ ⊠, with M
only WE BH | without M ∷ per day
| with M ∴ per day | B L ♥ D (not
Tu) | ⚲ ⛾ ♩ | M 750 | TR WE | S
★★★*Crest, Maidstone Rd, Rochester.
T:(0634) 687111. 105rm* ⇄

GIRTON
Cambridgeshire
Map IV E6

Girton Dodford Ln, Girton (NW
side of village)
T:(0223) 276169
*Flat open course with easy walking.
Some trees and bushes. Societies
welcome by arrangement. 18 | 5810 yds
| Par 69 | SSS 68*
Visitors welcome | ✳ | B ♥ not Mon
| L D prior arrangement (not Mon) |
⚲ ⛾ ∝ by arrangement ╲ | ♩ |
M 600 | S
★★★★*Cambridge Post House,
Lakeview, Bridge Rd, Impington.
T:(022023) 7000. 120rm* ⇄

GIRVAN
Strathclyde, *Ayr*
Map VI C5

Girvan Golf Course Rd, Girvan (N
side of town off A77)
T:(0465) 4272
*Municipal seaside and parkland course
(private club). Testing 17th hole
223 yds uphill par 3. Societies by
arrangement not July or Aug. Good
views. 18 | 5078 yds | Par 64 | SSS 65*
Visitors welcome | B L ♥ D prior
arrangement | ⚲ | ⛾ | ∝ often
available | ④ WE before 1200 | TR
competition days | ♩ | M 175
★★*Kings Arms, Dalrymple St.
T:(0465) 3322. 26rm (8 ⇄ 2 🍴)*

GLASGOW
Strathclyde, *Lanarkshire*
Map VI E2

Cowglen 301 Barrhead Rd,
Glasgow (4½m SW of city centre on
B762)
T:041-632 0556
*Parkland course with good views over
Clyde valley to Campsie Hills. 18 |
6006 yds | Par 69 | SSS 69*
Visitors welcome only with M | ✳ | B
L ♥ D | ⚲ ⛾ ╲ | ♩ | M 800 | S
★★★*Tinto Firs Thistle, 470
Kilmarnock Rd, Glasgow. T:041-637
2353. 27rm* ⇄

Haggs Castle Dumbreck Rd,
Dumbreck, Glasgow (2½m SW of
city centre on B768)
T:041-427 0480
*Wooded parkland course where Scottish
National Championships and the
Glasgow Golf Classic have been held.
Quite difficult. Societies by
arrangement August and September
only. 18 | 6464 yds | Par 72 | SSS 71*
Visitors welcome only with M ☎ | B
L ♥ D (not Mon) | ⚲ ⛾ ╲ | ♩ |
M 1000 | S
★★*Sherbrooke, 11 Sherbrooke Av,
Pollokshields, Glasgow. T:041-427
4227. 9rm (5 ⇄ 3 🍴)*

Kings Park Croftpark Ave,
Glasgow (4m S of city centre off
B766)
T:041-637 1066
*Municipal parkland course on the edge
of the city. Fairly hard walking. 9 |
2056 yds | Par 32 | SSS 32*
Open to public
★★★*Macdonald Thistle, Eastwood Toll

*Roundabout, Giffnock. T:041-638
2225. 56rm* ⇄ 🍴

Knightswood Park Lincoln Av,
Glasgow W3 (4m NW of city centre
off A82)
T:041-959 2131
*Parkland course within easy reach of
Glasgow. 2 dog legs. 9 | 4825 yds |
Par 66 | SSS 66*
Visitors welcome | M 105
★★★*Stakis Pond, Great Western Rd.
T:041-334 8161. 137rm* ⇄

Lethamhill Cumbernauld Rd,
Glasgow (3m NE of city centre on
A80)
T:041-770 6220
*Municipal parkland course. 18 |
5859 yds | Par 70 | SSS 68*
Open to public | B ♥ (summer only)
★★*Garfield House, Cumbernauld Rd,
Stepps. T:041-779 2111. 27rm* ⇄ 🍴

Linn Park Simshill Rd, Glasgow
(4m S of city centre off B766)
T:041-637 5871
*Municipal parkland course with 6 par
3's in outward half. 18 | 4832 yds |
Par 64 | SSS 63*
Open to public | B | ⚲ | ④
(probable) | M 80
★★★*Bruce, Cornwall St, East Kilbride.
T:(03552) 29771. 84rm (32 ⇄ 52 🍴)*

Pollok 90 Barrhead Rd, Glasgow
(4m SW of city centre on A762)
T:041-632 1080
*Parkland course with woods and river.
18 | 6257 yds | Par 71 | SSS 70*
Visitors welcome weekdays only
with M or ⊠ ☎ | ∷ per day | with
M no charge | B L ♥ (not Sun) | D
prior arrangement (not Sun) | ⚲ |
TR WE and 2nd & 4th Tu in month
| M 460
★★★*Tinto Firs Thistle, 470
Kilmarnock Rd, Glasgow. T:041-637
2353. 27rm* ⇄ 🍴

Williamwood Clarkston Rd,
Glasgow G44 (5m S of city centre
on B767)
T:041-637 2715
*Inland course, fairly hilly with wooded
areas with a small lake and pond.
Parties only by prior arrangement. 18 |
5377 yds | Par 67 | SSS 68*
No visitors unless introduced | ∷
per day | B L ♥ D | ⚲ ⛾ | TR
competition days only | ♩ | M 450
approx | S

★★★*MacDonald Thistle, Eastwood
Toll Rbt. T:041-638 2225. 56rm* ⇌ 🏠

GLENLUCE
Dumfries and Galloway,
Wigtownshire
Map **VI**   C6

Wigtownshire County Glenluce
(1½m W of Glenluce off A75)
T:(05813) 420
*Seaside links course, easy walking. 9 |
5826 yds | Par 70 | SSS 68*
Visitors welcome | .. per day WE |
B L ♥ prior arrangement | ⚒ Ⴈ |
TR WE (eve) and competitions |
M 200
★*Kings Arms, 31 Main St, Glenluce.
T:(05813) 219. 8rm (2 🏠)*

GLENROTHES
Fife, *Fife*
Map **VI**   G1

Glenrothes Golf Course Rd,
Glenrothes (W side of town off
B921)
T:(0592) 758686
*Testing and hilly parkland course with
burn crossed 4 times. Good views. 18 |
6449 yds | Par 71 | SSS 71*
Visitors welcome with M .. per
round | B L ♥ D prior arrangement
| ⚒ Ⴈ ⋈ | TR S 0730-0945,
1200-1430 | M 800
★★★*Balgeddie House, Leslie Rd.
T:(0592) 742511. 18rm (16 ⇌ 2 🏠)*

GLENSHEE (SPITTAL OF)
See Spittal of Glenshee
Tayside, *Perthshire*
Map **VII**   H7

GLOSSOP
Derbyshire
Map **V**   E7

Glossop and District Hurst Ln, off
Sheffield Rd (1m E of Glossop off
A57)
T:(04574) 3117
*Moorland course in good position,
excellent natural hazards. 11 | 5723 yds
| Par 68 | SSS 68*
Visitors welcome, restricted BH |
without M ∴ per day | with M ..
per day | B L ♥ D prior
arrangement (not Th) | ⚒ | Ⴈ (not
Th in winter) ⋋ | ⋈ | TR S
(summer) | M 250 | S
★★*York House, York Place, off
Richmond St, Ashton-under-Lyne.
T:061-330 5899. 26rm (8 ⇌ 3 🏠)*

GLOUCESTER
Gloucestershire
Map **III**   H7

**Gloucester Hotel and Country
Club** Robinswood Hill, Gloucester
(2m SW of Gloucester off M5)
T:(0452) 25653
*Undulating, wooded course, built
around a hill with superb views over
Gloucester and the Cotswolds. The
12th is a drive straight up a hill,
nicknamed 'Coronary Hill'. 18 | White:
6135 yds (Yellow: 5849 yds) |
Par 70(69) | SSS 69(68)*
Visitors welcome ☎ | .. per round
weekdays ∴ WE | B ♥ | ⚒ Ⴈ ⋋ |
TR competition days | ⅃ | M 150 | S
★★★*Gloucester Hotel and Country
Club, Robinswood Hill. T:(0452)
25653. 73rm (72 ⇌ 1 🏠)*

GLYNNEATH
West Glamorgan
Map **III**   E8

Glynneath 'Pen-y-graig' (2m NE of
Glynneath at Pont Nedd Fechan off
B4242)
T:(0639) 720452
*Attractive hillside course overlooking
the Vale of Neath. 12 | 5354 yds |
Par 68 | SSS 68*
Visitors welcome | ⚒ Ⴈ | ⋈
possible | ④ | S 5 pm | M 180
★*Windsor Lodge, Mount Pleasant,
Swansea. T:(0792) 42158. 18rm (11 ⇌
3 🏠)*

GOLSPIE
Highland, *Sutherland*
Map **VII**   G3

Golspie Ferry Rd (½m S of Golspie
off A9)
T:(04083) 3266
*Seaside course, with easy walking and
natural hazards including beach
heather and whins. Good views.
Societies welcome by arrangement.
Children allowed if with parents. 18 |
5763 yds | Par 68 | SSS 68*
Visitors welcome | B ♥ L D | ⚒ Ⴈ |
⋋ prior arrangement | ⋈ evngs WE
| ④ after 1700 | TR 1700-1830 |
M 160 | S
★★*Golf Links. T:(04083) 3408. 10rm
(5 ⇌ 2 🏠)*

GORLESTON-ON-SEA
Norfolk
Map **IV**   K4

Gorleston Warren Rd, Gorleston-
on-Sea (S side of town centre)
T:(0493) 661911
*Seaside course. 18 | 6279 yds | Par 70 |
SSS 70*
Visitors welcome ⋈ | ∴ per day WE
| B ♥ (not Mon) | L D prior
arrangement (not Mon) | ⚒ Ⴈ ⋋ ⋈
④ starting times published on tees |
TR Sun (1st and 3rd monthly)
ladies W | ⅃ | M 830 | S
★★★*Cliff, Cliff Hill, Gorleston-on-Sea.
T:(0493) 662179. 30rm (24 ⇌ 6 🏠)*

GOSFORTH
Tyne and Wear
Map **VI**   K6

Gosforth Broadway East, Gosforth
(N side of town centre off A6125)
T:091-285 3495
*Parkland course with natural water
hazards, easy walking. Societies
welcome by arrangement. 18 | 6030 yds
| Par 69 | SSS 69*
Visitors welcome ☎ parties
restricted Mon Tu WE BH | without
M ∴ per day WE | with M .. per
day WE | B L ♥ D prior
arrangement (not Mon) | ⚒ Ⴈ ⋋ |
TR competition days Tu (Ladies
Day) | ⅃ | M 500 | S
★★★★*Gosforth Park Thistle, High
Gosforth Pk, Gosforth, Newcastle-
upon-Tyne. T:(0632) 364111.
178rm ⇌ 🏠*

Gosforth Park Golf Centre
Inc Wideopen Golf Club, High
Gosforth Park, Newcastle (2m N of
Gosforth on B1318 off A6125)
T:(0632) 364867
*A very flat course short in length, tree
lined with a burn running through
many holes, also there is 30 bay covered
floodlit driving range open until 9pm
each night and a 9 hole pitch-putt
course. 18 | 5007 yds | Par 70 | SSS 68*
Visitors welcome without M | L
D B | ♥ ⚒ Ⴈ S ⋋ ⋈ TR when
required | M 350
★★★★*Gosforth Park Thistle, High
Gosforth Park, Gosforth, Newcastle-
upon-Tyne. T:(0632) 364111.
178rm ⇌ 🏠*

GOSPORT
Hampshire
Map **II**   B7

Gosport and Stokes Bay Military
Rd, Haslar, Gosport (S side of town
centre)
T:(07017) 581625

KEY

(IA1)	*atlas grid reference*
T:	*telephone number*
☎	*advance letter/telephone call required*
✉	*introduction from own club sec/handicap certificate/club membership card required*
..	*low fees*
∴	*medium fees*
::	*high fees*
*	*green fees not confirmed for 1987*
B	*light lunch*
L	*full lunch*
☛	*tea*
D	*dinner*
☖	*changing rooms/showers*
♈	*bar open mid-day and evenings*
⦚	*clubs for hire*
⋈	*partners may be found*
④	*restricted time for 4 balls*
TR	*times reserved for members*
ℐ	*professional*
Ⓢ	*well-stocked shop*
M	*member*
Mon Tu W Th F S Sun	
WE	*weekend*
BH	*bank holiday*

A testing seaside course with plenty of gorse and short rough. Changing winds. 9 | 5856 yds | Par 72 | SSS 69 Visitors welcome restricted WE BH | .. per day WE | B ☛ | L D prior arrangement | ☖ ♈ | ⋈ TR Sun (am) | M 370
★★*Anglesey, Crescent Rd, Alverstoke, Gosport. T:(0705) 582157. 18rm (5 ⇄ 14 ▥)*

GOUROCK
Strathclyde, *Renfrewshire*
Map **VI**   C2

Gourock Cowal View, Gourock (SW side of town off A770)
T:(0475) 31001
Moorland course. Testing 8th hole par 5. Magnificent views over Firth of Clyde. 18 | 6492 yds | Par 72 | SSS 71 Visitors welcome, ✉ or with M | ∴ per day | B L ☛ D | ☖ ♈ ⦚ ⋈ | TR WE and Mon, W | ℐ | M 730 | Ⓢ
★★★*Stakis Gantock, Cloch Rd. T:(0475) 34671. 63rm ⇄ ▥*

GRANGE-OVER-SANDS
Cumbria
Map **V**   C4

Grange-over-Sands Meathop Rd (NW of town centre off B5277)
T:(04484) 3180
Parkland course with trees, ditches and easy walking. 18 | 5660 yds | Par 69 | SSS 68 Visitors welcome | B (not Tu) | L ☛ D prior arrangement | ☖ ♈ ⦚ | ⋈ (not Tu) | TR 0830-0930, 1230-1400 | ℐ | M 425 | Ⓢ
★★*Netherwood, Lindale Rd. T:(04484) 2552. 23rm (15 ⇄ 2 ▥)*

GRANTHAM
Lincolnshire
Map **IV**   C3

Belton Park Londonthorpe Rd,

GRANGE-over-SANDS
Cumbria
Map **V**   C4

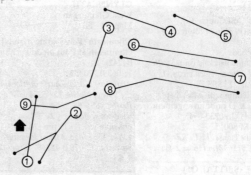

Grange Fell Fell Rd (1m W of Grange-over-Sands)
T:(044 84) 2536
Society meetings of limited numbers welcome by arrangement. 9 | 5278 yds | Par 68 | SSS 66 Visitors welcome | .. per day WE | ☖ ♈ (Nov to March WE only) | TR competitions (Sun) | M 300
★★*Netherwood, Lindale Rd, Grange-over-Sands. T:(04484) 2552. 23rm (15 ⇄ 2 ▥)*
Hillside course with magnificent views over Morecambe Bay and the surrounding lakeland mountains.

GRAVESEND
Kent
Map **II**   G4

Mid Kent Singlewell Rd, Gravesend (S side of town centre off A227)
T:(0474) 68035
Societies by arrangement. 18 | 6221 yds | Par 70 | SSS 70 Visitors welcome, with M only | WE ☎ preferred | ∴ per day | B L ☛ | ☖ ♈ ⦚ | TR WE | ℐ | M 1200 | Ⓢ
★★★*Inn on the Lake, Watling St, (A2, Shorne). T:(047 482) 3333. 78rm ⇄ ▥*
A well-maintained downland course with some easy walking and some excellent greens. The first hole is short, but nonetheless a real challenge. The slightest hook and the ball is out of bounds or lost.

Belton Ln (1½m NE of Grantham off A607)
T:(0476) 67399/63355/63911
Parkland course, wooded, with deer park and Canadian Geese Reserve. Famous holes: 5th, 12th, 16th and 18th. A 27-hole championship course, there are three 18-hole combinations. Societies welcome by arrangement. 18 | 6420/6101/5857 yds | Par 71/70/69 | SSS 71/69/68 Visitors welcome ✉ ☎ in advance | ∴ per day | B ☛ | L D prior arrangement | ☖ ♈ ⦚ | ⋈ (usually) | ℐ | M 750 | Ⓢ
★★★*George, High St. T:(0476) 63286. 46rm (40 ⇄ 6 ▥)*

GRANTOWN-on-SPEY
Highland, *Morayshire*
Map **VII**   G5

Grantown-on-Spey Golf Course
Rd, Grantown-on-Spey (E side of
town centre off A939)
T:(0479) 2079
*Moorland and woodland course. Part
easy walking, remainder hilly. Parties
accepted by arrangement. Ideal holiday
centre.* 18 | 5745 yds | Par 70 | SSS 67
Visitors welcome | ✳ | B L ☎ D prior
arrangement | ⚘ ♉ ↘ | ⋈
(probable) | TR medal days
0900-0930, 1330-1400 | M 200
★★*Seafield Lodge, Woodside Av.
T:(0479) 2152. 14rm (3 ⇋ 6 ⌂)*

GREAT
Places incorporating the word
'Great' - eg. Great Driffield, Great
Yarmouth - are listed under
Driffield, Yarmouth, etc.

GREENFORD
Greater London
Map **II**   E3

Horsenden Hill Woodland Rise (3m
NE of Greenford on A4090)
T:01-902 4555
A well-kept, tree-lined short course. 9 |
1618 yds | Par 28 | SSS 28
Visitors welcome | ☎ L | ⚘ ↘ ⋈ |
M 135 | S
★★★*Master Brewer Motel, Western
Av, Hillingdon. T:(0895) 51199.
64rm ⇋*

Perivale Park Ruislip Rd East,
Greenford (E side of town centre
off A40)
T:01-578 1693
Parkland course. 9 | 2600 yds | Par 68 |
SSS 65
Visitors welcome | B | ☎ | ⚘ ↘ ⋈ |
M 180 | S
★★★*Carnarvon, Ealing Common.
T:01-992 5399. 145rm ⇋*

GREENOCK
Strathclyde, *Renfrewshire*
Map **VI**   C2

Greenock Forsyth St, Greenock
(SW side of town off A770)
T:(0475) 20793/26819
*Testing heathland course with
panoramic views of Clyde Estuary.
There is also a 9-hole course. Societies
welcome mid-week (not Th). Children
with adults welcome.* 18 | 5838 yds | ➡

GUERNSEY
Channel Islands
Map I   A4

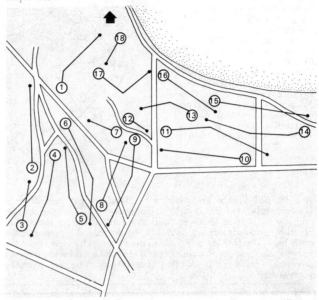

Royal Guernsey L'Ancresse Vale, Guernsey (3m N of St Peter Port)
T:(0481) 47022
18 | 6143 yds | Par 70 | SSS 70
Visitors welcome ⊠,not Th (pm) S (pm) Sun | ∴ per day | ∴ per round | ☎ |
B (not W) | L D prior arrangement | ⚘ ♉ ↘ | ⋈ prior arrangement | TR Th
and S pm, Sun before 1700 | ④ ☎ | M 1000 | S
★★★★*St Pierre Park, Rohais, St. Peter Port. T:(0481) 28282. 135rm ⇋ ⌂*
See advertisement on page 71.
Not quite as old as its neighbour Royal Jersey, Royal Guernsey is a
sporting course which was redesigned after World War II by
Mackenzie Ross, who has many fine courses to his credit. It is a
pleasant links well-maintained and administered by the States of
Guernsey in the form of the States Tourist Committee. The 8th hole,
a good par four, requires an accurate second shot to the green set
amongst the gorse and thick rough. The 18th, with lively views,
needs a strong shot to reach the green well down below. The course
is windy, with hard walking. There is a junior section.

GUILDFORD
Surrey
Map **II**   D5

Guildford High Path Rd, Merrow, Guildford (E side of town centre off A246)
T:(0483) 575243
Societies welcome by arrangement. 18 | 6080 yds | Par 69 | SSS 70
Visitors welcome, with M only WE BH | without M ⁞⁞ per day | with M ⁚⁚ per
day WE | B L ☎ ⚘ ♉ | TR W am, WE BH | ♩ | M 600 | S
★★*Angel, High St. T:(0483) 64555. 27rm ⇋ ⌂*
A downland course but with some trees and much scrub. The holes
provide an interesting variety of play, an invigorating experience.

GULLANE
Lothian, *East Lothian*
Map **VI** H2

Gullane Gullane (In centre of
village on A198)
T:(0620) 843115
3 courses. 18 | No 1 6491 yds, No 2
6127 yds, No 3 5035 yds | Par 71, 70,
65 | SSS 71, 69, 64
Visitors welcome, ☎ for courses 2
and 3 | Course 1 ∷ per day WE;
Course 2 ∴ per day ∷ WE; Course
3 ‥ per day ∴ WE | B L ☙ D prior
arrangement (not Mon) | ▵ ⅄ ⤸ |
④ (1) before 1030 | ⅃ | M 1200 | Ⓢ
★★★*Marine, Cromwell Rd, North
Berwick.* T:(0620) 2406.
86rm (76 ⇆ 10 🍴

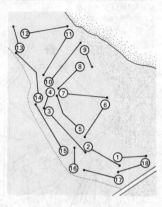

A delightful village and one of Scotland's great golf centres.
Gullane club was formed in 1882. There are three Gullane courses
and the No 1 is of championship standard. It differs from most
Scottish courses inasmuch as it is of the downland type and really
quite hilly. The first tee is literally in the village. The views from the
top of the course are magnificent and stretch far and wide in every
direction — in fact, it is said that 14 counties can be seen from the
highest spot.

Par 68 | *SSS 68*
Visitors welcome, only withM WE
BH | ∴ per day WE | B L ☙ D prior
arrangement (not Th) | ▵ ⅄ ⤸ | ⋈
| ④ TR S | ⅃ | M 790 | Ⓢ
★★★*Tontine, 6 Ardgowan Sq.*
T:(0475) 23316. *32rm (20* ⇆*)*

Whinhill Beith Rd, Greenock (1½m
SW of Greenock off B7054)
T:(0475) 210641
Picturesque heathland public course. 18
| 5454 yds | Par 66 | SSS 68
Visitors welcome to play on
municipal course | Private club
facilities with M only ⋈ ☎
★★★*Tontine, 6 Ardgowan Sq.*
T:(0475) 23316. *32rm (20* ⇆*)*

GRIMSBY
Humberside
Map **V** J7

Grimsby Littlecoates Rd, Grimsby
(W side of town centre off A1136)
T:(0472) 42823
Parkland course with easy walking. 18 |
6058 yds | Par 70 | SSS 69
Visitors welcome ⋈ restricted WE |
☎ | B ☙ | L D prior arrangement

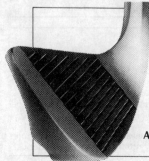

GULLANE
Lothian, *East Lothian*
Map VI   H2

Honourable Company of Edinburgh Golfers Muirfield, Gullane
(NE side of village)
T:(0620 84) 2123
18 | 6601 yds | Par 70 | SSS 73
Visitors welcome with M | without M Tu, Th, F am only ∷ per day | L ⊻ ☙⚲
⚲ | ✉ ☎ | | ⟦TR⟧ Mon, W, F, WE | ④ am | M 550
❀★★★⚌ *Greywalls, Duncar Rd, Gullane. T:(0620) 842144. 18rm (3 ▦)*
A prestigious links course with undulating grounds, no trees and
no water hazards, tenacious rough and 148 bunkers. Many of the
premier golfing tournaments are staged here.

(not W S) | ⚲ ⊻ ✉ | ⌡ | ④ ☎ for
details | M 725 | ⟦S⟧
★★★ *Humber Royal Crest, Littlecoates
Rd. T:(0472) 50295. 52rm ⇌*

GUERNSEY
Channel Islands
Map I   A4

St Pierre Park Rohais, St Peter Port
(1m W of town centre off Rohais
Rd)
T:(0481) 27039/28282
*Parkland course in delightful setting,
with lakes, streams and many tricky
holes. 9 | 1136 yds | Par 27*
Visitors welcome | ✳ | B L D ☙ ⊻ |
⚲ ✉ ✉ | ⟦S⟧
★★★★ *St Pierre Park, Rohais,
St Peter Port. T:(0481) 28282.
135rm (135 ⇌ ▦)*

GUISELEY
West Yorkshire
Map V   F6

Bradford Hawksworth Ln,
Guiseley, Leeds (SW side of town
centre off A6038)
T:(0943) 75570

*Moorland course with eight par 4 holes
of 360 yds or more. Many trees have
been planted recently. Societies welcome
by arrangement. 18 | 6259 yds | Par 71
| SSS 70*
Visitors welcome (Mon W Th Fri)
but with M ✉ WE BH | ☎ | without
M ∴ per day ∷ WE | with M .. per
day WE | B ☙ L D prior
arrangement | ⚲ | ⊻ | ✉ | ⌡ | ✉ |
M 560 | ⟦S⟧
★★★ *Craiglands, Cowpasture Rd,
Ilkley. T:(0943) 607676.
73rm (53 ⇌ 5 ▦)*

GURNEY SLADE
Somerset
Map I   H3

Mendip Bath (1½m S of Gurney
Slade off A37)
T:(0749) 840570
*Undulating downland course offers an
interesting test of golf on superb
fairways. 18 | 5958 yds | Par 69 |
SSS 69*
Visitors welcome, ✉ ☎ advisable.
Must belong to affiliated club. | ∴
per day WE, juniors half-rate | B | L

D prior arrangement (not Mon) | ☙
⚲ ⊻ ✉ | ✉ by arrangement ⟦TR⟧ ☎
advisable | M 600 | ⟦S⟧
★★ *Crown, Market Pl, Wells. T:(0749)
73457. 18rm (11 ⇌ 7 ▦)*

HADDINGTON
Lothian, *East Lothian*
Map VI   H2

Amisfield (1½m W of town centre)
T:(062082) 3627
*An inland course with lush fairways in
summer, trees and bunkers. 18 |
6280 yds | Par 71 | SSS 70*
Visitors welcome | B L D | ⊻ ☙ ⟦S⟧ ✉
✉ | ⟦TR⟧ S, Sun 0700-1000 | M 390
★★ *George, 91 High St. T:(062082)
3372. 4rm ⇌*

Haddington Amisfield Park (E side
of Haddington off A6137)
T:(062082) 3627
*Inland course with trees & bushes. 18 |
6280 yds | Par 71 | SSS 70*
Visitors welcome ☎ | ∴ per day
WE | B L ☙ D prior arrangement |
✉ ⚲ ⊻ ✉ | ⟦TR⟧ WE before 1000 |
M 375 | ⟦S⟧
★★ *George, 91 High St. T:(062082)
3372. 4rm ⇌*

HALE
Cheshire
Map V   D8

Hale Rappax Rd, Hale, Altrincham
(1¼m SE of Hale)
T:061-980 4225
*Beautiful undulating parkland course,
with River Bollin winding round
fairways. 9 | 5241 yds | Par 70 | SSS 68*
Visitors welcome ☎ | WE only with
M | restricted Th | without M ∴ per
day | with M .. per day WE | B L ☙,⟼

HADLEY WOOD
Hertfordshire
Map **II** E2

Hadley Wood Beech Hill (E side of village)
T:01-449 4328
18 | 6473 yds | Par 72 | SSS 71
Visitors welcome weekdays ⊠ | ☎ preferred | without M ∷ weekdays | with M ∴ weekdays | B L D prior arrangement (not Mon) | ☕ (not Mon) | △ 🍸 | ℨ | [TR] WE ④ ☎ for details | M 550 | [S]
★★★★West Lodge Park, Cockfosters Rd, Hadley Wood. T:01-440 8311. 50rm ⇄

A parkland course on the north-west edge of London at Barnet, easily accessible. The gently undulating fairways have a friendly width inviting the player to open his shoulders, though the thick rough can be very punishing to the unwary. The course is pleasantly wooded and there are some admirable views.

D prior arrangement (not Tu) | △ 🍸 prior arrangement | [TR] Th ladies day (until 1630) | M 305
★★★Bowdon, Langham Rd, Bowdon, Altrincham. T:061-928 7121. 41rm (38 ⇄)

HALESOWEN
West Midlands
Map **III** H5

Halesowen The Leasowes (1m E of Halesowen, off A458)
T:021-501 3606
Parkland course in convenient position. Societies by special arrangement. 18 | 5673 yds | Par 69 | SSS 68
Visitors welcome but with M only WE ☎ | ∴ per day WE | B L D (not Mon) | ☕ △ ╲ 🍸 ⋈ | [TR] WE and BH | M 500 | [S]
★★Norfolk, 257-267 Hagley Rd, Edgbaston, Birmingham. T:021-454 8071. 175rm (32 ⇄ 56 🚿)

HALIFAX
West Yorkshire
Map **V** E6

Halifax Bob Hall, Union Ln, Ogden (4m NW of Halifax off A629)
T:(0422) 244171
Moorland course crossed by stream, natural hazards, fine views. Testing 172-yd 17th hole (par 3). Societies welcome (Tu to F) WE by arrangement. 18 | 6034 yds | Par 70 | SSS 70
Visitors welcome, parties restricted Mon WE | ☎ preferred | without M ‥ per round ∴ WE | with M ‥ per round WE | B (not Mon) | L ☕ D prior arrangement (not Mon) | △ | 🍸 (not Mon) | ⋈ ╲ prior arrangement | ④ [TR] WE competition days | ℨ | M 400 | [S]
★★★Holdsworth House, Holdsworth Ln, Holmfield. T:(0422) 240024. 40rm (28 ⇄ 12 🚿)

Lightcliffe Knowle Top Rd, Lightcliffe (3½m E of Halifax on A58)
T:(0422) 202459
Heathland course. Societies welcome by arrangement. 9 | 5388 yds | Par 68 | SSS 68
Visitors welcome, restricted W (1130-1630) competition days | without M ‥ per round ∴ WE | with M ‥ per day WE | B ☕ (not Th) | L D prior arrangement (not Th) | △ 🍸 | ⋈ (possibly) | [TR] W (1130- 1630) competition days | M 487 | [S] ℨ
★★★Holdsworth House, Holdsworth Ln, Holmfield, Halifax. T:(0422) 240024. 40rm (28 ⇄ 12 🚿)

West End Paddock Ln, Highroad Well, Halifax (W side of town centre off A646)
T:(0422) 53068
Semi-moorland course. Societies welcome by arrangement. 18 | 6003 yds | Par 68 | SSS 69
Visitors welcome | without M ∴ per day WE | with M ‥ per day WE | B L ☕ D (not Mon) | △ 🍸 | ℨ | ④ competition days | [TR] competition days | M 600 | [S]
★★★Holdsworth House, Holdsworth Ln, Holmfield. T:(0422) 240024. 40rm (28 ⇄ 12 🚿)

HALTON
Buckinghamshire
Map **II** C2

Chiltern Forest Aston Hill, Aylesbury (1m NE of Halton, off A4011)
T:(0296) 630899 Sec. (0296) 631267
Hilly wooded parkland course on two levels. Testing uphill 7th hole (par 3). Ladies tees. 9 | 5298 mtrs | Par 68 | SSS 69
Visitors welcome | ∴ per day | B L ☕ D | △ | 🍸 | ⋈ | [TR] WE | M 450
★★Bell, Market Sq, Aylesbury. T:(0296) 89835. 17rm (16 ⇄ 1 🚿)

HAMILTON
Strathclyde, *Lanarkshire*
Map **VI** E3

Hamilton Riccarton, Ferniegair
(1½m SE of Hamilton on A72)
T:(0698) 282872
*Beautiful parkland course. Societies
welcome by arrangement.* 18 | 6281 yds
| Par 70 | SSS 70
Visitors welcome with M only | B
(not Th) | L ☻ D prior arrangement
(not Th) | ⚠ Υ | TR W WE | Ͽ |
M 480 | S
★★*Silvertrees, Silverwells Cres,
Bothwell. T:(0698) 852311. 7rm* ⇌ ▦
Annexe: 19rm ⇌ ▦

Strathclyde Park Mote Hill,
Hamilton (N side of town off B7071)
T:(0698) 66155
Municipal parkland course. 9 |
3147 yds | Par 35 | SSS 70
Visitors welcome | B L ☻ D (bar
meals until 2100) | ⚠ Υ | ⋈
sometimes | TR every 2nd S in
summer and medal days from 0700-
1200 | M 220 | S
★★*Silvertrees, Silverwells Cres,
Bothwell. T:(0698) 852311. 7rm* ⇌ ▦
Annexe: 19rm ⇌ ▦

HAMPTON WICK
Greater London
Map **II** E4

Home Park Hampton Wick,
Kingston-upon-Thames (off A308
on W side of Kingston Bridge)
T:01-977 2423
*Flat parkland course with easy walking.
Societies welcome by arrangement.
Children under 12 not permitted in
clubhouse.* 18 | 6497 yds | Par 71 |
SSS 71
Visitors welcome ☎ | B L ☻ not F |
⚠ Υ | ⋈ | Ͽ | TR competitions |
M 500 | S
★★★*Richmond Hill, 146-150
Richmond Hill, Richmond. T:01-940
2247. 125rm (110* ⇌ 4 ▦*)*

HARLECH
Gwynedd
Map **III** D3

Royal St Davids Harlech (W side of
town on A496)
*Championship links, with easy walking
and natural hazards.* 18 | 6495 yds |
Par 69 | SSS 72
Visitors welcome | ∴ per day ::
WE | B ☻ | L D prior arrangement

HARROGATE
North Yorkshire
Map **V** F5

Harrogate Forest Ln Head, Starbeck (2¼m E of Harrogate on A59)
T:(0423) 863158
Societies welcome by arrangement. 18 | 6204 yds | Par 69 | SSS 70
Visitors welcome, restricted Tu (am) S | ☎ advisable for parties | without M ∴
per day :: WE | B ☻ | L D prior arrangement (not F) | ⚠ Υ ⤬ | ⋈
(sometimes) | TR most S | Ͽ | M 600 | S
★★★*Cairn, Ripon Rd. T:(0423) 504005. 140rm (116* ⇌ 3 ▦*)*
One of Yorkshire's oldest and best courses, Harrogate was
designed in 1897 by 'Sandy' Herd. A perfect example of golf
architecture, its greens and fairways offer an interesting but fair
challenge. The course once formed part of the ancient Forest of
Knaresborough.

Oakdale Kent Rd, Harrogate (N side of town centre off A61)
T:(0423) 67162
18 | 6456 yds | Par 71 | SSS 70
Visitors welcome | without M ∴ per day :: WE | with M .. per day WE | B ☻
L D | ⚠ Υ ⤬ | ⋈ | TR before 0930 and 1230-1400 | M 700 | S
★★★★*Old Swan, Swan Road. T:(0423) 500055. 137rm (115* ⇌ 12 ▦*)*
A pleasant, undulating parkland course which provides a good test
of golf for the low handicap player without intimidating the less
proficient. A special feature is an attractive stream which comes in
to play on four holes. Excellent views from the Clubhouse which
has excellent facilities. Recent developments have considerably
enhanced the course from both a playing and scenic point of view.

(clubhouse closed Tu in winter) | ⚠
Υ ⋈ | TR competition days |
M 700 | S
★★*Ty Mawr, Llanbedr. T:(034123)
440. 10rm (2* ⇌ 4 ▦*)*

HARPENDEN
Hertfordshire
Map **II** E2

Harpenden Hammonds End,
Redbourn Ln (1m S of Harpenden
on B487)
T:(05827) 2580
*Gently undulating parkland course,
easy walking.* 18 | 6363 yds | Par 70 |
SSS 70
Visitors welcome WE | with M only
and ⋈ | ☎ preferred | B ☻ | L D
prior arrangement | ⚠ Υ | Ͽ | M 750
| S | TR 1st tee until 0930
★★★★*Harpenden Moat House, 18
Southdown Rd. T:(05827) 64111.
16rm (13* ⇌ 3 ▦*) Annexe: 30* ⇌

Harpenden Common Cravells Rd,
East Common (1m S of Harpenden
on A1081)
T:(05827) 5959
*Flat, easy walking, good greens, typical
common course.* 18 | 5613 yds | Par 68 |

SSS 67
Visitors welcome, restricted Mon-F
☎ | ✳ | B L ☻ (not Mon) D prior
arrangement | ⚠ Υ (1100-1500) |
TR WE | Tu Ladies Day | Ͽ | M 700 |
Ͽ | S
★★★*Glen Eagle, 1 Luton Rd,
Harpenden. T:(05827) 60271. 51rm
(48* ⇌ 3 ▦*)*

HARTLEPOOL
Cleveland
Map **V** F2

Castle Eden & Peterlee Castle
Eden, Hartlepool (2m S of Peterlee
on B1281, off A19)
T:(0429) 836510
*Beautiful parkland course alongside a
nature reserve. Hard walking, trees
provide wind shelter. Parties welcome
Th.* 18 | 6339 yds | Par 70 | SSS 70
Visitors welcome, no parties after
1600 | without M ∴ per day WE |
with M .. per day WE | B L ☻ D |
⚠ Υ | ⤬ ⋈ prior arrangement | Ͽ |
M 675 | S
★★★*Norseman, Bede Way, Peterlee.
T:(0783) 862161. 26rm* ▦

HARTLEPOOL
Cleveland
Map **V**   G2

Hartlepool Hart Warren (N side of Hartlepool off King Oswy Drive)
18 | 6218 yds | Par 70 | SSS 70
Visitors welcome ⊠ restricted WE BH | without M ∴ per day WE | with M ..
per day WE | ♥ (not Mon) | B L D prior arrangement (not Mon) | ♨ ⛾ ⚲ | ⋈
| TR Sun (am) | ⅃ | M 500 | Ⓢ
★★★*Hardwick Hall, Sedgefield. T:(0740) 20253. 16rm* ⇄
A seaside course, half links, overlooking the North Sea. A good test
and equally enjoyable to all handicap players. The 10th, par 4,
demands a precise second shot over a ridge and between sand
dunes, to a green down near the edge of the beach, alongside which
several holes are played.

HARTLEY WINTNEY
Hampshire
Map **II**   C4

Hartley Wintney London Rd,
Hartley Wintney (NE side of village
on A30)
T:(025126) 4211/3779
*Easy walking parkland course in
countryside. Testing par 4 at 4th and
13th. Societies welcome.* 9 | 6082 yds |
Par 70 | SSS 69
Visitors welcome, restricted W BH
WE | without M ∴ per day | with M
.. per day | B L ♥ D (societies only)
| ♨ ⛾ ⋈ ⚲ | TR ☎ for details |
M 400 | Ⓢ
★★★*Lismoyne, Church Rd, Fleet.
T:(02514) 28555. 40rm (29 ⇄ 3 ⋔)*

HARWICH
Essex
Map **IV**   J8

Harwich & Dovercourt Station Rd,
Parkeston, Dovercourt (W side of
Harwich ¼m from docks on A120)
T:(0255) 503616
*Flat moorland course with easy
walking.* 9 | 2931 yds | Par 68 | SSS 68
Visitors welcome with M ⊠ |
restricted WE | B ♥ L D prior
arrangement | ♨ ⛾ ⚲ | TR WE |
M 315 | Ⓢ
★★*Cliff, Marine Pde, Dovercourt.
T:(0255) 503345. 35rm (21 ⇄ 2 ⋔)*

HARWOOD, GREAT
Lancashire
Map **V**   D6

Great Harwood Harwood Bar,
Whalley Rd (E side of town centre
on A680)
T:(0254) 884391
*Flat parkland course with fine view of
the Pendle regions.* 9 | 6411 yds |

Par 73 | SSS 71
Visitors welcome weekdays |
restricted BH WE | .. per day ∴
WE | B L ♥ (not Mon) | ♨ ⛾ | TR
WE Tu | ⅃ | M 300 | Ⓢ
★★*Shireburn Arms, Hurst Green.
T:(025486) 518. 11rm (6 ⇄ 1 ⋔)*

HASLINGDEN
Lancashire
Map **V**   D6

Rossendale Ewood Ln Head,
Haslingden, Rossendale (1½m S of
Haslingden off A56)
T:(0706) 213056
*Testing, and usually windy
meadowland course.* 18 | 6262 yds |
Par 72 | SSS 70
Visitors welcome ☎ | Sun ⊠ | S
only with M | without M .. per day
∴ WE | with M .. per day WE | B L
♥ D prior arrangement (not Mon) |
♨ ⛾ TR WE, S | M 700 | Ⓢ
★★★*Blackburn Moat House, Preston
New Rd, Blackburn. T:(0254) 64441.
98rm* ⇄

HASTINGS
East Sussex
Map **II**   H7

Beauport Park St Leonards-on-Sea
(3m N of Hastings on A2100)
T:(0424) 52977
*Play over Hastings Public Course.
Undulating parkland course with
stream. Fine views. Societies welcome.*
18 | 6325 yds | Par 71 | SSS 70
Visitors welcome | B L ♥ | D prior
arrangement | ♨ ⛾ ⚲ | M 200 | Ⓢ
★★★*Beauport Park, Battle Rd,
Hastings. T:(0424) 51222. 23rm* ⇄

HAVERFORDWEST
Dyfed
Map **III**   B7

Haverfordwest Arnolds Down (1m
E of Haverfordwest on A40)
T:(0437) 3565
*Downland course in countryside,
exposed and windy. Societies welcome
by arrangement.* 18 | 5915 yds | Par 70
| SSS 70
Visitors welcome anytime | without
M .. per day ∴ WE | with M .. per
day | B L ♥ D prior arrangement
(not F) | ♨ ⛾ ⚲ ⋈ possible | TR
competition days | M 370 | Ⓢ
★★*Mariners Inn, Nolton Haven.
T:(0437) 710469. 11rm (4 ⇄ 7 ⋔)*

HAVERHILL
Suffolk
Map **IV**   F7

Haverhill Coupals Rd (1m SE of
Haverhill, off A604)
T:(0440) 61951
*Private parkland course with small
river crossing 3 times each 9 holes.* 9 |
5708 yds | Par 68 | SSS 68
Open to public | ∴ per day | ♥ | ♨
⛾ | TR ☎ for details | ⅃ | M 230 | Ⓢ
⋈
★★*Bell, Market Hill, Clare. T:(0787)
277741. 18rm (2 ⇄ 1 ⋔) Annexe: 11* ⇄

HAWARDEN
Clwyd
Map **III**   F2

Hawarden Groomsdale Ln,
Hawarden (W side of town off
B5125)
T:(0244) 531447
*Parkland course with comfortable
walking and good views. Societies
welcome by arrangement.* 9 | 5728 yds |
Par 68 | SSS 68
Visitors welcome restricted W pm |
WE BH only with M | ✳ | B ♥ (not
Tu) | L D prior arrangement
(not Tu) | ♨ ⛾ | ⋈ by arrangement |
TR 0800-0900, 1230-1330 | ⅃ | M 328
| Ⓢ
★★★*Chequers, Northophall. T:(0244)
816181. 29rm (27 ⇄ 2 ⋔)*

HAWICK
Borders, *Roxburghshire*
Map **VI**   H4

Hawick Vertish Hill, Hawick (SW
side of town)
*Windy hill course, with hard walking.
Good views.* 18 | 5929 yds | Par 68 |
SSS 69
Visitors welcome | B L ♥ D | ⛾ ⋈ |
M 500 | Ⓢ

HAYLING ISLAND
Hampshire
Map II C7

Hayling Ferry Rd, Hayling Island (SW side of island at West Town)
T:(0705) 464446
18 | 6489 yds | Par 71 | SSS 71
Visitors welcome, restricted BH competition days | ✉ | ☎ advisable | ∴ per
day | :: WE | B ☎ (not Mon) | L D prior arrangement (not Mon) | ⚐ Ⴤ ⚲ | TR
competition days, ladies 2nd and 4th Th | ♩ | M 900 | S
**✶✶*Newtown House, Manor Rd. T:(0705) 466131. 28rm (19 ⇄ 9 ♨)*
A delightful links course among the dunes offering fine sea-scapes
and views of the Isle of Wight. Varying sea breezes and sometimes
strong winds ensure that the course seldom plays the same two
days running. Testing holes at the 12th and 13th, both par 4. Club
selection is important.

✶✶*Kirklands, West Stewart Pl.*
T:(0450) 72263. 6rm (2 ⇄ 1 ♨)

HAWKHURST
Kent
Map II H6

Hawkhurst High St, Hawkhurst (W
side of village off A268)
T:(058058) 2396
*Undulating parkland course. Societies
welcome (Mon to F by arrangement. 9 |
5769 yds | Par 72 | SSS 68*
Visitors welcome, restricted WE BH
| without M .. per day ∴ WE |
with M .. per day | B | ☎ | ⚐ Ⴤ | ♩
| M 300 | S | TR competitions
✶✶*Tudor Arms, Rye Rd. T:(05805)
2312. 14rm (6 ⇄ 3 ♨)*

HAYWARDS HEATH
West Sussex
Map II F6

Haywards Heath High Beech Ln
(1¼m N of Haywards Heath off
B2028)
T:(0444) 414457
*Parkland/heathland course. Societies
welcome by arrangement. 18 | 6202 yds
| Par 71 | SSS 70*
Visitors welcome | ✳ | B ☎ (not Tu) |
L D prior arrangement (not Tu) | ⚐
Ⴤ ⚲ TR Tu am, competition days |
④ not before 0930 | ♩ | M 660 | S
✶✶✶*Ockendon Manor, Ockendon Ln,
Cuckfield. T:(0444) 416111. 10rm ⇄ 4 ♨*

HAZEL GROVE
Greater Manchester
Map V E8

Hazel Grove Buxton Rd, Hazel
Grove, Stockport (1m E of Hazel
Grove off A6)
T:061-483 3217
Moorland course. 18 | 6300 yds |

Par 71 | SSS 70
Visitors welcome | B L ☎ D prior
arrangement (not Mon) | ⚐ Ⴤ | ✕ |
TR competitions (usually S) | ♩ |
M 550 | S
✶*Acton Court, Buxton Rd, Stockport.
T:061-483 6172. 24rm (6 ⇄)*

HAZEL SLADE
Staffordshire
Map III J4

Beau Desert (½m NE of village)
T:(05438) 2626/2773
*Woodland course. Societies welcome by
arrangement. 18 | 6285 yds | Par 70 |
SSS 71*
Visitors welcome | :: per day WE |
B L D ☎ (parties prior
arrangement) | ⚐ Ⴤ ⚲ | ♩ | TR WE
| M 450 | S
✶✶✶*Roman Way, Watling St,
Hatherton, Cannock. T:(05435) 72121.
24rm (20 ⇄ 4 ♨)*

HEBDEN BRIDGE
West Yorkshire
Map V E6

Mount Skip Wadsworth (1½m E of
Hebden Bridge off A6033)
T:(0422) 842896
*Moorland course with splendid views.
Societies welcome by arrangement. 9 |
5202 yds | Par 68 | SSS 66*
Visitors welcome | B L ☎ D | ⚐ Ⴤ |
TR competition days | M 150
✶*Sun, Featherstall Rd, Littleborough.
T:(0706) 78957. 8rm*

HELENSBURGH
Strathclyde, *Dumbartonshire*
Map VI D2

Helensburgh 25 East Abercromby
St, Helensburgh (NE side of town
off B832)

T:(0463) 4173
*Sporting moorland course with superb
views of Loch Lomond and River Clyde.
18 | 6058 yds | Par 69 | SSS 69*
Visitors welcome ☎ only with M
WE | without M ∴ per day | with M
.. per day WE | B ☎ | L D prior
arrangment | ⚐ Ⴤ ⚲ | TR varies
☎ for details | ♩ | M 800 | S
✶✶✶*Commodore, 112 West Clyde St.
T:(0436) 6924. 45rm ⇄*

HELMSDALE
Highland, *Sutherland*
Map VII G3

Helmsdale Strath Rd, Helmsdale
(NW side of town on A897)
T:(04312) 224
*Sheltered, undulating 9 hole course
following the line of the Helmsdale
River. 9 | 1825 yds | Par 31(62) |
SSS 31(62)*
Visitors welcome without M | ..
per day | M 80
✶✶🏊*Navidale House, Helmsdale.
T:(04312) 258. 11rm (1 ⇄)*

HELSBY
Cheshire
Map III G2

Helsby Towers Ln (1m S of Helsby
off A56)
T:(09282) 2021
*Quiet parkland course with natural
hazards. 18th hole is testing 240 yds
par. Societies welcome by arrangement.
18 | 6262 yds | Par 71 | SSS 70*
Visitors welcome restricted WE BH |
☎ preferred | without M ∴ per day
WE | with M .. per day WE | B ☎
(not Tu) | L D prior arrangement
(not Tu) | ⚐ Ⴤ ✕ | ♩ | ④ ☎ | M 550
| S
○○○○*Chester Grosvenor, Eastgate St,
Chester. T:(0244) 24024. 98rm ♨*

HEMEL HEMPSTEAD
Hertfordshire
Map II D2

Boxmoor 18 Box Ln, Boxmoor (2m
SW of Hemel Hempstead on B4505)
T:(0442) 42434
*Challenging moorland course, fine
views, hard walking. Testing holes: 3rd
(par 3), 4th (par 4). Societies welcome
by arrangement. Children welcome. 9 |
4302/4834 yds | Par 62/64 | SSS 62/64*
Visitors welcome, not Sun | Ⴤ ☎ ⚐
✕ (probable) | TR Sun | M 250
✶✶✶*Post House, Breakspear Way,* ➥

KEY

(IA1)	*atlas grid reference*
T:	*telephone number*
☎	*advance letter/telephone call required*
⊠	*introduction from own club sec/handicap certificate/club membership card required*
..	*low fees*
∴	*medium fees*
::	*high fees*
*	*green fees not confirmed for 1987*
B	*light lunch*
L	*full lunch*
☛	*tea*
D	*dinner*
⚇	*changing rooms/showers*
☗	*bar open mid-day and evenings*
⟍	*clubs for hire*
⋈	*partners may be found*
④	*restricted time for 4 balls*
TR	*times reserved for members*
ꓰ	*professional*
S	*well-stocked shop*
M	*member*
Mon Tu W Th F S Sun	
WE	*weekend*
BH	*bank holiday*

Hemel Hempstead. T:(0442) 51122. *Annexe: 107rm* ⇄

Little Hay Box Ln, Bovingdon
(1½m SW of Hemel Hempstead on
B4505 off A41)
T:(0442) 833798
*Semi-parkland inland links. 18 |
6610 yds | Par 72 | SSS 70*
Visitors welcome .. per day WE | B
L ☛ | ⚇ Y ⟍ | ⋈ possible | ꓰ | S
★★★*Post House, Breakspear Way.*
T:(0442) 51122. *Annexe: 107rm* ⇄

HENLEY-ON-THAMES
Oxfordshire
Map **II**   C3

Badgemore Park (1m W of Henley)
T:(0491) 572206
*Parkland course with many trees and
easy walking. Societies welcome by
arrangement. 18 | 6112 yds | Par 69 |
SSS 69*
Visitors welcome ⊠ restricted WE
BH | ☎ | B | L D (by arrangement)
☛ | ⚇ Y | ⟍ | TR Tu (Ladies have
priority) | M 750 | S④ WE, BH
★★★*Red Lion, Henley-on-Thames.*
T:(0491) 572161. *28rm (19* ⇄)

Henley Harpsden (1¼m S of
Henley off A4155)
T:(0491) 575742
*Undulating parkland course. 6th hole
blind (par 4) with steep hill.
18 | 6329(White) 6130(Yellow)
5902(Green) yds | SSS 70/69/68*
Visitors welcome, with M only WE
BH | ☎ advisable | without M ::
per day | with M .. per day WE | B
☛ (not Mon) | L D prior
arrangement (not Mon) | ⚇ Y ⟍ |
TR ④ ☎ | ꓰ | S
★★★*Red Lion, Henley-on-Thames.*
T:(0491) 572161. *28rm (19* ⇄)

HERNE BAY
Kent
Map **II**   J4

Herne Bay Thanet Way (1m S of
Herne Bay on A291)
T:(0227) 373964
*Parkland course with bracing air. 18 |
5403 yds | Par 68 | SSS 66*
Visitors welcome restricted WE
(am) | ∴ per round/day weekdays
∴ per round :: per day after 1030
WE | B L ☛ D prior arrangement |
⚇ Y ⋈ | TR WE before 1030 | ꓰ |
M 350 | S
★★*Marine, Marine Parade, Tankerton,
Whitstable.* T:(0227) 272672. *20rm (4
⇄ 16* 🏠)

HESSLE
Humberside
Map **V**   H6

Hessle Westfield Rd, Raywell,
Cottingham (4m NW of Hessle, off
A164)
T:(0482) 650171
*Well-wooded downland course, easy
walking, windy. Societies welcome by
arrangement. 18 | 6638 yds | Par 72 |
SSS 72 or 6290 yds | Par 72 | SSS 70*

Visitors welcome | ☎ advisable |
without M ∴ per day WE | with M
.. per day WE | B ☛ | L D prior
arrangement (not Mon) | ⚇ Y ⋈ |
④ ☎ | TR Tu 0915-1300 (ladies) ☎
competition days | ꓰ | M 500 | S
★★★*Crest Hotel Humber Bridge,
Ferriby High Rd, North Ferriby.*
T:(0482) 645212. *102rm* ⇄

HEXHAM
Northumberland
Map **VI**   J6

Tynedale Tyne Green, Hexham
(N side of town)
*Flat easy moorland course. Bounded by
river and railway. 9 | 5643 yds | Par 69
| SSS 67*
Visitors welcome, restricted Sun |
⋈ | TR Sun 0730-1030 | M 275
★★*Beaumont, Beaumont St.* T:(0434)
602331. *22rm (2* ⇄ *14* 🏠)

HEYSHAM
Lancashire
Map **V**   C5

Heysham Trumacar Park (¾m S of
Heysham off A589)
T:(0524) 51011
*Seaside course. 18 | 6224 yds | Par 69 |
SSS 70*
Visitors welcome | with M .. per
day ∴ without M | B | L | ☛ D | ⚇
Y ⟍ | TR 1300-1345 | ꓰ | M 500 | S
★★*Clarendon, Promenade, West End,
Morecambe.* T:(0524) 410180. *31rm
(19* ⇄ *6* 🏠)

HICKLETON
South Yorkshire
Map **V**   G7

Hickleton Hickleton, nr Doncaster
(½m W of Hickleton on B6411)
T:(0709) 892496

HEXHAM
Northumberland
Map **V** E1

Hexham Spital Park (1m NW of Hexham on B6531)
T:(0434) 603072
Societies welcome (not Sun F) by arrangement.
18 | 6272 yds | Par 70 | SSS 70
Visitors welcome ☎ advisable | without M ∴ per day WE | with M ‥ per day WE | B L ☕ (not F) | D △ Y | [TR] Tu Th 1300-1400 | ℑ | M 700 | [S]
★★Beaumont, Beaumont St. T:(0434) 602331. 22rm (2 ⇌ 14 🚿)

SCORE CARD:

1	503	10	192
2	170	11	496
3	405	12	434
4	182	13	144
5	365	14	414
6	458	15	502
7	383	16	120
8	438	17	405
9	359	18	347

A very pretty undulating parkland course with interesting natural contours. From parts of the course, particularly the elevated 6th tee, there are the most exquisite views of the valley below. As good a parkland course as any in the North of England.

HINDHEAD
Surrey
Map **II** D5

Hindhead Churt Rd (2m NW of Hindhead on A287)
T:(042873) 4614
18 | 6349 yds | Par 70 | SSS 70
Visitors welcome ✉ | ☎ advisable | without M ∷ per day ∷ WE | with M ‥ per day ∴ WE | B ☕ L | △ Y ↘ | ⋈ (possible) | ④ [TR]☎ | ℑ | M 550 | [S]
★★★Frensham Pond, Churt. T:(025125) 3175. 7rm ⇌ Annexe: 12rm ⇌

A good example of a Surrey heath and heather course, and most picturesque. Players must be prepared for some hard walking. The first nine fairways follow narrow valleys requiring straight hitting; the second nine are much less restricted.

Undulating parkland course with stream running through, designed by Neil Coles and Brian Huggett. Societies welcome by arrangement. 18 | 6400 yds | Par 71 | SSS 71
Visitors welcome ☎ | restricted WE | without M ‥ weekdays WE | with M ‥ per day WE | B ☕ | L D prior arrangement | △ Y | ⋈ | [TR] S pm Sun am | ℑ | M 400 | [S]
★★★Danum Swallow, High St, Doncaster. T:(0302) 62261. 66rm (59 ⇌ 7 🚿)

HIGHCLIFFE
Dorset
Map **I** K5

Highcliffe Castle Lymington Rd, Highcliffe-on-Sea (SW side of town on A337)
T:(04252) 72953/72210
Parkland course with easy walking. Societies welcome by arrangement. 18 | 4732 yds | Par 64 | SSS 63
Visitors welcome without M ∴ per day ∷ WE | with M ‥ per day | B ☕ L D prior arrangement (not Tu) | △ Y ↘ | [TR] before 0930 | ℑ | M 450 | [S]⋈
★★Dan Cooks, Lyndhurst Rd, Christchurch. T:(04252) 3202. 19rm (3 ⇌ 10 🚿)

HIGH GREEN
South Yorkshire
Map **V** F7

Tankersley Park High Green, Sheffield (1m NE of High Green)
T:(0742) 468247
Parkland course, hilly, windy, with good views. Societies welcome by arrangement. 18 | 6212 yds | Par 69 | SSS 70
Visitors welcome (WE only with M) | B ☕ | L D prior arrangement (not Mon) | △ Y | ⋈ prior arrangement | [TR] Tu (Ladies Day) | M 430 | [S]
★★Rutland, 452 Glossop Rd, Broomhill, Sheffield. T:(0742) 664411. 73rm (68 ⇌ 1 🚿). Annexe: 17rm (15 ⇌ 2 🚿)

HILLINGDON
Greater London
Map **II** D3

Hillingdon Dorset Way, Vine Ln, Uxbridge (W side of Hillingdon off A4020)
T:(0895) 33956
Parkland course west of London. Societies welcome by arrangement. 9(x2) | 5459 yds | Par 68 | SSS 67
Visitors welcome weekdays | with M only WE BH | without M ∴ per day | with M ‥ per day | B ☕ | △ Y | ↘ prior arrangement | [TR] Th pm (ladies) | ℑ | M 375 | [S]
★★★Master Brewer Motel, Western Ave, Hillingdon. T:(0895) 51199. 64rm ⇌

HIMLEY
West Midlands
Map **III** H5

Himley Hall Golf Centre Log Cabin, Himley Hall Park, Dudley (½m E of Himley on B4176)
T:(0902) 895207
Parkland course with lovely views set in 70 acres, large practice area including a Pitch and Putt. 9 | 3090 yds | Par 70 | SSS 69
Visitors are welcome without M | ☎ at WE | ‥ per round | B ☕ ↘ | [S]
★★★Goldthorn, Penn Rd, Wolverhampton. T:(0902) 29216. 70rm (62 ⇌ 4 🚿) Annexe: 16rm (8 ⇌ 3 🚿)

HINCKLEY
Leicestershire
Map **III** K5

Hinckley Leicester Rd (1½m NE of Hinckley on A47)
T:(0455) 615124
Rolling pastureland with lake feature, tight gorse and lined fairways. The 8th and 17th are testing. 9 | 6578 yds (Championship) 6478 (Medal) | Par 72 | SSS 71
Visitors welcome with M only WE | B L prior arrangement (not W) D | ☕ (not W) | △ Y | [TR] Tu, WE (am) | ℑ | M 450 | [S] ⋈ | ④ ☎ for details
★★Longshoot Motel, Watling St, Nuneaton. T:(0203) 329711. Annexe: 47rm ⇌ 🚿

HINDLEY
Greater Manchester
Map **V** D7

Hindley Hall Hall Ln, Hindley,
Wigan (1m N of Hindley off A58)
T:(0942) 55131
*Parkland course with mostly easy
walking. Societies welcome by
arrangement.*
18 | 5875 yds | Par 69 | SSS 68
Visitors welcome ⊠ 🕿 restricted W
S Sun | without M ∴ per day WE |
with M .. per day WE | B L prior
arrangement (not Mon) | 🍷 D prior
arrangement (not Mon F) | ⚖ ⟡ | ╲
(prior arrangement) | ④
TR competition days | ♩ | M 450 | S
★★★*Brocket Arms, Mesnes Rd,
Wigan. T:(0942) 46283. 27rm (25 ⇄ 2
🍺)*

HOLLYWOOD
Hereford and Worcester
Map **III** J5

Gay Hill Alcester Rd, Hollywood
(N side of village)
T:021-474 6001
*A meadowland course some 7m from
Birmingham. Societies welcome by
arrangement.*
18 | 6532 yds | Par 72 | SSS 71
Visitors welcome but with M only
WE | ∴ per day | B L 🍷 (not Mon) |
D (not Mon-Th) | ⚖ | ⟡ | ╲ ⋈ | ♩ |
M 715 | S
★★★*George, High St, Solihull.
T:021-704 1241. 46rm (41 ⇄)*

HOLYHEAD
Gwynedd
Map **III** C1

Holyhead Trearddur Bay (1¼m S of
Holyhead on B4545)
T:(0407) 3279
*Societies welcome by arrangement (not
July Aug). 18 | 6081 yds | Par 71 |
SSS 70*
Visitors welcome 🕿 ⊠ | B L 🍷 D |
⚖ ⟡ | TR competitions | M 339 | S
★★★*Trearddur Bay, Trearddur Bay.
T:(0407) 860301. 28rm (19 ⇄)*

HOLSWORTHY
Devon
Map **I** D5

Holsworthy Killatree, Holsworthy
(1½m W of Holsworthy on A3072)
T:(0409) 253177
*Parkland course. 18 | 5894 yds | Par 70
| SSS 68*
Visitors welcome except Sun am |
.. per day | B 🍷 | ⚖ ⟡ | ⋈ | TR
competition days | M 250 | S
(limited)
★★★*Woodford Bridge, Woodford
Bridge. T:(040926) 481. 12rm (9 ⇄ 3
🍺) Annexe: 9rm*

HOLTYE
Kent
Map **II** F5

Holtye Holtye Common, Cowden
(N side of village on A264)
T:(034-286) 635
*Heathland course with tree-lined
fairways, providing testing golf,
especially 4th & 13th (both par 3).
Small societies welcome (Mon to F) by
arrangement. 9 | 5265 yds | Par 66 |
SSS 66*
Visitors welcome, please 🕿, with
M only WE | without M ∴ per day
∴ WE | with M .. per day WE | 🍷 |
⚖ ⟡ | ⋈ sometimes | TR WE and
matches | ♩ | M 420 | S
★★★*Felbridge Hotel and Health Club,
London Rd, East Grinstead. T:(0342)
26992. 48rm ⇄ 🍺*

HOLYWELL
Clwyd
Map **III** F2

Holywell Brynford (1¼m SW of
Holywell off B5121)
T:(0352) 710040
*Exposed moorland course, with easy
walking. 720ft above sea level. Societies
welcome by arrangement. 9 | 6353 yds |
Par 70 | SSS 70*
Visitors welcome weekdays | WE
BH only with M | .. per day WE | B
L 🍷 D | ⚖ ⟡ | ⋈ | M 370 | TR WE
★★*Stamford Gate, Halkyn Rd.
T:(0352) 712942. 12rm ⇄ 🍺*

HOLYWELL GREEN
West Yorkshire
Map **V** E6

Halifax Bradley Hall Holywell
Green, Halifax (½m N of Holywell
Green off B6112)
T:(0422) 74108
*Moorland course, easy walking. Junior
section. Societies welcome, restricted
WE.*
18 | 6213 yds | Par 70 | SSS 70
Visitors welcome | .. per day ∴
WE | with M ∴ WE | B 🍷 | L D prior
arrangement | ⚖ | ⟡ | ╲ (from pro)
| ⋈ by arrangement | ♩ | TR
competitions | M 530 | S
★★★*Ladbroke, Ainley Top,
Huddersfield. T:(0422) 75431. 118rm
⇄ 🍺*

HONITON
Devon
Map **I** G5

Honiton Middlehills (1¼m SE of
Honiton)
T:(0404) 44422
*Level parkland course with easy
walking and good views. 4th hole is a
testing par 3. Touring caravan site
attached to Club. 18 | 5900 yds | Par 69
| SSS 68*
Visitors welcome | ∴ per day WE |
.. per day after 1600 ∴ WE | B 🍷 |
L D prior arrangement | ⚖ | ⟡
1200-1430 | ╲ ⋈ | TR Sun until
1000 | M 650 | S
★★★🍴*Deer Park, Weston, Honiton.
(2½m W off A30). T:(0404) 2064.
17rm (13 ⇄) Annexe: 14rm ⇄*

HOPEMAN
Grampian, *Morayshire*
Map **VII** H4

Hopeman Hopeman (E side of

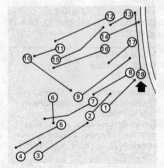

Completely treeless, undulating seaside course which provides a
varied and testing game, particularly in a south wind. The fairways
are bordered by gorse, heather and rugged outcrops of rock.

village off B9012)
T:(0343) 830578
Links course. 18 | 5439 yds | Par 67 | SSS 66
Visitors welcome | • • per day | B ☕ | 🍸 | M 300
★★★*Eight Acres, Sheriff Mill, Elgin. T:(0343) 3077. 57rm (33 🛁 24 🚿)*

HORNSEA
Humberside
Map **V** J5

Hornsea Rolston Rd (1m S of Hornsea on B1242)
T:(04012) 2020
Parkland course. Societies welcome (Mon to F) by arrangement. 18 | 6470 yds | Par 71 | SSS 71
Visitors welcome, restricted WE | ∴ per day ∷ WE | B L ☕ D (not F) | △ 🍸 ⟍ | [TR] Sun am | ℑ | M 500 | [S] ⋈
★★★*Beverley Arms, North Bar Within, Beverley. T:(0482) 869241. 61rm 🛁*

HORWICH
Greater Manchester
Map **V** D7

Horwich Victoria Rd (SE side of village A673)
T:(0204) 696980
Moorland course with natural hazards and generally windy. Hard walking. Society meetings by arrangement. 9 | 5404 yds | Par 66 | SSS 67
Visitors welcome, only with M | B ☕ (evening only) | △ 🍸 | ⋈ ④ not S | [TR] S | M 180
★★★*Crest, Beaumont Rd, Bolton. T:(0204) 651511. 100rm 🛁*

HOUGHTON-le-SPRING
Tyne and Wear
Map **V** F2

Houghton-le-Spring Copt Hill (1m E of Houghton-le-Spring on B1404)
T:(0204) 841198
Hilly downland course with natural slope hazards, windy. Testing 2nd hole (par 5). 18 | 6300 yds | Par 71 | SSS 70
Visitors welcome with M only, restricted WE BH | 🍸 △ | B (not Tu) | L ☕ D prior arrangement (not Tu) | ⟍ | ⋈ prior arrangement | [TR] competition days | ℑ | M 600 | [S]
★★★*Ramside Hall, Belmont, Durham. T:(0385) 65282. 11rm (6 🛁)*

HOWDEN
Humberside
Map **V** H6

Boothferry Spaldington Ln, Goole (2½m N of Howden, off B1228)
T:(0430) 30364
A heavily bunkered meadowland course with several dykes. 18 | 6651 yds | Par 73 | SSS 72
Visitors welcome ∴ per day | B L D ☕ | △ 🍸 | [S] ⟍ | ⋈ | M 500 | ℑ
★★*Bowmans, Bridgegate, Howden. T:(0430) 30805. 13rm 🛁*

HOYLAKE
Merseyside
Map **V** B8

Hoylake Municipal Carr Ln, Hoylake (SW side of town off A540)
T:051-632 2956
Flat, generally windy course. Very tricky fairways. 18 | 6312 yds | Par 70 | SSS 70
Visitors welcome, ☎ essential | • • per round WE | B L prior arrangement | ☕ 🍸 | △ ⟍ | ⋈ | ℑ | M 225 | [S]
★★★*Bowler Hat, Talbot Rd, Oxton, Birkenhead. T:051-652 4931. 29rm 🛁*

Royal Liverpool Meols Dr, Hoylake, Wirral (SW side of town on A540)
T:051-632 3101
A world famous seaside links course, windswept. 18 | 6737 yds | Par 72 | SSS 74
Visitors welcome, ☎ ✉ restricted club fixtures | ∷ per day WE | B L D ☕ | △ 🍸 ⟍ | ⋈ | [TR] 1230-1355 | M 632 | [S]
★★★*Bowler Hat, 2 Talbot Rd, Oxton, Birkenhead. T:051-652 4931. 29rm 🛁*

HUDDERSFIELD
West Yorkshire
Map **V** E7

Bradley Park Off Bradley Rd (3m N of Huddersfield on A6107)
T:(0484) 539988
Parkland course, challenging with good mix of long and short holes. Superb views. 18 | 6157 yds | Par 70 | SSS 69
Visitors welcome • • per round WE BH | 🍸 B L D ☕ | △ | [S] ⟍ | ⋈ | M 250 | ℑ
★★★*George, St. George's Sq, Huddersfield. T:(0484) 25444. 62rm (38 🛁)*

Huddersfield Fixby Hall, Lightridge Rd, Huddersfield (2m N of Huddersfield off A641)
T:(0484) 26203
A testing parkland/moorland course of championship standard laid out in 1891. Societies welcome by arrangement. 18 | 6424 yds | Par 71 | SSS 71
Visitors welcome | without M ∷ per day WE BH | with M • • per day WE BH | B L ☕ D (not Mon) | △ 🍸 ⟍ | [TR] S before 0930 and 1230-1330 | ℑ | M 600 | [S]
★★★**Ladbroke** *(& Conferencentre), Ainley Top, Nr Huddersfield. T:(0422) 75431. 119rm 🚿*

Longley Park Maple St, Off Somerset Rd, Huddersfield (½m SE of town centre off A629)
T:(0484) 22304
Lowland course. 9 | 5324 yds | Par 66 | SSS 65
Visitors welcome • • per day WE | B L D ☕ | △ 🍸 ⟍ | ⋈ | ④ 1st S in the month | [TR] WE and competition days | ℑ | M 380 | [S]
★★★*George, St George's Sq, Huddersfield. T:(0484) 25444. 62rm (38 🛁)*

HULL
Humberside
Map **V** J6

Ganstead Park Longdales Ln, Coniston (6m NE of Hull off A165)
T:(0482) 811121/811280
Parkland course, easy walking. 9 | 5769 yds | Par 70 | SSS 68
Visitors are welcome with M | • • per day not Wed or Sun am ∴ WE | L D B ☕ | △ 🍸 [S] ⟍ [TR] ladies (Sun am) | ℑ | ⋈ | M 300
★★★*Stakis Paragon, Paragon St, Hull. T:(0482) 26462. 125rm 🛁*

Hull (1921) The Hall, 27 Packman Ln, Kirk Ella, Hull (5m W of city centre off A164)
T:(0482) 658919
Parkland course. Societies welcome by arrangement. 18 | 6242 yds | Par 70 | SSS 70
Visitors welcome WE with M only | without M ∴ per day WE | with M • • per day WE | B ☕ | L | △ 🍸 ⋈ | M 760 | [S]
★★★*Willerby Manor, Well Ln, Willerby. T:(0482) 652616. 41rm (27 🛁 14 🚿)*

Springhead Park Willerby Rd (5m
W of Hull off A164)
T:(0482) 656309
*Municipal parkland course with
undulating fairways. 18 | 6439 yds |
Par 73 | SSS 71*
Course open to public. Club
facilities with M only | .. per round
| B L ☛ prior arrangement (not Tu)
| ⚊ ☩ ⚬ ∞ | ❎ | ⟦TR⟧ Sun
0700-1100, 1200-1500 | M 570 | Ⓢ
★★★*Willerby Manor, Well Ln,
Willerby. T:(0482) 652616. 41rm (27
⇌ 14 🏠)*

Sutton Park Salthouse Rd (4m NE
of Hull on B1237 off A165)
T:(0482) 781954
*Municipal parkland course. Societies
welcome by arrangement. 18 | 6295 yds
| Par 72 | SSS 70*
Visitors welcome to play on course,
☎ essential WE | with M to visit
club | B ☛ | L D prior arrangement |
⚊ ☩ ⚬ ∞ | ⟦TR⟧ ☎ WE | M 900 | Ⓢ
★★★*Stakis Paragon, Paragon St.
T:(0482) 26462. 125rm ⇌*

HUNSTANTON
Norfolk
Map **IV**   F3

Hunstanton (1½m N of
Hunstanton, off A149)
T:(04853) 2811
*Links course. 18 | 6670 yds | Par 72 |
SSS 72*
Visitors welcome, restricted WE BH
| ☎ advisable | without M :: per
day WE | with M ∴ per day :: WE
| B ☛ | L D prior arrangement | ⚊
☩ ⚬ ∞ | ④ ☎ for details | ⟦TR⟧
competitions | ❎ | M 600 | Ⓢ
★★★*Le Strange Arms, Golf Course Rd,
Sea Front, Old Hunstanton. T:(04853)
34411. 30rm (23 🏠 2 🏠)*

HUNTLY
Grampian, *Aberdeenshire*
Map **VII**   J5

Huntly Cooper Park (¼m through
School Arch on N side of Huntly)
T:(0466) 2643
*A parkland course lying between the
Rivers Deveron and Bogie. 18 |
5399 yds | Par 67 | SSS 66*
Visitors welcome without M .. per
day | B L D prior arrangement | ☩
⚊ ⟦TR⟧ W 1700-1830, Th 1630-1830,
competitions | M 495 | Ⓢ
★★🏠🏠*Castle. T:(0466) 2696. 27rm
(7 ⇌ 2 🏠)*

HUYTON
Merseyside
Map **V**   C8

Bowring Bowring Park, Roby Rd,
Huyton (On A5080 adjacent M62 Jct
5)
T:051-489 1901
*Flat parkland course. 9 | 2009 yds |
Par 34*
⚊ | ❎ | ∞ | M 80 | Ⓢ
★★★*Crest Hotel, Liverpool City, Lord
Nelson St, Liverpool. T:051-709 7050.
160rm ⇌*

Huyton & Prescot Hurst Park,
Huyton Ln, Huyton (1½m NE of
Huyton off B5199)
T:051-489 3948
*Reconstructed parkland course, easy
walking, excellent golf. Society
meetings by arrangement. 18 |
5738 yds | Par 68 | SSS 68*
Visitors welcome, WE by
arrangement | ∴ per day | ∴ per
round | B | L ☛ | D prior
arrangement | ⚊ ☩ ⚬ | ∞ | ❎ |
M 700 | Ⓢ
★*Rockland, View Rd, Rainhill.
T:051-426 4603. 12rm (2 ⇌) Annexe:
10rm (4 ⇌ 6 🏠)*

HYDE
Greater Manchester
Map **V**   E7

Werneth Low Werneth Low, Hyde
(2m S of town centre)
T:061-368 2503
*Hard walking but good views from this
moorland course. Exposed to wind.
Societies welcome weekdays by
arrangement. 9 | 5734 yds | Par 70 |
SSS 68*
Visitors welcome Mon to S except
Tu | B L ☛ D (not W) | ⚊ | ☩
evening only after 2000 (not W) |
⟦TR⟧ Sun, Mon, Tu | ❎ | M 250 | Ⓢ
★★★*Alma Lodge, 149 Buxton Rd,
Stockport. T:061-483 4431. 70rm (53
⇌)*

HYTHE
Kent
Map **II**   J5

Hythe Imperial Princes Parade,
Hythe (SE side of town)
T:(0303) 67441
*This course on the coast is flat and well
bunkered. 9 | 5583 yds | Par 67 | SSS
67*
Visitors welcome without M | ✳ | ☛
| ⚊ ☩ Ⓢ⚬ ∞ ⟦TR⟧ S Sun 0800-0900
| ❎ | M 250

★★★★*Hotel Imperial, Princes Pde,*
Hythe. T:(0303) 67441. 83rm (81 ⇄ 2
🛏)

ILFORD
Greater London
Map II   F3

Ilford Wanstead Park Rd, Ilford
(NW side of town centre off A12)
T:01-554 2930
Fairly flat parkland course intersected 5
times by river. Societies welcome by
prior arrangement. 18 | 5710 yds |
Par 68 | SSS 68
Visitors welcome | 🎣 | ∴ per day | B
🍴 | L D Th S | ⚐ ⚑ | TR 🕾 for
details | M 590 | S
★★★*Woodford Moat House, Oak Hill,*
Woodford Green. T:01-505 4511. 99rm
(69 ⇄ 30 🛏)

ILKLEY
West Yorkshire
Map V   E5

Ben Rhydding High Wood, Ben
Rhydding, Ilkley (SE side of town)
T:(0943) 608759
Moorland course with splendid views
over the Wharfe valley. 9 | 4711 yds |
Par 65 | SSS 64
Visitors welcome, not Sun (am) | ..
per day WE | ⚐ | ⚑ (not lunchtimes
Mon to F) | TR Sun am W
1200-1500 | M 300
★★★*Craiglands, Cowpasture Rd,*
Ilkley. T:(0943) 607676. 73rm (53 ⇄ 5
🛏)

INNERLEITHEN
Borders, *Peeblesshire*
Map VI   G3

Innerleithen Innerleithen Water
(1½m N of Innerleithen on B709)

T:(0896) 830951
Moorland course, with easy walking.
Burns and rivers as natural hazards.
Testing 5th hole 100 yds par 3.
Societies welcome by arrangement.
Children welcome. 9 | 5820 yds |
Par 68 | SSS 68
Visitors welcome | ⚑ evngs 🍴 ⚐ |
∞ probably | TR competitions 🕾 |
M 240
★★🛏*Tweed Valley, Galashiels Rd,*
Walkerburn. T:(089687) 220. 16rm (12
⇄ 4 🛏)

INVERGORDON
Highland, *Ross and Cromarty*
Map VII   F4

ILFRACOMBE
Devon
Map I   E4

Ilfracombe Hele Bay (1½m E of Ilfracombe off A399)
T:(0271) 62176
Societies welcome weekdays and WE. 18 | 5857 yds | Par 68 | SSS 68
Visitors welcome | ∴ weekdays WE | B 🍴 | L D | ⚐ ⚑ ∖ | ∞ ⊕ S am | 🎣 | TR
Ladies W 1100-1300, Veterans Tu 0845-0930 | M 430 | S
★★★*Lee Bay Hotel, Lee Bay. T:(0271) 63503. 48rm ⇄ 🛏*
A sporting clifftop downland course several hundred feet above the
Bristol Channel, with views of the sea from every tee.

ILKLEY
West Yorkshire
Map V   E5

Ilkley Middleton, Ilkley (W side of town centre off A65)
T:(0943) 600214/607277
18 | 6249 yds | Par 69 | SSS 70
Visitors welcome 🕾 advisable | without M :: per day | with M .. per day | B
L 🍴 D prior arrangement | ⚑ ∖ ⚐ | | TR 0830-0930, 1230-1330 | M 380 | S
★★★*Craiglands, Cowpasture Rd. T:(0943) 607676. 73rm (53 ⇄ 5 🛏)*
This beautiful parkland course is situated in Wharfedale and the
Wharfe is a hazard on each of the first five holes. In fact, the 3rd is
laid out entirely on an island in the middle of the river.

Invergordon King George St,
Invergordon (W side of town centre
on B817)
T:(0349) 852715
Fairly easy but windy parkland course,
with good views over Cromarty Firth.
Very good greens. Clubhouse situated
1m from course close to middle of town.
9 | 3000 yds | Par 34 | SSS 69
Visitors welcome | B (not Sun) | ⚐ |
🍴 ⚑ (not Sun) | ∞ | TR subject to
club fixture list | M 300
★★*Royal, Marine Ter, Cromarty.*
T:(03817) 217. 12rm (3 ⇄ 2 🛏)

INVERNESS
Highland, *Inverness-shire*
Map **VII** F5

Inverness Culcabock, Inverness (SE side of town centre on B9006)
T:(0463) 239882
Fairly flat parkland course with burn running through. Windy in winter. Societies welcome by arrangement. 18 | 6226 yds | Par 69 | SSS 70
Visitors welcome | ∴ per day WE | B ☙ | L D prior arrangement | ⚐ ⏣ ↘ | M 1100 | ⓢ
★★★*Kingsmills, Culcabock Rd.* T:(0463) 237166. *59rm (54 ⇄)*

Torvean Glenurquhart Rd, Inverness (1½m SW of Inverness on A82)
T:(0463) 237543
Municipal parkland course, easy walking, good views. 18 | 4308 yds | Par 62 | SSS 62
Visitors welcome, restricted competition days | .. per round | ⏣ ⚐
★★**Dunain Park.* T:(0463) 230512. *6rm (4 ⇄)*

INVERURIE
Grampian, *Aberdeenshire*
Map **VII** J5

Inverurie Davah Wood, Blackhall Rd, Inverurie (W side of town off A96)
T:(0467) 24080
Parkland course, part of which is exposed and windy, and part through wooded area. 18 | 5703 yds | Par 71 | SSS 68
Visitors welcome | B L ☙ (not W) | ⏣ ↘ | TR Tu W eves, WE to 1000 | ④ WE before 1000 | M 560 | ⓢ
★*Gordon Arms, The Square, Inverurie.* T:(0467) 20314. *11rm (6 ⋔)*

IPSWICH
Suffolk
Map **IV** H7

Rushmere Rushmere Heath, Ipswich (2m E of Ipswich off A12)
T:(0473) 77109
Heathland course with much gorse, prevailing winds. Testing 5th hole - dog leg 419 yds (par 4). Societies welcome by arrangement. 18 | 6287 yds | Par 70 | SSS 70
Visitors welcome, restricted WE BH until 1030 | ✉ | ☎ advisable | without M ∴ per day WE | with M

.. per day WE | ☙ | B L D prior arrangement | ⚐ ⏣ | ∝ | TR WE BH before 1030 and competition days. Ladies' tee restricted 0815-1030 W | M 750 | ⓢ
❀★★★*Marlborough, 73 Henley Rd.* T:(0473) 57677. *22rm ⇄*

IRVINE
Strathclyde, *Ayr*
Map **VI** D3

Irvine Bogside, Irvine (N side of town off A737)
T:(0294) 78139

Testing links course. Societies welcome (Mon Tu Th) by arrangement. 18 | 6454 yds | Par 71 | SSS 71
Visitors welcome ☎ | B L ☙ D (WE only) | ⚐ ⏣ ∝ | ♩ | M 450 | ⓢ
❀◊◊◊**Chapeltoun House, Stewarton.* T:(0560) 82696. *6rm (4 ⇄ 2 ⋔)*

Irvine Ravenspark Kilwinning Rd, Irvine (N side of town on A737)
T:(0294) 79550
Parkland course. 18 | 6429 yds | Par 72 | SSS 71

INGRAVE
Essex
Map **II** G3

Thorndon Park Ingrave Road, Brentwood (W side of village on A128)
T:(0277) 811666
Societies welcome by arrangement. 18 | 6455 yds | Par 71 | SSS 71
Visitors welcome weekdays ☎ | without M ∷ per day | B L ☙ prior arrangement (not Mon) | D parties only by arrangement | ⚐ ⏣ | TR ☙ 0915-1100 (Ladies Day) | ④ ☎ | ♩ | M 650 | ⓢ
★★★★*Brentwood Moat House, London Road.* T:(0277) 225252. *3rm (2 ⇄ 1 ⋔). Annexe: 34 ⇄ ⋔*
Among the best of the Essex courses with a fine new purposebuilt clubhouse and a lake. The springy turf is easy on the feet. Many newly planted young trees now replace the famous old oaks that were such a feature of this course.

IPSWICH
Suffolk
Map **IV** H7

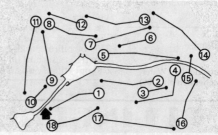

Ipswich Purdis Heath, Ipswich (E side of town centre off A1156)
T:(0473) 78941
Societies welcome (Mon to F) by arrangement. 18(9) | 6405 yds (3860) | Par 71(62) | SSS 71(59)
Visitors welcome ✉ ☎ advisable | ∴ per round ∷ per day (9 hole .. per day) | B ☙ | L D ⚐ ⏣ | TR ☎ for details | ♩ | M 700 | ⓢ
★★*Great White Horse, Tavern St.* T:(0473) 56558. *55rm (10 ⇄)*
Many golfers are suprised when they hear that Ipswich has, at Purdis Heath, a first-class golf course. The club has been in existence for almost 100 years. In some ways it resembles some of Surrey's better courses; a beautiful heathland/parkland course with two lakes and easy walking.

IRVINE
Strathclyde, *Ayr*
Map VI D3

Glasgow (Gailes) Irvine (2m S of Irvine off A737)
T:(0294) 311347
Restricted facilities for ladies. No children. Organised parties by arrangement. 18 |
6447 yds | Par 71 | SSS 71
Visitors welcome ☎ ✉ restricted WE BH | without M :: per day | B ☞ | L D
(high tea) | ♣ ♟ | ♪ | M 1020 | | ⓢ Basic clothing only
★★★★*Hospitality Inn, Roseholm, Annickwater. T:(0294) 74272. 128rm* ⇔ ▦
A lovely seaside links. The turf of the fairways and all the greens is
truly glorious and provides tireless play. Established in 1787 this is
the 8th oldest course in the world and is a qualifying course for the
Open Championship.

Western Gailes Gailes-by-Irvine (2m S of Irvine off A737)
T:(0294) 311357
Societies welcome by arrangement. 18 | 6833 yds | Par 71 | SSS 72
Visitors welcome | WE only with M, no ladies Tu | ☎ | B L ☞ | D prior
arrangement | ♣ ♟ | ✕ ☎ | TR ⓢ | M 430
★★★★*Marine, Crosbie Rd, Troon. T:(0292) 314444. 69rm* ⇔
A magnificent seaside links with glorious turf and wonderful
greens. The view is open across the Firth of Clyde to the
neighbouring islands. It is a well-balanced course crossed by 3
burns. There are 2 par 5s, the 6th and 14th, and the 11th is a testing
454-yd par 4 dogleg.

Visitors welcome | .. per day | L B
D ☞ ♟ | ♣ ✕ ✕ | M 400 | ⓢ
🏵○○○♨*Chapeltoun House,
Stewarton. T:(0560) 82696. 6rm (4* ⇔
2 ▦ *)*

ISLAY, ISLE OF
Strathclyde, *Argyllshire*
Map VI
See Port Ellen

ISLE OF ARRAN
Strathclyde, *Bute*
Map VI
**See Blackwaterfoot, Brodick,
Corrie, Lochranza and Whiting Bay**

ISLE OF BUTE
Strathclyde, *Bute*
Map VI
See Bute and Port Bannatyne

ISLE OF LEWIS
Western Isles, *Ross and Cromarty*
Map VII
See Stornoway

ISLE OF MAN
Map V
**See Douglas, Onchan, Peel, Port
Erin and Ramsey**

ISLE OF MULL
Strathclyde, *Argyllshire*

Map VII
See Craignure and Tobermory

ISLES OF SCILLY

Isles of Scilly St Mary's (1m N of
Hugh Town)
T:(0720) 22692
Links course, glorious views. 9 |
2987 yds | Par 36 | SSS 69 (18)
Visitors welcome | ∴ per day | B ☞
L D | ♣ ✕ | ✕ | M 300
★★*Godolphin, Church St, Hugh
Town. T:(0720) 22316. 31rm (25* ⇔ *2*
▦ *)*

ISLE OF SKYE
Highland, *Inverness-shire*
Map VII
See Sconser

ISLE OF WIGHT
Map II
**See Cowes, East Cowes,
Freshwater Bay, Newport, Ryde,
Sandown and Ventnor**

ISLEWORTH
Greater London
Map II E3

Wyke Green Syon Ln, Isleworth
(1½m N of Isleworth on B454 off
A4)
T:01-560 8777

*Fairly flat parkland course. Societies
welcome by arrangement.* 18 | 6242 yds
| Par 69 | SSS 70
Visitors welcome Mon to S | Sun
BH after 1500 | ☎ | :: per day | B ☞
| L D prior arrangement | ♣ ♟ ✕ |
✕ usually | ♪ | M 600 | ⓢ
★★★*Master Robert Motel, 366 Great
West Rd, Hounslow. T:01-570 6261.
Annexe: 63rm* ⇔

IVER
Buckinghamshire
Map II D3

Iver Hollow Hill Ln, Langley Park
Rd (1½m SW of Iver off B470)
T:(0753) 655615
Parkland course. 9 | 3018 yds | Par 74 |
SSS70
Visitors welcome without M .. per
day | B L D ☞ | ♣ ♟ ✕ | ♪ | ✕ |
M 150 | ⓢ
★★★★*Holiday Inn, Ditton Rd,
Langley. T:(0753) 44244. 308rm* ⇔ ▦

IVINGHOE
Buckinghamshire
Map II D2

Ivinghoe Wellcroft, Ivinghoe (N
side of village)
T:(0296) 668696
Parkland course, easy walking. 9 |
4508 yds | Par 62 | SSS 62
Visitors welcome | B L ☞ D (not
Mon) | ♣ ♟ ✕ | ✕ | ♪ | M 200 | TR
before 0900, WE 0800 | ⓢ
★★★*The Bell Inn, Aston Clinton.
T:(0296) 630252. 21rm* ⇔

JEDBURGH
Borders, *Roxburghshire*
Map VI H4

Jedburgh Dunion Rd (1m W of
Jedburgh on B6358)
T:(08356) 3587
Parkland course, windy, easy walking.
9 | 2760 yds | Par 68 | SSS 67
Visitors welcome | .. per day
(reduced with M) | D S. Sun only
prior arrangement | ♣ ♟ | TR
competitions ☎ | M 300 | ⓢ
★★*Jedforest Country House. T:(08354)
274. 7rm. Annexe: 4* ▦

JERSEY
Channel Islands
Map I B5

Jersey Recreation Grounds St
Clements, Jersey (E side of St
Helier on A5) ➡

KEY
(IA1) *atlas grid reference*
T: *telephone number*
☎   *advance letter/telephone*
       call required
✉   *introduction from own club*
       sec/handicap
       certificate/club
       membership card required
..   *low fees*
∴   *medium fees*
::   *high fees*
*   *green fees not confirmed for*
       1987
B   *light lunch*
L   *full lunch*
☕   *tea*
D   *dinner*
🛆   *changing rooms/showers*
🍸   *bar open mid-day and*
       evenings
✎   *clubs for hire*
⋈   *partners may be found*
④   *restricted time for 4 balls*
TR   *times reserved for members*
ʃ   *professional*
S   *well-stocked shop*
M   *member*
Mon Tu W Th F S Sun
WE   *weekend*
BH   *bank holiday*

T:(0534) 21938
Very tight moorland course. Holes cross over fairways, impossible to play to scratch. Suitable for middle and high handicaps. 9 | 4303 yds | Par 60 | SSS 61
Visitors welcome except Sun am | B L ☕ | 🛆 ⋈ | TR Sun until 1300 | M 450 | S
★★★*Ambassadeur, Greve d'Azette. T:(0534) 24455. 41rm ⇄*

La Moye La Moye, St Brelade (W side of village off A13)
T:(0534) 43401
Seaside championship course. 18 | 6267 yds | Par 72 | SSS 70
Visitors welcome ✉, restricted WE BH competition days | B ☕ | L D prior arrangement | 🛆 ✎ | ④ until 0930 | TR before 0930 and 1200-1330 | ʃ | M 1250 | S
★★*Les Arches, Archirondel Bay, Archirondel. T:(0534) 53839. 54rm (35 ⇄ 19 🏠)*

JOHNSTONE
Strathclyde, *Renfrewshire*
Map **VI**   D2

JERSEY
Channel Islands
Map I B5

Royal Jersey Grouville (3m E of St Helier)
T:(0534) 54416
18 | 6106 yds | Par 70 | SSS 69
Visitors welcome ✉ | B ☕ | L D prior arrangement | 🛆 🍸 ✎ | TR before 1000, Mon-F before 1430, WE comp times | M 700 | S
🏵○○○○🏌*Longueville Manor, St Saviour, (off St Helier/Grouville rd, A3). T:(0534) 25501. 33rm ⇄*
A seaside links, historic because of its age: its centenary was celebrated in 1978. It is also famous for the fact that Britain's greatest golfer, Harry Vardon, was born in a little cottage on the edge of the course and learned his golf on the course.

Cochrane Castle Scott Av, Johnstone (1m SW of Johnstone off A737)
T:(0505) 20146
Moorland and parkland in places, wooded with two small streams running through the course. 18 | 6227 yds | Par 70 | SSS 70
Visitors welcome without M | ∴ per day | L D B ☕ | 🛆 🍸 S ✎ ⋈ TR ☎ | M 400 | ④ S competition days
★★★*Glynhill, Paisley Rd, Renfrew. T:041-886 5555. 80rm ⇄*

Elderslie 63 Main Rd, Elderslie (E side of town on A737)
T:(0505) 22835
Parkland course, undulating, with good views. Parties accepted by arrangement. 18 | 6004 yds | Par 69 | SSS 70
Visitors welcome with M | B L ☕ (not Th) | D prior arrangement (not Th) | 🛆 🍸 | TR public holidays | M 440
★★★*Glynhill, Paisley Rd, Renfrew. T:041-886 5555. 80rm ⇄*

KEIGHLEY
West Yorkshire
Map **V**   E6

Keighley Howden Park, Utley,

Keighley (NW side of town centre off A629)
T:(0535) 603179
Parkland course. 18 | 6134 yds | Par 69 | SSS 70
Visitors welcome ☎ advisable | without M ∴ per day WE | with M .. per day WE | B ☕ D L | 🛆 🍸 | ʃ | M 500 | S
★★*Beeches, Bradford Rd. T:(0535) 607227. 10rm (2 ⇄) Annexe: 14rm (9 🏠)*

KEITH
Grampian, *Banffshire*
Map **VII**   H4

Keith Fife-Keith, Keith (NW side of town centre off A96)
T:(05422) 2469
Parkland course, with natural hazards over 1st 9 holes. Testing 7th hole 232 yds par 3. 18 | 5745 yds | Par 69 | SSS 68
Visitors welcome | without M .. per day WE | with M .. per round | B ☕ prior arrangement | 🛆 🍸 | M 300
★★*Royal, Church Rd. T:(05422) 2528. 12rm (3 ⇄)*

KEDLESTON
Derbyshire
Map III K3

Kedleston Park Kedleston Quarndon, Derby (2m SE of Kedleston)
T:(0332) 840035
Societies welcome by arrangement. 18 | 6636 yds | Par 72 | SSS 72
Visitors welcome ☎ ✉ | * | B L ☕ D | 🛆 🍸 ✎ | ʃ | ⋈ | ☎ TR for details | M 860 | S
★★*Meynell Arms, Ashbourne Rd, Kirk Langley. T:(033124) 515. 9rm (4 ⇄ 1 🏠)*
The course is laid out in mature parkland with fine trees and background views of historic Kedleston Hall. Many testing holes are included in each nine and there is an excellent modern clubhouse.

KELSO
Borders, *Roxburghshire*
Map **VI** H3

Kelso Racecourse Rd, Kelso (N side of town centre off B6461)
T:(0573) 23009
Parkland course. Easy walking. Parties by arrangement. 18 | 6066 yds | Par 70 | SSS 69
Visitors welcome | B ♣ D L (W-Sun) | ⚐ ⵊ | ⋈ | ⟍ | TR
competition days ☎ for details | M 310 | S
★★★*Cross Keys, 36-37 The Square.* T:(0573) 23303. 25rm (9 ⇌ 9 ♨)

KEMNAY
Grampian, *Aberdeenshire*
Map **VII** J5

Kemnay Monymusk Rd, Kemnay (W side of village on B993)
9 | 1792 yds | Par 28
Visitors welcome | ⚐ | TR Mon and Th eves | M 270
★★★*Westhill Inn, Westhill.* T:(0224) 740388. 38rm ⇌. Annexe: 14rm (6 ⇌ 8 ♨)

KENDAL
Cumbria
Map **V** C4

Kendal The Heights, Kendal (W side of town centre)
T:(0539) 24079
Moorland course. 18 | 5483 yds | Par 66 | SSS 67
Visitors welcome | B L ♣ D | ⚐ ⵊ ⟍ | M 400 | S | TR Tu 1300-1430, 1630-1800. Other days 1230-1330
★★★*Woolpack Inn, Stricklandgate.* T:(0539) 23852. 57rm (36 ⇌ 21 ♨)

KENILWORTH
Warwickshire
Map **III** K5

Kenilworth Crew Ln (½m NE of Kenilworth)
T:(0926) 58517
Parkland course in open hilly situation. Modern clubhouse. 18 | 6408 yds | Par 72 | SSS 71
Visitors welcome | B L ♣ D | ⚐ ⵊ ⟍ | J | M 725 | S
★★*Clarendon House, Old High St.* T:(0926) 57668. 24rm (10 ⇌ 14 ♨)

KENMORE
Tayside, *Perthshire*
Map **VII** G7

Taymouth Castle Kenmore (1m E of Kenmore on A827)
T:(08873) 228
Parkland course set amid beautiful mountain and loch scenery. Easy walking. 18 | 6061 yds | Par 69 | SSS 69
Visitors welcome ☎ | ∴ per round ∴ per day weekdays | ∴ per round ∷ per day WE | B L ♣ D | ⚐ ⵊ ⟍ J | ⋈ (sometimes) | TR Tu (1630-1830) W (1440-1520) | M 400 | S
★★★*Kenmore, Village Sq.* T:(08873) 205. 24rm (23 ⇌ 1 ♨) Annexe: 14rm (13 ⇌ 1 ♨)

KESWICK
Cumbria
Map **V** B3

Keswick Threlkeld Hall (5m E of Keswick off A66)
T:(0596) 83324
Varied fell and tree-lined course with commanding views of Lakeland scenery. 18 | 6175 yds | Par 71 | SSS 72
Visitors welcome | ∴ per day | B L by arrangement ♣ | ⚐ ⵊ ⟍ | ⋈ | TR occasional WE | M 420 | S
★★★*Borrowdale.* T:(059684) 224. 35rm (31 ⇌ 4 ♨)

KETTERING
Northamptonshire
Map **IV** C6

Kettering Headlands (S side of town centre)
T:(0536) 512074
A very pleasant, mainly flat meadowland course with easy walking. 18 | 6035 yds | Par 69 | SSS 69
Visitors welcome ⋈ but with M only WE BH | ☎ (if more than 4 players) | B L ♣ D prior arrangement (not Mon) | ⟍ ⋈ prior arrangement | TR WE BH | J |

M 500 | S
★★*George, Sheep St.* T:(0536) 518620. 50rm (21 ⇌)

KEYWORTH
Nottinghamshire
Map **IV** A3

Stanton on the Wolds Keyworth (E side of village)
T:(06077) 2044
Parkland course. Societies welcome by arrangement, juniors Mon, W F in holidays. 18 | 6379 yds | Par 73 | SSS 70
Visitors welcome (with M only at WE BH) ☎ | B (not F) prior arrangement | L ♣ D prior arrangement | ⚐ ⵊ ⟍ | ⋈ (see pro) | ④ | TR ☎ for details | M 965 | S J
★★*Edwalton Hall, Edwalton, Nottingham.* T:(0602) 231116. 12rm (2 ⇌ 1 ♨)

KIBWORTH
Leicestershire
Map **IV** B5

Kibworth Weir Rd, Kibworth, Beauchamp (S side of village)
T:(053753) 2301
Parkland course with easy walking. A brook affects a number of fairways. Societies welcome by arrangement. 18 | 6298 yds | Par 71 | SSS 70
Visitors welcome | without M ∴ per day | with M .. per day WE | B ♣ L D | ⚐ ⵊ ⟍ | J | M 500 | S
★★★*Three Swans, High St, Market Harborough.* T:(0858) 66644. 18rm (12 ⇌ 6 ♨)

KIDDERMINSTER
Hereford and Worcester
Map **III** H5

Habberley Habberley (2m NW of
Kidderminster)
T:(0562) 745756
Very hilly parkland course. 9 |
5406 yds | *Par 68* | *SSS 67*
Visitors welcome ⊠ | with M only
WE | without M .. per day | B L ♥
D prior arrangement (not Tu) | ⚲ Ⴤ
| M 400
★★*Gainsborough House, Bewdley Hill,
Kidderminster. T:(0562) 754041. 42rm*
⇄

Kidderminster Russell Rd,
Kidderminster (SE side of town
centre)
T:(0562) 2303
*Parkland course with natural hazards
and some easy walking. 18* | *6156 yds* |
Par 71 | *SSS 69*
Visitors welcome ⊠ | B ♥ (not
Mon) | L D prior arrangement (not
Mon) | ⚲ Ⴤ | ʃ | M 900 | ʂ
★★*Gainsborough House, Bewdley Hill.
T:(0562) 754041. 42rm* ⇄

KILBIRNIE
Strathclyde, *Ayr*
Map **VI** D3

Kilbirnie Place Largs Rd, Kilbirnie
(1m W of Kilbirnie on A760)
T:(0505) 684444
Easy walking parkland course. 18 |
5400 yds | *Par 69* | *SSS 67*
Visitors welcome | ♥ B L WE only |
⚲ Ⴤ | ᴛʀ S | M 300
★★*Elderslie, John St, Broomfields,
Largs. T:(0475) 686460. 25rm (9* ⇄ *4*
▥ *)*

KILLIN
Tayside, *Perthshire*
Map **VII** F8

Killin (1m N of Killin on A827)
T:(05672) 312
*Parkland course with good views.
Parties catered for April May Sept Oct
by arrangement. 9* | *2508 yds* | *Par 66* |
SSS 65
Visitors welcome | .. per day WE |
B | ♥ | ⚲ Ⴤ ⟍ | ᴛʀ weekday eves |
M 150 | ʂ
★★*Bridge of Lochay. T:(05672) 272.
17rm (4* ⇄ *3* ▥ *)*

KILMACOLM
Strathclyde, *Renfrewshire*
Map **VI** D2

Kilmacolm Porterfield Rd (SE side
of town off A761)

T:(050587) 2139
*Moorland course, easy walking, fine
views. Testing 7th, 13th and 14th
holes. 18* | *5964 yds* | *Par 69* | *SSS 68*
Visitors welcome WE with M only |
B ♥ L | ⚲ Ⴤ | M 800 | ʂ
❀★★★▲Gleddoch House, Langbank.
T:(047554) 711. 20rm ⇄ ▥

KILMARNOCK
Strathclyde, *Ayr*
Map **VI** D3

Annanhill Irvine Rd (1m W of
Kilmarnock on A71)
T:(0563) 21644
*Private golf club and municipal
parkland course. 18* | *6269 yds* | *Par 71*
| *SSS 70*
Visitors welcome ☎ | .. per day ∴
WE | B L ♥ | ⚲ Ⴤ ⋈ ʃ | M 300 | ʂ
★★★*Howard Park, Glasgow Rd.
T:(0563) 31211. 46rm* ⇄ ▥

Caprington Ayr Rd, Kilmarnock
(1½m S of Kilmarnock on B7038)
T:(0563) 23702
Municipal parkland course. 18 |
5718 yds | *Par 69* | *SSS 68*
Visitors welcome | ⊠ or with M for
club facilities | restricted F (pm) | ✳ |
B L ♥ D | ⚲ Ⴤ ⋈ ᴛʀ mainly WE |
ʃ | M 400 | ʂ
★★★*Howard Park, Glasgow Rd,
Kilmarnock. T:(0563) 31211. 46rm* ⇄
▥

KILSYTH
Strathclyde, *Stirlingshire*
Map **VI** E2

Kilsyth Lennox Tak Ma Doon Rd,
Kilsyth (N side of town off A803)

Kent
Map **II** K5

Walmer & Kingsdown The Leas, Kingsdown, Deal
(½m S of Kingsdown off B2057)
T:(0304) 373256
Societies welcome by arrangement. 18 | *6451 yds* | *Par 72* | *SSS 71*
Visitors welcome ⊠ | without M ∴ per day WE | with M .. per day WE | B ♥
| L prior arrangement (not Th) | D prior arrangement | ⚲ Ⴤ ⟍ | ⋈ | S (from
1st tee until 1130) | ᴛʀ WE BH (until 1130) | M 570 | ʂ
★★★*Dover Motel, Whitfield, Dover. T:(0304) 821222. 67rm* ⇄ ▥
This course near Deal has through the years been overshadowed by
its neighbours at Deal and Sandwich yet it is a testing circuit with
many undulations. The course is famous as being the one on which,
in 1964, Assistant Professional, Roger Game became the first golfer
in Britain to hole out in one at two successive holes; the holes were
the 7th and 8th. The course is situated on top of the cliffs, with fine
views.

T:(0236) 822190
Hilly moorland course, hard walking. 9
| *5944 yds* | *Par 70* | *SSS 69*
Visitors welcome weekdays | B L ♥
D | ⚲ Ⴤ | ᴛʀ Mon-F after 1700, Sun
before 1600, Sun before 1400 | ʃ |
M 400 | ʂ
★★*Kirkhouse Inn, Strathblane.
T:(0360) 70621. 16rm (10* ⇄ *)*

KINCARDINE
Fife, *Fife*
Map **VI** F1

Tulliallan Alloa Rd, Kincardine on
Forth (1m NW of Kincardine on
A977)
T:(0259) 30396
*Partially hilly parkland course with
testing 3rd hole (par 4). Societies
welcome (not S) by arrangement. 18* |
5982 yds | *Par 69* | *SSS 69*
Visitors welcome, restricted WE | ✳
| B L D ♥ prior arrangement | ⚲ Ⴤ
⟍ ⋈ | ④ | ᴛʀ ☎ for details | ʃ |
M 525 | ʂ
★★★*Inchyra Grange, Grange Rd,
Polmont. T:(0324) 711911. 30rm* ⇄ ▥

KINGHORN
Fife, *Fife*
Map **VI** G2

Kinghorn Kinghorn (S side of town
on A92)
T:(0592) 890345
*Municipal course 300 ft above sea level
with views over Firth of Forth and
North Sea. Undulating and quite
testing. Facilities shared by Kinghorn
Ladies. Societies welcome by
arrangement. 18* | *5246 yds* | *Par 65* |
SSS 67

Visitors welcome | B L ♨ D prior arrangement | ⚴ ⏃ ⋈ | M 200
★★*Station, 4 Bennochy Rd, Kirkcaldy.* T:(0592) 262461. 34rm (5 ⇌ 4 ⌑)

KINGSDOWN
Wiltshire
Map **I** J3

Kingsdown Kingsdown, Corsham (W side of village)
T:(0225) 742530
Fairly flat heathland course with surrounding wood. 18 | 6265 yds | Par 72 | SSS 70
Visitors welcome except on competition days | without M ∴ | with M ∴ | B ♨ | L D | ⚴ ⏃ | ⋋ | TR competition days | M 625 | S
★★*Stagecoach Motel, Park Ln, Pickwick.* T:(0249) 713162. 21rm (20 ⇌ 1 ⌑)

KINGSLEY
Hampshire
Map **II** C5

Dean Farm (W side of village off B3004)
T:(0420) 2313
Undulating downland course. 9 | 1350 yds | Par 27
Visitors welcome | .. per round | ⋋

KINGSTON
Greater London
Map **II** E4

Coombe Hill Golf Club Drive, Kingston Hill (1¾m E of Kingston on A238)
T:01-942 2284
Limited capacity for societies. 18 | 6286 yds | Par 70 | SSS 71
Visitors welcome with ✉ ☎ | ∷ per day | B L D ♨ | ⚴ ⏃ | TR 1015-1100 | ⏉ | M 540 | S
★★★★★*Hyatt Carlton Tower, 2 Cadogan Pl, SW1.* T:01-235 5411. 228rm ⇌ ⌑
Splendid course in wooded terrain. In fact one has difficulty in imagining the course is so near London, so isolated does it seem once you step on the first tee. The undulations and the trees make it an especially interesting course of great charm. There is a lovely display of rhododendrons in May and June.

KINGTON
Hereford and Worcester
Map **III** F6

Kington Bradnor Hill, (½m N of Kington off B4355)
T:(0544) 230340
18 | 5820 yds | Par 70 | SSS 68
Visitors welcome | B ♨ L D | ⚴ ⏃
★★*Burton, Mill St.* T:(0544) 230323. 10rm (5 ⇌ 1 ⌑)
The highest golf course in England and Wales, with views over 7 counties. A natural heathland course with easy walking on mountain turf cropped by sheep. There is bracken to catch any really bad shots but no sand traps.

★★★*Swan, High St, Alton.* T:(0420) 83777. 38rm (33 ⇌ 5 ⌑)

KINGS LYNN
Norfolk
Map **IV** F4

Kings Lynn Castle Rising (4m NE of Kings Lynn off A148)
T:(055387) 654
Woodland course. Societies welcome (Mon to F) by arrangement. 18 | 6552 yds | Par 72 | SSS 71
Visitors welcome ☎ advisable | ∷ per day WE | B ♨ | L D prior arrngement | ⚴ ⏃ | ⋈ | ⏉ | M 950 | TR ☎ for details | S
★★★*Duke's Head, Tuesday Market Pl.* T:(0553) 774996. 72rm ⇌

KINGSTON
Greater London
Map **II** E4

Coombe Wood George Rd (1¼m NE of Kingston on A308)
T:01-942 0388
Parkland course. 18 | 5210 yds | Par 66 | SSS 66
Visitors welcome | ∷ per day | B L D prior arrangement | ♨ | ⚴ ⏃ ⋋ | S | ⋈ possible | TR WE | M 600
★★*Haven, Portsmouth Rd, Esher.*

T:01-398 0023. 16rm (2 ⇌ 4 ⌑).
Annexe: 4rm (2 ⇌ 2 ⌑)

KINGSWOOD
Surrey
Map **II** E5

Kingswood Sandy Ln, Kingswood, Tadworth (S side of village off A217)
T:(0737) 832188
Flat parkland course, easy walking. 18 | 6821 yds | Par 72 | SSS 73
Visitors welcome except WE | ∷ per day | B ♨ | L D | ⚴ ⏃ | ⋈ | ☎ | ⏉ | M 700 | S
★★*Heathside, Brighton Rd, Burgh Heath.* T:(07373) 53355. 44rm ⌑

KINGUSSIE
Highland, *Inverness-shire*
Map **VII** G6

Kingussie Gynack Rd (¼m N of Kingussie off A86)
T:(05402) 374
Hilly parkland course with natural hazards and views. Society meetings by arrangement. 18 | 5504 yds | Par 66 | SSS 67
Visitors welcome | .. per day ∴ WE | B | ⚴ April to Oct | M 450 | S
✿✿*Osprey, Ruthven Rd, Kingussie.* T:(05402) 510. 8rm (1 ⇌ 1 ⌑)

KINROSS
Tayside, *Kinross-shire*
Map **VI** F1

Green Hotel, The Kinross (NE side of town on B996)
T:(0577) 63467
Parkland course, with easy walking. Parties by arrangement. 18 | 6124 yds | Par 70 | SSS 70
Visitors welcome | B | L ♨ | D in hotel | ⚴ ⏃ ⋋ | ⋈ prior arrangement | TR WE and eve | M 450 | S
★★★*Green, 2 The Muirs, Kinross.* T:(0577) 63467. 45rm (39 ⇌ 6 ⌑)

Kinross Beeches Park, Kinross (NE side of town on B996)
T:(0577) 62237
Parkland course on the banks of Loch Leven. 18 | 6124 yds | Par 70 | SSS 70
L D B ♨ | ⚴ ⏃ ⋋ | ⋈ (prior arrangement) | ⏉ | TR WE ☎ | M 540 | S
★★★*Green, 2 The Muirs, Kinross.* T:(0577) 63467. 45rm (39 ⇌ 6 ⌑)

KIRBY MUXLOE
Leicestershire
Map **IV**   A4

Kirby Muxloe Station Rd, Kirby
Muxloe (S side of village off B5380)
T:(0533) 393457
*Parkland course. 18 | 6303 yds | Par 71
| SSS 70*
Visitors welcome but with M only
WE BH | without M ∴ per day ∷
WE | ♥ | B L D | ⚐ ♈ ↘ | TR ☎ |
⅃ | M 610 | S
★★★★*Holiday Inn, St Nicholas Circle,
Leicester. T:(0533) 531161. 188rm ⇄
🍴*

KIRKBY IN ASHFIELD
Nottinghamshire
Map **IV**   A2

Notts Hollinwell (1½m SE of
Kirkby in Ashfield off A611)
T:(0623) 753225
*Undualating moorland; Championship
course. 18 | 7020 yds | Par 72 | SSS 74*
Visitors welcome but with M only
⊠ WE (not after 1000) ☎ | without
M fees on application | ✳ | B | L (not
Mon) | ♥ | D prior arrangement | ⚐
♈ ↘ | TR 1230-1430 F (pm) | M 500
| S
★★★★*Swallow, Carter Ln East, South
Normanton. T:(0773) 812000. 123rm
⇄ 🍴*

KIRKBY LONSDALE
Cumbria
Map **V**   D4

Kirkby Lonsdale Sedburgh Rd,
Casterton (1m N of Kirkby
Lonsdale on A683)
*Meadowland with splendid views. 9 |
2014 yds | Par 31 | SSS 60*
Visitors welcome | TR competitions
| M 200
★★*Pheasant Inn, Casterton. T:(0468)
71230. 10rm (9 ⇄ 1 🍴)*

KIRKBYMOORSIDE
North Yorkshire
Map **V**   G4

Kirkbymoorside Manor Vale,
Kirkbymoorside (N side of village)
T:(0751) 31525
*Parkland course. 18 | 5958 yds | Par 70
| SSS 69*
Visitors welcome | without M ..
per day ∴ WE | with M .. per day
WE | B ♥ L D | ⚐ ♈ | TR Medal &
competition days | M 400

★★*George & Dragon, Market Pl.
T:(0751) 31637. 14rm (10 ⇄ 4 🍴)
Annexe: 6rm ⇄*

KIRKCALDY
Fife, *Fife*
Map **VI**   G1

Dunnikier Park Dunnikier Way,
Kirkcaldy (2m N of Kirkcaldy off
A988)
T:(0592) 261599
*Parkland, rolling fairways, not heavily
bunkered, views of Firth of Forth. 18 |
6601 yds | Par 72 | SSS 72*
Visitors welcome, without M .. per
day ∴ WE | B | L ♥ D prior
arrangement | ⚐ ♈ | ⋈ | TR S
0830-0945, 1230-1400, Sun 1200-1400
| M 550 | S
★★*Station, 4 Bennochy Rd. T:(0592)
262461. 34rm (5 ⇄ 4 🍴)*

Kirkcaldy Balwearie, Kirkcaldy
(SW side of town off A910)
T:(0592) 260370
*Parkland course. 18 | 6004 yds | Par 71
| SSS 70*
Visitors welcome | without M ∴ per
day WE | B (not Th) | B L ♥ D prior
arrangement (not Th) | ⚐ ♈ ↘ | ④
at all times | TR S | ⅃ | M 660 | S
★★★*Dean Park, Chapel Level.
T:(0592) 261635. 19rm (13 ⇄ 6 🍴).
Annexe: 12rm 🍴*

KIRKCUDBRIGHT
Dumfries and Galloway,
Kirkcudbrightshire
Map **VI**   E6

Kirkcudbright Stirling Crescent,
Kirkcudbright (NE side of town off
A711)
*Parkland course. Hilly, with hard
walking. Good views. 18 | 5598 yds |
Par 67 | SSS 67*
Visitors welcome | ⚐ ♈ | ⋈ | TR
Tu W evenings and competitions |
M 300
★★*Selkirk Arms, Old High St,
Kirkcudbright. T:(0557) 30402. 15rm
(2 🍴). Annexe: 11rm (4 ⇄)*

KIRKINTILLOCH
Strathclyde, *Dumbartonshire*
Map **VI**   E2

Hayston Campsie Rd (1m NW of
Kirkintilloch off A803)
T:041-776 1244
*An undulating course with a sandy
subsoil and some wooded areas. 18 |*

6042 yds | Par 70 | SSS 69
Visitors welcome without M before
1630 ∴ per day | B L D ♥ | ⚐ ♈ |
TR after 1630 | M 440 | S
★★★*Black Bull Thistle, Main St,
Milngavie. T:041-956 2291. 28rm (27
⇄)*

Kirkintilloch Campsie Rd
(1m NW of Kirkintilloch off A803)
T:041-776 1256
*Parkland course. 18 | 5269 yds | Par 70
| SSS 66*
Visitors welcome with M only | B L
D ♥ | ⚐ ♈ | TR all times | M 650
★★★*Black Bull Thistle, Main St,
Milngavie. T:041-956 2291. 28rm (27
⇄)*

KIRKWALL
Orkney Islands
Map **VII**   K3

Orkney Grainbank (½m W of
Kirkwall off A965)
T:(0856) 2457
*Easy parkland course with few hazards,
superb views over Kirkwall and islands.
18 | 5406 yds | Par 70 | SSS 68*
Visitors welcome | .. per day WE |
⚐ ♈ | TR ④ 1700-1900 | M 150
★★*Ayre, Ayre Rd, Kirkwall. T:(0856)
2197. 31rm (3 ⇄ 6 🍴)*

KIRRIEMUIR
Tayside, *Angus*
Map **VII**   H7

Kirriemuir Northmuir (1m N of
Kirriemuir off B955)
T:(0575) 72144
*Parkland and heathland course with
good view. Parties by arrangement
Mon to F. 18 | 5591 yds | Par 68 |
SSS 67*
Visitors welcome, ☎ only with M
WE | ✳ | B L ♥ D prior arrangement
| ⚐ ♈ ↘ | ⋈ sometimes | TR WE |
M 600 | S
★★*Royal, Castle St, Forfar. T:(0307)
62691. 22rm (8 ⇄)*

KNARESBOROUGH
North Yorkshire
Map **V**   F5

Knaresborough Boroughbridge Rd
(1½m N of Knaresborough on
A6055)
T:(0423) 863219
*Parkland course. 18 | 6254 yds | Par 70
| SSS 70*
Visitors welcome ☎ for large

KNUTSFORD
Cheshire
Map **V**   D8

Knutsford Mereheath Ln, Knutsford (N side of town centre off A50)
T:(0565) 3355
9 | 6328 yds | Par 70 | SSS 70
Visitors welcome ☎ ⊠ restricted W pm | without M ∴ per day ∴ WE | with M
.. per day WE | B L ☛ D prior arrangement | ⚲ ⟙ | TR W (Ladies Day) |
M 135 | S
★★★*Swan, Bucklow Hill. T:(0565) 830295. 70rm (44 ⇌ 26 ⌘)*
A good 9-hole parkland course set in a beautiful old deer park. It
demands some precise iron play.

Mere Golf and Country Club	SCORE CARD: White Tees		
Chester Road, Knutsford	1	530	10	427
(N side of town centre off A50)	2	409	11	401
T:(0565) 830155	3	174	12	188
18	6723 yds	Par 70	SSS 72	4	357	13	467
Visitors welcome Mon, Tu, Th	B L	5	408	14	169
☛ D	⚲ ⟙ ⤢ ⤡ ⊠	TR W, F, S,	6	437	15	393
Sun, BH	M 300	S	7	434	16	441
★★★*Swan, Bucklow Hill. T:(0565)*	8	195	17	349
830295. 70rm (44 ⇌ 26 ⌘)	9	500	18	444

A gracious parkland championship course designed by James Baird
in the Cheshire sand belt, with several holes close to a lake. The
round has a tight finish with four testing holes.

parties | ∴ per day ∷ WE | ∴ per
round | B L ☛ D prior arrangement
parties only (not Tu) | ⚲ ⟙ ⤡ |
M 750 | S
★★★*Hospitality Inn, Prospect Pl, West
Park, Harrogate. T:(0423) 64601.
71rm ⇌*

KNEBWORTH
Hertfordshire
Map **II**   E1

Knebworth Deards End Ln (N side
of village off B197)
T:(0438) 812752
*Parkland course, easy walking. 18 |
6428 yds white (6052 yellow) |
Par 71(70) | SSS 71(69)*
Visitors welcome, except WE |
without M ∷ per day | with M ∴
per day | B L ☛ D prior
arrangement | ⚲ ⟙ ⤢ | TR WE | ⤡ |
M 800 | S
★★★*Roebuck Inn, Old London Rd,
Broadwater, Stevenage. T:(0438)
65444. 54rm ⇌*

KNIGHTON
Powys
Map **III**   F5

Knighton The Frydd (½m S of
Knighton off B4355)
T:(0547) 528646
Hill course with hard walking. 9 |

5320 yds | Par 68 | SSS 66
Visitors welcome ☎ | .. per day
WE | B ☛ | ⚲ | ⟙ evngs only | TR
W evng Sun (pm) | M 100
★★*Radnorshire Arms, High St,
Presteigne. T:(0544) 267406. 6rm ⇌
Annexe: 10rm ⇌*

KNOTT END-on-SEA
Lancashire
Map **V**   C5

Knott End Wyre Side, Knott End-
on-Sea (W side of village off B5377)
T:(0253) 810576
*Pleasant course on banks of River Wyre
open to sea breezes. 18 | 5852 yds |
Par 69 | SSS 68*
Visitors welcome ☎ restricted WE |
without M ∴ per day | B L ☛ D
prior arrangement (not Mon) | ⚲ ⟙
| ⤡ possible | TR until 0930,
1230-1330 | ⤢ | M 700 | S
★★★★*Imperial, North Promenade,
Blackpool. T:(0253) 23971. 159rm (146
⇌ 13 ⌘)*

LADYBANK
Fife, *Fife*
Map **VI**   G1

Ladybank Annsmuir, Ladybank (N
side of village off B9129)
T:(0337) 32075
Picturesque heath/moorland course,

*popular with visitors. 18 | 6617 yds |
Par 71 | SSS 72*
Visitors welcome | ∷ per day WE |
B ☛ L D | ⚲ ⟙ ⤢ | TR S | M 700 |
⤡ | S
★★★*⚲Fernie Castle, Letham.
T:(033781) 381. 15rm (6 ⇌ 9 ⌘)*

LAMBERHURST
Kent
Map **II**   G5

Lamberhurst Church Rd, (N side of
village on A21)
T:(0892) 890241/890591
*Parkland course crossing river twice,
fine views. 18 | 6277 yds | Par 72 |
SSS 70*
Visitors welcome, restricted WE BH
(am) ☎ | without M ∴ per day ∷
WE | with M .. per day WE | B L ☛
D prior arrangement (no food Mon)
| ⚲ ⟙ ⤢ ⤡ | ⤡ sometimes | TR
WE until 1200 | M 600 | S
★*Green Cross Inn, Goudhurst.
T:(0580) 211200. 6rm*

LAMLASH
Isle of Arran, *Strathclyde*
Map **VI**   C4

Lamlash Brodick Rd (¾m N of
Lamlash on A841)
T:(07706) 296
*A hilly course with magnificent views
of the mountains and sea. 18 | 4681 yds
| Par 64 | SSS 63*
Visitors welcome without M .. per
day | ⟙ B L ☛ | ⚲ ⤢ ⤡ | S | TR
Sun medal | M 400
★*Cameronia, Whiting Bay. T:(07707)
254. 6rm*

LANCASTER
Lancashire
Map **V**   C5

Lansil Caton Rd, Lancaster (N side
of town centre on A683)
T:(0524) 39269
*Parkland course. 9 | 5608 yds | Par 70 |
SSS 67*
Visitors welcome, restricted WE
before 1300 | .. per day | B L ☛ | ⚲
⟙ | ⤡ | TR S and Sun 0800-1300 |
M 375
★★★*Midland, Marine Rd, Morecombe.
T:(0524) 417180. 46rm (31 ⇌ 12 ⌘)*

LANGBANK
Strathclyde, *Renfrewshire*
Map **VI**   D2

Gleddoch Golf and Country Club ➥

LANARK
Strathclyde, *Lanarkshire*
Map **VI** F3

Lanark The Moor (E side of town centre off A73)
T:(0555) 3219
18 | 6416 yds | Par 70 | SSS 71
Visitors welcome Mon to F until 1630, with M only WE or ⊠ | B L ♥ D | ⚐ ⊽
⤡ | ⋈ | [TR] Mon-F (after 1630), WE | M 800 | [S]
★★★*Popinjay, Rosebank. T:(055586) 441. 36rm (29 ⇆ 7 ⋒)*
Chosen as one of the pre-qualifying tests for the Open
Championship held at Lanark from 1977 to 1983. The address of the
club, 'The Moor', gives some indication as to the kind of golf to be
found there. Golf has been played at Lanark for well over a century
and the Club dates from 1851.

LANCASTER
Lancashire
Map **V** C5

Lancaster Golf and Country Club Ashton Hall, Ashton with Stodday
(3m S of Lancaster on A588)
T:(0524) 751247
18 | 6422 yds | Par 71 | SSS 71
Visitors welcome ⊠ restricted WE (subject to starting sheet) | ∴ per day WE |
B L ♥ D | ⚐ ⊽ | ⤡ ⋈ prior arrangement | [TR] ④ ☎ for details | M 850 | [S]
★★★*Midland, Marine Rd, Morecombe. T:(0524) 417180. 46rm (31 ⇆ 12 ⋒)*
This course is unusual for parkland golf in being exposed to the
winds coming off the Irish Sea. It is situated on the Lune estuary
and has some natural hazards and easy walking. There are however
several fine holes among woods near the old clubhouse.

Langbank (1m S of Langbank off
B789)
T:(047554) 304
*Parkland and heathland course with
other sporting facilities available to
temporary members. Good views over
Firth of Clyde. 18 | 5661 yds | Par 68 |
SSS 67*
Visitors welcome ☎ ⊠ only with M
WE | B L ♥ D | ⚐ ⊽ ⤡ | ⋈ prior
arrangement | ④ WE [TR] WE | ⅃ |
M 300 | [S]
⑱★★★⚊*Gleddoch House, Langbank.
T:(047554) 711. 20rm ⇆ ⋒*

LANGHOLM
Dumfries and Galloway, *Dumfries*
Map **VI** G5

Langholm Whiteside, Langholm,
Dumfries & Galloway (E side of
village off A7)
*Hillside course with fine views, hard
walking. Society meetings by
arrangement. 9 | 2623 yds | Par 68 |
SSS 66*
Visitors welcome | .. per day WE |
⚐ | ⋈ | [TR] competitions | M 130
★★*Eskdale, Market Pl. T:(0541)
80357. 14rm (5 ⋒)*

LARBERT
Central, *Stirlingshire*
Map **VI** F2

Falkirk Tryst 86 Burnhead Rd,
Larbert (1m NE of Larbert off
A88/B905)
T:(0324) 562415
*Moorland course, fairly level and well
bunkered. Winds can affect play.
Visiting societies accepted Mon Tu Th
F by arrangement. 18 | 6053 yds |
Par 70 | SSS 69*
Visitors welcome, only with M WE
and W ⊠ | without M ∴ per day
WE | with M .. per day | B L ♥ D
(not F) | ⚐ ⊽ | ⋈ | [TR] competition
days | M 650 | [S]
★★★*Inchyra Grange, Grange Rd,
Polmont. T:(0324) 711911. 30rm ⇆ ⋒*

Glenbervie Glenbervie Clubhouse,
Stirling Rd, Larbert (2m NW of
Larbert on A9)
T:(0324) 562605
*Parkland course with good view. 18 |
6452 yds | Par 71 | SSS 71*
Visitors welcome by appointment,
☎ ⊠ or with M | B L ♥ prior
arrangement (not Mon) D | ⊽ ⚐ ⤡

| [TR] various | M 600 | [S]
★★★*Stakis Park, Arnot Hill, Camelon
Rd, Falkirk. T:(0324) 28331. 55rm ⇆*

LARGS
Strathclyde, *Ayr*
Map **VI** C3

Largs Irvine Rd (S side of town
centre on A78)
T:(0475) 673594
*A parkland, tree-lined course with
views to the Clyde coast and Arran
Isles. 18 | 6220 yds | Par 70 | SSS 68*
Visitors welcome without M ∷ per
day B L D ♥ | ⊽ ⚐ ⤡ | [S] ⋈ |
M 430
★★*Elderslie, John St, Broomfields.
T:(0475) 686460. 25rm (9 ⇆ 4 ⋒)*

Routenburn Routenburn Road,
Largs (1m N of Largs off A78)
T:(0475) 673230
*Heathland course with magnificent
view over Firth of Clyde. 18 | 5675 yds
| Par 68 | SSS 67*
Visitors welcome | B L ♥ D prior
arrangement | ⚐ ⊽ | [S] [TR] Sun
0830-1000 competition days | M 350
★★★⚊*Manor Park, Skelmorlie.
T:(0475) 520832. 7rm (5 ⇆ 1 ⋒)*

LARKHALL
Strathclyde, *Lanarkshire*
Map **VI** F3

Larkhall Burnhead Rd, Larkhall (E
side of town on B7019)
T:(0698) 881113
*Small inland hill course. 9 | 6968 yds |
Par 72 | SSS 72*
Visitors welcome | B L ♥ D | ⚐ ⊽ |
⋈ | [TR] S 1500-1700, Th 1700-1900,
Tu 1700-2000 | M 180
★★★*Popinjay, Rosebank. T:(055586)
441. 36rm (29 ⇆ 7 ⋒)*

LAUDER
Borders, *Berwickshire*
Map **VI** H3

Lauder (½m S of Lauder off A68)
*Moorland course, lovely views, with
some long interesting holes. 9 |
6002 yds | Par 72 | SSS 69*
Visitors welcome | M 100
★★*Carfraemill, Carfraemill. T:(05785)
200. 11rm (2 ⇆)*

LAUNCESTON
Cornwall
Map **I** D6

Launceston St Stephens (NW side

of town centre on B3254)
T:(0566) 3442
*Undulating parkland course with views
over Tamar Valley to Dartmoor and
Bodmin Moor. Societies welcome by
arrangement. 18 | 6409 yds | Par 70 |
SSS 71*
Visitors welcome | B L ☞ | D prior
arrangement | ⚘ ⅄ | ∖ | ⋈ prior
arrangement | 𝔍 | M 875 | S |
★★*White Hart, Broad St. T:(0566)
2013. 28rm (13 ⇄ 5 🍴)*

LEADHILLS
Strathclyde, *Lanarkshire*
Map **VI**   F4

Leadhills Leadhills, Biggar (E side
of village off B797)
T:(06594) 222
*Testing hilly course with high winds.
It is the highest golf course in Great
Britain. 9 | 2030 yds | Par 64 | SSS 62*
Visitors welcome | without M ▪▪
per day | ⋈ | 1300-1600 ladies only
★★*Mennockfoot Lodge, Mennock,
Sanquhar. T:(06592) 382. 1rm ⇄
Annexe: 8rm (2 ⇄)*

LEAMINGTON SPA
Warwickshire
Map **III**   K6

Leamington & County Golf Ln,
Whitnash, Leamington Spa (S side
of town centre)
T:(0926) 25961
*Undulating parkland course with
extensive views. 18 | 6430 yds | Par 71
| SSS 71*
Visitors welcome | ✳ | B L ☞ D | ⚘
⅄ | M 600 | S |
★★★*Manor House, Avenue Rd.
T:(0926) 23251. 53rm (47 ⇄ 6 🍴)*

Newbold Comyn Newbold Terrace
East, Leamington Spa (¾m E of
town centre, off B4099)
T:(0296) 21157
*Municipal parkland course with hard
walking in parts. The par 4 9th is a
467-yd testing hole. 18 | 6221 yds |
Par 70 | SSS 70*
Played over by club but course

LEEDS
West Yorkshire
Map **V**   F6

open to public | B ⅄ L D ☞ | ⚘ ∖ |
⋈ probable | 𝔍 | M 350 | S |
★★★*Manor House, Avenue Rd.
T:(0926) 23251. 53rm (47 ⇄ 6 🍴)*

LEATHERHEAD
Surrey
Map **II**   E4

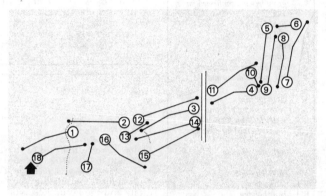

Headingley Back Church Ln, Adel, Leeds (5½m N of city centre off A660)
T:(0532) 675100
18 | 6238 yds | Par 69 | SSS 70
Visitors welcome | without M ∴ per day | ∷ WE | with M at reduced rate | ☞ |
B L D prior arrangement | ⚘ ⅄ | ⋈ (possible) | ④ TR competition days,
1200-1400 | 𝔍 | M 375 | S |
★★★*Post House, Otley Rd, Bramhope. T:(0532) 842911. 122rm ⇄*
Headingley is perhaps better known for its cricket ground than for
its golf course, but the members one and all will tell you that it is a
course which provides enjoyable golf. An undulating course with a
wealth of natural features offering fine views from higher ground.
Leeds's oldest course, founded in 1892.

Leatherhead Kingston Rd (1¼m N of Leatherhead on A244)
T:(0372) 3966
Parkland course with numerous ditches and only two hills, so walking is easy.
18 | 5701 yds | Par 69 | SSS 68
Visitors welcome | ☎ advisable | ∴ per day :: WE | B L 🍵 | ⚂ Ⴌ ↘ ⋈ | TR Sun am | ᴶ | M 480 | S
★★★★*Burford Bridge, Box Hill, Dorking. T:(0306) 884561. 48rm* ⇌

Tyrrells Wood Leatherhead (1½m SE of Leatherhead)
T:(0372) 376025
Parkland course with easy walking. Societies welcome (not Mon) by arrangement. 18 | 6022 yds | Par 70 | SSS 70
Visitors welcome ✉ but with M only WE | B L 🍵 (not Mon) | ⚂ Ⴌ ↘ | TR WE until 1200 competition days | ④ ladies' medal days | ᴶ | M 600 | S
★★★★*Burford Bridge, Burford Bridge, Box Hill, Dorking. T:(0306) 884561. 48rm* ⇌

LECKFORD
Hampshire
Map II   A5

Leckford Leckford, Stockbridge (1m SW of Leckford off A3057)
T:(0264) 810710
A testing downland course with good views. 9 | 6444 yds | Par 70 | SSS 71
Visitors welcome with M only restricted WE ☎ | ⚂ | ⋈ TR ☎ for details | M 200
★★*Grosvenor, High St, Stockbridge. T:(0264) 810606. 25rm* ⇌

LEEDS
West Yorkshire
Map V   F6

Gotts Park Armley Ridge Rd, Leeds (3m E of city centre off A647)
T:(0532) 638232
Municipal parkland course. 18 | 4594 yds | Par 65 | SSS 62
Course open to public | B 🍵 for parties | ⚂ ↘ ⋈ | Ⴌ eve M only | ᴶ | M 300 | S | TR Sun until 1000

LEEDS
West Yorkshire
Map V   F6

Moor Allerton Coal Rd, Wike, Leeds (5½m N of city centre on A61)
T:(0532) 661154
27 | 6935 yds | Par 72 | SSS 72
Visitors welcome | without M :: per day WE | with M .. per day ∴ WE | B 🍵 | L (not F) | D prior arrangement | ⚂ Ⴌ | ᴶ | TR 1230-1330 | M 1200 | S
★★★*Stakis Windmill, Mill Green View, Seacroft, Leeds. T:(0532) 732323. 100rm* ⇌ 🍴
The Moor Allerton Club has 27 holes set in 220 acres of undulating parkland, with magnificent views extending across the Vale of York to Sutton Bank. The Championship Course was designed by Robert Trent Jones, the famous American course architect and is the only course of his design in the British Isles. The well- appointed club house has many amenities, including tennis, bowls and sauna and the complex is considered to be second to none in the North of England.

LEEDS
West Yorkshire
Map V   F6

Sand Moor Alwoodley Ln, Leeds (6m N of city centre off A61)
T:(0532) 685180
18 | 6429 yds | Par 71 | SSS 71
Visitors welcome, restricted Tu Th WE | * | 🍵 | B L D (not Mon) | ⚂ Ⴌ ↘ | TR
Tu 0930-1030, Th 0912-1200, S 0800-1600, Sun 0800-1030 | S
★★★*Post House, Otley Rd, Bramhope. T:(0532) 842911. 122rm* ⇌
A beautiful, undulating course overlooking Lord Harewood's estate and the Eccup Reservoir. The course is wooded with some holes adjacent to water; most of the greens are large. The 12th is perhaps the most difficult where the fairway falls away towards the reservoir. Short straight shots might be the policy here!

★★★*Hotel Metropole, King St, Leeds. T:(0532) 450841. 113rm (96* ⇌ *6* 🍴 *)*

Horsforth Layton Rise, Layton Rd, Horsforth, Leeds (6½m NW of city centre off A65)
T:(0532) 585200
Moorland course overlooking airport. Societies welcome by arrangement. 18 | 6293 yds | Par 71 | SSS 70
Visitors welcome, restricted WE ☎ preferred | without M ∴ per day WE | with M .. per day WE | B L 🍵 (not Mon) | D prior arrangement (not Mon) | ⚂ Ⴌ ↘ | TR competition days ④ when 3 balls in play | M 600 | S
★★★*Post House, Otley Rd, Bramhope. T:(0532) 842911. 122rm* ⇌

Leeds Elmete Ln, Leeds (5m NE of city centre on A6120 off A58)
T:(0532) 658775
Parkland course with pleasant views. 18 | 6097 yds | Par 69 | SSS 69
Visitors welcome WE & BH with M

only | ✱ | B L ☕ D | △ Y ⟍ ⋈ (usually) | [TR] 1300-1400, 1630-1800 | M 600 | [S]
★★★★Ladbroke Dragonara, Neville St. T:(0532) 442000. 234rm (204 ⇄ 30 ⍓)

Middleton Park Municipal Middleton Park, Leeds (3m S of city centre off A653)
T:(0532) 700449
Parkland course. 18 | 5400 yds | Par 67 | SSS 66
Visitors welcome | Y B | △ | ⋈ | ⟍ | ℑ | M 150 | [S]
★★★★Ladbroke Dragonara, Neville St. T:(0532) 442000. 234rm (204 ⇄ 30 ⍓)

Moortown Harrogate Rd, Allwoodley, Leeds (5½m N of city centre off A61)
T:(0532) 686521
Heathland course, easy walking. 18 | 6606 yds | Par 69 | SSS 72
Visitors welcome, restricted WE BH ☎ advisable | ∷ per day WE | B L ☕ D | △ Y ⟍ | ⋈ (possible) | [TR] until 0915 daily, 1230-1400 WE | M 500 | [S]
★Hartrigg, Shire Oak Rd, Headingley, Leeds. T:(0532) 751568. 28rm

Roundhay Park Ln, Leeds (4m NE of city centre off A58)
T:(0532) 662695
Attractive municipal parkland course, natural hazards, easy walking. 9 | 5186 yds | Par 68 | SSS 65
Open to public ‥ per day | B ☕ weekends only | L D prior arrangement (not Mon) | △ | Y (members and guests only) ⟍ | ⋈ | [TR] 3rd Sun each month (0730-1030) | M 300 | [S]
★★★Stakis Windmill, Mill Green View, Seacroft. T:(0532) 732323. 100rm ⇄ ⍓

South Leeds Gipsy Ln, Beeston, Leeds (3m S of city centre off A653)
T:(0542) 700479
Parkland course, windy, hard walking, good views. Societies welcome by arrangement. Juniors welcome. 18 | 5835 yds | Par 69 | SSS 68
Visitors welcome | ✱ | B L ☕ D prior arrangement (not Tu) | △ Y ⟍ | ⋈ | [TR] WE competition days | M 400 | [S]
★★★★Queen's, City Sq. T:(0532) 431323. 195rm ⇄

Temple Newsam Temple-Newsam, Leeds (3½m E of city centre off A63)
T:(0532) 645624
Two parkland courses. Testing long 13th (563 yds) on second course. 36 | 6448 yds (6029) | Par 72(72) | SSS 71(72)
Visitors welcome | B L ☕ D (WE only) | △ Y ⟍ | ℑ | M 600 | [S]
★★★Ladbroke, Wakefield Rd, Garforth Roundabout. T:(0532) 866556. 143rm ⇄ ⍓

LEEK

Staffordshire
Map **III** J2

Leek Birchall (½m S of Leek on A520)
T:(0538) 384779
Undulating challenging moorland course. 18 | 6229 yds | Par 70 | SSS 70
Visitors welcome | ∴ per day ∷ WE | B ☕ L D | △ Y ⋈ | ℑ | M 700 | [S]
★★★Stakis Grand, 66 Trinity St, Hanley, Stoke-on-Trent. T:(0782) 22361. 93rm ⇄

LEICESTER

Leicestershire
Map **IV** A4

Humberstone Heights Gypsy Ln, Leicester (2½m NE of city centre)
T:(0533) 764674
Municipal parkland course with 9 hole pitch & putt. 18 | 6444 yds | Par 72 | SSS 71 (Ladies course 5404 yds | Par 72 | SSS 71)
Open to public ☎ essential WE | ‥ per round | B ☕ | D L prior arrangement | △ Y ⟍ | ⋈ | ℑ | [S]
★★★Ladbroke International, Humberstone Rd. T:(0533) 20471. 218rm ⇄

Leicestershire Evington Ln (2m E of city centre, off A6030)
T:(0533) 738825
Pleasantly undulating parkland course. 18 | 6312 yds | Par 68 | SSS 70
Visitors welcome ☎ WE (S by arrangement only) | B ☕ | L D (prior arrangement) | Y △ | ℑ | [TR] 1230-1330 except Sun; Tu Ladies' Day | M 750 | [S]
★★★Leicestershire Moat House, Wigstone Rd, Oadby, Leicester. T:(0533) 719441. 29rm ⇄ ⍓

Western Park Scudamore Rd, Braunstone Frith, Leicester (1½m W of city centre off A47)
T:(0533) 876158
Pleasant undulating parkland course with open aspect fairways. 18 | 6629 yds | Par 72 | SSS 72
Visitors welcome | B L ☕ D prior arrangement | △ Y ⟍ | [TR] WE ☎ for times | ℑ | M 350 | [S]
★★★Post House, Braunstone Ln East. T:(0533) 896688. 182rm ⇄

LEIGH

Greater Manchester
Map **V** D7

Pennington St. Helen's Rd, Leigh (SW side of town centre off A572) Gtr Manchester
Municipal parkland course, with natural hazards of brooks, ponds and trees and easy walking. 9 | 3104 yds | Par 36 | SSS 35
Open to public ‥ per day WE
★★★Greyhound, Warrington Rd. T:(0942) 671256. 54rm ⇄ ⍓

LEIGHTON BUZZARD

Bedfordshire
Map **IV** C8

Leighton Buzzard Plantation Rd, ➡

LEE-ON-SOLENT

Hampshire
Map **II** B7

Lee-on-Solent Brune Ln (1m N of Lee-on-Solent off B3385)
T:(0705) 551170
18 | *5978 yds* | *Par 68* | *SSS 69*
Visitors welcome except WE | ∴ per round/day | B ☕ | △ ☕ | [TR] WE | ℑ | M 700 | [S]
★★Red Lion, East St, Fareham. T:(0329) 239611. 33rm ⇄

A modest parkland/heathland course yet a testing one. The five short holes always demand a high standard of play and the 13th is rated one of the best in the country. Visitors can be sure of a warm welcome, and being a flat course it is not tiring.

Leighton Buzzard (N side of town centre off A418)
T:(0525) 373811
Parkland course with easy walking. 18 | 5366 yds | Par 69 | SSS 68
Visitors welcome but with M only WE BH | :: per day | ∴ per round | B ♛ L D | ⚐ ∖ | ♟ (not Mon) | ∞ prior arrangement | Ⓢ
★★★Swan, High St. T:(0525) 372148. 35 ⇄

LENNOXTOWN
Strathclyde, Stirlingshire
Map VI   E2

Campsie Crow Rd, Lennoxtown (½m N of Lennoxtown on B822)
T:(0360) 310244
Scenic hillside course. 18 | 5517 yds | Par 70 | SSS 67
Visitors welcome, restricted until 1600 | B ♛ | L (WE only) | ⚐ ♟ | ④ WE | M 330 | ⓉⓇ WE 0800-1000 | Ⓢ
★★Kirkhouse Inn, Strathblane.

LELANT
Cornwall
Map I   A8

West Cornwall Lelant, St Ives (N side of village off A3074)
T:(0736) 753401
18 | 5839 yds | Par 69 | SSS 68
Visitors welcome ✉ | ☎ advisable | ∴ per day WE BH | B ♛ | L D prior arrangement (not Tu) | ⚐ ♟ ∞ ∖ | ⓉⓇ W pm | 𝕁 | M 850 | Ⓢ
★★Boskerris, Boskerris Rd, Carbis Bay. T:(0736) 795295. 20rm (15 ⇄)

T:(0360) 70621. 16rm (10 ⇄)

LENZIE
Strathclyde, Dumbartonshire
Map VI   E2

Lenzie 19 Crosshill Rd, Lenzie (S side of town on B819)
T:041-776 1535
Parkland course near Glasgow. 18 | 5982 yds | Par 69 | SSS 68
Visitors welcome with M or ☎ | B L ♛ (not Mon) | D prior arrangement (not Mon) | ⚐ ♟ | ⓉⓇ ☎ | M 700 | Ⓢ
★★Garfield House, Cumbernauld Rd, Stepps. T:041-779 2111. 27rm ⇄ 🍴

LEOMINSTER
Hereford and Worcester
Map III   G6

Leominster Ford Bridge (3m S of Leominster on A49)
T:(0568) 2863
Sheltered parkland course. 9 | 5249 yds | Par 68 | SSS 66

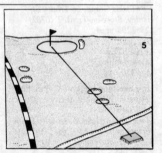

A seaside links with sandhills and lovely turf adjacent to the Hayle estuary and St Ives Bay. A real test of the player's skill, especially 'Calamity Corner' starting at the 5th on the lower land by the River Hayle. A small 3 hole course is available for practice and children.

Visitors welcome | without M .. per day ∴ WE | with M .. per day WE | B L ♛ D | ⚐ ♟ ∖ | ⓉⓇ Sun (until 1130) competition days | M 350 | Ⓢ
★★Royal Oak, South St. T:(0568) 2610. 16rm (15 ⇄ 1 🍴)

LERWICK
Shetland Islands
Map VII   J2

Dale (3½m NW of Lerwick on A970)
T:(059584) 369
Challenging moorland course, hard walking. This is the most northerly course in Britain. A burn runs the full length of the course and provides a natural hazard. Testing holes include the 3rd (par 4), 5th (par 4). Societies welcome (Mon to F) by arrangement. Children welcome. 18 | 6110 yds | Par 69 | SSS 71
Visitors welcome | B ♛ | ⚐ ♟ ∖ ∞ | ⓉⓇ as per notice board | M 265 | Ⓢ
★★★Lerwick Thistle, South Rd, Lerwick. T:(0595) 2166. 60rm ⇄ 🍴

LESLIE
Fife, Fife
Map VI   G1

Leslie Balsillie Laws, Leslie (N side of town off A911)
Challenging parkland course, par unbroken throughout course's long history. 9 | 4940 yds | Par 62 | SSS 64
Visitors welcome | .. per day WE | B ♛ | ⚐ ♟ | ∞ | S 0800-1000, 1300-1400 | M 200
★★★Balgeddie House, Leslie Rd, Glenrothes. T:(0592) 742511. 18rm (16 ⇄ 2 🍴)

LESMAHAGOW
Strathclyde, *Lanarkshire*
Map **VI**   E3

Holland Bush Acretophead,
Lesmahagow (2m SW of
Lesmahagow off A74)
T:(055) 893484
*Fairly difficult tree-lined municipal
parkland and moorland course. 1st half
is flat, while 2nd half is hilly. No
bunkers.* 18 | 6110 yds | Par 71 |
SSS 70
Open to public | B L ♥ D prior
arrangement | ⚐ ♈ | ↘ ⋈ prior
arrangement | TR during medals -
advisable ☎ | ④ during medals - ☎
| ♩ | M 500 | S
★★★*Popinjay, Rosebank. T:(055586)
441. 36rm (29 ⇄ 7 ▥)*

LEUCHARS
Fife, *Fife*
Map **VII**   H8

St Michaels Leuchars (NW side of
village on A919)
T:(033483) 365
*Parkland course with out of bounds at
every hole.* 9 | 5510 yds | Par 70 |
SSS 67

LETCHWORTH
Hertfordshire
Map **IV**   D8

Letchworth Letchworth Ln (S side of town centre off A505)
T:(0462) 683203
Societies welcome by arrangement. 18 | 6082 yds | Par 70 | SSS 69
Visitors welcome WE by invitation | ∷ per day ∴ per round | B ♥ L D | ⚐ ♈
| TR WE, Tu am | M 850 | S
★★*Broadway, The Broadway. T:(0462) 685651. 37rm (22 ⇄)*
Planned more than 50 years ago by Harry Vardon, this adventurous
course is set in a peaceful corner of Norman England. To its variety
of natural and artificial hazards is added an unpredictable wind.

LEVEN
Fife, *Fife*
Map **VI**   G1

Leven Thistle 3 Balfour St, Leven (NE side of town off A955)
T:(0333) 26397
Societies by arrangement. Club plays over Leven Links. 18 | 6500 yds | Par 71 |
SSS 71
Visitors welcome | ∴ per day ∷ WE | with M .. per day | B L ♥ D | ⚐ ♈ ↘ |
⋈ | TR Mon-F summer (1700-1900) | ♩ | M 500 | S
★★*Greenside, High St, Leslie, Glenrothes. T:(0592) 743453. 16rm (10 ⇄ ▥)*
Golf has been played here since early last century. Leven has the
classic ingredients which make up a golf links in Scotland;
undulating fairways with hills and hollows, out of bounds and
again a 'burn' or stream. A top class championship links course
used for British Open final qualifying stages.

LEVEN
Fife, *Fife*
Map **VI**   G1

Leven Golfing Society Links Rd,
Leven
T:(0333) 26096
*Plays over Leven Links (see Leven
Thistle). Societies welcome by
arrangement.* 18 | 6434 yds | Par 71 |
SSS 71
Visitors welcome ☎ | restricted S | B
♥ | L D prior arrangement | ⚐ ♈
⋈ | TR ④ ☎ | M 400
★★★*Balgeddie House, Leslie Rd,
Glenrothes. T:(0592) 742511. 18rm
(16 ⇄ 2 ▥)*

LEWES
East Sussex
Map **II**   F7

Lewes Chapel Hill, Lewes (E side of
town centre off A26)
T:(0273) 473074

*Downland course, fine views. Societies
welcome (Mon to Fri) by arrangement.*
18 | 5951 yds | Par 71 | SSS 69
Visitors welcome | ✳ | B ♥ | ⚐ ♈ ↘
⋈ | TR WE 0700-0930 | M 300 | S
★★*White Hart, High St. T:(0273)
474676. 19rm (13 ⇄ 1 ▥). Annexe:
14rm ⇄*

LEWIS, ISLE OF
Western Isles, *Ross & Cromarty*
Map **VII**
See Stornoway

LEYLAND
Lancashire
Map **V**   C6

Leyland Wigan Rd, Leyland (E side
of town centre on A49)
T:(0772) 436457, Preston, Lancs
*Parkland course, fairly flat, usually
breezy. Society meetings by
arrangement.* 18 | 6105 yds | Par 70 |
SSS 69
Visitors welcome, ☎ advisable,
restricted WE BH | without M ∴
per day | with M .. per day WE | B
L ♥ D prior arrangement (no
catering Mon) | ⚐ ♈ | ↘ ⋈ limited
| ④ TR ☎ | M 860 | S
★★★*Pines, Clayton le Woods. T:(0772)
38551. 25rm ⇄*

LILLESHALL
Shropshire
Map **III**   H4

Lilleshall Hall Newport (3m SE of
Lilleshall)
T:(0952) 603840
Heavily wooded parkland course. 18 |
5891 yds | Par 68 | SSS 68
Visitors welcome with M only WE |
∴ per day | B ♥ L D | ⚐ ♈ | TR Tu
1030-1200 | ♩ | M 600 | S
★★*Royal Victoria, St Mary's St,
Newport. T:(0952) 810831. 21rm (10
⇄ 5 ▥)*

LIMPSFIELD
Surrey
Map **II**   F5

Limpsfield Chart (1m E of
Limpsfield on A25)
T:(088-388) 2106
*Tight inland course set in National
Trust land.* 9 | Par 70 | SSS 68
Visitors welcome | ∴ per day ∷
WE | B L D ♥ | ⚐ ↘ ♈ | TR Th &
WE | ♩ | M 350 | S
★★*Reigate Manor, Reigate. T:(07372)* ➡

LICHFIELD
Staffordshire
Map III J4

Whittington Barracks Tamworth Rd (2½m SE of Lichfield on A51)
T:(0543) 432317
Societies welcome (W and Th only) by arrangement. 18 | 6457 yds | Par 70 | SSS 71
Visitors welcome but restricted WE BH (and day after) ☎ | without M :: per
day | with M .. per day | B ☛ (not Mon) | L D prior arrangement (not Mon) |
⚠ ♈ | TR ☎ for details | ♩ | M 500 | S |
★★★*George, Bird St. T:(0543) 414822. 39rm (34 ⇌ 4 🅐)*
18 magnificent holes winding their way through heathland and
trees, presenting a good test for the serious golfer. Leaving the
fairway can be severely punished. The dog-legs are most tempting,
inviting the golfer to bite off a little more than he can chew. Local
knowledge is a definite advantage. Clear views of the famous three
spires of Lichfield Cathedral.

LITTLEHAMPTON
West Sussex
Map II D7

Littlehampton Rope Walk, West Beach (1m W of Littlehampton off A259)
T:(09064) 717170
Societies welcome by arrangement (Mon Tu F). 18 | 6145 yds | Par 70 | SSS 68
Visitors welcome | B ☛ L D | ⚠ ♈ | ④ ☎ for details | TR before 0900 | ♩ |
M 650 | S |
★★★*Norfolk Arms, High St, Arundel. T:(0903) 882101. 21rm ⇌. Annexe: 13rm ⇌*
A delightful seaside links in a delightful setting — and the only links
course in the area. At Littlehampton you are soon among sand
dunes, golf's original backcloth where the best holes on the course
are to be found.

40125. 15rm (2 ⇌ 13 🅐) Annexe:
12rm (11 ⇌ 1 🅐)

LINCOLN
Lincolnshire
Map V H8

Canwick Park Canwick Park,
Washingborough Rd, Lincoln (1½m
SE of Lincoln on B1190)
T:(0522) 22166
*Parkland course. Testing 14th hole (par
3). 18 | 6257 yds | Par 70 | SSS 70*
Visitors welcome, restricted WE BH
☎ | ✳ | B L ☛ D prior arrangement
(not Mon) | ⚠ ♈ (not Mon
lunchtime) ↘ | TR S, Sun | M 600 |
S |
★★★*Eastgate Post House, Eastgate.*
T:(0522) 20341. 71rm ⇌

Carholme Carholme Rd, Lincoln
(1m W of city centre on A57)
T:(0522) 23725
*Parkland course where prevailing west
winds can add interest. New tree
planting in progress. Good views. 18 |
6086 yds | Par 71 | SSS 69*
Visitors welcome, restricted Sun
0730-1430 | .. per day ∴ WE | B L

(not Mon) ☛ | D prior arrangement
(not Mon) | ⚠ ♈ ↘ | ♩ | M 620 | S |
★★★★*White Hart, Bailgate. T:(0522)*
26222. 52rm (50 ⇌ 10 🅐)

LINLITHGOW
Lothian, West Lothian
Map VI F2

Linlithgow Braehead, Linlithgow
(1m S of Linlithgow, off Bathgate
Road, off A803)
T:(0506) 842585
*Parkland course in beautiful setting. 18
| 5858 yds | Par 70 | SSS 68*
Visitors welcome | .. per day ::
WE | with M .. per day WE | B | L
Sun only | ⚠ ♈ | TR W-S | M 425 |
S |
★★★*Inchyra Grange, Grange Rd,*
Polmont. T:(0324) 711911. 30rm ⇌ 🅐

West Lothian, The Airngath Hill,
Linlithgow (1½m N of Linlithgow
off A706)
T:(0506) 826030
*Hilly parkland course with superb
views of River Forth. Societies welcome
by arrangement. 18 | 6629 yds | Par 71
| SSS 72*

Visitors welcome, restricted WE,
competitions | .. per day ∴ WE | B
L ☛ | ⚠ ♈ | ⋈ | ④ up to 1500 | TR |
WE and selected competition dates
| M 500
★★★*Inchyra Grange, Grange Rd,*
Polmont. T:(0324) 711911. 30rm ⇌ 🅐

LIPHOOK
Hampshire
Map II C6

Liphook Wheatsheaf Enclosure
(1½m SW of Liphook off A3)
T:(0428) 723271
*Heathland course with easy walking
and fine views. 18 | 6207 yds | Par 70 |
SSS 70*
Visitors welcome ⋈ ☎ | ∴ per
round :: per day weekdays | :: per
round/day WE | B ☛ | L | D prior
arrangement | ⚠ ♈ | ④
1030-1230 and after 1500 | M 800 | S |
★★★*Lythe Hill, Petworth Rd,*
*Haslemere. T:(0428) 51251. 38rm (34
⇌ 2 🅐)*

Old Thorns London Kosaido Golf
and Country Club, Longmoor Rd
(1m W of Liphook on B2131)
T:(0428) 724555
*A challenging 18-hole championship
course designed around magnificent
oaks, beeches and Scots pine. 18 |
Par 72 | SSS 70*
Visitors welcome | ♈ B L D ⚠ ☛ ↘
⋈ S |
★★★*Lythe Hill, Petworth Rd,*
*Haslemere. T:(0428) 51251. 38rm (34
⇌ 2 🅐)*

LITTLE CHALFONT
Buckinghamshire
Map II D2

Little Chalfont Lodge Ln, Nr
Amersham (1m S of Little Chalfont
off B4442)
T:(02404) 4877
*Flat course surrounded by woods. 9 |
5852 yds | Par 68 | SSS 68*
Visitors welcome | .. per day ∴
WE | B L D ☛ | ⚠ ♈ ↘ | ♩ | M 400 |
S |
★★*Crown, High St, Amersham.*
T:(02403) 21541. 19rm (6 ⇌)

LITTLE GADDESDEN
Hertfordshire
Map II D2

Ashridge The Clubhouse, Little
Gaddesden (4m N of Berkhamsted
on B4506)

T:(044284) 2244
Good parkland course, tricky for the
average player but fair to all. Excellent
clubhouse facilities. Societies welcome
(Tu-F) March-Oct. 18 | 6508 yds |
Par 72 | SSS 71
Visitors welcome ⊠ ☎ | ∷ per day
| L ♞ | ⚐ ♟ | ⚲ ☎ | ∞ usually |
[TR] WE BH 𝄇 | M 680 | [S]
❀○○○*Bell Inn, Aston Clinton.*
T:(0296) 630252. 21rm ⇄

LIVERPOOL
Merseyside
Map **V**   C7

Allerton Park Allerton Manor Golf
Estate, Allerton Rd (5½m SE of city
centre, off A562 and B5180)
T:051-428 1046
Parkland course. 18 | 5459 yds | Par 67
| SSS 67
Visitors welcome | .. per round | B
L ♞ D | ⚐ ♟ ⚲ 𝄇 | M 650 | [S]
★★*Grange, Holmfield Rd, Aigburth.*

LITTLESTONE
Kent
Map II   J6

Littlestone St Andrews Road,
Littlestone (N side of village)
T:(0679) 63355
18(9) | 6424 yds (3996) | Par 71(64) |
SSS 71(64)
Visitors welcome | B L D ♞ | ⚐ ♟ |
④ 1030-1130 | [TR] 0830-0930 | M 450
| [S]
★★★★*Hotel Imperial, Princes Pde,*
Hythe. T:(0303) 67441. 83rm (81 ⇄ 2
▯)

SCORE CARD:				
1	296		10	422
2	398		11	355
3	395		12	396
4	375		13	405
5	492		14	180
6	162		15	371
7	510		16	476
8	373		17	179
9	178		18	490

Located in the Romney Marshes, this flattish seaside links course
calls for every variety of shot. The 8th, 15th, 16th and 17th are
regarded as classics by international golfers. Allowance for wind
must always be made. Additional facilities include 5 grass tennis
courts and an extensive practice area.

LIVERPOOL
Merseyside
Map V   C7

Childwall Naylors Rd, Gateacre (7m E of city centre off B5178)
T:051-487 0654
18 | 6425 yds | Par 72 | SSS 71
Visitors welcome, restrictions on juveniles | ∴ per day WE | B L ♞ D prior
arrangement (not Mon) | ⚐ ♟ | ⚲ ∞ | [TR] Tu W (usually midday) | 𝄇 | M 630
| [S]
★*Rockland, View Rd, Rainhill. T:051-426 4603. 12rm (2 ⇄) Annexe: 10rm (4 ⇄ 6*
▯)
Parkland golf is played here over a testing course, where accuracy
from the tee is well rewarded. The course is very popular with
visiting societies for the clubhouse has many amenities.

T:051-427 2950. 25rm (19 ⇄ 2 ▯)

Lee Park Childwall Valley Rd,
Liverpool (7m E of city centre off
B5178)
T:051-487 0268
Flat course with ponds in places. 18 |
6024 yds | Par 71 | SSS 69
Visitors welcome | B L ♞ | ⚐ | ∞ ♟
| 𝄇 | M 500 | [S]
★★★★*Liverpool Moat House, Paradise*
St, Liverpool. T:051-709 0181. 258rm
⇄ ▯

Liverpool Municipal Ingoe Ln,
Kirkby, Liverpool (7½m NE of city
centre on A506)
T:051-546 5435
Flat easy course. 18 | 6555 yds | Par 72
| SSS 71
Visitors welcome | B L ♞ | ⚐ ⚲ ♟
∞ | 𝄇 | [S]
★★★*Park, Park Lane West, Netherton,*
Bootle. T:051-525 7555. 60rm (23 ⇄
37 ▯)

Woolton Speke Rd, Liverpool (7m
SE of city centre off A562)
T:051-486 2298
Parkland course providing a good round
of golf at all standards. 18 | 5706 yds |
Par 69 | SSS 68
Visitors welcome ☎ | B L D ♞ (not
Mon F) | ⚐ ♟ ⚲ | ∞ | [TR]
(1300-1400 daily) | [S]
★★*Grange, Holmefield Rd, Aigburth.*
T:051-427 2950. 25rm (19 ⇄ 2 ▯)

LIVINGSTON
Lothian, *West Lothian*
Map **VI**   F2

Livingston Carmowdean,
Livingston (N side of town off
A809)
T:(0506) 38843
Long testing course, fairly flat,
championship standard. 18 | 6636 yds |
Par 71 | SSS 72
Visitors welcome | L D B ♞ | ⚐ ⚲
♟ | ∞ | 𝄇 | [TR] competition days
0800-1000 | M 500 | [S]
★★★▟▟*Houstoun House, Uphall.*
T:(0506) 853831. 30rm (27 ⇄ 3 ▯)

Pumpherston Drumshoreland Rd,
Pumpherston, Livingston (1m E of
Livingston, off B8046)
T:(0506) 32869
Undulating parkland course with
testing 8th hole (par 3), and view of
Pentland Hills. 9 | 5154 yds | Par 64 |
SSS 65
Visitors welcome with M only ⊠ |
.. per day WE | B ♞ | ⚐ ♟ | M 370
★★★▟▟*Houstoun House, Uphall.*
T:(0506) 853831. 30rm (27 ⇄ 3 ▯)

LLANDRINDOD WELLS
Powys
Map **III**   E6

Llandrindod Wells (1m SE of
Llandrindod Wells off A483)
T:(0597) 2010
Moorland course with easy walking and
panoramic views. Societies welcome by
arrangement. 18 | 5719 yds | Par 69 |
SSS 68
Visitors welcome | B ♞ (not Tu) | L
D prior arrangement (not Tu) | ⚐ |
♟ (not Tu) | ⚲ | [TR] WE 0800-0930,
1300-1400 | M 290
★★★*Hotel Metropole, Temple St.*
T:(0597) 2881. 121 (114 ⇄ 7 ▯)

LLANDYBIE
Dyfed
Map **III**   D7

LIVERPOOL
Merseyside
Map **V**   C7

West Derby Yew Tree Ln, West Derby (4½m E of city centre off A57)
T:051-228 1540
Societies welcome by arrangement. 18 | 6333 yds | Par 72 | SSS 70
Visitors welcome ⊠ ☎ restricted WE | without M ∴ per day WE | with M .. per day WE | B L ♥ | D prior arrangement | ⚒ ⟆ | TR Tu 1100-1330 (ladies) | J | M 600 | S
★★★*Crest Hotel-Liverpool City, Lord Nelson St, Liverpool. T:051-709 7050. 170rm* ⇄

A parkland course always in first-class condition, and so giving easy walking. The fairways are well wooded. Care must be taken on the first nine holes to avoid the brook which guards many of the greens. A modern well-designed clubhouse with many amenities overlooks the course.

Glynhir Glynhir Rd (2m NE of Llandybie)
T:(0269) 850472
Parkland course with good views, later holes close to Upper Loughor River leading down to the river. The 14th is 405-yd dog leg. Societies welcome (Mon to F) by arrangement. 18 | 6090 yds | Par 69 | SSS 70
Visitors welcome | without M .. per day ∴ (.. winter) WE | with M .. per day WE | B ♥ (not Mon) | L D prior arrangement (not Mon) | ⚒ | ⟆ (not Mon) | ⋈ by arrangement | TR competitions | M 500 | S
★★*Mill at Glynhir, Llandybie, Ammanford. T:(0269) 850672. 8rm (5* ⇄ 3 🍴)

LLANFAIRFECHAN
Gwynedd
Map **III**   D2

Llanfairfechan Fford Llannerch (W side of town on A55)

T:(0248) 680144
Hillside course with panoramic views of the coast. 9 | 3119 yds | Par 54 | SSS 57
Visitors welcome | ⟆ ⚒ | TR Sun am | M 120
★★★*Sychnant Pass, Sychnant Pass Rd, Conwy. T:(049263) 6868. 10rm (8* ⇄ 2 🍴)

LLANGATTOCK
Powys
Map **III**   F7

Old Rectory Llangattock, Crickhowell (SW side of Llangattock)
T:(0873) 810373
Sheltered course with easy walking. Swimming pool. 9 | 2225 yds | Par 53 | SSS 54
Visitors welcome | .. per day | B L ♥ D | ⚒ ⟆ ⋈ | M 200
★★🏟*Gliffaes, Crickhowell. T:(0874) 730371. 19rm (14* ⇄ 2 🍴)

LLANGOLLEN
Clwyd
Map **III**   F3

Vale of Llangollen Holyhead Rd, Llangollen (1½m E of Llangollen on A5)
T:(0978) 860040
Parkland course, set in superb scenery by the River Dee. Societies welcome by arrangement. 18 | 6017 yds | Par 72 | SSS 72
Visitors welcome | ∴ per day WE | B | L ♥ D prior arrangement | ⚒ ⟆ | ⟍ few | ⋈ (possibly) | M 580 | S
★★★*Bryn Howel. T:(0978) 860331. 37rm (31* ⇄ 🍴)

LLANGYBI
Dyfed
Map **III**   D9

Cilgwyn Llangybi, Lampeter (½m NW of Llangybi, off A485)
T:(0570) 45286
Parkland course. 9 | 5318 yds | Par 68 | SSS 67
Visitors welcome | B ♥ L D (except Mon) | ⚒ ⟆ ⟍ | ⋈ | M 100
★★*Black Lion Royal, High St, Lampeter. T:(0570) 422172. 16rm (6* ⇄ 1 🍴)

LLANIDLOES
Powys
Map **III**   E5

St Idloes Penrhallt, Llanidloes (1m N of Llanidloes off B4569)
T:(05512) 2559
Hill course which is undulating but walking is easy. Good view. 9 | 5320 yds | Par 66 | SSS 66
Visitors welcome, restricted Sun am | ⚒ | ⟆ evenings only | TR Sun |

LLANDUDNO
Gwynedd
Map **III**   D1

Llandudno (Maesdu) Hospital Rd,
Llandudno (S side of town centre
on A546)
T:(0492) 76450
18 | 6513 yds | Par 73 | SSS 72
Visitors welcome | without M ∴ per
day WE | with M .. per round | B L
♞ D | ♠ ⅄ ⋈ ⚲ | TR WE before
0945 and 1200-1345 | ♪ | M 500 | S
**Bryn Creigin Garden Hotel, Ty*
Mawr Rd, Deganwy. T:(0492) 83402.
16rm (12 ⇌ 4 ⌂)

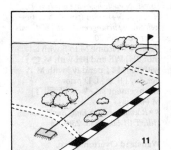

11

Part links, part meadowland, this championship course starts and finishes on one side of the main road, the remaining holes, more seaside in nature, being played on the other side. The holes are pleasantly undulating and present a pretty picture when the gorse is in bloom. Often windy, this varied and testing course is not for beginners.

LLANDUDNO
Gwynedd
Map **III**   D1

North Wales 72 Bryniau Rd, West
Shore, Llandudno (W side of town
on A546)
T:(0492) 75325
18 | 6132 yds | Par 71 | SSS 69
Visitors welcome | without M ∴ per
day WE | with M .. per day WE | B
♞ L D | ♠ ⅄ ⚲ | TR before 0945
daily | ♪ | M 720 | S
∘∘*St Tudno, North Pde, Llandudno.*
T:(0492) 74411. 21rm (19 ⇌ 2 ⌂)

SCORE CARD:			
1	344	10	400
2	359	11	420
3	338	12	359
4	200	13	182
5	490	14	530
6	385	15	334
7	498	16	141
8	352	17	100
9	317	18	383

This course is across the railway from Maesdu and is more of a seaside links with several extremely fine holes.

M 150
Red Lion, Longbridge St. T:(05512)
2270. 6rm

LLANWERN
Gwent
Map **I**   G2

Llanwern Golf House, Tenyson
Ave (½m S of Llanwern off A455)
T:(0633) 2029
*Meadowland course. Societies welcome
by arrangement. 18 | 6202 yds | Par 70*
Visitors welcome | B ♞ L D | ♠ ⅄
⚲ ⋈ | TR WE | ④ WE | M 829 | S
***Ladbroke, The Coldra, Newport.*
T:(0633) 412777. 119rm ⇌

LOCHGELLY
Fife, *Fife*
Map **VI**   G1

Lochgelly Cartmore Rd, Lochgelly
(W side of town off A910)
T:(0592) 780174
*Parkland course with easy walking and
often windy. 18 | 5491 yds | Par 68 |
SSS 67*
Visitors welcome, restricted
competition days | B ♞ L D | ♠ ⅄
⋈ TR competition days | M 400
***Dean Park, Chapel Level,*
Kirkcaldy. T:(0592) 261635. 19rm (13
⇌ 6 ⌂) Annexe: 12rm ⌂

Lochore Meadows Lochore
Meadows Country Park, Crosshill
(2m N of Lochgelly off B920)
T:(0592) 860086
*Lochside course with natural stream
running through and young woodland
nearby. Societies welcome by*

*arrangement. 9 | 6244 yds | Par 72 |
SSS 71*
Visitors welcome | B ♞ L | ♠ |
M 200
***Green, 2 The Muirs, Kinross.*
T:(0577) 63467. 45rm (39 ⇌ 6 ⌂)

LOCHMABEN
Dumfries and Galloway,
Dumfriesshire
Map **VI**   F5

Lochmaben Castlehill Gate,
Lochmaben (S side of village off
A709)
T:(038781) 552
*Comfortable walking parkland course
between two lochs with fine old trees
and 22 sand bunkers. 9 | 5304 yds |
Par 66 | SSS 66*
Visitors welcome | .. per day WE |
B L ♞ (limited catering) | ♠ | ⅄ ⋈ |
TR Mon-F after 1700 | M 550
**Dryfesdale, Lockerbie. T:(05762)*
2427. 11rm (8 ⇌ 1 ⌂)

LOCHRANZA
Strathclyde, *Bute*
Map **VI**   B3

Lochranza Isle of Arran (1m SE of
Lochranza on A841)
T:(077083) 273
*Parkland course. 9 | 1815 yds | Par 29 |
SSS 40*
Visitors welcome | B ♞ ♠ ⚲ ⋈ |
S (small)
**Kinloch, Blackwaterfoot.*
T:(077086) 286. 49rm ⇌

LOCHWINNOCH
Strathclyde, *Renfrewshire*
Map **VI**   D3

Lochwinnoch Burnfoot Rd,
Lochwinnoch (W side of town off
A760)
T:(0505) 842710
*Parkland course with hard walking and
testing golf. Overlooks bird sanctuary
and boating loch. Societies welcome
(Mon to F) by arrangement. 18 |
6241 yds | Par 70 | SSS 70*
Visitors welcome | L D ♞ B | ⅄ ♠ |
⋈ (usually) | M 380
**Elderslie, John St, Broomfields,*
*Largs. T:(0475) 686460. 25rm (9 ⇌ 4
⌂)*

LOCKERBIE
Dumfries and Galloway,
Dumfriesshire
Map **VI**   F5

KEY

(IA1)	*atlas grid reference*
T:	*telephone number*
☎	*advance letter/telephone call required*
✉	*introduction from own club sec/handicap certificate/club membership card required*
..	*low fees*
∴	*medium fees*
::	*high fees*
*	*green fees not confirmed for 1987*
B	*light lunch*
L	*full lunch*
☛	*tea*
D	*dinner*
⚐	*changing rooms/showers*
⛾	*bar open mid-day and evenings*
↘	*clubs for hire*
⋈	*partners may be found*
④	*restricted time for 4 balls*
TR	*times reserved for members*
⅃	*professional*
S	*well-stocked shop*
M	*member*
Mon Tu W Th F S Sun	
WE	*weekend*
BH	*bank holiday*

Lockerbie Corrie Rd, Lockerbie (E side of town centre off B7068)
T:(05762) 3363
Parkland course with fine views. 18 | 5434 yds | Par 67 | SSS 66
Visitors welcome | * | ☛ prior arrangement | ⚐ ⛾ | TR Sun | M 350
★★★*Lockerbie House. T:(05762) 2610. 27rm (23 ⇌ 1 ⅏)*

LONDON
Greater London
Map II   F3

Places within the London postal area are listed below in postal district order commencing East, then North, South and West. Other places within Greater London are listed under their respective place names and are shown on the main map section.

West Essex Bury Rd, Sewardstonebury, Chingford, London E4
T:01-529 7558
Off N Circular Rd at Chingford on M25 for Waltham Abbey

Testing parkland course within Epping Forest. Notable holes are 8th (par 4), 16th (par 5/4), 18th (par 5). Societies welcome by arrangement. 18 | 6342 yds | Par 70 | SSS 70
Visitors welcome M to F with ✉ (not BH) WE and BH with M ☎ | without M :: per day | with M ∴ per day | B ☛ | L D prior arrangement | ⚐ ⛾ ↘ | TR | ⅃ | M 600 | S
★★*Roebuck, North End, Buckhurst Hill. T:01-505 4636. 23rm ⇌*

Wanstead Overton Drive, Wanstead, London E11
T:01-989 3938
From central London A11 NE to Wanstead
A flat picturesque parkland course with many trees and shrubs and providing easy walking. The par 4 16th involves driving across a lake. Societies welcome by arrangement. No facilities for children. 18 | 6211 yds | Par 70 | SSS 70
Visitors welcome weekdays ✉ | ∴ per round :: per day | B L ☛ D | ⚐ ⛾ | TR WE BH | ⅃ | M 350 | S
★★★*Woodford Moat House, Oak Hill, Woodford Green. T:01-505 4511. 99rm (69 ⇌ 30 ⅏)*

Hampstead Winnington Rd, London N2
T:01-455 0203
Parkland course. 9 | 5812 yds | Par 68 | SSS 68
Visitors welcome ☎ | ∴ per day | B ☛ | L prior arrangement | ⚐ ⛾ ↘ | ④ TR ☎ | ⅃ | M 500 | S
★★★*Post House, Haverstock Hill. T:01-794 8121. 140rm ⇌*

Highgate Denewood Rd, London N6
T:01-340 3745
Parkland course. 18 | 5964 yds | Par 69 | SSS 69
Visitors welcome weekdays | with M only WE | restricted W WE BH | B ☛ | L D prior arrangement | ⚐ ⛾ ↘ | TR W am (ladies) | ⅃ | M 630 | S
★★★*Hendon Hall, Ashley Ln, NW4. T:01-203 3341. 52rm (49 ⇌ 3 ⅏)*

Picketts Lock Picketts Lock Sports Centre, Edmonton, London N9
T:01-803 3611
Municipal parkland course with the River Lea providing a natural hazard. Putting green and practice ground available. 9 | 2496 yds | Par 64 | SSS 64
Visitors welcome | B ☛ L | ⚐ ⛾ ↘ | ⅃ | S
★★★*Royal Chace, The Ridgeway, Enfield. T:01-366 6500. 92rm (51 ⇌ 41 ⅏)*

Leaside Picketts Lock Sports Centre, Edmonton, London N9
T:01-803 3611
Flat parkland course with River Lea running alongside several holes. 9 | 2496 yds | Par 32 | SSS 32
Visitors welcome | ⛾ B ☛ | ⚐ ↘ | ⋈ usually | S ⅃
★★★*Prince Regent, Woodford Bridge. T:01-504 7635. 10rm ⇌ ⅏*

Trent Park Bramley Rd, Southgate, London N14
T:01-366 7432
Parkland course with blue and white tees set in 150 acres of green belt area. 7 holes played across Merryhills brook.

LONDON
Greater London
Map II   F3

South Herts Links Dr, Totteridge, London N20
T:01-445 2035
Societies welcome (W Th F) by arrangement. 18 (also 9 hole short course) | 5748 yds | Par 72 | SSS 71
Visitors welcome ✉ ☎ (not WE) | with M only WE | ∴ per round :: per day | B L ☛ (not Mon) | D prior arrangement (not Mon) | ⚐ ⛾ ↘ | ④ | TR ☎ for details | M 830 | S
★★★Royal Chace, The Ridgeway, Enfield. T:01-366 6500. 92rm (51 ⇌ 41 ⅏)
An open undulating parkland course officially in Hertfordshire, but now in a London postal area. It is, perhaps, most famous for the fact that two of the greatest of all British professionals, Harry Vardon and Dai Rees CBE were professionals at the club. The course is testing, over rolling fairways, especially in the prevailing south-west wind.

LONDON
Greater London
Map **II** F3

Royal Blackheath The Club House, Court Rd, Eltham, London SE9
T:01-850 1795
18 | 6246 yds | Par 70 | SSS 70
Visitors welcome ✉ | ☎ advisable | :: per day | B L ☕ prior arrangement (not Mon) | △ 🍸 ⟍ | [4] not permitted | M 750 | [S]
★★★Bromley Court, Bromley Hill, Bromley. T:01-464 5011. 130rm ⇌

A pleasant, parkland course of great character as befits the antiquity of the Club: the clubhouse dates from the 17th century. Many great trees survive though a great number were lost to the Dutch Elm disease. The 18th is quite a gimmick requiring a pitch to the green over a thick clipped hedge.

LONDON
Greater London
Map **II** F3

Royal Wimbledon 29 Camp Rd, London, SW19
T:01-946 2125
Societies welcome (Tu to F) by arrangement. 18 | 6300 yds | Par 70 | SSS 70
Visitors welcome ✉ | restricted WE BH | without M :: per day | with M ∴ per day WE | L on certain days only check | ☕ △ | 🍸 until 2000 | ⟍ | [TR] Sun before 0900 daily, Tu ladies WE & BH | M 780 | [S]
★★★Richmond Hill, 146-150 Richmond Hill, Richmond. T:01-940 2247. 125rm (110 ⇌ 4 🚿)

SCORE CARD:

1	405	10	476
2	426	11	421
3	382	12	455
4	401	13	161
5	164	14	455
6	261	15	421
7	500	16	390
8	221	17	138
9	282	18	341

A club steeped in the history of the game, it is also of great age, dating back to 1865. Although it is so near London it is of the sand and heather type like so many of the Surrey courses. The course was once the site of a Roman encampment on which the 7th, 10th and 11th holes are now situated. The following hole, the 12th (par 4) is rated as the best on the course.

Testing holes are 2nd (405 yds) over brook 190 yds from the tee and up to plateau green. 7th (435 yds) dog-leg over brook par 4. 11th (131 yds) plateau to valley par 3. Considerable practice facilities. 18 | 5971 yds | Par 69 | SSS 69
Visitors welcome | ☎ for WE BH | B L ☕ D | △ 🍸 ⋈ | 🏌 | [TR] ☎ for details | M 500 | [S]
★★★★West Lodge Park, Cockfosters Rd, Hadley Wood. T:01-440 8311. 50rm ⇌

North Middlesex The Manor House, Friern Barnet Ln, London N20
T:01-445 1604
Short parkland course with tricky greens. 18 | 5611 yds | Par 69 | SSS 67
Visitors welcome | ☎ | without M :: per day | 🍸 L B (no catering Mon) ☕ △ [S] ⟍ ⋈ [4] possibly ☎ | M 500
★★★Hendon Hall, Ashley Ln, NW4. T:01-203 3341. 52rm (49 ⇌ 3 🚿)

Bush Hill Park Bush Hill Rd, Winchmore Hill, London N21
T:01-360 5738
Pleasant parkland course surrounded by trees. Societies welcome (Tu Th F) by arrangement. 18 | 5809 yds | Par 69 | SSS 68
Visitors welcome with M or ✉ | WE BH only with M | ☎ advisable | * | B L prior arrangement (not Mon) | D ☕ | △ 🍸 ⟍ | 🏌 | M 650 | [S]
★★★Royal Chace, The Ridgeway, Enfield. T:01-366 6500. 92rm (51 ⇌ 41 🚿)

Muswell Hill Rhodes Ave, Wood Green, London N22
T:01-888 2044
Off N Circular Rd at Wood Green
Narrow parkland course, popular with societies (book in advance). 18 | 6441 yds | Par 71 | SSS 71
Visitors welcome restricted Tu am, WE BH ☎ | B ☕ (not Mon) | L D prior arrangement (not Mon) △ 🍸 ⟍ | [TR] Tu am (ladies) | 🏌 | M 500 | [S]
★★★Royal Chace, The Ridgeway, Enfield. T:01-366 6500. 92rm (51 ⇌ 41 🚿)

Finchley Nether Court, Frith Ln, London NW7 (near Mill Hill East station)
T:01-346 2436
Easy walking on wooded parkland course. Societies welcome by arrangement. 18 | 6411 yds | Par 72 | SSS 71
Visitors welcome restricted Tu WE BH | with or without M :: per day | B L ☕ (not Mon) | D prior arrangement | △ 🍸 ⟍ | [4] ☎ for details | [TR] WE (am) | 🏌 | M 500 | [S] ⋈
★★★Hendon Hall, Ashley Ln, NW4. T:01-203 3341. 52rm (49 ⇌ 3 🚿)

Hendon Sanders Ln, London NW7
T:01-346 6023
Easy walking parkland course which provides good golf. Societies welcome Tu and Th. 18 | 6241 yds | Par 70 | SSS 70
Visitors welcome weekdays ☎ | restricted WE | B ☕ | D prior arrangement (not Mon) | △ 🍸 ⟍ ⋈ | 🏌 | M 425 | [S]
★★★Hendon Hall, Ashley Ln, NW4. T:01-203 3341. 52rm (49 ⇌ 3 🚿)

Mill Hill 100 Barnet Way, Mill Hill, London NW7 (On A1 (S bound carriageway) between Apex Corner and Stirling Corner)
T:01-959 2339
Parkland course with easy walking. 18 | 6286 yds | Par 69 | SSS 70
Visitors welcome restricted WE BH ☎ advised | without M :: per day WE | with M ‥ per day WE | B L ☕ D | △ 🍸 | [TR] WE & BH before 1130 | M 400 | [S]
★★★Hendon Hall, Ashley Ln, NW4. T:01-203 3341. 52rm (49 ⇌ 3 🚿)

Eltham Warren Bexley Rd, Eltham,
London SE9
T:01-850 1166
*Easy walking on parkland course. 9 |
5800 yds | Par 69 | SSS 68*
Visitors welcome weekdays with M
or ⊠ | ∴ per day | B L prior
arrangement (not Mon or F) | ☎ | D
prior arrangement (not Mon or F) |
⚐ | ⚑ (not Mon) ↘ | ☐TR☐ WE BH | ♪
| M 400 | ☐S☐
★★★*Bromley Court, Bromley Hill,
Bromley. T:01-464 5011. 130rm* ⇌

Shooters Hill Eaglesfield Rd,
Shooters Hill, London SE18
T:01-854 6368
Shooters Hill Rd from Blackheath
then left to Eaglesfield Rd
*Hilly parkland course with good view
and natural hazards. Small societies
welcome by arrangement. Societies Tu
& Th only. 18 | 5736 yds | Par 69 |
SSS 68*
Visitors welcome weekdays with M
or ⊠ | WE with M | ☎ advisable | ∷
per day | B ☎ | L D prior
arrangement | ⚐ ⚑ | M 850 | ☐S☐ ♪
★★★*Bromley Court, Bromley Hill,
Bromley. T:01-464 5011. 130rm* ⇌

Dulwich & Sydenham Hill Grange
Ln, College Rd, London SE21
T:01-693 3961
*Parkland course, overlooking London,
hilly with narrow fairways. Small
societies by arrangement. 18 | 6192 yds
| Par 69 | SSS 69*
Visitors welcome weekdays ⊠ | WE
with M | ∷ per day | B L ☎ | ⚐ ⚑
↘ | ♪ | M 575 | ☐S☐
★★★*Bromley Court, Bromley Hill,
Bromley. T:01-464 5011. 130rm* ⇌

Aquarius Beechcroft Reservoir,
Marmora Rd. Off Forest Hill Rd,
London SE22
T:01-693 1626
*Course laid out on two levels over a
covered reservoir; hazards include air
vents and bollards. 9 | 5178 yds |
Par 66 | SSS 65*
Visitors with M only | restricted WE
and competition days | B L D prior
arrangement ☎ (not Mon Tu) | ⚐ |
⚑ (not Mon Tu) | ♪ | M 400 | ☐S☐
★★★*Bromley Court, Bromley Hill,
Bromley. T:01-464 5011. 130rm* ⇌

Richmond Park Roehampton Gate,
London SW15
T:01-876 1795

*2 public parkland courses. No caddies,
spectators, dogs or children under 12
allowed. New sports complex being
built (tennis, badminton, sauna etc).
Princes 18 | 5978 yds | Par 70 | SSS 69
| Dukes 18 | 5960 yds | Par 68 |
SSS 69*
Open to public | WE ☎ | B L D ☎ |
⚐ ⚑ ↘ | ⋈ | ☐S☐
★★★*Richmond Hill, 146-150
Richmond Hill, Richmond. T:01-940
2247. 125rm (110* ⇌ *4* 🍴)

White Lodge Richmond Park,
London SW15
T:01-876 3205
*Municipal parkland courses played over
by White Lodge club (private
clubhouse). Princes 18 | 5978 yds |
Par 70 | SSS 69 | Dukes 18 | 5960 yds |
Par 68 | SSS 69*
Open to public ☎ WE
★★★*Richmond Hill, 146-150
Richmond Hill, Richmond. T:01-940
2247. 125rm (110* ⇌ *4* 🍴)

Wimbledon Park Home Park Rd,
Wimbledon, London SW19
(400 yds from Wimbledon Park
station)
T:01-946 1250
*Easy walking on parkland course.
Sheltered lake provides hazard on 3
holes. Societies welcome by
arrangement. No children. 18 |
5465 yds | Par 66 | SSS 66*

LONG ASHTON
Avon
Map I H3

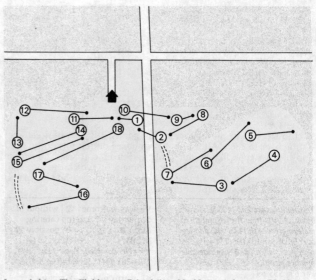

Long Ashton The Clubhouse, Bristol (½m N of Long Ashton on B3128)
T:(0272) 392316
18 | 6051 yds | Par 70 | SSS 70
Visitors welcome weekdays ⊠ | ∴ per day ∷ WE | B ☎ L | ⚐ ⚑ ↘ | ⋈ | ☐TR☐
WE | M 750 | ☐S☐
★★★*Redwood Lodge, Beggar Bush Ln, Failand, Bristol. T:(0272) 393901. 72rm* ⇌
🍴

A high downland course with nice turf, some wooded area and a
spacious practice area. The short par 3 2nd, with its drop shot on to
the green below closely backed by the wall of an old quarry, requires
good judgment as does the two-shot 16th with its diagonal sloping
fairway. Good drainage ensures pleasant winter golf. Additional
facilities are a large putting green and a billiard room.

Visitors welcome ⊠ | ☎ advisable |
restricted WE BH | ∷ per day
weekdays | B L ☙ (not Mon), prior
arrangement if more than 8 people |
⚥ (not WE BH) | Ⴈ | ⋈ | TR WE |
ʃ | M 450 | Ⓢ
★★★*Richmond Hill, 146-150
Richmond Hill, Richmond. T:01-940
2247. 125rm (110 ⇄ 4 ⚒)*

Hounslow Heath Municipal
Staines Rd, Hounslow
T:01-570 5271
*Parkland course in a conservation area,
planted with an attractive variety of
trees. The 15th hole lies between the
fork of two rivers. 18 | 5820 yds |
Par 69 | SSS 68*
Visitors welcome ☎ WE | .. per
round/day ∴ WE (reduced rates for
senior citizens and juniors
weekdays) | B (not Th) ☙ | ⚥ ＼ | ⋈
| TR WE competitions | ʃ | M 300 |
Ⓢ
★★★*The Post House, Sipson Rd, West
Drayton. T:01-759 2323. 597rm ⇄*

Ealing Perivale Ln, Greenford,
Middlesex
T:01-997 0937
*Flat parkland course relying on natural
hazards, trees, tight fairways, and the
River Brent which affects 9 holes. 18 |
6216 yds | Par 70 | SSS 69*
Visitors welcome weekdays with M
or ⊠ | ☎ preferred | B L ☙ | D prior
arrangement | ⚥ Ⴈ ＼ ⋈ usually |
④ | TR WE, competition days |
M 600 | Ⓢ
★★*Osterley, 764 Great West Rd,
Osterley. T:01-568 9981. 60rm (56 ⇄)*

Brent Valley 138 Church Rd,
Hanwell, London W7

T:01-567 1287
*Municipal parkland course with easy
walking. The River Brent winds
through the course. 18 | 5426 yds |
Par 67 | SSS 66*
B L ☙ D (with M only) | ⚥ Ⴈ (with
M only) ＼ | ⋈ | ʃ | M 350 | Ⓢ
★★★*Master Robert Motel, 366 Great
West Rd, Hounslow. T:01-570 6261.
Annexe: 63rm ⇄ ⚒*

LONGRIDGE PRESTON
Lancashire
Map **V**   D6

Longridge Fell Barn, Jeffrey Hill
(2m NE of Longridge)
T:(077478) 3291
*Moorland course 850ft high with views
of Ribble Valley. Trough of Bowland,
The Fylde and Welsh Mountains.
Societies welcome by arrangement. 18 |
5735 yds | Par 70 | SSS 68*
Visitors welcome | without M ..
per day ∴ WE BH | B L ☙ D | ⚥ |
M 400 | Ⓢ
★★*Shireburn Arms, Hurst Green.
T:(025486) 518. 11rm (6 ⇄ 1 ⚒)*

LONGNIDDRY
Lothian, *East Lothian*
Map **VI**   G2

Longniddry Links Rd, Longniddry (W side of village off A198)
T:(0875) 52141
18 | 6210 yds | Par 68 | SSS 70
Visitors welcome | without M ∷ per day WE | B ☙ | D L (not F) | ⚥ Ⴈ ＼ ⋈ |
④ | TR ☎ for details | ʃ | M 755 | Ⓢ
★★*Kilspindie House, Main St, Aberlady. T:(08757) 319. 12rm (8 ⇄ 4 ⚒)*
*Seaside and parkland undulating course. One of the numerous
courses which stretch east from Edinburgh right to Dunbar. The
inward half is more open and less testing than the wooded outward
half.*

LOOE
Cornwall
Map **I**   D7

Looe Bin Down (3½m NE of Looe
off B3253)
T:(050 34) 247
*Exposed and somewhat windy course
on high moorland and with easy
walking. Fine views over Looe
coastline. Societies welcome (not WE)
by arrangement. 18 | 5875 yds | Par 70
| SSS 68*
Visitors welcome | B L ☙ | ⚥ Ⴈ ＼
⋈ | ʃ | M 300 | Ⓢ
★★★*Hannafore Point, Marine Dr,
Hannafore, Looe. T:(05036) 3273.
40rm (39 ⇄ 1 ⚒)*

LOUTH
Lincolnshire
Map **V**   J8

Louth Crowtree Ln, Louth (SE side
of town centre off A157)
T:(0507) 603681
*Undulating parkland course, fine
views. 18 | 6502 yds | Par 71 | SSS 71*
Visitors welcome | ∴ per day WE |
B L ☙ D | ⚥ Ⴈ ＼ ⋈ | ʃ | M 500 | Ⓢ ➡

LOSSIEMOUTH
Grampian, *Morayshire*
Map VII H4

Moray Stotfield Rd, Lossiemouth (W side of town on B9040)
T:(034 381) 2018
18(18) | 6643 (Old) 6258 (New) yds | Par 71(70) | SSS 72(71)
Visitors welcome | :: per day WE | B L ♥ D | ♨ ⟆ | M 1043 | Ⓢ
***Mansion House, The Haugh, Elgin. T:(0343) 48811. 12rm ⇌*
Two fine Scottish links courses, known as Old and New Moray, and
situated on the Moray Firth away in the North-East where the
weather is unusually mild.

LOUGHBOROUGH
Leicestershire
Map IV A4

Longcliffe Snell's Nook Lane, Nanpantan
(3m SW of Loughborough off B5350)
T:(0509) 239129
Societies welcome. 18 | 6551 yds | Par 72 | SSS 71
Visitors welcome | without M :: per day | with M .. per day WE | B ♥ L D | ♨
⟆ | Ⓣ Ⓡ (1200-1400) | M 550 | Ⓢ
***Kings Head, High St, Loughborough. T:(0509) 233222. 86rm (69 ⇌ 9 ㎙)*
A re-designed course of natural heathland with outcrops of granite
forming natural hazards especially on the 1st and 15th. The course
is heavily wooded and has much bracken and gorse. There are a
number of tight fairways and one blind hole. The 7th is considered
one of the best par 4s in the Midlands.

White Hart, Tetford. T:(065883) 255.
6rm

LOWESTOFT
Suffolk
Map IV K5

Rookery Park Carlton Colville,
Lowestoft (3½m SW of Lowestoft
on A146)
T:(0502) 60380
Parkland course. Societies welcome
(Mon to F) by arrangement. 9-hole par
3 course adjacent. 18 | 6649 yds |
Par 72 | SSS 72
Visitors welcome, ⊠ restricted WE
BH | without M ∴ per day WE |
with M ∴ per day WE | B ∴ ♥ (not
Mon) | L D prior arrangement (not
Mon) | ♨ ⟆ ⟍ | ⋈ prior
arrangement | Ⓣ Ⓡ WE BH (until
1100) | M 1000 | Ⓢ
**Wherry, Bridge Rd, Oulton Broad.*
T:(0502) 3521. 23rm (20 ⇌ 3 ㎙)

LUNDIN LINKS
Fife, *Fife*
Map VI G1

Lundin Ladies Woodielea Rd,
Lundin Links (W side of village off
A915)
T:(0333) 320022

LUDLOW
Shropshire
Map III G5

Ludlow Bromfield (2m N of Ludlow off A49)
T:(977) 285
Societies welcome by arrangement. 18 | 6239 yds | Par 70 | SSS 70
Visitors welcome | ✻ | B ♥ L D | ♨ ⟆ ⟍ | ⋈ | ♩ | M 420 | Ⓢ
***Feathers, Bull Ring. T:(0584) 5261. 37rm ⇌ ㎙*
A long-established parkland course in the middle of the racecourse.
Very flat, quick drying, with little variance between summer and
winter play. Pleasant surroundings with adequate clubhouse. A
quarry is involved with 2 holes. The par 3 15th is testing.

LUNDIN LINKS
Fife, *Fife*
Map VI G1

Lundin Lundin Links (W side of village off A915)
T:(0333) 320202
18 | 6377 yds | Par 71 | SSS 71
Visitors welcome with M only Sun | B L ♥ prior arrangement (not Mon) | ♨
⟆ ⟍ | Ⓣ Ⓡ (before 0930, before 1430) Sun (all day) | ♩ | M 700 | Ⓢ
***Old Manor, Leven Rd, Lundin Links. T:(0333) 320368. 19rm (15 ⇌)*
The Leven Links and the course of the Lundin Club adjoin each
other. This course is part seaside and part inland. The holes which
can be described as seaside holes are excellent. The others no less
so, but of a different nature. Lundin Links, a popular holiday
village, has for long drawn golfers from all parts of Scotland and
beyond.

Short, lowland course with Roman
stones on the second fairway, and
coastal views. 9 | 2365 yds | Par 67 |
SSS 67
Visitors welcome | .. per day WE |
M 200 | Ⓣ Ⓡ W summer
***Old Manor, Leven Rd. T:(0333)*
320368. 19rm (18 ⇌ 1 ㎙)

LUTON
Bedfordshire
Map II D1

South Beds Warden Hill, Barton
Rd, Luton (3m N of Luton off A6)
T:(0582) 591500
Parkland course with rather mixed
going and very rough rough. Strong
winds are an additional hazard. 18(9) |
6341(4914) yds | Par 70(33) |
SSS 70(32). We have additionally a
9-hole course. 4914 yds | SSS 64 | Few
restrictions
Visitors welcome but with M only |
⊠ ☎ preferred | without M ∴
(main course) per day | with M ..
per day WE | B ♥ | L D prior
arrangement | ♨ ⟍ ⟆ |
sometimes | Ⓣ Ⓡ medal days, Tu pm
(ladies day) | M 700 | Ⓢ
***Strathmore Thistle, Arndale*
Centre. T:(0582) 34199. 151rm ⇌ ㎙

Stockwood Park Stockwood Park,
Luton (1m S of Luton on A6)
T:(0582) 413704
*Municipal parkland course. Societies
welcome by arrangement. 18 | 6276 yds
| Par 69 | SSS 69*
Open to public | B L ♥ | D prior
arrangement | ⚒ ☂ ⚲ | ✗ | TR WE
competitions | M 500 | S | ☇
★★★*Chiltern, Waller Ave, Dunstable
Rd, Luton. T:(0582) 575911. 99rm* ⇌

LUTTERWORTH
Leicestershire
Map **IV** A5

Lutterworth Rugby Rd (½m S of
Lutterworth on A426)
T:(04555) 2532
*Hilly course with River Swift running
through. 18 | 5570 yds | Par 67 |
SSS 67*
Visitors welcome | WE with M only
| without M ∴ per day | with M ..
per day | B L D ♥ | ⚒ ☂ | TR WE |
☇ | M 400
★★*Moorbarns, Watling St. T:(04555)
2237. Annexe: 11rm (6 ⇌ 5 ▥)*

LYBSTER
Highland, *Caithness*
Map **VII** H2

Lybster Main St, Lybster (E side of
village)
*Picturesque short heathland course,
easy walking. 9 | 3770 yds | Par 62 |
SSS 62*
Visitors welcome | .. per day WE |
⚒ ✗ | TR S pm for competitions |
M 45
★★★*Ladbroke, Riverside, Wick.
T:(0955) 3344. 48rm* ⇌

LYNDHURST
Hampshire
Map **II** A7

New Forest Southampton Rd (½m NE of Lyndhurst off A35)
T:(042128) 2450/2752
Societies welcome by arrangement. 18 | 5748 yds | Par 71 | SSS 68
Visitors welcome, restricted Sun (am) | ✳ | B L ♥ D | ⚒ ☂ ⚲ ✗ | TR Sun
until 1230 | ☇ | M 500 | S
★★★*Crown, High St, Lyndhurst. T:(042128) 2722. 42rm* ⇌
This picturesque heathland course is laid out in a typical stretch of
the New Forest on high ground a little above the village of
Lyndhurst. Natural hazards include the inevitable forest ponies.
The first two holes are somewhat teasing, as is the 485-yard par 5
9th. Walking is easy and there are 10 starting points.

LYDNEY
Gloucestershire
Map **III** G8

Lydney Lakeside Ave, Lydney (SE
side of town centre)
T:(0594) 42614
*Flat parkland-meadowland course with
prevailing wind along fairways. 9 |
5382 yds | Par 66 | SSS 66*
Visitors welcome WE with M only |
✳ | ⚒ ☂ ✗ | M 280
★★*Speech House, Forest of Dean,
Coleford. T:(0594) 22607. 13rm (6 ⇌)*

LYME REGIS
Dorset
Map I G6

Lyme Regis Timber Hill (1½m N of Lyme Regis on A3052)
T:(02974) 2043
Downland course with extensive views from 500ft over Lyme Bay and Dorset and Devon coast. Societies welcome by arrangement. 18 | 6262 yds | Par 71 | SSS 70
Visitors welcome ☎ advisable | without M ∴ weekdays WE | B ☞ L D | ⚲ ▼ ✓ | TR Th 0950-1315 Sun until 1130 | ♪ | M 670 | S
★★★*Devon, Lyme Rd.* T:(02974) 3231. 21rm (18 ⇄ 3 ♨)

LYMM
Cheshire
Map V D8

Lymm Whitbarrow Rd (½m N of Lymm off A6144)
T:(092 575) 5020
Flat course with natural water hazards. 18 | 6330 yds | Par 71 | SSS 70
Visitors welcome | ∴ per day WE | B L D ☞ | ⚲ ▼ ✓ ⋈ | M 700 | S
TR competition days ☎

LYTHAM ST ANNES
Lancashire
Map V C6

Fairhaven Lytham Hall Park, Ansdell, Lytham St Annes (E side of town centre off B5261)
T:(0253) 736741
Societies accepted by arrangement. 18 | 6810 yds | Par 74 | SSS 73
Visitors welcome ☎ advisable | restricted WE BH | without M ∷ per day WE | B L ☞ prior arrangement (not Mon) | D prior arrangement | S only | ⚲ | ▼ variable | ✓ | TR 1200-1330 | ♪ | M 800 | S
★★★★*Clifton Arms, West Beach, Lytham.* T: (0253) 739898 45rm (41 ⇄ 4 ♨)

SCORE CARD:			
1	513	10	213
2	186	11	498
3	501	12	378
4	446	13	378
5	189	14	366
6	378	15	494
7	348	16	497
8	396	17	161
9	357	18	511

A flat, but interesting course of good standard. There are natural hazards as well as numerous bunkers and players need to produce particularly accurate second shots. Testing holes at the 15th (par 5) and 17th (par 3).

★★★*Lymm, Whitbarrow Rd.* T:(092575) 2233. 69rm (38 ⇄ 31 ♨)

LYTHAM ST ANNES
Lancashire
Map V C6

Lytham Green Drive Ballam Rd, Lytham St Annes (E side of town centre off B5259)
T:(0253) 737390
Pleasant parkland course, ideal for holidaymakers. Societies welcome by arrangement, numbers restricted WE. 18 | 6013 yds | Par 70 | SSS 69

Visitors welcome | ∴ per day | B ✿
L D | ♠ ♈ ⚲ | ⋈ TR Mon-F
1300-1400, WE all day | M 750 | S
★★★★*Clifton Arms, West Beach.*
T:(0253) 739898. 45rm (41 ⇄ 4 ⌘)

Royal Lytham & St Annes Links
Gate, Lytham St Annes on Sea
(½m E of St Annes on Sea town
centre)
T:(0253) 724206
*Famous links. 18(9) | 6673 yds | Par 71
| SSS 73*
Visitors welcome, ☎ ⊠ or with M
TR check beforehand | ⋮⋮ per day |
B L ✿ D prior arrangement | ♠ ⚲ |
⋈ possibly | ⅃ | M 850 | S
★★*New Glendower, North Prom, St
Annes. T:(0253) 723241. 68rm (65 ⇄)*

MACCLESFIELD
Cheshire
Map III   H2

Macclesfield The Hollins (SE side
of town centre off A523)
T:(0625) 23227
*Very hilly heathland course situated on
the edge of the Pennines. Excellent
views. Societies welcome by
arrangement. 12 | 5974 yds | Par 69 |
SSS 69*
Visitors welcome | without M ∴
WE BH | with M .. per day | B ✿ |
L D (except Tu) | ♠ ♈ | TR S on
competition days ☎ | ⅃ | M 350 | S
★*Ellesmere, Buxton Rd. T:(0625)
23791. 10rm (1 ⇄ 3 ⌘)*

MACDUFF
Grampian, *Banffshire*
Map VII   J4

Royal Tarlair Buchan St, Macduff
(¾m E of Macduff off A98)
T:(0261) 32897
*Seaside clifftop course so can be windy.
Testing 13th Cuvet (par 3). 18 |
5866 yds | Par 71 | SSS 68*
Visitors welcome ☎ parties | B L |
✿ D prior arrangement (club closed
Tu Th winter) | ♠ ♈ ⋈ | M 400 | S
★★*County, 32 High St, Banff.
T:(02612) 5353. 6rm ⇄*

MACHRIHANISH
Strathclyde, *Argyll*
Map VI   A4

Machrihanish Machrihanish,
Campbeltown (on B843 from
Campbeltown)
T:(058681) 213

*Magnificent seaside links of
championship status. The 1st hole is
the famous drive across the Atlantic.
Sandy soil allows for playing all year
round. Large greens, easy walking,
windy. 18 | 6228 yds | Par 70 | SSS 70.
Ladies' course: 9 | 4780 yds | Par 68 |
SSS 68*
Visitors welcome | ∴ per day WE,
Ladies' course .. per day WE | B L
✿ D (not Tu) parties by prior
arrangement | ♠ ♈ ⚲ | ⋈ | TR
competition days | ⅃ | S
★*Ardshiel, Kilkerran Rd,
Campbeltown. T:(0586) 52133. 16rm
(8 ⇄ 4 ⌘)*

MACHYNLLETH
Powys
Map III   D4

Machynlleth Newtown Rd, Maes Y
Gollen (½m E of Machynlleth off
A489)
T:(0654) 2000
*Lowland course with mostly natural
hazards. 9 | 5734 yds | Par 68 | SSS 67*
Visitors welcome | ∗ | ♠ ♈ | TR
Sun am | M 190
★★*Wynnstay, Maengwyn St. T:(0654)
2941. 31rm (10 ⇄ 1 ⌘)*

MAESTEG
Mid Glamorgan
Map I   F2

Maesteg Mount Pleasant (½m W of
Maesteg off B4282)
T:(0656) 732037
*Mountainside course. 18 | 5845 yds |
Par 69 | SSS 69*
Visitors welcome .. per day WE | B
✿ | L D prior arrangement | ♠ ♈
⋈ | TR 1630-1730 Tu (ladies),

MAIDENHEAD
Berkshire
Map II   D3

Maidenhead Shoppenhangers Rd, Maidenhead
(S side of town centre off A308)
T:(0628) 24693
Societies welcome by arrangement. 18 | 6300 yds | Par 70 | SSS 70
Visitors welcome ⊠ | ☎ advisable | without M ⋮⋮ per day | B ✿ L D | ♠ ♈ ⚲
| ⋈ | M 650 | S
⑧★★★★*Fredricks, Shoppenhangers Rd, Maidenhead. T:(0628) 35934. 13rm (4 ⇄ 9
⌘). Annexe: 22rm (21 ⇄ 1 ⌘)*

A pleasant parkland course on level ground with easy walking to
good greens. Perhaps a little short but there are many natural
features and some first-rate short holes. The club is an old one (1898)
and somehow one feels that here is golf as the pioneers intended it
to be played. That is not to say it does not provide a good test under
modern conditions.

1630-1730 W, 0845-0915 S (juniors) |
④ ☎ | M 700 | S
★★★*Ladbroke Twelve Knights,
Margam Rd, Margam, Port Talbot.
T:(0639) 882381. 11 ⇄*

MAESYCWMMER
Mid Glamorgan
Map I   G2

Bryn Meadows The Bryn, Hengoed
(1m E of Maesycwmmer, off A472)
T:(0495) 225590
*A heavily wooded parkland course with
panoramic views. Testing 3rd, 12th
and 15th holes. 18 | 6003 yds | Par 71 |
SSS 69*
Visitors welcome | B L (not Mon) ✿
D | ♠ ♈ ⚲ ⋈ | ⅃ | TR Sun | M 500
| S
★★★*Maes Manor, Blackwood.
T:(0495) 224551. 10rm (7 ⇄ ⌘)
Annexe: 16rm (10 ⇄ 3 ⌘)*

MAIDSTONE
Kent
Map II   H4

Cobtree Manor Park Chatham Rd,
Sandling, Maidstone (on A229 ¼m
N of M20 Jct 6)
T:(0622) 53276
*An undulating parkland course with
some water hazards. 18 | 5701 yds |
Par 68 | SSS 68*
Visitors welcome | ∗ | B L D ✿ | ♈
♠ S ⚲ ⋈ | M 400 | ⅃
★★*Boxley House, Boxley Rd, Boxley,
Maidstone. T:(0622) 52226. 10rm (4
⇄ 6 ⌘). Annexe: 5rm (4 ⇄ 1 ⌘)*

MALDON
Essex
Map II   H2   ➥

KEY

(IA1)	*atlas grid reference*
T:	*telephone number*
☎	*advance letter/telephone call required*
✉	*introduction from own club sec/handicap certificate/club membership card required*
..	*low fees*
∴	*medium fees*
::	*high fees*
*	*green fees not confirmed for 1987*
B	*light lunch*
L	*full lunch*
✆	*tea*
D	*dinner*
♨	*changing rooms/showers*
♈	*bar open mid-day and evenings*
⤸	*clubs for hire*
⋈	*partners may be found*
④	*restricted time for 4 balls*
TR	*times reserved for members*
'J	*professional*
S	*well-stocked shop*
M	*member*
Mon Tu W Th F S Sun	
WE	*weekend*
BH	*bank holiday*

Forrester Park Beckingham Rd, Gt Totham, Nr Maldon (3m SE of Witham on A12)
T:(0621) 891406/891903
Tight, undulating parkland course with tree-lined fairways and good views over the Blackwater estuary. Easy walking. Attractive 16th-century clubhouse. Other facilities include tennis courts and a children's room. Societies welcome by arrangement. 9 | 5350 yds | Par 66 | SSS 66
Visitors welcome ☎ WE | .. per 18 weekdays ∴ WE | B L | ✆ D by prior arrangement | ♨ ♈ ⤸ | TR WE before 1230 | M 430
★★*Rivenhall Motor Inn, Rivenhall End, Witham. T:(0376) 516969. 3rm (1 ♨). Annexe: 40rm* ⇄ ♨

Maldon Beeleigh Langford (1m NW of Maldon off B1018)
T:(0621) 53212
Flat parkland course in a triangle of land by the River Chelmer, the Blackwater Canal and an old railway embankment. Alternate tees on 2nd 9. Societies welcome by arrangement only. 18 | 6197 yds | Par 71 | SSS 69

Visitors welcome except WE | ∴ per day | ✆ ♨ ♈ ⤸ | M 420 | S
★★*Blue Boar, Silver St, Maldon. T:(0621) 52681. 18rm* ⇄ *Annexe: 5rm* ⇄

MALTON
North Yorkshire
Map **V** H5

Malton & Norton Welham Park, Norton (1m S of Malton)
T:(0653) 2959
Parkland course with fine view from 4th tee. Very testing 1st hole (564 yds dog leg left). Societies welcome by arrangement. 18 | 6411 yds | Par 72 | SSS 71
Visitors welcome | without M ∴ per day WE | with M .. per day WE | B L D ✆ | ♨ ♈ ⤸ ⋈ | TR before 0915, Th ladies day | 'J | M 700 | S
★★*Talbot, Yorkersgate. T:(0653) 4031. 23rm (7* ⇄)

MALVERN WELLS
Hereford and Worcester
Map **III** H6

Worcestershire Wood Farm, Malvern Wells (2m S of Gt Malvern on B4209)
T:(06845) 5992
Fairly easy walking on windy downland course with trees, ditches and other natural hazards. 17th hole (par 5) is approached over small lake. No children allowed; societies welcome by arrangement. 18 | 6449 yds | Par 71 | SSS 71
Visitors welcome ✉, restricted WE before 1000 | without M ∴ per day :: WE | with M .. per day WE | B ✆ (not Mon) | L D prior arrangement (not Mon) | ♨ ♈ ⤸ | ⋈ prior arrangement | TR competition days ④ ☎ | 'J | M 650 | S
★★★*Foley Arms, Worcester Rd, Gt Malvern. T:(06845) 3397. 26rm (19* ⇄ 7 ♨)

MAN, ISLE OF
Map **V**
See **Douglas, Onchan, Peel, Port Erin and Ramsey**

MANCHESTER
Greater Manchester
Map **V** D7

Didsbury Ford Ln, Northenden (6m S of city centre off A5145)

T:061-998 2743
Parkland course. 18 | 6273 yds | Par 70 | SSS 70
Visitors welcome | without M ∴ per day WE | with M .. per day WE | B ✆ (not Mon) | L D prior arrangement (not Mon) | ♨ prior arrangement | ♈ (not Mon) | ⤸ TR 1230-1330 competitions Sun (until 1100) | 'J | M 365 | S
★★★*Post House, Palatine Rd, Northenden, Manchester. T:061-998 7090. 200rm* ⇄

Fairfield Booth Rd, Audenshaw (1½m W of Audenshaw off A635)
T:061-370 1641
Parkland course with reservoir (sailing available). Course demands particularly accurate placing of shots. 18 | 5654 yds | Par 70 | SSS 68
Visitors welcome | ✆ (not Mon) | B L ✆ | D prior arrangement (not Mon) | ♨ ♈ ⤸ | ⋈ | ④ S | TR Th (ladies day) | M 300
★★★★*Portland Thistle, 3/5 Portland St, Piccadilly Gdns, Manchester. T:061-228 3567. 219rm* ⇄ ♨

Houldsworth Wingate House, Higher Levenshulme (4m SE of city centre off A6)
T:061-224 5055/4571
Flat meadowland course, treelined and with water hazards. Testing holes 9th par 5 and 13th par 5. Societies welcome Mon to F. 18 | 6078 yds | Par 70 | SSS 69
Visitors welcome, restricted W pm WE before 1500 | without M .. per day WE | with M .. per day WE | B (not Mon) | L ✆ D prior arrangement (not Mon) | ♨ ♈ ⤸ | ⋈ prior arrangement | TR Tu 1330-1530, WE BH until 1500 | 'J | M 314 | S
★★★*Willow Bank, 340-342 Wilmslow Rd, Fallowfield, Manchester. T:061-224 0461. 123rm (104* ⇄ 9 ♨)

Northenden Palatine Rd, Manchester 22 (6½m S of city centre on B1567 off A5103)
T:061-998 4738
Parkland course. Societies welcome by arrangement. 18 | 6435 yds | Par 72 | SSS 71
Visitors welcome | B ✆ L D | ♨ ♈ | TR S competition days, Tu & F society days | M 700 | S
★★★*Post House, Palatine Rd, Northenden. T:061-998 7090. 200rm* ⇄

Withington Palatine Rd, West Didsbury (6m S of city centre off B5167)
T:061-445 9544
Parkland course. Societies welcome by arrangement Mon Tu W F. 18 | 6410 yds | Par 72 | SSS 71
Visitors welcome 🐾 | ∴ per day WE | B 🍴 (not Mon) | L D prior arrangement (not Mon) | 🏌 Y | ʃ | TR 1200-1330 | M 550 | S |
★★★*Post House, Palatine Rd, Northenden, Manchester. T:061-998 7090. 200rm* ⇌

Worsley Monton Green, Eccles (6½m NW of city centre off A572)
T:061-789 4202
Well-wooded parkland course. Societies welcome (Mon W Th). 18 | 6217 yds | Par 72 | SSS 70
Visitors welcome ✉ | B L 🍴 D | 🏌 Y | TR 0900-1000, 1200-1400 | ʃ | M 600 | S |
★★★★*Hotel Piccadilly, Piccadilly Plaza, Manchester. T:061-236 8414. 255rm* 🍴

MANNINGS HEATH
West Sussex
Map II E6

Mannings Heath Goldings Ln, Mannings Heath, Horsham (N side of village)
T:(0403) 66217
The course meanders up hill and down dale over heathland with streams affecting 11 of the holes. Wooded valleys protect the course from strong winds. Famous holes at 12th (the 'Waterfall' par 3) 13th (the 'Valley' par 4). Societies welcome on weekdays but should book at least a year in advance. 18 | 6402 yds | Par 73 | SSS 71
Visitors welcome weekdays | without M ∴ per day WE | B 🍴 L D

MANSFIELD
Nottinghamshire
Map IV A2

Sherwood Forest Eakring Rd, Mansfield (2½m E of Mansfield)
T:(0623) 26689
18 | 6796 yds | Par 72 | SSS 73
Visitors welcome restricted Mon Th F | ✉ | ✳ | B L 🍴 D prior arrangement (not Mon) | 🏌 Y | TR 1200-1400 | M 650 | S |
★★★Post House, Bostocks Ln, Sandiacre. T:(0602) 397800. 107rm ⇌
As the name suggests, the Forest is the main feature of this heathland course with heather-lined fairways. The homeward nine holes are particularly testing. The 11th and 14th are notable par 4 holes on this well-bunkered course.

| 🏌 Y | ④ visitors | TR Th am and WE | ʃ | M 700 | S |
★★*Ye Olde King's Head, Horsham. T:(0403) 53126. 41rm (5 ⇌ 32 🍴)*

MANSFIELD WOODHOUSE
Nottinghamshire
Map IV A1

Mansfield Woodhouse Leeming Ln North, Mansfield Woodhouse (N side of town centre off A60)
T:(0623) 23521
Easy walking on heathland. Societies welcome. 9 | 2150 yds | Par 62 | SSS 60
Open to public .. per round | B L | 🏌 Y ⤫ | ✖ | M 100 | S |
★*Hop Pole, Ollerton. T:(0623) 822573. 11rm (5 ⇌)*

MARKET DRAYTON
Shropshire
Map III G3

Market Drayton Sutton (1m S of Market Drayton)
T:(0630) 2266
Parkland course in quiet, picturesque surroundings providing a good test of golf. Societies (up to 40 players) welcome midweek by arrangement. Bungalow on course is made available for golfing holidays. 13 | 6520 yds | Par 71 | SSS 71
Visitors welcome, not Sun 🐾 | Y | 🍴 | B L | D prior arrangement | ⤫ (probably) | TR Sun | ʃ | M 300 | S |
★★*Corbet Arms, High St. T:(0630) 2037. 12rm (10 ⇌ 2 🍴)*

MARKET HARBOROUGH
Leicestershire
Map IV B5

Market Harborough Oxendon Rd (1m S of Market Harborough on A508)
T:(0858) 63684

A parkland course situated close to the town. There are wide- ranging views over the surrounding countryside. 9 | 6080 yds | Par 71 | SSS 69
Visitors welcome Mon to F, with M S & Sun | without M .. per day weekdays | 🏌 Y | ʃ | TR WE | S |
★★★*Three Swans, High St, Market Harborough. T:(0858) 666444. 18rm (12 ⇌ 6 🍴)*

MARKET RASEN
Lincolnshire
Map V J8

Market Rasen & District Legsby Rd (2m SE of Market Rasen)
T:(0673) 842416
Picturesque well-wooded heathland course, easy walking, breezy, becks form natural hazards. Good views of Lincolnshire Wolds. 18 | 6031 yds | Par 70 | SSS 69
Visitors welcome | ∴ per day | 🍴 | B L | D | 🏌 Y ⤫ | ✖ | ʃ | M 475 | S |
★★★*Limes, Gainsborough Rd. T:(0673) 842357. 13rm (10 ⇌ 3 🍴) Annexe: 4rm ⇌*

MARLBOROUGH
Wiltshire
Map I K3

Marlborough The Common, Marlborough (N side of town centre on A345)
T:(0672) 52147
Downland course open to prevailing wind. Extensive views. Societies welcome weekdays by arrangement. 18 | 6440 yds | Par 72 | SSS 71
Visitors welcome | without M ∴ per day WE | B 🍴 L D | 🏌 Y ✖ | M 700 | S |
★★*Castle & Ball, High St. T:(0672) 52002. 28rm (6 ⇌)*

MARSDEN
West Yorkshire
Map V E7

Marsden Mount Rd, Hemplow, Huddersfield (S side of Marsden off A62)
T:(0484) 844253
Moorland course with good views, natural hazards, windy. 9 | 5702 yds | Par 68 | SSS 68
Visitors welcome not permitted S in summer | .. per day WE | B | L 🍴 D | 🏌 Y | TR competition days | ④ WE | ʃ | M 200 | S |
★★★*Durker Roods, Bishops Way, Meltham. T:(0484) 851413. 32rm (25 ⇌ 🍴)*

MARYPORT
Cumbria
Map **V** B2

Maryport Bank End (2m N of Maryport on B5300)
T:(0900) 812605.
A tight seaside links course exposed to Solway breezes. Fine views across Solway. 11 | 6272 yds | Par 71 | SSS 70
Visitors welcome | ‥ per day WE | ⛳ 🍸 🍴 ⋈ | [S]
★Waverley, Curzon St. T:(0900) 812115. 20rm (1 ⇌ 4 🚿)

MASHAM
North Yorkshire
Map **V** F4

Masham Swinton Rd, Burnholme (1m SW of Masham off A6108)
T:(0765) 89379
Flat parkland course crossed by small river, easy walking. 9 | 5142 yds | Par 66 | SSS 65
Visitors welcome, with M only WE BH ☎ advisable | ⛳ | 🍸 ☕ | [TR] WE BH | M 280
★★🌳Jervaulx Hall, Masham. T:(0677) 60235. 8rm ⇌ 🚿

MATLOCK
Derbyshire
Map **III** K2

Matlock Chesterfield Rd (1m NE of Matlock on A632)
T:(0629) 2191
Moorland course with fine views of the beautiful Peak District. 18 | 5871 yds | Par 70 | SSS 68
Visitors welcome but restricted WE BH | ∴ per day | B L ☕ | D prior arrangement (no catering Mon) | ⛳ 🍸 🍴 | ⋈ usually | [TR] competitions | M 400 | [S]
★★★New Bath, New Bath Rd, Matlock Bath. T:(0629) 3275. 56rm ⇌

MAUCHLINE
Strathclyde, *Ayr*
Map **IV** D4

Ballochmyle Ballochmyle (1m SE of Mauchline on B705)
T:(0290) 50469
Parkland course. 18 | 5952 yds | Par 70 | SSS 69
Visitors welcome ☎ ✉ or with M | ∴ per day | B ☕ | L D prior arrangement | ⛳ 🍸 | [TR] S until 1600, and competition days | M 500
★Royal, 1 Glaisnock St, Cumnock. T:(0290) 20822. 12rm

MAWNAN SMITH
Cornwall
Map **I** B8

Budock Vean Hotel Mawnan Smith, Falmouth (1½m SW of Mawnan Smith)
T:(0326) 250288
Undulating parkland course. 9(18 tees) | 5222 yds | Par 68 | SSS 65
Visitors welcome | B L D ☕ | ⛳ 🍸 | [S] 🍴 | M 150 | [TR] competitions
★★★Budock Vean, Mawnan Smith. T:(0326) 250288. 53rm ⇌

MAYBOLE
Strathcylde, *Ayr*
Map **VI** D4

Maybole Municipal Memorial Park, Maybole, (S side of town off A77)
Parkland course, heavy walking. Course 6m from Robert Burns' cottage. 9 | 5270 yds | Par 66 | SSS 65
Visitors welcome | M 60
★★★★Turnberry, Turnberry. T:(06553) 202 due to change to (0655) 31000. 130rm ⇌ 🚿

MELLOR
Stockport
Map **V** E8

Mellor & Townscliffe Gibb Ln, Tarden (½m S of Mellor)
T:061-427 2208
Parkland and moorland course, undulating with some hard walking. Good views. Testing 200 yd 9th hole par 3. Societies welcome by arrangement. 18 | 5925 yds | Par 70 | SSS 69
Visitors welcome | without M ∴ per day WE | with M ‥ per day WE | B L ☕ D (not Tu) | ⛳ 🍸 | [TR] S (competitions) | M 450 | [S]
★Springfield, Station Rd, Marple. T:061-449 0721. 7rm (5 ⇌ 2 🚿)

MELROSE
Borders, *Roxburghshire*
Map **VI** H3

Melrose Dingleton, Melrose (S side of town centre on B6359)
T:(089682) 2855
Undulating parkland course with splendid views. 9 | 5464 yds | Par 70 | SSS 68
Visitors welcome | ‥ per day WE | B | ⛳ 🍸 | [TR] S and competition days | M 300
★★Burt's, The Square. T:(089682) 2285. 22rm (6 ⇌ 3 🚿)

MELTHAM
West Yorkshire
Map **V** E7

Meltham Thick Hollins Hall, Huddersfield (SE side of Meltham village off B6107)
T:(0484) 850227
Parkland course with good views. Testing 548-yd 13th hole (par 5). Societies welcome by arrangement. 18 | 6145 yds | Par 70 | SSS 70
Visitors welcome | without M ∴ per day WE | with M .. per day WE | B ☎ (not Tu) | L D prior arrangement (not Tu) | ⚲ ♈ ⚲ | ⋈ (lunchtime) | TR W (pm), S (pm) | M 500 | S ♃
★★★*Durker Roods, Bishops Way.*
T:(0484) 851413. 32rm (25 ⇌ 🏠)

MELTON MOWBRAY
Leicestershire
Map **IV**   B4

Melton Mowbray Thorpe Arnold (2½m NE of Melton Mowbray on A607)
T:(0664) 62118
Downland but flat course providing easy walking. Open to the wind. 9 | 6190 yds | Par 70 | SSS 69
Visitors welcome | ⚲ | ♈ | B ☎ WE only | TR competitions | M 415 | S
★★★*Harboro', Burton St. T:(0664) 60121. 28rm (24 ⇌ 4 🏠)*

MEOLE BRACE
Shropshire
Map **III**   G4

Meole Brace Meole Brace, Shrewsbury (NE side of village off A49)
T:(0743) 64050
Pleasant parkland municipal course. 12 | 3066 yds | Par 43 | SSS 42
Visitors welcome | B ☎ | ⚲ | S ⚲ | ⋈ | ♃
★★★*Lord Hill, Abbey Foregate, Shrewsbury. T:(0743) 52601. 22rm (10 ⇌ 12 🏠) Annexe: 24rm ⇌ 🏠*

MERIDEN
West Midlands
Map **III**   J5

Forest of Arden Maxstoke Ln (1m SW of Meriden on B4102)
T:(0676) 22118
Two courses; one 18-hole parkland and moorland offering a fine test of golf and a 9-hole beginners' course. Societies welcome by arrangement. 18(9) | 6962(1890) yds | Par 72(29) | SSS 72
Visitors welcome ☎ WE M only | ∷ per day WE (.. 9 hole) | with M .. per day WE | B L ☎ D | ⚲ ♈ ⚲ ⋈ | TR WE, Wed (ladies only) | ♃ |

M 500 | S
★★★*Manor. T:(0676) 22735. 32rm ⇌*

North Warwickshire Hampton Ln (1m SW of Meriden on B4102)
T:(0676) 22259
Downland course with easy walking. 9 | 3181 yds | Par 72 | SSS 70
Visitors welcome restricted WE & Th until 1430 - ladies BH | .. per day | ⚲ ♈ | B ⋈ TR WE | ♃ | M 400 | S
★★★*Manor, Meriden. T:(0676) 22735. 32rm ⇌*

MERTHYR TYDFIL
Mid Glamorgan
Map **III**   E8

Merthyr Tydfil Cilsanws, Cefn Coed (2m NW of Merthyr Tydfil off A470)
T:(0685) 3308
Hilly mountain course with good views and water hazards. 12(6) | 2898/5794 yds | Par 70 | SSS 68
Visitors welcome | .. per day WE | B ☎ D L prior arrangement | ⚲ | ♈ | ⋈ | TR Sun competitions | M 240
★★*Nant-ddu Lodge Country House, Cwm Taf, Nant-ddu. T:(0685) 79111. 7rm (4 ⇌ 3 🏠). Annexe: 1rm ⇌*

Morlais Castle Pant, Dowlais (2½m N of Merthyr Tydfil off A465)
T:(0685) 2822
Beautiful course in National Park adjacent to Brecon Beacons. Testing course since it is rocky off the fairways. 9 | 6356 yds | Par 72 | SSS 71
Visitors welcome | B L ☎ | ⚲ ♈ | TR S pm, Sun am | M 320
★★*Nant-ddu Lodge Country House, Cwn Taf, Nant-ddu. T:(0685) 79111. 7rm (4 ⇌ 3 🏠). Annexe: 1rm ⇌*

MICKLEOVER
Derbyshire
Map **III**   K3

Pastures Pastures Hospital, Mickleover (1m SW of Mickleover off A516)
T:(0332) 513921
Course laid out on undulating meadowland in the grounds of this psychiatric hospital with good views across the Trent valley. 9 | 5005 yds | Par 64 | SSS 64
Visitors welcome | with M only .. per day WE | ⋈ | ⚲ ♈ | TR competition days (most WE in summer) | M 300
★★★*International, 288 Burton Rd, Derby. T:(0332) 369321. 44rm (42 ⇌ 2 🏠)*

MIDDLESBROUGH
Cleveland
Map **V**   G3

Middlesbrough Brass Castle Ln, Marton (5m S of Middlesbrough off A172)
T:(0642) 316430/311515
Undulating parkland course, prevailing winds. Testing 9th, 16th and 17th holes. 18 | 6106 yds | Par 70 | SSS 69
Visitors welcome | ∴ per day WE | B L ☎ D | ⚲ ♈ | ♃ | TR Tu ladies priority | M 900 | S
★★★*Marton Hotel & Country Club, Stokesley Rd, Marton. T:(0642) 317141. 52rm ⇌*

Middlesbrough Municipal Ladgate Ln, Middlesbrough (2½m S of town centre on B1380 off A172)
T:(0642) 315533
Parkland course with stream running through and good views. 18 | 6314 yds | Par 71 | SSS 70   ➥

MIDDLETON
Greater Manchester
Map **V**   D7

Manchester Hopwood Cottage, Manchester (2½m N of Middleton off A664)
T:061-643 2718
Societies welcome by arrangement. 18 | 6450 yds | Par 72 | SSS 72
Visitors welcome ☎ advisable | B ☎ | L D prior arrangement | ⚲ ♈ ⋈ sometimes | TR S and 1200-1400 daily | M 420 | S
★★*Midway, Manchester Rd, Castleton. Rochdale. T:(0706) 32881. 30rm (2 ⇌ 20 🏠)*
Moorland golf of unique character over a spaciously laid out course with generous fairways sweeping along to large greens. One of the best inland tests in this part of Britain. A wide variety of holes will challenge the golfer's technique, particularly the testing last three holes.

Visitors welcome | B ♥ L | D (except
Sun & Mon) | ⊺ ♨ ⤬ ⋈ | TR WE
BH | M 400 | S
★★★Ladbroke Dragonara (&
Conferencentre), Fry St. T:(0642)
248133. 140rm (126 ⇄ 14 ⋔)

MIDDLETON
Greater Manchester
Map V   D7

North Manchester Rhodes House,
Middleton, Manchester (W side of
town centre off A576)
T:061-643 7094
*A long, tight course with natural water
hazards.* 18 | 6527 yds | Par 72 |
SSS 72
Visitors welcome | L D B (except Tu)
♥ | ⊺ ♨ ⤬ | TR Th 1200-1430 |
M 300 | S
★★★Bower, Hollinwood Av,
Chadderton, Oldham. T:061-682 7254.
66rm (42 ⇄ 24 ⋔)

MIDHURST
West Sussex
Map II   D6

Cowdray Park (1m NE of Midhurst
on A272)
T:(073 081) 3599/2088
Parkland course, hard walking up to

4th green, 4th and 11th very good par
4s. Societies welcome by arrangement.
18 | 6212 yds | Par 70 | SSS 70
Visitors welcome ☎ advisable WE |
without M ∴ per day WE | with M
.. per day WE | ♥ | B L D prior
arrangement | ♨ ⊺ ⤬ | ⋈ | ④ WE
(before 1030) and BH | ⅃ | M 600 | S
★★★Spread Eagle, South St,
Midhurst. T:(073081) 2211. 25rm ⇄
Annexe: 4rm

MIDSOMER NORTON
Avon
Map I   J3

Fosseway Country Club Charlton
Ln, Norton Hill, Midsomer Norton
(SE of town centre off A367)
T:(0761) 412214
*Parkland course, club has indoor
swimming pool, sauna baths, squash
courts.* 9 | 4246 yds | Par 62 | SSS 61
Visitors welcome, restricted W after
1700, Sat 1300-1600, Sun 0800-1300 |
B L ♥ D | ♨ ⊺ ⋈ | TR W from
1700 Sun am | M 240 | S
★★Court, Emborough. T:(0761)
232237. 9rm (5 ⇄ 4 ⋔)

MILFORD HAVEN
Dyfed
Map III   B8

Milford Haven Woodbine House,
Hubberstone (1½m W of Milford
Haven)
T:(06462) 2368
Parkland course. 18 | 6158 yds | Par 71
| SSS 70
Visitors welcome | B ♥ L D | ♨ ⊺ |
⋈ prior arrangement | TR club
competitions | S
★★Lord Nelson, Hamilton Ter.
T:(06462) 5341. 24rm (22 ⇄ 3 ⋔)

MILLBROOK
Bedfordshire
Map IV   C7

Mill Brook Millbrook, Ampthill (E
side of village off A507)
T:(0525) 404683
*Parkland course, hilly in places with
several water hazards. Club closed Th.*
18 | 6650 yds | Par 72 | SSS 72
Visitors welcome ∴ per day WE | S
⤬ | ④ ☎ | M 300 | ⅃
★★★♨Flitwick Manor, Church Rd.
T:(0525) 712242. 6rm (4 ⇄ 2 ⋔)

MILNATHORT
Tayside, *Kinross-shire*
Map VI   F1

Milnathort South St, Milnathort (S
side of town on A922)
T:(0577) 64069
Parkland course. 9 | 5818 yds | Par 70 |
SSS 68
Visitors welcome | B L ♥ D | ♨ ⋈ |
TR competitions | M 360
★★★Green, 2 The Muirs, Kinross.
T:(0577) 63467. 45rm (39 ⇄ 6 ⋔)

MILNGAVIE
Strathclyde, *Dumbartonshire*
Map VI   D2

Clober Craigton Rd, Milngavie,
Glasgow (NW side of town)
T:041-956 1685
*Parkland course. Testing 5th hole par
3.* 18 | 5068 yds | Par 66 | SSS 65
Visitors welcome, restricted after
1630 Mon to F WE BH | without M
.. per day | with M .. per day WE |
B (not Mon Th) | L (not Mon Th) ♥
D prior arrangement (not Mon Th)
| ♨ ⊺ | ⋈ | TR after 1630 daily WE
BH competitions | ⅃ | M 650 | S
★★★Black Bull Thistle, Main St.
T:041-956 2291. 28rm (27 ⇄)

Dougalston Strathblane Rd,
Milngavie (NE side of town on A81)
T:041-956 5750

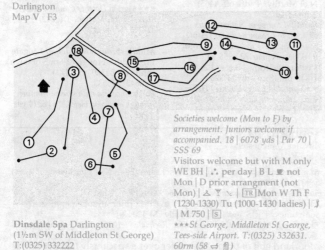

MIDDLETON ST GEORGE
Darlington
Map V   F3

*Societies welcome (Mon to F) by
arrangement. Juniors welcome if
accompanied.* 18 | 6078 yds | Par 70 |
SSS 69
Visitors welcome but with M only
WE BH | ∴ per day | B L ♥ not
Mon | D prior arrangment (not
Mon) | ♨ ⊺ ⤬ | TR Mon W Th F
(1230-1330) Tu (1000-1430 ladies) | ⅃
| M 750 | S
★★★St George, Middleton St George,
Tees-side Airport. T:(0325) 332631.
60rm (58 ⇄ ⋔)

Dinsdale Spa Darlington
(1½m SW of Middleton St George)
T:(0325) 332222
A mainly flat, parkland course on high land above the River Tees
with views of the Cleveland Hills. Water hazards front the 8th 9th
and 18th tees and the prevailing west wind affects the later holes.
There is a practice area by the clubhouse.

Tree-lined with water features. 18 |
6683 yds | *Par 72* | *SSS 72*
Visitors welcome ☎ advisable | ..
per day | B L ♥ D | ᕦ ヽ | ⟟ (not
Sun) | ⋈ | TR some S (am)
★★★*Black Bull Thistle, Main St.*
T:041-956 2291. 28rm (27 ⇄)

Hilton Park Stockiemuir Rd,
Milngavie, Glasgow (3m NW of
Milngavie on A809)
T:041-956 4657
*Windswept moorland courses with some
hills and good views. Visiting parties
considered on application. Hilton
course: 18* | *6002 yds* | *Par 70* | *SSS 70*
| *Allander: 18* | *5361 yds* | *Par 69* |
SSS 67
Visitors welcome weekdays | ✳ | B L
D prior arrangement | ♥ | ᕦ ⟟ |
TR WE | 🄹 | M 1200 | S
★★★*Black Bull Thistle, Main St,
Milngavie. T:041-956 2291. 28rm (27
⇄)*

Milngavie Laigh Park, Milngavie,
Glasgow (1¼m N of Milngavie)
T:041-956 1619
*Moorland course, hard walking,
sometimes windy, good views. Testing
1st and 4th holes (par 4). Parties by
arrangement. 18* | *5818 yds* | *Par 68* |
SSS 68
Visitors welcome with M only ⋈ ☎
| ✳ | B ♥ | L D prior arrangement |
ᕦ ⟟ | 🄹 | M 700 | S WE only
★★★*Black Bull Thistle, Main St.
T:041-956 2291. 28rm (27 ⇄)*

MILNROW
Greater Manchester
Map **V**   E7

Tunshill Kiln Ln, Milnrow (1m NE
of Milnrow off B6225)
T:(0706) 342095
*Testing moorland course, particularly
6th, 15th (par 5s). Societies welcome by
arrangement. 9* | *5800 yds* | *Par 70* |
SSS 68
Visitors welcome, restricted WE ⋈
☎ (Sun) | .. per day WE | B ♥ L
prior arrangement | ᕦ ⟟ | TR Tu
pm, WE see above | M 240 | S
★*Sun, Featherstall Rd, Littleborough.
T:(0706) 78957. 8rm*

MILTON KEYNES
Buckinghamshire
Map **IV**   B7

Abbey Hill Two Mile Ash (2m W of
new town centre, off A5)

MINEHEAD
Somerset
Map **I**   F4

Minehead & West Somerset The Warren, Minehead
(E side of town centre)
T:(0643) 2057
Societies welcome by arrangement. 18 | *6130 yds* | *Par 70* | *SSS 69*
Visitors welcome | B ♥ L D prior arrangement | ᕦ ⟟ ヽ ⋈ | M 400 | S
★★★*Northfield, Northfield Rd, Minehead. T:(0643) 5155. 28rm (24 ⇄ 4 🄳)*
Flat seaside links, very exposed to wind, with good turf set on a
shingle bank. The last five holes adjacent to the beach are testing.
The 218-yard 18th is wedged between the beach and the club
buildings and provides a good finish.

T:(0908) 563845
*Municipal course within the new city.
Societies welcome by arrangement. 18* |
6505 yds | *Par 69* | *SSS 71*
Open to public | B L ♥ D | ᕦ ⟟ ヽ |
🄹 | M 600 | S
★★*Swan Revived, High St, Newport
Pagnell. T:(0908) 610565. 31rm (12 ⇄
19 🄳)*

MINCHINHAMPTON
Gloucestershire
Map **III**   H8

Minchinhampton New Course
(1½m W of Minchinhampton)
T:(045383) 3866
Old Course T:(045383) 2642
*Cotswold upland course in rural
surroundings. Societies welcome by
arrangement. 18* | *6675 yds* | *Par 72* |
SSS 72
Visitors welcome | ∴ per day WE |
B ♥ L D | ⟟ ᕦ ヽ | TR WE | ④ WE
| M 1120 | S
★★★*Burleigh Court, Brimscombe,
Stroud. T:(0453) 883804. 11rm (8 ⇄ 3
🄳)*

MINTO
Borders, *Roxburghshire*
Map **VI**   H4

Minto Minto, Hawick (S side of
village)
T:(0450) 72267
*Parkland course in wooded
surroundings, easy walking. 18* |
5459 yds | *Par 68* | *SSS 68*
Visitors welcome | .. per day WE |
B L ♥ | ᕦ ⟟ ⋈ | TR Medal
competition days | M 300
★★*Kirklands, West Stewart Pl,
Hawick. T:(0450) 72263. 6rm (2 ⇄ 1
🄳)*

MIRFIELD
West Yorkshire

Map **V**   F6

Dewsbury District Sands Ln,
Mirfield (1m S of Mirfield off A644)
T:(0924) 492399
*Heathland/parkland course with
panoramic view from top, hard
walking. Ponds in middle of 3rd
fairway, left of 5th green and 17th
green. 18* | *6256 yds* | *Par 71* | *SSS 70*
Visitors welcome, restricted WE BH
(no parties) | B (not Mon) | L ♥ D
prior arrangement (not Mon) | ᕦ ⟟
ヽ ⋈ | TR WE ☎ for details | 🄹 |
M 350 | S
★★★*George, St George's Sq,
Huddersfield. T:(0484) 25444. 62rm
(38 ⇄)*

MITCHAM
Greater London
Map **II**   E4

Mitcham Carshalton Rd (1m S of
Mitcham on A237 at Mitcham
Junction Station)
T:01-648 4197
*Heathland course (gravel base),
wooded. 18* | *5931 yds* | *Par 69* |
SSS 68
Visitors welcome ☎ advisable |
restricted WE | .. per day WE | B ♥
L | ᕦ ⟟ | TR ④ ☎ | 🄹 | M 500 | S
★★★*Croydon Court, Purley Way,
Croydon. T:01-688 5185. 86rm ⇄*

MOFFAT
Dumfries and Galloway,
Dumfriesshire
Map **VI**   F4

Moffat Coatshill (1m SW of Moffat
off A701)
T:(0683) 20020
*Scenic hill course. Testing 9th Port
Arthur (par 3). Societies welcome by
arrangement. 18* | *4881 yds* | *Par 67* |
SSS 64

Visitors welcome | B ♥ | ⅄ ⅂ | TR |
WE (until 0900, 1230, 1330) | M 288 |
S |
★★*Annandale, High St. T:(0683)
20013. 19rm Annexe: 5rm ⇄*

MOLD
Clwyd
Map III   F2

Old Padeswood Station Rd,
Padeswood (3m SE of Mold off
A5118)
T:(0244) 547401
*Meadowland course, undulating in
parts. Societies welcome. 18 | 6728 yds
| Par 72 | SSS 74*
Visitors welcome | without M ..
per day WE | D (prior arrangement)
| B ♥ | ⅂ ⅄ | TR | competitions
(usually at WE) | M 350
★★★*Chequers, Northophall. T:(0244)
816181. 29rm (27 ⇄ 2 🏠)*

Padeswood & Buckley The Caia,
Station Ln, Padeswood, nr Mold
(3m SE of Mold off A5118)
T:(0244) 542537
*Gently undulating parkland course,
with natural hazards and good views of
the Welsh Hills. 18 | 5746 yds | Par 68
| SSS 68*
Visitors welcome except Sun ☎ | ..
per day ∴ WE | B ♥ | L D (not Mon
& Tu unless by arrangement) | ⅄ ⅂
⅂ ⋈ | ④ ☎ for details | TR | Sun,
Mon-S before 0900 and after 1630,
competition days | M 575 | S |
★★★*Chequers, Northophall. T:(0244)
816181. 29rm (27 ⇄ 2 🏠)*

MONIFIETH
Tayside, *Angus*
Map VII   J8

Ashludie & Medal Monifieth (E
side of town, off A930)
T:(0382) 532767
*Links course. Societies welcome
weekdays by arrangement. ☎ Sec
(0382) 533300. 18 | (Ash) 5123 yds,
(Med) 6657 yds | (Ash) Par 68, (Med)
Par 71 | (Ash) SSS 66, (Med) SSS 72*
Visitors welcome | ∴ per day WE |
B L ♥ D prior arrangement (not Tu)
| ⅄ ⅄ ⅂ | S | TR | ☎ for details
★★*Earlston, Church St, Carnoustie.
T:(0241) 52352. 17rm (2 ⇄ 5 🏠)*

Broughty Princes St, Monifieth
(½m E of Monifieth on A930)
*Two seaside courses. 18 | 6700/5200 yds
| Par 71/68 | SSS 72/66*

Visitors welcome | ∴ per day WE |
B (not Tu) | L ♥ prior arrangement
(not Tu) | ⅄ ⅂ | TR | S am,
weekdays 1630-1800 May and June |
M 400 | S |
★★★*Angus Thistle, 10 Marketgait,
Dundee. T:(0382) 26874. 58rm ⇄ 🏠*

MONMOUTH
Gwent
Map III   G7

Monmouth Leasebrook Ln, (1½m
NE of Monmouth off A40)
T:(0600) 2212
*Downland course, in scenic setting.
High, undulating land with good
views. Testing 1st and 4th holes. 9 |
5424 yds | Par 68 | SSS 66*
Visitors welcome, restricted Sun,
competitions | * | B L D ♥ | ⅄ ⅄ ⅂
| TR | Sun 0800-1100 | M 450 | S |
★★★*Kings Head, Agincourt Sq.
T:(0600) 2177. 25rm (19 ⇄ 6 🏠)
Annexe: 3rm ⇄*

MONIFIETH
Tayside, *Angus*
Map VII   J8

Monifieth Princes St, Monifieth (NE side of town on A930)
T:(0382) 532767
*Two courses: Medal and Ashludie. Five clubs with playing rights. 18(18) | M:
6657 yds (A: 5123) | Par 71(68) | SSS 72(66)*
Visitors welcome WE ☎ preferred | B L ♥ D by arrangement with clubs | ⅄ ⅄
⅂ | TR | WE | ⅂ | M 1200 | S |
★★*Carlogie House, Carlogie Rd, Carnoustie. T:(0241) 53185. 11rm (1 ⇄ 10 🏠)*
The chief of the two courses at Monifieth is the Medal Course. It has
been one of the qualifying venues for the Open Championship on
more than one occasion. A seaside links, but divided from the sand
dunes by a railway which provides the principal hazard for the first
few holes. The 10th hole is outstanding, the 17th is excellent and
there is a delightful finishing hole.

Rolls of Monmouth The Hendre
(4m W of Monmouth on the B4233)
T:(0600) 5353
*This spacious parkland course has an
arboretum close to the first tee and a
natural division between the first and
second nine holes. Several lakes and
ponds add interest. 18 | 6723 yds |
Par 72 | SSS 72*
Visitors welcome without M ∶∶ per
day | B L D ♥ | ⅄ ⅄ ⅂ ⋈ | S |
★★★*Kings Head, Agincourt Sq.
T:(0600) 2177. 25rm (19 ⇄ 6 🏠)
Annexe: 3rm ⇄*

MONREITH
Dumfries and Galloway,
Wigtownshire
Map VI   D7

St Medan Monreith, Port William
(1m SE of Monreith off A747)
T:(09885) 555
*Moorland/seaside course, fine views. 9 |
4554 yds | Par 64 | SSS 62*

MONTROSE
Tayside, *Angus*
Map VII   J7

Montrose (Medal & Broomfield courses), Starter's Box, Triall Drive,
Montrose (NE side of town off A92)
T:(0674) 70674
*Municipal courses played on by 5 clubs (one ladies). 18(18) | 6451(4815) yds |
Par 71(66) | SSS 71(63)*
Visitors welcome with M | B L ♥ D | ⅄ ⅄ ⅂ | ④ S 0700-1500 | M 750 | S |
★★★*Links, Mid Links. T:(0674) 72288. 22rm (18 ⇄)*
The links at Montrose like many others in Scotland are on common
land and are shared by several clubs. The oldest of the Montrose
clubs is the Royal Albert which began in 1810. The Medal course at
Montrose is typical of the seaside links to be found in Scotland, with
narrow, undulating fairways. The less spectacular but harder half of
the course is the second, but golfers will find problems from the first
hole to the last.

Visitors welcome | .. per day WE |
B L ♥ D (Apr-Sept) | ⚐ ⍟ ↘ |
M 175
★★★⚌*Corsemalzie House, Port
William. T:(098886) 254. 15rm (10 ⇄
5 ⚏)*

MONTROSE
Tayside, *Angus*
Map **VII** J7

Royal Montrose Montrose
T:(0674) 72376
*Club plays over Montrose municipal
course. Societies welcome by
arrangement.* 18 | 6451 yds | Par 71 |
SSS 71
Visitors welcome ☎ | ✳ | B L ♥ D
prior arrangement (not Th) | ⚐ ⍟
↘ | ⋈ by arrangement | TR ☎ for
information | M 300
★★★*Park, John St. T:(0674) 73415.
59rm (43 ⇄ 6 ⚏)*

MORFA NEFYN
Gwynedd
Map **III** C3

Nefyn & District Pwllheli (¾m NW
of Morfa Nefyn)
T:(0758) 720218
*Seaside course, with parkland fairways
and good views. Testing golf along cliff
edge. Large clubhouse with excellent*

MORECAMBE
Lancashire
Map **V** C5

Morecambe The Club House, Bare, Morecambe
(N side of town centre on A5105)
T:(0524) 412841
18 | 5766 yds | Par 67 | SSS 68
Visitors welcome ☎ | without M ∴ per day WE | with M .. per day WE | B ♥
| L D | ⚐ ⍟ ↘ | ⋈ | TR 0800-0930 | ʒ | M 950 | S
★★★*Elms. T:(0524) 411501. 39rm (29 ⇄ 3 ⚏)*
Holiday golf at its most enjoyable. The well-maintained, seaside
course is not long but full of character. Even so the panoramic views
across Morecambe Bay and to the Lake District make concentration
difficult. The 4th is a testing hole.

MORETONHAMPSTEAD
Devon
Map **I** E6

Manor House Hotel (3m W of Moretonhampstead off B3212)
T:(06474) 0355
18 | 6016 yds | Par 69 | SSS 69
Visitors welcome | B L ♥ D | ⚐ ⍟ ↘ | ʒ | TR Sun 0800-0900, competition
days | M 200 (no club house) | S
★★★⚌*Hotel Bel Alp House, Haytor. T:(03646) 217. 9rm (7 ⇄ 2 ⚏)*
This enjoyable parkland course is a sporting circuit with just
enough hazards (most of them natural) to make any golfer think.

*facilities. Societies welcome by
arrangement.* 18 | 6335 yds | Par 72 |
SSS 71
Visitors welcome ☎ | without M ∴
per day WE | B L ♥ D ↘ prior
arrangement (not Tu) | ⚐ prior
arrangement | ⍟ | ⋈ prior
arrangement | TR occasionally | ʒ |
M 800 | S
★★*Linksway. T:(0758) 720258. 26rm
(22 ⇄)*

MORLEY
Derbyshire
Map **III** K3

Breadsall Priory Moor Rd, nr Derby
(¾m W of Morley)
T:(0332) 832235
Wooded parkland course. 18 | 6422 yds
| Par 72 | SSS 71
Visitors welcome without M ∴ per
day WE | with M ∴ per day :: WE |
B L ♥ D | ⚐ ⍟ ↘ (by arrangement)
| ④ W, Sun (am) | TR competition
days | ʒ | M 450 | S
★★★*Breadsall Priory, Morley, Derby.
T:(0332) 832235. 23rm (20 ⇄ 3 ⚏)*

MORLEY
West Yorkshire
Map **V** F6

Howley Hall Scotchman Ln, Leeds

(1½m S of Morley on B6123)
T:(0924) 478417/472432
*Parkland course with easy walking and
good views.* 18 | 6420 yds | Par 71 |
SSS 71
Visitors welcome | ∴ per round ∴
per day WE | B L ♥ | ⚐ ⍟ | TR S |
ʒ | M 500 | S
★★★*Hotel Metropole, King St, Leeds.
T:(0532) 450841. 113rm (96 ⇄ 6 ⚏)*

MORPETH
Northumberland
Map **VI** K5

Morpeth The Common, Morpeth (S
side of town centre on A197)
T:(0670) 519980
*Parkland course with views of the
Cheviots.* 18 | 5671 yds | Par 72 |
SSS 70
Visitors welcome restricted WE BH
☎ | B ♥ D prior arrangement (not
Mon Tu) | ⚐ ⍟ ⋈ | TR ☎ | ʒ |
M 700 | S
★★★★*Linden Hall, Longhorsley.
T:(0670) 56611. 45rm ⇄*

MOTHERWELL
Strathclyde, *Lanarkshire*
Map **VI** E3

Colville Park New Jerviston House,
Motherwell (1¼m NE of
Motherwell on A723)
T:(0698) 63017
*Parkland course. 1st 9 holes tree-lined,
2nd 9 more exposed. Testing 10th hole
par 3, 16th hole par 4.* 18 | 6213 yds |
Par 71 | SSS 70
Visitors welcome, only with M
party bookings midweek by prior
arrangement only | B L ♥ | D prior
arrangement | ⚐ ⍟ ⋈ | TR
competitions | M 750
★★★*Garrion, Merry St. T:(0698)
64561. 52rm (28 ⇄ 8 ⚏)*

MOUNTAIN ASH
Mid Glamorgan
Map **I** F2

Mountain Ash Cefnpennar (1m
NW of Mountain Ash off A4059)
T:(0443) 472265
Mountain course. 18 | 5579 yds |
Par 69 | SSS 68
Visitors welcome, without M .. per
day ∴ WE | with M .. per day WE |
B L ♥ | ⚐ ⍟ ⋈ daily 1200-1400,
1600-1800 (except Mon) | TR Sun
sometimes for competitions ☎ | ʒ |
M 300 | S ➥

KEY

(IA1)	*atlas grid reference*
T:	*telephone number*
☎	*advance letter/telephone call required*
✉	*introduction from own club sec/handicap certificate/club membership card required*
..	*low fees*
∴	*medium fees*
::	*high fees*
*	*green fees not confirmed for 1987*
B	*light lunch*
L	*full lunch*
☛	*tea*
D	*dinner*
⚐	*changing rooms/showers*
ⵖ	*bar open mid-day and evenings*
↘	*clubs for hire*
⋈	*partners may be found*
④	*restricted time for 4 balls*
TR	*times reserved for members*
J	*professional*
S	*well-stocked shop*
M	*member*
Mon Tu W Th F S Sun	
WE	*weekend*
BH	*bank holiday*

★★*Nant-ddu Lodge Country House, Cwn Taf, Nant-ddu. T:(0685) 79111. 7rm (4 ⇄ 3 🍴) Annexe: 1rm ⇄*

MUCKHART
Clackmannanshire
Map VI F1

Muckhart Drumburn, Muckhart, Dollar (SW of village off A91)
T:(025 981) 423

Heathland/downland course. Testing 5th Firehill (par 4). Societies welcome by arrangement. 18 | 6115 yds | Par 71 | SSS 70
Visitors welcome, restricted WE | without M ∴ per day WE | with M .. per day WE | B L ⵖ D | ⚐ ⵖ | TR WE BH (before 0945, 1200-1430) | M 500 | S
★★★*Green, 2 The Muirs, Kinross. T:(0577) 63467. 45rm (39 ⇄ 6 🍴)*

MUIRHEAD
Strathclyde, *Lanarkshire*
Map VI E2

Crow Wood Garnkirk Estate, Muirhead, Chryston, Glasgow (½m W of Muirhead on A80)
T:041-779 2011
Parkland course. 18 | 6209 yds | Par 71 | SSS 70
Visitors welcome, only with M | B L ⵖ D (not Mon) | ⚐ ⵖ | ④ competition days | J | M 600 | S
★★*Garfield House, Cumbernauld Rd, Stepps. T:041-779 2111. 27rm ⇄ 🍴*

MUIR OF ORD
Highland, *Ross and Cromarty*
Map VII F4

Muir of Ord Great North Rd, Muir of Ord (S side of village on A862)
Old established (1875) heathland/moorland course with tight fairways, easy walking. Testing 11th Castle Hill (par 3). Societies welcome by arrangement. 18 | 5022 yds | Par 66 | SSS 63
Visitors welcome | B L ⵖ | D prior arrangement | ⚐ ⵖ ↘ ⋈ | TR Mon 1700-1845, Tu, Th 1700-1900, Sun 0800-1100 | M 519 | S

★★*Ord Arms, Great North Rd. T:(0463) 870286. 12rm (3 ⇄ 3 🍴)*

MULL, ISLE OF
Strathclyde, *Argyllshire*
Map VII
See **Craignure and Tobermory**

MULLION
Cornwall
Map I B8

Mullion Cury, Helston (1½m NW of Mullion)
T:(0326) 240276
Links course with panoramic views on sea edge. Well-known ravine hole (7th). Societies limited (not June-September) by arrangement. 18 | 5616 yds | Par 69 | SSS 67
Visitors welcome ✉ | ☎ advisable | ∴ per day WE | B ⵖ L D (no food Tu) | ⚐ ⵖ ↘ ⋈ | J | TR competitions ☎ | M 700 | S
★★★*Polurrian Hotel, Mullion. T:(0326) 240421. 43rm (38 ⇄)*

MUNDESLEY
Norfolk
Map IV J3

Mundesley Links Rd, Mundesley-on-Sea (W side of village off B1159)
T:(0263) 720095
Seaside course, good views, windy. 9 | 5410 yds | Par 68 | SSS 66
Visitors welcome, restricted W | without M ∴ per day WE | with M .. per day WE | ⵖ B L D (no catering Tu) | ⚐ ⵖ ↘ ⋈ (possible) | TR Sun (0800-1100) W (1230-1530) | M 400 | S
★★*Manor, Mundesley-on-Sea. T:(0263) 720309. 26rm (9 ⇄ 12 🍴)*

MUSSELBURGH
Lothian, *Midlothian*
Map **VI** G2

Musselburgh Monktonhall (1m S of Musselburgh on B6415)
T:031-665 2005
Testing parkland course with natural hazards including trees and a burn, easy walking. 18 | 6614 yds | Par 69 | SSS 72
Visitors welcome | * | B L ♥ D | ᗄ
♈ ↘ | ⋈ (possible) | TR ☎ for details | ⅃ | M 500 | S
★★★*Donmaree, 21 Mayfield Gdns, Edinburgh. T:031-667 3641. 9rm (4 ⇄ 5 ▦). Annexe: 8rm (3 ⇄ 2 ▦)*

Musselburgh Links Linkfield Rd (1m E of town off A1)
A links type course. 9 | 2710 yds | Par 33 | SSS 33
Visitors welcome, restricted WE | ♈ ᗄ | TR WE | M 70
★★★*Donmaree, 21 Mayfield Gdns, Edinburgh. T:031-667 3641. 9rm (4 ⇄ 5 ▦). Annexe: 8rm (3 ⇄ 2 ▦)*

MUTHILL
Tayside, *Perthshire*
Map **VII** G8

Muthill Peat Rd, Muthill (W side of village off A822)
T:(0764) 3319
Parkland course with fine views. 9 | 2371 yds | Par 66 | SSS 63
Visitors welcome, restricted match nights | .. per day WE | ♥ | ᗄ ↘ (limited) | TR ④ club medals and matches, eves | M 300
★*George, King St, Crieff. T:(0764) 2089. 30rm (4 ⇄)*

NAIRN
Highland, *Nairnshire*
Map **VII** G4

Nairn Seabank Rd, Nairn (NW side of town)
T:(0667) 53208
Championship seaside links. Societies welcome by arrangement. 18(9) | 6540(2035) yds | Par 72(31) | SSS 71
Visitors welcome ☎ ∴ per round :: per day WE | B (not Th) | L ♥ D prior arrangement (not Th) | ᗄ ♈ ↘ | ⋈ (possible) | ④ after 0930 | ⅃ | M 850 | S
★★★★*Golf View, Seabank Rd. T:(0667) 52301. 55rm (45 ⇄ 10 ▦)*

Nairn Dunbar Lochloy Rd, Nairn (E side of town off A96)
T:(0667) 52741
Seaside course with sea views and breezy at holes 6, 7, 8. Testing hole: Long Peter (527 yds). 18 | 6431 yds | Par 71 | SSS 71
Visitors welcome | with M .. per day ∴ WE | ♈ B | ᗄ ⋈ prior arrangement | ↘ | TR competition days, 1700-1900 | M 600 | S
★★★*Royal Marine, Marine Rd. T:(0667) 53381. 43rm (28 ▦ 5 ▦)*

NANTYGLO
Gwent
Map **III** F8

West Monmouthshire Pond Rd, Nantyglo (¼m W of Nantyglo off A467)
T:(0495) 310233
Mountain and heathland course with hard walking and natural hazards. Testing 3rd hole par 5, and 7th hole par 4. 18 | 6097 yds | Par 71 | SSS 69
Visitors welcome | B (not Th) | L ♥ D ᗄ ♈ ⋈ | M 200
★★★*Angel, Cross St, Abergavenny. T:(0873) 7121. 29rm ⇄*

NEATH
West Glamorgan
Map I E2

Neath Cadoxton (2m NE of Neath off A4230)
T:(0639) 3615
Mountain course, with hard walking and spectacular views. Testing holes: 10th par 4; 12th par 5; 15th par 4. Facilities available for societies by arrangement. 18 | 6436 yds | Par 72 | SSS 72
Visitors welcome, restricted WE | B (not Mon) | L D ☘ prior arrangement (not Mon) | ⚐ ⚑ ⚘ | ∞ prior arrangement | ⚑ | M 500 | ⓢ
★★*Glyn Clydach House, Longford Rd, Neath Abbey.* T:(0792) 813701. 8rm (1 ⇌ 4 🕮)

Swansea Bay Jersey Marine, Neath (4m SW of Neath off A48)
T:(0639) 814153
Fairly level seaside links with part sand dunes. 18 | 6302 yds | Par 71 | SSS 70
Visitors welcome | B | L ☘ D (not W) | ⚐ ⚑ ⚘ | ∞ | M 400 | ⓢ
★★★★*Dragon, Kingsway Circle, Swansea.* T:(0792) 51074. 118rm ⇌

NELSON
Lancashire
Map V D6

Marsden Park Nelson Municipal Golf Course, Townhouse Rd, Nelson (E side of town centre off A56)
T:(0282) 67525
18 | 5806 yds | Par 70 | SSS 68
Visitors welcome, ☎ WE | .. per day | B L D WE only | ⚐ ⚘ | ∞ usually | ⚑ | M 150 | ⓢ
★★*Great Marsden, Barkerhouse Rd, Nelson.* T:(0282) 64749. 14rm (3 ⇌ 3 🕮)

Nelson King's Causeway, Brierfield (1½m SE of Nelson)
T:(0758) 64583
Hilly moorland course, usually windy, with good views. Testing 8th hole par 4. 18 | 5962 yds | Par 70 | SSS 69
Visitors welcome, restricted Th pm WE BH | without M ∴ per day WE | with M .. per day WE | ⚐ B ☘ (not Mon W) | L D prior arrangement (not Mon W) | ⚐ | TR Th, Sat | M 500 | ⓢ
★★★*Oaks, Colne Rd, Reedley, Burnley.* T:(0282) 414141. 32rm ⇌

NELSON
Mid Glamorgan
Map I G2

Whitehall The Pavilion, Nelson (2m W of Nelson off A470)
T:(0443) 740245
Windy mountain course. Testing 4th hole 235-yds par 3, and 6th hole 408-yds par 4. 9 | 5400 yds | Par 68 | SSS 68
Visitors welcome | B L ☘ D prior arrangement (not W) | ⚘ (not W) | ⚑ 1200-1600 (not W) | TR competition days | M 300
★★*Griffin Inn Motel, Rudry, Caerphilly.* T:(0222) 869735. *Annexe:* 23rm (20 ⇌)

NETHYBRIDGE
Highland, *Inverness-shire*
Map VII G5

Abernethy (N side of village on B970)
T:(047982) 204
Picturesque moorland course. Societies by arrangement. Families with children welcome. 9 | 2484 yds | Par 33 | SSS 33
Visitors welcome | B ☘ | ⚘ ⚘ | ∞ | TR competitions | M 220
★★★*Nethy Bridge.* T:(047982) 203. 63rm (62 ⇌ 1 🕮)

NEWARK-ON-TRENT
Nottinghamshire
Map IV B2

Newark Coddington (4m E of Newark on A17)
T:(063 684) 282
Parkland course in secluded situation with easy walking. No facilities for children. Societies welcome by

Many golf courses have been sited inside racecourses, although not so many survive today. One which does is the Northumberland Club's course at High Gosforth Park. Naturally the course is flat but there are plenty of mounds and other hazards to make it a fine test of golf. It should be said that not all the holes are within the confines of the racecourse, but both inside and out are some good holes. This is a Championship course.

arrangement. 18 | 6486 yds | Par 71 | SSS 71
Visitors welcome restricted Tu (ladies day) ☎ | B ☘ (not F) | L D prior arrangement (not F) | ⚐ ⚑ ⚘ | ∞ | TR WE | ⚑ | M 550 | ⓢ
★*Ram, Newark-on-Trent.* T:(0636) 702255. 21rm (1 ⇌)

NEWBIGGIN-BY-THE-SEA
Northumberland
Map VI K5

Newbiggin-by-the-Sea (N side of town)
T:(0670) 817344
Seaside course. 18 | 6444 yds | Par 72 | SSS 71
Visitors welcome | ☎ for parties | without M .. per day WE | with M .. per day WE | B L ☘ | D prior arrangement (not Tu) | ⚐ ⚑ | ⚘ ∞ prior arrangement | TR competition days | ⚑ | M 500 | ⓢ
★★★★*Linden Hall, Longhorsley.* T:(0670) 56611. 45rm ⇌

NEWBURGH on YTHAN
Grampian, *Aberdeenshire*
Map VII K5

Newburgh on Ythan Ellon (E side of village on A975)
Seaside course adjacent to bird sanctuary. Testing 550-yd dog leg (par 5). 9 | 2879 yds | Par 72 | SSS 70
Visitors welcome | TR Tu after 1530 | M 160
★*Buchan, Ellon.* T:(0358) 20208. 17rm (1 ⇌)

NEWBURY
Berkshire
Map II B4

Newbury & Crookham Bury's Bank Rd, Greenham (2m SE of Newbury off A34)
T:(0635) 40035
A well laid out course running mostly through woodland, and giving more of a challenge than its length suggests. 18 | 5883 yds | Par 68 | SSS 68
Visitors welcome, with M only WE BH | ☎ advisable summer | ∴ per day WE | B ☛ (not Mon) | L D prior arrangement (not Mon) | ⚤ ⅄ | TR | WE Tu (am) | M 500 | S |
★★★*Chequers, Oxford St, Newbury. T:(0635) 38000. 59rm (53 ⇄ 6 ᨈ)*

NEWCASTLETON
Borders, Roxburghshire
Map VI   H5

Newcastleton Holm Hill (W side of village)
T:(054121) 257
Hill course. 9 | 2896 yds | Par 70 | SSS 68
Visitors welcome | without M ..
per day | ⚤ ⋋ ⋈ | M 70
★★*Eskdale, Market Pl, Langholm. T:(0541) 80357. 14rm (5 ᨈ)*

NEWCASTLE-UNDER-LYME
Staffordshire
Map III   H3

Newcastle Municipal Keele Rd (2m W of Newcastle on A525)
T:(0782) 627596
An open course on the side of a hill without any mature trees. 18 | 6302 yds | Par 72 | SSS 70
Visitors welcome without M .. per round | ⅄ L D B ☛ ⚤ | ⋋ ⋈ | TR |
Sun am | M 195 | S |
★★★*Clayton Lodge, Clayton Rd, Clayton, Newcastle-under-Lyme. T:(0782) 613093. 50rm ⇄*

Newcastle-under-Lyme Whitmore Rd (1m SW of Newcastle on A53)
T:(0782) 617006
Parkland course. Societies welcome (W) by arrangement. Children not allowed. 18 | 6315 yds | Par 72 | SSS 71
Visitors welcome but with M only WE | ∴ per day | B ☛ (not Mon) | L D prior arrangement (not Mon) | ⚤ ⅄ | TR competition day matches etc | ⋈ | ᒎ | M 550 | S |
★★★*Clayton Lodge, Clayton Rd, Clayton, Newcastle-under-Lyme. T:(0782) 613093. 50rm ⇄*

NEWCASTLE UPON TYNE
Tyne and Wear
Map VI   K6
(See also Dudley)

City of Newcastle Three Mile Bridge, Great North Rd, Gosforth (3m N of Newcastle on A1)
T:091-285 1775
A well-manicured parkland course in the Newcastle suburbs, subject to wind. 18 | 6492 yds | Par 72 | SSS 71
Visitors welcome restricted F | ☎ | without M ∴ per day ∷ WE | with M .. per day WE | ☛ | B L D prior arrangement (not Mon) | ⚤ ⅄ ⋋ | ⋈ | ④ | TR competition days | M 580 | S |
★★★*Stakis Airport, Woolsington. T:(0661) 24911. 100rm ⇄ ᨈ*

Newcastle United Ponteland Rd, Cowgate, Newcastle upon Tyne (1¼m NW of city centre off A6127)
T:091-286 4693
Moorland course with natural hazards. Societies welcome by arrangement. 18 | 6484 yds | Par 72 | SSS 71
Visitors welcome, with M only WE BH | B L ☛ (not Mon) | ⚤ ⅄ | M 500 | S |
★★★*Imperial, Jesmond Rd. T:(091) 2815511. 133rm ⇄ ᨈ*

Westerhope Bowerbank, Whorlton Grange, Westerhope, Newcastle upon Tyne (4½m NW of city centre off B6324)
T:091-286 9125
Attractive parkland course with tree-lined fairways, and easy walking. Good open views towards the airport. Societies welcome by arrangement. 18 | 6468 yds | Par 72 | SSS 71
Visitors welcome | .. per day ∴ WE | B L ☛ prior arrangement (not Mon) | ⚤ ⅄ | TR WE as per starting sheet | ᒎ | M 875 | S |
★★★★*Gosforth Park Thistle, High Gosforth Park, Newcastle upon Tyne. T:(091) 2364111. 178rm ⇄ ᨈ*

NEW CUMNOCK
Strathclyde, Ayrshire
Map VI   E4

New Cumnock Lochhill, New Cumnock (¾m N of New Cumnock on A76)
Parkland course. 9 | 2365 yds | Par 66 | SSS 63

Visitors welcome | ④ competitions | M 152
★*Royal, 1 Glaisnock St, Cumnock. T:(0290) 20822. 12rm*

NEW GALLOWAY
Dumfries and Galloway, Kirkcudbrightshire
Map VI   E5

New Galloway New Galloway, Castle Douglas (S side of town on A762)
No telephone
Set on the edge of the Galloway Hills and overlooking Loch Ken, the course is located in the smallest Royal Burgh in Scotland. 9 | 2509 yds | Par 68 | SSS 65
Visitors welcome | .. per day WE | ⚤ ⅄ ☛ ⋈ (probable) | M 176
★★*King's Arms, St Andrew's St, Castle Douglas. T:(0556) 2626. 15rm (5 ⇄ 3 ᨈ)*

NEWHAVEN
East Sussex
Map II   F7

Peacehaven Brighton Rd, Newhaven (¾m W of Newhaven on A259)
T:(0273) 514049
Downland course, sometimes windy. Testing holes: 1st (par 3) 4th (par 4) 9th (par 3) 10th (par 3) 18th (par 3). Societies welcome by arrangement. 9 | 5235 yds | Par 69 | SSS 65
Visitors welcome | B ☛ L D | ⚤ ⅄ ⋋ | ⋈ | TR WE before 1100 | M 200 | S |
★★★*Star Inn, Alfriston. T:(0323) 870495. 32rm ⇄*

NEW MALDEN
Greater London
Map II   E4

Malden Traps Ln, New Malden (N side of town centre off B283)
T:01-942 0654
Parkland course with the hazard of the Beverley Brook which affects 4 holes (3rd, 7th, 8th and 12th). Societies welcome by arrangement. 18 | 6315 yds | Par 72 | SSS 70
Visitors welcome | B ☛ L | D prior arrangement | ⚤ ⅄ ⋋ | TR WE | ᒎ | M 650 | S |
★★★*Petersham, Nightingale Ln, Richmond Hill. T:01-940 7471. 56rm ⇄*

NEWMARKET
Suffolk
Map **IV** F6

Links Cambridge Rd (1m SW of
Newmarket on A1034)
T:(0638) 663000
*Gently undulating parkland. Societies
welcome by arrangement. 18 | 6402 yds
| Par 72 | SSS 71*
Visitors welcome restricted Sun am
| ∴ per round ∴ per day
weekdays ∷ per round WE | B ☛ |
L (not Mon) D prior arrangement |
⚖ ⛳ | ⋈ (possibly) | TR Sun
(before 1130) | ♩ | M 750 | S
★★★*Newmarket Moat House, Moulton
Rd. T:(0638) 667171. 49rm ⇄*

NEW MILLS
Derbyshire
Map **V** E8

New Mills Shaw Marsh, New
Mills, Stockport (½m N of New
Mills off B6101)
T:(0663) 43485
*Moorland course with panoramic views
and first-class greens. 9 | 5707 yds |
Par 68 | SSS 68*
Visitors welcome but with M only S
(after 1030) Sun, special days |
without M ·· per round | with M ··
per round | B L ☛ D | ⚖ ⛳ ⤡ | ⋈ |
♩ | M 260 | S
★★★*Belgrade, Dialston Ln, Stockport.
T:(061-483) 3851. 160rm ⇄*

NEWPORT
Dyfed
Map **I** G2

Newport (Pemb) The Golf Club
(1¼m N of Newport)
T:(0239) 820244
*Seaside course, with easy walking and
good view. Societies welcome by
arrangement. 9 | 3089 yds | Par 36 |
SSS 69*
Visitors welcome | B ☛ L D | ⚖ ⛳
⤡ ⋈ | ♩ | M 150 | S
★★*Fishguard Bay, Goodwick,
Fishguard. T:(0348) 873571. 62rm (27
⇄)*

NEWPORT
Isle of Wight
Map **II** B8

Newport St George's Down (1½m
S of Newport off A3020)
T:(0983) 525076
*Downland course, fine views. Societies
(limited) by arrangement. 9 | 5704 yds |*

Par 68 | SSS 68
Visitors welcome | ·· per day ∴
WE | B L ☛ prior arrangement D |
⚖ ⛳ | TR WE until 1200 | M 200
★★⚎*Padmore House, Beatrice Ave,
Whippingham. T:(0983) 293210. 11rm
(6 ⇄ 1 🛁)*

NEWQUAY
Cornwall
Map **I** B7

Newquay Tower Rd, Newquay (W
side of town)
T:(06373) 4354
*Seaside course close to the beach and
open to wind. Tennis courts. 18 |
6140 yds | Par 69 | SSS 69*
Visitors welcome | ☎ advisable WE
∴ per round | with M ·· per round
| B L ☛ D prior arrangement (not
Mon) | ⚖ ⛳ | ⤡ ⋈ limited | TR
competition days | ♩ | M 850 | S
★★★*Hotel Mordros, 4 Pentire Av.
T:(06373) 6700. 30rm ⇄ 🛁*

NEW SCONE
Tayside, *Perthshire*
Map **VII** H8

*Murrayshall House Hotel and Golf
Club* Murrayshall, Scone (E side of
village off A94)
T:(0738) 51171
*This course is laid out in 130 acres of
parkland with tree-lined fairways. 18 |
6416 yds | Par 73 | SSS 71*
Visitors welcome | B ☛ L D | ⚖ ⛳
⤡ ⋈ | TR WE 0800-0930, 1200-1400
| ④ WE 0930-1030, after 1400 |
M 400 | S
❀○○○⚎*Balcraig House, New Scone,
Perth. T:(0738) 51123. 10rm ⇄*

NEWTON
Suffolk
Map **IV** G7

Newton Green Sudbury Rd,
Newton (W side of village on A134)
T:(0787) 77501
*Flat, commonland course. 9 | 5448 yds |
Par 68 | SSS 66*
Visitors welcome, restricted WE
with M only | B L ☛ | ⚖ ⋈ ⛳ | ♩ |
M 360 | S
★★★*Bull, Long Melford. T:(0787)
78494. 27rm ⇄*

NEWPORT
Gwent
Map **III** F8

Newport Great Oak, Rogerstone, Newport (3m NW of city centre off B4591,
1m from M4 (Junc 27))
T:(0633) 894496
Societies welcome by arrangement. 18 | 6370 yds | Par 72 | SSS 71
Visitors welcome ⊠ | without M ∷ per day WE | with M ∴ per day WE | B ☛
not F | L D prior arrangement | ⚖ ⛳ ⤡ | ⋈ by arrangement | ♩ | M 650 | S
★★★★*Celtic Manor, The Coldra. T:(0633) 413000. 17rm ⇄ 🛁*
An undulating downland course, part wooded. The 2nd hole is
surrounded by bunkers — a difficult hole. The 11th hole is a bogey 4
and the fairway runs through an avenue of trees, making a straight
drive preferable. Practice grounds are also available.

NEWPORT
Gwent
Map **III** F8

Tredegar Park Bassaleg Rd, Newport (2m SW of Newport off A467)
T:(0633) 894433
18 | 6044 yds | Par 71 | SSS 70
Visitors welcome ⊠ | ∴ per day WE BH | B ☛ (not F) | L D prior arrangement
| ⚖ ⛳ ⤡ | ⋈ | TR club competitions | M 820 | S
★★★*Ladbroke, The Coldra, Newport. T:(0633) 412777. 119rm ⇄*
A parkland course with river and streams as natural hazards. The
ground is very flat with narrow fairways and small greens. The 17th
hole (par 3) is played on to a plateau where many players spoil their
medal round if they do not play on top of the bank.

NEWTON ABBOT
Devon
Map I   F6

Newton Abbot (Stover) Bovey Rd
(2½m NW of Newton Abbot on
A382)
T:(0626) 2460
*Parkland-heathland course with brook
meandering through. 18 | 5724 yds |
Par 68 | SSS 68*
Visitors welcome ⊠ | * | B L ♥ D |
♨ ⋎ ⚲ | ⋈ | 🗓 | TR competition
days | M 550 | S
★★★♨Bel Alp House, Haytor.
T:(03646) 217. 9rm (7 ⇄ 2 ⓜ)

NEWTON MEARNS
Strathclyde, *Renfrewshire*
Map VI   D3

East Renfrewshire Pilmuir, Newton
Mearns (3m SW of Newton Mearns
on A77)
T:(03555) 258
*Undulating moorland course with loch,
prevailing SW wind. 18 | 6097 yds |
Par 70 | SSS 70*
Visitors welcome Tu Th ☎
secretary T:041-226 4311 | * | B L ♥
D prior arrangement | ♨ ⋎ | S
★★★*MacDonald Thistle, Eastwood
Toll Rbt, Giffnock. T:041-638 2225.
56rm ⇄ ⓜ*

Eastwood Muirshield, Loganswell
(2½m S of Newton Mearns on A77)
T:035-55 261280
*Moorland course. 18 | 5864 yds |
Par 68 | SSS 68*
Visitors welcome | B ♥ L D | ♨ ⋎ |
TR competition days | ④
competition days | M 450 | S
★★★*MacDonald Thistle, Eastwood
Toll Rbt, Giffnock. T:041-638 2225.
56rm ⇄ ⓜ*

Whitecraigs 72 Ayr Rd,
Whitecraigs, Giffnock, Glasgow
(1½m NE of Newton Mearns on
A77)
T:041-639 2140
*Beautiful parkland course. 18 |
6230 yds | Par 70 | SSS 70*
Visitors welcome ☎ with M, ⊠
without M, restricted competition
days | ∷ per round | B ♥ | L D (not
Mon) | ♨ ⋎ | 🗓 | M 1000 | S
★★★*MacDonald Thistle, Eastwood
Toll Rbt, Giffnock. T:041-638 2225.
56rm ⇄ ⓜ*

NEWTONMORE
Highland, *Inverness-shire*
Map VII   F6

Newtonmore Golf Course Rd,
Newtonmore (E side of town off
A9)
T:(05403) 328
*Inland course beside the River Spey.
Beautiful views and easy walking.
Testing 17th hole (par 3). Societies
welcome by arrangement. 18 | 5890 yds
| Par 70 | SSS 68*
Visitors welcome | .. per day WE |
B L ♥ | ♨ ⋎ ⚲ ⋈ | TR |
occasionally at WE, ☎ for details |
④ when tee is booked | M 242
★★*Ard-Na-Coille, Kingussie Rd.
T:(05403) 214. 10rm (1 ⇄ 3 ⓜ)

NEWTON STEWART
Dumfries & Galloway, *Wigtownshire*
Map VI   D6

Newton Stewart Kirroughtree
Avenue, Minnigaff (½m N of town
centre)
T:(0671) 2172
*Flat course with much rough, making
every hole a challenge.
9 | 5512 yds | Par 68 (18 holes |*

SSS 67 (18 holes)
Visitors welcome | B L D ♥ | ⋎ | ♨ |
⋈ | TR competition days, and Tu
1700-1900 | M 300
★★★*Kirroughtree, Minnigaff,
Newton Stewart. T:(0671) 2141. 21rm
⇄ ⓜ. Annexe: 2rm ⇄*

NEWTOWN
Powys
Map III   F5

St Giles Pool Rd, Newtown (½m
NE of Newtown on A483)
T:(0686) 26844
*Inland country course with easy
walking. Testing 2nd hole par 3, and
4th hole par 4. River Severn skirts 4
holes. Societies welcome Mon to F by
arrangement. 9 | 5864 yds | Par 70 |
SSS 68*
Visitors welcome | B ♥ (not Mon) |
L D prior arrangement (not Mon) |
♨ ⋎ ⚲ | ⋈ | M 200 | S
★★★*Bear, Broad St. T:(0686) 26964.
36rm (26 ⇄ 10 ⓜ)*

NORMANTON
West Yorkshire
Map V   F6

Normanton Snydale Rd (½m SE of
Normanton on B6133)
T:(0924) 892943
*A pleasant, flat 9-hole course with tight
fairways in places and an internal out of
bounds requiring accuracy. 9 | 5284 yds
| Par 66 | SSS 66*
Visitors welcome | B ♥ | ♨ ⋎ ⋈ |
TR all day Sun | M 200 | S(WE
only)
★★★*Swallow, Queens St, Wakefield.
T:(0924) 372111. 64rm (60 ⇄ 4 ⓜ)

NEWTON-LE-WILLOWS
Lancashire
Map **V**   C7

Haydock Park Golborne Park, Rob Ln (¾m NE of Newton-le-Willows off A49)
T:(09252) 28525
18 | 6043 yds | Par 70 | SSS 69
Visitors welcome until 1600 ☎ | restricted Tu WE BH | only with M WE | ✳ | B L ☞ D prior arrangement | ⅄ | ⅄ (not Mon) | ↘ | ⋈ | ④ ☎ for details | 🥄 | TR 1245-1345 | M 510 | S
★★★*Brocket Arms, Mesnes Rd, Wigan. T:(0942) 46283. 27rm (25 ⇌ 2 ⋔)*
A well-wooded parkland course, close to the well-known racecourse, and always in excellent condition. The pleasant undulating fairways offer some very interesting golf. The clubhouse is very comfortable having all modern facilities.

NORTHAMPTON
Northants
Map **IV**   B7

Delapre Golf Complex Eagle Drive, Nene Valley Way (2m SE of Northampton)
T:(0604) 63957/64036
Municipal golf complex, also includes two 9 hole par 3 courses, pitch and putt, 33 bay driving range. 18 | 6293 yds | Par 70 | SSS 70
Open to public ‥ per round | B L ☞ D | ⅄ ↘ | ⋈ | TR Sun (0700-1000) ⅄ | 🥄 | M 500 | S
★★★*Northampton Moat House, Silver St, Town Centre. T:(0604) 22441. 134rm* ⋔

Kingsthorpe Kingsley Rd, Northampton (N side of town centre on A5095)
T:(0604) 711173
Parkland course. Societies by arrangement. No facilities for children. 18 | 6006 yds | Par 69 | SSS 69
Visitors welcome but with M only WE BH | without M ∴ per day | with M ‥ per day WE | B | ☞ | L D | ⅄ ⅄ | ⋈ | TR WE | 🥄 | M 325 | S
★★★*Northampton Moat House, Silver St, Town Centre. T:(0604) 22441. 134rm* ⋔

Northampton Kettering Rd, Northampton (2m NE of town centre)
T:(0604) 711054
Parkland course with comfortable walking. Societies welcome by arrangement. 18 | 6002 yds | Par 69 | SSS 69
Visitors welcome, with M only WE | ∴ per day | B L ☞ D | ⅄ ⅄ | TR W pm (ladies) | 🥄 | M 600 | S

★★★*Northampton Moat House, Silver St, Town Centre. T:(0604) 22441. 134rm* ⋔

Northamptonshire County Church Brampton, Northampton (4m NW of town centre off A50)
T:(0604) 843025
Undulating heathland course with gorse, heather and fine pine woods. Societies welcome by arrangement. 18 | 6509 yds | Par 70 | SSS 71
Visitors welcome ⊠ | without M ∷ per day WE | with M ‥ per day WE | B ☞ L D | ⅄ ⅄ ↘ | ④ ☎ for details | TR competition days | 🥄 | M 810 | S
★★★*Westone Moat House, Ashley Way, Weston Favell, Northampton. T:(0604) 406262. 30rm ⇌ Annexe: 34rm* ⇌

NORTH BERWICK
Lothian, *East Lothian*
Map **VI**   H2

NORTH BERWICK
Lothian, *East Lothian*
Map **VI**   H2

North Berwick West Links, New Clubhouse, Beach Rd, North Berwick (W side of town on A198)
T:(0620) 2135
18 | 6298 yds | Par 70 | SSS 70
Visitors welcome ☎ advisable | ✳ | B L ☞ prior arrangement (not Th) | ⅄ ⅄ ↘ | D prior arrangement | TR S (competition days) Sun 0800-1000 | 🥄 | M 550 | S
★★★*Marine, Cromwell Rd. T:(0620) 2406. 86rm (76 ⇌ 10 ⋔)*
Another of East Lothian's famous courses. Years ago golfers used to flock to the pretty little town and stay in one of the hotels or lease a house for a month — it became the fashionable thing to do. Those days have gone, but the links at North Berwick is still popular. The great hole on the course is the 15th, the famous 'Redan', selected for the television best 18 in the UK. There is also a 9-hole course for children.

East Links North Berwick (E side of town off A198)
T:(0620) 2726
Coastal course on the south shores of Firth of Forth, opposite the famous Bass Rock Island. 18 | 6086 yds | Par 69 | SSS 69
Visitors welcome | ⅄ B L D (high tea) by arrangement | ☞ | ⅄ | S summer only | ⋈ | TR WE am | M 350
★★*Point Garry, West Bay Rd. T:(0620) 2380. 15rm (2 ⇌ 6 ⋔)*

Glen East Links (E side of town centre)
T:(0620) 2221
An interesting course with a good variety of holes. The view of the town, the Firth of Forth and the Bass Rock are breathtaking. 18 | 6079 yds | Par 69 | SSS 69
Visitors welcome without M ‥ per day ∴ WE | B L (also high tea) ☞ | ⅄ ⅄ ↘ | ⋈ | 🥄 | TR 0800-0930 WE | M 300 | S
★★*Nether Abbey, Dirleton Ave. T:(0620) 2802. 16rm (4 ⇌ 6 ⋔)*

NORTHWOOD
Greater London
Map **II**   D3

Haste Hill The Drive (½m S of Northwood off A404)
T:(09274) 22877
Parkland course with stream running through, excellent views. 18 | 5787 yds | Par 68 | SSS 68
Visitors are welcome without M | L B ☞ | ⅄ ⅄ | TR occasionally | ↘ ⋈ | M 350 | S

★★*Harrow, Roxborough Bridge, 12-22 Pinner Rd, Harrow. T:01-427 3435. 64rm (12 ⇌ 52 ⏚)*

Sandy Lodge Sandy Lodge Ln, Northwood (N side of town centre off A4125)
T:(09274) 25429
Heathland course; links-type, very sandy. Societies welcome by arrangement. 18 | 6340 yds | Par 70 | SSS 70
Visitors welcome, restricted WE BH | without M ∷ per day | with M .. per day | B ☎ | L D prior arrangement | ⚤ ⏂ ↘ | ④ TR ☎ for details | M 500 | Ⓢ
★★★*Ladbroke, Elton Way, Watford-by-Pass, Bushey. T:(0923) 35881. 155rm ⇌*

NORWICH
Norfolk
Map **IV** J4

Eaton Newmarket Rd, Norwich (2½m SW of city centre off A11)
T:(0603) 51686
An undulating, tree-lined parkland

course. 18 | 6105 yds | Par 70 | SSS 69
Visitors welcome with M or with ⊠ | ∴ per day ∷ WE | B L (not WE) ☎ | ⏂ | TR WE (0745-1130) | ⌡ | M 885 | Ⓢ
★★★*Post House, Ipswich Rd, Norwich. T:(0603) 56431. 120rm ⇌*

Royal Norwich Hellesdon, Norwich (2½m NW of city centre on A1067)
T:(0603) 49928
Undulating parkland course. 18 | 6603 yds | Par 72 | SSS 72
Visitors welcome, restricted WE BH | ⊠ ☎ advisable | ＊ | B ☎ | ⚤ ⏂ ↘ | M 650 | Ⓢ
★★★*Hotel Norwich, 121-131 Boundary Rd. T:(0603) 410431. 102rm ⇌ ⏚*

NOTTINGHAM
Nottinghamshire
Map **IV** A3

Beeston Fields Beeston (4m SW of Nottingham off A52)
T:(0602) 257062
Parkland course with sandy subsoil and

wide, tree-lined fairways. The par 3 14th has elevated tee and small bunker guarded green. 18 | 6404 yds | Par 71 | SSS 71*
Visitors welcome, restricted Tu until 1430 Th pm WE BH | without M ∴ per day | B ☎ ⏂ L | D prior arrangement | ⚤ ↘ | TR Tu S | ⌡ | M 650 | Ⓢ
★★★*Post House, Bostocks Ln, Sandiacre. T:(0602) 397800. 107rm ⇌*

Bulwell Forest Hucknall Rd, Bulwell (4m NW of city centre on A611)
T:(0602) 278008
Municipal heathland course with many natural hazards. Very tight fairways and subject to wind. 18 | 5606 yds | Par 68 | SSS 67
Open to public .. per round | B L ☎ | D prior arrangement | ⏂ | TR WE | ⏂ | ⌡ | M 420 | Ⓢ
★★★*Savoy, Mansfield Rd. T:(0602) 602621. 125rm ⇌*

Bulwell Hall Bulwell Hall Park, Nottingham (4m NW of city centre off A6002)
T:(0602) 278021
A pleasant municipal parkland course on the city outskirts. 18 | 6210 yds | Par 69 | SSS 70
Visitors welcome .. per day | B L ☎ D | ⚤ ⏂ ↘ | M 325 | Ⓢ
★★★*Savoy, Mansfield Rd. T:(0602) 602621. 125rm ⇌*

Chilwell Manor Chilwell (4m SW of Nottingham on A6005)
T:(0602) 257050
Flat parkland course. 18 | 6345 yds | Par 70 | SSS 70
Visitors welcome | with M only | ∴ per day WE | B ☎ | L D prior arrangement | ⚤ ⏂ | ⏂ | ⌡ | M 600 | Ⓢ
★★*Europa, 20 Derby Rd, Long Eaton. T:(0602) 728481. 18rm (6 ⇌ 8 ⏚)*

***Mapperley** Central Avenue, Mapperley Plains, Nottingham (3m NE of city centre off B684)
T:(0602) 265611
Hilly meadowland course but with easy walking. 18 | 6224 yds | Par 71 | SSS 70
Visitors welcome | B ☎ L | ⚤ ⏂ | TR S | ⌡ | M 600 | Ⓢ
★★★★*Albany, St James' St. T:(0602) 470131. 161rm ⇌*

KEY
(IA1) *atlas grid reference*
T: *telephone number*
☎   *advance letter/telephone call required*
✉   *introduction from own club sec/handicap certificate/club membership card required*
..   *low fees*
∴   *medium fees*
::   *high fees*
*   *green fees not confirmed for 1987*
B   *light lunch*
L   *full lunch*
♥   *tea*
D   *dinner*
⚖   *changing rooms/showers*
♈   *bar open mid-day and evenings*
✎   *clubs for hire*
⋈   *partners may be found*
④   *restricted time for 4 balls*
TR   *times reserved for members*
𝕁   *professional*
S   *well-stocked shop*
M   *member*
Mon Tu W Th F S Sun
WE   *weekend*
BH   *bank holiday*

NUFFIELD
Oxfordshire
Map II C3

Huntercombe Nuffield, Henley-on-Thames (N side of Nuffield, off A423)
T:(0491) 641207
Societies welcome by arrangement. 18 | 6257 yds | Par 70 | SSS 70
Visitors welcome ☎ advisable | without M :: per day WE | with M .. per day WE | B ♥ | L prior arrangement | D ⚖ ♈ | ✎ prior arrangement | 𝕁 | ④ not allowed | M 600 | S
***Shillingford Bridge, Shillingford, Wallingford. T:(086 732) 8567. 25rm (24 ⇄ 🛁)*

Huntercombe 5th hole

This heathland/woodland course overlooks the Oxfordshire plain and has many attractive and interesting fairways and greens. Walking is easy after the 3rd which is a notable hole. The course is subject to wind and grass pot bunkers are interesting hazards.

NUNEATON
Warwickshire
Map III K5

Nuneaton Golf Drive, Whitestone (2m SE of Nuneaton off B4114)
T:(0203) 347810
Parkland course. 18 | 5431 yds | Par 71 | SSS 71
Visitors welcome, with M only WE ∴ per day without M | B ♥ L D | ⚖ ♈ | ④ as starting board | TR club competitions | 𝕁 | M 550 | S
**Chase, Higham Ln. T:(0203) 383406. 28rm ⇄

OADBY
Leicestershire
Map IV A4

Oadby Leicester Rd (W side of town centre off A6)
T:(0533) 700326. Pro shop 709052
Municipal parkland course. Societies may reserve tees on application to Oadby and Wigston Council. 18 | 6228 yds | Par 71 | SSS 69
Open to public .. per round | B L ♥ D | ⚖ ♈ ✎ | 𝕁 (R Adams) | M 400 | S
***Leicestershire Moat House, Wigston Rd, Oadby, Leicester. T:(0533) 719441. 29rm ⇄ 🛁

OCKLEY
Surrey
Map II E5

Gatton Manor nr Dorking (1½m SW of Ockley off A29)
T:(030679) 555
Undulating course through woods and over many challenging water holes. Games room. 18 | 6906 yds | Par 72 | SSS 73
Visitors welcome WE | .. to ∴ per round | B L ♥ D | ⚖ ♈ ✎ | ⋈ by arrangement | 𝕁 | TR Sun am | M 300 | S
***White Horse, High St, Dorking. T:(0306) 881138. 38rm (36 ⇄ 🛁)
Annexe: 32rm ⇄

OGBOURNE ST GEORGE
Wiltshire
Map I K2

Swindon Ogbourne St George (N side of village on A345)
T:(067284) 327
Downland turf and magnificent greens. Societies welcome by arrangement. 18 | 6226 yds | Par 71 | SSS 70
Visitors welcome weekdays ☎ | without M ∴ weekdays WE | with M .. per day | B (not Mon) | ♥ L D prior arrangement (not Mon) | ⚖ ♈ ✎ | ④ competition days | S
***Crest Hotel, Oxford Rd, Stratton St. Margaret, Swindon. T:(0793) 822921. 98rm ⇄

OKEHAMPTON
Devon
Map I E5

Okehampton Tors Rd (1m S of Okehampton off A30)
T:(0837) 2113
Interesting moorland course with true Dartmoor turf. Societies welcome by arrangement. 18 | 5300 yds | Par 68 | SSS 67
Visitors welcome ☎ preferred | .. per day ∴ WE | B ♥ | L D prior arrangement | ⚖ ♈ ✎ | TR 0800-1000 competition days ☎ | 𝕁 | M 400 | S
**Oxenham Arms, South Zeal. T:(0837) 840244. 8rm (6 ⇄)

OLDHAM
Greater Manchester
Map V E7

Crompton & Royton Highbarn, Oldham (½m NE of Royton)
T:061-624 2154

OBAN
Strathclyde, *Argyllshire*
Map **VII**   D8

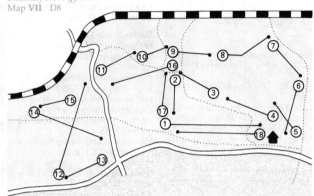

Glencruitten Glencruitten Rd, Oban (NE side of town centre off A816)
T:(0631) 62868
Parties accepted by prior arrangement. 18 | 4452 yds | Par 61 | SSS 63
Visitors welcome, restricted during competitions, Th pm, S | ∴ per day WE | B (not Mon) | L ☻ D prior arrangement | ⚘ ↘ | ⋈ usually | TR Th 1200-1400, 1730-1830 S 0800-1100, 1300-1530 | 🎽 | M 640
★★★*Caledonian, Station Sq, Oban. T:(0631) 63133. 69rm ⇌*
There is plenty of space and considerable variety of hole on this downland course — greatly popular with holidaymakers. In a beautiful, isolated situation, the course is hilly and testing-particularly the 1st and 12th, par 4s, and 10th and 15th, par 3s.

Moorland course. 18 | 6187 yds | SSS 69
Visitors welcome ☎ | .. per day | B (not Mon) | L ☻ D prior arrangement (not Mon) | ⚘ ⋈ | TR 1200-1400 and S or competition days | 🎽 | M 600 | S
★★*Midway, Manchester Rd, Rochdale. T:(0706) 32881. 30rm (2 ⇌ 20 🍴)*

Oldham Lees New Rd (2½m E of Oldham off A669)
T:061-624 4986
Moorland course, with hard walking. 6th and 10th holes par 4. 18 | 5045 yds | Par 66 | SSS 65
Visitors welcome, ☎ restricted Tu pm and WE | .. per day WE BH | B L ☻ D | ⚘ ⵕ | TR Tu, WE ☎ for times | 🎽 | M 250 | S
★★*York House, York Pl, off Richmond St, Ashton-under-Lyne. T:061-330 5899. 26rm (8 ⇌ 3 🍴)*

Werneth Green Ln, Garden Suburb, Oldham (S side of town centre off A627)
T:061-624 1190

Moorland course, windy, with a deep gulley and stream crossing 8 fairways. Testing hole: 3rd (par 3). Societies welcome by arrangement. 18 | 5363 yds | Par 68 | SSS 66
Visitors welcome, weekdays only | .. per day | B ☻ | L D prior arrangement | ⚘ ⵕ ↘ ⋈ | 🎽 | M 400 | S
★★*York House, York Pl, off Richmond St, Ashton-under-Lyne. T:061-330 5899. 26rm (8 ⇌ 3 🍴)*

ORMSKIRK
Lancashire
Map **V**   C7

Ormskirk Cranes Ln, Lathom (1½m NE of Ormskirk)
T:(0695) 72112
Societies by arrangement. 18 | 6333 yds | Par 70 | SSS 70
Visitors welcome | without M ∷ per day WE | B L ☻ D | ⚘ ⵕ | ④ Competition days | TR 1200-1430 | 🎽 | M 300 | S
★★*Bold, Lord St, Southport. T:(0704) 32578. 23rm (18 ⇌)*
A pleasantly secluded, fairly flat, parkland course with much heath and silver birch. Accuracy from the tees will provide an interesting variety of second shots.

OLD MELDRUM
Grampian, *Aberdeenshire*
Map **VII**   J5

Old Meldrum Old Meldrum (E side of village off A947)
Generally narrow downland course requiring accuracy rather than long hitting, superb views. 9 | 2567 yds | Par 68 | SSS 65
Visitors welcome | ⚘ | TR competition days | M 200
★*Gordon Arms, The Square, Inverurie. T:(0467) 20314. 11rm (6 🍴)*

ONCHAN
Isle of Man
Map **V**   A6

Howstrake Groudle Rd, Onchan (E side of town off A11)
T:(0624) 24299
Hilly seaside course, perfect for beginners, with natural hazards. Good views. 14 | 5243 yds | Par 68 | SSS 66
Visitors very welcome | .. per day WE including clubs, balls and tees | ☻ ↘ | ⋈ possible | TR Sun 0815-0930, after 1400 | 🎽 | M 350 | S
★*Woodbourne, Alexander Dr, Douglas. T:(0624) 21766. 12rm*

ORKNEY
Map **VII**
See Kirkwall, Stromness and Westray

ORPINGTON
Greater London
Map **II**   F4

Cray Valley Sandy Ln (2m NE of Orpington off A224)
T:(0689) 37909
An open parkland course with two man-made lakes and open ditches. 18 (9) | 5624 yds (1773) | Par 69 (29) | SSS 68
Visitors welcome without M | L D B ➡

ORSETT
Essex
Map **II**   G3

Orsett Brentwood Rd (1½m SE of Orsett off A128)
T:(0375) 891352
Societies welcome by arrangement. 18 | 6621 yds | Par 72 | SSS 72
Visitors welcome with M or ✉ | ☎ | restricted WE Ladies day Thurs am | B L
♥ (not F) | D prior arrangement (not F) | ⚘ ♈ (not Fri) | ↘ (clubs for hire) | ♪
| M 800 | ⓢ
**Ye Olde Plough House, Brentwood Rd, Bulphan. T:(0375) 891592. Annexe:*
77rm (67 ⇔ 10 🚿)
A very good test of golf — this heathland course with its sandy soil
is quick drying and provides easy walking. Close to the Thames
estuary it is seldom calm and the main hazards are the prevailing
wind and thick gorse. Any slight deviation can be exaggerated by
this wind and a ball lost in the gorse results. The clubhouse has been
modernised.

OTLEY
West Yorkshire
Map **V**   F6

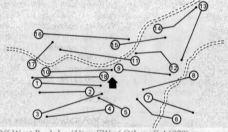

Otley Off West Busk Ln (1½m SW of Otley off A6038)
T:(0943) 461015
18 | 6229 yds | Par 70 | SSS 70
Visitors welcome ☎ advisable | ∴ per day ∷ WE (summer), ∴ per day WE
(winter) | B L ♥ D | ⚘ ♈ ↘ ⋈ | TR 1200-1400 | ♪ | M 600 | ⓢ
***Post House, Otley Rd, Bramhope. T:(0532) 842911. 122rm ⇔*
An expansive course with magnificent views across Wharfedale.
The course is well wooded with streams crossing the fairway. The
4th is a fine hole which generally needs two woods to reach the
plateau green. The 17th is a good short hole with a bunker-guarded
green.

OTTERSHAW
Surrey
Map **II**   D4

Foxhills Stonehill Rd (1m NW of Ottershaw)
T:(093287) 2050
Societies welcome. 36 | 6880 yds (6747) | Par 73(72) | SSS 73(72)
Visitors welcome with M only ∷ per day | B L ♥ | D prior arrangement | ⚘ ♈
↘ | TR WE (one course) | ♪ | M 600 | ⓢ
***Ladbroke Seven Hills, Cobham. T:(0932) 64471. 90rm ⇔ Annexe: 25rm ⇔*
A pair of parkland courses designed in the grand manner and with
American course design in mind. One course is tree-lined, the
other, as well as trees, has massive bunkers and artificial lakes
which contribute to the interest. Both courses offer testing golf and
they finish on the same long 'double green'.

♥ | ⚘ ♈ ↘ | ⋈ | TR S/Sun am, BH |
④ S/Sun | M 800 | ⓢ
***Bromley Court, Bromley Hill,*
Bromley. T:01-464 5011. 130rm ⇔

Ruxley Sandy Ln, St Paul's Cray,
nr Orpington, Kent (2m NE of
Orpington on A223)
T:(0689) 71490
Parkland course with public driving
range. Difficult 6th hole, par 4. Easy
walking and good views. Reductions in
green fees for children. Societies
welcome by arrangement. 18 | 4964 yds
| Par 65 | SSS 65
Visitors welcome, restricted WE am
| .. per day | B L ♥ D prior
arrangement | ♈ ↘ | ⋈ by
arrangement | ④ ☎ | TR WE BH
until 1130 | M 250 | ⓢ
***Bromley Court, Bromley Hill,*
Bromley. T:01-464 5011. 130rm ⇔

OSSETT
West Yorkshire
Map **V**   F7

Low Laithes Parkmill Ln,
Flushdyke (1½m NE of Ossett off
A638, Junc 40 M1)
T:(0924) 273275
Testing parkland course with short
holes. 18 | 6448 yds | Par 71 | SSS 71
Visitors welcome | without M ..
per day ∴ WE BH | ♥ B L D | ⚘ ♈
↘ ⋈ | M 450 | ⓢ
***Post House, Queens Dr, Ossett.*
T:(0924) 276388. 96rm ⇔

OSWESTRY
Shropshire
Map **III**   F3

Oswestry Aston Park (3½m SE of
Oswestry on A5)
T:(0691) 221
Parkland course laid out on undulating
ground. Societies welcome (W F) by
arrangement. 18 | 6046 yds | Par 70 |
SSS 69
Visitors welcome but restricted
competition days ☎ | ∴ per day | B
L ♥ | D prior arrangement | ⚘ ♈ |
TR competition days | ♪ | M 700 | ⓢ
***Wynnstay, Church St. T:(0691)*
655261. 31rm (17 ⇔ 2 🚿)

OUNDLE
Northamptonshire
Map **IV**   C5

Oundle Benefield Rd (1m W of
Oundle on A427)
T:(0832) 73267

OXFORD
Oxfordshire
Map **II**   B2

Southfield Hill Top Rd, Oxford (1½m SE of city centre off B480)
T:(0865) 242158
Societies welcome by arrangement. 18 | 6230 yds | Par 70 | SSS 70
Visitors welcome weekdays ☎ preferable | WE only with M | B ♥ (not Mon) | L D prior arrangement (not Mon) | ⅄ | ☿ ⟍ | TR WE | 🍴 | M 850 | S
★★★⚑*Studley Priory, Horton-cum-Studley. T:(086735) 203. 19rm (15 ⇄ 4 ⋒)*
Home of both the City and University Clubs and well-known to graduates throughout the world. A challenging course, in varied parkland setting, providing a real test for players.

Undulating parkland course close to the town. A small brook affects some of the approaches to the greens. 18 | 5507 yds | Par 70 | SSS 67
Visitors welcome except WE | ∴ per day WE | B L ♥ D | ⅄ ☿ ⋉ | TR
Ladies only 0930-1030 Tu | M 500
★★★*Talbot, New St. T:(0832) 73621. 39rm ⇄*

OUTLANE
West Yorkshire
Map **V**   E7

Outlane Slack Ln, Outlane, nr Huddersfield (S side of village off A640)
T:(0484) 74762
Moorland course. 18 | 5590 yds | Par 69 | SSS 67
Visitors welcome | ✳ | B L ♥ D | ⅄ ☿ ⋉ | TR WE | M 230 | S
★★★*Ladbroke, Ainley Top, Huddersfield. T:(0422) 75431. 118rm ⇄ ⋒*

OXFORD
Oxfordshire
Map **II**   B2

North Oxford Banbury Rd, Oxford (3m N of city centre on A423)
T:(0865) 54415
Parkland course with easy walking. Societies welcome by arrangement. 18 | 5805 yds | Par 67 | SSS 67
Visitors welcome | ∴ per day | ⁚⁚ WE | B ♥ L D | ⅄ ☿ ⋉ | TR Sun am | 🍴 | M 500 | S
★★★*Oxford Moat House, Godstow Rd, Wolvercote Rbt, Oxford. T:(0865) 59933. 155rm ⇄*

OXTON
Nottinghamshire
Map **IV**   A2

Oxton Oaks Ln, Nottingham (1m NW of Oxton off A6097)
T:(0602) 653545

PAINSWICK
Gloucestershire
Map **III**   H8

Painswick Painswick (1m N of Painswick on A46)
T:(0452) 812180
Downland course set on Cotswold Hills at Painswick Beacon with fine views. Short course more than compensated by natural hazards and tight fairways. Societies welcome by arrangement. 18 | 4895 yds | Par 67 | SSS 64
Visitors welcome | .. per day WE | B L ♥ D | ⅄ ☿ ⟍ | TR Sun | M 150
★★★*Painswick, Kemps Ln. T:(0452) 812160. 15rm (14 ⇄)*

PAISLEY
Strathclyde, *Renfrewshire*
Map **VI**   D2

Barshaw Barshaw Park, Paisley (1m E of Paisley off A737)
T:041-889 2908
Municipal parkland course. 18 | 5703 yds | Par 68 | SSS 67
Open to public | .. per day | ⅄ ♥
★★★*Glynhill, Paisley Rd, Renfrew. T:041-886 5555. 80rm ⇄*

Paisley Braehead, Paisley (S side of town off B774)
T:041-884 2292
Moorland course, windy but with good view. Societies welcome by arrangement. 18 | 6424 yds | Par 71 | SSS 71

Visitors welcome not WE, with M ✉ 🏠 | .. per round ∴ per day WE | B ♥ | L D prior arrangement | ⅄ ☿ | TR 1230-1400 | M 700
★★★*Glynhill, Paisley Rd, Renfrew. T:041-886 5555. 80rm ⇄*

Ralston Strathmore Av, Ralston, Paisley (2m E of Paisley off A737)
T:041-882 1349
Parkland course. 18 | 6071 yds | Par 71 | SSS 69
Visitors welcome with M only | B L ♥ D prior arrangement (not Mon) | ⅄ ☿ | M 750 | S
★★★*Bellahouston Swallow, 517 Paisley Rd West, Glasgow. T:041-427 3146. 120rm ⇄ ⋒*

PANT
Shropshire
Map **III**   F3

Llanymynech nr Oswestry (½m SW of Pant off A483)
T:(0691) 830542
Downland course on the site of an early British encampment with far-reaching views. The 4th fairway crosses the Welsh border. 18 | 6114 yds | Par 70 | SSS 69
Visitors welcome | without M .. per day ∴ WE | with M .. per day WE | L D B ♥ | ⅄ ☿ ⟍ ⋉ | M 600 | S
★★★*Wynnstay, Church St, Oswestry. T:(0691) 655261. 31rm (17 ⇄ 2 ⋒)*

PANT-Y-MWYN
Clwyd
Map **III**   F2

Mold Pant-y-mwyn (E side of village)
T:(0352) 740318
Meadowland course with some hard walking and natural hazards. Fine views. Society meetings by arrangement. 18 | 5521 yds | Par 69 | SSS 69
Visitors welcome | ✳ | B L ♥ D | ⅄ ☿ ⟍ | ⋉ | TR competitions | M 320 | S
★★★*Chequers, Northophall. T:(0244) 816181. 29rm (27 ⇄ 2 ⋒)*

PEEBLES
Borders, *Peebleshire*
Map **VI**   G3

Peebles Municipal Kirkland St, Peebles (W side of town centre off A72)
➥

Exposed and very testing quick drying heathland course with easy walking. The par 3 16th and par 4 1st are notable. 18 | 6630 yds | Par 72 | SSS 72
Visitors welcome | ✳ | B L ♥ D | ⅄ ☿ ⟍ | ④ WE and BH | TR WE 0730-1200 | 🍴 | M 520 | S
★★★*Saracens Head, Market Pl, Southwell. T:(0636) 812701. 23rm ⇄ ⋒*

PANNAL
North Yorkshire
Map V F5

Pannal Follifoot Road, Pannal, Harrogate (E side of village off A61)
T:(0423) 871641
Societies welcome by arrangement. 18 | 6573 yds | Par 72 | SSS 71
Visitors welcome 🕿 ✉ | ✳ | B 🏌 L D | 👜 ⛳ ╲ ✕ | TR until 0930, 1230-1330 |
J | M 700 | S
✳✳✳*Hospitality Inn, Prospect Pl, West Park, Harrogate. T:(0423) 64601. 71rm ⇔*
A fine championship course. Moorland turf but well-wooded with
the trees closely involved with the play.

T:(0721) 20197
*Parkland course with fine views. 18 |
6137 yds | Par 70 | SSS 69*
Visitors welcome | B L 🏌 | 👜 ⛳ ╲
✕ | TR competitions 🕿 | M 250 | S
★★★*Tontine, High St. T:(0721)
20892. 37rm (36 ⇔ 1 🛏)*

PEEL
Isle of Man
Map V A6

Peel Rheast Ln, Peel (SE side of
town centre on A1)
T:(0624) 4842227
*Moorland course, with natural hazards
and easy walking. Good views. 11th
hole par 4 dogleg. 18 | 5907 yds |
Par 69 | SSS 68*
Visitors welcome | .. per day WE |
B L 🏌 prior arrangement | 👜 ⛳
Pro. (Tel. 3514) | ✕ | TR WE before
1030 🕿 (0830-1000, 1230-1430,
1530-1700) | M 574
★*Woodbourne, Alexander Dr, Douglas.
T:(0624) 21766. 12rm*

PEMBROKE DOCK
Dyfed
Map III B8

South Pembrokeshire Defensible
Barracks, Pembroke Dock (SW side
of town centre off B4322)
T:(0646) 683817
*Downland course overlooking Milford
Haven with easy walking and little
rough. Suitable for beginners. Societies
welcome by arrangement. 9 | 5804 yds |
Par 70 | SSS 69*
Visitors welcome | .. per day | B L
🏌 D prior arrangement | 👜 ⛳ | ✕ |
TR after 1630 | M 275
★★*Old King's Arms, Main St,
Pembroke. T:(0646) 683611. 21rm ⇔*

PENARTH
South Glamorgan
Map I G3

Glamorganshire Lavernock Rd,

Penarth (S side of town centre on
B4267)
T:(0222) 701185
*Parkland course, overlooking the Bristol
Channel. Societies welcome by
arrangement. 18 | 6342(Blue boxes)
5769(Yellow boxes) yds | Par 70(B)
70(Y) | SSS 70(B) 68(Y)*
Visitors welcome 🕿 ✉ | restricted
Tu ladies day | B L prior
arrangement (not Mon) | 🏌 D prior
arrangement | 👜 ⛳ ╲ | ✕ | ④ 🕿
for details | TR competitions and
matches | J | M 1000 | S
★*Walton House, 37 Victoria Rd.
T:(0222) 707782. 12rm (4 ⇔ 1 🛏)*

PENICUIK
Lothian, *Midlothian*
Map VI G3

Glencorse Milton Bridge, Penicuik
(1½m N of Penicuik on A701)
T:(0968) 77177
*Picturesque parkland course with burn
running through and many interesting
holes. Testing 5th hole 237 yds par 3.
Parties accepted by arrangement Mon
to F except Tu. 18 | 5205 yds | Par 64 |
SSS 66*
Visitors welcome, restricted WE | B
L 🏌 D | 👜 ⛳ ╲ ✕ prior
arrangement | TR Sun before 1430 |
J | M 400 | S
★★★*Braid Hills, 134 Braid Rd, Braid
Hills, Edinburgh. T:031-447 8888.
68rm (47 ⇔ 21 🛏)*

PENMAENMAWR
Gwynedd
Map III D2

Penmaenmawr Cae Maen Pavilion,
Penmaenmawr (1½m NE of
Penmaenmawr off A55)
T:(0492) 623330
*Hilly course with magnificent views
across the bay to Llandudno and
Anglesey. Dry stone wall natural
hazards. Societies welcome by
arrangement. 9 | 5171 yds | Par 66 |*

SSS 65
Visitors welcome | B L 🏌 D | 👜 ⛳ |
TR competitions | M 500
★★*Castle, High St, Conwy.
T:(049263) 2324. 25rm ⇔*

PERRANPORTH
Cornwall
Map I B7

Perranporth Budnick Hill,
Perranporth (¾m NE of
Perranporth on B3285)
T:(087257) 2454
*There are two testing par 5 holes on the
links course (11th & 14th) and a fine
view over Perranporth Beach from all
holes. Societies welcome by
arrangement. 18 | 6208 yds | Par 72 |
SSS 71*
Visitors welcome | without M ∴ per
round WE | with M .. per round | B
🏌 L D | 👜 ⛳ ╲ ✕ | TR WE am |
M 450 | S
★*Beach Dunes, Ramoth Way, Reen
Sands. T:(087257) 2263. 7rm (2 ⇔ 1
🛏) Annexe: 3rm ⇔*

PERTH
Tayside, *Perthshire*
Map VII H8

Craigie Hill Cherrybank, Perth (1m
SW of city centre off A9)
T:(0738) 24377
*Slightly hilly, parkland course. Good
views over Perth. 18 | 5379 yds |
Par 66 | SSS 66*
Visitors welcome 🕿 restricted WE |
∴ per day WE | B L 🏌 D prior
arrangement | 👜 ⛳ ✕ | TR 🕿 for
details | M 600 | S
★★★*Stakis City Mills, West Mill St,
Perth. T:(0738) 28281. 78rm (77 ⇔ 🛏)*

King James VI Moncrieffe Island,
Perth (SE side of city centre)
T:(0738) 25170
*Parkland course, situated on island in
the middle of River Tay. Easy walking.
Societies welcome by arrangement. 18 |
6037 yds | Par 70 | SSS 69*
Visitors welcome restricted S | B L
🏌 D | 👜 ⛳ | ✕ ╲ possible | TR S |
M 500 | S
★★*Salutation, South St, Perth.
T:(0738) 22166. 66rm (58 ⇔)*

PENRITH
Cumbria
Map **V** C3

Penrith Salkeld Rd, Penrith (¾m N of Penrith off A6)
T:(84) 62217
18 | 6020 yds | Par 69 | SSS 69
Visitors welcome ☎ ✉ | ✳ | B ✿ D | L (not Mon and Tu) | ⚐ ▼ ⚲ | ④
competitions | TR ☎ | M 850 | S
✱✱*George, Devonshire St. T:(0768) 62696. 32rm (11 ⇄ 20 ⏏)*

A beautiful and well-balanced course, always changing direction, and demanding good length from the tee. It is set on rolling moorland with occasional pine trees and some fine views.

PETERBOROUGH
Cambridgeshire
Map **IV** D5

Peterborough Milton Milton Ferry, Peterborough (3m W of Peterborough on A47)
T:(073121) 489
Well-bunkered parkland course on part of Earl Fitzwilliam's estate with easy walking. Societies welcome by arrangement. 18 | 6431 yds | Par 71 (69) | SSS 71 (69)
Visitors welcome ✉ | ✳ | B ✿ L D |
⚐ ▼ | ④ Tu after 1600 | M 780 | S
✱✱*Haycock Inn, Wansford. T:(0780) 782223. 21rm (14 ⇄)*

Thorpe Wood Thorpe Wood, Peterborough (2m W of city centre off A1260)
T:(0733) 267701
A municipal course with associated club, parkland. 18 | 7086 (medal tees) 6595 (forward tees) | Par 73 | SSS 74 (medal) 72 (forward)
Open to the public | ⚬⚬ per day WE
| B L ✿ | ⚐ ▼ ⚲ ✕ | TR
competition days | ♪ | M 350 | S
✱✱✱*Bull, Westgate, Peterborough. T:(0733) 61364. 114rm (107 ⇄)*

PETERHEAD
Grampian, *Aberdeenshire*
Map **VII** K5

Peterhead Craigewan Links, Peterhead (N side of town centre off A952)
T:(0779) 72149
Seaside course. 9-hole course for children. Societies welcome (Mon to F) by arrangement. 18 | 6070 yds | Par 70 | SSS 69
Visitors welcome, advisable to ☎
WE | B ✿ | L D prior arrangement |
⚐ ▼ 1100-1330 S, competition days | M 550
✱✱✱*Waterside Inn, Fraserburgh Rd.*

T:(0779) 71121. 80rm ⇄ ⏏ *Annexe: 40rm ⇄ ⏏*

PETERSFIELD
Hampshire
Map **II** C6

Petersfield The Heath, Petersfield (E side of town centre off A3)
T:(0730) 63725
Part heath, parkland course with a lake, and good views. Societies welcome by arrangement. 18 | 5422 yds | Par 68 | SSS 66
Visitors welcome | ⚬⚬ per round ∴ per day weekdays, ∴ per round ⠶ per day WE | B ✿ L | ⚐ ▼ ⚲ ✕ | TR before 1030 WE | ♪ | M 400 | S
✱✱✱*Spread Eagle, South St, Midhurst. T:(073081) 2211. 25rm ⇄ Annexe: 4rm*

PINNER
Greater London
Map **II** E3

Grims Dyke Oxhey Ln, Hatch End (3m N of Pinner on A4008)
T:01-428 4539
Parkland course. Societies welcome by arrangement. 18 | 5598 yds | Par 69 | SSS 67
Visitors welcome weekdays | WE BH with M | without M ∴ per day | with M ⚬⚬ per day | B ✿ | L prior arrangement (not Mon) | D ⚐ ▼ ⚲ | TR S pm, Sun | ♪ | M 575 | S ✕
✱✱✱*Grims Dyke, Old Redding, Harrow Weald. T:01-954 4227. 8rm ⇄ Annexe: 40rm ⇄*

Pinner Hill Southview Rd, Pinner Hill (2m NW of Pinner off A404)
T:01-866 0963
Wooded parkland course. 18 | 6260 yds | Par 72 | SSS 70
Visitors welcome, except Sun | without M ∴ per day ⠶ WE | L D B ✿ | ⚐ ▼ ⚲ | ✕ | TR Sun until 1200 | M 530 | S
✱✱✱*Grims Dyke, Old Redding, Harrow Weald. T:01-954 4227. 8rm ⇄ Annexe: 40rm ⇄*

PIRBRIGHT
Surrey
Map **II** D5

Goal Farm Gole Rd (1½m NW of Pirbright on B3012)
T:(04867) 3183/3205
Beautifully landscaped parkland 'Pay and Play' course with excellent greens. 9 | 1273 yds | Par 54 | SSS 54
Visitors welcome with M not S am |

PITLOCHRY
Tayside, *Perthshire*
Map **VII** G7

Pitlochry Pitlochry Estates Office, Pitlochry (N side of town off A924)
T:(0796) 2114
Societies welcome by arrangement (no parties before 0930). Reduced fees available for children. 18 | 5811 yds | Par 69 | SSS 68
Visitors welcome ☎ preferred | ✳ | B ✿ | L D (prior arrangement) | ⚐ ▼ ⚲ ✕ | ♪ | M 300 | S
✱✱*Burnside, West Moulin Rd, Pitlochry. T:(0796) 2203. 17rm (12 ⇄ 5 ⏏) Annexe: 6rm (1 ⇄ 1 ⏏)*

A varied and interesting heathland course with fine views and posing many problems. Its SSS permits few errors in its achievement.

SCORE CARD:

1	398		10	432
2	408		11	194
3	320		12	411
4	166		13	375
5	372		14	284
6	378		15	300
7	277		16	184
8	329		17	291
9	364		18	328

PLEASINGTON
Lancashire
Map **V** D6

Pleasington nr Blackburn (W side of village)
T:(0254) 22177
Society meetings by arrangement Mon W F. 18 | 6417 yds | Par 71 | SSS 71
Visitors welcome, ☎ restricted Tu Th WE BH | B ♛ | L (not Mon) | D prior
arrangement (not Th) | ⚒ ⅄ | TR Tu 1030-1400, Mon W F 1315-1400, Th
1315-1430 | ♖ | M 500 | S
★★★*Blackburn Moat House, Preston New Rd, Blackburn. T:(0254) 64441. 98rm* ⇥
♨ ♪
Plunging and rising across lovely moorland turf this course tests
judgement of distance through the air to greens of widely differing
levels. The 11th and 17th are testing holes.

B L ♛ | ↘ ⋈ | TR S am | M 400 | S
★★★★♨♨*Pennyhill Park, College Ride,*
Bagshot. T:(0276) 71774. 19rm ⇥
Annexe: 31rm ⇥

PLYMOUTH
Devon
Map **I** D7

Elfordleigh Plympton (8m NE of
Plymouth off B3416)
T:(0752) 336428
Charming saucer-shaped parkland
course with alternate tees for 18 holes.
Fairly hard walking. 9 | Par 67 |
SSS 67
Visitors welcome | B L ♛ D | ⚒ ⅄
↘ | ⋈ | TR S competition days &
monthly medals | M 300
★★★*Novotel Plymouth, Marsh Mills*
Rbt, 270 Plymouth Rd. T:(0752)
21422. 100rm ⇥ ♨

Staddon Heights Plymstock,
Plymouth (5m SE of Plymouth)
T:(0752) 42475
Seaside course can be windy, walking
easy. Societies welcome by
arrangement. 18 | 5861 yds | Par 68 |
SSS 68
Visitors welcome ⊠ | ∴ per day WE
| B ♛ L (not Mon) | D prior
arrangement (not Mon) | ⚒ ⅄ ↘ ⋈
| TR competition days | M 540 | S
★★★*Astor, Elliot St, The Hoe,*
Plymouth. T:(0752) 25511. 58rm (54
⇥ *4* ♨ *)*

POLMONT
Central, *Stirlingshire*
Map **VI** F2

Grangemouth Polmont Hill,
Polmont (On unclass rd, ½m N of
M9 Jct 4)
T:(0324) 711500
Windy parkland course. Testing holes:

3rd, 4th (par 4's), 5th (par 5), 7th (par
3) 216 yds over reservoir elevated
green, 8th, 9th, 18th (par 4's).
Societies welcome by arrangement. 18 |
6339 yds | Par 71 | SSS 71
Visitors welcome ☎ advisable | L ♛
D B | ⚒ ⅄ ⋈ | M 700 | S
★★★*Inchyra Grange, Grange Rd.*
T:(0324) 711911. 30rm ⇥ ♨

Polmont Manuelrigg Maddiston,
Polmont (E side of village off A803)
T:(0324) 711277
Parkland course, hilly with few
bunkers. Views of the River Forth and
Ochil Hills. 9 | 6088 yds | Par 72 |
SSS 69
Visitors welcome | without M ..
per day | L D B ♛ | ⚒ ⅄ ⋈ | TR
Sat 0830-1000 | M 130
★★★*Inchyra Grange, Grange Rd.*
T:(0324) 711911. 30rm ⇥ ♨

PONTARDAWE
West Glamorgan
Map **III** D8

Pontardawe Cefn Llan,
Pontardawe, Swansea (N side of
town centre off A4067)
T:(0792) 863118
Meadowland course situated on plateau
600 ft above sea level with good views
over Bristol Channel and Brecon
Beacons. 18 | 6061 yds | Par 70 |
SSS 69
Visitors welcome | without M ..
per day ∴ WE | B L ♛ | ⚒ ⅄ ⋈ |
TR WE and competition times.
Visitors can usually play between
1200-1400 ☎ advisable | M 280 | S
★★*Glyn Clydach House, Longford Rd,*
Neath Abbey. T:(0792) 813701. 8rm (1
⇥ *4* ♨ *)*

PONTEFRACT
West Yorkshire
Map **V** F6

Pontefract & District Park Ln,
Pontefract (1½m W of Pontefract on
B6134)
T:(0977) 792241
Parkland course. Societies welcome by
arrangement. 18 | 6227 yds | Par 72 |
SSS 70
Visitors welcome | ∴ per day WE |
B ♛ L D | ⚒ ⅄ | ⋈ | M 700 | S
★★★♨♨*Wentbridge House, Wentbridge.*
T:(0977) 620444. 17rm (10 ⇥ *7* ♨ *)*
Annexe: 3rm

PONTELAND
Northumberland
Map **VI** K6

Ponteland 53 Bell Villas, Ponteland,
Newcastle (½m E of Ponteland on
A696)
T:(0661) 22689
Open parkland course, good views and
testing golf. Societies welcome by
arrangement. 18 | 6512 yds | Par 72 |
SSS 71
Visitors welcome, with M only WE
BH ☎ preferred | ✳ | B ♛ L D | ⚒ ⅄
↘ | TR WE BH | M 1100 | S
★★★*Stakis Airport, Woolsington,*
Newcastle upon Tyne. T:(0661) 24911.
100rm ⇥ ♨

PONTYGWAITH
Mid Glamorgan
Map **I** F2

Rhondda Golf Club House,
Pontygwaith, Ferndale, Rhondda
(½m W of Pontygwaith off B4512)
T:(0443) 433204
Mountain course with good views. 18 |
6428 yds | Par 70 | SSS 70
Visitors welcome | B ♛ (not Mon) |
L D prior arrangement (not Mon) |
⚒ ⅄ ↘ | ⋈ prior arrangement | TR
WE Sun am & competitions | M 500
| S
★★*Bear, High St, Cowbridge.*
T:(04463) 4814. 21rm (18 ⇥*) Annexe:*
10rm ⇥

PONTYPOOL
Gwent
Map **I** G2

Pontypool Trevethin, Pontypool
(1½m N of Pontypool off A4043)
T:(04955) 3655
Undulating, hill-course with
magnificent views. 18 | 6058 yds |

Par 69 | *SSS 69*
Visitors welcome | without M **..**
per day **∴** WE | with M **..** per day |
B L ☙ D | ⚲ ⛳ | TR competition
days | M 500 | S
★★★*Hotel Commodore, Mill Ln,*
Llanyravon, Cwmbran. T:(06333)
4091. 60rm (47 ⇌ 11 ⚑)

PONTYPRIDD
Mid Glamorgan
Map I F2

Pontypridd Ty Gwyn, Pontypridd
(E side of town centre off A470)
T:(0443) 402359
Well-wooded mountain course with
springy turf. Good views of the
Rhondda Valleys and coast. Societies
welcome. 18 | *5650 yds* | *Par 69* |
SSS 68
Visitors welcome | **..** per day **∴**
WE | B ☙ L D | ⚲ ⛳ ⛌ |⊠
sometimes | **⅃** | M 480 | S
★★★*Crest, Westgate St, Cardiff.*
T:(0222) 388681. 160rm ⇌

POOLE
Dorset
Map I K6

Parkstone Links Rd, Parkstone,
Poole. (E side of town centre off
A35)
T:(0202) 707138
Heathland course. 18 | *6250 yds* |
Par 72 | *SSS 70*
Visitors welcome ⊠ | without M **::**
per day | with M **::** per day | B ☙ L
D | ⚲ ⛳ ⛌ | ⊠ (occasionally) | TR
until 0930, 1230-1400, after 1600 | ④
☎ | M 800 | S
★★★★*Hospitality Inn, The Quay,*
Poole. T:(0202) 671200. 68rm (65 ⇌ 3
⚑)

PORT BANNATYNE
Strathclyde, *Bute*
Map VI C2

Port Bannatyne Bannatyne Mains
Rd, Port Bannatyne, Bute (W side
of village off A844)
T:(0700) 2009
Seaside hill course with panoramic
views. Difficult hole: 4th par 3. 13 (18)
| *4589 yds* | *Par 67* | *SSS 63*
Visitors welcome | **..** per day | ⚲ |
M 155
★*St Ebba, 37 Mountstuart Rd,*
Craigmore. T:(0700) 2683. 15rm (1 ⇌
8 ⚑)

PORT ELLEN
Strathclyde, *Argyllshire*
Map VI A3

Machrie Hotel Machrie, Isle of Islay
(4m N of Port Ellen off A846)
T:(0496) 2310
Seaside course playable all year, many
blind holes. Testing holes: Heather hole
Par 4, Scotsman's Maiden Par 4. 18 |
6226 yds | *Par 71* | *SSS 69*
Visitors welcome | **∴** per day WE |
B ☙ | L D | ⛳ ⛌ | ⊠ | S
★*Dower House, Kildalton, Port Ellen.*
T:(0496) 2425. 7rm (6 ⇌ 1 ⚑)

PORT ERIN
Isle of Man
Map V A6

Rowany Rowany Dr, Port Erin (N
side of village off A32)
T:(0624) 834108
Undulating seaside course with testing
later holes. 18 | *5757 yds* | *Par 70* |
SSS 69
Visitors welcome | **..** per day WE |
B L D ☙ | ⛳ ⛌ | ⊠ by arrangement |
④ | TR competition days | M 350 | S
★★★*Golf Links, Fort Island,*
Castletown. T:(0624) 822201. 75rm
(26 ⇌ 20 ⚑)

PORT GLASGOW
Strathclyde, *Renfrewshire*
Map VI D2

Port Glasgow Devol Rd (1m S of
Port Glasgow)
T:(0475) 704181
A moorland course set on a hilltop
overlooking the Clyde, with
magnificent views from Dunbarton to
the Cowal hills. 18 | *5712 yds* | *Par 68* |
SSS 68
Visitors welcome **∴** per day | B ⛳ |
TR Sat until 1700 | ④ not after 1600
| M 300
★★★*Tontine, 6 Ardgowan Sq,*
Greenock. T:(0475) 23316. 32rm (20
⇌)

PORTHCAWL
Mid Glamorgan
Map I F2

Royal Porthcawl (1½m NW of town
centre)
T:(06571) 2251
This championship-standard
heathland/downland links course is
always in sight of the sea. 18 | *6605 yds*
| *Par 72* | *SSS 74*

Visitors welcome with M ⊠ | B L D
prior arrangement | ⚲ ⛳ ⛌ | TR
W, WE BH | ④ W, WE BH | M 815 |
S
★★*Maid of Sker, West Rd, Nottage,*
Porthcawl. T:(065671) 2172. 10rm ⇌

PORTHMADOG
Gwynedd
Map III D3

Porthmadog Morfa Bychan,
Porthmadog (1½m SW of
Porthmadog)
T:(0766) 2037
Seaside links, with easy walking and
good views. Societies welcome by
arrangement. 18 | *5900 yds* | *Par 68*
Visitors welcome | **..** per day WE |
B L ☙ | ⚲ ⛳ | M 150 | S
★★*Royal Sportsman, High St.*
T:(0766) 2015. 20rm (7 ⇌)

PORTMAHOMACK
Highland, *Ross and Cromarty*
Map VII G3

Tarbat Portmahomack, Tain (E side
of village)
T:(086287) 519
Easy seaside links course with
magnificent views. 9 | *4657 yds* |
Par 64 | *SSS 63*
Visitors welcome, no Sun play | **..**
per round | ⚲ | M 150
★★★*Royal, High St, Tain. T:(0862)*
2013. 25rm (15 ⇌ 7 ⚑)

PORTPATRICK
Dumfries and Galloway,
Wigtownshire
Map VI C6

Portpatrick (Dunskey) Portpatrick
(NW side of village)
T:(0776) 81725
Seaside course with some natural
hazards, easy walking, fine views. Also
9-hole par 3 course. Parties welcome
(July Aug) by arrangement. 18 |
5640 yds | *Par 71* | *SSS 67*
Visitors welcome | ✳ | B L ☙ high
tea (not Mon) | ⚲ ⛳ | ⊠ | ④ July-
Aug (until 1000) | S WE
0900-0930, 1300-1330 and
competition times | M 280 | S
★★★*Fernhill. T:(077681) 220. 11rm (7*
⇌) Annexe: 4rm (1 ⇌ 3 ⚑)

PORTSMOUTH
Hampshire
Map II B7

Great Salterns Public Course ➠

KEY
(IA1) atlas grid reference
T: telephone number
☎   advance letter/telephone
          call required
✉   introduction from own club
          sec/handicap
          certificate/club
          membership card required
..   low fees
∴   medium fees
::   high fees
*   green fees not confirmed for
          1987
B   light lunch
L   full lunch
♥   tea
D   dinner
♨   changing rooms/showers
Ⴘ   bar open mid-day and
          evenings
↘   clubs for hire
∞   partners may be found
④   restricted time for 4 balls
[TR]   times reserved for members
'ʃ   professional
[S]   well-stocked shop
M   member
Mon Tu W Th F S Sun
WE   weekend
BH   bank holiday

Eastern Rd, Southsea (NE of
Portsmouth town centre on A2030)
T:(0705) 664549
*Flat seaside course known as Great
Salterns. Easy walking. Testing 13th
hole approx 130 yds across lake (no
alternative). 18 | 5855 yds | Par 71 |
SSS 68*
Open to public | B L ♥ D | Ⴘ ↘ ∞ |
M 700 | [S]
★★★Hospitality Inn, South Pde,
Southsea. T:(0705) 731281. 111rm ⇆

PORTWRINKLE
Cornwall
Map I   D7

Whitsand Bay Hotel Portwrinkle,
Crafthole, nr Torpoint (E side of
village off B3247)
T:(0503) 30276
*Seaside course laid out on cliffs
overlooking Whitsand Bay. Easy
walking after 1st hole. The par 3 3rd
hole is well known. 18 | 5612 yds |
Par 68 | SSS 67*
Visitors welcome | * | B L ♥ D prior
arrangement | ♨ | Ⴘ variable | ↘ ∞
| [TR] ☎ for details | 'ʃ | M 300 | [S]

★*Whitsand Bay, Portwrinkle, Crafthole.*
T:(0503) 30276. 27rm (24 ⇆)

POTTERS BAR
Hertfordshire
Map II   E2

Potters Bar Darkes Ln, Potters Bar
(N side of town centre)
T:(0707) 52020
*Parkland course. 18 | 6273 yds | Par 71
| SSS 70*
Visitors welcome, with M only WE
| B L ♥ D | ♨ Ⴘ | [TR] W (Ladies
Day) | 'ʃ | M 450 | [S]
★★★Crest, Bignells Corner, South
Mimms. T:(0707) 43311. 120rm ⇆

POULTON-le-FYLDE
Lancashire
Map V   C6

Poulton le Fylde Breck Rd, Poulton
le Fylde (N side of town)
T:(0253) 893150
*Municipal parkland course, with easy
walking. 9 | 2979 yds | Par 35 | SSS 69*
Open to public | .. per round WE |
B L ♥ | ♨ Ⴘ ↘ ∞ | 'ʃ | M 220 | [S]
★★★★Imperial, North Prom. T:(0253)
23971. 159rm (146 ⇆ 13 ♨)

POWFOOT
Dumfries and Galloway,
Dumfriesshire
Map VI   F6
See entry for Cummertrees

POYNTON
Cheshire
Map V   E8

Davenport Worth Hall,
Middlewood Rd, Poynton (1m E of
Poynton off A523)
T:(0625) 877321
*Undulating parkland course. Extensive
view over Cheshire Plain from elevated
5th tee. Testing 17th hole par 4.
Societies by arrangement on Tu and
Th. 18 | 6006 yds | Par 69 | SSS 69*
Visitors welcome | without M ∴ per
day WE | with M .. per day | B ♥
(not Mon) | L D prior arrangement |
♨ Ⴘ ↘ | ∞ | [TR] WE | 'ʃ | M 600 | [S]
★★★Alma Lodge, 149 Buxton Rd,
.Stockport. T:061-483 4431. 70rm
(53⇆)

PRAA SANDS
Cornwall
Map I   A8

Praa Sands Germoe Crossroads,

Penzance (N side of village on
A394)
T:(0736) 763445
*A parkland course with sea views. 9 |
4036 yds | Par 60 | SSS 60*
Visitors welcome | B L ♥ D | ♨ Ⴘ
↘ | ∞ | [TR] Sun am, F eve | M 330 |
[S]
★♨♨Nansloe Manor Country, Meneage
Rd, Helston. T:(0326) 574691. 6rm (3
⇆)

PRESTATYN
Clwyd
Map III   E1

Prestatyn Marine Rd East,
Prestatyn (½m N of Prestatyn off
A548)
T:(07456) 4320
*Very flat seaside links exposed to stiff
breeze. Testing holes: 9th par 4 green
bounded on 3 sides by water; 10th par
4; 16th par 4. Juniors welcome. 18 |
6214 yds | Par 72 | SSS 70*
Visitors welcome | B L ♥ D | ♨ Ⴘ
↘ ∞ | [TR] S until 1530 | M 520 | [S]
★★Kimmel Manor, St Georges Rd,
Abergele. T:(0745) 822014. 22rm (20
⇆ 2 ♨)

St Melyd The Paddock, Meliden
Rd, Prestatyn (½m S of Prestatyn
on A547)
T:(07456) 4405
*Parkland course with good views of
mountains and Irish Sea. Testing 1st
hole 415 yds par 4. Society meetings by
arrangement. 9 (18 tee positions) |
5805 yds | Par 69 | SSS 68*
Visitors welcome | ✉ | * | B L ♥ D
(not Tu) | ♨ | Ⴘ (not Tu) | [TR]
competition days (usually WE) |
M 580 | [S]
★★★Oriel House, Upper Denbigh Rd,
St Asaph. T:(0745) 582716. 18rm (12
⇆ 6 ♨)

PRESTBURY
Cheshire
Map III   H2

Prestbury Macclesfield Rd,
Prestbury (S side of village off
A538)
T:(0625) 828241
*Rather strenuous parkland course,
undulating, with many plateau greens.
Good views. Society meetings by
arrangement. 18 | 6359 yds | Par 71 |
SSS 71*
Visitors welcome ☎, only with M
WE BH | * | B L ♥ D | ♨ Ⴘ | [TR] Tu

0930-1400, W 1200-1600 | ♪ | M 415 |
Ⓢ
★★★*Mottram Hall, Mottram St
Andrew. T:(0625) 828135. 72rm (69
⇆ 3 ⌘)*

PRESTON
Lancashire
Map **V** C6

Ashton & Lea Tudor Ave, Lea (3m
W of Preston on A5085)
T:(0772) 726480

PRESTON
Lancashire
Map **V** C6

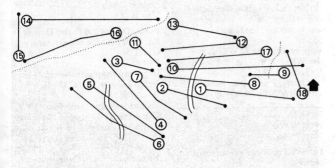

Penwortham Blundell Ln, Penwortham, Preston
(W side of town centre off A59)
T:(0772) 744630
*Society meetings by arrangement. No children under 11. 18 | 5915 yds | Par 69 |
SSS 68*
Visitors welcome, | without M ∴ per day WE | with M .. per day WE | B L ♥
D | ⚥ Υ | TR before 1000 and 1230-1400 | M 875 | Ⓢ
★★★*Tickled Trout, Preston New Rd, Samlesbury, Preston. T:(077 477) 671. 66rm
⇆*
A progressive golf club set close to the bank of the River Ribble. The
course has tree-lined fairways, excellent greens, and provides easy
walking. Testing holes include the 178-yd par 3 3rd, the 480-yd par
5 6th, and the 398-yd par 4 16th.

PRESTON
Lancashire
Map **V** C6

Preston Fulwood Hall Ln, Fulwood, Preston (N side of town centre)
T:(0772) 700011
Societies welcome by arrangement. 18 | 6267 yds | Par 71 | SSS 70
Visitors welcome ☎ preferable | without M ∴ per day ∷ WE | with M .. per
day WE | B L ♥ D | ⚥ Υ | TR 1300 to 1400 daily | ♪ | M 500 | Ⓢ
★★★*Broughton Park, Garstang Rd, Broughton. T:(0772) 864087. 63rm (52 ⇆ 11
⌘)*
Pleasant inland golf at this course set in very agreeable countryside.
There is a well-balanced selection of holes undulating amongst
groups of trees and not requiring great length. The course begins
with a testing short hole reminiscent of the 'Postage Stamp' at Royal
Troon.

*Semi-parkland course offering pleasant
walks and some testing holes. 18 |
6286 yds | Par 71 | SSS 70*
Visitors welcome | restricted Th WE
| ∴ per day | B L ♥ D | ⚥ Υ ∿ ⋈ |
TR 0815-0915, 1215-1315 and
competitions | ♪ | M 600 | Ⓢ
★★★*Crest, The Ringway. T:(0772)
59411. 126rm ⇆*

Fishwick Hall Glenluce Dr,
Farringdon Park, Preston (E side of
town centre off A677)
T:(0772) 798300
*Meadowland course situated
overlooking River Ribble. Natural
hazards. 18 | 6203 yds | Par 71 |
SSS 70*
Visitors welcome | ＊ | B ♥ L D | ⚥ |
Υ (except Mon) | ∿ ♪ ⋈ prior
arrangement | ④ Sun am | TR
competitions | M 350 | Ⓢ
★★★*Crest, The Ringway. T:(0772)
59411. 126rm ⇆*

Ingol Tanterton Hall Rd, Ingol (3m
NW of Preston off B5411)
T:(0772) 734556
*Long, high course with natural water
hazards. 18 | 6345 yds | Par 72 |
SSS 71*
Visitors welcome .. per day ∴ WE
| B L D ♥ | ⚥ Υ ∿ | ⋈ usually | ♪
| M 500 | Ⓢ
★★★*Crest, The Ringway, Preston.
T:(0772) 59411. 126rm ⇆*

PRESTONPANS
Lothian, *East Lothian*
Map **VI** G2

Royal Musselburgh Prestongrange
House, Prestonpans (W side of
town off A198)
T:(0875) 276
*Parkland course. No facilities for
children. 18 | 6250 yds | Par 70 |
SSS 70*
Visitors welcome | with M only WE
| ☎ booking essential | B L (not Tu)
♥ D prior arrangement (not Tu) | ⚥
Υ | M 700 | Ⓢ
★★*Kilspindie House, Main St,
Aberlady. T:(08757) 319. 12rm (8 ⇆ 4
⌘)*

PRESTWICH
Greater Manchester
Map **V** D7

Prestwich Hilton Ln, Prestwich (N
side of town centre on A6044)
T:061-773 2544 ➡

Parkland course, near to Manchester city centre. Societies welcome. 18 | 4712 yds | Par 64 | SSS 63
Visitors welcome | •• per day ∴ WE | B L ☕ D | ⛳ 🍸 ⚑ | [TR] WE, Tu Ladies Day | [S]
★★*Racecourse, Littleton Rd, Salford. T:061-792 1420. 20rm (5 ⇌)*

PRESTWICK
Strathclyde, *Ayrshire*
Map **VI** D4

Prestwick 2 Links Rd, Prestwick (In town centre off A79)
T:(0292) 77404
Seaside links with natural hazards, fine views. 18 | 6544 yds | Par 71 | SSS 72
Visitors welcome, ✉ ☎ | ∷ per day | ☕ | B L | D prior arrangement for parties only | ⛳ 🍸 ⚑ | [TR] 0900-1000, 1230-1500 daily | 🔑 | M 425 | [S]
★*Auchencoyle, 13 Links Rd, Prestwick. T:(0292) 78316. 6rm (3 🏨)*

Prestwick St Cuthbert East Rd, Prestwick (SE side of town off A79)
T:(0292) 77107
Parkland course with easy walking, natural hazards and sometimes windy. 18 | 6470 yds | Par 71 | SSS 71
Visitors welcome, with M only WE | without M ∴ per day | with M •• per day WE | B L ☕ D | ⛳ 🍸 | [TR] WE BH | M 500
★★*St. Nicholas, 41 Ayr Rd. T:(0292) 79568. 16rm (7 🏨)*

Prestwick St Nicholas Grangemuir Rd, Prestwick (S side of town off A79)
T:(0292) 77608
Seaside course with whins, heather and tight fairways. It provides easy walking and has an unrestricted view of Firth of Clyde. 18 | 5864 yds | Par 68 | SSS 68
Visitors welcome | without M ∷ per day WE | B L ☕ (not Mon) | ⛳ 🍸 ⚑ | [TR] WE | 🔑 | M 700 | [S]
★★*Parkstone, Esplanade, Prestwick. T:(0292) 77286. 28rm (6 ⇌ 9 🏨)*

PRINCES RISBOROUGH
Buckinghamshire
Map **II** C2

Whiteleaf Whiteleaf (1¼m NE of Princes Risborough off A4010)
T:(08444) 3097
Short parkland course requiring great accuracy, fine views. 9 | 5391 yds | Par 66 | SSS 66
Visitors welcome | without M ∴ per day | with M ∴ per day WE | B (not Mon) | L ☕ D prior arrangement (not Mon) | ⛳ 🍸 | ④ not Tu | [TR] Tu (Ladies Day) | 🔑 | M 285 | [S]
❀○○○*Bell, Aston Clinton. T:(0296) 630252. 21rm ⇌*

PRUDHOE
Northumberland
Map **VI** K6

Prudhoe Eastwood Pk, Prudhoe (E side of town centre off A695)
T:(0661) 32466
Parkland course with natural hazards, easy walking. Societies welcome by arrangement. 18 | 5812 yds | Par 69 | SSS 68
Visitors welcome ☎ WE | •• per day WE | B L ☕ D | ⛳ 🍸 | ⋈ | ④ [TR] WE | M 390 | [S]
★★*County, Priestpopple, Hexham. T:(0434) 602030. 10rm (4 🏨)*

PUDSEY
West Yorkshire
Map **V** F6

Fulneck Pudsey (S side of town centre)
T:(0532) 565191
Picturesque hilly parkland course. 9 | 5432 yds | Par 66 | SSS 67
Visitors welcome, restricted W, with M only WE BH | ⛳ 🍸 evening | [TR] competition days | 🔑 | M 160
★★★*Novotel Bradford, Merrydale Rd, Bradford. T:(0274) 683683. 136rm ⇌*

Woodhall Hills Calverley, Pudsey (2½m NW of Pudsey off A647)
T:(0532) 564771
Meadowland course, prevailing SW winds, fairly hard walking. Testing holes: 8th 377 yds (par 4), 14th 233 yds (par 3). Societies welcome by arrangement. 18 | 6200 yds | Par 70 | SSS 69
Visitors welcome | ∴ per day WE | •• per round per day | ∴ per round WE | B L ☕ (not Mon) | D (not Mon Tu W) | ⛳ ⚑ ⋈ | 🍸 | 🔑 | M 300 | [S]
★★★★*Stakis Norfolk Gardens, Hall Ings, Bradford. T:(0274) 734734. 126rm ⇌*

PULBOROUGH
West Sussex
Map **II** D6

West Sussex Hurston Ln, Pulborough (2m SE of Pulborough off A283)
T:(07982) 2563
Heathland course. Societies welcome by arrangement. No children allowed. 18 | 6156 yds | Par 68 | SSS 70
Visitors welcome ✉, ☎ (48 hours notice) | without M ∷ per day | with M •• per day ∴ WE | ☕ B L | ⛳ 🍸 | [TR] Tu | 🔑 | M 780 | [S]
★★*Roundabout, Monkmead Ln, West Chiltington. T:(07983) 3838. 21rm (18 ⇌ 3 🏨)*

PURLEY
Greater London
Map **II** F4

Purley Downs 106 Purley Downs Rd, Purley (E side of town centre off A235)
T:01-657 8347
Hilly downland course. Notable holes are 6th and 12th. 18 | 6237 yds | Par 70 | SSS 70
Visitors welcome | with M only WE ☎ preferred | without M ∷ per day | with M •• per day | B ☕ L D | ⛳ 🍸 | [TR] WE, Tu (Ladies Day) | 🔑 | M 650 | [S]
★★★*Croydon Court, Purley Way, Croydon. T:01-688 5185. 86rm ⇌*

PUTTENHAM
Surrey
Map **II** D5

Puttenham nr Guildford (1m SE of Puttenham on B3000)
T:(0483) 810498
Picturesque tree-lined heathland course offering testing golf, easy walking. Societies welcome (W and Th) by arrangement. 18 | 5367 yds | Par 69 | SSS 66
Visitors welcome | without M ∴ per day WE | with M •• per day WE | B L ☕ prior arrangement D prior arrangement | ⛳ 🍸 ⚑ | [TR] WE | M 500 | [S]
★★★*Hog's Back, Hog's Back, Seale. T:(02518) 2345. 50rm ⇌ 🏨*

PWLLHELI
Gwynedd
Map **III** C3

Pwllheli Golf Rd, Pwllheli (½m SW of Pwllheli off A497)
T:(0758) 612520
Easy walking on flat seaside course with outstanding views of Snowdon, Cader Idris and Cardigan Bay. Societies welcome by arrangement. 18 | 6110 yds

| Par 69 | SSS 69
Visitors welcome | .. per day ∴
WE | B ☙ L D | ⚓ ⅄ | ⋈ | TR Tu,
Th and S 1245-1400, Sun 0830-0930 |
ℐ | M 760 | Ⓢ
★Caeau Capel, Rhodfar Mor, Nefyn.
T:(0758) 720240. 23rm (6 ⇄)

PYECOMBE
West Sussex
Map II E6

Pyecombe Clayton Hill, Pyecombe
(E side of village on A273)
T:(07918) 5372
Typical downland course on the inland
side of the South Downs. 18 | 6207 yds
| Par 71 | SSS 70
Visitors welcome, restricted WE BH
| without M ∴ per day WE | with
M .. per round WE | B ☙ | L
(except Th and WE) D (except Tu,
Th and WE) | ⚓ ⅄ ⤢ | TR Mon-F
before 0915, S BH before 1000, Sun
before 1100 | ④ | ☎ for details | ℐ |
M 550 | Ⓢ
★★★Courtlands, 22 The Drive, Hove.
T:(0273) 731055. 55rm (44 ⇄ 6 ⓕ)
Annexe: 5rm ⇄

PYLE
Mid Glamorgan
Map I F2

Pyle & Kenfig Waun-Y-Mer (S of
Pyle off A4229)
T:(065671) 3093
Links course, with sand-dunes. Easy
walking. Often windy. Society
meetings by arrangement. 18 |
6640 yds | Par 71 | SSS 73
Visitors welcome, only with M WE
BH | :: per day WE | B L ☙ D | ⚓
⅄ ⤢ | ⋈ | ℐ | M 835 | Ⓢ
★★★Seabank, The Promenade,
Porthcawl. T:(065671) 2261. 64rm (42
⇄)

RADCLIFFE-ON-TRENT
Nottinghamshire
Map IV A3

Radcliffe on Trent Cropwell Rd
(1m SE of Radcliffe on Trent off
A52)
T:(06073) 3125
Parkland course with 3 good finishing
holes: 16th 426 yds (par 4), 17th
181 yds through spinney (par 3), 18th
336 yds dog leg (par 4). 18 | 6423 yds |
Par 70 | SSS 71
Visitors welcome ☎, restricted Tu |
B ☙ | L D prior arrangement | ⚓ ⅄

RADLETT
Hertfordshire
Map II E2

Porter Park Shenley Hill, Radlett (NE side of village off A5183)
T:(092 76) 4366
18 | 6313 yds | Par 70 | SSS 70
Visitors welcome, with M only WE | without M :: per day | with M .. per day
| ☙ B L | D prior arrangement | ⚓ ⅄ | ④ | TR ☎ for details | ℐ | M 700 | Ⓢ
★★★Noke Thistle, Watford Rd. T:(0727) 54252. 57rm ⇄ ⓕ
A splendid parkland course with fine trees, lush grass and easy
walking. The holes are all different and interesting — on many
accuracy of shot to the green is of paramount importance.

⤢ | TR Tu ④ (Ladies) | ⋈ | ℐ |
M 600 | Ⓢ
★★Edwalton Hall, Edwalton,
Nottingham. T:(0602) 231116. 12rm
(2 ⇄ 1 ⓕ)

RAMSEY
Cambridgeshire
Map IV D5

Ramsey 4 Abbey Terrace, Ramsey
(S side of village)
T:(0487) 812600, Huntingdon
Parkland course with brook hazards.
Societies welcome by arrangement. 18 |
6136 yds | Par 71 | SSS 70
Visitors welcome, restricted
competition days | without M ∴
per day :: WE | with M .. per day
WE | ☙ | B (not Sun BH) | L D prior
arrangement | ⚓ ⅄ | ④ until
1030 medal days | TR WE BH until
1030 | ℐ | M 620 | Ⓢ
★★★Old Bridge, Huntingdon.
T:(0480) 52681. 22rm (21 ⇄ 1 ⓕ)

RAMSEY
Isle of Man
Map V B5

Ramsey Brookfield, Ramsey (SW
side of town)
T:(0624) 812244
Parkland course, with easy walking.
Windy. Good views. Testing holes: 1st
par 5; 18th par 3. 18 | 6003 yds |
Par 70 | SSS 69
Visitors welcome | .. per day WE |
B L ☙ D prior arrangement (not Th)
| ⚓ ⅄ ⤢ ⋈ | ④ ☎ | TR until 1000 |
ℐ | M 850 | Ⓢ
★Woodbourne, Alexander Dr, Douglas.
T:(0624) 21766. 12rm

RATHO
Lothian, Midlothian
Map VI F2

Ratho Park Ratho, Newbridge,
Midlothian (¾m E of Ratho, N of

A71)
T:031-333 1406
Undulating parkland course, easy
walking. Societies welcome by
arrangement. 18 | 6028 yds | Par 71 |
SSS 69
Visitors welcome | without M ∴ per
day :: WE | with M .. per round
WE | B L ☙ (not F) | D prior
arrangement (not F) | ⚓ ⅄ | ⤢ ⋈
(possible) | ④ ☎ for details | TR ☎
| M 600 | Ⓢ
★★★Post House, Corstorphine Rd,
Edinburgh. T:031-334 8221. 207rm ⇄

RAWDON
West Yorkshire
Map V F6

Rawdon Golf & Lawn Tennis Club
Buckstone Drive, Rawdon (S side of
town off A65)
T:(0532) 506040
Undulating parkland course. Grass and
hard tennis courts. 9 | 5902 yds |
Par 72 | SSS 68
Visitors welcome, with M only WE
| B ☙ L D (not Mon) | ⅄ ⤢ | M 500
| Ⓢ
★★★Post House, Otley Rd, Bramhope.
T:(0532) 842911. 122rm ⇄

RAWMARSH
South Yorkshire
Map V F7

Wath Abdy, nr Rotherham (2½m N
of Rawmarsh off A633)
T:(0709) 878677
Parkland course, not easy in spite of
short length, 17th hole a difficult
240 yds with narrow driving area.
Societies welcome by arrangement (not
WE). 9 | 5606 yds | Par 66 | SSS 67
Visitors welcome, with M only WE |
B L prior arrangement | ⚓ ⤢ | ⅄
(evening only) | ⋈ | ④ Sat | ℐ | TR
competitions, F (ladies day) | M 200
| Ⓢ   ⮕

RAMSGATE
Kent
Map II K4

St Augustine's Cottington Rd, Cliffsend, Ramsgate (3m SW of Ramsgate off A256)
T:(0843) 590333
18 | 5138 yds | Par 69 | SSS 65
Visitors welcome ✉ ☎ | without M ∴ per day | with M .. per day | B L ♟ | D prior arrangement | ⚲ ⛨ | ⋈ (possibly) | ⟨TR⟩ Sun until 1100 | M 650 | ⟨S⟩
★★*Savoy, Grange Rd. T:(0843) 592637. 14rm (1 ⇄ 2 ⋔). Annexe: 11rm (2 ⇄ 1 ⋔)*
A comfortably flat course in this famous bracing Championship area of Kent. Neither as long nor as difficult as its lordly neighbours, St Augustine's will nonetheless extend most golfers. Dykes run across the course.

READING
Berkshire
Map II C4

Calcot Park Bath Rd, Calcot (2½m W of Reading, on A4)
T:(0734) 427124
18 | 6283 yds | Par 70 | SSS 70
Visitors welcome, except BH WE | ☎ | * | B L ♟ (not Mon) | ⚲ | ⟨TR⟩ competition days | ⛨ | M 700 | ⟨S⟩
★★★*Copper Inn, Pangbourne. T:(07357) 2244. 21rm ⇄*
A delightfully sporting parkland course just outside the town. Hazards include a lake and many trees. The 6th is the longest, 497 yards par 5, with tee-shot hit downhill over cross-bunkers to a well-guarded green. The 13th (188 yards) requires a big carry over a gully to a plateau green.

★★*Brentwood, Moorgate Rd, Rotherham. T:(0709) 382772. 14rm (3 ⇄ 5 ⋔) Annexe: 20rm (16 ⇄ 4 ⋔)*

READING
Berkshire
Map II C4

Reading Kidmore End Rd, Emmer Green, Reading (2m N of Reading off B481)
T:(0734) 472909
Meadowland course. Societies welcome by arrangement. 18 | 6204 yds | Par 70 | SSS 69
Visitors welcome, restricted WE BH | ☎ | without M ∷ per day | with M .. per day | ♟ (not Mon) | B L D prior arrangement (not Mon) | ⚲ ⛨ | M 650 | ⟨S⟩
★★★★*Ramada, Oxford Rd. T:(0734) 598753. 200rm ⇄ ⋔*

REAY
Highland, *Caithness*
Map VII G1

Reay Reay (½m E of Reay off A836)
T:(084781) 288
Picturesque seaside links with natural hazards. Junior tees. Testing 1st, 4th,

6th, 7th, 14th holes. 18 | 5865 yds | Par 69 | SSS 68
Visitors welcome | .. per day | ⚲ ⋈ sometimes | ⛨ (evng) | ⟨TR⟩ competition days | M 300
★★*Pentland, Princes St, Thurso. T:(0847) 63202. 57rm (17 ⇄ 9 ⋔)*

REDBOURN
Hertfordshire
Map II D2

Redbourn Kinsbourne Green Lane, Redbourn (1m N of Redbourn off A5183)
T:(058 285) 3493, nr St Albans
Testing parkland course (5 par 3's over 400 yds). Also short 9-hole course. Societies welcome by arrangement. 18(9) | 6407(1360) yds | Par 70(27) | SSS 71
Visitors welcome, restricted WE BH | ☎ advisable | B L ♟ | D prior arrangement | ⚲ ⛨ ⟍ | ⋈ ⟨TR⟩ WE | ⛨ | ⟨S⟩
★★★★*Harpenden Moat House, 18 Southdown Rd, Harpenden. T:(05827) 64111. 16rm (13 ⇄ 3 ⋔) Annexe: 30rm ⇄*

REDCAR
Cleveland
Map V G3

Wilton Wilton Castle, Redcar (3m W of Redcar on A174)
T:(0642) 465265
Parkland course with some fine views. 18 | 6104 yds | Par 70 | SSS 69
Visitors welcome, restricted S | without M ∴ per day | with M .. per day WE | B D | L ♟ | ⚲ ⛨ | ⟨TR⟩ S (all day) Sun (until 0900) | ⛨ | M 750
★★★*Royal York, Coatham Rd, Redcar. T:(0642) 486221. 51rm (50 ⇄ 1 ⋔)*

REDDITCH
Hereford and Worcester
Map III J6

Abbey Park Golf and Country Club Dagnell End Rd, Redditch (1¼m N of Redditch off A441, on B4101)
T:(0527) 63918
A newly-built parkland course with rolling fairways. A Site of Special Scientific Interest, the course includes two fly-fishing lakes and is pleasant to play. Societies are welcome. 18 | 6300 yds | Par 71 | SSS 71
Visitors welcome, ☎ WE | .. per day WE | Refreshments available when hotel/clubhouse opens early 1987 | ⚲ ⛨ early 1987 | ⟍ ⋈ | ⛨ | ⟨S⟩
★★★*Southcrest, Pool Bank, Redditch. T:(0527) 41511. 34rm (29 ⇄ 5 ⋔)*

Pitcheroak Plymouth Rd, Redditch (SW side of town centre off A448)
T:(0257) 41064
Woodland course, hilly in places. 9 | 4584 yds | Par 66 | SSS 62
Visitors welcome | ⚲ ⛨ ⟍ | B L D ♟ | ⋈ | ⛨ | M 120 | ⟨S⟩
★★★*Southcrest, Pool Bank, Redditch. T:(0527) 41511. 34rm (29 ⇄ 5 ⋔)*

Redditch Lower Grinsty Ln, Callow Hill, Redditch (2m SW of Redditch)
T:(0527) 43309
Parkland course, the hazards including woods, ditches and large ponds. The par 4 14th is testing hole. 18 | 6671 yds | Par 72 | SSS 72
Visitors welcome ✉ ☎ advisable | without M ∴ per day | with M .. per day | B ♟ D (not Mon) | L prior arrangement (not Mon) | ⚲ ⛨ ⟍ | ⋈ | ⛨ | M 733 | ⟨S⟩
★★★*Perry Hall, Kidderminster Rd,*

Bromsgrove. T:(0527) 31976 due to change to 579976. 53rm (36 ⇌ 17 ⋔)

REDHILL
Surrey
Map **II** E5

Redhill & Reigate Pendleton Rd, Redhill (1m S of Redhill on A23)
T:(07372) 44626
Parkland course. Societies welcome by arrangement. 18 | 5193 yds | Par 67 | SSS 65
Visitors welcome restricted WE (am) | .. per day WE | B ☛ | L D prior arrangement (not Mon) | ⚥ Υ ∖ | ⟨TR⟩WE (0800-1030) | M 400 | ⟨S⟩
★★*Reigate Manor, Reigate Hill, Reigate. T:(07372) 40125. 15rm (2 ⇌ 13 ⋔) Annexe: 12rm (11 ⇌ 1 ⋔)*

REIGATE
Surrey
Map **II** E5

Reigate Heath Reigate (1½m W of Reigate off A25)
T:(07372) 42610
Heathland course. Societies (up to 30) welcome by arrangement. 9(14 tees) | 5554 yds | Par 67 | SSS 67
Visitors welcome, restricted match and competition days, with M only Sun BH | ☎ advisable | without M ∴ per day ∷ S | with M .. per day WE | D prior arrangement | B L ☛ | ⚥ Υ | ⟨TR⟩Sun am | ④ ☎ | M 300 | ⟨S⟩
★★*Reigate Manor, Reigate Hill. T:(07372) 40125. 15rm (2 ⇌ 13 ⋔) Annexe: 12rm (11 ⇌ 1 ⋔)*

RENFREW
Strathclyde, *Renfrewshire*
Map **VI** D2

Renfrew Blythswood Estate, Inchinnan Rd (¾m W of Renfrew off A8)
T:041-886 6692
Tree-lined parkland course. Societies welcome by arrangement. 18 | 6818 yds | Par 72 | SSS 73
Visitors welcome with M only or ⊠ | ∴ per round ∷ per day | B L ☛ D prior arrangement | ⚥ Υ | M 700 | ⟨S⟩
★★★*Stakis Normandy, Inchinan Rd. T:041-886 4100. 142rm ⇌ ⋔*

RENISHAW
Derbyshire
Map **III** K2

Renishaw Park Golf House, Renishaw, Sheffield (½m NW of Renishaw on A616)
T:(0246) 432044
Part parkland and part meadowland with easy walking. 18 | 6253 yds | Par 71 | SSS 70
Visitors welcome restricted Th WE | ⟨TR⟩WE Sat & Sun until 1430 | ☎ advisable | B L D prior arrangement (not F) | ☛ (not F) | ⚥ Υ | ⊠ prior arrangement | Ɉ | M 350 | ⟨S⟩
★★*Royal Victoria, Victoria Station Rd, Sheffield. T:(0742) 768822. 66rm (37 ⇌ ⋔)*

RHOSNEIGR
Gwynedd
Map **III** C2

Anglesey Station Rd (NE side of village, on A4080)
T:(0407) 810219
Seaside course with easy walking. Societies by arrangement. 18 | 5700 yds | Par 69 | SSS 69
Visitors welcome | B not Mon in winter | L ☛ D | ⚥ Υ ∖ | ⊠ | ④ 0900-1000, 1400-1500 | Ɉ | M 400 | ⟨S⟩
★★★*Trearddur Bay, Trearddur Bay. T:(0407) 860301. 28rm (19 ⇌)*

RHOS-ON-SEA
Gwynedd
Map **III** E1

Rhos on Sea Penryhn Bay, Llandudno (½m W of Rhos-on-Sea off A546)
T:(0492) 49641
Seaside course, with easy walking and panoramic views. Societies welcome by arrangement. 18 | 6064 yds | Par 69 | SSS 69
Visitors welcome | B ☛ D prior

arrangement | ⚥ Υ ∖ ⊠ | M 300 | ⟨S⟩
★★★*Gogarth Abbey, West Shore, Llandudno. T:(0492) 76211. 41rm (30 ⇌ 5 ⋔)*

RHUDDLAN
Clwyd
Map **III** E2

Rhuddlan Rhuddlan (E side of town on A547)
T:(0745) 590217, Rhyl
Parkland course with easy walking and both artificial and natural hazards. 18 | 6038 yds | Par 70 | SSS 69
Visitors welcome | without M ∴ per day WE | B L ☛ D prior arrangement | ⚥ Υ ⊠ ∖ | ⟨TR⟩Sun & Tu am (ladies) (☎ for times) | Ɉ | M 950 | ⟨S⟩
★★★*Oriel House, Upper Denbigh Rd, St Asaph. T:(0745) 582716. 18rm (12 ⇌ 6 ⋔)*

RHYL
Clwyd
Map **III** E1

Rhyl Coast Rd, Rhyl (1m E of Rhyl on A548)
T:(0745) 53171
Seaside course. 9 | 3109 yds | Par 35 | SSS 70
Visitors welcome, restricted Sun summer, advisable to check | .. per day | ☛ B L Υ | D prior arrangement | M 350 | ⟨S⟩ ∖
★★★*Oriel House, Upper Denbigh Rd, St. Asaph. T:(0745) 582716. 18rm (12 ⇌ 6 ⋔)*

RICHMOND
North Yorkshire
Map **V** F4 ➽

RICHMOND
Greater London
Map **II** E4

Richmond Sudbrook Park, Richmond (1½m S of Richmond off A307)
T:01-940 4351
Societies welcome by arrangement. 18 | 6020 yds | Par 70 | SSS 69
Visitors welcome | ❋ | B ☛ Υ | D for members or visiting parties prior arrangement | ⚥ Ɉ | ⟨S⟩
★★★Richmond Hill, 146-150 Richmond Hill, Richmond. T:01-940 2247. 125rm (110 ⇌ 4 ⋔)
A beautiful and historic wooded, parkland course on the edge of Richmond Park, with six par 3 holes. The 4th is often described as the best short hole in the south of England. Low scores are uncommon because cunningly sited trees call for great accuracy. The clubhouse is one of the most distinguished small Georgian mansions in England.

Royal Mid-Surrey Old Deer Park, Richmond (½m N of Richmond off A316)
T:01-940 1894
*Societies welcome (Tu to F) by arrangement. 36 | 6331 yds (5446) | Par 69 |
SSS 70(71)*
Visitors welcome ⊠ | but with M only WE | ∷ per day and per round | B | L
(not Mon) | D societies only ♨ | ⚲ ↘ | ④ prior reference to secretary | TR
early mornings comp days ☎ | ④ ☎ | M 700 | S
***Richmond Hill*, 146-150 Richmond Hill, Richmond. T:01-940 2247. *125rm
(110 ⇌ 4 ▥)*
A long playing parkland course. The flat fairways are cleverly
bunkered. The 18th provides an exceptionally good par 4 finish
with a huge bunker before the green to catch the not quite perfect
long second.

Richmond Bend Hagg, Richmond
(¾m N of Richmond)
T:(0748) 2457
*Parkland course. 18 | 5704 yds | Par 70
| SSS 68*
Visitors welcome | B L ♨ D | ⚲ | ♟
(evng only) | TR 0800-0900,
1200-1400 Sun | M 450 | S
★★*King's Head*, Market Sq. T:(0748)
2311. *25rm (17 ⇌)*

RICKMANSWORTH
Hertfordshire
Map **II**   D2

Moor Park (1½m SE of

Rickmansworth off A4145)
T:(0923) 773146
*Two parkland courses. Societies
welcome by arrangement. 18(18) |
6675(High) 5815(West) yds |
Par 72(69) | SSS 72(68)*
Visitors welcome ☎ preferred |
restricted WE BH | without M ∷
per day WE | with M ∴ per day WE
| B L ♨ | ♟ ⚲ ↘ ⋈ | ℑ | M 1800 | S
★★★*Ladbroke*, Elton Way, Watford by-
Pass. T:(0923) 35881. *155rm ⇌*

RIDDLESDEN
West Yorkshire
Map **V**   E6

Riddlesden Howdenrough,
Riddlesden, Keighley (1m NW of
Riddlesden)
T:(0535) 602148
*Undulating moorland course with two
quarry hazards, prevailing W winds,
some hard walking, beautiful views.
Short par 3 course with some very
testing holes. 18 | 4247 yds | Par 62 |
SSS 61*
Visitors welcome | ‥ per day WE |
B (WE only) | ♨ | ⚲ | ♟ (not winter
evng) | ⋈ (possible some WE) | TR
Sun before 1000 | M 220
★★*Beeches*, Bradford Rd, Keighley.
T:(0535) 607227. *10rm (2 ⇌) Annexe:
14rm (9 ▥)*

RIPON
North Yorkshire
Map **V**   F5

Ripon City Palace Rd, Ripon (1m N
of Ripon on A6108)
T:(0765) 3640
*Hard walking on parkland course; 2
testing par threes at 5th and 7th. 9 |
5752 yds | Par 70 | SSS 68*
Visitors welcome | without M ‥
per day ∴ WE BH | with M ‥ per
day | ♨ | ⚲ | ♟ WE, not mid-week

mornings except Th \ | ⋈ | TR 🕾
| ④ competition days | M 350 | S
★★★*Ripon Spa, Park St. T:(0765)*
2172. 41rm (35 ⇄ 6 🛏)

RISHTON
Lancashire
Map **V**   D6

Rishton Eachill Links, Rishton,
Blackburn (S side of town off A678)
T:(0254) 884442
Moorland course recovering from recent
dissection by the M65. 9 | 5568 yds |
Par 70 | SSS 69
Visitors welcome | ⚲ | ⅄ | ⋈
(sometimes) | M 140
★★★*Blackburn Moat House, Preston*
New Rd, Blackburn. T:(0254) 64441.
98rm ⇄

ROCHDALE
Greater Manchester
Map **V**   E7

Rochdale The Clubhouse,
Edenfield Road, Bagslate, Rochdale
(1¾m W of Rochdale on A680)
T:(0706) 46024
Parkland course with enjoyable golf. 18
| 5981 yds | Par 70 | SSS 69

Visitors welcome restricted
competition days. Tu May to
August: S Th March to October | ✳ |
B ♟ | L D prior arrangement (not
Mon) | ⚲ ⅄ | ⅃ | TR 1200-1400 ④
🕾 | M 625 | S
★★*Midway, Manchester Rd,*
Castleton. T:(0706) 32881. 30rm (2 ⇄
20 🛏)

Springfield Park 11 Marland Fold,
Rochdale (1½m SW of Rochdale off
A58)
T:(0706) 49801
Parkland-moorland course situated in a
valley. The River Roch adds an extra
hazard to the course. 18 | 5209 yds |
Par 67 | SSS 66
Visitors welcome | ⚬⚬ per round | \
⋈ | M 200 | S
★★*Midway, Manchester Rd,*
Castleton. T:(0706) 32881. 30rm (2 ⇄
20 🛏)

ROCHFORD
Essex
Map **II**   H3

Rochford Hundred Hall Rd,
Rochford (W side of Rochford on
B1013)

T:(0702) 544302
Parkland course with ponds and ditches
as natural hazards. Societies welcome
by arrangement. 18 | 6255 yds | Par 70
| SSS 69
Visitors welcome most weekdays ⋈
🕾 | ✳ | L ♟ (Tu-F by arrangement) |
⚲ ⅄ \ | TR Tu WE | M 800 | S
★★*Roslin, Southend-on-Sea. T:(0702)*
586375. 39rm (26 ⇄ 13 🛏)

ROCK
Cornwall
Map **I**   C6

St Enodoc Rock, nr Wadebridge (W
side of village)
T:020-886 3216
Seaside course with natural hazards.
18(x2) | 6188 (4151) yds | Par 69(61) |
SSS 70
Visitors welcome | ⋈ for main
course | ⁚⁚ per day (main), ∴ per
day (short) | B L ♟ (not F) | ⚲ ⅄ \
⋈ | ④ before 1030 on 1st tee, before
0930 on 10th tee | TR competition
days | M 850 | S
★★*St Enodoc. T:020-886 3394. 14rm*
(6 ⇄ 2 🛏)

ROCHESTER
Kent
Map II G4

Rochester & Cobham Park Park Pale, nr Rochester
(2½m W of Rochester on A2)
T:(047 482) 3411
18 | 6467 yds | Par 72 | SSS 71
Visitors welcome, with M only WE (before 1700) | ∷ per round | B ♥ | L prior
arrangement | D prior arrangement (not Mon and F) | ⚐ Ⴤ | ④ 0800-0930,
12th; 1030-1130, 1st; 1300-1430, 12th; 1530-1630, 1st; 1630-1800, 12th. | M 725
| Ⓢ
***Inn on the Lake, Watling St (A2), Shorne. T:(047 482) 3333. 78rm ⇄*
A first-rate course of challenging dimensions in undulating
parkland. All holes differ and each requires accurate drive placing
to derive the best advantage. The clubhouse and course are situated
on the south side of the A2 a quarter of a mile from the western end
of the M2.

ROMFORD
Essex
Map II F3

Romford Heath Drive, Gidea Park, Romford (1m NE of Romford on A118)
T:(0708) 40986
18 | 6378 yds | Par 72 | SSS 70
Visitors welcome but with M only WE BH | ☎ | without M ∷ per day | with
M ∴ per day | ✉ | B L D prior arrangement | ⚐ Ⴤ | M 660 | Ⓢ
****Brentwood Moat House, London Road, Brentwood. T:(0277) 225252. 3rm (2
⇄ 1 ♨) Annexe: 34rm ⇄ ♨*
A many-bunkered parkland course with easy walking. It is said
there are as many bunkers as there are days in the year. The ground
is quick drying making a good course for winter play when other
courses might be too wet.

ROMFORD
Greater London
Map II F3

Maylands Colchester Rd, Harold
Park (NE side of Romford off A12)
T:(04023) 42055
*Picturesque undulating parkland
course. Societies welcome by
arrangement. 18 | 6182 yds | Par 71 |
SSS 69*
Visitors welcome, restricted Tu WE
BH | ✉ ☎ essential | B L ♥ | D prior
arrangement | ⚐ Ⴤ | Ⴈ | M 700 | Ⓢ
***Post House, Brook St, Brentwood.
T:(0277) 210888. 120rm ⇄*

ROMILEY
Greater Manchester
Map V E8

Romiley Goose House Green,
Romiley, Stockport, Cheshire (E
side of town centre off B6104)
T:061-430 2392
*Parkland course, well wooded. 18 |
6325 yds | Par 70 | SSS 70*
Visitors welcome, restricted Th | B L

(not Mon) ♥ D prior arrangement
(not Mon) | ⚐ Ⴤ | ④ ⬚TR⬚ until 1000,
1200-1400 | M 700 | Ⴈ
***Belgrade, Dialston Ln, Stockport.
T:061-483 3851. 160rm ⇄*

ROSS-ON-WYE
Hereford and Worcester
Map III G7

Ross-on-Wye Two Park, Gorsley
(On B4221, N side of M50, Jct 3)
T:(098 982) 267
*Societies welcome (W Th F) by
arrangement. 18 | 6500 yds | Par 72 |
SSS 73*
Visitors welcome ✉ ☎ | ∴ per day
∷ WE | B | ♥ (not Mon) | L D prior
arrangement (not Mon) | ⚐ Ⴤ ⵒ |
⨉ by arrangement | ④ ☎ for
details | ⬚TR⬚ medal days and some
WE | M 660 | Ⓢ
***Chase, Gloucester Rd. T:(0989)
63161. 40rm ⇄*
The undulating, parkland course has been cut out of a silver birch
forest, the fairways being well-screened from each other. The
fairways are tight, the greens good.

ROMSEY
Hampshire
Map II A6

Dunwood Manor Shootash Hill
(4m W of Romsey off A27)
T:(0794) 40549
*Parkland course, fine views. Testing
hole: Reynolds Leap (par 4). Societies
welcome by arrangement. 18 | 5959 yds
| Par 70 | SSS 69*
Visitors welcome | .. per round .∴.
per day WE | B ♥ | L D prior
arrangement | ⚐ Ⴤ ⵒ | ⨉ | ⬚TR⬚ WE
| Ⴈ | M 560 | Ⓢ
***Potters Heron, Ampfield.
T:(04215) 66611. 60rm ⇄*

Romsey Romsey Rd, Nursling (3m
S of Romsey on A3057)
T:(0703) 734637
*Parkland/woodland course with narrow
tree-lined fairways. 6 holes are
undulating, rest are sloping. There are
superb views over the Test valley. 18 |
5740 yds | Par 69 | SSS 68*
Visitors welcome, with M only WE
| B L ♥ (not Th) | D prior
arrangement (not Th) | ⚐ Ⴤ | M 650
| Ⓢ
***White Horse, Market Pl. T:(0794)
512431. 33rm ⇄*

ROTHBURY
Northumberland
Map VI K5

Rothbury Old Race Course,
Rothbury (S side of town off B6342)
T:(0669) 20718
Very flat downland course with natural

SCORE CARD:

1	313	10	448
2	455	11	355
3	284	12	135
4	394	13	346
5	477	14	437
6	536	15	326
7	147	16	295
8	498	17	429
9	218	18	407

*hazards. 9 | 5108 metres | Par 68 |
SSS 67*
Visitors welcome | without M ‥
per day WE | ⟨TR⟩ S 0830-1000,
1300-1430 | M 200
★★★*White Swan, Bondgate Within,
Alnwick. T:(0665) 602109. 41rm (40
⇄)*

ROTHERHAM
South Yorkshire
Map **V** F7

Grange Park Upper Wortley Rd
(3m NW of Rotherham off A629)
T:(0709) 559497
*Parkland/meadowland course, with
panoramic views especially from the
back nine. The golf is testing,
particularly at the 1st, 4th and 18th
holes (par 4) and 8th 12th and 15th
holes (par 5). 18 | 6461 yds | Par 71 |
SSS 70*
Visitors welcome | ‥ per day WE |
B ⬤ L D (not WE) | ⚘ ⟐ ⟍ | ⟍ | ⟐ |
M 830 | ⟨S⟩
★★*Brentwood, Moorgate Rd. T:(0709)
382772. 14rm (3 ⇄ 5 ⬤) Annexe:
20rm (16 ⇄ 4 ⬤)*

Phoenix Pavilion Ln, Brinsworth,
Rotherham (SW side of town centre
off A630)
T:(0709) 363864
*Undulating meadowland course with
variable wind. 18 | 6041 yds | Par 71 |
SSS 69*
Visitors welcome | ✳ | B L D ⬤ prior
arrangement | ⚘ ⟐ ⟍ | ⟨TR⟩ Th
1300-1430 (Ladies Day) | M 750 | ⟨S⟩
★★*Brentwood, Moorgate Rd. T:(0709)
382772. 14rm (3 ⇄ 5 ⬤) Annexe:
20rm (16 ⇄ 4 ⬤)*

Rotherham Golf Club Ltd
Thrybergh Park, Thrybergh,
Rotherham (3m NE of Rotherham
on A630)
T:(0709) 850812
*Parkland course with easy walking
along tree-lined fairways. Societies
welcome by arrangement. 18 | 6375 yds
| Par 70 | SSS 70*
Visitors welcome ☎ | ⬤ | B L D
prior arrangement | ⚘ ⟐ | ⟨TR⟩
W:ladies before 1030 Mon-Fri.
Between 1200-1430 Mon-F. Before
1000 WE & BH | M 500 | ⟨S⟩
★★*Brentwood, Moorgate Rd. T:(0709)
382772. 14rm (3 ⇄ 5 ⬤) Annexe:
20rm (16 ⇄ 4 ⬤)*

Sitwell Park Shrogs Wood Rd,
Rotherham (SE side of town centre
off A631)
T:(0709) 541046
*Parkland course with easy walking. 18 |
6203 yds | Par 71 | SSS 70*
Visitors welcome restricted
competition days | ☎ for parties | ∴
per day WE | B ⬤ (not Tu) | L D
prior arrangement (not Tu) | ⚘ ⟐

⟍ | M 500 | ⟨S⟩
★★*Brentwood, Moorgate Rd. T:(0709)
382772. 14rm (3 ⇄ 5 ⬤) Annexe:
20rm (16 ⇄ 4 ⬤)*

ROTHERWICK
Hampshire
Map **II** C5

Tylney Park Rotherwick, Hook, nr
Basingstoke, Hants (½m SW of
Rotherwick)
T:(72) 2079
*Parkland course. Practice area. 18 |
6150 yds | Par 70 | SSS 69*
Visitors welcome, handicap
certificate requested WE | B ⬤ | L D
prior arrangement | ⚘ ⟐ ⟐ | ⟍ |
⟨TR⟩ competitions | M 500 | ⟨S⟩
★★*Raven, Station Rd, Hook.
T:(025672) 2541. 46rm (28 ⇄ 18 ⬤)*

ROTHLEY
Leicestershire
Map **IV** A4

Rothley Park Westfield Ln, Rothley
(¾m W of Rothley on B5328)
T:(0533) 302019 ➠

KEY

(IA1) *atlas grid reference*
T: *telephone number*
☎ *advance letter/telephone call required*
✉ *introduction from own club sec/handicap certificate/club membership card required*
.. *low fees*
∴ *medium fees*
:: *high fees*
* *green fees not confirmed for 1987*
B *light lunch*
L *full lunch*
☙ *tea*
D *dinner*
⚄ *changing rooms/showers*
Y *bar open mid-day and evenings*
⚲ *clubs for hire*
⋈ *partners may be found*
④ *restricted time for 4 balls*
TR *times reserved for members*
ʝ *professional*
S *well-stocked shop*
M *member*
Mon Tu W Th F S Sun
WE *weekend*
BH *bank holiday*

Parkland course in picturesque situation. Children not allowed. Societies welcome by arrangement. 18 | 6487 yds | Par 71 | SSS 71
Visitors welcome ✉ | without M ∴ per day :: WE | with M .. per day WE | B ☙ (not Mon) | L D prior arrangement (not Mon) | ⚄ Y ⚲ | TR ④ ☎ | M 500 | S
★★★*Rothley Court Hotel, Westfield Ln. T:(0533) 374141. 14rm ⇌ Annexe: 20rm (18 ⇌)*

ROYSTON
Hertfordshire
Map **IV** E7

Royston Baldock Rd, Royston (½m W of town centre)
T:(0763) 42177
Heathland course. Societies welcome by arrangement. 18 | 6032 yds | Par 70 | SSS 69
Visitors welcome, Sun not until 1200, restricted WE ✉ | ☎ preferred | * | B L ☙ D prior arrangement | ⚄ Y ⚲ | TR Sun am | M 650 | S
★★★*Blakemore, Little Wymondley, Hitchin. T:(0438) 355821. 70rm ⇌*

RUGBY
Warwickshire
Map **III** K5

Rugby Clifton Rd, Rugby (1m NE of Rugby on B5414)
T:(0788) 75134
Parkland course with brook running through the middle and crossed by a viaduct. 18 | 5457 yds | Par 68 | SSS 67
Visitors welcome weekdays | ∴ per day or round .. after 1500 | Y B L D prior arrangement ☙ | ⚄ ⚲ | S
✉ | TR WE | M 550 | ʝ
★★★*Clifton Court, Lilbourne Rd, Clifton-upon-Dunsmore. T:(0788) 65033. 14rm (10 ⇌ 4 ⌠)*

RUISLIP
Greater London
Map **II** D3

Ruislip Ickenham Rd, Ruislip (½m SW of Ruislip on B466)
T:(08956) 32004
Municipal parkland course. Many trees. 18 | 5346 yds | Par 67 | SSS 66
Club playing over municipal course open to public | * | B L ☙ | ⚄ Y ⚲ | ⋈ | M 300 | S
★★★*Master Brewer, Western Ave, Hillingdon. T:(0895) 51199. 64rm ⇌*

RUNCORN
Cheshire
Map **V** C7

Runcorn Clifton Rd, Runcorn (1¼m S of Runcorn Sta)
T:(09285) 72093
Parkland course, with easy walking. Fine views over Mersey and Weaver valleys. Testing holes: 7th par 5; 14th par 5; 17th par 4. 18 | 6012 yds | Par 69 | SSS 69
Visitors welcome ✉ | without M ∴ per day WE | with M .. per day WE | B ☙ | L D prior arrangement | ⚄ Y | TR competition days | M 375 | S

RYTON
Tyne and Wear
Map V E1

Tyneside Westfield Ln, Ryton (NW side of town)
T:(091) 4132742
Societies welcome by arrangement. 18 | 6055 yds | Par 70 | SSS 69
Visitors welcome ✉ | ∴ per day | B L ☙ D | ⚄ Y ⚲ | TR (1130-1330) | ʝ | M 350 | S
★★County, Priestpopple, Hexham. T:(0434) 602030. 10rm (4 ⌠)
Open parkland course, not heavily bunkered. Water hazard, hilly, practice area.

★★★*Crest, Wood Ln, Beechwood. T:(0928) 714000. 130rm ⇌*

RUTHIN
Clwyd
Map **III** F2

Ruthin-Pwllglas Pwllglas, nr Ruthin (2½m S of Ruthin, off A494)
T:(08242) 4658
Moorland course in elevated position with panoramic views. Undulating, except for one stiff climb to 3rd and 9th holes. 10 | 5306 yds | Par 66 | SSS 66
Visitors welcome ☎ | .. per day | ⚄ | Y variable | TR competition days | M 330 | S Sun only
★★★*Ruthin Castle. T:(08242) 2664. 58rm (56 ⇌ 2 ⌠)*

RYDE
Isle of Wight
Map **II** B7

Ryde Binstead Rd, Ryde (1m W of Ryde on A3054)
T:(0983) 614809
Parkland course with wide views over the Solent. 9 | 5266 yds | Par 66 | SSS 66
Visitors welcome ✉ restricted W (pm) WE BH | .. per day | B L ☙ | ⚄ Y mid-day only ⚲ | ⋈ | TR Sun am | TR 1200-1600 W ladies | M 250 | S
★★*Yelfs, Union St. T:(0983) 64062. 21rm ⇌*

RYE
East Sussex
Map **II** H6

Rye Camber, Rye (2¾m SE of Rye off A259)
T:(0797) 225241
Links course. 18(9) | 6301(3306) yds | Par 68(36) | SSS 71(36)
Visitors welcome only with M, or introduction from M ☎ | B ☙ L | ⚄ | ⚲ | S M 900 | S

★★*George, High St. T:(0797) 222114.
17rm* ⇄ 🍴

RYTON
Tyne and Wear
Map **V**   K6

Ryton Clara Vale, Ryton (NW side
of town off A695)
T:(091) 4133737
*Parkland course. 18 | 5968 yds | Par 70
| SSS 68*
Visitors welcome, with M only WE
(until 1700) | without M . . per day |
with M . . per day WE | B L D ☎ |
⚿ ⛳ | TR WE (0800-1000, 1200-
1400) | M 400
★★*County, Priestpopple, Hexham.
T:(0434) 602030. 10rm (4 ⇄)*

SAFFRON WALDEN
Essex
Map **IV**   F7

Saffron Walden Windmill Hill,
Saffron Walden (NW side of town
centre off B184)
T:(0799) 22786
*Undulating parkland course, beautiful
views. Lessons for juniors S (am).
Societies welcome (Mon to F) by
arrangement. 18 | 6608 yds | Par 72 |
SSS 72*
Visitors welcome, with M only WE |
∴ per day | B ☎ | L D prior
arrangement | ⚿ ⛳ ↘ | TR Tu, WE
| M 800 | S
★★*Saffron, 10-18 High St. T:(0799)
22676. 18rm (4 ⇄ 2 🍴)*

ST ALBANS
Hertfordshire
Map **II**   E2

Batchwood Hall Batchwood Hall

(1m NW of St Albans off A5183)
T:(0727) 33349
*Municipal parkland course, 18 |
6463 yds | Par 71 | SSS 71*
Open to public | . . weekdays WE
(per round) | B | L ☎ D prior
arrangement | ⚿ ⛳ ↘ | ✕ | TR WE
am | ⛳ | M 300 | S
★★★*St Michael's Manor, Fishpool St,
St Albans. T:(0727) 64444. 26rm (13
⇄ 9 🍴)*

ST ANDREWS
Fife, *Fife*
Map **VII**   J8
St Andrews Links Management
Committee, St Andrews
T:(0334) 75757
*4 public links courses played over by
local clubs. Royal & Ancient, New, St
Andrews, St Rule, St Regulus Ladies'.
Old: 18 | 6566 yds (medal tees) | Par 72
| SSS 72*
Reservations 6 weeks in advance (at
an additional fee) ☎ for details of
TR | ∷ per round
*New: West Sands Rd. 18 | 6604 yds
(medal tees) | Par 71 | SSS 72*
Reservations can be made 6 weeks
in advance at additional fee ☎ for
details of TR | ∴ per round
*Eden: Dundee Rd. 18 | 5971 yds
(medal tees) | Par 69 | SSS 69*
Reservations can be made 6 weeks
in advance at additional fee ☎ for
details of TR | . . per round
*Jubilee: West Sands Rd. 18 | 6284 yds
(medal tees) | Par 69 | SSS 70*
Reservations can be made 6 weeks
in advance at an additional fee ☎
for details of TR | . . per round
B L ☎ D | ⛳ ⚿ ↘ | ✕ | S(various)
★★*Russell, 26 The Scores. T:(0334)
73447. 7rm (1 ⇄ 4 🍴)*

St Regulus Ladies St Andrews
T:(0334) 74699
Plays over all four St Andrews courses.
Visitors welcome only with M | ⚿ |
M 220
★★★★*Old Course & Country Club,
Old Station Rd. T:(0334) 74371.
150rm* ⇄

St Rule 12 The Links, St Andrews
T:(0334) 72988
*Ladies club which plays over all four St
Andrews courses.*
Visitors welcome ☎ | B L ☎ prior
arrangement (not Sun) | ⚿ | ⛳ (not
Sun) | M 250
★★★★*Old Course & Country Club,
Old Station Rd. T:(0334) 74371.
150rm* ⇄

ST ANNES-ON-SEA
Lancashire
Map **V**   C6

St Annes Old Links Highbury Rd,
St Annes on Sea (N side of town
centre off A584)
T:(0253) 723597
*Seaside links qualifying course for Open
Championship, compact and of very
high standard, particularly greens.
Windy, only long 5th, 17th 18th holes.
Famous hole: 9th 171 yds Par 3.
Practice ground, exceptional club
facilities. Societies by arrangement. 18 |
6616 yds | Par 72 | SSS 72*
Visitors welcome ☎ | ∷ per day | B
L ☎ D (not Thu Nov to March) | ⚿
⛳ ↘ | TR until 0915, 1200-1400 |
M 900 | S
★★*Fernlea, 15 South Prom, Lytham St
Annes. T:(0253) 726726. 95rm* ⇄

ST AUSTELL
Cornwall
Map **I**   C7

St Austell Tregongeeves Ln, St
Austell (1m SW of St Austell off
A390)
T:(0726) 72649
*Very interesting inland course designed
by James Braid. Undulating, well
covered with tree plantations and well
bunkered. Notable holes are 8th (par 4)
and 16th (par 3). Special rates for
societies by arrangement. Juniors under
14 must play with an adult.* 18 |
5875 yds | Par 69 | SSS 68
Visitors welcome except
competition days | ☎ ⊠ | B L ♥ | ⚖
| ⛳ | ⚲ | TR competition days |
M 800 | S
★★★*Porth Avallen, Sea Rd, Carlyon
Bay. T:(072681) 2802. 25rm (19 ⇌ 2
⌘)*

ST BEES
Cumbria
Map **V**   A3

St Bees St Bees (½m W of village
off B5345)
T:(0946) 812105
*Links course down hill and dale with
sea views.* 9 | 5082 yds | Par 64 |
SSS 65
Visitors welcome ‥ per day WE |
⋈ | TR competition days | ④
competition days S (1400-1445) |
M 275
★★*Roseneath Country House, Low
Moresby, Whitehaven (3m NE off
A595). T:(0946) 61572. 8rm (4 ⇌ 3
⌘)*

ST BOSWELLS
Borders, *Roxburghshire*
Map **VI**   H4

St Boswells Boswells (N side of
village off B6404)
T:(0835) 22359
*Attractive parkland course, easy
walking.* 9 | 2527 yds | Par 66 | SSS 65
Visitors welcome | ‥ per day WE |
TR competition times | M 200
★★*Buccleuch Arms, The Green.
T:(0835) 22243. 16rm (10 ⇌)*

ST DAVIDS
Dyfed
Map **III**   A7

St Davids City Whitesands
(2m NW of St Davids on B4583)
T:(0437) 721620
*The course overlooks Whitesands beach
and bay.* 9 | 5172 yds | Par 66 | SSS 65
Visitors welcome without M ‥ per
day | ⚖ ⋈ | (catering facilities
available at the hotel) | M 105
★★★⚕*Warpool Court. T:(0437)
720300. 25rm (16 ⇌ 9 ⌘)*

ST ENODOC
Cornwall
Map **I**   C6
See Rock

ST HELENS
Merseyside
Map **V**   C7

Grange Park Toll Bar, Prescot Rd (1½m SW of St Helens on A58)
T:(0744) 26318
Societies welcome by arrangement. 18 | 6429 yds | Par 72 | SSS 71
Visitors welcome ⊠ | ☎ preferable | without M ∴ per day ∷ WE | with M ‥
weekdays WE | B L ♥ D prior arrangement | ⚖ ⛳ ⚲ | ⋈ | ④ Tu | TR 0930-
1015, 1300-1415 | ⛳ | M 700 | S
★★★*Post House, Lodge Ln, Newton-le-Willows. T:(0942) 717878. 98rm ⇌*
A course of Championship length set in pleasant country
surroundings — playing the course it is hard to believe that
industrial St Helens lies so close at hand. The course is a fine test of
golf and there are many attractive holes liable to challenge all grades
of player.

ST FILLANS
Tayside, *Perthshire*
Map **VII**   F8

St Fillans St Fillans (E side of
village off A85)
T:(076485) 312
*Fairly flat beautiful parkland course,
with facilities for children.* 9 | 2634 yds
| Par 68 | SSS 66
Visitors welcome | ‥ per day WE |
B ♥ | ⚖ ⚲ | TR ☎ for details |
M 350 | S
★★*Drummond Arms. T:(076485) 212.
31rm (14 ⇌)*

ST HELENS
Merseyside
Map **V**   C7

Sherdley Park Sherdley Rd, St
Helens (2m S of St Helens off A570)
T:(0744) 813149
*Fairly hilly course with ponds in
places.* 18 | 5941 yds | Par 70 | SSS 69
Visitors welcome | ‥ ⚲ | TR
WE am 0700-0930 | ⛳ | M 160 | S
★★★*Post House, Lodge Ln, Newton-le-
Willows. T:(0942) 717878. 98rm ⇌*

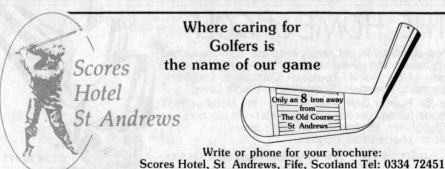

ST IVES
Cambridgeshire
Map **IV** E6

St Ives (Hunts) Westwood Rd
(W side of town centre off A1123)
T:(0480) 68392
Picturesque parkland course. 9 |
3302 yds | *Par 68* | *SSS 69*
Visitors welcome, restricted WE
until 1100 (Oct-April) Sun until
1100 (May-Sept), ✉ juniors |
without M ∴ per day WE | with M
.. per day WE | B ☻ (not Mon) | L
D prior arrangement (not Mon) | ⚘
🍸 ✕ | TR WE up to 1100 | M 305 |
S
★★★*Slepe Hall, Ramsey Rd. T:(0480)
63122. 14rm (10 ⇄)*

ST MARY'S
Scilly, Isles of
See Isles of Scilly

ST MELLION
Cornwall
Map **I** D6

St Mellion Golf and Country Club
St Mellion, Saltash (½m NW of St
Mellion off A388)
T:(0579) 50101
*Downland-parkland course of
championship quality. Testing holes
8th, 11th, 15th. Facilities for squash,
badminton, snooker, table tennis and
trout fishing. Also sauna and solarium.*
18 | *5927 yds* | *Par 70* | *SSS 68*
Visitors welcome weekdays | ✉ ☎ |
∷ per day | B L ☻ | D prior
arrangement | ⚘ 🍸 ✕ | ✕ | M 600 |
S
★★★*St Mellion. T:(0579) 50101.
Annexe: 24rm ⇄ 🏚*

ST MELLONS
South Glamorgan
Map **I** G2
See Cardiff

ST NEOTS
Cambridgeshire
Map **IV** D6

Eynesbury Hardwicke (2m SE of St
Neots)
T:(0480) 215153/217951
*Attractive parkland course with
pleasant views. Floodlit driving range.*
18 | *6179 yds* | *Par 70* | *SSS 71*
Visitors welcome without M ∴ per
day ∷ WE BH | M 580 | ☻ B L D
prior arrangement | ⚘ 🍸 S ✕
TR competitions and society
bookings
★★*George, High St, Buckden.
T:(0480) 810307. 12rm (4 ⇄)*

St Neots Crosshall Rd, St Neots,
Huntingdon (W side of town centre
on A45)
T:(0480) 72363
*Parkland course close to the Kym and
Great Ouse rivers with easy level
walking.* 18 | *6027 yds* | *Par 69* |
SSS 69
Visitors welcome restricted WE BH |
☎ advisable | without M ∴ per day
∷ WE | B L ☻ D | ⚘ 🍸 ✕ | ✕ by
arrangement | TR WE | M 560 | S
★★*George, High St, Buckden.
T:(0480) 810307. 12rm (4 ⇄)*

SALE
Greater Manchester
Map **V** D7

Ashton on Mersey Church Ln, Sale
(1m W of M63, Jct 7)
T:061-973 3220

Parkland course with easy walking. 9 |
6242 yds | *Par 72* | *SSS 70*
Visitors welcome but with M only
Sun BH (not S) | without M ∴ per
day | with M .. per day WE | L ☻
(not Mon) D prior arrangement (not
Mon) | ⚘ 🍸 ✕ | ✕ | TR Tu (Ladies)
1030-1330 | M 321 | S
★★★*Cresta Court, Church St,
Altrincham. T:061-928 8017. 139rm
⇄ 🏚*

Sale Golf Rd, Sale (NW side of
town centre off A6144)
T:061-973 3404
Parkland course. Societies welcome. 18 |
6358 yds | *Par 71* | *SSS 70*
Visitors welcome | without M ∴ per
day ∷ WE | with M .. per round |
B L ☻ (not Mon) | D (not Mon)
prior arrangement | ⚘ 🍸 ✕ | TR
S and competitions | M 530 | S ♪
★★★*Cresta Court, Church St,
Altrincham. T:061-928 8017. 139 ⇄
🏚*

SALINE
Fife, *Fife*
Map **VI** F1

Saline Kinneddar Hill, Saline (½m
E of Saline at jct B913/B914)
T:(0383) 852591
*Hillside course with panoramic view of
the Forth Valley.* 9 | *5302 yds* | *Par 68* |
SSS 66
Visitors welcome except S | .. per
day WE | B ☻ | L prior arrangement
| ⚘ 🍸 | ✕ | TR S | M 350
★★★*King Malcolm Thistle,
Queensferry Rd, Wester Pitcorthie,
Dunfermline. T:(0383) 722611. 48rm
⇄ 🏚*

SALISBURY
Wiltshire
Map I K4

Salisbury & South Wilts
Netherhampton, Salisbury (2½m W
of Salisbury on A3094)
T:(0722) 2645
*Gently undulating downland course in
country setting. Societies welcome by
arrangement. Also a 9-hole course.
18(9)│6140 (4848) yds│Par 70(66)│
SSS 70(64)*
Visitors welcome│∴ weekdays ∴
WE│B L ☎ (not Tu)│D prior
arrangement (not Tu Sun)│⚘ ☈ ↘
│④ ⊺ʀ M and Th before 1000, WE
before 1000, 1200-1400│M 800│Ⓢ
★★★*Rose & Crown, Harnham Rd.
T:(0722) 27908. 28rm ⇄ 🍴*

SALTBURN-BY-THE-SEA
Cleveland
Map V G3

Saltburn by the Sea Hob Hill,
Guisborough Rd, Saltburn-by-the-
Sea (S side of town centre on
B1268)
T:(0287) 22812
*Undulating meadowland course
surrounded by woodland, which is
particularly attractive in autumn.
There are fine views of the Cleveland
Hills and of Tees Bay. Societies
welcome by arrangement. 18│5803 yds
│Par 70│SSS 68*
Visitors welcome ⊠│B ☎ (not
Mon)│L D prior arrangement (not
Mon)│⚘ ⊺ ↘ ⋈ (possible)│④ S
(not before 1015 or between 1200
and 1430│⊺ʀ S│M 850│Ⓢ
★★★*Royal York, Coatham Rd, Redcar.
T:(0642) 486221. 51rm (50 ⇄ 1 🍴)*

SALTFORD
Avon
Map I J3

Saltford Golf Club Lane, Saltford
(S side of village)
T:(02217) 3220
*Parkland course with easy walking. The
par 4 2nd and 13th are notable.
Societies welcome (Th) by arrangement.
18│6081 yds│Par 69│SSS 69*
Visitors welcome ☎│without M ∴
per day WE│with M .. per day WE
│B L ☎ D prior arrangement│⚘ ⊺
↘ by arrangement│ ⫟ │M 800│Ⓢ
❀○○○*Hunstrete House, Chelwood,
Hunstrete. T:(07618) 578. 13rm ⇄
Annexe: 8rm ⇄*

SANDBACH
Cheshire
Map III H2

Malkins Bank Municipal Betchton
Rd, Sandbach (1½m SE of
Sandbach off A533)
T:(09367) 5931
*Parkland course. Tight 13th hole with
stream running through. 18│6071 yds
│Par 70│SSS 69*
Visitors welcome│.. per day WE│
⊺ B L ☎│⚘ ↘│⋈│M 250│⫟│Ⓢ
★★★*Saxon Cross, Holmes Chapel Rd,
Sandbach. T:(0270) 763281. 52rm ⇄*

Sandbach Middlewich Rd,
Sandbach (½m W of Sandbach on
A533)
T:(09367) 2117
*Meadowland, undulating course with
easy walking. Limited facilities but
societies accepted by arrangement. 9│
5533 yds│Par 67│SSS 67*
Visitors welcome, not Tu, WE BH│
∴ per day│B ☎ (not Mon Th)│L D
prior arrangement (not Mon Th)│
⚘ ⊺│M 370
★★★*Saxon Cross, Holmes Chapel Rd,
Sandbach. T:(0270) 763281. 52rm ⇄*

SANDOWN
Isle of Wight
Map II B8

Shanklin & Sandown Fairway,
Lake, Sandown (1m NW of
Sandown)
T:(0983) 403217
*Links course. Societies welcome by
arrangement. 18│6000 yds│Par 70│
SSS 69*
Visitors welcome│☎│B L (not
Mon)│D prior arrangement (not
Mon)│⚘ ⊺ ↘│⊺ʀ major
competitions│④ ☈ for details│
M 650│Ⓢ
★★★*Cliff Tops, Park Rd, Shanklin.
T:(0983) 863262. 102rm (80 ⇄ 3 🍴)*

SANDWICH
Kent
Map II K4

Royal St George's Sandwich (1½m
E of Sandwich)
T:(0304) 613090
*Links course, men only. 18│6857 yds
(championship) 6534 yds (medal)│
Par 70(76)│SSS 74(72)*
Visitors welcome, not WE BH│☎│

✳ | B L ⚑ | ⚹ ♈ ⚲ | ④ not
permitted | TR 0830-0945,
1315-1415 | M 700 | S
★★*Savoy, Grange Rd, Ramsgate.*
T:(0843) 592637. 14rm (1 ⇄ 2 ⌂)
Annexe: 11rm (2 ⇄ 9 ⌂)

SANDY
Bedfordshire
Map **IV**　D7

John O'Gaunt Sutton Park, Sandy
(3m NE of Biggleswade on B1040)
T:(0767) 260360
Two tree-lined parkland courses. 18x2 |
6505 (5882) yds | Par 71(69) |
SSS 71(68)
Visitors welcome ✉ | without M ⠢
per day | B L D ⚑ | ⚹ ♈ ⚲ | ✉ |
M 1050 | S
★★★*Woodlands Manor, Green Ln,*
Bedford. T:(0234) 63281. 18rm (8 ⇄
10 ⌂) Annexe: 3rm ⇄

SANQUHAR
Dumfries and Galloway,
Dumfriesshire
Map **VI**　E4

Sanquhar Euchan Golf Course,
Sanquhar (½m SW of Sanquhar off
A76)
T:(065 92) 577
Moorland course, fine views. Play park
nearby. 9 | 5144 yds | Par 70 | SSS 68
Visitors welcome | ⠢⦁ per day ∴
WE | ⚹ ♈ | all catering prior
arrangement | TR 1st tee Sun
(1400-1420) Tu Th (1800-1820) |
M 120
★*Nithsdale, High St, Sanquhar.*
T:(06592) 506. 6rm

SAUNTON
Devon
Map **I**　D4

Saunton Saunton, Braunton (S side
of village off B3231)

T:(0271) 812436
Two traditional links courses (one
championship), (East and West).
Windy, natural hazards. Championship
standard course. Societies welcome by
arrangement. 18(18) | 6703 yds
(6322 yds) | Par 71(70) | SSS 73(71)
Visitors welcome ☎ helpful,
restricted only during
championships | ⠢⠢ per day (East
course) ∴ per day (West course) | B
⚑ | L D prior arrangement | ⚹ ♈ ⚲
| ⋈ (usually, prior arrangement) |
⅃ | TR comp days | M 950 | S
★★★★*Saunton Sands, Saunton.*
T:(0271) 890212. 102rm ⇄

SCARBOROUGH
North Yorkshire
Map **V**　H4

Scarborough North Cliff North
Cliff Av, Scarborough (N side of
town centre off A165)
T:(0723) 360786　➥

Seaside parkland course with good views. 18 | 6425 yds | Par 71 | SSS 71 Visitors welcome | without M ∴ per day ∷ WE | with M ‥ per round | ♛ | B L D prior arrangement | ⚤ ♈ ⚲ ∝ | ⟨TR⟩ Sun S and competition days | M 800 | ⟨S⟩ ♩ ★★*Esplanade, Belmont Rd.* T:(0723) 360382. 81rm (53 ⇌ 12 ⚏)

SCARCROFT
West Yorkshire
Map **V**   F6

Scarcroft Scarcroft, Leeds (½m N of village off A58) T:(0532) 892263 *Parkland course, prevailing W wind, easy walking. Societies welcome by arrangement.* 18 | 6426 yds | Par 71 | SSS 71 Visitors welcome, restricted WE | without M ∴ per day ∷ WE | with M ‥ per day WE | B ♛ | L D prior arrangement (not Mon) | ⚤ ♈ | ⟨TR⟩ 1230-1330 | M 600 | ⟨S⟩ ★★★*Stakis Windmill, Mill Green View, Seacroft, Leeds.* T:(0532) 732323. 100rm ⇌ ⚏

SCILLY, ISLES OF
See Isles of Scilly

SCONSER
Highland, *Inverness-shire*
Map **VII**   C5

Sconser Sconser, Isle of Skye (½m E of village on A850) *Seaside course, often windy, splendid views.* 9 | 4798 yds | Par 66 | SSS 63 Visitors welcome, no Sun play | B ♛ L D ♈ all available in adjacent hotel | ⟨TR⟩ S (pm) in summer | M 100 ★★*Broadford, Broadford.* T:(04712) 204. 20rm (3 ⇌ 6 ⚏) *Annexe:* 9rm (2 ⇌ 7 ⚏)

SCRAPTOFT
Leicestershire
Map **IV**   A4

Scraptoft Beeby Rd, Scraptoft (1m NE of Scraptoft) T:(0533) 419000 *Pleasant inland country course. Societies welcome by arrangement.* 18 | 6146 yds | Par 70 | SSS 69 Visitors welcome with M only WE | B L ♛ D (not Mon) prior

arrangement for parties | ♈ ⚲ | ⟨TR⟩ competition days | M 550 | ⟨S⟩ ★★★*Leicestershire Moat House, Wigston Rd, Oadby, Leicester.* T:(0533) 719441. 29rm ⇌ ⚏

SCUNTHORPE
Humberside
Map **V**   H7

Holme Hall Holme Ln, Bottesford (3m SE of Scunthorpe) T:(0724) 840909 *Heathland course, easy walking. Attractive 4th pond hole. Societies welcome by arrangement.* 18 | 6475 yds | Par 71 | SSS 71 Visitors welcome, restricted WE BH | without M ∴ per day | with M ‥ per day ∴ WE | B ♛ (not F) | L D prior arrangement (not F) | ♈ ⚤ ⚲ ∝ | ♩ | M 480 | ⟨S⟩ ★★★*Royal, Doncaster Rd, Scunthorpe.* T:(0724) 868181. 33rm (31 ⇌ 2 ⚏)

Kingsway Kingsway, Scunthorpe (W side of town centre off A18) T:(0724) 840945 *Parkland course with many par 3's.* 9 | 1915 yds | Par 30 | SSS 29

Visitors welcome | ⚐ ⋈ | [S] ⚲
★★★*Royal, Doncaster Rd, Scunthorpe.*
T:(0724) 868181. 33rm (31 ⇄ 2 ▥)

Scunthorpe Ashby Decoy, Burringham Rd, Scunthorpe (2½m SW of Scunthorpe on B1450)
T:(0724) 842913/866561
Very tight parkland course, easy walking. Testing dog leg (par 4).
Societies welcome by arrangement. 18 | 6281 yds | Par 71 | SSS 71

Visitors welcome, restricted WE ☎
✉ | without M .. per day ∴ WE | with M .. per day | B L ♥ D prior arrangement | ⚐ Ⴃ ⚲ | ⋈ prior arrangement | M 700 | [S]
★★★*Royal, Doncaster Rd. T:(0724) 868181. 33rm (31 ⇄ 2 ▥)*

SEAHAM
Durham
Map **V** F2

Seaham Dawdon, Seaham (S side of town centre)

SEAFORD
East Sussex
Map **II** F7

Seaford Firle Rd, East Blatchington, Seaford (1m N of Seaford)
T:(0323) 892442
18 | 6241 yds | Par 69 | SSS 70
Visitors welcome ☎ | without M :: per day WE | with M .. per day WE | B L ♥ | D prior arrangement | ⚐ Ⴃ | ④ after 0930, and after 1300 WE | [TR] until 0930 weekdays, WE until 1300 | M 770 | [S]
★★★*Star Inn, Alfriston. T:(0323) 870495. 32rm ⇄*
The great J H Taylor did not perhaps design as many courses as his friend and rival, James Braid, but Seaford's original design was by Taylor. It is a splendid downland course, in fact one of the best downland courses in the country with magnificent views and some fine holes such as the 6th, the 11th and the 18th.

SEAL
Kent
Map **II** G4

Wildernesse Park Lane, Seal, Sevenoaks (½m S of Seal off A25)
T:(0732) 61199
Societies welcome by long prior arrangement. 18 | 6478 yds | Par 72 | SSS 72
Visitors welcome, with M only WE BH | ✉ ☎ | B L ♥ prior arrangement | ⚐ Ⴃ ⚲ | [TR] before 0900 | ④ at all times | ℐ | M 800 | [S]
★★*Sevenoaks Park, Seal Hollow Rd. T:(0732) 454245. 16rm (3 ⇄ 3 ▥)*
A fine, tight inland course heavily wooded with attractive tree-lined fairways. Straight driving is called for with attention to the many well-placed bunkers. Easy walking with few slopes, but it is difficult to beat par.

T:(0783) 812354
Undulating heathland course. 18 | 5972 yds | Par 70 | SSS 69
Visitors welcome, with M only WE
BH | B L ♥ D | ⚐ Ⴃ | M 600 | [S]
★★★*Norseman, Bede Way, Peterlee. T:(0783) 862161. 26rm ⇄ ▥*

SEAHOUSES
Northumberland
Map **VI** K4

Seahouses Beadnell Rd, Seahouses (S side of village on B1340) ➟

SEASCALE
Cumbria
Map **V**   B4

Seascale The Banks, Seascale (NW side of village off B5344)
T:(0940) 28202
18 | 6396 yds | Par 71 | SSS 70
Visitors welcome, restricted WE BH | without M ∴ per day WE | B L ♛ D prior arrangement | ⚬ ☂ ⤢ | ∞ | TR comp days W & Sun — Summertime | ♪ | M 550 | S
Wansfell, Drigg Rd. T:(0940) 28301. 14rm (2 🛏)

A tough links requiring length and control. The natural terrain is used to give a variety of holes and considerable character. Undulating greens add to the challenge.

T:(0665) 720794
Seaside course. Easy walking. Societies welcome by arrangement. 18 | 5399 yds | Par 66 | SSS 66
Visitors welcome | ‥ per day WE | B L ♛ D | ⚬ ☂ ⤢ | ∞ | M 260 | S
★★*Olde Ship. T:(0665) 720200. 10rm (2 ⇔ 5 🛏)*

SEDBERGH
Cumbria
Map **V**   D4

Sedbergh The Riggs, Sedbergh (¾m S of Sedbergh off A683)
T:(0587) 20993
Open fell course, very hilly. Rough, with natural hazards, and hard walking. 4 short par 3's. 9 | 4134 yds | Par 64 | SSS 61
Visitors welcome, pay green fees at Midland Bank, Sedbergh | ‥ per round | ∞ | M 70
Barbon Inn, Barbon. T:(046836) 233. 10rm

SELBY
North Yorkshire
Map **V**   G6

Selby Brayton Barff, Brayton, Selby (2¾m SW of Selby off A19)
T:(075782) 622
Mainly flat links course, prevailing SW wind. Testing holes including the 3rd, 7th and 16th. 18 | 6246 yds | Par 70 | SSS 70
Visitors welcome | with M ∴ per day ∷ WE | B L ♛ D prior arrangement (not Mon) | ⚬ prior arrangement (not Mon) | ☂ | ∞ | ④ ☎ for details | M 685 | S
★★★🛏🛏*Monk Fryston Hall, Monk Fryston. T:(0977) 682369. 24rm ⇔*

SELKIRK
Border, *Selkirkshire*
Map **VI**   H4

Selkirk Selkirk Hills, Selkirk (1m S of Selkirk on A7)
T:(0750) 20621.

Heathland course, windy, fine views. 9 | 5560 yds | Par 68 | SSS 67
Visitors welcome, restricted S competitions ☎ parties | ⚬ ∞ ⤢ | ☂ B | L | D food by prior arrangement | ♛ | ④ S competitions | TR | M 200
Heatherlie House, Heatherlie Park. T:(0750) 21200. 7rm (1 ⇔)

SELSEY
West Sussex
Map **II**   C7

Selsey Golf Links Ln, Selsey (1m N of Selsey off B2145)
T:(0243) 602203
Fairly difficult seaside course, exposed to wind and has natural ditches. Societies welcome by arrangement. 9 (playing 18) | 5402 yds | Par 68 | SSS 68
Visitors welcome | ✳ | B (not Th) | L ♛ D prior arrangement (not Th) | ⚬ ☂ ⤢ | ∞ | TR Sun | M 300 | S
★★★*Dolphin & Anchor, West St, Chichester. T:(0243) 785121. 54rm ⇔ 🛏*

SERLBY
Nottinghamshire
Map **V**   G8

Serlby Park Serlby, Bawtry, Doncaster (E side of village off A638)
T:(0777) 818268
Parkland course. 9 | 5325 yds | Par 66 | SSS 66
Visitors welcome only with M | ♛ | ⚬ ☂ WE & special occasions only |

SEATON CAREW
Cleveland
Map **V**   G3

Seaton Carew Tees Rd, Seaton Carew, Hartlepool (SE side of village off A178)
T:(0429) 266249
22 | 6613 yds | Par 72 | SSS 72
Visitors welcome | without M ∴ per day ∷ WE | with M ‥ per day WE | B L ♛ D | ⚬ ☂ ⤢ | ∞ | TR parties and competitions ☎ for details | M 500 | S
★★★*Billingham Arms, Town Sq, Stockton-on-Tees. T:(0642) 553661. 62rm (41 ⇔ 12 🛏)*

A championship links course enjoyable to tiger and tyro alike, taking full advantage of its dunes, bents, whins and gorse. Renowned for its par 4 17th, a two-shotter from a tee over dunes and bents with just enough fairway for an accurate drive, to be followed with another precise shot to a pear-shaped, sloping green, severely trapped and named 'Snag'. There is also a junior green.

SEVENOAKS
Kent
Map II F5

Knole Park Seal Hollow Rd,
Sevenoaks (SE side of town centre
off B2019)
T:(0732) 452150
Societies welcome by arrangement. 18 |
6249 yds | Par 70 | SSS 70
Visitors welcome, restricted WE BH
☎ | ⠿ per round ⠿ per day | B ♣ L
prior arrangement | ⚘ ⛳ | ④ | TR ☎
for details | ♪ | M 850 | S
**Sevenoaks Park, Seal Hollow Rd.*
T:(0732) 454245. 16rm (3 ⇄ 3 ∰)

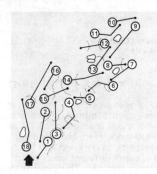

The course is set in a majestic park with many fine trees and deer
running loose. It has a wiry turf seemingly impervious to rain.
Certainly a pleasure to play on. Excellent views.

M 300 | S
Fourways, Blyth. T:(090976) 235.
12rm

SETTLE
North Yorkshire
Map V D5

Settle Giggleswick, Settle (1m NW
of Settle on A65)
T:(07292) 3912
Picturesque parkland course. 9 | 4088
metres | Par 64 | SSS 62
Visitors welcome, restricted WE BH
| .. per day WE | ⚘ | M 120
***Falcon Manor, Skipton Rd.*
T:(07292) 3814. 16rm (13 ⇄ 2 ∰)

SEVENOAKS
Kent
Map II F5

Sevenoaks Town Knole Park,
Sevenoaks (SE side of town centre
off B2019)
T:(0732) 452150
Plays over Knole Park Course. 18 |
6249 yds | Par 70 | SSS 70
Visitors welcome weekdays ✉ ☎ |
B ♣ | L D prior arrangement | ⚘ ⛳ |
♪ | M 45 | S
**Sevenoaks Park, Seal Hollow Rd.*
T:(0732) 454245. 16rm (3 ⇄ 3 ∰)

SHEERNESS
Kent
Map II H4

Sheerness Power Station Rd,
Sheerness (1½m SE of Sheerness
off A250)
T:(0795) 662585
Seaside course, subject to wind. 18 |
6500 yds | Par 72 | SSS 71
Visitors welcome but with M only
Sun BH | ☎ | without M ∴ per day
⠿ WE | with M .. per day WE | B L
♣ D (not Mon) | ⚘ ⛳ ⋈ | TR Sun |
M 400 | S
***Great Danes, Ashford Rd,*
Hollingbourne. T:(0622) 30022. 127rm
⇄ ∰

SHEFFIELD
South Yorkshire
Map V F8

Abbeydale Twentywell Ln, Dore
(4m SW of city centre off A621)
T:(0742) 360743
Parkland course, well kept, wooded.
Testing hole: 12th par 3. 18 | 6410 yds
| Par 72 | SSS 71
Visitors welcome ☎ advisable,
restricted W from 1100-1400 | ∴ per
day ⠿ WE | B L ♣ D prior
arrangement (not Mon) | ⚘ ⛳ | TR
0800-0900, 1200-1330 | ♪ | M 690 | S
****Hallam Tower Post House,*
Manchester Rd, Broomhill. T:(0742)
686031. 136rm ⇄

Beauchief Municipal Abbey Ln,
Sheffield (4m SW of city centre on
A621)
T:(0742) 360648
Municipal course with natural water
hazards. The rolling land looks west to
the Pennines and a 12th-century abbey
adorns the course. 18 | 5470 yds |
Par 67 | SSS 66
.. per day | B ♣ L | ⚘ ⛳ ⅍ | M 350
| S ⋈
**Manor, 10 High St, Dronfield.*
T:(0246) 413971. 10rm (1 ⇄ 9 ∰)

Birley Wood Birley Ln, Sheffield
(4½m SE of city centre off A616)
T:(0742) 397979
Undulating meadowland course with
well varied features, easy walking and
good views. Practice range and green.
Societies welcome by arrangement. 18 |
6257 yds | Par 72 | SSS 70
Visitors welcome | ✳ | L D (W F WE)
♣ | ⚘ ⛳ ⋈ ♪ | S
****Grosvenor House, Charter Sq.*
T:(0742) 20041. 103rm ⇄

Concord Park Shiregreen Ln,
Sheffield (3½m N of city centre on
B6086 off A6135)
T:(0742) 613605
Hilly municipal parkland course with
some fairways wood-flanked, good
views, often windy. 18 | 4276 yds |
Par 65 | SSS 61
Open to public | .. per round | ⚘
⛳ | ⋈ | TR S morning | M 85
****Hallam Tower Post House,*
Manchester Rd, Broomhill. T:(0742)
686031. 136rm ⇄

Dore & Totley The Clubhouse,
Bradway Rd, Sheffield (7m S of city
centre on B6054 off A61)
T:(0742) 360492
Flat parkland course. 18 | 6301 yds |
Par 70 | SSS 70
Visitors welcome ✉ ☎ restricted
WE BH | ∴ per day | B L ♣ D prior
arrangement (not Mon) | ⚘ ⛳ | ⋋
⋈ prior arrangement | ♪ | M 600 | S
****Hallam Tower Post House,*
Manchester Rd, Broomhill. T:(0742)
686031. 136rm ⇄

Hillsborough Worrall Rd, Sheffield
(3m NW of city centre, off A616)
T:(0742) 343608
Beautiful moorland/woodland course
500ft above sea level, reasonable
walking. 18 | 5672 metres | Par 71 |
SSS 70
Visitors welcome ✉ restricted WE |
∴ per round ∴ per day | ⠿ WE | L
D prior arrangement | B ♣ | ⚘ ⛳ |
♪ | M 500 | S
**Rutland, 452 Glossop Rd,*
Broomhill. T:(0742) 664411. 73rm (68
⇄ 1 ∰) Annexe: 17rm (16 ⇄ 1 ∰)

Lees Hall, The Hemsworth Rd,
Norton, Sheffield (4m S of city
centre off A6102)
T:(0742) 554402
Parkland/meadowland course with
panoramic view of city. Societies ➥

SHEDFIELD
Hampshire
Map **II** B7

Meon Valley Hotel, Golf and Country Club Sandy Ln, Shedfield, Southampton (1m NW of Shedfield off A334)
T:(0329) 833455
18 | 6519 yds | Par 71 | SSS 71/69
Visitors welcome ☎ advisable | ∷ per day | B L ☕ D | △ 🍸 ↘ | [4] WE | [TR] ☎ | ☽ | [S]
❀★★*Old House, Wickham. T:(0329) 833049. 10rm ⇨ ⌂*

This course is situated in the triangle — Southampton, Winchester and Portsmouth. It has been said that a golf course architect is as good as the ground on which he has to work. Here Hamilton Stutt had magnificent terrain at his disposal and a very good and lovely course is the result. There are trees of many different kinds which, incidentally, help to provide plenty of hazards. The hotel is of modern design and provides many amenities.

SHEFFIELD
South Yorkshire
Map **V** F8

Hallamshire Golf Club Ltd. The Club House, Sandygate, Sheffield (3m W of city centre, off A57)
T:(0742) 302153
Societies welcome by arrangement. 18 | 6396 yds | Par 71 | SSS 71
Visitors welcome ☎ | ∴ per day | B L ☕ D prior arrangement (not Sun Tu) | △ 🍸 ↘ | ⋈ | [TR] until 0930 | ☽ | M 600 | [S]
★★★★*Hallam Tower Post House, Manchester Rd, Broomhill, Sheffield. T:(0742) 686031. 136rm ⇨*

Situated on a shelf of land at a height of 850 ft. Magnificent view to the west—Moorland turf—Good natural drainage.

SHERBORNE
Dorset
Map **I** H5

Sherborne Higher Clatcombe, Sherborne (2m N of Sherborne off B3145)
T:(0935) 814431
18 | 5776 yds | Par 70 | SSS 68
Visitors very welcome ☎ preferable | B ☕ | L D prior arrangement | △ 🍸 ↘ | ⋈ possible | [TR] until 1000 | M 700 | [S]
★★★*Post House, Horsecastles Ln. T:(0935) 813191. 60rm ⇨*

SCORE CARD:

1	407	10	155
2	513	11	459
3	436	12	115
4	479	13	334
5	189	14	256
6	489	15	160
7	194	16	368
8	298	17	281
9	289	18	346

A sporting course of first-class fairways with far-reaching views over the lovely Blackmore Vale and the Vale of Sparkford. Parkland in character the course has many well-placed bunkers. The dog-leg 2nd calls for an accurately placed tee shot, and another testing hole is the 7th, a 194-yard par 3. There is a practice area.

welcome by arangement. 18 | 6137 yds | Par 71 | SSS 69
Visitors welcome, restricted Sun | without M ∴ per day WE | with M ⁚ per day WE | B ☕ | L D (not Tu) | △ 🍸 | ⋈ | [TR] 1200-1300 | M 500 | [S]
★★★★*Grosvenor House, Charter Sq. T:(0742) 20041. 103rm ⇨*

Tinsley Park Municipal High Hazels Park, Darnall, Sheffield (4m E of city centre off A630)
T:(0742) 42237, S Yorks
Woodland course. 18 | 6000 yds | Par 69 | SSS 69
Visitors welcome | B L ☕ (no catering Tu) | D prior arrangement | △ | 🍸 (lunch only) | ↘ ⋈ | M 475 | [S]
★★★★*Grosvenor House, Charter Sq. T:(0742) 20041. 103rm ⇨*

SHEFFORD
Bedfordshire
Map **IV** D7

Beadlow Manor Hotel and Golf Club (2m W of Shefford on A507)
T:(0525) 60800
Undulating parkland course with water hazards on four holes. 9 hole course suitable for beginners. 18(9) | 6231(3297) yds | Par 71(34) | SSS 70(34)
Visitors welcome (handicap required WE) | B L ☕ D | △ 🍸 ↘ ⋈ | ☽ | M 750 | [S]
★★*Broadway, The Broadway, Letchworth. T:(04626) 685651. 37rm (22 ⇨)*

SHETLAND
Map **VII**
See Lerwick

SHEVINGTON
Greater Manchester
Map **V** C7

Gathurst 62 Miles Ln, Shevington, Wigan (W side of village on B5375)
T:(02575) 2861
Testing parkland course, with easy walking. 9 | 6308 yds | Par 72 | SSS 70
Visitors welcome ☎ ✉ restricted W WE BH | ∴ per day | B L ☕ D (not Mon) prior arrangement | △ 🍸 | [TR] W WE BH | ☽ | M 350 | [S]
★★*Cassinellis Almond Brook Motor Inn, Almond Brook Rd, Standish. T:(0257) 425588. 43rm (42 ⇨) Annexe: 16rm ⌂*

SHIFNAL
Shropshire
Map **III** H4

Shifnal Decker Hill, Shifnal (1m N of Shifnal off B4379)
T:(0952) 460330
Well wooded parkland course. Walking is easy and an attractive country mansion serves as clubhouse. Societies welcome by arrangement (Tu W). 18 | 6422 yds | Par 71 | SSS 71
Visitors welcome but with M only Sun ☎ preferred | ∴ per day | B L ☕ D | △ 🍸 | ↘ ⋈ prior arrangement | M 500 | [S]
★★★*Park House, Park St. T:(0952) 460128. 19rm (16 ⇨ 3 ⌂)*

SHERINGHAM
Norfolk
Map **IV** H2

Sheringham Weybourne Road, Sheringham (W side of town centre off A149)
T:(0263) 822038
18 | 6430 yds | Par 70 | SSS 71
Visitors welcome ⊠ ☎ | without M ∴ per day ∷ WE | with M .. per day | B
☙ | L D prior arrangement | ⚠ ⏶ ⤫ | ④ TR ☎ | M 650 | S
★★Beaumaris, South St. T:(0263) 822370. 25rm (15 ⇄ 2 ▥)
Splendid cliff-top links with good 'seaside turf' and plenty of space.
Straight driving is essential for a low score. The course is close to the
shore and can be very windswept.

SHIPLEY
West Yorkshire
Map **V** E6

Northcliffe High Bank Ln, Shipley,
Bradford (1¼m SW of Shipley off
A650)
T:(0274) 584085
*Parkland course with magnificent views
of moors. Testing 1st hole (18th green
between and 100 feet below tee has to be
driven over to the fairway). Societies
welcome by arrangement. 18 | 6093 yds
| Par 71 | SSS 69*
Visitors welcome | without M ∴ per
day WE | with M .. per day WE | B |
☙ | L D | ⚠ ⏶ ⤫ prior
arrangement | TR match days | 𝄞 |
M 250 | S
*★★★Bankfield, Bradford Rd, Bingley.
T:(0274) 567123. 69rm (67 ⇄ 2 ▥)*

Shipley Beckfoot Ln, Cottingley
Bridge, Bingley (2½m W of Shipley
off A650)
T:(0274) 568652
*Parkland/meadowland course, good
views, easy walking. Several long par
4's and interesting par 3's. Societies
welcome by arrangement. 18 | 6203 yds
| Par 71 | SSS 70*

Visitors welcome, with M only WE
| B ☙ (not Mon) | L D prior
arrangement (not Mon) | ⚠ | ⏶ (not
Mon) | ⤫ | ⤫ prior arrangement |
TR competition days | M 500 | S
*★★★Bankfield, Bradford Rd. T:(0274)
567123. 69rm (67 ⇄ 2 ▥)*

SHIRLAND
Derbyshire
Map **III** K2

Shirlands Golf & Squash Club
Lower Delves Shirland (S side of
village off A61)
T:(0773) 834935
*Rolling parkland course with extensive
views of Derbyshire countryside. 18 |
6021 yds | Par 71 | SSS 69*
Visitors welcome | ⏶ B L | D by
arrangement | ⚠ ⤫ ⤫ | 𝄞 | TR
comp. times at WE - check | M 350 |
S
*★★★★Swallow, Carter Ln East, Sth
Normanton. T:(0773) 812000. 123rm
⇄ ▥*

SHOREHAM
Kent
Map **II** F4

Darenth Valley Station Rd (1m E of
Shoreham on A225)
T:(09592) 2944
*Easy walking parkland course in
beautiful valley. Testing 12th hole par
4. Societies welcome (not Sun) by
arrangement. 18 | 6356 yds | Par 72 |
SSS 71*
Visitors welcome, prior
arrangement only at WE | ∴ per
day | B | L 🐝 D prior arrangement |
⚠ | ♈ (not winter evngs) | ⚲ | 🕱 | S
★★★*Bromley Court, Bromley Hill,
Bromley. T:01-464 5011. 130rm* ⇆

SHREWSBURY
Shropshire
Map III   G4

Shrewsbury Condover (4m S of
Shrewsbury off A49)
T:(074372) 2955
*Parkland course. 18 | 6212 yds | Par 70
| SSS 70*
Visitors welcome ✉ | B L 🐝 D (not
Mon) | ⚠ ♈ | TR competition days
| M 700 | S
★★★*Ainsworth's Radbrook Hall,
Radbrook Rd, Shrewsbury. T:(0743)
4861. 43rm (35 ⇆ 8 🔔) Annexe: 5rm
🔔

SHRIVENHAM
Berkshire
Map II   A3

Bremhill Park Shrivenham (½m
NE of town centre)
T:(0793) 782946
*Parkland course with easy walking. The
par 4 15th is a difficult dog leg through
woods. Societies welcome. 18 | 6040 yds
| Par 71 | SSS 71*
Visitors welcome 🕿 for Sun play | B
L D 🐝 | ⚠ ♈ ⚲ ⚮ | 🕱 | M 650 | S
★★★*Crest, Oxford Rd, Stratton St
Margaret, Swindon. T:(0793) 822921.
98rm* ⇆

SIDCUP
Greater London
Map II   F4

Sidcup Golf Club 1926 Ltd 7 Hurst
Rd, Sidcup (N side of town centre
off A222)
T:01-300 2864
*Easy walking parkland course with
natural water hazards. 9 | 5692 yds |
Par 68 | SSS 67*
Visitors welcome weekdays | with
M only WE BH | 🕿 advisable |
without M ∴ weekdays | with M ..

per day | B L | D prior arrangement
(not Mon) | 🐝 WE only | ⚠ | ♈ (not
Mon) | TR competition days |
M 450 | S
★★★*Bromley Court, Bromley Hill,
Bromley. T:01-464 5011. 130rm* ⇆

SIDMOUTH
Devon
Map I   G6

Sidmouth Cotmaton Rd, Peak Hill,
Sidmouth (W side of town centre)
T:(03955) 3451
*Situated on the side of Peak Hill offers
good views. Societies welcome by
arrangement. 18 | 5188 yds | Par 66 |
SSS 65*
Visitors welcome | ∴ per day WE
BH | B prior arrangement | L D prior
arrangement (not Tu) | 🐝 ⚠ ♈ ⚲ |
∞ by arrangement | TR 0915-1015,
1215-1415 W | M 580 | S
★★★★*Victoria, Esplanade. T:(03955)
2651. 61rm* ⇆

SILECROFT
Cumbria
Map V   B4

Silecroft Silecroft (1m SW of
Silecroft)
*Seaside course. Often windy. Easy
walking. 1st and 10th holes parallel to*

SILLOTH
Cumbria
Map VI   F6

Silloth on Solway The Clubhouse, Silloth (S side of village off B5300)
T:(0965) 31304
18 | 6400 yds | Par 72 | SSS 70
Visitors welcome, 🕿 WE | ∴ per day ∴ WE BH | B L 🐝 D prior arrangement
| ⚠ ♈ ⚲ ⚮ | TR Sun (am) | M 650 | S
★★*Golf, Criffel St. T:(0965) 31438. 23rm (11 ⇆ 11 🔔)
Billowing dunes, narrow fairways and constant subtle problems of
tactics and judgment make these superb links on the Solway an
exhilarating and searching test. The 13th is a good long hole.

SITTINGBOURNE
Kent
Map II   H4

Sittingbourne & Milton Regis Wormdale, Newington (3m W of
Sittingbourne off A249)
T:(0795) 842261
Societies welcome by arrangement. 18 | 6121 yds | Par 70 | SSS 69
Visitors welcome | with M only Sun 🕿 advisable | B D prior arrangement | 🐝
coffee only | ⚠ ♈ | ∞ | possibly | TR Sun & comp. days | M 630 | S
★★★*Great Danes, Ashford Rd, Hollingbourne. T:(0622) 30022. 127rm* ⇆ 🔔
A downland course with pleasant vistas. There are a few uphill
climbs, but the course is far from difficult. The 166-yard 2nd hole is
a testing par 3.

beach. 9 | 5627 yds | Par 68 | SSS 66
Visitors welcome | .. per day WE |
⚠ | ♈ prior arrangement | M 360
★*Old King's Head, Station Rd,
Broughton in Furness. T:(06576) 293.
9rm

SILKSTONE
South Yorkshire
Map V   F7

Silkstone Field Head, Silkstone (1m
E of Silkstone off A628)
T:(0226) 790328
*Parkland/downland course, fine views
over the Pennines. Testing golf.
Societies welcome by arrangement. 18 |
6045 yds | Par 70 | SSS 70*
Visitors welcome, with M only WE
BH | without M ∴ per day | with M
.. per day WE | B 🐝 (not F) | L D
prior arrangement (not F) | ⚠ ♈ | 🕱
| M 500 | S
★★★*Ardsley Moat House, Doncaster
Rd, Ardsley, Barnsley. T:(0226)
289401. 62rm* ⇆

SILSDEN
West Yorkshire
Map V   E6

Silsden High Brunthwaite, Silsden,
Keighley (1m E of Silsden)
T:(0535) 52998

Tight downland course which can be windy. Good views of the Aire Valley. 14 | 4870 yds | Par 65 | SSS 64 Visitors welcome, restricted Sun until 1400 | . . per day WE | ♿ | ⚐ (evng only) | TR S all day, Sun am | M 260 ★★*Beeches, Bradford Rd, Keighley. T:(0535) 607227. 10rm (2 ⇔) Annexe: 14rm (9 🍴)*

SILVERDALE
Lancashire
Map **V** C5

Silverdale Red Bridge Ln, Silverdale, Nr Carnforth (opposite Silverdale Station) T:(0524) 701300 *Difficult heathland course with rock outcrops. Excellent views.* 9 | 5256 yds (white) 4996 yds (yellow) | Par 70 | SSS 67 (white) 65 (yellow) Visitors welcome | without M . . per round WE | with M . . per day | B ⚑ | ♿ ⚐ | TR competition days | M 440 ★*Wheatsheaf, Beetham. T:(04482) 2123. 8rm (2 ⇔)*

SINDLESHAM
Berkshire
Map **II** C4

Bearwood Mole Rd (1m SW of Sindlesham on B3030) T:(0734) 760060 *Parkland course. Societies welcome.* 9 | 2499 yds | Par 35 | SSS 33 Visitors welcome | B ⚑ | ⚐ ⚲ ⋈ | ♩ | M 350 | S ★★*Cantley House, Milton Rd, Wokingham. T:(0734) 789912. 19rm ⇔*

SKEGNESS
Lincolnshire
Map **IV** F1

North Shore North Shore Rd, Skegness (1m N of town centre off A52) T:(0754) 3298 *A half links, half parkland course with easy walking and good sea views. Societies welcome by arrangement.* 18 | 6129 yds | Par 70 Visitors welcome | ∴ per day WE | B ⚑ L D | ♿ ⚐ ⋈ occasionally | M 500 ★★*Links, Drummond Rd, Seacroft. T:(0754) 3605. 21rm (2 ⇔ 4 🍴)*

SKEGNESS
Lincolnshire
Map **IV** F1

Seacroft Seacroft, Skegness (S side of town centre) T:(0754) 3020 *Societies welcome by arrangement.* 18 | 6478 yds | Par 71 | SSS 71 Visitors welcome ✉ | without M ∴ per day ∷ WE BH | with M . . per day | ⚑ B | L D prior arrangement (not Sun Tu) | ♿ ⚐ | TR until 0930 | ♩ | M 620 | S ★★*County, North Pde, Skegness. T:(0754) 2461. 44rm (33 ⇔ 11 🍴)* A typical seaside links with flattish fairways separated by low ridges. Easy to walk round. To the east are sandhills leading to the shore. Southward lies Gibraltar Point Nature Reserve.

SKELMORLIE
Strathclyde, *Ayrshire*
Map **VI** C2

Skelmorlie Skelmorlie (E side of village off A78) T:(0475) 520152 *Parkland/moorland course with magnificent views over Firth of Clyde. Societies (up to 24 M) welcome (Mon to F) by arrangement.* 18 | 5056 yds | Par 64 | SSS 64 Visitors welcome, restricted S (March to Oct) | with M . . per day WE | with M . . per day WE | B ⚑ | L D prior arrangement Tu Th | ♿ ⚐ | ⋈ | TR S Apr to Oct | M 260 ★★★🍴*Manor Park. T:(0475) 520832. 7rm (5 ⇔ 1 🍴)*

SKIPTON
North Yorkshire
Map **V** E5

Skipton Grassington Rd, Skipton (1m N of Skipton on A65) T:(0756) 3922 *Grassland course with panoramic views.* 18 | 6191 yds | Par 71 | SSS 70 Visitors welcome | B L ⚑ D (not Mon) | ♿ | ⚐ (not Mon) | ♩ | ④ WE mornings | TR WE mornings | M 300 | S ★ *Midland, Broughton Rd. T:(0756) 2781. 10rm*

SKYE, ISLE OF
Highland, *Inverness-shire*
Map **VII**
See Sconser

SLEAFORD
Lincolnshire
Map **IV** C2

Sleaford South Rauceby, Sleaford (2½m SW of Sleaford off A153) T:(05298) 273 *Flat, dry course in winter, appearance*

of links course. 18 | 6443 yds | Par 72 | SSS 71 Visitors welcome without M ∴ per day | B L ⚑ D prior arrangement | ♿ ⚐ | ♩ | TR ladies Tu, 0930-1015, 1430-1515 comp times | M 650 | S ★★*Carre Arms, Mareham Ln, Sleaford. T:(0529) 303156. 15rm (3 ⇔)*

SOLIHULL
West Midlands
Map **III** J5

Olton Mirfield Rd (1m NW of Solihull off A41) T:021-705 1083 *Parkland course, prevailing SW wind. Societies welcome by arrangement.* 18 | 6229 yds | Par 69 | SSS 71 Visitors welcome, restricted WE BH Tu (ladies day) ☎ recommended | B ⚑ L D prior arrangement (not Mon) | ♿ ⚐ | ♩ | M 600 | S ★★★*St Johns Swallow, 651 Warwick Rd. T:021-705 6777. 213rm (192 ⇔)*

Robin Hood St Bernards Rd, Solihull (2m W of Solihull off B4025) T:021-706 0061 *Pleasant parkland course with easy walking and open to good views.* 18 | 6609 yds | Par 72 | SSS 72 Visitors welcome but with M only WE BH ☎ | without M ∴ per day | with M . . per day | B (not Mon) | L D prior arrangement (not Mon Th) | L B ⚑ prior arrangement | ♿ ⚐ | ④ two ball competition days | TR WE | ④ competition days | M 600 | S ★★★*St John's Swallow, 651 Warwick Rd. T:021-705 6777. 213rm (192 ⇔)*

Shirley Stratford Rd, Monkspath, Shirley, Solihull (3m SW of Solihull off A34) T:021-744 6001

KEY

(IA1) *atlas grid reference*
T: *telephone number*
☎   *advance letter/telephone call required*
✉   *introduction from own club sec/handicap certificate/club membership card required*
..   *low fees*
∴   *medium fees*
::   *high fees*
*   *green fees not confirmed for 1987*
B   *light lunch*
L   *full lunch*
☛   *tea*
D   *dinner*
⚐   *changing rooms/showers*
⚑   *bar open mid-day and evenings*
⚒   *clubs for hire*
∞   *partners may be found*
④   *restricted time for 4 balls*
TR   *times reserved for members*
J   *professional*
S   *well-stocked shop*
M   *member*
Mon Tu W Th F S Sun
WE   *weekend*
BH   *bank holiday*

Fairly flat parkland course. 18 | 6445 yds | Par 72 | SSS 71
Visitors welcome | without M Mon-F only | ✉ required ☎ | without M :: per day | B ☛ (not Mon) | L D prior arrangement (not Mon) | ⚐ ⚑ | ④ check beforehand | ⚒ limited supply | M 300 | S
★★★*George, High St, Solihull. T:021-704 1241. 46rm (41 ⇌)*

SOUTHALL
Greater London
Map II   E3

SONNING
Berkshire
Map II   C3

Sonning Duffield Rd, Sonning (1m S of Sonning off A4)
T:(0734) 693332
Societies welcome by arrangement. 18 | 6310 yds | Par 70 | SSS 70
Visitors welcome | ✉ | with M only WE BH | without M :: per day | with M .. per day WE | B L ☛ D prior arrangement (not Th) | ⚐ ⚑ | ∞ | M 600 | S
★★★*White Hart, Sonning. T:(0734) 692277. 10rm ⇌. Annexe: 15rm (14 ⇌ 1 ⌂)*
A quality parkland course and the scene of many county championships. Wide fairways, not overbunkered, and very good greens. Holes of changing character through wooded belts.

SOUTHAMPTON
Hampshire
Map II   A6

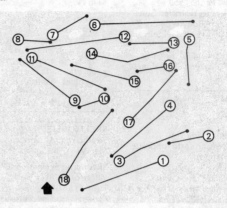

Stoneham Bassett Green Rd, Southampton (4m N of city centre off A27)
T:(0703) 768151
Societies welcome (Mon Th F) by arrangement. 18 | 6310 yds | Par 72 | SSS 70
Visitors welcome ☎ advisable | ∴ per day :: WE | B ☛ | L (not Sun) | ⚐ ⚑ ⚒ | TR competition days and before 0930 Sun | M 550 | S
★★★★*Polygon, Cumberland Pl. T:(0703) 226401. 119rm ⇌*
A hilly heather course with sand or peat sub-soil, the fairways separated by belts of woodland and gorse, presenting a varied character of terrain. The interesting 4th is a difficult par four, the long-hitter having the advantage of a down slope. The very fine 11th has cross-bunkers about 150 yards from the tee.

West Middlesex Greenford Rd, Southall (W side of town centre on A4127 off A4020)
T:01-574 3450
Gently undulating parkland course. Clubhouse includes 3 squash courts. Societies welcome weekdays by arrangement. 18 | 6242 yds | Par 69 | SSS 70
Visitors welcome weekdays | restrictions WE BH | without M .. Mon W :: Tu Th F per round :: WE | with M .. per day ∴ WE | B L ☛ (not Mon) | D prior arrangement | ⚐ ⚑ | ④ possible | TR WE | J | M 500 | S
★★★*Master Robert Motel, 366 Great West Rd, Hounslow. T:01-570 6261. 63rm ⇌*

SOUTHAMPTON
Hampshire
Map II   A6

Southampton Bassett, Southampton (4m N of city centre off A33)
T:(0703) 760472/768407
This beautiful municipal parkland course always ensures a good game, fast in summer, slow in winter. Three par 4's over 450 yds. Societies welcome. 18 | 6400 yds | Par 69 | SSS 70. Separate 9 hole course.
Open to public | .. per round (9-hole half fees) | B L ☛ D | ⚐ ⚑ ⚒ | ∞ | M 500 | S
★★*Albany, Winn Rd, The Avenue. T:(0703) 554553. 32rm (12 ⇌ 20 ⌂) Annexe: 2rm (1 ⇌ 1 ⌂)*

SOUTH BRENT
Devon
Map I E7

Wrangaton (S Devon) Wrangaton,
South Brent (2¼m SW of South
Brent off A38)
T:(03647) 3229
*Moorland course within Dartmoor
National Park. Spectacular views
towards sea and rugged terrain.
Natural fairways and hazards include
bracken, sheep, ponies. 9 | 5871 yds |
Par 68 | SSS 68*
Visitors welcome | B ⚑ | ⚴ ⛾ | ✕ |
M 250
★★🛦*Grazebrook House, South Brent.
T:(03647) 3322. 12rm (6 ⇄ 1 🛋)*

SOUTHEND-ON-SEA
Essex
Map II H3

Belfairs Park Eastwood Rd, Leigh-
on-Sea (3m W of Southend, N of
A13)
T:(0702) 525345
*Municipal parkland course run by
Southend-on-Sea Borough Council.
Tight second half through thick woods,
easy walking. 18 | 5857 yds | Par 70 |
SSS 68*
Open to public | licensed cafe under
club house generally open during
day | 🎾 | M 300 | Ⓢ
★*Balmoral, 34 Valkyrie Rd, Westcliff-
on-Sea, Southend. T:(0702) 342947.
19rm (14 ⇄ 5 🛋)*

Thorpe Hall Thorpe Hall Av,
Thorpe Bay (2m E of Southend off
A13)
T:Sec (0702) 582205. Pro (0702)
588195
*Parkland course. Societies welcome by
arrangement. 18 | 6259 yds | Par 71 |
SSS 71*
Visitors with accredited handicap
welcome, restricted WE (am) BH
(am), with M only or ✉ | without M
:: per round WE | with M .. per
day WE | B | ⚑ (not Mon) | L prior
arrangewment (not Mon) | D prior
arrangement (not Mon) | ⚴ ⛾ ⚲ |
④ early am and pm from 1st | TR
WE (am) | 🎾 | M 750 | Ⓢ
★★*Roslin, Thorpe Esp, Thorpe Bay.
T:(0702) 586375. 39rm (24 ⇄ 15 🛋)*

SOUTHERNESS
Dumfries
Map VI F6

Southerness Southerness (3½m S
of Kirkbean off A710)
T:(038788) 677
*Seaside course, windy and flat, with
magnificent views. Societies welcome by
arrangement. 18 | 6548 yds | Par 69 |
SSS 72*
Visitors welcome | ∴ per day WE |
B L D ⚑ prior arrangement (not W)
| ⚴ ⛾ ✕ | TR Ⓢ Sun before 1000 |
M 530

SOUTHPORT
Merseyside
Map V C7

The Hesketh Golf Club Cockle Dick's Ln, off Cambridge Rd, Southport (1m
NE of town centre off A565)
T:(0704) 36897
Societies welcome by arrangement. 18 | 6478 yds | Par 71 | SSS 72
Visitors welcome ☎ | without M :: per day WE | B L ⚑ D prior arrangement
| ⚴ ⛾ ⚲ doubtful | TR ☎ | 🎾 | M 550 | Ⓢ
★★*Bold, Lord St, Southport. T:(0704) 32578. 23rm (18 ⇄)*
Hesketh is the senior club in Southport, founded in 1885. The
course comprises much of the original territory plus a large area of
reclaimed land on the seaward side—essentially 'Links' in
character.

★★★🛦*Baron's Craig, Rockcliffe.
T:(055663) 255. 26rm (20 ⇄)*

SOUTHGATE
West Glamorgan
Map I E2

Pennard 2 Southgate Rd, Southgate
(NW side of village)
T:(044128) 3131
*Undulating seaside links with good
coastal views. Societies welcome by
arrangement. 18 | 6266 yds | Par 71 |
SSS 71*
Visitors welcome | without M ∴ per
day | with M .. per day WE | B ⚑ |
L D prior arrangement (not Mon) |
⚴ ⛾ ⚲ ✕ | 🎾 | M 270 | Ⓢ
★*Windsor Lodge, Mount Pleasant,
Swansea. T:(0792) 42158. 18rm (11 ⇄
3 🛋)*

SOUTH OCKENDON
Essex
Map II G3

Belhus Park Municipal Belhus
Park, South Ockenden (½m N of M
25 Jct 30 on B1335)   ➤

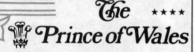

T:(0708) 854260
*Flat parkland, easy going. 18 |
5501 yds | Par 68 | SSS 68*
Visitors welcome .. per day WE
BH | B L D ♥ | ᴧ ↘ | [S] | ⋈ | ♪
★★★*Stifford Moat House, North
Stifford. T:(0375) 71451. 64rm* ⇆ 🍴

Thurrock Belhus Park Belhus Park,
South Ockendon (2m SW of South
Ockendon off B1335)
T:(0708) 854260
*Municipal parkland type course with
easy walking. Council- sponsored club.
Swimming pool. 18 | 5701 yds | Par 68
| SSS 68*
Private club but course open to
public | B ♥ L | ᴧ Ɏ ↘ | | ⋈ | [TR]
certain WE | ♪ | M 250 | [S]
★★★*Stifford Moat House, North
Stifford. T:(0375) 71451. 64rm* ⇆ 🍴

SOUTHPORT
Merseyside
Map **V** C7

Hillside Hastings Rd, Southport
(2m SW of town centre on A565)
T:(0704) 67169
*Links course with natural hazards open
to strong wind. Societies by
arrangement. 18 | 6850 yds | Par 72 |
SSS 74*
Visitors welcome restricted Tu (am)
WE BH | 🕿 | without M :: per day
WE | with M .. per day WE | ♥ B |
L D prior arrangement (not F) | ᴧ
Ɏ | [TR] 1200-1400, 1630-1830 | ♪ |
M 840 | [S] ↘ ⋈
★★★*Royal Clifton, Promenade.
T:(0704) 33771. 115rm (104* ⇆ 2 🍴*)

Park Park Rd, Southport (N side of
town centre off A565)
T:(0704) 30133, Merseyside
*Very flat municipal parkland course. 18
| 6200 yds | Par 70 | SSS 70*
Open to public 🕿 restricted WE
1100-1400 | B L ♥ from cafe | Ɏ M
only | ↘ | M 400 | [S]
★★★★*Prince of Wales, Lord St,
Southport. T:(0704) 36688. 101rm (82
⇆ 18 🍴)*

Royal Birkdale Waterloo Rd,
Southport (1¾m S of town centre
on A565)
T:(0704) 69903
*Championship Links. 18 | 6711 yds |
Par 72 | SSS 73*
Visitors welcome 🕿 ⊠ | fees on
application | B L ♥ D prior

SOUTHPORT
Merseyside
Map **V** C7

Southport & Ainsdale Bradshaws Ln, Ainsdale, Southport (3m S of
Southport off A565)
T:(0704) 78000
18 | 6603 yds | Par 72 | SSS 73
Visitors welcome (except WE, BH) 🕿 | ✳ | B L ♥ | D prior arrangement | ᴧ Ɏ
↘ | ④ Th morning | [TR] before 0920, 1200-1424, after 1600 | ♪ | M 800 | [S]
★★★★*Prince of Wales, Lord St. T:(0704) 36688. 101rm (82 ⇆ 18 🍴)*
S and A, as it is known in the North is another of the fine
Championship courses for which this part of the country is famed.
This Club has staged many important events, the qualifying rounds
of the 1971, 1976 and 1983 Open Championships, the British Ladies
Open and other professional and amateur tournaments. Seaside
golf of the highest order includes a testing par 3 1st hole and the
famed Gumbley's bunker at the par 5 16th.

SOUTH SHIELDS
Tyne and Wear
Map **V** F2

South Shields Cleadon Hills, South
Shields (SE side of town centre off
A1300)
T:(0632) 568942
*Societies welcome (Th) by arrangement.
18 | 6295 yds | Par 71 | SSS 70*
Visitors welcome | without M ..
per day ∴ WE | with M .. per day
WE | B L ♥ | D prior arrangement |
ᴧ Ɏ ↘ | ♪ | M 800 | [S]
★★*New Crown, Mowbray Rd. T:(0632)
4553472. 11rm (3 ⇆ 2 🍴)*
A slightly undulating downland course on a limestone base
ensuring good conditions underfoot. Open to strong winds, the
course is testing but fair. There are fine views of the coastline both to
the north and the south.

SCORE CARD:			
1	183	10	179
2	348	11	328
3	387	12	494
4	427	13	151
5	187	14	459
6	516	15	286
7	437	16	373
8	490	17	387
9	305	18	327

arrangement | ᴧ Ɏ ↘ | [TR] 1230-
1330 | [S]
★★★★*Prince of Wales, Lord St.
T:(0704) 36688. 101rm (82 ⇆ 18 🍴)*

Southport Municipal Park Rd
West, Southport (N side of town
centre off A565)
T:(0704) 35286
*Municipal seaside links course. Played
over by Alt Golf Club. 18 | 5900 yds |
Par 70 | SSS 69*
Open to public | .. per day WE | B
L ♥ D | ᴧ Ɏ ↘ ⋈ | [TR] 🕿 | [S]
★★★★*Prince of Wales, Lord St.
T:(0704) 36688. 101rm (82 ⇆ 18 🍴)*

Southport Old Links Moss Ln,
Churchtown, Southport (NW side
of town centre off A5267)
T:(0704) 28207
*Seaside course, easy walking. 9 |
6486 yds | Par 72 | SSS 71*

Visitors welcome, restricted W BH
⊠ 🕿 preferred | B L ♥ D prior
arrangement (not Mon) | ᴧ Ɏ | [TR]
competition days (Ladies Day) |
M 370
★★*Bold, Lord St. T:(0704) 32578.
23rm (18 ⇆)*

SOUTH QUEENSFERRY
Lothian, *East Lothian*
Map **VII** F2

Dundas Parks South Queensferry
(1m S of Queensferry on A8000)
Secretary J C Davidson
T:031-331 1902
*Parkland course situated on the estate
of Lady Jane Stewart- Clark. For 18
holes the 9 are played twice, yardage
and par doubled. 9 | 3013 yds | Par 35*
Visitors welcome with M .. per
round | ᴧ | [TR] competition days |
M 500 (restricted) ➥

★★★*Forth Bridges Moat House, Forth Road Bridge, South Queensferry. T:031-331 1199. 108rm ⇄*

SOUTH SHIELDS
Tyne and Wear
Map **V** F2

Whitburn Lizard Ln (2½m SE of South Shields off A183)
T:(0683) 292144
Parkland course. 18 | 6035 yds | Par 70 | SSS 69
Visitors welcome | ‥ per day or per round ∴ per round WE | B ☕ | L D prior arrangement | ⛺ 🍸 ↘ | ⋈ | Ȝ | M 500 | [S]
★★★*Seaburn, Queen's Pde, Seaburn, Sunderland. T:(0783) 292041. 82rm (79 ⇄ 3 🚿)*

SOUTH UIST, ISLE OF
Western Isles, *Outer Hebrides*
Map **VII** A5
See Askernish

SOUTHWICK
Hampshire
Map **II** B7

Southwick Park Naval Recreation Centre Pinsley Dr, Southwick, Fareham (½m SE of Southwick off B2177)
T:(0705) 380131
Set in 100 acres of parkland. 18 | 5855 yds | Par 69 | SSS 69
Visitors welcome, restricted WE | ∴ per round ∴ per day | L D prior arrangement | B ☕ | ⛺ 🍸 ↘ | ⋈ sometimes | [4] ☎ | M 570 | [S]
❀★★*Old House, Wickham. T:(0329) 833049. 10rm ⇄ 🚿)*

SOUTHWOLD
Suffolk
Map **IV** K6

Southwold The Common, Southwold (½m W of Southwold off A1095)
T:(0502) 723234
Commonland course with 4 acre practice ground and panoramic views of the sea. 9 | 6001 yds | Par 70 | SSS 69
Visitors welcome | * | B L ☕ D by arrangement | ⛺ | 🍸 (not Mon) | ↘ | [TR] competition days | Ȝ | M 450 | [S]
★★★*Swan, Market Pl. T:(0502) 722186. 34rm (9 ⇄ 10 🚿) Annexe: 8rm ⇄*

SOWERBY
West Yorkshire
Map **V** E6

Ryburn The Shaw, Norland, Sowerby Bridge (1m S of Sowerby Bridge off A58)
T:(0422) 831355
Moorland course, easy walking. Societies welcome by arrangement. 9 | 5002 yds | Par 66 | SSS 65
Visitors welcome | B L ☕ D (not Mon) | ⛺ 🍸 | ⋈ | [TR] competition days | M 217
★★★*Ladbroke, Ainley Top, Huddersfield. T:(0422) 75431. 118rm ⇄*

SPALDING
Lincolnshire
Map **IV** D3

Spalding Surfleet, Nr Spalding (5m N of Spalding off A16)
T:Pro (077585) 474, Sec (077585) 386
A pretty, well laid-out course in a fenland area. The River Glen runs beside the 1st and 2nd holes, and streams, ponds and new tree plantings add to the variety of this well-maintained course. The new clubhouse has good modern facilities. Societies welcome Th by arrangement. 18 | 5807 yds | Par 68 | SSS 68 | Ladies' 18 | 5295 yds | Par 73 | SSS 71
Visitors welcome ✉ | without M ‥ per round ∴ per day weekdays, ∴ per round/day WE BH | with M ‥ per round/day weekdays, ‥ per round ∴ per day WE BH (reduced rates for juniors) | ☕ B L D by prior arrangement (not Tu) | ⛺ 🍸 | Ȝ | M 500 | [S]
★★*Dembleby, Broad St, Spalding. T:(0775) 67060. 8rm (6 🚿)*

SPEY BAY
Grampian, *Moray*
Map **VII** H4

Spey Bay Spey Bay, Fochabers (4½m N of Fochabers on B9104)
T:(0343) 820424
Seaside course, easy walking, good views. 18 | 6059 yds | Par 71 | SSS 69
Visitors welcome, restricted Sun ☎ advisable | * | B L ☕ D | ⛺ 🍸 | [TR] competitions | M 320 | [S]
★★*Spey Bay. T:(0343) 820424. 9rm (5 ⇄ 4 🚿)*

SPITTAL OF GLENSHEE
Tayside, *Perthshire*
Map **VII** H7

Dalmunzie Dalmunzie Estate (2m NW of Spittal of Glenshee)
T:(025085) 226
Grassy moorland course, highest in Britain, difficult walking. Testing 5th hole. Small but good greens. 9 | 2200 yds | Par 64 | SSS 62
Visitors welcome | ‥ per day under 15s half rate | B L ☕ D prior arrangement | 🍸 | ⋈ (probable) | M 22
★★♣♣*Dalmunzie House, Spittal of Glenshee. T:(025085) 224. 19rm (10 ⇄)*

STAFFORD
Staffordshire
Map **III** H4

Stafford Castle Newport Rd, Stafford (SW side of town centre off A518)
T:(0785) 3821
Meadowland course. 9 | 6347 yds | Par 71 | SSS 71
Visitors welcome except S and Sun am, BH | without M ‥ per day ∴ WE | with M ‥ per day | B L ☕ D prior arrangement (not Tu Th) | ⛺ ⋈ | 🍸 | M 350 | [S]
★★*Swan, 46 Greengate St. T:(0785) 58142. 31rm ⇄*

STALYBRIDGE
Greater Manchester
Map **V** E7

Stamford Huddersfield Rd (2m NE of Stalybridge off A635)
T:(045 75) 2126
Moorland course. Extremely hilly, with hard walking. 18 | 5619 yds | Par 70 | SSS 67
Visitors welcome, restricted Tu (Ladies day) WE (competitions) | ‥ per day ∴ WE | B L ☕ D prior arrangement (not Mon) | ⛺ ↘ ⋈ | 🍸 (not Mon) | M 310 | [S]
★★*York House, York Pl, Ashton-under-Lyne. T:061-330 5899. 26rm (8 ⇄ 3 🚿)*

STAMFORD
Lincolnshire,
Map **IV** C4

Burghley Park St Martins (1m S of Stamford on B1081)
T:(0780) 53789

Short flat parkland course with superb greens situated in the grounds of Burghley House. Societies welcome midweek by arrangement. 18 | 6236 yds | Par 71 | SSS 70
Visitors welcome ☎ preferred | without M ∴ per day WE | with M .. per day | B L D ☕ | △ | 🍸 | ⟍ ⋈ | ⟆ | M 800 | [S]
★★★*George of Stamford, St Martins, Stamford. T:(0780) 55171. 44rm (43 🛁 1 🚿)*

STANLEY
Durham
Map **VI** K6

South Moor The Middles, Craghead, Stanley (1½m SE of Stanley on B6313)
T:(0207) 232848
Moorland course with natural hazards. Dances and social functions. 18 | 6550 yds | Par 72 | SSS 71
Visitors welcome | without M .. per day ∴ WE | with M .. per day ∴ WE | B ☕ L D | △ | 🍸 | ⟍ | M 450
★★★*Lumley Castle, Chester-le-Street. T:(0385) 891111. 8rm 🛁 Annexe: 42rm (33 🛁 9 🚿)*

STANMORE
Greater London
Map **II** E3

Stanmore Gordon Ave, Stanmore (S side of town centre)
T:01-954 2599
North London parkland course. 18 | 5982 yds | Par 68 | SSS 68
Visitors welcome ☎ preferred | restricted WE BH | ∴ per round ∷ per day | L (not Mon) | B ☕ | D prior arrangement | △ 🍸 ⟍ | [TR] WE | M 528 | [S]
★★★*Grim's Dyke, Old Redding, Harrow Weald. T:01-954 4227. 8rm 🛁 Annexe: 40rm 🛁*

STANTON-BY-DALE
Derbyshire
Map **III** K3

Erewash Valley nr Ilkeston (1m W of Stanton-by-Dale)
T:(0602) 323258
Parkland/meadowland course. 8 new holes overlooking valley and M1. Unique 4th and 5th in Victorian quarry bottom; 5th testing par 3. Societies by arrangement. 18 | 6436 yds | Par 72 | SSS 72
Visitors welcome ☎ advisable | ∴ per day WE | B L ☕ | D (prior arrangement) (not F Sun) | △ 🍸 ⟍ ⋈ | ⟆ | [TR] Tu (ladies day), WE ☎ for details | [4] ☎ | M 650 | [S]
★★★*Post House, Bostocks Ln, Sandiacre. T:(0602) 397800. 107rm 🛁*

STAPLEFORD ABBOTTS
Essex
Map **II** F3

Skips Horsemanside, Tysea Hill, Stapleford Abbotts (1m E of Stapleford Abbotts off B175)
T:(04023) 48234
Level course, testing in places. 18 | 6146 yds | Par 71 | SSS 71
Visitors welcome | △ | [S]
★★★*Prince Regent, Woodford Bridge. T:01-504 7635. 10rm 🛁 🚿*

STAVERTON
Northamptonshire
Map **IV** A6

Staverton Park (¾m NE of Staverton on A425)
T:(03272) 705911
Open course, fairly testing with good views. 18 | 6574 yds | Par 71 | SSS 71
Visitors welcome without M ∴ per day | B L ☕ D | △ 🍸 ⟍ ⋈ | ⟆ | M 410 | [S]
★★★*Crossroads, Weedon. T:(0327) 40354. 28rm 🛁*

STEVENAGE
Hertfordshire
Map **IV** D8

Stevenage Aston Ln, Stevenage (4m SE of Stevenage off A602)
T:(043888) 424
Natural water hazards designed by John Jacobs with some wooded areas. 18 | 6451 yds | Par 72 | SSS 71. Driving range | Par 3 course
Visitors welcome without M | * | B L ☕ D | △ 🍸 ⟍ ⋈ | ⟆ | [TR] Sun morning | M 350 | [S]
★★★*Roebuck Inn, London Rd, Broadwater. T:(0438) 65444. 54rm 🛁*

STEVENSTON
Strathclyde, *Ayr*
Map **VI** C3

Ardeer Greenhead (½m N of Stevenston, off A78)
T:(0294) 64542, Ayrshire
Parkland course, with natural hazards. 18 | 6630 yds | Par 72 | SSS 72
Visitors welcome restricted WE | without M .. per day ∴ WE | with M .. per day WE | B L ☕ (not Th) | D prior arrangement (not Th) | △ 🍸 | [TR] S (Sun ☎ for details) | ⟆ | M 500 | [S]
★★★★*Hospitality Inn, Roseholm, Annickwater, Irvine. T:(0294) 74272. 128rm 🛁 🚿*

STIRLING
Central, *Stirlingshire*
Map **VI** E1

Stirling Queens Rd (W side of town on B8051)
T:(0786) 64098
Undulating parkland course with magnificent views. Testing 15th Cotton's Fancy 395 yds (par 4). 18 | 6409 yds | Par 72 | SSS 71
Visitors welcome, restricted WE ☎ advisable | ∴ per round or per day weekdays ∴ per round ∷ per day WE | with M .. per day WE | B | L ☕ prior arrangement | D prior arrangement (not Tu Sun) | △ 🍸 ⟍ | [TR] WE | M 950 | [S]
★★*King Robert, Glasgow Rd, Bannockburn. T:(0786) 811666. 21rm 🛁*

STOCKPORT
Greater Manchester
Map **V** E8

Heaton Moor Heaton Mersey, Stockport (N of town centre off B5169)
T:061-432 2134
Parkland course, easy walking. Societies welcome by arrangement. 18 | 5907 yds | Par 70 | SSS 69
Visitors welcome, restricted Tu BH | B ☕ | L D prior arrangement (not Mon) | △ 🍸 ⟍ | [TR] Tu (ladies day) W 1130-1400 (members have preference), summer competitions | ⟆ | M 400 | [S]
★★★*Belgrade, Dialston Ln, Stockport. T:061-483 3851. 160rm 🛁*

Marple Barnsfold Rd, Marple, Stockport (S side of town centre)
T:061-427 2311
Parkland course. 18 | 5506 yds | Par 68 | SSS 67
Visitors welcome | ∴ per day WE | B L (not Mon) ☕ D | △ 🍸 | M 250 | [S] (WE only)
★★★*Belgrade, Dialston Ln, Stockport. T:061-483 3851. 160rm 🛁*

STOCKPORT
Greater Manchester
Map **V**   E8

Stockport Offerton Rd, Stockport (4m SE of Stockport on A627)
T:061-427 2001
18 | 6290 yds | Par 71 | SSS 70
Visitors welcome | without M ∴ per day : : WE | with M . . per day WE | B L
♀ (not Mon) | D prior arrangement (not Mon) | ⚘ ♈ | TR 1230-1345 daily |
M 500 | S
***Alma Lodge, 149 Buxton Rd. T:061-483 4431. 70rm (53 ⇌)
A beautifully situated inland course in wide open countryside. It is
not too long but requires that the player plays all the shots, to
excellent greens.

Mirrlees Hazel Grove, Stockport
(2m SE of town centre off A6)
T:061-449 9513
A flat parkland course, easy walking. 9
| 6102 yds | Par 69 | SSS 69
Visitors are welcome with M | B ♀ |
♈ ⚘ S TR Tu WE | M 400
***Alma Lodge, 149 Buxton Rd,
Stockport. T:061-483 4431. 70rm (53
⇌)

STOCKSBRIDGE
South Yorkshire
Map **V**   F7

Stocksbridge & District Royd Ln,
Townend, Deepcar, Sheffield (S
side of town centre)
T:(0742) 882003
Hilly moorland course undergoing
extension from 15 to 18 holes.
Visitors welcome | without M . .
per day ∴ WE | with M . . per day |
B | L ♀ | ⚘ ♈ | ⋈ probably | TR
competitions | M 200
***Ardsley Moat House, Doncaster
Rd, Ardsley. T:(0226) 289401. 62rm ⇌

STOCKSFIELD
Northumberland
Map **VI**   K6

Stocksfield New Ridley Rd,
Stocksfield (2½m SE of Stocksfield
off A695)
T:(0661) 843041
Challenging parkland (9 holes)
woodland (9 holes) course. Societies
welcome by arrangement. 18 | 5626 yds
| Par 68 | SSS 68
Visitors welcome, restricted W
(am), with M only WE | without M
. . per day ∴ WE | with M . . per
day WE | B ♀ prior arrangement |
⚘ ♈ | M 750 | S
**Beaumont,. Beaumont St, Hexham.
T:(0434) 602331. 22rm (2 ⇌ 14 ♨)

STOCKTON-ON-TEES
Cleveland
Map **V**   F3

Teesside Acklam Rd, Thornaby
(1½m SE of Stockton on A1130)
T:(0642) 676249
Parkland course, easy walking. 18 |
6472 yds | Par 72 | SSS 71
Visitors welcome, but with member
only weekdays after 1630 WE until
1100 | without M ∴ per day : : WE |
with M . . per day WE | B L ♀ D
prior arrangement | ⚘ ♈ | ⋈ | ④
when singles competition is being
played | M 450 | S
***Post House Hotel, Low Ln,
Thornaby-on-Tees. T:(0642) 591213.
136rm ⇌

STOKE-ON-TRENT
Staffordshire
Map **III**   H3

Burslem Wood Farm, High Ln,
Tunstall, Stoke-on-Trent (4m N of
city centre on B5049)
T:(0782) 87006
A moorland course on the outskirts of
Tunstall with hard walking. Societies
welcome by arrangement. 9 | 5615 yds |

Par 66 | SSS 66
Visitors welcome with M or ⊠ | . .
per day WE | B ♀ | L D prior
arrangement (not W) | ⚘ ♈ | ⋈ | TR
S am | M 230
***Stakis Grand, 66 Trinity St,
Hanley. T:(0782) 22361. 93rm ⇌

Greenway Hall Stanley Rd,
Stockton Brook (5m NE of Stoke-
on- Trent off A53)
T:(0782) 503158 (Club) 503095 (Mgr)
Moorland course with fine views of the
Pennines. 18 | 5802 yds | Par 68 |
SSS 68
Visitors welcome with M Tu W F,
without M except S Sun am |
without M ∴ per day | with M . .
per day | L D 24 hours' notice | B ♀
prior arrangement on day | ⚘ ♈ | ⋈
| M 400
****North Stafford, Station Rd,
Stoke on Trent. T:(0782) 48501. 70rm
(42 ⇌ 28 ♨)

Trentham Barlaston Old Rd,
Trentham, Stoke-on-Trent (3m S of
Stoke-on-Trent off A5035)
T:(0782) 658109
Parkland course. The par 3 4th is a
testing hole. Societies welcome by
arrangement. Squash courts. 18 |
6523 yds | Par 72 | SSS 71
Visitors welcome ☎ | : : per day
WE | B L ♀ D prior arrangement
(not Sun Mon F) | ⚘ ♈ ⚲ | ④ 0900-
1000, 1330-1430 | TR 1230-1400 and
competition days | ④ 0900-1000,
1330-1430 | ♊ | M 733 | S
****North Stafford, Station Rd.
T:(0782) 48501. 70rm (42 ⇌ 28 ♨)

Trentham Park Trentham Park,
Stoke-on-Trent (3m SW of Stoke-
on-Trent off A34 adj. to Junction 15

of M6)
T:(0782) 658800
Fine parkland course. Societies welcome
by arrangement (well in advance) (W
and F only). 18 | 6403 yds | Par 71 |
SSS 71
Visitors welcome ✉ | ☎ for WE BH
| * | B L ☞ (not Mon) D | (book
before play not Mon) parties by
arrangement | ♨ Ⴤ ⟍ | TR |
competition days | ϑ | M 600 | Ⓢ
★★★*Clayton Lodge, Clayton Rd,*
Newcastle-under-Lyme. T:(0782)
613093. 50rm ⇄

STOKE POGES
Buckinghamshire
Map II   D3

Farnham Park Park Rd, Stoke
Poges (W side of village off B416)
T:(02814) 3332
Public parkland course in a pleasing
setting. 18 | 5847 yds | Par 69 | SSS 68
Visitors welcome without M | D L B
☞ | ♨ Ⴤ Ⓢ⟍ | ⋈ | M 500
★★*Ethorpe, Packhorse Rd, Gerrards*
Cross. T:(0753) 882039. 29rm (28 ⇄ 1
🛏)

STONE
Staffordshire
Map III   H3

Stone The Filleybrooks, Stone (1m
W of Stone on A34)
T:(0785) 813103
Parkland course with easy walking.
Societies welcome by arrangement. 9 |
6272 yds | Par 71 | SSS 70
Visitors welcome but with M only
WE BH | without M .. per day |
with M .. per day WE | B ☞ (not
Mon) | L D prior arrangement (not
Mon) | ♨ Ⴤ | ⋈ | TR WE | ϑ |
M 350 | Ⓢ
★★★*Crown, High St. T:(0785)*
813535. 13rm ⇄ *Annexe: 16rm* 🛏

STONEHAVEN
Grampian, *Kincardineshire*
Map VII   K6

Stonehaven Cowie, Stonehaven
(1m N of Stonehaven off A92)
T:(0569) 62124
Challenging meadowland course
overlooking sea with 3 gullies and
splendid views. Children (accompanied
by adults) welcome. 18 | 5103 yds |
Par 66 | SSS 65
Visitors welcome, restricted
competition days | .. per day ∴
WE | B L ☞ D prior arrangement
(no catering Mon Th, except BH) |
♨ Ⴤ | ⋈ (usually) | Tu Th 0930-
1015 (Ladies), W 1215-1315, WE
until 1600, first W of month
(competitions) | ④ ☎ | M 800 | Ⓢ
★★★*Commodore, Cowie Pk. T:(0569)*
62936. 40rm ⇄ 🛏

STORNOWAY
Western Isles, *Isle of Lewis*
Map VII   C2

Stornoway Lady Lever Park,
Stornoway (N side of town centre

off A857)
T:(0851) 2240
Picturesque tree-lined parkland course,
fine views. Dardanelles - most difficult
par 5 in Europe. 18 | 5120 yds | Par 68
| SSS 66
Visitors welcome, no Sun play | ..
per round per day | B ☞ L D prior
arrangement | ♨ Ⴤ ⟍ | ⋈ | TR W
(eve) S | M 200 | Ⓢ
★★★*Caberfeidh. T:(0851) 2604. 39rm*
⇄

STOURBRIDGE
Worcestershire
Map III   H5

Hagley Country Club Wassell
Grove, Hagley (1m E of Hagley off
A456)
T:(0562) 883701
Parkland course set beneath the Clent
Hills; there are superb views. 18 |
6298 yds | Par 72 | SSS 72
Visitors welcome | B ☞ | L (not
Mon) | D (prior arrangement) | Ⴤ ♨
⋈ | ϑ | TR W morning, S and Sun
morning | M 450 | Ⓢ
★★*Talbot Hotel, High St, Stourbridge.*
T:(0384) 394350. 21rm (6 ⇄ 1 🛏)

STRANRAER
Wigtownshire
Map VI   C6

Stranraer Creachmore by Stranraer
(2½m NW of Stranraer on A718)
T:(0776) 87245
Parkland course with beautiful view of
Lochryan. 18 | 6300 yds | Par 70 |
SSS 71
Visitors welcome | ☎ parties |
without M ∴ per day WE | B L ☞ D
prior arrangement | ♨ Ⴤ | TR WE
until 1930, 1230-1330 | M 450 | Ⓢ
★★★*North West Castle, Stranraer.*
T:(0776) 4413. 74rm ⇄ *Annexe: 3rm*
⇄

STREATLEY-ON-THAMES
Berkshire
Map II   B3

Goring & Streatley Rectory Rd, Streatley-on-Thames (N of village off A417)
T:(0491) 873229
Societies welcome by arrangement. 18 | 6255 yds | Par 71 | SSS 70
Visitors welcome, with M only WE BH | B ☞ | D L (not Mon) | ⋈ ☎ | ♨ Ⴤ ⟍
(limited) | ϑ | M 740 | Ⓢ
★★★Swan, Streatley. T:(0491) 873737. 25rm ⇄ 🛏
A parkland/moorland course that requires 'negotiating' with four
well-known first holes separating the men from the boys up to the
heights of the 5th tee to which there is a 300ft climb. Wide fairways,
not overbunkered, with nice rewards on the way home down the
last few holes.

STRATFORD-ON-AVON
Warwickshire
Map **III** J6

Stratford-on-Avon Tiddington Rd,
Stratford-on-Avon (¾m E of
Stratford-on-Avon on B4086)
T:(0789) 205749
*Beautiful parkland course. The par 3
16th is tricky and the par 5 17th and
18th provide a tough end. Societies
welcome (Tu Th) by arrangement.
Juniors welcome if introduced.* 18 |
6309 yds | Par 72 | SSS 69
Visitors welcome ☎ | WE limited |
without M ∴ per day WE | B ♥ | L
D prior arrangement (not Mon) | ⚘
Ⴤ ↘ | ✕ prior arrangement | TR W
(Ladies) competitions | M 750 | S
★★★*Alveston Manor, Clopton Br.*
T:(0789) 204581. *112rm* ⇄

Welcombe Hotel Warwick Rd,
Stratford-on-Avon (1½m NE of
Stratford-on-Avon off A46)
T:(0789) 295252
*This wooded parkland course has great
character and boasts superb views of the
River Avon, Stratford and the
Cotswolds. It is a good test for all
standards.* 18 | 6202 yds | Par 70 |
SSS 70

Without M ∴ per day ∶∶ WE | with
M ∙∙ per day | B L ♥ D | ⚘ Ⴤ ↘ ✕
| TR WE BH (am) | M 300 | S
★★★★*Welcombe, Warwick Rd.*
T:(0789) 295252. *85rm* ⇄

STRATHAVEN
Strathclyde, *Lanarkshire*
Map **VI** E3

Strathaven Overton Av, Glasgow
Rd, Strathaven (NW side of town
on A726)
T:(0357) 20421
*Parkland course with panoramic views
over town and Avon valley.* 18 |
6226 yds | Par 71 | SSS 70
Visitors welcome | without M ∶∶
per day WE | with M ∙∙ per day | B
L ♥ D (not Tu) | ⚘ Ⴤ ↘ | ✕ | ④ W
| TR WE BH | M 900 | S
★★★*Stuart, 2 Cornwall Way, East
Kilbride.* T:(03552) 21161. *30rm* (26
⇄ 4 🛁)

STRATHPEFFER
Highland, *Ross and Cromarty*
Map **VII** F4

Strathpeffer Spa Strathpeffer (N
side of village off A834)
T:(0997) 21219

*Moorland course with many natural
hazards (no sand bunkers), hard
walking, fine views. Testing 3rd hole
(par 3) across loch. Societies welcome
by arrangement.* 18 | 4813 yds | Par 65
| SSS 65
Visitors welcome | ∙∙ per day WE |
B ♥ L D (high tea) not catering
Mon | ⚘ Ⴤ ↘ ✕ ☎ | TR Tu S
0800-1000, 1300-1430, 1600-1930 Sun
(until 1000) | M 360 | S
❀★*Holly Lodge.* T:(0997) 21254. *7rm*
(2 ⇄ 3 🛁)

STROMNESS
Orkney Islands
Map **VII** J3

Stromness Stromness (S side of
town centre off A965)
T:(0856) 850245
*Testing parkland/seaside course with
easy walking. Beautiful holiday course
with magnificent views of Scapa Flow.
Table tennis, bowling green, tennis
court.* 18 | 4762 yds | Par 65 | SSS 64
Visitors welcome | B (evenings) ♥ |
⚘ | Ⴤ (evenings) | ↘ ✕ | TR
1730-1830 competitions | M 120 | S
★★*Stromness, Victoria St.* T:(0856)
850298. *40rm* (12 ⇄ 21 🛁)

★★★★ H

WELCOMBE HOTEL & GOLF COURSE
STRATFORD-UPON-AVON
Warwickshire
Telephone: (0789) 295252 Telex 31347

The Welcombe Hotel is situated in 150 acres of wooded parkland and boasts
its own private golf course but only 1½ miles from Shakespeare's Stratford.
A four star luxury Jacobean style hotel where the 1st tee is only a few yards
from the restaurant terrace. An ideal base for touring the Cotswolds.

Special golfing packages throughout the year —

Rates and brochure on request.

VENICE SIMPLON-ORIENT-EXPRESS HOTEL

SUNDERLAND
Tyne and Weir
Map **V** F2

Wearside Coxgreen, Sunderland
(3½m W of Sunderland off A183)
T:(0783) 342518
18 | 6248 yds | Par 71 | SSS 70
Visitors welcome, restricted WE | ∴
per day | B ☕ (not Mon) | L D prior
arrangement (not Mon) | ⚲ ╲ | ♈
(not lunchtime Mon) | ♪ | M 600 | Ⓢ
★★★*Seaburn, Queen's Pde, Seaburn.
T:(0783) 292041. 82rm (79 ⇄ 3 ∰)*

SCORE CARD:

1	172	10	390
2	371	11	352
3	502	12	365
4	347	13	224
5	570	14	150
6	350	15	303
7	160	16	417
8	375	17	351
9	339	18	476

Open undulating parkland course rolling down to the River Wear and beneath the shadow of the famous Penshaw Monument, a folly erected by a past Lord Lambton. Two ravines cross the course presenting a variety of challenging holes.

SUNNINGDALE
Berkshire
Map **II** D4

Sunningdale Ridgmount Rd,
Sunningdale (1m S of Sunningdale
off A30)
T:(0990) 21681
*Heather and pine course. 2 18-hole
course | Old 6341 yds, New 6676 yds |
Par 70(70) | SSS 70(72)*
Visitors welcome midweek ☎ ⊠ |
with M only WE BH | ✳ | B | L ☕
(not Mon) | ⚲ ♈ ╲ | Ⓣ︎Ⓡ︎ 1200-1330 |
M 450 | Ⓢ
★★★★*Berystede, Bagshot Rd,
Sunninghill, Ascot. T:(0990) 23311.
88rm ⇄*

Sunningdale Ladies Cross Rd,
Sunningdale (1m S of Sunningdale
off A30)
T:(0990) 20507
*Heathland course. 18 | 3622 yds |
Par 60 | SSS 60*
Visitors welcome ⊠ ☎ | ladies ∴

per day WE | men ∷ per day WE | B
L ☕ (usually) | ⚲ ♈ | ④ 0900-1100
WE BH competitions | Ⓣ︎Ⓡ︎
competition days | M 350
★★★★*Berystede, Bagshot Rd,
Sunninghill, Ascot. T:(0990) 23311.
88rm ⇄*

SUTTON COLDFIELD
West Midlands
Map **III** J4

Sutton Coldfield Thornhill Rd, Streetly, Sutton Coldfield (3m NW of Sutton Coldfield on B4138)
T:021-353 9633
18 | 6541 yds | Par 72 | SSS 71
Visitors welcome restricted Tu (0900-1100) and limited WE BH ☎ | without M
∴ per day ∷ WE BH | with M ∴ per day WE | B ☕ not F | L D prior
arrangement | ⚲ ♈ | Ⓣ︎Ⓡ︎Tu 0830-1100 (ladies), competition and medal days |
M 500 | Ⓢ
★★*Parson & Clerk Motel, Chester Rd, Streetley. T:021-352 1747. 30rm ∰*
A fine natural, heathland course, which is surprising when the high-rise buildings of Birmingham are not far away. It is a course on which good driving from the tee is essential. If that department of the game is weak then the golfer can expect plenty of trouble.

SURBITON
Greater London
Map **II** E4

Surbiton Woodstock Ln,
Chessington (2m S of Surbiton off
A3)
T:01-398 3101
*Parkland course with easy walking.
Societies welcome by arrangement. 18 |
6211 yds | Par 70 | SSS 70*
Visitors welcome but with M only
WE BH | B ☕ | L D prior
arrangement | ⚲ ♈ ╲ | ⋈ prior
arrangement | M 550 | Ⓢ
★★★*Richmond Hill, 146-150
Richmond Hill, Richmond. T:01-940
2247. 125rm (110 ⇄ 4 ∰)*

SUTTON BRIDGE
Lincolnshire
Map **IV** E3

Sutton Bridge New Rd, Sutton
Bridge (E side of village off A17)
T:(0406) 350323
Parkland course. 9 | 5804 yds | Par 70 |

SSS 68
Visitors welcome with M only WE |
without M **..** per day | with M **..**
per day | B ♨ | L | D prior
arrangement (no catering Mon) | ⚗
| ⚲ (not Mon) | ⬉ | TR WE | M 330
| S |
★★*Red Lion, Market Pl, Spalding.*
T:(0775) 2869. 27rm (4 ⇌ 1 ⌂)

SUTTON COLDFIELD
West Midlands
Map **III** J4

Belfry Lichfield Rd, Wishaw (4m E
of Sutton Coldfield at junction of
A446/A4091)
T:(0675) 70301
*The headquarters of the PGA, situated
in a 370-acre park, only 10 miles north
east of Birmingham. The two 18-hole
courses, the Brabazon and Derby have
been designed by Peter Alliss and Dave
Thomas. The Brabazon, a demanding
championship course, has eleven holes
on which one has to negotiate water.
Streams and lakes are features of the
courses and spectators have been taken
into account. Societies are welcome.*
Brabazon: 18 | 6975 yds | Par 73.
Derby: 18 | 6077 yds | Par 70
Visitors welcome ☎ 2 weeks in
advance | ✉ for Brabazon course |
Brabazon **::** per day, Derby **∴** per
day WE | B L ♨ D prior
arrangement | ⚗ ⚲ ⬉ | TR ⋈
residents only before 1000. | ⅃ | S |
★★★★*Belfry, Lichfield Rd, Wishaw.*
T:(0675) 70301. 170rm ⇌ ⌂

Little Aston Streetly (3½m NW of
Sutton Coldfield off A454)
T:021-353 2066

*Societies welcome weekdays by
arrangement. 18 | 6724 yds | Par 72 |
SSS 73*
Visitors welcome ☎ ✉ essential, or
with M | B ♨ | L D prior
arrangement (not Mon) | ⚗ ⚲ |
M 340 | S |
★★*Parson & Clerk Motel, Chester Rd,
Streetley (junc A452/B4138).
T:021-353 1747. Annexe: 30rm* ⌂

Moor Hall Moor Hall Dr, Sutton
Coldfield (2½m N of town centre
off A453)
T:021-308 6130
*Parkland course. The 14th is notable
hole. Societies welcome (Tu W) by
arrangement. 18 | 6249 yds | Par 70 |
SSS 70*
Visitors welcome restricted WE BH
☎ | B ♨ | L D prior arrangement |
⚗ ⚲ ⬉ ⋈ | TR Th (ladies) WE |
M 690 | S |
★★★*Moor Hall, Moor Hall Dr, Four
Oaks, Sutton Coldfield. T:021-308
3751. 50rm* ⇌

Pype Hayes Eachelhurst Rd,

SUTTON-IN-ASHFIELD
Nottinghamshire
Map **IV** A2

Coxmoor Coxmoor Rd (2m SE of Sutton-in-Ashfield off A611)
T:(0623) 557359
Societies by arrangement. 18 | 6501 yds | Par 72 | SSS 71
Visitors welcome without M **∴** per day | **::** WE | with M **..** per day WE | B L ♨
D prior arrangement | ⚗ ⚲ ⬉ | ⅃ | TR Ladies day Tu | M 650 | S |
★★★★*Swallow, Carter Ln East, South Normanton. T:(0773) 812000. 123rm* ⇌ ⌂
Undulating moorland course with easy walking and excellent
views. The clubhouse is modern with a well-equipped games room.
The course lies adjacent to Forestry Commission land over which
there are several footpaths and extensive views.

Walmley (2½m S of Sutton
Coldfield off B4148)
T:021-351 1014
*Attractive, fairly flat course with
excellent greens. 18 | 5811 yds | Par 70
| SSS 68*
Visitors welcome | **..** per day | B L
♨ D | ⚗ ⬉ | ⋈ | ⅃ | TR |
occasionally, ☎ | M 300 | S |
★★★★*Penns Hall, Penns Ln,
Walmley, Sutton Coldfield. T:021-351
3111. 120rm* ⇌

Walmley Brooks Rd, Wylde Green
(2m S of Sutton Coldfield off
A5127)
T:021-373 0029
*Pleasant parkland course with many
trees. The hazards are not difficult.
Societies welcome by arrangement. 18 |
6340 yds | Par 70 | SSS 70*
Visitors welcome, with M only WE
BH | ✉ ☎ | without M **∴** per day |
with M **..** per day WE | ♨ | B L D
prior arrangement (not Mon) | ⚗ ⚲
⅃ | M 700 | S |
★★★★*Penns Hall, Penns Ln.
T:021-351 3111. 120rm* ⇌

SUTTON-ON-SEA
Lincolnshire
Map **V** K8

Sandilands Sutton on Sea (1½m S of Sutton-on-Sea off A52)
T:(0521) 41432
Flat seaside course. Societies welcome anytime by arrangement. 18 | 5984 yds | Par 69 | SSS 69
Visitors welcome ✉ | .. per round ∴ per day ∴ per round WE | with M .. per day ∴ WE | B | ☕ prior arrangement | △ 🍸 ⟍ | ⋈ | M 450 | [S]
★★*Grange and Links, Sea Ln, Sandilands. T:(0521) 41334. 16rm (11 ⇄ 3 🚿)*

SWAFFHAM
Norfolk
Map **IV** G4

Swaffham Cley Rd, Swaffham (1½m SW of Swaffham)
T:(0760) 21611
Heathland course, societies by arrangement, no dogs, no facilities for children. 9 | 6252 yds | Par 72 | SSS 70
Visitors welcome Mon to F, with M WE pm only | without M .. per day | with M .. per day | B (not Mon, Th) | L ☕ D prior arrangement (not Mon Th) | △ 🍸 ⋈ | [TR] Sun am | M 450 | [S]
★★*George, Station St. T:(0760) 21238. 32rm (17 ⇄)*

SWANSEA
West Glamorgan
Map **I** E2

Clyne 120 Owls Lodge Ln, The Mayals, Blackpyl (3½m SW of Swansea on B4436, off A4067)
T:(0792) 401989
Course of heath and moor - very open to the wind. 18 | 6312 yds | Par 70 | SSS 71
Visitors welcome | without M ∴ per day WE | with M .. per day WE | B L (not Mon F) | ☕ D (not Mon) | △ 🍸 | ℨ | M 500 (approx) | [TR] competition days | [S]
★★★★*Dragon, Kingsway Circle. T:(0792) 51074. 118rm ⇄*

Langland Bay Langland Bay, Swansea (6m W of Swansea on A4067)
T:(0792) 61721
Parkland course overlooking Gower coast. The par 4 6th is an uphill dog-leg open to the wind, and the par 3 16th 151 yds is aptly named 'Death or Glory'. Societies welcome by arrangement. 18 | 5812 yds | Par 70 | SSS 69
Visitors welcome, restricted WE BH Tu pm | ∴ per day WE | B ☕ L D by prior arrangement | △ 🍸 ⟍ | ⋈ | [TR] WE competitions | ℨ | M 750 | [S]
★★★*Osbourne, Rotherslade Rd, Langland Bay. T:(0792) 66274. 37rm (30 ⇄)*

Morriston 160 Clasemont Rd, Morriston (5m N of Swansea on A48)
T:(0792) 71079
Parkland course. 18 | 5734 yds | Par 68 | SSS 68
Visitors welcome | without M .. per day WE | with M .. per day WE | B L | △ 🍸 ⟍ | [4] | [TR] WE competitions ☎ for details | ℨ | M 400 | [S]
★★★★*Dragon, Kingsway Circle, Swansea. T:(0792) 51074. 118rm ⇄*

SWINDON
Wiltshire
Map **I** K2

Broome Manor Golf Complex Pipers Way, Swindon (1¾m SE of town centre, off B4006)
T:(0793) 32403
Two courses and a 20-bay floodlit driving range. Parkland course with water hazards, requires accuracy. Walking is easy on gentle slopes. Societies welcome on weekdays. 18(9) | 6359 (2805) yds | Par 71(68) | SSS 70(68)
Visitors welcome | ☎ for WE booking 2 weeks in advance | .. per day | B L ☕ D | △ 🍸 ⟍ ⋈ | ℨ | M 350 | [S]
★★★*Post House, Marlborough Rd. T:(0793) 24601. 104rm ⇄*

TADLEY
Hampshire
Map **II** B4

Bishopswood Bishopswood Ln, nr Basingstoke (1m W of Tadley off A340)
T:(07356) 5213
Wooded course, fairly tight, with stream and natural water hazards. Societies welcome by arrangement. 9 | 3237 yds | Par 72 | SSS 71
Visitors welcome | .. per day | B L ☕ | △ 🍸 | ⋈ (possible) | ℨ | M 325 |

SWANAGE
Dorset
Map **I** K6

Isle of Purbeck (2½m N of Swanage on B3351)
T:(09244) 210
Societies welcome by arrangement (not Sun). 18(9) | 6283(2022) yds | Par 70(30) | SSS 71(30)
Visitors welcome | without M :: per day | B ☕ | L D prior arrangement | △ 🍸 ⟍ ⋈ | ℨ | M 650 | [S]
★★★*Knoll House, Ferry Rd, Studland. T:(092944) 251. 104rm (83 ⇄). Annexe: 7rm*
A heathland course sited on the Purbeck Hills with grand views across Swanage, the Channel and Poole Harbour. Holes of note include the 5th, 8th, 14th, 15th and 16th where trees, gorse and heather assert themselves. The very attractive clubhouse is built of the local stone.

SWINTON
Greater Manchester
Map **V** D7

Swinton Park East Lancashire Rd, Swinton (1m W of Swinton off A580)
T:061-794 1785
Societies welcome by arrangement. 18 | 6628 yds | Par 73 | SSS 72
Visitors welcome weekdays ✉ with M only WE | without M ∴ per day | with M .. per day | B L ☕ D prior arrangement (not Mon) | △ 🍸 (not Mon) ⟍ | [TR] 1200-1330 daily, Th (ladies day) | M 750 | [S]
★*Beaucliffe, 254 Eccles Old Rd, Pendleton, Salford. T:061-789 5092. 22rm (2 ⇄ 20 🚿)*
One of Lancashire's longest inland courses. Recent clubhouse extensions have greatly improved the facilities at this club.

[S]
★★*Red Lion, London St, Basingstoke. T:(0256) 28525. 63rm (31 ⇌ 32 🚿)*

TAIN
Highland, *Ross and Cromarty*
Map **VII** G4

Tain The Clubhouse, Tain (E side of town centre off B9174)
T:(0862) 2314
Heathland/seaside course with river affecting 3 holes, easy walking, fine views. 18 | 6322 yds | Par 70 | SSS 70
Visitors welcome | B ☕ L (not Mon) | D prior arrangement | △ 🍸 | ⋈ prior arrangement | [TR] competition days | M 400 | [S]
★★★*Royal, High St. T:(0862) 2013. 25rm (15 ⇌ 7 🚿)*

TALBOT GREEN
Mid Glamorgan
Map I F3

Llantrisant & Pontyclun Llanelry Rd, Talbot Green (N side of village off A473)
T:(0443) 222148
Parkland course. 12 (18 played) | 5712 yds | Par 68 | SSS 68
Visitors welcome | without M ∴ per day | L ☕ D by arrangement B | △ 🍸 | ⋈ ⟍ | 🏌 | [TR] competitions only | M 500 | [S]
★★*Bear, High St, Cowbridge. T:(04463) 4814. 21rm (18 ⇌) Annexe: 10rm ⇌*

TAMWORTH
Staffordshire
Map **III** J4

Tamworth Municipal Eagle Drive, Tamworth (2½m E of Tamworth off B5000)
T:(0827) 53850
First-class parkland course and a good test of golf. Societies welcome by arrangement. 18 | 6691 yds | Par 73 | SSS 72
Visitors welcome | B L ☕ | △ 🍸 ⟍ ⋈ | 🏌 | M 300 | [S]
★*Old Red Lion, Atherstone. T:(08277) 3156. 10rm (5 🚿)*

TANDRIDGE
Surrey
Map **II** F5

Tandridge Oxted (1m NE of Tandridge off A25)
T:(08833) 2273
Rolling parkland course, good views. 18 | 6260 yds | Par 70 | SSS 70
Visitors welcome Mon W Th ☎ essential | L ☕ | △ 🍸 ⟍ | ④ not Sun after 1130 | [TR] Tu F WE | M 400 | [S]
★★*Hoskins, Station Rd West, Oxted. T:(08833) 2338. 10rm 🚿*

TANWORTH-IN-ARDEN
Warwickshire
Map **III** J5

Ladbrook Park Poolhead Ln, Tanworth in Arden, Solihull (1m NW of Tanworth in Arden on A4023)
T:(05644) 2220
Parkland course lined with trees. 18 | 6407 yds | Par 71 | SSS 71
Visitors welcome | without M ∴ per

TADMARTON
Oxfordshire
Map **III** K7

Tadmarton Heath Wigginton, nr Banbury (1m SW of Lower Tadmarton off B4035)
T:(0608) 737278
Parties by arrangement. 18 | 5917 yds | Par 69 | SSS 69
Visitors welcome | without M ∷ per day | with M ‥ per day WE | B L ☕ D (not Mon) | △ 🍸 | ⟍ ⋈ prior arrangement | 🏌 | [TR] WE | M 600 | [S]
★★*The Olde School, Church St. T:(0295) 720369. 11rm (4 ⇌ 7 🚿)*
A mixture of heath and light land, the course, which is open to strong winds, incorporates the site of an old Roman encampment. There is an annual open 36-hole scratch competition. The clubhouse is an old farm building with a 'holy well' from which the greens are watered. The 7th is a testing hole over water.

TAVISTOCK
Devon
Map I D6

Tavistock Down Rd, Tavistock (1m SE of Tavistock)
T:(0822) 2049
18 | 6250 yds | Par 70 | SSS 70
Visitors welcome ☎ advisable | ∴ per day WE BH | with M ‥ per day ∴ WE | B L ☕ D prior arrangement | △ 🍸 ⟍ ⋈ | 🏌 | ④ WE ☎ | M 800 | [S]
★★★*Bedford, Plymouth Rd. T:(0822) 3221. 32rm (30 ⇌ 2 🚿)*
Set on Whitchurch Down in south-west Dartmoor with easy walking and magnificent views over rolling countryside and into Cornwall. Downland turf with some heather, and interesting holes on undulating ground.

TAYPORT
Fife, *Fife*
Map **VII** J8

Scotscraig Tayport (S side of village off B945)
T:(0382) 552515
Societies welcome by arrangement. 18 | 6486 yds | Par 71 | SSS 71
Visitors welcome weekdays | ☎ WE only with M | without M ∴ per day | with M ‥ per day | B L ☕ D prior arrangement △ 🍸 | [TR] after 1630 Mon-F WE | M 600
★★*Queen's, 160 Nethergate, Dundee. T:(0382) 22515. 56rm (11 ⇌ 1 🚿)*

SCORE CARD:

1	397	10	404
2	373	11	460
3	209	12	388
4	355	13	170
5	391	14	476
6	151	15	173
7	400	16	481
8	388	17	385
9	488	18	397

A rather tight course on downland-type turf with an abundance of gorse. The sheltered position of the course ensures good weather throughout the year.

round | with M .. per day | B ♥ L
D (not Mon) | ⚬ ♈ | TR Tu until
1400, WE BH | ④ Th after a BH
until 1200 | ♉ | M 700 | S
★★★*George, High St, Solihull.*
T:*021-704 1241. 46rm (41 ⇄)*

TARBERT
Strathclyde, *Argyllshire*
Map **VI** B2

Tarbert Tarbert, Kintyre (1m W of
Tarbert off A83)
T:(08802) 565
Beautiful moorland course. 9 | 4404 yds
| Par 66 | SSS 64
Visitors welcome | without M ..
per day | ♈ | TR competition days |
M 100
★*West Loch, Tarbert.* T:*(08802) 283.
6rm*

TARLAND
Grampian, *Aberdeenshire*
Map **VII** J6

Tarland Aberdeen Rd, Tarland (E
side of village off B9119)
T:(033981) 413
*Difficult parkland course but easy
walking.* 9 | 5320 metres | Par 66 |
SSS 68
Visitors welcome ☎ | B ♥ | ⚬ ♈ |
⚬⚬ | ④ after 1300 | TR medal days
(0800-1100) | M 300
★★*Birse Lodge, Aboyne.* T:*(0339)
2253. 12rm (11 ⇄ 1 ⓯) Annexe: 4rm
⇄*

TAUNTON
Somerset
Map **I** G4

Taunton & Pickeridge Corfe,
Taunton (4m S of Taunton off
B3170)

T:(082342) 537
Downland course with extensive views.
18 | 5927 yds | Par 69 | SSS 68
Visitors welcome | B ♥ (not Mon) |
L D prior arrangement (not Mon) |
⚬ ♈ ⚬ (limited) | TR Tu (ladies)
WE (am) | M 600 | S
★★★*County, East St, Taunton.*
T:*(0823) 87651. 68rm (60 ⇄)*

Vivary Park Municipal Fons
George, Taunton (S side of town
centre off A38)
T:(0823) 73875
A parkland course, tight and narrow

TEIGNMOUTH
Devon
Map I F6

Teignmouth Exeter Rd, Teignmouth (2m NW of Teignmouth off B3192)
T:(06267) 4194
18 | 6200 yds | Par 71 | SSS 69
Visitors welcome ⊠ | ∴ weekdays WE | B ♥ | L prior arrangement | D prior
arrangement | ⚬ ♈ ⚬ | ⚬⚬ | ④ alternate starting times on 1st and 10th tee |
M 900 | S
★★*Venn Farm Country House, Higher Exeter Rd.* T:*(06267) 2196. 10rm (7 ⇄ 2 ⓯)*
This fairly flat heathland course is high up with a fine seascape from
the clubhouse. Good springy turf with some heather and an
interesting layout makes for very enjoyable holiday golf.

TENBY
Dyfed
Map I C2

Tenby The Burrows, Tenby (S side of town)
T:(0834) 2978
Societies welcome by arrangement. 18 | 6232 yds | Par 69 | SSS 71
Visitors welcome ☎ preferred | ∴ (summer) .. weekday WE (winter) | B ♥
(not Tu) | L D prior arrangement (not Tu) | ⚬ ♈ ⚬ | ⚬⚬ | M 460 | S
★★★*Imperial, The Paragon.* T:*(0834) 3737. 48rm (38 ⇄ 8 ⓯)*
A fine old seaside links, 'The Burrows', so called, with sea views
and natural hazards. It provides good golf, and is a popular holiday
course.

*with ponds on course. Pro/Am
championship held here each year. 18 |
4620 yds (being extended) | Par 63 |
SSS 63*
Visitors welcome ☎ on day. With
M only | without M Wed pm 1630
onwards | ✳ | B ♥ ⚬ ♈ | ⚬ ⚬⚬ | TR
W 1630 onwards | M 400
★★*Falcon, Henlade, Taunton.*
T:*(0823) 442502. 10rm (8 ⇄ 2 ⓯)*

TELFORD
Shropshire
Map **III** H4

TEWKESBURY
Gloucestershire
Map **III** H7

Tewkesbury Park Hotel Lincoln Green Ln, Tewkesbury (1m SW of Tewkesbury off A38)
T:(0684) 295405
18 | 6197 yds | Par 73 | SSS 69
Visitors welcome ⊠ ☎ | without M ∴ per day ∷ WE | with M ‥ per day WE | B L ☙ D | ⚘ ☂ ⤫ ⤬ | ④ WE TR WE ☎ for details | M 550 | S
★★★*Royal Hop Pole Crest, Church St. T:(0684) 293236. 29rm (28 ⇄)*
A parkland course in a sheltered situation beside the River Severn. The par 3 5th is an exacting hole calling for accurate distance judgment. Tewkesbury Park Hotel Golf and Country Club is centred in an attractive 18th-century mansion house and there are many facilities: heated swimming pool, squash courts, billiards.

THETFORD
Norfolk
Map **IV** G5

Thetford Brandon Rd, Thetford (¾m W of Thetford on B1107)
T:(0842) 2169
Societies welcome by arrangement. 18 | 6499 yds | Par 71 | SSS 71
Visitors welcome ⊠ ☎ restrictions WE | without M ∴ per day ∷ WE | with M ‥ per day WE | B L ☙ not Tu | D prior arrangement (not Tu) | ⚘ ☂ ⤫ | ⤬ ☎ | TR competitions | M 550 | S
★★★*Bell, King St, Thetford. T:(0842) 4455. 43rm ⇄*
This is a course with a good pedigree. It was laid out by a fine golfer, C H Mayo, later altered by James Braid and then again altered by another famous course designer, Mackenzie Ross. It is a testing heathland course with a particularly stiff finish. The fairways are lined with trees and a road forms a hazard on several holes. It deserves to be better known than it is.

Telford Hotel Sutton Hill, Telford (4m S of Telford town centre off A442)
T:(0952) 585642
Parkland course with easy walking. Three lakes and large sand traps are hazards to the fine greens. Societies and parties welcome. 18 | 6228 yds | Par 70 | SSS 70
Visitors welcome ⊠ certificate of handicap requested | B ☙ L D prior arrangement | ⚘ ☂ ⤫ | M 450 | S
★★★*Telford Hotel Golf & Country Club, Great Hay, Sutton Hill, Telford. T:(0952) 585642. 58rm ⇄*

TENTERDEN
Kent
Map **II** H6

Tenterden Woodchurch Rd, Tenterden (¾m E of Tenterden on B2067)
T:(05806) 3987
Attractive parkland course, last 3 holes hilly. 9 | 5119 yds | Par 69 | SSS 65
Visitors welcome, restricted WE BH (until 1200), no juniors WE BH | without M ‥ per day ∴ WE | with M ‥ per day WE | B L ☙ | ⚘ ☂ | TR Sun am | M 350 | S
★★*White Lion, High St. T:(05806) 2921. 12rm (8 ⇄ 2 ⋒)*

THIRSK
North Yorkshire
Map **V** F4

Thirsk & Northallerton Thornton-Le-Street, Thirsk (2m N of Thirsk on A168)
T:(0845) 22170
The course has good views of the nearby Hambleton Hills. 9 | 6259 yds | Par 72 | SSS 70
Visitors welcome with M only Sun | without M ‥ per day ∴ WE | with M ‥ per day WE | B L D ☂ ☙ prior arrangement (not Tu) | ⤬ | ④ for small parties (prior arrangement) | TR 0830-0930, 1230-1330 | ♩ | M 300 | S weekends
★★*Golden Fleece, Market Pl, Thirsk. T:(0845) 23108. 22rm (6 ⇄)*

THORNHILL
Dumfries & Galloway, *Dumfriesshire*
Map **VI** E5

Thornhill Blacknest, Thornhill (¾m NE of Thornhill off A76)
T:(0848) 30546
Course with fine views. 18 | 6011 yds | Par 71 | SSS 69
Visitors welcome | ‥ per day ∴ WE | B L ☙ D prior arrangement | ⚘ ☂ ⤬ | ♩ | TR ④ medal and competition days | M 360 | S
★★*Buccleuch & Queensberry. T:(0848) 30215. 11rm (4 ⇄ 1 ⋒)*

THORNTON
Fife, *Fife*
Map **VI** G1

Thornton Station Rd, Thornton (E side of town off A92)
T:(0592) 771111
Flat but fairly difficult parkland course. Testing holes: 3rd (par 3), 5th (par 4), 12th (par 4), 14th (par 3). 18 | 6177 yds | Par 70 | SSS 69
Visitors welcome | ‥ per day ∴ WE | B L ☙ by arrangement | ⚘ ☂ ⤬ | TR WE 0730-0930, 1245-1400, Tu 1700-1800 | ④ ½ before TR | M 536
★★★*Balgeddie House, Leslie Rd, Glenrothes. T:(0592) 742511. 18rm (16 ⇄ 2 ⋒)*

THURSO
Highland, *Caithness*
Map **VII** H1

Thurso Newlands of Geise, Thurso (1½m SW of Thurso on B874)
T:(0847) 63807
Parkland course, windy, fine view. Societies welcome by arrangement. 18 | 5818 yds | Par 69 | SSS 69
Visitors welcome, restricted Tu Th (pm) | ‥ per day | ⤫ ⚘ ☂ | L B WE | ⤬ prior arrangement | TR Tu Th (eves) S (am) | ④ ☎ | M 250 | S
★★*Pentland, Princes St. T:(0847) 63202. 57rm (17 ⇄ 9 ⋒)*

TICEHURST
East Sussex
Map **II** G6

Dale Hill Wadhurst (N side of Ticehurst off B2087)
T:(0580) 200112
Parkland course. Societies welcome by arrangement. 18 | 6035 yds | Par 69 | SSS 69 (Also 9-hole par 3 course)
Visitors welcome ⊠ | ☎ WE (am) |

THEYDON BOIS
Essex
Map II   F2

Theydon Bois Theydon Rd, Epping (1m N of Theydon Bois)
T:(0378) 881
18 | 5472 yds | Par 68 | SSS 68
Visitors welcome with M only WE | without M ∴ per day ∷ WE (pm) | with M
•• per day | B L D prior arrangement | ᐃ Υ ⟍ | TR Th (am) | ④ am | M 625 | S
★★★*Post House, High Rd, Bell Common, Epping. T:(0378) 73137. 82rm ⇔*
A new nine holes have been added to the old nine built into Epping
Forest. They are well planned and well bunkered but are situated
out in the open on the hillside. The old nine in the Forest are short
and have three bunkers among them, but even so a wayward shot
can be among the trees. The autumn colours here are truly
magnificent.

THORPENESS
Suffolk
Map IV   K6

Thorpeness Thorpeness (W side of village off B1353)
T:(072 885) 2176
Societies welcome by arrangement. 18 | 6241 yds | Par 69 | SSS 71
Visitors welcome ☎ | ∷ per day WE | ☕ | B L D prior arrangment | ᐃ Υ ⟍ |
∝ | 𝕵 | M 350 | S
★*White Horse, Station Rd, Leiston. T:(0728) 830694. 9rm (1 ⇔)*
The holes of this moorland course are pleasantly varied with several
quite difficult par fours. Natural hazards abound. The 15th with its
sharp left dog-leg is one of the best holes.

without M ∴ per day WE | with M
•• per day WE | B ☕ | L D prior
arrangement | ᐃ Υ ⟍ | ∝ prior
arrangement | 𝕵 | TR WE until 1030
| M 500 | S
★★*Tudor Arms, Rye Rd, Hawkhurst.*
T:(05805) 2312. 14rm (6 ⇔ 3 🛁)

TIGHNABRUAICH
Strathclyde, *Argyllshire*
Map VI   B2

Kyles of Bute Tighnabruaich (1¼m
S of Tighnabruaich off B8000)
T:(0700) 811355
*Moorland course which is hilly and
exposed to wind. Good views.* 9 |
2379 yds | Par 33 | SSS 32
Visitors welcome | without M ••
per day | B ☕ | ᐃ | M 175
❀❀★★*Kilfinan, Kilfinan. T:(070082)*
201. 11rm (10 ⇔)

TILLICOULTRY
Central, *Clackmannanshire*
Map VI   F1

Tillicoultry Alva Rd, Tillicoultry (W
side of town on A91)
T:(0259) 50741/51337
Parkland course at foot of the Ochil ➡

Take a new look at the Thurlestone Hotel.

You'll love the Thurlestone. It's a little
exclusive but very friendly and extremely
comfortable. If you've stayed at the Thurlestone
before you'll find the same welcoming faces,
but there have been many changes in the hotel
to make your stay more enjoyable still.

Come to the Thurlestone for peaceful
relaxation on the lovely South Devon Coast,
superb food, and every recreation including a
golf course — all within the magnificent grounds.
Find out why the Thurlestone is that much
different — send for our folder.

Thurlestone Hotel

Thurlestone, Near Kingsbridge, South Devon   Telephone: Kingsbridge (0548) 560382

KEY
(IA1) *atlas grid reference*
T: *telephone number*
☎   *advance letter/telephone call required*
✉   *introduction from own club sec/handicap certificate/club membership card required*
..   *low fees*
∴   *medium fees*
::   *high fees*
*   *green fees not confirmed for 1987*
B   *light lunch*
L   *full lunch*
♟   *tea*
D   *dinner*
♨   *changing rooms/showers*
♟   *bar open mid-day and evenings*
↖   *clubs for hire*
∞   *partners may be found*
④   *restricted time for 4 balls*
TR   *times reserved for members*
♩   *professional*
S   *well-stocked shop*
M   *member*
Mon Tu W Th F S Sun
WE   *weekend*
BH   *bank holiday*

Hills entails some hard walking. 9 |
4616 yds | Par 68 | SSS 66
Visitors welcome | .. per day WE |
B L D ♟ prior arrangement | ♨ ♟
(evng only Mon to F) | TR
competitions only | M 300
★★★*Royal, Henderson St, Bridge of Allan. T:(0786) 832284. 33rm (25 ⇔)*

TILSWORTH
Bedfordshire
Map IV   C8

THURLESTONE
Devon
Map I   E7

Thurlestone Thurlestone (S side of village)
T:(0548) 560405
18 | 6337 yds | Par 71 | SSS 70
Visitors welcome with handicap certificate ✉ ☎ | without M ∴ per day | with
M ∴ per day | B ♟ | L prior arrangement | ♨ ♟ Mon, W, Th | ∞ possible | ④
TR ☎ for details | ♩ | M 1000 | S
★★★★*Thurlestone. T:(0548) 560382. 68rm (65 ⇔ 3 ⏦)*
Situated on the edge of the cliffs at Thurlestone with typical
downland turf and good greens. The course, after an interesting
opening hole, rises to higher land with a fine seaview, and finishes
with an excellent 502 yard downhill hole to the clubhouse.
See advertisement on page 213.

TIDWORTH
Wiltshire
Map I   K3

Tidworth Garrison Bulford Rd, Tidworth (W side of village off A338)
T:(0980) 42321
18 | 5990 yds | Par 69 | SSS 69
Visitors welcome ☎ | without M ∴ per day | with M .. per day | B L ♟ D prior
arrangement | ♨ | ♟ | ④ WE BH until 1345 | TR WE 0830-1045, and major
competition days until 1500 | ♩ | M 550 | S
★★*Antrobus, Church St, Amesbury. T:(0980) 23163. 20rm (12 ⇔)*
A breezy, dry downland course with lovely turf, fine trees and
views over Salisbury Plain. The 393-yard 3rd and the 173-yard 12th
are notable. The 564-yard 13th going down towards the clubhouse
gives the big hitter a chance to let fly. The belts of beech and fir trees
protect players from winter winds.

Tilsworth Dunstable Rd, Tilsworth
(½m NE of Tilsworth off A5)
T:(0525) 210721
A moorland course. 9 | 5443 yds |
Par 70 | SSS 67
Visitors welcome without M | ..
per day | L D B ♟ | ♨ ♟ ↖ | ♩ | TR
Sun am | M 200 | S
★★★*Old Palace Lodge, Church St, Dunstable. T:(0582) 62201. 50rm ⇔*

TOBERMORY
Strathclyde, *Argyllshire*
Map VII   C7

Western Isles Tobermory, Isle of
Mull (½m N of Tobermory off
A848)
T:(0688) 2020
*Hilly seaside course, no sand bunkers,
hard walking, superb views over the
Sound of Mull. Testing 3rd hole (par
3). Keys to clubhouse obtainable from*

TILFORD
Surrey
Map II   C5

Hankley Common Tilford, Farnham (¾m SE of Tilford)
T:(948 25) 2493
Societies welcome by arrangement. 18 | 6403 *yds* | *Par 71* | SSS 71
Visitors welcome ✉ and restricted W alternate WE | ☎ | ∷ per day WE | ∴
after 1300 | B ☎ D prior arrangement | L prior arrangement (not F) | ⚘ Υ ④ ☎
[TR] Tu, W (societies) Th (ladies) ☎ | 𝕁 | M 700 | [S]
**Pride of the Valley, Jumps Rd, Churt. T:(042873) 5799. 13rm (9 ⇌ 1 🍴)*
A natural heathland course subject to wind. Greens are first rate.
The 18th, a long par 4, is most challenging, the green being beyond
a deep chasm which traps any but the perfect second shot.

TIVERTON
Devon
Map I   F5

Tiverton Post Hill, Tiverton (2½m E of Tiverton on B3391)
T:(0884) 252187
18 | 6227 *yds* | *Par 71* | SSS 70
Visitors welcome with M or ✉ | ☎ advisable | without M ∴ per day | with M
. . per day | B L prior arrangement (not Mon) | ☎ ⚘ Υ ✵ | [TR] ☎ for details
| ④ 10th | 𝕁 | M 740 | [S]
***Tiverton Hotel, Blundells Rd. T:(0884) 256120. 29rm ⇌ 🍴*
A parkland course where the many different species of tree are a
feature and where the lush pastures ensure some of the finest
fairways in the SW. There are a number of interesting holes where
visitors will find a real challenge.

Mssrs A Brown, Stronsaule. 9 |
2460 *yds* | *Par 32* | SSS 64 *(18 holes)*
Visitors welcome | . . per day WE |
✵ | ⋈ (sometimes) | M 60
*Mishnish, Main St, Tobermory.
T:(0688) 2009. 14rm (6 ⇌)*

TODMORDEN
West Yorkshire
Map V   E6

Todmorden Rive Rocks, Cross
Stone Rd, Todmorden (NE side of
town off A646)
T:(070681) 2986
*Pleasant moorland course. Society
meetings by arrangement.* 9 | 5818 yds
| *Par 68* | SSS 68
Visitors welcome, restricted S pm
competition days | B (not Mon) | L
☎ D prior arrangement (not Mon) |
⚘ Υ | ⋈ | [TR] competitions | M 140
| [S]
*Sun, Featherstall Rd, Littleborough.
T:(0706) 78957. 8rm*

TOLLESHUNT D'ARCY
Essex
Map II   H2

Manifold Colchester Rd, Maldon
(1¾m NE of Tolleshunt D'Arcy on

B1026)
T:(0621) 860410
*Parkland course. Societies welcome by
arrangement.* 18 | 6450 yds | *Par 72* |
SSS 71
Visitors welcome but restricted Sun
(am) | B L ☎ D | ⚘ Υ ✵ | ⋈ | [TR]
Sun (am) | ④ ☎ for details | 𝕁 | [S]
**Kings Ford Park, Layer Rd,
Colchester. T:(0206) 34301. 14rm (11
⇌ 2 🍴)*

TONBRIDGE
Kent
Map II   G5

Poultwood Higham Ln, Tonbridge
(3m N of Tonbridge off A227)
T:(0732) 364039
*Public woodland/parkland course. Easy
but varied walking, water hazards.
Societies welcome by arrangement.* 18 |
5569 yds | *Par 68* | SSS 67
Open to public ☎ WE BH | . . per
day | B L ☎ | D prior arrangement
(not Mon) | ⚘ Υ ✵ | ⋈ prior
arrangement | ④ until 1200 WE | 𝕁 |
[S]
**Rose & Crown, High St. T:(0732)
357966. 52rm ⇌*

TORKSEY
Lincolnshire
Map VI   H6

Lincoln Torksey (SW side of
village)
T:(042771) 210
*A testing inland course with quick
drying sandy subsoil and easy walking.*
18 | 6400 yds | *Par 70* | SSS 70
Visitors welcome with M or ✉ ☎ |
WE BH only with M | ∴ per day | ∷
WE | ☎ | B L D prior arrangement |
⚘ Υ | ⋈ by arrangement | [TR] Tu
0900- 1230 (ladies), competition
days | 𝕁 | M 600 | [S]
****White Hart, Bailgate, Lincoln.
T:(0522) 26222. 52rm (50 ⇌ 10 🍴)*

TORPHINS
Grampian, *Aberdeenshire*
Map VII   J6

Torphins Golf Rd, Torphins (NW
side of village off A980)
T:033-982 493
*Heathland course built on hill with
views of Cairngorms, Grampians etc.* 9
| 4660 yds | *Par 64* | SSS 63
Visitors welcome | ☎ ⚘ | ⋈ | [TR]
competitions and WE mornings |
M 200
***🍴🍴Raemoir, Banchory. T:(03302)
4884. 18rm (14 ⇌) Annexe: 6rm (4 ⇌
2 🍴)*

TORQUAY
Devon
Map I   F6

Torquay 30 Petitor Rd, St
Marychurch, Torquay (1½m N of
Torquay off A379)
T:(0803) 37471
*Parkland course between sea and
Dartmoor. Societies welcome (not
beginners).* 18 | 6251 yds | *Par 70* |
SSS 70
Visitors welcome (regular players)
✉ | ∴ per day WE | B ☎ | L prior
arrangement (not M) | ⚘ Υ ✵ | ⋈
sometimes | [TR] competitions | 𝕁 |
M 850 | [S]
**Norcliffe, Babbacombe Downs Rd.
T:(0803) 38456. 20rm (9 ⇌ 1 🍴)*

TORRINGTON
Devon
Map I   D5

Torrington Weare Trees, Great
Torrington (1¼m NW of Great
Torrington)

Hard walking on hilly commonland course but views outstanding. 2nd hole is a testing 230 yd par 3. Societies welcomed by arrangement. 9 | 4410 yds | Par 64 | SSS 63
Visitors welcome except Sun am | ▪▪ per day WE BH | ▪ B | ⚲ Y | ⋈ | ⟨TR⟩ Sun 0800-1200 | M 350
★★*Beaconside, Monkleigh. T:(02372) 77205. 9rm (4 ⇄ 2 ⌂)*

TREDEGAR
Gwent
Map **III**   F8

Tredegar and Rhymney
Cwmtysswg, Rhymney (1¾m SW of Tredegar on B4256)
T:(0685) 840743
Mountain course with lovely views of the surrounding area. 9 | 5564 yds | Par 34 | SSS 33
Visitors welcome | Y B ⚲ ⋈ | M 146
★★★*Maes Manor, Blackwood. T:(0495) 224551. 10rm (7 ⇄ ⌂) Annexe: 16rm (10 ⇄ 3 ⌂)*

TROON
Strathclyde, *Ayrshire*
Map **VI**   D4

Royal Troon Craigend Rd, Troon (S side of town on B749)
T:(0292) 311555
Societies welcome by arrangement. Medal course 18 | 6641 yds | Par 71 | SSS 73. *Portland course* 18 | 6274 yds | Par 70 | SSS 71
Visitors welcome except S | ☎ ✉ | Ladies only Mon W F | without M :: per day | B L prior arrangement (not S) | ▪ prior arrangement | ⚲ Y ⟍ | ⟨TR⟩ before 0930, 1100-1430,

after 1530 | M 800 | ⟨S⟩
★★★★*Marine, Crosbie Rd. T:(0292) 314444. 69rm ⇄*

TRURO
Cornwall
Map **I**   B7

Truro Treliske, Truro (1½m W of Truro on A390)
T:(0872) 72640
Parkland course. 18 | 5347 yds | Par 66 | SSS 66
Visitors welcome except on competition days | without M ∴ weekdays WE | with M ▪▪ weekdays WE | B | L D prior arrangement | ▪ ⚲ Y ⟍ | ⟨TR⟩ competitions | ♃ | M 800 | ⟨S⟩
★★★*Brookdale, Tregolls Rd. T:(0872) 73513. 21rm (17 ⇄ 4 ⌂) Annexe: 18rm (6 ⇄ 2 ⌂)*

TUNBRIDGE WELLS
Kent
Map **II**   G5

Tunbridge Wells Langton Rd,

TUNBRIDGE WELLS
Kent
Map **II**   G5

Nevill Benhall Mill Rd (1¾m SE of Tunbridge Wells off B2169)
T:(0892) 25818
Societies welcome (W Th) by arrangement. 18 | 6336 yds | Par 71 | SSS 70
Visitors welcome ✉ ☎ advisable | without M :: per day WE | with M ▪▪ per day WE | Y ▪ prior arrangement | B L D prior arrangement (not Mon F) | ⚲ | ⟨TR⟩ Ladies day Tu, major competitions | M 850 | ⟨S⟩
★★★*Spa, Mount Ephraim, Tunbridge Wells. T:(0892) 20331. 70rm (67 ⇄ 3 ⌂)*
Just within Sussex, the county boundary runs along the northern perimeter of the course. Open undulating ground, well wooded with much heather and gorse for the first half. The second nine holes slope away from the clubhouse to a valley where a narrow stream hazards two holes.

Tunbridge Wells (1m W of Tunbridge Wells on A264)
T:(0892) 23034
Somewhat hilly parkland course with lake; trees form natural hazards. 9 | 4684 yds | Par 65 | SSS 62
Visitors welcome, with M only W (pm) WE BH | without M ∴ per day | with M ▪▪ per day | B L ▪ D | ⚲ Y ⟍ ⋈ | ♃ | M 495 | ⟨S⟩
★★★*Spa, Mount Ephraim. T:(0892) 20331. 70rm (67 ⇄ 3 ⌂)*

TURNBERRY
Strathclyde, *Ayrshire*
Map **VI**   C4

Turnberry Turnberry (N side of village on A719)
T:(06553) 202
Societies welcome by arrangement with Turnberry Hotel. Ailsa course championship and medal tees. 18 | 6948 yds | Par 71 | SSS 71 | *Arran course* 18 | 6276 yds | Par 69 | SSS 70
Visitors welcome ☎ | without M :: per day | B L ▪ D | ⚲ Y ⟍ | ⟨TR⟩

Priority to hotel guests | 𝟑 | M 435 |
ⓢ
★★★★*Turnberry. T:(06553) 202.
130rm* ⇄ ▥

TURRIFF
Grampian, *Aberdeenshire*
Map **VII**   J4

Turriff Rosehall (1m W of Turriff
off B9024)
T:(0888) 62745
*A well-maintained inland course
alongside the River Deveron in
picturesque surroundings. Friendly
clubhouse. 18 | 6105 yds | Par 69 |
SSS 69*
Visitors welcome | without M ..
per day ∴ WE | ⚤ ⼂ | ④ not
permitted | M 540
★★*The County, 32 High St, Banff.
T:(02612) 5353. 6rm* ⇄

TWICKENHAM
Greater London
Map **II**   E4

Fulwell Wellington Rd, Hampton
Hill (1½m S of Twickenham on
A311)
T:01-977 1833
*Championship-length parkland course
with easy walking. The 575-yd 17th is
notable. Societies welcome (W Th F) by
arrangement. 18 | 6490 yds | Par 69 |
SSS 71*
Visitors welcome with M ⊠ |
restricted WE BH | ∴ per day WE |
B ▼ | L (not Mon) | D prior
arrangement | ⚤ ⼂ ⼂ | TR Thu am
| 𝟑 | M 600 | ⓢ
★★★*Richmond Hill, 146-150
Richmond Hill, Richmond. T:01-940
2247. 125rm (110* ⇄ *4* ▥ *)*

Strawberry Hill Wellesley Rd,
Twickenham (S side of town centre
off A311)
T:01-894 1246
*Parkland course with easy walking. 9 |
4762 yds | Par 64 | SSS 62*
Visitors welcome but with M only
WE BH | * | B L (not Mon) ▼ | ⚤ ⼂
⼂ | TR WE and competitions |
M 350 | ⓢ
★★★*Richmond Hill, 146-150
Richmond Hill, Richmond. T:01-940
2247. 125rm (110* ⇄ *4* ▥ *)*

Twickenham Staines Rd,
Twickenham (2m W of
Twickenham on A305)
T:01-941 0032

*Municipal commonland course. 9 |
3180 yds | Par 72 | SSS 71*
Open to public | B L ▼ D | ⚤ ⼂ ⼂
⼂ | 𝟑 | TR competitions | M 250 | ⓢ
★★★*Richmond Hill, 146-150
Richmond Hill, Richmond. T:01-940
2247. 125rm (110* ⇄ *4* ▥ *)*

TYNEMOUTH
Tyne and Wear
Map **V**   F1

Tynemouth Spital Dene,
Tynemouth, North Shields (½m W
of Tynemouth)
T:(0632) 2574578
*Well drained parkland/downland
course, easy walking. 18 | 6403 yds |
Par 70 | SSS 71*
Visitors welcome, restricted WE BH
| without M ∴ per day | with M ..
per day WE | B ▼ (not Mon) | L
prior arrangement (not Mon) | D
prior arrangement (S only) | ⚤ ⼂
⼂ | ⼂ | TR competition days |
M 740 | ⓢ
★★★*Grand, Grand Pde. T:(0632)
572106. 39rm (33* ⇄ *)*

UCKFIELD
East Sussex
Map **II**   F6

Piltdown Uckfield (3m NW of
Uckfield off A272)
T:(082572) 2033
*Heathland course, no bunkers, windy,
easy walking, fine views. 18 | 6059 yds
| Par 68 | SSS 69*
Visitors welcome, restricted Sun
BH ☎ | ∴ per day WE (winter | : :
per day .. after 1600 (summer) | ▼
B L | ⚤ ⼂ ⼂ | TR Sun am,
competition days | ④ | 𝟑 | M 350 | ⓢ
★★★*Roebuck, Wych Cross, Forest
Row. T:(034282) 3811. 31rm* ⇄

ULVERSTON
Cumbria
Map **V**   B4

Ulverston Bardsea Park, Ulverston (2m S of Ulverston off A5087)
T:(0229) 52824
Society meetings by arrangement. 18 | 6122 yds | Par 71 | SSS 69
Visitors welcome ☎ ⊠ | B ▼ (not Mon) | L D prior arrangement (not Mon) | ⚤
⼂ ⼂ | ⋈ generally | 𝟑 | TR Tu (ladies priority) | M 700 | ⓢ
★★*Sefton House, Queen St, Ulverston. T:(0229) 52190. 11rm (2* ⇄ *5* ▥ *)*
Inland golf of a comparatively quiet nature with many medium
length holes on undulating parkland. The two-shot 3rd will stand
comparison anywhere and the 17th is a testing par 4.

UDDINGSTON
Strathclyde, *Lanarkshire*
Map **VI**   E3

Calderbraes 57 Roundknowe Rd,
Uddingston, Glasgow (1½m NW of
Uddingston off A74)
T:(0698) 813425
*Parkland course with good view of
Clyde Valley. Testing 4th hole par 4
hard uphill. 9 | 5046 yds | Par 66 |
SSS 67*
Visitors welcome only with M | * | B
| L ▼ D prior arrangement | ⚤ ⼂ |
④ Medal days | TR WE | M 230
★★*Silvertrees, Silverwells Cres,
Bothwell. T:(0698) 852311. 7rm* ⇄ ▥
Annexe: 19rm ⇄ ▥

ULLESTHORPE
Leicestershire
Map **IV**   A5

Ullesthorpe Frolesworth Rd,
Ullesthorpe, Lutterworth (½m N of
Ullesthorpe off B577)
T:(0455) 209023
*Parkland course. 18 | 6048 yds | Par 70
| SSS 69*
Visitors welcome without M .. per
day ∴ WE | L D B ▼ | ⚤ ⼂ ⼂ | 𝟑 |
TR Sun am | M 500 | ⓢ
★★*Moorbarns, Watling St,
Lutterworth. T:(04555) 2237. Annexe:
11rm (6* ⇄ *5* ▥ *)*

UPAVON
Wiltshire
Map **I**   K3

RAF Upavon Upavon, Pewsey (2m
SE of Upavon on A342) Enquire at
RAF guardroom
T:(0980) 630787
*Downland course set on sides of valley,
with some wind affecting play. The
2nd, 9th, 11th and 18th are all par 3 to
small greens. 9 | 5116 metres | Par 69 |
SSS 67*   ➡

UPHOLLAND
Lancashire
Map **V**   C7

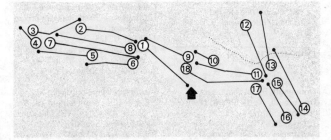

Dean Wood Lafford Ln, Upholland (½m NE of Upholland off A577)
T:(0695) 622219
Societies welcome by arrangement Th. No children. 18 | 6129 yds | Par 71 | SSS 70
Visitors welcome Mon to F restricted WE BH | ☎ | without M ∴ per day WE
| with M .. per day WE | B (not Th) | L ☙ D prior arrangement (not Th) | ⚖ ⏱
⋈ | TR 1215-1345 | 🍴 | M 800 | S
**Holland Hall*, 6 Lafford Ln. T:(0695) 624426. 11rm (4 ⇄ 7 🍴)*
This parkland course has a varied terrain. Beware the par 4 17th
which has ruined many a card. If there were a prize for the best
maintained course in Lancashire, Dean Wood would be a strong
contender.

Visitors welcome but with M only
WE BH | ⚖ | ⏱ evng Mon-F,
midday WE | TR | B ☙ | M 230
**Antrobus, Church St, Amesbury.*
T:(0980) 23163. 20rm (12 ⇄)

UPHALL
Lothian, *West Lothian*
Map **VI**   F2

Uphall Uphall (W side of village on
A899)
T:(0506) 852414
Windy parkland course, easy walking.
18 | 5567 yds | Par 69 | SSS 67
Visitors welcome, restricted WE
(until 1100) ☎ | B L ☙ D prior
arrangement | ⚖ ⏱ ⋈ | M 500
***💢Houstoun House. T:(0506)*
853831. 30rm (27 ⇄ 3 🍴)

UPLAWMOOR
Strathclyde, *Ayrshire*
Map **VI**   D3

Caldwell Uplawmoor (½m SW of
Uplawmoor off A736)
T:(050 585) 329
Parkland course. Societies welcome
Mon-F prior arrangement. 18 |
6102 yds | Par 71 | SSS 69
Visitors welcome Mon-F ✉
restricted Sun BH | ∴ per round ∴

per day | B L ☙ D prior
arrangement (not Mon) | ⚖ ⏱ ⋈ |
🍴 | TR WE | M 600 | S
**Dalmeny Park, Lochlibo Rd,*
Barrhead. T:041-881 9211. 20rm (10
🍴)

UPMINSTER
Greater London
Map **II**   G3

Upminster 114 Hall Ln, Upminster
(N side of town centre)
T:(04022) 22788
Parkland course adjacent to river.
Societies welcome by arrangement. 18 |
5951 yds | Par 68 | SSS 69
Visitors welcome weekdays ✉ | ☎
advisable | WE only with M | B L ☙
(not Mon) | ⚖ ⏱ | TR ☎ for details
| 🍴 | M 800 | S
***Ladbroke, Southend Arterial Rd,*
Hornchurch. T:(04023) 46789. 136rm
⇄ 🍴

UPPER KILLAY
West Glamorgan
Map **I**   E2

Fairwood Park Black Hills Rd,
Upper Killay, Swansea (1½m S of
Upper Killay off A4118)
T:(0792) 203648

Parkland course on Gower coast with
good views and easy walking. Societies
welcome by arrangement. 18 | 6661 yds
| Par 72 | SSS 72
Visitors welcome ☎ | without M ∴
per day WE | with M .. per day,
not BH | B L ☙ | ⚖ ⏱ ⋌ | 🍴 | S
**Windsor Lodge, Mount Pleasant,*
Swansea. T:(0792) 42158. 18rm (11 ⇄
3 🍴)

UPPERMILL
Greater Manchester
Map **V**   E7

Saddleworth Uppermill, Nr
Oldham (E side of town centre off
A670)
T:(04577) 2059
Moorland course, with superb views of
Pennines. Societies welcome by
arrangement. 18 | 5976 yds | Par 71 |
SSS 69
Visitors welcome | ∴ per day WE |
.. per day after 1600 ∴ WE after
1500 | B L ☙ D prior arrangement
(not Mon) | ⚖ ⏱ 🍴 | ⋈ occasionally
| M 530 | S
**York House, York Pl, Ashton under*
Lyne. T:061-330 5899. 26rm (8 ⇄ 3
🍴)

URMSTON
Greater Manchester
Map **V**   D7

Flixton Church Rd, Flixton,
Urmston (S side of town centre on
B5213)
T:061-748 2116
Parkland course bounded by River
Mersey. Society meetings by
arrangement. 9 | 6441 yds | Par 71 |
SSS 71
Visitors welcome, restricted W |
without M .. per day ∴ WE | with
M .. per day WE | B ☙ (not Tu) | L
D prior arrangement (not Tu) | ⚖ ⏱
| ⋈ sometimes | 🍴 | M 190 | S
***Ashley, Ashley Rd, Hale,*
Altrincham. T:061-928 3794. 49rm ⇄
🍴

UTTOXETER
Staffordshire
Map **III**   J3

Uttoxeter Wood Ln, Uttoxeter (1m
SE of Uttoxeter off B5017)
T:(0893) 4884
Downland course with open aspect. 9
(work in progress to extend to 18 holes)
| 5460 yds | Par 67 | SSS 67

Visitors welcome but with M only WE BH | .. per day ∴ WE | B L ☛ D | ⚲ ♈ (not Mon) | TR ☎ for details | M 200 | S
★★★Ye Olde Dog & Partridge, High St, Tutbury. T:(0283) 813030. 4rm (1 ⇌) Annexe: 14rm (12 ♨ 2 ♨)

UXBRIDGE
Greater London
Map II D3

Harefield Place The Drive, Harefield Place (2m N of Uxbridge off B467)
T:(0895) 37287
Municipal parkland course. 18 | 5737 yds | Par 68 | SSS 68
Open to public | B ☛ | L D prior arrangement | ⚲ ♈ ꞉ | ⋈ sometimes | ℑ | M 500 | S
★★★Master Brewer, Western Ave, Hillingdon. T:(0895) 51199. 64rm ⇌

VENTNOR
Isle of Wight
Map II B8

Ventnor Steep Hill Drive Rd, Ventnor (1m NW of Ventnor off B3327)
T:(0983) 853326
Downland course subject to wind. Fine seascapes. New yardage planned at going to press. 9 | 5772 yds | Par 70 | SSS 68
Visitors welcome restricted Sun am | .. per day WE | ♈ not evenings | ⚲ ꞉ (limited) ⋈ sometimes | TR
Sun am | M 170
★★★Ventnor Towers, Madeira Rd. T:(0983) 852277. 30rm (17 ⇌ 5 ♨)

VIRGINIA WATER
Surrey
Map II D4

Wentworth Virginia Water (W side of town centre off B389)
T:(09904) 2201
Heathland/wooded courses. 18 (18) | West 6945 yds, (East 6176 yds) | Par 72 (68) | SSS 74 (70) | Short 9 | 1731 yds | Par 31
Visitors welcome weekdays only ☎ | :: per day | B L ☛ D (parties only) | ⚲ ♈ ꞉ | ④ daily course allocation | TR 1230-1400 daily, WE | ℑ | M 1900 | S
★★★★Berystede, Bagshot Rd, Sunninghill, Ascot. T:(0990) 23311. 88rm ⇌

WADDINGTON
Lincolnshire
Map IV C1

RAF Waddington Lincoln E side of village off A607)
T:(0522) 720271
Heavily bunkered course with unusual hazards such as real bunkers. Aircraft have right of way on some holes. 9 | 5223 yds | Par 69 | SSS 66
Visitors welcome ☎ | ♈ | ⋈ | M 40
★★Moor Lodge, Branston, Lincoln. T:(0522) 791366. 34rm (13 ⇌ 2 ♨)

WAKEFIELD
West Yorkshire
Map V F6

City of Wakefield Lupset Park, Horbury Rd, Wakefield (1¼m SW of city centre on A642)
T:(0924) 376214
Parkland course. 18 | 6405 yds | Par 72 | SSS 71
Visitors welcome | ✳ | B L ☛ (not Th) | D prior arrangement (not Th) | ⚲ ♈ ꞉ | ⋈ TR summer: WE 0800-1000, 1200-1400 | M 800 | S
★★★Post House, Queens Dr, Ossett. T:(0924) 276388. 96rm

Painthorpe House Painthorpe Ln, Painthorpe, Crigglestone, Wakefield (2m S of Wakefield off A636)
T:(0924) 255083
Meadowland undulating course, easy walking. 9 | 4060 yds | Par 62 | SSS 60
Visitors welcome | ✳ | B L ☛ D | ⚲ ♈ ꞉ ⋈ | M 150 | S
★★★Post House, Queens Dr, Ossett. T:(0924) 276388. 96rm

Wakefield Woodthorpe Ln, Sandal (3m S of Wakefield off A61)
T:(0924) 255104
A well-sheltered parkland course with easy walking. Good views. 18 |

WALLASEY
Merseyside
Map V C7

6626 yds | Par 72 | SSS 72
Visitors welcome restricted Tu | ⊠ | ☎ for parties | ⚲ ♈ ꞉ | B L ☛ D prior arrangement (not Mon) | TR 1200-1400 | ℑ | M 500 | S
★★★Post House, Queens Dr, Ossett. T:(0924) 276388. 96rm ⇌

WALKDEN
Greater Manchester
Map V D7

Brackley Municipal Walkden, Salford (2m NW of Walkden on A6)
T:061-790 6076
Mostly flat course. 9 | 3003 yds | Par 35 | SSS 70
Visitors welcome | .. per day WE/BH | B ☛ ⚲ | S ꞉ | ⋈ | M 90 | ℑ
★★Racecourse, Littleton Rd, Salford. T:061-792 1420. 20rm (5 ⇌)

WALLASEY
Merseyside
Map V C7

Bidston Scoresby Rd, Leasowe, Moreton (½m W of M53 Jct 1 entrance off A551)
T:051-638 3412
Parkland course, with westerly winds. Society meetings by arrangement. 18 | 6207 yds | Par 71 | SSS 70
Visitors welcome with M or ⊠ | WE ☎ | B L ☛ D ♈ | ⋈ generally | TR WE | ℑ | M 400 | S
★★★Bowler Hat, 2 Talbot Rd, Oxton, Birkenhead. T:051-652 4931. 29rm ⇌

Leasowe Moreton, Wirral (2m W of Wallasey on A551)
T:051-677 5852
Seaside course. Societies welcome by arrangement. No facilities for children. 18 | 6204 yds | Par 71 | SSS 70
Visitors welcome but with M only Sun am | without M ∴ per day | :: WE | with M .. per day WE | B | ☛ ➥

WALLASEY
Merseyside
Map V C7

Wallasey Bayswater Rd, Wallasey (N side of town centre off A554)
T:051-639 3700
Society meetings by arrangement. 18 | 6607 yds | Par 72 | SSS 73
Visitors welcome ☎ | ⊠ | B L ☛ (not Mon) | D prior arrangement (not Mon) | ⚲ ♈ | TR before 0930; 1300-1430 Sun am competition days | M 700 | S
*Grove House, Grove Rd. T:051-630 4558. 14rm
A well-established sporting links with huge sandhills and many classic holes where the player's skills are often combined with good fortune.

L D prior arrangement | ⚏ ♟ | ∞
↘ | M 450 | Ⓢ
★★★*Bowler Hat, 2 Talbot Rd, Oxton,
Birkenhead. T:051-652 4931. 29rm* ⇌

Warren Grove Rd, Wallasey (N side
of town centre off A554)
T:051-639 8323
*Short, undulating links course with a
first-class green. 9 | 2863 yds | Par 35 |
SSS 68*
Visitors welcome | B L ♟ D (from
cafe adjoining club) | ♟ ↘ ∞ ♪ |
Ⓣ Ⓡ S 0700-0800 | M 150 | Ⓢ
★*Grove House, Grove Rd, Wallasey.
T:051-630 4558. 14rm*

WALLSEND
Tyne and Wear
Map VI K6

Wallsend Rheydt Av, Bigges Main,
Wallsend (NW side of town centre
off A193)
T:(091) 2628989
*Parkland course. 18 | 6601 yds | Par 72
| SSS 72*
Visitors welcome | without M ..
per day WE | with M .. per day | ⚏
↘ | ④ competition days | Ⓣ Ⓡ WE
am | ♪ | M 850 | Ⓢ
★★★*Newcastle Moat House, Coast Rd.
T:(091) 2628989. 162rm* ⇌ 🍴

WALSALL
West Midlands
Map III J4

Bloxwich Stafford Rd, Bloxwich,
Walsall (3m N of town centre on
A34)
T:(0922) 751
*Undulating parkland course with
natural hazards and subject to strong
north wind. Societies welcome by
arrangement. 18 | 6286 yds | Par 71 |
SSS 70*
Visitors welcome but with M only
WE ✉ | ☎ for parties | B ♟ | L D
prior arrangement | ⚏ ♟ ↘ | ∞ by
arrangement | ④ | Ⓣ Ⓡ competition
days | ♪ | M 426 | Ⓢ
★★*County, Birmingham Rd, Walsall.
T:(0922) 32323. 47rm (11* ⇌ *3* 🍴*)*

Walsall The Broadway, Walsall (SE
side of town centre off A34)
T:(0922) 613512
*Parkland course with easy walking. The
greens are very extensive. 18 | 6232 yds
| Par 70 | SSS 70*
Visitors welcome (Mon to F) WE by
arrangement with M | ☎ | without

M ∴ per day | with M .. per round
| B L ♟ D prior arrangement (not
Mon) | ⚏ ♟ ↘ | ∞ | Ⓣ Ⓡ WE | ♪ |
M 700 | Ⓢ
★★★*Crest, Birmingham/Walsall,
Birmingham Rd. T:(0922) 33555.
100rm* ⇌

WALTON ON THE HILL
Surrey
Map II E5

Walton Heath Walton on the Hill
(SE side of village off B2032)
T:(073781) 2060
*Two fast-running heathland
championship courses, exposed to wind.
Societies welcome (Mon to Fri) by
arrangement. 36 | Old 6813 yds (New
6659) | Par 73(72) | SSS 73(72)*
Visitors welcome ✉ weekdays,
with M only WE ☎ | ∷ per day | B
L ♟ | ⚏ ♟ ↘ | ④ various times |
Ⓣ Ⓡ WE BH | M 800 | Ⓢ
★★*Heathside, Brighton Rd, Burgh
Heath. T:(07373) 53355. 44rm* 🍴

WARE
Hertfordshire
Map II F2

Chadwell Springs Hertford Rd
(¾m W of Ware on A119)
T:(0920) 3647

*Quick drying moorland course on high
plateau subject to wind. The first two
holes are par 5 and notable. Societies
welcome by arrangement. 9 | 6042 yds |
Par 72 | SSS 69*
Visitors welcome but with M only
WE | B ♟ | L D prior arrangement |
⚏ ♟ ↘ | M 400 | Ⓢ
★★★*Ware Moat House, Baldock St,
Ware. T:(0920) 5011. 50rm (44* ⇌ *6*
🍴*)*

WAREHAM
Dorset
Map I J6

Lakey Hill Hyde (6½m W of
Wareham)
T:(0929) 471776
*Country course with a profusion of
rhododendrons. 18 | 6146 yds | Par 70 |
SSS 69*
Visitors welcome | B L ♟ | ⚏ ↘ | ∞
♟ | M 600 | Ⓢ | ♪
★★★*Priory, Church Green. T:(09295)
2772. 15rm (11* ⇌ *4* 🍴*)*

WARKWORTH
Northumberland
Map VI K4

Warkworth The Links, Warkworth
(½m E of village off A1068)
T:(0665) 711596

Seaside course, good views. 9(18 tees) |
5817 yds | *Par 70* | *SSS 68*
Visitors welcome | without M ..
per day WE | with M .. per day WE
| ⚤ | ⛛ (WE) | M 400
★★★*White Swan, Bondgate Within,
Alnwick. T:(0665) 602109. 41rm (40
⇥)*

WARRINGTON
Cheshire
Map **V** D8

Birchwood Kelvin Cl, Birchwood
(4m NE of Warrington on A574)
T:(0925) 818819
*Very testing course with natural water
hazards. The 11th hole is particularly
challenging. Societies welcome. 18* |
6810 yds | *Par 71* | *SSS 73*
Visitors welcome | ∴ per day ::
WE | B L ♥ D | ⚤ ⛛ ＼ ⋈ | TR

WARRINGTON
Cheshire
Map **V** D8

Leigh Kenyon Hall, Kenyon (5m
NE of Warrington off A579)
T:(092 576) 3130
18 | *5861 yds* | *Par 69* | *SSS 68*
Visitors welcome ☎ | without M ∴
per day WE | with M .. per day WE
| B L ♥ D | ⚤ ⛛ ＼ | TR | W, Th,
WE | ♩ | M 550 | S
★★*Patten Arms, Parker St,
Warrington. T:(0925) 36602. 43rm (29
⇥ 14 ⓐ)*

competition days | M 700 | S
★★★*Post House, Lodge Ln, Newton-le-
Willows, Haydock. T:(0942) 717878.
98rm ⇥*

Walton Hall Warrington Rd,
Higher Walton (2½m S of
Warrington off A56)
T:(0925) 630619
*Municipal parkland course on Walton
Hall estate. Societies welcome by
arrangement. 18* | *6810 yds* | *Par 72* |
SSS 73
Open to public | B L ♥ D ⛛ (not
Mon) | ⚤ ＼ ⋈ | ♩ | TR | Sun before
0900 | M 200 | S
★★*Patten Arms, Parker St,
Warrington. T:(0925) 36602. 43rm (29
⇥ 14 ⓐ)*

Warrington, The Hill Warren,
London Rd, Appleton (2½m S of

SCORE CARD:

1	411	10	359
2	284	11	301
3	346	12	155
4	501	13	271
5	192	14	390
6	391	15	189
7	132	16	445
8	305	17	338
9	434	18	417

A pleasant parkland course with a fair number of trees. Any discrepancy in length is compensated by the wide variety of golf offered here. The course is well-maintained and there is a comfortable clubhouse.

WATFORD
Hertfordshire
Map **II** E2

West Herts Cassiobury Park, Watford (W side of town centre off A412)
T:(0923) 36484
18 | *6488 yds* | *Par 72* | *SSS 71*
Visitors welcome, restricted Th (ladies) Wed F (societies), with M only WE BH
| B L ♥ (not Mon) | D societies only (not Mon) | ⚤ ⛛ ＼ | TR | Th (1030-1300)
WE BH | ♩ | M 700 | S
★★★*Ladbroke (& Conferencentre), Elton Way, Watford-by-Pass, Bushey. T:(0923)
35881. 155rm ⇥*

Another of the many clubs which were inaugurated in the 1890s when the game of golf was being given a tremendous boost by the performances of the first star professionals, Braid, Vardon and Taylor. The West Herts course is close to Watford but its setting is beautiful and tranquil. Set out on a plateau the course is exceedingly dry. It also has a very severe finish with the 17th a hole of 386 yards the toughest on the course. The last hole measures over 500 yards

Warrington on A49)
T:(0925) 65431
*Meadowland, with varied terrain and
natural hazards. Societies by
arrangement W and Th (25 max on
Th). No children under 10. 18* |
6305 yds | *Par 72* | *SSS 70*
Visitors welcome ☎ | without M ::
per day WE | with M .. per day WE
| B prior arrangement 4 or more
(not Mon) | ♥ (not Mon) | L D prior
arrangement (not Mon) | ⚤ | ⛛ (not
Mon lunchtime) | ④ ☎ for details |
TR 1245-1330) | ♩ | M 400 | S
★*Rockfield, 3 Alexandra Rd,
Grappenhall. T:(0925) 62898. 7rm (3
⇥) Annexe: 8rm (2 ⇥)*

WARWICK
Warwickshire
Map **III** K6

Warwick The Racecourse, Warwick
(W side of town centre)
T:(0926) 494316
*Parkland course with easy walking.
Driving range with floodlit bays.
Societies by arrangement. 9* | *2612 yds* |
Par 34 | *SSS 66*
Visitors welcome .. per round | ♥
(not Sun) | ⚤ ⛛ ＼ ⋈ | ④ Sun
(0745-1100) | ♩ | M 90 | S
★★*Warwick Arms, High St. T:(0926)
492759. 29rm (11 ⇥ 18 ⓐ)*

WATERLOOVILLE
Hampshire,
Map **II** B7

Waterlooville Idsworth Rd,
Cowplain (NE side of town centre
off A3)
T:(0705) 263388
*Parkland course, easy walking.
Societies welcome (Th) by arrangement.
18* | *6647 yds* | *Par 72* | *SSS 72*
Visitors welcome, with M only WE
BH | without M ∴ per day | with M
.. per day | B L ♥ | D prior
arrangement | ⚤ ⛛ ⋈ | TR | ladies
Sun Tu (1200-1330) | ♩ | M 600 | S
★★★*Post House, Northney Rd,
Hayling Island. T:(0705) 465011.
Annexe: 96rm ⇥*

WELLINGBOROUGH
Northamptonshire
Map **IV** C6

Rushden Kimbolton Rd,
Chelveston, Wellingborough (2½m
NE of Rushden on A45)
T:(0933) 312581

KEY
(IA1) *atlas grid reference*
T: *telephone number*
☎ *advance letter/telephone call required*
✉ *introduction from own club sec/handicap certificate/club membership card required*
•• *low fees*
∴ *medium fees*
∷ *high fees*
* *green fees not confirmed for 1987*
B *light lunch*
L *full lunch*
☕ *tea*
D *dinner*
⧋ *changing rooms/showers*
Y *bar open mid-day and evenings*
⟍ *clubs for hire*
⋈ *partners may be found*
④ *restricted time for 4 balls*
[TR] *times reserved for members*
ʃ *professional*
[S] *well-stocked shop*
M *member*
Mon Tu W Th F S Sun
WE *weekend*
BH *bank holiday*

Parkland course. 9 | 6381 yds | Par 71 | SSS 70
Visitors welcome ✉ | with member only WE | without M ∴ per day | with M •• per day | B L ☕ D prior arrangement (not Mon) | ⧋ | Y (not Mon) | ⋈ | [TR] W pm | M 400
★★★*Hind, Sheep St, Wellingborough. T:(0933) 222827. 32rm* ⇄ ⌂

Wellingborough Gt Harrowden Hall, Wellingborough (2½m N of Wellingborough on A509)
T:(0933) 677234
An undulating parkland course with many trees. The 514 yd 14th is a testing hole. Societies welcome (W Th only) by arrangement. Outdoor pool. 18 | 6604 yds | Par 72 | SSS 72
Visitors welcome weekdays, with M only WE BH | ∷ per day | B (not Sun) | L D prior arrangement (not Sun) | ☕ | ⧋ Y ⟍ | ʃ | M 550 | [S]
★★★*Hind, Sheep St. T:(0933) 222827. 32rm* ⇄ ⌂

WELLINGTON
Shropshire
Map **III** G4

Wrekin Ercall Woods, Wellington (1¼m S of Wellington off B5061)
T:(0952) 44032
Downland course with some hard walking but rewarding views. 18 | 5690 yds | Par 66 | SSS 67
Visitors welcome ☎ advisable | restricted WE BH | without M ∴ per day WE | with M •• per day WE | B L ☕ D prior arrangement (not Mon) | ⧋ Y | ⋈ | [TR] competitions | ʃ | M 600 | [S]
★★★*Buckatree Hall, Ercall Ln, Wellington. T:(0952) 51821. 37rm* ⇄

WELLS
Somerset
Map **I** H4

Wells (Somerset) East Horrington Rd, Wells (1m E of Wells off B3139)
T:(0749) 72868
Beautiful wooded course. The prevailing SW wind complicates the 445-yd 3rd. Societies welcome by arrangement. 18 | 5300 yd | Par 67 | SSS 66
Visitors welcome | •• per day WE | B L D ☕ (not W) | ⧋ Y ⟍ ⋈ | ʃ | [TR] competitions | M 550 | [S]
★★★*Swan, Sadler St. T:(0749) 78877. 32rm (27 ⇄ 5 ⌂)*

WELSHPOOL
Powys
Map **III** F4

Welshpool Y Golfa Hill, Welshpool (5m W of Welshpool off A458)
T:(0938) 83249
Undulating heathland course with bracing air. Testing holes are 2nd par 5, 14th par 3, 17th par 3. 18 | 5708 yds | Par 70 | SSS 69
Visitors welcome restricted Mon BH | B L ☕ prior arrangement (not Mon) | ⧋ Y (not Mon) | [TR] competition days | ʃ | M 250
★★*Royal Oak, The Cross. T:(0938) 2217. 25rm (14 ⇄ 5 ⌂)*

WELWYN GARDEN CITY
Hertfordshire
Map **II** E2

Panshanger Golf and Squash Complex Hernes Ln, Welwyn Carden City (N side of town centre off B1000)
T:(07073) 33350
Municipal parkland course overlooking Mimram Valley. 18 | 6638 yds | Par 72 | SSS 70
Visitors welcome | B L ☕ D | ⧋ Y ⟍ ⋈ | ʃ | [S]
★★★*Crest, Homestead Ln. T:(07073) 24336. 58rm* ⇄

Welwyn Garden City Mannicotts, Welwyn Garden City (W side of town centre off B195)
T:(07073) 25243
Undulating parkland course with ravine, 14th hole 'The Dell' par 4

across the ravine. 18 | 6029 yds | Par 70 | SSS 69
Visitors welcome except Sun ∷ per day | B ☕ (not Mon) | L D prior arrangement (not Mon) | △ 🍸 ⟍ | ℷ | M 650 | [S]
★★★*Crest, Homestead Ln. T:(07073) 24336. 58rm* ⇄

WEMBLEY
Greater London
Map **II** E3

Sudbury Bridgewater Rd, Wembley (SW side of town centre on A4090)
T:01-902 3713
Parkland course very near centre of London. 18 | 6282 yds | Par 69 | SSS 70
Visitors welcome weekdays | ☎ preferred | * | B L D prior arrangement (not Mon) | ☕ prior arrangement (not Mon and F) | △ 🍸 ⟍ ⋈ | [TR] Tu WE | M 600 | [S]
★★★*Grims Dyke, Old Redding, Harrow-weald. T:01-954 4227. 8rm* ⇄ *Annexe: 40rm* ⇄

WENVOE
South Glamorgan
Map **I** G3

Wenvoe Castle Wenvoe (1m S of Wenvoe off A4050)
T:(0222) 594371
Parkland course which is hilly for 1st 9 holes. Pond situated 280 yds from tee at 10th hole is a hazard. Society meetings by arrangement Mon Th. 18 | 6422 yds | Par 72 | SSS 71
Visitors welcome ☎ ✉ | restricted WE BH | B ☕ | L D prior arrangement | △ 🍸 ⟍ ☎ | ℷ | M 610 | [S]
★★★*Crest, Westgate St, Cardiff. T:(0222) 388681. 160rm* ⇄

WEST BROMWICH
West Midlands
Map **III** J5

Dartmouth Vale St, West Bromwich (E side of town centre off A4041)
T:021-588 2131
Well-wooded parkland course with undulating but easy walking. The 615 yd Par 5 first hole is something of a challenge. Societies welcome by arrangement. 9(with 18 tees) | 6060 (3089/2971) yds | Par 71 | SSS 69
Visitors welcome but with M only WE BH | without M ‥ per day | with M ‥ per day WE | B L ☕ D 🍸 prior arrangement (not Tu) | △ ⟍ | ⋈ | [4] [TR] Medal Days (1st WE in month) | ℷ | M 310 | [S]
★★★*West Bromwich Moat House, Birmingham Rd. T:021-553 6111. 181rm* ⇄ ⌂

Sandwell Park Birmingham Rd, West Bromwich (SE side of town centre off A4040)
T:021-553 4637
Undulating heathland course close to the Motorway. 18 | 6500 yds | Par 71 | SSS 71
Visitors welcome restricted WE and BH ☎ advisable | without M ∴ per day | with M ‥ per round | B L ☕ (not Mon) | D prior arrangement (not Mon) | △ | 🍸 | ⋈ | [TR] WE | M 500 | [S]
★★★*West Bromwich Moat House, Birmingham Rd, West Bromwich. T:021-553 6111. 181rm* ⇄ ⌂

WEST CALDER
Lothian, *Midlothian*
Map **IV** F2

Harburn West Calder (2m S of West Calder on B7008)
T:(0506) 871256
Moorland, reasonably flat. 18 | 5843 yds | Par 69 | SSS 68
Visitors welcome | without M ∴ per day WE | with M ‥ per round | B L ☕ D prior arrangement | [S] ⋈ | △ 🍸 | M 623
★★★*Golden Circle, Blackburn Rd, Bathgate. T:(0506) 53771. 75rm* ⇄ ⌂

WEST DRAYTON
Greater London
Map **II** D3

Holiday Stockley Rd (1m SE of West Drayton off A408)
T:(0895) 444232
Fairly large, testing, hilly course suitable both for beginners and scratch players. 9 | 3900 yds | Par 30 | SSS 32
Visitors welcome, restricted 1st Sun each month 0800-1200 | ‥ per day | L D in hotel | B ☕ | 🍸 | ⟍ | M 280 | [TR] Sun am
★★★★*Holiday Inn, Stockley Rd, W Drayton. T:(0895) 445555. 400rm* ⇄ ⌂

WEST END
Surrey
Map **II** D4

Windlemere Windlesham Rd, West End, Woking (N side of village off A319)
T:(09905) 8727
A parkland course, undulating in parts with natural water hazards, there is a floodlit driving range also. 9 | 2673 yds | Par 34 | SSS 33(66)
Visitors welcome without M ‥ per day | B ☕ L D | △ 🍸 ⟍ | ⋈ | ℷ | [S]
★★★★*Pennyhill Park, College Ride, Bagshot. T:(0276) 71774. 19rm* ⇄ *Annexe: 31rm* ⇄

WESTGATE-ON-SEA
Kent
Map **II** K4

Westgate and Birchington Westgate on Sea (E side of town centre off A28)
T:(0843) 31115
Seaside course. 18 | 4926 yds | Par 64 | SSS 63
Visitors welcome ✉ | ☕ | B L prior arrangement | △ | 🍸 (limited to evenings) | ℷ | [TR] Tu, Th, WE before 1100 | M 320 | [S]

WEST BYFLEET
Surrey
Map **II** D4

West Byfleet Sheerwater Rd, West Byfleet (W side of village on A245)
T:(093 23) 45230
18 | 6211 yds | Par 70 | SSS 70
Visitors welcome, restricted Th WE BH | ✉ ☎ | ∷ per day | B ☕ | L prior arrangement | D societies only | △ 🍸 | ⟍ ⋈ | [4] ☎ for details | [TR] competition days and WE | ℷ | M 600 | [S]
★★★*Thatchers, Epsom Rd, East Horsley. T:(04865) 4291. 6rm* ⇄ *Annexe: 24rm* ⇄
An attractive course on quick-drying sandy sub-soil set against a background of woodland and gorse. The 13th is the famous 'pond' shot, the water hazard and two bunkers fronting the green being much less formidable than at first appears. No less than five holes of 420 yards or more will provide testing long two-shotters for the strong player.

★★*Savoy, Grange Rd, Ramsgate.*
T:(0843) 592637. 14rm (1 ⇄ 2 ⌘)
Annexe: 11rm (2 ⇄ 9 ⌘)

WESTHOUGHTON
Greater Manchester
Map **V**   D7

Westhoughton Long Island,
Westhoughton (½m NW of
Westhoughton off A58)
T:(0942) 811085
*Dowland course. 9 | 5772 yds | Par 70 |
SSS 68*
Visitors welcome, with M only WE
| ☎ if without M | ⚑ ⛾ | TR
competition days | 🍴 | M 300 | S
★★★*Crest, Beaumont Rd, Bolton.*
T:(0204) 651511. 100rm ⇄

WEST KILBRIDE
Strathclyde, *Ayrshire*
Map   VI C3

West Kilbride Fullerton Drive,
Seamill, West Kilbride (W side of
town off A78)
T:(0294) 833128
*Seaside links course, fine view of Isle of
Arran from every hole. 18 | 6235 yds |
Par 71 | SSS 70*
Visitors welcome except WE ✉ | B
⚑ | L D prior arrangement | ⚑ ⛾ |
TR WE | 🍴 | M 960 | S
★★*Elderslie, John St, Broomfields,
Largs. T:(0475) 686460. 25rm (9 ⇄ 4
⌘)*

WEST KINGSDOWN
Kent
Map **II** G4

Woodlands Manor Woodlands,
West Kingsdown (2m S of West
Kingsdown off A20)
T:(09592) 3806

*Interesting undulating parkland course
with testing 1st 9th 15th holes.
Societies welcome by arrangement.
Billiard table. 18 | 5858 yds | Par 69 |
SSS 68*
Visitors welcome weekdays ☎ with
member only WE pm | B ⚑ | L D
prior arrangement (not Mon) | ⚑ ⛾
⛾ | ④ by arrangement | TR Tu
(ladies day) ④ ☎ | 🍴 | M 550 | S
★★*Sevenoaks Park, Seal Hollow Rd,
Sevenoaks. T:(0732) 454245. 16rm (3
⇄ 3 ⌘)*

WEST LINTON
Borders, *Peeblesshire*
Map **VI** F3

West Linton West Linton (NW side
of village off A702)
T:(0968) 60589
*Moorland course with beautiful views
of Pentland Hills. Societies welcome
(Mon to S) by arrangement. 18 |
5835 yds | Par 70 | SSS 68*
Visitors welcome | ⛾ per round ∷ |
WE | B L ⚑ D (not Tu) | ⚑ ⛾ ⋈ |
TR ☎ for details | M 450 | S

Weston-super-Mare Uphill Rd North, Weston-super-Mare (S side of town
centre off A370)
T:(0934) 26968
Societies up to 60 welcome by arrangement. 18 | 6279 yds | Par 70 | SSS 70
Visitors welcome except on competition days | ☎ advisable | without M ⛾ |
with M ⛾ per day | B ⚑ D | L (not F) | ⚑ ⛾ | ⋈ prior arrangement | TR
competition days | 🍴 | M 400 | S
★★★*Grand Atlantic, Beach Rd, T:(0934) 26543. 79rm ⇄*
A compact and interesting layout with the opening hole adjacent to
the beach. The sandy links-type course is slightly undulating and
has beautifully maintained turf and greens. The 15th is a testing
455-yard par 4.

★★★*Tontine, High St, Peebles.
T:(0721) 20892. 37rm (36 ⇄ 1 ⌘)*

WESTON
Staffordshire
Map **III** J3

Ingestre Park Stafford (2m SE of
Weston off A51)
T:(0785) 270845/270061
*Parkland course set in the grounds of
Ingestre Hall, former home of the Earl
of Shrewsbury. 18 | 6376 yds | Par 70 |
SSS 70*
Visitors welcome, with M only WE
BH | ∴ per day | B L ⚑ D | ⚑ ⛾ ⛾
| 🍴 | M 500 | S
★★★*Tillington Hall, Eccleshall Rd,
Stafford. T:(0785) 53531. 93rm (90 ⇄
3 ⌘)*

WESTONBIRT
Gloucestershire
Map **I** J2

Westonbirt Westonbirt, Tetbury (E
side of village off A433)
*A parkland course with good views. 9 |
2252 yds | Par 32 | SSS 32*   ➥

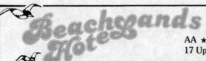

Visitors welcome without M
★★★*Hare & Hounds, Westonbirt,*
Tetbury. T:(066688) 233. 23rm (19 ⇄)

WESTON-SUPER-MARE
Avon
Map **I** **G3**

Worlebury Worlebury Hill Rd,
Weston-Super-Mare (2¾m NE of
Weston-Super-Mare off A370)
T:(0934) 25789
Fairly easy walking on seaside course

situated on the ridge of Worlebury Hill.
No children under 8. 18 | 5945 yds |
Par 70 | SSS 68
Visitors welcome | B ☎ | D L prior
arrangement | ⚠ ♈ | ↘ ✕ prior
arrangement | ④ TR competitions |
⅃ | M 600 | S
★★★*Royal Pier, Birnbeck Rd. T:(0934)*
26644. 41rm (33 ⇄ 2 ⌘)

WESTON TURVILLE
Buckinghamshire
Map **II** **C2**

Weston Turville New Rd, Weston
Turville, nr Aylesbury (½m N of
Weston Turville off B4544)
T:(0296) 24084
Parkland course, easy walking. 13 |
6782 yds | Par 73 | SSS 72
Visitors welcome | without M ∴ per
day ∷ WE | with M ‥ per day WE |
B ☎ L | ⚠ ♈ ↘ | TR Sun (am) Th
1700-1830 | M 325 | S
❀○○○*Bell Inn, Aston Clinton.*
T:(0296) 630252. 21rm ⇄

WESTON-UNDER-REDCASTLE
Shropshire
Map **III** **G3**

Hawkstone Park Hotel Weston-under-Redcastle, Shrewsbury (N side of
village, ¾m E of A49)
T:(093 924) 611
2 courses. 18(18) | 6203(5063) yds | Par 72(66) | SSS 70(65)
Visitors welcome | ☎ advisable. | Hawkstone ∷ per day WE, Weston ∴ per
day WE | B L ☎ D (food/drink voucher included in green fee) | ⚠ ♈ ✕ ↘ |
TR 0815-1035 (hotel residents only) | ⅃ | M 450 | S
★★★*Hawkstone Park, Weston. T:(093 924) 611. 43rm ⇄ Annexe: 16rm ⇄*
Two courses in a beautiful setting, both with natural hazards and
good views. Hawkstone Course has been established for over 50
years and enjoys a superb setting whilst the Weston course has
developed well over the last 10 years.

SCORE CARD:

1	322	10	356
2	370	11	476
3	330	12	310
4	433	13	255
5	480	14	365
6	167	15	390
7	486	16	148
8	410	17	363
9	139	18	403

WESTRAY
Orkney Islands
Map **VII** K2

Westray Westray, Orkney (1m NW of Pierowall off B9066)
Interesting, picturesque seaside course, easy walking. 9 | 2405 yds | Par 33
Visitors welcome, no Sun golf | ⟍ ⋈ | M 30
★★*Ayre, Ayre Rd, Kirkwall. T:(0856) 2197. 31rm (3 🛁 6 🚿)*

WEST RUNTON
Norfolk
Map **IV** J2

Links Country Park West Runton, Cromer (S side of village off A149)
T:026-375 691
Parkland course 500 yds from the sea, superb views overlooking West Runton. 9 | 2407 yds | Par 33 | SSS 64
∴ per day ∴ WE | 🍸 B L D ☕ | △ | [S]⟍ | ⋈ | M 270 | ℨ
★★★*Links Country Park Hotel & Golf Club, West Runton. T:(026375) 691. 22rm (20 🛁 2 🚿)*
See advertisement on page 225.

WESTWARD HO
Devon
Map **I** D4

Royal North Devon Westward Ho (N side of village off B3236)
T:(02372) 73817
Links course with sea views. 18 | 6644 yds | Par 71 | SSS 72
Visitors welcome ∴ per day | 🍸 B L D ☕ | △ | [S]⟍ | ⋈ | M 550 | [TR] Tu Th | ℨ
★★*Culloden House, Fosketh Hill. T:(02372) 79421. 9rm (2 🛁 5 🚿)*

WETHERBY
West Yorkshire
Map **V** F5

Wetherby Linton Ln, Wetherby (1m W of Wetherby off A661)
T:(0937) 62527
Parkland course with fine views. Parties over 12 in number welcome on W Th F by arrangement only. 18 | 6244 yds | Par 71 | SSS 70
Visitors welcome | without M ∷ per day WE | with M ∴ per day WE | B L ☕ D prior arrangement (not Mon) | △ 🍸 | [TR] until 0930, 1200-1400 | ℨ | M 550 | [S]
★★★*Ladbroke Wetherby, Leeds Rd. T:(0937) 63881. 72rm 🛁*

WEXHAM STREET
Buckinghamshire
Map **II** D3

Wexham Park Wexham St, Wexham, nr Slough (½m S of Wexham Street)
T:(02816) 3271
Gently undulating parkland course. 18 | 5424 yds | Par 67 | SSS 67
Visitors welcome without M | B L ☕ D | △ 🍸 ⟍ ⋈ | ℨ | M 500 | [S]
★★★★*Holiday Inn, Ditton Rd, Langley, Slough. T:(0753) 44244. 308rm 🛁 🚿*

WEYMOUTH
Dorset
Map **I** J6

Weymouth Links Rd, Westham, Weymouth (N side of town centre

WEYBRIDGE
Surrey
Map **II** D4

St George's Hill Weybridge (2m S of Weybridge off B374)
T:(0932) 42406
Societies welcome (W Th) by arrangement. No children. 18(9) | 6492(2360) yds |
Par 70(32) | SSS 71(35)
Visitors welcome to 18-hole course, with M only WE | ✉ ☎ at all times |
without M ∷ per day (.. 9-hole) | with M ∷ per day WE | B L ☛ prior
arrangement (not Mon) | ⚥ ☥ ↘ | ④ ☎ for details | TR Tu (ladies day), WE &
BH also ½ hour each day | M 600 | Ⓢ
★★★*Ship Thistle, Monument Gn.* T:(0932) 48364. 39rm ⇌ 🍴
Comparable and similar to Wentworth, a feature of this course is the
number of long and difficult par 4s. To score well it is necessary to
place the drive — and long driving pays handsomely. Walking is
hard on the undulating, heavily wooded course.

off B3157)
T:(0305) 773981
*Seaside course. At 5th play off elevated
green over copse.* 18 | 5961 yds | Par 70
| SSS 69
Visitors welcome weekdays and
WE | ✉ ☎ advisable | B L D prior
arrangement (not Mon) | ☛ ⚥ ☥ ↘
| ∞ usually | TR Ladies Day Th 1st
tee 1245-1400 9th tee 1400-1530,
competitions | ☥ | M 600 | Ⓢ
★★*Hotel Rex, 29 The Esplanade.*
T:(0305) 773485. 21rm (14 ⇌ 7 🍴)

WHALLEY
Lancashire
Map **V** D6

Whalley Long Leese Barn, Portfield
Ln (1m SE of Whalley off A671)
T:(025482) 2236
*Parkland course on Pendle Hill,
overlooking Ribble Valley. 9th hole over
pond.* 9 | 5913 yds | Par 70 | SSS 69
Visitors welcome | ✳ | B L ☛ D (no
catering Mon) | ⚥ | ☥ (not Mon) ↘
(possible) | TR Th 1200-1600 (ladies

day) competitions | ☥ | M 475
★★★*Blackburn Moat House, Preston
New Rd, Blackburn.* T:(0254) 64441.
98rm ⇌

WHEATHAMPSTEAD
Hertfordshire
Map **II** E2

Mid Herts Gustard Wood (1m N of
Wheathampstead on B651)
T:(058283) 2242
*Commonland, wooded with heather and
gorse-lined fairways. Reduced fees for
children. Societies welcome by
arrangement.* 18 | 6094 yds | Par 69 |
SSS 69
Visitors welcome, restricted Tu and
with M only WE BH | ☎ essential |
without M ∷ per day | with M ..
per day WE | B L ☛ D (no catering
Mon) | ⚥ | ☥ certain times | ④ ☎
for details | TR Tu am (ladies) |
M 600 | Ⓢ
★★★*Harpenden Moat House, 18
Southdown Rd, Harpenden.* T:(05827)
64111. 16rm (13 ⇌ 3 🍴) Annexe:
30rm ⇌

WHETSTONE
Leicestershire
Map **IV** A5

Whetstone Cambridge Rd, Cosby
(1m S of village)
T:(0533) 861424
*Small and very flat parkland course
adjacent to motorway. Small societies
welcome by arrangement.* 9 | 6212 yds |
Par 72 | SSS 69
Visitors welcome | B ☛ | ⚥ ☥ ↘ ∞
(sometimes) | ☥ | M 70 | Ⓢ
★★★*Post House, Braunstone Ln East,
Leicester.* T:(0533) 896688. 182rm ⇌

WHICKHAM
Tyne and Wear
Map **VI** K6

Whickham Hollinside Park,
Newcastle upon Tyne (1½m S of
Whickham)
T:(091) 4887309
*Parkland course, some uphill walking,
fine views.* 18 | 6129 yds | Par 68 |
SSS 69
Visitors welcome | without M ..
per day ∴ WE | B ☛ | L D prior
arrangement | ⚥ ☥ ↘ | TR S | ☥ |
M 500 | Ⓢ
★★★*Five Bridges, High West St,
Gateshead.* T:(091) 4771105. 106rm ⇌

WHITBURN
Lothian, *West Lothian*
Map **VI** F2

Polkemmet Country Park
Whitburn, Bathgate (2m W of
Whitburn off B7066)
T:(0501) 43905
Parkland course very picturesque. 9 |
3216 yds | Par 37
Public course .. per round | B L D
☛ | ☥

WHITCHURCH
Shropshire
Map III G3

Hill Valley Terrick Rd (1m N of Whitchurch)
T:(0948) 3584
18 | 6884(6050) yds | Par 72(72) | SSS 71(69)
Visitors welcome | .. per day ∴ WE | B L ♥ D | ⚘ ⛳ ⚲ | TR 0900-1015 (hotel residents only) | ♪ | M 400 | S
∗∗∗Terrick Hall Country Hotel, Hill Valley. T:(0948) 3031. 10rm ⇌
This parkland course was opened in 1975, providing a very good test of golf. The course was designed to championship standard by Peter Allis and Dave Thomas. The hilly terrain is enhanced by many glorious views over 6 counties. There are natural water hazards on 10 holes.

WHITEFIELD
Greater Manchester
Map V D7

Stand The Dales, Ashbourne Grove, Whitefield, Manchester (1m W of Whitefield off A667)
T:061-766 2388
18 | 6411 yds | Par 72 | SSS 71
Visitors welcome ☎ ⊠ | restricted WE | B ♥ (not Mon) | L D prior arrangement (not Mon) | ⚘ ⛳ | TR 1230 to 1400 daily | ⚲ | ⋈ | M 700 | S
∗Woolfield House, Wash Ln, Bury. T:061-764 7048. 13rm (1 🅿)
A fine test of golf; accuracy from the tee is the key to success here. A very demanding finish commences at the delightful short 13th hole.

WHITTLE-LE-WOODS
Lancashire
Map V C7

Shaw Hill Golf and Country Club Whittle-le-Woods, Chorley (S side of village off A6)
T:(02572) 69221
Society meetings by arrangement Tu Th F. 18 | 6467 yds | Par 72 | SSS 71
Visitors welcome | without M ∴ per day | with M .. per day WE | B L ♥ D | ⚘ ⛳ ⚲ | ⋈ | TR 0830-0915, 1200-1300, 1630-1730 midweek; 0830-0930, 1200-1330, 1630-1730 WE | M 600 | S
∗∗∗Shaw Hill Golf and Country Club, Preston Rd. T:(02572) 69221. 18rm ⇌
Undulating, attractively wooded parkland golf, never severe but with several narrow drives and two difficult par 5s with which to contend. Seven lakes add interest.

∗∗∗♨Houstoun House, Uphall. T:(0506) 853831. 30rm (27 ⇌ 3 🅿)

WHITBY
North Yorkshire
Map V H3

Whitby Low Straggleton (1½m NW of Whitby on A174)
T:(0947) 602768
Seaside course on cliff top. Good views and fresh sea breeze. Ravine to cross on course. Societies welcome by arrangement. 18 | 5980 yds | Par 69 | SSS 67
Visitors welcome | ∗ | B ♥ L (not Mon) | D prior arrangement (not

Mon) | ⚘ ⛳ ⚲ ⋈ | TR WE until 1030 | ♪ | M 650 | S
∗∗Royal, West Cliff. T:(0947) 602234. 134rm (23 ⇌ 44 🅿)

WHITEFIELD
Greater Manchester
Map V D7

Whitefield Higher Ln, Whitefield (N side of town centre on A665)
T:061-766 3096
Fine sporting parkland course with well watered greens. Societies welcome on application. 18 | 6041(5714) yds | Par 69(68) | SSS 69(68)
Visitors welcome | fees on

application | B ♥ L D | ⚘ ⛳ ⚲ ⋈ | TR 1200-1400 | ♪ | M 500 | S
∗∗∗∗Portland Thistle, 3/5 Portland St, Piccadilly Gdns, Manchester. T:061-228 3567. 219rm ⇌ 🅿

WHITING BAY
Strathclyde, Bute
Map VI C4

Whiting Bay Whiting Bay, Isle of Arran (NW side of village off A841)
T:(07707) 516
Heathland course. 18 | 4405 yds | Par 63 | SSS 63
Visitors welcome | ⛳ | ⋈ by arrangement | M 290 | S
∗Cameronia, Whiting Bay. T:(07707) 254. 6rm

WHITLEY BAY
Tyne and Wear
Map V F1

Whitley Bay Claremont Rd, Whitley Bay (NW side of town centre off A1148)
T:(091) 2520180
Downland course close to the sea. A stream runs through the undulating terrain. 18 | 6712 yds | Par 73 | SSS 72
Visitors welcome but with M only WE BH | without M ∴ per day | with M .. per day WE | B ♥ (not Mon) | L D prior arrangement (not Mon) | ⚘ ⛳ | ♪ | M 700 | S
∗∗Holmedale, 106 Park Ave. T:(091) 2513903. 23rm (5 ⇌)

WHITSAND
Cornwall
Map I D7
See entry for Portwinkle

WHITSTABLE
Kent
Map II J4

Chestfield 103 Chestfield Rd (2m SE of Whitstable off A299)
T:(022779) 2365
Parkland course with sea views. 18 | 6068 yds | Par 70 | SSS 69
Visitors welcome weekdays ⊠ | with M .. per round | without M ∴ per round | B L ♥ D prior arrangement | ⚘ ⛳ | TR competitions | ♪ | M 630 | S
∗∗Marine, Marine Pde, Tankerton. T:(0227) 272672. 20rm (4 ⇌ 16 🅿)

Whitstable & Seasalter Collingwood Rd, Whitstable (W

side of town centre off B2205)
T:(0227) 272020
*Links course. 9 | 5276 yds | Par 66 |
SSS 63*
Visitors welcome without M .. per
round | B ♥ | L prior arrangement |
⚘ ? | TR WE | M 250
★★*Marine, Marine Pde, Tankerton.
T:(0227) 272672. 20rm (4 ⇌ 16 ⋔)*

WHITWORTH
Lancashire
Map **V**   D7

Lobden Lobden Moor, Whitworth,
nr Rochdale (E side of town centre
off A671)
T:(0706) 343228
*Moorland course, with hard walking.
Windy. 9 | 5770 yds | Par 70 | SSS 68*
Visitors welcome, restricted Tu W
Th pm | B L (WE only) ♥ D prior
arrangement | ⚘ ? | TR Tu W Th
(eve) S (all day) | M 245
★★*Midway, Manchester Rd,
Castleton, Rochdale. T:(0706) 32881.
30rm (2 ⇌ 20 ⋔)*

WICK
Highland, *Caithness*
Map **VII**   H2

Wick Reiss (3½ m N of Wick off A9)
T:(0955) 2726
*Seaside course, windy, easy walking.
18 | 5976 yds | Par 69 | SSS 69*
Visitors welcome | ⚘ ? | TR W
1630-1900, Th 1630-1900 | M 250
★★★*Ladbroke, Riverside. T:(0955)
3344. 48rm ⇌*

WIDNES
Cheshire
Map **V**   C8

St Michael Jubilee Dundalk Rd,
Widnes (W side of town centre off
A562)
T:051-424 6230
*Recently extended municipal parkland
course, dominated by the Stewards
Brook. The old and the new sections are
split by the main road and joined by an
underpass. 18 | 2991 yds | Par 69 |
SSS 35*
Visitors welcome without M .. per
round | ⚘ ⟍ ⋈ | ⫂ | S
★★*Hillcrest, 75 Cronton Ln, Widnes.
T:051-424 1616. 46rm (28 ⇌ 18 ⋔)*

Widnes Highfield Rd, Widnes (W
side of town centre on B5178)
T:051-424 2995

*Parkland course, easy walking.
Societies welcome weekdays (not Tu).
18 | 5171 yds | Par 69 | SSS 68*
Visitors welcome 🕮 | B ♥ | L D
prior arrangement | ⚘ ? | TR 🕮
for details | ⫂ | M 800 | S
★*Rockland, View Rd, Rainhill.
T:051-426 4603. 12rm (2 ⇌) Annexe:
10rm (4 ⇌ 6 ⋔)*

WIGAN
Greater Manchester
Map **V**   C7

Haigh Hall Haigh, Gtr Manchester
(2m NE of Wigan off B5238)
T:(0942) 831107
*Municipal parkland course, with hard
walking and a canal forms the west
boundary. Adjacent to Haigh Country
Park with many facilities. 18 | 6423 yds
| Par 70 | SSS 71*
Open to public | * | reduction
juniors | L B ♥ | ⚘ ⟍ ⫂ | TR
competitions | S
★★★*Brocket Arms, Mesnes Rd,
Wigan. T:(0942) 46283. 27rm (25 ⇌ 2
⋔)*

WIGHT, ISLE OF
Map **II**
See Cowes, East Cowes,
Freshwater Bay, Newport, Ryde,
Sandown and Ventnor

WIGTOWN
Dumfries and Galloway,
Wigtownshire
Map **VI**   D6

Wigtown & Bladnoch Wigtown
(SW side of village on A714)
T:(09884) 3354
*Slightly hilly parkland course with fine
views over Wigtown Bay to Galloway
Hills. 9 | 5160 yds | Par 68 | SSS 67*
Visitors welcome 🕮 parties | .. per
day WE | ♥ B | ⚘ ? | ⋈ | TR
competitions | M 150
❀★★★⚘Kirroughtree, Minnigaff,
Newton Stewart. T:(0671) 2141. 21rm
⇌ Annexe: 2rm ⇌*

WILPSHIRE
Lancashire
Map **V**   D6

Wilpshire 72 Whalley Rd,
Wilpshire, Blackburn (E side of ⮫

WICK
Avon
Map I   J3

Tracy Park Tracy Park, Wick (S side of village off A420)
T:(027 582) 2251
*Societies welcome by arrangement 27 | 7152 yds (1st and 2nd 9) | Par 74/73/73 |
SSS 74/73/72*
Visitors welcome weekdays 🕮 | B L (not Mon) | ♥ | D prior arrangement | ⚘
? ⟍ | ⫂ | M 600 | S
★★★*Lansdown Grove, Lansdown Rd, Bath. T:(0225) 315891. 41rm (38 ⇌ 3 ⋔)*
A new club at Wick, near Bristol. The course, situated on the south-
western escarpment of the Cotswolds is undulating with fine
views. The clubhouse dates back to 1600 and is a building of great
beauty and elegance, set in the 220-acre estate of this golf and
country club. Natural water hazards affect a number of holes.

WIGAN
Greater Manchester
Map V   C7

Wigan Arley Hall, Haigh (3m NE of Wigan off B5238)
T:(0257) 421360
Societies welcome by arrangement. 9 | 6058 yds | Par 70 | SSS 69
Visitors welcome, visiting parties only on prior arrangement | B (not Mon) ♥
| L D prior arrangement | ⚘ ? | TR Tu Ladies day, S Men only | M 330
★★★*Brocket Arms, Mesnes Rd, Wigan. T:(0942) 46283. 27rm (25 ⇌ 2 ⋔)*
Among the best of Lancashire's 9-hole courses. This parkland
course has a ravine at the 9th hole crossed by a timber bridge. The
fine old clubhouse is the original Arley Hall and is surrounded by a
moat.

KEY
(IA1) *atlas grid reference*
T: *telephone number*
☎   *advance letter/telephone*
      call required
✉   *introduction from own club*
      sec/handicap
      certificate/club
      membership card required
..   *low fees*
∴   *medium fees*
::   *high fees*
*   *green fees not confirmed for*
      1987
B   *light lunch*
L   *full lunch*
▼   *tea*
D   *dinner*
⚐   *changing rooms/showers*
Ⴘ   *bar open mid-day and*
      evenings
↘   *clubs for hire*
∞   *partners may be found*
④   *restricted time for 4 balls*
TR   *times reserved for members*
Ј   *professional*
S   *well-stocked shop*
M   *member*
Mon Tu W Th F S Sun
WE   *weekend*
BH   *bank holiday*

WILMSLOW
Cheshire
Map **V** D8

Wilmslow Great Warford, Mobberley (2m SW of Wilmslow off B5085)
T:(056587) 2148
18 | 6500 yds | Par 71 | SSS 71
Visitors welcome ☎ ✉ | restricted W WE | without M : : per day WE | with M
.. per day WE | B ▼ prior arrangement (not Mon) | D L prior arrangement
(not Mon) | ⚐ Ⴘ | TR W until 1430 (ladies day) | Ј | M 660 | S
❀****Belfry, Stanley Rd, Handforth. T:061-437 0511. 92rm ⇄
A fine parkland championship course, of middle length, fair to all
classes of player and almost always in perfect condition.

WINCHESTER
Hampshire
Map **II** B6

Royal Winchester Sarum Rd, Winchester (1½m W of Winchester off A3090)
T:(0962) 52462
Societies welcome (Mon Tu W) by arrangement. 18 | 6021/6218 yds | Par 71 | SSS 70
Visitors welcome ✉, with M only WE BH | ☎ (for parties over 4) | without M
∴ per day | with M .. per day WE | B | ▼ | L prior arrangement | D prior
arrangement | ⚐ Ⴘ | ∞ probably | M 600 | S
***⚏Lainston House, Sparsholt. T:(0962) 63588. 32rm ⇄ 🍴
The Royal Winchester Club must be included in any list of notable
clubs, because of its age (it dates from 1888) and also because the
Club was involved in one of the very first professional matches. The
adversaries were J H Taylor and the club's professional Andrew
Kirkaldy. It was a 36 hole match, half being played at Burnham and
the other half at Winchester. Taylor proved the victor by 4 up and 3
to play. There have been many changes since that match in 1891 but
the club still flourishes on its present sporting downland course.

village off A666)
T:(0254) 48260
*Semi-moorland course. Testing 17th
hole 219 yds par 3. Good views of
Ribble Valley. Societies welcome by
arrangement Mon W Th F. 18 |
5911 yds (5424 ladies) | Par 69 |
SSS 68*
Visitors welcome ☎ | without M ∴
per day WE BH | with M .. per day
WE | B L ▼ D prior arrangement
(not Mon) | ⚐ Ⴘ (not Mon
lunchtime) | ∞ (usually) ↘ | ④ WE
| TR ☎ | Ј | M 600 | S
***Blackburn Moat House, Preston
New Rd. T:(0254) 64441. 98rm ⇄

WINCHESTER
Hampshire
Map **II** B6

Hockley Twyford, Hants (2m S of
Winchester on A333)
T:(0962) 713165
*High downland course with good
views. 18 | 6260 yds | Par 71 | SSS 70*
Visitors welcome except WE BH |
without M ∴ per day : : WE | with
M .. per day | B ▼ | L D prior

arrangement (not Tu) | ⚐ Ⴘ | Ј |
M 800 | S
****Wessex, Paternoster Row,
Winchester. T:(0962) 61611. 94rm (91
⇄ 3 🍴)

WINSFORD
Cheshire
Map **III** G2

Knights Grange Sports Complex (N
side of town off A54)
T:060-65 52780
*A nine hole municipal course. 9(18) |
3105(6210) yds | SSS 70*
Visitors welcome without M | B L D
▼ | ⚐ Ⴘ ↘ ∞ | TR Sun am
monthly | M 100
**Woodpecker, London Rd,
Northwich. T:(0606) 45524. 34rm (28
⇄ 1 🍴)

WISHAW
Strathclyde, *Lanarkshire*
Map **VI** E3

Wishaw 55 Cleland Rd, Wishaw
(NW side of town off A721)
T:(0698) 372869

*Parkland course. 18 | 6160 yds | Par 69
| SSS 69*
Visitors welcome, restricted Mon to
F Sun S | without M ∴ per day WE
| with M .. per day WE | B | L ▼ D
prior arrangement (limited catering
Mon W) | ⚐ Ⴘ | ∞ sometimes | TR
midweek (after 1600) S, Sun (until
1130) Ј | M 1000 | S
***Popinjay, Rosebank. T:(055586)
441. 36rm (29 ⇄ 7 🍴)

WITHERNSEA
Humberside
Map **V** J6

Withernsea Chesnut Ave,
Withernsea (S side of town centre
off A1033)
T:(09642) 2258
*Exposed seaside links with bunkers.
Societies welcome by arrangement. 9 |
5112 yds | Par 66 | SSS 64*
Visitors welcome | .. per day | ⚐ |
Ⴘ (evenings and S Sun lunchtime) |
TR Sun (am) | Ј | M 280
**Pearson Park, Pearson Park, Hull.
T:(0482) 43043. 39rm (23 ⇄ 2 🍴)

WOKING
Surrey
Map II D4

Worplesdon Heath House Rd, Woking (3½m SW of Woking off B380)
T:(04867) 2277
Societies welcome by arrangement. 18 | 6422 yds | Par 71 | SSS 71
Visitors welcome ⊠ with member only WE BH | ☎ advisable | :: per day | B
♥ | L D prior arrangement | ⚖ ♈ ⬝ | ④ ☎ for details | TR competitions | ♪ |
M 600 | S
★★*Angel, High St, Guildford. T:(0483) 64555. 27rm ⇌ ⌗*
The scene of the celebrated mixed-foursomes competition. Accurate
driving is essential. The short 10th across a lake from tee to green is
a notable hole, and the 18th provides a wonderfully challenging
par 4 finish.

WOODBRIDGE
Suffolk
Map IV J7

Woodbridge Bromeswell Heath, Woodbridge (2½m NE of Woodbridge off
A1152)
T:(03943) 2038
18(9) | 6314 yds (4486) | Par 70(31) | SSS 70(31)
Visitors welcome ☎ ⊠ | :: per round | No visitors WE, BH | B ♥ | L D prior
arrangement | ⚖ | ④ S am | TR before 0930 | ♪ | M 800 | S
★★★*Melton Grange. T:(03943) 4147. 38rm (35 ⇌ 1 ⌗)*
A beautiful course, one of the best in East Anglia. It is situated on
high ground and in the different seasons present golfers with a
great variety of colour, from gorse especially. Some say that of the
many good holes the 14th is the best.

WOKING
Surrey
Map II D4

Hoebridge Golf Centre The Club
House, Old Woking Rd, Old
Woking (1m SE of Woking on B382)
T:(04862) 22611
*This public course is set in parkland.
2x18 holes | 2298(6587) yds |
Par 72(54) | SSS 71(N/A)*
Visitors are welcome without M ..
per round | L D B ♥ | ⚖ ♈ ⬝ ⊠ |
TR WE | ④ WE only | M 400 | S
★★★★⚏*Pennyhill Park, College Ride,
Bagshot. T:(0276) 71774. 19rm ⇌
Annexe: 31rm ⇌*

WOKINGHAM
Berkshire
Map II C4

Downshire Easthampstead Park,
Wokingham (3m SW of Bracknell)
T:(0344) 424066
*Municipal parkland course with many
water hazards, easy walking. Testing
holes: 7th (par 4), 15th (par 4), 16th
(par 3). Societies welcome by
arrangement. 18 | 6382 yds | Par 73 |
SSS 70*

Open to public .. per round | B | L
(not Sun) | ♥ prior arrangement | D
prior arrangement (F S only) | ⚖ ♈
⬝ | ♪ | S
★★★★*Berystede, Bagshot Rd,
Sunninghill, Ascot. T:(0990) 23311.
88rm ⇌*

WOLDINGHAM
Surrey
Map II F5

North Downs Northdown Rd,
Woldingham, Caterham (¾m S of
Woldingham)
T:088-385 3298
*Downland course 850ft above sea level,
with several testing holes. Societies
welcome by arrangement. No facilities
for children. 18 | 5787 yds | Par 69 |
SSS 68*
Visitors welcome, with M only WE
BH | .. to :: according to season/
day/round with/without M | ♥ (not
Mon) | B | L prior arrangement (not
Mon) | D prior arrangement | ⚖ ♈ |
⊠ by prior arrangement | ♪ | TR
WE until 1230 ☎ | M 700 | S
★★*Sevenoaks Park, Seal Hollow Rd,
Sevenoaks. T:(0732) 454245. 16rm (3
⇌ 3 ⌗)*

WOLVERHAMPTON
West Midlands
Map III H4

Oxley Park Stafford Rd, Bushbury,
Wolverhampton (N of town centre
off A449)
T:(0902) 20506
*Parkland course with easy walking on
the flat. Societies welcome by
arrangement. 18 | 6128 yds | Par 71 |
SSS 69*
Visitors welcome ☎ preferred | B | L
♥ (at certain times) D | ⚖ ♈ | TR
competition days ☎ | M 530 | S
★★★*Mount Hotel, Mount Rd,
Tettenhall Wood, Wolverhampton.
T:(0902) 752055. 58rm (57 ⇌ ⌗)*

Penn Penn Common, Penn,
Wolverhampton (SW side of town
centre off A449)
T:(0902) 341142
*Heathland course just outside the town.
18 | 6449 yds | Par 70 | SSS 71*
Visitors welcome | .. per day WE |
B L D ♥ | ⚖ ♈ | ④ TR WE
competitions | ♪ | M 600 | S
★★★*Goldthorn, Penn Rd. T:(0902)
29216. 70rm (62 ⇌ 4 ⌗). Annexe:
16rm (8 ⇌ 3 ⌗)*

South Staffordshire Danescourt
Rd, Tettenhall (2m NW of
Wolverhampton off A41)
T:(0902) 751065
*A parkland course. Societies welcome by
arrangement. 18 | 6538 yds | Par 71 |
SSS 71*
Visitors welcome, with M only WE |
∴ per day WE | B L ♥ | D (prior
arrangement) | ♈ ⚖ | ♪ | ⊠
(possibly) | ⬝ (by arrangement) |
TR Tu mornings, WE | M 600 | S
★★★*Mount Hotel, Mount Rd,
Tettenhall Wood, Wolverhampton.
T:(0902) 752055. 58rm (57 ⇌ ⌗)*

WOODFORD
Cheshire
Map V D8

Avro Old Hall Ln, Woodford,
Cheshire (W side of village on
A5102)
T:061-439 2709
*An attractive, tight and challenging
9-hole course. Societies welcome by
arrangement. 9 | 5318 yds | Par 68 |
SSS 66*
B ♥ | ⚖ | ♈ (M) | TR Sun am, W
pm | M 250

★★★*Bramhall Moat House, Bramhall Ln South, Bramhall. T:061-439 8116. 40rm* ⇄ 🄵

WOODFORD GREEN
Greater London
Map **II** F3

Woodford Sunset Ave, Woodford Green (NW side of town centre off A104)
T:01-504 0553
Forest land course where grazing cattle create natural hazards. 9 | 2900 yds | Par 35 | SSS 68
Visitors welcome weekdays except Tu am | WE BH with M | ☎ advisable | B L ☙ | ⚺ | ⵑ (not Sun pm) ⌇ | ⋈ | ⟦TR⟧Tu am | ⅉ | M 400 | ⒮
★★★*Woodford Moat House, Oak Hill. T:01-505 4511. 99rm (69 ⇄ 30 🄵)*

WOODHALL SPA
Lincolnshire
Map **IV** D1

Woodhall Spa The Broadway, Woodhall Spa (NE side of village off B1191)
T:(0526) 52511
Flat heathland course with easy walking. 18 | 6866 yds | Par 73 | SSS 73
Visitors welcome ☎ essential | without M ∷ per day WE | with M ∴ per day ∴ WE | B L ☙ | D ⚺ ⵑ | ⟦TR⟧S, Sun 0800-0945 | ⅉ | M 400 | ⒮
★★★*Golf, The Broadway. T:(0526) 53535. 51rm (41 ⇄ 10 🄵)*

WOODHAM
Surrey
Map **II** D4

WOODHAM WALTER
Essex
Map **II** H2

Warren Woodham Walter, Nr Maldon (½m SW of Woodham Walter)
T:(0621) 3258
Parkland course with natural hazards and good views. Societies welcome (not W WE) by arrangement. 18 | 6211 yds | Par 70 | SSS 69
Visitors welcome without M if member of another golf club | ⊠ | without M ∷ per day | with M ∴ per day WE | B L ☙ | D prior arrangement | ⚺ ⵑ ⌇ ⋈ | ⟦TR⟧WE | ⅉ | M 650 | ⒮
★★*Blue Boar, Silver St, Maldon. T:(0621) 52681. 18rm ⇄ Annexe: 5rm ⇄*

WOODHOUSE EAVES
Leicestershire
Map **IV** A4

Charnwood Forest Breakback Ln, Loughborough (¾m NW of Woodhouse Eaves off B591)
T:(0509) 890259
Hilly heathland course with hard walking. Children are not allowed on course. 9 | 6202 yds | Par 70 | SSS 70
Visitors welcome ⊠ ☎ restricted WE BH | ☎ for groups of more than 4 players | B ☙ L D prior arrangement (not Tu) | ⚺ ⵑ | ⟦TR⟧ competition days WE (am) Tu | M 200

★★★*Kings Head, High St, Loughborough. T:(0509) 233222. 86rm (69 ⇄ 9 🄵)*

Lingdale Joe More's Ln, nr Loughborough, Leics (1½m S of Woodhouse Eaves off B5330)
T:(0509) 890035
Parkland course located in Charnwood Forest with some hard walking at some holes. The par 3 3rd and par 5 8th are testing holes. The 4th and 5th have water hazards. Societies welcome (Mon to Th) by arrangement. 9 | 3057 metres | Par 72 | SSS 72
Visitors welcome ⊠ ☎ restricted WE BH and competition days | B ☙ (not Mon) | L D prior arrangement (not Mon) | ⚺ | ⵑ (not Mon) | ⋈ | M 450 | ⒮
★★★*King's Head, High St, Loughborough. T:(0509) 233222. 86rm (69 ⇄ 9 🄵)*

WORCESTER
Hereford and Worcester
Map **III** H6

Tolladine The Fairway, Tolladine Rd, Worcester (1½m E of Worcester)
T:(0905) 21074
Parkland type course with excellent views of the surrounding hills and Worcester city. 9 | 5662 yds | Par 68 | SSS 67
Visitors welcome ☎ advisable, restricted WE BH | ∴ per day | B ☙ (not Mon) | ⚺ | ⵑ (not Mon) | ④ Mon-F 1700-1800 | ⅉ | M 300 | ⒮
★★★*Giffard, High St. T:(0905) 27155. 104rm ⇄*

Worcester Boughton Park, Worcester (SW side of city centre off A4103)
T:(0905) 422555
Fine parkland course with many trees and views of the Malvern Hills. Societies by arrangement. 18 | 5890 yds | Par 68 | SSS 68
Visitors welcome but with M only WE BH ☎ | without M ∴ per day | with M ∴ per day | B ☙ (not Mon) | L D prior arrangement (not Mon) | ⚺ ⵑ ⌇ ⋈ | ⅉ | ⟦TR⟧WE | M 1150 | ⒮
★★★*Giffard, High St. T:(0905) 27155. 104rm ⇄*

WORKINGTON
Cumbria
Map **V** A3

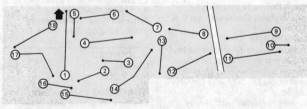

New Zealand Woodham Ln, Woodham, Weybridge (½m W of Woodham on A245)
T:(09323) 45049
Societies welcome (Tu W Th F) by arrangement. 18 | 6012 yds | Par 68 | SSS 69
Visitors welcome, restricted WE BH | ☎ | ∷ per day ∷ per round | L ☙ prior arrangement (not Mon) | ⚺ ⵑ | ⅉ | M 350 | ⒮
★★★*Ship Thistle, Monument Gn, Weybridge. T:(0932) 48364. 39rm ⇄ 🄵*
A very beautiful heathland course with many pine and other trees.

Workington Braithwaite Rd,
Workington (1¾m S of Workington
off A596)
T:(0900) 3460
*Meadowland course, undulating, with
stream. Good views of Solway Firth
and Lakeland Hills. Society meetings on
application Mon to F.* 18 | 6202 yds |
Par 71 | *SSS 70*
Visitors welcome | without M ∴ per
day WE | with M •• per day WE | B
☛ (not Mon) | L D prior
arrangement (not Mon) | ⚑ Υ ❖ |
⋈ | 𝔍 | M 650 | Ⓢ
★★★*Westland, Braithwaite Rd.*
T:(0900) 4544. 50rm (46 ⇌)

WORKSOP
Nottinghamshire
Map **V**   G8

Kilton Forest Blyth Rd, Worksop
(NE side of town centre on B6045)
T:(0909) 472488
*On the north edge of Sherwood Forest.
New course opened in 1977.* 18 |
6772 yds | *Par 73* | *SSS 73*
Visitors welcome | •• per day.
Parties welcome, restricted some
WE | B ☛ L D by arrangement | ⚑
Υ ❖ ⋈ | TR certain Sun | 𝔍 |
M 400 | Ⓢ
★*Fourways, Blyth. T:(090976) 235.*
12rm

Lindrick Lindrick Common,
Worksop (3m NW of Worksop on
A57)
T:(0909) 472120
*Heathland course with some trees and
masses of gorse.* 18 | 6615 yds | *Par 71* |
SSS 72
Visitors welcome ☎ ✉ essential |
without M ∷ per round ∷ per day
WE | with M •• per round any day |
B ☛ L D | ⚑ Υ | ❖ ⋈ prior
arrangement | ④ Daily (1 hr
between 1230-1430 depending on
time of year), WE BH | TR Daily (1
hr 1230-1430) | 𝔍 | M 472 | Ⓢ
★★★*Ye Olde Bell, Barnby Moor.*
T:(0777) 705121. 58rm (46 ⇌)

WORLINGTON
Suffolk
Map **IV**   F6

Royal Worlington & Newmarket
Worlington, Bury St Edmunds (½m
SE of Worlington)
T:(0638) 712216
*Excellent downland course. Societies
(up to 30 M) welcome by arrangement.*
9 | 3105(x2) yds | *Par 70* | *SSS 70*
Visitors welcome ☎ advisable | B ☛
| L prior arrangement | ⚑ Υ ❖ |
TR matches only | ④ not permitted

WORKSOP
Nottinghamshire
Map **V**   G8

Worksop Windmill Ln, Worksop (1¾m S of Worksop off A620)
T:(0909) 477731/477732
Societies welcome by arrangement. 18 | 6651 yds | *Par 72* | *SSS 72*
Visitors welcome ☎ | B L ☛ D prior arrangement | ⚑ Υ ❖ ⋈ | TR until 0930,
after 1600 | 𝔍 | M 500 | Ⓢ
★*Fourways, Blyth. T:(090976) 235. 12rm*
Adjacent to Clumber Park this course has a sandy subsoil and
drains well, a valuable asset for winter golfers. The par 3 3rd is a
fine test early in the round. The 11th, 12th and 13th are three testing
par 4s on the new part of the course.

| M 325 | Ⓢ
★★★*Angel, Angel Hill, Bury St
Edmunds. T:(0284) 3926. 38rm (37 ⇌
1 🏛)*

WORTHING
West Sussex
Map **II**   E7

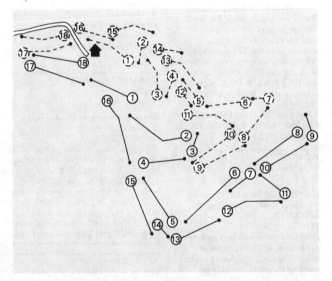

Worthing Links Rd, Worthing (N side of town centre off A27)
T:(0903) 60801
Societies welcome by arrangement. 18 (18) | 6519(5243) yds | *Par 71(66)* | *SSS 71(66)*
Visitors welcome ✉ | without M ∴ per day ∷ WE | with M •• per day WE | B
☛ | L prior arrangement (not Mon S) | D prior arrangement (not Mon Th) | ⚑
Υ ❖ | ④ | TR ☎ for details | 𝔍 | M 1000 | Ⓢ
★★*Ardington, Steyne Gdns. T:(0903) 30451. 55rm (22 ⇌ 22 🏛)*
The High Course, short and tricky and with entrancing views will
provide good entertainment. But the tiger may well prefer the
Lower Course which after various improvements and alterations, is
considered to be one of the best downland courses in the country.

WORMSLEY
Hereford and Worcester
Map **III** G6

Herefordshire Ravens Causeway, Wormsley (E side of village)
T:(0432) 71219
Undulating parkland course with expansive views. 18 | 6300 yds | Par 70 | SSS 69
Visitors welcome, restricted WE BH ☎ | without M .. per day WE | with M .. per day WE | B L ☎ D prior arrangement | ☘ ⍟ ⤬ ⋈ | TR ☎ for details | ♪ | M 475 | S
★★★*Green Dragon, Broad St, Hereford. T:(0432) 272506. 88rm* ⇄

WORSLEY
Greater Manchester
Map **V** D7

Ellesmere Old Clough Ln, Worsley (N side of village off A580)
T:061-790 2122
Parkland course with natural hazards. Testing holes: 3rd, par 5; 9th, par 3; 13th par 4. Hard walking. 18 | 5957 yds | Par 69 | SSS 69
Visitors welcome ☎ | restricted during club competitions | without M ∴ per day WE | with M .. per day WE | ⍟ B L ☎ D | ☘ ⤬ prior arrangement | TR competitions | ♪ | M 500 | S
★*Beaucliffe, 254 Eccles Old Rd, Pendleton, Salford. T:061-789 5092. 22rm (2 ⇄ 20 ⌂)*

WORTHING
West Sussex
Map **II** E7

Hill Barn Hill Barn Ln, Worthing (N side of town, at junction of A24/A27)
T:(0903) 33918
Downland course with easy walking and views to Brighton and Isle of Wight. The Par 3 11th has 11 bunkers guarding the green. 18 | 6224 yds | Par 70 | SSS 70
Visitors welcome | B L ☎ D prior arrangement | ☘ ⍟ ⤬ ⋈ | ♪ | TR WE | M 300 | S
★★★*Beach, Marine Pde, Worthing. T:(0903) 34001. 90rm (70 ⇄ 9 ⌂)*

Hill Barn Municipal Hill Barn Ln, Worthing, Sussex (N side of town, at junction of A24/A27)
T:(0903) 37301
Downland course with views to both

Isle of Wight and Brighton. 18 | 6224 yds | Par 70 | SSS 70
Visitors welcome without M .. per day ∴ WE | L D prior arrangement B ☎ | ☘ ⍟ ⤬ | TR matches & societies booking sheet S Sun | M 300 | S
★★★*Chatsworth, The Steyne. T:(0903) 36103. 97rm (76 ⇄ 3 ⌂)*

WORTLEY
South Yorkshire
Map **V** F7

Wortley Hermit Hill Ln, Wortley, nr Sheffield (½m NE of village off A629)
T:(0742) 882139
Well-wooded, parkland course, sheltered from prevailing wind, undulating. 18 | 5960 yds | Par 68 | SSS 69
Visitors welcome | ☎ for parties (W and F) | ⍟ | B L ☎ D prior arrangement (not Mon) | ☘ ⍟ ⤬ | ♪ | M 300 | S
★★★★*Hallam Tower Post House, Manchester Rd, Broomhill, Sheffield. T:(0742) 686031. 136rm* ⇄

YARMOUTH, GREAT
Norfolk
Map **IV** K4

Great Yarmouth & Caister Beach House, Caister on Sea (½m N of Great Yarmouth off A149)
T:(0493) 728699
Societies welcome by arrangement. 18 | 6235 yds | Par 70 | SSS 70
Visitors welcome, restricted Sun until 1130 ✉ | without M ∴ per day WE | with M ∴ per day | B ☎ D | L (not Mon) | ☘ ⍟ ⤬ (probable) | TR Sun (until 1130) | ♪ | M 650 | S
★★*Imperial, North Dr, Great Yarmouth. T:(0493) 851113. 41rm (30 ⇄ 11 ⌂)*
This great old club which celebrated its centenary in 1982, has played its part in the development of the game. It is a fine old-fashioned links where not many golfers have bettered the SSS in competitions. The 468-yard 8th, par 4, is a testing hole.

YELVERTON
Devon
Map **I** E6

Yelverton Golf Links Rd, Yelverton (1m S of Yelverton off A386)
T:(0822) 852824
Societies welcome by arrangement. 18 | 6288 yds | Par 70 | SSS 70
Visitors welcome except W pm and WE am ☎ ✉ | without M ∴ per day WE | with M .. weekdays ∴ WE | B ☎ | L D prior arrangement (not Tu F) | ☘ ⍟ ⤬ | ⋈ occasionally | ♪ | TR competition days | M 700 | S
★★★*Moorland Links. T:(0822) 852245. 30rm* ⇄
An excellent course on the moors with virtually no trees. It is exposed to high winds. The fairways are tight but there is plenty of room. The longest hole is the 8th, a 573-yard par 5.

WREXHAM
Clwyd
Map **III** F3

Wrexham Holt Rd, Wrexham (1¾m NE of Wrexham on A534)
T:(0978) 364268
Inland sandy course with easy walking. Testing doglegged 7th hole par 4, and short 14th hole par 3 with full carry to green. 18 | 6137 yds | Par 70 | SSS 69
Visitors welcome, restricted competitions | ⍟ | B L ☎ D (not Th) | ☘ ⍟ ⤬ | TR competition days | ♪ | M 500 | S
★★★*Wynnstay Arms, High St/Yorke St. T:(0978) 353431. 80rm* ⇄

WYBOSTON
Bedfordshire
Map **IV** D7

Wyboston Lakes Wyboston (NE side of village off A1)
T:(0480) 219200/212501
Parkland course, with narrow fairways, small greens, set around 4 lakes and a river. 18 | 5688 yds | Par 68 | SSS 68
Visitors welcome to this 'pay and play' course | ⍟ | B L ☎ D | ☘ ⍟ ⤬ | M 100 | S

YEOVIL
Somerset
Map I   H5

Yeovil Sherborne Rd, Yeovil (1¼m E of Yeovil off A30)
T:(0935) 75949
18 | 6139 yds | Par 71 | SSS 69
Visitors welcome ☎ advisable | restricted competition days | ∴ per day WE |
B ☛ (not Mon) | L D prior arrangement (not Mon) | ⚓ ☖ ↘ | TR ☎ | ♩ | M 500
| S |
★★★Manor Crest, Hendford. T:(0935) 23116. 42rm (42 ⇄)
The opener lies by the River Yeo and then the course climbs gently
for four holes to high downs with good views. The outstanding
478-yard 14th, and the 250-yard 15th present a challenge being
below the player with a deep railway cutting on the left of the green.

YORK
North Yorkshire
Map V   G5

Fulford Heslington Ln (2m SE of York)
T:(0904) 413579
Societies welcome by arrangement. 18 | 6809 yds | Par 72 | SSS 72
Visitors welcome ✉ ☎ | :: per day | B ☛ (not Mon) | L D prior arrangement
(not Mon) | ⚓ ☖ ↘ | TR 1230-1330 | ♩ | M 600 | S |
★★★★Viking, North St, York. T:(0904) 59822. 187rm ⇄
A flat, parkland/moorland course well-known for the superb
quality of its turf, particularly the greens, and now famous as the
venue for some of the best golf tournaments in the British Isles.

YORK
North Yorkshire
Map V   G5

York Lords Moor Lane, Strensall,
York (6m NE of York, E of Strensall
village)
T:(0904) 490304
18 | 6275 yds | Par 70 | SSS 70
Visitors welcome | ∴ per day :: |
WE | B L ☛ D (not F) | ⚓ ☖ | TR |
0830-0915 | ♩ | M 625 | S |
★★★Dean Court, Duncombe Pl.
T:(0904) 25082. 36rm (34 ⇄ 2 ⌂)

SCORE CARD: White Tees

1	437		10	409
2	153		11	122
3	514		12	352
4	344		13	371
5	381		14	372
6	423		15	502
7	155		16	381
8	466		17	184
9	337		18	369

A pleasant, well-designed, heathland course with easy walking.
The course is of good length but being flat the going does not tire.
There are two testing pond holes.

★★★Woodlands Manor, Green Ln,
Clapham, Bedford. T:(0234) 63281.
18rm (10 ⇄ 8 ⌂)

WYTHALL
Hereford and Worcester
Map III   J5

Fulford Heath Tanners Green Ln,
nr Birmingham (1m SE of Wythall
off A435)
T:(0564) 822806
Heathland course in two parts either
side of the River Cole. Societies

welcome by arrangement. 18 | 6256 yds
| Par 70 | SSS 70
Visitors welcome by arrangement
and with M only WE BH | ∴ per
round :: per day | ☖ B ☛ (not
Mon) | L D prior arrangement (not
Mon) | ⚓ ↘ | ✉ | TR WE | ♩ | M 700
| S |
★★★St John's Swallow, 651 Warwick
Rd, Solihull. T:021-705 6777. 213rm
(192 ⇄)

YORK
North Yorkshire
Map V   G5

Heworth Muncaster House,
Muncaster Gate, York (1½m NE of
city centre on A1036)
T:(0904) 424618
Parkland course, easy walking. 11 |
6091 yds | Par 69 | SSS 69
Visitors welcome ☎ for parties |
without M .. per day ∴ WE | with
M .. per day | B L ☛ D | ⚓ ☖ ↘ |
✉ (possible) | TR Sun (am) | M 440
| S |
★★★Dean Court, Duncombe Pl, York.
T:(0904) 25082. 36rm (34 ⇄ 2 ⌂)

YSTALYFERA
West Glamorgan
Map III   D8

Palleg Lower Cwm-twrch,
Ystalyfera, Swansea (1½m N of
Ystalyfera off A4068)
T:(0639) 842193
Heathland course liable to become heavy
going after winter rain. Societies
welcome by arrangement. 9 | 3200 yds |
Par 36 | SSS 72
Visitors welcome | B ☛ | L D WE
(prior arrangement otherwise) | ⚓
☖ ✉ | M 120
★★Glyn Clydach House, Longford Rd,
Neath Abbey. T:(0792) 813701. 8rm (1
⇄ 4 ⌂)

Golf driving ranges

ASCOT Berks
Lavender Park Golf Range,
Swinley Road. T:(0344) 884074.
Daily 1000–2200

CHATHAM Kent
Chatham Golf Centre Ltd,
Street End Road. T:(0634)
48925. Daily 1000–2200

COBHAM Surrey
Fairmile Golf Range,
Portsmouth Road. T:(093 26)
4419. Mon–F 1000–2200. WE
BH 0900–2100

COVENTRY W Midlands
Coventry Golf Drive, Sandpits
Lane, Keresley. T:(020 333)
3405. Mon–F 1000–2200, WE
1000–1800

CRAWLEY Sussex
Fairway Golf Driving Range,
Horsham Road, Pease Pottage.
T:(0293) 33000. Daily 0900–2230

CROYDON Surrey
Croydon Golf Range, 175 Long
Lane, Addiscombe. T:01-654
7859. Daily 0900–2200, WE
0900–2100

ESHER Surrey
Sandown Golf Centre,
Sandown Park, More Lane.
T:(0372) 65921. Mon–F
0800–2230, WE BH 0700–2230

FINCHLEY London
Finchley Golf Range, High
Road. T:01-445 0411. Daily
1000–2200

HALESOWEN W Midlands
Halesowen Golf Range,
Quarry Lane. T:021-550 2920.
Daily 0930–dusk

HULL Humberside
Hull Golf Centre, National
Avenue. T:(0482) 492795.
Mon–F 0900–2100, WE
0900–1930

IPSWICH Suffolk
Ipswich Golf Range Ltd, Shaw
Ground Car Park, Bucklesham
Road. T:(0473) 76821. Mon–F
0900–1930, WE 0800–1930

LEICESTER Leics
Bass Leisure Golf Range and
Putting Course, Melton Road.
T:(0533) 664400. Daily
1000–2200

LEICESTER Leics
Whetstone Golf Driving
Range, Cambridge Road,
Whetstone. T:(0533) 861424.
Daily 0800–dusk

NEWCASTLE UPON TYNE
Tyne & Wear
Gosforth Park Golf Centre,
Gosforth Road. T:(0632)
364867. Daily 0930–2230
WE 0930–1800

NORTHAMPTON Northants
Delapre Golf Complex, Nene
Valley Way. Floodlit. T:(0604)
64036. Daily 1000–2200

NORTHOLT Middlesex
Ealing Golf Driving Range,
Rowdell Road, Northolt.
T:01-845 4967. Mon–F
1000–200, WE BH 1000–2100

NOTTINGHAM Notts
Carlton Forum Golf Range,
Foxhill Road, Carlton. T:(0602)
872333 ext 12. Mon–F
1000–2200, WE 1000–1700

REDRUTH Cornwall
Radnor Golf Centre, Radnor
Road, Treleigh. T:(0209)
211059. Mon–F 1000–2100, WE
BH 1000–1800

RENFREW Strathclyde
Normandy Golf Range,
Normandy Hotel. T:041-886
7477. Mon–F 0930–2100. WE
(summer) 0930–1800, WE
(winter) 0930–1730

RICHMOND Surrey
Richmond Athletic Assn. Golf
Driving Range, Kew Foot
Road. T:01-940 5570. Mon–F
0900–2100, WE 0900–1800

ST PAUL'S CRAY Kent
Ruxley Golf Centre, Sandy
Lane. T:(0689) 71490. Daily
0900–2200

SAFFRON WALDEN Kent
Saffron Walden Golf Driving
Range, Little Walden Road.
T:(0799) 23339. Daily 1000–2200

SHEFFIELD S Yorks
Arnold Palmer Golf Range,
Bradway Road, Bradway.
T:(0742) 361195. Daily
1000–2200

STOCKPORT Gtr Manchester
Cranford Driving Range,
Harwood Road, Heaton,
Mersey. T:061-432 8242. Daily
1030–2230

TILSWORTH Beds
Broad Range Golf and Leisure
Centre, Dunstable Road.
T:(0525) 210721. Mon–F
1000–2100, WE 1000–1800

WARWICK Warwick
Warwick Golf Centre, Warwick
Racecourse. T:(0926) 494316.
Mon–F 1000–2100, WE
0900–dusk. Closed for horse
race meetings

WATFORD Herts
Watford Driving Range,
Sheepcoat Lane, Garston.
T:(0923) 675560. Daily
1000–2200

WELWYN GARDEN CITY
Herts
Welwyn and Hatfield Sports
Centre, Stanborough Road.
T:(070 73) 31056. Daily
1000–2200

WOLVERHAMPTON
W Midlands
Three Hammers Golf Centre,
Coven. T:(0902) 790220.
Mon–F 0930–2200, WE
0830–1730

YORK Yorks
Gallery Golf Ltd, White Hall,
Wiggington Road. T:(0904)
59421. Daily 1030–1700 (Tu,
Thu 2030)

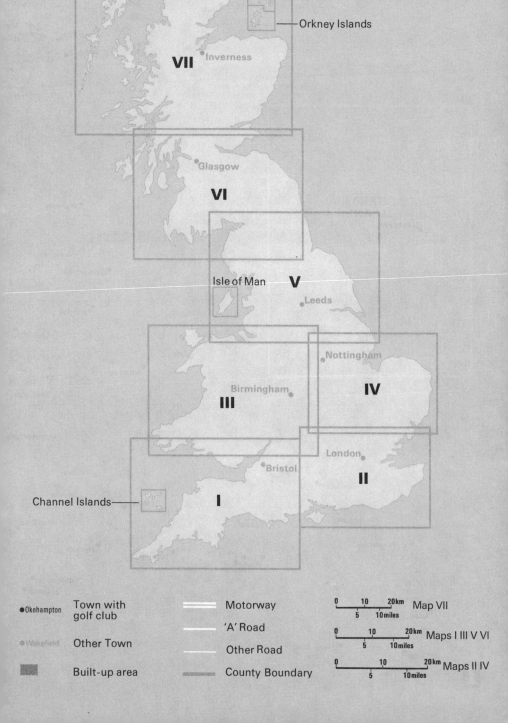

Shetland Islands

Orkney Islands

VII

Inverness

VI

Glasgow

Isle of Man

V

Leeds

Nottingham

Birmingham

III

IV

London

Channel Islands

Bristol

I

II

●Okehampton — Town with golf club

Wakefield — Other Town

Built-up area

Motorway

'A' Road

Other Road

County Boundary

| 0 | 10 | 20km | Map VII |
| 5 | 10miles | | |

| 0 | 10 | 20km | Maps I III V VI |
| 5 | 10miles | | |

| 0 | 10 | 20km | Maps II IV |
| 5 | 10miles | | |

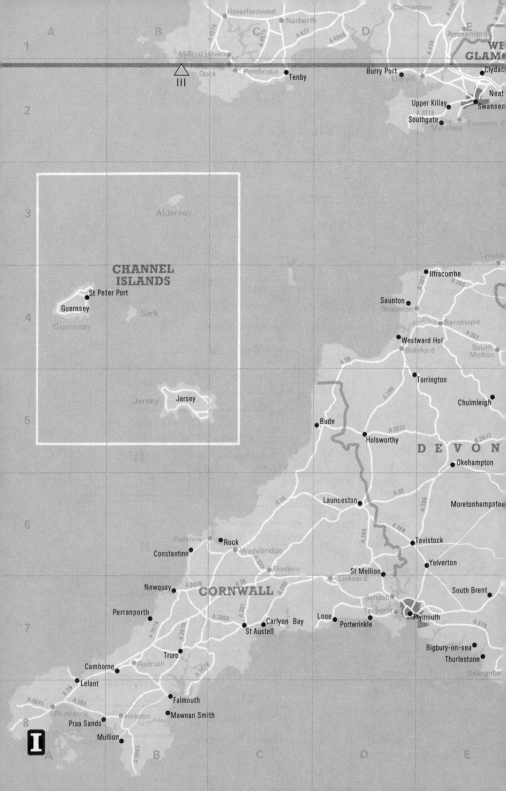

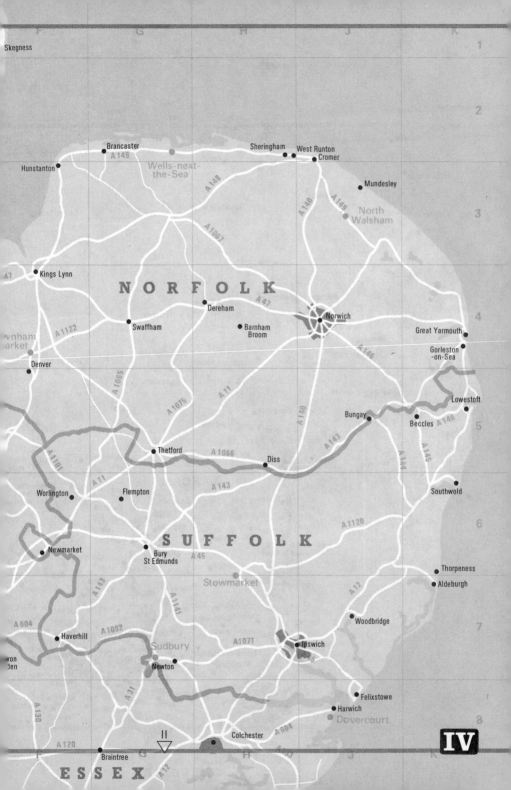

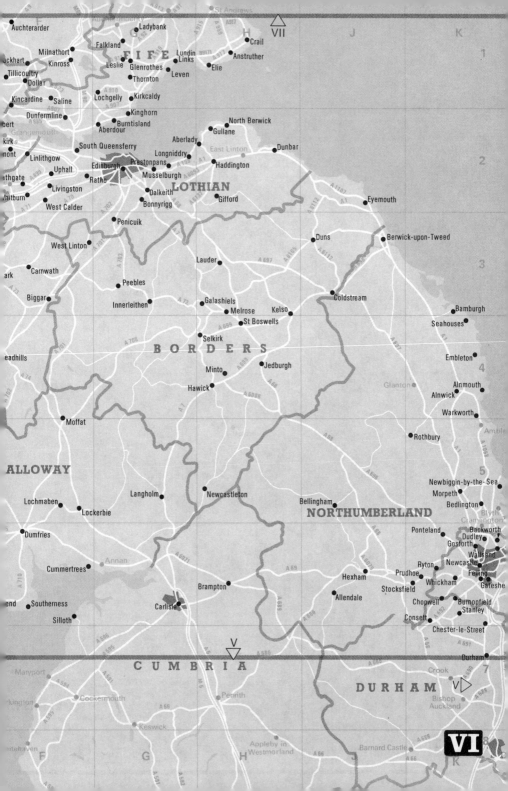

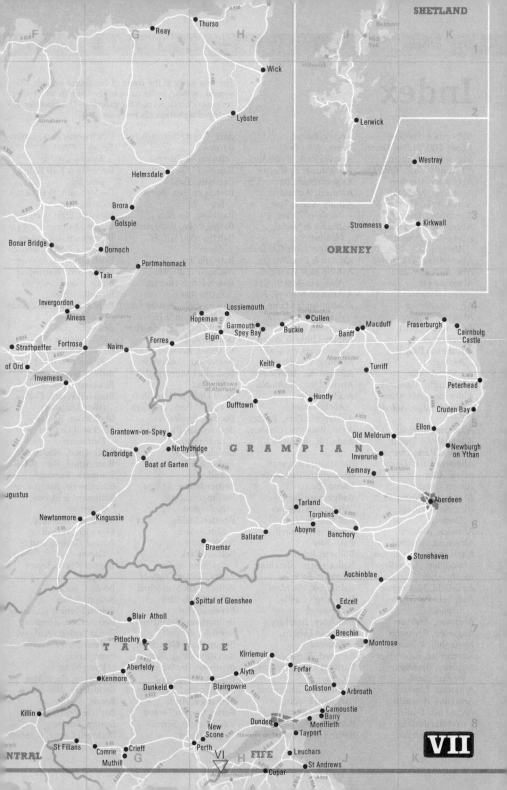

Index

The first name is the name of the course or club; the second (*in italic*) is the name of the town in which the course or club appears in the gazetteer. The gazetteer is arranged alphabetically by town.

ACKNOWLEDGEMENTS

The Automobile Association wishes to thank the following libraries for their assistance in the
compilation of this book.

BBC Hulton Picture Library 9 Alfred Perry, 14 Michael Bonallack; *Peter Dazeley* 4 Severiano Ballesteros,
6 Muirfield, 10 British Open Trophy, Muirfield; 13 Walker Cup, Old course, Sunningdale;
17 Prestwick; *Phil Sheldon* Cover Lee Trevino at Woburn

AFTER SHADOW

AFTER SHADOW

KIM PRITEKEL

SAPPHIRE BOOKS

SALINAS, CALIFORNIA

Cover Design by Christine Svendsen

Sapphire Books
Salinas, CA 93912
www.sapphirebooks.com

Printed in the United States of America
First Edition – 2013

Dedication

For Rebecca. Thank you for all you've shown me. It's been a wild ride, but well worth the price of admission.

Prologue

1980: Denver, Colorado

Clara Greenwold could hear noises coming from the basement. Her mother had gone down there awhile ago to get hamburger from the freezer for their dinner. Clara walked into the kitchen, tentatively placing a hand on the partially open basement door and looking down into the deep, inky depths of the steep, narrow stairwell.

"Mama?" she called, her four-year-old voice high-pitched and unsure. "Are you comin' back up?"

"Yeah, honey," Stephanie Greenwold called back through the gloom. And then, "Clara, come down here for a minute. I want to show you something."

The child felt panicked butterflies battering her ribcage at the request. She chewed uncertainly on a finger, then, never removing the digit, placed one foot on the naked wood of the top stair. The sole of her tennis shoe thudded dully. Her hand never left the rail alongside the stairs, her saucer-size eyes trying desperately to adjust to the darkness that was quickly engulfing her. "Mama?" she called out again, needing the reassurance that her mother was really there at the end of the dark tunnel.

"I'm here, sweetie."

As Clara moved further into the basement, she felt the thickness in her belly; she always did when heading down into the darkness. She hated it when her mother asked her to go downstairs for *anything*. She didn't understand why her sister — older by three years — was never asked to go.

Finally, the dim light from the naked bulb, which hung in the unfinished space, came into view. Clara hit the cement floor of the basement and scurried over to where her mother knelt. As long as the girl could remember, there had always been a large wooden box against the far wall. Her mother called it a hope chest. Clara wasn't sure what that was but never went near it. Whenever she did, she got a funny feeling in her tummy.

"What are you doing, Mama?" Clara asked, copying her mother's kneeling position on the floor. It occurred to the young girl just how much smaller she was than the woman who was her mama.

"I'm looking through some of Grandma and Grandpa Holridge's things, sweetie," Stephanie said absently, looking into the depths of the cedar hope chest. The chest had belonged to her mother, who'd had it since she was a small girl, growing up in rural Colorado in the 1930s and 1940s. When she'd married in her late teens, it had changed from holding the dreams of a young girl to the memories of a young bride.

"How did they die again, Mama?" Clara picked up a small Indian girl doll. The clothing and moccasins were elegant with their colorful beads and ribbon work.

"I've told you this story a hundred times, Clara." Stephanie smiled, leaning over to kiss the top of her youngest daughter's head. "They were killed in a car accident when I was just a little older than you are now."

"Oh," the girl said, as though hearing the details for the very first time. She put the doll aside and picked up a long violin bow.

"Oh! No, Clara, don't touch that." Stephanie took the bow away from the child and placed it lovingly beside the violin in the opened black, velvet-lined case. She snapped the aged case shut and moved it out of a questing four-year-old's reach. "My mother used to play for us when we were little," Stephanie remembered. She sighed, sifting through some clothing.

Clara's wide, violet eyes fell upon something else. She reached both hands in and came out with a strange object. It was cloth that had been cinched inside a round, wooden frame, the cloth stretched taut across its face. On the stretched part of the cloth, a design of flowers and a bird had been done in needlepoint, the bird not completed. All across one entire side of the cloth was something that was a brownish color, making the material stiff.

A small, curious finger reached out and touched the hardened brownish stuff, and the girl gasped. She felt the butterflies from moments before turn into screeching eagles, battering the insides of her entire body. She began to sweat, her head throbbing with the pounding of every heartbeat. She felt a sense of dread wash over her. Fear clenched her guts, followed by a deep sorrow and regret.

Stephanie gasped in shock as her daughter burst into hysterical tears, dropping the needlepoint to the floor and plowing up the stairs at a dead run.

"Clara!"

Clara ran to her bedroom, throwing herself on the pretty white and green canopy bed that she'd just started sleeping in the previous spring. She couldn't hold back the hot tears as they streamed down her face and onto the pink comforter, along with dribbles from her nose.

"Clara!" Stephanie, out of breath and filled with fear, nearly bypassed her daughter's open bedroom door in her haste to get to the girl. "What is it, honey?" She hurried over to the bed, sitting beside her sobbing daughter. "What happened?"

Clara allowed herself to be cuddled by her mother, grabbing onto the older woman as if for her very life. "She was so sad!" she cried, the emotions still coursing through her like an electric shock.

"Who?" Stephanie ran her fingers through soft, brown hair, kissing the top of Clara's head.

"Grandma."

Stephanie stopped dead, a chill trickling through her body. "Your Grandma Greenwold?" Clara shook her head no. "Honey, my mom is dead. She's not sad anymore."

Clara wiped her nose with her arm, leaving a slime trail behind. She looked up at her mother with big, sad eyes and nodded. "She told me she was."

Stephanie felt herself go cold, and she shook her head, getting to her feet. "That's not funny, Clara, and I don't want to hear you talk that way about your Grandma Holdridge again. Do you understand?"

"But Mama—"

"I'm going to get you a Kleenex for your nose."

The girl watched her mother leave her bedroom, a sinking feeling replacing the battering wings of the eagles.

Chapter One

1986

Clara had to admit: up close and personal, butterflies had the strangest faces. Quite ugly, in fact. She gasped as the winged insect took flight off the girl's finger, where it had landed a few moments before. Violet eyes watched it go until it was out of sight.

"So, what do you wanna do now?" Jason Rugby asked, sitting cross-legged on Clara's back lawn, picking at a scab on his knee. He winced as the roughened patch peeled back, revealing a less-than-healed scrape.

Clara sighed and flung herself back on the lawn, hands cupping the back of her head. She looked up at the blue, July sky. Fat, white clouds drifted by, forming and reforming into crazy patterns. Her father, Max, had told her it was called matrixing, where the mind would try to make sense and patterns out of just about anything. Including clouds. If that were true, then she was matrixing a rabbit hopping toward the Seller's place.

"Clara?"

"What? Oh. Sorry. I don't know. I could get some money from my mom and we could ride down to the store. Get a Slurpee."

Jason lay down next to his best friend, head slightly cocked to the side as he tried to make out what the cloud above him was turning into. "Lotsa clouds today."

"My mom said we're in for a summer storm."

"That sucks. I'll have to go home early, then."

They lay in silence for a long minute, listening to the summer day. School had let out a month ago, and the friends were already bored, running out of ideas to fill their days.

Jason and his father had moved into the house at the end of the cul-de-sac the previous Christmas, and Clara had been drawn to the boy. She'd promptly taken over in showing him around Mason Elementary School, and they'd become inseparable. This was their first summer together, and Clara was excited to spend it with him.

"Kids! Lunch!" Stephanie called from the open sliding glass door, stepping out onto the small patio.

"Mom?" Clara called, lifting her head just enough to see her mother. "Can me and Jason ride down to the store after we eat?"

Stephanie studied her daughter for a moment, hand on hip. "Are you going to be careful this time?" she asked, raising a pale eyebrow at the girl. "I don't need another call from Mr. Struthers telling me how he nearly ended up in the ditch to avoid hitting you because you weren't paying attention."

"Mom! That was like, months ago!" Clara sat up, indignant at the memory.

"It doesn't matter if it was three years ago, Clara. I don't want you getting hurt."

Jason glanced back and forth between mother and daughter. He'd heard the entire story at school the following day, hearing how upset the old man had gotten, actually getting out of his car to yell at Clara.

"Yes, Mom. I promise," Clara said, rolling her

eyes.

"You don't make faces at me, and I'll think about it," Stephanie warned, heading back inside, effectively ending negotiations.

"Your mom's strict," Jason whispered, his friend nodding. "My dad lets me do whatever I want."

"That's 'cause he's never home," Clara grumbled, getting to her feet. "Come on before she changes her mind."

☙ ☙ ☙ ☙

Clara sat on the seat of her blue and white Huffy dirt bike, a foot resting on one of the pedals. She rested the large blue, white, and red Slurpee cup on her raised knee. The neighborhood convenience store was bustling as the noon hour passed. The local workers had come out to gas up or grab a quick lunch at the Wendy's on the opposite end of the convenience store parking lot.

"This is so good," Jason murmured around the straw, the other end creating a tunnel of juice in his cherry Slurpee. He sucked greedily then pulled quickly away from the drink. "Ah! Brain freeze!"

Clara giggled at her friend. He did that every time and never seemed to learn. She watched as he set the cup down on the lid of a nearby trash can then grabbed his head. *As if that'll do you any good, you goof,* she thought, rolling her eyes.

She glanced across the parking lot, sucking slowly at her drink when she noticed someone standing near the corner of the fast-food place near the busy street beyond. He wore blue jeans, a white T-shirt and high-topped tennis shoes. He was looking right at her.

Clara felt her stomach grow tight, a wave of nausea brushing through her. She couldn't take her eyes off the man, who looked to be in his twenties. He smiled at her then walked away, heading toward the street. She glanced further up the street, noting that a red truck was headed right for him. The man didn't slow or even seem to notice.

Clara's heart began to pound, a sense of urgency gripping her. She took a step forward, about to cry out a warning, when the man faded into the warm afternoon. She started, blinking several times — still no one. The red truck blew by harmlessly.

"Hey, you okay?" Jason asked, looking from his friend to the restaurant and back again. "You look like you just saw a ghost."

"I did," Clara muttered then turned back to her cold treat.

Soon the pair was on their way back toward their neighborhood, racing each other with the sudden burst of energy from the sugar-filled Slurpee. Clara jumped the curb, her Huffy taking to the air in an impressive arc before she landed on the street, her tires and pedaling feet never missing a beat. Jason was right behind her, trying to accomplish the same trick, but instead nearly falling head first into Sylvia Tanner's prized rose bushes. He cursed softly then hurried after his friend.

❧ ❧ ❧ ❧

The dinner table was quiet, only the scraping of forks across plates, which grated on Clara's nerves. Her parents sat on either side of her, her older sister, Kerri across from her. She glanced at the pre-teen, only to be nailed to the spot with a glare. To say Clara and Kerri were close would be a complete lie.

Clara was a smaller girl with the build of a beanpole, while Kerri was bigger — in every way — and used that size to her advantage. At least once a week Clara found herself stuffed in the trash can outside or some possession of hers ripped out of her hands by the bully she lived with.

Clara's gaze drifted away from the brown eyes trying to intimidate her and turned to her father, instead. Max was Clara's hero. He worked long, hard hours for a trash pick-up company. He left before dawn and sometimes got home after dark, usually carrying some sort of "treasure" he'd found during his daily rounds. Stephanie never saw his finds the same way, and more often than not the item found its way back into the trash.

Max Greenwold was a handsome man with Clara's same brown hair — unlike Kerri and Stephanie's dark blonde. He had sparkling blue eyes and a dimpled smile. He looked older than his thirty years, but Clara figured that was from his long days. It was important to him that Stephanie stay home with their daughters, so he put in upward of fifty to sixty hours a week. Clara adored her father.

"How was your day, sweet pea?" he asked, sipping from his milk.

"Good. I managed to jump higher on my bike than Jason. He wasn't thrilled." Clara played with her mashed potatoes with her fork.

"Don't play with your food, Clara. Eat it," Stephanie said absently, scooping up the last of her peas with a spoon. It was a nightly game to try and get the youngest Greenwold to eat.

"I bet Jason didn't like that. Maybe he'll get you tomorrow."

"Dad! Whose side are you on?"

Max grinned. "Yours, sweet pea."

Clara glanced around the table at her family, chewing on her lower lip. "Did you know there was a guy who died on Rigby Road?"

Even the silence seemed to screech to a halt. Three pairs of eyes were on her — one blue, two brown.

"What?" Max asked, setting his fork down.

"You're such a freak," Kerri muttered, turning back to her dinner.

"I said there is a guy who died on Rigby Road." Clara looked at both her parents, her courage beginning to wane, especially as she took in the look of disapproval from her mother. "By Wendy's. I think he was hit by a car or something..." her voice trailed off.

"Kerri, how did your first day go, babysitting Ross and Jenny's girls?" Stephanie asked, not even bothering to hide her discomfort with Clara's words.

Clara felt her heart drop as did her head. She looked at her plate, no longer hungry. Anger mixed with fear topped by hurt began to fill her eyes.

"You can tell me about it later, sweet pea," Max said softly, patting the girl's leg under the table.

Clara looked up at him briefly before nodding and looking back at her plate.

ဆလါဆလါ

The room was dark, only the light shining in from the streetlight at the corner — one house down — broke through the gloom. Clara lay on her bed, one hand tucked behind her head, the other resting casually across her stomach. She connected the glow-in-the-dark stars that her mother had allowed her to put on the ceiling a couple years before. They'd made constellations as well as silly designs. She smiled as she picked out her name, literally written in the stars.

Summer was almost over; it had gone so quickly. It seemed just yesterday she and Jason were wasting a day, trying to figure out what to do with their time. Jason and his father had headed out to North Dakota to see Jason's grandparents. They had already been gone for a week, though it felt more like a year.

The day before Stephanie had taken Clara and Kerri to shop for school clothes. Clara was proud to say that she'd grown two inches over the summer. That was happy news. She wondered if she was finally taller than her friend, Michelle. Michelle and her family had left for the entire summer, so they wouldn't see each other until the first day of school, in a week and a half.

Clara's thoughts stopped as she felt a strange wave hit her in the stomach. She took a deep breath, then looked away from the ceiling. Her eyes were drawn to the corner between her window and the closed closet door. She swallowed, as the shadows were thick as ever.

"Is somebody there?" she whispered, barely audible. There was no noise, no movement. Nothing. Just the nausea in her stomach, and she knew what that meant. The room was quiet, but she was still drawn to that corner.

Clara took another deep breath, then pushed the sheet off her body, sliding her legs off the side of the bed, feet hitting the carpet beneath. She stared, her breathing beginning to get heavier. She could feel her palms sweating, and rubbed them on the bedding. She fought the urge to call for her father, knowing that she'd have to deal with this herself.

"Is there—" she gasped, muffling a soft cry when she saw movement. A shadow — quick and dark — seemed to scamper from the corner to the closet and disappear. "I can do this," she whispered to herself, closing her eyes for a moment and taking several breaths.

Clara pushed off the bed, her hands trembling as she took a slow step toward the closet. Her heart was pounding so loudly she was worried she'd wake her parents and sister. Another step. Her scalp began to itch as it, too, began to sweat. She was truly frightened.

She reached out a hand, her fingers grasping the handle of her closet door before, with one last punch of courage, she pulled it open. Clothing on hangers swayed gently from the sudden exposure, but nothing else seemed amiss. Clara looked inside, pushing shirts and pants aside, only to see the white wall of the back of the closet.

Clara let out a breath, a hand gripping her chest. "This sucks," she muttered, closing the closet door and hurrying back to her bed, where she pulled the sheet up over her head.

꧁꧂

Weeks later, Clara was in the kitchen, preparing lunch for herself on a Sunday afternoon. Her parents were out, leaving Kerri to watch her younger sister. The older girl was in her room, reading one of the books in her endless Stephen King collection.

Clara licked the knife clean of grape jelly, then

tossed it into the dishwasher. She grabbed her plate and cold can of Coke, and headed toward the round kitchen table that was tucked into a nook in the kitchen near the sliding glass doors.

Plate and can set down, she pulled out a chair ready to sit when something caught her attention. She had no idea what it was, but she found herself standing in front of the sliding glass door, looking into the backyard. Their house backed up to an open field, a distant stream and trees beyond the open space. Her gaze fell upon their six-foot privacy fence.

Barely rising above it was a face. Clara, unable to take her eyes off it, was riveted to the spot. She felt a strange mixture of fear and power surge through her. She couldn't get a set fix on the face's features, almost as though they were blurred somehow.

The face was attached to a figure, which began to climb the backside of the fence. Clara's gaze moved to the support boards to the fence, which were on her side, meaning the side the figure climbed was smooth, nothing to hold on to. She felt her heartbeat quicken, the pulse in her throat throbbing.

Clara wanted nothing more than to slam the door shut and close the vertical blinds. She wanted to sit down and enjoy her peanut butter and jelly sandwich and Coke.

"Go away," she whispered. She sensed the face was smiling at her. Grinning, evil. "Please. Just go away." Clara suddenly felt something charge through her, making her stand taller, and she found herself taking a step toward the sliding glass door. She met the blurred gaze of the figure. "You will not touch me," she said, her voice strong, filled with a conviction she didn't understand. She felt as though someone was talking through her. "Leave this place. Now!"

"Who are you talking to?"

Clara whipped around to see Kerri standing just inside the kitchen, looking at her with a mixture of irritation and unease.

"No one." Clara felt ashamed as she stepped away from the door, slamming it shut. A quick glance into the backyard proved the figure was gone. "No one," she said again, sitting down to eat her lunch.

Chapter Two

1989

God, this is so disgusting," Clara muttered, finishing her business, then washing her hands with soap and water. She grabbed the little toilet paper-wrapped bundle, and headed out to the garage, where the big trash can was kept. She and Kerri were not allowed to leave used sanitary products in the house trash, which Clara thought was crap. Their mother had had a partial hysterectomy after Clara was born, so she hadn't had a period in thirteen years. She had forgotten what it was like to scurry outside in arctic temperatures just to toss a used tampon.

Her bare feet pounded down the three short garage stairs, she dumped her package, then scurried back into the warm house. It was late October, and temperatures had begun to sink into the low depths of cold. The first snow was predicted for the following night.

"Hey, freak, help me clear the table," Kerri said as Clara passed by the dining room door.

"Kerri, don't call your sister names!" their dad called from the family room, where he was taking in the news.

Clara stuck her tongue out at her sister, glad her father had stepped in for her. The older girl glared and continued to do her job.

The girls had what was officially called the Work

Chart, but the Greenwold sisters secretly called it the Slave Chart. They had assigned duties that had to be completed before bed — before homework, even — every night. This week Kerri had dishes duty while Clara had to vacuum the house and clean the bathroom the girls shared.

"Sorry," Clara said sweetly. "Not my job. So says the Work Chart." She chuckled as she heard Kerri outright growl at her. The teen continued into the family room, plopping down next to Max. "Hey. What's up?"

"Hey, sweet pea. Just more bad news." Max Greenwold sighed, watching Tom Brokaw explain about a failing economy and vicious attacks in foreign lands.

"Sounds interesting, I guess. Why aren't you watching TGIF?"

"Uhh..." Max looked at his daughter in confusion.

"Thank God It's Friday. All the good shows are on. *Family Matters. Mr. Belvedere...* Ring a bell?"

"Not exactly, Clara. This is the first night I've been home before nine this month. I'm watching the news."

"Okay." Clara sighed, knowing from his tone that she wasn't going to win this battle with her father. The family room television being the only one in the house, she was either stuck watching Tom Brokaw or she would have to entertain herself in another way. She was about to choose "another way" when a story came on the news about a young mother who had been missing for nearly a month; speculation was that she'd run away with an old boyfriend.

Clara watched the images and listened to the

details of the case, riveted. Deep in her mind, she heard a voice. It was almost like her own thought but not, somehow. *She's dead. The little baby, too.*

Max glanced over at his youngest, noting the look of pure concentration on her face. "What's wrong, sweet pea?"

"She's dead. The woman. She didn't run off with the guy. Her baby, too," Clara said. It was only after she uttered the words that she realized she'd even spoken.

"What? Who? That lady?" Max pointed to the screen, which was changing from a picture of the young woman back to Tom Brokaw. Clara nodded. "How do you know that?"

Clara realized what she'd said and realized it was wrong. "Nothing! Never mind, Dad, I'm sorry. Forget I said anything."

"Wait, no." Max turned in his seat so he was facing the girl, his gaze focused only on her. "How do you know that, Clara?"

Clara felt awkward under his close scrutiny, and though she loved and trusted her father above anyone else — except maybe Jason — she knew she couldn't fully trust him with this. "Dad, please just forget I said anything." She looked down at her hands, which fidgeted in her lap.

Instead of answering, Max got up from the couch and left the room, leaving his daughter to breathe a sigh of relief. It was short-lived, however, as he returned within moments. He held a deck of playing cards.

"Uh, rummy?" Clara asked, feeling nerves begin to nip at her.

"Honey, I want to try something. Okay?"

Clara nodded, uneasy. She eyed the cards, which he'd removed from the box and had begun to shuffle in large, hard-worked hands.

"Okay. Here we go." Max had had his suspicions about Clara for years and wanted to prove something to himself — and to her — that night. He shuffled the deck to his liking, then set them down on his thigh, facedown. Plucking the top card in his fingertips, he looked at it, sure to keep it so Clara couldn't see the face. "What's this card, Clara?" he asked, his voice quiet. He wasn't worried about Stephanie walking in on them, as she wasn't home tonight, having gone to help a neighbor bake for the woman's daughter's upcoming wedding, so they were safe; he knew how she felt about all this. He just hoped if Kerri came into the room, she'd keep her mouth shut.

Clara took a deep breath and looked at the card, noting the picture on the back: a half-naked woman grinning rakishly. She grinned, blushing slightly as she looked away. She pushed the image out of her mind and tried to concentrate on what her father was asking her to do. Closing her eyes, she pushed open her mind, trying to stare into the deep black void she saw there. A void that she knew would open up and show her things. Images, voices, information. All she had to do was listen.

"It's the ace of spades," she said quietly, still seeing the bold card before her mind's eye.

Max knew what the card was, but he couldn't help but look at it again. He was amazed when he spotted the large, proud black ace. "Okay. This one?" He didn't react, not wanting to frighten the girl. Holding up another card, he studied the thirteen year old.

Clara saw the card form in her mind. "Two of hearts," she said, not even bothering to open her eyes.

"And this?" Max was trying to keep the excitement

out of his voice as he held up a third card.

"Nine of diamonds."

Max's grin was a mile wide. He decided to try something. Grabbing the box the cards had come in, he tipped it until a card slid into his palm. He held it up. "This?"

Clara's brow creased as she tried to get a feel for the new card. Nothing would come to her mind. Eyes still closed, she reached out and took it, holding it sandwiched between her palms. She'd found that it was easier to pick up on an object's energy if she touched it. She concentrated, waiting for the images to come. Her eyes opened, a smirk on her lips. "Very funny, Dad." She handed the card back to him, the face of it facing him. "It's one of the jokers."

"Yes!" Max took the card, the colorful image of a man juggling while riding a unicycle grinning at him. He grabbed the girl in his excitement, hugging her tight.

Clara took in the affection and approval like a starving man dying for food.

"What's all the excitement about?" Kerri asked, stepping into the room, drying her hands on a dishtowel.

"Kerri! Come here, watch this."

≈≈≈≈

Stephanie Greenwold dried the last pan. Personally, she thought her friend was nuts for volunteering to bake all the goods for her daughter's wedding, but to each their own. Stephanie swore that in another life she had been a baker or chef. She loved to cook and was pretty damn good at it.

"Is that the last of it?" Paula Abbott asked, looking around her kitchen, hands on hips.

"Yep. We've got it all." Stephanie sighed, tired from the long day. She was just glad her girls were older now, and at sixteen, Kerri could easily watch Clara. "I better get home, though."

"Okay. Thank you so much for your help." Paula gave her friend a quick hug then walked her to the door. "You guys are still coming Saturday, right?"

"After all this baking," Stephanie said, indicating the piled containers of baked goods, "you bet your ass we'll be there!"

Paula was still chuckling as she closed and locked the door behind the other, younger woman.

Stephanie walked across the street, slightly irritated to see every light on in her house. Extra electricity cost money they didn't have. She wished Max would back her up on some of these things. He was just as wasteful as the girls, though. Undoubtedly, he's where they got it.

Letting herself into the house, Stephanie turned off lights as she went, noting the kitchen wasn't finished yet, and it was nearly nine thirty! They'd eaten at seven. She heard laughter and clapping from the family room and, curious, went to check it out.

"That's amazing!" Kerri laughed, shaking her head in stunned shock. Her little sister had just found out what Ryan's, Kerri's boyfriend, favorite color was, what he ate for breakfast, and where his parents bought his car, just from holding the letterman jacket he'd given to Kerri. "How do you do that?"

"I don't know." Clara grinned, handing the heavy jacket back to her sister. "Things just come to me."

"Try these." Max had bundled the playing cards

back into their box, and handed it to Clara just as Stephanie made her presence known.

Clara took the cards in her hand, but before she could fully concentrate on what she was seeing, she looked up to meet the hardened gaze of her mother. She felt panicky butterflies begin to fly around and her heart sink. She knew it was time to head back into the closet.

"Hey," Max said, trying to sound as nonchalant as he could. Kerri gathered up her boyfriend's letterman jacket, sheepishly heading upstairs with it to put it away. "How was the baking?"

"It was good." Stephanie took in the room. "What's going on here? Why didn't Kerri finish with the dishes?"

"Aw, honey, we were just having some fun. No biggie."

Stephanie felt a pang of panic and fear niggle at her gut, but swallowed it down. There was no reason to make a fuss over things. "Kerri," she said, as the older girl came back down the stairs, "please finish the dishes. Clara, finish up your homework. I know you have that big report due Wednesday. I doubt you want homework over the weekend."

"Okay." Silently, Clara headed up the stairs, deck of cards still in her hand. She wanted to look at the pictures.

Max couldn't meet his wife's eyes as he turned his attention to the muted television. He grabbed the remote, turning the sound back on, and continued watching his program.

Stephanie sat beside him in silence until Kerri finished up with the dishes, then reported she was heading over to her friend Kathy's house for the night.

Stephanie glanced over at her husband and could tell he was angry at her. She chewed on her bottom lip before taking a deep breath and speaking her mind.

"What were you doing, Max? Why are you encouraging this?"

"I'm not encouraging anything, Steph." He met her gaze. "The girl has a gift. Why do you refuse to see that?"

"Because it's not a healthy one. It'll cause her pain and fear in the end, Max, and you know that."

"No, I don't know that. And you don't, either. She's not you, Stephanie. She's not you, living with an aunt and uncle who didn't want you in the first place and called everything you did evil. She has a mother and a father who love her, who support her — at least *should* support her," he said, eyeing his wife, "and who has a right to be who she is. It's not fair what you're doing, and it's not right."

Stephanie lowered her voice, not wanting to chance Clara hearing. "Max, I know what she's capable of. What she sees, and what she can do. It can be very dark, and I will not encourage that in my house. In our house, with our family. We've got Kerri to think about, too."

"Steph," Max said, taking on his wife's lowered tone, "she did nothing tonight but a few cool parlor tricks. It's not like the kid was about to start vomiting pea soup with her head spinning."

"It's all connected, Max. You don't know the kinds of dark forces that can come through with her fun 'parlor tricks'. It all comes from the same place. The same source."

"Well," Max said, pushing to his feet and clicking off the TV with the remote. "I'm not going to damn her. But, I am going to bed. Good night, Stephanie."

❧ ❧ ❧ ❧

Clara sat on her bed, the deck of cards tossed to the comforter beside her, forgotten. Though she was slightly nervous about what her mom would say, she couldn't help but think back to the surprising turn of the evening and smile. For the first time she was able to use her abilities in front of her family, without them calling her names or rolling their eyes or flat-out changing the subject altogether.

It had felt wonderful! She felt exhilarated, validated, and completely happy. Even Kerri — who thought she was a waste of human space — had been impressed. What Clara hadn't told her sister and father was that she had seen much, *much* more when holding Ryan's jacket. Clara's grin widened: great blackmail material.

Clara reached out blindly until she felt the cool cardboard box the deck of cards was wrapped in, and grabbed it. She held it up, looking at the woman on the front of the box. She couldn't help but wonder where her father had gotten the cards, and why she'd never seen them before. The half-naked woman looked like a pinup girl from the 1940s — blonde hair, voluptuous curves.

"Dad, you devil," she grinned, enjoying the view. She held the cards between her palms, concentrating on what she felt and what images were brought to mind. She relaxed, allowing her mind to once more reach out, feeling the energy that was left upon the cards by their owner.

Clara sensed her father's energy, could almost

smell his cologne. A quick flicker of an image raced across her mind — his smile. She saw the dimples winking before they vanished. Clara's breathing hitched a bit as she felt a warm blush flow through her, and for a moment she felt embarrassed, as though she had inadvertently stumbled across a memory between her parents that she really did *not* want to see. But then it occurred to her that it wasn't her mother's energy she felt at all.

Dark hair. Long, dark hair.

Stephanie Greenwold had medium-length blonde hair.

Clara's eyes flew open, the cards tumbling from her fingers. She sat up, staring at them with wide eyes. She nearly jumped out of her skin when she heard a knock at her door. Taking a deep breath, she called out an invite to enter. The door opened, her father's head peeking around it.

"Hey, sweet pea. You still up?"

"Uh, yeah, Dad. It's barely ten."

"True." Max opened the door wide enough to step through and moved to the side of Clara's bed. She was unable to look him in the eye as the truth of what she'd seen from his cards hit her. *Dad's been with another woman.* "I just wanted to stop by and say goodnight. And to thank you."

She looked at him, surprised. "Thank me? For what?"

"For sharing that with me tonight. Definitely more entertaining than Tom Brokaw."

Clara couldn't help but smile at that. "Yeah, but not as entertaining as TGIF."

"I don't know about that." Max sat on the edge of her bed, his youngest scooting over to make room. "But

I do appreciate it. I know your mom can be difficult about this stuff, and I know she doesn't understand it." He met her gaze, his blue eyes filled with love and caring. "I don't understand it, either, really, but I do understand that it's a part of you. You don't have to hide it from me. Okay?"

She nodded, nearly moved to tears. "Thank you." She sat up fully and gave him a big hug, staying in his arms and resting her cheek on his shoulder. "Dad?"

"Hmm?" Max asked, relishing the feel of the daughter that he knew in his heart would always be his favorite, no matter how wrong it was to choose between the two.

"Are you and Mom okay? Like, doing okay?"

Max felt his blood run cold. He pulled back, concern in his eyes and studied Clara for a moment. "Yeah, we're fine. Why?"

Clara smiled, not wanting him to feel bad, or to worry. "No reason. Just wondering, is all." She reached behind herself and grabbed the cards, holding them out to him. "Here are your cards."

"Thanks." He tucked them into the pocket of his shirt then looked deeply into the girl's eyes. "You always had the most beautiful eyes, Clara. Your grandma used to say you had eyes the color of Elizabeth Taylor's. She was a huge fan."

"Of my eyes or of Liz Taylor?"

Max chuckled. "Both. I think you got such a different shade because it matches you. What you see."

"I see a lot, Dad," Clara said softly, looking him in the eye.

Max had to look away. He wasn't sure if guilt was eating at him or the intensity of Clara's stare was making him uncomfortable. "I know you do." He gave her a quick kiss on the top of her head then got to his feet. "I'm beat. I'll see you in the morning."

"I love you, Dad."

"I love you, too, sweet pea." With a final smile and wave, Max was gone, leaving his daughter to wonder at life.

Chapter Three

1990

"Heads!"

Clara heard the warning too late as the soccer ball sailed through the air into the stands, smacking her dead center in the back of the head. She fell face-first, barely having the clarity to land on her hands and knees on the hard cement of the high school stadium.

"Ah, shit, Clara! You okay?" Jason hurried over to his friend, squatting beside her.

"Jason, I think the sky is falling," she muttered, sitting back on her knees and bringing a hand to the throbbing goose egg that was already forming on the back of her head. She looked at her fingers, relieved to see there was no blood.

"Oh my god! Are you okay?"

Clara looked up to see who was speaking to her, but instead what she saw was the face of an angel. She stood next to the speaker, her blonde hair pulled back into a tight ponytail. Green eyes surveyed the scene, then landed on Clara.

"Are you okay?" the girl asked again.

Clara realized there was a tall African American girl standing next to the blonde, who was looking at Clara with deep brown, concerned eyes.

"I think so," Clara said, falling back onto her butt. The world seemed to get a little fuzzy around the

edges as she teetered on the edge of consciousness.
"Clara!"

⚘⚘⚘⚘

Stephanie and Kerri Greenwold ran down the
hospital corridor, the younger still dressed in her soccer
practice outfit. Since she'd borrowed her mother's car
that day, she had left the high school fields as soon as
Clara had been loaded into the ambulance and had
run home to gather their mother and take them to St.
Mary's.

The woman at the ER counter was less than
helpful, but then Kerri spotted her teammates, Tanisha
and Abby, as well as Clara's friend Jason.

"Over here, Mom." Kerri led her shaken mother
over to the friends who sat quietly together, though
Jason looked about as uncomfortable as a cat in a room
full of rocking chairs.

Stephanie was relieved to see her younger
daughter's friend, knowing he'd know what happened.
"Jason!" She hurried over to the boy, sitting next to
him while Kerri joined her friends. "What happened?"

"A missile — otherwise known as a well-kicked
soccer ball — hit her in the head. She passed out on
us," he explained calmly.

Stephanie breathed a sigh of relief, flopping back
in the chair. "Is she all right?"

Jason shrugged. "Guess so."

"I am so sorry," Tanisha said to Kerri, her eyes
filling with tears. "I didn't mean to hit her."

"I know. It's okay." Kerri squeezed the frightened
girl's hand in understanding and support.

༄༅༄༅

Clara looked around, not sure where she was. She found herself in a strange place, not really inside, but not exactly outside, either. The air around her was light with a golden, rose-hued tint to it. Looking around, she could see nothing around her. No objects, no furniture, no scenery. Nothing.

Voices. She tried to figure out which direction they were coming from. A woman. No, two women, but she sensed a man, too.

"I think it's time. I'm going to take her to the next level," one woman said, her voice soft and pleasing to the ear.

"I think that's wise. A good plan," said the other, her voice a bit deeper, words somewhat clipped.

Clara walked toward where she thought the voices came from, realizing there was a wall there. She almost had the feeling she wasn't supposed to be hearing those words, or wasn't supposed to be where she was, though she had no idea where she was. Footfalls. Clara froze, listening as someone approached her.

Crap! She tried to find a place to hide, not wanting to be found lurking and listening. She stopped again, becoming aware of her body.

Clara felt torn, lying on the hospital gurney in the ER, well aware of her body lying there, her head pounding where it *had* been hit by the soccer ball; even so, she was very well aware of the other place, with its golden rose hue. She could still hear the footfalls, yet she could hear the nurse moving around in her little curtained off cubicle.

What the heck?

Clara became aware that the person — one of the

women, she suspected — was about to round the corner and show herself from behind the wall. She glanced down to the floor, noting the beginning of a foot.

"Welcome back, Clara. You gave us quite a scare."

Clara blinked several times, disoriented, her stomach feeling slightly nauseous. She glanced to her right and saw the nurse standing next to her bed, smiling down at her, even as she scribbled something onto a chart.

"Do you know where you're at?"

"Not really," Clara muttered, bringing a hand up to rub at her eyes. "The ER."

"Good. How many fingers am I holding up?" the nurse asked, holding up three fingers.

"Three."

"Excellent." The older woman smiled then pushed the curtain aside to leave. "The doctor will be with you in a sec." Then she was gone.

Clara lifted her head to look around her, but regretted it immediately. She groaned, lying it back down on the thin, paper-covered pillow. "Ow."

As she lay there, she thought back to what she'd just experienced. Somehow she felt like she either should know where she'd been or *did* know where she was. She could see it all very clearly: the space she'd been in, the voices she'd heard, the feel of the environment, and she also knew that she hadn't been dreaming. Her thoughts were interrupted when she heard her mother's voice getting closer.

The curtain spread open as Stephanie made her way into the cubicle, followed by a worried-looking Kerri.

"They said you were awake," Stephanie said,

leaning down and kissing her daughter's forehead then taking her hand. Kerri took up residence on the opposite side of the gurney. "How are you, sweetie?"

"I'll live. I think. Head hurts pretty bad, though."

"Yeah, you got hit pretty hard," Kerri said. "Tanisha is here. She feels terrible."

"Eh. I got a hard head." Clara tried to dismiss the injury, even though she felt like she wanted to puke.

"The nurse said she thinks you've got a concussion." Stephanie peered into her daughter's violet eyes, judging one against the other. "Your pupils are dilated."

"She probably does, then," Kerri assessed, also looking into her sister's eyes.

Their speculations were cut short when the curtain was once again moved aside as the doctor entered. He smiled and greeted everyone before turning his attention to the patient lying in the middle of the bed.

Clara endured his attention, her mother doing her best to hold her hand the entire time. She found out she would live, though Stephanie was instructed to keep Clara in bed for the rest of the day, and to keep an eye on her, waking her every hour to ensure no damage was done from the concussion.

Armed with a prescription for a good pain medication, Clara was released from the care of St. Mary's ER.

The entire group sat at Dairy Queen, Tanisha insisting on buying Clara ice cream as a peace offering. Clara sat across from Kerri and Tanisha's friend and teammate, Abby Jensen. The blonde had barely said two words during their entire visit, instead concentrating on picking at her Oreo Blizzard. Once in a while she'd glance up, her green gaze catching Clara's shy smile. The girl obviously had something on her mind.

Before Clara could censor her thoughts, her mouth opened and she spoke, the words soft. "I know you're worried, but your grandma will be fine."

Abby's head flew up, her eyes wide. "What?"

"She'll pull through the surgery just fine."

"How did you know about that?" she demanded, her eyes narrowing.

Silence filled the table for a moment as everyone stared at Clara. She felt herself shrink, wanting to fit inside her Peanut Buster Parfait cup.

"Ignore her, Abby. She's a freak," Kerri said.

Clara glared at her sister, hurt and embarrassed. How could Kerri sit there so smug, calling her names when she'd enjoyed Clara's gifts more than once to get answers or clarification on things? It stung.

"We all ready to go, here?" Stephanie asked brightly.

Clara dumped her half-eaten treat, following the group out to the parking lot, Jason walking beside her.

"It's okay," he whispered. "Kerri's the freak, not you."

Clara nodded, less than convinced. She had shared some of her abilities with her best friend over the past year, as they'd developed more and more. He knew how her family was about them — well, her mother, anyway — and he never judged her or called her down.

"Thanks, Jason." He rammed his shoulder playfully into her, eliciting a small smile.

࿇࿇࿇࿇࿇

Very few knew that Clara was quickly coming to a realization; she liked girls. She'd kept it to herself, not even telling Jason about it. Girls occupied her thoughts day and night. She would listen to Jason extolling the virtues of "this hot chick" or "that hot chick" and wonder why she couldn't extol away with him.

What was wrong with her? Why so much... *different*. Clara felt like she carried a big burden in her young life, then in the same instant, thought she was being quite melodramatic. The hardest part of the whole thing was she had no one to talk to. About either thing!

Sometimes — at the risk of her own life — she'd sneak into Kerri's room and snag one of her romance novels. While under the cover of darkness, Clara would read the stories by moonlight, skipping over the boring parts so she could have the book done in a night and returned to Kerri's room. Her older sister thus far was none the wiser. The thing was, when she'd look at the covers of the cheesy Harlequin novels, she would take in the pictures of the half-naked women with huge, feasting eyes. She'd take in their heaving breasts, bodices of their dress usually torn open, or they were so "distraught" that their garments seemed to strain at the seams. Never once would she spare a glance for the handsome pirate or rogue who was essentially molesting them.

Instead, what she'd do was finish the book, return it to Kerri's room as she slept, then head back to her own bed, lie there, and stare up at her ceiling. She'd replay the steamiest scenes in her mind's eye, replacing the gallant hero with herself. Then, somehow it made sense that she'd lust after the buxom beauty. If she could transform herself into the pirate or the scoundrel trying to take over the beauty's family land, or even if she saw herself as the sweet, caring sheriff in a town full of bad guys, who finally wins the hand of the new veterinarian in town, her own feelings could make more sense to her. That is, until the light of day made her hide in the corners of the locker room at school, her back intentionally to her classmates so she wouldn't feel awkward or embarrassed.

Clara felt very alone in a world of fourteen-year-old girls who seemed to know who they were, for the most part. Seemed to know where they fit in their families, in school, and even in their after-school activities. It seemed the only two people in Clara's world who halfway understood her — or tried — were Jason and her father.

Max. Clara sighed, sitting alone in a park on a swing. She absently twisted the swing to and fro, resting her head against her hand that gripped the thick chain. She had pushed out of her mind what she'd discovered the year before, while holding his deck of cards. She'd never said anything, had never touched the cards again, even though she knew where he kept them — out in his workshop in the garage.

Why would he do something so awful to his family? To his wife? She thought of her mother, was able to see her smile in her mind's eye. She knew that Stephanie Greenwold wasn't always the easiest person to deal with: she could be narrow-minded, stubborn, and certainly a forceful clean freak, but when it boiled down to it, Stephanie loved her family. She loved her daughters, and she loved her husband. She was big-hearted. So why was Clara's father cheating with another woman?

He had started coming home from work later and later. He'd always been a hard worker, working long days. But, last year, or even months before, he'd never taken clothes with him to change into. He said it was because he was tired of smelling like a trash heap, and didn't want the car to smell, either.

Clara knew better. She thought her mother did too. She would see the look on Stephanie's face when she glanced at the clock as the time would get later and later. Her lips would purse, and the little crinkle of anxiety would form between her brows.

"He'll be home soon," she'd say, almost as if to convince herself. "I just know it."

It was getting late, so Clara jumped off the swing and picked up her ten-speed from where she'd laid it on the ground. She looked around the park, marveling at the beautiful colors in the sky as the sun began to set. She knew without glancing at her watch that it was nearly seven thirty. Would her father beat her home?

⁂

Clara used the sprayer to clean out the sink then wiped down the counters and kitchen table. It was her week on dish duty. She noticed the garbage sitting in the corner of the room and groaned inwardly. It was her father's job to take it out, but he wasn't home yet, and she knew her mother would make her do it anyway.

The neighborhood was well dark by the time she heaved the Hefty sack over her shoulder and headed outside. The garbage cans were out by the curb, as garbage day was the following morning. She held her breath as she lifted the can lid, then tossed the bag inside, slamming the plastic lid back down into place.

She started back up the driveway to the house when she stopped, perking her ears to listen. There it was again... Clara whirled around, looking to see if Jason was hiding somewhere, whispering her name. His house was darkened, as it should have been, considering he and his dad were in North Dakota with Jason's grandparents.

Clara...

"What? Who's there?" She felt a chill run down the length of her spine, settling in the pit of her stomach, which began to flow with slight nausea.

Clara...

Beginning to feel really frightened, Clara turned back toward the house, intending to run full speed ahead. She stopped dead in her tracks. In the shadows, near the gate that led to the backyard, a woman stood, looking at her. Clara felt her heart clench and her legs grow weak.

I won't hurt you, Clara.

The woman was beautiful, with dark hair — nearly black — that just barely reached her shoulders. It was all one length, the bangs pulled back away from her face. Her eyes were dark, the skin seemingly smooth and somewhat pale. She held no malice in her gaze, but Clara still felt an acute need to run.

Clara...

Not willing to stay for a second longer, Clara barely touched the ground as she ran for the front door, her heart pounding painfully in her chest, every hair on her body standing on end. It was only when she had the front door safely closed and locked behind her that she was able to take a full breath.

"You okay?" Kerri asked, passing on her way

toward the staircase. Clara couldn't speak so she merely nodded. Kerri shrugged, figuring it was just another moment of weirdness from her sister, and continued on her way.

ৰ্থ,ৰ্থ,৵,৵

It was after eleven, and Clara was still waiting on the stairs. Stephanie and Kerri had gone to bed more than an hour before, but Clara knew she wouldn't be able to sleep. Not until he was home. She sat with her knees spread, her hands dangling between them, her father's deck of cards in her hands. She shuffled and reshuffled, trying to keep her hands busy and her mind blank.

Finally, the familiar sound of her father's car pulling into the drive. The engine cut out, a door opened then slammed shut, and finally, his key in the front door lock. The door swung open, and a slightly disheveled Max stepped through. He looked very surprised to see his youngest waiting for him.

"Hey, sweet pea," he smiled, heading toward her. "What are you still doing up? Don't you have a test tomorrow or something?"

"That's kind of hard when we're on summer break, Dad," she said dryly, not willing to latch on to his lame attempt at a joke. She stopped shuffling the cards and fanned them out, offering one to him. "Pick one."

Max looked slightly annoyed, as he was tired, but humored Clara and studied the cards before picking one, just to the left of the center of the semicircle of cards. He knew the drill, so he pressed the face of the card against his leg so Clara couldn't sneak a peek.

"My guess is you drew the Queen of Hearts," Clara drawled, unable to find any satisfaction in her father's shock as he looked at his card. "Or should I say, Queen of *broken* Hearts?" She was tired of seeing the pain in her mother's eyes, and the humiliation and embarrassment Clara herself felt every time she saw her parents together. Why pretend?

"What?" Max asked, handing the card back.

"You wanna know what card I think you should have drawn instead?" Clara asked, ignoring her father's confusion.

"What's that?" he asked, unsure how to take his daughter's low, quiet tone. It seemed very unlike her.

"Not a heart, not a diamond, not a spade, or a club. You should have drawn from the suit they forgot to add to the deck. You should have drawn the Jack of Assholes card."

Max was taken aback, mouth falling open. "Who do you think you are, Clara? Talking to me that way. What did I do?"

Clara once again ignored his words, and handed him the deck of cards for a second time. "Do the right thing, Dad," she said softly, standing from the step. "Win back my respect." She turned to head upstairs. "And Mom's." With that, she headed down the upstairs hall to her bedroom, closing the door softly behind her.

Chapter Four

*C*areful what you wish for. Those words kept going round and round in Clara's head. *Careful what you wish for, because you might just get it.* She sat on the porch swing, watching as box after box was carried out of the house and set in the bed of her father's truck.

It had been two weeks since Clara had confronted her father on the stairs. They had avoided each other for a few days after that, but then by the following weekend, she had come home to find her parents sitting at the dining room table, a wad of used tissues lying on the table between them.

As Clara watched her mother carrying one last box out to the waiting truck, she knew that the woman wanted nothing more than to break down and beg Max to stay. Ultimately, as much as Stephanie might be hurting right now, Clara knew she'd been hurting a hell of a lot more knowing that her husband was unhappy and that unhappiness had driven him to stray.

Kerri hurried out of the house, down to her father, nearly knocking him over with her hug, clinging to him. Clara watched, almost feeling detached, as the scene unfolded. She could tell Kerri was crying, and their father was doing his best to try to soothe her. He gently pushed Kerri into the care of her mother's awaiting arms, Max's gaze finding Clara's.

Clara felt herself grow cold as he made his way

to where she sat, legs curled up against her chest. She wanted to pretend she didn't see him, but knew that would only buy her a couple moments before she had to face him.

"Hey," he said, his voice quiet. Clara looked up at him, but said nothing. He sat on the swing beside her, the chair wobbling crazily for a moment at his added weight. "I know you're mad at me, and I understand that." He paused, studying his beloved Clara's face, trying to get her to meet his gaze. When she wouldn't, he continued. "I'm really sorry, sweet pea. I know it doesn't make a whole lot of sense to you right now, but I promise — someday it will."

Clara said nothing, biting her tongue so hard it nearly burst. She was trying to keep her emotions in, not wanting to cry in front of him, even though what she wanted most was for her daddy to hold her and tell her everything would be okay.

"Aren't you going to say goodbye?" Max asked, his voice catching slightly.

Clara looked at him, her face reddening as she tried to hold in her heartbreak. "Goodbye."

Max bit his lower lip, able to feel the hurt washing off his daughter in waves. He knew better than to push her so simply nodded and pushed up from the swing. "Take care, Clara. I love you."

Clara forced her lips to stay closed, as she felt he didn't deserve to know she loved him too. She watched as he walked away from her, heading toward his truck. The image began to wash away as her tears finally fell.

෴෴෴

Dinner was a somber affair as Clara picked at

her food. Stephanie had been softly crying off and on all day, and Kerri tried to ignore it all, her nose stuck in one of her books.

Clara chased her carrots around her plate before dunking them in her mashed potatoes. Meatloaf, carrots, and mashed potatoes — with tons of butter — was her favorite dish of her mother's, and the one she'd requested for that night, yet she couldn't make herself eat it. She gave a surreptitious glance at her father's empty chair then quickly looked away again. Was all of this her fault? Maybe if she hadn't said anything to him; if she hadn't given him an ultimatum. Would he still be there? Late, but at least he'd be there. Right?

"Can I be excused?" she asked softly, glancing at her mother. Stephanie, never taking her eyes off her own barely touched plate, simply nodded. Clara carried her plate to the kitchen, dumped the remains into the trash, and placed the plate in the sink.

Clara was glad to get away from the doom and gloom that had permeated her childhood home. Her father had been gone for an entire day, and his absence was felt acutely. Flopping down on her bed, Clara stared at the ceiling, covered in shadows as the sun fell to end another day. Clara's only solace was that Jason and his dad would be heading home the following morning. She needed him.

❧ ❧ ❧ ❧

The road was long, the pavement beginning to come to life as the day begun. Mile after mile, the dotted white lines blurred into a fuzzy line between the lanes. Content with a just eaten fast-food breakfast in his belly, he looked out the passenger window, watching the scenery as it flew by.

"Can I change the radio station, Dad?" he asked, tired of listening to his father's favored country music.

"Sure, Jay. Go for it. Just none of that rap crap. 'Cause remember—"

"I know, I know. You can't have C-R-A-P without R-A-P."

"You got it."

He fiddled with the radio knob, getting a whole lot of static. "I think we're between areas where I can get a signal."

"All right. Put in a tape."

He unbuckled his seatbelt, twisting his body so he could reach between the bucket seats of the Buick, and grabbed the cassette tape holder — a black, plastic case that held twenty tapes — and dragged it onto his lap as he got resettled in the front seat.

"Buckle up, kid."

"Yeah, hang on. I'm trying to find that Ozzy Osborne tape."

A loud POP rocked the early morning, the car suddenly jerking violently to the left as the shredded tire tossed pieces of rubber onto the highway. He tried to hold onto the wheel, but the car was out of his control and sliding along sideways.

Weightlessness.

The crash of glass.

Sudden flight...

≈≈≈≈

Clara bolted awake, her eyes wide, sweat soaking her T-shirt to her chest. She was gasping for breath as she looked around her bedroom. She tried to calm herself when memory came back to her, and she saw the dream all over again.

"Jason!" she gasped, throwing the sheet off her and hitting the floor at nearly a dead run. She pounded down the stairs, tripping over a throw rug placed at the bottom. She hissed at the rug burn on her knees, but was immediately up and running again.

Stephanie nearly jumped out of her skin, dumping coffee from the cup that had been raised halfway to her mouth in the process. "Clara! Slow down! Where's the fire?"

"Where's the phone?" Clara hurried over to where the cordless phone was usually kept. Not there. She turned, frantically looking around the kitchen. "Where's the phone?"

"What's wrong, Clara? You're scaring me." Stephanie put her coffee cup down and was about to get out of her seat in concern.

"Jason. I gotta call Jason," Clara said absently, hurrying out of the room to check the family room.

"Wait! Why?" Stephanie followed Clara's panicked trail. "Honey, do you have any idea what time of the morning it is?"

Clara glanced at the grandfather clock standing in the corner of the dining room. "Yeah, it's four-ten," she said resuming her search.

"Exactly. You're not calling Jason in the middle of the night."

"But, I have to!" the girl cried, turning on her mother. "I have to warn him."

"About what?"

"I just...damn it! Where's the phone?!"

"I think Kerri had it last." Stephanie put a hand on Clara's arm, stopping her from jetting back up the stairs. "Clara, stop. Stop right now." She waited until she had the girl's attention. "Now, like a human being, tell me what's going on."

Clara took several deep breaths then looked at her mother, trying to keep her irritation in check. "I had a dream. Their tire blew, and Jason wasn't wearing his seatbelt because he hates country music. I have to warn him!"

Stephanie blinked several times, trying to figure out what her daughter was talking about. "Honey, it was just a dream. A *bad* dream, but a dream. Okay?"

"No, Mom. I need to call him. I have to warn them." Clara tried to get past her again, but Stephanie tightened her hold.

"Clara, stop! You had a nightmare, and you need to calm down. You're going to scare the hell out of Jason and his dad, calling them this early to tell him about bad country music."

"And what if the dream is true? What if it was real?"

"It wasn't, honey." Stephanie brushed a strand of brown hair out of Clara's eyes. "It's been a bad couple of days, sweetie, and you're tired. I don't think any of us have had a good night's sleep in a week. Obviously, I'm up at four in the morning."

Clara sighed, calmed. Her mother was probably right, although she still had a sick feeling in her stomach. "Can I call him when I get up?"

"Yeah, sweetie. You can call him then." Stephanie placed a kiss on her daughter's forehead. "Go to bed, Clara. Get some rest."

❧ ❧ ❧ ❧

The phone rang for the fourth time, Clara's impatient foot tapping along with the irritating shrillness. "Come on," she muttered. "Answer, already." She glanced at the torn piece of paper Jason had given her before he left, his grandparents' number scrawled on it. She checked the number for the third time, as she hadn't gotten an answer yet. She'd been trying for the past hour. "Damn."

Clara clicked the power button on the cordless and tossed the handset to the couch. Kerri, who was sprawled out on the loveseat reading, glanced over at her.

"No answer?"

"No."

"Maybe they took Jason and his dad to breakfast before they left or something," Kerri offered during a rare time of actually trying to be helpful.

Clara glanced at her, a tiny amount of relief flooding into her, as what her sister said actually made sense. "Maybe." She glanced at the clock to see that it was eleven o'clock "You'd think they'd be back by now, though. The grandparents. Jason and his dad have a long drive ahead of them. Wouldn't you think they'd be gone by now?"

Kerri shrugged. "Who knows, Clara. Maybe the grandparents had stuff to do after they left. Did you leave a message?"

"No. I think they're the only people left on the planet who don't have an answering machine."

"Oh. That sucks." With those last brilliant words of observation, Kerri turned back to her reading.

Clara rolled her eyes and left the room. She couldn't shake the unease of her dream, but knew there was nothing she could do about it, so she went in search of her mother. It wasn't long before she found her, sitting at the kitchen table, the newspaper spread out before her. She held a red ink pen in one hand, the other wrapped around the handle of a mug of coffee.

"What are you doing?" Clara asked, plopping down in a chair across from her mother.

"Looking for a job," Stephanie said absently, bringing the pen to a midway point on the page and drawing a quick red circle around a squared off ad.

"Why?" Clara felt a sudden surge of panic rush through her. In all her fourteen years, her mother had never worked. She'd always been there when they'd left for school in the morning, and then when they'd returned at night. At one time the girl had thought it might be kind of cool to have that time alone after school, like a lot of her friends did, but now, faced with it, she wasn't so sure.

Stephanie looked at her daughter. She looked about as awful as she felt: hair hanging around her face in unwashed strands. Her eyes were puffy and red, the skin of her face pale and tight from too many nights of crying. As was typical for her when stressed, she'd lost her appetite, so her T-shirt hung on her shoulder blades, almost as though it had been draped over a chair.

"Because we need money, Clara," she said, a tad more harshly than she'd intended. Immediately she felt bad. She dropped the pen and reached across the table to cover her youngest daughter's hand with her own. "I'm sorry. I didn't mean to snap. Your dad has always been the breadwinner, honey, but now he's gone."

"You know he's not going to let us go under," Clara pointed out, trying to sound every bit the wise adult that she was not.

Stephanie shrugged. "So he says, but these situations can get nasty. I don't want you girls to think badly of your dad, but you just never know. I'd rather play it safe than sorry. Besides," she said with a heavy, coffee-scented sigh, "I think it's best for me to get out of this house." She ran a hand through her hair, grimacing at the oily feel.

"Probably best," Clara agreed. An idea hit her. She pushed back from the table, the chair screeching against the tile. Grabbing her mother's coffee cup, she took it to the sink, dumping the cold contents and rinsing it out. She then gathered up the newspaper, ignoring her mother's protests. "Come on, Mom." She grabbed Stephanie's hand, tugging her out of the chair. "Go get showered and dressed. We're going out."

Stephanie got to her feet, but pulled her hand away. "Sweetie, that's sweet, but we can't. I need to conserve—"

"Conserve money, yes I know." Clara grinned devilishly. "Good thing I still have the birthday money from Grandma, huh?"

The Russett Mall was busy, as was to be expected during summer break. Typically not one for shopping, Clara knew her mother was. Her mother rarely was able to buy herself anything nice: they usually didn't have the money, and there were far too few occasions for Stephanie to dress up. Usually when Max came home from work, she was in a pair of shorts or jogging pants that she'd been in all day. Maintaining a house didn't require dress-up clothes.

"Oh! Look at that one!" Clara exclaimed, pointing at a sword that was in a window display in a shop called *Sharp, Pointy Things*. Stephanie stepped up beside her daughter, the straw of her Orange Julius pressed between her lips. "Wow."

"Honey, what in the world would you do with a sword?"

Clara shrugged. "I don't know, but wow..." Her gaze drank in the sight of the polished steel, her mouth nearly leaking drool at the thought of holding something like that in her hands. "Some day, though. I'll have me one."

"Oh, I'm sure you will. In your own place," Stephanie emphasized, earning a rueful grin from her daughter. They walked on down the main hall of the mall complex. "You'll have those things hanging all over your walls, and then some idiot will decide to break into your house and run screaming into the night."

Clara laughed. "Yeah, either that or I'll be totally screwed!"

They checked out a few more display windows before deciding to take a rest and sit on a bench near a potted plant. Clara played with her drink for a moment, her mother people watching.

"Mom?"

"Hmm?"

"What do you think happened?"

Stephanie glanced at her daughter, brows creased in question. "With what?"

"You and Dad." Clara looked into her mother's eyes for a moment, chewing on her bottom lip as she tried to decide how much she should divulge. "I know about the other woman."

Stephanie's eyes opened wide in surprise, then filled with pain. "How? I know you guys are close, but... Did he tell you?"

Clara shook her head.

"Then, how do you know about that?"

"I'm going to tell you, but you can't get all weird on me. Okay?" When she had her mother's nod of consent, Clara continued. "That night you came home and found us all in the family room, Kerri and Dad were testing my abilities."

"Right. I remember."

"Well, he gave me a deck of cards that night. That's how we started it. He was holding up a card to see if I'd know what it was and all that. Well, after you broke it up, I went upstairs to my room, still holding the cards," she explained. "Mom, I get... Well, when I hold things, sometimes I can pick up memories from them. Like, read their energy."

When Clara didn't continue, Stephanie pressed. "And you felt something?" At Clara's nod, Stephanie turned away. "I see. Clara, that was almost a year ago. Why didn't you *say* anything?"

Clara couldn't stand to see the hurt in her mother's eyes. She wanted to plead for her mother to understand. "What was I supposed to say? 'Hey, Mom, guess what Dad's doing'. I couldn't say anything. For one, I wasn't sure, and I didn't want to believe it. For two..." her voice trailed off.

Stephanie held back her tears, the wounds still so fresh. She nodded in understanding, giving Clara a one-armed hug and placing a kiss on the side of her head. "I'm sorry. You're right."

Clara felt her heart needing to purge itself, the emotions beginning to really rise to the surface. "This is my fault, Mom."

"What? How do you mean?"

"About two weeks ago, I confronted him." Clara wiped angrily at the tears that had begun to fall. She felt stupid, having already seen some kids from her school wandering through the shops.

"About his affair?"

Clara nodded. "I called him an asshole."

Stephanie tried to hide her slight amusement at her brave little girl, instead giving her a full hug. "Oh, honey," she cooed. "It's not your fault. Your dad has his own demons to battle, and the majority of them deal with me. Not you girls." She rocked the crying girl, running a hand through her thick, brown hair. "Don't take this burden on, Clara. Please don't. Your father loves you more than anything."

"Maybe if I hadn't said anything. Or maybe—"

"Stop it!" Stephanie pulled away, cupping her daughter's face between her palms and looking into her eyes. "Stop it, Clara. There is *nothing* you could have done. Nothing you did wrong. Okay? Do you understand me?"

Clara nodded, sniffling like a child. Stephanie reached into her purse to pull out an ever-present packet of tissues and handed one to the girl.

"Come on. Let's get you to the bathroom so you can wash your face, and let's go see that movie. It starts in twenty minutes."

Clara nodded and opted to go to the restroom alone. She found one near the food court and pushed the heavy door open, stepping inside the large, somewhat odorous space.

She gave the room a casual glance, noting the five stalls — all of which were empty — to the right and a counter that ran along the left-hand wall, sinks spaced intermittently, separated by wall-mounted soap dispensers. The far wall held two hand dryers.

She headed further into the room, walking

toward the farthest stall.

"That one's broken."

Clara jumped as the voice practically whispered in her ear, the source behind her. She whirled around to see a grinning girl behind her. She looked a bit older than Clara, her long hair dyed black. Dark makeup made her dark eyes seem to disappear. Her lips were a slash of red lipstick, her face pale. She wore the uniform of one of the fast-food restaurants in the food court, her nametag clipped just above her left breast: *Erica*.

"Oh. Thanks." Clara moved away from the girl, ducking into one of the other four stalls. She wasn't entirely sure the girl was real until she heard her step into her own stall, pants unbutton and unzip, and then the familiar *tinkle* of bathroom business.

❧❧❧

No matter how much Clara had wanted to see the movie she and her mother sat watching, she couldn't stay focused. Jason kept creeping into her mind, as well as images from her dream the night before. She felt uneasy and slightly agitated. She glanced at her watch for the fourth time, groaning when she realized that only six and a half minutes had gone by since she'd checked it last.

"See? I told you he'd come back to her," Stephanie whispered, completely unaware of her daughter's anxiety.

Clara nodded absently, not a clue what her mother was talking about.

An hour and a half later, Clara and Stephanie were making their way up the driveway, their few purchases in hand, when Kerri burst out of the front door. Her eyes were red from crying. Clara felt her heart begin to pound as her older sister made her way over to her.

"What happened?" Clara whispered, barely able to speak over the lump that had begun to form in her throat.

Chapter Five

The bird perched on the tree for only a moment before flapping colorful wings, and once more taking flight. Clara watched until it disappeared from sight, catching a leaf falling from the tree branch as her gaze slid back down to the backyard. She followed the leaf's progress until it, too, was out of sight.

She brought up a hand, brushing her bangs out of her eyes. The day beyond the window was bright, the sun high in the sky. She rested her head against the cool glass as she studied the clouds. She followed the lines of the witch's profile she saw, her nose pointy, complete with a wart at the tip.

A knock sounded at her closed bedroom door, which Clara gave no notice to.

"Clara? Come on. You have to eat something," Kerri's muffled voice said. "Please?"

Clara said nothing, instead continuing to study the clouds. Eventually she heard her sister give a frustrated sigh, then walk away.

"I don't want food, Kerri," Clara whispered.

She turned away from the window and lay on her bed, legs stretched out and her hands tucked behind her head. She glanced at her desk and the corkboard mounted above it. Pinned dead center was a picture of her and Jason, big goofy smiles on their unsuspecting faces, an arm draped over the other's shoulder. She looked at his young, handsome face, meeting his twinkling eyes. The picture had been snapped a few months back while Max had been fooling around with a Polaroid camera.

Clara climbed off her bed, walked to the desk and plucked the picture from its moorings. She realized Jason hadn't even known about what had happened between her parents. She hadn't had a chance to tell him.

"Now you'll never know," she said, tracing a finger across the image that was her best friend. "Either that or you're sitting up there watching. A good show, I'm sure."

☙ ☙ ☙ ☙

Max's brow creased as he tried to figure out why the burner wasn't heating up. "What the hell," he murmured, passing a hand back and forth over it as he adjusted the turn dial. There was a brief ticking noise, then the unmistakable stench of natural gas. "Shit!" He turned the dial to the "off" position. He stepped back, studying the stove, then decided to use the microwave instead.

The apartment he'd been able to rent was small — two tiny bedrooms (in case the girls wanted to ever spend the night), a tiny bathroom, decent-sized living room, and a hallway kitchen. The furnishings were sparse, as he hadn't wanted to take anything from the house. He'd managed to buy an old couch from a buddy at work, as well as a horribly scarred kitchen table with three matching chairs. The fourth, apparently, had been thrown out years ago.

Boxes were still stacked everywhere, Max not

having the energy or enthusiasm to unpack. Instead, he used a can opener to wrench open a can of Spaghetti-O's. He dumped the noodles and sauce into a bowl and shoved it into the microwave he'd picked up at Walmart for $29.95.

As his lunch heated up, Max walked into the living room, picking up the remote to turn on the TV. He hadn't just sat and watched TV on a Saturday in years. Typically, they headed out as a family and did something. Or just him and Clara.

Max sighed as he leaned against the counter, his thoughts going to his youngest. He thought back to the day he'd left and the way his heart had broken when he'd had to leave her. He hadn't asked either of the girls if they wanted to go with him, not wanting to do that to Stephanie. But, deep in his heart, he had hoped that Clara would speak up and ask to go. If he were honest with himself, he'd looked for a two-bedroom with the expectation that she'd be with him.

The microwave beeped, alerting him that his lunch was ready. He pushed off the counter, and was about to grab the handle of the appliance when the phone rang. Only Stephanie and the girls had his number at the moment, so he ran toward the phone in the living room, hurdling a stack of boxes in his haste.

"Hello?" he said, nearly out of breath.

"Hey, Dad."

"Hi, sweetie." Max's brow drew in concern. "What's wrong, Kerri?"

❧ ❧ ❧ ❧ ❧

The sun was setting. Clara rolled onto her side, her pillow tucked up against her chest as she got settled.

She'd been asleep for the majority of the day, not bothering to come out of her bedroom except to use the restroom. Even then, it was only when she saw the coast was clear. She didn't want to see anyone. Didn't want to talk to anyone. She didn't...*want.*

Her eyes blinked open when she heard some noise from downstairs, though couldn't tell what it was. Soon after, footfalls fell upon the hallway carpet, leading up to her closed bedroom door. There were muffled voices outside, then a soft, but firm knock.

"Hey, you in there, sweet pea?"

Her eyes shot open, glancing at the barrier that kept her father from view. She longed to run to him, but allowed her stubbornness to speak for her. "Go away!" There was more muffled talking, then the door clicked open. *Damn. Why didn't I lock it?* "I *said*, go away!" she called out again, her father's head peeking around the opened door. He smiled at her, though it was a sad smile. Clara's heart leapt at the sight of him.

"Hey, you." He closed the door gently behind him, trying not to step on anything in the darkened room, knowing his daughter's propensity for leaving things wherever they fell.

"I don't wanna see you."

"Yeah, well, that's too bad. I wanna see *you*." Max sat on the edge of Clara's bed, a smile on his lips. Despite her words, he recognized Clara's tone. That was her I'm-angry-at-you-but-don't-want-you-to-leave tone. So be it.

Clara felt her stomach clench with building emotion, and she tried to fight it down. She honestly didn't think she was capable of any more tears, but apparently she was wrong. Her eyes stung, her head hurt from the abundance of emotion shed over the past two days. She just couldn't seem to stop, except for when she was asleep.

Max placed a hand on her shoulder, gently rolling her to her back. He studied her pale, tear-streaked face, and it made his heart break. "How are you?" he asked softly.

"Had better days."

"I bet. Kerri says you haven't been out of this room in two days. Haven't eaten. Nothing." Max waited for a response and continued when there was none. "You can't do this to yourself, Clara. Jason wouldn't want this for you."

At the mention of her best friend's name, Clara burst into near hysterical tears. Max was taken aback, but recovered quickly, gathering her up and pulling until she curled up in his lap, just like when she was a little girl.

"It's okay, sweet pea," he whispered, rocking her as she cried. "I'm here now. I'm here."

For the first time in two days, Clara felt as though she was really, *finally* able to let it go. She'd done her fair share of crying, but never felt very satisfied from it. But now, in the arms of her father, she really let go. She was comforted by the soft words he murmured, most of which she couldn't understand nor did it matter what they were. He was there, and that's what mattered.

Max was relieved when Clara's tears began to slow then subside altogether. Kerri and Stephanie had filled him in on what had happened to Jason, as well as how hard Clara had taken it. Kerri had mentioned that Clara had had a bad dream about it, and had been worried. Max said nothing, but his jaw had clenched, and the way his wife refused to meet his eyes, he knew they would need to have a talk later. But for now, Clara needed him. He smoothed back the girl's hair from her face, wiping her tears away.

Clara pulled away slightly, just enough to grab a tissue from the box on her bed, and blew her nose and wiped her face and neck. "Did you hear what happened?" she asked at length.

Max nodded. "Kerri and your mom told me."

She looked up at him with big, tearful eyes. "Was he wearing his seatbelt?" she asked. "Kerri didn't tell me any details."

Max sighed then shook his head. "No, he wasn't. He was thrown out when the car rolled."

Clara squeezed her eyes shut trying to block out images that she realized now had been a vision, not a nightmare. "And his dad?"

"He's in serious condition in the hospital. He's alive."

Clara was silent for such a long time Max thought she'd drifted off to sleep. "Dad?" she finally said.

"Yeah, honey?" he murmured, leaning down to kiss the top of her head.

"I saw it happen. I knew it was going to."

Max had dreaded this, but knew it was coming. He tried to swallow down his anger for Clara's sake. "Tell me about it."

Clara took a long moment before she recounted the dream to him. "I knew it, Dad," she whispered, staring off into the memory of her vision. "I knew it. I knew that if I could just warn him. Warn his dad to check their tires..."

Max felt cold inside, as he knew that likely the boy's life could have been saved with one phone call. "Why didn't you?" he asked. "Call, I mean."

"I tried. Mom wouldn't let me." Clara felt Max

tense beneath her, and she held up a hand to forestall his anger. "Wait, before you get upset. It was four in the morning. She thought it could wait until morning."

Max said nothing, instead pulling his daughter back to him, placing a kiss on the top of her head. He didn't want her to see the anger building in him. His eyes were sharp, his jaw clenching and unclenching.

"Will you go to the funeral with me?"

"Of course, sweet pea. Of course."

❧❧❧❧❧

"What the hell is wrong with you?" Max fired, getting dangerously close to invading Stephanie's personal space. He was having a hell of a time keeping his rage in check.

"How was I supposed to know it was a vision she had, Max?" she raged back. "It was four in the morning! Was I supposed to just let her call and wake up Jason's dad because of a bad dream? Be realistic."

Max lowered his voice as he took a step closer to Stephanie. "You know damn well that Clara isn't a regular kid, Stephanie. You also know damn well that when she is that passionate about something, there's usually a reason. She's a sensible kid. She doesn't just go off on a lark on a regular basis." He turned away from her, running a hand through his hair. "You should have listened to her."

Stephanie was near tears. Since Kerri had run out and told her and Clara what had happened two days ago, she had been riddled with guilt and shame. "I didn't know," she whispered. "I really didn't know. I never would have wished anything bad to happen to that boy, Max. You have to know that."

"I *do* know that, Steph, but I also know that you refuse to see what Clara is capable of. You had a bad experience when you were a kid. You were haunted by a fucking spirit." He whirled on her. "Does that mean you have to deny Clara her own gifts, which from what I hear, likely came from *you!*"

Stephanie bristled at the reminder of her terrifying childhood. "That's not fair, and you know it. I'm not an oracle. I don't know what to believe as pure fact and what to believe is simply a bad dream. We all have them! How was I supposed to know?!" Her grief and anger at herself came out in a room-shattering yell, which startled Max.

"Well, now maybe you know." Max tried to reign in his temper, able to fully see how badly Stephanie was suffering. Though he was terribly angry with her, he knew she would feel guilty about it for the rest of her life. He sighed, once again running a hand through his hair, making it stand up on end. "This is part of the problem with us, Stephanie. You see what you want to see; not what's right in front of you. When it was just mainly with me, fine, I'm an adult, I can handle it. But Clara is a fourteen-year-old girl. A child! She needs to know that she can go to you. She can confide in you and feel safe that you won't turn her away, or ignore her, or pretend her abilities don't exist. 'Cause I got news for you, Stephanie, she does. Clara is special, and nothing you say or do will *ever* change that. Get used to it."

Chapter Six

The sky was a curious shade of gray. Clara had never seen anything quite like it. Clouds were indeed moving in, but they didn't look threatening. There wasn't the smell of rain in the air. It was just a gray sky. She heard a bird squawk somewhere off in the distance, which brought her numbly back to the reason for being out in the gray day.

The crowd at the cemetery wasn't nearly as large as it had been at the church, but it was still huge, mourners trampling over graves, trying not to run into headstones and monuments as they gathered as closely as they could to the green tent covering Jason's place of rest.

Jason's father had not been able to attend, as he was still in a hospital in the Midwest. Jason's mother, whom Clara had never met, sat in the first row. Her quiet sobs could be heard above the minister's words. Clara didn't care what the minister had to say anyway, as it was all flowery sentiment. She knew it had no bearing on where Jason had gone or how quickly he got there. What was done was already done.

Max stood behind his daughter, his hands on her shoulders. He had been keeping a careful eye on her all day, somewhat concerned with her extreme calm. Stephanie and Kerri had joined them, though Stephanie had kept her distance somewhat from Clara. She knew Clara was deeply, profoundly touched by

what had happened, and felt that she had no place at
the moment to offer condolences or comfort. She just
hoped that, in time, her daughter could forgive her.

Clara glanced beyond the gathered mourners,
looking out into the rest of the beautifully maintained
cemetery. She noticed a woman sitting on one of
the many stone benches scattered throughout the
grounds. At first, she thought the woman was visiting
a grave then realized she recognized the woman. She
recognized her dark hair, the bangs pinned back away
from her face. She sat quietly, one leg crossed over the
other, her gaze fixed on Clara. The woman smiled, and
Clara wasn't sure what to think.

She looked away, turning her attention back to
the situation at hand, but again felt her eyes pulled
away from Jason's services, and back toward the stone
bench. The woman was still sitting there. Clara knew
it was the same woman she'd seen standing in front of
the backyard gate the night she took the trash out.

I'll come to you when you're ready.

Clara heard the words as clear as day in her mind
yet knew they weren't her thoughts. She watched as
the woman raised her hand in a quick wave then stood
from the bench, walking off into the cemetery, fading
out of sight as she got further away.

"Everything okay?" Max asked, glancing over to
where Clara seemed to be visually riveted.

Clara nodded. "Fine."

Max squeezed her shoulders as the minister
continued.

After the services, everyone reconvened in the
church basement for a dinner held in Jason's honor.
The space was a big, open room where folding tables
and chairs had been set up. A buffet-style lunch was

being served at the front of the room, people talking to each other as they stood in line, waiting for their turn, many with plastic Dixie plates in hand.

Clara and her family had taken a table about halfway down the rows. Stephanie had disappeared to find the restroom while Kerri had found a couple of her friends who had come in support. Max sat across from his youngest, holding her hands in his. He studied her face — a poker face. Completely expressionless. He was very worried about her; at least when she was crying he knew what she was feeling. But this...

"Hey, guys. Mind if my friend Abby joins us?"

Max and Clara looked up to see Kerri standing at the head of the table, her blonde soccer teammate in tow. Clara felt her breath catch and nervous butterflies take flight.

"No, hon, that's fine. You girls have a seat," Max said unaware of the state of turmoil Clara's emotions had suddenly become. To make things worse, Abby sat in the chair to Clara's left.

Clara looked straight ahead, unable to meet the older girl's intense, green gaze, which she could feel on her.

"Listen, Clara, um," Abby said, her voice soft. "I wanted to say I'm really sorry about your friend. It's terrible what happened to him." She paused, sipping from the plastic Dixie cup filled with iced tea. "I also thought you should know that you were right. About my grandma."

That got Clara's attention. She looked over at the girl, taking a huge gulp of air first to settle her nerves. It didn't work. "Thank you — for Jason. And, she's okay?"

Abby nodded enthusiastically. "Not only is she

okay, but after the surgery we had to put her in one of those homes. She met Jed there."

"Jed?"

"Her new boyfriend. See, my grandfather died back in the seventies, and she's been alone. They're very happy."

Clara's grin was small, but genuine. "I'm so glad. Thanks for telling me."

"Come on, Abby. The line has gone down. Let's get some food."

Clara watched as Abby joined her friend, and they pushed through the waves of people and to the food line.

"You hungry? Want to get some food?" Max asked, nodding toward the laden tables.

"Not really," Clara muttered.

"Honey, you've barely eaten since all this happened. You really need to eat." He met her gaze with a steady one of his own. "Okay?"

"Here we go," Stephanie said, suddenly materializing, seemingly from nowhere. She had a heaped plate balanced on either palm, setting one down in front of Max and a second in front of Clara.

"This is a ton of food, Mom," the girl complained, noting the pasta, salad, roll with butter, small piece of carrot cake, and huge meatball. She quickly glanced up to see if she could catch another glimpse of Abby in the food line, but her mother inadvertently sat in the exact spot that would block her view. Clara turned her attention back to her food.

"I know it is, but I wasn't sure what you'd want. Just eat what you want." Stephanie, not all that hungry herself, picked a carrot off her daughter's plate and took a roll she'd put on Max's plate for herself.

Clara felt horrible, knowing that her mother was doing all she could to make it up to her. During the past couple days, having her dad back in her life, Clara had made a decision, and she knew it would break her mother's heart. It was a much easier decision to make when she was angry with Stephanie. She wanted to live with her dad.

☙☙☙☙

Clara kept her attention on her packing, neatly folding a T-shirt before settling it inside the suitcase with the others. Her mother stood on the other side of her bed, doing the same. Things had been tense in the Greenwold house for the past week, since the night of Jason's funeral when Clara had made her intentions known. Just as she'd feared, her mother had been deeply hurt, and Kerri hadn't spoken to her all week.

"Is it something I did, Clara?" Stephanie asked, suddenly breaking the silence.

Clara glanced at her mother, who refused to meet her daughter's gaze. "No," she said, her voice quiet.

"Then why, Clara?" Stephanie asked, slamming down the pair of shorts she had been folding. "Why are you breaking up your family?"

"Mom, I can't talk to you about this," Clara said, feeling defensive.

"Why?" Stephanie's anger and hurt was full-blown now. "Why can't you talk to me? Why *won't* you talk to me? Am I that bad?"

Clara felt her heart pounding, but let her own anger get her through. "Because you'll judge me!" she cried, glaring. "You judge everything I do. You don't accept me for me, and I can't stand it! You didn't listen to me, and now Jason is dead because of it. Dad listens! He understands, or at least tries to!" Clara was trembling as years of rage and hurt came out in one huge burst.

A pregnant silence filled the room, both looked away, unable to meet the other's gaze for their own reasons. Finally Stephanie headed toward the door. "You'd better hurry. Your dad will be here soon." With that, she left, slamming the door behind her.

Clara collapsed on the bed, feeling bad, but knowing she had to be honest. She had to finally say what had been bothering her for years. Unexpectedly, she felt a short, but intense wave of emotion engulf her, and then silent tears sprang from her eyes. She was utterly baffled as she tried to wipe them away. She felt fine — other than really angry — and had no need to cry. As soon as she'd wipe a tear away, two more came to take its place. It was almost as though she was someone else for a moment, and the tears were from that person, not from Clara.

Finally the emotion subsided, and Clara shook herself. "That was weird," she whispered.

≫ ≫ ≪ ≪

Parting certainly was sweet sorrow — as Clara had read in a Shakespeare play — as she left her mother's house and the home she'd grown up in. All of her family memories were in that house, basically. All of her belongings had been loaded into her father's truck, and now she stood at the front door, Max behind her, looking at an obviously angry Kerri and her mother, who could barely hold her gaze.

"If you need anything, you call me. Okay?"

Stephanie said quietly, doing her best to hold in her tears. Her youngest nodded, and Stephanie took the girl in for a tight hug.

Clara couldn't help but feel like a traitor of some sort. Especially with the way Kerri was shooting her daggers. She hugged her mother then stepped away, glancing at Kerri, who promptly turned and left the room. *Well, guess that's that.*

"I love you, Clara," Stephanie whispered.

"I love you, too." With that, Clara turned and followed her father out the door, unable to be in the house for a moment longer.

Chapter Seven

1991

Clara chewed on her bottom lip, shrugging her backpack higher onto her shoulder. She took a deep breath, her gaze scanning the much larger campus than the high school that was close to her mom's house; the one where Kerri was a senior. Now, Clara would start her high school career as a freshman at John Freed High School.

At one time she had looked forward to high school. At least she had Jason to start the new phase in their lives. She sighed, sad. Now, she was completely alone. Not only in a new school level, but a new side of town! She'd had very few friends in middle school, but at least she knew her peers. Not so much now. Yes, she'd done it to herself by moving in with her dad. But still...

She was dressed in brand-new clothes, a new backpack, carrying her new school supplies — pens (she hated pencils), notebooks, a calculator, and folders — and a new haircut. She'd always worn her brown hair long, mostly because Kerri did, but she decided she needed a change. When Clara had first looked in the mirror at the hair salon, she'd nearly swallowed her tongue. It was now short, though not boyish. It was cut in lots of layers so it looked messy and daring. Completely opposite of what Clara really was.

Max had driven her to the school over the

weekend, so she could see how to get there and how to get home. The school was less than a mile from her dad's apartment, so she opted to walk. That is, until he bought her a car the following year. He'd flatly said no, but she intended to work on him over the next year.

The school itself looked like any other high school: long halls with cinderblocks painted obnoxious colors of pastel and highly polished linoleum floors. The lockers were painted in alternating green and gold, the school colors, and a huge hornet was painted on one wall of the gymnasium. *Who the hell had a bug as their school mascot?* Clara wondered more than once.

Students plowed down the halls in groups and singles, most yelling after-summer greetings to each other. Clara couldn't help but feel very alone and small in a sea of people who all seemed to know each other, even though she knew there was no way that was true. It sure felt that way, though.

Her locker was found easily enough. It was one that was painted green, as opposed to the gold on either side. The lock was set firmly in place, and she had to dig out the piece of paper that had been mailed to her, the six-digit locker combination written on it. She tried it a couple of times, her hands trembling from nerves, making her miss the correct number several times before the lock clicked, the heavy padlock falling away from the metal ring that held it in place.

Clara pulled open the metal door, taking in the shelf toward the top, giving a smaller space to put books, the long, lower part for hanging jackets, thus spoke the brass hooks affixed to the side wall of the locker. She let her backpack slide off her shoulder, squatting to unzip it and pull everything out. She only kept one notebook, two pens and a folder in the backpack, stowing the extras on the top nook. She had no jacket so the rest of the locker remained empty.

She felt somewhat safe, almost able to hide behind the opened door of the locker, able to shut out the rest of the activity around her. A glance at her watch told her she had to be in first period — Italian — in six minutes. With a final sigh, she shouldered her now-lighter backpack and slammed the locker shut, sliding the lock into place and snapping it home.

༄ ༄ ༀ ༀ

The one part of her day that Clara had always hated most was lunchtime. It had always been a lonely, isolated part of her day. Well, since middle school, anyway. Their school had been a large one and had to divide the students into two different lunch periods. All three years — sixth, seventh, and eighth grades — she and Jason had opposite lunches. She'd had a few casual friends or acquaintances who would take pity on her from time to time, but overall, she'd always eaten alone; just as she was now.

The lunchroom was large, much larger than what she was used to from middle school. Much larger than the high school Kerri went to. Her father had given her money to buy a lunch, but instead she had used the five dollars to buy a Coke and a bag of chips from the small cantina. She had very little appetite and didn't want to stand in line with all the strangers.

The cafeteria was in an open area, near banks of lockers. Tables were set up at the center of the large room, a padded bench running in a semi-circle around the area. On the outside of the benches was more space for people to gather and talk, as well as trash cans, and the cantina. Clara found herself a spot on the outskirts, her back resting against the cold metal of a locker. She watched all the activity, absently sipping her drink, the chips opened but untouched.

She noticed a couple standing over by the bathrooms, obviously in some sort of lover's quarrel. The girl looked as though she were ready to bolt, the boy looking as though he were trying desperately to explain something. Perhaps some bad behavior, Clara reasoned. As she watched the pair, an image came into mind:

The boy held a beer in his hand, his eyes unsteady and bloodshot. He was sitting in the driver's seat of a pickup truck. He was amorous. His face was flushed with arousal or anger, but whichever, it was strong and leading his thoughts.

The girl sat in the passenger seat, her hand on the door handle, about to push the door open. She looked angry, her hair mussed, lipstick smeared. Some heavy kissing and petting had happened.

The boy spoke, his mouth moving, yet no words escaping. The girl shook her head, glaring at him. She pulled on the door handle, the door about to open when the boy suddenly reached across the truck cab, closing and locking the door. The girl pushed him away, speaking in that strange, soundless talk. He grabbed her, cupping the back of her head, and trying to force her face down into his crotch.

The girl fought him, finally getting away from him and leaving him with a hard slap before letting herself out of the truck. She slammed the door, yelled something at him, then stomped away.

Clara blinked several times, trying to clear her head and get the images out of her head. She focused once more on the couple, able to tell now that he was trying to apologize. The girl looked as though she might cave, but Clara wasn't sure.

"So, do you want to get your ass out of my way today, or should I wait for tomorrow?"

Clara's attention was ripped from the fighting couple, and to a girl standing a few feet away, her arms crossed over her chest, a foot tapping. She made her way from black combat boots up baggy, torn black pants to a fitted black tee. Finally, Clara looked into the owner's face. Her long hair was down, hanging in her pale face. Her dark eye makeup made her look dangerous, completely creepy and unforgiving.

"Do I know you?" Clara asked, a memory sparking somewhere. The girl rolled dark eyes.

"I don't give a shit. Move!" She yanked on the lock attached to the locker Clara sat against, indicating it was her locker.

Clara scrambled out of the way, barely grabbing her bag of Doritos before a combat boot would have smashed them into powder. She gathered up her backpack and stood, holding the chips protectively to her chest. "Jesus," she muttered, stunned at the girl's nonchalance as she casually got into her locker. "You're rude."

The girl smirked, never taking her eyes off the tiny magnetic mirror mounted to the inside of her door. She was applying more blood-red lipstick. "Been called worse." She puckered then closed the cap on the lipstick, sliding it into her backpack and slamming her locker shut. Without another glance at Clara, she closed the locker, locked it, and walked away.

❧❧❧❧

"I hate it!" Clara exclaimed, slamming two plates onto the table, the already-placed forks jumping at the action.

"Oh yeah?" Max asked, eyeing his daughter as he put the finishing touches on the Hamburger Helper he'd prepared. "Why's that?"

"The kids there are mean. The school is friggin' huge, and I got lost four times. My lock only opens half the time, and I didn't make a single friend." She collapsed into her chair, feeling quite sorry for herself. "I think I want to go to South High."

"Oh, no, Clara," Max said, taking his seat to Clara's left. "We're not going to play this game." He popped open the can of Pepsi. "You are not going to play this back-and-forth stuff. I love you, sweet pea, but it was too hard on your mom the first time. I won't allow you to put her through that again, unless you plan to stay there until you're married."

"But, can't I just get a ride there? Live here and go to South?" Clara asked, her hopes not totally dashed.

"And who's gonna drive you? I have to be at work by crack-of-dawn a.m., and your mom is working now too. You know damn well Kerri won't do it, and she shouldn't have to. No," he shook his head, taking a sip from his drink. "You made your choice."

Clara looked at him, stunned. "But, Dad!" she whined.

"But, what?" he whined back, dishing out Hamburger Helper to her and himself. He was determined to keep the tone light on what he knew could potentially be a very heavy subject. "Clara, you've given it one day. One." He held up a finger to emphasize his point. "Nobody can make up their mind based on one day, I promise you."

Clara sat back in her chair, arms crossed stubbornly over her chest. She watched him out of the corner of her eye, both irritated and amused as she realized he wasn't going to give in to her pout. They both knew each other all too well. "Fine," she sighed — for the sake of dramatics, of course — and began to eat her dinner.

❧❧❧❧

Though she wasn't thrilled about it, Clara decided to give John Freed High School one more try. After all, she had to admit, even if begrudgingly so, it had been only one day. Starting any type of new situation wasn't easy for her. She was shy and quiet by nature: more of an observer than a participant. Though that would help her later in life, as a teenager it was hell. She never quite felt like she fit in anywhere, or with any group of people.

Clara walked through the halls, headed to lunch, and looked around at her peers. She looked at them all, *really looked* at them, and saw, to her amazement, some miserable faces in the crowd. Though she felt bad for those kids who, like herself, were singled out, it somehow made her feel a little better to know they were there. Though none of them knew each other or hung out per se, they were bonded together by some sort of strange glue of exceptionism.

That was somewhat fascinating to her, in some weird, warped way. Was it with humans like it was in nature? Survival of the strongest, the weak found out then mauled by the mighty lion? As she looked around, she had to smirk to herself. Despite appearances, it was quite obvious to her who the actual "strong" and "weak" were. The popular, desired kids hung around in packs — safety in numbers, whereas the supposed weaker of the specimen were alone, strong enough to be themselves, without the support of the masses.

Philosophizing done for the day, Clara headed to her math class.

≈≋≋≋

A month into Clara's stay at John Freed High School, she sat outside, enjoying the last of the warm weather before autumn began to rear its head. She sat with her back against the three-story brick building, her lunch bag sitting between her spread feet, a half-eaten apple in her hand. She sat at the back of the building where an area had been set up for outdoor lunchers. Stone tables and benches dotted the area, as well as trash cans. Beyond the lunch area was fenced off, separating those eating from those who had gym class. The sports field was circled with a track for runners.

Clara watched the current class that stood around in small groups on the sports field. Their teacher, Coach Raybrush, was talking to a couple students, leaving the others to mill around or talk, all looking bored. Something caught Clara's eye, making her turn to her left. She saw a man walking away from the parking lot that ran along the back of the stadium seating that was on either of the long sides of the track. He was walking toward the side of the building, carrying something in his hand.

She dropped her apple in the brown paper bag, leaving it with her backpack as she got to her feet. The man was dressed in brown, baggy pants, nearly covering the tops of the brown leather shoes he wore. His white button-up shirt was smudged, the sleeves rolled up to his elbows; the outfit topped off by a worn, wool flat cap.

Clara felt a strange wave rush through her insides as she began to follow. His pace was brisk, seemingly unaware of anyone or anything around him. As Clara rounded the side of the building, she caught a glimpse of him, walking right toward the brick wall. She realized that what he carried in his hand was a giant wrench, nearly three feet in length. It looked lethal. She gasped softly as she watched him walk right through the wall.

Trying to calculate what lay on the other side of that wall, Clara hurried into the school, making her way down a long, quiet hall. She could hear the murmurings of teachers behind the closed doors that lined the corridor. In a distant hall, she heard laughter from a girl, joined by that of a second.

Trying to stay unnoticed, Clara got her mental bearings, closing her eyes as she mapped out the layout of the school, compared to where she'd seen the man outside. She hurried down an adjacent hall to where she had been, finding herself at a dead end, with stairs going up, and stairs going down. At a crossroads, she looked in either direction, chewing on her bottom lip as she tried to decide where to go.

Down.

Clara was startled by the voice in her head, but decided to follow it. Glancing around to make sure no one was watching, she scurried down the stairs. The short staircases led to a landing, then anther set, leading her into the bowels of the building. She had never been there, and immediately felt a sense of unease. The corridor wasn't extremely well lit, the bulbs overhead flickering in some cases or completely burnt out in others. She knew the building was old, but had been added to over the years. It seemed the basement was part of the original structure.

Closed doors lined the hall, each with a labeling plaque: STORAGE, MAINTENANCE, ELECTRICAL, BOILER, and finally, OFF LIMITS! She looked at each door in turn, trying to decide where to go. She felt drawn to the door marked boiler.

"Damn," she murmured, noting the deadbolt lock — shiny and new against the backdrop of old wood and an old, brass knob. Logic told her that the guy was probably long gone, and she should just get out of there and go finish her lunch. Then she reasoned, in an illogical situation, logic isn't the best tool to use. In her mind, this was anything but a logical situation, so she tried the knob. To her surprise, not only did it turn but the door pushed open.

Immediately Clara was hit in the face with the smell of old, stale air. A low-toned, throbbing hum could be heard deep inside the room. She pushed the door open just enough to slip inside, once again, making sure she hadn't been spotted. The door closed behind her, Clara looked around the room she'd just entered. Too late, she realized that she had no flashlight, matches, nothing. There were lights on in the large, dank room, but they were naked bulbs, and only a handful at best. They gave off a dim, buttery light that set Clara's nerves on end.

She stopped to look around and get her bearings. The floor of the room was poured cement only for the first ten feet or so from the door then ended in packed dirt. It looked as though the outskirts of the room was the walkway, the center filled with huge machinery, the oiled parts moving and purring with a rumble that Clara could feel in the pit of her stomach.

Looking left then right, she settled on heading right, careful to keep away from anything that could potentially catch her clothing or hurt her. She understood mechanics about as much as she understood how to jump off a cliff and fly to Tahiti with only the flapping of her bare arms.

As she made her way around, she saw something in a dim corner. It looked as though something — some sort of paper — had been taped to the brick wall. She walked over to it, and realized it was, in fact, a newspaper. A very *old* newspaper. Not wanting to destroy the paper, she peered at it closely, trying to discern what the picture was and the words that accompanied it.

The faded image on the severely yellowed paper was of a brick structure, a third the size of the current one. Clara wasn't sure where it was until she noted a familiar-looking patch of trees. The article was dated June 10, 1896.

"Wow," Clara whispered, her eyes roving over the somewhat fuzzy picture. A group of people stood in front of it, smiling proudly. Most looked to be officious types, dressed in fine clothing: ladies in larger-than-life gowns of gorgeous fabrics and styles, the men in top hats and gloves.

Dead center of the posing crowd was an older man, distinguished and very wealthy looking. On his arm was a lovely young woman, at least twenty years younger than the man, a partial smile on her lips. Clara's gaze was drawn to a figure standing away from the others. His features were far too blurry to be able to discern, but he was dressed in a button-up shirt, the sleeves rolled to the elbows, and a flat cap on his head. He seemed to be looking at the pretty woman standing with the gentleman in the center of the photograph.

"Oh, that's cool," she murmured, grinning. She felt in her gut that the man was the same man she'd seen earlier and was chasing. Her head whipped around when she heard a bang — metal on metal. She peered into the dimness, trying to make her eyes focus. The bang came again, this time clearly coming from the back of the room.

Clara turned away from the newspaper article, trying to be as quiet as she could, in case it was a maintenance guy working. She was pretty sure she'd be in trouble if she got caught in the boiler room of her high school. She inched closer, listening and trying to keen all her senses. She heard the banging again, a hollow *ping, ping, ping.* She could see a dark corner, but the shadows were complete, and she could see just enough to know there was no one there, though the sound seemed to originate from there.

What the...?

There was a slight pause in the banging, Clara's heart was pounding in her ears as she held her breath, waiting to see what would happen next. Her entire body was in a state of alert, her nervous system primed and ready for anything. So she thought.

As the pounding continued, the figure of the man slowly faded into view. He was swearing as he used the wrench in his hand to bang on something that was no longer there. He stopped, squatting as though examining something, not paying a bit of attention to his audience of one. He stood, about to start his pounding again when he stopped, looking to his left, which was right where Clara was standing. She was about to run, but then realized he wasn't seeing her at all.

His face spread into a grin, and Clara nearly gasped when suddenly a young woman was standing next to him, out of breath as though she'd just run a great distance. Clara's entire body felt as though it had just been shocked by electricity, her heart pounding, every hair standing on end.

When she looked closer, Clara realized it was the same woman from the newspaper article, in her Sunday best. Their figures seemed solid in the dim light, though Clara had the feeling if lights were turned on, they would fade into the brightness.

The couple embraced, then, with heads lowered together, seemed to engage in a serious conversation, though no sound could be heard. Clara's heart continued to pound, and for a moment she felt as though she were witnessing something she shouldn't, as though she were intruding.

She began to feel incredibly uneasy as the temperature around her began to drop significantly. The entire atmosphere of the boiler room changed, and Clara felt a strong need to run, never to look back. Foreboding and dread prickled along her arms. A huge bolt of energy rushed through her, making her take several steps back. Hand to her chest, she saw two men seem to burst from the shadows of where she'd just been standing moments before, their intent obvious as they grabbed the young man. His flat cap fell to the floor as the three began to fight. The woman was knocked down, her hand held to her mouth in terror as she watched.

Clara's eyes grew huge as she saw the man in the brown pants use all his strength, managing to push one of the assailants off of him, then taking his wrench in both hands and swinging with all his might. He hit one of his attackers in the stomach, doubling him over, while the other went at him again. The man swung the wrench one more time, again aiming at his attackers, but the attacker jumped out of the way of the heavy, lethal tool.

Clara gasped in horror as she saw the metal slam into the fallen woman's head. As if choreographed in some play, the two attackers disappeared, the man falling to his knees. The next thing Clara saw was that the wrench had seemingly disappeared, leaving the man in brown sitting on the ground, holding the woman in his arms. Her eyes were closed, a bloody gash at her temple. Clara figured she was probably dead. The man was crying, his entire body shaking with the force of his sobs.

Reaching a hand up, Clara wiped away her own tears, unknowingly leaving a smudge mark on her cheek, her hands dirty from trying to feel her way along the time-dirtied walls. Her heart felt heavy as she saw the man raise his face to the Heavens, eyes squeezed shut, mouth opened as an anguished cry slipped out, filling the small space, and completely startling Clara. As the echoes died away, so did the figures.

She shook herself out of it when she realized that his flat cap still lay where it had fallen. Wiping at her tears again, she walked over to it. As she was about to reach for it, it slowly faded away leaving only hard-packed earth, littered with greasy stains.

Chapter Eight

Clara made her way back to the main floor of the school, glad that the halls were quiet. They must not have passed for lunch, yet, which meant she could sneak back outside, grab her backpack and hurry to her locker before she had to head to her next class.

She absently beat her fingertips against the sides of her thighs as she thought over what she'd just witnessed. She'd heard of that kind of thing before, and knew it was referred to as a "residual haunting," which meant it was — in theory, anyway — the residual energy from a traumatic event that kept it happening again and again. The spirits aren't even really there, but the memory of them was.

What a horrible thing to happen! She wondered what the story was and decided she wanted to do some research on the school: the history of the building, the history of the people associated with it. She imagined the library downtown might have something on that. Or, maybe even the school library. If she had time after school, maybe she'd duck inside and see what there was to be found.

"You are in some pretty big trouble, my friend."

Clara jumped at the unexpected voice and the unexpected presence of someone suddenly walking beside her. She glanced over to see Mr. Estrata, her English teacher.

That's odd, she thought, I don't have his class until last period.

"Why?" she asked, about to take a turn at the end of the hall, which would lead to the doors headed outside. She just wanted to grab her backpack and get back to her day.

"Nope. Come with me." He guided her to the main hall where the main office was. To her shock, two uniformed policemen were standing just outside the office, one speaking with Max.

"What the...?" A sense of dread fell over Clara. "Oh my god! Is everything okay?" she asked, bursting into a run to get to her father. She was stunned cold in her tracks when he looked at her, his face going from shock to relief to rage.

"Where the hell have you been?!" he demanded, hurrying over to her. "Do you have *any* idea how worried everyone has been? Any idea at all?"

It was then that Clara realized one of the policemen was holding her backpack, his hands covered in latex gloves.

"No. I didn't know. What's going on?"

"You've turned this school upside down, *that's* what's going on!" Max was trembling, his face red, the vein at the center of his forehead popping. "I get a call at work from your principal asking me if I know where the hell you're at. That's what's going on. No one had seen you since lunch, you missed all your classes, and then someone found your bag outside, half the stuff inside spilled out on the ground."

Alexander Estrata could see that things might get out of hand, so he stepped in. "Mr. Greenwold," he said quietly, partially stepping in front of the irate man. He knew Clara's dad was far less likely to try anything with him than with the girl. "Let's everyone calm down."

Max wanted to rip the man's face off, but realized he was right, and grounding Clara for the rest of her life wouldn't change how afraid he'd been. He took a deep breath and a step away from the man in the dress pants, blue button-up shirt, and blue- and gray-stripe tie.

"I'm sorry, Dad," Clara said, her voice quiet. A glance at the office clock told her it was nearly four thirty. Where had the time gone? How was it possible she'd been in the boiler room for four hours? She felt terrible, and had never seen her father so upset before. Certainly not at her!

"My name is Alex Estrata," the English teacher said. "I teach one of Clara's classes." He turned to his student. "Clara, what happened? Are you okay?" His brows drew when he noticed a smudge on her cheek, and what appeared to be tear tracks through it.

Max noticed at the same time. "Oh my god! Clara!" He grabbed both shoulders in large hands, leaning in to get a closer look. "Are you okay? What happened? Who hurt you?"

Completely baffled, Clara could only stare at her frantic father. "What? Hurt me? No one did." She shook her head to emphasize her claim. "I..." Her voice trailed off as she realized she wasn't entirely sure what to tell them, especially when she had five pairs of expectant eyes on her, now that Mr. Swan, the John Freed High School principal, had joined them. Suddenly she felt as though the weight of the world was on her shoulders.

"Clara?" Max asked. He knew his daughter well enough to know that she had been doing something she maybe shouldn't have. He could tell she was fine and unharmed, and though it was a great relief, it almost made his anger return full force. That, however, could wait.

"I fell asleep," she said, knowing it sounded as lame as it felt.

"You fell asleep," Mr. Swan repeated, arms crossed over his chest. It was obvious he didn't believe her. "Where?"

"Listen, Mr. Swan," Max interjected, "it's been a long day. Why don't you let me get her home and cleaned up, then I can talk to her. I know you fellas probably want to get home."

The principal and English teacher glanced at their watches. "You *will* talk to her?" Mr. Swan asked, eyeing Max with a raised brow.

Max nodded. "You bet your butt I will." He looked at Clara with a stern gaze. "As soon as we get home."

Feeling somewhat mollified, the principal nodded, then turned to the officers, thanking them for their time, then headed into the office.

Alex Estrata was amused, though very curious. He liked the quiet girl, and felt there was a lot more to her than most people thought or saw. "See you tomorrow, kid," he said, squeezing Clara's shoulder, then heading back to his classroom to pack up for the night.

Left with her father, Clara looked up at him with big, sheepish eyes. "Let's go."

Clara took her backpack, which one of the officers had handed to Max, and dutifully followed him out to his car.

≈≈≈≈≈

Clara could feel Max's eyes on her as she poked at her baked chicken. Feeling bad, she'd made an attempt at making her father's favorite dish, using her mother's recipe. She assumed it must have tasted good, as her father had gotten a second helping, but she was barely able to get through her first.

"So?" Max asked after a long silence. "Are you going to tell me what happened?"

"What if I said you wouldn't believe me if I told you?" Clara countered, pushing her peas into the scalloped potatoes, watching the gooey mixture.

"What if I said you're just as grounded either way, so you might as well tell me."

Clara had to stop herself from smirking at that. *Grounded.* It wasn't like there was anything to ground her *from.* She didn't do anything to be grounded from. Finally she sighed, setting her fork down to stop the pretense that she was going to actually eat anything. She met her father's curious gaze.

"You have to promise not to laugh."

"Okay." Max continued to eat, knowing what he was about to hear would be good. He was just glad he hadn't called Stephanie yet when Clara showed up. The girl's mother would have needed counseling to get over the trauma.

"I was sitting at lunch, outside, when I saw a guy walk through the wall of the building."

Max stopped eating and stared at his daughter.

"You said you wouldn't laugh!" Clara complained, feeling insecure.

"I hardly think I'm laughing," he said quietly.

She gave a dramatic sigh. "Anyway, I was curious, so I ran inside the building, trying to figure out where he'd walked to. I ended up in the basement, in the boiler room, where I saw him." Clara paused, unsure how to continue her story. Should she tell him everything she saw? Should she just glaze over it, keeping the details to herself?

Max could see the indecision on his daughter's face and knew she had seen something that had either bothered her or had touched her in some way. "What did you see, Clara?" he asked, setting his own fork aside. He had the feeling she needed his whole, undivided attention.

"I...I think something really terrible happened in that basement, Dad. I think a woman was killed."

"A woman? You just said you saw a man."

"I did. But there was a woman too. She was accidentally hit in the head." Clara told her father the entire story, not passing over one detail. She could see it fresh in her mind again as she told the tale, and it made her hunger to find out what had actually happened there that much stronger.

"So," Max said, after he'd heard the entire incredible story. "You're telling me that you saw an event that happened almost a hundred years ago?" At his daughter's nod, he took a drink from his Pepsi, taking a moment to gather his thoughts. Letting out a loud belch, he continued. "How is that possible?"

Clara shrugged. "I'm not sure. I do have a theory, though. I think it was something so traumatic that happened in that boiler room that the energy was somehow... I don't know...trapped, I guess. Doomed to replay the events over and over again."

"That sounds a little far-fetched, sweet pea. Even for you." Max crushed the empty soda can, doing an overhead toss, the can clanging into the open trash can near the back door.

"I know it's crazy, but I swear every word is true."

"So then explain why you were away for four hours. Where did you go?"

"I was down there the entire time. I truly thought I'd only been down there for maybe thirty minutes. Forty-five, tops."

Max looked at her, boring his unbelieving gaze into her until it burned. "Clara, don't lie."

"I'm not!" She was hurt he didn't believe her. She knew her story was crazy, and even sounded like she'd made the entire thing up, but surely he knew she'd never lie to him about something like that.

"Okay, okay. I surrender," Max said, holding his hands up. He sighed, sitting back in his chair. "So, what are you going to tell that principal of yours tomorrow?"

"Can I be sick tomorrow?" Clara muttered, looking down at her plate, which had become a lot more appetizing now that she had gotten everything out, and knew her father believed her.

Max laughed. "Hardly. But you need to come up with something. Somehow I don't think the truth in this case is the wisest course of action."

Clara grinned. "Why, Dad, are you telling me to *lie*?"

Max's grin matched that of his daughter. "Yep. Pretty much."

Chapter Nine

The microfiche rolled by, Clara watching intently, pen between her teeth. She scanned the articles, looking for anything dealing with the building that had once stood at 2500 E. Parker Street, but then had been expanded to John Freed High School.

She'd been at the downtown library for over an hour, her focus on only one thing. It had been a week since her boiler room adventure, and it was the first day her father had allowed her out of the house, other than for school purposes, or to see her mom. Kerri had swung by earlier that Saturday morning to spend some time with their dad and volunteered to drop Clara off at the library on her way to work. Her mother would pick her up when she got *off* work, and mother and daughter would head to dinner, and then Clara would be spending the weekend with Stephanie. The whole "parents separated" thing kind of sucked, in Clara's humble opinion.

"Here are those articles you requested, miss."

Clara looked up to see the elderly librarian standing next to her, a folder in her outstretched hand.

"Oh! Thank you." She took the folder and immediately began to finger through them. They were photocopies made from old, bound newspapers that the public had no access to, for fear the delicate pages would be destroyed through handling and misuse.

Clara put aside several of the articles until one caught her eye. She was face-to- face with the same newspaper page she'd seen in the boiler room. She studied the faces of the players once more: the man in the brown pants and flat cap and the beautiful young woman who had been so brutally — and accidentally — murdered. Looking at her face, Clara was once again able to see her lifeless body held in the young man's arms, the blood gushing down the side of her face from the horrible head gash. Flipping to the page behind the one with the picture on it, she read the article.

June 10, 1896: In a lavish ceremony this morning, Senator John Freed and his new bride, Josie, led the excitement of the opening of the John Freed Conservatory.

Clara read on, learning that John Freed — age 53 at the time of the opening of the building — had been a steel baron from Pittsburgh, and after the death of his wife Mildred the previous spring, he'd married 19-year-old Josie Rasputin, the daughter of a successful local merchant. Nowhere could Clara find out who the young man was.

She put the article aside, and soon had an answer to her question. The front page of the June 11, 1896 edition of the *Daily Record*, boasted a haunting photo of the young man being led toward a building, the word JAIL displayed above the door. Flanked by uniformed officers, their billy clubs in hand, he was looking down, refusing to look into the lens of the camera, nor the crowd that had gathered outside the jail.

She read the accompanying article, shocked to find out that the man — William Compton, age 23 — was actually John Freed's nephew, whom he was trying to help, and had recently moved into the Freed estate. William and Josie had apparently fallen in love and had made plans to run away together. Though the article mentioned nothing of it, Clara knew instinctively that Freed had hired two thugs to either kill William or beat some sense into him. According to the article, William had gotten angry when Josie refused to go through with the plan, instead choosing her love for her husband. William became angry and, in a violent rage, murdered the young woman in cold blood.

Clara gasped when she looked at the next page, which was an article from three days later and a newspaper man's sketch of events. William had been found guilty of the crime of murder and hanged. His lifeless body was seen hanging from the gallows, the crowd drawn in as cheering and throwing unidentifiable objects at the corpse.

"God, that's horrible," she said, a hand covering her mouth.

"What's horrible?"

Clara whipped around, surprised to see her mom setting her purse down on the table next to the microfiche machine Clara had been using and sinking into a chair next to her daughter. Stephanie looked tired, her hair slightly disheveled from a long day. She was putting in long hours at her new job at a bakery in town.

Stunned into silence by the sudden arrival of her mother, Clara could only stare. "Hi," she finally managed.

"Hey, sweetie." Stephanie was so happy to see her youngest. She felt a bit self-conscious, as she knew she stunk from a day in front of a hot oven, but she reached over and gave Clara a tight hug, anyway. Once they parted, she indicated all the pages in Clara's lap, as well as the old newspaper article on the microfiche reader screen. "What's all this?"

"Oh, um." Clara chewed on her bottom lip for a moment, trying to think quickly. "I have a research paper to do for school. I'm doing it on the history of the John Freed High School building."

"Very cool. Well, are you ready, honey? I'm tired."

"Yeah. Let me get this stuff cleaned up and returned."

Clara agreed to help her mother make dinner, rather than go out somewhere. Though Max was helping financially, money was tight, and Stephanie was exhausted working so many extra hours. The night had gone well, thus far, both mother and daughter talking freely as they prepared Clara's favorite meatloaf together.

Clara was filled completely with mixed emotions, standing hip to hip with the woman she'd seen every day of her life up to a month and a half ago. She still was ravaged with guilt for moving in with her father, though she still knew in her heart it was the best thing for her. Was it the best thing for her mom, though? She knew her mom was also filled with conflicting emotions, as Kerri had told her that their mom felt her own guilt over Jason and blamed herself for pushing Clara away because of that. Kerri went on, telling her about late night conversations with their mom, and how she felt betrayed mostly, however. Max had screwed up. He'd been the one fucking some nameless woman, and then he'd been the one who'd left. Yet, Clara had chosen to go live with him instead of staying at home and supporting her mother. Kerri had admitted their mother was somewhat bitter at times.

"Do you still like living with your dad?" Stephanie asked quietly.

Clara sighed softly, knowing that the conversation would come up eventually. "Yeah, Mom, I do. Besides," the girl grinned, trying to add a bit of levity to the situation, "I think you've ruined him for life. If I weren't there, I'm not sure he'd know which was his head and which was a hole in the ground."

"Not spoiled enough to not fuck around though, huh?" Stephanie snapped, regretting the comment the moment it was out of her mouth. She couldn't stand to see the stung expression on Clara's face. "I'm sorry, sweetie. I promised you I wouldn't talk about it, and I won't." She gave the girl a brave smile. "Subject closed."

Clara was relieved, and just hoped that her mother would abide by it. She wanted very much to spend time with the older woman, but couldn't do it if it was going to be a slam-her-father marathon. "How are things at the bakery? Kerri said they're already talking about training you to be an assistant manager."

Stephanie's smile lit up her entire face. Stephanie Greenwold was a naturally beautiful woman with blonde hair and brown eyes. Her skin was like peaches and cream, and she had a wonderful smile. It wasn't hard to see what Max had seen in her twenty years before. "That they are." The pride was evident in her voice, which made Clara automatically proud, too.

"Mom, that's great!" She reached over and gave her mother a one-armed hug. "I'm so happy for you!"

"Thanks." Stephanie stuck her tongue out between her teeth in a mischievous grin. "Someday I'll own that place."

"Oh, I have *no* doubts, whatsoever."

They continued on in silence until Stephanie spoke again. "So, any cute guys at your new school?" She glanced over at her daughter, who she thought looked decidedly uncomfortable.

Clara *was* uncomfortable. She had to bite the inside of her cheek when Abby Jensen popped into her mind's eye at the question. *Behave.* "Well, you know, Mom," she stuttered, "new school and all. I think I want to get my bearings before I worry about that stuff."

Stephanie studied her daughter for a moment and turned back to the salad she'd begun to toss. She thought back for a moment and realized that she'd never heard Clara talk about any boys. Except... She gasped, a hand covering her mouth. "Clara," she whispered. "Were you and Jason...you know."

Clara looked at her mother, stunned, and then she saw the grief and realization on Stephanie's face. Her mind whirled, trying to decide what she should say. It would certainly get her off the hook as far as the boy topic went. *Forgive me, Jason.* "Well, kind of," she muttered.

"Oh, honey!" Stephanie grabbed her daughter in a tight hug, holding her close. She'd never fully been able to get over her guilt over what had happened to the boy and his father. She would forever feel that somehow she was responsible. If only she'd let Clara call...

"It's okay, Mom," Clara murmured, allowing herself to get lost in the hug. Every girl needed a good hug from their mom, and she didn't get those all that often anymore. She gave her mother one final squeeze then let her go with a smile. "Come on. Let's eat."

꒰ঌ꒰ঌ꒱ৡ꒱ৡ

Clara walked into the living room, Stephanie insisting on doing the dishes while the girl got herself comfortable. She walked around the room she knew as well as the back of her own hand. Fourteen years spent in a house, all gone. Down the drain. There were times when she wanted to go to her father and grab him by the ears, shake him until he got some sense back into him. Though part of her did understand why he left, a bigger part didn't and hated it. Standing in her childhood home, she realized that she wanted nothing more than for her family to be put back together again.

She noted that the house wasn't as clean as it used to be. She knew her mom wasn't home as much anymore, and Kerri had a full schedule — soccer, school (senior year, no less), and a new boyfriend. There were unread magazines scattered across the living room table, as though thrown there when they'd come in with the mail. A small stack of old newspapers sat on one of the chairs, and a thin layer of dust covered the top of the TV.

Clara's eye was caught by a framed picture which had sat on the mantel for as long as she could remember. Walking over to it, she reached out, brushing her fingertips across the smooth glass. Ironically, it seemed as though the wood frame was dust free, as was the glass. The picture inside was old, yellowed with age. In it a young woman, maybe in her mid-twenties, sat, three young children grouped around her — two girls and a boy — and a fourth child, a toddler — the youngest daughter — on her lap.

Taking hold of the frame, Clara brought it off the mantel, closer to her, her eyes raking over the children, intentionally avoiding the woman for the moment. She easily found her mother, all blonde hair and frilly dress. She was standing next to the oldest child, her sister, Carol Ann, who was also killed in the car accident that happened little more than a year after the photo had been taken. The only boy, James — named after his father — knelt in front of his mother, a cute boy with a slightly perplexed look on his face. He was, after all, only around three years old.

Clara's gaze reluctantly traveled to the woman, her grandmother. She was beautiful, her hair in the typical style of the 1950s, her dress just so. Clara brought the picture closer, looking into her grandmother's eyes. She felt a chill run down her spine, as though those eyes were looking right into her soul and not out of a simple piece of photo paper.

She shivered, looking away with great effort. Clara tried to swallow the lump that had formed in her throat, her stomach roiling with a strange nervousness. It was the same every time she dared look at that photograph and had been since she was a small child. She took several deep breaths, pushing a strange sense of grief away, and setting the frame back in its place. She looked at it once more, then turned away.

⚜ ⚜ ⚜ ⚜

It had been a good night. The smile on Clara's face was certainly indicative of that. She lay in her old bed, the familiar shadows all around her, as well as her posters and glow-in-the-dark stars. She stared up at those, reacquainting herself with them, just as she did every time she spent the night at her mom's. And, to make things even better, Kerri had spent the night with a friend, so Clara and her mom had the place to themselves.

Clara did have to admit that things between her and her sister had gotten better once she moved out, though. She and Kerri just weren't meant to live together. Living in separate households, Kerri wasn't able to boss Clara around and actually seemed somewhat happy to see her younger sister when they saw each other. Perhaps there was hope for them yet. Maybe Kerri wasn't such a pain in the ass after all.

"Nah," Clara said, conviction in her voice. "She still is." There was a soft knock at the closed bedroom door. "Come in."

The door opened and Stephanie stepped inside the dark room. "Hey. Were you asleep?" She walked over to Clara's bed, looking down at her.

Clara shook her head. "No. Just contemplating what level of a pain Kerri still is."

Stephanie looked confused for a moment but shrugged it off. "Okay. Well, I hope you came to some sort of conclusion." She sat down on the edge of the bed.

"Yeah. I concluded that she is still a pain, but it's easier to handle not living with her."

Stephanie tried not to smile, knowing that her girls had never fully gotten along. She knew they loved each other, but two people couldn't possibly be any more different than Clara and Kerri. She knew from her own troubled relationship with her younger sister that siblings weren't always the easiest.

"What's up?" Clara asked, knocking Stephanie from her train of thought.

"I wanted to talk to you about something. Something I should have told you a long time ago."

Stephanie sighed, looking out the moonlight-filled window. "I just hope you're not mad at me when I've finished."

"Is it bad?" Clara asked, scooting over a bit further in her bed to make more room for her mother.

Stephanie shook her head. "Not exactly. But you might call me quite the hypocrite."

"Oh! Something to hold over your head!"

Stephanie chuckled. "Maybe." She cleared her throat and her thoughts. "As you know, I've always been uncomfortable with your abilities."

Clara was stunned by the topic of conversation, but remained quiet, very curious to hear what her mother had to say.

"I knew when you were very young that you had a gift, Clara. Several gifts, I'd wager." She continued to look out the window, unable to look her daughter in the eye. "There's a reason it makes me uncomfortable." She finally did look at Clara, barely able to see her face in the shadows that bathed Clara Maybe that was for the best. "When I was a little girl, living with Aunt Bess and Uncle George, I always used to see a man standing in the closet of the room I shared with my cousin Gail." She grew silent, shooting back in time to the bedroom of a terrified young girl. "He'd always stare at me," she whispered, lost in memory. "I was so afraid of him."

Clara was stunned, not only by what she was hearing, but also by the fear she could hear in her mother's voice. She reached out and took a trembling hand in hers. Stephanie didn't even notice, so lost was she in events long past.

"He started moving things in the house. Hiding things. Making noises — bangs, crashes, footsteps." Her voice trailed off.

Clara studied her mother's face, well illuminated by the moonlight, able to see not only fear, but also angry bitterness. "They blamed you, didn't they?"

Stephanie was pulled back to the present by Clara's perceptiveness. She nodded. "Yeah, they did. Life with them was hard enough after our parents were killed, but then to add that on top of it, too... I don't know." She shrugged. "Aunt Bess made me feel like I was crazy and dirty when I'd tell her about the man. I'd try to defend my brother and sister, but she never believed me on that, either. She said I was wicked, and it was all my fault."

"I'm so sorry, Mom. What do you think the man was?"

Stephanie looked at Clara for a long moment, trying to think of a way to answer that. What indeed? She'd never been asked that question before and wasn't sure how to answer it. "I guess I think he was a mean spirit. He enjoyed taunting us, especially me, because he knew I could see him."

Clara allowed what she'd been told to process, mentally filling in spaces that had been left blank by many years of confusion. "So, after the way you were treated, why did you keep yourself in denial about me?"

Stephanie shook her head. "I wasn't in denial, Clara. I was hoping that if I didn't encourage it, maybe you would grow out of it, or block it out. Something. It's not an easy road to take, and I didn't want to see you get hurt. I don't want to see you afraid of a boogie man in the closet of your own."

"Actually," Clara said gently, "she stays in the corner over there."

Stephanie followed where her daughter pointed,

seeing nothing but empty space. She turned back to Clara. "Is she there now?"

Clara shook her head. "No. I haven't seen anyone here all evening. Maybe I left them back at Dad's." They both chuckled at that.

"Well, I hope so. I don't need anything moved around in this house. I have a hard enough time keeping everything straight as it is — including my head."

"I'm really glad you told me, Mom. I wish you would have before now, but I'm glad you did. I needed to know that." She chewed on her lower lip for a moment, unsure whether to continue.

"What, honey? Tell me." Stephanie raised their joined hands and kissed her daughter's knuckles. "I don't want any more secrets between us. This was bad enough."

"Okay." Clara was filled with a mixture of uncertainty and relief. She hoped her mom was telling her the truth that she was, in fact, willing to finally listen. "I see stuff a lot, now. When I was younger, it was sporadic, or I'd just see vague shadows. Something to catch out of the corner of my eye, that kind of thing. Now," she began to whisper, "I see dead people."

Stephanie broke into laughter, Clara grinning at the wonderful sound. It had been awhile since she'd heard a full-out guffaw from her mother. "Well, I'd love to hear all about it, but not tonight." She gave Clara's hand one final squeeze then let go of it as she stood. "I'm exhausted. Guess confessing can do that to a person." She stretched and yawned.

"Yeah, either that or working fifty hour weeks, one or the other," Clara said dryly.

"You can say that again. Okay." Stephanie sighed, dead on her feet. She turned toward the bedroom door.

"Good night, sweetie. I love you."

"I love you, too, Mom." Stephanie was halfway out into the hallway when Clara had the urge to blurt, "Your mom misses you and loves you."

Stephanie stopped in her tracks, a slight chill running down her spine. She turned back to look at her daughter, who was now sitting up in bed. "What?"

Clara looked as though she were a deer caught in headlights. She had no idea why she'd said that or where it had come from. "Uh, I imagine she would. Don't you think?" she said weakly, hoping to cover up for her blunder.

"Yeah. I suppose so," Stephanie said softly, a gentle smile curving her lips. "I love and miss her too." And with that, she quietly closed Clara's bedroom door, and headed off to bed.

Chapter Ten

S he hated the stares. Why did people have to stare? It was rude, disconcerting, and it really ticked Clara off. She sat with her back against the wall, as was her lunch habit, watching her fellow high school students. She was baffled as to why she'd been going to John Freed for nearly half a semester and yet hadn't made one friend. There had to be something terribly wrong with that picture.

She bit into her egg salad sandwich, relishing the tangy taste of lots of Miracle Whip. That had always been one problem when her mom made it: too much egg, not enough of the good stuff.

Clara had tried to get a table, since it was far too cold to eat outside anymore, and she had learned from that first day not to sit against the lockers anymore. She had found herself a fairly clean spot on the floor, which was cold tile and was giving her chills through the seat of her jeans. She glanced down at her half-eaten sandwich as she chewed, fingering a large chunk of egg before plucking it out and popping it into her mouth. It was then that she noticed a pair of black combat boots standing not three feet from her.

The Goth girl from the locker incident looked down at her, a smirk on her red-slashed lips. "Hey," she said.

"I'm not in front of your locker," Clara said defensively. The girl had never spoken a word to her, other than to be incredibly rude.

"Very observant." The girl squatted down to Clara's level and looked into her eyes, leaning in a bit to get a better look. "You have got some wicked eyes," she said. "Like the color of twilight or something."

Clara felt uncomfortable at the up close and personal scrutiny and looked away. "Thanks."

"You're Clara," the girl pointed out, a self-satisfied smile on her face.

"Yes. I know." Clara wasn't sure what to think of this girl. She looked at her face, what she could see beneath the black hair that hid a lot of it.

"I'm Erica." Without invitation, she sat down where she'd been squatting. "You're the one who got 'lost' right?"

Clara grimaced. *Lost? Was that the rumor?* "I didn't get lost," she muttered, tossing the rest of her sandwich into the brown paper lunch sack.

A grin split Erica's face wide open. "That's what I thought." She leaned forward, her dark eyes boring into Clara's. "You saw him, too, didn't you?"

Clara could only stare back at the girl. She was trying to read her, get a vibe off her. Was Erica playing a game with her? Trying to make her look stupid? Would she run back to her friends and tell them all about the "freak"? "Saw who?" she asked, deciding to play it safe.

"The man. He has one of those little paperboy hats," she said, demonstrating with her hand. "My mom used to work here in the lunchroom. She used to see him all the time. Said he carried a big hammer, too."

"It's a wrench," Clara said automatically.

Erica got excited. "I *knew* it! I knew you saw him

too!"

Clara mentally smacked herself upside the head. "Yes, I did. I followed him."

"My mom would love to hear the story. She's a witch and gets into all that shit." Erica reached into her backpack and pulled out a notepad. She spoke as she scribbled something on it. "She owns this shop now. It's down on Prairie." She tore off the sheet and handed it to Clara. "You should go there sometime. She'd like to meet you. I told her all about you." Erica grinned wickedly.

Clara felt a flush of heat wash over her and quickly pushed it aside, unsure of where it stemmed from and feeling uncomfortable with it. "Why?"

Erica zipped her backpack up and slung it over a shoulder as she was about to stand. "Because she's interested in new talent." Getting to her feet, she ran a hand through her hair, pushing it away from her face, only for it to fall back. "I'm having a party at my place next weekend. You should come."

Clara felt her heart stop, and a cold sweat break out over her body. She swallowed. "What kind of party?"

"The fun kind. I wrote my address on that paper I gave you along with my mom's store. If you want to come, it's Saturday night, around nine thirty or ten." With that, she walked away.

Clara watched her go, her stomach in knots at the prospect — part excitement, part dread of having to meet new people in a completely unfamiliar environment. "Man, I wish you were here, Jason," she muttered, and got up to throw her lunch away.

☙ ☙ ☙ ☙

"If you need anything, you call me. Okay?" Max looked at his daughter through the darkness of the cab of the truck. He could tell she was scared but truly thought it was a good idea for her to go. She hadn't made much of an attempt at making any new friends since Jason's death, and even when he'd been alive, hadn't had many. He didn't understand it: Clara was a beautiful young girl with a wonderful intellect and sense of humor. What wasn't to like? Granted, he might be a bit biased.

Clara blew out a long breath, rubbing her palms on the thighs of her jeans. She nodded, glancing at the house they were parked in front of. It was a modest home, nothing huge or too small. It looked average, sitting in an average neighborhood. "It'll be fine," she blew out, more to convince herself than her father.

"Of course it will, sweet pea." He reached over and squeezed her hand. "Go have a good time. Just be smart. I'll be back at midnight."

Clara nodded again, then gathering her courage, reached for the door handle and let herself out, stepping into the cold, October air. She knew her dad was watching her as she made her way up the walk. In one way she wished he'd just go, as she felt like a dork having her dad drop her off. But, on the other side of that very nervous token, she was glad. What if it was a joke after all, and nobody was even home, and Erica had given her a bogus address?

"Stop it, stop it, stop it," she muttered angrily to herself, trying not to let the butterflies in her stomach get the best of her. Before she could take another step, the porch light flicked on and the front door opened. Erica was standing in the warm entrance dressed in her usual all-black attire, a welcoming smile — as much as she was seen giving, anyway — on her lips.

"Hey. Come in."

Clara heard the loud engine of her father's truck rumble off into the night as the front door closed behind her. The inside of the house was dim as they entered what looked to be a typical family room: TV, sofas, low wooden and glass tables, and framed pictures on the walls, though it was entirely too dim to see them.

"Can I take your coat?" Erica asked, tugging at the lapel of Clara's leather jacket. She took it once Clara shrugged out of it. Erica folded it over an arm and headed down a hallway that Clara figured was probably toward the bedrooms.

She walked further into the house, realizing the single light source was coming from the kitchen, and that was a lamp that had dark red cloth covering its shade. There was a breakfast bar where two teenaged boys were sitting, each sipping from a beer. Clara thought she recognized one of them from the halls at school, but wasn't sure on the other. Like Erica, they were dressed in dark clothing, one wearing dark eyeliner.

"Hey," one said; the other raising his beer in salute.

"Hi." Clara felt nearly nude standing there, unsure why she was even there.

"Want a beer?" Erica asked, entering the room and heading to the fridge.

"Um, sure." Clara had never had a beer before and didn't really want one, but figured she might as well try to fit in as much as possible. She took the cold bottle that was handed to her, trying to ignore the jolt that passed through her hand and up her arm as Erica's fingers grazed hers during the transfer.

"Is Richard coming?" the boy Clara recognized asked, finishing his beer and setting the empty bottle next to two others. He accepted the fresh drink Erica offered him, with a huge belch.

"Gross. Yep. He's bringing the twins with him too."

Clara made her way to the opposite side of the kitchen, leaning back against the stove so she could observe. Her gaze scanned the outfits the boys were wearing — black pants with chains hanging off them, the legs so huge she couldn't even tell what kind of shoes they were wearing. One was wearing a black concert tee, the other a black tank top. She glanced at Erica, who was resting her folded arms on the breakfast bar countertop. Her pants were her usual baggy black ones with the heavy combat boots. Her shirt, however, was a deep purple in the dim light of the lamp. It was tight and very fitted to her breasts and flat stomach.

She tore her eyes away only to find she met the other guy's dead on. He smirked at her and took a drink from his beer. It wasn't long before people began to show up — more Goth, Morticia Addams types. Clara felt like she was completely out of her element and wasn't entirely sure what to do about it. She had finished her first beer and was starting on her second, which one of the guys had so kindly brought to her, the cap already popped.

The people around her were laughing and talking, enjoying each other's company. Clara stood back, watching and listening, amused a few times at some of the snippets of conversation she'd been able to take in. Erica zoomed back and forth from the main area of the house where her friends were gathered and the back bedroom, putting away and grabbing coats as people came and went.

As Clara took a long swallow from her second beer, she began to feel a bit dizzy, as though her head were filled with cotton. She set the bottle of beer down, reaching out to grab onto the breakfast bar counter. She blinked several times, finally squeezing her eyes shut and shaking her head, trying to shake off the effects of the moderate, inexperienced drinker-buzz she was having.

She turned and looked at the covered lamp in the kitchen and realized that instead of the muted red light it had once been, it was now a strange gray light, as though the color had been bled from it. She looked around the room, trying to focus. It wasn't exactly black and white but more like what the room would look like if moonlight shining in through a window were the only light during a dark night.

She made her way toward the dining room table, seeing that it was still there, though now it had a strange shape to it, was smaller, and not dark wood. Her footfalls echoed off of wood flooring rather than the carpet, which she'd been walking on all night.

Looking up, Clara gasped, as there was a figure standing not two feet from her. He was a tall man, maybe in his fifties. His face was heavily lined, and the stench of cigarettes clung to him. He said nothing, simply looked at her, his eyes hard and unfeeling. She staggered back, away from him, reaching back to catch herself on the breakfast bar counter, only to fall to the ground. She looked up and saw there was no breakfast bar counter. Only open space leading into the kitchen.

Quickly getting to her feet, she made her way toward the living room, bumping into something she couldn't see. Feeling hands on her, she screamed out, lurching away from those hands, nearly running over a small boy who looked up at her with sad eyes. He wore knickers and leather buckle shoes. He reached for her, but Clara was too terrified to take his hand.

Relax. It's okay. Just relax.

Clara wondered if those were her thoughts or did she just hear that in her head?

Erica's party guests watched Clara with fear and confusion. She seemed to be on some sort of bad trip,. She was screaming out at something, lashing out at thin air. She had run into a couple of the gathered group, and when they'd tried to help her, she only screamed and tried to get away. The girl's eyes were wide and wild, filled with absolute terror.

"What the hell did you put in her drink?" Jacob Phillips asked his friend, Derrick.

"Nothing, I swear. I chickened out." He saw the doubtful look on his friend's face. "I swear, dude. I didn't."

Clara found herself in an open room, which she knew had been the living room of Erica's house. The furniture was gone, as was the TV. She saw looming shadow groups, and felt her heart begin to race when she saw them move toward her. She felt like she was trapped in a horror movie.

She had to run! She darted down a long, narrow hallway, throwing herself into the first open door she found, slamming the door behind her. She pressed her forehead into the cool wood, crying out when she felt hands on her shoulders.

Erica barely missed being slugged by a terrified Clara. "Hey!" she said, shaking the girl to try and get her attention. Clara's eyes were huge, the pupils dilated. She looked through Erica as though she didn't even realize she was there. "Hey, hey, hey. Clara. Come back. It's Erica."

Clara heard her name and stopped, listening to the voice. *Clara. Erica. I know that name.* She blinked, trying to focus, seeing her new friend when she did.

"Hey," Erica cupped Clara's face in her hands, holding the trembling girl's face still. "It's okay. What's wrong? What happened?" Erica's own heart was pounding in her chest.

"I wasn't here," Clara cried, her voice a high-pitched rush. "There was a man. And a boy. It wasn't here. It was so scary. Dark."

Erica listened, remembering her own mother talking about that very place. She grinned, taking a half step away from Clara. "Sounds like you ended up in the after shadow."

Clara took several cleansing breaths, then looked at Erica for the first time since she'd crashed into the room. "What?"

"Come on. Sit."

Clara looked around for the first time and figured she'd stumbled into Erica's bedroom. The overhead light was on, but the walls were draped in black fabric, and the window had a heavy, black drape over it. Candles were placed on just about anything that would sit still, though none were lit.

She was led to a double bed, and with gentle pressure put on her shoulder, sat down.

"I'll be right back. Stay here, okay?" At Clara's nod, Erica left the room, closing the door securely behind her.

Erica marched up the hall, turning on every light she passed until the entire house was lit up like a Christmas tree. Noticing the new atmosphere, the party guests stopped talking, turning to see a seething Erica standing in their midst.

"All right, which of you fuckers did it?" she asked, arms crossed over her chest.

Everyone looked at her, then at each other, confused. "What are you talking about?" a girl named Lacey asked.

"Which one of you put something in Clara's drink?"

Jacob looked at Derrick. He smacked him with his shoulder. "Derrick did."

"What?" Derrick sputtered, his face turning crimson. "I didn't! I swear it, Erica. I was going to, but I totally chickened out. I swear!" He reached into his pocket, pulling out the tiny plastic bag with the white powder in it. The bag was still obviously full.

"I think this was her drink, and it smells fine," someone else said, holding up the mostly full beer Clara had left on the breakfast bar.

Still doubtful and a little worried, Erica decided to call it a night. "Everyone out."

Groaning and muttering their disapproval, the crowd filtered out, plans to continue the party at someone else's house called out to a rush of cheers of agreement. Once the place was empty, Erica went back to her bedroom, closing the door behind her. Clara was exactly where she'd left her, though she'd fallen back on the bed, her feet still on the floor, one forearm resting over her eyes.

"You okay?" She sat down next to her, putting a hand on Clara's leg.

"Fine, other than feeling like I was stepped on by a moose. On my head."

Erica smiled at that. "Listen, I need to ask you something, and need you to answer honestly, okay?"

Clara blew out a breath and nodded, pulling herself to sit up. "Okay."

"Did you take anything, or do you remember anyone offering you anything, or giving you anything?"

Clara shook her head immediately. "No. Nothing like that."

"You're sure? Did your drink taste funny? Like, kind of bitter, maybe?"

Clara thought about it for a moment then shook her head again. "No."

"You don't do drugs on your own, do you?" Erica was baffled. She kicked off her combat boots, curling her legs up as she turned to face Clara on her bed.

"God, no. I never have. I don't believe in them." Clara looked at her with innocent eyes, not sure why Erica looked so confused. "What?"

"So, you're telling me that you got to the after shadow without the help of drugs of any kind?" The doubt in her voice was obvious.

"Well, I don't know. I think you should tell me what the after shadow is before I can answer that question."

"You don't know what that is?" Erica was stunned when Clara shook her head. She could tell the girl was telling the truth. "It's the spirit realm. Well, actually, they say we all live in the after shadow all the time, and that's how people see ghosts, and that kind of stuff. But, where you went was the dark side of the after shadow. It's the place where spirits get stuck. My mom says it's creepy as shit. Was it?"

Clara nodded, a shiver passing through her.

"Yes." She hugged herself.

"Man, that's cool. My mom always takes some sort of herb to get there. I can't believe you went on your own! What was it like?"

Clara closed her eyes, trying to bring back the moment and remember how it started. Her head felt fuzzy, her memory seemingly affected by what had happened to her moments before. "I don't know," she murmured, staring up at the darkened ceiling, trying to bring back the moments. "I guess it felt like being a stranger in a very strange land, and I didn't belong there. It was almost like being awake and trapped in a nightmare. Very strange," she whispered, her thoughts drifting off, back to what Erica called the after shadow.

"You've got to meet my mom. She will absolutely *love* you!"

"I don't know." Clara sighed, sitting up. She ran her hands through her hair, brushing her bangs out of her eyes. A glance at Erica's bedside alarm clock told her it was nearly midnight. Her father would be here any moment. "I need to go. My dad will be here in three minutes."

Erica glanced at the clock then back to the girl sitting on her bed. "Will you hang out with me tomorrow?" she asked, trying to mask the hope in her voice, but not doing a stellar job of it.

Clara was surprised by the invitation. She got to her feet and stretched. "Um, sure. What do you want to do?"

Erica shrugged, also standing. "I don't know." A wicked grin spread across her face. "I'm sure we'll think of something."

❧❧❧❧

Clara finished picking her clothes up off the floor of her bedroom — something she had promised her father she would do before bed — and then stripped out of her clothing from that day, leaving it trailed on the floorboards leading to her bed. The night was cold, so she decided to forgo her usual tank top and panties and put on her flannel pajama bottoms and a T-shirt. The bed was beginning to warm up, as she had turned on her electric blanket before she began to clean up her bedroom.

As she lay in the dark, she thought back over the night at Erica's. She didn't want to think about the beer, or the friends, and certainly not the after shadow. Instead, her thoughts drifted to more pleasurable thoughts. Erica. A small smile spread across her face as she pictured the pretty girl. Erica was a junior — an upper-classmen — and she wanted to spend time with *her*, a lowly freshman!

As Clara thought about her and pictured her, she felt a flush wash through her, as she suddenly knew that Erica liked her. But, what was she supposed to do with that? The topic of Clara's sexuality had never come up with her parents.

"Oh, boy," she murmured, then with a sigh, rolled over to her side and closed her eyes.

❧❧❧❧

Her sleep was somewhat restless, and Clara couldn't stop fidgeting. She was in a strange place between sleep and awake, where strange dreams and visions came at her, yet she was not fully resting, and somewhere inside she was very aware of the surroundings of her bedroom.

Clara.

Clara wrestled with the sheets, her body reacting to hearing her name.

Clara. Open your eyes.

Fear swept through her. She knew she was not alone in the room, yet didn't feel that she was in any danger, per se. She just knew that something was very off.

Clara. Open your eyes for me.

Outside the window a car backfired as it drove down the street. Clara was ripped out of her state of delirium. She sat up, chest heaving. Looking around the dark bedroom, she saw nothing, not even in the corner. She ran a hand through her hair, leaving it to stand on end.

"God, what was that about?" She glanced at her alarm clock and groaned when she saw it was only just after four in the morning. She felt exhausted; her eyes felt like sandpaper had been rubbed into them. She flopped back into the pillow and took a deep breath. Closing her eyes, she decided to give it another try, this time pushing the blankets off her. She always slept better cold, so maybe that would help.

Within minutes, Clara grabbed her covers, bringing them up to her chin. She felt incredibly exposed and vulnerable, and had no idea why. Closing her eyes, she tried to relax herself enough to fall back to sleep. She felt her body begin to calm, her chest rising and falling under soft, even breaths. She could feel her body beginning to float off into relaxation and down into sleep.

Clara. Open your eyes for me. Open your eyes.

Clara wasn't sure if she was dreaming or not. She felt her body react, a thrill of fear and uncertainty reaching into the very depths of her soul.

Don't be afraid, Clara. Open your eyes...

Clara wasn't entirely sure what state she was in. Was she awake? Was she asleep? Wherever she was, she opened her eyes, and standing beside her bed was the beautiful woman with the dark hair that she'd seen twice before.

"Who are you?" she asked, looking into dark, twinkling eyes.

It's time for us to begin, Clara.

"Begin what?" Clara sat up, pulling her knees to her chest and wrapping her arms around her legs.

Your destiny.

The woman's voice was soft, filled with kindness. "I've seen you before."

The woman smiled, nodding.

Many times. More than you realize. I need you to have faith.

Clara felt fuzzy and confused. She was so tired. "Faith? In what?"

The woman smiled again then began to back away from the bed.

Have faith, Clara. I'll be back soon.

Clara found herself staring into a dark bedroom, completely alone. She blinked several times in utter confusion. Had she just seen a woman standing next to her bed? A woman dressed in a simple black dress, her hair pinned back away from her face. Or was she just simply crazy? She buried her face in her hands.

"I'm so confused."

Chapter Eleven

I have to say," Max said, amusement in his voice, "you look like shit."

Clara glared at him, then turned back to her cereal, head resting against the palm of her hand. "Thanks."

"Look, I'm not going to yell at you for drinking, because I know you'll do it anyway. But," he said, pointing his spoon at her, a small chunk of Chex cereal sticking to the rounded back, "don't you ever come to my breakfast table hungover again." Feeling his fatherly duty was done, he tucked back into his cereal.

"I'm not hungover, Dad."

Max looked at her, surprised at Clara's denial. He thought he'd been pretty easy on her. "That's a load of crap."

"I had two beers, yes. Well, one and part of another one, but that's it."

"Then why do you look like hammered shit?"

"Sorry. I was born with this face."

Max threw his head back and laughed, loud and deep. "Oh, you're priceless, kid." He got up, taking his empty coffee cup with him, refilling it, and returning to the table. "If you're not hungover, what's wrong with you?"

"I didn't sleep very well." Clara dug through her bowl of Lucky Charms until she had plucked out all of the rainbow marshmallow pieces.

"That mattress again, huh? We can get you another one—"

"Try some lady was bugging me all night. 'Clara, open your eyes. Open your eyes'," she whispered, wiggling her fingers in a show of monstrous creepiness.

Max looked at her, a brow raised. "What?"

The girl nodded. "Yep. Some woman — a spirit — was in my room most the night." She took a bite of her cereal and chewed, her brow creased in thought. "You know, I think she's been haunting me my whole life."

Max stared at his daughter, coffee cup halfway to his mouth. There she sat, talking about some ghost woman who stays in her room at night like she was talking about what she should do with her Sunday afternoon. "That's creepy, Clara."

Clara shrugged, taking a drink of her orange juice. "Not really. I think she's fairly harmless."

"Did she tell you who she is?"

Clara shook her head. "Nope. We didn't get to formal introductions."

Max smirked and turned back to his breakfast.

"Dad?"

"Yeah, sweet pea?"

"Does it bother you? This stuff that I do?" Clara indicated the space around her with her spoon. Her father looked up, meeting her gaze. "You know, the spirits and stuff."

"No. Should it?"

"Well, no. But, does it creep you out at all? Make you uncomfortable?" Clara nearly held her breath. She wasn't sure why she was asking, because she'd never gotten that feeling from him before. In fact, he'd always seemed interested in what she did and saw. But, somehow she had the feeling that her abilities, or "gifts" as she'd heard them referred to, would become even more a part of her life soon. Very soon.

"Not at all. In fact, I think it's great. I admire you for what you can do."

Clara looked away, feeling suddenly shy by the compliment. "I don't do anything," she muttered. "It just happens."

"That may be, but you've got the guts to go for it. You don't block it out like your mom did." Max's eyes grew big and he tucked his lower lip into his mouth.

Clara grinned. "It's okay. We had a talk. She told me about everything."

"Oh. Okay. Good. I never knew why she didn't want me to say anything." Max sipped his coffee.

"Because she was ashamed. Her aunt and uncle made her feel like she was doing something wrong. She was weird, or a *freak* as Kerri is so fond of saying."

"Eh, Kerri's the freak," Max said, winking with a devilish grin.

"I agree. I've been saying that for years, but no one would listen."

Max got quiet for a moment, deep in thought. There had been something he'd wanted to ask Clara for a week, but had chickened out every time. He glanced at her, saw that she was thoroughly engaged in her own thoughts and her Lucky Charms, so turned back to his own breakfast. Finally he sighed, putting his spoon down. "Clara, I need to ask you something."

"Shoot," she said, shoving a large spoonful of cereal into her mouth.

"How would you feel if I started dating?"

Clara stopped chewing and looked up at him.

"You mean that woman you were fucking before?"

Max sighed, holding his temper down. "I'm going to give you one free pass with a comment like that because I know what I did was crappy. But only one." He held up a finger to emphasize his point. "And you just used it up, kiddo. Got it?"

Clara nodded, trying to stamp down her own anger. She swallowed the rest of the food that was in her mouth and washed it down with a gulp of orange juice. She was trying to stall for time before she had to answer. She could feel his eyes on her, though. Finally she sighed, running a hand through her already morning-mussed hair.

"Why are you asking me?" she asked.

"Because I respect you, and your opinion. I don't want to hurt you any more than I already have. Or Kerri. But, what's done is done, and I've made my decisions in life, and I want to move on."

"So, there's no chance that you and Mom will ever get back together, is there?" Clara tried to be brave, tried to be the little adult she knew her father needed her to be.

"Clara, there were a lot of problems between your mom and me. We didn't share them with you girls because we wanted to protect you." He sighed and shrugged his shoulders. "Maybe that was a mistake. But, we did what we thought was right at the time. The problems had been there for years. It wasn't just something that popped up overnight."

"A guy said that when someone cheats it's because there's something at home they're not getting. Is that true?"

Max smiled. "Who said that? You been watching *Oprah* again?"

"*Montel Williams*, actually."

Max chuckled. "Yeah, I'd say that's about right. There was something missing in your mom's and my relationship."

"Was she a bad wife?" Clara asked, pushing her nearly finished cereal away.

Max shook his head. "No. And it's not that simple. You'll understand more once you get into a relationship of your own. Sometimes," he sighed and shrugged,, "sometimes it just doesn't work. People grow apart."

Clara knew he was right; there was no way she could fully understand without experiencing it herself. It still made her sad, though. "Well, I guess then you have to do what you have to do." She pushed back from the table and stood up. "I need to get in the shower." She cleaned her dishes and stowed them in the dishwasher, then turned to her father. "If you want to date, Dad, I'm not going to stand in your way."

Max watched his daughter leave the room, feeling the resigned sadness radiate off her. It made him feel sad, too. Sad for her and Kerri, sad for Stephanie. And sad for himself. He so often wondered what went so wrong. Where had his life slid off course from what he saw for himself over twenty years ago, when he'd proposed to Stephanie Holdridge. Back then she had been a young, beautiful, vibrant girl of seventeen, just about to graduate from high school. He'd fallen in love with her spirit the first time he'd seen her. Despite the harsh hand life had dealt her already by that time, she hadn't lost her spunk for life, nor her hope for the future.

"What happened, Steph?" he muttered to the empty kitchen.

⚙️⚙️⚙️⚙️

"Are you sure you don't mind? I don't want to push you, or anything," Erica said, her eyes never leaving the road.

"No, that's fine. I'm cool with it." Clara held her hands in her lap, looking every bit the polite little girl as she sat in the passenger seat of Erica's 4Runner. Her emotions were tied up in a mixture of nerves and excitement. She was nervous as hell because Erica made her nervous for some reason, and she was excited, because it felt good to be out with a friend again. It had been a very long time since Jason's death.

"I figure we can kill two birds with one stone." Erica stopped for a red traffic light, only then glancing over at her passenger. She grinned. "Lighten up, Clara. You look scared to death over there, huddled next to the door." She pushed playfully at Clara's shoulder. "I won't hurt you, I promise."

Clara took a deep breath, nodding as she slowly let it out. "Sorry. Guess I'm just a little keyed up."

"It's okay. I just don't want you to be afraid. No reason. I'm perfectly harmless." She grinned and laughed. "For the most part. Anyway, I figured we'd kill two birds with one stone by dropping by my mom's shop so I can deliver that package I told you about, and introduce you to her. She's dying to meet you."

"Okay. I'm fine with that, really."

"Cool." They drove on in silence for several blocks before Erica spoke again. "Listen, about last night. I was thinking a lot about it today before I picked you up. I think it's pretty amazing what you did. Have you ever done that before?"

Clara shook her head. "No. Never. And I've never heard of the after shadow before, either."

"Well, if you're interested, my mom can fill you in a lot more than I can. Did I tell you she's a witch?" At Clara's nod, she continued. "I don't fully understand all that stuff," Erica said, waving off the idea. "I think it's cool and stuff, but I don't really like the spells and all that. Just creeps me out. But you..." She glanced at her passenger. "You're the *real* deal, I think. Like, the real deal."

Clara felt slightly uncomfortable at Erica's enthusiasm. She really didn't want to be the focus of the discussion anymore, and she certainly didn't want their entire day to revolve around what she could or couldn't do. "Erica, would you think I was a total bitch if I asked that we don't talk about my abilities?" She saw the confusion on Erica's face.

"Why? I don't think you're a bitch, but why? It's so cool! You're very special, Clara."

Clara shrugged. "Maybe today I just don't want to be special."

Erica studied her for a long moment then smiled with a nod. "Okay. I'm sorry. I'm just excited."

"It's okay. I'm excited about myself just about every other day, too."

Erica burst into laughter, turning onto Prairie, which would lead to her mother's store.

The Pagan was located off the busy intersection of Prairie and Thorp streets. The squat brick building was nestled between two taller ones. The storefront was made up of two huge windows, posters and coverings blocking the view of the inside. A bell jangled softly as Erica pushed the glass door open. As they walked in, Clara's senses were immediately assaulted by strong incense and soft Indian music.

The walls of the shop were painted a deep purple, much of the wall space covered by hangings of deep red sheer material, much like the walls of Erica's bedroom. Shelves displayed various candles, books and canisters of incense. Pagan jewelry and symbols were also offered under the glass of a locked case.

A tall, rail-thin woman was draped in a material that Clara supposed would be called a dress. The free-flowing material billowed around her every time she moved. Her deep red hair was piled on top of her head, large earrings batted against her long neck with every movement of her head.

"Hey, Cassandra," Erica said, walking over to the woman, who stood behind the counter. "Here's your package."

Clara followed Erica, but continued to look around. She could immediately feel eagle-like eyes on her. She turned to find the woman Erica called Cassandra eyeing her. Her eyes were dark and sharp, much like Erica's.

"Cassandra, this is Clara. Clara, this is my mom." Erica made the introductions casually. Clara was surprised, wondering why Erica called her mother by her first name.

"Nice to meet you, my dear." Cassandra breezed out from behind the counter, never taking her eyes off Clara. "I've heard so much about you." Clara could hear a slight accented lilt to the woman's voice. Romanian, perhaps? Cassandra placed heavily ringed hands on either side of Clara's face, her touch gentle. She looked deeply into the girl's eyes, causing Clara to want badly to squirm. "You have the gift, that is for sure," she said at last.

"How do you know?" Clara asked, taking an unconscious step back from the woman once she was released.

Cassandra went back behind the counter, taking a very sharp dagger and slicing into the tape on the box Erica had brought her. "I see it in your eyes, child. Such beautiful eyes. The soul of one whose subconscious mind has been unlocked. That's what I see." She gave an approving sigh as she unpacked several silver candleholders shaped in the form of a praying goddess.

Clara also looked at the candleholders, thinking them beautiful, if a bit gaudy.

"Well, Cassandra, we're going to head out," Erica announced, grabbing Clara's hand and tugging her toward the door.

"You girls have fun," the older woman said, eyeing the two for a moment before her gaze locked on Clara. "You come back, Clara. I'd love to speak with you."

"Okay. Um, it was nice to meet you," Clara said before she was yanked out into the cold day. Erica let go of her hand as they headed toward her car. "Your mom seems nice." She buckled herself in. "Why do you call her Cassandra, though?"

"Because that's her name," Erica said simply, as though that answered everything.

"Oh." Clara was quiet for a moment, chewing on her lower lip as they merged into traffic. "But, why don't you call her 'Mom'?"

"Because she's not."

"What? Wait. Now I'm really confused."

Erica grinned, never taking her eyes off the road. "You hungry? Want some lunch?"

"Yeah. My Lucky Charms didn't last long, I'm afraid," Clara said, placing a hand on her stomach.

For anyone who was lucky enough to watch Clara eat a sandwich, it was a real interesting experience. Erica sat across from her at a sub shop, one dark brow raised in question. Clara had picked her turkey and American cheese sandwich apart, smearing onto the bread mayo, ketchup and a dab of honey. The stems of the three jalapeños she'd added could be seen sticking out the sides. She put the whole concoction back together, and happily took a bite.

"What?" she managed around the food in her mouth.

"That was disgusting," Erica said, her own sandwich still in its wax paper wrapper. "Do you actually kiss someone after you've eaten something so gross?"

Clara grinned, shaking her head. "Can't say as I've had to worry about that, no."

"Well," Erica said, sipping from her Coke. "You sure as hell wouldn't be kissing *me* after that."

Clara looked down at the table, her face flushed with excited embarrassment. She finally managed to mutter, "I'll remember that."

"Good. You do that." Erica was amused as she watched Clara's flush deepen. *Bingo.* "Does it bother you?" she asked, intentionally being vague. She ripped a bite from her meatball sandwich.

"Does what bother me?" Clara finally was able to make eye contact with the Goth girl.

"When I flirt with you?" Erica popped a Lay's potato chip into her mouth, never taking her eyes off Clara.

Clara swallowed, butterflies doing battle in her

stomach. She shook her head. "No."

"Good." Erica turned her attention fully on her lunch, intentionally leaving Clara to ponder over that little bit of conversation. She had liked Clara since the first time she'd seen her wandering around the mall the summer before. Erica had been working, so hadn't been able to talk to the beautiful girl, but had gotten — and blown — her chance in the restroom later that same day.

Erica had thought that was pretty much it, and Clara was one that got away until she saw her sitting against her locker during lunch on the first day of school. Almost like a gift, all wrapped up and delivered. Then she'd blown it again, by being aggressive. Now here was, hopefully, another shot. She didn't want to blow this, especially since she could sense that Clara was, if not interested, could definitely be persuaded to be. After the boiler room incident at school, which everyone knew about, Erica knew her best chance to get in might be Cassandra and Clara's own abilities. It had worked, and here they were, eating lunch together and whiling away a Sunday.

Clara was caught up in her own thoughts as she forced the rest of her sandwich down. She felt nervous, her stomach tied up in knots. Though Erica was fully engaged in eating her lunch, Clara could still feel a strong energy coming from her. It was like a heat wave washing over her.

While Erica was busy eating, Clara took the chance to really study her new friend. She wondered what color Erica's hair actually was. She tried to tell by the roots, but wasn't able. Maybe her hair was naturally dark? Clara didn't think so. Her gaze traveled to what she could see of Erica's face, made more possible as

Erica tucked one side behind her ear so it wouldn't get into her food. Clara was able to study her face. Dark eyes were topped by delicate arched brows, which, if used correctly, could seem quite sexy or quite bitchy. Erica's features were small and petite, much like her body structure.

Clara's inspection was cut short when her gaze was met by twinkling dark eyes.

"Tell me about you. Are you new to the area?" Erica sat back in her chair, her appetite sated. "I don't remember you from any of the schools around here."

"I was born and raised here, but I used to live on the south side. My parents split over the summer, and I live with my dad now. That's why I go here. My sister is a senior at South."

"Oh wow. That sucks. I'm sorry to hear that. You and your dad close?"

"Yeah. Used to be more so, but..." Clara picked at her Lay's chips, deciding she didn't want them, "something happened over the summer that made me go live with him."

Erica could tell by Clara's expression that it was painful for her. "Hey," she said, reaching across the table and lightly touching Clara's arm. "You don't have to tell me if you don't want to."

"No, it's okay." Clara took a deep breath and let it out before taking a quick sip of her drink. "My best friend Jason was killed this past summer, and I saw it all happen in a dream. I was warned, and my mom wouldn't let me call him or his dad to tell them."

"Jeez! What a bitch!" Erica exclaimed, disgust on her face.

"Well, hold on a sec." Clara explained the talk she'd had with her mother, and though it didn't fix what had happened with Jason and the dream she'd had, it helped Erica to understand.

"Wow. You must have gotten your abilities from your mom, then. It's usually hereditary, and through the mom. So I hear, anyway," Erica amended. "It's still not right, though. Your mom not letting you call, knowing how gifted you are."

Clara shrugged. "Nothing I can do about it, you know? I have to think that maybe Jason was supposed to die. I wasn't supposed to be able to help him." She sighed, playing with her straw. "That's how I sleep at night, anyway."

Chapter Twelve

Clara leaned against the post that held the *No Parking* sign, her bottom lip tucked between her teeth. She stared at the storefront, the CLOSED sign staring back at her. According to the posted store hours, Cassandra would be opening the shop any minute.

She put her hands in her coat pockets, her fingers wrapping around the bus ticket she'd bought. She couldn't wait until she turned sixteen over the summer. Her father kept telling her there was no car in her near future, but she somehow doubted that. Maybe she could get a job and help pay for it.

"Good morning, Clara."

Clara jumped in surprise at the voice that suddenly appeared to her right. She looked to see Cassandra smiling in greeting. "Good morning."

"Early-bird shopper?" the older woman asked, teasing in her voice. She dug out a heavy key ring and slid a silver key into the lock of the store. She held the door open for Clara to follow her inside.

"Yeah. Guess so," Clara said, closing the door behind her and turning the lock as instructed. She was grateful to get out of the bitter cold of the October day, her cheeks red and nose running. Unsure what to do or where to do it, she stood in the center of the store, hands still in her pockets. Cassandra unwrapped her scarf and unbuttoned her coat as she made her way around the counter and through a darkened doorway that led to an unseen room.

"Come back here, Clara," she called.

Clara did as she was asked, and found herself in a small room with a desk and computer, tall filing cabinets, and a coffeemaker. She watched as Cassandra booted up a computer and checked the calendar hung on the wall.

"I wasn't sure if you'd come back or not," she said, never taking her attention from her opening duties.

"Why?" Clara leaned back against the open doorway to the small room, feeling somewhat uncomfortable in such a small space with a total stranger.

"Well," Cassandra said, gracefully lowering herself into the desk chair. "Because you looked frightened the last time you were here." She spared a glance and a smile. "I thought you would run fast and far. Either that or Erica would have scared you away." She smiled. "She can be a scary girl."

Clara smiled and looked away, her cheeks flushing slightly. "No. Not yet."

Cassandra studied the slightly flustered girl. "Hmm. Perhaps not." She slapped her palms on her skirted thighs. "So, dear Clara, what can I do for you that got you out of bed so early? I know how you young girls work. You all love your sleep."

Clara chuckled. "Yes, we do." She felt slight panic for a moment. *Why am I here?* "I was wondering if maybe you could give me some advice. Maybe tarot cards... I'm not really sure."

Cassandra turned the desk chair away from the desk and her opened e-mail and faced Clara, giving the girl her full attention. "You wish to learn," she said simply. At Clara's nod, Cassandra smiled. "Then I will teach you. I will learn much from you in return, I suspect."

"Oh, I don't know about that," Clara hedged, shifting nervously where she stood. "I don't know anything, Cassandra. That's part of the problem."

"No, the problem is you do not understand that a natural gift is just that — natural. A musician, for instance, if he is a natural talent with a guitar will pick up the instrument and begin to play. It may take time and certainly practice, but he will master it soon, yes?" she asked, her accent giving a pleasing spin to her words.

"True."

"Same with a cook. Or an actor. The same is true with you, young Clara. You have a natural gift, and one that should not be taken lightly. Or wasted." She stood, breezing past Clara into the main room of the store, Clara at her heels. "I have many questions for you."

"Like what?" Clara asked, moving to the customer side of the counter as Cassandra began to prepare to open. She headed back to the office for a moment, returning with a money tray which she began to count.

"Well, for instance, Erica told me what happened at her party the other night. Unfortunate in front of a group of teenagers, no doubt, but a wonder all the same." She glanced up at Clara, her hand filled with the stack of one-dollar bills she was counting. "She told you about the after shadow, yes?"

"Yes, she did. Before that, I'd never even heard of it." Clara leaned on the counter, her chin resting in her palm.

"No? Have you gone back since?"

"God, no! It scared the hell out of me!"

Cassandra laughed, a soft musical sound. "It is nothing to fear. The after shadow is a part of life. It can be a dark side of life, but it is part of life, all the same." She inserted the money drawer into the cash register, slamming the cash drawer closed. "Get the sign, will you?" she asked, indicating the CLOSED sign on the door. "Turn the lock, too."

Clara did as she was told, the store officially open for business. She made her way back to Cassandra. "Why is it scary? And, Erica mentioned something about we live in the after shadow now, but there's a dark side to it."

"And she is right. So she does listen, eh?" Cassandra smiled, her dark eyes twinkling. "We do live in the after shadow. The dark side is for those who are lost. It serves as a sort of bridge to the other side. You see, young Clara, the other side — where we go when we die — is actually where life is. This world," she said, indicating the store around them, "is simply a place to learn. School, if you will. Our souls are learning through life, through adversity, and through pain. Negativity is the greatest of all teachers, and there is no negativity on the other side. Only love."

Clara tried to absorb all that she had just been told. Her mind somersaulted over the information, her brain trying to fit it into the world of understanding she'd been given: Christian beliefs, Heaven, Hell, God. "What about God?"

"He exists, but not in the traditional teachings. He is all-knowing, all-powerful, but very different from what the Christians would like to claim. He does not punish. He does not put demands on us."

"Then who does? There's got to be a price for everything, right?"

"Of course. We put the demands on ourselves, Clara. Our souls. We determine what our lives will be, who we'll be, and what we'll learn before we ever make the journey back to this realm."

"Back? As in reincarnation?"

"Exactly. But," Cassandra said, placing heavily ringed fingers on Clara's arm, "these are only my beliefs, Clara. I do not expect you to follow them. You must follow your own heart and your own gift. All right?"

Clara nodded, not entirely sure what to think. "Okay. I do want to learn." They were interrupted when the bells above the door announced the entrance of a small group of older women.

"Do me a favor, Clara, and go light the incense." Cassandra handed the girl a box of matches.

⁂

Clara had found an interesting book, which she read while tucked away in an out-of-the-way corner of the store. The three ladies who had come in were still with Cassandra, the four chatting away about candles and the importance of colors and duration of burn. Clara had long ago stopped listening, instead reading about tarot cards and their many uses. She had always found tarot cards interesting but had never owned a deck, and wasn't entirely sure she wanted one. The cards and their uses just didn't call to her. All the same, it was an interesting intermission while Cassandra was busy.

"Psst..."

Clara jumped, startled. She saw a grinning Erica squatting beside her. "That wasn't very nice. You scared me."

"That was the point." Erica got herself settled on the floor beside her. "What are you reading?" she asked, lifting the book so she could see the cover. "*Tarot and You.* Gonna get a deck?"

Clara shrugged. "I don't know. Just passing time while Cassandra deals with those women."

Erica followed Clara's gaze to see the three women speaking with the shop owner. "Ah. You'll be waiting awhile. Those are the Frank sisters. They'll keep Cassandra busy for hours." She checked her watch. "And I'd guess they already have. When did you get here?"

"Awhile ago," Clara hedged, slightly embarrassed to admit she'd been waiting for Cassandra before the shop even opened.

"Well, I just got off work, thus the smell of greasy fries. Want to go grab something to eat?"

Clara was amused by the hope she saw in Erica's dark eyes and utterly charmed by it. She nodded. "Okay."

≈≈≈≈≈

Even with the light of day shining in through the windows in the rest of the house, Erica's room didn't look much different. Clara wandered around the small room, the sound of Erica's shower running in the distance. She reached out, touching the material that was draped on the walls, its softness gliding against her fingertips. She wondered why Erica had created a virtual tomb for herself as a sanctuary. The material covering the window above the bed had been so completely covered that not even one tiny lick of sunlight managed to sneak in.

She noticed the candles that were placed all over, most well used with frozen droplets of melted wax running down the sides. Most of the candles were black, though some were red and a few were white. Her gaze wandered to Erica's bed, bringing back memories of the party. She remembered lying on that bed, trying to get her bearings after her strange trip into the after shadow.

The bedding was a dark purple, the bed not made, so the grape-colored sheets were visible. The two pillows were askew, as though Erica had been lying on one while hugging the other in her sleep. In her mind's eye, she could almost see Erica lying there. She wondered if she even slept in black pajamas. This thought was interrupted by the sound of someone entering the room.

"Thanks for waiting. I really appreciate it."

Clara turned to see Erica standing just inside her bedroom doorway, her hair still wet, a towel vigorously rubbing through it to dry the dark strands. Erica didn't have a bit of makeup on, and Clara was amazed at just how beautiful the girl really was. Without all the heavy darkness around her eyes, and the slash of red across her lips, she had a youthful, innocent look to her. The black hair looked horribly out of place with that face, convincing Clara that Erica's natural hair color must be a lighter shade of brown, or perhaps even blonde.

Her gaze fell from Erica's face and hair to the white tank top she wore, a bit short and showing creamy white stomach with the movement of Erica's hair-drying. Erica didn't wear a bra, and her nipples stood erect under the thin white cotton of her tank. Clara swallowed. Hard.

Erica stopped her drying, her gaze finding Clara's eyes, and realizing where those twilight eyes were latched onto. She looked down at herself then back at Clara, a smirk firmly planted on her lips. "Like what you see?" she asked, tossing the wet towel to her laundry pile in the corner.

Clara nearly choked over her tongue at being caught. She looked into Erica's eyes, expecting to see her angry or offended at such crass behavior, but what she saw couldn't be further from offended. She swallowed again, her hands finding their way into the back pockets of her jeans as she began to shift nervously.

"It's okay, Clara," Erica said, slowly making her way to her fidgety friend. "You can look all you want."

Clara couldn't look at Erica as she advanced, instead her eyes finding perch anywhere else they could. She could feel the girl's body heat getting closer, could smell her freshly washed skin and hair. It was all intoxicating. Clara's heart began to pound in her chest, nearly painful in its excited cadence.

"I really like you, Clara," Erica said softly, brushing Clara's forearm with her fingertips, marveling at the soft skin she found there. "A lot."

Clara took several deep breaths, wanting to speak, but unable to say a word. Nothing could get past her frantic heart or her dry throat. Instead, she found the courage to look into Erica's eyes.

"I think you like me too. Am I right? If I'm wrong, it's okay," Erica said, for just a moment her slight insecurity showing through, which, though she didn't realize it, made Clara feel better.

Clara still couldn't speak, so she simply nodded her head.

Erica stopped her advance, their breasts nearly touching. "I'd really like to kiss you. Can I?"

Clara felt a wave of heat wash through her, her stomach dropping south. She nodded again, her body trembling a bit.

"Why are you shaking?" Erica asked, bringing up a hand and cupping Clara's chin. "Are you afraid?" At Clara's nod, she smiled. "You don't have to be. I'm not going to hurt you." She ran her fingers through soft, brown hair, brushing long bangs out of beautiful twilight eyes. "You've never kissed anyone, have you?"

"No," Clara whispered, her gaze falling from Erica's eyes to her lips, then back to dark eyes. "Never."

"That's okay." Erica smiled with understanding. "We all have our first."

"Have you? Kissed someone before?"

Erica nodded. Her hand left Clara's hair and slid to cup her jaw. "I'll go easy," she promised.

Clara thought her heart was going to pound right out of her chest as Erica got closer. She'd seen enough in movies and TV to know to close her eyes. As darkness filled her visual world, her sensory one exploded with color and sensation. Erica brushed her lips against Clara's, the other girl so soft and gentle. Clara immediately wanted her to return, which she did. The second pass had a bit more pressure but was still infinitely soft.

"You okay?" Erica whispered against Clara's mouth. At the younger girl's nod, she moved in a bit closer, pulling Clara to her with an arm around her back. Their bodies made full contact with a gasp from Clara. Erica smiled then deepened the kiss. She knew she'd have to take it slow, as she didn't want to scare her before they'd even started.

Clara tried to follow Erica's lead, afraid she'd screw it up and the older, experienced girl wouldn't like her anymore. She tentatively reached out a hand, resting her palm against Erica's waist. The warm skin beneath the thin cotton nearly burned her at the touch. A small sigh escaped her as yet another wave of warmth flowed through her, landing squarely between her legs.

Erica gently stroked the side of Clara's face and neck, tilting her head so their lips would fit better. Within moments she'd coaxed Clara's lips open, and she gently stroked the inside of the other girl's mouth. She deepened the kiss as she pressed their bodies even closer, her hand sliding down Clara's back until finally it rested just above her ass, unsure how far she'd be allowed to go.

Clara started, realization dawning on her: she was kissing a girl, and that girl's hand was nearly on her butt. It wasn't that she wasn't enjoying it, because she was. Thoroughly. But, a trip of fear and uncertainty made her push lightly against Erica's shoulder.

"Wait," she said, her voice breathy from her excitement.

"Are you okay?" Erica dropped her hands from Clara's body, taking a half step back. "Did I do something wrong?"

"No! No. Not at all. I just..." Clara blew out a breath, running a trembling hand through her hair. "I just need a minute."

"Okay." Erica's insides were flying, her heart

pounding, inner thighs slick. She could tell by the flushed cheeks of Clara that she had enjoyed it just as much. "Are you okay?" she asked again.

Clara nodded. "Yes, I'm fine." Clara took a deep breath then grinned at Erica. "That was nice. Can we do it again, sometime?"

Kim Pritekel

Chapter Thirteen

Max rubbed the back of his neck as he paced once more across the living room of his estranged wife's home. Stephanie sat on the couch, sipping a cup of coffee. Max had been there less than twenty minutes, just long enough to get out the reason for his visit.

"So?" he asked, stopping his pacing just long enough to spare her a glance. "What do you think?"

"Well, do you think she'll be able to handle it and her school work?" Stephanie asked, pushing to her feet to head to the kitchen. She could hear Max following her.

"I'm not sure. She's doing well. She's gotten A's and B's on her reports and school work so far this semester."

Stephanie refilled her mug. "Are you sure you don't want some?" she asked, raising the half-filled pot. When Max shook his head, she refilled her own, adding cream and sugar. "What about waiting until the semester ends? That's only in what, just over six weeks?"

"She's not going to like that," Max warned, leaning his backside against the counter, arms crossed over his chest.

"Well, then I'd say it's a good thing you're the parent then, wouldn't you?" Stephanie drawled, blowing on her coffee to cool it down.

"I'm very aware of my role, Stephanie," Max bit back. "You don't have to live with her. She chose to stay with me, remember?" Max regretted the words the moment they were out of his mouth, and felt even worse when he saw the tears that immediately welled up in his wife's eyes. For some reason he hadn't been able to go down to the courts and draw divorce papers yet. "Aw jeez, Steph, I'm sorry. That was a really shitty thing to say."

"Yeah Max, it was." She angrily wiped at her tears before they could fall. She didn't want to give him that satisfaction. Not anymore. "Well, if she's your daughter, staying at your place, then why the hell are you here? I couldn't possibly be any help to you."

"Stop it. Just stop the damn theatrics right now!" Max could feel his anger rising. He hated the passive-aggressive stuff, and it was a big reason for his leaving in the first place. "I said I was sorry and that's the end of that. It was shitty, and I admit it. I came here to talk to you about *our* daughter. Now, can we please continue like adults?"

Stephanie took a moment to gather herself then nodded, knowing full well he was right. She was angry at herself for falling back into her old patterns. Her counselor, Brittany St. James, had been talking a lot about that with her. "I'm sorry too. I'm trying to break myself of that," she said softly, staring into her coffee. "Brittany has been working with me on it."

"Brittany? Is that the lady you've been seeing?"

Stephanie nodded, blowing out a long breath. "Okay, so where were we?"

"I was about to tell Clara that she has to wait until winter break before she can begin working at that metaphysical store, and I was about to have to hear an earful of whining protest."

Stephanie grinned. "Better you than me, bucko. Guess that's what you get for charming our daughter away from me."

Max was about to let loose when he saw the twinkle in her eyes. "Cute," he said instead. "All right. I agree with you. I think right now — her freshman year, she's only fifteen — waiting till winter break is the best way to go."

"Okay. I'll back you up." Stephanie set her mug down, imitating Max's position. "How is she doing? She talks to me, but I'm never sure if she tells me everything that's going on in her life. Is she making any friends?"

"Did she tell you about Erica?" Max walked over to the fridge, suddenly in the mood for a beer. He had his hand on the handle when he remembered it was no longer his house. He stopped, awkward. "Um, do you mind...?"

"No. There's Miller Light in the door." Stephanie watched as Max got himself a beer, her heart hurting at a sight that was once so familiar. She cleared her throat to clear away the memory. "Erica?"

"Yeah. Some little Goth girl she met. A junior. Seems nice enough. I guess her mom owns the shop where Clara wants to get the job."

"She hasn't mentioned her." There was hurt in Stephanie's voice.

"Eh, it's a pretty recent thing. I think the only reason I know about it is because I dropped her off at the girl's house one night."

Stephanie was silent for a long moment. Even though her youngest was upstairs, asleep in her old bedroom, she felt so removed from her. It varied how often she saw Clara. Sometimes it was twice a month, sometimes twice a week, sometimes she'd go an entire month without seeing her at all. It was all up to Clara, which made it so difficult. The times when she didn't see Clara at all, or saw her less, she couldn't help but wonder if it was something she'd done wrong. Had she let the girl down as a mother somehow? Never-ending questions and doubts. She wondered if she'd ever get used to it, and, in some ways, hoped she wouldn't. If she got used to it, would that mean she no longer cared as much?

Max watched Stephanie, paying careful attention to her expression as her emotions changed with her thoughts. He'd known the woman for more than half of her life and knew well what was going on inside her mind. No matter how many problems they'd had as a couple, there was never any doubt about how much she loved her children.

"This is harder on her than you think, Steph," he said softly. "I think Clara is very confused by all this. It doesn't help that she's never even so much as had a boyfriend, let alone a husband to understand what can happen between two people. She loves you, and she hurts."

"How did we mess it up so badly, Max?" she asked, her hand covering her mouth as she tried to keep her emotions under control. There was no answer from Max, which she didn't expect there to be. It had mostly been a rhetorical question, anyway.

"What's important is that no matter what, we've got to keep the girls in mind first. We decided to bring them into this world, and very fucked-up situation, so now we've got to protect them."

"Yeah." Stephanie blew out a breath, suddenly feeling very tired. "You're right."

Max threw back the rest of his beer, then tossed the bottle in the trash. "I should go." He grabbed his keys off the counter. "If you need me to pick Clara up Sunday let me know."

"Okay. I should be able to get her home. Or Kerri can. But thanks." Stephanie followed him to the door, watching as he stepped onto the front porch. He turned and gave her a smile and a small wave. "Be careful. Are you okay after drinking that beer?"

"Yeah, fine," he called as he made his way down the path toward his truck. "'Night."

Stephanie watched him climb in and turn on the engine. "Good night, Max," she sighed and closed and locked the front door.

❧❧❧❧

Clara stopped talking, bringing a hand up to cover the phone as she thought she heard footsteps in the hall outside her door. She was right; she heard Kerri's bedroom door open then close.

"I'm going to have to go soon," she said, uncovering the phone. "My sister will want to use the phone."

"When can I see you again?" Erica asked, impatience in her voice. "How long are you stuck at your mom's?"

"I'm here until Sunday." Clara tried to fight her sadness, as she wanted to see Erica in the worse way. It had been a whole day! She brightened as an idea hit her. "I'm going to a movie with my mom and Kerri tomorrow. Why don't you come over after? We can hang out here."

"Will your mom mind? I mean...you know."

Clara grinned. "We're not going to make out in the living room or anything," she said, then immediately blushed. She could hear Erica's laughter on the other end of the line.

"You're all flushed, aren't you?"

"No," she lied.

"Yes you are. You're blushing! You're blushing!"

"Stop!" Clara buried her face in her hand.

Erica laughed. "Okay, okay. I have to work until three. What time is your movie?"

"Noon."

"Okay. I'll call you when I get home and showered. What's your mom's number?"

Clara gave her the familiar digits then quickly hung up the phone as the line had already been picked up twice in just the five minutes since Kerri had gone into her room.

"Phone's free!!" she yelled out.

She plopped onto her back on her bed, staring at the ceiling, a hand resting on her stomach. She felt giddy and goofy all at the same time. *I kissed someone! Better yet, someone kissed me!*

"That is *so* cool," she whispered.

They had spent the rest of that day together, hanging out at the mall for a while then going to see a movie. They'd glance at each other shyly then laugh at their own antics. Clara felt her heart flutter every time she had seen Erica at school over the previous week. They were in different grades, which meant their classes were in different halls and typically different levels of the building. Seeing each other was rare, though Erica had given her a ride home the one day that Erica didn't have to report immediately to work.

They hadn't really talked about the kiss since it happened, but Clara could feel the same intense energy coming off Erica in waves ever since. She felt the older girl wanting to find a way to do it again, and Clara was more than willing to give it another round, but wasn't sure how to go about it. She figured Erica knew more about that kind of stuff so she would leave it to her.

⁂

Clara found herself sitting on a stone bench, which was cold beneath her. She looked around, noting the sky was a strange yellow-gold, rose hue in color. No clouds floated by, only the bright purity of color. The ground at her feet was inlaid stones, cut into geometric shapes, the bench sat in the circle they created. Behind her was a hedge, probably at least five feet high, thick, and lush. The hedge wall formed a horseshoe-shape, leaving an opening, which Clara looked out of.

A pathway led from the circle of stones to a small knee-high maze of cut hedges, which she could see was in some sort of Celtic knot pattern. Beyond that was another path, which connected to another circular setting of the inlaid stones and a bench similar to the one she sat on. Instead of a hedge wall around that circle, there was a huge X-shaped sculpture behind the bench.

"Beautiful, isn't it?"

Clara whipped around, shocked to find the dark-haired woman sitting next to her. "You scared me."

"I'm sorry." She smiled, bringing a hand up and gently caressing the side of Clara's face. "You've turned into such a beautiful young woman, Clara. Like your

mother." Her dark hair was pulled back away from her face, her dark eyes with the ever-present twinkle in them. She wore dark clothing, fitted close to a petite frame.

"Who are you?"

"My name is Rebecca. But you can call me Grandma."

Clara was confused as she looked at the woman who couldn't be any more than thirty. "Grandma?" she asked. The woman nodded. Before Clara could say anything else, the woman changed. Her dark eyes turned green, black hair brown, cut in a style that Clara was very familiar with. Suddenly, before her sat her grandmother, her mother's long-dead mother. She gasped, tears springing to her eyes.

"Shhh. It's okay," Rebecca said, wiping away a few stray tears, even as her appearance slowly faded back to that of the woman with dark hair and eyes. "I've been watching you for a very long time. Your whole life, actually."

"Why do you look like this? I don't understand..."

"This," Rebecca said, looking down at herself, "is what my soul looks like. You know me by what I looked like in my last life. But, I assure you, I'm one and the same." Her smile was contagious, and Clara felt herself return it, if shyly. "I've been waiting a long time to talk to you. But first, there's someone who wants to say hello."

Clara followed her grandmother's pointing finger, a gasp and a cry escaping her throat. She was on her feet and running toward the Celtic hedge maze. Jason wrapped his arms around her, holding her tightly against him as she cried.

"I'm so sorry," she sobbed into his shoulder. "I

wanted to warn you."

"Shh. Hey, I know," he soothed, rubbing her back. "It's okay. Everything happens as it's supposed to, Clara."

She pulled away from him just enough to look up into his eyes. She studied his face, pulling away a bit more to look him over. He looked as young and strong as ever. "Why do you look like you and she doesn't?" she asked, indicating Rebecca, who still sat on the bench, patiently waiting.

"How else were you going to recognize me?" he asked, a brow raised in question. Clara half-laughed, half-sobbed as she hugged him close again.

"God, I've missed you." She pulled away after a long moment, wiping her eyes with the sleeve of her shirt.

"I've missed you too. I have to go now, Clara, but please tell my dad that I love him, and I don't blame him, okay?" He looked her dead in the eyes, making sure she fully understood. "Okay?"

"Okay. I promise."

Jason squeezed her arm as he began to back away, never taking his eyes off her. "And Clara, look for the birds."

Clara stared after him as he turned and walked toward the X sculpture, fading into the bench until he was gone. "The birds?" she asked, confused.

"Come sit with me, Clara. We have a lot to talk about," Rebecca called softly from the bench.

Clara turned to face her, a flutter of love in her belly. As she looked at the woman sitting there, her youthful face and eyes, somehow she knew that Rebecca was telling the truth. In her eyes she saw the truth, and she saw the love she always felt when she looked at the *picture in the living room of her mother's house. Though this time there wasn't the grief and heartache to go along with it.*

"Where is this place?" she asked, once again sitting next to Rebecca.

"This is the other side. The place where you'll return to when you die."

Clara looked around, stunned. "Is this Heaven?"

Rebecca chuckled. "If you want to call it that, but that's not entirely correct." She shrugged. "It's the other side."

Clara studied her for a long time, her grandmother's gaze unwavering. "You are my grandmother, aren't you?"

Rebecca smiled. "Yes, Clara. I am. I died in that car accident in 1958 with your grandfather and your aunt, Carol Ann. Your mother, her younger brother, and sister were the sole survivors."

Clara could hear sadness in Rebecca's voice, as well as a slight hitch. "I'm sorry," she whispered, wanting badly to give Rebecca a hug. "Can I..." she chewed on her bottom lip. Without having to say anything else, Rebecca opened her arms. Clara's eyes slid closed as she felt herself engulfed in warmth and love like she'd never known. It was beyond unconditional. It was beyond motherly and beautiful. It was a truly religious experience.

"I love you, little Clara," Rebecca whispered. "I always have. Your mother too. Will you tell her that for me? That I love her and I'm sorry?"

Clara nodded, her eyes closed as she allowed herself to be rocked and caressed.

ॐ ॐ ॐ ॐ

Clara's eyes opened wide as she was pulled into the world of the wakened. She looked around the bedroom, trying to figure out what had woken her. The knock sounded again on the door.

"Clara, honey, are you awake? I need you to open the door." Stephanie's muffled voice came from the hall.

Groggy, Clara pushed the covers off and made her way to the door, rubbing the sleep out of her eyes.. She pulled the door open to find her mother standing there with a tray laden with steaming pancakes, freshly cooked bacon and eggs, and tall glasses of orange juice and milk, and a smile.

Stephanie hurried past her daughter, about to drop the heavy tray. "Come on. Have breakfast with me."

Clara walked back to the bed, sitting cross-legged as her mother got everything organized and ready for consumption.

"I know damn well that you're surviving off Lucky Charms at your dad's," she continued, preparing everything exactly how her daughter liked it. "So," she said, finally meeting Clara's gaze, "I wanted to make you something special this morning."

"Grandma says she loves you and she's sorry," Clara blurted out, having no idea where that had come from. Since opening the door for her mother, the strange dream she was having had already begun to fade into strange images of hedges and X-shaped sculptures. And Jason. Oh, Jason. She felt tears sting at the backs of her eyes as she cut herself a fluffy bite of pancake.

"She did?" Stephanie asked, fighting her knee-jerk need to deny what Clara said. "When?" She slid a bite of scrambled egg into her mouth.

"I'm not sure," Clara said, brows drawn. "I just know that she told me to tell you that."

Stephanie forced a smile. The subject of her dead parents had always been a difficult one for her. It brought back memories of a cruel aunt and uncle, and the feeling of being abandoned her entire life. "I'm glad you did, sweetie. Thank you."

Clara nodded, tucking into her breakfast with vigor.

⁂

The movie and day spent with her mother was a good one. The movie had sucked, but Stephanie was always fun to hang around with, though Clara would never admit that aloud. She was grateful that she had gotten permission for Erica to come over, which she did around six thirty that night.

"And," Clara said with a flourish, flinging her door open, "this is my room."

Erica stepped inside, looking around with open curiosity. She wondered what the sleeping digs of the younger girl would look like. Clara was a bit of a mystery to her. One minute she was quiet and introspective, the next she was jabbering on about whatever came to her mind. But, all in all, she found her to be a quiet, shy girl who was filled with unwitting charm and definite beauty.

"Very nice." Erica walked over to a poster of a famous singer. "I wouldn't have placed you in the Jon Bon Jovi fan camp," she said, tapping the poster with a finger.

"Yeah, well," Clara said, feeling shy and extremely nervous at having her new friend in her bedroom. She'd already given her the tour of the rest of the house, purposely leaving the room for last. "I don't seem like a *lot* of things."

"This is very true," Erica said, walking back over to Clara. "I missed you this week," she said, her voice low. She took hold of Clara's hand as she walked past her just far enough to push the bedroom door closed, then she tugged the girl until they were nearly body to body. "A lot."

Clara felt her heart begin to do a jig in her chest. "I missed you too." She swallowed, feeling her breathing begin to pick up just a bit. Erica let go of her hand, sliding her palm up Clara's arm, over her shoulder, and finally to the back of her neck and head.

"God," Erica whispered, her lips nearing Clara's. "I've been wanting to do this all week."

Clara's eyes slid closed, only to pop open when there was a loud knock at the door. "Shit!" Clara hissed, jumping away from Erica and heading to the door. Kerri stood on the other side.

"Hey," the older girl said. "I'm going to Abby's for a party tonight and don't know if I'll be back before you leave tomorrow."

Clara felt her stomach clench slightly at the mention of her sister's blonde friend, and then felt immediately guilty, as Erica stood next to her. "Okay. Have fun and it was good to see you."

Kerri gave her a half-hearted, one-armed hug then headed out, never giving Erica the time of day.

"That was my sister Kerri," Clara explained, her hand on the doorknob to close it when she heard her mother's voice.

"Hey girls?" Stephanie called from the bottom of the stairs. "You want some popcorn and a movie?"

Clara glanced at Erica. "You hungry?"

※ ※ ※ ※

Stephanie was completely unaware of the longing looks tossed back and forth between her movie mates. She sat on the couch, feet up on the coffee table and happily munched on popcorn. Clara sat next to her, Erica on the comfortable chair that matched the sofa and loveseat. She liked Clara's new friend, but didn't understand why she'd cover up her natural beauty underneath all that heavy makeup and dark, creepy eye shadow.

Clara was miserable. She wanted nothing more than to grab Erica by the hand and run upstairs to her bedroom with her and be kissed again. She felt guilty, knowing that she saw her mother so rarely and didn't have the heart to decline Stephanie's invite to them. Her only solace was that the movie was almost over. On the flip side, it was nearly ten, and she wasn't sure how long Erica would be allowed to stay.

Erica, for her part, wanted nothing more than to grab Clara, throw her down onto her bed, and undress her with her teeth. She glanced over at the center of her carnal interest, her gaze falling to Clara's breasts, hugged tight in a knit sweater. She groaned inwardly. *Goddess, give me patience.*

The movie came to end and the credits began to roll. Stephanie stretched, smiling at her daughter. "Did you like it? The girl at the rental place said it was good. She was right."

"Yeah. It was great, Mom. Thanks." Clara gave her

mother a smile, which she hoped Stephanie believed. She glanced at Erica, silent communication passing between them just before Clara glanced at the clock. "Mom, it's getting kind of late, and I was wondering if maybe Erica could just stay the night."

Erica was stunned — though secretly thrilled — at the prospect. She looked from Clara to Mrs. Greenwold, trying to give her best, most innocent look.

Stephanie looked from one hopeful face to the other, then back again. "Sure, sweetie." She smiled and leaned over to kiss her daughter goodnight. "You guys keep it down." She looked at Erica. "Please make sure it's okay with your mom, okay?"

"Sure thing, Mrs. Greenwold," Erica said, taking the cordless phone that Clara passed to her.

Clara climbed the stairs, easily picking up on Erica's energy behind her. Once they entered her bedroom, she closed the door, but before turning around, she said, "Can we maybe talk for a while?" She was nearly trembling, wanting Erica to kiss her again, but she didn't want it to just be that. Plus, she was nervous and worried about where the kissing would lead. She could sense how excited Erica got and had no doubt the older girl wasn't new at all of this.

"Sure," Erica said, sitting on the edge of Clara's bed. "What do you want to talk about?" Erica tried to keep the disappointment out of her voice, knowing she had to take it easy with Clara.

"Well," Clara said, walking over to her friend. She pushed her back on the bed, positioning Erica so her head rested on one of the pillows. She walked over to the light switch and flicked it off, the glow-in-the-dark stars coming to life. She lay down next to Erica, her hands resting safely on her stomach. "I don't know.

Anything."

Erica stared at the solar system above her. "Wow. That's really cool." As she stared at the stars, she felt like she could reach up and touch them. Doing just that, she could barely make out her raised arm in the darkness, her fingertips only touching air.

"Thanks. I've been staring at those most of my life." Clara glanced over at Erica, not able to see her profile just yet, her eyes not adjusted to the darkness of her bedroom. Slowly, however, her friend began to come into shadowy focus. "How long have you been into girls?" she nearly whispered.

Erica turned her head, looking where she figured Clara's face should be. "All my life, I think. I was pretty young when I knew. That much I know for sure."

"Does Cassandra know?" Clara turned to her side, sliding her arm underneath her pillow and head.

Erica nodded, but then remembered Clara likely couldn't see the gesture. "Yeah. I think she knew before I did, actually."

"Is she cool with it?"

Erica smirked. "There's very little I could do that Cassandra wouldn't be cool with." She also turned to her side, able to see a bit more of the younger girl. "Have you always known you were into girls? Or are you even into girls? Are you just into me?"

Clara smiled. "No. I like girls. I think I figured it out — well, was able to admit it to myself, anyway — last year. I never told anyone. Not even Jason."

"Why?"

Clara shrugged the shoulder that wasn't pressed into the mattress. "I don't know. Afraid, I guess. I'm not sure what my parents will say. My sister will call me a freak, I'm sure." She sighed, feeling somewhat sorry for herself. "I don't know if I can ever tell them."

"Give it time. I'm sure it'll be fine."

They lay in contemplative silence for a moment before Clara spoke. "If Cassandra isn't your mother, who is she?"

"It's a long story, Clara," Erica said, feeling somewhat protective of her past.

Clara grinned. "Good thing we've got all night then, huh?"

Erica returned the grin, able to almost totally make out Clara's features now. "Cute. Okay, fine."

"If you don't want to tell me, don't."

"No. I'll tell you, though I doubt you'll believe me. My mother and Cassandra were girlhood friends, growing up in a tiny town in Romania. They belonged to a gypsy family. One day my mother got pregnant — raped — and guess what? Poof! Here I come." There was slight bitterness in her voice. "She died during childbirth and made Cassandra promise she'd take me to America and raise me. So, she did."

"If she raised you from birth, why don't you just call her mom?" Clara asked, unable to stop herself as she reached out and touched Erica's arm.

"Because she didn't want me to. She always told me about my mom and what she was like. Gave me pictures of her. Cassandra didn't want me to forget her or try and replace her, so I've always called my mother Mom and Cassandra by her name."

Clara was quiet for a moment. "You're right. I don't believe you." She giggled as she suddenly found herself the victim of very fast and very *strong* tickling fingers.

"You don't, huh?" Erica said through clenched teeth, grinning as she pinned Clara to the bed with her playful assault.

"No!" Clara cried, though Erica wasn't sure if she was telling her to stop tickling her or that she didn't believe her.

"'No' what? Huh?" She had moved so she was straddling the younger girl, who continued to squeal at her attack.

"Okay!" Clara cried, trying desperately to grab Erica's hands so she'd stop tickling her. "I believe you! I believe you!"

Erica stopped, nearly panting from the exertion. She chuckled as she moved off Clara, lying on her side next to the girl who was sprawled on her back. "You're fun," she said, brushing some bangs out of Clara's eyes.

Clara got herself under control. "You, too." She rolled onto her side, holding herself up on one elbow so she could look down at her friend. "Is that true about your mom?"

"Yes," Erica said, her voice soft. She looked up into Clara's eyes, mesmerized by their color and depth. "Come here."

Clara leaned down, one of Erica's hands finding its way to the back of her head, fingers losing themselves in the short locks of her hair. The kiss was immediate, both girls sighing into the contact. Clara loved the feel of Erica's tongue moving against her own, and opened her mouth a little wider, accepting more inside.

Erica slowly urged Clara closer, until finally she had gotten her to lie atop her. Clara wasn't sure what to think. The feel of Erica's length against her own was sending shooting waves of pleasurable heat between her legs. At the same time, it felt incredibly bizarre to lie on top of another person's body. She was worried she would hurt Erica, whose frame was petite, but with enough of Erica's urging, she finally lowered herself completely, resting her weight on her forearms on either side of Erica's head.

Erica was anxious to feel Clara's body and ran her hands down and over her shoulders and back as the kissing continued. She was so turned on and could tell Clara was too. She ran her hands down Clara's sides, able to feel her breasts. She was pleased by the surprised little gasp that incited, as well as the way Clara's hips bucked slightly, completely involuntarily. Erica took that opportunity to shift their positions slightly.

Clara wasn't sure what Erica was doing and nearly moved off her when she felt a thigh come in contact with her center, sending shocking jolts throughout her entire body. She broke the kiss, her forehead finding Erica's shoulder as she pressed down against the pressure.

"That feels so good," she breathed, her breaths ragged and hot against Erica's neck as she placed a kiss there.

"I know," Erica whispered, her hands finding Clara's backside and grabbing hold, pressing Clara more firmly into her thigh. "Ride it, baby," she whispered.

Clara couldn't stop. It was as though her body had totally gone out of her control. The pleasure was coursing through her, and she couldn't stop it, didn't want to stop it. She buried her face in Erica's neck as her orgasm exploded. Erica held on as Clara's body shook violently, her own arousal pushed back by the surprise of how hard the other girl's body had reacted.

Clara felt immense shame as she pulled away from Erica, tears running down her face. She moved away, curling up on the edge of the bed.

"Hey," Erica said, moving behind her, utterly confused. "What's the matter? Why are you crying?"

"I'm so embarrassed," Clara whispered.

"Why?" Erica leaned over her, brushing bangs out of closed, wet eyes. "Why are you embarrassed, Clara? That was amazing. Really beautiful."

Clara didn't know how to respond. How could she tell Erica that she had just experimented with masturbation three weeks before, only reaching orgasm twice? She felt ashamed and bad, like a very young girl playing a very big girl's game.

"I'm sorry, Clara," Erica said, spooning Clara's body. "I didn't mean to push you too far. I'm really sorry." She rested her cheek against Clara's shoulder, letting the younger girl work through her own emotions, meanwhile letting her know that she was there with her.

After a few moments Clara got herself under control. "It's not your fault, Erica. I'm sorry I'm such a baby." She sniffled, reaching over to the nightstand to snag a tissue from the box next to her alarm clock. She wiped at her face and chin then blew her nose.

"You're not a baby. I'm just really sorry. I don't ever want to make you feel uncomfortable or embarrassed again."

Clara turned over to her back. Erica moved to give her the space, her head in her hand as she looked down at Clara. She was amazed all over again at just how beautiful Clara really was, made even more so by the fact that the girl had no idea.

Clara stared into Erica's face. "What did we just do?" she asked, truly baffled. She felt a new wave of embarrassment wash through her as Erica chuckled softly. "What? I'm sorry, okay? I'm new at all this."

"I know. It's fine. I'm sorry." Erica cleared her throat, trying to calm herself even though what she really wanted to do was burst into hysterical laughter at the innocent comment, as well as to release a bit of her pent-up arousal. "It's called dry fucking."

Clara scrunched up her nose. "Dry fucking? Sounds painful."

"And anything but dry," Erica said with a wink. Certainly not according to her absolutely saturated Calvin Klein's. "It's when you have sex with your clothes on," she explained.

Clara's eyes got huge. "We had *sex*?" she whispered.

Erica suppressed another laugh. She nodded. "Essentially. But, it's all up to what you define as sex."

Chapter Fourteen

Clara was on top of the world! She swore she heard Frank Sinatra singing in her head. "'Start spreading the news...'" she sang along, humming the rest of the crooner's famous song. There was pep in her step and smile on her face. *I have a girlfriend!* It had been two weeks since Erica had spent the night, and that night they had decided to officially go out. They had done more kissing and more messing around after Clara had gotten over her initial embarrassment, but she hadn't let it go much beyond that. She wanted it to be special and not "dry fucking."

Her parents, of course, had no idea what was going on between the two. All Max knew was that Clara spent a great deal of time either with her "new friend," or at The Pagan. Clara was still miffed that she wasn't allowed to accept Cassandra's offer of a job until winter break, but that was coming up in a month, so she was looking forward to it.

She made her way to the kitchen for breakfast, her left eye twitching slightly from the new makeup she'd applied moments before. She had no idea what her father was going to say and didn't much care.

"Good morning, sweet pea," Max said to his daughter, dropping the last scoopful of grounds into the coffeemaker.

"Morning, Dad." Clara poured herself a bowl of Lucky Charms and grabbed the milk from the fridge.

Within a few moments her father had joined her at the table, spreading strawberry jam on his toast.

Max glanced over at his daughter then did a second take. "What is that shit on your face?" he asked, peering at the eyeliner and dark shadow that covered her lids more closely.

"It's called makeup," she drawled, feeling somewhat defensive because she wasn't entirely secure in wearing it. After all, Erica had just shown her how to apply it the weekend before.

"I know *that*, smartass. Why are you wearing it? You hate makeup."

Clara shrugged, shoveling a spoonful of cereal into her mouth so she wouldn't have to answer verbally right away.

Max shook his head. "Whatever, kid. Just don't go too far with it."

"Yes, master," Clara muttered, rolling her eyes.

"Hey. What's with the attitude?" He stared at the top of her head as she continued to eat. Shaking his head, and not wanting to deal with teenage 'tude before work, he finished his breakfast then cleaned up his mess. "I gotta go. Remember, I'll be home late tonight." He gave the girl a kiss on her head. "Erica is giving you a ride home, right?"

Clara nodded, perking up at the mention of Erica's name. "Can she hang out for a while?" she asked, hope in her eyes.

"Sure. She's not spending the night, though. You got school tomorrow."

"Okay."

꙰ ꙰ ꙰ ꙰

"Damn, you've gotten good at that," Erica said, looking into her rearview mirror to reapply her lipstick after a heated make-out session. After picking Clara up for school, she'd parked around the corner so she could give her a proper "hello."

Clara grinned, quite proud of herself, judging by Erica's flushed face. She wasn't sure about the rest yet, but she knew she *loved* kissing. "So, my dad is going to be late tonight, and he said you can hang out after school if you want."

Erica glanced at her girlfriend, a smile spreading across her newly painted lips. "Really?" she drawled.

"Yes. Really." Clara pulled down the passenger seat visor and looked into the mirror mounted on the underside. She had done a good job with the eye makeup. She was amazed at how it made her eyes stand out even more. She wasn't so sure about the lipstick, but Erica said she liked it. She puckered up, blowing a kiss at herself as Erica got the car started and headed toward John Freed High School.

❧❧❧❧

"All right, guys. Get outta my class!" Mr. Estrata called out, his students already packing away their books as the bell continued to shriek. He sat behind his desk in his regular position: seat slightly tilted back, hands clasped behind his head. He loved his job and genuinely cared about his students. He'd been teaching for seventeen years, and it never got old. He knew he'd been born to teach and was thankful every day he had the chance.

It had been a good year so far. Most of his students — though he cared about them and wanted them all to do well — were just a blur to him. There were usually only one or two who passed through his classroom every year who really got his attention. Clara Greenwold was one of them. He watched as she shoved her textbook into her backpack, about to zip it up and sling it over her shoulder.

"Clara," he called, never stopping the casual rocking of his chair.

"Yeah, Mr. Estrata?"

"Can you hang for a second after all these guys leave?" the English teacher asked, indicating the students filtering out of the room in a loud burst of excitement that another day was over.

"Okay." Clara sat back down worried that maybe she'd done something wrong. She'd noticed all day that she was getting stares with her new look, though wasn't sure if they were positive or negative ones. She wasn't entirely sure about her new look, either, and hoped her teacher wasn't going to tell her she looked ridiculous. She rolled her eyes at her own thoughts. *No. It's none of his business. That's not what he wants to talk about.*

When the room was empty, Clara made her way to Alex Estrata's desk, leaning a hip against it, her arms crossed over her chest. She looked at him expectantly.

The teacher sat up in his chair, not sure how to go about the discussion he'd wanted to have with his student for three weeks. He rubbed his palms on the legs of his trousers and finally just blurted it out. "Clara, what really happened that day?"

Clara looked at him, confused. "Huh?" she said, not sure she'd understood correctly.

"The correct response would be: Excuse me, Mr. Estrata? I didn't understand your question."

Clara grinned, unable to be irritated at her

favorite teacher. "Okay, fine. Excuse me, Mr. Estrata? I didn't understand your question because your question was so friggin' vague."

The teacher burst into laughter. "I like you, Greenwold. Here," he stood and pulled a chair around to sit beside his desk, "have a seat. I won't keep you long because I know the weather is getting bad, so…" Once his student was seated and comfortable he continued. "That day you scared the bejesus out of all of us when you disappeared." He faced her, leaning forward so his elbows rested on his knees. "What happened? Where did you go? I've heard the rumors, but I want to hear it from you."

Clara studied him, not sure what to say or how honest she should be. His dark eyes held nothing but curiosity and something else that she couldn't quite define. She felt he had something more to say or ask but was working his way up to it. "I saw a spirit and I followed it," she said simply.

Alex Estrata nodded. "That's what I thought. So, you speak to ghosts, then?"

"I can see the dead, yes. I've never spoken to them. And," she faltered, her grandmother coming back to her in a quick flash, "they don't *always* speak to me."

He nodded. "I see. Have you ever tried? To speak to them? Or is it just not possible?"

Clara shrugged. "I haven't really tried, I guess. It usually happens so fast that I'm either startled or too scared to speak to them. Or try, anyway."

Alex nodded again with a small smile. "Okay. Thanks, Clara. You can go." He began to turn away when she stopped him, a hand on his arm.

"Wait, something's up. What is it that you *really*

kept me here to ask, Alex?"

He stopped dead in his tracks, looking at the girl who suddenly sounded very much like a grown adult, in full charge of her abilities. His first name from her lips surprised him, as well. One look in her eyes and he knew that she could help him. He changed his tone to match hers: deeper, calmer, and dead serious. "My wife died three years ago when she committed suicide. The problem is, I don't believe she *did* commit suicide. Something tells me you can help me."

"Yes. I can." Clara had no idea where the words were coming from, but she felt them from the bottom of her soul. "Tell me what you want me to do."

Mr. Estrata smiled shyly feeling like what he was about to ask was completely inappropriate. "I'd really like you to come to my home and see what you feel. But," he said, holding up a hand to forestall a response, "I want your dad to come with you. I don't need stories swarming through this place about me inviting a fifteen-year-old student to my house."

Clara nodded. "Okay. I'll tell him. Just tell me when and where."

༄ ༄ ༖ ༖

Clara found Erica waiting for her in her car, the heater and music blasting. "Hey," she said, climbing into the 4Runner.

"Hey. Where were you?" Erica turned down the radio and buckled up.

"Mr. Estrata wanted to talk to me about something." Clara tossed her backpack into the backseat and settled in for the short drive to her house.

"What did he want to talk to you about?" Erica

waited for a school bus to pull out of the circular drive then merged onto the street that ran in front of the school. Snow was coming down in earnest, which caused her to slow her speed.

Clara chewed on her bottom lip, debating how much to tell her girlfriend. Her English teacher had asked her to keep it between the two of them, and she respected him too much to blab. She settled on the partial truth. "He wanted to know what happened to me that day, the day I saw that guy."

"Boiler Room Ghost?" Erica clarified.

"Yep. So, I told him the whole sordid tale."

"Wow. Really?" Erica spared a glance at her passenger. She reached over and grabbed Clara's hand, entwining their fingers.

Clara grinned at her, squeezing her fingers in appreciation. "Yeah. He's a cool teacher. I knew he'd be cool about it."

The rest of the drive to her house was made in relative silence. Clara absently stroked the back of Erica's hand with her thumb, her mind back on her conversation with her teacher. He had asked if she and her dad could be at his house over the weekend. The alleged suicide had happened there. No investigation had been done, the medical examiner declaring it suicide.

Clara's mind raced, her thoughts a jumbled ball of images and sounds. She wasn't entirely sure what she was picking up, as little of it made sense, but she knew they weren't her own thoughts, and certainly not her own memories.

"Clara?"

"Huh?" She looked at Erica, thrown at hearing Erica's voice.

"I asked if you wanted to get something to eat. Are you hungry?"

"Oh. Yeah. Sorry."

❧ ❧ ❧ ❧

An hour later they lay on Clara's bed, Erica exploring the younger girl's neck with her mouth. Clara's eyes were closed, her body alive with sensations. She gasped softly when a hand covered her left breast, and of its own volition, her back arched, pressing herself further into Erica's palm. Erica groaned in approval, nipping at the skin of Clara's throat.

"I really want to see you naked," Erica murmured, using her thumb and index finger to tease the nipple, which had begun to push against Clara's bra and shirt.

The words both infused Clara with heat, and frightened her at the same time. She pushed the fear away but did not encourage Erica's statement, either. Instead, she buried her fingers into the dark strands of Erica's hair, pressing Erica's face further into her neck. She was on fire! The insides of her thighs were slick with what her body wanted, but her mind wasn't entirely ready for it, yet.

Erica's need for more was building quickly. The night at Clara's mom's house had been an anomaly, apparently. Clara had made no move to go much further than they were at the moment since. Erica had not seen the younger girl naked at all nor had she been invited to touch. Covering the breast that she held in her hand was the first time she'd ventured there. After Clara's dramatic reaction to what happened at her mother's house, she'd been careful.

"You okay?" she murmured against Clara's throat.

Clara could only nod, her mind a haze of lust and want. She gasped as sensation flew from her nipple to between her legs. "God, that feels so good, Erica," she moaned.

Despite all her good intentions, Erica couldn't help herself. She reached down and grabbed the hem of Clara's shirt. She waited a brief moment for any signs of protest. Getting none, she lifted the shirt up and over Clara's bra-clad breasts. She took in the sight like a dying man looking at his last meal. Her mouth watered.

Clara's breath caught, her stomach roiling with knots of arousal, nerves, and the knowledge that her dad could be home at any minute. That thought flew out of her mind as she felt a wet tongue glaze across the bare skin of her right nipple.

"Oh, god," she breathed, her hands flying to Erica's head, fingers burying themselves in her hair to hold her in place. She'd never experienced anything like it! "Please don't stop."

Sweeter words Erica had never heard. She shoved Clara's bra out of the way, fully exposing her girlfriend's breasts to her. They were absolutely gorgeous. She covered one with her hand, her mouth the other. She lost herself in what she was doing, the little sounds of pleasure Clara was making were making her more and more wet.

She began to kiss her way back up to Clara's mouth. "What time does your dad get home?" she asked against her lips.

"I don't know," Clara panted, her hands clutching Erica to her. "An hour. Maybe two."

Erica pushed up, holding herself up on her hands. Looking down into Clara's face, she could see how turned on she was, her arousal visible in her flushed cheeks and heavy-lidded eyes. "I really want you, Clara," she whispered, pressing her hips into Clara for emphasis. She smiled when she felt hands on her ass cheeks, pulling her down . "I don't want to scare you, but I really, really want you right now."

Clara met her gaze, spreading her legs a bit so Erica would fit better between them. "What do you want to do?" she asked, her voice quiet. She asked partly out of pure ignorance of what was possible, and because she wanted to hear what Erica would say and how it would make her feel.

Erica lowered herself just a bit, only so she could hold herself up on one forearm. With her free hand, she pulled up her own shirt, as well as unhooked her front-clasp bra. Pushing the open sides apart, she lowered herself fully, bare breasts lying atop of Clara.

Clara's eyes slid closed, her mouth opening in a silent gasp. Hot fluids saturated her panties all over again.

Erica pressed a little harder between her legs. Her voice was trembling from controlled want as she spoke. "I want to feel that all over. Naked skin to naked skin." She pressed her hips a little harder, both moaning at the sensation. "I want my mouth on you," she punctuated that statement with a passionate kiss. "On your mouth. On your breasts, and here." She reached down, lifting herself just enough to slide her hand between their bodies. She cupped Clara's crotch, amazed at how much heat she could feel through the denim of Clara's jeans.

Baffled, Clara looked at her through her arousal.

"You want your mouth down *there?*"

Erica grinned as she nodded. "Oh, yeah. You'll love it. It feels awesome." Erica moved off just enough so that she could easily reach the buttons of Clara's jeans. "Will you let me do that to you some time?" she asked, tugging at the button fly.

Clara couldn't think, could only nod as she found herself mentally willing Erica to touch her. She couldn't believe she was allowing to happen what was potentially about to happen.

Erica groaned in approval as she pushed past the waistband of Clara's panties, her fingers sinking into the saturated flesh between her legs. "Jesus, you're so wet," she whispered, finding Clara's mouth.

Clara was overwhelmed with what she was feeling as Erica's fingers slid through her sex. No one had ever been there before. Hell, *she'd* barely been there! She closed her eyes, allowing herself to just feel. Her mind was a million miles away as wave after wave rushed through her, sending her off on a roller coaster of both physical and emotional feelings. She cried out as Erica began to rub her clit in quick circles, her body already nearly poised for release.

"That's it, baby," Erica whispered, sensing that Clara was close. "Come for me..."

Clara tried to keep it in, but it was impossible as her body exploded, sending her hips up off the bed with each spasm as Erica continued to rub her until finally Clara pushed her hand away, unable to take anymore.

Erica was painfully aroused. She grabbed Clara's hand, not even bothering to undo her pants. She pressed the younger girl's palm hard between her legs, sending her crashing over the edge. She pressed herself down hard on Clara's hand, rocking until the pressure subsided.

It took a moment for them to get themselves together, but finally Clara pulled down her bra and shirt and sat up. Her hair was a mess, sticking up all over her head, which made Erica chuckle.

"Well, it's your fault!" She grinned, slapping her girlfriend playfully.

"And I'd happily do it again." Erica kissed her quickly then stood. The afternoon's events weren't exactly what she had wanted and certainly not what she'd planned, but it would have to do for now. She got off the bed and got her clothing back in place. She looked down at Clara, who still sat on the bed. "You really are gorgeous, you know that?"

Clara blushed, not sure what to say to such a compliment. She muttered a thank you and rebuttoned her jeans. She ran her hands through her hair and got to her feet. She walked over to Erica, putting her arms around the older girl's neck. "You are too," she murmured against her lips.

Erica kissed her, long and deep. "What are your thoughts on cemeteries?" she asked once they'd come up for air.

Clara looked at her. "Why?"

"Just tell me. Do you like them?"

"I don't know. I've only been to them for funerals."

"Will you come with me to one? Over the weekend, maybe?"

Clara felt unsure, but nodded anyway. "Okay. Sure."

"Cool." They kissed again. "I should go. Your dad will be home soon."

"Okay." Clara walked Erica to the front door

then watched as she got in her car and drove away. Clara was filled with a tempest of different emotions and sensations as she headed back to her room. She groaned softly when she saw the rumpled bed, her body reacting to what had just occurred there. "Jesus."

Chapter Fifteen

Max glanced down at the page in hand then back to the house he'd stopped the truck in front of. "Guess this is it."

Clara also took in the small, two-story house, the address her teacher had given her clearly marked on the mailbox. The house was white with dark green trim. A Ford Explorer was parked in the driveway, and the untouched morning newspaper still sat on the walkway where it had been thrown early that morning.

Together they walked up the path, which had been cleared of snow, and stepped onto the wide front porch. It was a nice house, but the closer they got to it, the more Clara's heart began to pound, and her stomach was tied in knots. She felt definite energy coming from the place and wasn't sure what to make of it. She just hoped she could help her English teacher, though she wasn't entirely sure how she was going to do that.

"Hey, guys," Alex Estrata said with a welcoming smile. He held the front door open for Clara and Max. "Welcome."

"Hi, Mr. Estrata."

"Good to see you, Clara." Alex turned to her father. "Mr. Greenwold, it's nice to see you again. We met at the school that day. I'm Alex Estrata."

"Right, I remember. Nice to meet you, Alex. Call me Max."

Clara stopped paying attention as the men shook hands, her focus solely on the house. She walked further inside, the entryway connected to a short hall where straight ahead was the kitchen; to the right was the living room; to the left stairs led to the second floor.

She walked into the living room, looking around, but not really seeing the well-kept furniture or the Oriental rug in the center of the room that covered the hardwood flooring. She didn't see the game that was playing on the television, nor the half-empty Coke can resting on a mahogany coaster on the coffee table. The stack of graded papers on the couch meant nothing to her as she absorbed the energy in the room, instinctually letting it flow through her.

Max was silent as he stood next to the teacher in the archway of the room. They watched Clara, neither sure what she was doing as she walked around the room slowly, almost as though in a daze. She didn't seem to settle her attention on any one thing. She didn't touch anything, nor linger at any spot.

"What is she doing?" Alex whispered.

Max shook his head, a sense of wonder and pride filling him. "I don't know."

Clara almost felt as though there was a beacon calling for her, a ping in the air that only she could hear. She glanced toward the small doorway — which something told her would lead to another small hallway, which would end up in the kitchen and a bathroom — something catching her eye. She barely caught the movement of someone passing through, headed toward the kitchen.

"Mr. Estrata?" she said, her voice quiet, eyes riveted to the spot as she followed the shadow.

"Yeah?" Alex asked, following his student.

"Is there anyone else here today?" Clara asked, ending up in the kitchen, which was empty. She noticed a bowl, a coffee cup, and spoon in the drainer, long-since dry.

"No. My son is with my girlfriend, and they are visiting her parents this weekend."

Clara didn't respond, her attention drawn to the back door next to the kitchen counter, the filmy curtains over the small, square window blowing slightly back as though from a breeze. "You have activity here a lot, don't you?" she said, turning to her teacher, and really seeing him for the first time since she'd arrived. He looked tired and sad. And surprised.

"What do you mean?" he asked warily.

"Things moving. Disappearing only to show up somewhere you never left them." She had a snapshot image of Alex searching the entire house for his car keys and knew that it had happened earlier that morning. She then saw a quick snapshot of the keys, hidden in a toy box. "You might want to check for your keys in your son's toy box." Clara chuckled at the look of utter shock on her teacher's face. He stared at her, mouth opening then closing, then opening again to speak, though no sound was made. Max smirked.

"I... Okay. I'll check," Alex finally managed.

Clara turned her focus back to where she was being called. "Can I go where I need to go?" she asked absently, her gaze following the energy trail back toward the living room.

"Of course," Alex said, stepping out of her way as she breezed past him and her father. Alex stood, stunned as he watched her go.

"Are you okay?" Max asked, a hand on the teacher's shoulder.

Alex nodded. "Yeah. I think so."

Clara walked through the living room, drawn to the stairs and the second floor. She felt a flutter in the pit of her stomach, though she couldn't quite identify what it was. She stood at the bottom of the stairs, hand on the balustrade, looking up. At the top she saw a woman appear. She was dressed in shorts and a T-shirt. Her red hair was pulled back in a ponytail, tennis shoes firmly tied.

"Your wife. Was she into fitness? Aerobics, maybe?" Clara asked Mr. Estrata, who stood a few feet behind her.

"Yeah. She was a runner. Why?"

"Okay," Clara breathed out, ignoring Alex's question. "I've got the right person." She took a deep breath then began to climb the stairs. She felt a heavy sense of dread with every step, but knew she had to continue.

Just tell what you see, Clara. Trust yourself.

Clara faltered, the voice in her head clear. Somehow she knew it was the voice of...the voice of her grandmother! She had a quick scene pop into her head: *a garden, stone bench. The woman with the dark hair.* Rebecca! She smiled, a sense of comfort enveloping her. She felt at peace and safe as she began to climb the stairs once more.

At the top of the stairs, she could go immediately right, which looked to be the bedroom of a small child, likely Alex's son; straight, which was the master suite; or further right, past the boy's room, which was a bathroom then a third bedroom. She didn't care about the bathroom or smaller bedrooms. Her focus was solely on the master bedroom.

Alex and Max followed at a distance as Clara

headed down the hall with purpose in her steps. She slowed as she neared the large bedroom, one hand resting on the doorframe, the other resting lightly on her stomach.

The bedroom was large with lots of windows letting in sunlight to brighten the space. A cream-colored spread on the massive four-poster bed helped to reflect the light, making some parts nearly blinding. Clara saw none of that as her gaze was drawn to a spot in the corner. She gasped, making the two men behind her start in concern.

The woman she had seen at the top of the stairs was hanging, a rope around her neck, her still body swinging slightly. Clara looked up into her face, horrified to see the look of fear and desperation on the redhead's pretty face. Blue eyes opened, making Clara take a slight step back.

"Help me," the woman begged, her voice coarse and strained from the rope. "Help me. Find him." Then she was gone.

Clara was shaken to her core by what she'd just seen. All she could do was stare at the spot where the woman had been hanging, her eyes riveted to what was now a large plant hook.

Alex watched the girl carefully, his heart in his throat as memories flooded him. Clara was staring at the exact spot where Debra had been found. He watched as she turned around, tears in her twilight eyes, which looked up at him.

"She died here," Clara said softly, reaching up a hand to wipe away a tear that had started to roll down her cheek. "She was hung."

Alex nodded, unable to say anything. He'd never forget that as long as he lived.

"This wasn't suicide, Mr. Estrata. Your hunch is right. She said a man did this to her."

"What man?" Alex finally managed to speak. "Who murdered Deb?"

"I'm not sure yet." Clara turned away from her teacher and looked around the room, trying to see where else she felt drawn. Immediately she stopped by the double closet doors, their mirrored surfaces reflecting the curious faces of Alex and her father. She ignored them, instead seeing an image come into focus. Debra was getting dressed, having just put on her panties and bra. She was pulling clothing out of the closet — shorts and a T-shirt — when she was grabbed from behind.

A hand flew to Clara's hand flew to her mouth as she watched the brutal assault, unable to shake the feeling that Debra knew the man. She knew him, and he knew his way around the house. Had access to get in. She could only see him from the back, but his blond hair was in direct opposition to Mr. Estrata's dark, Spanish heritage.

When it was all over, the room became quiet again. Or, better yet, Clara's mind became quiet, a calm settling over her. She could feel Debra's presence in the room strongly and could nearly pinpoint her exact location without seeing her. She took several deep breaths, trying to decide how to tell Alex what she'd seen. Again, her grandmother's voice in her head: *Just tell what you see, Clara...*

"Okay," she blew out, turning to face the men. If the situation hadn't been so sad, she would have burst into laughter. Both full-grown men were looking at her as though they were waiting for Christmas morning, bright-eyed and curious. She sobered her thoughts and turned to Alex Estrata. "Here's what I saw. Your wife was getting ready for her day, picking out her clothes, that kind of thing. She was..." Her voice faltered, not wanting to tell him such a horrible thing. Clearing her throat, she continued. "She was attacked from behind. Raped. Then murdered."

Alex turned away, not wanting his student to see the instant emotion that filled his eyes. He took a deep breath, his hand on the back of his neck. "I knew it," he blew out, looking up at the ceiling, as though asking for strength. "Who did this to her, Clara?"

"I'm not sure. I sense it's someone she knew. I think he had a key. He was blond. Medium build, though kind of on the short side." She trailed off, seeing Alex go pale at her description. "You know who it was, don't you?"

Alex sighed. "I'm not sure. Listen, I have some calls to make..."

Understanding, Clara nodded. "Okay." She walked over to him, placing a tentative hand on his arm. "If you need anything else, just ask. Okay? I'd be happy to try again. Maybe get more for you."

Alex stared down into the eyes of Clara Greenwold, entirely too ancient for those of a fifteen-and-a-half-year-old kid. He smiled, pulling her to him in a tight hug. "Thank you, Clara. You've given me a lot of closure today."

Clara hugged him back, a sense of pride and relief washing through her. She felt like she'd just run a marathon, filled with both the exhaustion and elation of such an event. But most of all, she just felt at peace. "You're welcome." She sensed someone watching her, and looked into the corner of the room, under the plant hook. Debra Estrata stood there, watching, a smile on her face.

"Thank you." Then she was gone.

Clara raised a hand, offering a small wave.

Chapter Sixteen

Clara took a deep breath, inhaling the cold air as they left Alex Estrata's house. She felt her chest puff out with pride and gratitude, though what she was grateful for she wasn't entirely sure.

"Aw, jeez!" Max exclaimed, bringing a hand up to his cheek, his finger coming back with a white substance on it.

Clara looked at it then glanced up into the sky. She barely caught the tail feathers of a bird as it squawked into the cold day.

"What the hell is a bird doing out this time of year?" Max asked, wiping his face on the sleeve of his jacket.

Clara ignored her father's question, her mind reeling. She heard a voice in her head. A very *familiar* voice: *And Clara, look for the birds.* She looked up again, the sky clear and gray.

Max was surprised to hear a burst of laughter from his daughter. What was it, a delayed reaction? He glanced at her, realizing that she wasn't even looking at him, but seemed to be staring off into some distant future. She met his gaze, a pleased smile on her lips.

"He's proud of me, Dad," she said, her voice trembling with emotion. "Jason's proud."

Max was utterly baffled, but didn't get to ask about it as Clara climbed into the truck, slamming the door securely behind her and seemingly on the topic at hand. Shaking his head, he followed.

❧❧❧❧

"I did it! I actually *did* it!" Clara exclaimed, throwing herself into Erica's arms. The older girl was taken aback, stunned by Clara's exuberance, and merely tried to hold on. "Can you believe it? Can you *fucking believe it?*"

"Well, I'm sure I could if I knew what you were talking about," Erica said, releasing Clara just long enough to push her bedroom door closed. She walked back over to her girlfriend, other ideas in mind. She grabbed Clara, intending to kiss her but Clara resisted.

"Wait. No. Erica, I need to tell you something."

"You can tell me in a minute," Erica said, grabbing Clara and pulling her in for a deep kiss. Clara shoved her away, hard.

"Damn it, Erica, I said *no*." They looked at each other for a long moment, Clara's heart pounding in her chest. "God, do you ever think about anything else?"

Erica was angry but pushed it away. She walked over to a chair that was buried beneath clothing, throwing them harshly to the floor and sitting down in their place. "I'm sorry. What happened?"

Clara didn't think Erica really cared to hear what she had to say at that exact moment but didn't care. She needed to talk about it. Say it out loud. "I went to Mr. Estrata's house today," she began, forgetting she had never told her girlfriend about her teacher's request in the first place. "I did it! His wife came to me, and she told me what happened. She actually *showed* me, Erica! She showed me!" Clara was nearly vibrating with her excitement, getting in Erica's face to emphasize her point. She pushed away from the older girl, standing in the center of Erica's bedroom and whirling in a circle, her adrenaline making her nearly manic.

Erica was completely confused, and still irritated at Clara's rebuff. "What the hell are you talking about, Clara? Why did you go to your English teacher's house, and what the hell did his wife show you?"

Clara realized her mistake and chewed on her bottom lip. *Shit.* She let out a breath and walked over to Erica. Feeling bad for not giving her girlfriend a proper hello she decided to try and kill two birds with one stone. She climbed up into Erica's lap, facing her. Erica automatically placed her hands on Clara's hips. Clara leaned in, placing a soft kiss on Erica's lips. "Hi. I'm sorry, I was just really excited."

"It's okay. And, just so you know, yes I do think of other things." She grinned rakishly. "Just not much else."

Clara rolled her eyes. "God, you're just like a boy."

"Worse. Unlike them, I can shoot more than once."

"Ew! God, that's so gross, Erica." Clara wrinkled her nose, eliciting a laugh from the older girl. She quickly got serious. "Okay. Now, I'm going to tell you something that is really private, okay? Promise me you won't say anything to anyone."

"I promise," Erica pledged as her hands slid down to cup Clara's ass, pulling the girl closer. She smirked when Clara reached around, grabbed both hands and forced them back to her hips.

"Behave. I need you to really listen to me. I'm excited."

"Obviously. So tell me."

"Okay." Clara blew out a breath, bringing her mind back to what had happened earlier. "What Mr. Estrata really wanted to talk to me about the other day after school was his wife. I didn't tell you because he asked me to keep it between him and I. Three years ago she died. It was declared suicide, but he always felt that wasn't the whole story. He knew what had happened with me and Boiler Room Boy, so he asked if I'd be willing to go to his house and see what — if anything — I could find out."

Erica was stunned, her attention and interest completely piqued. "Whoa."

"Yeah. That's where I just was. My dad went with me."

"What happened?"

"She was murdered, Erica," Clara said, her voice quiet, but filled with the awe of what she'd just experienced. "I saw it all happen. She actually showed me. God." She blew out. "It was amazing." The images came back to her, and she felt a chill run down her spine and sadness fill her heart. "It was awful." She lowered her head, not wanting Erica to think she was weak as her eyes filled with tears, finally able to feel all the emotions of the afternoon.

"Hey," Erica tipped her chin up with two fingers. "Why are you crying?" She brushed strands of brown hair out of twilight-colored eyes.

"It was terrible what happened to her, Erica," Clara whispered, meeting the dark, concerned gaze. "She was raped first. Then ..." her voice broke as she saw Debra hanging in the corner again. She was gathered in tender arms and encouraged to cry against Erica's shoulder. She did, letting out everything she'd witnessed, her youth making it difficult to handle.

"It's okay," Erica cooed, resting her head against Clara's, her arms holding the girl tightly against her. "It's okay."

After long moments, Clara's tears subsided and eventually died. She stayed where she was, basking in the soft warmth of Erica's body against hers. It felt good to be held and comforted. Still, it didn't take long before she felt Erica's mouth on her neck. "Hey," she said, pulling gently away. "Are we still doing the cemetery thing tonight?"

Erica looked up at Clara, successfully distracted from her task. She grinned, nodding. "Oh yeah. We're going to do a memorial visit."

"What's that?" She played with Erica's necklace as she spoke.

"Well, it's where you and me and a few friends hit the cemetery and celebrate life."

"Celebrate life?" Clara asked, uncertain, and feeling a little nervous knowing that they wouldn't be alone. Clara hadn't spent a lot of time with Erica's friends and wasn't keen on starting now.

"Yeah. It'll be fun, I promise." Erica kissed Clara then nudged her off her lap. She dropped to her hands and knees and finally to her belly as she dug around under her bed, grunting as she stretched her arm as far as she could. She hooted in victory, pulling herself to her knees, a clear plastic bag in her hand.

"What's that?" Clara asked, a little nervous.

Erica grinned, wiggling her eyebrows. "A celebration of life, baby!"

❧❧❧❧❧

It was extremely dark, and it was even colder. Clara held her jacket close to her body, looking around as she followed Erica and four of her friends — two guys and their girlfriends — through the darkened graveyard. She did her best not to bang her shins on the low stones that dotted the landscape.

"This is kind of creepy, Erica," she whispered, feeling as if she were to speak at regular volume, she'd shatter the night.

"I know. Isn't it great?" Erica whispered back, excitement in her voice.

Just ahead, they could hear the laughter and speaking voices of Erica's friends, as well as the flicker of a lighter's flame. Clara watched as cigarettes were lit and bottles opened. She began to feel uneasy as the party got started.

"Erica..." she said, her voice trailing off.

Sensing what her girlfriend was about to say, Erica said, "It's okay. It's a celebration, Clara. A celebration of life and fun. Being alive and free." She smiled at Clara, her charm coming through. The explanation made sense to Clara, so she smiled back, though she was still unsure about what was about to happen.

Erica and Clara finally caught up to their friends, and a bottle was passed to them. Erica raised it and a questioning brow, but Clara immediately declined. She remembered what had happened last time, and that had only been while drinking beer, let alone something much stronger.

"Are you sure, baby?" Erica asked after taking a swig. Her breath in Clara's ear smelled of Jack Daniels.

"I'm sure." Clara moved away slightly, uncomfortable with the intimacy in their position.

Erica's friends were watching them, knowing grins plastered on their faces.

"Here you go, guys," Erica said, handing the bottle back to her friend, Jeff. Hands free, she reached inside her jacket and pulled out the plastic bag from under her bed. There was a round of cheers as she held it up for all to see. "Give me a lighter, Jeff." Erica removed a small, thin cigarette from the bag and put it between her lips. As the flame flickered to life, a sweet smoke began to rise from the cherry tip, making Clara's nose twitch.

The joint was passed around, once again Clara declining. She was beginning to feel more and more uncomfortable, but said nothing. She was afraid to look around, afraid of what or *who* she might see.

As the liquor and drugs began to flow more freely, the group of six formed a circle next to a large crypt, everyone joining hands. Clara held Erica's hand in her left hand, a girl named Corey's hand in her right. She looked around the group, taking in each person's face as they all closed their eyes. Erica began to speak, her voice loud and clear in the quiet, cold night.

"We come here tonight to rejoice the dead. We raise our hands," the group raised their arms, hands linked in the air, "and celebrate! Watch us now. Watch as we relish life, and the living, among the dead."

Clara's right hand was dropped as Corey turned to her boyfriend and Erica pulled Clara to her. She found herself in a deep kiss, Erica's body pressed into her. Breathless, she pulled away. "Whoa," she panted, a hand on Erica's chest. "What was that for?"

Instead of an answer, Erica pushed her own jacket open then began to unbutton her shirt. Clara watched, stunned as Erica's breasts came into view, the nipples darkened and painfully hard from the intense cold that surrounded them. Erica backed up until her back came into contact with the cold stone of the crypt.

"Come here, baby," Erica whispered, taking Clara's hand and tugging until their bodies were pressed together. "I want you to fuck me," she hissed, taking Clara in a hard kiss.

Clara was excited and frightened at the same time. She kissed Erica back, realizing that a beautiful, half-naked woman was begging her to take her. But, then she realized that a beautiful, half-naked woman was begging her to take her in a dark, cold cemetery!

All thoughts of quick sex with Erica were interrupted when she heard something behind her. She glanced over her shoulder and gasped, shocked to see that Corey was seated atop a headstone, her skirt pushed up, and her boyfriend between her legs, his pants down far enough to reveal half of his naked ass. They kissed and moaned as he continued to thrust into her.

"Isn't it hot?" Erica asked, bringing Clara's face back to her with her hand cupping her jaw. "Watching him fuck her like that." She kissed Clara again then whispered against her lips. "I want you to fuck me like that, Clara."

Erica took Clara's hand and thrust it under the skirt she wore. Clara gasped, realizing her girlfriend wore no underwear, her sex hot and wet. Three of her fingers were guided inside Erica's scorching sex making Erica cry out, her head falling back against the crypt. Even though she was incredibly uncomfortable, Clara got so caught up in what she was doing: the fact that she was literally inside Erica, quickly thrusting inside her sex.

Hot juices nearly burned Clara's hand as Erica came hard, her inner walls and muscles clenching and unclenching around her fingers. Erica's mouth fell open, a heavy sigh of relief escaping as a look of pure euphoria crossed her features.

"Oh, baby," she moaned, grabbing the back of Clara's head and pulling her in for a long, lazy kiss. "God, that was wonderful. You are so fucking good." She tried to reach for the zipper of Clara's coat, but the younger girl backed away, shaking her head. "What? What's wrong?"

"I can't do this, Erica," Clara said, looking around. The other two couples were still heavily involved. "This is so wrong," she whispered, disgusted.

"What's the matter?" Erica shoved her skirt down and zipped her coat, leaving her shirt unbuttoned beneath it. She grabbed the smoldering joint from the top of a headstone and took a deep drag, blowing the smoke into the cold night. "Enjoy yourself, baby. Don't be such a fucking stick in the mud."

"It's not about being a 'stick in the mud', Erica." Clara felt anger clutch at her, still able to feel Erica's juices on her fingers. "God, this is just really messed up! What's wrong with you guys?"

"Let her walk home, Erica," the other boy, who Clara thought was called Mason, said. His girlfriend was on her knees, enthusiastically giving him a blow job.

"Fuck off," Erica said to him, then turned back to Clara. "This is part of what it's like to be with me, Clara. This is part of who I am." She indicated the cemetery around them, then walked up to her, caressing the side of her face with cool fingers. "Baby, this isn't wrong. We are celebrating life, not trying to disrespect the dead. I swear. I have the ultimate respect for what you do, baby. I think it's fucking hot."

Clara accepted Erica's kiss but still wasn't convinced. When Erica pulled away, Clara wrapped her arms up around Erica's neck, deciding to try and use a weapon she knew Erica's weakness. "Then why don't we leave and be alone," she said, leaning up to lay kisses on Erica's neck. "We can be alone, and I know you want to see me." She took Erica's hand and slid it up under her coat, resting the palm on one of her breasts. She could hear Erica's breathing hitch and quicken. *Bingo.* She just wanted to get out of the cemetery and take Erica with her. She had a really bad feeling.

Erica could feel her blood begin to boil once more. "Okay.

Later that night they lay in Erica's bed, Clara's naked body spooned by her sleeping girlfriend. Clara stared into the darkness, wondering if she'd just made a huge mistake. There was no questioning just exactly what they'd done so far was called. She'd given herself to Erica that night, completely and totally. Was she a woman now? Maybe. It was a stiff price to pay, but it got them out of the cemetery.

They would find out the next day that a gang had been trolling the graveyard, and had come upon Erica's friends. The boys had been beaten within an inch of their lives, and one of the girls had nearly been raped.

Chapter Seventeen

Clara tried to focus on the TV program she was watching, but it wasn't working so great. She could hear the flirtatious voice of her father on the phone in the kitchen. He was talking to Kathy, his new squeeze. She'd met the woman once, and didn't like her from the outset. Max said it was because Kathy wasn't her mother, but Clara felt it was more than that. She sensed the woman was after something, but didn't know exactly what it was. It sure as hell wasn't his money.

Clara smirked at that thought as she finished eating her TV dinner. It was a Thanksgiving turkey surprise. The surprise was, the meat wasn't real and what *was* real was the asshole of the turkey. Clara set her half-eaten dinner aside.

"Disgusting," she muttered. Tomorrow was the big day, Turkey Day, and she'd be spending it with her mom and Kerri. Her father had been invited, but he'd opted to spend it with Kathy. Clara had been invited to the woman's house, but there was no way in hell she was going to miss dinner with her mother for dinner with Kathy.

Clara was angry. She was *really* angry. She slumped farther down in her chair, not even paying attention to the channels she surfed through. Her father hated it when she did that, as he was one of the only males in North America who didn't channel surf, which was exactly why she *was* doing it.

"Hey, kiddo, grab a station and leave it," Max said, entering the room with his own dinner. Clara ignored him, continuing to channel surf with even more vigor than she was before. "Clara," Max said, his voice sharp.

"What?" she said not even bothering to look at him. She could tell he was trying to hold in his irritation, as they both knew damn well what she was angry about.

"So," he said, trying to break the heavy tension in the air. "You looking forward to turkey and your favorite — mashed potatoes and gravy — tomorrow?"

"Yep."

"And pumpkin pie..."

"Yep."

"And then Christmas is just around the corner."

"Yep."

Max threw his fork down, setting his untouched dinner aside. "Damn it, Clara. We talked about this." He looked at his daughter, getting only her profile. "I asked you how many weeks ago if you were okay with the fact that I'd be dating? You said you were fine with it."

"No, what I said was, if you want to date then do what you have to do, and I wouldn't stand in your way. Very different from being 'fine with it'." She glared at him, unable to hide her hurt. "I was never *fine* with it."

"Clara, I'm doing what I have to do to be happy. Why can't you understand that?" he pleaded, wishing there was some way he could get her to understand.

"You've always done what *you* needed to do to make yourself happy, Dad," Clara said, her voice wavering as unshed tears threatened. "That's the problem. That's why we're here," she indicated the small apartment around them. "That's always been the problem with you." She shot up from her chair and grabbed her coat, slamming the front door behind her.

Max was stunned, sitting on the couch in the quiet apartment, only the sound of a commercial on the TV for company. He felt sick. He knew Clara was angry and hurt both at him and by the situation — considering the upcoming holidays would be the first since the family split. Somehow, though, he knew that what she'd said wasn't all about emotions and anger. She'd meant it.

He put a hand to his chest, covering his heart, which hurt. It felt like it was broken. Was he truly the selfish bastard she all but said he was? Max couldn't help but think back over his life, and his marriage to Stephanie. Yes, she was certainly part of their problems, but had he ever truly stopped to think about his part in things? Had he ever once taken responsibility for some of the bad times?

Stephanie Holdridge had been one of his first girlfriends and certainly his first serious one. First love. Hell, he'd taken her virginity. They'd been so happy for such a long time. Many, many years had gone by before he'd begun to feel stifled and trapped. The hard part was, he loved his family. He loved Stephanie, and he adored his daughters. So, what had gone wrong? Which turn had he taken that was the wrong one, pointing him in the wrong direction?

Max's thoughts were interrupted by the sound of the ringing phone. He grabbed the cordless and couldn't help but smile when he saw Kathy's number.

Thoughts of the past were replaced with thoughts of an exciting night with the fiery redhead.

᧖ᦲ᧖ᦲ

Clara wiped angrily at her tears, which she feared would freeze on her cheeks if she wasn't careful. The temperature outside was bitterly cold, and fresh snow had fallen the night before. The streets — regardless of the bad weather — were filled with traffic, people trying to get their last-minute details worked out for the following day's holiday feast.

She pulled her jacket closer, zipping the coat with trembling hands. She cursed silently when she didn't find her gloves in the pockets, remembering she'd tossed them on her chair when she'd gotten in from school the day before. It was certainly days and times like this that she wished she had a car.

Clara had walked for more than twenty minutes when she saw the lights blazing in a small coffee shop, which she'd never been to or even known was there. Relieved to find a wadded up ten-dollar bill in her pants pocket, she headed inside.

The coffee shop was a typical one: scattered tables and an ordering area. She looked in the glass cases at the goodies displayed, though she didn't have much of an appetite for anything. She only wanted something hot to warm her up from the inside out.

"Can I help you?" the girl behind the counter asked, a friendly smile on her face.

Clara ordered a large hot chocolate with extra whipped cream, paid for it then went to find herself a table where she could be by herself. She didn't fully trust her emotions at the moment, and didn't want to be around people, but didn't want to freeze to death outside, either. Going home at that moment wasn't an option even to consider.

Shedding her coat, she laid it across the back of a chair. She sat down, blowing on her red, chapped hands and rubbing them together. She sat in a corner across from the large, plate glass window. She watched cars chug by, careful to keep enough distance between each other to avoid weather-related accidents. Some braver souls walked along the sidewalks, bundled up like Randy in *A Christmas Story*. She smiled at that thought and image.

"Hot chocolate, extra whipped cream?"

Clara looked up at the clerk who'd brought her drink to her, shocked to see Abby Jensen looking down at her. She had a nametag pinned to the dark green coffee shop polo, and a maroon apron tied around her waist.

"Hey," she said, setting the cup down. "You're Kerri's sister, aren't you? Clara?"

Clara nodded, unable to form words for a moment. She hadn't seen the blonde since Jason's funeral, nearly six months earlier, and was at a loss for words. She felt stupid: there she was, on the verge of tears, half frozen, and unable to say a damn word.

"Okay. Well, enjoy." Abby left her alone, walking back behind the counter, not giving her another look as she started on another customer's drink order.

Clara let out a long breath, flopping her forehead down on the hard wood of the table, feeling like a complete idiot. "I am a complete idiot," she muttered, finally pulling herself together and sipping at her drink. The inner warmth helped clear her head a bit, enough to lose the Abby haze and get her thoughts back to why she was out in the Arctic-like weather in the first place.

Her dad. Her mom. Thanksgiving.

Clara felt her emotions rise once again and tried her best to swallow them. She wasn't entirely successful. As she stared out the large window, she saw couples and families scurry by, laughing and talking. She felt an emptiness inside her that was like a black hole. She knew she was being dramatic, but her fifteen-year-old mind couldn't help but wonder if her life would ever feel normal again. Would she ever have her family around her? It's amazing just how much is taken for granted in life. Nothing is ever missed until it's gone.

Clara bit her lip as tears began to trickle down her cheeks. She was mortified as a quiet sob escaped and she really began to cry. She felt like her world was in a state of flux, and it hurt.

"Are you okay?"

Clara looked up, even more mortified to see Abby standing next to her table, wiping her hands on a white towel, which she flicked to her shoulder once they were dry. Clara nodded, even as fresh tears began to flow. She didn't know what to think or say as the older girl sat in the chair next to hers, concern in her green eyes.

"You don't look okay, Clara." Abby scooted her chair a bit closer, leaning in. "Is everything okay? Did something happen?"

Clara shook her head, snagging a napkin from the silver dispenser on the table. She wiped her eyes and nose, shaking her head. "No. Everyone's fine." She looked down at her hand which clutched the napkin. "I think I'm just being a baby," she managed with a watery smile.

"About what?"

Abby's soft voice and genuine concern brought fresh emotion to the surface. "Tomorrow. My parents' split." Clara let out a breath, wiping uselessly at the tears in her eyes, which just kept leaking out.

"I can't imagine how hard this must be on you, Clara. I know Kerri has struggled with it too."

"She has?"

Abby nodded. "Sure. And don't tell her I said this or I'll have to kill you," Abby said with a smile, "but she really had a hard time when you moved out too."

"Really?" Clara was stunned to hear that.

Abby glanced over her shoulder and saw that a line had begun to form at the counter. "Hey, I gotta go, but we close in thirty minutes. I'll give you a ride home." Without waiting for a response, Abby was up and headed back behind the counter.

≈≈≈≈

"Are you hungry?" Abby asked, glancing over at her passenger as they drove away from the coffee shop.

Clara nodded, unable to look at the girl sitting next to her. She was so nervous! Her palms were sweating, even as she continually rubbed them on the thighs of her jeans. "That TV dinner was gross," she said absently.

"What?"

Clara realized she'd spoken out loud. She grinned, shaking her head. "Never mind."

"Okay. Well, where do you want to go? Our choices are limited because everything is closing up early for the holiday."

"How about Burger King?" Clara said, noting the fast food restaurant at the end of the block.

"Burger King it is."

Fifteen minutes later they were seated with their food in front of them, tucked away in a corner booth to get away from the hungry, shopping crowds. Abby prepared her sandwich and squirted a healthy amount of ketchup on the wrapper for her fries. "So tell me what's going on," she said, not looking at her dinner companion. "What has you so upset tonight?"

Clara took a bite of her Whopper and chewed thoughtfully as she contemplated her answer. She tried to forget that she was having dinner with Abigail Jensen and tried to focus on the fact that Abby was trying to be nice, undoubtedly because Clara was Kerri's sister. Otherwise, the popular older girl would never have given her a second glance, let alone have a Whopper with her.

Clara blew out a breath and just began to talk. She figured things happen for a reason, and if Abby was willing to listen to her sob story, she might as well tell it and get it out. Maybe she'd actually feel better in the end.

"My dad is dating some bimbo named Kathy, who I can't stand. He wanted me to go with him to her house for dinner tomorrow, and that's like, no way! How the hell can he expect me to not spend Thanksgiving Day at my mom's? I mean, come on! So, anyway, he was invited to mom's but, as usual, he let his dick do the thinking for him, so he's not coming. Our first holiday since the split, and our family won't be together. I know what you're thinking — a split is a split, but still! You know?" She didn't give Abby a chance to respond as she continued. "And, then to top it all off, I have no money to buy Christmas presents, and I can't even buy something for my girlfriend 'cause my parents won't let me work at Cassandra's shop until winter break. I mean, hello! Christmas will be over by then! And, speaking of my girlfriend, we're having problems because I think there's only two things she's interested in when it comes to me." She ticked them off on her fingers, "sex and the dead."

Clara stopped herself, realizing what she'd just said, what she'd just admitted, and to *whom. Oh shit.* What would stop Abby from running straight to Kerri and telling her that her little sister was gay?

Abby blinked several times, trying to straighten out in her head everything that she'd just been told in nearly one, long, breathless sentence. "Okay," she said, "let me try to piece this together. You're hurt because your dad's dating someone you don't like. You're also angry at him because you guys won't have a family holiday tomorrow, because he wants to spend the day with his new girlfriend, and even though he invited you, there's no way you're going to go. You're hurt because the family is torn apart, and you blame him for it. You're also angry because you have no money to buy gifts because your folks won't let you work for some lady, and then your girlfriend isn't being there for you. Did I get it all?"

Clara stared at the blonde for a moment, unable to speak. She took a drink from her Coke to wash down her shock. Finally she nodded. "Yeah, that about covers it."

"Okay. Good." Abby wiped her mouth and got ready for a long discussion. "Let's go through these an issue at a time, okay?" At Clara's nod she continued.

"Okay. Let's start with your parents and your dad, the split, all that. I think it can be handled in one, fell swoop."

"All right." Clara was nervous. How was she going to handle this business about just outing herself to one of her sister's best friends? Internally she cringed. She waited for Abby to speak, feeling like she was a damned prisoner, waiting on the chopping block.

"Okay. Let's start with your parents' marriage. What are your thoughts on it? I mean, when you look back, if you have to describe it in one word, what would that word be?"

Clara wanted to say happy, but she knew that wasn't true. Well, not accurate, anyway. She gave it real thought, wanting to be completely honest with Abby. "I guess I'd have to say separate." She remembered so many times over the years when her mother would be either at a neighbor's house or by herself, and Max would be either spending time in his shop in the garage or he and Clara would go do something. She knew they spent time together as a family during the weekends sometimes, but usually it was her father and her and her mother and Kerri, almost like two different parties in one trip.

"Why do you say that?" Abby asked, munching on a ketchup-drenched fry.

"I don't know why I never saw that before or thought it was odd," Clara said, absently playing with the straw in her drink. "But they were." She met Abby's gaze. "They didn't really spend much time together. If they did, it was still, somehow, like they weren't really together. My mom would try, maybe make some sort of comment, trying to bind the family together. But, ultimately it was like it was me and my dad and her and Kerri."

"Do you think your mom was happy with that arrangement? Always trying to bring you guys together?"

"I doubt it, knowing her."

"Okay, let's move on to something else real quick, and we'll circle back. You mentioned your girlfriend, and that there's a problem. What's her name?"

"Um," Clara said quietly, almost like a frightened child. "I'd really rather not tell you that, if that's okay."

Abby stared at her for a moment, confused, but then understanding dawned in her eyes. "Oh, okay. Well, however you want to play it, but I'll tell you this, Clara," Abby pointed at her with a fry, "nothing that is said here is going anywhere beyond this table. So, you don't have to worry about me telling Kerri, if that's what you're worried about."

Clara smiled, a little sheepish. "Yeah. Nobody knows."

"And they won't find out from me."

"Thanks, Abby. I really appreciate that." Clara took a deep breath and a leap of faith. "Erica."

"Okay. Erica. So, as I was saying, you're having problems with Erica, saying that she only wants to take from you and obviously not give you what you need from her."

"How do you know that?" Clara asked, knowing she hadn't made it all that clear in her babbling.

"Well, if she was, wouldn't you be sitting here having this conversation with her and not me?" Abby asked with a raised brow.

"Oh. Yeah, I guess so," Clara said, seeing the logic.

"Okay, so tell me more about the problems with her. What isn't Erica giving you?"

Clara sighed, tossing the wadded up paper that had once protected her straw. "I don't know, exactly. I mean, when I first met her, it was amazing and exciting. Someone *wanted* me. That blew my mind. And then we...well, you know, and now it's like that's all she wants from me. That or to bring me into her weird world of the dead. Abby, she has no respect for the spirit world at all. None! She thinks it's some sort of weird game or like it's taboo to mess with it or something. I'm not comfortable with it."

"What aren't you comfortable with?" Abby asked, confused. "Don't you dabble in that stuff, yourself?"

"I don't dabble," she said, unable to keep the defensive tone out of her voice. "This came to me, not the other way around. I take it very seriously. It's no game."

Abby was surprised by the intensity in Clara's eyes. "I'm sorry, Clara. I didn't mean to offend. Just trying to understand."

"It's okay. I'm sorry. I don't mean to preach. I think it boils down to Erica having this weird fascination with anything macabre and she saw me as the perfect conduit to that world." She sighed again, her shoulders slumping. "Sometimes I wonder if she even likes me for me at all."

"I'm really sorry, Clara. I know what that's like." Abby smiled with understanding. "Okay, so now you've got that out, tell me this: you're unhappy in your relationship with Erica. She doesn't give you the support you need for your gifts or seem to have any other purpose for being in a relationship with you. Right?"

"Right," Clara drawled, not entirely sure where the conversation was going.

"Okay, so can you imagine staying in this thing with her throughout the rest of high school? That's another three and a half years, Clara. Can you see it?"

Clara immediately shook her head. "God, no. Not the way it is now. Not a chance."

"Okay, so — forgive me, because I'm not entirely sure how this works with girls, so I'm going to have to go with what I know — I imagine that at one time Erica was all you thought about. The only girl in the world for you, right?"

Clara blushed and looked away. *The only girl except for you.* "Right," she muttered.

"Now that you're unhappy, do you find yourself looking at other girls? Wondering what it would be like to be with them?"

Clara was beginning to catch on. She nodded. "Yeah. Okay, I see your point. You're saying that where I'm at is where my dad was with my mom. He was unhappy for whatever reason, so instead of basically settling in his unhappiness, he had to get out. Well, he moved on *before* he got out, really."

"Yeah. I heard about that, and I'm really sorry, Clara. But, yes. That's what happened with your dad. He's moved on, trying to find his own happiness, and he's hoping that this new girlfriend might give it to him."

"I see your point, but he had two kids, Abby. Doesn't he care? Doesn't he care what it's doing to us?" Clara asked, emotion beginning to rise again. She tried quickly to swallow it down.

"Of course he cares!" Abby said, her gaze boring into Clara's trying to make the younger girl understand.

"If he didn't care, do you really think he would have let you move in with him? Do you think he would be sticking around? Hell, Clara, this was his escape! It was his chance to move on and leave the unhappiness behind." She paused, waiting for Clara to reign in her emotions, which she was making a valiant effort to do. "Give him a chance. He loves you and Kerri, and I bet he loves your mom too. He just wasn't happy where he was, and by him being unhappy, he was making everyone unhappy. You may not realize it right now, but he actually did all of you a favor by leaving."

"I remember how hurt my mom was, knowing that when he was out late, what he was doing. That he was lying to her."

"Exactly. Now your mom can also move on and try to find her happiness too."

Clara wiped away a few stray tears that had managed to find their way to her cheeks. She smiled through her tears. "I hate it when people make sense like this."

Abby grinned, taking a drink from her Coke. "I try not to do it too often, but sometimes I'm just brilliant that way."

Clara laughed, and it felt really good. "You know, the funny thing is, Dad told me that I'd never really be able to understand until I was in a relationship of my own."

"And he was right. Nothing is as black and white as it seems, Clara. Nothing." She loaded all her dinner trash onto the tray. "I should get you home." She scooted out of the booth and dumped the tray, refilling her drink before returning to the table, where Clara sat, looking exhausted. "As for tomorrow, I know it hurts, but give your dad some slack. He wants you with him, but you made the choice to go to your mom's." She bent down just enough to catch Clara's gaze. "Give him credit for that. Okay?"

Clara nodded, again trying to hold her tears in.

"Come here."

Clara was tugged to her feet engulfed in a warm hug. She couldn't resist and laid her head down on Abby's shoulder, her eyes closing as the blonde's scent filled her soul. Nothing had ever felt as right as getting a hug from Abby Jensen.

Abby pulled away after a long moment. "Are you okay?"

Clara nodded. "Yes. Thank you so much. This really meant a lot to me tonight, you listening to me and talking to me like this."

"Sure. Any time."

Chapter Eighteen

1992

Clara grunted as she tried to hold up the glass shelving, Cassandra working as quickly as she could to bolt it into place.

"Okay. I think you can let it go," Cassandra said, taking a slight step back, looking from one end to the other.

Clara slowly began to remove her hands, but then felt the entire thing about to go. She quickly put her hands back under it. "Or not."

"Shit! Sorry, Clara." Cassandra immediately went to work to try and secure the new shelving that had just arrived that morning. Within a few moments it was secured and both stood back, checking out their handiwork. "Not bad, kiddo." Cassandra gave her employee a one-armed hug. "Looks good."

"Yeah. Those new candles will look great there." Clara began to gather up the packaging the shelving had come in, crushing it all into a compact bundle that she'd take out with the rest of the trash.

"I agree."

Clara headed to the back room to start closing procedures. She'd been working at The Pagan for three months and loved it! She had been working day shifts mainly since she started working on weekends, but her dad had given her permission to work two nights a week after school. Cassandra was teaching her how to close up shop, and Clara suspected that fairly soon she would be left to work alone. She knew Cassandra was looking forward to actually having time off.

The trash gathered, Clara pushed open the store's back door, which led into the alley where the trash bin was. With a grunt, she heaved the bag and boxes into the huge, metal container. She was wiping her hands on her jeans when Erica's 4Runner pulled up. Clara groaned inwardly but waited.

"Hey," Erica said, climbing out of the SUV. She walked up to Clara, her hands tucked into the back pockets of her jeans. She only wore a light jacket, the March air hinting at the coming warmer weather.

"Hi, Erica." Clara waited until her ex reached her. After her talk with Abby, Clara had given things a lot of thought and decided that Erica wasn't what she wanted. The sex was great, but it wasn't everything. At least not like it was to Erica. She wanted someone she could talk to, could share things with, and who would try and understand her — not change her.

"How's it going?" Erica nodded toward the back of the shop, bringing up a hand to brush some dark strands of hair out of her eyes.

"Good. That new shelving finally came in."

"Cool. Well, I was just coming by to pick up Cassandra. Is she finished yet?"

"No. We just started closing the place up. Those shelves took us forever to install."

Erica nodded, then chewed on her lower lip for a moment, trying to decide whether to say what was on her mind or not. Finally she blew out a breath. "I really miss you, Clara." She ran a hand through her hair. "A lot. I'm sorry for how things went."

Clara felt a slight tug in Erica's direction but

quickly shoved it aside. She knew Erica wasn't in her future. Not in the way she had been in her past. "I'm sorry, too."

"Well," Erica said, feeling slightly uncomfortable and surprised. She had hoped that her simple declaration would give her some idea that Clara wanted to get back together, but it was more than obvious that wasn't the case. "I'll see you around."

Clara watched her enter through the store, leaving her alone in the alley. She blew out a loud breath, feeling somewhat bad. Finishing her task, she headed back into the store, knowing that she couldn't do what she wanted to do, which was just walk out the alleyway and head home. She had to stay and finish helping Cassandra.

Erica was reclining in the back office as Clara replaced the trashcan in there. Cassandra was talking to a last-minute customer who had come in while she was outside. Clara wandered out to the main room of the store — not wanting to stay in the back with Erica — and began to clean up.

"So, you think the amethyst will help?" the woman asked, holding up a large, purple stone Cassandra had removed from the glass countertop case.

"It should. The purpose of the amethyst is to help bring peace to the home," Cassandra explained.

Clara wasn't paying any attention to them as she straightened the gift cards they'd begun to carry, but which people felt a strange need to destroy. Suddenly she had the image of a race car in her head zooming around and around an oval track. She pushed the image away, continuing her task but it came back, followed by the sight of a blue bicycle. She stopped what she was doing and focused on the image. One thing she'd learned over the last several months was when an image wouldn't go away, and she knew it wasn't anything that registered in her own personal life, it typically meant she was picking up on something or getting a message.

When she turned to look at the two women at the counter the race car reappeared in her head. She looked at Cassandra, who was still talking about the power of stones and crystals, and somehow it just didn't feel right. When she turned her attention on the other woman the race car stopped, almost parking itself directly in front of her mind's eye. She clearly saw the colorful details on the car including a bright yellow number fourteen.

Clearing her throat, Clara walked over to the women. "Excuse me," she said to the customer, "I'm sorry to interrupt, but does a race car mean anything to you?"

The woman looked at her, the polite smile she'd worn at the interruption sliding off her face. "Excuse me?"

"A race car. Number fourteen. And a blue bicycle." Another image popped into her head: a little boy, maybe six or seven, was riding the blue bicycle round and round a fire hydrant. "I feel drawn to you; that this information is for you. A little boy is riding a blue bicycle." She smiled at the image, amused. "He keeps riding circles around a yellow fire hydrant."

"How do you know about Lewis?" the woman asked, a hand to her chest.

"I don't."

"She's a medium, Margaret," Cassandra said softly to the woman.

The woman named Margaret looked from the

shop owner then back to Clara. "Yes. Lewis had a blue bicycle, and the fire hydrant was just down the street from our house."

"Did he used to play with a race car that was blue, yellow, and purple? With a number 14 on the door and hood? Maybe like a matchbox car or something?"

The woman took a deep breath, seeming to try and get her balance back. "No. But I think I know what that means."

Before the woman could explain further, she had another image. Lewis was leaving the fire hydrant and was about to head across a residential intersection on his bike. The race car image came again, the car tires screeching to life, smoke in their wake as the car shot off. Clara had a horrible feeling in the pit of her stomach.

"Lewis was struck by a speeding car. He was killed."

"Oh, Margaret, I didn't know," Cassandra said, placing a consoling hand on the woman's arm.

"It was a long time ago," she said softly.

"What about the number fourteen?" Clara asked, unsure if it had significance, or if it was just simply part of the image. The number was so bright, though, she felt it had something to do with it.

"It happened fourteen years ago." The woman thought for a moment, a bright albeit sad smile gracing her lips. "Lewis would be twenty-two today. Today is his birthday."

Clara felt like she'd just been struck in the head with a brick.

"Oh, Margaret!" Cassandra exclaimed, her hands to her mouth. "That is wonderful! Maybe he is trying to tell you hello."

Clara noted that even Erica had come out to see what was happening, but that was soon interrupted by more images. "I'm seeing some sort of flower," she said, closing her eyes to see the image better. "Like a dandelion, maybe?" She was brought out of her concentration by the sound of a soft cry. She looked at the woman to see that she was on the verge of tears.

"He used to pick those for me all the time and bring them to me," she whispered, unable to take her eyes off Clara.

Clara smiled, understanding filling her. "He's saying hello and that he loves you." She heard something: *I love you, Momma.* "'I love you, Momma', I just heard."

Margaret was crying now, Cassandra had moved around the counter to stand next to her customer, an arm around her waist for support. "Is he okay? Is he happy?"

Clara smiled. "Oh, yes." She chuckled as she suddenly saw an image of a little boy running and playing. He stopped for a moment, gave her an enthusiastic wave then faded. "Very much so." The energy gone, Clara focused on Lewis's mother. "He doesn't want you to worry or be sad anymore."

Margaret hurried over to Clara, giving her a huge hug. "Oh, thank you, honey," she murmured before pulling away, a smile on her tear-streaked face. "That was incredible, and it means the world to me that my baby came to me on his birthday. Thank you."

"You're very welcome. I'm glad I could help."

With a few quiet words, Margaret bought the stones she wanted then with a warm smile, left the shop. Clara felt eyes on her and turned to see both Cassandra and Erica staring at her, mouths open.

"What?"

～～～～

She wasn't sure how it happened, but the next thing Clara knew, she was holding weekly readings at The Pagan, sometimes two or three a week. The craziest part was that she was being *paid* to do it. There she was, almost 16 years old, sitting at a table behind a newly curtained off area, her "client" sitting across from her with either great expectation or total skepticism on their faces.

Before every reading, whether it was a scheduled one or simply someone who had wandered into the shop, Clara felt nauseous. What if she was wrong? What if nothing came to her? What if the person thought she was a quack? Not only that, but a lot of times, it was emotionally taxing on her. Not only did she see images, hear voices — and sometimes the spirit standing in the corner — but she'd also feel what they were feeling. They'd get their message through to her via their emotional state at the time of a traumatic event, or she'd actually feel the physical pain of whatever had happened to them. The worst was when a grandfather, who had committed suicide, explained what had happened by a sudden and very sharp pain in Clara's temple. It was disturbing, and sometimes downright creepy.

Despite the toll on her, Clara enjoyed the readings. It felt like a part of her was now complete, somehow, like she was beginning to do what she'd been born to do. The downside was that word had begun to spread through the small town she lived in and inevitably to her school.

Because of the spread of that word, Clara was anxious for the school year to be over with, which would be in six weeks. Kerri would be graduating from South High in a month. She hefted her backpack higher onto her shoulder and walked down the hall, headed to her last — and favorite — class of the day, Mr. Estrata's English class. English wasn't a particularly favorite subject of hers, but she loved the way her teacher went about it, his passion for the subject coming through in every lesson. So, though he couldn't make her any better at English than she already was, he at least made her have an appreciation for it and for reading.

On her way to Mr. Estrata's room, she saw a group of upper-class boys walking toward her, but didn't give it another thought until she found herself shoved into a row of lockers she was passing.

"Outta the way you fuckin' dyke witch!" one of them said, his friends laughing and tossing high-fives through the group.

Saying nothing, Clara took several deep breaths and gathered her courage, forcing herself to continue on her way to class. She was beginning to hate school and most of her peers. Every day somebody said something, either about her being a "dyke" or "lezbo" or about her abilities as a medium. A few would actually take time to ask her about it out of curiosity and not fear or spite.

She sighed heavily, glad the day was almost over.

"Clara?" Alex Estrata said, erasing the chalkboard after class had ended. He'd barely caught his favorite student before she made her way with the flow of her peers who were pouring out into the hall.

Clara battled her way upstream until she was

back in the classroom. "What's up?"

"I've heard a lot about you lately," Alex said, leaning against his desk, arms crossed over his chest. "Congratulations, Clara. Sounds like you're finally able to use your gift for the good of others."

Clara grinned, it was an "aw-shucks" moment for her. "Thanks, Mr. Estrata. I love it, but some people here aren't too thrilled."

The teacher waved her words off. "What do they know? This is a short time of your life, Clara. You'll have many, many years ahead of you where you'll help people and they'll respect and understand your gift."

"Do you think so?"

Alex nodded. "I do. That's why I asked you to stay behind. I thought you might like to know that an investigation into Deb's death has finally been opened. I can't talk much about it, but I think I know who Deb showed you in your vision."

"Oh, Mr. Estrata, that's awesome!" Clara was immediately giddy with excitement. "Please let me know how it goes. I really hope that your wife can finally find some peace."

Alex nodded with a smile. "Me, too."

Clara slapped her teacher affectionately on the arm and turned to leave. "Oh, Alex?" she said, glancing at him over her shoulder. "Did you ever find your keys?"

The English teacher grinned. "They were in my son's toy box. Just like you said."

Chapter Nineteen

1995

Clara kept her patience, letting her mother fuss over her. After all, it *was* her day. Well, her day and three hundred and ten of her fellow classmates, anyway. She was graduating from John Freed High School at long last! She had never thought it would come and had never thought she'd get out of school.

"Okay, are you ready for your mortarboard?" Stephanie asked, unable to believe her baby was graduating!

"No, not yet. I'll just carry it with me for now." Clara looked at herself, secretly very pleased to see the gold gown she wore, the sunlight making it shine.

"Okay." Stephanie was nearly beside herself, so proud of Clara. She would never tell her youngest, but she and Max had talked about it over the past four years, whether Clara would graduate or not. She hated school even though she was so intelligent. They never truly understood what the problem was, and Clara had never been open about it. It had been beyond a fight to get her to register for college classes in the fall.

"I think you guys are supposed to be lining up," Kerri said, indicating a woman who was trying to get the seniors — boys in green, girls in gold — in order for the march inside the stadium.

"Oh. Okay." Stephanie gave her daughter one final hug and a kiss on the cheek, careful not to leave a lipstick smudge. Max stood back, videotaping the entire thing. The smile of pride wouldn't leave his face.

Clara was nervous as she hurried to join her fellow classmates. She couldn't believe the day had finally come and was beyond excited. Even so, she knew this momentous occasion meant something bigger: real life. Well, almost. She'd be heading to college in the fall, though she looked forward to that almost as much as she looked forward to her period each month.

⁂

Family and friends gathered at Stephanie's house, where tables had been set up in the backyard and loaded with food. People stood around with plastic plates balanced on their hands, talking as they ate. Clara wasn't entirely sure who everyone was, so she just figured they must be cousins or something. She wasn't all that close to her family outside the circle of her parents, Kerri, and her grandparents. She knew her mother had invited them hoping maybe their monetary gifts would help Clara during the next stage of her life.

"Did you find the coleslaw?" Stephanie asked, working shoulder to shoulder with Max to try and make their youngest child's day as special as possible.

"Yeah, it was behind the pickles." Max tore into another package of raw meat patties then got them going on the grill. He felt a hand on his back, rubbing affectionately. He couldn't help but smile, but then turned with surprise to see that Florence had walked up to him. "Hey."

"Hi. Looks good," his newest girlfriend said, eyeing the plate full of grilled burgers.

"Thanks."

Florence walked away, her hips swaying in the denim shorts she wore. He tore his eyes off them and turned to speak to Stephanie, but she was nowhere to be found.

༄༅ ༅ ༄

"So, I was thinking," Kerri said, sitting on a blanket under the huge cottonwood tree in the backyard, the same one she and Clara used to play on all the time when they were kids. The same one Jason fell out of when he was ten.

"That's a scary thought," Clara muttered, having just joined her sister and her long-time boyfriend, Zane.

"I know. You'd better run," he snickered, getting a playful backhand to his stomach.

"Since there isn't a kitchen, or anything like one, in the attic apartment, why don't you just use ours?" She turned to her sister, taking a bite out of her hot dog as she waited for Clara's response.

Clara glanced at her, uneasy at the sudden generosity. "Are you sure? I don't want to encroach..."

"Don't be silly. Trust me, Clara, once you're in college, you won't be able to afford to eat out all the time. You'll need a kitchen. I've been there. Let me help you out."

Clara stared at her for a long moment, finally drawling, "Okay."

The deal had been made that if Clara would go to college, she could move out. She wasn't all that keen on living in the dorms, and Kerri and Zane had managed to find an old Victorian with a small attic apartment. Clara would live in the apartment, rent free, as long as she helped out in the massive, quarter-acre yard.

Clara was still trying to understand how the whole sister thing worked. Ever since they'd been children they'd never gotten along, both girls far too different to even live in the same house, let alone on the same planet. But, something had happened over the past couple years. Once Kerri got into college — which she'd graduate from six months early, the following winter — they had formed some sort of bond.

She had no fantasies of them ever being close, or "best friends," but was glad that they had reached some sort of silent understanding: yes, Kerri was older, would always be older, and therefore she had the right to boss Clara around at will. The flip side of that coin was that: yes, Clara was younger, would always be younger, but was a human being with a brain and a purpose, other than to stuff into trash bins.

"Hey, guys. We're ready to cut the cake," Max said, strolling over to the three sitting under the tree. He reached down to help Clara up as Zane did the same for Kerri. "Come on, kiddo." He swung an arm over her shoulders, holding her to his side as they walked toward the patio where Stephanie was busy placing and lighting candles into the huge sheet cake. A picture of a smiling, gap-toothed, nine-year-old Clara was done in rice paper on top.

Clara held onto her father's waist, which she noticed had slimmed down considerably since he wasn't eating her mother's home-cooked meals anymore. The other women who had come and gone in his life over the past four years had gone sooner than they'd been kept around. Clara never understood that.

"Um, Mom?" Clara said, watching as her mother lit the last candle, twelve in all. "It's not my birthday. I only graduated from high school."

"*Only?*" Stephanie said, hands on hips. "You accomplished something, sweetie, and I want to give you all the luck I can. There are twelve candles here, one for every year of school you've been in so far." She smiled, proud of herself. "Make a wish!"

Clara decided to play along, scanning the rooms of her brain for what she wanted most. She leaned over, holding her newly grown-out hair out of the way and blew out all the candles. The gathered guests clapped.

๛๛๛๛๛

The party was a success, Clara walking away with just over two hundred dollars and lots of well wishes. Everyone had gone home. Max and the girls were helping clean up. Florence had gone home almost an hour before, irritated that Max wanted to stay and help.

He sat on the front stoop of the house that he hadn't lived in for four years. He'd been there hundreds of times for various occasions, never again missing a holiday after the first year, when Clara had been so upset at him. He took a drag from his cigarette, blowing smoke out into the early evening of a warm, summer night. He sat on the front stoop, feet spread, a bottle of beer dangling from his fingers between his knees.

The moon was beginning to show itself over the roof of the neighbor's house across the street. Max watched it, its bright yellow color and size indicative of the brilliant full moon it would become. He felt a certain level of peace as he sat there, for the first time in long time, a feeling of family love around him. He still couldn't believe both of his daughters had now graduated high school — one graduating college in December. Where had the time gone? Had he been everything they needed him to be, or had he failed them, the way he'd failed their mother?

Max's thoughts were interrupted when the screen door opened, then softly closed. The person who had entered his solitude sat on the stoop next to him, taking his beer from his fingers and taking a quick swig before giving it back.

"Good stuff," Clara said, looking out over the falling night.

"That it is." Max took one final drag of the cigarette, swallowed the last of his beer, and tossed the cigarette butt inside the bottle. The cherry fizzled in the tiny bit of liquid at the bottom of the brown glass bottle. "You got everything packed?" he asked, unable to look at his daughter. They'd been a team — through good and bad — for four years. He couldn't imagine his life — or his house — without her.

"Yeah." Clara was silent for a long moment, her thoughts running very much along the lines of her father's. She was filled with a strange mixture of elation and loss. "Guess you'll finally get to have that home office you always wanted," she said, playfully bumping his shoulder with her own.

"Goodie." Max smiled, no real enthusiasm behind it.

Clara looked at her father, gazing into his sad eyes. "Dad, I'll be back. I promise."

He nodded. "I know you will, sweet pea. I just hate seeing you go. All grown up, now." He looked at her, taking in the breathtaking young woman she'd turned into. "No matter what happens — you and Kerri get into it, whatever — you've got a place to come back to." He looked into her eyes, making sure she was really hearing him. "Okay?"

Clara nodded, a sudden lump forming in her throat. "Okay." Her voice had become that of the child Max used to hold in his arms. She lost control of her emotions when she saw tears glisten in his eyes.

"Come 'ere," he murmured, pulling her against him in a one-armed hug. They sat in silence for a long moment, just absorbing the warmth and love of the other. Together they watched the sun set.

≈≈≈≈≈

Clara never thought it would be scary to have her own apartment. To move to a place where neither her father nor her mother lived. It helped immensely to know that Kerri and Zane were two floors below, but still...

She sat on her bed, looking around the space. It was actually a really nice — albeit small — apartment. It was essentially a studio apartment, everything in the larger, main space, while the bathroom had been partitioned off for privacy. She had everything there that she owned: all her clothing, her minimal movie collection, and her CDs and stereo, a gift for graduation.

A few movie posters were tacked to the slanted ceiling by the two windows that allowed minimal light into the space. All her clothes were neatly tucked away in the dresser set her mother had bought for her, as well as the simple closet space her father had built in the corner. She was set.

She flopped back onto the comforter, hands above her head as she stared up at the ceiling, not really seeing the plaster and paint, but instead a future that was yet to be determined. She knew the future her parents wanted for her: go to college, do her best, and earn her degree, just as Kerri was doing. Max had worked for the garbage company for more years than Clara could remember, and Stephanie had been at the bakery for almost four years. Both her parents wanted more for their daughters than the hard, day-to-day life of someone "uneducated."

Clara understood and respected that, but she wished they understood and respected what *she* wanted and what *she* knew of her future. She knew her future didn't lay in the corporate world or as some bigwig in business. Her place in the world was to help people through her gifts. Her family refused to see this, worried that she'd never be able to make a living at it. Clara understood their fears, as she had the same fears herself. Even so, she was drawn.

Clara sighed heavily, glancing over at the backpack — already loaded with books bought for her upcoming semester — that sat on the floor by the wall. She didn't look forward to her college career, at all. Yet another way she and Kerri were complete opposites. One of Kerri's first words had been college.

"Shit," she blew out. "I dread this."

Chapter Twenty

The campus of State was huge — much, much larger than John Freed High School, for certain. It had taken Clara several weeks to truly get her bearings in the place. Now, nearly through her first six weeks in college, she had found all her hangout and hideout spots. One of which, she was currently sitting in.

On the fifth floor of the library, which was a study floor with a few stacks of books, Clara sat in a cubby at the back of the large room, "reading." In truth, she was peering over the top of her text at the girl who was shelving books. She'd noticed Shelby the first week of classes and hadn't been able to take her eyes off her since. Shelby had short, blonde hair, cut in a sporty style, and smiling blue eyes. Dimples teased every time she spoke or smiled, which was often. She was adorable. She seemed to have a natural glow about her that drew Clara in like a bug to the zapper.

Clara had no idea what year Shelby was or what she was taking. She'd never so much as spoken to her, but she had figured out what her work schedule typically was, and made sure to be on the library's fifth floor on Tuesday nights. Thus, she was tucked away, watching.

Shelby pulled a two-level metal cart with her, books set in two neat rows on the top and on the lower shelf. She took her time, reading the Library of

Congress code on the spine then finding the correct location for the book before moving on to the next.

She wore black mesh shorts and a tank top. Her tanned skin looked pale and sickly under the fluorescent lights, but Clara had seen her on campus under the bright sun. She was stunning, her arms and legs well toned, as though Shelby had played soccer or volleyball or some other sport, for many years. Clara's eyes followed the movement of her body, her stomach awash with nervous butterflies of excitement.

Shelby pushed her cart toward the cubby where Clara sat, making Clara want to vomit with anxiety. She turned her attention back to her book, though she couldn't recall a single thing she'd read on the page she'd been on for the past twenty-seven minutes. She had been trying to figure out a good way to talk to the blonde for six weeks, but had no idea what to say, or how to go about it. Sometimes — most times — she cursed her quiet nature.

Clara peeked over her book, only to find herself meeting Shelby's gaze. She gave the girl a quick smile of acknowledgment. As she went to bury her nose back into her book, she stopped. Sitting at the table Shelby was about to pass was a woman, her gaze locked onto Shelby. Clara looked from the library worker to the woman, but the woman had vanished.

"How's it going?" Shelby asked politely as she began to push her cart past Clara.

"Fine. Um, hey," Clara felt a bit devilish as she realized the woman she'd seen was a perfect segue into conversation with the gorgeous blonde. "Do you believe in psychics and mediums?"

Shelby stopped, her brows drawn in confusion. "What?"

Clara opened herself up, reaching out toward the spirit of the woman she knew was still with them. She could feel her energy, and it was close to Shelby. "You know, people who speak to spirits."

Shelby stopped, one hand resting on her cart, the other on her hip. "I guess. Why?"

Clara had to stop herself from grinning, proud of taking advantage of the opportunity. "Well, there was a woman sitting over at that table," she said, nodding toward the one in question. Shelby glanced over her shoulder to see it was empty. "She was looking at you, and I feel strongly she's here for you."

Shelby looked at Clara as though she wasn't sure whether to tell Clara to go fly a kite or to ask for more information. "Okay," she said slowly, waiting for Clara to continue.

Clara listened for a moment, nodding slightly at the information she'd just heard in her mind. She also saw the woman again, this time standing just on the other side of Shelby's cart. "I'm sensing a mother-figure. Has your mom crossed?" Shelby nodded, but said nothing. "About this tall," she held up a hand to just a wee shorter than herself, "blonde hair, longer than yours. And..." Clara looked at the woman, watching as the older blonde opened her shirt just enough to bare her upper chest and an ugly scar that ran the length across from her right collarbone across her heart, and disappearing into the shirt. "And a really bad scar." Clara used her finger to draw an imaginary scar across her own chest.

Shelby could only stare, her blue eyes wide. "Who are you?" she asked, about to run in the opposite direction.

Clara could tell the blonde was getting more and

more skittish. "I'm sorry. I'm not trying to freak you out. It's just that, when they come to me, I feel kind of obligated to pass on the message, you know?"

Shelby nodded, rattled. "All right. So, what's the message?"

Clara glanced back to the woman, Shelby, following her gaze, was baffled to see just empty space. Clara could see the woman's lips moving, but the words came to her in her own mind. "Okay," she murmured, nodding. She turned to Shelby. "She said to tell you that it wasn't your fault that she passed. Does that make sense? She's saying that it would have happened whether you'd hit it or not." Clara's brows drew, not understanding, but simply repeating.

Shelby apparently understood, as her hand flew to her mouth, a soft sob escaping her throat. "Oh, god," she whispered.

"She also says that she knows about the kiss on her forehead."

Tears began to fall down Shelby's cheeks.

"Aw, jeez. I'm sorry." Clara rifled in her backpack, finding a travel-size pack of Kleenex. She handed them to the blonde. "I didn't mean to make you cry." What she had viewed as a great way to pick up a woman a few moments ago now made her feel terrible!

"No, no!" Shelby exclaimed, wiping at her eyes and laughing nervously. "This is amazing." She glanced over to where Clara had been staring. "Is she here still, or something?"

Clara nodded. "Yeah. She's standing about four feet away from you."

Shelby looked at the spot, trying desperately to catch a glimpse, but it was impossible. She looked away, instead studying the wadded up Kleenex in her hand. "Is she saying anything else?"

Clara glanced over to the woman, sad to see she was beginning to fade, though her lips were moving again. "She said she loves you and Monkey. Don't forget about her, but she said you need to move on with your life too."

Shelby's eyes got huge. "There's no possible way you could know about Monkey," she said, looking at Clara with almost accusing eyes. "How do you *know* this stuff?"

Clara shrugged. "I just repeat what I'm told or shown."

"Wow." Shelby blew out a long breath, wiping her face and blowing her nose. She took a moment to get herself together; Clara remained quiet to give her time. "That woman was my mother," Shelby began to explain softly, her focus once again on the Kleenex in her hands. "Lucy. She died last year from breast cancer." She took a deep breath, trying to keep the emotions down that insisted on rising. "She was really sick, and I was driving her to the hospital. We got stuck in traffic, and um..." She looked up at the ceiling, her blue eyes vibrant from unshed tears. She cleared her throat, trying to get herself under control. "She died before we got there."

"Oh, wow," Clara whispered, shoving her hands into the pockets of her shorts so she wouldn't reach out to Shelby and comfort her. She'd already freaked her out enough for one day. "Um," she said, feeling rather sheepish. "Can I ask you who Monkey is?"

Shelby let out a bark of nervous laughter. "My dog. He was actually hers, but Monkey and I kind of had a love-at-first-sight moment, so she let me take him with me."

Clara smiled, amused. "Well, I truly *am* sorry for making you cry, but I hope it helped. She obviously needed to talk to you, or you needed to hear from her."

Shelby leaned back on the table behind her, needing the sturdy support. "I've been thinking about her a lot, lately. The year anniversary is coming up next month."

"Ouch."

"Yeah. So," she shrugged, a smile on her lips. "Guess I really did need that. Thank you...?"

"Clara."

"Thank you, Clara. That was really amazing, even if it was a little freaky."

Clara was amused. "Yeah, well, what can I say?"

"Have you been doing this for a long time? Talking to dead people, I mean?"

Clara nodded. "Since I was a kid."

"Wow." Shelby sat on the table for a moment, her head shaking slowly side-to-side. "Wow." She hopped off the table and walked over to her book cart. "I need to get these finished before I close up the library for the night." She put a hand on the cart, about to start pushing it when she thought better of it. She moved over to Clara, taking her in a tight, and all too quick, embrace. "Thank you, Clara."

Clara hugged her back, releasing her as soon as Shelby showed signs of letting go. She smiled as she met her gaze once they parted. "You're welcome. I'm glad I could help."

"You really did." She took hold of her cart. "I'll see you around, Clara." She left with a brilliant smile, disappearing into the stacks.

Clara tried not to react to the shiver that traveled

down her spine at the smile she'd just received, coupled with the memory of the feel of Shelby's body against hers. After she'd broken up with Erica during the second semester of her freshman year, Clara hadn't bothered to date. She'd concentrated most of her energy into The Pagan — which she still worked at — and honing her gift. She didn't have time for love, or for schoolwork, for that matter.

She sighed as she watched the last of Shelby disappear. How wonderful it would be to feel that body again. She gathered her things together, noting that the library would be closing in forty-five minutes, anyway. She heaved her backpack on her shoulder and headed for the elevators.

ॐॐ৺৺

Clara ignored the couple eating dinner on the couch. She kept her place in the La-Z-Boy chair in the corner, her gaze on the TV, listening to Peter Jennings as he rattled off the nightly news.

"Hey, Clara, how did you do on your paper?" Zane asked, shoveling a forkful of spaghetti in his mouth. A noodle and sauce fell onto his chin. Kerri rolled her eyes as he wiped it off on the sleeve of his shirt.

"You're doing laundry next," she stated drily.

"I did good." Clara turned to face her sister's boyfriend, a sweet smile plastered on her face. "So how many of my firstborn would I have to sacrifice to have you write *all* my papers this semester?"

Zane looked her in the eye. "You couldn't breed enough for that, kid."

"Damn." Clara turned back to the TV, only to

have her sister grab her attention. "What time is Tory coming over?" Kerri asked, setting her plate aside and wiping her mouth on the napkin in her lap.

Clara glanced at her. "Any time." Though Kerri had stopped calling her a freak long ago, they'd never talked about her abilities. Kerri certainly had not requested them before, so Clara had been stunned when Kerri asked if she'd do a reading for one of her co-workers at the hospital, where Kerri was working while finishing up her nursing education. Zane rolled his eyes, getting up to put his dish and Kerri's in the kitchen.

"Crazy-ass voodoo shit," he muttered as he walked by.

Clara ignored him. "Where do you want me to do it? Want me to take Tory up to my room?" she asked, nodding in the direction where Zane had just disappeared. "Don't want him to be uncomfortable.

"Eh, he'll survive," Kerri said, waving off her boyfriend's attitude, which was even worse than Stephanie's had been for most of Clara's life. She'd never spoken with him about it and hadn't exposed him to much of what her sister was capable of, either.

"Okay," Clara said skeptically, finishing her dinner.

☙ ☙ ☙ ☙

Tory Amberson arrived fifteen minutes later, nervous about getting her first reading with a medium, but open-minded, and apparently needing something from Clara. Clara wouldn't allow her to give her any information about whom she wished to connect with, instead just letting the threads of information come to her naturally.

They sat in the front room of the Victorian, Tory sitting anxiously on the couch while Clara perched casually on the window seat. Eyes closed, Clara took in several deep breaths, trying to open herself up for the connection she could feel was beginning to come. She could feel energy beginning to gather around her, the coolness touching her leg. It was male energy that much she could tell, and told Tory as much. She couldn't quite make anything out about him and asked silently if he'd give her some sort of clue as to his age at death.

"Okay," Clara finally said, "he's showing me baggy jeans. A flannel shirt..." her voice trailed off as she tried to focus on the image in her brain. "Long hair. A younger man. Twenties, maybe?"

Tory nodded, trying to hold in any reactions as she still wasn't entirely a believer, yet. Not to mention, part of her was hoping Clara would truly be gifted, and part of her hoped she was a fraud. She was only there because her mother needed some answers, anyway.

"I'm seeing a...something silver." Clara tried to focus harder on the object that glittered in front of her mind's eye. "A keychain. Shaped like a skull."

"Sapphire eyes?" Tory asked, her heart beginning to pound.

Clara nodded. "Yes. It says Brandon on it."

"Oh my god," Tory gasped. Clara met her shocked gaze. "That's my brother."

"Is that who you were wanting to connect with today?" At Tory's nod, Clara continued. Her brows drew as she could feel Brandon's energy even stronger. "I'm feeling something very, very negative around him," she explained, shivering slightly. She couldn't see Brandon very clearly anymore — some spirits stuck around in a visual sense, others preferred to identify themselves only once, then disappeared again — but she could feel him intensely. And it was incredibly unsettling.

Tory was shocked, but still wanted more confirmation that it was, in fact, her brother. "Can you maybe tell me a little more? About him, I mean."

Clara nodded, amused. She never blamed her clients for their skepticism. She turned inward, focusing on Brandon again, mentally asking him to give her more information about him. She gasped, a snapshot entering her head that chilled her blood. She saw two figures — neither in clear focus — in a struggle then the echoing BOOM of a gunshot reverberated in her mind. At first she thought that perhaps Brandon was showing her how he'd died, but somehow that didn't feel right. She then saw his eyes: black as night, and threatening to stare a hole in her. She shivered again.

"What is it?" Tory asked, her heart beginning to pound again. Clara had gone pale, and Tory couldn't help but wonder if she knew why.

"Um," Clara said, clearing her throat and trying to get the chill out of her spine. "Was Brandon part of something..." she was trying to decide the most tactful way to say it. Thinking of none, she just blurted out what she'd seen. "Was he part of a murder? A shooting death?"

Tory stared at her, mouth hanging open. Kerri, who had been asked by Tory to witness the reading, stared slack-jawed from her sister to her friend and back to her sister. She knew the details of Tory's family's history, and couldn't believe Clara had picked up on it.

"Yes. He was. He—"

Clara cut her off. "No details, please. It makes it more difficult to do this if I know stuff beforehand."

"Okay. Sorry. Yes, he was involved in a shooting death."

"Okay. Was the victim a woman? I'm getting a female energy, like a girlfriend or wife."

"His ex-girlfriend," Tory validated. "The mother of his child."

Clara pushed down her reactions. She had to try and stay somewhat detached on this one because she had the distinct feeling she wasn't going to like this guy very much. "Okay. He's here, so what did you want to say or ask?"

"I want to know why. I want to know why he did it to Lisa. Why he did what he did in prison." Tory couldn't keep her anger at bay. Though she'd never been close to her older brother, she still loved him.

"Okay." Clara waited, knowing that Brandon was able to hear his sister. She didn't have to wait long before the answers began to come. "I'm getting something about Brandon's past." Clara looked the older woman in the eye. "Do you want to know everything, Tory?"

"Yes. I think so. Yes. Yes, I do."

"Okay. Were you aware that your brother was involved with..." Clara saw a large number two appear in her mind, "with two situations?"

"Situations? What do you mean?" Tory asked, feeling slightly nervous at the answer. Her parents had denied for years that Brandon had been involved in anything dark, but Tory had always suspected something. She just never knew what.

"Yeah. I'm seeing two girls. He uh...um. He—"

"Raped them, didn't he?" She blew out a long breath at Clara's nod. "I knew it. Danielle and Lee

Ann." Tory shook her head. "I always knew something happened that night." She looked at Clara. "Lisa knew about it, didn't she? Is that why she was killed?"

Clara turned her attention back inward to Brandon. She saw a struggle. Shapes fighting, yelling. "I think it was more of a fight. I think it came out, and her death was basically accidental, on purpose."

Tory nodded her understanding. "I see. So what about what happened in prison?" she asked, still not wanting to lead Clara on with information.

Clara could hear Brandon in her thoughts: *Pressure. Too much pressure and guilt.* She tried to make sense of the words, but decided it wasn't hers to figure out. "He said, and I quote: 'Pressure. Too much pressure and guilt'."

"Coward," Tory said, her voice bitter. "Thank you, Clara. I don't really want to know anything else."

Clara nodded. "Sure. I hope it helped."

"Oh," Tory said, shouldering her purse strap and rising to her feet. "It did. I'll let my mother know."

Clara stayed where she was as Kerri walked her friend to the front door. The two women stood in the entryway talking for a few minutes, then Tory was gone, and Kerri returned to the front room, taking Tory's seat.

"That was really impressive, Clara."

"He was a real bastard," Clara said, a chill racing down her spine. "God, his energy was just...dark."

"He was a bastard. Tory didn't like him, and used to try and stay away from him. Her mother wanted this reading tonight. She never wanted to see Brandon for what he was. He was put in prison for Lisa's death, then hung himself there."

"Wow. I didn't like that at all. Really, *really*

creepy feel to him."

"So, how did it go?" Zane asked from the archway leading into the room, a glass of iced tea in hand. "Is 'this house clean'?" he asked, imitating the voice of Zelda Rubinstein as her character in the film *Poltergeist*.

"Don't be an ass, Zane," Kerri said, shooting a glare at her boyfriend.

"This stuff is so creepy, Kerri." He turned to Clara. "I like you Clara, but I don't want you doing that voodoo stuff in this house. You got me?"

Clara could only stare at him, surprised and hurt.

"Zane!" Kerri said, again glaring at him. "What is your deal? She didn't do anything wrong."

"I didn't say she did. This shit is creepy, and I don't want it here," he said, pointing to the floor at his feet.

Clara was embarrassed and hurt. She pushed up from the window seat. "Whatever," she muttered, breezing past him and up to her apartment.

"What the hell is the matter with you?" Kerri asked, walking over to him. "That was really rude."

"Doesn't that shit make you feel uneasy?" he asked, crossing his arms over his chest. "Does she even know what she's doing?"

"Yes. She does. She's not doing anything wrong, and you owe her an apology."

"No." He looked down at Kerri, jaw set stubbornly. "I meant it. I don't want that shit here."

Kerri shook her head, pushing past him. "Jerk."

Chapter Twenty-one

"Damn." Clara stopped at the stop sign, chewing on her lower lip as she noted the orange construction signs on the next block, as well as the detour sign that would lead her to the university in another route. She was already running late, and now would be even later. "Damn, damn, damn!"

Clara had actually been up late studying for the test, overslept, and now was going to be late for that test. When she awoke and realized how light it was out, she panicked, not even bothering to shower as she threw on some clothes, tugged her hair into a ponytail, and flew out the door.

As she sped down a side street, she noticed a small army of police cars parked outside of a house, as well as an ambulance. There was no activity outside, all apparently inside. She shrugged it off and hurried on to school.

✺✺✺✺✺

Clara was in another of her hiding places, the Cantina — an underground cafeteria for the university — eating a slice of greasy pepperoni pizza when her eyes alighted on an angelic sight. She was surprised, as she'd never seen Shelby in the Cantina before, and couldn't pull her gaze away. The blonde library worker was talking to a black guy as they stood in line for

Subway. Their conversation was animated, both all smiles, which made Clara immediately feel an uneasy jealousy just under the surface.

She had very little time to stew over the thought because Shelby spotted her and raised a hand in greeting. Clara swallowed her nervousness — after all, the woman was half a room away — and waved back with what she hoped was a friendly smile.

Shelby continued her conversation with her companion, but then moved away from him when she ordered her meal. Clara watched — with no small relief — when a Hispanic girl hurried over to them, immediately planting a kiss on the tall black man. Shelby greeted the girl and gave her a hug, accepted her food, paid for it, then walked over toward Clara's table.

"Oh, shit," Clara whispered, panic setting in.

"Hey," Shelby said. "Are you here alone? Mind if I join you?"

"No," Clara said, tugging her heavy backpack off the table and to one of the other chairs. "Help yourself."

Shelby got situated and began to prepare her salad. "So, how have you been? I didn't see you at the library the other day." She squirted a liberal amount of ranch dressing over her greens.

"Oh, yeah. I had to work Tuesday night. Usually I have that night off, but Cassandra — my boss — wasn't feeling so hot, so she asked if I'd be willing to work for her." Clara quickly shut her mouth, realizing she was babbling, and that the explanation of her job had been entirely unnecessary.

Shelby smiled, as though realizing the very same thing. "Where do you work?" She stabbed a carrot with her plastic fork.

Clara picked one of the few pieces of pepperoni off her pizza and popped it into her mouth. "The Pagan. It's a metaphysical shop downtown," she explained, seeing the look of unfamiliarity on her dinner companion's face. "We sell tarot cards, crystals, incense. That kind of thing."

"Gotcha. Guess it makes sense, with what you do and all." Shelby chewed her food, studying Clara thoughtfully for a moment. "I've thought a lot about what happened. With my mom and everything. I've taken her advice. Now I only go to the cemetery once a week instead of almost every day." Her smile was mischievous.

"Well, it's a good start, I suppose," Clara said, returning the humor, then quickly sobered. "I'm really glad, Shelby. You can't let grief run your life. That's one thing I've learned in all this. They may be gone, as in you can't see them anymore, but they're never truly gone."

"Yeah, but you can see them and talk to them. It's different for us mere mortals."

Clara chuckled, shaking her head in disagreement. "Not really. I mean if you pay attention, and I mean *really* pay attention, you'll see that they actually find ways to get into contact with you all the time."

"Like how?" Doubt was obvious on Shelby's beautiful features. She sat back in her chair, forgetting about her food for a moment.

"Well, as an example, I know a lady who loves music, and music was a huge part of her relationship with her mom when her mom was alive. My friend was driving down the street one day, having a hard time with missing her mom. She felt compelled to turn on her radio, and when she did, it was a song her mom used to love and listen to all the time."

"Oh, come on, Clara," Shelby said, leaning forward slightly. "That kind of thing has got to be just coincidence."

"I don't believe in coincidence," Clara said, complete certainty in her voice. "Nothing is by accident. Nothing."

"Like us meeting? You think there was some sort of purpose in it?" she asked, a brow rising in challenge.

Is she flirting? Clara was doing a little happy dance inside. "Your mom needed to give you a message, and it was one you needed to hear. I've been in that library how many Tuesday nights, and not once have you said a word to me. The one night that your mom has a message for you, you do. Coincidence? I think not."

Shelby grinned, nodding. "Okay. But I still think most things in life are pure chance."

"And that's cool. You're certainly entitled to your beliefs." She held her pizza up to her mouth, about to take a bite, pausing for effect. "Even if they're wrong."

"Oh, nice!" Shelby laughed, playfully tossing a carrot piece at Clara. They ate in silence for a moment, then, "Doesn't it bother you? Seeing the dead people?"

Clara shook her head. "No, not at all. It used to. It used to scare the hell out of me, but now... Nah."

"I don't know. It's just kinda...creepy."

Clara shrugged. "That's not the first time I've heard that, and it won't be the last, I'm sure. When I was in high school, and really figuring this stuff out, I would ask friends, even my parents' friends, if I could do a practice reading for them. I was surprised by the number of people who weren't cool with it."

"Yeah. The peanut gallery is still out on that one for me, I think." Shelby took a few bites of her salad, chewing thoughtfully before asking, "Are you from here?"

Clara nodded, recognizing the change of subject for what it was. At the moment, Shelby wasn't comfortable with what she did. She hoped that would change in time. "Born and raised. You?"

Shelby shook her head. "No. I was born in New York City, but we left when I was still in diapers. We moved around a lot. I counted it one time. I went to thirteen different schools, and that was *before* high school!"

"Good god! That had to suck."

Shelby shrugged, pushing her lunch away. "Sometimes. It was harder on my older brother, Dennis. He's pretty shy, so I think the constant new people kind of threw him into even more isolation."

"It would have done the same thing to me," Clara admitted, tossing the remaining crust of her pizza to the paper plate it had been served on.

"Why? Are you shy?"

"Extremely." Clara smiled sheepishly.

"Really?" Shelby asked, swinging her arm casually over the back of her chair. "So, what does it take to get to know you, then?"

Okay, she is definitely flirting. Clara took a deep breath. "Well, why don't you go to dinner with me and I'll tell you?"

Chapter Twenty-two

Clara breezed into the store. If it had been a cartoon, birds carrying a silken scarf in their beaks would have flown in before her, announcing her ridiculously happy mood.

"Good afternoon, Cassandra," she hummed, heading around the counter and the older woman to the back room to drop off her backpack. She had some studying to do later so didn't want to leave the bag in her car.

"Good afternoon to you, too." Cassandra followed her one employee to the back, amused. "How's the new girlfriend?" She leaned against the doorframe, arms crossing over her chest with a jingle of bracelets.

Clara's spreading grin spoke louder than anything she might say. Her boss chuckled. "So how has business been today? We gonna be busy tonight?" Clara donned her apron and nametag.

"You're the psychic. You tell me."

Clara followed Cassandra to the main part of the store. As she walked, she pulled her hair into a loose bun. "What's on the agenda tonight?"

"You have a reading at seven, and then one at nine," Cassandra said, looking at her daily log of appointments.

Since Clara had started doing regular readings at the shop, business had nearly tripled. Clara kept all the money for her readings, but more often than not the clients would either come in early and shop or stay to purchase something that Clara would recommend: often sage to cleanse their homes of unwanted spirits or energies. Usually after the sage the customers found themselves drawn to the books, and then the decks of tarot. It was a win-win situation for both.

"Sounds good." Clara knew she had stocking to do, as Thursdays were their delivery date. She quickly set about pulling the product from the stockroom before her first reading.

Clara had just found the new shipment of candles when she felt a presence behind her. She knew immediately who it was without turning around. "Hi," she tossed over her shoulder.

"What's up?" Erica asked, hoisting herself up on a stack of boxes. The heels of her shoes beat a light rhythm on the boxes beneath her.

"Just working. You?" She turned to her old flame, arms crossed over her chest. It had taken some time for her to adjust to Erica's dirty blonde hair, long ago freed of damaging dyes. She had lost the Goth façade a couple years before, instead allowing her true beauty to come through. Even still, Clara had to fight hard against Erica's natural charm, and it didn't stop Erica from trying, though. Far from it.

"So, I was thinking of heading to the cemetery tonight," she said, brushing dirty blonde hair off her shoulder. "Wanna come?"

Clara glanced at the young woman, now twenty. "Not really."

"Come on, Clara. You know I don't do that stuff anymore. I just want to go. It's so peaceful."

Clara leaned against the wall, studying her old friend. "Erica, we've been through this. I'm not your personal spirit guide."

Erica snickered, knowing Clara's beliefs in such things. "I know that. Guess I just hoped for old time's sake." She shrugged, playing the rejection off like no big deal. "We had some fun."

"We did," Clara agreed, though reluctantly.

"Clara, have you got those new candles, yet?" Cassandra asked, stopping when she stepped into the back room. She could feel the tension in the air. Looking from one young woman to the other, she decided she should leave them be.

Erica still carried a torch for Clara, and Cassandra knew she regretted the way she'd treated the younger girl four years before. They'd had many a discussion about it over the years. Erica had moved on, had dated this one and that, graduated high school, and had gone off on her own. Even still, Clara had never been far from Erica's thoughts.

Grateful for the interruption, Clara pushed away from the wall and grabbed the box of candles in question. "I need to get back to work."

ᘔᘓ᙮ᘓ᙮ᘔ᙮ᘔ

Two weeks had gone by and Clara couldn't be happier. She spent as much time with Shelby as she could, though their work hours tended to get in the way. Cassandra was asking Clara to work more and more nights, especially after the older woman started to teach a tarot class on Tuesday and Thursday nights and couldn't mind the shop.

It hadn't been firmly established just exactly *what* Clara and Shelby's relationship was, though Clara saw the blonde as her girlfriend, and anyone who knew that she was gay — all three people — believed the same thing. Except for Shelby. She was afraid to bring it up to Shelby. What if Shelby didn't feel the same way? What if she freaked out? What if Shelby just thought they were really, really, *really* good friends, and if Clara said anything, that friendship would begin to deteriorate because Shelby would feel pressured, or threatened, or...

Clara took a deep breath, trying to calm herself so she wouldn't hyperventilate. She was at home, up in her small studio apartment, thinking. She was supposed to be studying, but it wasn't happening. Her mind had been in turmoil over Shelby for well over a week, now. What should she do? Should she say anything? Should she just kiss Shelby and let things happen as they would? Oh, so many choices!! None of them felt right to her or seemed appealing.

Clara had thought about talking to Kerri and trying to get her advice, but she hadn't even told her older sister yet that she was a lesbian. What would Kerri do? Would she run off and tell their parents? What would they say if they knew?

"Shit!" Clara flopped back on her bed, a headache beginning to creep up with all the thoughts and uncertainty whirling around in her mind. She groaned when she heard scratching on the door. "Moses!" she whined, throwing her legs off the bed and following suit as she got to her feet.

Kerri's cat loved to sleep in the open area that was the closet Max had made for her. She padded over to the door and opened it, letting the black and gray feline run inside. She knew better than to close the door again, as he would meow and whine until she opened the door again. And, if she were to dare close it once more, he wouldn't quit. He wanted to come and go as he pleased. Even if he chose to stay in her apartment all day, it didn't matter, he wouldn't want out until she closed the door.

Heading back to her bed, Clara plopped down, staring down at the sea of papers and books scattered on her bed. She had no desire to work on any of it, but knew she had to. Distantly she heard the doorbell, and a glance at the alarm clock on the dresser made Clara smile. Shelby had gotten off work and come right over, just as she did every Monday night.

Clara felt her heart pound a little faster with every footfall that brought Shelby up one more stair toward her apartment. The blonde peeked her head into the opened door.

"Hey."

"Hi. Come on in." Clara shoved her books and papers to one side of the double bed, making room for Shelby to sit down. The blonde looked around the room that she'd been in dozens of times before.

"You really need to get some furniture in here, Clara," she said, sitting down, bouncing slightly on the mattress.

"Yes, yes, so you say every time you're here."

"And yet you still haven't done it." Shelby raised a challenging brow.

Clara rolled her eyes in the familiar game they played. They both grinned. "How was your day?"

"It was good." Shelby flopped back across the bottom of the bed looking at Clara's calculator before moving it so she could rest her head in its place. "Long." She sighed tiredly. "Caleb called off again, so I ended up working two extra hours today. I went in this morning before class then worked my normal shift tonight. God!" she exclaimed, slamming a fist into the comforter. "Why the hell doesn't my boss do something about him? You know?" She turned to look at Clara, who quickly looked away. She'd been studying the blonde's profile, marveling at just how gorgeous Shelby really was. She had nearly gotten caught.

"Yeah, I know exactly what you mean. We had someone like that down at the shop for a while, too, then Cassandra and I realized that we did better with just the two of us and got rid of Tammy."

"I don't want them to get rid of him, I just want them to hire someone who actually gives a crap and wants to work. I can't keep putting in the extra hours like this."

"I'm sorry." Clara shoved the books off the bed totally and lay across her bed on her side, facing Shelby. She pillowed her head in the palm of her hand. With a slight grunt, Shelby repositioned herself to mirror Clara.

"What do you want to do tonight?" the blonde asked, her tone turning from hard frustration to the soft, gentle tones always reserved for Clara. Or so Clara hoped.

"I don't know. I don't have a lot of money. I had to get that damn radiator fixed. Again." She sighed in her own frustration.

"Honey, why don't you just get rid of that clunker?"

Clara's heart leapt in her chest. She wondered if Shelby realized she'd just called her "Honey." "I know. I just don't want to have to deal with it. Grrr!" She flopped onto her back, warm fuzzies forgotten as she remembered that her bank account was nearly dry after the four hundred and seventy-nine dollar bill she'd received from the garage. "I hate my car."

Shelby scooted over closer, looking down at her. "At least you don't have huge bills to pay," she pointed out, indicating the space around them. "You've actually got a pretty sweet deal right here."

Clara looked up at her. "You think so?"

Shelby nodded. "Oh, yeah. No rent. Only have to water the lawn. I'd say you've got it made in the shade."

Clara grinned. "Yeah, maybe. But I do have my books every semester. You've got that covered from your scholarship."

"True," Shelby conceded. "But I've got rent." She poked at Clara with a finger. "And food," poke, "and I've got to put up with Jasper."

"The evil roommate."

"Yes. The evil roommate." She poked one last time, grinning at Clara's response. "I still say you should move in so I can kick him out."

Clara looked into Shelby's face, trying desperately to read her eyes. Shelby had said things like that before, but Clara always prayed and hoped that one of these days she would finish it with "we should move in together" rather than just Clara taking over for the roommate Shelby didn't want in her apartment anymore.

The energy in the room began to change as Shelby continued to look down at Clara. She searched the younger woman's face, though for what Clara wasn't sure.

"Can I tell you something, Clara?" Shelby asked, her voice growing softer. Clara nodded. "I really like you. A lot." She grew very shy as she played with the comforter that they lay on. "I've been having some pretty strange thoughts lately. I was hoping that maybe you could help me out a little." She glanced at Clara.

"Okay," Clara said, her chest beginning to rise faster and her heart sped up. "Tell me what you've been thinking. I'll see what I can do."

"Okay." Shelby reached out and touched a long strand of Clara's hair, wrapping it around one of her fingers. "I've been thinking about you. About your eyes." She looked into them. "They're so beautiful. Really unusual color." She brought up a finger, tracing a brow. "I've also been thinking about..." her words trailed off as her gaze settled onto Clara's mouth. Her eyes flicked back to Clara's, almost as though to see what her reaction would be to what she had insinuated.

"Have you ever kissed a girl before, Shelby?" Clara asked, her heart about to speed right out of her chest. Shelby shook her head. "But you want to. Right?"

Shelby nodded. "Yeah. Very much so. But only if it's you."

"Come here. Let me show you."

Shelby's were the softest lips Clara had ever touched. She sighed into the kiss, as did Shelby. She didn't even notice when her slightly ajar apartment door was pushed a bit further open. Kerri peeked her head in to see if the girls wanted to join her and Zane for dinner. Quietly, she closed the door and crept down the stairs.

❧ ❧ ❧ ❧

She sat across from Clara, a stern look on her face. "No, you need to say it like you always say it, Clara," she said.

Clara was confused, and getting frustrated. Every time she tried to say it just like she was being asked, it came out wrong. "Okay. Let me try again." *She cleared her throat and opened her mouth, intending to say it, just like she'd been asked.* "I washed the dog." *She heard it in her head, knew that was what she was supposed to say, but still it came out wrong: Save me.*

"No, Clara! That's wrong! Say it right!"

"I'm trying!"

Save me...

❧❧❧❧

Clara gasped as she awoke, looking around her room.

Save me...

She heard it again. This time it wasn't a strange hiccup in a dream. She could feel that she wasn't alone and knew Shelby's sleeping form had nothing to do with it.

Save me...

She pushed the covers off, ignoring the cool chill in the night air, and padded across her living space. The tank top and panties she wore did little to protect her from the cold or from the fear that niggled at her brain.

Save me...

She stood in the center of her apartment, turning in a slow circle, trying to figure out where she felt the presence. Her senses landed on the area near the curtained-off bathroom, and she stared, trying to see through the inky blackness, but she could make nothing out.

"Clara?"

Clara was startled by Shelby's sleepy voice. She'd never had anyone stay overnight before. "Yeah. Just gotta pee," she said, as she forced herself to walk to the very spot where she felt the hairs on the back of her neck prickle to life.

Once behind the curtain, she closed her eyes and took several deep breaths, trying not to let the fear and uncertainty get to her. Instead, she sent her thoughts drifting to Shelby, who had fallen back to sleep in her bed. They had kissed a lot throughout the evening, never even leaving Clara's room, but had done nothing else. Clara knew how it felt; that want and desire coupled with the fear of going too far, so had let Shelby lead. When the blonde had reached her limit, she had let Clara know, but had asked if she could stay. Clara wasn't about to say no.

She decided to go ahead and pee, since she was there anyway, then headed back to the bed. She felt a shiver run down her spine as she thought of the sound of the woman's voice in her head. It hadn't exactly been an audible voice, but it sure had been clear in her mind.

Save me...

Save who? From what? She had no idea, but knew the woman wasn't going to go away until Clara did something. The voice had sounded pleading, yet utterly tired and defeated. Maybe she'd see if her grandmother could help, tell her what to do. It had been a long time since she'd seen her grandmother and wasn't entirely positive how to reach her. Rebecca just seemed to show up whenever the mood struck.

Clara climbed back in bed, and was immediately glad she did. Shelby rolled over to her and cuddled up against her, placing a soft kiss on Clara's neck. "Sleep," she moaned, half-asleep. "Stay here."

Clara nodded, knowing there was no other place

she wanted to be.

❧❧❧❧

"Damn it, Kerri, this isn't funny!" Zane exclaimed, glaring at his girlfriend, who was most amused.

"I know it's not, but what do you want me to do about it, babe?" she asked, clipping her hospital badge to the scrubs top she wore.

"I don't know," he blew out, hands on hips as he looked around the kitchen.

"What's up?" Clara asked as she bounded into the room.

"Zane lost his pocketknife. Again."

"This isn't funny, Kerri," he whined.

"So you've said." She got up from where she'd been reading the morning paper and began to look through the kitchen drawers again. "You're sure you left it in here?"

"Positive."

Clara joined the search, knowing that her sister's boyfriend was less-than-careful where he put things. She opened the fridge, more to grab some orange juice than to look for the wayward knife and started. Sitting atop the lid of the butter container was the pocketknife that Zane's grandfather and namesake had given him as a boy. She held it up.

"Would this be it?"

Zane's brows drew. "Where the hell did you find it?" He snatched it out of her fingers.

"Sitting on top of the Parkay."

Kerri tried to hide her snicker but wasn't entirely successful at it. With an irritated growl, Zane shoved the folded knife into his back pocket and stormed out of the room.

"Did he have a late night or something?" Clara asked, sitting in the chair her sister had just vacated.

"No. I honestly don't know why it was in there, but," she said, shrugging, "so be it."

"Crazy." Clara drank her juice, sensing her sister's gaze hot on the back of her head. "Yes, Kerri?" she drawled.

Kerri chewed on her bottom lip, not sure what to say, or if she should say anything at all. Finally she took a deep breath and blew it out. "Why didn't you tell me you were gay?"

Clara choked on the drink she'd just taken, reaching for a napkin from the wooden holder at the center of the table to wipe at her mouth. "What?"

Kerri sat across from her. "Why did you never tell me you were into girls?" she asked, her voice soft.

"I guess I never thought it was your business, just like it isn't now." Clara pushed back from the table, her defenses on high alert. Kerri grabbed her wrist, stopping her from escaping the kitchen.

"Wait, Clara. I want to talk to you about this."

"How the hell do you know?" Clara demanded, slamming the single-serving-sized bottle on the counter.

"I saw you and Shelby the other night. I went upstairs to ask if you guys wanted some pizza. Your door was open, and..."

"And you saw us." Clara sighed at Kerri's nod. "Your cat is evil," she muttered, ignoring her sister's confused look. "I didn't tell you because I didn't know what you would do. I didn't know if you'd freak."

"Why would I freak?"

"Because I love girls!" Clara said, as though it

were the most obvious thing in all the world.

"Jeez, Clara," Kerri laughed. "We're almost at the new millennium, for crying out loud! I'm open-minded. Besides," Kerri said, taking a relaxed, casual pose in her chair, despite the fact that she was a little uncomfortable with her little sister being a lesbian, "you've always been odd, doing your own thing, so why should this be any different?"

Clara rolled her eyes. "Great. Thanks."

Kerri laughed. "I'm kidding. It's okay, really. Just be careful."

"Of?" Clara leaned against the counter, still not sure what to think. She wasn't entirely sure if she should believe Kerri's supposed acceptance of her. She'd always felt judged by her older sister, and this was no different.

Kerri shrugged, slightly exasperated. "I don't know! I guess who you end up with. What you do. Whatever."

"Let me ask you something. Would you be telling me the same thing if I dated guys? To be careful, I mean?"

Kerri had to think about that one, realizing that Clara might have gotten her there. "I don't know, Clara. All I know is that I love you, and I want to see you happy. If dating girls does that, then what can I say?"

Clara sighed, still not completely convinced. She chewed on her bottom lip for a moment, grabbing the juice bottle in sweat-slicked palms. "What about Mom and Dad? Are you going to tell them?"

"Are you?"

"I hadn't really planned on it." Clara sighed, draining the last of the juice then tossing the empty bottle into the trash. "Would you?"

Kerri sighed. "I don't know. I'm not entirely sure how they'll take it. You know Grandma will blow a gasket."

"Of course she will. Everything is the end of the world with her."

Kerri chuckled, nodding in agreement. "Mom will probably be okay. I don't know about Dad, though you guys are really close. If it were me who was gay, I'm sure he'd blow a gasket, too. But with you..."

"Stop. That's not true and you know it." Protective of her father to the end, Clara glared at her sister.

"Whatever. Either way, I'm not sure what to tell you where they're concerned. Who knows," she snickered, "maybe you should just show up with Shelby at Thanksgiving dinner."

Chapter Twenty-three

Clara stared out the window of Shelby's small, two-bedroom apartment. The snow was falling hard outside, the murmur of the stereo in the corner blocking the sound of the driving November winds. The holiday season was nearly upon them, and Old Man Winter was making his presence known.

Shelby chewed on the tip of her pen as she tapped some numbers into her calculator, glancing every so often at her girlfriend, who was less-than-interested in her own homework. Clara was watching the snow fall, staring up at the ceiling, the floor, or at her.

"You're not in homework mode, are you?" she finally asked.

Clara looked at her, surprised to hear Shelby's voice, as neither of them had said anything in well over three hours. She shrugged. "Not in the mood, I guess."

"I can't recall a time when you are in the mood."

Clara sighed, pushing herself up off the couch, where she'd been lounging with her head in Shelby's lap. "Not really." She indicated the books around them. "This just isn't my thing, I guess. I never wanted to go to college, Shelby." She ran a hand through her hair, messing up an already messy ponytail.

"Then why are you here?" Shelby put her textbook aside, tossing her pen to the coffee table.

"Because my parents made me, to be perfectly honest." Clara looked away, not wanting to see the disapproval she knew she'd see in Shelby's face. The blonde was dead set on making her mark in the world, and doing it through business.

"They didn't exactly hold a gun to your head, did they?" Shelby pulled her legs up, resting her chin on her knee.

"No." Clara shook her head. "Not exactly. But I knew my dad would be disappointed. I told him I'd make a go at it."

"But have you?" Shelby watched Clara, who still looked away from her. "Clara? What do you want for your life?"

"I don't know," Clara blew out. She walked over to the window that had had her attention all night. The street, two floors below, was nearly empty at the eleven o'clock hour. Tracks made from earlier car tires were nearly gone, fresh snow in their place. "I wish someone could tell me."

"No one can but you. Why don't you give school a chance? You barely study. I don't know how many classes you go to, let alone if you pay attention during them..." Shelby's voice trailed off as she saw Clara's body stiffen as her anger built.

Clara whirled on her, arms crossed protectively over her chest. "Whose side are you on, Shelby?" she demanded. "I'm sorry if I'm not the academic like you or like Kerri. I'm a different person than either of you. Maybe my interest doesn't lie within academia."

"Then what will you do? Work some nine-to-five somewhere? Maybe buy a house in ten years? If you're lucky, that is. You have to think ahead, Clara. I mean, jeez." She got to her own feet. "You speak to dead people, for crying out loud. I'm sure they've told you that you don't live forever. You have to start planning now."

Clara shook her head, feeling sick to her stomach. "Jesus," she whispered. Was there no one in the world who understood her? Anyone who would even try? "I gotta go." She gathered her books, shoving them angrily into her backpack, looking for her pencil, which somehow had escaped during her hours of relaxing. "Shit, where's my pencil?" she demanded, falling to her knees to look under the couch.

"Hey," Shelby said, her voice soft as she rested a hand on Clara's shoulder. "Wait." She waited until she had Clara's attention. "You can't drive in this, Clara. Please don't leave."

Clara, on her knees, glanced out the window again. The snow was beginning to come down even harder, threatening an all-out blizzard. "Damn." She knew Shelby was right, but didn't have to like it. Getting to her feet, pencil forgotten, she zipped her backpack, finished with homework for the night. "I'll stay until the storm begins to slow, then I'm gone."

Shelby nodded, not wanting to fight with Clara. She knew the brunette could be extremely stubborn when she wanted to be. "Okay."

❧❧❧❧

It was growing colder in the small apartment as Clara huddled on the couch, wrapped in the blanket Shelby had provided. She could hear the blonde moving around in her bedroom, the door not completely closed. She glanced down the hall to see the sliver of golden light that emanated from the crack along three sides of Shelby's door.

"Shit," she hissed. She was cold, she was tired, and she was being stubborn. She knew that although she didn't agree with Shelby's tactics, she truly was just trying to be practical. It amazed Clara on a fairly regular basis just how different the two of them really were. Even so, it seemed to work.

Trying to decide what she wanted to do, Clara wrapped the blanket tighter around herself as she stood and shuffled her way over to the windows, pushing the closed blinds aside. The storm had yet to lighten, and she knew it wasn't going to.

"Still snowing," Shelby said softly from behind Clara, nearly making Clara jump out of her skin. Shelby grinned. "Oops."

"God, don't *do* that!"

"I'm sorry about earlier, Clara." Shelby stood a few feet away, shivering in her sweats and tank top. "Know that I wasn't trying to judge you. I know you've had a lot of that. I just worry about you. That's the honest truth."

Clara looked at Shelby, and knew that what she had said was, in fact, the honest truth. She felt a warmth spread throughout her entire body. There had been very few people in her life who had only been looking out for Clara's benefit. She was touched, and felt a sense of something that baffled her. Maybe it was even love.

"You're freezing," she said in lieu of a response. She opened her arms, the blanket spreading out almost like wings as she engulfed Shelby in the cocoon of warmth.

"God, this feels so good," Shelby moaned, nuzzling even closer as Clara's arms, and the blanket, enclosed around her. "I don't want you to go," she murmured against Clara's neck, where she was warming up her chilled nose.

"I'm not," Clara whispered, eyes closed as she rested her head against Shelby's. "The storm's too bad."

Shelby shook her head, still half-buried under the blanket cocoon. "No, I mean ever." She raised her head, looking at Clara. "I want you to move in here with me, Clara."

Clara studied her gaze, trying to read what wasn't being said. "You mean as a roommate?"

Shelby smiled, finding Clara's insecurity cute at times. "I mean as in my girlfriend." She couldn't hold it in anymore and wanted to finally complete what they'd started.

Clara was startled by the power and passion of Shelby's kiss, which she returned with equal vigor. She moaned as Shelby's hand made its way up her shirt, cupping her breast over her bra.

"Come to bed with me," Shelby said, her mouth already laying a trail of kisses along Clara's neck.

Clara didn't have to be asked twice. The cold was forgotten as the blanket landed on the floor in a pile of blue fleece.

Chapter Twenty-four

Kerri closed her eyes, enjoying the feel of the hot water streaming down her body. A cold spell had hit, and the entire city was under dangerous-temperature warnings.

It had been a long day at the hospital, and she was looking very forward to a quiet night at home alone. Zane was working late, and Clara was upstairs packing. Kerri thought about that as she grabbed the bottle of Pantene, squirting a glob of the ivory-colored shampoo into her palm. Her little sister had gone and fallen in love. Clara had been overjoyed as she'd gushed about her plans to move in with Shelby. Kerri was happy for her and to be perfectly honest, was kind of glad about getting the house back to just her and Zane. It had been a true joy having Clara around, but she looked forward to the total privacy.

Kerri's thoughts were interrupted when she saw the shadow of a figure walk quickly by the closed shower curtain, the form distorted by the folds of the vinyl. She felt her blood turn to ice and her heart stop as the figure seemed to vanish as quickly as it had come.

Taking a deep breath, she peeked her head around the curtain, thinking that maybe Zane had come home early to surprise her. Or maybe Clara had come in to get something. The bathroom was exactly as she'd left it, including the door being securely closed.

Letting out a shaky breath, she pulled the curtain back into place and began to rub the shampoo into her hair. She wanted to forget about what she *thought* she saw. Perhaps she hadn't seen it at all, and it had simply been a figment of her imagination. Closing her eyes, she raised her face, allowing the water to wash the soap away before turning around and rinsing the shampoo out of her hair.

Kerri couldn't stop feeling like she was being watched. She peeked around the curtain again, wiping at her eyes with the edge of her bath towel.

"Clara?" she called out, wondering if maybe her sister was just outside the bathroom. Perhaps while packing, she had realized that some of her things were in the main bathroom, where Kerri was showering. There was no response.

Kerri pulled the curtain fully closed again, then screamed out as the shadow moved across the front of the curtain in the opposite direction from where it had started moments before.

⁂

Clara stopped, blood freezing in her veins as her sister's scream reached her ears. She threw the T-shirt she'd been folding to the floor and ran out of the studio, running down the stairs. She was nearly out of breath when she reached the second-floor bathroom.

"Kerri?" she called, banging on the door. She tried the doorknob but found it locked. "Kerri!" She pounded a few more times when the door flew open, a towel-wrapped Kerri flying into her arms and startling Clara.

Kerri clung to Clara, trembling as her panic

turned into emotional release. She tried to stop the tears that flowed down her cheeks but was unable.

Clara held on, frightened and totally bewildered. She looked into the bathroom, not seeing anything out of the ordinary. The shower was still running, water beginning to drench the toilet seat and rug on the floor in front of the tub.

"Hey," she finally said, her wits returning to her. She pushed Kerri away from her just enough to look into her pale face. "What happened?"

Kerri couldn't speak. She was still trembling and wanted to get away from the bathroom.

"You're cold. Can you go to your bedroom and put something on and I'll turn the water off?" Clara asked softy, rubbing her sister's naked shoulder. Numbly, Kerri nodded, scurrying off to the bedroom she shared with Zane down the hall.

Clara took a deep breath, running a shaky hand through her hair as she headed into the bathroom. She looked around, trying to see if maybe Kerri had seen some sort of bug, spider, or mouse. There didn't seem to be anything. Nothing under the pile of neatly folded clothes on the vanity counter. Nothing in the tub or near the drain.

"What the hell?" she muttered, reaching into the shower stall to turn the water off. She wiped her wet arm off with a hand towel then headed to Kerri's room.

Kerri sat curled up on her bed, dressed in a matching pair of sweatpants and sweatshirt with her university logo running down along the right thigh of the pants. Clara sat next to her.

"Are you okay?" she asked.

Kerri blew out a breath then nodded. She was

lost in her own head, remembering again what she'd seen. She couldn't shake the image, no matter how she tried. Tears began to slowly slide down her cheeks once more.

"Hey," Clara said, rubbing a hand across Kerri's back. She was beginning to fill with true concern. This was completely unlike her sister. "What happened?"

"I was taking a shower," Kerri began, her voice shaky. She brought a trembling hand up to rub at her cheek. "I saw..." her voice trailed off, once again the image before her mind's eye.

"You saw what? What happened, Kerri?" Clara asked, her voice more firm as she got a bad feeling in the pit of her stomach.

"I saw a shadow. I thought maybe it was you or maybe Zane, but it wasn't. I thought maybe I was crazy." Kerri wiped at her tears as she tried to keep a sob in. "Then I saw it again. I pulled open the curtain, and... and..." She broke down.

Clara hugged her, trying to decide what to do. She knew there was more to this for Kerri to be so shaken by it. She looked around the room as she hugged her sister close, trying to decide what to do.

"It was terrible, Clara." Kerri sniffled, her head resting on Clara's shoulder. "She was so awful. Her face was all bloody. She kept staring at me, her mouth moving but nothing came out. I think she was saying, 'Save me'."

Clara pulled away, nearly knocking Kerri over with the movement. "She said what?"

"Save me."

Clara felt dizzy, her stomach turning in knots. Those words echoed in her head, the tone still fresh in her head, though she'd heard it more than a week before.

"What's wrong?" Kerri asked, wiping at her eyes and nose with the sleeve of her sweatshirt. "You look like you're the one who saw the ghost."

Clara smiled at her sister's weak attempt at humor. "Maybe. Are you okay?"

Kerri nodded. "Yeah. It just really scared me." She got herself under control, taking a steadying breath. "Who do you think that was?"

Clara shrugged, shaking her head. "I'm not sure. I think it may be the same woman who came to me at night, once. Scared the hell out of me."

"Was she all bloody?"

"I didn't see her. I heard her. She was saying 'save me'."

A visible shiver raced through Kerri as she wrapped her arms around herself in a protective hug. "Why didn't you say anything?"

"I didn't know there was anything to say, really. I don't know who she is, and I guess I just figured maybe she would go away."

"Obviously not. You've got to get her out of here, Clara," Kerri said, her voice pleading. "I don't care what you have to do, but you need to get her out."

Clara nodded, sighing heavily. "Okay." *How the hell am I going to do that?* "I'll do what I can."

"Are you going to Shelby's tonight?" At Clara's nod, Kerri put on her best sheepish smile. "I need to ask a favor."

❧❧❧❧❧

Shelby closed the bedroom door softly, turning to see Clara already beginning to undress. "Do you think she'll be okay out there?" she asked, sitting on the end of the bed to untie her shoes.

Clara nodded. "I think so. She had a pretty bad scare." Clara looked at her girlfriend, walking over to her and placing a kiss on her lips. "I really do appreciate this," she nodded toward the door. "I know she'll feel a lot better sleeping out there on the couch than she will at home tonight. Zane won't be home till later, so..."

"No problem. I don't mind. I like Kerri." She finished undressing, throwing on a T-shirt and boxers, as she wasn't entirely comfortable sleeping naked while Clara's sister slept on the couch just down the hall.

They were quiet for a moment as they slipped into bed and settled in. Clara sighed in contentment, Shelby resting her head on her shoulder. She kissed the blonde head and reached to turn out the lamp.

"I probably don't want to know what happened, do I?" Shelby asked at length.

"That's up to you. I'll tell you if you want me to, but..." Clara's voice trailed off. Truth be told, she wanted nothing more than to be able to share with Shelby what had happened, and maybe try and get some advice.

Shelby raised herself to her elbow, looking down at Clara. She could see that Clara wanted to talk about it, but she truly wasn't sure if she could listen. She understood what her girlfriend did, but she'd be lying if she said she was comfortable with it.

"Well—"

Shelby was interrupted by violent banging on the front door of the apartment. Both women jumped out of bed, startled and already shaken from the unusual events of the night. Clara quickly pulled on the jeans and sweater she had taken off only moments before and hurried out of the bedroom and to the living room, Shelby hot on her heels.

Kerri was sitting up in the bed she'd made on the couch, her eyes wide with fear and surprise. "Are you guys expecting someone?" she asked as Clara and Shelby hurried into the living room.

"No," Shelby said. She was about to look into the peephole on the door when the person banged again. She nearly hugged the door to see who was on the other side, visibly relaxing. "It's Zane."

Clara and Kerri both breathed a sigh of relief as Shelby released the lock and safety chain. The door wasn't fully opened when Zane pushed his way inside. He looked around the room until he spotted Kerri standing by the couch.

"What are *you* doing here, Zane?" she asked, moving toward him.

"I think the better question is what are you doing here?" he asked, angry eyes finding Clara.

"I left you a note—"

"I got your damn note." He moved into Clara's personal space. "I told you I didn't want your crazy voodoo shit in my house, Clara!" he boomed.

"Zane!" Kerri rushed between them, pushing her boyfriend out of Clara's face. "Stop this."

"Well, she brings all this crazy shit into our house and our lives, Kerri!" he said, glaring at Clara. "I don't know what you did to scare your sister so bad, but I want you to fix it. I want it, and *you*, out of my house. You got me?"

Clara took a step back, intimidated by Zane's temper and larger size. She could only stare, stunned by his outburst. Kerri helplessly watched, looking to Shelby for support. They exchanged a look of anger then Kerri took action.

"Zane, quit it right now."

Zane was about to continue, but Kerri was yanking his arm to pull him away from Clara, who looked like she wanted to cry. He took a deep breath, trying to let his anger and fear go. "Let's go," he said, grabbing Kerri by the hand.

"I'm not going, Zane," Kerri said, pulling her hand away. "I'm staying here tonight." She took a step back, inadvertently forming a female triangle of strength and support with Shelby and Clara.

Zane looked from one face to the other. "Are you shitting me? Why?"

"Because I'm not comfortable there right now. I want a good night's sleep, and I won't get it there. I got really scared tonight."

Zane glared at Clara once more. "I hope you're happy, Clara," he said then slammed out the front door.

Stunned silence filled the room as everyone tried to reconcile what had just happened, and Kerri tried to figure out where Zane's irrational anger stemmed from. She shook herself out of it and turned to her sister. "Are you okay, Clara? I don't know what set him off like that."

Clara could only nod. She was hurt by Zane's words, and frightened by the power of his anger, which had come off him in waves. She fell back into the warm comfort of Shelby, who had walked up behind her and wrapped protective arms around her waist.

"Are you okay, Kerri?" Shelby asked softly.

Kerri nodded. "Yes. I don't know where that came from. I've never seen him like that before."

There was awkward silence as all three tried to

think of what to say or do. Finally Shelby spoke. "Well, I guess we should all get back to bed." After forty-five seconds, no one had moved a muscle. Shelby broke into laughter, followed by Clara and Kerri. "Or not."

༄.༄.༄.༄

Twenty minutes later the three sat around the kitchen table, a cup of hot tea for Shelby, a beer for Clara, and milk for Kerri.

"What do you think it is?" Shelby asked. She hadn't wanted to know what happened, but Zane's enraged appearance had piqued her interest, despite her own internal warnings. She knew she'd be having nightmares that night.

"I don't know. I need to ask my grandmother." The words were out of Clara's mouth before she could stop them. She could feel Kerri's eyes on her. She took a sip of beer before meeting her sister's gaze. "She's my spirit guide."

Kerri stared at her for a long moment. "Grandma Greenwold is your spirit guide?" she asked, incredulous. "I didn't even know she believes in this stuff."

Clara slowly shook her head. "Not Grandma Greenwold." She waited for the light bulb to switch on.

"Wait, what?" Kerri leaned forward in her chair, utterly baffled. "Do you mean..."

"Yes," Clara nodded. "Mom's mom."

"That's not funny, Clara."

"It's not meant to be, Kerri." Clara kept her voice soft and on an even keel, even as she felt her defenses begin to rise. She absolutely hated having to defend herself and her abilities.

Shelby was confused, as she'd heard none of this. "What's the catch?"

"Our mom's mom has been dead for thirty-five years."

Shelby looked from Kerri to Clara then to her tea. "Oh."

"I don't understand. What do you mean 'spirit guide'? What is that? Why Grandma? You've never even met her, Clara. How the hell can she be your spirit anything?"

"Because she's a spirit herself, mainly," Clara answered, looking her sister dead in the eye, daring her to a challenge. It worked, as Kerri began to back down.

"Can you explain it to me?" she asked, her voice noticeably softer, less confrontational.

"I've always felt a connection with her. I've told you that before," Clara explained. At her sister's nod, she continued, Shelby's attention bouncing back and forth between the sisters, like she was watching a tennis match. "She came to me one night a few years ago. Said she's been guiding me this whole time. She helps me when I'm stuck. Like right now."

"So, she comes to you?"

Clara nodded. "Sometimes. I need to figure out how to...summon, I guess the word would be...her. I haven't really messed with it."

"Why?" Shelby asked, intrigued despite herself.

Clara shrugged, finishing off her drink. "I don't know. Sounds stupid, but guess I don't want to bug her."

Kerri chuckled. "I doubt that." She played with her half-empty glass of milk for a moment, chewing on her bottom lip in thought. "What is she like?" Stephanie had said little about her mother, and Kerri wasn't entirely sure that she remembered much, considering how young she'd been when the accident happened.

Clara's smile was immediate. "She gives me a sense of calm. I don't know. It's like...it's like she gives me complete and total unconditional love. There's no judgment. Just love."

"All of this from your dead grandmother?" Shelby asked, the doubt obvious in her voice. At Clara's nod, she scooted back from the table, images of her mother — cold and in the ground — entering her mind. "I'm going to bed. I have class early tomorrow."

Kerri watched as her sister watched her girlfriend leave the room. She remained silent waiting to see what Clara would say or do. It was obvious Shelby was uncomfortable.

Clara cleared her throat, taking Shelby's abandoned teacup to the sink, rinsing it out and putting it in the dishwasher. "She doesn't like to talk about this kind of stuff," she said, her voice quiet. Clara tried to push it out of her mind, push out the fact that she was defending her girlfriend's absence.

"Not everyone does, Clara." Kerri dumped out the rest of her milk, the glass taken from her by Clara. Kerri rested a hand on the counter as she watched her little sister rinse the glass. "How are *you* with *that*?"

Clara shrugged after a moment. "What can I do? If she's not comfortable, she's not comfortable. Her mom died last year, and I think it messes with her pretty bad." She finally met Kerri's penetrating gaze. "What?"

Kerri shook her head. It wasn't her place to judge or question. Clara had always been strong enough to walk away from people who didn't accept her for all that she was. The older sister just hoped Clara wasn't making an exception for love.

"So," Kerri blew out, attempting to lighten the darkening mood. "What's your plan to get that woman out of my house?"

"I'm not sure." Clara hopped up onto the countertop, her bare heels bumping lightly against the cabinets below. "This woman is obviously in some sort of trauma. Have you ever noticed any activity in your house before?"

Kerri thought for a minute then shook her head. "Nope. Nothing out of the ordinary."

"What about Zane constantly losing things? Have you ever lost anything there? Or something been misplaced."

"Actually, now that you mention it, yes." Kerri leaned against the counter, arms crossed over her chest.

"I don't think that was random, Kerri. I think this woman has been trying to get your attention."

"But it all seemed to start when you moved in," Kerri said, not meaning to sound accusatory, but a fact was a fact.

Clara shrugged. "That may be. See, we all have a light, Kerri. A living light. People like me — those who can communicate with them, psychics, that kind of thing — have a living light that is nearly blinding. Spirits are drawn to it, like a moth to a flame."

"Is that why weird shit seems to follow you around?" Kerri grinned.

Clara nodded, amused. "Exactamente. They know I can 'hear' them, so to speak." She rested her head against the cabinet behind her. "So, now I just have to try and figure out how to help her. How to reach her."

They were quiet for a moment, both lost in the situation. Finally Kerri spoke. "I'm really sorry about how Zane reacted. That was completely uncalled for, and very much not like him."

Clara looked at Kerri for a long moment. "Why are you with him?"

Kerri was taken aback. "Because I love him."

Clara nodded, but hopped down from the counter. "I'm tired. Gonna head to bed."

Kerri followed her out of the small kitchen. "Why did you ask that, Clara?"

Clara looked at her for a long moment. "Because he's an ass, Kerri. I'm sorry to say that, but he is." With that, she headed down the short hall to the bedroom she shared with Shelby, passing the empty bedroom where Jasper used to sleep.

༄ ༄ ༄ ༄

Shelby was lying on her side, facing Clara's side of the bed. Clara stood next to the bed for a few moments, looking down at the sleeping blonde. With a heavy sigh, feeling as though a weight had been placed on her shoulders — though she wasn't sure from what — Clara turned and walked over to the window. Pushing the gauze-like curtains aside, she stared down at the winter wonderland below. She loved the snow. Loved how pure it was.

Resting her forehead against the cool glass, she sighed, her breath leaving a circle of condensation on the pane. She thought about her conversation with Kerri and Shelby, and then her thoughts roamed to her grandmother. She hadn't seen her in a long time, though she felt that the voice of reason or suggestion she often heard in her head was likely her. One thing, though, ever since she'd been shown that Rebecca was indeed in her life, she had felt a feeling of love and well-being. It was almost as though no matter what, no matter where she went or what she did, someone was there for her. An ally. It was comforting.

"Baby?" Shelby mumbled. "Come to bed."

Clara glanced over her shoulder into the darkness of the bedroom, able to make out Shelby's still form beneath the covers. With one final sigh, Clara undressed and slid into bed.

Chapter Twenty-five

Clara lay in bed, staring at the ceiling. She could hear the quiet, even breathing of her girlfriend next to her, as well as soft snorts from Monkey, who slept on the floor. She'd been lying there for more than an hour, unable to fall asleep. Thoughts of her grandmother kept racing through her mind, wishing that she'd show up, sit on the edge of the bed, and tell her what to do.

Close your eyes...

Clara looked around the room, halfway sitting up in search of the source of the voice. They were alone.

Close your eyes, Clara. See my face...

Clara's heart began to pound, even as she lay back down, letting her eyes slip closed.

Deep, even breaths. Think of me. See me...

Clara did as she was told, feeling her body begin to relax, even feel lighter. She tuned out the sound of snow hitting the window. She tuned out the sound of Shelby's breathing. She tuned out the sound of her own. At first what she saw behind her eyes was a swirl of blackness, the blood flowing to create crazy shapes and images. As she felt herself fall deeper, the blackness began to part, like a shroud, conveying her from one world to the next.

❧ ❧ ❧ ❧

She found herself in a cave, a massive waterfall to the left. She quickly realized she was in the space behind the waterfall. Looking around, it was dark, but light seemed to emanate from an unknown source, giving everything a bit of a surreal, ethereal quality.

She decided to look around the cavern, noting there seemed to be carvings in the stone of the walls. She reached out a hand, amazed to find she could actually feel the coolness of the stone against her fingertips. There were indeed carvings, wonderful designs that pitted the stone. She was following one with her index finger when she realized she wasn't alone.

Turning, she saw someone standing not more than ten feet away. The silent figure began to come into focus. Clara's smile was immediate when she realized Rebecca stood there, watching her. She looked as she remembered: young and beautiful, her own natural light making her absolutely breathtaking. Her shoulder-length dark hair was pulled back from her face, but left long in the back.

"Welcome," Rebecca said, her voice soft, soothing. She held out her arms. Clara needed no other invitation. She found herself engulfed in the warmest, most comforting embrace she ever remembered having. Even more than a hug from her own mother. "I've missed you, Clara," she said into the hug.

Clara rested her head on her grandmother's shoulder, eyes closed. "Me, too. Crazy since I don't really know you."

"Not crazy. Your soul does know me." Rebecca pulled back, looking into Clara's eyes. "Do you remember this place?"

Clara looked around. Though she thought the cave was beautiful and very interesting, she knew she didn't know it. She shook her head.

"*It's a favorite spot of yours here. We used to come here a lot before you incarnated.*"

"*So, we are close. Over here. Where am I, anyway?*"

Rebecca smiled. "The other side, and yes, we're very close. Come on," she said, taking Clara's hand in her own, "we have a lot to talk about."

The next thing Clara knew, she was standing in the middle of what looked to be a very small cabin. The room was a rectangle, no halls or doorways leading to other parts. In front of her was a massive fireplace, which took up the entire wall, behind a green sofa, where Rebecca sat, waiting. She patted the cushion next to her.

Clara sat down, relaxing into the softness of the couch and basking in the warmth of the fireplace and her grandmother.

"*Come here, Clara," Rebecca said, gently pulling Clara down until her head was resting in her grandmother's lap. Clara sighed as she felt gentle fingers run through her hair. "We need to talk about this little problem you have.*"

"*What problem?" Clara muttered, barely able to think straight, Rebecca's ministrations felt so good.*

Rebecca chuckled. "Don't fall asleep on me. I'll lose you. We have limited time."

Clara nodded. "Okay." She focused on her grandmother's voice instead of her fingers. "I don't know what to do about that woman. How do I reach her?"

"*You'll have to go to her, Clara.*"

Clara sat up, looking at the soft serenity of Rebecca's face. "You mean..."

Rebecca nodded. "The after shadow, yes." Clara

began to shake her head, fear creeping into her eyes. "Clara, listen to me." Rebecca cupped her face in her palms. "You can't be afraid of it. You shouldn't go there often, but there are times when you have to. This woman is stuck. She needs you to help her."

Clara took a deep breath, turning to look at the fire, marveling at the brilliance of the colors of the flames. So much more vivid than anything she'd see on her plane. "Okay. Tell me how."

"I will. When the time is right, I'll be there." She pulled Clara's head into her lap once more. "For now, you need to rest."

Clara sighed, content as once more Rebecca's fingers began to sweep through her hair. Rebecca leaned over her, placing a soft kiss to her cheek.

"Tell your mother I love her," she whispered.

❧❧❧❧

Clara nodded, feeling her body begin to drift, as though on a sea of clouds. Contentment and peace filled her, sending her off into the land inside her head, deep into sleep.

Chapter Twenty-six

I didn't mean it literally, Clara," Kerri hissed as they walked up to their mother's house, Shelby locking the car.

Clara grinned. "What, you mean I shouldn't tell Mom and Dad I'm gay by bringing my girlfriend to Thanksgiving dinner?"

"Yes! They're gonna freak."

Clara chuckled. "I guess Dad's already here," she observed, noting his truck parked at the curb in front of the house.

"Want some help?" Shelby asked, reaching for the large bowl Clara carried of the family's favorite: a mixture of fruit, whipped cream and tiny acini noodles, which gave the frog-eyed salad its name. Clara also carried two loaves of bread.

"Sure." Clara readjusted her load, handing her the bowl.

The house smelled wonderful as they walked inside, and Clara felt like drooling. One memory she had through all of her childhood years was the smell of turkey the nights before Christmas and Thanksgiving. Her mother would put the bird in her big, white metal roaster late the night before, letting it cook slowly all night. Stephanie Greenwold was a wonderful cook, and Clara's mouth was already watering at the thought of all the wonderful food that had been prepared. She knew her mother had spent a small fortune on the feast.

Max greeted his daughters with a wide smile and even wider hug. He was overjoyed to see them, especially his Clara girl, whom he didn't get to see very often, with her busy school and work schedule. He was, however, surprised to see the cute blonde who stood behind her.

"Hi. I'm Max," he said, holding his hand out. He hadn't been told one of Clara's friends would be joining them for the family dinner.

"Hi. Shelby." Shelby shook his hand, returning his warm smile of welcome. She wondered if his smile would be as welcoming once he found out she was sleeping with his daughter.

"Nice to meet you. Do you go to school with Clara, or...?"

"Actually, Dad," Clara said, moving to Shelby's side. She took a deep breath, knowing this was the moment of truth. She just hoped she'd still be able to have her mother's famous mashed potatoes *after* that truth. "Shelby and I live together."

Max's smile froze on his lips, unsure what to make of the statement. He looked at Kerri, confused. "When did you move out of Kerri's house?"

"Hey, girls!" Stephanie gushed, grabbing Kerri in a ferocious hug, followed quickly by Clara. She sensed something was up and looked from Max to her daughters, to the blonde stranger. "What's going on?"

"Did you know Clara had moved out of Kerri and Zane's?" Max asked.

Stephanie shook her head, looking at her youngest. "No. No idea. Everything okay?" she asked, looking back and forth between her girls.

Kerri took a step back, not wanting to get in the middle of this. She thought it was nuts for Clara to spring it on their parents the way she was about to, but it was her deal.

"No, everything's fine. Shelby and I just decided we wanted to live together." Clara grabbed the blonde's hand, holding it securely in her own, leaving nothing to the imagination of the manner of their relationship. Max had to tear his eyes away from the sight of the clasped hands, anger beginning to build at being ambushed. He looked at Stephanie. "What the hell is going on?" he asked. Stephanie shrugged, shaking her head. "What the hell is going on?" he asked again, this time the question aimed at Clara.

"Dad, Mom, I know this is kind of an awkward time—"

"Awkward?" Max boomed. "It's Thanksgiving, for Christ's sake!"

"Max, calm down," Stephanie said, taking hold of his arm. "Keep a cool head." She turned to Clara. "Clara, could you come talk to me and your dad in the kitchen for a minute, please?"

Clara looked at Shelby, her heart pounding. The blonde nodded her consent and let go of Clara's hand, stepping over by Kerri. Clara held her head up high, exuding a confidence she did *not* feel as she headed into the kitchen. She looked with wistfulness at the bounty of food spread out over the kitchen counter and table.

"Okay, before we begin," Stephanie said, turning pointedly to Max, "no one will lose their temper or say anything they might regret." She turned to Clara, who stood dead center, arms crossed protectively over her chest. "Explain this to us, Clara. What's going on?"

"I'm gay," Clara said with a shrug of indifference.

"You are not gay." Max laughed, thinking the whole thing was ludicrous.

"Max," Stephanie warned. He shut his mouth, taking a similar position to that of his daughter. "Clara, why do you think you're gay?"

Clara smirked. "Because I have sex with women."

"Clara Jane Greenwold!" Stephanie scolded, angry at the flippant way her daughter was handling this. "This isn't a joke. You need to have some respect for your parents."

"I'm sorry," Clara said quietly, dully chastised. "This isn't new, guys. I knew back in high school."

"And Erica?" Max asked, doing his best not to sound like Clara was in the middle of the Spanish Inquisition. He wasn't entirely successful. The squeeze on his bicep from Stephanie helped keep him calm.

"She was my first girlfriend." Clara tried to physically relax, even if inside she was a molten core of worry and confusion. Why couldn't they just understand she liked girls and leave it at that?

"I see," he said, bringing up a hand to stroke the stubble that marred his chin, as he'd recently begun growing a goatee.

"So, what does this mean, exactly?" Stephanie asked, resting her hand on the butcher-block island at the center of the kitchen.

Clara shrugged. "It means that I'm in love with Shelby, like Kerri is with Zane, and we're making a life together."

Stephanie walked over to her daughter, eyes hurt. "Why didn't you ever say anything to either of us about this, honey?"

"Because I knew I would get the third degree."

Clara's defiance wasn't helping her father's mood.

"We have a right to know," he said, no longer able to hold his tongue. "Instead, you bring your girlfriend here, during a *family* holiday, embarrassing us by blurting out this unbelievable news!"

"Max!" Stephanie turned on him then, glaring. "Please go set the table."

"Forget it," Clara said, slamming by her father and into the living room. "Kerri, can Zane give you a ride home later?" she asked, not even bothering to wait for her sister to respond. Shelby, stunned, looked from Kerri to Clara, who was hurrying out of the house, then to Stephanie who was running from the kitchen following.

"Clara, wait!" she called.

"What do I do?" Shelby whispered to Kerri, who simply shrugged her shoulders.

Clara dug her keys out of the pocket of her jeans, tears making it difficult to find the right one. Finally she got the car unlocked and slid behind the wheel. There was a tapping on the passenger-side window. She saw Shelby standing there, and leaned over the front seat, unlocking the door for her.

"Clara, don't do this," Stephanie said, knocking on Clara's window.

Clara looked up at her, rolling the window down just enough to be heard. "Enjoy your holiday, Mom. I'll call you later." She started the engine and backed out of the driveway.

❧❧❧❧

Shelby stirred in the chocolate powder, leaving the spoon on a folded napkin as she carried the mug of hot cocoa to where Clara sat on the couch. Her twilight-colored eyes were puffy and red from the crying she'd done once they'd reached the apartment.

"Here you go, sweetie," Shelby said softly, setting the mug down on the end table next to Clara. She sat next to her. She studied Clara's profile, not sure what to do. The day's events had been a surprise to everyone, and she could tell Clara's heart was broken. She hadn't said much, but Shelby knew how close she was to her father. Apparently what he'd said had hurt her deeply. "He called again," Shelby said softly, brushing a few stray strands of hair out of Clara's face. "He said he's going to keep bugging you until you talk to him."

Clara took a deep, shaky breath, finally looking at her girlfriend. "I really didn't think he'd do that, Shel," she said. "I figured if anyone would be okay with it, he would. He always supported me on what I am, who I am. Why is this any different?"

"Because I think he felt cornered. Today may not have been the best time to break the news to them, baby. A little warning might have been better."

"Why didn't you tell me that?" Clara asked.

Shelby smiled, leaning in to place a small kiss on Clara's lips. "I did. So did Kerri." She poked her playfully. "You're just too stubborn."

"Like him," Clara said, trying to hide a slight smile.

"You should talk to him, Clara. He sounds pretty broken up about this. He even offered to bring you a plate of mashed potatoes. Not sure what that means, but...he did offer."

"I love my mom's mashed potatoes. He knows that." She let out a loud breath, which blew her long bangs. Sipping her hot cocoa, she thought about what

Shelby had said. They'd been at the apartment for less than three hours, and the phone had rung nearly off the hook. She'd spoken briefly to Kerri, but refused to speak to either of her parents.

"Listen, I can't make this decision for you, but I'd do anything to have my mom here to spend the holiday with. Monkey just doesn't cut it, you know?" Shelby said, indicating the dog who slept undisturbed on the chair across the room. "Don't take time with your parents for granted. They're not perfect, just like you're not. They make mistakes too." Shelby placed a solid kiss on Clara's cheek then left her alone, heading off to shower and give Clara some privacy to think.

Clara took that time, sprawling out on the couch and sipping her hot drink. It was colder than a witch's tit outside, and more snow was predicted for the coming night. Shelby had wanted to start her Christmas shopping on the traditional day after Thanksgiving, but Clara wasn't sure anything would be open. She was just glad that The Pagan wouldn't be.

She was about to take another drink when the phone rang once more. She glanced at the cordless on the coffee table as if it were a snake that would bite her hand should she reach for it. She could hear Shelby in the bedroom rifling through her dresser drawers. The movement stopped, as did the ringing. Distantly Clara could hear her voice, low and calm. Pleasantries were exchanged then Shelby padded down the hall until she reached the mouth of the living room.

"That was your mom. She said your dad has asked for you to come to his place and talk to him when you're ready. She said he's off for the next four days and said you have a key, so let yourself in if he happens to not be home." Message delivered, Shelby turned and retraced her steps, ending in the bathroom with a soft closing of the door.

࿇ ࿇ ࿇ ࿇

Max sat in his recliner, the neck of a beer bottle dangling from between his fingertips. He watched the fire dancing in its brick prison, his thoughts troubled. Soft fingers trailed through his hair, even softer lips grazing his cheek.

"It'll be okay, Max."

"I just hope I didn't mess up bad," he said, taking a swig of the beer. A feminine hand reached down, taking the bottle from him. The diamond on a brand-new engagement ring glinted in the firelight.

"Drinking yourself into oblivion isn't going to help. You've done what you can, and the rest is up to her." Another kiss was placed on his other cheek. "Come to bed. She'll come around when she's ready."

Max blew out a breath, nodding his agreement. Even so, his stomach was tied up in knots. He followed where he was being led, eyes firmly glued to the shapely ass of the woman he loved. She glanced at him over her shoulder.

"You really should tell her, Max."

He nodded again. "I will. When I see her."

Chapter Twenty-seven

Zane chewed on a fingernail, his nerves nearly getting the best of him. Clara had been at the house for less than ten minutes, and he was already getting a creeped-out feeling in his gut. The ghost stuff freaked him out, and he just wanted Clara out. She had been officially moved out for a week, and he was glad. He liked the kid well enough, but something about her set him on edge.

Clara, for her part, was ignoring Zane. He and Kerri sat in the front room of the large, somewhat rundown Victorian, allowing her to wander through all the rooms and floors at will. She was trying to get a feel for the place, and much like Alex Estrata's house, allowing herself to be led by the energy. The house had a heavy feel to it that she didn't remember feeling before.

When she'd arrived, she'd asked Kerri in depth about what had been happening — if anything — over the past week. Nothing quite as traumatic as the night she'd been in the shower, Kerri said, but she also felt the heaviness in the air, and Zane seemed to be even more moody than usual. Things continued to disappear or move, seemingly of their own accord.

As Clara made her way through the house, she couldn't shake the feeling that whatever was in the house didn't originate there. It didn't feel as if it were someone who used to live in the house, or even on the land, as it had been in her English teacher's house.

She needs help...

Clara stopped, her hand on the banister about to make her way downstairs from the second floor. She looked around, expecting to see her grandmother standing behind her.

She followed you...

"Who is she?" Clara asked softly, eyes scanning the hall and opened doorways around her. She very much felt as though she were being watched. Though she didn't feel she was in danger, or the source had any sort of malicious intent, she felt uneasy, all the same.

Susannah...

Clara heard the name as clear as if someone three feet away had said it, and it wasn't the voice of her grandmother. She turned away from the stairs, deciding to stay on the second floor, as that's where she felt Susannah's presence.

"Are you stuck here, Susannah?" Clara asked conversationally, walking toward Kerri and Zane's bedroom, eyes ever on the lookout. "Do you need my help?" She heard nothing. "Susannah? Are you here? I can't help you if you won't help me."

The bedroom was empty, as Clara expected, and the energy wasn't as heavy. She left it, heading into one of the two guest bedrooms. She found herself drawn to the one piled with boxes and old, unused furniture. It had effectively been turned into a storage space, since the attic had been in use by her.

"Wow," she whispered, almost able to feel the air clinging to her skin. Her solar plexus was wide open, accepting the energy in such large quantities that it was making Clara feel nauseous. She put her hand over her stomach, trying in vain to block it.

Save me...

Clara whirled around, instantly stopping cold. Halfway across the small room she saw the vision of a tall woman, her dark hair cropped short and curly. The figure of what looked to be a man was with her. Clara knew instinctively that she was seeing Susannah, and was about to see what had happened to her. She tried to prepare herself for the worst.

Susannah raised her arms, trying to ward off the myriad blows that were being rained down upon her head, face, and shoulders. It looked as though he were beating her with either a pipe or a candlestick, Clara couldn't tell. She gasped in horrified wonder as blow after blow was dealt until finally the image faded.

"Jesus, Susannah," she whispered, her voice shaky with emotion. "What do I do, Grandma?"

Kerri...

Clara turned to see Kerri peeking into the room, looking unsure, almost like a child creeping into her parents' room in the middle of a thunderstorm. "Everything okay?"

Clara nodded. "I think so. I've made contact." Something occurred to her. She realized that Rebecca hadn't mentioned Kerri's name to alarm her of her presence, but had said it as a guide. She wanted Kerri there, and Clara understood why. "Bring Zane in here."

Kerri shook her head. "He won't come, Clara."

"Do it."

Kerri, surprised by the hard, authoritative tone of her little sister's voice nodded without further argument and left the room. Minutes later the couple appeared. Zane hung back while Kerri entered, stopping halfway between him and Clara. Clara reached for them both.

"I need you both to come here."

"Nah, that's okay," Zane said, sounding just like a little boy. If the situation hadn't been so serious Clara would have laughed.

"Zane, take my hand," she said instead, holding out her left hand to him. Reluctantly he took it in his much bigger one. Kerri took Clara's right hand and took Zane's in her other hand. "Do you guys feel it?" Clara asked, looking at them both.

"It feels so heavy in here," Kerri said. She looked at her boyfriend to see he was nodding.

"Because that's where she stays. Her name is Susannah."

"Why in here?" Zane asked, looking around uncomfortably.

"Because this room isn't used that much," Clara said.

After shadow, Clara. Go find her in the after shadow...

Clara closed her eyes, not entirely sure why she did. "I need you guys to stay quiet," she said, her voice low and soft. "I need you to trust me, and no matter what, do not let go of my hands." She truly had no clue what she was saying and why but decided to go with it.

Find her. Find Susannah...

As the darkness behind Clara's lids began to clear, she found herself in a backward world. It was the same world where she'd been the night of Erica's party, almost five years before. She took a deep breath, trying to calm herself and push away the panic. She could see the room they were standing in, but it was as though the sun had gone out, leaving eternal moonlight to guide her way.

Looking to her left, Clara saw the ghoulish outline of Zane: dark and featureless, though seeming larger than life. She shivered. To her right was the figure of her sister, just as dark and sinister as Zane's. They didn't belong in this world. The living had no rights. This was a place for the dead.

The room began to recede, and Clara could see Susannah standing not far from her. She looked frightened, so very, very frightened. Clara walked toward her, reaching out a hand.

"*I need you to come with me, Susannah,*" *she said, her voice soft. Susannah could only stare, not sure what to do.* "*I can help you. I can free you.*" *She reached the much taller woman and looked up into her face, eyes so filled with the shadows of her violent death.* "*You came to me for help. Let me help you.*"

"Clara? What's going on?" Kerri asked, feeling a change in the room. It was as though some sort of energy was gathering right in the center of the circle the three of them had created with their linked hands.

"Don't be afraid," Clara said, eyes still closed.

Clara realized they were in some sort of hallway, the walls seemed to be painted black. It was eerie, though not exactly threatening. Even so, Clara knew she had to get Susannah and herself out of there.

"Grandma, help me," Clara whispered, never seeing her sister's and Zane's eyes on her.

At the end of the long hallway a door opened. Beyond the opened entrance — or was it an exit? — Clara could see Rebecca's silhouette against the golden light that she knew was the other side.

"*Come with me,*" *she said, holding tightly to Susannah's hand as she began to make her way down the hallway and toward her grandmother, who had entered the hall, but only by about ten feet.*

"Who is that?" Susannah whispered, her voice shaky with fear.

"She'll help you. I promise." Clara smiled at the frightened woman, holding tight to her hand.

Kerri felt her heart beginning to pound as a coldness began to envelope the space the three of them had created between them. It wasn't cold coming from the windows or the cold November day beyond. It was a cold that seemed to have its source between them, and it started from the inside and worked its way out, not the other way around. She shivered, as did Zane, who met her gaze.

"What is that?" he mouthed.

Kerri shook her head with a slight shrug.

Clara led Susannah to where her grandmother waited, then gently placed the frightened woman's hand in Rebecca's.

"I'll take her from here, Clara."

Clara stood back, watching as Susannah literally put her soul in Rebecca's hands. They made their way toward the open doorway, stepping across. The tall woman turned back once, gave Clara a large, grateful smile then passed through, vanishing into the light of the other side.

Clara felt a coldness wash over her, bringing her back to the guest room in her sister's house. She gasped, almost as if taking a breath for the first time in minutes. The air in the room seemed to get extremely heavy, and then, without warning, the coldness washed over all of them, dissipating, leaving a calm in the room that was palpable.

Zane looked around, stunned. The room was lighter, and seemed to be brighter too, though he imagined that had to be his own imagination talking. He felt that the heavy presence that had been in his house was gone, and he truly had no words for how that felt. He felt frightened, grateful, and very humbled to have witnessed something that he felt at a gut level was extraordinary.

Kerri let go of Clara's hand, wiping at a tear that was about to escape her left eye. She felt emotionally drained and had no idea why. She looked at her boyfriend and saw he was equally affected.

"She's gone, isn't she?" she asked Clara, who simply nodded. "I can tell. God, it feels so different in here." She looked around the room, as if seeing it for the first time in a month. "What happened?"

Clara shook her head, not wishing to share it. "Just know that Susannah has found peace, and it was beautiful."

☙☙☙☙

Clara sat on the front porch of the apartment building where she lived with Shelby. She didn't even feel the cold as she stared sightlessly into the night. Her mind was still back in the bedroom. She once again saw the pain and torture Susannah went through before she finally found the relief of death, only to be lost, trapped between two worlds.

She shivered, hugging herself tightly. She closed her eyes as she felt a tear make its way down her cheek, just about freezing on her chilled skin. She absently wiped it away.

"Hey." Shelby sat on the stoop next to her, tugging her jacket tightly around her. "I was wondering if you'd used taking out the trash as an excuse to run off with the circus or something."

Clara smiled, though she didn't look at the blonde. "No. Just sitting out here thinking."

"About what?"

"Nothing." Clara looked at Shelby, a sad smile on her face. She wanted so badly to talk to her about it, to be rocked and held and told she'd done good. Instead, she kept it inside, saying nothing. "Today at Kerri's was just a little emotional, that's all."

"I bet. I'm glad you were able to help them out. I'll have to start calling you Dr. Venkman?" she teased, referring to Bill Murray's character in Ghostbusters.

Clara nodded with a weak smile. "You do and I'll never answer."

Shelby chuckled, unaware of the emotional turmoil inside her girlfriend. She gave her a quick kiss on the cheek. "Well come on in. It's freezing out here." She pushed up from the stoop and headed inside.

Clara looked up at the sky, the moon long hidden by the winter clouds, tears slowly sliding down her cheeks.

Chapter Twenty-eight

Clara glanced over at the building, seeing her father's truck parked out back. At least he was home. She hadn't spoken to him since the whole Thanksgiving fiasco and felt nervous sweat licking her palms. At first she hadn't called because she was angry, but then she began to think maybe she was wrong and had overreacted then she felt guilty.

"Shit," she blew out, resting her head against the seat, hands with a white-knuckled grip on the steering wheel. She hoped her father would listen to her and just accept her like he always had. The only area of her life they'd ever disagreed on was whether or not she went to college. She'd ultimately given in, but not with this. He had no say in this, and his opinions couldn't matter.

Finally gathering her courage, she unbuckled her seat belt and let herself out of her car. Shoving her hands into the pockets of her jacket, she bent her head to avoid getting hit full-force by the wind. Shelby had offered to go with her for moral support, and now there was a part of her that wished she'd taken her up on that.

She made her way to his doorstep, grudgingly pulling a hand out of her pocket to knock. She waited, bouncing slightly on her heels as she waited for him to answer.

"Come on, Dad," she muttered, looking around

the parking lot of the building. Nothing. She knocked again, this time louder. After another moment of silence, she pulled out her key chain, picking out the key that would open the door and let her into the warmth of his apartment. He was probably showering, the CD player volume at ridiculous decibels, per usual. He was worse than any teenager.

The living room was an absolute disaster — far more than usual. Magazines were spread all around the floor next to the coffee table. Two wineglasses sat on an end table, one still with the lipstick mark on it. There was a trail of clothing leading from the couch down the hall, and ending at the opened bedroom door with a red, satin thong.

Clara immediately felt embarrassment flushing her cheeks as she heard obvious sounds of some serious passion coming from down the hall.

"Ah, Jesus, Dad," she muttered. She was about to backtrack when she heard:

"Do you hear something?" Her father's voice.

"I think someone is here," a woman whispered.

"Hello?" Max called out.

Clara buried her face for a moment. "It's me, Dad. Um, I'll come back later," she called out, her hand already on the doorknob of the front door.

"No!" he called. "I'll be there in a sec!"

"Oh. Okay. Um. I'll wait for you on the front porch."

Clara couldn't get out of there fast enough, having already seen and heard enough to traumatize her for life. She closed the door behind her and sat down, already beginning to shiver. "I cannot believe my dad was in there getting it on," she muttered to herself, her words coming out in white puffs.

She heard movement behind her and turned as the door opened. Max was wearing a pair of jeans and a hastily thrown on shirt. His hair was mussed, and the stubble from Thanksgiving had turned into a nearly full, though still short, beard.

"I'm sorry about that," he said, apology in his voice.

"Hey, it's your deal," Clara said, getting to her feet and shoving her hands back into her pockets. "Just like it's mine."

"Come inside, Clara," he said, opening the door wider in invitation. "We have a lot to talk about."

Clara walked toward him, ready to pass him when he stopped her. He looked into her eyes for a long moment, love radiating from him. He took her in a tight hug, as though his very life depended on it. Clara clung to him, her head resting against his chest. She could hear his heart beating solidly in his chest, a large hand gently cupping the back of her head to hold her in place.

He kissed the top of her head then released her. He kept his hand on her shoulder as she stepped away to face the rest of the room. She was stunned to see her mother sitting on the couch, a smile on her face.

All she could do was stare, her mouth hanging open.

"We've been meaning to tell you," Max said from beside her.

"So why didn't you?" Clara asked, finally pushing her shock aside.

"We were going to over Thanksgiving, honey," Stephanie said, rising from the couch and walking over to her youngest. "It didn't work out that way." She took her daughter in a tight hug, looking into her stunned face as she released her. "We're sorry we didn't tell you sooner."

Clara looked from one parent to the other. "What does this mean? Are you guys just gettin' it on, or is there something substantial actually behind this?"

Stephanie looked at Max, a moment of silent communication before she turned back to their daughter. She raised her left hand, showing off the new engagement ring Max had given her two weeks before. "We're giving it a second chance."

"I could never fully walk away from your mom," Max explained, his arm around her waist. He shrugged. "We both made some mistakes in the past, but it's time to put it all behind us and look to the future."

"As a family," Stephanie added.

Clara shook her head, stunned. "Why do I feel like I'm stuck in some after-school special, or something? A family. Another shot. Mistakes. What?"

"We never stopped loving each other, honey," Stephanie said, her tone soft with understanding.

"That's why neither of us ever filed. Just couldn't bring myself to do it." Max smiled down at Stephanie, getting a girlish googly-look back.

"Whoa." Clara moved away from them, running a hand through her hair. "I feel like I'm in the *Twilight Zone*." A thought occurred to her, and she turned on them. "Does Kerri know?"

Max nodded. "We told her and Zane during Thanksgiving dinner."

Clara truly wasn't sure what to feel. Should she feel betrayed that no one had told her? Should she feel hopeful that her parents were getting back together? Or, should she simply run and not allow herself to get caught up in hope. Hope was a dangerous, scary thing. "Okay," she finally said, not coming to any sort of decision within her own torn emotions. "Okay. So, I guess congratulations are in order." She hugged each in turn.

"Thank you." Stephanie kissed her cheek then led her to the couch. Clara sat down, flanked by her parents. "So, let's talk about you."

Clara blew out a breath, nodding. For a moment she'd forgotten all about why she was there, but the realization came crashing quickly down upon her, bringing kamikaze butterflies with it. "Right. From your love life to mine. I think I pretty much said all I needed to say at Thanksgiving. I'm a lesbian, am in love with Shelby, and we live together." She shrugged. "End of story."

"When did this happen?" Stephanie asked.

"When did *what* happen?"

"When did you become gay?" Max asked.

Clara felt like she was in either a tennis match or an intense interrogation as she looked back and forth between her parents. She certainly knew that she felt trapped sitting between them.

"I didn't *become* anything, Dad. It's not like *becoming* a diabetic, or *becoming* pregnant. I've always been gay. I'm just allowing myself to be me."

"Honey," Stephanie began, choosing her words carefully. "We're not trying to pick on you or make you angry. We're just trying to make sense of this. You have to admit, it's pretty sudden."

"Not really. I came out at fifteen."

Max looked away, running a hand across his beard. "Was it because Jason was killed?" he finally asked.

"What does Jason have to do with this?"

"Well, it seems that after he died, you went pretty quickly to Erica," Stephanie said, picking a small piece of lint off of Clara's coat.

"That's when I met her, Mom." No longer able to take the squeeze, Clara shot up, moving to pace in front of the coffee table, putting the low piece of furniture between them. "Guys, you can't just boil this down to nuts and bolts, parts and pieces. It just is. I'm not gay to piss you off. I'm not even gay to rebel. I like girls. I always have, I always will." She held up a hand to forestall what she knew her mother was about to say. "I don't need to date guys to see if I'm gay any more than you needed to date girls to see if you were straight. I'm asking you both to please respect me enough to know that *I* know what's best for me. Okay?"

Stephanie and Max stared up at their daughter, too stunned to say anything. All they could do was nod dumbly.

"Good. Now," Clara blew out, "tell me about this remarriage business."

Chapter Twenty-nine

1996

Winter came, bringing the holidays with it, and then they went, bringing the end of a semester and sunny skies. Clara tossed her keys into the air, catching them with gusto as she made her way to her car. Classes were officially over, and she felt great about how she'd done. Over the past semester she'd decided to listen to Shelby, and buckle down.

After everything that had happened at Kerri and Zane's house, Clara had been rocked to the core. Her emotional center had been hit hard, and she hadn't fully bounced back from it. So, she decided that maybe Shelby had something with the whole school thing. Maybe she did need to put the medium stuff aside, and concentrate fully on her future. On *their* future. Shelby was the one, she was sure of it!

Finals were over, and she couldn't wait to get the results back. She had pretty much bombed her first semester in college. Nothing had to be retaken, but she could have done monumentally better. The second go around, well, the smile that spread across her face said it all.

The drive to the apartment was slow, as midday traffic clogged the arteries of the city. They had begun to pack the previous weekend. They had decided a bigger place was in order. Clara had left her job with Cassandra at The Pagan, deciding to completely cut her ties with her old life. She needed space and distance from all of it. She no longer did readings for clients, instead redirecting her focus.

She had gotten a job with a hardware store chain close to where their new place was and was making two dollars more an hour there. The bigger wage had allowed her and Shelby to get a nice two-bedroom apartment that was nearly double the size of their old one and was in a better neighborhood.

The past seven months had flown by, it seemed. Clara had finally gotten used to the idea of her parents being back together, though it was strange to go home and see them both there, and not just a matter of her father over fixing something for Stephanie. Zane and Kerri still lived in the old Victorian over on Seacrest, and nothing had been said since the situation the previous fall. Zane certainly treated Clara better, but it was never talked about exactly why.

She was just about to her exit when she decided to stop downtown and get Shelby something nice for the weekend. They had planned a couple of romantic days, both having taken time off work for it.

Clara parked off of Main, deciding to walk down the main drag, which was lined with locally owned shops that carried things which couldn't typically be found in a Walmart or mall.

The sidewalks were busy, other people getting the same idea as spring fever hit the city. Clara managed to avoid being gutted by a couple whose hands seemed to be welded together, and they weren't budging. She saw a small shop that sold lingerie and immediately got a mischievous grin on her face. Shelby had a magnificent body, and Clara loved to see it in satin.

She was about to push open the door when she

noticed a woman out of the corner of her eye. Turning, she saw that the woman was balancing a package on one hip while trying to dig her keys out of her purse with her one free hand. Her car, an expensive-looking sports car, sat at the curb, its glossy red finish glittering in the sun.

Clara was about to turn away to head into the shop, but something stopped her. She turned back to the woman and, for no reason that she could figure, ran over to her. She grabbed her, and with a scream from the startled woman, threw her back away from the street and her car. The woman landed on one knee, her package falling to the ground with the sound of breaking glass.

"What are you *doing*?!" she demanded, about to get to her feet.

Clara looked at the woman, just as startled as she was. She was about to apologize profusely when she felt a strange sensation along her right side — the side closest to the street — then a shove. She stumbled a few feet toward the shop front when a screeching sound rent the air. A moment later, the woman's sports car was an explosion of glass and metal as an out-of-control pickup truck smashed into it, pushing the car onto the sidewalk, exactly where the woman had been standing.

Clara and the woman watched in stunned silence, neither able to do much more than take their next breath. No one moved in the truck, the horn blaring, along with the sound of a distant car alarm.

"Oh my god," Clara breathed, finally getting her bearings. She ran to the truck, shouting to anyone who was listening, "Call nine-one-one!"

The man in the truck was knocked unconscious,

a nasty gash on his forehead bleeding profusely. Clara grimaced as the smell of blood assailed her senses. She reached in, checking for a pulse, relieved to find one. Past the driver, scattered on the floor of the large truck, were empty bottles of beer and a few hard liquor bottles. She looked back to the man unable to hide her feelings of disgust.

"Is he dead?" someone asked, standing behind Clara.

She shook her head. "No. Just unconscious." Hearing the wailing sirens getting closer, she took a step back, body trembling from the rush of adrenaline and fear. She could see the woman still standing on the sidewalk, her face pale. "Are you okay?" she asked. The woman looked at her blankly for a moment, then slowly nodded. It was only then that Clara noticed the expensive rings and clothing the woman wore. She looked to be in her late thirties, forty at most, though little telltale signs of wrinkles in her neck teased of age in the fifties. Her auburn hair was piled high on her head, her gold and diamond earrings dangling like ice from her ears.

The woman seemed to finally really see Clara. "How did you know?"

"Know what?"

"What was about to happen. I assume that's why you threw me onto the sidewalk like so much trash."

"I'm sorry about that. Something just told me to get you out of the way. I'm sorry—"

"You saved my life, and that's not something I take lightly," the woman interrupted. She reached for her purse, which had also been thrown to the ground, digging until she found a piece of paper and pen. She looked at Clara expectantly. "Name?"

"Uh, Clara Greenwold," Clara said automatically, unsure what the woman was doing.

"And your phone number?"

Clara hesitated, but the look on the woman's face told her there was no room for argument. She gave her the number. "Why?"

"I'll be in touch," the woman said, holding her heavily ringed hand out. "My name is Isabelle Van Wurt. I'm in town with my husband. He's doing business. I'll be in touch so I can take you to dinner and thank you." With that, the woman turned and walked away, not even bothering to salvage what was left of her package.

⚜⚜⚜⚜

"Do you think she intends to sue you or something?" Shelby asked, winding noodles around her fork, splattering spaghetti sauce on her placemat with the action.

Clara shrugged. "I sure as hell hope not. But, you can't get blood from a turnip, so..."

"What a strange lady," Shelby muttered, placing her fork in her mouth.

What a strange incident, Clara thought to herself, but said nothing, instead focusing her attention on her dinner as Shelby changed the subject, prattling on and on about the project she had done for her spring semester class. Clara half-listened, half-shut down. She had learned how to put herself into autopilot mode: she got up every morning, went to class without fail, listened and took notes, then came home and did homework, or did homework at the library. Every day. Not thinking, and not really feeling.

She glanced up at her girlfriend — who was still talking — and studied her. Shelby was beautiful, no one could deny that, including Clara. But as she looked at her, *really* looked at her, she saw a woman who was ambitious and a bit controlling. She saw a woman who wanted the best for Clara, but on Shelby's terms. She saw a woman who perhaps didn't accept Clara as much as Clara thought she did.

Clara was amazed at how quickly her life could swing from happier than she'd ever been to feeling stifled and shut out from her own life. How was that possible?

Looking back down at her dinner, Clara's mind began to wander, reliving the events of earlier in the day once more. She hadn't allowed herself to feel or open up in such a long time that it had felt strange when she'd pushed Isabelle Van Wurt out of harm's way. She had to admit — if only to herself — that it had felt good. She had been holding herself back, trying to pretend her "gift" didn't exist. It was almost like someone who was drawn to numbers, a math genius; it was like that person trying to suppress their natural talents and abilities and inclinations by never looking at numbers, and if they did, they simply saw them as one, two, and three, and not a puzzle to be solved by a brilliant mind that was wired to do just that.

She thought back to a few times at school when she'd seen a spirit walking through the trees or when she'd heard her own name spoken softly on the breeze. She'd ignored it, pushed it aside like it wasn't there. She smiled to herself as she suddenly had a mental image of herself, eyes squeezed shut, hands over her ears, "La la la la la, I can't hear you!" echoing in her mind.

"What's so funny?" Shelby asked, realizing Clara wasn't listening, but instead chuckling at her plate of pasta.

Clara looked at her with a small smile, shaking her head. "Nothing. Nothing's funny at all." She grabbed her napkin and wiped her mouth before pushing back from the table.

"Where are you going?" Shelby asked, dinner forgotten.

Clara didn't look at her as she scraped the remnants of her dinner into the trash then rinsed her dish and loaded it into the dishwasher. "Out for a while. I need some alone time."

Shelby was very aware of her girlfriend's need for personal time and space, though it was never easy to deal with. She didn't understand it, but knew there was nothing she could say without starting a fight. She'd learned that the hard way. Even so, she felt this time it was different; something was wrong.

"Did I make you mad or something?" she asked, pushing back from the table, her chair screeching against the linoleum.

Clara sighed, not in the mood to do this now. She shook her head, looking at her from across the small kitchen. "No. I just need—"

"To be by yourself, I know." Shelby couldn't keep the bitterness out of her voice. "You've needed to be by yourself more and more." She paused, hands on hips as she stared Clara down. "Is there someone else?"

Clara was taken aback by the question, and she immediately shook her head. "Not even close. I swear."

"Then what is it?"

"I need to go where I can be myself!" Clara yelled, shocking both of them with the anger behind her words. She didn't want to say anything she'd regret, so she grabbed her keys and wallet and headed out the front door.

The city was quiet as she drove around, her head wrapped in a fog. She wasn't sure where she was going, she just drove. Something was wrong inside, something was missing. She couldn't put a finger on it, but it was beginning to haunt her, which she couldn't help but see as ironic since she'd left the ghosts behind.

She thought about school, which she was doing well in, but didn't like. She'd allowed herself to be talked into getting a business degree, as Shelby said that no matter what Clara did in life, knowing how the business world worked would always come in handy. It seemed to make sense at the time, so Clara had gone with it. Now, as she drove around, she wondered if she was masochistic. She *hated* the business classes, even though she was taking them at a freshman level. How would she feel as she got further into the program? They'd get harder and far more complex and in depth than what she was doing now. Not only that, but she didn't want to just do well because she had a good brain in her head and could go on autopilot and do the work. She wanted to actually *enjoy* what she was doing.

She stopped at a red traffic light, tapping her fingers on the wheel as she waited. She could change her major; maybe keep business as a minor, perhaps?

"I hate business!" she yelled in the empty car, slamming the steering wheel for emphasis. "So what *do* I like?" she pondered. She felt compelled to talk to her grandmother, get her advice, but she stopped herself. Part of her knew exactly what Rebecca would tell her. "No," she said, shaking her head. "I can't go back there again. It's not healthy for me. Shelby's right about that."

Clara heard a soft scraping sound and watched in astonishment as a small, bluebird landed on the hood of her car, its beady black eyes staring at her, first left, then right. She immediately felt Jason's presence with her, as though he were sitting in the passenger seat next to her.

"What?" she asked the bird, who did not react, nor did it fly away, even as Clara tried to shoo it away with a wave of her hand out her window. It continued to stare at her. Clara stared back, almost losing herself in the heat of the strange connection. She heard a car honk behind her, the bird flying away as she realized the traffic light had turned green.

Shaken, Clara drove on.

≈≈≈≈

Shelby was long asleep by time Clara made her way to the bedroom. She undressed quietly, not wanting to wake her. She slid under the sheets, tired, but completely discontent. She lay in the dark for a long while, staring at the ceiling, hands behind her head. She had noticed the note left by Shelby on the kitchen table when she came in. So Isabelle Van Wurt had called, huh? Clara had wadded the page up and tossed it into the trash.

She turned to her side, facing the window and nearly jumped out of her skin. Her grandmother stood there, looking down at her. Clara sat up, unable to take her eyes off of her. Rebecca smiled, amused before sitting on the edge of the bed.

"Don't worry," she said in her usual soft tone. "Shelby can't hear me. I need you to listen to me now, Clara, and take what I say to heart." Clara opened her mouth, but was silenced. "No," Rebecca said, shaking her head. "You listen now. You were given a gift for a reason, and it's not to be wasted. Do you know why you're so unhappy?"

Clara shook her head. "No."

"Because you're following the wrong path. Always remember that, Clara. You have a path, as does everyone. When you fall off that path or go the wrong direction, depression and uncertainty will soon follow." She smiled, reaching a hand out to caress Clara's hair. "You don't need to search anymore, my love. You found your path and your path found you."

Clara felt her heart swell with comfort and confusion at her grandmother's visit. "It's unhealthy for me, Grandma. Seeing dead people, talking to them..."

"Says who? It's all about perspective. No one ever dies. The soul can't. The time in this life has simply finished. It doesn't mean that person doesn't still have a role to fulfill for those here on the earthly plane." She dropped her hand, standing. "Don't let others tell you what you should or shouldn't be doing. That, my love is what's unhealthy. You have a wonderful gift, and during this life you're meant to use it."

Clara jerked up in bed, realizing she was alone. Her heart pounded with the adrenaline of the dream she'd just had. She was completely alone in the bedroom, save for the sleeping form next to her. She looked over at Shelby, noting the way some of her hair had fallen onto her forehead.

Blowing out a breath, Clara laid back down, turning onto her side to face the window. She started when she noticed something on the nightstand beside the bed. She reached over to take it between her fingers, gasping quietly when she saw that it was Shelby's note about Isabelle Van Wurt.

Chapter Thirty

Clara looked around the long car, never having been in a limo before. The tan interior was leather, the bar mahogany. Isabelle Van Wurt sat next to her on the long bench seat, her manicured hands clutched in her lap and legs crossed like a proper lady. To say Clara felt like a hick from the sticks was as much of an understatement as there ever was.

"You didn't have to go to so much trouble, Mrs. Van Wurt," she said, breaking the silence. The wealthy socialite looked over at her.

"Well, I couldn't very well pick you up in my little car, now could I? I'm afraid the damage was far more than the most talented mechanic could handle."

Clara smiled, but said nothing more. She wished she could have just met Isabelle and her husband — who would be joining them — in her own car. The limo pulled up in front of one of the most expensive hotels in town. Clara looked up at the giant building, trying to keep her reactions to a minimum. She remembered always looking at the gorgeous building when she passed it, wondering what it looked like inside and what it would be like to stay in such a place.

"My husband, Raymond, is waiting upstairs for us in our suite. I hope you don't mind, but we've ordered dinner to arrive there in...," Isabelle checked her lady's Rolex, "fifteen minutes."

"Um, no. That's fine." Clara smiled, but was

actually about to choke on her nervousness.

The door next to Isabelle opened and the uniformed chauffeur extended a gloved hand to help her out of the car. Next he helped Clara, who smiled shyly at him. Once out in the mild May air, Clara looked around, bending her neck back as she took in the ornate building that rose seventy stories above the sidewalk.

She followed Isabelle into the building, marveling at the marble floors — highly polished — and the expensive, heavy furnishings and décor. They made their way to the elevators, where a tuxedoed man asked which floor.

"The penthouse, please," Isabelle said, digging her key card out of her purse.

Within moments they were walking down a dimly lit hallway, where only two doors adorned either side. Isabelle led the way to the one on the left, inserting the key card in the door, which beeped softly with a blinking green light.

The suite was larger than Clara and Shelby's entire apartment. She looked around, owl-eyed at the size and sophistication of the rooms. There was a huge bedroom, dining room, and living room area, as well as two bathrooms. Further inside Clara could hear a deep, male voice talking. From the one-sidedness of the conversation, she figured he was on the phone.

"Darling, we're here," Isabelle called out, dropping her purse on the bar and making her way around to the business side. "Would you care for a drink, Clara?" she asked.

"Oh, uh, no. I'm not old enough," Clara said, feeling immediately stupid.

Isabelle, on the other hand, was completely

amused. "That's not what I asked now, is it?"

Clara grinned. "Whatever you're having."

"That's more like it." Isabelle began to bring out bottles of various sizes and shapes and shades of liquor within. Clara had no idea what she was making, as she'd never been much of a drinker.

"Well, hello there!" Raymond Van Wurt boomed from the opened doorway of the bedroom. His deep baritone filled the entire suite. He walked over to the bar where Clara had settled onto a padded stool. His gelled hair shone in the overhead lights of the bar area. "I'm Raymond Van Wurt. You must be our new friend, Clara Greenwold." His extended hand was large and tan, a heavy gold pinky ring winking at her.

"Yes, sir. Nice to meet you." Clara shook his hand, hiding her reaction at the tight grip he had. She wasn't entirely sure what to make of the Van Wurt couple. She'd never met anyone so rich before.

"None of that. Call me Raymond or Ray." He made his way around the bar and placed a kiss on Isabelle's cheek. "Hello, sweetheart. Yes, perfect," he said to the drink she offered him. He took a long sip. "I hope you ladies are hungry. I wasn't sure what you liked, Clara, so I've ordered enough food to feed a small army." His laugh was as demanding as his voice. "Come!" He walked to the living room and sat on one of the massive leather sofas.

Doing as asked, Clara mirrored his position, drink in hand. She sipped it, recoiling from the strong taste of vodka. She heard Raymond chuckle.

"Careful with that. My wife has been known to add gasoline to her drinks."

"Oh, stop," Isabelle said, sitting next to her husband. The couple looked at Clara, making her want to squirm in her seat.

"So," Raymond began, getting down to business. It seemed that it was always business for him. "I understand you saved my wife's life from what could have potentially been a very messy situation. Quite lethal too." He studied her, his head slightly cocked to the side. He didn't even flinch when someone knocked on the door to the suite. Without a word Isabelle got up to retrieve their dinner. "Tell me, Clara. How did you know that truck was coming?"

Clara swallowed heavily, setting her drink down on the glass-topped table in front of her. She used the motion to stall for time to decide. She could tell him she simply heard or saw the truck coming. She could tell him she had a random hunch. She could tell him that she was simply crazy and felt the need to tackle his wife to the ground, and got lucky that there happened to be an out-of-control truck coming at the same time.

Tell him the truth...

Or she could tell him the truth.

"I knew she was about to be hit," she finally said, catching Raymond's gaze.

"How did you know that?" he asked, sitting back and casually crossing one leg over the other.

"I have abilities that...tell me things."

Raymond sat forward, completely intrigued. He raised a hand to ward off Isabelle's invitation to dinner. "Tell me more."

Clara took a deep breath and started at the beginning, from her earliest memories of her gift as a child. Isabelle had taken her seat next to her Raymond again, both engrossed in what they were being told. None of the three cared that their dinner was cooling. Raymond didn't say a word or ask a question until

Clara had finished her story.

He cleared his throat and sipped his drink. "Who can you see around me?" he asked, eyeing her in a challenge.

Clara was taken slightly aback, not expecting to do a reading, which she hadn't done in many months. "Now?"

"Now."

Clara resettled herself, the hunger pangs in her stomach replaced by nervous butterflies. She felt a great deal of pressure suddenly, as though what she was about to do had high stakes for her future. She closed her eyes for a moment, concentrating on getting focused and opening up. *Grandma, keep me strong and focused*, she asked. As she took another cleansing breath, she felt a peace wash over her, as if she'd done a reading only yesterday.

Looking at Raymond once again, she felt her mind opening up as information began to come in. Raymond and Isabelle watched, as it seemed Clara was having a conversation with herself. She'd nod and mutter, "Okay. Wait, say again?" Isabelle looked at her husband only to get a shrug in return.

"Okay," Clara said to Raymond. "What is your connection to a red wagon? You know, the kind with a metal body, big black and white wheels with the little red knobs holding them on." She described the wagon she was seeing in her mind.

Raymond looked at her for a long moment, trying to figure out what she was talking about. He was coming up blank. "I haven't the slightest."

"Okay." The wagon image faded, one of a big brown dog in its place. "I'm seeing a dog. A very..." her voice trailed off as she got a better fix on it, "big dog.

Floppy ears with a blue collar."

Raymond's face paled slightly. "That was my son's dog, Archie. He died when RJ was eleven." Then it hit Raymond. "The wagon! I used to take RJ to the park in that wagon."

Clara barely noticed as Isabelle got up from the couch, leaving the room. "Okay, good. Whoever is coming in keeps telling me to tell you about peach cobbler. With raisins."

Raymond let out a bark of laughter, nodding vigorously. "RJ loved the stuff. My mother used to make it for him every time he went to her house."

"Has your son crossed, Raymond?" Clara asked gently, trying to get a hold on the situation. Raymond looked away for a moment, clearing his throat before nodding. "All right. Well, I think it's him, then. RJ, give me one more thing to verify that it's you."

Raymond watched anxiously. His son had been dead for thirteen years, and he hadn't expected to hear from him that day. In truth, as a skeptic, he hadn't expected to hear from *anyone*. His thoughts were interrupted by Clara's next comment.

"I'm hearing jangling, like either change in a pocket or keys." Clara made the sound she was hearing as best she could. "Does this ring any bells for you?" She made the noise again.

Raymond nodded slowly. "RJ always carried around a ring of keys, He worked in corrections."

"I see." Clara stopped, another image taking over her entire focus. "I'm seeing a large tree. I mean this thing is huge." She opened her arms to emphasize, still focused on the image in her mind. "What does this tree have to do with anything? I can't get it out of my head."

Raymond shook his head, unsure.

"Did he have a big tree in his yard? Like, dead center in the front?"

"Yes!" Raymond said, remembering.

"Okay, that must be it." Clara waited for the tree to disappear, but it didn't. Her brows drew. "Something with this tree, Raymond. Typically when an image won't leave it's because it has some sort of significant meaning that I'm not getting." She looked at Raymond, hoping he could tell her something so she could move on. "Was there someone hiding behind this tree?"

Once again Raymond's face paled. He took a long swallow from his drink, nearly finishing it. "The police said he was possibly taken by surprise."

Clara nodded. "He was ambushed. Someone was hiding behind that tree, waiting for him." She felt her stomach clench as she realized where the reading was headed. "Raymond, you're aware your son was murdered, right?"

"Yes. We never knew all the details, but we knew it was murder, yes."

Isabelle returned to the room, standing behind the couch her husband sat on, her hands resting on his shoulders. Her eyes were slightly red, as though she'd been crying.

Clara didn't notice Isabelle's return as her focus again turned inward. The tree faded, to her relief. She'd gotten it right. A very sudden, and very *painful*, phantom blow hit her in the back of the head. Her hand immediately went back to feel the spot, almost expecting blood to come back on her hand. She grimaced at the shock then the pain disappeared as quickly as it had started. "Did he have any bumps or cuts on the back of his head?"

Isabelle nodded. "Yes. He had extensive bruising at the back of the skull."

"He was hit there. I'd say knocked out."

Isabelle and Raymond looked at each other. "That was never released in the media," she said quietly.

"What else can you tell us about it?" Raymond asked. He wasn't interested in new details, as he felt he knew enough to know what had happened to his son that night, but he wanted to know more Clara's capabilities. A plan was already hatching in his head.

❦❦❦❦❦

Kerri and Zane watched Clara pace back and forth, her excitement palpable. Kerri's head was spinning from all she was being told. "Wait, wait," she said, waving her hands to get Clara's attention.

"What?" Clara stopped her pacing, looking down at her sister.

"Let me get this straight. You're telling me that this rich business guy from Los Angeles wants you to go back with them so you can do readings for his rich friends?"

Clara stopped to think about it in such simplified terms. "Yeah," she said, nodding. "That's about it."

"That's crazy, Clara," Zane said. "What about here? School, your family—"

"Shelby?" Kerri finished.

Clara plopped down on the couch, not wanting to think about any of those things, but she knew she had to. She'd made commitments to both her girlfriend and her classes. She ran a hand through her hair as she looked at her sister. "I'm torn," she finally admitted, slapping her hands on her thighs.

"What are you torn about?" Zane asked. "You've got it pretty good here."

"But I'm not happy," she countered. "I haven't been for a while, Zane. I'm trying to live a life that isn't meant for me."

"Leaving your family and everything you've ever known to move to California is?" Kerri asked, her brows raised in challenge.

"I can't stay here forever, Kerri. I happen to know for fact that you and Zane have wanted to move to Oregon for years."

"That's different. We both have college degrees and jobs to go to."

"And I don't?" Clara asked, hand to her own chest. "Isn't that what Raymond Van Wurt offered me?"

Kerri was silent, knowing Clara had gotten her on that one. She looked to Zane, hoping he could maybe talk some sense into her little sister. It wasn't that she didn't want her to find her happiness, but she had hoped she could find it locally.

"That's crazy," Zane said. "You don't even really know this guy, Clara. He could be a nut, or he could totally stand you up once you get there. Besides," he said, brows drawn, "I thought you were a dyke?"

Clara rolled her eyes. "He wants to get me jobs, Zane, not fuck me." She was amused. Zane turned away, embarrassed.

"Regardless, he has a point, Clara. Who is this guy? How do you know he won't hurt you, or get you into a bad situation?"

"I don't," Clara said simply, meeting Kerri's gaze head on.

"Then why consider it?"

"Why not? Besides," Clara said, popping up from the couch again. "Who's to say what I'll end up doing at all." She grabbed her keys from the coffee table where she'd dropped them when she'd come in thirty minutes before. She'd had Isabelle drop her off at her sister's house after the evening ended. "Kerri, can you give me a ride home?"

⁂

Kerri was quiet on the way to the apartment. Clara glanced over at her from time to time, but said nothing either. Kerri pulled up in front of the apartment complex and turned to her little sister.

"You're not happy, are you?"

Clara shook her head. "No."

"Is this really the right thing to do? It's a huge chance you'd be taking."

Clara sighed heavily. "I don't know, Kerri. I'm not telling you I'm going to do it, but tonight made me realize that I need to do something. I'm not happy: I hate school, I hate my job, and I'm not happy with Shelby anymore." She looked at her sister. "She doesn't get it. Doesn't get me."

Kerri chuckled. "Very few do, Clara. I do hope you can find someone someday who does. Maybe go find another psychic or something."

"Medium, thank you very much. I'll try that. Maybe there's a Medium's 'R Us chat room or something." The sisters laughed at that. "No, but seriously. I'm not happy with one single aspect of my life. You know the crazy thing? Just a few days ago I thought I was. I really, really thought I was, Kerri." She snapped her fingers. "Like that, something in me changed. It all started that day with Isabelle."

"What do you think happened?" Kerri asked.

Clara shrugged. "Honestly, I'm not sure, but I think I had just convinced myself. You know?" She looked at her sister, truly hoping Kerri would understand or at least try. "I tried to be something I'm not."

Kerri blew out a breath and was silent for a moment. "I don't know. Maybe heading out is the right thing for you. Maybe you need to go out and find yourself somewhere, other than here."

Clara looked at her. "Do you mean that?"

Kerri nodded. "Yeah. Dad will be pissed, and Mom will be devastated if you leave. You do know that, right?"

Clara nodded. "It'll be a fight with him, I know." She chuckled. "He had to fight so hard to get me to go to school, and now I just want to leave it all behind. I don't belong there, Ker. I never did. It was a waste of time and money." She scrubbed her face with her hands. "Ugh. I don't know. I think the answer will just come to me one day. Until then," she shrugged. "I think I'm pretty much stuck."

"You're never stuck, kiddo. Well, at least no more than you make yourself be. Ultimately you hold the reins. No one else."

Clara leaned over and hugged her sister. "Thank you."

♠♠♥♥

The apartment was quiet as Clara made her way inside. A glance at the clock on the wall told her it was nearly eleven. She headed to the bedroom, surprised to see the bed made. She turned on the light, looking for any sign that Shelby had been there recently, but found none. Nor did she find a note anywhere in the apartment.

Clara felt numb as she walked through the empty rooms, looking at a sea of material things that meant little to her. As she walked back into the bedroom, she realized that it all seemed so foreign to her. Like somehow she'd gone to meet with the Van Wurts and came back a stranger in a strange land.

Reaching into her pocket, Clara pulled out the piece of paper Raymond had given her, his personal phone number scribbled on it. She studied the unfamiliar numbers for a moment then grabbed the cordless phone off the dresser.

She waited for several moments until the line was picked up. "Okay, Raymond. I accept your offer."

ꙮ ꙮ ꙮ ꙮ

"Absolutely not!" Max Greenwold roared, face red. He shook his head. "It's not going to happen, Clara."

Clara looked at her father, her own anger building. "Says who?" she asked. "I'm twenty years old. Hardly your ward anymore."

"No, but you did ask for my blessing in this," he retorted, hands on hips.

Clara shook her head. "No. I asked your *opinion*. Very different thing than your blessing."

Max threw his hands up in exasperation, storming from the room, leaving a hurt and angry Clara and a calm Stephanie behind. Stephanie moved over to where her daughter sat on the couch, her face as red as her father's had been. Sitting next to her, she knocked her playfully with her shoulder until Clara met her gaze.

"You have no idea how much the two of you are alike," she said. "Or how much he loves you."

"He can't control me, Mom," Clara said, doing her best to bring her tone down a notch. Her anger wasn't directed at Stephanie, and she had no desire to inadvertently pass it to her.

"I know, and I don't think that's what his intention is. Your dad has never been good at talking things out, Clara. You know that. The problem is, not only is he worried about you, but he's about to lose his baby girl."

Clara stared at her mother, surprised. That had never even entered her mind. "What?"

"You two got pretty close when you were living with him, honey. He doesn't want to lose you, and he feels that by you moving to another state — regardless of the reason — he'll be losing you. You could be moving because you got a job as an aerospace engineer, making two hundred thousand dollars a year, and he still wouldn't want you to go."

"Then why doesn't he just say that?" Clara asked, exasperated.

Stephanie grinned. "Because he's a man, Clara. That would make far too much sense."

Clara burst into laughter, glad to be letting go of some of the tension inside her. She nodded in understanding. "So what do I do?"

"Nothing." Stephanie hugged her and placed a kiss on her forehead. "Just let him come to you. I don't want to see you go, either, but you're a big girl. I know better than to try and stop you. All I can do is pray we've taught you enough for you to make smart decisions, and that you know you have somewhere to come back to if things don't work out as you hope they will."

Clara felt her chest expand with love and gratitude as she hugged her mother tight. They clung to each other for long moments, knowing this was it. Tomorrow Clara would be driving her loaded car halfway across the country to an unknown future.

Chapter Thirty-one

Clara looked on in amazement as the palm trees passed by, their huge fronds dancing slightly in the late spring ocean breeze. She was in good company of average cars, such as her own, as well as BMWs, expensive sports cars, and even a Rolls Royce, as she drove along the Pacific Coast Highway. She couldn't help but wonder what Shelby would think. Her mind raced back to the day she'd left.

Shelby had sat quietly on the couch, her hands tucked into her lap. Clara could tell she was doing her best not to cry.

"Are you sure this is what you want?" Shelby had asked, looking up at Clara finally.

Clara sat on the coffee table, their knees almost touching. She nodded. "Yeah. This is what I want."

Shelby had nodded, taking a deep breath. "Well, I can't stop you." The tears had begun to shimmer in her eyes. "I guess that's it, then."

Shelby hadn't been around when Clara had pulled away from the apartment for the last time. She said she couldn't watch Clara leave, and Clara had no choice but to respect her wishes. Parting, after all, was such sweet sorrow.

Clara took several deep breaths, pushing down the building emotions. She wasn't sad to leave the relationship with Shelby, but she was scared as hell to leave life as she'd known it. She was starting over, and it was a mixed bag of emotions.

She reached over to the passenger seat and grabbed the page that had the scribbled directions to the house on it. She was headed to the Van Wurts' home in Malibu.

She passed by houses to her left that lined the coast, deceiving in the size as seen from the PCH side. On the beach below, their true splendor was revealed. Clara slowed, pulling off the side of the road to let a cab-yellow Ford Escalade pass that had been riding her tail as she'd slowed to try and read the house addresses. Once the SUV had passed — with the blare of a frustrated horn — she continued, eventually finding what she'd been looking for.

The Van Wurts' house was amazing, even from the PCH! The two-story structure was gated, so Clara stopped in front of the wrought iron gate, looking inquisitive as she studied the speaker box with a keypad built in.

"Can I help you?" a disembodied voice squawked, making Clara jump.

"Yes. Clara Greenwold," she said, hoping she didn't have to push any sort of button to allow her to communicate.

"One moment."

There was a moment of silence before the gate slowly swung open, allowing her to pull onto the grounds of the estate. The front of the house was all glass and modern steel. There was an orange Ferrari parked to one side and a black Mercedes next to it.

Clara blew out a breath, feeling quite unsubstantial in her beat-up old Honda. She unbuckled her seat belt and drew her courage around her and headed out of the car.

A woman answered the ring of the doorbell within moments, smiling graciously at Clara, who stood on the massive front stoop, feeling very small.

"Good afternoon, Miss Greenwold," the woman said, stepping aside to allow her in. "My name is Margaret, and I'll take you to Mr. Van Wurt."

"Thank you," Clara said quietly, following whom she assumed was the maid. The inside of the house was just as grandiose and contemporary as the outside. Metal sculptures dotted the hall and rooms, along with modern art: huge canvases filled with raucous color that made absolutely no sense to Clara.

She was led through a maze of rooms and stairwells, the sound of surf getting closer with every corner turned. It wasn't long before the booming voice of Raymond Van Wurt could be heard, as well. He was talking to someone, their quieter, higher-pitched tone heard from time to time, though it was obvious Raymond held the lion's share of the conversation.

Clara stepped out onto what was the top level of a multilevel deck made of steel that led down to the private beach below. Raymond sat in a chair, bare feet up on the matte-finished rail, sunglasses hiding his dark, watchful eyes. The sun made his gelled hair gleam as it beat down on the top of his head. His companion, however, sat underneath the slate-gray umbrella, his face in shadow, though Clara could tell he was much younger than the fifty-something Raymond.

"Mr. Van Wurt, Miss Greenwold has arrived," Margaret announced, heading back into the coolness of the house, her job complete.

Raymond's feet hit the floor of the deck with a slap of bare skin against rubber — meant to keep the metal cool on hot days. "Clara!" he boomed, pushing up from his chair and hurrying over to her.

Clara accepted his enthusiastic hug. "Sorry I'm a little late. Got lost."

"No worries, no worries. Tanner, I'd like you to meet my newest find, Clara Greenwold." Clara and the visitor shook hands. "Clara, this is Tanner Roth, star of my newest venture, *Starplay*, airing on Sci-Fi next month."

"Nice to meet you, Clara," Tanner said, looking her up and down from behind the mirrored lenses of his Oakley's.

"Nice to meet you too," she said, feeling somewhat shy and on display. He was handsome enough, certainly with the good looks of a starring role, but she got the slime factor from him. Once they'd shaken hands, she stuck her hands in the pockets of her jeans and took a step back.

"I'll let you get to it, Ray," Tanner said, turning to the older man. "Thanks for the chat."

"Absolutely." He turned to Clara. "Make yourself comfortable. I'll send Margie out to get your order." He turned to Tanner, slapping him on the shoulder. "I'll walk you out."

Clara walked to the railing, leaning her forearms on it. She had expected the metal to be hot, but it was cool. Looking down at it, she realized it was treated with some sort of plastic coating, which left it smooth and shiny, even though it had the matte finish beneath it.

"Are you hungry, Miss Greenwold?" Margaret asked from behind her. She had her hands clasped together, head slightly tilted to the side as she waited patiently for Clara's order.

"Um, yeah. Actually I am."

"What can I get you?"

"Do you have lunchmeat?" Clara asked, somewhat unsure of what to say.

The older woman hid a smile as she nodded. "What kind, Miss?"

"Clara. Please call me Clara. And turkey? Maybe wheat bread, turkey and American cheese?"

"Mayonnaise, mustard, relish...?"

"Um, mayo and mustard, hold the relish," Clara said, scrunching her nose.

This time Margaret did smile. "Lettuce, tomato? Pickles? Sprouts?"

"Oh. Lot of choices. Um, put whatever you want on there, I guess."

Margaret nodded, her blue eyes twinkling in amusement as she headed back inside. Clara turned her attention back to the view beyond the house and deck. Below, down the beach, she could see two people throwing a Frisbee around, a large black dog barking as it tried to chase the bright orange disc. Clara smiled, amused by the animal's antics. She turned her focus back to the water, having never been to the ocean before.

"Pretty amazing, isn't it?" Raymond asked, stepping up beside her.

Clara nodded then turned to her host. "It's nice to see you again, Raymond."

"You, too," he said with a genuine smile. "I'm also very glad you've taken me up on my offer. I think we could be good for each other." He leaned one forearm on the railing, turning to look at Clara's profile. "Did you have a good drive out?"

Clara nodded. "Yeah. I think it was good for me, helped to clear my head and prepare."

"Prepare? Do you think you need to prepare to do what you were born to do?"

Clara shook her head, mirroring Raymond's position. "No, but I do need to prepare for the fact that I've uprooted my entire life, packed everything that would fit into my car, and got rid of everything else. It's a huge step for me."

Raymond nodded, taking his sunglasses off and tucking them into the loose-fitting button-up shirt he wore. "It reminds me of when I was about your age. Isabelle and I packed up our VW van and drove from New Jersey to Santa Barbara. Scariest thing I've ever done, to be honest."

"And it worked out?" Clara asked, her voice small.

Raymond nodded. "In time, yes. I've had some of the best moments of my life here in California, and some of the worst, as you can attest to by what you saw during my reading."

Clara nodded, remembering all too well what Raymond and Isabelle had endured by the murder of their son.

"But that's life, isn't it?"

"That it is."

"Your lunch, Clara," Margaret said, setting down an elaborate sandwich, piled high with fixings, as well as a chilled can of Coke next to a tall glass of ice. "Would you care for chips, veggies, or anything on the side?" the older woman asked, taking the same stance of hands clasped, head slightly tilted to the side.

"Chips, please."

With a nod, Margaret hurried into the house, happy to serve.

"She's been with us for eighteen years now,"

Raymond said, joining Clara at the table. "Can you believe that?"

Not sure what to say, Clara merely smiled, trying to figure out how she was going to get the sandwich into her mouth.

Raymond took his former position of bare feet on the rail, though this time he was under the shade of the umbrella with his guest. He watched her eat for a moment, then got down to business. "As promised in the deal, the guest house is all set up for you, so you can move in today if you like. As I recall, the deal was for you stay there as you build your clientele, then it's up to you where you'd like to go. I have a list of people for you, which I'll share with you later."

Clara nodded, butterflies settling in her stomach at the thought of doing readings for a bunch of rich, famous people. She had to force herself to swallow the large bite she'd taken. Wiping her mouth with the napkin Margaret had left when she'd brought a separate bowl of chips, Clara prepared to speak.

"Do you want me to do the readings in the guesthouse?"

Raymond shook his head, running a manicured hand across the soft cotton of his pants. "Nope. I've set aside space in the offices of Van Wurt Industries in downtown L.A. You can go in with me every morning or go in when you have an appointment. Up to you. From what I've heard, it's not a good idea to have readings in someone's personal living quarters." He rested his gaze on her. "Is that true?"

Clara thought about it for a moment then nodded. "Makes sense. I'll go in with you, if that's okay."

"Sure."

⁂

The guesthouse was nearly as large as Clara's childhood home, though all on one level instead of three. She tried to hide her reactions as Margaret showed her around. Two employees of the Van Wurts were busy carrying in everything from her car, placing them in the rooms Clara directed them to.

"Is there anything else I can get for you?" Margaret asked expectantly.

Clara shook her head. "Thank you."

Left alone in her new home, she turned in a slow circle, not sure what to feel or think. Should she think she was the luckiest woman in the world, with the chance of a lifetime at her feet? Or, was she simply a fool walking into a viper pit? She liked Raymond a lot, and Isabelle was okay too, but something told her they were only nice when they were getting what they wanted out of someone or something. Would they tire of her?

Clara pushed negative thoughts out of her head as she made her way to the bedroom, which overlooked the ocean. She pushed the windows wide open, allowing the evening breeze to wash over her. She wrinkled her nose at the strong smell of saltwater and sea life. She hoped she'd get used to it.

The guesthouse was decorated in muted yet tasteful colors and fabrics, meant to be neutral enough for anyone's tastes, yet remain elegant in their appointment. She wandered into the kitchen, somewhat smaller in proportion to the rest of the house, but still filled with all the latest gadgets and gizmos that made modern-day cooking easy and efficient. The cabinets were filled with the basic staples, leaving room for anything special Clara might want.

Impressed, but completely full from Margaret's Dagwood-like sandwich, Clara left the room, curious to check out the rest of the house without Margaret's watchful gaze on her. Not that she intended on doing anything wrong, but she'd always prized her privacy above just about all else.

That had been one argument Kerri had made against Clara taking Raymond's offer. In the life she had now launched herself into, there would be little privacy or alone time. Raymond had made it very clear that she was there as a business prospect to him, and though he'd help her a great deal to get settled and established, he expected complete loyalty to him and his business. She would single-handedly be establishing a new area of his entertainment division for Van Wurt Industries. He had mentioned a television series in passing once, which, of course, brought to mind images of the Medium Sylvia Brown on Montel Williams every Wednesday afternoon.

"Grandma, that would just be cruel," she muttered having no interest in sharing such a personal thing with millions of people at once. What she did was part of a gift, not a spectacle.

❧ ❧ ❧ ❧

The offices of Van Wurt Industries in downtown Los Angeles were impressive: all modern steel and glass, much like the house in Malibu. She rode the elevator with an Armani-suited Raymond. She felt rather underdressed in a simple pair of slacks and blouse, though he told her she looked fine. She wasn't, after all, there for a board meeting, he reminded her.

The area that had been set up for her readings was a modest, but nice office with a seating area: couch and overstuffed chair. A desk was set in the corner, next to the large window. There was nothing on the desk, as the office was unused.

"Will this do?" Raymond asked, giving a hopeful look to his newest acquisition.

Clara looked around and nodded. "Yeah. It's perfect."

"Great. Oh! I almost forgot." He reached into the inside pocket of his suit jacket, retrieving a black cell phone with a yellow sticky note attached. "This is for you. Your new number is written on the sticky. Don't worry about the time you use it." He smiled charmingly. "I figured you might want a way to call your family, as well as any new friends you make here. Also, this will be your business phone. Clients can call you at that number."

Clara took the phone, never having used a cell phone before in her life. "Wow," she breathed. "Thank you."

"Absolutely! Good luck today, and do me proud." Raymond gave her a smile and a wink then was out the door, leaving her alone in her new office to contemplate her new position.

She walked over to the window, looking down at the busy streets far below. "Damn, that's far," she whispered. Turning away, she looked out over the office again, deciding how she would handle the readings. Her gaze was drawn to the seating area with the designer furniture that looked about as comfortable as the futon she and Shelby had at the old apartment.

Shelby. She sank down onto the chair as she thought about her ex. For just a moment she wished she were back at the apartment with her. Clara felt terribly out of her element in Lost Angeles with Raymond and Isabelle and all their flashy cars and houses. At least with Shelby, she knew where she stood and who she was.

"No you didn't, Clara," she whispered to herself, setting the cell phone down on the glass table next to the chair. "You only thought you did." She blew out a breath along with thoughts of Shelby and being homesick. She'd made her choice and had to stand with it. Give it a chance.

"Excuse me?" said a soft, male voice followed by a knock on the opened office door.

Clara shot to her feet to see a slight man standing in the doorway. He looked to be around thirty, his black hair cut short and stylishly flopping over his forehead. Smiling blue eyes met her gaze. "Hi." Clara felt a bit sheepish, taken by surprise.

"Hi. I think I'm your next appointment," the man said, taking a hesitant step into the room.

"Well, you're my first, actually," Clara said with a small smile. "Please come in. Close the door."

The man did as asked, then turned to her for further instructions. She could tell he was very nervous, which actually helped her to feel a bit better about the situation.

"My name is Mike James," he said, holding out a pale hand toward Clara, who took it. She looked him in the eye; he wasn't much taller than she was.

"Nice to meet you, Mike. I'm Clara." They sat down, Mike on the couch, Clara in the chair. She couldn't help but feel as if she was about to facilitate a psychiatric therapy session. She pushed the thought away with a small smile. "So, what can I help you with today?"

❧❧❧❧

Forty-three minutes later, Clara sat on the couch next to Mike, a Kleenex held lightly between her fingers. He smiled gratefully as he plucked the tissue from her and wiped his eyes and blew his nose.

"Are you okay?" she asked softly, wanting to give the poor guy a hug.

Mike nodded, giving her a weak smile. "I didn't expect him to come through. I've always felt so guilty about what happened." He blew out a loud breath, much of the tension and emotion from the reading leaving his body. "I can tell you I never played ball next to an ocean again."

Clara smiled with a small nod. "I'm sure. Your brother knew you never meant to send him running into the undercurrent, Mike. He flat out said so."

Mike raised his face to the ceiling for a moment, eyes closed as if in silent conversation with a brother long dead. He nodded, seeming to get himself together. "Yes. He forgives me, regardless of how much he said there was nothing to forgive." He looked at Clara again. "I needed to hear that from him."

"He knew that. That's why he came today, instead of your grandfather, who you expected."

Mike studied her for a long moment, then a smile lit up his handsome features, baby blues sparkling. "You want to get a beer with me tonight?"

Clara stuttered, not sure what to say. "Uh, well. My girlfriend is at home, waiting, you know..." her voice trailed off.

A bark of laughter erupted from him. "That's

okay. So is my boyfriend."

Clara joined him in laughter, now wondering why she hadn't sensed it in him. "Well, in that case, I was lying about a girlfriend, and I'd love to have a beer with you." She leaned into him to whisper conspiratorially, "But I'm only twenty."

Mike grinned. "I don't have a boyfriend, either, and that's okay. We'll get a Coke." He pushed up off the couch, rubbing his eyes with his fingers. "It was a pleasure to meet you, Clara, and you're a very gifted medium."

"Thank you." Clara also stood, extending her hand out to him.

Mike looked down at her hand then ignored it, grabbing her in a tight hug, his slight form stronger than it appeared. "Thank you so much," he whispered into the hug.

Clara nodded, a feeling of satisfaction and contentment spreading through her. They parted and Mike handed her a business card.

"Call me when you're finished here. There's a great little place around the corner."

Clara glanced down at the card before tucking it into her pants pocket. "Will do." She walked him to the door of the office, surprised to see a woman with a raised hand, about to knock on the other side.

"Guess your next client is here," Mike said with a wink then stood aside, allowing the woman to enter. With a final smile and a wave, he was gone.

Chapter Thirty-two

The noise level was high as Clara and Mike found themselves a table. Happy hour had started, so the pub was filling up quickly. Clara looked around, noting the Old West-style theme of the pub, which amused her. So much of what she'd seen during her short time in the area was very new and contemporary. Modern in every way. It was kind of nice to see a bit of a throwback.

"What will you have?" Mike asked, leaning in close to be heard over a raucous group of men who had just passed.

"A Coke is fine," Clara said, which Mike relayed to the waiting waitress, who quickly disappeared in the gathering throngs. Clara wasn't sure why Mike had brought her to such a busy, loud place. As though reading her thoughts, he leaned toward her again.

"It quiets down fast."

They sat in silence for a moment as their drinks arrived. Mike outfitted his Bloody Mary with pepper as Clara watched, a little disgusted. She hated tomato juice by itself, let alone with alcohol thrown in. As promised, the noise began to calm a bit, so Mike began to talk.

"So, how long have you known Ray and Belle?"

Clara chuckled. "Just a little longer than I've known you."

Mike stared at her. "Are you crazy? Didn't you

move here from the Midwest, or something?"

"Yep. I packed up my little piece of crap car and drove out after Raymond offered me a job to do the readings." She shrugged. "It felt like the right thing to do, crazy or not."

"I must say, I think you have bigger balls than I do."

Clara laughed. "I certainly hope not, or you're pretty much screwed."

They talked on, Clara learning that Mike had been born and raised in the area, his father a real estate mogul, which left Mike with a pretty charmed life, though he didn't go into the family business. Instead, after college, he struck out on his own path, finding success in the art world. Though not an ounce of artistic creativity in his fingers, his mind was brilliant, and his creative talent was in the art of making money. He had opened his first gallery in New York in 1989 and had since opened one in San Francisco, Ft. Lauderdale, and finally one in West Hollywood. He'd lived in New York and then Florida to get the two galleries going, but had finally come home to California, where he now lived.

"So, let me get this straight," Mike said, pushing aside the empty glass of his second Bloody Mary. He was leaning forward on his crossed forearms. "You're telling me you walked away from a college education — flat walked away from it — to come out here?" he asked. "To fulfill a job offer from a man you don't even know?"

"That would be correct," Clara nodded, sipping from her third Coke and nabbing a chip from the basket of nachos they'd ordered to share. She had filled him in on the past twenty years of her history.

"Why?" his question was filled with the passion

of a slightly buzzed man, passionate about education and building a future. Clara couldn't help but think that Mike and Shelby would get along wonderfully.

"Because that's not what I wanted," she said simply, popping a fallen black olive into her mouth. "I wasn't happy in school, wasn't happy with my girlfriend, and knew I needed to make a change. I was squashing too much of myself trying to fit into other people's views of what my life should be." She shook her head. "Never again."

Mike thought for a moment, mulling over what he'd just been told, then smiled, nodding with approval. "Good for you, Clara! That took guts." He raised his glass in salute, Clara clinking her own against it.

"Cheers."

✥ ✥ ✥ ✥

Weeks turned into months as Clara was set up with client after client. Most — at first anyway — were people Raymond knew. They were people with lots of money who wanted a shot at the new show in town. Many were skeptics at the start, but Clara took personal delight in changing that within moments. Sometimes she would even show off a bit, share embarrassing little snippets that were whispered in her ear, or things that she'd pick up from handling a personal item of the person.

One thing she had to say about the rich and powerful, they certainly tipped well. She made more on their tips in one day than she had in a month working long hours at either of her jobs back home.

After a while Clara began to bring in her own clientele, either people Mike knew, or the lady she would happen to start talking to in line at the grocery store. Those were her favorite clients. They were the Everyman; the ones who couldn't afford much, but who needed the comfort more than anyone else. So many needed to know that they would be okay, and that their sometimes stark, difficult lives were worth it in the end. Clara often spent her weekends with these clients, and sometimes during the nine-to-five weekdays. She had to be careful with that, though.

She was never given an actual schedule for the day, per her request. She didn't want to know names or any information of who was to visit her. Her readings tended not to go as well when she knew more about the client, as typically the spirit would give what she called identifiers. Those were small tidbits for the client to identify the person who had come to speak to them. The more she knew, the harder she and the spirit had to work for the identifiers.

Before Clara knew it, the holidays were once again coming around. She thought about where she'd been the previous Thanksgiving, the day she'd come out to her parents in a big way. She smiled at the memory as she sat in the guesthouse she was staying in. She relaxed on the couch, looking out over the ocean. The moonlight had turned the crashing waves into blue and white-crested beings that pounded the shore, as though battling an unknown foe.

Her thoughts drifted away from the sea to her family. She hadn't seen any of them in four months, though she kept in weekly phone contact with them. Her father was still angry with her, but she hoped he'd get over it and try to understand. Though she was miles from home and in a world unlike anything she'd ever known, she was happier than she'd ever been.

Clara was brought out of her musings by a knock at her door. She set down the cup of coffee she'd been drinking and padded over, unlocking and pulling the door open. Raymond stood on the other side, still dressed in the slacks and shirt from his suit that day, though the jacket and tie were gone.

"Hi," he said.

"Hey, Ray. Come on in." Though it was hers for the time being, Clara always felt like she had to defer to Ray when he showed up at the guesthouse. He'd never said or done anything to make her feel that way, but there was an air of power and control to him that made her uncomfortable. She didn't like controlling people nor to be controlled, but she had to admit Raymond did intimidate her.

On the flip side of that coin, Raymond stepped just inside the door, looking around the room, but going no further, trying to respect Clara's privacy. "Mind if I come in for a minute?" he asked, indicating the couch.

"Please." Clara led the way, Raymond's Gucci shoes clapping softly on the hardwood floor. "Can I get you something?"

"No, that's okay," he said, waving off her offer.

"Okay." Clara sat on the chair while Raymond sat dead center in the couch. He clapped his hands on his knees, smiling brightly. "Is everything okay?" she asked, feeling somewhat nervous.

"Yes. Fine. We haven't had much of a chance to speak lately, what with me being in Tokyo for the past month and everything. I just wanted to touch base with you, see how things are going." He eyed her expectantly, his dark eyes missing nothing.

"It's going well. Steady clients, and I've been

seeing a few on my own—"

"I heard about that," he interrupted, voice still light. "That's actually one thing I wanted to talk to you about, but we'll get to that." Again he waved off the topic as though it were an annoying housefly. Clara really began to feel nervous. "Tell me about this wedding. Your parents second I hear."

Clara nodded, surprised to be asked about it. She realized in that moment that she'd best not talk to anyone in Raymond's office about anything remotely serious. She'd mentioned the wedding to a woman she'd met in the cafeteria the week before. She had no idea where the woman worked or what she did, just that they'd chatted while they ate. "Yes," she finally said.

"That's great news. I wish them well. I'm assuming you'll want to go back for the event?"

"Yes. I was going to talk to you about that when you got back from your trip."

"Here I am!" Raymond smiled, opening his arms wide. "Let's talk about it. When do you need to go, and for how long?" He pulled a small tablet of paper from his pocket, clicking the pen he'd grabbed off her coffee table.

"Oh, uh," Clara stuttered, glancing at his waiting hand. "The actual wedding day is December twentieth. I was hoping that maybe I could just stay the whole week, have Christmas with my family."

Raymond had begun to write before Clara was even finished, her gaze following the marks. "Clara will be gone December," he glanced up at her, brows raised in approval, "fifteenth, perhaps? Give you a chance to be fitted, as I'm sure you'll be part of the wedding party." At Clara's nod he returned to his notes. "Back on December twenty-sixth." Again he glanced up at her, as though he really needed to ask her permission. "Doable?"

Clara nodded, thrilled that he was being so understandable about it. "That's great, Raymond, thank you."

He gave her an encouraging smile as he clicked the pen and handed it to her, tucking the pad back into his pocket. "I'm a businessman, Clara. Not a monster." He reclined back onto the couch, one arm running the length of the back and an ankle brought over one knee. "Now, that said, let's talk about your extra clients."

"Is it a problem?" she asked, her palms suddenly beginning to sweat.

"I think problem is entirely too strong of a word, but perhaps concern might be a bit more accurate."

Clara swallowed, waiting for whatever Raymond would send her way. She felt like she'd been called to the principal's office, caught ditching class or something.

"You see, Clara, as I said, I *am* a businessman, which means I provide various types of business to clients. Your gifts happen to be one of those types of services that I deal in. When I hear that one of those clients has to wait outside your office for fifteen minutes while you finish up with one of your personal pet projects, that concerns me." He paused, making sure he had her full attention. Though he'd never once raised his voice above a conversational tone, Clara felt like she was being fully and truly chastised. "Now, you look like you're about to tremble out of your socks, but let me reassure you; that's not necessary." His smile returned. "This is the first time it's happened, and I'm confident it's the last."

Clara nodded, swallowing again. "I'm sorry,

Raymond."

He held up a large hand. "No need to apologize. I know you're a very generous person who only wants to help people. After all, that's how you ended up here with us, isn't it?"

Again Clara nodded.

"All right, then. It's been discussed, all's well, no harm. So," he said, tone bright and filled with question, "I understand you've been spending a great deal of time with Michael James. I have to say, since you bought your own car, I've missed driving into work together. I don't get to hear the — what do kids call it today — *skinny* on what's going on in your life."

Other than what you hear from your spies, Clara couldn't help but think, her thoughts tinged with the bitterness of betrayal. She shoved it down, knowing Raymond wasn't the man to complain to. "Yeah, Mike and I spend a lot of time together. Is that okay?"

"Of course! Michael is a great guy. I've done lots of business with him over the years. I wouldn't get your hopes up, though," he said, voice dropping conspiratorially. "He's gay." He winked at Clara, and something inside her told her he knew damn well that she was too.

"I'll keep that in mind," she said instead.

"Wise. I've gone to dinner with him several times, and even to a few sporting events. The man *loves* boxing. I do dislike it when he gets into one of his depressed modes, however," he said, brows drawn in thoughtful contemplation. "But, I'm sure you have more patience for that kind of thing than I do." He slapped his hands on his knees again, marking his intent to leave. "So, anything else?"

Clara shook her head. "Nope. I think that just

about covers everything."

"Excellent." Raymond got to his feet and headed for the door, followed by Clara. He turned to her before stepping out. "You're doing a wonderful job for me, Clara. I've heard many, many wonderful things about you and your marvelous gifts." He smiled, kind and genuine. "I'm glad I managed to snag you before anyone else found you."

Clara smiled back, feeling warm and fuzzy at such a wonderful compliment. "Thank you, Raymond. I am, too."

"Good night, Clara."

Chapter Thirty-three

For the fifth time in as many minutes Clara adjusted the pearl choker she wore with her dress. Not only was she not used to wearing dresses, she wasn't used to wearing necklaces, either. Especially ones that threatened to cut off her air supply.

"Stop fidgeting," Kerri admonished through a clenched-teeth smile.

Clara forced herself to stop messing with the necklace. She had this horrible vision of inadvertently breaking the strand, sending hundreds of tiny pearls sweeping across the sanctuary. She cleared her throat, instead focusing on the couple walking toward them now.

Stephanie was breathtaking in her ivory satin gown, simple yet elegant. After all, she said, they'd been there before, so didn't need anything over the top. She was on the arm of her brother, who looked proud and handsome in his black tux. The man of the hour, however, was Clara's father. Max stood proud and strong, awaiting his bride. Again. He was clean cut, hair trimmed, and looking more handsome than ever.

Max Greenwold was a bittersweet thing for Clara at the moment. She'd gotten into town five days before, and though Kerri and her mother had been overwhelmed in their excitement to see her and welcome her home, Max had been quiet and somewhat distant. Clara had hoped that the time apart would help him overcome his issues, but it didn't seem to be. Clara knew they needed some serious one-on-one time, and she intended to do just that after the wedding. Her parents weren't leaving on their weeklong honeymoon for another two weeks, so she had time before she headed back to California.

In the meantime, she cleared her mind of anything negative, as she wanted the day to be special for her parents, and wanted them to have as good a shot — as it would probably be their last — at making it this time.

Stephanie reached her husband-to-be looking like a young and fresh woman, looking forward to the rest of her life. At nearly forty-four years old, Stephanie was still beautiful and vibrant.

Out of the corner of her eye Clara saw Kerri wipe at a tear, which of course made Clara nearly lose it herself. She turned her focus back to her parents, who now were instructed to join hands. As she watched the beautiful ceremony unfold, Clara couldn't help but feel almost wistful. She wondered if she'd ever get a chance for such love. She'd struck out twice already, though she did realize she was still very young. All the same, she wished she knew exactly where her future lay.

No sooner did the thought cross her mind than she felt compelled to look to her right into the crowd of well-wishers. A small gasp escaped Clara's lips when she saw Abby Jensen sitting in the third row, a peaceful smile on her face. Her eyes were riveted on the happy couple, as were everyone's — including the dark-haired man who sat very close to her.

Clara was jolted from her shock when Kerri gave her a small nudge. Clara looked at her only to feel embarrassment as quiet laughter filled the sanctuary. She turned to see her mother and the minister looking at her expectantly.

"The ring?" the minister asked, a smile in his voice.

"Oh." Feeling oh-so-stupid, Clara took a step forward, holding out her father's heavy gold band to her mother. Stephanie smiled and kissed her lightly on the cheek, laughing nervously at the lipstick smear she'd left. She wiped it off with her fingertips, leaving a small, loving caress on her youngest's cheek. She mouthed 'thank you,' then turned to Max.

Clara didn't dare take her eyes off the proceedings again, though she could still feel the shock of seeing Abby after so many years.

≈≈≈≈≈

Clara reveled in the snow that was falling steadily, though not dangerously. She was also grateful to be out of that awful dress her mother made her wear. She was honored to be co-maid of honor with Kerri, but still... She shoved her hands a little deeper into the pockets of her jacket as she hurried inside the hall where the wedding reception was being held.

She had been asked to drive a few of the guests home from the church, so after that little chore, she'd hurried to her parents' house and changed before arriving at the reception hall. Loud music could already be heard pulsing in the cold night, the parking lot filled with cars that were already covered with a light dusting of powdered sugar-like snow.

As she gazed over the cars, she wondered which one — if any — belonged to Abby. Was she just inside?

Who was the man she'd left the church with? Kerri hadn't mentioned Abby in a long time, so she hadn't been aware if the two high school buddies were still friends. What other reason would Abby have for coming to the wedding?

The night wore on, everyone having a good time during the reception. Even Clara managed to laugh and dance, even if it was with Zane and a few cousins. All the while, though, she continued to look for Abby, but had yet to see her. She was pretty sure the blonde wasn't there, which for some reason filled her with deep disappointment and relief.

"May I have this dance?"

Clara turned, surprised to hear the request asked in her left ear. A wide smile immediately split her face at the sight of her father. "You may," she said with a vigorous nod.

Max took her hand and led her onto the dance floor; the crowd seemed to part for father and daughter. Clara felt her heart begin to melt when the DJ played "Unforgettable" with Natalie Cole and her father, Nat King Cole. Max smiled down at her as he gracefully led her around the dance floor.

"Why did you change your clothes?" he asked, twirling her.

"I hate dresses."

Max laughed, nodding. "Yes, I remember. You were almost as beautiful as the bride today, Clara. Almost," he said with a wink.

"And you were the most handsome guy in the entire place."

"Why, thank you."

They danced on in silence for a long moment before Max brought her in close again. "I've missed you, sweet pea."

Clara nearly burst into tears at the sound of the endearment Max had used for her entire life — until she left school and went to California. "I've missed you too," she said, her voice nearly breaking. "Don't be mad at me, Dad," she pleaded, looking up into his face, his own eyes a bit more moist than they should be.

Max shook his head. "I'm not. I can't be. I love you too much." The song ended. He cupped her face in large hands. "You're too unforgettable."

The dam burst and the tears flowed. Clara was taken into a strong embrace, her daddy back in her life.

"I love you, little one," Max whispered, kissing the top of her head.

"I love you too, Dad." They shared one more tight hug then walked hand-in-hand off the dance floor.

⁂

Clara glanced over at her father several times, often met with a return glance or smile from him. They had decided to take a walk around the neighborhood, neither saying much. She was due to head back to California in two days. Though the dance during the wedding reception had been special to both, they hadn't talked much since.

"Want to go to the pond?" Max asked, words coming out in white puffs. At his daughter's nod of consent, they turned left at the corner and headed to the small park where they used to feed the ducks when Clara was a small child. After a long moment, Max spoke again. "Are you happy?"

Clara chewed on her ChapStick-slathered bottom

lip before answering. "I needed to do this, Dad."

Max stopped them with a hand to her arm. "That's not what I asked."

"I know. Like anything, there's good and bad. I do love what I'm doing, and I've made a really good friend. Is this where I want to be for the rest of my life? Probably not. But for right now, it's what I need to do, and where I need to be."

"Why?" he asked, genuine curiosity replacing what was once bitter accusation.

"Because I needed some distance from what was safe: you guys, Shelby, doing things I never wanted to do."

"Like school," he finished, defeated.

"Yes, Dad. Like school. Listen," she said, putting a hand on his arm. "I know you want the best for me and Kerri and don't want to see us struggling like you and Mom have. But you have to understand something: College isn't always the answer to every question or problem."

"But without an education—"

"What about people who have natural gifts and talents?" Clara interrupted. "What if I was a writer? A painter or an actor? Would we be standing here having the same conversation?"

Max chuckled. "Probably."

Clara smiled. "Probably," she agreed. "But the fact of the matter is, I *do* have a gift or talent, and my path in this life is to use it, Dad. To help people."

"I know that, Clara, and I've always supported and respected you for it. You know that. But you're not some teenager anymore. You're growing up, and have to make it on your own. Eventually I'm sure you'll have a mortgage, a family hopefully. Is this stuff *really* going to pay for all that?"

Clara shrugged. "Maybe. Maybe not. I don't know, but right now I'm not worried about that. I need to do this, Dad." She looked him in the eye, wanting him to fully understand what she was saying. "It's a part of me. A *very* big part of me."

"And I know that. But, why can't you get something — the normal nine-to-five — that's stable and you can count on? You can do this stuff on weekends, or after work, or whatever," Max said, his voice hopeful.

Clara shook her head. "It doesn't work that way. When you're programmed to do something, regardless of what that something is, you have to do it. Like I said, if I were a writer or an artist, it would be the same thing. I just really need you to understand that, and to have enough faith in me that I'll be okay. And, if it doesn't work out, have the faith in me to know that I'll walk away. I'm not a stupid person, Dad, nor do I consider myself terribly foolish. I really need you to trust me. Okay?"

Max met her gaze for a long moment before finally giving in. He didn't like it, but he nodded and began walking again.

༄ༀ༄

The visit home and Christmas had gone entirely too quickly, and now Clara sat on an airplane headed west to her new home. The time with her family and all that was familiar had been harder to leave than she ever dreamed it would.

Her life in California was about as opposite from back home as night was from day. In Malibu she was surrounded by some of the richest people in the world, certainly the United States, and many were filled with purpose and pomp. Back home, people worked hard for what they had, and the smallest of luxury was hard won.

Then there was her family. There was a small ache in her heart from seeing her mother's tears as she and Kerri waited with her at the gate until her flight boarded. Stephanie had tried to stay strong, but hadn't been entirely successful, and it broke Clara's heart. She was, however, glad that she and her father had come to some peace. She felt they were pretty much back on as solid of ground as they were before she made the big announcement. At least he understood, anyway. She knew, though, that if he had his way, she would be heading back to pack up and drive back home. They both knew that wasn't going to happen. She was happy where she was. Clara knew she'd know when it was time to go.

Chapter Thirty-four

1999

Mike set down the last box, his pale face ruddy from the exertion of carrying everything Clara owned. Hand on hip, he took a deep breath and looked around the small loft apartment she'd decided to rent.

"Is that it?" she asked, making a pathway between the boxes so she could reach the bathroom.

"I sure as hell hope so," Mike said, plopping down on top of a plastic tub that held Clara's books. "'Cause I'm done."

Clara laughed. "Get yourself a beer. I put some in the fridge to chill last night."

"Oh, you are a doll!" he exclaimed, pushing to his feet and picking his way to the small kitchen. "So, was Ray pissed at you?" he called out, hoping to be heard through the closed bathroom door.

"Kind of," was called back, though muffled.

"I bet," he muttered, heaving himself up on the countertop, letting the flip-flops drop from his feet. He knew Raymond Van Wurt well. Ray said jump, you asked how high. He said stay, you asked how long. The fact that his pet had moved out had undoubtedly not gone over so well.

"He didn't understand," Clara explained, buttoning her shorts as she made her way into the living room. "He thought Isabelle had pissed me off."

Mike chuckled. "Did she?"

"No more than usual," Clara said, beginning to slice into the tape that held the boxes shut. "Isabelle is a woman with more money than sense who likes martinis a little too much."

"I'll drink to that," Mike said, holding his beer up in salute before taking a long pull. He wiped his mouth with the back of his hand. "I think I'm going to ask Jeff to move in," he said, staring off into what he hoped would be a future with the gorgeous blond. "What do you think?"

Clara kept her back to him, knowing full well that question was coming. Mike had struck out more often than he'd made home runs in love. He was a good guy with a sweet face and beautiful eyes, but few saw him as more than a twink with lots of money. He'd met Jeff Stanley four months before at a party, and in Clara's opinion, the only thing Jeff had done for Mike was introduce him to Valium and better oral sex.

"Clara?" Mike said, hopping down from the cabinet and sauntering into the living room. He leaned against the wall, waiting for an answer.

Clara sighed, finally turning to face him. "You sure you want to know what I think?"

"Why? Is it bad?"

"I don't know about bad, but I don't know about good, either."

"Damn it, Clara!" Mike threw the cap to his beer across the room where it bounced off the huge windows that fronted the building. "I am thirty-three, almost thirty-four years old! I'm going to end up some creepy old eccentric with a million cats!"

"No you're not." Clara chuckled, tossing the newly emptied box aside. "That's not old, Michael, and you know it. Well," she said on second thought, "not ancient, anyway."

"Nice. Just because you haven't even reached your mid-twenties yet doesn't mean you can't be sympathetic to my plight." Mike flopped down onto the floor, a pout on his face.

Clara managed to hide her smile as she sat on a box in front of him. "Listen, Mike, I think Jeff is a nice guy, but I don't think he's the nice guy for you."

"Why?" he asked, his eyes beginning to fill as he looked up at her.

Clara slid off the box and sat next to him. Her heart broke for him. The one thing Michael James had never experienced in a pampered life was true love. He'd had lovers, and he'd had users, but never a man who loved him for who he was as a person, and not how much money was in his wallet. The problem Clara knew was that he lured men to his table or his house with the size of his bank account. For whatever reason, men just weren't interested in anything else he had to show them. Including a massively large heart.

"I don't know, sweetie," she said softly, reaching out to intercept a tear as it fell from one eye. "I wish I did. I wish I could call my grandmother here right now and ask her, but the truth is, she wouldn't tell me if I did. It's something in your plan this go round, and it's something you must have to learn from."

"Fuck lessons!" Mike roared, jumping to his feet and stumbling over boxes as he tried to pace. "Damn it, Clara! All I want is someone to love me. Me!" He pounded his own chest. "Is that too much to ask?"

"I've been asking myself that very same question for the past seven years, Mike. I understand."

"Clara," he pleaded, kneeling in front of her. "I

want a home. I want a family. I even want a damn dog, even though I'm allergic!"

Clara smiled.

"Am I asking for too much? Why don't you like Jeff? Why isn't he the one?"

"Do *you* think he's the one, Mike?" she asked, taking his hand in hers. "Because honestly, it doesn't matter diddly what I think. It only matters what you think."

Mike sighed, swiping angrily at another falling tear. "I don't know." He looked down at his fingers, the tip of his index finger wet with his frustration. "I think he might be. Maybe."

Clara nodded, though red flags were flying all over the place in her head. "Then you need to do what you need to do. If you feel it's right, I support you one hundred thousand percent. I'll help you guys move him in. Just," she brought his face up with a finger under his chin, "promise me you'll think about it first, okay? Be sure."

Mike nodded, smiling in gratitude. He hugged her tightly to him, whispering into her ear. "Thank you, Clara. Thank you."

⁂⁂⁂⁂

Clara got the office ready, lighting a few candles to bring some warmth to what used to be a cold, rather sterile room. The blinds were closed, allowing the candlelight to filter throughout the room, barring the harsh brightness of the sunny day, which she felt gave things an artificial, impersonal feeling.

The coffee was brewing, though it was specifically for the client. Two years ago Rebecca had urged Clara to make a drastic change in her diet and food intake. She was asked to purify her system, ridding herself and her diet of sugars, caffeine, and fatty foods. Rebecca had explained that they were toxic to what she called the "energy highway" that everyone possessed, causing not only blockage in arteries but also in clarity. Especially sugar. It had been a *very* difficult row for her to hoe, and the caffeine headaches had been murder, but she'd gotten through it.

Her first client of the day was due in three minutes, so Clara quickly straightened the throw pillows she'd bought for the couch, and opened up a new box of Kleenex to put on the glass top table. More often than not readings got emotional for the client.

At nine a.m. on the button there was a knock on the door.

"Come in," Clara called out, making sure her cell phone was turned off and left out of sight.

The office door opened, and Clara was surprised to see one of her favorite singers walk through the door. She walked over to her, professionalism as firmly in place as her friendly smile.

"Hi. I'm Clara," she said, extending a hand, which was quickly taken.

"Christine Gray."

"Welcome. Please, come in." Clara and the singer got themselves situated, Christine declining a cup of coffee. "Okay, do you know anything about me? What I do, who I am, what you're in for?"

Christine smiled, pushing a long, dark strand of hair out of sky-blue eyes. The white tank top she wore hugged her firm torso nicely, as did the well-ventilated pair of jeans. "I know you talk to dead people, but beyond that," she shook her head, "not a clue."

"Okay. Well, yes, you're right. I do talk to dead people, and lucky me, they talk back." Both women smiled. "So, I only ask a few things of you before we begin. Please give me no names, no details of any events or person. And, during the reading, if you could refrain from expounding on anything I tell you, but keep it simple to what I ask. Okay?"

Christine nodded, sitting back in the cushions. She casually crossed one leg over the other, swinging a long leg lazily to and fro. Clara cleared her throat, trying to ignore just how gorgeous her current client was, and closed her eyes.

Grandma, help me get through this without looking like an idiot, please.

She took several deep breaths, opening her mind to connect to the spirit world. Within a few moments information began to come. She opened her eyes, watching as the scene unfolded seemingly in her office. She was looking so intently into the past that Christine glanced over her shoulder to try to find what Clara was so focused on. Seeing nothing, she waited in silence for Clara to speak.

"Okay, I'm seeing what looks to be an empty room. White walls. A window, sunlight on the floor." She saw something in the corner and tried to focus on it. "It looks like there's...orange juice?" Her attention was caught by Christine's gasp. She glanced at the singer. "Do you know what I'm talking about?"

"Yes. Very much so." Christine tried to keep the bitterness out of her voice, but wasn't entirely successful. She wanted to explain, but remembered Clara's words of warning not to expound. Instead she blew out a breath.

"This feels like a scary place, Christine," Clara

said, unconsciously hugging herself. "Very dark. Can I ask you where this is?"

"It's the apartment in Queens where I lived with my parents." She bit her tongue to stop any more information from coming. The ironic thing was, her parents were an off-limits topic with everyone else, but for some reason she felt like talking to Clara about it.

"Okay. That's fading. Now I'm seeing containers of Chinese food, it looks like. Chopsticks."

Christine chuckled and nodded. "Yep. I used to eat Chinese food with my mother." She stopped cold, realization coming to her. "Wait, if you're seeing someone, does that mean they're dead?"

Clara could see the pain in the singer's eyes, and her heart reached out to her. "Typically," she acknowledged. "But maybe not in this case. Let's see what else I get. Okay?"

Christine nodded. When she was just a child, she'd come home from school to find her home empty: no furniture, no belongings, no parents. Her father had been in trouble with shady characters her entire short life at that time, so Christine had always just assumed they'd gone on the run. She hadn't seen them in more than twenty years, never hearing from them again.

"Okay, let's see." Clara blew out a breath, feeling somewhat under pressure now. "Who had blue eyes? Same color as yours."

"My mother."

"Okay, that's who I've got with me, Christine. I'm so sorry."

Christine was silent for a long moment, trying to absorb what she'd just been told. She swallowed several times, not wanting the emotions to rise any more than they had to. She'd been abandoned by the woman; left to fend for herself at nine years old. She felt the woman who'd given birth to her didn't deserve her tears.

"Take your time," Clara said softly, able to feel the battle waging inside her client. She wanted to cry herself, able to feel the anguish held within the spirit who stood to her left.

"What does she want?" Christine finally managed to ask.

"Let's find out. Okay?" Clara reached across the narrow table and touched the singer lightly on the knee. "She's telling me she was forced to leave. She had no choice. Does that make sense to you?"

Christine nodded, not sure she wanted to believe it. "Yes, it does."

"Good. Okay, wait, say again?" Clara asked the woman who seemed so anxious to finally say what had been on her mind for so many years. "She says she was messed up. In the head." Clara demonstrated what she was being shown by moving her finger in a circle next to her head. "She said tried to get Carla to take you—"

"That drunk old hag?!" Christine erupted, her hands fisted at her sides. "I'm sorry," she nearly whispered, trying to force her anger down and away from herself and certainly Clara.

"That's okay. Hold on. She's talking again. Talkative, this one." Clara held up her hands, "Whoa, wait. Slow down." Her head was a jumbled mess of messages, images, and sounds. It was almost as if the woman only had a few precious seconds to get out everything she'd needed to get out for so long. From the looks of Christine's fidgeting body, that was probably fairly accurate. "Okay. Okay, I've got it. She wants you to know that she loves you, she's sorry, and that it was quick. Your father is still alive. She was killed in an accident, Christine. She was crossing a street when a car ran a red."

Christine nodded, finally giving in and letting her tears come. They were slow, but there. She wiped at them with the edge of the tissue she'd pulled from the box.

"She also said you should make time for Adam."

Christine's head shot up at that one. "Why? Is he okay? How the hell does she know about Adam?"

Clara couldn't help but smile. "On the other side they know about everything. She won't say. Just that you should see him." She smiled. "She also said you'll make a wonderful mother."

Christine's dark brows drew. "A wonderful mother? I don't have any kids, nor any plans for them."

Clara shrugged. "I just tell you what I hear. I feel her energy fading," she said, the signal growing weaker and weaker as her head became more her own rather than the temporary home of Christine's mother. "Anything else before I lose her?"

Christine opened her mouth, the words I love you nearly falling out. She clamped her mouth shut and shook her head.

"She's gone," Clara said softly. "And, Christine? She can hear you any time. Okay?"

Christine smiled, a little sheepish. "Thank you so much. That was...wow. Really amazing."

"You're welcome. Any time."

They both stood and Clara offered a hug, which Christine returned. "Powerful stuff, Clara. Powerful stuff." They walked to the door. "I'm very impressed with you. Guess what they say is right."

"What's that?" Clara asked, her hand on the

doorknob as her client stepped out into the hall.

"You *really* can talk to dead people." With a megawatt smile, Christine was gone.

"And it's true what they say about you too," Clara muttered as she closed the door. "You're hotter than hell!"

Chapter Thirty-five

2000

"...three, two, one, Happy New Year!" A crowd of voices cheered, noisemakers going crazy. All around the huge beach house in Malibu happy couples found each other and kissed to bring in the new millennium.

Clara received a sloppy kiss from her drunk girlfriend. Well, girlfriend may have been slightly too strong of a word for what Leah was. More like bed warmer. Clara turned her head after the kiss, wiping her mouth with her sleeve, trying to hide her disgust. The woman spent most of her time drunk, and if she was sober, she liked to call herself a model. Clara never said anything; after all, it was good to have a dream.

"Happy New Year, baby," the drunk woman slurred in Clara's ear, leaving the remnants of their shared kiss on her lobe.

Clara pulled away, yet again keeping her revulsion in check. "I think you've had a little too much to drink, Leah," she said, holding the already-tall woman steady on her four-inch heels.

"No way!" Leah said, pulling away so fast that she toppled over backwards, nearly knocking the beverage table over.

Embarrassed, Clara looked around to see who all had seen. Glad to be in the clear, as everyone was still busy celebrating, she helped Leah to unsteady legs and eventually out of the house altogether.

"Where we goin', baby?" Leah asked, folding herself into Clara's car, one of her heels snapping in the process. "Goddamn motherfucking cocksucker!" she cried, throwing the now-useless shoe outside of the car.

"Damn it, Leah!" Clara yelled, hurrying back around her car to snag the discarded shoe and tossing it back inside with her girlfriend. She got back and started the car, making sure Leah's door was locked using the child safety locks.

"Why the hell did'ju take me there, anyways?" Leah asked, turning angry hazel eyes on Clara.

"Because you wanted to go," Clara said, steamed.

"Nah uh!"

"Don't start this shit with me again, Leah," Clara warned, her voice dangerously low. "I'll leave you on the side of the road so fast..."

"I told you I didn't wanna go—"

"No, that is not true and you know it. *I'm* the one who didn't want to go to some party at your friend's. *I'm* the one who suggested a quiet New Year's at my place. *I'm* not the one who is drunk out of my fucking mind!" When there was no response, Clara glanced over to see that Leah had passed out, her mouth hanging open and saliva beginning to dribble out. "God, you're so pathetic," she muttered. "And I'm pathetic for staying."

Clara pulled up in front of the bungalow Leah shared with three other people, one of the roommates helping her get the tall woman inside. Once inside Leah's dark bedroom, Clara got the unconscious woman settled on the mattress, the other high heel off, and a sheet covering her sleeping form.

She stood next to the bed and stared down at her. Though it had only been a few months that they'd been together, they had been disastrous ones. More times than not Clara had picked Leah up from a bar or a party, either drunk or stoned out of her mind. When she was sober, Leah could be a lot of fun and was great in bed, but those times were becoming fewer and fewer in between. Clara wondered why it was that such a beautiful woman was destroying herself from the inside out.

"Hey," Jules Gilbredth said from the kitchen as Clara made her way toward the front door. Jules had been roommates with Leah the longest, the two models having known each other for five years.

"Hi," Clara replied, stopping a few feet shy of the door.

"Tough one tonight?" Jules asked, raising her coffee mug in invitation.

Clara thought about it for a moment, looking into Jules' deep blue eyes. She smiled, deciding that she would definitely like some.

꙼꙼꙼꙼

Clara realized she was sitting in a rowboat, her grandmother behind her. They were on a lake, a small island far off to the left, the mainland to the right.

"Row, Clara," Rebecca ordered.

Clara tried to turn back to look at her guide, but a stern "Row" stopped her. She grabbed the oars in either hand, trying to figure out the mechanics of rowing a boat, which she'd never done before. It took a moment, but then she had them moving.

"Where am I going?" she asked, the wooden oars chopping cleanly into the water that lapped at the sides of their boat.

"I'll tell you when to stop."

Clara had the distinct feeling that further conversation was not welcome, so remained silent in her task. The day was beautiful, the sky above the wonderful golden hue that she'd grown accustomed to during her trips to see her grandmother. They were alone on the lake, and it seemed they were alone period. No one could be seen on the small tropical island, and the mainland was too far away to see anything other than the large and small structures scattered about.

"Pull in here," Rebecca said, pointing toward a dock that seemed to have come out of nowhere.

Clara managed to maneuver the boat until they were right alongside. She jumped out and quickly tied off the boat, as though she'd done it a million times before. Reaching a hand down, she intended to help Rebecca from the boat, but the dark-haired woman only shook her head. Confused and slightly hurt by her seemingly distant demeanor, Clara simply nodded and backed away. She had no idea where she had been directed to go or why, as Rebecca had never done anything like that before.

Soon the dock ended and Clara stepped onto land, though as soon as she stepped down, she was no longer on that land, she had entered the after shadow. Darkness encroached around her, along with sounds of far-off humming and a distant cry. She walked down a hallway, wide yet seeming to close in around her. Aimless spirits walked toward her, their large, fearful eyes staring at her, silently pleading for her help.

Clara ignored them, knowing that her grandmother

had sent her there to do something, and she just hoped she would know what it was when it happened, or when she came upon...whatever. Ahead of her was a door, closed, the handle bright silver among the gloom. Clara stood before it, taking a deep breath before entering. Somehow she knew the other side was her destination.

The room beyond was dark, as though the walls had been painted a dark gray. It was square and empty, except for the woman who sat dead center. Her hair was long, acting as a shield completely obscuring her from whatever might frighten her.

Clara took a careful step closer to the woman, noting the woman's thin frame and the clothing that hung from her limbs in tattered remnants of what used to be jeans and a T-shirt.

"Hello," Clara said, unsure of what to do or say. The woman looked up and Clara gasped. She immediately recognized her as Nancy August, mother of Rachel August, a girl Clara hade gone to middle school with. "Nancy?" she whispered, slowly lowering herself so she was kneeling in front of the woman. She knew Nancy had committed suicide during their eighth-grade year. Rachel and her sister had then moved to Arkansas to live with an aunt.

Nancy looked into Clara's face, her own pale eyes large and frightened. She said nothing, nor did she have to. The fear was quickly replaced with absolute despair. Her head slowly fell again, her hair re-forming its shield.

"Nancy, I have to get you out of here," Clara said, reaching out a hand to gently brush strands of stringy hair aside. "Will you come with me?" Clara almost couldn't look into those unbelievably sad eyes as Nancy looked at her again. She shook her head.

"I can't," she whispered, her voice barely audible.

"Yes, you can." Clara took one of Nancy's hands, so cold and limp, within her own. She stood, Nancy's arm rising with the movement, her hand still clutched in Clara's. Satisfied that she had her, Clara turned, still holding Nancy's hand and began to head for a second door that nearly blended in with the wall. "See? I told you—" Clara turned, shocked to see Nancy still sitting in a defeated heap at the center of the room. She looked down at her hand, stunned to see it was empty, as she swore she had still been able to feel Nancy's hand within her own.

She hurried back to Nancy, determination dogging her steps. She squatted in front of the woman again, brushing long strands of hair aside.

"You can do this, Nancy. You have to do this. Do you understand?"

Nancy looked at her, slowly shaking her head. It was as if every movement the woman made was in slow motion. "I can't. I can't go."

"Yes. With me, you can go. Let me take you from this place. This awful, awful place you've put yourself." Clara looked around the room, feeling a thrill of fear race down her spine, feeling like the walls were beginning to push in on her. She felt suffocated and sad. "Come on." She took her hand again, this time taking them both and holding on tight. Holding on for dear life.

Clara got to her feet, gently tugging and stepping back to encourage Nancy to move. It was as though the sitting woman were ninety years old and stepping out of her wheelchair for the first time in twenty years.

"That's it." Clara smiled, taking another step back.

Nancy groaned as one foot hit the ground, pushing

enough to get the other foot flat on the floor. She rested, her head lolling forward with the exertion. Her legs nearly gave out as she began to stand.

"Don't give up, Nancy. You're doing it..."

Nancy grunted as she got to her feet, her legs weak; arms so very thin. "It's so hard," she whispered. "So hard."

"I know it's hard. God, you've been here so long. Come on. Keep it coming." Clara took another step backward, not daring to take her eyes off Nancy, who was still slowly coming. Together they made slow progress, coming closer and closer to the door. "Almost there," Clara said, dropping one of Nancy's hands to grab the doorknob behind her. Nancy's arm fell limply to her side, as did her head. She began to turn into dead weight as Clara tugged the door open. "Oh no you don't!" she cried, grabbing the woman in her arms before Nancy fell to the floor.

Arms dangling limply over Clara's own, Nancy was nearly dragged over to the door where Clara turned so her back was to the room and all but pushed Nancy through to the golden light of the other side.

Clara watched in awe as Nancy stood straight as she hit the light, her head flung back, arms wide as she was filled with and then surrounded by the healing magic of the light. It was nearly blinding, but utterly beautiful to watch. When it all cleared, a young, radiant woman with short red hair stood in Nancy's place. Her green eyes sparkled as she smiled at Clara.

"Thank you so much," she said, taking both of Clara's hands in hers once more.

Clara could only smile and nod, truly astonished by what she'd just witnessed and been part of. Nancy's soul was truly beautiful. "You're welcome." She watched *as Nancy hurried off, finally finding peace.*

ཨ༅ཨ༅ཨ༅ཨ༅

Clara's eyes flew open, a gasp torn from her lungs. She sat up in bed, the sheet falling to reveal her naked breasts. She looked around, disoriented and wondering why there was a sleeping woman lying beside her. A sleeping, *naked* woman. It took her a moment to realize it was Jules.

"Shit," she blew out, scrubbing her face with her hands. Everything came back to her, and she felt a shiver pass through her and down her spine. She remembered Nancy, and the amazing moment when she'd crossed. Incredible. Now if only she knew how to find her daughter, Rachel, and tell her.

Clara drove home in the early morning hours of 2000. Everything looked fine, so she assumed Y2K hadn't struck, ending the world as everyone knew it. She actually knew people who had gathered bottled water and nonperishable foods, stockpiling them "just in case." The city was still asleep, dead after a night of bringing in the New Year. Clara just wondered how in the world she was going to remember to write a new millennium on her checks.

Her mind drifted back to the disaster of a party she'd attended — against her better judgment — with Leah. Disaster wasn't even the word for it, and she felt foolish for even bothering. It was definitely over between them and in her mind, good riddance. This, of course, led to the stupidity of sleeping with Leah's roommate, Jules.

"Ah, hell," she blew out, running a hand through her hair, which was a mess without a brush. "Did I just do a clichéd lesbian thing or what?" Pretty much. She thought about Jules and wondered if maybe there could be something more between them than just a night of really good sex. "No," she said aloud, knowing better than to go there. Jules wasn't much different than Leah, except maybe with a few less drugs. Her life was just as much about drama as anyone else's in that house. A very unhealthy environment.

As she pulled into the parking lot of her building, Clara let out a heavy, tired sigh. She hadn't gotten much sleep and felt emotionally exhausted, though she wasn't entirely sure why. Sure, the incident with Leah had been draining and completely embarrassing, but nothing out of the ordinary with the difficult model. Then Nancy August's face popped in front of her mind's eye. She once again recalled the entire thing from start to finish, and felt it had to be one of the most profound things she'd ever experienced in all her years in the spiritual world.

She pushed open her car door and climbed out, her entire body aching from lack of sleep and enthusiastic sex. Thoughts crept back into her mind as she dug her house key from the ring. The lock clicked open, and she pushed into her apartment.

Was that what happened to souls when they committed suicide? Were they lost forever, or at least until someone like her could rescue them? Rebecca had once told her that those who took what she called 'an early exit' were destined to turn right back around and live a similar life to what they'd just escaped. They'd planned it for themselves and had to keep going until they finished it and learned whatever was to be learned from it.

So, what happened with Nancy? Did she fall

through the cracks? Did her fear and pain in life keep her trapped within that fear and pain, keeping her from crossing, from finding that door that was just within arm's reach?

Clara had no idea as she tossed her keys to the coffee table and kicked her shoes off. She padded off to the bathroom, desperately wanting a shower. She wanted to wash off the stupidity of her night with Jules and the disgust of her night with Leah. Stripping her clothes off, she left them in a pile on the bathroom floor as she turned the shower on, nice and hot.

The water blasted over Clara's skin and hair, causing a deep, satisfied groan to escape her throat. She pushed her hair off her face, surprised at how long it had gotten. It was past her bra strap, and she tinkered daily with the idea of cutting it. Mike had threatened to kill her if she did. She took her time, allowing the heat to relax her tension-filled body. She had a few readings to do that day. More than once she'd patted herself on the back for moving out of Malibu and closer to the office. She had grown to despise the long commute every day, which made for some really long days.

Dressed in a white terrycloth robe, Clara rubbed the water out of her hair as she padded down the hall toward the kitchen. She was starving and had a hankering for a banana-nut muffin. A bite of muffin in her mouth, she grabbed a bottled water from the fridge and prepared to go sit in the living room when a knock on her door startled her, making her nearly drop her water.

Cautiously, she walked over to the front door, wondering who in the world would be knocking at her door at five-thirty in the morning. Relief filled her when, through the fisheye, she saw Mike standing in the hall. She quickly unlocked the door and opened it, concern taking the place of fear.

"Hey. What are you doing here so early?" she asked, ushering him inside so as not to awaken any of her neighbors.

"Hi. I'm sorry. Did I wake you?" he asked, then noting the muffin and water she held. "I guess not."

"No. I actually just got home not too long ago. Sit down. Want me to make you some coffee or something? Decaf, but..."

"Yeah. Sounds good, actually." Mike followed her into the kitchen where she set about making him coffee. She rarely made the stuff, but kept a one-cup maker and a can of decaf around just in case the mood struck. He hopped up onto the counter, reaching into the cabinet beside him to grab a mug. "How was your New Year's?" he asked, trying to keep the hurt from his voice.

"I'm an idiot, that's how it was," Clara said, leaning against the opposite counter where Mike sat, picking chunks off her muffin and popping them into her mouth. "I never should have gone with her, Mike." She shook her head in disgust. "God, it was awful."

"No sympathy from here, sweets," he said, playing with the handle on his mug.

"I know, I know. I should have gone to William's with you and Jeff." She let out a long breath. "It was stupid. Mike, she was loaded when I picked her up. Why the hell did I not just turn right then and there and leave?"

"Because you're a fool," Mike said with a tired sigh.

Clara stopped, realizing she had asked a question that was never answered. "Mike, why are you here so early?"

Mike didn't answer for a long moment, his expression troubled. "I'm actually glad you didn't go with us last night," he finally said, voice quiet. "Very glad, in fact."

"Why?" Clara grabbed the creamer and sugar container she kept around specifically for her friend.

"Because you would have said I told you so, and I didn't much want to hear that last night."

Clara took the mug from him, pouring him a cup of coffee before handing it back to him, as well as the creamer and sugar. "How do you mean?"

"I mean about Jeff. He's an asshole, and I've known it all along. I just didn't want to face that, yet again, I'd made a grave mistake."

"Oh, Mike," Clara said, suddenly feeling her exhaustion creeping back in. "What happened?"

"I lost track of him for a while at the party; Larry kept me company. Well, finally I went to find him and saw him with Deaton Wagner's dick up his ass." The words were said with such calm, so matter-of-factly.

"Oh no," Clara said, covering her mouth with her hand to stop herself from saying those very words: I told you so.

"Oh yes. And it gets even better from there." Mike hopped down from his seat on the counter and readied his coffee. "It seems my dear Jeff has sucked off just about every man at that party over the past year. The funny thing is, he was sucking off *my* dick during the past year, too. Well, when he was 'in the mood' that is."

"Mike, I'm so sorry—" she put a hand to his shoulder but he shrugged her away.

"No. No, you were right all along, and I'm man

enough to admit that. I was a fool, Clara, and the worst part was I knew it. But," he said with a big smile, "that's okay. It's truly okay. I spent the entire night fighting with the son-of-a-bitch and I'm exhausted, but I've come to a decision."

"What is that?"

"That Jeff Stanley can kiss my ass. I don't need him to make me happy. I don't need anyone to make me happy. All my life I've been thinking that it would take Prince Charming on a white horse to gallop in wearing leather chaps and only that would make me happy." He shook his head. "No more. No man can bring me that kind of happiness."

Clara grinned from ear to ear, glad to hear it. Mike had always put his happiness in other's hands and had constantly been hurt because of it. It was about time he realized that true happiness had to come from within. Others simply were accessories in life. She hugged him tight, wanting to express to him just how proud of him she truly was.

Mike clung to his friend, one of the only people in his life who had truly accepted him for all of him. He ran his hand over her back, placing a kiss at her temple.

"What do you say to some breakfast and shopping this morning?" he asked, pulling slightly away.

"Oh, I'm sorry Mike, I can't. I have some readings, but," she said at his look of disappointment, "I'll be done by eleven. I'll tell you what. You look absolutely exhausted, so why don't you crash in my bed and get some good sleep, okay? It'll be quiet and safe. Take yourself a nice, long hot bath and be ready by eleven-fifteen at the latest. Then, we'll go grab something to eat and shop our hearts out. Okay?"

Mike nodded, taking a slight step back from her to grab his coffee. "Okay. All that sounds wonderful."

"Awesome! It'll be fun." Clara gave him her best smile. "But, in the meantime, I need to get ready for my run, then I'm heading into the office, okay?"

Chapter Thirty-six

Clara waited for her client to quit with the explanations, wanting nothing more than to throttle the woman. She'd been told explicitly to keep her comments and/or stories to herself, but that didn't seem to matter. Glancing at the clock on the wall above her client's head, Clara was irritated to find that the woman had been yapping on and on for nearly twenty-two minutes. Finally, the woman slowed down to take a breath. Clara took her opening.

"Okay, so what I'm hearing in my head is: ask about Saturday spaghetti dinners — "

"Oh my goodness, yes! We had the most wonderful dinners! You should have seen..."

Another twenty-minute story began, Clara's mind started to drift. Suddenly she saw a clear picture of Nancy August sitting in that dark room, hair hanging in her face, body limp and defeated.

The woman was startled from her rambling when Clara gasped, her eyes opening wide in shock and fear.

"What is it?" the client asked, sitting forward on the couch hoping for some good gossip from her mother.

"I'm so sorry, Mary, but I need to reschedule our appointment," Clara said, her hands trembling as she managed to get to her feet. "I've just remembered something very important I need to do."

"What? Wait a minute, I paid for a full hour, and I want my hour today!" Mary demanded, her diamond-covered fingers glinting in the candlelight as she waved them at Clara.

"I'll give you two hours next week, I promise. I have to go." Clara grabbed her keys and hurried out the door.

It took three tries to get the key into the lock on her car door. Finally successful, she climbed in and the car roared to life. Followed by a chorus of angry horns, she plowed into the busy late morning traffic. Grabbing her cell phone out of her bag, she tried to dial with one hand and drive with the other. The call finally went through, but went straight to voice mail.

"Shit!" She threw the phone to the passenger seat and sped off toward home.

❧❧❧❧

Mike's car was still parked out front, the hood cool. She jogged up the path past it to the front door of the building and pushed inside. She ran up the stairs until she reached her door, panting and out of breath. She tried the knob and found it locked, so she inserted her key and pushed the door open.

"Mike?" she called out, tossing her keys to the coffee table and heading farther into the apartment. She stopped in front of the closed bathroom door: music was playing. Clara kept a small CD stereo in the bathroom, which she figured Mike must have decided to use.

Blowing out a relieved breath, Clara headed into her bedroom and changed her shirt. She'd gotten herself so freaked out about Mike she'd saturated her T-shirt with perspiration.

"Disgusting," she muttered with wrinkled nose, tossing the shirt to the laundry basket.

Feeling better, she made her way to the kitchen, grabbing a bottled water from the fridge and turning on the TV. Mike was notorious for his long soaks, so she knew she was in for the long wait. Part of her felt guilty, like maybe she should get hold of Mary Walker and continue their session over the phone. She thought back to the annoying older woman with all her diamonds and pearls and never-ending stories, and thought better of it.

"Hey, Mike, I'm going to head out for a minute. I'll grab some of that fudge you like," she called out, grabbing her keys again. "Be back in a few. Be ready, I'm hungry!"

Without waiting for a reply, Clara bounced out of the apartment, her relief turning to a state of near giddiness. She walked down to the market around the corner, which had some of the most wonderful organic fudge she'd ever eaten. She loaded up the basket she carried with all kinds of munchies, as she had the feeling there would be a lot of discussions throughout the day with Mike.

He would be starting his life over again, essentially. He and Jeff had lived together for more than a year, and their lives and finances had become entangled. That would not bode well for Mike's many businesses. But, Clara reasoned, he was incredibly intelligent when it came to money, so she knew he likely had something in place already. At least she hoped he did.

"Honey, I'm home!" she called, setting the paper sack down on the kitchen counter. She hummed along with the music that was blasting from the bathroom. "You'd think he would've gotten over Bon Jovi back in 1987," she muttered, putting the groceries away.

She munched on a carrot stick, trying to find something that would take the edge off her hunger as she waited. A glance at the stove clock told her she'd been waiting for forty minutes.

"Okay, this is ridiculous," she muttered, leaving the half-eaten carrot on the counter and heading down the hall to the bathroom. "Shot Through the Heart" had just begun to play. She knocked on the door. "Mike? Come on, man. I'm about to start eating the couch. Are you almost done?" Nothing. "Mike?"

Fear began to seize Clara's gut once more, her intuition telling her that something was terribly wrong. She tried the door handle only to find it locked. She pounded on the door.

"Mike! Michael! Don't you dare do this to me!" She pounded again, rattling the knob with so much force she felt it coming loose. "Michael!" She pounded against the door with her shoulder but was getting nowhere.

Trying to decide what to do, Clara took a step back and using her foot and all the force she could muster, she kicked the door. The door splintered enough for her to reach inside and unlock the knob. She sliced her hand open on a jagged piece of wood but didn't care. All that mattered was getting to her friend.

The walls in the bathroom nearly vibrated with the loud music, which Clara immediately turned off. The room was cool, the once-hot water long gone cold. She cried out when she looked at the tub.

"No! Mike, no!"

She fell to her knees beside it, taking her friend's

pale face between her hands. His eyes were unfocused, lids at half-mast. His lips were slightly opened, a tiny smile curling up the corners, lips blue. The water that reached his mid-chest was an eerie pinkish red color. His left hand was in the water, palm up and resting on his thigh. The wicked cut could be seen through the bloody water. His other arm rested along the side of the tub, a blood trail leading from it down to the floor.

Clara didn't know what to do first. See if he had a pulse? Cry? Scream? Call for help? Nothing? She didn't have to try for a pulse, as she knew in her heart that he was already gone, but she tried anyway. Two fingers to his throat, she felt across the cold, clammy skin, desperately hoping she was wrong. Nothing.

"God damn you, Mike," she whispered, a sob tearing from her throat. The tears fell in to mix with the ruby water. "Damn you!" she screamed, shaking his lifeless body like a rag doll, head lolling to the side. Her sobs were uncontrollable now as she hugged his head to her chest, blood smearing the clean T-shirt she'd put on an hour before. "Oh, Mike."

❧ ❧ ❧ ❧

Clara sat numbly as the paramedics placed Mike's body on a gurney, covered him with a sheet and tied him down. She sat on the couch, watching with red, swollen eyes as he was removed from her apartment. A police officer was asking her questions, a small notepad in his hand.

"Ma'am, I know this is hard, but I really need you to answer these questions," he was saying, though Clara could barely hear him, his voice seeming to come from a far distance. She stared at him, not even registering the color of his hair or eyes. He sighed, getting to his feet from where he'd been squatting next to the couch. "She's in shock," he explained to another officer.

Clara wasn't sure where she was. All she knew was she couldn't get the vision of her best friend out of her mind. She kept seeing his eyes, dead and glazed over. She thought of her grandmother and the previous night when all Rebecca would say was, "Row." She'd led Clara to Nancy August, where she'd saved her from her own devastation. That thought made her come to life, especially when she saw Rebecca standing over in the corner of the room.

"Why didn't you warn me?" Clara yelled, jumping to her feet and scaring the hell out of the personnel in the room. "Why, Grandma?!" she demanded, walking over to where Rebecca patiently stood.

Officers looked at her, seeing absolutely nobody in the corner of the room where Clara was screaming. They exchanged glances, wondering if the woman had lost her mind.

Clara didn't care, nor did she see them. "Why? Why did you let this happen! You knew, didn't you? You fucking knew!"

Rebecca remained silent, but tried to send as much love and comfort to Clara as she could.

"Nothing to say? Fine. Well fuck you, Grandma. Fuck you."

Chapter Thirty-seven

Here, drink this." Isabelle placed a snifter of warmed brandy in front of Clara, who had been sitting on the uppermost portion of their deck for hours. She hadn't spoken a word since breaking the news the previous afternoon. Hell, she'd barely breathed, from what Isabelle could tell.

Clara heard the older woman's voice, but had a hard time responding to it. She could smell the strong odor of even stronger alcohol. She glanced at the dark liquid, turning her gaze back to the sea.

"Honey, you're not going to do yourself any good if you let yourself fade away." She studied Clara's profile, unsure what to do. Clara hadn't wanted to go back to her apartment, so she'd been given a room in the main house so Isabelle could watch over her. She was very worried about the young woman. "Clara," she began again, placing a warm hand on Clara's arm. "Please talk to me. Tell me what happened." All they'd been told was that Mike had died in her apartment yesterday morning.

Clara cleared her throat, which had become raw and tight from lots of tears and no talking. She reached out absently until she felt the warm snifter, taking a small sip. She nearly choked on the strong taste, but decided that maybe a little numbness was what she needed. Finally she turned to face Isabelle.

"He slit his wrists in my bathtub while I was

working."

Isabelle gasped softly, covering her mouth with a heavily ringed hand. "I was afraid it had been something like that. I know Mike was rather unsteady."

"Says who?" Clara demanded, anger rising as she wanted to protect the memory of her friend.

"Says everyone, sweetheart. Between his drinking and valium use..." her voice trailed off.

Clara said nothing. She knew Isabelle was right, but didn't want to go there. "I honestly didn't think he'd hurt himself when I left that morning," she said, her voice barely a whisper. "I swear."

Isabelle listened, her own pain dulled slightly by the two snifters of brandy she'd had before bringing Clara her own. Even still, she could see the terrible pain in those strange-colored eyes.

"I raced home at one point because I had a bad feeling," Clara continued, taking another sip, feeling her emotions begin to rise. "I thought everything was okay." Her face fell as fresh tears stung her eyes during their escape. They plopped on the metal table with hollow notes. "He might have still been alive then," she cried, her words nearly unintelligible.

Unsure what else to do, Isabelle left her seat and went to Clara, pulling her into as much of a maternal embrace as she could muster. Though grateful for the comfort, Clara wished it were coming from someone else. She had no idea who, but she had a craving for affection and comfort from someone who knew her as well as she knew herself. Her soul cried out for it. If only she knew where to find it.

❧❧❧❧❧

The funeral was on Tuesday, January 5th. Clara would never forget that because it landed on Jason's birthday. He would have been twenty-five that day. Clara looked up into the sky, the minister's words turning into mumbling in her mind. She didn't care what he had to say. His words had no bearing on her life or Mike's. She doubted he even *knew* Mike.

A testament to Michael James and his business practices was the amount of people who had shown up, very few in tears, but all in expensive suits. She looked around at them, wondering if any of them had any clue just what a wonderful human being he'd been. Did they know anything about him, outside of the newest artist he had been sponsoring? Did they know about his warm heart? Or his desperate need for acceptance and love? Likely not, she figured. Very few knew the Mike that she did, and it had cost him his life.

Her attention was caught by something further off in the cemetery. She wasn't entirely surprised to see Rebecca standing next to a large tree, her eyes focused on Clara. The irony wasn't lost on Clara, as her grandmother had shown up at Jason's funeral too. Two men in her life whom she could have helped. Two young lives that were taken in the blink of an eye, both of which she could have prevented.

She turned away from Rebecca, not wanting to see her or talk to her. She shut her mind down: nobody's home.

≈≈≈≈≈

A huge crowd had gathered at Mike's downtown gallery, the art cleared out to make room for the celebration that had been planned. Clara didn't want to go, truth be told. What she wanted to do was pack up and head home. She had never felt so alone in all her life. She knew many of the people who were talking and eating, most of them Mike's business associates and customers whom she'd met at one function or another. Others were Raymond's friends and colleagues. None were friends of Clara's.

She nursed a glass of wine, foregoing food, as she hadn't had an appetite in the four days since it had all happened. She wandered, looking at the pictures that still adorned the walls, only the more massive pieces having been removed. Half the time she didn't know what she was looking at, her mind wandering.

"How are you holding up?" Raymond asked, stepping up beside her. His tie was loosened, top button unbuttoned on his shirt. She was surprised to see the casual dress.

Shrugging, Clara sighed. "Okay, I guess. I'm just trying to wrap my mind around all this, I guess."

Raymond nodded in understanding. He set his empty wineglass on a passing waiter's tray. "I understand that very much. I liked Mike, and I am sorry for your loss, Clara. I know you two were close."

"Yes, we were." Making a decision, she turned to her boss. "Ray, I'd like to take some time off."

"Oh? How much? Are you going somewhere?"

"I'm not sure how much, to be honest. I want to head back home for a little while. I need to get away for a bit, you know?"

Ray's brows drew. "You're not planning to come back, are you?"

Clara blinked at him, surprised. She hadn't even given that thought very serious interest, but now that he had... "I don't know. I mean, I know we all lost him, and I'm not trying to be melodramatic about all this, but I really need to get away and think about a few things."

"Here's the problem with that, Clara," he said, turning to fully face her, all business. "If you decide to go back to that tiny town you came from, you might as well stay there."

Clara stared at him, stunned.

He continued, "This is a business, and I can't very well decide to just go hopping off somewhere to think. I have to be there to run my business. You're it, Clara. It's not like I can call in someone to take your place while you decide what you're going to do. Do you understand what I'm saying?"

Anger began to fill her as she stared into dark, uncaring eyes. "I understand perfectly. Then I guess consider this my two weeks notice." She set her wineglass on a low table and walked out of the gallery.

∿∿∿∿∿

Clara felt like an indulgent teenager as she cruised along the interstate, sipping her first mocha breve with extra whipped cream in more than two years. Fuck the "energy highway." She was going to do her own thing now, and the spirit world be damned. She sipped, moaning at the strong taste of espresso and mocha, licking the whipped cream off her upper lip. She turned her car stereo up louder, enjoying herself and the freedom she felt as she headed toward her hometown, all that she owned loaded into her car. What wouldn't fit had been left. Just like old times.

The farther away from California she got, the more snow lined the landscape. Though she had enjoyed her time in the California sun, she had missed truly inclement weather: cold nights and fires in the fireplace. Even so, she knew she wasn't going to enjoy scraping her windows in the morning, once she stopped for the night at a hotel in New Mexico, which she would be reaching within two hours.

It had been a wonderful day's drive, though it hadn't started out great. Clara had left the gallery during Mike's funeral reception and forced herself to go back to the apartment. She'd packed up her car, left a note with keys under the landlord's office door, and left town. She'd driven to a small town in Arizona where she'd gotten herself a room and had hidden out to think. Had she done the right thing? Was it time to leave California and the life she'd created there? Would she find that Raymond was taking some sort of action against her? Wouldn't surprise her if he did.

She had sat in that hotel room with its double bed, scarred dresser, and black-and-white TV, and had stared at the ceiling as she lay on the bed. She'd contemplated calling her parents, but then realized she'd left the cell phone Raymond had given her at the gallery. She didn't want to pay crazy charges in the room to make a call so had tried to sort it all out on her own.

She'd thought of her grandmother, her abilities, and Mike. In the end she'd come to the realization that what was the good of being able to communicate with the spirit world and help those in it if she couldn't even help save those in her own world? Every time she saw Mike's face she saw Jason's. She knew nothing in life was arbitrary or coincidence, but still. Why had two men who had been her closest friends died in such horrible ways? Both times she knew, but was still unable to stop it?

Somewhere inside she heard "because you weren't meant to," but she couldn't believe that. *Wouldn't* believe that. In her mind there was no reason for that to happen. No excuse. She was done. Going home was the best thing she could do for herself. She planned to leave every part of her life back in California where it belonged.

❧❧❧❧

Night had already fallen when Clara pulled into the parking lot of a Motel 6. She had stopped during the day and bought a new cell phone and plan. She unloaded any valuables from the car and then carried in the dinner she'd picked up before checking into the motel. It was almost cold by now, but she didn't care; she was famished.

After she got settled and had eaten, she pulled her new phone out of the box and began to play with all the new features. She loved fun gadgets. Satisfied with her new ringtone, she dialed her parents' house. After three rings, the line was picked up by her mother.

"Hey, sweetie," Stephanie said, glad to hear her daughter's voice. "Where are you? This is a Denver number."

"I'm in New Mexico, but I'm coming home."

Stephanie felt her heart fill with gratitude, but kept it low-key. She closed the newspaper she'd been reading and tossed it aside. "I'm so glad to hear that, Clara. You know you have a place to come."

"Thanks, Mom. I appreciate that."

"Are you okay? How did the Van Wurts take your leaving?"

Clara blew out a breath, focusing on a water stain in the ceiling by the corner. "Not thrilled, but Raymond didn't exactly give me a choice. I told him I was coming home for a while to try and deal with what happened with Mike, and he all but said, 'you leave, you stay gone'."

"Oh, honey. I'm sorry." Stephanie leaned back into Max who remained quiet, trying to figure out what was being said from his wife's responses. "I think it's wonderful and a smart move for you to come home."

"Do you?" Clara asked, for some reason filled with doubt, despite knowing it was the right choice.

"Yes. Very much so."

"Okay. I'll be home tomorrow sometime. Probably afternoon, but it depends on how early I get out of here."

"Okay, sweetie. We'll be waiting for you. Still have your old room too."

"Good thing I brought my bed back, huh?" Clara smiled, feeling better just hearing her mother's voice. "Is Dad there?"

"He sure is. Want to talk to him?"

Max took the phone from his wife, glad to speak to his youngest. "Hey, sweet pea. Coming back home, huh?"

"Yep. I've had enough."

"I'm glad. And, Clara? I'm so sorry we couldn't make it to your friend's funeral. There was just no way with work."

"I know, Dad. Thank you. I'll see you tomorrow."

Clara slapped her cell phone shut and tossed it onto the comforter beside her. She felt an unusual loneliness embrace her. Always one to spend time alone, and rarely needing the presence of another, she felt uneasy with the feeling. Like when Mike died, she felt a craving for something she just couldn't put her finger on. A craving for someone to hold her and let her know it would all be okay. She needed to be comforted in a way she'd never been before, but knew there was no one in her life who could do that. Once upon a time her grandmother could offer that kind of comfort, but not anymore. Besides, what she wanted was comforting of the physical body, not her soul.

Chapter Thirty-eight

Clara stepped out of her car, her breath coming in white puffs as the chilled, early spring air whirled around her. Soon the snows would be disappearing, bringing green grass and blooming flowers with it. For the time being, it was a bitterly cold March afternoon.

She walked between the rows of knee-high stones, her boots crunching on the snow-packed grass. It was a gray day, the sky heavy and pregnant, threatening more snow. She inhaled the clean, cold air, allowing it to fill her lungs and remember the reason she was there.

Clara hadn't been to Jason's grave since the day he was buried, ten years before. She wasn't sure what had brought her there, but felt compelled to see him. She knew that cemeteries were essentially for the living, as the dead were long gone, but still. She needed to talk to him.

Someone had recently visited Jason's grave, fresh flowers adding color to the otherwise dreary landscape. She cleared a small patch of grass to sit on then sat down cross-legged.

"Hi, Jay," she began, feeling stupid talking to a stone. Looking at the date of his death brought the dream from that night back to her mind all over again. She remembered seeing the accident, watching as Jason catapulted out of the car. She could recall the fear and panic like it had all just happened yesterday. "Been a long time."

Clara sighed, feeling a weight on her shoulders trying to push her down. She didn't even bother looking around, as she didn't want to see anything. Or anyone. She had been back in her hometown for three months, living the ordinary life of a woman in her mid-twenties who worked at the bakery her mother managed. She had turned a blind eye to anything remotely out of the ordinary. She wanted to be like everyone else.

"I'm not sure why I'm here, Jay, but I am. I know you know what's been going on with me. My life in L.A. What a crazy place that is." She shook her head with a small chuckle. "Crazy indeed. Complete opposite of here. You know, Jay, I wanted to get out of here so badly that it never *ever* occurred to me that I'd want to come back." She stopped, looking at the stone, seeing Jason's young face in it. "You think I ran, don't you?" Only the gently falling snow — which had been promised in the weather report — answered her question. Everything was so calm, so still. Not even any animals made a sound. "I don't want to think that about myself, though. I do think it was time to go. Most the time I think that, anyway."

She raised her face to the sky, allowing a few flakes to land on her tongue. "I do like working at the bakery, though. It's different. Never done anything like that before." She shrugged. "It's nice. I think I've gained ten pounds since working there, which sucks." Her smile was met with the distant barking of a dog.

"I'm thinking of buying a house. I was smart in L.A. and managed to save a lot of money. Never done that before. I've got more than enough for a down payment on something small. I'm not real keen on staying with my parents anymore." She grimaced at the thought. "Definitely time to move on from there. Oh, Jason," she blew out, reaching out to touch the cold granite of his headstone. "I miss you. After all these years, I still miss you."

With a heavy sigh, she pushed to her feet, kissing two fingers and laying them on Jason's name. "Take care my friend. I don't think I'll be seeing you over there anymore. I hope you can understand and forgive me. It's time I moved on. Lived a normal life for the first time in my life. I love you."

Clara shoved her hands into the pockets of her coat, trying to shrug off the cold. She was about to pass through the wrought iron gate that surrounded the cemetery when something caught her eye. Looking down she saw a white feather. Looking up into the sky, she saw no birds, and there were no trees nearby. A soft smile tucked up the corners of her mouth as she picked it up, tucking it carefully into her wallet.

≈≈≈≈≈

"Well, what do you think?" Stephanie asked, opening and closing the cabinet doors, both above and below the kitchen counters. The small house had two medium-sized bedrooms and a tiny third that would make a great home office, Clara thought. The living room was a nice size: not huge, but not small. The yard was small, which was a plus as Clara wasn't huge on yard work.

"I like it," Clara said, standing in the empty space and turning in a small circle to look everything over one more time. They'd already spent thirty minutes there. She looked at her mother. "What about you?"

"I think it's great," Stephanie said, nodding in approval as she checked out the fridge. "They left the fridge, which is a plus. That way you'll only have to buy a stove and washer and dryer."

Clara nodded in agreement. "And a couch. And a bed. And a—"

"I got it," Stephanie laughed, walking over to her daughter. The fact that Clara was looking to buy a house made her happier than she'd been in a long time. To her that meant her youngest was intending to finally stay put. She put an arm around Clara's shoulders. "Verdict?"

Clara let out a long breath, nervous but very excited. "I'm going to take it."

❧ ❧ ❧ ❧

2001

A hand snaked out from under a layer of blankets — SMACK! The beeping finally stopped, but it was replaced by a groan.

"Too fucking early to go make the doughnuts," Clara muttered. She slipped her hand back underneath the covers, pretending she hadn't heard or turned off her alarm. BUZZZZZZZZZZZZZZZZZZZZZZ! "Damn it!" She exploded out from underneath the heavy bedding, bare feet slapping against the wood floor as she hurried to her dresser, stubbing her toe on a bed leg along the way, and shut off her second alarm. She'd been working at the bakery for more than a year and still was unable to wake up at three forty-five in the morning with just one alarm.

Clara rubbed at her eyes as she padded her way

to the bathroom to do her morning business and get ready for work. She was now the chief baker, so had to be there at what she called ass crack a.m.

Within moments the sound of running water filled the small house, along with a loud, low throaty groan of approval. Clara stood under the spray, letting the warmth fill her in the cold, early autumn morning.

❧ ❧ ❧ ❧

The drive to the bakery was an uneventful one. She let herself in, flicking on the lights as she made her way through the building until she was in the back room. The smells of sugar and flour always hung in the air, no matter how well the place was cleaned. The bakery had been in that same building for more than sixty years. It wasn't likely the smell would *ever* go away.

When Clara had first started working at the bakery, she'd tried and sampled everything the store had to offer. That was mainly when she'd gained those extra ten pounds. Now, she'd grown fairly immune to the temptations of pastries and pies. Over the past six months she'd been feeling a need to cleanse. She wasn't sure why, and was actually fighting it. The thought of going back to the strict diet she was on in California brought back too many memories, and made her feel that she would once again be slave to the whims of the spirit world. She didn't want to go back there.

Clara turned on the stereo, music filling the kitchen area as she began to prepare the goods for the day. Soon she was stripped down to a tank top and jeans from her bundled clothing to block out the cold.

It got downright hot once those ovens were fired up.

Raw doughnut dough laid out, another batch in the oven, Clara peeled off her latex gloves and grabbed the paint chips out of her backpack, sitting on a stool as she sorted through them. She had decided to do an overhaul to her house: new paint, new rugs and decorative accessories. She'd been in the house for more than a year but had yet to really make it her own. Sure, she had bought furniture and had hung pictures on the walls, but somehow it didn't feel much like a home to her. Part of her felt she'd kept somewhat of an emotional distance from the place because her heart wasn't totally set on the path she'd set herself on. Part of her still wasn't. At least revamping the house would give her something to do.

Since coming back into town, Clara had kept mostly to herself. She saw her parents and sister regularly, of course. The friends she'd had in school had either moved on from their hometown, or she had lost touch and wasn't entirely keen on reconnecting. Even so, she felt a restlessness setting in that she wasn't entirely sure what to do with. How to make it go away. What to think about it. What did she want? The answer to that question eluded her to the point of frustration.

❧❧❧❧

Soon the snow began to clear completely, fresh flowers blooming in the manicured garden of Stephanie Greenwold. Birds had come back, their cheerful songs filling the air, and their little gifts littering car windows and hoods. Time marched on, and so did Clara's many home repairs.

It was mid-May when Kerri caught Clara up on

a ladder, studiously painting the outside of her house, a brush in hand as she worked on the trim.

"Wow. I must say, you are quite ambitious," she said, walking across the thick, lush lawn toward her sister.

Clara glanced down to see Kerri many feet below her. "Well, somebody's gotta do it. Don't have anyone to give a honey-do list to." Kerri matched her grin. "What's up?" She stuck the brush into the paint tray that was attached to the ladder, and then carefully climbed down, rubbing her hands on the thighs of her sweat shorts.

"I came by to see the new place."

"New place?" Clara asked, twisting the cap off her bottle of water.

"Yeah. Mom says you've done a lot of remodeling. Show me."

The sisters headed inside the small house, which Clara had been working on nearly nonstop for the past two months. The entire inside had been painted, new light fixtures installed and thick floor rugs gave the hardwood personality.

"Very nice, I must say," Kerri said, peeking her head into the larger of the two spare bedrooms. "I may have to hire you for our place." She grinned at her sister.

"There is no way in hell I'm climbing a ladder tall enough to reach the trim on that monstrosity," Clara declared, leading the way into the kitchen where she poured her sister a glass of decaf iced tea.

"Thanks." Kerri added two bags of sweetener to it before sipping. "I recall you actually *liked* that monstrosity when you lived there."

"Yeah, well I was a teenager and didn't know

better. I didn't have to clean it all."

Kerri laughed, joining Clara at the kitchen table. They sat across from each other, Kerri playing with her wedding ring as she tried to decide the best way to approach the two reasons she'd actually come. She decided on the good news first, news that she knew Clara would be excited about. She wasn't so sure on the second bit.

"Zane and I have actually decided on a new purpose for your old apartment," she began, eyeing her sister.

"Oh yeah?" Clara asked. "What's that? A torture chamber? Maybe a BDSM room? You could call it Den of Sin."

Kerri grinned. "Maybe someday, but for now we're turning it into a playroom. Well, it will be baby storage for a little while until—"

Catching on, Clara was out of her chair in three point five, grabbing her sister in a furious hug. "Oh my god! When?!"

"I'm due in November."

"That's wonderful news!" She moved back to her own chair, feeling exhilarated. "I wondered if you guys were ever going to reproduce."

Kerri rolled her eyes at her sister's choice of words. "Yes, Clara, the *breeders* will reproduce."

Clara snickered, finishing her water and tossing the bottle in the garbage. "I'm very happy for the two of you. I'm sure mom was beside herself when you told her."

"Well, actually I haven't, yet. I wanted to wait until their barbeque this weekend."

For some reason a thrill traveled through Clara at knowing that she was the first to know. "Then I can't wait to see her and Dad's faces. I'm glad I'll be there to see it."

"Clara," Kerri began, her voice losing the excitement of baby news. "I need to ask you for a favor."

"Sounds serious. Go ahead." Clara readied herself, unsure what her sister would ask of her. She could count on one hand the times Kerri had asked anything of her, and was curious, though for some reason had a sense she wasn't going to like it.

"Before I ask, I want you to know that I understand how you feel about things. I understand why you've walked away from your gifts. I have a friend—"

"No," Clara said, scooting back from the table to grab an apple from the basket on the recently installed butcher block. She kept her back to her sister, not wanting to see her face.

Kerri had expected that kind of reaction so had come prepared to plead her case. She walked over to Clara, leaning against an adjacent counter as Clara cut the apple into slices.

"Do you want one?" Clara asked, clearly trying to change the subject before it had even begun.

"No. Clara, what happened to you in California was awful. I know Michael meant a lot to you, and I know his death — and how it happened — has hit you hard. I see a change in you. It's almost like before you were filled with this wonderful light, and since you've come back home, it's gone. Or at least very dim."

"Yes, Kerri, it is. I'm done with all that, and I ask that you respect me enough to drop it."

Kerri sighed, knowing there was nothing more she could say. Clara was right: she had to respect her enough to take to heart what she said. She nodded, giving her sister a small hug. "Okay. I'm sorry. I'll tell her you can't."

"Thank you."

Chapter Thirty-nine

The bakery was busy, everyone coming in to grab bags and boxfuls of goodies for the upcoming weekend. Typically Clara was out of there by eleven, or noon at the latest, but they had a call-off, and her mother had begged her to stay and help out. It was nearly five o'clock, and she was about to fall over dead from a fourteen-hour shift, with a two-hour lunch to take a power nap.

She had just boxed up a birthday cake, ordered a week ago, and was ringing up the sale when the bells above the door jingled the entrance of yet another customer. Internally she sighed. *People! Go home and bake for yourself!* She glanced up, a forced smile of welcome in place, becoming *frozen* in place when she saw Abby Jensen step up to the counter.

"Thanks, Clara," the birthday cake customer said, gathering the cake and her purse and moving out of Abby's way.

"Welcome," Clara said, trying not to stare. She hadn't seen Abby since her parents' wedding years before, and certainly hadn't seen her close up since Abby and Kerri were still in high school.

"Hi, Clara. How are you? I heard you were back in town," Abby said, her voice filled with the friendly smile that was on her face. It was a genuine smile that reached her bright green eyes.

"I'm doing well. You heard that, huh?" Clara

smiled, feeling like she could float off the ground.

"Yep. Kerri has filled me in over the years on where you'd run off to, or what you were doing."

"I see," Clara said, trying her best to not break anything by the sizeable grin that threatened to split her face. "What can I help you with?"

"Well, actually, I was hoping to be able to talk to you for a few minutes."

"Oh. Um," Clara glanced behind her to see who was available to take over at the register. Luckily the place was beginning to clear, the Friday afternoon rush slowing. "Jill, can you take over for a few?" she called to the teenager who was helping Stephanie load doughnuts into the day-old rack that would be rolled into the main lobby of the bakery.

"Sure." The perky teen took over, allowing Clara to slip away.

"Want to step outside?" Clara asked, looking at the small space available in the store, as a few customers still waited for assistance.

"Sure."

The air outside smelled fresh and clean, the trees swaying in the slight breeze. Clara led them to the corner where a bench was placed in front of a jewelry store. They sat down, Clara nervous, though trying her best not to show it. She got a good look at Abby as the blonde got settled. Abby had cut her hair, now in a cute, somewhat sporty style. She was wearing jeans and a cap-sleeved tee that showed off toned arms and a very cute figure.

"Well, first of all, welcome back," Abby began, placing her sunglasses over her eyes to block out the late afternoon sun.

"Thank you. I guess it's nice to be back, though

it was nice to be away too."

"Yes, it is. My ex-husband and I moved to Ohio for a few years to be closer to his family, which was nice. But I have to say, it was nice to come back too."

Clara's mind raced back to the wedding and the man with dark hair who had been with Abby. She wondered if that was her ex.

"The second reason I came today is I want to talk to you. I need your help, Clara, and I hear Kerri wasn't very successful in talking to you about it."

Clara stared at her, stunned. Had Kerri been asking on Abby's behalf that day, two weeks ago in her kitchen? "That was about you?" she blurted.

Abby nodded. "I don't know what happened to you — Kerri never told me — but I do understand that you no longer dabble in the supernatural stuff anymore. If you won't help me, then is there maybe someone you know who can? Or can I plead my case with you myself, directly?"

Clara could almost hear her grandmother laughing at the position she'd been put in. Before her sat the woman she'd been obsessed with since she was fourteen years old, asking for her help. She was asking her to reclaim a life that she no longer wanted, a gift that had been wasted on the wrong person. Clara felt she was no good for anyone.

"Let me think about it, okay?" she asked, truly unsure what to do.

"Okay. I can take that. But," Abby said, pleading in her voice, "whether you decide to help me or refer someone to me, I need help pretty soon. Here." She reached into her purse and brought out a ready-printed piece of paper, an address and phone number on it. "I own this place, and this is where the trouble is."

Clara looked at the address, unsure exactly where it was. "Okay." She tucked the paper away and stood up. "I need to get back. I'll contact you within a couple days, okay?"

"Fair enough," Abby said, also standing, a bright smile on her face. "Thank you so much, Clara. I've never forgotten that day you told me my grandmother would be okay after her surgery. That meant the world to me." With that, she turned and walked down the street to a bright blue SUV. She climbed in and drove away.

Clara walked back to the bakery, feeling a new kind of fatigue wash over her. Indecision weighed heavily on her shoulders.

❧ ❧ ❧ ❧

Clara found herself standing on the banks of a river she'd seen before. Across the lake was a beautiful, snow-capped mountain range, the reflection rippling in the gentle waves in the water. The golden sky above calm and peaceful. The pebbled beach spanned out to the right, curving around to fold the lake in a small pocket. To the left the beach disappeared into a thick wood that also lined the backside of the beach, opposite the water.

Looking down into the sand, Clara saw obvious footprints, which led toward the wooded area to her left. She followed, unsure of where she was going. She hadn't been to the other side for well over a year and felt a curious mixture of joy and anger. The trees were thick and beautiful, their full branches reaching toward the sky in graceful arcs.

Up ahead and to the left she saw what appeared to

be glass, light glinting off its smooth surface. She brushed a few low branches out of her way and was startled to find herself standing directly in front of a cabin. The structure was so well hidden that she almost missed it. The glass she'd seen was actually the front windows of the two-story cabin. A large front porch stretched the full length of the building, two rocking chairs straddling the front door.

Clara felt pulled to the cabin. She climbed the three stairs to the porch, running her hand along the smooth log rail. At the front door, she wasn't sure whether to knock, just help herself inside, or... It didn't matter as the door slowly swung open, its beveled glass panes reflecting Clara's face for a brief moment.

Directly inside was a small sitting area, a ruggedly built couch and chair inviting someone to sit and relax. The couch was along the wall to the right, the chair against a small portion of the staircase that ran behind it and up to a small landing before heading up the other direction to finally reach the second floor. To the left was the rest of the front — and what looked to be main — room. The wall was made entirely of stone, a massive fireplace burning brightly at the center of the wall.

The room was empty, so Clara turned her attention to the stairs. She slowly made her way up, heart pounding. Why was she so nervous? She knew who would be waiting for her, but somehow she felt anxious. Was it anger? Was it guilt?

The upstairs was one large space, windows lining the walls, almost giving the appearance of a glass room. Light streamed in, bathing everything in the golden hue of the outside world of the other side. A bed was tucked into one corner, dwarfed by the sheer size of the room. To the far right was a small nook where Rebecca sat in a chair, waiting.

"Welcome home, Clara," she said softly, studying her granddaughter.

Clara said nothing, instead sitting next to her grandmother She could still feel her heart pounding in her chest. She couldn't bring herself to look at Rebecca.

"You don't need to be afraid or nervous. You know I won't hurt you."

"I know," Clara said, sparing a glance at the beautiful brunette. She blew out a breath, finally meeting the dark, penetrating, yet understanding eyes. "Why am I here?"

"Because we need to talk. I've sent you messages for the past year, all of which you've ignored, and that's fine. I understand what you've gone through. I've listened to you curse me and your gifts; now I get to tell my side of the story, and you will sit and listen."

Clara felt almost as though she were paralyzed to do anything else. She nodded, feeling the stern strength coming from her Spirit Guide.

"Mike."

Clara took a deep breath at the mention of his name, trying to keep the images that haunted her still out of her head.

"You had no control over that. You could have never left your apartment that day, and it likely still would have happened. Mike was set on his own path, Clara. That is a path you were never meant to intervene with. He set his own obstacles for himself long before you knew him. He couldn't handle those and chose to exit early. That is his fate to deal with, not yours, and don't take it upon yourself.

"I know," Rebecca continued, "that your anger at me was actually anger for yourself that you didn't know

how to direct properly. You allowed your anger and grief to cloud your judgment. You made the right choice by going home, as that is where the rest of your path leads, Clara. But," she held up one finger to emphasize her point, "you have made the wrong choice in turning your back on who and what you are. You feel that loss, don't you?"

Clara didn't answer, instead, sitting quietly, hands tucked in her lap.

"Your restlessness. Going back to the diet I asked you to follow. Your soul is crying out for you to be true to your path, Clara. You have the perfect opportunity now."

Clara truly looked at her for the first time. "Abby?"

Rebecca nodded, a knowing smile on her lips. "Abby."

Chapter Forty

C lara glanced at the paper in her hand, making sure the address did, in fact, match that of the Stoney Brook, which she stood in front of. The pub was in one of the beautiful historical buildings downtown. Brick and masonry work gave the old building character.

She pushed through the glass and brass front door, which led into a small area where coats could be hung to allow the patrons free movement while they socialized inside. The bar, itself was a dimly lit room, old Tiffany lamps hung over the booths that lined the wall, the bulbs within a low wattage to keep the atmosphere intimate and low-key. The bar, which took up much of the center of the room with its horseshoe shape, had a highly polished mahogany finish with brass fittings and padded stools.

At the center of the horseshoe was a mirrored divider wall where row after row of bottled alcohol was kept on wooden racks. Low music was piped through the room. At the back of the long room was a staircase, leading to whatever was on the second level. From the distant sounds of clanking balls, Clara guessed there were pool tables up there.

A few patrons meandered around the classy place, some talking in booths, others sitting at the bar chatting with Abby, whose easy laughter could easily be heard. It made Clara smile. She walked over to the bar, taking a seat at the rounded hoop of the horseshoe. A redheaded man of maybe twenty-two walked over to her, a white towel flipped over his shoulder.

"How can I help you?" he asked.

"A water, please. I'm actually here to talk to Abby."

"Water it is." He quickly had her drink in front of her then sauntered over to his boss, tapping her on the shoulder to get her attention. He spoke quietly to her, pointing in Clara's direction. Abby immediately excused herself from the couple she'd been talking to and walked over to where Clara sat.

"Hey there!" she said, leaning against the bar.

"Hi. Okay, so I lied, and it took me three days to contact you."

Abby smiled, waving off her words. "It's okay. I *was* beginning to wonder, though."

"Yeah, sorry. So, you own this place?"

"I do," Abby said, obvious pride in her voice. She looked around, seeing it through the eyes of someone seeing it for the first time, as she guessed Clara was. "My ex-husband had the harebrained idea of buying this place two years ago, then got bored with it, while I fell in love with it. It's all I wanted out of the divorce decree."

"Good for you. It's really a nice place."

"Thanks. Want the tour?"

"Yes, please."

Clara slid off the stool, leaving her water on the bar as she followed Abby around, trying to pay attention to the history of the building and not stare at Abby's very shapely behind.

"This," Abby said, indicating the small office she'd led her to on the second floor, "is where the majority of things happen."

"What happens in here?" Clara asked, walking in and looking around. She noted the old wood desk, a new Dell computer on top of the scarred surface. The roof sloped down slightly, so Clara ducked as she made her way toward the solitary window. Looking out, she found herself looking down into an alley. She ran her fingers across the faces of the metal filing cabinets that lined the wall opposite the desk.

"Lots of sounds. I'll be closing up at night and will hear something thud in here. Maybe voices, like actual conversation between two people. I come in — after I *unlock* the door, might I add — and find nothing. I've come in here in the morning or afternoon when I do inventory, and the chair will be on the other side of the room, over by the window or file cabinets. Sometimes the computer will have magically turned itself on."

"Okay," Clara said, keeping any thoughts or impressions to herself. She still wasn't positive she was going to help. She still could refer Abby to someone else. Maybe Cassandra knew of someone local. "What else?"

Abby leaned against the wall, her hands pinned between her body and the wall. "I didn't talk about this downstairs because I didn't want to scare anyone — customers, Ryan, anything. A lot happens down there too, Clara. Glasses will fall and break. I smell cigar smoke a lot, which seems strange to me as I've never seen anyone smoke them here, but it's always possible that a customer has. Um," she glanced off toward the window as she thought of other things that had happened. "Oh! The jukebox up here will start up on its own sometimes. Scares the hell out of pool players." She grinned.

"I bet." Clara shoved her hands in the pockets of her jeans, looking everywhere but at Abby. The blonde still made her as nervous as she had eleven years ago. "What exactly are you wanting to happen here, Abby?" she asked quietly.

"I want it to stop. It's gotten worse in the past year or so, ever since we moved in a couple of the pool tables. I don't know why, and I'm not sure that I care. It's scaring my patrons. It's scaring my employees, and honestly, it's scaring the hell out of me." Pleading green eyes looked into Clara's. "Will you help me, Clara? Please? I don't know where else to go."

Clara looked into her eyes for a long moment, knowing full well she had to help her. She nodded, letting out a long breath. "Okay. I'll help you. I'm a little rusty, so no guarantees, but I'll help you."

"Thank you so much, Clara. You have no idea how much I appreciate it. I'll pay you, of course. How much?" Abby walked over to the desk and pulled out a drawer, plucking a checkbook out and tossing it to the top of the desk.

"No. I don't want you to pay me," Clara said, waving the idea away. "No money."

"Why?" Abby's brows drew together. "Isn't this what you do for a living?"

"Not anymore. I'm just doing it to help you. Put that away."

Abby shut the drawer but did not put the checkbook away. "All right. For now. So, how do we start?"

❧❧❧❧❧

Clara sat in a mess that had been taken out of

the two boxes she'd pulled out from her crawl space. She dug through the debris, looking for something she hadn't seen or touched since she'd left California. She rooted through papers, books and random odds and ends. Finally she spotted what she'd been looking for.

"Ha!" she exclaimed in victory, snatching the tiny velvet ring box, setting it next to the tiny leather bag she'd already found.

After cleaning up her mess and stacking the two repacked boxes in the hall to put back into the crawl space later, Clara returned to her office, picking up the bag and box, setting them on the computer desk. She sat in the leather desk chair and stared at the two items for a moment, as though she could see the contents inside.

Letting out a long breath, she grabbed the bag first. Inside was a small yellowish colored stone. She held it between her fingers, feeling the cold smoothness against her skin. Holding the calcite up to the light, she could see all the imperfections inside the stone, as well as the flecks of mineral imbedded in the fragile sheets.

"Long time since I've seen you," she said softly, rubbing the marble-sized stone between her palms. "Let's hope you still work, hmm?"

Setting the stone aside, she grabbed the ring box, opening the creaking lid. Inside was the silver ring she once wore on her middle finger, the small amethyst stone gleaming up at her. She plucked the ring from its satin prison, sliding the cool silver onto her right middle finger. She gasped slightly, feeling the familiar energy of the stone pulse weakly through her finger.

It was said that Archangel Azrael oversaw all mediums, as he was known as the Angel of the Dead. Azrael was responsible for crossing the dead, as well as for helping people grieve after losing someone to death. The amethyst and calcite were his stones, encapsulating his energy and power. The energy between the stones helped to regulate the energy within Clara's own body, making it flow easier, and with more clarity.

She swore she'd never use them again. As she stared down at her finger, then took the calcite in her hand, she knew that vow was broken.

ฆ ฆ ฌ ฌ

Stoney Brook was truly a creepy place at night when it was closed and most of the lights were off. Abby had given her the keys and let Clara roam as she pleased. The pub owner had asked to join her, but Clara declined. She felt it best if she could just walk around the place and get a vibe for it, let her mind reach out and see what it could find — what would reveal itself.

She walked through the main room of the pub, only the lights in the bar illuminated the large area. She didn't want lighting to interfere with her impressions. She could feel the calcite in her pocket and the silver and amethyst ring on her finger. Her own energy was strong as it surged throughout her body, reaching out into the room to see what she would find.

One thing Abby had asked for was some sort of proof of what was in her building. Clara knew she wouldn't be able to do that with her gifts alone, so she had arranged for the CPS — Colorado Paranormal Society — to come do an investigation the following night.

In the meantime, she was on her own. She made her way toward the stairs at the back of the room when she heard something behind her. Stopping, Clara held her breath, listening, able to hear the blood pounding through her ears. The sound of glass hitting glass caught her ear.

Turning slowly, Clara peered through the dimness, trying to spot the source. She saw nothing at the bar, the only places where any glasses were. Walking toward the bar, she was startled when one of the stools — stacked pad-down on the bar top — fell to the floor. Hand to her heart, Clara took a deep breath and blew it out.

"Are you letting me know you're here?" she asked, something inside her beginning to feel nervous. She felt as though there was something in the pub with her, watching her. No matter how much she tried to reach out with her senses, she couldn't quite grasp what it was. It almost felt as though whatever it was, was hiding from her.

Clara decided to head upstairs to see what else she could find,, as well as do some comparison with what she'd been told by Abby. The stairs creaked with every step, the stairway dark. She could feel the darkness all around her, weighing in on her. She could feel a presence with her, watching her, almost as though it were stalking her.

Clara had barely reached the top of the stairs when she heard a loud thud, as though something had been thrown or dropped. She flicked on the first of the three light switches, which only lit two of the six hanging lights above the pool tables. The two lights sent a bright patch of light on the green felt of the tables, but left the rest of the room in relative darkness.

She made her way carefully through the room, not familiar enough with the layout to not whack a leg on something. The last thing she wanted to do was break something in the pub, or something on her. Just ahead she could see the blackness that was the office doorway, left open for her convenience. Abby had said that a good deal of the activity happened in that office, so Clara knew she had to give it a lot of attention.

She stopped at the opened door, looking inside the inky blackness. A chill traveled first up, then back down her spine as she felt the air within the room. She had noticed on her tour with Abby that the room was heavy and made her feel slightly uncomfortable, but now, in the dark, in the territory of whatever lurked there, she felt downright afraid.

About to turn and head out for the night, basically seeing and feeling what she needed to feel, she heard the same bang within the office that she'd heard when she was by the pool tables. She reached a hand inside the room, gasping as a wisp of very cold air washed over her hand. She drew her hand back, holding it within her other hand. She had been touched by a spirit and never liked the feeling. Within her life, and certainly within her spiritual life, she'd felt a spirit's energy many, many times. It was never easy to get used to, especially when it was unexpected and uninvited. It was a cold unlike any other kind. Rather than starting from the outside and working its way in, as a cold breeze would, the chill from a spirit started from the inside and worked its way out. The feeling lingering for many minutes.

She reached into the room again, this time finding the light switch and flicking it on. She looked around the room, seeing nothing out of the ordinary: computer desk replete with computer, filing cabinets, open window—

Clara's attention was drawn back to the open

window. As she watched, the window slammed down to the sill below, making Clara jump in surprise. She studied the window, curious to see if it would move again. It was possible Abby had opened the window earlier in the day, as it was a warm day, and had forgotten to close it. After all, it was a second-story window, so maybe she hadn't worried about it.

Stepping further into the room, Clara walked over to the desk, looking to see if anything looked out of place. Everything had been put away, the desk clear and clean. About to turn, something caught the corner of her eye. Turning back to the desk, Clara leaned over it, surprised to see the contents of one of the drawers dumped on the floor, the drawer itself lying on its side next to the rolling feet of the desk chair.

Bending down, Clara gathered the items and put them back into the drawer, about to slide the drawer back into its slot when the office door moved. Her head whipped up at the sound — a low creak. She thought for a moment that she'd imagined it and turned back to her task. The drawer had just slid into place when she heard the creaking again.

Getting out from behind the desk, she watched for a moment, waiting for movement. Her heart was pounding, the room growing even heavier than before, a cold chill washing through her. Whatever was there did not want her there.

"I'm leaving," she said quietly, "but I will be back."

The journey downstairs was fairly uneventful, though Clara swore she heard voices from time to time. If she didn't know better, she'd almost think someone had broken into the place and was hiding, watching her, talking to someone.

As she walked past the bar, she gasped softly, seeing the glittering pieces of glass on the bar top and floor. Looking up to the glass rack above, she saw that three beer steins had either fallen, or been pushed, only to shatter upon contact. Looking further over the floor, she saw little shards glittering like diamonds.

"My god."

"This has happened before."

Clara yelled out, her heart jumping to her throat when she whirled to see Abby standing behind her. The blonde gave her own little yelp and jumped back at Clara's violent reaction. Once their hearts began to beat again, they both burst into nervous, relieved laughter.

"You scared the hell out of me!" Clara said, hand still clutching her chest.

"I'm so sorry. I didn't think." Abby grabbed a napkin from a nearby dispenser to wipe at the tears from the laughter. "That was classic, though. Truly classic."

"Glad *you* thought so! I'm still waiting for my heart to slow."

Abby sobered, looking over the mess of broken glass. "This does happen a lot, though. I come in probably one to three times a week and find this," she indicated the glass shards scattered across the bar.

In response, Clara took one of the stools — which hadn't been bothered at all — down from the bar and climbed up onto the bar in its place.

"Be careful of the glass, Clara," Abby said, watching carefully to make sure Clara didn't stick her knee right onto a dagger-like piece.

Clara examined the glass rack, checking for any loose screws either in the rack itself or within the hanging mechanism. Nothing. The rack was completely solid, as were the glasses being held within.

She jumped down, her shoes crunching broken glass upon landing onto the floor. "That thing is solid."

Abby nodded, grabbing a broom and dustpan from behind the bar. "I know. I make sure all the time. The last thing I need is a lawsuit because this happens on some poor patron's head."

Clara helped by picking up the larger pieces, throwing them in the plastic trash can Abby provided. "The crazy thing is, I was just upstairs and never heard a thing down here. I'm sure that had to have sounded like a bomb going off when those fell. Look at the way they shattered." She held up a sliver of glass. "Those are some heavy-duty steins. Those things would have to have been literally thrown at the bar to shatter like that."

"I know. I don't understand this."

"We need to talk about some things, but I don't think this is the place to do it." Clara glanced at her watch. "It's almost midnight-thirty, and I'm beat. I appreciate you closing the place down early so I could do this, Abby."

"No," Abby said, shaking her head as she finished the last of the cleanup. "I appreciate you doing this. I still want to pay you."

Clara smiled. "Buy me a beer sometime."

"You got it. Okay, so when do you want to talk?"

"Are you available in the morning? I've got the next couple days off from the bakery to do this, so..." They cleaned up their mess, turned off the bar lights and walked to the door together. "We have the team coming in tomorrow night, and you won't be here for that—"

"Why won't I be?" Abby asked, stopping Clara with a hand to her arm.

Clara looked at Abby, her features lit only by the moonlight from outside. She could see the fear in her eyes, yet the determination on her face. She was amazed at just how much of the beautiful teenage girl she still saw in the twenty-eight-year-old woman before her. "Abby," she began, her voice soft and filled with understanding. "This is a really scary situation. I don't want you to be exposed to it anymore than you already are."

"And I do appreciate that, but Clara, this," she indicated the room they stood in, "is my livelihood. I've put my heart and soul into this business, not to mention a *lot* of money, and I'm not about to let some ghost destroy that."

Clara studied her for a long moment, gauging her earnestness. She could see the fire in those green eyes, and literally feel the energy coming off Abby in waves. Finally she nodded. "Okay. Come to my house in the morning, and we'll talk. Okay?"

Abby nodded vigorously. "Absolutely! Where do you live?"

Chapter Forty-one

Clara glanced at the clock above the stove as she brushed her hair back from her face, careful to pick out the few tangles from her recent shower. Abby was due at her house within five minutes. She had woken late, causing her to run around like a chicken with its head cut off, trying to get the house ready for Abby's arrival.

She had just poured herself a glass of orange juice when the doorbell rang.

"Good morning!" Abby chirped, after being let inside. She walked into the living room, taking a look around at the small, yet beautifully decorated, very comfortable room. "I like your house."

"Thank you. Can I offer you coffee or juice?" Clara asked, leading the way to the kitchen.

Abby followed. "Coffee, if you have it."

"I do. Leaded or unleaded?" she asked, opening the fridge door to show she had a canister of both.

"Mmm, better go with decaf."

"Decaf it is." Clara began to make the coffee, offering Abby a seat at the table. "Did you sleep?"

Abby sighed, sitting back in the chair and glancing out the window. A bird flew by, nearly hitting the window with its beating wings. "Not really. My mind is spinning right now, trying to figure out what I'm going to do about this problem at the Stoney Brook." She sighed, heavy and tired. "I'm just not sure."

"Well, then I guess it's a good thing you're not the one who has to worry about it. Right?" Clara said, sitting across from her sister's friend, whom she still couldn't believe was in her house.

Abby's smile was a bit sheepish, which Clara thought was adorable. "I guess not. I'm not a fan of asking for help, Clara. If I can't do it myself, it doesn't need to be done." She smiled ruefully. "My ex-husband hated that trait in me."

"Why? It's an admirable trait." Clara pushed back from the table and grabbed a mug for Abby, and poured her a cup. She delivered the coffee with the requested creamer and sugar. "Did your ex not like strong women?"

Abby shrugged, preparing her coffee. "He thought he did." Her grin was mischievous. "But, once we were actually married and he saw that it wasn't something that could simply be turned off, he wasn't such a fan."

"I see." Clara sat down again, sipping her orange juice. "Weak men usually don't like strong women." She thought for a moment. "Come to think of it, I don't think *any* man likes a strong woman."

"Amen to that." They were quiet for a moment before Abby broke the silence. "Can I ask you something, Clara?"

"Of course."

"Why did you stop using your gift?"

The question was asked with such genuine curiosity and without an ounce of judgment that Clara felt she had no choice but to answer honestly. "When I was in Los Angeles, my best friend's name was Michael James. I met him virtually the first day I arrived there, and we got close quick." She took a sip of her juice, stalling for a few moments reprieve of what was to come. "Mike had some issues with depression and finding love. Lethal combination. He hoped he'd finally maybe found someone, but Jeff was an asshole, like all the others. Wanted Mike's money, not his heart. I broke a door down in my apartment to find that Mike had slit his wrists in my bathtub."

Abby stared at her. She could tell Clara was trying to put on a brave face, her tone steady and devoid of emotion, but behind her twilight eyes, Abby could see the real story. "That absolutely devastated you, didn't it?" she asked quietly, wrapping her hands around her coffee mug to keep from squeezing one of Clara's hands. She wasn't sure how the younger woman would react to that kind of physical contact; Clara seemed a bit of a touch-me-not.

Clara nodded, blowing out a quiet breath. "It was rough."

"Why did that, as horrible as it was, make you give up your life's work?"

"What's the good of having this so-called gift if I can't even save those I love most? You were at Jason's funeral, Abby. You remember what happened to him. I couldn't save him, either."

"Maybe it was just Jason's time to go, Clara," Abby reasoned. "It may sound like a clichéd blanket statement, but I believe everything happens for a reason. There are no accidents or coincidences."

"But, I was shown both deaths in advance. Why? Why when I couldn't get there in time to stop it?"

"Because maybe you were never *meant* to stop it. Did you think of that?" Abby asked with a raised brow in challenge. "Maybe your grandmother was kind enough to show you those things so you'd be prepared when they happened. You were close to both of those guys, and likely she knew it. You think?"

Clara was quiet for a long moment, trying to wrap a stubborn mind around what she'd just been told. It made sense she had to admit, even if she didn't want it to. She sipped her juice in lieu of saying anything.

"Don't walk away from your gift." This time Abby did reach out and lightly touch one of Clara's hands, wanting to convey the seriousness of her plea. "There are so many that you've touched and helped. You must know that."

Taking a deep breath, Clara nodded. "I suppose."

Abby smiled, amused by the stubborn set of Clara's words and jaw. "Something tells me that's the best I'm going to get out of you, but I'll take it. For now." She put on a bright smile to show change of subject. "So, what are you going to do at my pub tonight?"

⁂

For the second night in a row, Abby closed the pub an hour early so the CPS could get in and set up. The Stoney Brook owner watched in amazement as four men and a woman walked in, each carrying sophisticated camera equipment and other technical devices that she had no clue what they were used for.

"Abby, this is Jordan Crossland. He's head of the CPS," Clara said, introducing them.

"Hi, Jordan. Welcome to the Stoney Brook." Abby shook the African American man's hand, giving him a friendly smile.

"Thanks. Great place," he said, looking around

the main bar room. "We'll get everything set up then I'll explain to you what we're doing, okay?"

"Sounds great. Anything I can do to help?"

"Nope. For now just sit tight." He flashed her a brilliant smile then hurried off to help his team, glancing once over his shoulder to get a second look at the beautiful blonde pub owner. He whistled quietly between his teeth in approval.

"This is quite the setup they've got here," Abby commented, not even noticing Jordan's obvious attraction to her.

"It is," Clara admitted, her gaze roaming to Jordan, who kept sneaking glances at Abby. "From everything I've seen and heard, these guys are good. They know what they're doing."

"Good." Abby blew out a nervous breath, feeling her heart begin to pound at the prospect of actually seeing something on tape.

Clara studied her for a moment, Abby was so caught up in her own nerves she didn't notice the scrutiny. "Abby?" Clara said softly, lightly touching the blonde's arm. "Are you okay to be here?" she asked once she had Abby's attention. "You can go, you know. I'll make sure these guys stay professional and nothing goes wrong."

"Oh, no. No, that's not why I'm here. I need to be here, Clara. Like I told you last night: I've put everything into this place, into making it a success. I mean, hell, I even survived an awful divorce to win it. I'm not letting something scare me out of here. Okay?"

Clara nodded, respecting Abby's gumption. "Okay."

"However," Abby added, a sheepish smile

in place. "Can I stick with you tonight? I *am* a little creeped out."

Clara chuckled with a nod. "Sure."

࿈࿈࿈࿈

By one a.m. the equipment had been placed and lights were out. Jordan and his second-in-command, Abraham Schwartz, decided to hit the pub with the thermal camera. It was a camera that detected its surroundings' heat sources, showing up on the screen in colored degrees of heat and cold. Jordan held the camera as Abe held the accompanying clamshell screen.

Tammy Boyd stayed at central command, set up in the CPS's van outside. The last two members of the team, Jerome Kyle and Juan Armijo, headed downstairs to do an EMF sweep. Clara and Abby were left on the main floor to do some EVP work.

Abby held her small flashlight tight in her hand. Though she'd been in the pub millions of times in all types of lighting — or lack thereof — she had never felt quite as uncomfortable as she did walking around during the CPS investigation.

"What is an EMF sweep?" she asked, referring to the two guys in the basement.

"It stands for Electromagnetic Field. You've talked about a lot of your employees feeling like they're being watched or really uncomfortable up here, so they're making sure you don't have a fear cage in the building," Clara explained.

"Um, can I have that in non-*Ghostbuster* lingo, please?"

Chuckling, Clara explained. "High EMF's can

cause those symptoms, plus nausea and some other nasties. Basically, wires that are old, copper, or lead can cause high EMF readings, and can cause what's referred to as a fear cage. It can affect the surrounding area, or if it's bad enough, sometimes the floor directly above."

Abby stared at her for a moment, a perplexed look on her face. "How the hell do you know this stuff?"

Clara grinned. "I've done a few of these. I used to work with a paranormal group from time to time in California."

"Ah. Gotcha." They headed to a small room off the main bar where tables were set up. During the day, the Stoney Brook served lunch, and many of the diners chose to eat in there. "So, what are we doing, then?"

"EVP." Clara held up a small tape recorder, the silver body glinting briefly in the beam of her flashlight. "Electronic Voice Phenomena. It's where you catch a voice on tape that you didn't hear with your own ears. Pretty soon we'll find a place to settle in and try some." She glanced at her companion. "You game?"

"My head is spinning, but yes, I'm game."

Amused, Clara led on.

≈≋≈≋≈

Upstairs Jordan and Abe made their way into the pool table room. Abraham studied the clamshell screen of the thermal. The pool tables appeared blue and green, no living heat radiating from them. Jordan swung the camera around, and Abraham nearly jumped out of his skin.

"Whoa! Wait, dude. What was that?"

Jordan walked over to him, Abe rewinding the tape to find the spot that had got his attention. As Jordan had swung the camera, a quick flash of a red and yellow object jumped in front of the lens before it was gone.

"What is that?" Abe asked, pausing on the object.

Jordan studied it for a moment, running a hand over his short-cropped hair then goatee. "Oh!" he chuckled, using his finger to point. "I caught your reflection in that mirror," he shined his flashlight up to catch the shiny surface in its beam. A long mirror ran along the length of the back of the room, STONEY BROOK etched into the glass.

Abe laughed. "Okay. Let's keep going."

They continued through the second floor at a slow pace, wanting to make sure Jordan was able to scan everything, as well as they didn't want to run into anything. Jordan had been in the pub a couple times before, but hadn't been upstairs. He did, however, wonder how he'd missed seeing Abby. He'd have to come in a little more often and talk with the pretty pub owner.

"Jordan," Abe hissed, stopping the larger man with a hand to his arm. "Did you hear that?"

Jordan instantly stopped, pulling his mind out of the gutter to listen. He could hear the blood pounding through his body, then breathing that was not his own. He glanced over at his friend, noting that Abe was standing to his right and slightly behind him. He listened harder, trying to figure out where the breathing was coming from.

"It's over there," he whispered, pointing off to their left. Abe nodded, though Jordan couldn't see it in the darkness. Jordan turned the camera, pointing it in the direction of the sound, which was back toward the two first pool tables. On top of one of the tables was a red and yellow smudge, almost as though something had just been sitting there and had gotten up.

"A heat signature," Abe commented, showing Jordan the screen.

"That is bizarre," Jordan murmured, studying the area around the heat signature, then comparing it to what his flashlight was showing him, which was nothing. No one there. "Why don't you get a roll call real quick."

Abe unclipped the radio from his belt and did a check to see where everyone else was in the building. He shook his head. "Nope. Everyone else is downstairs. No one has come up here at all."

"Okay. Let's go check it out." They walked to the pool table, the heat signature beginning to fade slightly. Jordan handed the camera to his friend.

Abe watched as Jordan stepped into view, his body a mass of red-hot heat with yellow signatures throughout. He could discern the big man's shape easily. He laid a hand on the green felt top, quickly removing it. Left behind was a signature mark in the perfect shape of a red and yellow handprint.

"It wasn't a hand," Abe said. "It's smaller than your hand, though."

"Smaller, huh? Hmm." Jordan stroked his goatee. "Okay. Well, we'll look at it later during analysis. Let's keep going."

꧁꧂꧁꧂꧁

Jerome held a flashlight in his right hand, the EMF detector in his left. The EMF was a simple black device with a gray readout screen. He swept it up toward the ceiling where he saw a lot of bundled wires clamped.

"Getting a base EMF of about 0.02," he said.

❧❧❧❧

Juan stood nearby, though he was only half-listening to his friend. He was beginning to get the heebie-jeebies as he shone the beam of his flashlight out across the basement. The large room wasn't finished, but was used for storage instead. The walls were brick, just like the rest of the place, the floor cement. Blacked-out windows lined one wall. At the end of the room were stacked crates filled with products for the pub upstairs. In the back corner was an old, burnt-out furnace; obviously not what kept the place warm. It looked like it hadn't been run in more than a hundred years.

"Man, this place is freaky," he muttered, turning back to his friend.

"Nah," Jerome said, aiming his EMF in a different direction. "Nuthin' here to be worried about, Johnny." He climbed down from the stepladder he'd been standing on to get a better reading of the wires. Putting the ladder back where he'd found it, he turned to face the rest of the basement. "Well, their EMF's are good, here. Nothing from that."

"Yeah, but there is something here, Jerry," Juan insisted. "Don't you feel it? Man, it's just like negative here."

"Pussy," Jerome chided, leading the way back

toward the stairs. "Come on, nothing down here but booze and cobwebs. Let's trade places with another team." He was turning to head toward the stairs when he jumped and whirled around to face empty space.

Juan nearly jumped out of his skin, his defenses already on high alert. "What?"

Jerome reached a hand up, touching the back of his neck and head then shone his flashlight to the spot where he'd felt the touch. He looked for the telltale glitter of a spider web. He saw nothing.

"What happened?" Juan asked, shining his flashlight nervously around their immediate surroundings. He'd gone on more than twenty investigations with CPS, but had yet to feel as uncomfortable as he did at the Stoney Brook.

"I don't know," Jerome said, once again running a hand over his hair. "I felt something." He jerked again, this time his flashlight nearly tumbling from his hand. "What the fuck!" He grabbed at his hair again, turning his back toward his fellow investigator. "Man, do I gotta bug or spider or something on me?"

Juan raised the flashlight to look, pushing Jerome's shaggy brown hair aside, but seeing nothing. He pulled the neckline of his T-shirt down, eyes widening in surprise. "Dude," he exhaled, shocked to see two parallel red lines running down the back right side of Jerome's neck. "Who scratched you?"

"What are you talking about?" Jerome moved away from Juan's prying eyes, feeling for himself. He whined at the sting. "I don't know. I didn't know I *was* scratched back there."

Juan turned his friend around once more to get a second look. "They're fresh, Jerry. I don't think the skin is broken, but them weren't there a few minutes ago, dude. Them are new."

※.※.※.※

Clara was impressed with how Abby had handled things over the investigation. They'd been sitting in the perfect darkness in the dining area for more than an hour. The flashlights had been turned off, Clara wanting to get a true reading of the room. Psychically, she could feel at least two presences near them. They'd heard a couple bumps, and a bump overhead, which they attributed to Jordan and Abe upstairs. Twenty minutes ago they'd started their EVP session. Abby had been a trouper the whole way.

"Why are you here?" the pub owner asked in the darkness, sitting no more than two feet away from Clara. She felt comfort in Clara's presence. Somehow there was a peace and a calm to the medium that helped immensely. When it was all said and done, and her pub was cleared of its uninvited guests, she hoped Clara would want to stay in contact. Since the first time she'd met the younger woman, way back when Clara couldn't have been more than thirteen or fourteen, she'd been intrigued by her. She had never liked it when Kerri had referred to Clara as a freak, as she'd always thought what Clara could do was wonderful, not freakish.

Clara waited a few moments then added her own question. "What is your name?" She waited a beat. "What do you want from Abby?"

"Do you ever get a response?" Abby asked, wrapping her arms around herself, feeling a chill in the air.

"Sometimes."

"What does an EVP sound like? Is it as clear as

you and me?"

Clara shrugged. "Not always. It really depends. It depends on how close the spirit was when they spoke, how far into the after shadow they are. There are a lot of considerations."

They sat in silence for a long moment, Abby glancing at her companion for a moment. She was curious about the medium. "Are you glad you moved back home?"

Clara was quiet for a moment, surprised at the change in topic. She looked in the blonde's direction, unable to see her in the dark. She thought about the question for a long moment, wanting to answer honestly. "In some ways, yes. In most ways, I guess."

"But?" Abby asked, sensing the hesitation in her voice.

"But, I hope I did it the right way. I hope I didn't do something rash when I left L.A. the way I did. You know, like I acted on emotion rather than logic. Or even practicality."

"Did you have a lot of friends there? A lot going for you?"

Clara shrugged. "Yes and no. Mike was my one *real* friend. I had acquaintances, people I'd read for. But nobody special."

"No girlfriends?" Abby asked, letting Clara know she knew she was gay.

Clara chuckled. "Guess Kerri filled you in pretty good, huh?"

Abby smiled, though it went unseen. "Yes, though you told me yourself that you were gay way back at Burger King, Clara. But yes, she told me a lot about you over the past ten years."

"Such as?"

Before Abby was able to answer, they heard footfalls on the stairs in the main room of the pub, followed by the voices of Jordan and Abraham.

"Come on," Clara said, rising to her feet from her chair. "Let's go meet the guys."

Chapter Forty-two

Clara woke up, disoriented, but well rested. The room was dim, and she realized why when she saw that the blinds had been drawn. Who did that? She knew she hadn't. Rolling over, she saw the bedside clock, and was surprised to see that it read 10:17.

"I haven't slept this late since college," she muttered, rubbing her eyes with the heels of her hands. Blinking several times, she took in her surroundings again. The bed was far too comfortable to be hers. It took a moment to remember that she was sleeping in Abby's guest room. Why? It had been a long night, and she had to think back over the events at the Stoney Brook.

They'd wrapped up the investigation at nearly four in the morning. Clara had been dragging, to say the least, considering she was used to going to bed at eight or nine at night and waking up at three in the morning. She'd been so tired she'd forgotten to grab her house and car keys from inside the pub. Rather than having to go and unlock the place, Abby had invited her to stay in her guest room.

"Oh," Clara muttered, sitting up. "That's why."

She pushed the sheet and light blanket off and swung her legs over the side of the bed, feet hitting the soft carpet. Beyond the door she could hear quiet music, muffled by distance. Figuring Abby was awake, she decided it was time to get her things together and get home.

Clara walked over to a hope chest that rested under the window, surprised to see her clothing folded in a neat pile, her keys on top of the clothing. Shaking her head in amusement and gratitude, she quickly pulled her jeans on, removing the T-shirt she'd slept in to put her bra on, then putting the shirt back in place. Keys in her pocket, she made up the bed and headed out of the room.

Following the sounds of Billie Holiday and the smell of bacon, Clara found Abby in the kitchen, softly humming to the sultry tones of "I'll Be Seeing You."

"Good morning!" Abby chirped, in a wonderful mood as she prepared breakfast.

"Morning." Clara looked around the large, open space, where she saw dishes filled with fragrant foods, covered to keep them warm until served. Abby was pouring herself a cup of coffee. "I'll get out of your way so you can eat your breakfast," she said, wincing at the very audible sound of her stomach growling in response to the most wonderful aromas.

Abby chuckled, pouring a second cup of the decaf brew. "Not if your stomach has anything to do with it. Sit down, Clara. You're not going anywhere."

With a sheepish smile, Clara did as she was told. "Can I help you?"

"Nope." Abby brought two mugs to the table, setting one in front of the medium, as well as a small container of skim milk and Splenda. "I remembered you can't have sugar," she explained.

Clara was stunned. "Did you get this stuff special?"

Abby shrugged, her own sheepish grin in place.

"I woke up early. Did you find your keys?"

"I did, thank you."

"Sure. I figure I can drop you off at the pub later so you can get your car. Unless, that is, you have somewhere you need to be?"

Clara shook her head. "No. You've got me for however long you want me."

"Excellent! Then I'd like to talk with you today. Feel like spending some time with me? I've never really gotten to just talk to you, pick your brain. Your gift fascinates me. Besides," Abby added, beginning to carry dishes to the table, "I want to hear all about your time in Los Angeles."

Clara nodded, thrilled at the prospect. "You got it. I'd like to catch up on what you've been up to for the past ten years too."

"Well, then we've got something in common. But, for now, eat! I made a feast."

Clara was in absolute bliss as she ate her breakfast. The food was amazing, and the wonderful, calm feel of Abby's two-story Victorian was a comfort to her. She was more curious than ever about the woman who sat across the table from her. The longest amount of time they'd ever really spent talking was that night when Clara had run out of her father's house when she was fifteen. Abby had taken the time to talk to her and try and help her through her teenage issues.

As though reading Clara's mind, Abby said, "So, did you ever find a way to deal with what happened between your parents when you were a kid? The breakup? I mean I know they obviously worked things out eventually, but..."

Clara nodded, pushing her plate away, full. She wiped her mouth before answering. "Yes. My dad and

I have had some tough times, though. The problem is, we're too much alike. Stubborn." Abby smiled at that. "We fought over my going to college, which I did for a whole whoppin' year. We fought about my being gay. We fought about my heading to California." She rolled her eyes as she sipped her coffee. "Finally, when I came back for their wedding we had a good heart-to-heart. I think he had to realize that I'm an adult and am going to do what I'm going to do. His blessings or no."

"I was at the wedding. I was surprised to see you. You'd kind of disappeared for a while, then poof! There you were."

"Yes, replete in dress and everything," Clara said ruefully.

"Hey, I thought you looked beautiful! You're too hard on yourself."

Clara took her time setting her mug on the table, a slight flush coloring her cheeks. "Thank you," she said quietly. "I saw you, and who I assume is your ex, sitting in the third row. I was pretty surprised to see you there."

"Why?"

Clara shrugged. "I guess I didn't realize you and Kerri had stayed friends after school. I wasn't sure what you had done: gone off to school. Moved away, whatever."

"I see." Abby leaned back in her chair, running a hand through short, blonde hair. "Nope. I met my ex a year after I graduated high school, and we got serious fairly quickly. I married him, against my better judgment, and even *more* against my better judgment, I moved to Ohio with him to be close to his family. That's when things really started to fall apart. I wasn't happy there, wasn't happy with him, so to try and save the marriage, he agreed to move back here. We did and bought the Stoney Brook. It was too late. I wanted out, and here I am."

"Is your ex still here? In town?"

Abby nodded. "I see him from time to time. For some reason he likes to parade his newest girlfriend in front of me and have a drink at the pub." She chuckled, shaking her head. "It's pretty stupid. I could honestly care less."

Clara was amused. "Sounds like something my first girlfriend would have done. Oh man, Erica. She wouldn't leave me alone. You know, even once I moved to California, and we'd been broken up for like five years, she still tried to get ahold of me. It was crazy." She drained her coffee, pushing the cup aside.

"Have you seen or spoken to her since you've come back?"

"Nope. No desire to either. Her mom is a really cool lady, though. She owns The Pagan down on Prairie. At least she did. Not sure if it's still there or not."

"I've driven past it, never been inside." Abby pushed away from the table, clearing their dishes and setting them in the sink. She returned with the coffee carafe, refilling both mugs. "So tell me about some of the people you read for while in California. Anyone famous?" she asked, sitting back down and fixing her coffee.

Clara put her hand to her chest in mock astonishment. "Are you asking me to divulge secrets of my business?"

Abby nodded. "Pretty much."

"Well, in that case. Yes. I did read for some famous people."

Abby was so intrigued by all the stories Clara

told about her adventures in L.A. that she totally forgot about her coffee. Before she knew it, it had grown cold and was pushed away.

"You're serious? *He* wanted a reading?!" she asked, astonished at the story of a famous rocker from the 1970s who had sat on Clara's couch.

"I'm very serious. Nice guy too." Clara sat back in her chair, satisfied to know that Abby had listened to every word she'd said, only interrupting to ask questions or to clarify something.

"Do you miss it? All the glitz and glam?" Abby asked, a conspiratorial grin on her face.

Clara shook her head. "No, to be honest. It's not a real world out there, Abby. It's fake. Yeah, people are nice, they're polite, but at the end of the day, it's all about business. It's all about connections. I had a hard time with that. I got mixed up in the party life for a while, because that's all I found. What really made me see what I had become was this woman I was seeing, Leah. She was a model. Well, in name only. Truth be told, she was so stoned or drunk all the time, she couldn't get or keep jobs. Pretty pathetic." She shook her head at the memory of the beautiful, yet hopelessly lost woman. "That wasn't long before Michael killed himself."

"Wow," Abby said, shaking her head sadly. "You hear stories like that on TV. You know, the *Entertainment Tonight* kind of shows. So it's all true, huh? The young people ruining themselves with too much partying."

"Young people, old people, you name it. Not my cup of tea."

"And this is?" she asked, indicating the kitchen around them and the town beyond.

Clara thought for a moment then nodded. "For now. I can't tell you this is where I want to retire, but for right now it works." She studied Abby for a moment, noting the blonde's features had taken on the look of someone very disturbed by something. "What's up? What's on your mind?"

Abby sat back in her chair, a heavy sigh escaping her lips. "Give me your expert opinion, Clara. What's going on in my pub?"

Clara rested her elbows on the table, chin on her folded hands. "Truthfully, I feel you've got several entities in your place. I want to do some research on the building, find out what purposes it's served since it was built, as well as the land around it. Get an idea for what's going on maybe. Do you know much of the details of the history, beyond what you've already told me?"

Abby shook her head. "Where can we go to find that out? I want to help you with this, so whatever we need to do, just say the word."

Clara nodded. "Excellent. We'll need to start at the library and Hall of Records."

"Let me clean this up, and we'll go today."

⁂

Four hours later, they sat across from each other at the very coffee shop Abby used to work at in high school. Each had a stack of printed pages in front of them.

"Okay," Abby said, sipping from her latte before setting it aside. "What I got from the Hall of Records is that the building was built in 1853 by Meyer Spence. It was originally used as a canning factory for his fruit preserves business. Later, it was taken over as a girl's boarding school, and finally in 1931 as the headquarters for a local Elks Club Chapter. It sat vacant for about twelve years before it was bought in 1955 by Reginald Beeman and turned into apartments. That lasted for almost thirty-seven years before it was turned into the Turnkey, who are the owners that my ex and I bought the place from."

"Okay. Good work, detective," Clara complimented, grabbing her own stack of research and preparing to present it. "What I found out at the library is as follows." She shuffled through the papers, looking for the juicier tidbits she'd found while Abby had been across the street at the Hall of Records.

"Like you, I found the Spence record, except one thing I did find was a woman by the name of Ruth Macon was killed there when the hem of her dress got caught in one of the machines."

Abby wrinkled her nose. "Ouch. That had to be messy."

"Undoubtedly. So, things were fairly quiet for about a hundred years or so, until 1971. Back then they were the Beeman apartments. A woman and her boyfriend — Scarlet Fisher, but I couldn't find his name — moved in that spring. There had been problems with them as tenants from the very beginning, according to the newspaper article. Scarlet's nephew Frederick moved in with them that summer when he was just seven years old.

"Well, I guess the boyfriend had a heroin habit, and liked to beat on his girlfriend and the kid whenever he couldn't find the money to get his fix." She tugged a sheet of paper out of the stack and slid it across the table for Abby to see.

"Oh wow," she blew out, taking the page between her fingers. The grainy black- and-white image showed a man with long, stringy hair being led away in handcuffs in the foreground. In the background a gurney was being rolled toward a waiting ambulance, a blood-soaked body on top. Following the gurney, two uniformed officers carried a small bundle zipped in a body bag. "How terrible."

"Scarlet died on the way to Park Meadow Hospital. Both she and her nephew had been bludgeoned. A Mrs.," she glanced down at another sheet, "Gertrude Whippley, the neighbor across the hall, called authorities, but when they arrived, Frederick was already dead."

"That's so tragic," Abby said absently, looking at the assortment of pictures Clara handed her. They were snapshots of the inside of the building at the time, when the apartments had originally been walled off. The walls were long gone, leaving only the open space of the second and third floors. She looked at a picture taken in the building hallway, outside of Scarlet's apartment. The door was open, police officers seen inside gathering evidence. From the far right corner of the picture she could barely make out a bit of light shining in, and knew it was from the window at the end of the hall.

Clara watched her carefully, curious to see if anything would ring with her. It appeared something had. "What is it?" she asked, slowly peeling the paper from the bottom of her banana nut muffin.

"This apartment," Abby said, turning the page so Clara could see where her finger tapped. "I bet you money where their apartment was is right where the office is upstairs. See? This is the window at the end of the hall, I think."

"Oh, wow." Clara took the page and sat back in her chair, examining it. Though Abby knew that building better than anyone, it didn't take a resident to see what she meant. "I think you're right." They exchanged a knowing look. Tossing the page to the table, Clara blew out a breath. "Jordan is supposed to get with me today about what was found last night. He and a couple of the guys were going to spend all day going over evidence. Once I go over that with him, I'll bring it over your house and we can go from there. Okay?"

Abby nodded, hugging herself, as she felt slightly uneasy. "Okay."

"There's nothing to worry about, Abby. All a spirit is, is a person without a body. They're just energy. They can't hurt you. When they do what they do, it's simply to get your attention. It wants help or simply wants to interact with you. Unfortunately, making noise and breaking glasses is part of what it's limited to do."

"But, why does it feel so negative?" Abby asked her brow creased in concern.

Clara thought about that for a moment, trying to think of what to say. She'd felt the same negative energy there, especially in the second-floor office. She wanted to be careful, scaring Abby or making her feel even more uneasy wasn't an option. She wanted to be honest with her, but there was a fine line.

"Well, I think the best way to think of it is in terms of people. As I said, spirits are essentially just that. There are negative people out there, or people who you just don't like or feel comfortable around. Usually because they've got a 'bad vibe'," she explained, using her fingers as quote marks. "Spirits are the same thing, except even more potent. All they are is energy, a vibe, so you're going to feel that amplified."

"Okay, I get that." Abby nodded, sipping from her latte. She stared into its creamy depths for a moment. "Have you managed to make contact with anything yet? Know who's there? You said you think there is more than one. Any ideas of who?"

"If you're asking if anything has come right out and introduced itself to me, the answer is no," Clara said, grinning.

"Cute." Abby threw the crinkled up wrapper from her sugar packet at the medium. "I don't know how all this stuff works — what you see, what you don't."

"I have no idea who they are. I'll have to go to the after shadow to do that."

"What's that?"

"The land of the dead."

Abby blinked at her several times, not sure what to say. "Okay," she drawled, shaking her head. "How exactly does one *get* to the after shadow?"

Clara smiled, amused by Abby's reaction. "A lot of concentration. And," she added, "a little help from my grandmother."

Chapter Forty-three

Clara sat on Jordan's couch, watching as he forwarded through footage, finally stopping on the spot he was looking for.

"This," he explained, pausing the image on the screen so he could explain what Clara was about to see, "was when me and Abe were up in the small attic area. She has mostly dust up there, a few mouse droppings. And this ..." he pushed play.

Clara studied the image. The room was basically bare, save for a few old boxes that were tucked toward the back. The rafters could be seen, and at the very end of the long attic was a window, the night obviously visible beyond.

"Now," he continued, "as you know, the cameras we use can see in total darkness. I had just climbed up there, Abe right behind me. He raised the FLIR just in time to catch this."

Clara's eyes were drawn to the window, then in a split second, something moved in front of it, completely blocking out the incoming moonlight, before it was gone again. "Whoa!" she exclaimed, sitting forward in her seat. "Can I see that again?"

"You got it." Jordan rewound the tape. This time when he played it, he played it in slow motion. "Watch this, Clara. You can actually see what looks to be an arm when you slow it down."

Attention fully caught, Clara watched as what appeared to be a full-bodied shadow ducked in front of the window then was gone as soon as it appeared. And, she also noted what Jordan saw. It was almost as though an arm had been swung out, like a person quickly moving out of the way of prying eyes.

Stunned, she sat back in her chair, staring at the paused image, frozen on the screen. "That is one of the creepiest things I've ever seen," she said at length, still staring at the figure. As she looked at where the head would be, she felt almost as if the shadow were looking directly back at her. A shiver passed through her spine. It was almost as if through the frozen image on the screen she could feel rage coming through.

"What do you think?" Jordan asked quietly.

Clara sighed heavily. "I think this is going to freak Abby out," she said, glancing at him. "Badly."

"I thought I'd go over there with you to share this with her."

"That won't be necessary," Clara snapped, immediately regretting the sharp tone in her voice. She smiled, trying to lighten the sudden tension. "I think she'll take it better from me, Jordan." *Not from some guy who wants to drool all over her.*

He stared at her for a moment then finally nodded, reluctantly agreeing. "I've got more to show you."

❧❧❧❧❧

Abby was nervous to see what had been caught in her pub, but knew she had to. She had asked for it, so now had to face it. She and Clara sat in Clara's living room, an array of electronic equipment spread out over Clara's coffee table.

"We can start with video, pictures, or EVPs. What's your poison?" As she looked at Abby, waiting for her answer, she could actually feel the waves of nervousness coming from her. She wanted so badly to find a way to comfort her but didn't know how. She knew she had to keep her distance, as she didn't want to get too attached. She had the sense that if she were she to spend a great deal of time with Abby, that's exactly what would happen.

"Let's start out small. Show me the pictures," Abby finally managed, rubbing her sweating palms on the thighs of her jeans.

"All right. Pictures it is."

Abby took the handful of printed images into her hands, slowly looking through them, sometimes unsure exactly what she was looking at.

"Okay, these," Clara explained, pointing at the white, seemingly glowing balls that were frozen in the image forever, "are orbs. There are varying theories on those. Personally, I'm not impressed by them. Some say they're bugs, some say they're dust, others say they're actually balls of energy caught floating around, while others still insist they're spirits."

"What do you think?" Abby asked, glancing over at Clara.

"I think they're either dust, bugs, or simply balls of energy. I have yet to experience a spirit showing itself to me in this form. But," she shrugged, "I could be wrong."

"I trust you, Clara. What you say goes."

"No, let your own mind make your decisions, Abby. I can try and guide you, but ultimately, you have to feel comfortable with what you see, learn, and experience."

Abby looked at Clara for a long moment, a slow smile spreading across her face. She handed the pictures back, all of which were filled with orbs. "What's next, Yoda?"

Clara chuckled. "Well, what gives you the heebie-jeebies more: to hear something and not see it, or to see it and not hear it?"

"Oh boy." Again, she ran sweaty palms on her thighs. "I guess to hear it would be a little less creepy for me."

"Okay." She opened the laptop Jordan had let her borrow. The program on the laptop had been able to take the EVPs from the small recorders used and digitally clean them up. "Here's the first one, which was caught between Juan and Jerome on the first floor. At first you'll hear them talking. It's right after Jerome says, 'Nice glasses'."

"Okay."

The laptop screen showed sound patterns, spiking at higher levels of sound. Clara tapped the touchpad to start the program. At first all they heard was mild static, picked up from air currents around them, as well as various miscellaneous noises. Juan and Jerome began to talk.

"*Hey, Juan, let's go over by the bar,*" *Jerome said, the sound of a chair being moved out of his way making the sound spike jump.*

"*Cool,*" *Juan said in answer.*

There was a pause for a moment as the men got settled in at the bar, where they'd pulled down stools and sat down. "*Nice glasses,*" *Jerome commented.*

"Mine. Not yours..."

Abby nearly jumped in surprise, her hands flying to cover her mouth. She looked at Clara wide-eyed. "Oh my god," she breathed.

Clara could only nod in understanding, knowing there was far more in their evidence that would upset the pub owner.

The two men continued to talk, oblivious to their gravelly-voiced companion.

"I wonder how much a stein like that costs," Juan asked.

"Dunno. More than you got." Both men chuckled. "Okay, let's get to work."

"Can you tell us your name?" Juan said, beginning the EVP session unaware that it had already begun.

"Leave me alone..."

"Are you a man or a woman?" Jerome asked. There was no verbal response, only a chilling bit of laughter.

"I have got the chills," Abby said, hugging herself.

"Are you okay?" Clara asked, stopping the program. She waited for a long moment, still getting no answer from the woman sitting beside her, who was obviously shaken up. "Abby?"

Abby looked at her, trying to keep the tears in her eyes from spilling onto her cheeks. She felt frightened, intrigued and angry, all at the same time. "I'm sorry. I just really don't know what to think. What to say."

"You don't have to say or think anything. I know this isn't easy, Abby. I'm here for you."

"I know. Thank you so much for that." Abby reached over and took Clara's hand, squeezing it tightly before letting it go. She took several deep breaths, determined to be strong. "Let's continue. What else?"

Clara studied her for a moment, seeing the steely

determination enter Abby's eyes. With a short nod, she turned back to the laptop. Loading up the next EVP found. She wasn't looking forward to Abby's reaction to this one, but it had to be done.

"This next one was when we were sitting in the dining area talking. We hadn't started an 'official' EVP session yet, but I was recording." She glanced over at Abby. "Are you okay to hear this?"

Abby nodded. "So, did we hear this when we were actually there?"

Clara shook her head. "No. It only appeared on the recording."

Abby blew out a loud breath. "Okay. Let's hear it."

Clara hit play on the program again, and they both sat back to listen.

The sound of someone resettling on a chair was the first thing heard, then the light tap, tap, tapping of Abby's flashlight against her leg.

"So, what do you think of my pub?" Abby asked.

"I think it's great. Beautiful place," Clara responded, a slight squeak of the chair as she adjusted her body in the seat. "What did this used to be? It's a neat building."

"You know, I'm not sure—"

"Mommy? Do they like us?"

"—probably a bordello." Both Clara and Abby laughed, completely unaware of the child's voice that had interrupted them.

"Wait," Abby said, putting a hand on Clara's wrist. "Play that again."

Clara directed the cursor over the STOP button then rewound a few seconds.

"...it's a neat building."

"You know, I'm not sure—"

"Mommy? Do they like us?"

Clara hit PAUSE, waiting for Abby's reaction. She studied the bar owner's profile, looking for any sign of how she was feeling.

Abby chewed on the inside of her bottom lip for a moment, trying to decide just exactly what she felt and thought. The child's voice was so clear in the EVP, almost as though he or she — though it sounded like a little boy — had been standing right next to the recorder, which she realized had been sitting on the table, right next to where her hand had been resting. She shivered.

"Is there more?"

Clara nodded, clicking the PLAY button.

"Is there anyone here with us tonight?" Clara asked, finally getting around to actually asking questions.

"If there is," Abby added, *"can you tell us your name?"*

"Alfred..."

Abby looked at Clara, brow creased in thought. "Who's Alfred? Did you get an Alfred in your research?"

Clara shook her head. "I wondered the same thing." She glanced over at Abby. "Want to continue?"

"Yes. Let's keep going."

"Okay. We're almost done with the EVPs. I think there's one or two more to go."

Abby clasped her hands in her lap as they continued.

"My name is Clara, and I'm sitting here with my friend, Abby. She owns this place, so I'm sure you've seen her around a lot before. She isn't here to hurt you,

and we aren't, either. We just want to better understand why you're still here, and how I may be able to help you." There was a short pause. "Are you okay with that?"

"No..."

"He's coming..."

Abby sat back, goose bumps erupting over her arms. She wasn't even sure what it was, but something was making her blood chill.

Clara said nothing, simply stopped the program, as that was the last of the EVPs, and waited for Abby to speak.

Abby was silent for a long moment then took a deep breath. "I'm okay, but I am somewhat disturbed." She looked at Clara. "There is definitely something there, isn't there?"

Clara nodded. "Appears to be, yes. I mean, I have felt things there personally, but I'm never comfortable with saying that in someone's home or business or whatever, until I have the scientific proof to back me up." She indicated the laptop with a wave of her hand. "The EVPs are good, yes, but are they totally solid?" she shrugged. "Depends on who you are, and your definition of a haunting."

"But, do *you* feel it's haunted? I trust you, Clara, and I trust you'll tell me the truth and won't try and bullshit me either way."

"Yeah, I do. I feel there is some definite energy in that pub, and it's not all residual. You've got something there, and I strongly feel it doesn't want *you* there, or anyone else."

Abby nodded, chewing on her lower lip. "I agree. That's the vibe I get too." She blew out a breath. "Okay, what else you got?"

Clara closed the audio program and brought up

the video. She pulled up the first of two visual pieces of evidence, starting with the one Jordan had shown her of the full-bodied apparition in the attic.

Abby watched saucer-eyed, sitting forward in her chair. Her mouth was still open a bit after the scene played out. Clara watched her again for reaction.

"Holy shit," Abby finally said, unable to take her eyes off the paused frame. She looked over at Clara. "Was that what I think it was?" At Clara's nod, she turned her attention back to the screen.

"Do you want to see it again?" Clara asked, fingers ready to deliver.

Abby shook her head. "No. Once was enough to give me nightmares."

"There's one more. Do you want to see it, or have you had enough? I mean, with what I've shown you, you have more than enough proof—"

"Show me," Abby insisted.

A newfound respect for the pub owner filled Clara as she switched the player to the second video Jordan had put on the computer for her. "This is in the main pub area downstairs. You can't see it with the angle of this camera, but the bar is off to the right, out of frame."

"Okay," Abby nodded, orienting herself with the area of the room she was looking at.

There were two tables, their chairs slid neatly underneath. It was quiet, no one seen in the room. She gasped and jumped, startled as one of the chairs rocked slightly, almost as though it were being wedged out from underneath the table, then flew backward, only stopping when it ran into another chair.

Clara's living room was silent as the footage came to an end, and the screen went dark. The medium studied her client for a moment, waiting, not daring to speak. After what seemed like an hour, but in actuality was only a few seconds, Abby glanced at her.

"That was interesting."

Clara nodded. "It was."

"Where do we go from here?"

Clara could hear the steely determination in Abby's voice, so decided to go with it, and follow her lead. "Well, I need to get—"

"We," Abby interrupted. "I want to be there too. I want to be involved and see what needs to be done."

Clara smiled, her gut telling her not to argue. "All right. *We* need to get in there, and I'll check out the situation from the after shadow. From there I'll either cross the spirits, or I'll make them leave. Either way, they'll be gone."

Abby's smile was bright and filled with bravery. "Let's do it."

Chapter Forty-four

Clara rolled the dough on the kitchen table, adding a bit more flour when needed. She'd been helping her mother all day with a private order for a woman, who needed three-dozen specially decorated cookies for her daughter's birthday. Though Stephanie put in tons of hours at the bakery, she'd never lost her love of baking, and had continued to do projects on the side for a number of clients who'd come back time and again for her wonderful creations.

Stephanie was on the phone with Kerri, holding the phone between cheek and shoulder, mixing a bowl of frosting.

"Yeah, from what I hear it's going well." Stephanie added a bit more almond extract as she listened to her older daughter. "Really? Her ex-husband has come back into the picture, huh?"

Clara's interest was piqued, as she knew they were talking about Abby. She didn't want to full-out eavesdrop, but wanted to hear more. She hadn't seen Abby in three days, not since the night they'd looked at the investigative footage at Clara's house. The plan was for Clara and Abby to go into the pub after closing in two nights. Abby couldn't afford to close early again. In the three days, they'd spoken briefly on the phone, but it had been all business. She couldn't explain it, but somehow she missed Abby's presence. It was a strange feeling.

"Wasn't he a real ass, or something?" Stephanie asked, oblivious to her younger daughter's interest in the one-sided conversation. "I thought so. Well, Abby better be careful not to let that guy back into her life. Sounds like trouble, to me."

Clara stopped rolling, using the excuse of stretching her back as she listened.

"Whatever happened with that restraining order she got last year?" Pause. "Yeah, I thought he'd broken it. Didn't he move away? No? Oh." To Clara's frustration, Stephanie left her mixing bowl and headed down the basement stairs, hot on the trail of a missing ingredient that would likely be in the pantry Max had built for her down there two years ago.

Clara turned back to her task, probably rolling out the dough with a bit more vigor than was necessary. She wanted to know the story, but didn't feel like she knew Abby well enough to ask, and didn't want Stephanie or Kerri wondering why she wanted to know and why she was listening in on other people's conversations by asking.

Stephanie's steps clanked on the wooden stairs as she hurried back to the kitchen, a small glass bottle of some secret spice in one hand, the phone in the other. She had finished her talk with Kerri and set the phone on the counter as she headed back to the mixing bowl.

"Did you ever meet James, Clara?" she asked, tapping in a bit of the sweet-smelling powder.

Clara did a mental happy dance. She could ask to her heart's content now that her mother had brought it up. "No. She's mentioned him a few times, though I never even knew what his name was." She set the rolling pin aside and began to cut the dough into their cookie-cutter shapes. "Was that him at your wedding?"

Stephanie paused in her mixing as she thought for a moment then nodded, continuing her labor. "That was him; a real prick, according to Kerri."

"What happened? All Abby has told me was they moved to Ohio to be closer to his family, then moved back here and bought the Stoney Brook. End of story."

"Well, from what Kerri told me over the years, he was a controlling ass. He tried to use that pub to keep tabs on her. When they bought the place, she took to bartending and being a business owner like a duck to water." She scraped the frosting into separate bowls, which would become the different colors used to decorate the cookies. "He, of course, didn't like that. Things began to fall apart. Hell, he even tried to get her to sell the place because she was doing so well there."

"She said it was the only thing she got out of the divorce," Clara said, placing her newly cut dough on a cookie sheet.

Stephanie nodded. "That's true. Even that was a fight." Stephanie sucked on the tip of her thumb as some frosting colored the skin white. "Mm, that's good. Anyway, James fought her tooth and nail for that, but eventually a judge awarded it to Abby since he already had a job. The pub was her job."

Clara nodded her understanding, taking the cookie sheet and sliding it into the preheated oven. "So, what's going on now?"

"Guess he's been coming back around. Asking about her."

"Does Abby know that?"

Stephanie shrugged. "I don't know. Your sister heard it from an old high school friend they all knew,

Anthony somebody."

"Anthony Fitzpatrick?"

"Yeah! That's him." Stephanie carried the bowls of frosting to the kitchen table, as well as the tiny bottles of food coloring. Clara brought the pan of cookies that had been cooling to the table, and together they began to mix colored frosting, and Stephanie created her masterpieces.

"I remember him. Didn't he date Abby for a while?"

Stephanie shrugged. "Hell if I know. It was hard enough to keep up with the *Days of Our Lives* that was you girls' lives back then, let alone to remember it all now."

Clara chuckled, tasting the frosting, eyes closing in pleasure.

"Good?" Stephanie asked expectantly.

"Oh, yeah! Very. However," Clara said, holding up a finger for emphasis, "I've had my sugar intake for the week."

Stephanie rolled her eyes, unable to understand her daughter's eating habits. Though she respected Clara's reasons, she felt life was too short to live off rabbit food alone.

Clara was amused as she watched her mother work her artistic culinary magic. "So, James. What does he want with her?"

"No idea, though Kerri's worried. She helped Abby through a lot of that stuff back then."

"You know, I had no idea they were such good friends."

"Oh, yeah. Ever since tenth grade."

"Oh."

"Has it gone pretty well? I mean, especially since

I know you never wanted to do the ghost stuff again," Stephanie asked, studying her daughter for a moment before turning her attention back to the tube of black frosting she was filling.

"Yeah. It's gone great. I think she's pretty disturbed by what the guys of CPS found."

"Who wouldn't be? Honestly, I think even I would be disturbed, and you're my daughter!" Stephanie turned her focus to the tiny designs she was making on the cookie.

"She's been wonderful. I admit, I wasn't looking forward to doing this, but I don't know," Clara shrugged, stealing another quick swipe of icing with her finger. "I've enjoyed my time with her. She's very curious about what I do and wants to be there when I clear her pub."

Stephanie stopped her art, smiling at her daughter. "Really? Oh, honey, that's great! It's about time someone truly respected what you do." She turned back to her design.

Clara watched, but her mind swam back to Abby. They seemed to get along great; that was true. She remembered the many conversations they'd had about the supernatural world, and what Clara did, and what it involved. She couldn't stop the smile from spreading across her lips as she thought back to the day they'd done research on Abby's building. How wonderful it had been, sitting in that coffee shop exchanging notes and bits of information. She was so lost in thought she didn't notice her mother watching her, a knowing smile on her face.

❧❧❧❧

The Stoney Brook was busy when Clara walked in. The sound of animated conversation filled the space, as well as glasses clinking and drinks being poured. Low music hung in the background, distant pool balls knocking into each other.

Clara looked around, trying to spot Abby, but didn't see her behind the bar. Deciding to get a glass of water, she found an empty stool at the bar and waited until the girl who was tending noticed her.

"Clara?"

Clara turned to see a completely unexpected face. "Shelby!'

Her ex smiled and they exchanged a tight, but brief hug. Shelby looked her over, noting Clara's hair, which was longer than she'd ever seen it, as well as a much more trim, womanly figure. "My god, you look great!" she said, sitting on the stool next to Clara's. "When did you get back into town? Are you visiting?"

Clara felt like an ass as she tried to think how best to answer Shelby's questions. She'd been back home for such a long time, yet had never once called Shelby, or tried to see if she was still even in town. She was given a moment to think when the girl behind the bar showed up, asking for her order and placing a beer in front of Shelby.

"Water?" Shelby asked, brows drawn. "I've never known you to drink a shot glass-full, let alone to actually order one on purpose."

Clara chuckled, nervously tucking her hair behind her ear. "Yeah, well, some things change." She looked her ex over, noting that Shelby was still a beautiful woman, and amused — and a bit disturbed — to realize just how much she reminded her of Abby. "You look great, Shelby." Her water arrived, and Clara took a long swig.

"Thanks! Want to join us?" Shelby pointed to a table near the back of the pub, two women seeming to be engaged in a deep conversation sitting there.

Clara glanced around the pub, looking one last time for Abby. She saw her coming out of the staircase leading from upstairs, and walking toward the bar. "Actually, I'd love to catch up with you, but the person I came here to talk to just got here."

Shelby glanced over her shoulder and saw Abby. She smiled and raised her hand in greeting. "Hey, Abby. Didn't know you were here."

Abby walked into the horseshoe that was the bar, and over to the two women. "Hey, Shelby." She turned, surprised to see Clara sitting next to the long-time patron, "Clara!"

Shelby curiously watched the interaction between the two women.

"Hey!" Clara grinned, glad to see the pub owner. "Just dropped by to talk about tomorrow night."

Shelby's brows and interest shot up, but she said nothing. When Clara turned to her, she decided it was time to take her leave. "Clara, it was great to see you again." She stood, giving her ex another tight hug then holding her by the shoulders. "I really do want to catch up, okay?"

Clara felt a little awkward, knowing Abby was watching her and Shelby's every interaction. She nodded. "Yeah. I would too."

"See you, Abby," Shelby said before grabbing her beer and weaving her way through the tables and patrons to her own party, Abby watching her go before turning back to Clara.

"You know her?"

Clara nodded. "She was my girlfriend in college."

"Really?" Abby was surprised, resting her folded arms on the polished bar. "Shelby's been coming here for a long time, now. I never even knew she was gay."

Clara chuckled. "Can't attest for now, but she sure was then."

For some reason that made Abby uncomfortable, and she couldn't help but glance at the table where Shelby sat with two friends. One of the women she had seen with her before many times. *So, is that a girlfriend, maybe?* Abby cleared her thoughts and returned her attention to her friend, glad to see her.

"So, this is a nice surprise. What can I get ya?"

"Got my water," Clara said, raising her bottle.

Abby was amused. "Don't you ever drink anything with a little more kick to it than that?"

"Orange juice. Even grape juice from time to time," Clara said, eyes twinkling.

Abby played along. "Oh my! Can your poor body handle so much acid?" she asked, hand to her heart.

"It does. Amazing, isn't it?"

"Oh, yes. Definitely!" They broke into laughter. "It's good to see you." She reached out and squeezed Clara's arm enthusiastically. "What brings you out?"

"Well, just wanted to say howdy, and I wanted to make sure everything was still a go for tomorrow night." *And I really missed you.*

"Howdy right back at'cha, and yes. We are very much still a go for tomorrow night. You said you can be here at two, right?"

"Yes, ma'am. Two a.m. it is."

"Wonderful." Abby said her goodbyes to a few patrons who were leaving, then turned her attention back to Clara. "Can I ask you something?"

"Of course."

"Do you do psychic stuff too?"

"As in, your future is..."

"As in, your ex-husband wants..."

Clara nodded in slow understanding. "I see. I can probably help you with that."

"Come upstairs with me."

The walk to the second floor was a quiet one, other than Abby's greetings to her pool-playing patrons, making sure everyone was comfortable and had everything they needed. Eventually they made it to Abby's office, the pub owner closing the door behind them.

"Have a seat," she offered, taking one behind the large desk.

Clara sat on the old, rickety chair, waiting for whatever Abby had to say. She studied her new friend, and could feel Abby's energy, which was coming off in waves of heat. Something was very wrong. As the silence continued, Clara got more concerned. Reaching across the desk, she took one of Abby's hands lightly in hers, offering friendly comfort.

"Abby?"

Abby took a deep breath then began to speak. "Jimmy is hanging around again," she began, her thumb absently running along the smooth skin of Clara's hand. The touch sent a slight shiver through the medium. "I haven't seen him yet, and he hasn't tried to contact me, but I know it's a matter of time. He'd actually left me alone for a while."

When there was nothing more forthcoming, Clara urged her on with questions. "And this is a bad thing? That he's back?"

Abby nodded. "Potentially. If I know him as well as I think I do, yes. After we split, as I told you, he'd come around off and on, usually with some new woman, but it was nothing major. Nothing threatening."

The fear in Abby's green eyes disturbed Clara greatly. "Can you tell me more?"

"Like what?" Abby released Clara's hand with a gentle squeeze, then hugged herself as she sat back in her chair.

Clara felt the loss immediately, but ignored it. "What happened in your marriage, Abby? What *really* happened?" She didn't want to tell her about the conversation she'd had with her mother just the day before, as she didn't want to break Kerri's confidences, or cause problems between the two friends. She decided playing dumb was the best route. "And, why is it bothering you so much this time, him coming around again?"

Abby blew out a breath, which disturbed her bangs. "What didn't happen is the question." She laughed, a bit self-consciously. "I hate talking about this, and really haven't told anyone the full truth." She looked into Clara's eyes, letting her know she meant to reveal her secrets to her. "This is hard."

"If you're not comfortable with this, Abby, I can just try and connect and see what I come up with. It may mean nothing to me, but may mean the world to you."

Abby smiled, genuine and beautiful. "I really appreciate the offer, Clara, but I want to talk. I feel I can trust you, and it's probably best for me to finally just talk it out, anyway."

"Okay." Clara settled in, waiting to hear the worst.

"Okay, here we go. I met Jimmy when I was pretty young, and we got married far too young. The problem was, I knew when we were dating things weren't cool."

Clara listened — trying to keep her expression clear — to a story of mental and verbal abuse, and even a time or two where the physical realm was breeched. She heard tales of Jimmy calling Abby names, and bringing her self-esteem down to the point of nonexistence. A brutal time in Abby's life, and one she was still very damaged from.

"I just remember the times when I'd come home from work, and he'd call me down for how fast or slow I had driven home — depending on what time I got back. God, Clara, he would make fun of me for the way I sounded when I cry! He'd say I sounded stupid or retarded."

Clara wasn't sure what to say. She could feel Abby's pain and devastation. She wasn't sure whether to say anything or just remain silent.

"You know," Abby said softly, near tears, "the day your parents got married I saw you, and really wanted to talk to you. I had planned to at the reception, but he insisted we not go. Hell." She laughed ruefully. "Getting him to even go to the wedding was a job."

"Oh, Abby." It took everything in her power to stay seated and not hurry around the desk and take Abby into her arms. She could feel that lost, very lonely young bride in the friend sitting across from her. "I'm so sorry."

Abby glanced at Clara, seeing the genuine caring in her face, and it finally did her in. She felt the first of many tears flow out of her eyes. She'd kept the tears locked away for such a long time, she felt ashamed to let them out now. "It was my cross to bear, I guess."

Clara gave in to her need and hurried around the desk and knelt in front of her friend, Abby immediately fell into the hug. They stayed that way for a long time, neither moving to break the embrace. Abby rested her head on Clara's shoulder, feeling so safe and warm.

"I was very stupid," she said softly. "I stayed far too long."

"You know," Clara said, rubbing small circles over Abby's upper back. "My grandmother tells me that everything in this life is planned for a purpose. One thing leads into the next."

Abby pulled away just enough to be able to look into Clara's face. Her eyes were a vibrant green from crying. "What do you mean?" she sniffled.

"Well," Clara said, reaching over to the desk and grabbing two tissues from the box there. She handed one to Abby and used the other to gently wipe away the tear streaks. "You've given him enough of these," she whispered, watching as Abby closed her eyes so Clara could wipe them dry.

Abby smiled with a small nod. "I have." She quickly blew her nose then looked back to Clara for answers.

"First of all," Clara said, feeling an intense need to kiss away any remaining tears that slipped out. She banished the thought as quickly as it had entered her mind. "What can you tell me about you now? How are you different from when you were with Jimmy?"

Abby blew out a watery laugh. "I don't take any shit from anyone anymore."

Clara smiled with a nod. "Okay. What else?"

"I'm a lot stronger than I was before. I'm not afraid to do it on my own."

"Is that something you could have ever done with him? Or, if you hadn't married Jimmy, would you have grown into such a strong woman?"

Abby thought for a long minute, then finally shook her head. "No."

"There you go, see?" She rested her hands on Abby's knees, squeezing slightly. "It was all for a reason. Don't regret the bad in life, because ultimately it leads to the good."

Abby looked at Clara for a long moment, a soft smile on her lips. She shook her head in wonder. "You sure did get wise, Clara."

Clara felt warmth spread through her at the compliment, and also the way Abby was looking at her. It was as though she felt nothing but respect and admiration for her, and it felt damn good. "Thank you." She smiled, feeling the air around them becoming heavy. Uncomfortable with what she was feeling, Clara got to her feet and made her way around the desk to her chair.

Abby took that moment to get herself together, trying to swallow down her emotions. The caring in Clara's touch and the warmth in her eyes had made Abby want to just flat out break down, as long as Clara held onto her, offering her warmth and the unbelievable comfort and calm she seemed so filled with. That wasn't an option, so she got herself together, blowing her nose one last time and then faced her friend.

"Okay," she blew out. "What do you see in your crystal ball, oh psychic one?"

"Let me see." Clara closed her eyes for a moment, opening her mind and reaching out mentally, trying to taste the energy around her and get an image from it. A picture began to form inside her head. "I'm getting something, hold on..."

When Clara used the psychic side of her talents, as opposed to the medium-ship, it was always a strange feeling when something was coming. It felt like a strange pressure was building in her head, almost as though something were trying to push the information in front of her mind's eye. It was a literal pressure that eased into either an image, word, or feeling.

Slowly, an image began to bleed in, the feel of a stuffy, dark space all around her. "Abby, do you have a basement in your house?"

"Yes."

"What's in the box with the Barbie doll on it?"

Abby stared at her, stunned. "How did you know about that?"

"I'm seeing it. It's near..." Clara concentrated a bit, trying to see further into the vision of Abby's basement. "...it's near the table. It's a dark table, can't tell if it's cherry or painted, but it's dark."

"It's mahogany. My grandmother gave me that table."

"Okay. It's by that. A big box is next to it." Clara held her hands up to the size of the box she was seeing, her gaze locked onto the picture in her mind.

"Yeah, I know exactly what you're talking about. The Barbie box; it's pink and yellow?" At Clara's nod she continued. "It's next to the box my microwave came in. I had to buy a new one last year."

"Why do I keep seeing this Barbie box? What's in it, Abby? Why do I feel so drawn to this box?" Clara opened her eyes and looked at Abby, waiting.

Abby was looking down at her desk, fingers playing with a pencil, trying to keep her emotions under control.

"Abby?" Clara said softly. "Why does he want this box?" She felt in her gut that was exactly why James had come back, for whatever was in it.

A single tear slipped from Abby's closed eyes and rolled gracefully down her cheek. She wiped it away, but it was replaced by another. "Our daughter's pictures and some of her clothing is in that box," she finally said, looking up at Clara with very sad eyes.

Clara was stunned. "I didn't know you had a daughter."

"She died when we were in Ohio. That was one of the reasons I wanted to come back. I needed to be close to my family after that."

"Oh, jeez." Clara felt her shoulders slump as the news hit her between the eyes. Once again she found herself kneeling in front of her friend.

"God, I'm sorry." Abby laughed nervously, trying to clear up her tears. "I'm sorry to unload this on you, Clara. You didn't ask for this."

"Hey, no. Don't worry. I'm here, and I don't mind. Okay?" She waited until Abby met her gaze. "Let's get this figured out."

Abby nodded, once again taking the tissue offered her, and wiping her face and eyes. "Okay."

"Is there a reason why he would want that stuff? I mean, other than the fact that she was his daughter, that is. But, enough of a reason to bring him back into your life?"

Abby nodded. "If anything, he'll do it to hurt me. By taking the last bit of Alison from me, it would destroy me and he knows it."

Clara sat back on her haunches. "Would he be that vindictive? After all this time?"

"Yeah. That's how he is. He fought the divorce

tooth and nail." Abby took a loud, cleansing breath. "For whatever reason, I guess something crawled up into a deep, dark place and so he's back."

"Well, before I get you upset — though I think it's too late for that, let's reason this out. You know him better than I do. Do you think Jimmy will even contact you? Maybe he's been snooping around for some other reason."

Abby shook her head. "No. The minute you mentioned Alison's box, I knew you had hit the nail on the head."

Clara was about to respond when there was a soft knock on the door.

"Come in," Abby called out. The door opened and one of her employees peeked her head inside.

"Abby, you have a visitor."

From the all-too serious look on the girl's face, Abby's stomach fell. She turned and looked at Clara. "He's here."

The three walked down to the first floor in silence, Clara bringing up the rear after Abby. She kept her focus on her friend, ready to be there for her in a heartbeat.

The noise level in the pub had risen as the lunch hour approached, and workers from local businesses poured in for business meetings, or simply to enjoy the pub's famous cheeseburgers during their lunch break.

Clara scanned the place, looking for the man she'd seen at the wedding with Abby so many years back. He wasn't hard to miss as he sat on one of the few empty stools at the bar, his voice loud as he chatted with one of the pub's workers.

Abby steeled her resolve and walked up to her ex-husband. "Hi, Jimmy," she said, her voice strong.

The man sitting at the bar, dark hair slicked back from his face, turned to look at her. "Well, hello," he said, a charming smile on his handsome face. Clara thought he looked like a snake sizing up his prey, dark eyes trailing over Abby's body and face.

"What can I do for you, Jimmy?" Abby asked, crossing her arms over her chest, no nonsense, even though Clara could sense she was very afraid of the man.

"Not much, except have dinner with me. I want to talk to you about something."

Abby shook her head. "No. I'm not comfortable with that and you know it."

Clara stood back watching, able to feel the level of tension rising with every tick of the clock. She looked to Jimmy, curious as to what his response would be.

He stood from his stool, looking around to see who was paying attention to their conversation, not even giving Clara a second glance. "Abby, don't be dramatic. What do you think I'm going to do?" he said, voice lowered.

Abby took a small step back, inadvertently showing her fear of him as he advanced. "It doesn't matter. We have nothing to talk about anymore. Please leave."

Jimmy stared her down for a moment, making it clear he was trying to show his dominance. To Abby's credit, she didn't flinch or cower, but did begin to tremble slightly.

"We need to talk," he said, voice still quiet, almost calm. "I'll come by your place later."

"Please don't, Jimmy. We have nothing to talk about," Abby said again, her fear beginning to seep into her voice.

After a tense moment, Jimmy finished the drink that had been placed on the bar before him and left, not another word or glance spared at Abby. The pub owner waited until he'd left the establishment then breathed out a sigh of relief.

Clara looked at her. "Are you okay?"

Abby nodded, rubbing her hands over her arms. "I'm fine. Glad he's gone." She looked at Clara. "I'm sorry you had to see that."

Clara shook her head. "No need to apologize, Abby. You didn't invite him in here. I thought you handled it well."

Abby laughed ruefully. "I felt like a coward. God," she blew out a breath, running her hand through her hair. "Why does he make me so crazy?"

"Because you have a lot of history with him, and from the sounds of it, a lot of it is unpleasant and very negative. That doesn't just go away because a judge signs a paper and calls you divorced." She studied her friend for a moment, squeezing a shoulder. "Do you need anything? A drink? A valium?"

Abby broke into relieved laughter and shook her head. "No. No valium, and no drink. What I need is for him to forget where I live and work."

"Well, good luck with that one, but if you find a way and need help, let me know and I'll be there."

Abby smiled, grateful to have Clara there. "Well, I better get back to things, I guess." She uncrossed her arms and took a step toward Clara. "Thank you so much for everything, Clara. Truly, it means the world to me."

Clara accepted the hug she was offered and nearly melted into it. As she felt Abby's arms tighten around her, their bodies coming into contact, she realized she finally knew what heaven felt like. She closed her eyes and inhaled all that was Abby, knowing the blonde's wonderful floral scent would be on her clothes all day.

After a moment Abby stepped back and gave her a quick, but genuine smile, then headed back toward the stairs that led up to the second floor.

Chapter Forty-five

Abby wasn't sure exactly what Clara was doing, but stood back, studying her every move. The medium had told her she wanted to get a "feel for things," whatever that meant, and for the past ten minutes had been walking around the second floor of the pub, eyes closed, almost as if in a daze. Her movements were slow and measured, almost as though she was waiting for something to step out of a wall in front of her.

Clara stopped suddenly, hands out in front of her then a soft gasp escaped her lips.

Clara could feel a presence close to her as she wandered through the mirror image of the pub in the after shadow. She scanned her surroundings, seeing the inanimate shapes and shadows of the pool tables and scattered chairs. She could make out the jukebox, now silent and dark. Abby's shape loomed large and black, unwelcome in this strange, spirit world.

She turned toward the feel of the presence, only to stop suddenly, hands out in front of her in a natural instinct of defense. Standing not a foot away was a figure, its dark eyes focused on her. She gasped in her surprise, heart pounding out of her chest. She could feel a negative energy flowing from the figure, even though she couldn't clearly see his face. All she knew was it was a he and he didn't want her there. She took a slight step back, stopping when, in the blink of an eye, the figure was gone, yet again startling her.

From what seemed like a far distance, she heard her name.

Abby started as Clara jumped, whirling around when the pub owner placed a tentative hand on her arm. They both cried out in surprise, Abby's heart racing.

"Whoa," Clara said, shaking her head and rubbing her eyes. She looked around, almost as though seeing her surroundings for the first time. "Sorry."

"It's okay. Are you okay? You looked like you... well...like you saw a ghost." Abby grinned sheepishly.

Clara chuckled. "I did." She looked around, now seeing the room as Abby saw it: Stoney Brook Pub. "I saw someone."

"In the after shield?" Abby asked, trying to remember what Clara had called that other world.

"After shadow," Clara corrected. "Yeah. He was quick too." She was trying to feel his energy, but couldn't. It was almost as though he had just transported himself to another planet or something. "He was quick. Very quick. I don't think I've seen anything like that before. I can't even feel him now, which is unusual. Typically even once a spirit has left the room I can still feel their lingering energy." She shook her head as she studied one of the pool tables. "Not with this guy."

"Who is it, do you think?"

Clara shook her head. "No idea yet."

No sooner were the words out of her mouth than they heard something fall in the office. With a quick glance at each other, both women hurried toward the small room, led by Clara.

The room lit up with the flick of a switch, everything seemingly in perfect order to Clara's eyes.

Abby squeezed past her into the office and headed straight to one of the filing cabinets.

"How the hell did this happen?" she asked, bending down to pick something up. When she stood and turned to Clara, she held the handle to one of the drawers in her hand. Clara took the metal object from her, studying it. It was almost as though one of the screws that had been holding the handle onto the drawer had been wrenched loose, the actual hole for the screw bent slightly out of shape. The second screw was nowhere to be found.

"That's very strange, I must say," Clara said, realizing the immense understatement of her comment. She looked at the drawer itself, then to Abby. "Someone's trying to get our attention."

"Or make us go away."

"No," Clara said. "Something wants our attention."

"Is it a bad something?"

"Not sure."

Clara set the handle on top of the filing cabinet and turned her attention to the rest of the room. She reached out energy feelers, trying to connect with anything that was near. Almost like the sonar that a bat sends out, Clara waited for her energy to bounce off that of another. It didn't take long.

Abby watched, part fascinated, part frightened, as Clara made a beeline for the area behind the desk. The pub owner stood back, hugging herself as she watched, fighting against an intense need to leave.

Clara could feel the pull of the energy, leading her to the corner. She stopped at the side of the desk, gently pushing the chair aside. She felt almost as though a child were hunkered down in the corner, hiding.

She had no idea where Abby was, but didn't want to chance frightening the spirit. Clara held up a hand. "Don't move, Abby. Just stay back."

Abby said nothing, but moved farther away from the desk, careful in her movements.

Clara became only aware of what was before her. She reached out a hand, able to feel the energy shift, the corner cold. Letting out a soft breath, she closed her eyes and entered the after shadow. After a moment's concentration, she saw what she was looking for.

Huddled in the corner was a small figure. His face was pale, and it was very difficult to discern his features. All she could tell was he had dark hair, and it was a bit shaggy, hanging in his eyes. His shoulders were narrow, and Clara guessed he was no older than six, seven at most.

"Hey," Clara said, using the power of her thoughts to communicate with him. He looked up at her, blinking a few strands of hair out of deep-set eyes. "How can I help you?"

"Mamma?" he said, the word almost hopeful.

Clara shook her head. "No, sweetie. I'm sorry, I'm not your mom, but I can help you. Want my help? Are you the one who was trying to get my attention a few minutes ago?"

The boy nodded, then his head drooped again, face completely hidden by his arms, which were folded atop his bent knees.

"Do you want my help? Is that why you made the big noise?"

Again, the boy nodded, though he didn't look up at her again.

Clara got to her feet and walked over to Abby. "There's a little boy over there. He's the one who tried to get our attention." She nodded toward the corner where the child still sat.

Abby swallowed a bit nervously, but nodded her understanding.

"I'm going to cross him. Do you want to help me?"

"Yeah. Whatever you need."

"Okay. Come with me," Clara said, holding out her hand for Abby to take, which she did. Still holding her hand, Clara led Abby over to the desk, close to the boy. She faced Abby and met her gaze. "Give me your other hand." Both hands clasped, Clara gave her friend a gentle smile. "It's okay. Don't be afraid. What we're about to do is beautiful, not scary. Okay?"

Abby nodded, though she didn't feel near the confidence that was in the nod. "Okay. Just tell me what you need me to do."

"Right now I just need you to concentrate. I want you to try and clear your head completely. No thoughts, no emotions. Just nothingness."

Abby nodded. "Okay. I can do that."

"Good." Clara squeezed Abby's hands in a quick show of understanding then closed her eyes.

All color began to dissolve as Clara re-entered the after shadow. Immediately she saw the little boy, exactly where she'd left him, though now he was looking up at her, then at Abby's shadowy form, then back to Clara.

"Did you find my mamma?" he asked, slowly rising to his feet.

"No, sweetie," Clara said, holding out her hand to him. "But I'm going to help you now."

Slowly, ever watchful, the little boy walked over to Clara. It was only then that Clara saw — for a split second — a huge gash in the side of the boy's head. Blood had spurted out, staining his ear, down the side of his neck, and had matted his hair.

Clara gasped, startled for a moment. She blinked, and the wound was gone, leaving only a sweet-faced boy looking expectantly at her.

Abby felt Clara jerk slightly. She opened her eyes to see if she was okay. Though Clara's eyes remained closed, her face had screwed up into a look of shock and disgust then once again became expressionless.

"Are you okay?" she whispered. It was only after she received Clara's nod that she once again closed her own eyes, returning to her concentration.

Clara took his hand in her own, relieved when she saw the hallway appear out of the darkness. At the other end of the hall a door opened, the silhouette of her grandmother breaking through the blinding light that gushed in from the other side.

"Clara," Rebecca said, her voice soft. "Be careful this time. Be very careful."

Clara nodded and led the little boy toward her. Another figure stepped into the hallway from the other side, a small figure, which looked female. The figure stepped around Rebecca, staring down the hall, her features blocked by the bright light behind her.

"Douglas!" the figure screamed then began to run toward Clara and the little boy.

"Mamma!" he cried, pulling free of Clara and running toward the woman who fell to her knees, collecting the child in her arms.

Clara stood back and watched the touching scene, Rebecca moved to stand next to her, both silent for a moment. The woman stood, picking the boy up and holding him close.

"Beautiful," Clara said, a satisfied smile on her

lips.

"*Yes. Be careful though, Clara,*" Rebecca warned. "*There are more in this place.*"

Abby felt a rush of cold air wash over and through her, almost to the point of causing her to release Clara's hands. Clara seemed to sense that, as she tightened her grip, even as her eyes remained closed. Abby's eyes had opened when she'd felt the cold, and studied Clara. The medium's concentration was complete, her focus palpable as her brows drew. Abby followed the lines of Clara's face with her gaze, taking in her features, the shape of her mouth and the way her dark brows arched. She hadn't noticed before just how beautiful Clara really was. She'd always found her attractive, maybe even cute, but hadn't thought about it beyond that.

Abby was startled out of her observations when twilight eyes were suddenly looking into her own gaze. Abby cleared her throat, feeling somewhat stupid at being caught staring.

So involved in what was happening, Clara didn't realize she'd been the center of such intense scrutiny. She was still half in and half out of the after shadow, her senses slowly coming back to her as she realized she was staring at Abby.

"Hey," she said, voice low, serene.

"Hi. How did it go?"

"It went well. He crossed. Douglas was his name." Without thinking, she gently rubbed her thumbs over Abby's soft skin. "I think he's been rejoined with his mother, which was amazing." Her grin was contagious as Abby returned it.

"Clara, that's wonderful!" Abby tugged on Clara's hands, bringing them together in a tight hug.

Clara allowed herself to dissolve into the embrace, Abby's warmth washing through her. She could sleep forever in that embrace. Deciding on propriety, she disengaged, giving Abby a quick smile. "We're not done, yet. Come on. Let's get this place cleaned out."

Chapter Forty-six

Clara lay in bed, hands tucked behind her head as she stared up at the ceiling. She was on a high, completely satisfied and content. It had been a long night at the Stoney Brook, but so worth it.

She and Abby had worked for more than four hours to clear out the pub, and Clara was mentally and emotionally exhausted. But, oh she was happy! She had been able to clear the place and had crossed three spirits. She hadn't seen the strange, elusive spirit that she'd first seen and figured he'd left when he saw that he would be next.

Her mind fast-forwarded to the end of the night when Clara had crossed the final spirit in the Stoney Brook. Abby had joined her in her excitement of being done and feeling as though they'd truly accomplished something. Abby was also excited at the prospect of having her pub back. They had hugged.

A small thrill spread throughout her body, leaving little goose bumps on her arms. There was something about a hug from Abby that she couldn't quite put her finger on. Something that felt so...*right*. Something about Abby had called to Clara since the day she'd met her as a young teenaged girl. The day she'd been hit in the head by the soccer ball; an event she wouldn't forget for a couple reasons.

Clara smiled, tracing her fingers over the spot where she'd been hit, and ultimately knocked out. She also thought back to when she'd first seen who had seemed, at the time, to be an indifferent Abigail Jensen. She'd been so beautiful. She still was. She damn near took Clara's breath away every time she saw her. Not good. Not good at all. Dangerous, in fact. Clara knew this would likely result only in heartbreak for her, if she didn't get her thoughts and feelings under control.

Clara turned onto her side, hoping sleep would soon come, when she was startled by the sound of the doorbell. Sitting up in bed, she waited, seeing if it would ring again. It did. Grabbing her cell phone, Clara padded to the front room and pushed the curtains aside, relieved at first to see Abby's car, then concerned.

She quickly unlocked the front door, Abby standing on the other side.

"Hey. Are you okay?" Clara asked, looking around to see if anyone else was around. She had a bad feeling.

"I'm so sorry to come here so late. I can leave. I'm sure I woke you up—"

"Get in here," Clara interrupted, tugging on Abby's wrist until she stepped inside the house. Clara closed and locked the door, turning to Abby for an explanation.

"When I was driving home from the Stoney Brook, I saw Jimmy's car in my neighborhood. I felt uneasy, so I went to an all-night diner, hoping to kill some time so he'd leave. He was still there, so I came here. I mean, I can go to Kerri's place, I'm so sorry I woke you up. It's just that I know he doesn't know you or where you live, so…"

"Hey, it's okay." Clara gave the flustered woman a quick hug then led her farther into the house to the kitchen. "What can I get you? Coffee? Water? Juice?"

Abby took a seat at the table. "Actually, do you

have anything stronger?" Abby ran a hand through her hair, looking tired and somewhat haggard. "I'm usually not a drinker, but I need one now."

"Sure. Let me see what I've got."

Within ten minutes, both women were seated on the couch, a glass of vodka and orange juice in hand. Abby hadn't said much as she stared straight ahead, sipping from her drink. Clara remained quiet, waiting for Abby to speak, as she sensed she needed to. She was obviously very bothered by the sudden appearance of her ex-husband in her life again.

"I'm really grateful for your kindness," Abby said at length, setting her drink down on the coffee table and turning on the couch to face her new friend.

"Absolutely. You're welcome here any time, Abby. Day or night."

"Thank you. I'm sure I'm overreacting, but I don't know. When I saw his car, I just kind of freaked out a little. I don't trust him."

"And it sounds like you've got good reason not to. When I met him the other day, I didn't like him immediately. I really felt a kind of sliminess to him."

Abby nodded, picking up her drink again. She took a sip, wincing as the vodka burned on the way down. "You're not the first person to say that. Hell, my own mother didn't like him." She smiled a bit at that, the alcohol beginning to loosen her emotions a bit. She thought for a moment. "Come to think of it, I don't think anyone did."

"Why did you marry him?" Clara asked, sipping her own drink. She knew the vodka would hit her hard, as she hadn't had alcohol in many years. The vodka had been a gift from Raymond when she was in California. She'd never opened it, but had carried it with her. Good thing.

"Because he was cute, to be honest. God, how bad is that?" Abby finished her drink and raised her glass, silently asking if she could have another.

"Help yourself."

Within a few moments she sat back down, her glass filled with a fresh drink. "He was cute, he was charming, and he won me over." She giggled. "I was so stupid, Clara. I mean really stupid."

"We all do stupid things, Abby. You've got to know that." Clara was feeling her own senses beginning to numb, the vodka making steady progress through her system.

They sat in silence for a long moment, a clock down the hall ticking away the seconds. Finally Abby glanced at her, a shy, somewhat mischievous look in her eyes.

"You know, I always wanted to know you better when we were younger. I wanted to talk to you. I was actually bummed when you went to another high school. I was a senior, and it was my only chance to really talk to you. To really get to know you."

Clara was surprised to hear it and leaned forward a bit. "Really? Are you serious?"

"Yes, ma'am. I am serious," Abby said with somewhat buzzed conviction. "I always thought you were fascinating!"

Clara's grin was wide, her eyes bright from both her drink and the new information she'd just heard. "Why? What was so interesting about me?"

"I don't know." Abby studied Clara for a moment, her head tilted slightly to the side in contemplation. "I guess it was just the way you looked at life. And, that day at Dairy Queen, when you told me my grandma would be okay, somehow it changed me. I became intrigued by you."

Clara burst into laughter. "Do you mean to tell me that you didn't see me as the freak Kerri did?"

Abby shook her head vigorously. "Never."

"I thought you were gorgeous." Clara regretted the words the moment they were out of her mouth. Her eyes got wide as she met Abby's surprised gaze, then quickly turned to her drink, taking a healthy gulp, the punishing burn sliding down her throat.

"Really?" Abby asked after a moment, a slow grin spreading across her face.

Clara could only nod, setting her near-empty glass aside. She finally found the courage to meet Abby's gaze. "Yep."

"Thank you. That's really cool to hear. But, I guess everyone is gorgeous at sixteen, huh? Young, in their prime." She snorted bitterly. "Now..."

"You're still gorgeous, Abby. Nothing's changed there."

Abby's smile was so pure, so sweet, it melted Clara's heart. "You are so sweet, Clara. I have to admit, after living with Jimmy for so long, I guess I just don't see it anymore. It makes me so angry because before, when I used to look in the mirror, I saw a woman who was maybe not a supermodel — too short to be one of those — but was pretty enough. Now." She sighed heavily. "Now I see a woman almost thirty, who has seen better days."

Clara could only stare, looking at the beautiful woman who sat just a few feet away, stunned to hear such defeat in her voice. "Oh, Abby. That is so not true! Don't you ever look in the mirror?"

Abby chuckled, shaking her head. "No more than

I have to, Clara. I'm afraid my self-confidence isn't what it used to be."

"That breaks my heart, Abby. It breaks my heart bad." The alcohol dumbed her senses enough to allow her to reach over and place a hand on her friend's leg. "You're beautiful, hot as hell even, and shouldn't hide away from that. Jimmy isn't worth doing that to you. He's an asshole of the lowest order and never deserved you in the first place."

Abby was surprised by Clara's impassioned speech, able to feel the heat of Clara's palm through the denim of her jeans. She looked into those twilight eyes and saw just how serious Clara really was.

"You are intelligent, kind, and sweet, and a wonderful woman who owns her own business — a *successful* business, I might add—who should be proud of who she's become. You're loved and respected within your community. I mean, hell, your customers absolutely adore you! Even my ex-girlfriend does, for crying out loud!"

Abby listened, feeling emotions rise within her. It had been far too long since she'd heard anyone talk to her like Clara was at that moment. She was building her up, making Abby feel better than she had in a long time. Overwhelmed, she stood, pulling Clara to her feet as well.

Clara went into the hug, surprised by the move, but then quickly fell into it, wrapping her arms around Abby's back as Abby's arms wrapped around her neck, holding her close. They stood in silence for nearly ten minutes, each just absorbing the warmth of the other. Clara could feel her heart pounding in her chest, nervous energy speeding through her body. But, on the other side of that token, she felt more at ease and comforted than she ever had in her life. The feel of Abby's arms, the feel of her body, the feel of her head resting on Clara's shoulder, was more wonderful than anything Clara had ever experienced before.

Abby, for her part, was lost in a sensation of absolute comfort. She could hear Clara's heart beating, and it put her at ease, somehow. She felt like in that moment, with Clara near to her, she could do anything. How was it that Clara could make her feel like everything would be okay? Make her believe that she *was* beautiful. Was worth something to someone else. The feeling was intoxicating.

இ.ஐ.

It had been three days since Abby had shown up on Clara's doorstep in the middle of the night, and the two women had shared some truths. Abby had spent the night sleeping in the guest room, and had been gone by the time Clara woke up the next morning. At first, she had been afraid that maybe she'd taken it too far, the things she'd admitted to Abby, and had been hesitant to contact her. Abby had contacted her, instead. They had had dinner the following night, and nothing they'd spoken about at Clara's house had come up. Other than some of Abby's fears of Jimmy, that is.

Now, three days later, Clara walked into the Stoney Brook. Her plan was to surprise Abby and take her to lunch. She spotted the pub owner immediately, standing behind the bar. She was leaning on the polished mahogany, a smile on her face and laughter in the air. When Clara saw who she was talking to, a stab of jealousy shot through her.

Jordan Crossland, head investigator of the CPS,

was sitting at the bar, doing his best to put the moves on Abby. Even from across the room, Clara could see he was flirting with his former client.

Instant irritation spread like wildfire, and Clara decided it wasn't wise for her to approach the two just yet. She didn't want to cause any problems or seem like she was overstepping bounds she had no right to even toe. Instead, she was grateful to see Shelby and the same two women sitting at a corner table. One of the women had noticed Clara, and had gotten Shelby's attention. The blonde waved Clara over.

"Hey!" Shelby jumped out of her chair and gave Clara a tight hug, which Clara happily returned. "Come sit with us."

Abby glanced past Jordan's shoulder, following Clara's progression across the bar to Shelby's table. She remembered the two women had once been in a relationship and felt a strange surge of discomfort as the two women embraced.

"What?" she said, her voice a bit harsher than it should have been. She missed what Jordan had said to her and forced her attention back to him.

"I said, we need to get some dinner some night," he said, flashing a charming smile her way.

Clara glanced over at the bar, watching as Jordan reached over and touched Abby's hand. It was all she could do to not growl. She hadn't cared much for Jordan Crossland the night of the investigation, and she was even less fond now.

"Clara? Are you okay?" Shelby asked, following her ex's line of sight to the beautiful pub owner. Her brows rose in recognition of the longing on Clara's face, as well as obvious jealousy. "Oh boy."

"Huh?" Clara asked, oblivious to Shelby's

realizations. "Sorry. Yeah, I'm fine." She turned and faced the three women at the table, deciding to forget about Abby and be social.

Abby watched as Clara spoke to the three women, her movements animated and excited. She often turned to speak to Shelby, at one point the former lovers leaning in close, Shelby bursting into laughter at something Clara said.

"You okay, boss?" asked one of Abby's employees, who was tending bar with the pub owner.

Abby nodded, turning away from Clara's side of the bar. "I'm fine." She smiled at the girl then went to help a customer who had just sat down. Jordan had left a few minutes before, and she was glad. She hadn't been thrilled to sit and talk to him as it was, let alone when she was feeling less than friendly.

After helping a line of customers who had come in for after-work drinks, she glanced over to where Clara had been sitting. All four women were standing, and Clara and Shelby were hugging, then Shelby placed a quick kiss on Clara's lips. Abby looked away, her blood heating. Within moments, Clara was standing at the bar; Shelby and her friends had left with Shelby raising a hand of greeting to Abby on her way out.

Clara took a deep breath, trying to get the vision of Jordan flirting with Abby out of her head. She rested her elbows on the bar, waiting for Abby to notice her.

"Hey," Abby said, forcing a smile onto her face and in her voice. She was unsettled by the feelings that had stirred when she saw Clara with Shelby.

"Hey, yourself. I had intended to come in to take you to lunch, but saw you were busy with Jordan, so..." Clara glanced at the clock on the wall, "guess we missed the lunch hour."

Abby was surprised by what sounded like bitterness in Clara's voice. She felt her own hackles rise, not only from the tone but the fact that maybe if Clara had said something to her, rather than spending her time laughing and talking with Shelby, they could have gone out.

She put a sweet smile on her lips. "Well, I guess losing yourself talking to friends didn't help either, did it?"

Clara looked at her for a moment, surprised by both the words, as well as the fact that Abby seemed bothered that Clara had been sitting with the women. Or was that just the hope of her imagination? Either way, she didn't want the day to turn bad. She'd come to be nice, not fight.

"Guess it was just a missed opportunity, huh?" She smiled, as genuine as she could, to try and take the sting out of the situation. "Not meant to be."

Abby chuckled, shaking her head at her own silliness. "Yeah. Not meant to be. That's too bad, because I would have loved to go with you." She leaned on the bar. "How about dinner instead?"

Clara's grin was blinding. "Yes! Absolutely."

"Excellent! Okay. I'm actually glad you came because I have something I want to ask you too."

"Oh?"

"Yep, but that'll wait until dinner. I want to be able to talk to you about it." Abby glanced over at a large group of patrons who had just entered the pub, laughing and talking and heading straight for the bar.

"Guess I should let you get to it. How about I pick you up at your place at around six thirty?"

"Perfect." Abby nodded her agreement, already making her way toward the new arrivals. "See you then!"

Chapter Forty-seven

Clara glanced once more at her list, making sure she'd gotten everything on it.

"Crap. Bagels."

She crumpled the piece of notebook paper and shoved it into her pocket on her way to the bakery area of the grocery store. She pushed her half-filled grocery cart down the aisle, the fluorescent lights above shining on the highly polished tile at her feet. She smiled at a young mom and her child as she passed them, then turned out of the aisle and into the main drag that ran along the dairy and meat counters.

She turned down the bread aisle, and when she stopped, she saw an elderly woman deciding on a loaf of bread for herself halfway down the aisle. Standing not far from the woman's near-empty cart was an elderly man dressed in golfing pants and shoes, his silver hair pushed back away from his heavily lined face. He looked at Clara, smiled then vanished before her eyes.

Clara stood rooted to the spot, gaze still frozen to where the man had stood not two seconds before. She wanted to turn and walk away, but knew she couldn't.

"Bagels," she muttered to herself. "I need bagels, then I can leave."

Heading down the aisle, she saw the bagels, which were just beyond the woman's cart. She hurried past the woman, turning to look at the array of differing brands and flavors. She was about to grab a package of cinnamon raisin bagels when she felt a presence behind her.

Levi... Tell her I love her...

Clara could hear the voice in her head, whispery and kind. She ignored it, tossing the package of bagels into her cart, ready to hurry out of the aisle.

Please tell her... Levi...

Clara stopped, eyes squeezing shut for a moment, as she wrestled with her indecision. She didn't want to get involved yet her conscience wouldn't allow her to walk away.

Turning back toward the older woman, she took a deep breath and backed her cart up until she was next to the woman. Clearing her throat, she spoke. "Hi, my name is Clara, and I have a really strange message for you."

The woman looked up at Clara, her blue eyes watery and dull. "Excuse me?"

"I know it sounds strange, but I have a message for you."

"From who? Do I know you, dear?"

"No, ma'am, you don't. And it's from Levi." Clara nearly took a step back as a look of shocked rage began to fill those pale blue eyes. "I mean no harm, ma'am, I swear. I'm a medium, and Levi asked me to tell you he loves you."

"Who are you?" the woman asked, her voice lowering in her anger. Her already watery eyes were beginning to fill even more.

"He looked like he was in the middle of a good golf game," Clara said, hoping the bit of detail would mean something to the woman and make her believe.

Almost as if beyond her control, the woman's

smile broke through the clouds. She brought a heavily veined hand up, wiping at a tear with her fingers. "Only Levi would come back wearing golf attire."

Clara smiled. "Cleats and everything."

"Does that mean they have a course in Heaven?" the old woman asked, her voice serious, questioning eyes hopeful.

"I guess so." Clara nodded. "He looked awfully happy, and he was standing here next to you while you were selecting your bread."

The woman seemed to take in what she'd been told, then looked up at Clara, a warm smile on her face. "Thank you for telling me, honey. My Levi always told me he'd come back and say hello. Guess he has."

"Yes, ma'am, he has. You're very welcome." Clara squeezed the woman's arm lightly, then turned and walked away, warmth spreading throughout her whole body, muttering to herself, "Okay, so that was nice, but I can't get back into this. I can't."

❧❧❧❧

Clara took Abby to a small café downtown that they both enjoyed. Typically, the best places to eat were the locally owned, hole-in-the-wall types. They found a table near the front windows and waited for someone to take their orders.

"So, how did your day go?" Clara asked, glancing through the plain paper menu. She glanced over the top at her friend before turning back to the sandwich listings.

"Pretty well. Busy." A moment of heavy silence hung between them. Each woman had questions about what had happened that day. Abby had tried to put it out of her mind after Clara had left the Stoney Brook, but hadn't been able to. She was deeply bothered by the hot jealousy that had grabbed her that day and could not figure out where it had come from. But how could she bring it up? How could she ask Clara about it, when she didn't understand it herself? It made no sense.

"Good. I assume busy is good anyway, right?" Clara asked, tossing her menu aside, having made her choice.

"Yes. It's definitely good."

Clara could feel the slight tension in the air and wasn't sure what to do about it. How could she possibly explain that her blood had run hot when she'd seen Abby talking to Jordan? How could she ask Abby why she'd been so snippy about Clara talking to Shelby? What a mess.

They sat in silence for a moment, both grateful when the waitress came and took their orders. Left alone once more, Abby decided to tell Clara about her planned trip.

"So, what I wanted to ask you was if you could possibly get your schedule free this weekend. With all this stuff happening with Jimmy — he drove by again last night, by the way — I just really feel the need to get away. My grandma lives in a gorgeous farmhouse up in the mountains."

Clara listened, wondering what this had to do with her. She had her hopes, but was afraid to really let herself think about what she wanted Abby to say.

"I've told her all about you too. My grandma has always been fascinated by the spirit world and wants to meet you."

"Is this the one who had the surgery?"

"Yes!" Abby brightened, nodding. "So? Are you

up for it? Want to head over the river and through the woods this weekend with me?"

"To grandmother's house we go?" Clara asked, finishing the Christmas song. Abby laughed, nodding. Clara's heart was pounding. "Yes. Absolutely!"

"Wonderful!"

After a moment, their food came and they ate in silence, both women yet again contemplating the same thing, yet neither willing to talk about it first or ask the first question. Instead, Clara decided to tell Abby about the incident in the grocery store. Abby was completely drawn in by the story, her eyes wide, never making a sound as she ate and listened. Finally when Clara was done, she grabbed her napkin and wiped her mouth.

"Clara," she said, tossing her napkin into her empty plate. "Why don't you go into business again? Call me crazy, but somehow I don't see your destiny as working behind the scenes in a bakery."

Clara shook her head, taking a bite of her own sandwich. "I can't, Abby. After Mike died, I gave it up."

"I know. But don't you think you're doing him an injustice by quitting? I mean, Clara, you've been given this unbelievable gift! How can you just walk away from that? You have the ability to help so many people. I mean, jeez, look what you did for me. You've given me peace. Made my pub safe again for my employees." She caught Clara's gaze and wouldn't let it go. "There's nothing in the world like being able to do something for people that no one else can. Please don't give that up on a principle."

Clara sat back in her chair, chewing the last bit of her food. She stared out the window into the darkening evening beyond. A few people walked by the café, but overall the streets and sidewalks were fairly quiet.

"You know, today, when I was walking up to the pub, I passed an empty building close to the Stoney Brook. A For Rent sign on the window." She sighed, sipping from her water. "For just a minute I had this fantasy of opening up a shop there. You know, doing readings for clients, plus maybe offering some products: candles, incense, books. That kind of thing."

Abby could see the war that was going on inside her friend. She could hear the longing in her voice and see the determination to stick by her guns in her eyes. "What made you think that?" she asked quietly, trying to play it nonchalant.

"I don't know. Opening a store like that has never even crossed my mind before." Clara grinned. "Maybe watching my mom slave at the bakery all these years has made me want to follow the same fate."

"Or, maybe you're finally seeing what your destiny is," Abby said, a challenge in her voice. She eyed Clara, daring her to disagree.

"You think so?"

"I do. I've always felt there was something special about you. Something that very few in this world have."

Clara thought for a long moment, playing with the straw in her water. She sighed, finally saying out loud what she'd barely dared say to herself. "You know, for about the past year I've felt lost. I basically got up, went to work, did what I was supposed to do, then went home. I rarely went out, rarely did anything. My family was even questioning why I didn't have any friends, didn't try to rekindle any old relationships." She sighed.

"Well, I don't know. Seems like you and Shelby

have rekindled something." Abby regretted the words as soon as they were out of her mouth. She knew she couldn't take them back, so she tried to cover it with a joking smile.

Clara saw right through the innocent, just-kidding act. She studied Abby for a moment, a slow smirk spreading across her lips. "You think so?"

"Well, I mean, I think it's great. You guys were together at one point, after all, and hey, why not, right? She's a pretty girl. So..." Abby let her voice trail off, already feeling stupid.

Clara leaned forward in her seat, pinning her friend with her gaze. "Abby, were you jealous?" she asked quietly, amused and extremely pleased.

Abby began to fidget slightly in her seat, feeling every ounce of the weight behind Clara's stare. She couldn't meet those eyes and instead focused on her napkin. "I think jealous is too strong of a word," she back-pedaled, but it was too late, and they both knew it.

"Is it?"

Abby decided to try another angle. "Well, it sounds like she hurt you. I mean, she wasn't exactly keen on your gift and not real supportive, so..." She shrugged. "I guess I just worry about you. I know right now you're pretty vulnerable with this stuff, just starting up with it again. I don't want her to dissuade you."

They both knew Abby was only telling a half-truth, but Clara decided to let it go. For now. They'd return to that subject again, and she'd make Abby squirm. However, since the subject had been brought up, she wanted to know the details about Jordan Crossland. "What was up with Jordan today? Does he come to see you a lot?"

Abby grinned, a twinkle entering her eyes. She definitely knew jealousy when she saw it, and she saw it in Clara's eyes. "He's come in a few times. He's a friend. He asked me to go to dinner with him."

Clara felt her blood begin to boil all over again. "Abby, he's a jerk! He's a player, and will only end up hurting you in the end. I hope you didn't tell him yes."

Abby's grin grew. "And what if I did?"

Clara shrugged, trying to act indifferent. "Then it's your broken heart. Don't say I didn't warn you."

"All right, I promise to not say you didn't warn me, especially since I told him no."

The relief that washed through Clara was palpable. She tried to hide it while taking a drink of her water. She heard Abby's soft chuckle. "What?"

Abby shook her head, thoroughly amused. "Nothing." She decided to change the subject. "So, will it be hard to get the time off this weekend?"

Clara shook her head. "Nah. Having your mother for your boss has its perks."

Abby smiled. "Brownnoser."

Chapter Forty-eight

As promised, Abby's grandmother's house was amazing. It was a two-story farmhouse, the type seen in any Norman Rockwell painting. It had actually been built in New Hampshire in the late 1840s, but Abby's great-grandparents had the ancestral home moved to the mountains of Colorado in the 1930s, where it had been ever since.

The house was white, all the windows framed in shutters painted a dark green, as was the trim on the house. It sat on three hundred and thirty-three acres of land, outbuildings scattered across the property.

"I spent a lot of my time as a kid in the Other House," Abby said as she maneuvered her way along the winding drive that was more than two miles long.

"The Other House? What is that? How many houses does your grandma have up here?"

"One." Abby smiled at Clara's confusion. "My grandma calls it the Summer Kitchen too."

"Okay, but what the hell is it?"

Abby laughed. "Ye of no farmer knowledge. It's a smaller, separate building from the main house that basically looks like a mini version. Inside are two main rooms, one a complete kitchen — stove, sinks, cabinets and all. And, below it is a root cellar."

"What is that?" Clara asked, having no clue what Abby was talking about. She'd heard of a root cellar before, but had no idea what one actually was.

"You store canned goods there. My grandma used to can jams and syrups, tomatoes, all kinds of stuff. Back in the days before electricity — which they didn't get up here until the 1960s, by the way — everything that needed to stay cool or be stored went below ground in the root cellar."

"Ah. So, it's cold down there?"

"Very."

Abby pulled up in front of the beautiful old house, a stone chimney rising proudly above the roofline. The car tires crunched their way to a stop on the gravel drive. Clara stepped out of the car, slinging her backpack over her shoulder and looked around. The house was beautiful, the scenery surrounding it even more so.

"Did you come up here often as a kid?"

"All the time," Abby said, leading the way toward the house. "This," she said, indicating a white building to their left, the main house to their right, "is the Other House. I'll take you in there. In fact, you might actually be staying in there tonight." They walked past it, Clara noting the small chimney that jutted up from the sloped roof. "A couple years before Grandpa died, they converted the kitchen area into a sort of living area for him. He couldn't climb the stairs in the main house anymore, so he slept out here, instead."

They entered through a door, which was actually the back door of the house. The front of the house, with its wraparound porch, faced the road, but to reach it required a trek across the beautifully manicured lawn, edged with a colorful rose garden.

The back door led to the kitchen, which was bursting with wonderful smells and the heat of a recently used oven and stove. An older woman dressed in the typical clichéd housedress was placing a steaming pot of something on the round oak kitchen table. When she turned around to greet the two women, her fire engine-red lipstick threw Clara for a loop. Perhaps there was more to her than a typical housewife/grandma. Clara could immediately feel her energy, which was wonderful.

"Grandma!" Abby exclaimed, hurrying across the small distance to the woman, who immediately engulfed her in a tight hug.

"Hello, my love!"

Clara stood back and watched with a mixture of joy and a small bit of envy at the beautiful reunion. She had never been terribly close to her living grandmother. Certainly not like Abby obviously was with hers. But then, who else could say they were so close with their *dead* grandmother?

Abby pulled away from her grandmother and turned toward Clara. "Grandma, I'd love for you to meet Clara. This is the friend I've told you about."

"Ah, yes. I definitely remember hearing about you." A much older version of Abby stepped over to Clara, extending a warm hug to her, as well. Clara accepted it, which surprised her, as it defied her usual touch-me-not attitude. "Your abilities have intrigued my granddaughter for quite a long time."

Abby looked away, suddenly very uncomfortable, which Clara found very interesting. "Well, things have just kind of slipped out from time to time when I've been around my grandma."

"Oh, I don't think so. I think it's far more than that, Clara." Abby's grandmother gave her a wide, brilliant smile. "Let's sit down and eat." She turned back to a somewhat-blushing Abby. "I made your favorite."

"Potato soup?" Abby asked with child-like glee.

Her grandmother chuckled. "Just for you. Come on, sit and eat. If I know you, you've worked yourself to the bone and not taken proper care of yourself. Look at you! You're all skin and bones!" She took one of Abby's slim wrists in her hand and held her arm out so she could get a better look at her. "Honey, why don't you eat?"

Abby looked embarrassed as she spared a glance to Clara before turning back to her grandmother. "I do! Grandma, I weigh more now than I have in four years." She looked down at herself. "Where do you see I'm skin and bones?" She slapped the itty-bitty tummy she'd gained. "Look at that! That is hardly skinny."

Grandma clucked her disapproval and turned to Clara for an ally. "Don't you think she's too thin, Clara?"

Put on the spot, Clara put her hands up in supplication. "No, no. I don't want to get pulled into a family dispute."

"Smart girl, that one," Grandma said, amused. She let the women sit down and began to fuss over them, making sure they had enough to eat, more bread, more milk, more water. Clara wasn't used to such treatment but had to admit that she enjoyed it. It was also the best potato soup she'd ever had!

༄༅།༄།

The Other House was a small space, almost like a studio cottage with two rooms and a basement, which as Abby had said, was basically a cold storage room. In the main room, which used to have a fridge and stove in it, now had only counters, cabinets, and a sink. The back wall was lined with built-in shelves, which were filled with boxed games such as checkers, chess, Monopoly, and Risk.

"I remember these games," Clara said, pulling The Game of Life from the shelf.

"I used to play Connect Four with my cousins all the time when I was a kid," Abby said, tapping the box with a finger. "My grandma has had these games forever. A lot of them clear back from when my dad was a kid, I think."

Clara looked around the room she'd be staying in for the night. A nice, comfy couch folded out into a double bed, which Abby walked over to, tossing the cushions onto the floor.

"This bed is so comfortable. After Grandpa died, Grandma put this couch in here for guests." She grinned at her friend. "I've slept on this couch many a night. Especially during the worst nights of my marriage."

"I'm glad you broke it in for me."

"Yes I did. Along with my Aunt Linda and her kids, that is." She began to make up the bed with the pile of linens Grandma had given her, Clara moving to the other side of the bed to help.

"Where will you sleep tonight, and why aren't you out here?"

"I'll be in the second bedroom upstairs in the main house. Grandma snores like a freight train, and I don't want you to have to deal with that. You'll have plenty of privacy out here."

There was a moment of silence and a growing tension that Clara could feel. They looked at each other then found other things in the room to keep their attention.

"Oh!" Abby said, excited to have found something else to show Clara. She hurried over to the fireplace, grabbing a small white remote from the mantle. "If you get cold — because it does get cold up here at night — feel free to start a fire." She pushed one of the two buttons on the remote, a fire whooshing to life in its brick prison.

Clara immediately felt the warmth against her skin and stared down into the flames for a moment. "So beautiful. You know, I've always wanted to have a fireplace in my room."

"Here's your chance. Even if it is only for a night."

Excitement of the fireplace fading, the tension returned. Clara held her hands down at her sides, her fingers wanting to reach out to Abby and touch something, *anything*.

"I suppose I should head to the house," Abby said, her voice soft. She looked over at Clara, the flames dancing in her beautiful eyes. "Is there anything else you need?"

Clara shook her head, not sure what else to say, or even if her voice would work.

"Okay." Abby reached for her, taking her in a tight hug, which Clara expected to pull away from within a few moments, but Abby stayed where she was, her head resting on Clara's shoulder.

They stood in front of the fireplace for what must have been five minutes or more, neither woman willing to relinquish the comfort and warmth of the other.

"I'm really glad you came up with me, Clara," Abby whispered, tightening the hug.

Clara's eyes fell closed, lost in the sensation of

Abby against her. She nodded, the fragrant blonde hair tickling her nose. "Me, too. Thanks for inviting me."

Abby smiled, looking down at the fire as Clara held her. "I thought you might think it odd that I invited you. I mean, here we've just barely become friends over the last few weeks, and then I go and ask you to come with me for a weekend at my grandma's house."

Unwittingly, Clara returned the smile. "I was happy. I like having you in my life." There was silence for a long moment, and Clara's heart clenched. She hoped she hadn't said too much or given too much away.

Abby pulled back from the hug, but stayed within Clara's personal space. She looked into Clara's eyes, studying her for a moment before a soft smile touched her lips.

"I am, too. I'm not sure how, but somehow you bring something to it, add a bit of sparkle that wasn't there before."

"It's all my wit," Clara joked, a nervous smile on her face. The tension seemed to double within the span of five minutes. It now hung heavily in the air around them.

"Maybe so." Abby squeezed Clara's arm playfully. "Or maybe it's all your scary ghost-spotting stories. It's not every day a girl gets to be regaled with such tales, you know."

"Well, it's not every day a girl gets to regale someone who appreciates such tales as much as you do."

"That I do." Abby knew she needed to just step away and go to bed, but she couldn't make her body obey. She didn't want to leave. She didn't want to

head to the main house and go to bed. She wanted...
She wasn't sure, but it had nothing to do with leaving
Clara.

"Are things pretty good at the pub?" Clara asked,
trying desperately to think of a topic that would keep
Abby there longer.

"Seems to be. I think you did the trick. I still wish
you'd let me pay you something for that."

Clara shook her head vehemently. "Not a chance.
I was glad to do it. And," she shrugged, "who knows.
Maybe you're helping me to get back to where I should
be. Maybe," she qualified with a raised brow at the
growing grin on Abby's face. "We'll see."

"I'm sure we will. You'll be back to doing readings
within a month."

"You think so, huh?"

"Yes, I do." Abby held out a hand. "Bet me you
don't."

"What's the bet?" Clara asked, knowing full well
that this was a bet she was likely to lose. The crazy thing
was, part of her was very okay with that.

"Okay, let's see." Abby thought for a moment. "I
bet you dinner and a movie that you do. You pay."

"And if I don't?"

"Then a movie, but I'll make you dinner."

"Deal." To Clara it was pretty much a win-win,
so she gladly took Abby's hand to shake on it.

"Excellent!" Abby held on to Clara's hand as
she grew serious. "I really do want to see you get back
into it, Clara. Nothing makes you look more alive than
when you're helping someone with this stuff. It's part
of you. In your heart and soul."

Clara looked away for a moment, looking into
the flames which continued to pop and sizzle. "You

know me far too well, Abby." She met her friend's smiling gaze.

"Of course I do. I look at you and it's like looking into glass. I don't know, somehow you're just very easy for me to read. I can see what Mike's death did to you, but I can also see what it's doing to you to be so far off your path." She reached a hand up, brushing some bangs out of Clara's eyes. "Those beautiful eyes of yours. They should only be filled with life and sparkle, not the drudgery of heading back and forth to a bakery all day." She shook her head. "It's not you."

Clara sighed, trying to hold back the sudden emotion that had built in her chest. To have someone truly see her, truly look at her and inside her soul, touched her far more than she could have imagined.

"Thank you," she said softly, taking Abby's hand in her own and bringing the knuckles to her mouth. She gently kissed them then held the joined hands to her chest. "It's nice for someone to see me. It hasn't happened in a very long time."

Abby stepped forward, intending to place a simple kiss on Clara's lips, a kiss of understanding, a kiss of friendship. Somehow, it became far more than that.

Clara was shocked when she felt the soft contact, which quickly became bolder. Within moments she had her arms around Abby, pulling her closer as Abby's hands wound themselves into her hair. The kiss quickly deepened, both women breathing hard as the fire began to rage.

Far too soon for Clara's liking, Abby pulled away, breathless and wide-eyed. She stared at Clara, her mouth opening and closing as she attempted to say something, but nothing came. Finally she cleared her throat, taking two steps back.

"I'm sorry, Clara. That was totally inappropriate of me." She quickly turned away, hurrying toward the door, tossing a "good night" over her shoulder.

Alone, Clara stood frozen in place, her skin still tingling from the feel of Abby's hands and mouth. She didn't know what to do or say, her heart still hammering in her chest.

Chapter Forty-nine

The early morning air was crisp and cold. Clara hadn't packed for it, so she had wrapped up in a crocheted blanket she'd found in the Other House. Abby's grandmother's land was gorgeous in the predawn hours; the wildlife could be heard in the distant forest lands, the moon beginning to fall as a new day readied to dawn.

She'd had little sleep, the events of the evening playing and replaying in her mind. She couldn't help but wonder if somehow she'd been responsible or could have maybe stopped it. She worried what Abby was thinking, and wondered if their fragile new friendship was forever damaged or ruined. So many questions, and a long drive back home too.

"You're out here early," came a soft voice from the darkness. Clara cried out in surprise as Abby's grandma appeared, seemingly out of nowhere. The old woman chuckled, amused. "Sorry. Didn't mean to scare you."

"No, it's okay, Mrs.—"

"Grandma. Everyone calls me that, and you will too," Grandma tsked, joining Clara as they began to make their way across the moon-swept yard.

"Grandma. It's your house, so by all means."

"Scare you all I want?" Grandma teased.

Clara chuckled with a nod. "I guess so."

They walked on in silence before Grandma

spoke. "Ever since my husband died I've had trouble sleeping. I come out here, usually around four thirty in the morning or so, and walk. Sometimes I can get back to sleep after, sometimes not."

"You miss him?"

"Very much. But, it's not why you'd think, sadly. I mean, yes, I do miss him, but our marriage was rocky for so many years that in some ways it was a relief." She glanced over at Clara. "That may sound pretty terrible to you."

Clara shook her head. "Everyone has their reasons for everything they do, Grandma. No one can say any different. You have your reasons."

"That I do. But, I won't bore you with that." She waved off the subject. "I can't sleep because for so many years he'd wake me up either coming in, or because of his emphysema. He had a horrible cough that always kept me awake. I guess I got so used to it that I can't stand the quiet now."

"I can understand that." Clara pulled the blanket a little tighter around her, the morning at its chilliest right before the sun rose.

"So, why are you out here, young Clara? What kept you from sleep?"

Clara wanted to laugh out loud at that question but decided against it. She didn't want to have to explain things to Abby's grandmother, especially since Abby may very well hate her come rise of the sun.

"Just can't sleep. That happens sometimes."

"Especially in your line of work, I imagine."

Clara smiled. "Yes. Sometimes they like to keep me up. Spirits can be rude that way."

"I'm very glad Abby brought you with her, Clara. I can see you have a good heart. Good soul, too." She was quiet for a moment, leading them back toward the house. "My mother was a seer. It used to downright give me the heebie-jeebies, what with some of the things she'd tell me. And dang it all if they didn't come true." She stopped them, smiling up at the taller woman. "You have that same sense of calm at your core that she did. It's almost an awareness that the rest of us don't have."

Grandma's gaze was so piercing Clara found it difficult to meet. It was almost as though she were looking into Clara's very soul. There was a part of Clara that felt that was exactly what she was doing.

"Yes. I see it in your eyes. Very old eyes. Your gaze makes me feel as though I'm looking into the eyes of a two-hundred-year-old woman, filled with all the knowledge and wisdom of living all those years. Heck, maybe even older than that." She smiled, a roadmap of lines and crow's feet erupting all over her features. "It's reassuring, somehow."

"Thank you. That's very kind of you, Grandma."

The old woman chuckled, beginning to walk again. "Not meant to be kind, young Clara. Just what I see." They stopped at the walkway that connected the Other House to the main house. "You get some sleep, honey. Whatever kept you awake will be better tomorrow." Grandma gave her a quick hug then headed to the kitchen door, disappearing inside the dark house.

Clara let out a long, deep breath. "I sure hope so, Grandma. I sure hope so."

꧁꧂꧁꧂

"Oh my god, Grandma, you should have seen it! It was so funny. Don't you remember her, Clara?" Abby asked, sandwich halfway to her mouth.

Clara had barely been able to keep up with Abby's nonstop babbling all afternoon. From the moment she'd first laid eyes on her that morning, all through their tour of Grandma's property by Grandma herself, and now during their picnic lunch.

"Uh, no. I don't think I went to school with her." She turned back to her macaroni salad as Abby continued with her story. Even her grandmother looked slightly confused. Clara was part relieved and part hurt. Abby hadn't mentioned the night before, hadn't been remotely personal at all. She had kept things on a cool surface level. Almost superficial. She told stories of her childhood at the house, told her grandmother stories about the Stoney Brook. Through it all, she hadn't once looked Clara in the eye. She didn't look forward to the ride home.

※.※.※.※

Clara tapped her fingers on her thigh in time with the beat of the song on the radio. The station had come in clear for ten whole minutes, as it had been going in and out as they drove the narrow mountain roads, the signal getting lost in the valleys they drove through. They'd been on the road for an hour, and not one word had been passed between them. Finally Abby broke the silence.

"What did you think of Grandma?"

Surprised to hear her voice, Clara glanced over at Abby, whose eyes were focused firmly on the winding road. "I thought she was great. I really enjoyed talking to her."

"Yeah. I do, too." Abby was quiet for a moment longer, her expression pensive, something obviously bothering her. "I'm sorry about last night, Clara." She still would not look at her.

Clara waited, but there was no more coming. "Why are you sorry?"

"Because I don't want you to get the wrong idea. I don't know why that happened, but I guess it did."

"What wrong idea would that be?" Clara was trying to keep her rising anger in check. It wouldn't do to end up in a fight while stuck in a car.

"The idea that I can do that. That *we* can do that." She finally managed a small glance at Clara, but the moment she saw the look in Clara's eyes she turned back to the road ahead.

"Though you were obviously able to do that last night."

"That was a mistake. Like I said, I don't know where it came from, or how it happened, but it did. That was wrong of me, Clara, and I hope you can forgive me." She spared another glance, her eyes filled with pain and confusion.

Clara felt her anger totally deflate at that look and simply nodded, looking out her window.

⁂

Stephanie watched her daughter dip the newly iced doughnuts into the colorful sprinkles. Clara's actions were slow, her mind seemingly somewhere else. She noticed it more and more in her and was beginning to get concerned.

"Clara?"

"Hmm?" Clara said absently, placing another doughnut on another tray for another day at the bakery. She peeled off her latex gloves, as the last of the doughnuts had been finished and glanced over at her mother, who was watching her, brows drawn.

"Are you all right?"

"Yeah. I'm good." Clara tried to give her mother as genuine a smile as she could. Her thoughts were scattered, and she was having a hard time staying focused.

"I need to ask you a favor. Plus, it'll give you extra money in your pocket."

Clara sighed. "Mom, I can't do a double again today."

"No, it has nothing to do with the bakery." Stephanie chuckled, finishing up the paperwork she'd been working on. She stacked the pages nicely, and set them aside, turning her full attention to her daughter. "Do you remember Linda Bethel?"

"The Girl Scout cookie lady?"

"Yes, Linda's the one who always bought cookies from Kerri. Well, this weekend she's having a birthday party, and she wants to hire you."

Clara's brows drew. "Hire me to do what?"

Stephanie hesitated a moment before answering. She wasn't entirely sure what Clara's reaction would be. "To do readings for her party guests." She chewed on her bottom lip, waiting for the fallout. She was pleasantly surprised when there wasn't any, just a curious glance from her youngest. "She wants psychic readings, medium readings, psychometry, all of it."

"How does she know I do all that?" Clara asked, sitting back in her chair, curious.

"Because I told her you do. Despite what you

might think, Clara, I'm proud of you and who you are."

Clara smiled, touched. "Thank you. But you know I've gotten out of the voodoo biz."

"Honey," Stephanie began, taking hold of one of her daughter's hands. "I've thought a lot about that over the past year, and I think you're wrong to have stopped. You've been given a gift by God, or by my mom, or whoever is in charge of that kind of thing. I truly think you're wasting it. And," she added, holding up a hand to forestall whatever Clara was about to say, "I don't feel you're happy here. I'm telling you this as a mother *and* as a boss. Your heart isn't in icing doughnuts," she indicated the trays Clara had filled. "This isn't what you're supposed to do with your life."

Clara could only stare at her mother in disbelief. Had she and Abby been talking or something?

"See, the thing is this. All of us — me, your dad, even Kerri — are doing what we can to get by in this world. We don't have any special gifts or talents. None of us can go write a novel. Can't go record a song or paint a painting. You, however, have got a golden ticket. Why would you let that pass you by?" There was so much earnestness in Stephanie's voice that Clara was touched all over again. "Don't let your life pass you by too. I don't want for you to wake up someday and realize you've wasted your life, working in a bakery and icing doughnuts at the ass crack of day."

All Clara could do was stare. She'd never heard her mother talk like this before and had no idea she felt that way. "I have to admit, I'm stunned. I honestly didn't think you supported me much in what I did."

Stephanie sighed, stung by the words, but knew they were true. "I didn't support you early on, that's no secret. I really regret that, honey, and I hope you know that. I know I should have been there more for you during this, and I have to live with myself knowing that. To be perfectly honest, I think I was jealous."

"Jealous?" Stephanie definitely had Clara's attention at that.

"Yeah. Not so much at what you can do. Lord knows *I* have no desire to see dead people." She smiled at that, as did Clara. "But you figure, my mother died when I was so young. You have no idea how much I would have done just to have her with me for one day during some hard times in my life. I've never really had a mom, Clara. Yet, I find out she was with you all along."

"I'm sorry, Mom. I never thought of it that way."

"You have nothing to be sorry for, sweetie. That's just how it was laid out to be. What are you always saying: our lives were mapped out before we got here? I did this to myself, for whatever reason, and so now I just have to be happy and proud that my mom is helping guide you."

Clara's eyes welled as she took her mother in a tight hug. "Thank you, Mom," she whispered into the embrace. "You have no idea how much I've needed to hear this from you."

"I'm sorry it took so long." Stephanie squeezed her daughter tight then let her go. "But I really do want you to think about what I said. If you need the bakery to help pay your mortgage, then work at the bakery to help pay your mortgage. Don't stay here because you've given up, or are being stubborn, or don't think there's anything else out there for you." She made sure she had Clara's full attention. "Okay?"

Clara nodded. "Okay. And yes, I'll be the Girl Scout cookie lady's party favor."

Stephanie grinned, pride shining in her eyes. "I'll let her know."

༄ ༄ ༄ ༄

Clara parked down the street, locking the car as she stepped up onto the sidewalk. She tried not to focus any attention on the few doors down from her destination, not wanting to think about it. About *her*. It had been nearly a week since she and Abby had arrived back in town from Grandma's house. Clara had heard nothing from Abby, nor had she tried to contact her.

The storefront was still empty, the lease sign where she had seen it last, hanging on the inside of the glass and wood door. She cupped her hands around her face against the glass and looked inside. The space was narrow, but went back far into the building. Signs and stickers from the previous leasers were still visible. From the looks of it, the shop had been a skateboard store.

As she looked into the store's depths, her mind began to show her images. She saw a big sign above the door and painted on the storefront glass: SOUL SEARCHER. Inside she could imagine anything that a searching soul would be looking for, whether it was spiritual needs, organic foods and teas, books on coming out, maybe...

She could see an archway leading into an adjacent room, which couldn't be seen from the sidewalk. Depending on the size, she could imagine a curtained-off area where she could do readings. Bring in a few glass cases to showcase jewelry and healing stones. Candles, maybe display some incense burners, the smell of incense wafting through the store.

Clara's daydream was interrupted when she saw the reflection of a familiar, but unwelcome face in the window next to her. She turned, doing her best to hide her annoyance.

"Hey, Jordan. How are you?"

"Hi. I thought that was you." The big man glanced into the empty store then at Clara curiously. "Window shopping?"

"Sort of." She gave him a sheepish smile. "What's going on?"

"Eh, just waiting for Abby." Clara's blood began to boil at the statement, but she said nothing. Jordan continued on, not realizing he was one step away from being star of a homicide scene. "I'm glad I saw you, actually. We did this amazing investigation over the weekend, and I want you to take a look at the footage." He grinned charmingly. "I had asked Abby to come with us, you know, get some more experience with paranormal research since she seems so interested in it, but she said she was going out of town."

Yeah, you prick. She was with me at her grandmother's house. She even kissed me! Clara kept a smile on her face, not letting on what she was really thinking.

Jordan shrugged, yet again oblivious of the rage he was causing inside Clara. "Next time, huh?"

"Hi, Clara."

Both turned to see Abby walking toward them. The pub owner eyed first Clara then Jordan, then her gaze turned back to the medium.

"Hey, Abby." Clara shoved her hands into the pockets of her shorts, trying to stop herself from throttling the pair. "How are you?" She felt so fake. Where once she had seen such warmth in Abby's green eyes, now she saw a stranger. Perhaps she'd never known Abby at all.

"I'm doing well. You?" Abby asked, her voice carefully controlled. She stepped up next to Jordan, who put a protective — or was that possessive? — hand on her back. Abby didn't lean into the touch, but she didn't pull away from it, either.

"Can't complain." Clara gave her a smile but felt her heart turning to ice. She couldn't take the pleasantries anymore, and the sight of Jordan's hand on Abby was making Clara crazy. "Well, you two kids have fun." She flashed them both one more smile, then turned and walked to her car, her pace picking up the closer she got, almost as though the confines of the vehicle would save her, somehow.

Once she slid behind the wheel, she let out a long, deep breath. The sting of tears to her eyes surprised her as she realized she felt like her heart was breaking. Seeing Abby standing there with Jordan, who obviously felt comfortable enough with Abby to be physical with her. What did that mean? Were they seeing each other? Why did she feel betrayed?

"Damn it, Abby," she whispered, smacking the steering wheel with the palm of her hand. She started the car and drove away, determined to never see Abby again.

Chapter Fifty

Thirteen pairs of eyes looked intently at Clara, who stood in the middle of the living room, the women seated on various pieces of furniture, waiting. Clara closed her eyes, listening to the energies that were swirling around her. Finally a bit of information stuck.

"Okay. Which one of you has something to do with a dog food making facility? Dog food, cat food..." She wrinkled her nose, able to smell the odors of the large plant, even as she saw a quick snapshot of it in her mind.

"Oh my god!" one of the ladies said, bringing her hands up to cover her mouth. "My father-in-law used to work at the Alpo plant in Tennessee for years."

Clara looked at her. "Did he like fast cars too? I'm seeing them going round and round and round the track." She moved her finger in a quick circle to help emphasize her vision.

The woman squealed again. "Yes! He used to restore cars during his off time. Muscle cars."

"Okay, ladies. I think we have a winner to start us off." Clara grinned, proud that she'd managed to connect so quickly.

The readings, and the information, flowed quick and strong. Clara made her way around the room, giving a little to each person there. Two of the women had no one they wished to connect with from the other side, but Clara was able to work with them too. One woman she dazzled by reading the memories from her wedding ring, while the second she worked on her health.

"Okay, Moira," she said, looking at the woman, though what she was seeing had nothing to do with the petite redhead sitting in front of her. In Clara's mind she saw the black silhouette of a human form. She saw no clothing, no internal organs, just the solid black form, almost like a target for a shooting range. She felt the need to concentrate on the legs. The area of the right knee began to glow red, getting brighter by the second, until it was an almost blinding, pulsing light.

"What do you see?" Moira asked, transfixed by the medium.

"What's going on with your right knee? You've got an injury there." Clara focused in on the pulsing red and was able to see a thin black line cross the reddened area. "You've had surgery there, and it still bothers you."

Moira and a couple of her close friends gasped quietly, murmurs spreading through the gathered group about the knee injury she'd received during a car accident ten years before, which had required surgery to correct.

"How did you know that?" Moira asked, a little disturbed.

"I see it." She reached down to the woman's skirt-covered knee. "It's about right here, your scar." She traced a curved line with her finger.

Moira pulled up the skirt just enough to reveal her bare knee, and a faded scar. Clara grinned, amazed herself at what she'd seen and what had been proven.

"Okay. Let me see what else." Again she studied

the figure — the knee still pulsing red — to see what, if anything she'd see. "Oh, Moira. You need to stop smoking." Again a murmuring of words and gasps; one woman laughed, claiming she'd been telling her friend to stop smoking for years.

"Why?" Moira said, somewhat defensive.

"Well, your lungs are beginning to glow a faint red, but I promise it'll get worse within the next—" Clara waited until she saw a number in her mind. "—five years." She shook her head to shake the focus from the black figure and looked at the real woman. "You can still stop it, if you stop now. If not," she shrugged. "It's not pretty."

❧❧❧❧

The party ended at nearly eleven o'clock, and Clara was exhausted. She'd given out her phone number to eight of the women, all of whom wanted to set up private readings with her. Clara was filled with mixed feelings at that. Did she want to go back into it? Yes, she'd heard what both Abby and her mother had said, and their words felt right. Even still, if she went back, she'd have to commit to it again, and possibly find more heartbreak, and possibly have to give bad news to the folks she read for. That didn't happen often, but it did happen enough to where it could be hard on her.

She turned out the light in her bedroom, getting herself settled in bed. The night was calm and peaceful, but she felt a mixture of glee and apprehension, though couldn't quite name the source. As she lay in bed, staring at the ceiling, she decided to do something she hadn't done in a very long time. She missed Rebecca and decided she wanted to go see her.

Taking several deep breaths, Clara relaxed herself, allowing her mind to flow into the altered state that would launch her soul to the other side, where she felt her grandmother's presence and anticipation of the visit. Closing her eyes, she allowed her thoughts to drift away, closing a gate behind them so her mind was clear and calm. It took a few tries, as it had been a long time since she'd meditated, and she'd had a lot of excitement that night at the party. Finally it began to take.

≈≈≈≈

The house, which Clara had come to know was her grandmother's house on the other side, was quiet, as usual. The front room was small, arched bookshelves built into two walls, an angled doorway connecting the two walls. A couch and two chairs were the furniture in the front room, while off to the right was a large archway that led to another room, which was like a kitchen with counters and cabinets, though no cooking surfaces existed, as eating wasn't a necessity there. On the back wall of the main room, was another archway that led to the bedroom.

Clara walked into that room, always loving the feel of the space. The room was very different than the other rooms of the house. The room was large, the outside wall reaching out in a semicircle and made almost entirely of windows. The room was always filled with golden light from the outside world with its golden skies. To the left, tucked back against the wall was a bed covered in white bedding, while a leather lounger was in front of the windowed wall. Clara knew this was where her grandmother did her own meditations, which was often how she communicated with Clara.

Rebecca was there now. She had been in deep meditation when Clara had entered, but opened her eyes and gave her granddaughter a warm smile.

"I've missed you, Clara."

"I've missed you too."

Rebecca patted the lounger beside her. Clara walked over to her, a bit hesitant, as she was mixed with a feeling of coming home, as well as not so sure this was her world anymore.

"Please sit," Rebecca said, feeling Clara's hesitation. She patted the lounger again.

The lounger almost looked like a deck lounger, except it was sturdy furniture made of wood and leather, and was nearly as wide as a double bed. Clara sat next to her grandmother, leaning back against the reclined back.

"How have you been?" she asked, trying to find her stride again on the other side.

"Good, though very sad." Rebecca glanced over at her granddaughter, her beautiful face filled with concern. "I was worried, Clara, I have to admit. I wasn't sure you would come back to me."

Clara felt a pang of guilt. "I know. I'm sorry. I wasn't really all that sure, either." She met her grandmother's gaze. "I feel so compelled to come back, though."

Rebecca's smile was brilliant. "I'm so happy to hear that. I know how you feel about all this, and I hear every single internal battle you have." She turned to face Clara. "I know this isn't easy for you, and I'm proud of you for coming. I love you so much, Clara, and I want you to be happy. I want you to follow your chosen path."

Clara mirrored her position. "I do too. I just don't know if I have the strength to do it."

"Oh, yes you do. You are so much stronger than you give yourself credit for. You can't lose sight of that wonderful inner strength you possess. You've been through so much in your life to give you that strength, Clara."

"But it got so hard!" Clara felt her frustration building, feeling like she was being a spoiled brat.

Rebecca smiled. "You're far too hard on yourself. Of course it's hard. But you wouldn't have this gift if you weren't strong enough to handle it and all the good and bad things that come with it. It's all part of it, sweetie."

Clara sighed. "I know." She felt defeated, knowing that everything Rebecca told her was dead on, but she was struggling with her decision.

"Clara," Rebecca said softly, reaching out and touching her granddaughter's arm. "You'll never find peace and happiness if you don't find your way back to your path. Something will always niggle at you; something will feel like it's missing. Trust me on this."

Clara looked into her grandmother's gaze for a long moment, feeling the truth in those words. "Okay. You're right." She sighed again. "Now, what about this Abby business? What the hell?"

Rebecca grinned, shaking her head. "I can't tell you that, but I promise everything will work out as it's supposed to. You will find your happiness."

Relieved to be with Rebecca again and feeling hope for the first time in a long time, Clara hugged her tightly, extremely grateful to have her in her life. "I love you, Grandma."

"I love you, too, Clara." Rebecca kissed the top of her head. "I promise. Everything will work out."

"Okay. I'm going to go. I'm tired."

"You had a big night. I'm very proud of you. You did good."

"Thanks." Clara couldn't keep the huge grin from her face, proud of herself and happy to hear her grandmother say it. "I'll come back soon."

"Good. Next time I'll show you what I've been working on in my gardens."

"Can't wait to see it."

Clara felt herself beginning to pull out of the deep meditation, her surroundings coming back into focus. She was about to open her eyes when she felt the pull to return to her meditation, feeling almost as though someone had a message for her.

She calmed her breathing and began to return, only to realize she wasn't heading back to her grandmother's house. Instead, she was at an ocean, and it was dark, which was confusing, as the other side was never dark. Curious, and a bit wary, she continued on.

The ocean was a dark entity spreading out far from the rocky beach, which white-capped waves pounded. Looking up into the dark sky, Clara saw the moon, which was full of shadows and omens. The rocky cliffs that surrounded the beach on three sides were steep and unforgiving. A fall would mean death.

"Where am I?" Clara felt uneasy, as though she were being watched. It felt as though she were in the

after shadow, but didn't know how she'd gotten there, nor where in the after shadow she was.

Turning in a full circle and feeling a strong need to leave and leave quickly, she looked for a way away from the beach. She saw an opening from a crag in the rock face, and began to walk toward it, hoping that the other side would be just that — the other side.

She got to the crag and was about to pass under it when she felt compelled to turn back to the beach. A dark figure stood at the shoreline, wrapped in a dark cloak. The figure's back was turned to Clara, so she couldn't see who it was. Long, black hair blew in the nonexistent breeze.

Feeling that perhaps this person was why she'd been called to the after shadow, she decided to see what the deal was. As she got closer to the figure, she felt more and more nervous, as though something bad were about to happen, or as if she were entering incredibly negative energy. Her steps slowed until she stopped about five feet from the figure. Part of her felt compelled to take another step, while another part of her wanted to flee.

The figure was thin, the cloak it wore outlining the shape of its body as the breeze, that seemed to be for the figure alone, blew the garment close to its frame. She saw no arms and felt as though the figure were actually hugging itself, bringing the cloak even closer to its thin body.

Clara stared, wanting to speak, but not having the first clue what to say. She took a tentative step closer but stopped, the figure turning its head just enough to show she'd been detected. Clara waited, unsure and uneasy.

The figure turned a bit more, this time its whole body and not just the head. As it turned to fully face Clara, she gasped as a nightmare image greeted her. The long, stringy hair was lost in an extremely high hairline, the sloped forehead half gray, mottled skin, half bone. The face was a partially grinning skull, the other part covered with the same gray skin, though flaps hung freely, including an eyeball that hung from the optic nerve.

Clara screamed, though nothing escaped her lips. She quickly backed away, the creature beginning to move toward her. The menace in its eyes was plain to see, even as one eye hung from an empty socket. She turned and began to run, not daring to look behind her to see if she was being pursued.

༄།༄།༄།༄།

Clara shot up in the bed, Abby's name on her lips. She was gasping for air, looking desperately around her bedroom for safety. Realizing she'd escaped, she placed a hand to her heart, which pounded painfully hard.

"Jesus Christ!" she gasped, still feeling on edge and as though the figure had followed her from her worst nightmare to infiltrate the waking light of day, or night as it was nearly two in the morning. She cried out again as the doorbell rang out, piercing the quiet of night.

Clara pushed the covers off and made her way to the living room and the front door. The doorbell rang again, then again. She felt a bit of panic seize her heart as she unlocked the door, worried there was bad news on the other side. Instead, a pale, frantic Abby stood on her doorstep.

"Abby!"

"Oh my god, I'm so sorry to be here so late. Oh my god, Clara." Abby began to sob. "I need your help."

"What's wrong?" She guided Abby inside the house, closing and locking the door behind her. "Are you okay? Is it Jimmy?"

Abby shook her head, trying to get her emotions under control, but Clara could tell she was terrified. "It's the pub. It's not gone, Clara. It's not gone!"

Clara stared at her in disbelief, truly worried. She'd never seen Abby so seemingly traumatized before. "What do you mean, it's not gone?" she asked, voice quiet as she was afraid to hear the answer.

"Whatever it is, it's not gone! I just left. I don't even know if I locked the door. I can't go back there." She shook her head violently. "I can't."

"Okay, okay. Hold on." Clara took a deep breath, still shaken from her own incident, which came back in all its scary-as-hell glory. Her eyes opened wide, mouth fell open as something occurred to her. "It was playing with me," she said absently, once again seeing the horrible face.

"What?"

Clara shook herself out of her thoughts. "Nothing. Come on." She led Abby to the couch and got her seated. "Tell me what happened."

Abby nodded, taking a very shaky breath. Her hands were shaking as she tried to take off the light jacket she was wearing. Clara stopped her with a hand to her arm and helped her. "Thank you," Abby whispered, running a hand through her hair. "Okay. I got a call tonight around ten from my bartender. He told me there was a problem with the shelving behind the bar. Bottles kept falling off, most breaking when they hit the floor. He and one of the waitresses had found some nails and a hammer, but it did no good.

More bottles fell as the night went on. I went in around eleven thirty to see what was going on. I mean, shit, I can't afford to lose that much liquor."

Clara nodded in understanding, her stomach beginning to turn as she saw where this was going. "Okay. Then what?"

"Everything seemed to calm down for a while, so I decided to head up to my office and do some scheduling since I was already there. We were busy tonight, so I went down to help during the one o'clock rush. Suddenly, the entire rack of bottles crashed to the floor. I got cut, my bartender got cut; Clara, it was awful."

"Oh, Abby." Clara could feel the fear in Abby.

"Oh, I'm not done yet. So, if we have no alcohol, we can't very well operate a bar. It was getting close to closing time anyway, so my waitresses began to clear people out while my bartender and I began to clean up the mess. The bar was nearly empty when the glass rack hanging above the bar explodes, Clara. Wood pieces went flying everywhere! Glasses fell, shattering on the bar, on the floor." Abby wiped at a tear with a trembling hand. "After that I told Ryan and the girls to leave. I came straight over here. Whatever that thing is in there, it was asleep for a little while, but it's awake now, and it's pissed!"

All Clara could do was stare at the other woman, astonished. "I don't know what to say," she finally managed. "God, I'm so sorry, Abby. I'm really, really sorry. I thought it was gone."

"It's not your fault, Clara. You did everything you could that night."

"Listen, I can see who I can get a hold of. Maybe I can bring in another medium for you—"

"No! I want you to do this. I only trust you, and I want you to get rid of this fucking thing. I'm not going to let it ruin my business. I've fought too goddamn hard for it!" Abby exclaimed, near hysterics.

"Hey, calm down." Clara let out a long breath, trying to think what to do. "Listen, I'm going to head over there. I want you to stay here. Okay?" She held up a hand as Abby began to protest. "Please, Abby. I need to know you're safe. Please stay here."

After a long moment, Abby nodded. "Okay. I'll stay."

Chapter Fifty-one

Clara jingled Abby's keys against her thigh nervously as she walked toward the Stoney Brook. The lights were still on, and she could hear music pounding from within. It looked almost as though the club were still open and rockin' with business.

Walking up to the front doors, Clara tried the handle, not entirely surprised to see that it opened. Now she had two jobs to do: go do a sweep of the entire building to make sure no one had decided to help themselves to the pub and get rid of the dark entity that awaited within.

She carefully made her way inside, cell phone in hand so she could call 911 at the first sign of mortal trouble. Her gaze was immediately drawn to the bar, and the unbelievable mess Abby had described. She could imagine how panicked and scared Abby and her employees must have been. The air inside the pub was heavy, the energy moving in waves. She could feel the energy rushing into her solar plexus, which was the chakra where energy began and ended, and as often happened when she was swarmed with energy — good or bad — she began to feel nauseous.

She made a quick sweep of the building, her heart pounding in her chest, though she wasn't sure what would scare her more: a normal person who had let themselves in or running into the nightmarish creature she'd seen in the after shadow. Satisfied that no one was in the building, Clara put her cell phone away and locked the front doors. No one could help her do this. Well, no one she could call on the earthly plane, that is.

Clara's heart was pounding as she stood in the center of the main room and closed her eyes. She felt so vulnerable and knew she was being watched. What had tormented Abby and her employees was still there, and it was angry that it had more company. Clara didn't want to go into the after shadow quite yet, knowing that it would do no good. No, what she felt as she reached out with her senses was that this thing was hiding. It was jumping back and forth between dimensions that Clara didn't fully understand. It was almost like it would peek its head around a corner, then it was gone, and by time Clara got to the room where it had been, it no longer existed.

"I'm going to need help," she said, blowing out a loud breath and looking around the room. "Grandma and anyone else you can bring to help you, I need you now."

Clara had started to walk toward the stairs leading to the second floor, not a clue as to what she was going to do once she reached the second level, but then stopped. She felt a presence in the room she was about to leave but knew that presence. A smile spread across her face as she turned back toward the bar. Standing next to three bar stools that had been gathered by patrons who'd been sitting on them, was Rebecca. As when Clara always saw a spirit, she saw her guide with her third eye, not her two visual eyes. It was almost as though Rebecca's form had been superimposed on the scene: she was there, but not there.

I've come to help you, Clara...

Clara heard the words so clearly in her mind.

"Thank you, Grandma. I don't know what to do about this."

I've brought help...

As Clara looked on, a bright light seemed to squeeze out of the air itself, nearly blinding. Stepping out of the light was a tall woman with blonde hair and a mischievous smile. After her came a man with dark hair, his dark eyes intense, yet exuding a wonderful sense of calm. Though the man and blonde woman were dressed in normal clothing, Clara couldn't help but feel something was different about them. One more figure appeared then. This one was a blond man, tall with broad shoulders and a kind face, though his blue eyes were piercing.

Clara felt a sense of awe as she looked at the three newcomers, speech leaving her at the beauty of them and their entrance. She looked to her grinning grandmother, hoping she'd give her some sort of clue as to who they were.

Clara, this is my help: Gabriel, Azrael, and Michael...

Clara didn't know what to say. She knew — though couldn't quite believe it — that she was standing in the presence of angels. Archangels for that matter.

"You don't have wings," Clara said stupidly, the first thing that came to mind.

The woman, Gabriel, smiled.

We come in the form you need us to. You would never have believed who we were had we come with wings and shining halos.

Clara shook her head, gaze riveted to the stunning woman. "No, I wouldn't have."

So, we've come like this, Azrael said, indicating

his black clothing. Even in street clothes, the Angel of the Dead kept his penchant for dark garments.

Rebecca spoke next. *The dark entity in here is too much for you to handle by yourself, Clara. We need you to concentrate and fill this entire building with the light of purity. We'll do the rest.*

Clara nodded, almost as though she understood what her grandmother had just told her to do. Somehow she knew it would come to her as she did it. After all, that's how she'd figured out most of her abilities. The same graceful way they'd come, the angels disappeared, followed by Rebecca, who gave her granddaughter an encouraging smile.

Clara shook herself free of her lingering shock and made her way toward the second-floor office, where she felt drawn. The upstairs area was calm, even peaceful as Clara walked through, running her fingertips along the felt of one of the pool tables. The office was dark, which surprised her, as she'd left the light on when she'd done her walk-through. Wary, she reached into the dark room, flicking the light switch. She gasped in surprise as she saw a dark figure vanish before her eyes in the corner. Hand to her heart, she forced herself to step inside the room. It was cold, the air filled with energy, all of which made just about every hair on Clara's body stand on end.

"I know you're here, you son of a bitch," she said, turning in a small circle in the room, trying to figure out where the presence had gone, and where the source of the energy was coming from. She knew she was being watched, and it took everything in her power to not run and get the hell out of the Stoney Brook, Abby or no Abby.

Clara whirled around to her right, feeling a quick

chill along that side of her body. She saw nothing. The scrape of one of the filing cabinet drawers being tugged open startled her. She looked at it, staring in disbelief as the drawer moved again, metal scraping on metal until the entire drawer was yanked free, landing on the carpeted floor with a loud crash, accompanied by Clara's cry of surprise.

Another crash rent the air as the handset of the telephone on the desk clattered to the desktop. Her heart was pounding, her breathing quick and labored as fear gripped her insides.

"Come out, you coward!" she yelled, voice echoing in the confines of the small office. She was tempted to go into the after shadow and find the presence, but something screamed inside her head not to do it. She realized it was the voice of her grandmother.

In the years since Clara had been dealing with the other side and the spirits that inhabited it, she'd never seen anything as negative and downright dangerous as the entity that seemed to be in Abby's pub. She'd never felt true terror in a haunted location before. Now, as she stood in the office, eyes darting around everywhere, trying to sense what would come next, she was nearly petrified with fear.

Clara gasped then cried out in pain as a searing hotness swept across her arm. She looked down, shocked to see two parallel angry welts across the side of her forearm. Taking a shaky breath she closed her eyes, trying to focus, even as her heart raced and sweat broke out all over her body.

A sense of peace began to steal over her as she began to thrust energy out into the room, visualizing in her mind's eye the entire room filling with a white light, which spread out into the main room of the second floor, then down the stairs, then crept into every nook and cranny of the pub. She spread her arms wide, allowing the energy to push out of her, cleansing the space with the light of life. She could feel others beginning to gather nearby, and knew it was Rebecca and the angels, joining her light with their own. The light in Clara's mind was becoming so blinding she could hardly stand to look at it anymore.

Clara felt the entity beginning to react, a dark push against the light. She could sense it nearby, almost as though it were trying to make its way back into the room after it had run from her, trying to combat the forces that were trying to dispel it.

In her mind she saw the small army of her grandmother and the three angels as well as the dark figure she'd seen in her meditation. The entity was waging a fierce war with its own dark energy, while the other four, and Clara, tried to bind it with white light and positive energy.

The figure stopped, standing in the wave of light it had been bathed in and looked at Clara. Its dark, sunken eye was filled with a hatred that made Clara shiver. The creature grinned, its skeletal features twisting in malice as it opened its mouth wide, a ball of black heat flying out and hitting Clara right in the solar plexus. She nearly doubled over, almost losing concentration as nausea like nothing she'd ever felt hit her. It began in her gut then radiated throughout her entire body, making her shaky and unsteady.

She almost lost the vision in her head but it all came back into focus soon enough for her to realize the creature was running right at her. She didn't know what to do, her body already trembling from the blast of energy he'd shot at her. She wasn't sure what would happen if she was hit head-on by this thing. It got closer and closer when suddenly Michael stepped in front of Clara, swinging a sword of light and catching the figure right at the neck, destroying it in one fell swoop, which released a blast of energy and a nearly deafening scream that shook the spiritual plane.

Clara was knocked to her butt as the creature seemed to explode, her body on overload as energy seeped from every pore. She blinked rapidly as the vision disappeared, leaving her alone in the office, a quiet calm filling the space. She looked around, almost as though seeing it for the first time.

After a moment Clara got up off the floor, wiping off the seat of her running pants as she did. She ran a still-trembling hand through her hair and took an uneven breath.

"My god," she muttered, unsure what had just happened.

You did me proud, sweetie...

Clara smiled as Rebecca's voice spoke softly in her head.

So proud. I love you.

"I love you too, Grandma."

ॐॐॐ

Clara was exhausted as she let herself into her house. After everything had come to a crashing end she had saged the entire pub, which involved lighting a bundle of sage and washing the space with the smoke, especially in the corners, as sprits enter and exit via corners, which people often forget to cleanse. She had filled the entire building with light, freeing the air of negative energy. She was satisfied that the Stoney Brook was completely clear now, and it had been spiritually locked, which meant spirit energy was neither welcome nor able to enter.

A lamp had been left on in the living room, but the sun was starting to come up, and Clara had no intention of staying up to need light. She flicked off the lamp and made her way toward her bedroom, ducking her head into every room along the way, yet to find Abby. She stopped in the doorway of her own bedroom, watching as Abby slept. She was curled up on the comforter, the paperback that had been on Clara's bedside table curled up in her arms.

Clara leaned her shoulder against the doorframe, sighing from extreme exhaustion, and completely charmed by the sight of Abby sleeping. For a moment she was undecided: should she wake Abby to either go home or move to the guestroom bed? Should she go sleep in the guestroom herself? Climb in to her own bed next to Abby?

Making up her mind, as she was entirely too exhausted to go anywhere else, she stepped out of her shoes and pants as she walked to the bed, shimmying out of her bra while keeping her T-shirt on. Only in a tee and undies, she climbed under the covers and promptly fell deeply asleep.

∾∾∾∾

Abby started, realizing the sun was blazing in through a window and right into her closed eyes. She found that confusing, considering her bedroom window was on the same wall as the bed, and the morning sun never woke her up. Then she realized she was not only in bed with someone but was cuddled up behind that person. She opened her eyes and saw brown hair and a lot of it. The body she was pressed to was warm and soft, her arm around the person's waist, and a hand resting on it.

It hit her. *Oh shit.* She lifted her head slightly to get a look at her surroundings and found that she was, in fact, in Clara's bedroom, in her bed. *Oh shit, oh shit, oh shit!*

As slowly and quietly as she could, she extricated herself from the warmth of Clara's body, immediately missing its softness and comfort. She climbed off the bed, realizing she had been sleeping on top of the covers, still in the clothes she'd been wearing all day the day before. She had to pee like mad, so hurried to the bathroom down the hall rather than using the one in Clara's bedroom. She didn't want to wake her.

🪶🪶🪶🪶

Clara rolled over onto her back, her shoulder screaming at her for lying on it so long. That had been the position she'd fallen asleep in, and she wondered if she'd ever moved. A glance out the window told her it was late morning, if not early afternoon. She felt groggy and sore and quickly realized she was not alone.

Abby sat on the chair in the corner, reading the paperback she'd started reading the night before, when she'd fallen asleep. Seeing that Clara was awake, Abby slapped the book closed and set it aside.

"Hey," she said, her voice soft.

"Hi." Clara sat up, still trying to blink the sleepies out of her eyes, which felt heavy and riddled with bits of sand. "What time is it?"

"Almost noon. What time did you get in?"

Clara thought for a moment, trying to think past her exhaustion. "I think it was almost five."

"Damn." Clara scrubbed her face with her hands, trying to wake herself up.

Abby stood and walked over to the bed, standing beside Clara. "Can I get you anything? Coffee? Water?"

Clara shook her head. "No. I gotta pee, then I'll fill you in on what happened."

"Okay. I'll meet you in the kitchen."

As Abby left the room, closing the door behind her, Clara got out of bed, looking out on the bright and sunny day before disappearing into the bathroom. She felt like she'd been run over by a truck. After taking care of her business, she washed her face and brushed her teeth. Feeling almost alive and refreshed, she put clean clothes on and padded out to the kitchen where a pot of coffee was beginning to perk to life.

Abby waited patiently at the table, feeling somewhat nervous about being in Clara's house again, even as she felt relief from the other woman's comforting presence. She hoped Clara wouldn't be angry she'd started a pot of coffee, but Abby knew she'd need something to concentrate on as she listened to what Clara had to say.

"Smells good," Clara said, padding into the kitchen and heading over to a cabinet to remove two coffee mugs.

"I hope you don't mind. I figured you'd probably want some to help wake you up." Abby smiled sheepishly. "Even if it is decaf."

"Hey, decaf has its purposes too." Clara put the bottle of Irish Cream creamer on the table, as well as a bowl of sugar and Equal. They were both quiet as coffee was poured and prepared. After a long, satisfying drink, Clara felt much more human. "Your pub is completely clear now. I know I said that before, but I have it on high authority this time."

"What happened?" Abby noticed something on Clara's arm. "Oh my god! What happened to you?"

Clara looked down at the double scratches she'd received, which were somewhat caked with dried blood. She'd been so tired when she got home that she'd forgotten to clean them out. "Battle scars," she said absently, taking another sip from her cup.

Not fully understanding, Abby said nothing. She waited patiently for Clara to continue.

"What you had in that place was a dark entity. Basically what that is, is a mass of negative, dark energy. It's not necessarily a 'spirit' in that it was once a living person. Dark entities usually hang around the after shadow, trolling to find spirits and humans to torment. I truly think it was using the other spirits in the Stoney Brook to cause problems. When I crossed those, I pissed it off."

"So, when it got angry, it reacted violently?"

Clara nodded. "Exactly."

"So, how did you get rid of it?"

Clara chewed on her bottom lip for a moment, unsure if she should tell Abby the entire story. How much would she believe? She put her coffee cup down, wanting to give all her attention to Abby. "You might think I'm nuts when I tell you this, Abby, but I swear it's the truth. I haven't lied to you yet, and I'm not about to start now. Okay?"

Abby could only nod, intrigued by the serious tone of Clara's voice.

"My grandmother brought a *few friends* to help

me get rid of this thing."

"A few friends," Abby said, feeling there was much more to the story than just simply a few friends.

"Yes. A few angelic friends." Clara studied Abby's face, carefully studying her reactions. She saw curiosity and intrigue but never disbelief or disapproval. "As in, *Archangels*. Gabriel, Michael, and Azrael came to help her. Help me. Well, I guess help *you*, get this thing out of your pub. I wasn't strong enough to do it myself."

Abby sat back in her chair, not doubting Clara's story for a minute, which she had a hard time understanding. Wasn't that absolutely absurd? Angels? Come on. How was that possible? And yet, she believed every word, felt everything Clara was telling her was nothing but the absolute truth. Her heart opened to Clara, as she could see the worry in her eyes. Without thinking, Abby reached across the table and took one of her hands.

"I believe you, Clara. Thank you for doing what you did. You have no idea how grateful I am."

Clara had to stop herself from blowing out a breath of relief. She was not only worried that Abby would not believe her but would once again walk out of her life.

"You're welcome. I'm glad I could help."

There was an uncomfortable moment of silence as Abby gently released Clara's hand and turned her attention back to her coffee. After a moment she asked, "Are my staff and I safe now?"

Clara nodded. "Yes."

Abby nodded, pleased. "Again, thank you." She felt her guilt beginning to gnaw at her, and she wasn't comfortable with that. It was time for her to go. She pushed away from the table and walked over to the sink, dumping out the rest of her coffee and rinsing the cup. "I should go."

Clara stood, feeling her heart sink. She had hoped that maybe they could reestablish some semblance of their friendship, but Abby obviously wasn't interested.

"Okay."

Abby gave her a shy smile, then turned and headed toward the door, Clara behind her. Suddenly she stopped, unaware of why. She turned and looked at Clara. "Come by the Brook tomorrow, Clara. I'll buy you lunch."

Surprised by the invite, Clara simply nodded. "Okay. I will."

Abby smiled, then quickly hurried out of the house.

Chapter Fifty-two

Clara pulled up in front of the Stoney Brook, not sure why she'd agreed to come at all. She felt somewhat apprehensive and just hoped it went well. When Abby had tossed out the invite the previous day, the look on her face had said it all. She wasn't even sure herself why she'd asked Clara to come for lunch. What did that mean? Did she not actually want Clara there?

"Shit," Clara muttered, turning off her car and climbing out. Her cell phone chirped to life as she locked her door. The display screen showed it was Kerri on the other end of the line. They had planned to get together later in the day. "Hey."

"Hey, Clara. Are we still on? I really want your help in deciding which color to choose."

Clara rolled her eyes. "Kerri, why don't you just wait until your fifth month ultrasound?"

"Because I want you to tell me, that's why. I want to know."

"Fine. Yes, we're still on. I'm at the Stoney Brook right now to have lunch with Abby, but I don't think that'll take all that long."

"Okay. How about I come around three?"

"Sounds good. See you then." The sisters said their goodbyes and Clara tucked her phone into her pants pocket as she pushed through the front doors of the pub. She was curious how it would feel after everything that had happened. She noticed an immediate difference in the atmosphere and air of the place. It was quiet and calm. Peaceful.

"Hey, you're the ghost lady, aren't you?" asked the bartender, whom Clara had seen there before. She walked over to him.

"Yep. Sure am."

"Well, then, let me buy you a drink. Anything you want. We're all so grateful for what you did. Scared the shit outta Abby and me the other night."

"Ah, so you were there, huh?"

He shivered, nodding. "Never been so scared." He rested his palms on the bar, leaning on her arms. "What can I get you?"

Clara studied the new shelving that had been installed, the bottles of various types of liquor placed in neat rows. "How about a chocolate martini?"

The bartender nodded. "Chocolate martini coming up."

"Thanks." She looked around the pub, looking for Abby as her drink was being made. Not seeing her, she decided to ask. "Hey, where can I find Abby?"

The barkeep paused in his task for a moment, thinking. "Upstairs in the office, I think. Least that's where she was off to about fifteen minutes ago."

"Okay, thanks. I'm going to head up there. Be back for my drink in a few."

"Sounds good." He gave her a charming smile then returned to making her drink.

Clara made her way up the stairs, flattening herself against the wall as two girls came down, the three unable to pass at the same time. The second floor was quiet, a lone man playing pool at the far table. He glanced in her direction as she headed his way on her way to the office. After a quick nod of greeting, he turned back to his game, concentrating on sacking the four ball in the corner pocket.

As Clara neared the office she heard voices — one of them was Abby, the other was that of a male. She was just positive it was Jordan's voice. She stopped short of the closed door to the office, trying to swallow her jealousy. She had no right or reason to feel it. Abby was a grown woman and could do what she wanted, with whomever she wanted. But then she decided she wanted to pull out Jordan's eyeteeth with pliers anyway.

Taking a deep breath, she tried to decide what she wanted to do. After a moment's indecision, she raised her fist and knocked on the hard wood. She could hear Jordan's voice rumbling low behind the door but had no idea what he was saying. Abby's voice followed, just as low, then, "Come in!"

Clara pushed the door open, and her stomach dropped as she saw Jordan grab Abby's hand and tug her toward him, lowering his head to quickly catch her in a kiss. He pulled away grinning.

"I'll see you later, then," he said to her, winking at Clara as he left the office.

Clara stood there stunned, unsure what to do or say. Abby stood by her desk, where Jordan had left her, shyly glancing at Clara. "Hey," she finally said, plastering a smile on her lips. The lips Jordan had just kissed. The kiss Abby hadn't fought.

Clara could feel her anger and jealousy beginning to rage within her, and she wasn't entirely sure she was going to be able to contain it. Jaw muscles clenching and unclenching, she stayed by the open door. "I'm sorry to interrupt," she finally managed, her voice low and strained.

"You weren't interrupting anything, Clara. He just showed up."

"I see. Should I leave? Maybe the two of you can finish what you started."

Abby stared at her for a moment, shocked at Clara's tone of voice. "Nothing was started, Clara," she said, somewhat on the defensive. Why did she feel such a strong need to have Clara believe her? "He came by to ask me to lunch, I told him I had other plans, and then you came."

"And he kissed you." Clara felt sick at the accusatory tone, but she couldn't help herself, or stop.

"I don't think it's any of your business what he does. Do you?" Abby placed a hand on her hip, feeling her anger beginning to bubble. In truth, she had been shocked when Jordan had done that, but now that she was getting pissed, she wasn't about to let Clara know that.

"Is that why you called me here? Right at that moment?" Clara moved into the office a bit farther, all rational thought leaving, which she knew was dangerous. If she were smart she would have turned right around and left the Stoney Brook, never to return. Too bad she wasn't smart.

"Clara, that's ridiculous."

"Is it? Gotta prove to me that you're that much more straight, huh?" Clara had no clue where the words were coming from. All she did know was that she couldn't stop them.

"Please don't do this," Abby begged, her head beginning to pound. She had the distinct feeling that things were about to get completely out of hand.

"Don't do what?" Clara took another step toward

her.

"Don't say something that we're both going to regret." Abby stood her ground, even as she wanted to take a step back with every step forward Clara took. Within moments they were nearly toe to toe.

"Oh, I don't have anything left to say. Except this," Clara grabbed Abby's face and brought it to her own. The kiss was heated and instantly deep, demanding, and harsh. Abby responded, about to grab Clara's hips, pulling her closer. Before she could, Clara pulled away, leaving them both breathless. "The next time he kisses you, ask yourself if it affects you like that."

With those words, she walked out of Abby's office and out of her life.

⚖⚖⚖⚖

Clara was having a hell of a time concentrating on what her sister was saying, which made her feel terrible, considering Kerri was droning on and on about what would eventually be Clara's first niece. Her mind was a fog of thoughts and snippets of conversations and images. She could still see Jordan kissing Abby and could still see the disapproving look in Abby's eyes when Clara had begun to get angry. She could still feel and taste Abby's mouth...

"Clara? Are you listening to anything I'm saying?" Kerri asked, obvious hurt in her voice.

"Huh?" Clara looked at her sister and was immediately washed over with guilt. "I'm sorry. What did you say?"

Kerri studied her for a moment, head slightly cocked to the side as she pondered. "What's gotten into you today? You've basically been on another planet since I got here. Do you want to talk about it?"

Clara immediately shook her head, a slight panic seizing her. What would her sister say if she knew that Clara had fallen in love with one of her best friends? "No, I'm okay. I'm sorry."

"It's all right. I was just going to ask you—"

Before Kerri could say another word there was a loud pounding at the door. The sisters looked at each other, Clara shrugging at Kerri's questioning look. She pushed up off the couch and walked to the door, pulling it open, shocked to see a very angry Abby standing on the doorstep. Without a word or a greeting, or any kind of explanation, Abby pushed past Clara, grabbing her by the hand and tugging her off toward the hall that led to the bedrooms.

"I'm sorry, Kerri, but we need to talk," Abby tossed over her shoulder as she marched them to her destination. Once inside Clara's bedroom, she slammed the door closed, whirling on a stunned Clara. "Why the hell did you do that?" she demanded, hands balled into fists at her sides. Clara had never seen her so upset and was completely taken aback.

"Which thing?" Clara asked, her own emotions turning her cocky. She crossed her arms casually over her chest, trying to hide the fiery emotions that were raging through her.

"Why did you leave?"

Clara was surprised, as she figured her leaving was the last thing Abby would be upset about. "Because there was nothing left for me to say or do. You've made it very clear since we got back from your grandmother's house that our friendship and anything else was officially over."

"Which was wrong of me," Abby admitted, her

anger only dimming a smidge.

"You're damn right it was! What the hell, Abby? You kiss me, then treat me as if I did something wrong? I can't play your games. I *won't* play your games." She glared at her, glad to finally say what she'd been dying to say all week.

Abby was quiet for a long moment, staring out the window, her jaw working as she thought of what to say to that. Finally she gave a heavy sigh, her shoulders slumping slightly. "Why can't I stay away from you?" she asked, her voice quiet, resigned.

"I don't know. I can't answer that other than to tell you that I've been in love with you since I was fourteen years old." Clara threw her hands up in resignation. "There, I said it."

Abby studied her for a long moment. "Is that what this is?" Clara only stared back at her, unable to answer that question for her. Abby shook her head, running a hand through her hair. "Since the day I met you, I've felt drawn to you. I never fully understood why. I thought maybe it was because of what you do. The medium stuff always fascinated me." She glanced at Clara. "*You* fascinated me. Why?" She rushed over to Clara, taking her by the shoulders. "*Why?* Damn it, Clara! Why the hell can't I get you out of my head? Why do I dream about you? Why does my heart always feel like it's about to pound out of my fucking chest when I see you?" She shook Clara with the passion of her words and confusion.

Clara remained calm, cupping Abby's face, holding her still until Abby met her gaze unflinchingly. "Because you're in love, Abby. Some things are meant to be." Clara had never felt so much conviction in anything she'd ever said.

Abby had nothing to say to that, so she decided to stop using her head and start using her heart. The kiss happened so quickly that Clara actually took a partial step backward. Abby followed, holding Clara's mouth to her own, their bodies finally meeting.

Clara bounced back quickly, sliding her hands to Abby's hips, pulling her as close into her body as she could. The passion inside her was fierce, and she could feel it coming off Abby in waves.

Abby felt overwhelmed and broke the kiss, wrapping her arms around Clara and burrowing her face in her neck. Her breathing was heavy, her heart thudding painfully fast. She sighed in relief as she felt Clara hold her, their breathing the only sound.

"I can hear your heart," Abby whispered, listening to the fast, but steady cadence.

"It's kind of pounding," Clara chuckled.

"That it is." Abby lifted her head, looking into Clara's eyes. She raised her hand, brushing her fingertips down Clara's cheek. "So beautiful," she whispered. Suddenly she felt shy. "Clara?"

"Yeah?" Clara basked in the affection, feeling like her soul was whole for the first time in her life.

"I don't know how, but I do love you. It makes no sense, but it's almost like somehow my soul knows. I'm drawn to you."

Clara smiled, Abby's words a balm for every bad thing that had ever happened to her — every heartbreak, every disappointment. She was far too touched to speak, so she let her kiss speak for her. It didn't take long before a fire had sparked into an explosion of pent-up feelings and need.

Abby moaned into the kiss, her hands finding their way to Clara's back, fingers clenching and unclenching as her want built, the fabric of Clara's shirt gathered into her fists.

Clara was surprised to feel her shirt being tugged upward, realization dawning on her as she allowed her T-shirt to be pulled off. She shook her hair free of the material, immediately returning to Abby's mouth, drawn like a drug.

Abby ran her hands over the softness of Clara's bare back, amazed at just how soft her skin truly was. Her fingers felt the material of the clasp on Clara's bra and suddenly panic set in. She broke the kiss, looking at Clara with sheepish eyes.

"I have no clue what I'm doing, Clara," she said, wishing so badly she knew how to work Clara's body.

Clara grinned then moved to suckle Abby's neck. "All you gotta do is feel," she said into the supple skin, her own hands working their way to the buttons on Abby's shirt.

"I hope you like what you see," Abby moaned, her eyes falling closed as the warmth of Clara's mouth moved to the hollow of her throat. "God, I hope so."

Clara was amused, and charmed by Abby's self-consciousness. As far as she was concerned, she'd been waiting for this her entire life. She moved away from her as the shirt completely opened, revealing Abby's bra-clad torso. Personally, she thought Abby was the most beautiful, precious thing she'd ever seen.

A shiver passed through Abby as her shirt whispered down her arms and finally fell to the floor in a silent pile. Her bra quickly followed, leaving her exposed from the waist up. She looked into Clara's eyes.

"Remember, I've given birth," she warned, hoping beyond hope that Clara would approve of her body. "It's not the body of a sixteen-year-old soccer player anymore."

Clara cupped her face, leaning in close. "Stop. You leave me breathless every time I see you, Abby. To me, you are absolute perfection. I love you." She sealed her promise with a kiss.

Abby was overwhelmed with emotion: love, lust, and absolute acceptance. She grabbed Clara in a fierce hug and kiss, needing so badly to be touched and to touch.

Clara backed them up toward her bed, unbuttoning Abby's jeans the entire time. The denim fell down Abby's legs, pooling at her feet. Abby skillfully kicked her shoes off, then stepped out of her pants, reaching down to tug her socks off. Left in her underwear, she finished undressing Clara with trembling hands.

Clara pulled Abby down onto the bed with her, moving on top of her, their mouths immediately making contact. Abby groaned at the feel of their naked skin pressed together, her fingers stretching out over the expanse of Clara's back, wanting to feel as much of that wonderful skin as she could.

"You feel so amazing," Clara moaned, again finding Abby's neck with her mouth, one of her hands moving up to capture one of her breasts. She could feel the turgid nipple against her palm.

Abby gasped, words leaving her as she arched her neck, trying to give Clara as much as she could. Sensations flew through her, far too many to decipher, so she just allowed herself to get lost in them.

Clara moved farther down Abby's body, leaving a wet trail as she went, until finally she found a small breast. She took the nipple into her mouth, sucking just hard enough to get a deep groan from Abby. Her body was pulsing with need. She needed to feel all of Abby against her again.

Abby welcomed Clara's mouth once more, gasping as Clara's thigh made contact with her sex. She opening her legs, giving Clara more room until she was settled, Abby's own thigh pressing up into an immensely hot wetness.

Clara moaned, pressing herself down onto Abby's thigh as she pushed herself into Abby. They continued to kiss as Clara set a slow, lazy rhythm, just enough to ease some of the ache while creating a hunger for more.

"God, yes," Abby sighed, the kiss breaking as both of their breathing began to quicken. "That feels so good."

"I have waited my whole life for you," Clara whispered, giving her a quick kiss, then making her way down again, needing to taste Abby. She settled herself between spreading legs, wanting so badly to give Abby pleasure.

Abby cried out as Clara began to love her, pleasure beginning to ripple through her with every pass and swipe of Clara's tongue. She reached down, burying her hands in Clara's dark hair as she got lost in sensation once more. She felt the build begin, slowly burning its way throughout her entire body, exploding in a cry that echoed throughout the room.

Clara lovingly kissed her way back up Abby's body, suckling a nipple on the return trip. She was surprised when she was pushed to her back, Abby climbing on top of her and kissing her with an almost animalistic intensity, which took Clara's breath away.

Abby wanted to make Clara feel as good as she had, as well as wanted to know what it was like to be inside her. She explored Clara's neck and face with kisses and small nips, her hands making their way down her body. The skin was smooth and warm. Heavenly.

Clara moaned as she was entered, her hand tugging on Abby's shoulder until their mouths met again. Abby found the soft wetness that enveloped her fingers intoxicating and knew it was a place she would want to visit again very soon. She set what she felt was a steady stroking rhythm, not sure what she was doing, but trying her best to listen to Clara's body.

It didn't take long at all before Clara felt her body bursting with pleasure, her sex clenching down on Abby's fingers as she gasped, her body trembling with the power of her climax. She could feel the tender, comforting caresses and kisses across her face and upper chest as she came back down to earth.

Abby smiled at Clara when those twilight eyes finally opened again. "Hey."

Clara swallowed, her mouth dry and cold from breathing so hard during the intensity of her experience. "Hi," she finally managed. "Wow."

Abby grinned, pleased. "That was pretty amazing, wasn't it?"

Clara nodded, her thoughts barely beginning to actually make sense. "What about Jordan?"

Abby shook her head, chuckling. "There was never anything going on between us, Clara. When he kissed me, I was just as surprised as you were." She placed a kiss on her lips. "I promise."

"Good." Clara pulled Abby down on top of her, hugging her close, their bodies molding together. "I love you."

"I love you too."

As they drifted off into a light sleep, neither had even noticed the sound of the front door closing.

Epilogue

2008

Clara stood on the sidewalk, looking up to make sure the sign was straight. She smiled when arms slid around her waist from behind, Abby's warmth against her back.

"It looks good, doesn't it?" Abby said, resting her chin on Clara's shoulder.

"Hmm. It does." She rested her head against Abby's. They both looked up at the brand-new sign, which read: SOUL SEARCHER. "I can't believe this is our second store."

"Eh, I always knew you'd be a success."

Clara smiled, feeling content and completely loved.

About the Author

Kim Pritekel was born and raised in Colorado and still lives there today, in love with the Rockies and simple beauty of home. She began writing at age 9 and has yet to stop, as writing a novel is more fulfilling than therapy. Cheaper, too. Kim embraces all forms of creativity, including filmmaking, which she has done as a writer, producer and director, since 2006. She can be reached on Facebook or by email at XenaNut@hotmail.com

You can also find Kim's other books at - www.sapphirebooks.com

Coming soon from Kim Pritekel - Shadow Box

Erin Riggs has played it safe her entire life. She's followed the stream of expectation rather than the beating of her own heart. After a most brutal - and unexpected - heartbreak, she decides to toss safe aside, and moves to a different town and wing it. Though she finds a nice, safe place to live and a nice, safe job, her life is about to be anything but nice and safe.

Tamson Robard has lived her entire life on the edge, guided only by her own anger and her very special invisible guide, Penny. One night Fate brings her to the door of the next phase of her life, where she's given choices to make that will determine the rest of her life, as well as unlock an unknown past.

Lightning Source UK Ltd.
Milton Keynes UK
UKOW042040260613

212875UK00001B/164/P